Handbook of the Nutritional Value of Foods

in Common Units

Prepared by Catherine F. Adams
for the United States Department of Agriculture

Dover Publications, Inc.
New York

Published in Canada by General Publishing Company, Ltd., 30 Lesmill Road, Don Mills, Toronto, Ontario.

Published in the United Kingdom by Constable and Company, Ltd., 10 Orange Street, London WC2H 7EG.

This Dover edition, first published in 1986, is an unabridged and unaltered republication of Agriculture Handbook No. 456 of the Agricultural Research Service of the United States Department of Agriculture, *Nutritive Value of American Foods: in Common Units,* 1975.

Manufactured in the United States of America
Dover Publications, Inc., 31 East 2nd Street, Mineola, N.Y. 11501

Library of Congress Cataloging-in-Publication Data

Adams, Catherine F., 1915–
Handbook of the nutritional value of foods.

Reprint. Originally published: Nutritive value of American foods in common units. Washington : Agricultural Research Service, U.S. Dept. of Agriculture, 1975.
Bibliography: p.
Includes index.
1. Food—Composition—Tables. I. United States. Dept. of Agriculture. II. Title.
TX551.A34 1986 641.1 86-2105
ISBN 0-486-21342-0

PREFACE

This publication provides values for calories and nutrients supplied by various household measures and market units of food. These values have been prepared to serve the needs of the growing number of research groups who conduct dietary surveys and nutritional status studies on individuals and household groups, as well as the needs of other professional and technical personnel who plan or evaluate diets and food supplies, including personnel in food industries and health-related professions.

Bernice K. Watt, formerly leader of the Nutrient Data Research Center, supervised the compilation of data and the presentation of the information.

CONTENTS

LIST OF TABLES

NOTE: Punched cards or magnetic tape of the data in tables 1 and 2 can be made available upon request.

NUTRITIVE VALUE OF AMERICAN FOODS
In Common Units

By CATHERINE F. ADAMS, *Consumer and Food Economics Institute, Northeastern Region, Agricultural Research Service*[1]

This publication has been prepared to serve as a basic reference for data on nutrients in frequently used household measures and market units of food. The data have been limited mostly to well-known basic measures. For many foods, however, a basis has been provided also to enable users of this type of information to calculate values for various additional measures and units as may be needed.

This handbook includes data on approximately 1,500 foods in the form of menu items, snacks, and market products, some as ready-to-eat foods, some that require preparation in varying degrees, and some that are used as ingredients in preparing other products. Although this information is primarily for use with retail supplies and foods used or prepared in the home, some of it applies to foods used in institutional and other large-scale operations.

The nutritive values on which data are provided include water, food energy, protein, fat, carbohydrate, five mineral elements (calcium, phosphorus, iron, sodium, and potassium), five vitamins (vitamin A, thiamin, riboflavin, niacin, and ascorbic acid), total saturated fatty acids, and two unsaturated fatty acids (oleic acid and linoleic acid). Except for water the food values shown are the amounts supplied by the edible part of the designated quantity of each product. Because water content often is helpful in identifying the different forms of a food, data for water have been expressed as the percentage of the edible part of each food listed. Edible part or portion refers to the part of a food item that is potentially edible and customarily eaten even though the product may require cooking or other preparation to render it edible.

Much of the information for nutritive values in the various measures and units of food is in the first two tables. It has been supplemented by explanatory material and some additional data in the appendixes.

Values for nutrients in this handbook have been calculated by applying the weight of the edible part of the food item to data for its nutrient composition. Except where noted, the bases of the data in this handbook were values previously published in Agriculture Handbook No. 8, "Composition of Foods . . . Raw, Processed, Prepared," revised 1963 (*28*).[2] Revisions made to update values and the substitution of other more appropriate data for those previously published in this 1963 handbook have been indicated in the present publication by tabular footnotes or explanations in Appendix A, "Notes on Selection of Items and Supplementary Data on the Composition of Foods." Information on kinds and proportions of ingredients in formulas for home-prepared food items, changes in weight between ingredients and prepared foods, and retention of vitamins during the preparation of these foods for serving is in ARS 62–13, "Procedures for Calculating Nutritive Values of Home-Prepared Foods" (*7*).

Development of suitable data on weight-volume relationships for the measures of the food items has been an essential part of the preparation of the information presented here. The weight in grams shown for each household measure or

[1] The author gratefully acknowledges the assistance and contributions of Annabel L. Merrill, Patricia M. Thomas, and Ruth M. Feeley, formerly of this Institute, Ruth G. Bowman and Ruth H. Matthews, of this Institute, and many individuals in industry.

[2] Italic numbers in parentheses refer to Literature Cited

market unit listed is considered reasonable for the item as described. Procedures and problems in arriving at the weight-volume relationships are discussed in Appendix B, "Notes on Weight and Volume Relationships."

Appendix B includes information about a few of the foods for which data are provided in the tables. However, background information about foods that may be helpful in using the data in the tables has been provided mostly in Appendix C, "Notes on Foods." Information about the energy values and nutrients for which data have been shown is in Appendix D, "Notes on Energy Values and Nutrients."

The measurements for specifying quantities of the food items are in the customary units now in use. Occasions may arise when the food values shown may need to be expressed for quantities of foods measured in metric units. Customary units used in this handbook for measuring amounts of foods, for energy values, and for temperature, with their metric system equivalents, are as follows:

Customary system (U.S.)	*Metric system equivalent*
Length	
1 inch	2.54 centimeters, 25.4 millimeters
Volume	
1 cubic inch	16.39 cubic centimeters
1 teaspoon	4.9 milliliters
1 tablespoon	14.8 milliliters
1 fluid ounce	29.573 milliliters
1 cup	236.6 milliliters
1 pint	473.2 milliliters, 0.473 liter
1 quart	946.4 milliliters, 0.946 liter
1 gallon	3,785.6 milliliters, 3.786 liters
Energy	
1 kilocalorie	4.184 kiloJoules
Temperature [1]	
1° Fahrenheit (F.)	5/9° Celsius (Centrigrade, C.)

[1] To convert °F. to °C., use formula (°F.—32°) × 5/9; to convert °C. to °F., use formula (9/5 × °C.) + 32°.

The equivalents shown here differ slightly from the rounded figures for the capacities of teaspoon (5 ml.), tablespoon (15 ml.), and cup (240 ml.) as used by the U.S. Food and Drug Administration in regulations for nutrient labeling.

EXPLANATION OF TABLES

For each food product in tables 1 and 2, the tabulated information includes the description of the item, the approximate measure or unit, the corresponding weight in grams, and the values for the edible part of the foods. Table 1 has data for energy values and all nutrients for which values are included except fatty acids.

Table 2 provides data for total fat and the amounts of total saturated, oleic, and linoleic fatty acids. Data on fatty acids are presented in table 2 for about half the foods listed in table 1. Foods were omitted from table 2 if data on the content of fatty acids were not available or if the content of total fat was 2 percent or less.

In both tables foods have been arranged mainly in alphabetical order according to their common name. Some foods have been grouped under a heading. For example, commercially prepared foods for infants and small children have been listed under Baby Foods and soft drinks and alcoholic beverages under Beverages. Cross references have been inserted to aid in finding data for items that might be designated by any of several terms.

Breakfast-type cereals with more than one grain ingredient are listed under the predominating grain in the product, that is, under the first-named grain. For example, a breakfast cereal with the ingredient clause on the package "contains sugar, wheat, corn sirup, and honey" is listed under Wheat; one described as containing yellow cornmeal, oat flour, sugar, and wheat starch will be found under Corn.

To insure identity of an item, it may be necessary at times to refer to the scientific name or to data on composition per 100 g. (type of information found in Handbook No. 8). To facilitate finding this additional information, the number for the item in Handbook No. 8 has been shown here in column A in tables 1 and 2 for those foods that have been included.

Letters have been added under the item numbers in column A of tables 1 and 2 to indicate that more than one quantity of a product has been listed, that data for a product are shown with and without an inedible component, or that the data are shown for the product in different conditions. For example, a cup of almonds in the shell is listed as 8a in table 1, a cup of whole almonds without shell as 8d, and a cup of chopped almonds as 8e. The letters do not necessarily connote the same meaning in table 2 as in table 1. The descriptions and the measures or units for a food product are shown in full in table 1 under column B but have been shortened in some instances in table 2.

Units for a few foods listed in the tables include some refuse. Examples are raw fruits served whole, fruits canned whole with pits, and meat with bone. The nature and content of the inedible material present in an item are specified in parentheses in column B following the description of the food. Figures for content of refuse have been adapted from data in table 2 of Handbook No. 8, Agriculture Handbook No. 102 (*12*), and from unpublished data.

For food items containing refuse, the weight shown in grams for the volume measure or unit includes the weight of the inedible material. The data in the tables for the nutrients in the food items are the amounts provided by the edible portion of the item. Should the weight in grams be needed for the edible part of an item containing refuse, the weight can be calculated by multiplying the figure for the percent edible (100 minus percent refuse) by the weight in grams shown for the item.

The terms "peeled" and "pared," applied throughout the tables to methods of removing exterior coverings of fruits and vegetables, have different meanings. "Peeled" refers to having stripped off the skin or peelings with a minimum of adhering flesh. "Pared" applies to having used some kitchen device to cut into the food, removing both skin and adhering flesh, or parings. Figures for refuse obtained by peeling are less than those obtained by paring.

Table 3, which is part of Appendix A, includes information referred to in footnotes to the items in tables 1 and 2 but too extensive to be put in the footnotes. Accompanying table 3 is a discussion of the selection of items for this publication and of the background leading to the revised values shown. For example, revised values for certain baby cereals and orange juice items are listed in table 3. Reasons underlying the changes to these new values are discussed in Appendix A. Data are shown in table 3 also for some new items closely related to those in tables 1 and 2 that may differ in form of marketing, proportion or kind of ingredients, and method of cooking. The items in table 3 are identified in the first column by the same numbers and the same footnotes assigned to these items in tables 1 and 2.

TABLE 1.—*Nutritive values for household measures and market units of foods*

[Item numbers correspond to those in table 1 of Handbook No. 8, revised 1963. Values in parentheses denote imputed values usually from another form of the food or from a similar food. Zeros in parentheses indicate that amount of a constituent, if present, is probably too small to be measured. Dashes (—) denote lack of reliable data for a constituent believed to be present in a measurable amount. Calculated values, as those based on a recipe, are not in parentheses]

Item No.	Food, approximate measures, units, and weight (edible part unless footnotes indicate otherwise)			Values for edible part of foods														
				Water	Food energy	Protein	Fat	Carbohydrate	Calcium	Phosphorus	Iron	Sodium	Potassium	Vitamin A value	Thiamin	Riboflavin	Niacin	Ascorbic acid
(A)	(B)			(C)	(D)	(E)	(F)	(G)	(H)	(I)	(J)	(K)	(L)	(M)	(N)	(O)	(P)	(Q)
			Grams	Percent	Calories	Grams	Grams	Grams	Milligrams	Milligrams	Milligrams	Milligrams	Milligrams	International units	Milligrams	Milligrams	Milligrams	Milligrams
3	**Acerola** (Barbados-cherry or West Indian cherry), raw, 1-in. diam. (refuse: stones, 18%).[1]	10 fruits	100	92.3	23	0.3	0.2	5.6	10	9	0.2	7	68	—	0.02	0.05	0.3	[2]1,066
4	**Acerola juice, raw, and acerola, raw, used for juice:**																	
a	Juice	1 cup	242	94.3	56	1.0	.7	11.6	24	22	1.2	7	—	—	.05	.15	1.0	[3]3,872
b	Acerola used for juice (refuse: stones, skins, residue, 32%).[1]	1 lb	454	94.3	71	1.2	.9	14.8	31	28	1.5	9	—	—	.06	.19	1.2	[3]4,934
	Albacore.[4] See Tuna (items 2323-2325).																	
	Ale. See Beverages, Beer (item 394).																	
	Alimentary pastes. See Macaroni, Noodles, Pastinas, Spaghetti.																	
	Almonds:[5]																	
8	Dried:																	
	In shell (refuse: shells, 60%):[1]																	
a	Cup	1 cup	78	4.7	187	5.8	16.9	6.1	73	157	1.5	1	241	0	.07	.29	1.1	Trace
b	Pound (yields 6.4 oz., approx. 1¼ cups, shelled whole nuts).	1 lb	454	4.7	1,085	33.7	98.3	35.4	424	914	8.5	7	1,402	0	.44	1.67	6.3	Trace
c	10 nuts	10 nuts	25	4.7	60	1.9	5.4	2.0	23	50	.5	Trace	77	0	.02	.09	.4	Trace
	Shelled:																	
d	Whole	1 cup	142	4.7	849	26.4	77.0	27.7	332	716	6.7	6	1,098	0	.34	1.31	5.0	Trace
	Chopped:																	
e	Cup	1 cup	130	4.7	777	24.2	70.5	25.4	304	655	6.1	5	1,005	0	.31	1.20	4.6	Trace
f	Tablespoon	1 tbsp	8	4.7	48	1.5	4.3	1.6	19	40	.4	Trace	62	0	.02	.07	.3	Trace
	Slivered:[6]																	
g	Cup, not packed	1 cup	115	4.7	688	21.4	62.3	22.4	269	580	5.4	5	889	0	.28	1.06	4.0	Trace
h	Cup, packed	1 cup	135	4.7	807	25.1	73.2	26.3	316	680	6.3	5	1,044	0	.32	1.24	4.7	Trace
i	Sliced (approx. 1/16 in. thick)	1 cup	95	4.7	568	17.7	51.5	18.5	222	479	4.5	4	734	0	.23	.87	3.3	Trace
j	Pound (yield from approx. 2½ lb., in shell[7])	1 lb	454	4.7	2,713	84.4	245.9	88.5	1,061	2,286	21.3	18	3,506	0	1.09	4.17	15.9	Trace
k	Ounce	1 oz	28	4.7	170	5.3	15.4	5.5	66	143	1.3	1	219	0	.07	.26	1.0	Trace
9	Roasted (in oil), salted:																	
a	Cup (approx. 120 nuts)	1 cup	157	4.7	984	29.2	90.6	30.6	369	791	7.4	311	1,214	0	.08	1.44	5.5	0
b	Pound	1 lb	454	.7	2,844	84.4	261.7	88.5	1,066	2,286	21.3	898	3,506	0	.23	4.17	15.9	0
c	Ounce (approx. 22 nuts)	1 oz	28	.7	178	5.3	16.4	5.5	67	143	1.3	56	219	0	.01	.26	1.0	0
	Sugar coated. See Candy (item 613).																	
10	**Almond meal,** partially defatted[5]	1 oz	28	7.2	116	11.2	5.2	8.2	120	259	2.4	2	397	0	.09	.48	1.8	0
11	**Amaranth,** raw, leaves	1 lb	454	86.9	163	15.9	2.3	29.5	1,211	304	17.7	—	1,864	27,670	.36	.73	6.4	363
12	**Anchovy,** pickled, not heavily salted, flat or rolled, canned:																	
a	Drained contents from can of net wt., 2 oz. (10-16 anchovies).	1⅗ oz	45	58.6	79	8.6	4.6	.1	76	95	—	—	—	—	—	—	—	—
b	Anchovy (flat, 4 in. long, ½ in. wide, ⅛ in. thick; rolled, ½- to ¾-in. diam., ½ in. thick).	5 anchovies	20	58.6	35	3.8	2.1	.1	34	42	—	—	—	—	—	—	—	—
c	Pound	1 lb	454	58.6	798	87.1	46.7	1.4	762	953	—	—	—	—	—	—	—	—
	Apples:																	
	Raw, commercial varieties:[8]																	
	Freshly harvested and stored, portion used:																	
13	Fruit with skin:																	
	Whole, good quality (refuse: core and stem, 8%):[1]																	
a	Fruit, 3¼-in. diam. (approx. 2 per pound)	1 apple	230	84.4	123	.4	1.3	30.7	15	21	.6	2	233	190	.06	.04	.2	8
b	Fruit, 3-in. diam. (approx. 2½ per pound)	1 apple	180	84.4	96	.3	1.0	24.0	12	17	.5	2	182	150	.05	.03	.2	7
c	Fruit, 2¾-in. diam. (approx. 3 per pound)	1 apple	150	84.4	80	.3	.8	20.0	10	14	.4	1	152	120	.04	.03	.1	6
d	Fruit, 2½-in. diam. (approx. 4 per pound)	1 apple	115	84.4	61	.2	.6	15.3	7	11	.3	1	116	100	.03	.02	.1	4
e	Quarters or finely chopped pieces	1 cup	125	84.4	73	.3	.8	18.1	9	13	.4	1	138	110	.04	.03	.1	5
f	Slices, ¼ in. thick, or diced pieces	1 cup	110	84.4	64	.2	.7	16.0	8	11	.3	1	121	100	.03	.02	.1	4
g	Pound	1 lb	454	84.4	263	.9	2.7	65.8	32	45	1.4	5	499	410	.14	.09	.5	18
14	Pared fruit:																	
	Whole, good quality (refuse: core, stem, thin parings, 14%):[1]																	
a	Fruit, 3¼-in. diam. (approx. 2 per pound)	1 apple	230	85.1	107	.4	.6	27.9	12	20	.6	2	218	80	.06	.04	.2	4
b	Fruit, 3-in. diam. (approx. 2½ per pound)	1 apple	180	85.1	84	.3	.5	21.8	9	15	.5	2	170	60	.05	.03	.2	3

(A)	(B)			(C)	(D)	(E)	(F)	(G)	(H)	(I)	(J)	(K)	(L)	(M)	(N)	(O)	(P)	(Q)
c	Fruit, 2¾-in. diam. (approx. 3 per pound)	1 apple	150	85.1	70	0.3	0.4	18.2	8	13	0.4	1	142	50	0.04	0.03	0.1	3
d	Fruit, 2½-in. diam. (approx. 4 per pound)	1 apple	115	85.1	53	.2	.3	13.9	6	10	.3	1	109	40	.03	.02	.1	2
e	Quarters or finely chopped pieces	1 cup	125	85.1	68	.3	.4	17.6	8	13	.4	1	138	50	.04	.03	.1	3
f	Slices, ¼ in. thick, or diced pieces	1 cup	110	85.1	59	.2	.3	15.5	7	11	.3	1	121	40	.03	.02	.1	2
g	Pound	1 lb	454	85.1	245	.9	1.4	64.0	27	45	1.4	5	499	180	.14	.09	.5	9
	Freshly harvested, portion used:																	
15	Fruit with skin:																	
	Whole, good quality (refuse: core and stem, 8%):[1]																	
a	Fruit, 3¼-in. diam. (approx. 2 per pound)	1 apple	230	84.8	118	.4	1.3	29.8	15	21	.6	2	233	190	.06	.04	.2	15
b	Fruit, 3-in. diam. (approx. 2½ per pound)	1 apple	180	84.8	93	.3	1.0	23.3	12	17	.5	2	182	150	.05	.03	.2	12
c	Fruit, 2¾-in. diam. (approx. 3 per pound)	1 apple	150	84.8	77	.3	.8	19.5	10	14	.4	1	152	120	.04	.03	.1	10
d	Fruit, 2½-in. diam. (approx. 4 per pound)	1 apple	115	84.8	59	.2	.6	14.9	7	11	.3	1	116	100	.03	.02	.1	7
e	Quarters or finely chopped pieces	1 cup	125	84.8	70	.3	.8	17.6	9	13	.4	1	138	110	.04	.03	.1	9
f	Slices, ¼ in. thick, or diced pieces	1 cup	110	84.8	62	.2	.7	15.5	8	11	.3	1	121	100	.03	.02	.1	8
g	Pound	1 lb	454	84.8	254	.9	2.7	64.0	32	45	1.4	5	499	410	.14	.09	.5	32
16	Pared fruit:																	
	Whole, good quality (refuse: core, stem, thin parings, 14%):[1]																	
a	Fruit, 3¼-in. diam. (approx. 2 per pound)	1 apple	230	85.3	105	.4	.6	27.5	12	20	.6	2	218	80	.06	.04	.2	8
b	Fruit, 3-in. diam. (approx. 2½ per pound)	1 apple	180	85.3	82	.3	.5	21.5	9	15	.5	2	170	60	.05	.03	.2	6
c	Fruit, 2¾-in. diam. (approx. 3 per pound)	1 apple	150	85.3	68	.3	.4	17.9	8	13	.4	1	142	50	.04	.03	.1	5
d	Fruit, 2½-in. diam. (approx. 4 per pound)	1 apple	115	85.3	52	.2	.3	13.7	6	10	.3	1	109	40	.03	.02	.1	4
e	Quarters or finely chopped pieces	1 cup	125	85.3	66	.3	.4	17.4	8	13	.4	1	138	50	.04	.03	.1	5
f	Slices, ¼ in. thick, or diced pieces	1 cup	110	85.3	58	.2	.3	15.3	7	11	.3	1	121	40	.03	.02	.1	4
g	Pound	1 lb	454	85.3	240	.9	1.4	63.1	27	45	1.4	5	499	180	.14	.09	.5	18
	Stored, portion used:																	
17	Fruit with skin:																	
	Whole, good quality (refuse: core and stem, 8%):[1]																	
a	Fruit, 3¼-in. diam. (approx. 2 per pound)	1 apple	230	83.9	127	.4	1.5	31.3	15	21	.6	2	233	190	.06	.04	.2	6
b	Fruit, 3-in. diam. (approx. 2½ per pound)	1 apple	180	83.9	99	.3	1.2	24.5	12	17	.5	2	182	150	.05	.03	.2	5
c	Fruit, 2¾-in. diam. (approx. 3 per pound)	1 apple	150	83.9	83	.3	1.0	20.4	10	14	.4	1	152	120	.04	.03	.1	4
d	Fruit, 2½-in. diam. (approx. 4 per pound)	1 apple	115	83.9	63	.2	.7	15.7	7	11	.3	1	116	100	.03	.02	.1	3
e	Quarters or finely chopped pieces	1 cup	125	83.9	75	.3	.9	18.5	9	13	.4	1	138	110	.04	.03	.1	4
f	Slices, ¼ in. thick, or diced pieces	1 cup	110	83.9	66	.2	.8	16.3	8	11	.3	1	121	100	.03	.02	.1	3
g	Pound	1 lb	454	83.9	272	.9	3.2	67.1	32	45	1.4	5	499	410	.14	.09	.5	14
18	Pared fruit:																	
	Whole, good quality (refuse: core, stem, thin parings, 14%):[1]																	
a	Fruit, 3¼-in. diam. (approx. 2 per pound)	1 apple	230	84.8	109	.4	.6	28.5	12	20	.6	2	218	80	.06	.04	.2	4
b	Fruit, 3-in. diam. (approx. 2½ per pound)	1 apple	180	84.8	85	.3	.5	22.3	9	15	.5	2	170	60	.05	.03	.2	3
c	Fruit, 2¾-in. diam. (approx. 3 per pound)	1 apple	150	84.8	71	.3	.4	18.6	8	13	.4	1	142	50	.04	.03	.1	3
d	Fruit, 2½-in. diam. (approx. 4 per pound)	1 apple	115	84.8	54	.2	.3	14.2	6	10	.3	1	109	40	.03	.02	.1	2
e	Quarters or finely chopped pieces	1 cup	125	84.8	69	.3	.4	18.0	8	13	.4	1	138	50	.04	.03	.1	3
f	Slices, ¼ in. thick, or diced pieces	1 cup	110	84.8	61	.2	.3	15.8	7	11	.3	1	121	40	.03	.02	.1	2
g	Pound	1 lb	454	84.8	249	.9	1.4	65.3	27	45	1.4	5	499	180	.14	.09	.5	9
	Canned. See Applesauce (items 28-29).																	
	Dehydrated, sulfured:																	
19	Uncooked:																	
a	Cup	1 cup	100	2.5	353	1.4	2.0	92.1	40	66	2.0	7	730	—	Trace	.06	.6	10
b	Pound	1 lb	454	2.5	1,601	6.4	9.1	417.8	181	299	9.1	32	3,311	—	.02	.27	2.7	45
20	Cooked with added sugar:[8]																	
a	Cup	1 cup	255	79.6	194	.5	.8	50.0	15	26	.8	3	270	—	Trace	.03	.3	3
b	Pound	1 lb	454	79.6	345	.9	1.4	88.9	27	45	1.4	5	481	--	Trace	.05	.5	5
	Dried, sulfured (rings):																	
21	Uncooked:																	
a	Container, net wt., 8 oz	1 container	227	24.0	624	2.3	3.6	163.0	70	118	3.6	11	1,292	—	.14	.27	1.1	23
b	Cup[10]	1 cup	85	24.0	234	.9	1.4	61.0	26	44	1.4	4	484	—	.05	.10	.4	9
c	Pound	1 lb	454	24.0	1,247	4.5	7.3	325.7	141	236	7.3	23	2,581	—	.27	.54	2.3	45
	Cooked:[9]																	
22	Without added sugar:																	
a	Cup	1 cup	255	78.4	199	.8	1.3	51.8	23	38	1.3	3	413	—	.03	.08	.3	Trace
b	Pound	1 lb	454	78.4	354	1.4	2.3	92.1	41	68	2.3	5	735	—	.05	.14	.5	Trace

[1] Measure and weight apply to food as it is described with inedible part or parts (refuse) included.

[2] Based on average value of 1,300 mg. per 100 g. for fully ripened fruit grown in Florida, Puerto Rico, Hawaii; range may be 1,000–2,000 mg. per 100 g. At firm-ripe stage, average is 1,900 mg.; range 1,200–2,700 mg. At partially ripe stage, average is 2,500 mg.; range 1,200–4,500 mg. For further information on classification and ascorbic acid content, see Appendix C, section on Acerola

[3] Based on average value of 1,600 mg. per 100 g. for juice from ripe fruit; range may be 2,400–5,300 mg. for 1 cup of juice (item 4a); 3,100–6,800 mg. for 1 lb. of fruit used for juice (item 4b).

[4] Almost all catch is canned as tuna.

[5] Most of phosphorus in nuts, legumes, and outer layers of cereal grains is present as phytic acid. See also Appendix D, section on Minerals and Oxalic Acid

[6] Slivered refers to almonds that are split in half, laid flat side down, and sliced into thin slices, approx. 3/16 in. wide.

[7] Yield applies to varieties marketed "in shell."

[8] For further information on ascorbic acid value for apples, see Appendix C, section on Apples

[9] For information on proportion of fruit, sugar, and water used, see ARS 62–13 (7), section on Fruits, Dried and Dehydrated, p. 7, and table 20, p. 24.

[10] Separated pieces when stuck together.

TABLE 1.—*Nutritive values for household measures and market units of foods*—Continued

[Item numbers correspond to those in table 1 of Handbook No. 8, revised 1963. Values in parentheses denote imputed values usually from another form of the food or from a similar food. Zeros in parentheses indicate that amount of a constituent, if present, is probably too small to be measured. Dashes (—) denote lack of reliable data for a constituent believed to be present in a measurable amount. Calculated values, as those based on a recipe, are not in parentheses]

Item No.	Food, approximate measures, units, and weight (edible part unless footnotes indicate otherwise)			Values for edible part of foods														
				Water	Food energy	Protein	Fat	Carbohydrate	Calcium	Phosphorus	Iron	Sodium	Potassium	Vitamin A value	Thiamin	Riboflavin	Niacin	Ascorbic acid
(A)	(B)			(C)	(D)	(E)	(F)	(G)	(H)	(I)	(J)	(K)	(L)	(M)	(N)	(O)	(P)	(Q)
			Grams	Percent	Calories	Grams	Grams	Grams	Milligrams	Milligrams	Milligrams	Milligrams	Milligrams	International units	Milligrams	Milligrams	Milligrams	Milligrams
	Apples—Continued																	
	Dried, sulfured (rings)—Continued																	
	Cooked [9]—Continued																	
23	With added sugar:																	
a	Cup	1 cup	280	69.7	314	0.8	1.1	81.8	22	36	1.1	3	403	—	0.03	0.08	0.3	Trace
b	Pound	1 lb	454	69.7	508	1.4	1.8	132.5	36	59	1.8	5	653	—	.05	.14	.5	Trace
24	Frozen, sliced, sweetened with nutritive sweetener, not thawed.	1 lb	454	75.1	422	.9	.5	110.2	23	27	2.3	[11] 299	308	90	.05	.14	.9	32
25	**Apple brown betty** (made with enriched bread) [12] [13]	1 cup	215	64.5	325	3.4	7.5	63.9	39	47	1.3	329	215	220	.13	.09	.9	2
26	**Apple butter:**																	
	Container and approx. contents:																	
a	Can, size 603 × 700 [14] (No. 10); net wt., 124 oz. (7 lb. 12 oz.).	1 can	3,515	51.6	6,538	14.1	28.1	1,645.0	492	1,265	24.6	70	8,858	0	.35	.70	7.0	70
	Glass jar:																	
b	Size, 12 oz.; net wt., 12 oz	1 jar	340	51.6	632	1.4	2.7	159.1	48	122	2.4	7	857	0	.03	.07	.7	7
c	Size, 28 oz.; net wt., 28 oz. (1 lb. 12 oz.)	1 jar	794	51.6	1,477	3.2	6.4	371.6	111	286	5.6	16	2,001	0	.08	.16	1.6	16
d	Size, 38 oz.; net wt., 38 oz. (2 lb. 6 oz.)	1 jar	1,077	51.6	2,003	4.3	8.6	504.0	151	388	7.5	22	2,714	0	.11	.22	2.2	22
e	Cup	1 cup	282	51.6	525	1.1	2.3	132.0	39	102	2.0	6	711	0	.03	.06	.6	6
f	Tablespoon	1 tbsp	17.6	51.6	33	.1	.1	8.2	2	6	.1	Trace	44	0	Trace	Trace	Trace	Trace
g	Pound	1 lb	454	51.6	844	1.8	3.6	212.3	64	163	3.2	9	1,143	0	.05	.09	.9	9
h	Ounce	1 oz	28	51.6	53	.1	.2	13.3	4	10	.2	1	71	0	Trace	.01	.1	1
27	**Applejuice,** canned or bottled:																	
	Container and approx. contents:																	
a	Bottle, net contents, 32 fl. oz. (1 qt.)	1 bottle or 1 qt.	993	87.8	467	1.0	Trace	118.2	60	89	6.0	10	1,003	—	.10	.20	1.0	[15] 10
	Can:																	
b	Size, 202 × 308 [14] (6Z); net contents, 5½ fl. oz.	1 can	171	87.8	80	.2	Trace	20.3	10	15	1.0	2	173	—	.02	.03	.2	[15] 2
c	Size, 404 × 700 [14] (46Z, No. 3 Cylinder); net contents, 46 fl. oz. (1 qt. 14 fl. oz.).	1 can	1,427	87.8	671	1.4	Trace	169.8	86	128	8.6	14	1,441	—	.14	.29	1.4	[15] 14
d	Glass jug, net contents, 1 gal. [16]	1 jug or 1 gal.	3,971	87.8	1,866	4.0	Trace	472.5	238	357	23.8	40	4,011	—	.40	.79	4.0	[15] 40
e	Cup [16]	1 cup	248	87.8	117	.2	Trace	29.5	15	22	1.5	2	250	—	.02	.05	.2	[15] 2
f	Glass (6 fl. oz.) [16]	1 glass	186	87.8	87	.2	Trace	22.1	11	17	1.1	2	188	—	.02	.04	.2	[15] 2
g	Fluid ounce [16]	1 fl. oz	31.0	87.8	15	Trace	Trace	3.7	2	3	.2	Trace	31	—	Trace	.01	Trace	[15] Trace
	Applesauce, canned, regular (comminuted) style:																	
28	Unsweetened:																	
	Container and approx. contents:																	
a	Can, size 211 × 304 [14] (8Z Tall, Buffet); net wt., 8 oz.	1 can	227	88.5	93	.5	.5	24.5	9	11	1.1	5	177	90	.05	.02	.1	[15] 2
b	Can, size 303 × 406 [14] (No. 303); net wt., 16 oz. (1 lb.).	1 can or 1 lb	454	88.5	186	.9	.9	49.0	18	23	2.3	9	354	180	.09	.05	.2	[15] 5
c	Glass jar, net wt., 7½ oz	1 jar	213	88.5	87	.4	.4	23.0	9	11	1.1	4	166	90	.04	.02	.1	[15] 2
d	Glass jar, net wt., 15 oz	1 jar	425	88.5	174	.9	.9	45.9	17	21	2.1	9	332	170	.09	.04	.2	[15] 4
e	Cup	1 cup	244	88.5	100	.5	.5	26.4	10	12	1.2	5	190	100	.05	.02	.1	[15] 2
29	Sweetened with nutritive sweetener:																	
	Container and approx. contents:																	
a	Can, size 303 × 406 [14] (No. 303); net wt., 16½ oz. (1 lb. ½ oz.).	1 can	468	75.7	426	.9	.5	111.4	19	23	2.3	9	304	190	.09	.05	.2	[15] 5
b	Can, size 603 × 700 [14] (No. 10); net wt., 108 oz. (6 lb. 12 oz.).	1 can	3,062	75.7	2,786	6.1	3.1	728.8	122	153	15.3	61	1,990	1,220	.61	.31	1.2	[15] 31
c	Glass jar, size 25 oz.; net wt., 25 oz. (1 lb. 9 oz.).	1 jar	709	75.7	645	1.4	.7	168.7	28	35	3.5	14	461	280	.14	.08	.8	[15] 7
d	Glass jar, size 35 oz.; net wt., 35 oz. (2 lb. 3 oz.).	1 jar	992	75.7	903	2.0	1.0	236.1	40	50	5.0	20	645	400	.20	.10	.4	[15] 10
e	Cup	1 cup	255	75.7	232	.5	.3	60.7	10	13	1.3	5	166	100	.05	.03	.1	[15] 3
f	Pound	1 lb	454	75.7	413	.9	.5	108.0	18	23	2.3	9	295	180	.09	.05	.2	[15] 5
	Apricots:																	
30	Raw:																	
	Whole (12 per pound) (refuse: pits, 6%): [1]																	
a	Pound	1 lb	454	85.3	217	4.3	.9	54.6	72	98	2.1	4	1,198	11,510	.13	.17	2.6	43
b	3 apricots	3 apricots	114	85.3	55	1.1	.2	13.7	18	25	.5	1	301	2,890	.03	.04	.6	11

(A)	(B)			(C)	(D)	(E)	(F)	(G)	(H)	(I)	(J)	(K)	(L)	(M)	(N)	(O)	(P)	(Q)
	Halves:																	
c	Cup	1 cup	155	85.3	79	1.6	0.3	19.8	26	36	0.8	2	436	4,190	0.05	0.06	0.9	16
d	Pound	1 lb	454	85.3	231	4.5	.9	58.1	77	104	2.3	5	1,275	12,250	.14	.18	2.7	45
	Canned, solids and liquid:																	
32	Water pack, without artificial sweetener, halved style:																	
	Can and approx. contents:																	
a	Size, 211 × 304 [14] (8Z Tall, Buffet); net wt., 8 oz.; 6–12 halves and approx. 5 tbsp. of drained liquid.	1 can	227	89.1	86	1.6	.2	21.8	27	36	.7	2	558	4,150	.05	.05	.9	9
b	Size, 303 × 406 [14] (No. 303); net wt., 16 oz. (1 lb.); 12–20 halves and approx. 9½ tbsp. of drained liquid.	1 can or 1 lb	454	89.1	172	3.2	.5	43.5	54	73	1.4	5	1,116	8,300	.09	.09	1.8	18
c	Size, 603 × 700 [14] (No. 10); net wt., 103 oz. (6 lb. 7 oz.); 85–108 halves and approx. 4 cups of drained liquid.	1 can	2,920	89.1	1,110	20.4	2.9	280.3	350	467	8.8	29	7,183	53,440	.58	.58	11.7	117
d	Cup	1 cup	246	89.1	93	1.7	.2	23.6	30	39	.7	2	605	4,500	.05	.05	1.0	10
e	Halves with drained liquid	3 halves; 1¾ tbsp. liquid.	84	89.1	32	.6	.1	8.1	10	13	.3	1	207	1,540	.02	.02	.3	3
35	Sirup pack, heavy (whole apricots with pits and halves, pitted):																	
	Can and approx. contents:																	
a	Size, 211 × 304 [14] (8Z Tall, Buffet); net wt., 8¾ oz.; halved style (6–12 halves and approx. 5½ tbsp. of drained liquid).	1 can	248	76.9	213	1.5	.2	54.6	27	37	.7	2	580	4,320	.05	.05	1.0	10
	Size, 303 × 406 [14] (No. 303); net wt., 17 oz. (1 lb. 1 oz.):																	
b	Whole style (8–14 apricots and approx. 10 tbsp. of drained liquid; refuse: pits, 6%).[1]	1 can	482	76.9	390	2.7	.5	99.7	50	68	1.4	5	1,060	7,880	.09	.09	1.8	18
c	Halved style (12–20 halves and approx. 10⅔ tbsp. of drained liquid).	1 can	482	76.9	415	2.9	.5	106.0	53	72	1.4	5	1,128	8,390	.10	.10	.19	19
	Size, 401 × 411 [14] (No. 2½); net wt., 30 oz. (1 lb. 14 oz.):																	
d	Whole style (15–18 apricots and approx. 18 tbsp. of drained liquid; refuse: pits, 6%).[1]	1 can	851	76.9	688	4.8	.8	176.0	88	120	2.4	8	1,872	13,920	.16	.16	3.2	32
e	Halved style (26–35 halves and approx. 19 tbsp. of drained liquid).	1 can	851	76.9	732	5.1	.9	187.2	94	128	2.6	9	1,991	14,810	.17	.17	3.4	34
	Cup:																	
f	Whole style (refuse: pits, 6%)[1]	1 cup	275	76.9	222	1.6	.3	56.9	28	39	.8	3	605	4,500	.05	.05	1.0	10
g	Halved style	1 cup	258	76.9	222	1.5	.3	56.8	28	39	.8	3	604	4,490	.05	.05	1.0	10
	Pound:																	
h	Whole style (refuse: pits, 6%)[1]	1 lb	454	76.9	367	2.6	.4	93.8	47	64	1.3	4	998	7,420	.09	.09	1.7	17
i	Halved style	1 lb	454	76.9	390	2.7	.5	99.8	50	68	1.4	5	1,061	7,890	.09	.09	1.8	18
	Fruit served with drained liquid:																	
j	Whole style (refuse: pits, 6%)[1]	2 apricots; 2 tbsp. liquid.	96	76.9	78	.5	.1	19.8	10	14	.3	1	211	1,570	.02	.02	.4	4
k	Halved style	3 halves; 1¾ tbsp. liquid.	85	76.9	73	.5	.1	18.7	9	13	.3	1	199	1,480	.02	.02	.3	3
	Dehydrated, sulfured, nugget type and pieces:																	
37	Uncooked:																	
a	Cup	1 cup	100	3.5	332	5.6	1.0	84.6	86	139	5.3	33	1,260	14,100	Trace	.08	3.6	15
b	Pound	1 lb	454	3.5	1,506	25.4	4.5	383.7	390	631	24.0	150	5,715	63,960	Trace	.36	16.3	68
38	Cooked, fruit and liquid, sugar added:[9]																	
a	Cup	1 cup	300	66.7	337	3.9	.6	91.5	60	99	3.9	24	897	8,400	Trace	.06	2.4	6
b	Pound	1 lb	454	66.7	540	5.9	.9	138.3	91	150	5.9	36	1,356	12,700	Trace	.09	3.6	9
	Dried, sulfured (large halves, 1½-in. diam.; medium halves, 1⅓-in. diam.):																	
39	Uncooked:																	
a	Container, net wt., 11 oz. (approx. 65 large halves or 90 medium).	1 container	312	25.0	811	15.6	1.6	207.5	209	337	17.2	81	3,054	34,010	.03	.50	10.3	37

[1] Measure and weight apply to food as it is described with inedible part or parts (refuse) included.

[9] For information on proportion of fruit, sugar, and water used, see ARS 62–13 (7), section on Fruits, Dried and Dehydrated, p. 7, and table 20, p. 24.

[11] Based on average value of 66 mg. per 100 g. weighted in accordance with commercial freezing practices. Values range from 9 to 907 mg. per pound. Values in upper part of range represent packs to which preservatives containing sodium have been added to prevent darkening of apple slices.

[12] Cup measure made on product after it had cooled. See also Appendix B, section on Home-Prepared Foods

[13] For information on ingredients used, see ARS 62–13 (7), table 18, pp. 22–23.

[14] Dimensions of can: 1st dimension represents diameter; 2d dimension, height of can. 1st or left-hand digit in each dimension gives number of whole inches; next 2 digits give additional fraction of dimension expressed as 16th of an inch.

[15] Applies to product without added ascorbic acid. For value of product with added ascorbic acid, refer to label.

[16] Weights of volume measures and nutritive values also apply to pasteurized apple cider.

TABLE 1.—*Nutritive values for household measures and market units of foods*—Continued

[Item numbers correspond to those in table 1 of Handbook No. 8, revised 1963. Values in parentheses denote imputed values usually from another form of the food or from a similar food. Zeros in parentheses indicate that amount of a constituent, if present, is probably too small to be measured. Dashes (—) denote lack of reliable data for a constituent believed to be present in a measurable amount. Calculated values, as those based on a recipe, are not in parentheses]

Item No.	Food, approximate measures, units, and weight (edible part unless footnotes indicate otherwise)			Water	Food energy	Protein	Fat	Carbohydrate	Calcium	Phosphorus	Iron	Sodium	Potassium	Vitamin A value	Thiamin	Riboflavin	Niacin	Ascorbic acid
				Values for edible part of foods														
(A)	(B)			(C)	(D)	(E)	(F)	(G)	(H)	(I)	(J)	(K)	(L)	(M)	(N)	(O)	(P)	(Q)
			Grams	Percent	Calories	Grams	Grams	Grams	Milligrams	Milligrams	Milligrams	Milligrams	Milligrams	International units	Milligrams	Milligrams	Milligrams	Milligrams
	Apricots—Continued																	
	Dried, sulfured (large halves, 1½-in. diam.; medium halves, 1⅓-in. diam.)—Continued																	
	Uncooked—Continued																	
b	Cup (approx. 28 large halves or 37 medium)[10]	1 cup	130	25.0	338	6.5	0.7	86.5	87	140	7.2	34	1,273	14,170	0.01	0.21	4.3	16
c	Pound (approx. 95 large halves or 130 medium)	1 lb	454	25.0	1,179	22.7	2.3	301.6	304	490	24.9	118	4,441	49,440	.05	.78	15.0	54
	10 halves:																	
d	Large	10 halves	48	25.0	125	2.4	.2	31.9	32	52	2.6	12	470	5,230	Trace	.08	1.6	6
e	Medium	10 halves	35	25.0	91	1.8	.2	23.3	23	38	1.9	9	343	3,820	Trace	.06	1.2	4
	Cooked, fruit and liquid:[9]																	
40	Without added sugar:																	
a	Cup	1 cup	250	75.6	213	4.0	.5	54.0	55	88	4.5	20	795	7,500	.01	.13	2.5	8
b	Pound	1 lb	454	75.6	386	7.3	.9	98.0	100	159	8.2	36	1,442	13,610	.02	.23	4.5	14
41	With added sugar:																	
a	Cup	1 cup	270	66.2	329	3.8	.3	84.8	51	84	4.3	19	751	7,020	.01	.11	2.4	5
b	Pound	1 lb	454	66.2	553	6.4	.5	142.4	86	141	7.3	32	1,261	11,790	.01	.18	4.1	9
42	Frozen, sweetened with nutritive sweetener, not thawed.	1 lb	454	73.3	445	3.2	.5	113.9	45	86	4.1	18	1,039	7,620	.09	.18	3.6	[17] 127
43	**Apricot nectar,** canned or bottled (approx. 40% fruit):																	
	Container and approx. contents:																	
a	Bottle, net contents, 30 fl. oz. (1 qt.)	1 bottle or 1 qt.	1,006	84.6	573	3.0	1.0	146.9	91	121	2.0	Trace	1,519	9,560	.10	.10	2.0	[15] 30
b	Can, size 202 × 308[14] (6Z); net contents, 5½ fl. oz.	1 can	173	84.6	99	.5	.2	25.3	16	21	.3	Trace	261	1,640	.02	.02	.3	[15] 5
c	Can, size 211 × 414[14] (12Z, No. 211 Cylinder); net contents, 12 fl. oz.	1 can	377	84.6	215	1.1	.4	55.0	34	45	.8	Trace	569	3,580	.04	.04	.8	[15] 11
d	Can, size 404 × 700[14] (46Z, No. 3 Cylinder); net contents, 46 fl. oz. (1 qt. 14 fl. oz.).	1 can	1,446	84.6	824	4.3	1.4	211.1	130	174	2.9	Trace	2,183	13,740	.14	.14	2.9	[15] 43
e	Cup	1 cup	251	84.6	143	.8	.3	36.6	23	30	.5	Trace	379	2,380	.03	.03	.5	[15] 8
f	Glass (6 fl. oz.)	1 glass	188	84.6	107	.6	.2	27.4	17	23	.4	Trace	284	1,790	.02	.02	.4	[15] 6
g	Fluid ounce	1 fl. oz	31.4	84.6	18	.1	Trace	4.6	3	4	.1	Trace	47	300	Trace	Trace	.1	[15] 1
45	**Artichokes, globe or French,** cooked (boiled), drained (refuse: stem and inedible parts of bracts and flower, 60%):[1]																	
a	Bud or globe (size or count, 24 per half box; net wt., approx. 20 lb.).	1 bud	380	86.5	([18])	4.3	.3	[19] 15.0	78	105	1.7	[20] 46	458	230	.11	.06	1.1	12
b	Bud or globe (size or count, 30 per half box; net wt., approx. 20 lb.).	1 bud	300	86.5	([18])	3.4	.2	[19] 11.9	61	83	1.3	[20] 36	361	180	.08	.05	.8	10
c	Bud or globe (size or count, 36 per half box; net wt., approx. 20 lb.).	1 bud	250	86.5	([18])	2.8	.2	[19] 9.9	51	69	1.1	[20] 30	301	150	.07	.04	.7	8
	Asparagus:																	
46	Raw spears (green):																	
a	Cup (cut spears, 1½- to 2-in. pieces)	1 cup	135	91.7	35	3.4	.3	6.8	30	84	1.4	3	375	1,220	.24	.27	2.0	45
b	Pound	1 lb	454	91.7	118	11.3	.9	22.7	100	281	4.5	9	1,261	4,080	.82	.91	6.8	150
47	Cooked spears (green) (boiled), drained:																	
	Spears:																	
a	Large, ¾- to ⅞-in. diam. at base	4 spears	100	93.6	20	2.2	.2	3.6	21	50	.6	[20] 1	183	900	.16	.18	1.4	26
b	Medium, ½-in. diam. at base	4 spears	60	93.6	12	1.3	.1	2.2	13	30	.4	[20] 1	110	540	.10	.11	.8	16
c	Small, ⅜-in. diam. at base	4 spears	40	93.6	8	.9	.1	1.4	8	20	.2	[20] Trace	73	360	.06	.07	.6	10
	Cup:																	
d	Whole	1 cup	180	93.6	36	4.0	.4	6.5	38	90	1.1	[20] 2	329	1,620	.29	.32	2.5	47
e	Cut (1½- to 2-in. pieces)	1 cup	145	93.6	29	3.2	.3	5.2	30	73	.9	[20] 1	265	1,310	.23	.26	2.0	38
f	Pound	1 lb	454	93.6	91	10.0	.9	16.3	95	227	2.7	[20] 5	830	4,080	.73	.82	6.4	118
	Canned spears:																	
	Green:																	
	Regular pack:																	
48	Solids and liquid:																	
	Can and approx. contents:																	
a	Size, 211 × 400[14] (No. 1 Picnic), whole	1 can	298	93.6	54	5.7	.9	8.6	54	128	5.1	[21] 708	495	1,520	.18	.27	2.4	45

(A)	(B)			(C)	(D)	(E)	(F)	(G)	(H)	(I)	(J)	(K)	(L)	(M)	(N)	(O)	(P)	(Q)
	or cut spears; net wt., 10½ oz.																	
b	Size, 300 × 407 [14] (No. 300), whole or cut spears; net wt., 14½ oz.	1 can	411	93.6	74	7.8	1.2	11.9	74	177	7.0	[21] 970	682	2.100	0.25	0.37	3.3	62
c	Size, 603 × 700 [14] (No. 10), cut spears; net wt., 103 oz. (6 lb. 7 oz.).	1 can	2,920	93.6	526	55.5	8.8	84.7	526	1,256	49.6	[21] 6,891	4,847	14,890	1.75	2.63	23.4	438
	Cup:																	
d	Whole spears with liquid	1 cup	244	93.6	44	4.6	.7	7.1	44	105	4.1	[21] 576	405	1,240	.15	.22	2.0	37
e	Cut spears with liquid	1 cup	239	93.6	43	4.5	.7	6.9	43	103	4.1	[21] 564	397	1,220	.14	.22	1.9	36
f	Pound, whole or cut spears with liquid	1 lb	454	93.6	82	8.6	1.4	13.2	82	195	7.7	[21] 1,070	753	2.310	.27	.41	3.6	68
49	Drained solids:																	
	Can and approx. drained contents:																	
a	Size, 211 × 400 [14] (No. 1 Picnic), whole spears; wt., 6¼ oz.	1 can	177	92.5	37	4.2	.7	6.0	34	94	3.4	[21] 418	294	1,420	.11	.18	1.4	27
b	Size, 300 × 407 [14] (No. 300), whole spears; wt., 8¾ oz.	1 can	248	92.5	52	6.0	1.0	8.4	47	131	4.7	[21] 585	412	1,980	.15	.25	2.0	37
c	Size, 603 × 700 [14] (No. 10), cut spears; wt., 60¼ oz. (3 lb. 12¼ oz.).	1 can	1,708	92.5	359	41.0	6.8	58.1	325	905	32.5	[21] 4,031	2,835	13,660	1.02	1.71	13.7	256
d	Spears, ½-in. diam. at base	4 spears	80	92.5	17	1.9	.3	2.7	15	42	1.5	[21] 189	133	640	.05	.08	.6	12
e	Spears, ⅜-in. diam. at base	4 spears	60	92.5	13	1.4	.2	2.0	11	32	1.1	[21] 142	100	480	.04	.06	.5	9
	Cup:																	
f	Whole spears	1 cup	242	92.5	51	5.8	1.0	8.2	46	128	4.6	[21] 571	402	1,940	.15	.24	1.9	36
g	Cut spears	1 cup	235	92.5	49	5.6	.9	8.0	45	125	4.5	[21] 555	390	1,880	.14	.24	1.9	35
h	Pound, whole or cut spears	1 lb	454	92.5	95	10.9	1.8	15.4	86	240	8.6	[21] 1,070	753	3,630	.27	.45	3.6	68
50	Drained liquid:																	
a	Pound	1 lb	454	95.6	50	3.6	Trace	10.9	68	109	6.4	[21] 1,070	753	Trace	.27	.32	3.6	68
b	Ounce	1 oz	28	95.6	3	.2	Trace	.7	4	7	.4	[21] 67	47	Trace	.02	.02	.2	4
	Special dietary pack (low sodium):																	
51	Solids and liquid (cut spears):																	
	Can and approx. contents:																	
a	Size, 300 × 407 [14] (No. 300); net wt., 14½ oz.	1 can	411	94.7	66	8.2	.8	11.1	74	177	7.0	12	682	2,100	.25	.37	3.3	62
b	Size, 603 × 700 [14] (No. 10); net wt., 103 oz. (6 lb. 7 oz.).	1 can	2,920	94.7	467	58.4	5.8	78.8	526	1,256	49.6	88	4.847	14,890	1.75	2.63	23.4	438
c	Cup	1 cup	239	94.7	38	4.8	.5	6.5	43	103	4.1	7	397	1.220	.14	.22	1.9	36
d	Pound	1 lb	454	94.7	73	9.1	.9	12.2	82	195	7.7	14	753	2,310	.27	.41	3.6	68
52	Drained solids (cut spears):																	
	Can and approx. drained contents:																	
a	Size, 300 × 407 [14] (No. 300); wt., 8½ oz.	1 can	241	93.6	48	6.3	.7	7.5	46	128	4.6	7	400	1,930	.14	.24	1.9	36
b	Size, 603 × 700 [14] (No. 10); wt., 60¼ oz. (3 lb. 12¼ oz.).	1 can	1,708	93.6	342	44.4	5.1	52.9	325	905	32.5	51	2,835	13,660	1.02	1.71	13.7	256
c	Cup	1 cup	235	93.6	47	6.1	.7	7.3	45	125	4.5	7	390	1,880	.14	.24	1.9	35
d	Pound	1 lb	454	93.6	91	11.8	1.4	14.1	86	240	8.6	14	753	3,630	.27	.45	3.6	68
53	Drained liquid:																	
a	Pound	1 lb	454	96.4	41	3.6	Trace	9.1	68	109	6.4	14	753	Trace	.27	.32	3.6	68
b	Ounce	1 oz	28	96.4	3	.2	Trace	.6	4	7	.4	1	47	Trace	.02	.02	.2	4
	White (bleached):																	
	Regular pack:																	
54	Solids and liquid:																	
	Can and approx. contents:																	
a	Size, 211 × 400 [14] (No. 1 Picnic), whole or cut spears; net wt., 10½ oz.	1 can	298	93.3	54	4.8	.9	9.8	45	98	2.7	[21] 703	417	150	.15	.18	2.1	45
b	Size, 300 × 407 [14] (No. 300), whole or cut spears; net wt., 14½ oz.	1 can	411	93.3	74	6.6	1.2	13.6	62	136	3.7	[21] 970	575	210	.21	.25	2.9	62
c	Size, 603 × 700 [14] (No. 10), cut spears; net wt., 103 oz. (6 lb. 7 oz.).	1 can	2,920	93.3	526	46.7	8.8	96.4	438	964	26.3	[21] 6,891	4,088	1,460	1.46	1.75	20.4	438
	Cup:																	
d	Whole spears with liquid	1 cup	244	93.3	44	3.9	.7	8.1	37	81	2.2	[21] 576	342	120	.12	.15	1.7	37
e	Cut spears with liquid	1 cup	239	93.3	43	3.8	.7	7.9	36	79	2.2	[21] 564	335	120	.12	.14	1.7	36
f	Pound, whole or cut spears with liquid	1 lb	454	93.3	82	7.3	1.4	15.0	68	150	4.1	[21] 1,070	635	230	.23	.27	3.2	68

[1] Measure and weight apply to food as it is described with inedible part or parts (refuse) included.

[9] For information on proportion of fruit, sugar, and water used, see ARS 62-13 (7), section on Fruits, Dried and Dehydrated, p. 7, and table 20, p. 24.

[10] Separated pieces when stuck together.

[14] Dimensions of can: 1st dimension represents diameter; 2d dimension, height of can. 1st or left-hand digit in each dimension gives number of whole inches; next 2 digits give additional fraction of dimension expressed as 16th of an inch.

[16] Applies to product without added ascorbic acid. For value of product with added ascorbic acid, refer to label.

[17] Based on average value of 28 mg. per 100 g. weighted in accordance with commercial freezing practices. For products without added ascorbic acid, average is about 41 mg. per pound; for those with added ascorbic acid, about 295 mg. See also Appendix C, section on Frozen Fruits and Vegetables

[18] Value for item 45a may range from 12 Cal., when prepared from freshly harvested artichokes, to 67 Cal., when prepared from stored artichokes; value for item 45b, 10–53 Cal.; value for item 45c, 8–44 Cal.

[19] If prepared from freshly harvested sample, large proportion of carbohydrate may be inulin, which is of doubtful availability. If prepared from stored sample, inulin may have been converted to available sugars.

[20] Value is for unsalted product. If salt is used, increase value by 236 mg. per 100 g. of vegetable—an estimated figure based on typical amount of salt (0.6%) in canned vegetables. See also Appendix C, section on Cooked Vegetables

[21] Estimated value based on addition of salt in amount of 0.6% of finished product.

TABLE 1.—*Nutritive values for household measures and market units of foods*—Continued

[Item numbers correspond to those in table 1 of Handbook No. 8, revised 1963. Values in parentheses denote imputed values usually from another form of the food or from a similar food. Zeros in parentheses indicate that amount of a constituent, if present, is probably too small to be measured. Dashes (—) denote lack of reliable data for a constituent believed to be present in a measurable amount. Calculated values, as those based on a recipe, are not in parentheses]

Item No.	Food, approximate measures, units, and weight (edible part unless footnotes indicate otherwise)			Water	Food energy	Protein	Fat	Carbohydrate	Calcium	Phosphorus	Iron	Sodium	Potassium	Vitamin A value	Thiamin	Riboflavin	Niacin	Ascorbic acid
				Values for edible part of foods														
(A)	(B)			(C)	(D)	(E)	(F)	(G)	(H)	(I)	(J)	(K)	(L)	(M)	(N)	(O)	(P)	(Q)
			Grams	Percent	Calories	Grams	Grams	Grams	Milli-grams	Milli-grams	Milli-grams	Milli-grams	Milli-grams	International units	Milli-grams	Milli-grams	Milli-grams	Milli-grams
	Asparagus—Continued																	
	Canned spears—Continued																	
	White (bleached)—Continued																	
	Regular pack—Continued																	
55	Drained solids:																	
	Can and approx. drained contents:																	
a	Size, 211 × 400 [14] (No. 1 Picnic), whole spears; wt., 7 oz.	1 can	198	92.3	44	4.2	1.0	7.1	32	81	2.0	[21] 467	277	160	0.10	0.12	1.4	30
b	Size, 300 × 407 [14] (No. 300), whole spears; wt., 9½ oz.	1 can	269	92.3	59	5.6	1.3	9.7	43	110	2.7	[21] 635	377	220	.13	.16	1.9	40
c	Size, 603 × 700 [14] (No. 10), cut spears; wt., 64½ oz. (4 lb. ½ oz.).	1 can	1,829	92.3	402	38.4	9.1	65.8	293	750	18.3	[21] 4,316	2,561	1,460	.91	1.10	12.8	274
d	Spears, ½-in. diam. at base	4 spears	80	92.3	18	1.7	.4	2.9	13	33	.8	[21] 189	112	60	.04	.05	.6	12
e	Spears, ⅜-in. diam. at base	4 spears	60	92.3	13	1.3	.3	2.2	10	25	.6	[21] 142	84	50	.03	.04	.4	9
	Cup:																	
f	Whole spears	1 cup	242	92.3	53	5.1	1.2	8.7	39	99	2.4	[21] 571	339	190	.12	.15	1.7	36
g	Cut spears	1 cup	235	92.3	52	4.9	1.2	8.5	38	96	2.4	[21] 555	329	190	.12	.14	1.6	35
h	Pound, whole or cut spears	1 lb	454	92.3	100	9.5	2.3	16.3	73	186	4.5	[21] 1,070	635	360	.23	.27	3.2	68
56	Drained liquid:																	
a	Pound	1 lb	454	95.4	50	3.2	Trace	11.3	59	82	3.2	[21] 1,070	635	Trace	.23	.18	3.2	68
b	Ounce	1 oz	28	95.4	3	.2	Trace	.7	4	5	.2	[21] 67	40	Trace	.01	.01	.2	4
	Special dietary pack (low sodium):																	
57	Solids and liquid (cut spears):																	
	Can and approx. contents:																	
a	Size, 300 × 407 [14] (No. 300); net wt., 14½ oz.	1 can	411	95.0	66	5.8	.8	12.3	62	136	3.7	16	575	210	.21	.25	2.9	62
b	Size, 603 × 700 [14] (No. 10); net wt., 103 oz. (6 lb. 7 oz.).	1 can	2,920	95.0	467	40.9	5.8	87.6	438	964	26.3	117	4,088	1,460	1.46	1.75	20.4	438
c	Cup	1 cup	239	95.0	38	3.3	.5	7.2	36	79	2.2	10	335	120	.12	.14	1.7	36
d	Pound	1 lb	454	95.0	73	6.4	.9	13.6	68	150	4.1	18	635	230	.23	.27	3.2	68
58	Drained solids (cut spears):																	
	Can and approx. drained contents:																	
a	Size, 300 × 407 [14] (No. 300); wt., 9 oz	1 can	255	94.0	48	4.8	.5	8.9	41	105	2.6	10	357	200	.13	.15	1.8	38
b	Size, 603 × 700 [14] (No. 10); wt., 64½ oz. (4 lb. ½ oz.).	1 can	1,829	94.0	348	34.8	3.7	64.0	293	750	18.3	73	2,561	1,460	.91	1.10	12.8	274
c	Cup	1 cup	235	94.0	45	4.5	.5	8.2	38	96	2.4	9	329	190	.12	.14	1.6	35
d	Pound	1 lb	454	94.0	86	8.6	.9	15.9	73	186	4.5	18	635	360	.23	.27	3.2	68
59	Drained liquid:																	
a	Pound	1 lb	454	97.2	36	2.7	Trace	8.2	59	82	3.2	18	635	Trace	.23	.18	3.2	68
b	Ounce	1 oz	28	97.2	2	.2	Trace	.5	4	5	.2	1	40	Trace	.01	.01	.2	4
	Frozen (green):																	
	Cuts and tips:																	
60	Not thawed:																	
a	Container, net wt., 10 oz	1 container	284	92.3	65	9.4	.6	10.2	65	187	3.7	6	679	2,410	.45	.40	3.4	71
b	Pound	1 lb	454	92.3	104	15.0	.9	16.3	104	299	5.9	9	1,084	3,860	.73	.64	5.4	113
61	Cooked (boiled), drained:																	
a	Cup	1 cup	180	92.5	40	5.8	.4	6.3	40	115	2.2	[20] 2	396	1,530	.25	.23	1.8	41
b	Pound	1 lb	454	92.5	100	14.5	.9	15.9	100	290	5.4	[20] 5	998	3,860	.64	.59	4.5	104
	Spears:																	
62	Not thawed:																	
a	Container, net wt., 10 oz	1 container	284	92.0	68	9.4	.6	11.1	65	196	3.4	6	736	2,220	.51	.43	3.7	82
b	Pound	1 lb	454	92.0	109	15.0	.9	17.7	104	313	5.4	9	1,175	3,540	.82	.68	5.9	132
63	Cooked (boiled), drained:																	
	Spears:																	
a	Large, ¾-in. diam. at base	4 spears	80	92.2	18	2.6	.2	3.0	18	54	.9	[20] 1	190	620	.13	.11	.9	21
b	Medium, ½-in. diam. at base	4 spears	60	92.2	14	1.9	.1	2.3	13	40	.7	[20] 1	143	470	.10	.08	.7	16
c	Small, ⅜-in. diam. or less at base	4 spears	40	92.2	9	1.3	.1	1.5	9	27	.4	[20] Trace	95	310	.06	.06	.4	10
d	Cup	1 cup	190	92.2	44	6.1	.4	7.2	42	127	2.1	[20] 2	452	1,480	.30	.27	2.1	49
e	Pound	1 lb	454	92.2	104	14.5	.9	17.2	100	304	5.0	[20] 5	1,080	3,540	.73	.64	5.0	118
	Avocados, raw:																	

(A)	(B)		(C)	(D)	(E)	(F)	(G)	(H)	(I)	(J)	(K)	(L)	(M)	(N)	(O)	(P)	(Q)
64	All commercial varieties: [22]																
a	Whole fruit (refuse: seed and skin, 25%); [1] wt., 10¾ oz.	1 avocado	302	74.0	378	4.8	37.1	14.3	23	95	1.4	9	1,368	660	0.25	0.45	8.6	82
b	Halved fruit served with skin (refuse: skin, 10%). [1]	½ avocado	125	74.0	188	2.4	18.5	7.1	11	47	.7	5	680	330	.12	.23	1.8	16
c	Cubes (½ in.)	1 cup	150	74.0	251	3.2	24.6	9.5	15	63	.9	6	906	440	.17	.30	2.4	21
d	Puree (mashed or sieved)	1 cup	230	74.0	384	4.8	37.7	14.5	23	97	1.4	9	1,389	670	.25	.46	3.7	32
65	California, mainly Fuerte (marketed in midwinter and late winter):																
a	Whole fruit (refuse: seed and skin, 24%); [1] wt., 10 oz.; diam., 3⅛ in.	1 avocado	284	73.6	369	4.7	36.7	12.9	22	91	1.3	9	1,303	630	.24	.43	3.5	30
b	Halved fruit, 3⅛-in. diam., served with skin (refuse: skin, 10%). [1]	½ avocado	120	73.6	185	2.4	18.4	6.5	11	45	.6	4	652	310	.12	.22	1.7	15
c	Cubes (½ in.)	1 cup	150	73.6	257	3.3	25.5	9.0	15	63	.9	6	906	440	.17	.30	2.4	21
d	Puree (mashed or sieved)	1 cup	230	73.6	393	5.1	39.1	13.8	23	97	1.4	9	1,389	670	.25	.46	3.7	32
66	Florida (marketed in late summer and fall):																
a	Whole fruit (refuse: seed and skin, 33%); [1] wt., 16 oz.; diam., 3⅝ in.	1 avocado or 1 lb.	454	78.0	389	4.0	33.4	26.7	30	128	1.8	12	1,836	880	.33	.61	4.9	43
b	Halved fruit, 3⅝-in. diam., served with skin (refuse: skin, 15%). [1]	½ avocado	180	78.0	196	2.0	16.8	13.5	15	64	.9	6	924	440	.17	.31	2.4	21
c	Cubes (½ in.)	1 cup	150	78.0	192	2.0	16.5	13.2	15	63	.9	6	906	440	.17	.30	2.4	21
d	Puree (mashed or sieved)	1 cup	230	78.0	294	3.0	25.3	20.2	23	97	1.4	9	1,389	670	.25	.46	3.7	32
	Baby foods: [23]																
	Cereals, precooked, dry, [5] [24] and other cereal products:																
67	Barley, added nutrients:																
a	Tablespoon	1 tbsp	2.2	6.8	8	.2	.1	1.7	[25] 20	18	2.1		8	[27] (0)	.05	.05	[28] .5	(0)
b	Ounce (approx. 13 tbsp.)	1 oz	28	6.8	102	3.1	.7	21.5	[25] 264	234	26.9		109	[27] (0)	.70	.60	[28] 6.3	(0)
68	High protein, added nutrients:																
a	Tablespoon	1 tbsp	2.5	6.6	9	.9	.1	1.2	21	22	[29] 2.0		32	[27] (0)	.06	.05	[28] .4	(0)
b	Ounce (approx. 11 tbsp.)	1 oz	28	6.6	101	9.9	1.3	13.2	239	247	[29] 22.7		357	[27] (0)	.67	.61	[28] 4.5	(0)
69	Mixed, added nutrients:																
a	Tablespoon	1 tbsp	2.6	6.9	10	.3	.1	1.8	[25] 25	20	[29] 2.1		8	[27] (0)	.07	.06	[28] .5	(0)
b	Ounce (approx. 11 tbsp.)	1 oz	28	6.9	105	3.7	1.1	20.2	[25] 277	221	[29] 22.7		88	[27] (0)	.73	.70	[28] 5.8	(0)
70	Oatmeal, added nutrients:																
a	Tablespoon	1 tbsp	2.2	6.8	8	.3	.2	1.5	[25] 18	17	[29] 1.8		8	[27] (0)	.06	.05	[28] .5	(0)
b	Ounce (approx. 13 tbsp.)	1 oz	28	6.8	109	4.0	2.0	19.1	[25] 233	218	[29] 22.7		105	[27] (0)	.73	.70	[28] 5.8	(0)
71	Rice, added nutrients:																
a	Tablespoon	1 tbsp	2.7	7.3	10	.2	.1	2.1	[25] 24	18	[29] 2.2		5	[27] (0)	.07	.07	[28] .6	(0)
b	Ounce (approx. 11 tbsp.)	1 oz	28	7.3	108	2.0	1.3	21.7	[25] 252	194	[29] 22.7		58	[27] (0)	.73	.70	[28] 5.8	(0)
72	Teething biscuit (approx. 3⅛ in. long × 1⅛ in. wide).	1 biscuit	12	5.6	45	1.3	.3	9.4	39	42	.6	[26]	30	—	.06	.07	.4	(0)
	Wheat. See also Farina, instant-cooking (items 995–996).																
	Desserts, canned:																
73	Custard pudding, all flavors:																
	Jar and approx. contents:																
a	Junior food, net wt., 7¾ oz	1 jar	220	76.5	220	5.1	4.0	40.9	141	136	.7		207	220	.04	.26	.2	2
b	Strained food, net wt., 4½ oz	1 jar	128	76.5	128	2.9	2.3	23.8	82	79	.4		120	130	.03	.15	.1	1
c	Ounce (approx. 1¾–2 tbsp.)	1 oz	28	76.5	28	.7	.5	5.3	18	18	.1		27	30	.01	.03	Trace	Trace
74	Fruit pudding with starch base, milk and/or egg (banana, orange, or pineapple):																
	Jar and approx. contents:																
a	Junior food, net wt., 7¾ oz	1 jar	220	75.7	211	2.6	2.0	47.5	59	75	.7		165	220	.07	.11	.2	7
b	Strained food, net wt., 4¾ oz	1 jar	135	75.7	130	1.6	1.2	29.2	36	46	.4		101	140	.04	.07	.1	4
c	Ounce (approx. 1¾–2 tbsp.)	1 oz	28	75.7	27	.3	.3	6.1	8	10	.1		21	30	.01	.01	Trace	1
	Dinners, canned:																
	Cereal, vegetable, meat mixtures (approx. 2–4% protein):																

[1] Measure and weight apply to food as it is described with inedible part or parts (refuse) included.

[5] Most of phosphorus in nuts, legumes, and outer layers of cereal grains is present as phytic acid. See also Appendix D, section on Minerals and Oxalic Acid

[14] Dimensions of can: 1st dimension represents diameter; 2d dimension, height of can. 1st or left-hand digit in each dimension gives number of whole inches; next 2 digits give additional fraction of dimension expressed as 16th of an inch.

[20] Value is for unsalted product. If salt is used, increase value by 236 mg. per 100 g. of vegetable—an estimated figure based on typical amount of salt (0.6%) in canned vegetables. See also Appendix C, section on Cooked Vegetables

[21] Estimated value based on addition of salt in amount of 0.6% of finished product.

[22] Values for nutrients, percent refuse, and weight of fruit are weighted according to production, estimated as 90% from California, 10% from Florida.

[23] Common-size jar listed for strained and junior foods is applicable to items in this group. Nutritive values for other sizes of jars may be calculated from values given for 1 oz.

[24] Nutritive values based on revised values per 100 g. of cereal. See also Appendix A, section on Baby Foods, p. 262, and table 3, p. 264.

[25] Value varies widely with brand. Amount in 1 tbsp. ranges from 15 to 26 mg. for item 67, 14–42 mg. for item 69, 13–24 mg. for item 70, 18–32 mg. for item 71. Values for 1 oz. range from 187 to 340 mg. for items 67 and 71, 150–454 mg. for item 69, 162–312 mg. for item 70.

[26] For further information, see Appendix A, section on Baby Foods, p. 262.

[27] For 1 brand with added vitamin A, value for 1 tbsp. is 5 I.U. for items 67, 70, and 71; 10 I.U. for items 68 and 69. Value for 1 oz. is 60 I.U. for items 67, 70, and 71; 110 I.U. for item 68; 90 I.U. for item 69.

[28] Value varies widely with brand. Amount in 1 tbsp. ranges from 0.3 to 0.7 mg. for items 67 and 70; 0.1–0.8 mg. for item 68, 0.4–0.8 mg. for items 69 and 71. Values for 1 oz. range from 4 to 9 mg. for items 67 and 69–71 and from 1 to 9 mg. for item 68.

[29] Value varies widely with brand. Amount in 1 tbsp. ranges from 1.3 to 2.5 mg. for item 68, 1.3–2.6 mg. for item 69, 1.1–2.2 mg. for item 70, 1.4–2.7 mg. for item 71. Values for 1 oz. range from 14 to 28 mg.

TABLE 1.—*Nutritive values for household measures and market units of foods*—Continued

[Item numbers correspond to those in table 1 of Handbook No. 8, revised 1963. Values in parentheses denote imputed values usually from another form of the food or from a similar food. Zeros in parentheses indicate that amount of a constituent, if present, is probably too small to be measured. Dashes (—) denote lack of reliable data for a constituent believed to be present in a measurable amount. Calculated values, as those based on a recipe, are not in parentheses]

Item No. (A)	Food, approximate measures, units, and weight (edible part unless footnotes indicate otherwise) (B)			Water (C)	Food energy (D)	Protein (E)	Fat (F)	Carbohydrate (G)	Calcium (H)	Phosphorus (I)	Iron (J)	Sodium (K)	Potassium (L)	Vitamin A value (M)	Thiamin (N)	Riboflavin (O)	Niacin (P)	Ascorbic acid (Q)
			Grams	Percent	Calories	Grams	Grams	Grams	Milligrams	Milligrams	Milligrams	Milligrams	Milligrams	International units	Milligrams	Milligrams	Milligrams	Milligrams
	Baby foods [21]—Continued																	
	Dinners, canned—Continued																	
	Cereal, vegetable, meat mixtures (approx. 2–4% protein)—Continued																	
75	Beef noodle dinner:																	
	Jar and approx. contents:																	
a	Junior food, net wt., 7½ oz	1 jar	213	88.2	102	6.0	2.3	14.5	26	62	1.1		339	1,320	0.04	0.11	1.1	4
b	Strained food, net wt., 4½ oz	1 jar	128	88.2	61	3.6	1.4	8.7	15	37	.6		204	790	.03	.06	.6	3
c	Ounce (approx. 1¾–2 tbsp.)	1 oz	28	88.2	14	.8	.3	1.9	3	8	.1		45	180	.01	.01	.1	1
76	Cereal, egg yolk, bacon: [5]																	
	Jar and approx. contents:																	
a	Junior food, net wt., 7½ oz	1 jar	213	84.7	175	6.2	10.4	14.1	62	128	1.7		77	1,110	.11	.13	.9	—
b	Strained food, net wt., 4½ oz	1 jar	128	84.7	105	3.7	6.3	8.4	37	77	1.0		46	670	.06	.08	.5	—
c	Ounce (approx. 1¾–2 tbsp.)	1 oz	28	84.7	23	.8	1.4	1.9	8	17	.2		10	150	.01	.02	.1	—
77	Chicken noodle dinner:																	
	Jar and approx. contents:																	
a	Junior food, net wt., 7½ oz	1 jar	213	88.5	104	4.5	2.8	15.3	58	64	.6		89	1,700	.06	.13	.9	2
b	Strained food, net wt., 4½ oz	1 jar	128	88.5	63	2.7	1.7	9.2	35	38	.4		54	1,020	.04	.08	.5	1
c	Ounce (approx. 1¾–2 tbsp.)	1 oz	28	88.5	14	.6	.4	2.0	8	9	.1		12	230	.01	.02	.1	Trace
78	Macaroni, tomatoes, meat, cereal: [5]																	
	Jar and approx. contents:																	
a	Junior food, net wt., 7½ oz	1 jar	213	84.5	143	5.5	4.3	20.4	45	75	1.1		164	1,070	.30	.26	2.1	2
b	Strained food, net wt., 4½ oz	1 jar	128	84.5	86	3.3	2.6	12.3	27	45	.6		99	640	.18	.15	1.3	1
c	Ounce (approx. 1¾–2 tbsp.)	1 oz	28	84.5	19	.7	.6	2.7	6	10	.1		22	140	.04	.03	.3	Trace
79	Split peas, vegetables, and ham or bacon:																	
	Jar and approx. contents:																	
a	Junior food, net wt., 7½ oz	1 jar	213	81.5	170	8.5	4.5	23.9	62	168	1.5		239	1,280	.17	.11	1.1	2
b	Strained food, net wt., 4½ oz	1 jar	128	81.5	102	5.1	2.7	14.3	37	101	.9		143	770	.10	.06	.6	1
c	Ounce (approx. 1¾–2 tbsp.)	1 oz	28	81.5	23	1.1	.6	3.2	8	22	.2		32	170	.02	.01	.1	Trace
80	Vegetables, bacon, cereal: [5]																	
	Jar and approx. contents:																	
a	Junior food, net wt., 7½ oz	1 jar	213	85.7	145	3.6	6.2	18.5	36	60	1.3		277	4,690	.15	.11	1.3	2
b	Strained food, net wt., 4½ oz	1 jar	128	85.7	87	2.2	3.7	11.1	22	36	.8		166	2,820	.09	.06	.8	1
c	Ounce (approx. 1¾–2 tbsp.)	1 oz	28	85.7	19	.5	.8	2.5	5	8	.2		37	620	.02	.01	.2	Trace
81	Vegetables, beef, cereal: [5]																	
	Jar and approx. contents:																	
a	Junior food, net wt., 7½ oz	1 jar	213	87.0	119	5.8	3.4	16.2	36	83	1.7		305	5,960	.06	.09	1.9	2
b	Strained food, net wt., 4½ oz	1 jar	128	87.0	72	3.5	2.0	9.7	22	50	1.0		183	3,580	.04	.05	1.2	1
c	Ounce (approx. 1¾–2 tbsp.)	1 oz	28	87.0	16	.8	.5	2.2	5	11	.2		41	790	.01	.01	.3	Trace
82	Vegetables, chicken, cereal: [5]																	
	Jar and approx. contents:																	
a	Junior food, net wt., 7½ oz	1 jar	213	87.8	111	4.5	3.0	16.4	70	70	.9		117	2,130	.06	.09	1.1	Trace
b	Strained food, net wt., 4½ oz	1 jar	128	87.8	67	2.7	1.8	9.9	42	42	.5		70	1,280	.04	.05	.6	Trace
c	Ounce (approx. 1¾–2 tbsp.)	1 oz	28	87.8	15	.6	.4	2.2	9	9	.1		16	280	.01	.01	.1	Trace
83	Vegetables, ham, cereal: [5]																	
	Jar and approx. contents:																	
a	Junior food, net wt., 7½ oz	1 jar	213	85.6	136	6.0	4.7	17.7	53	89	.6		192	2,130	.17	.11	1.1	6
b	Strained food, net wt., 4½ oz	1 jar	128	85.6	82	3.6	2.8	10.6	32	54	.4		115	1,280	.10	.06	.6	4
c	Ounce (approx. 1¾–2 tbsp.)	1 oz	28	85.6	18	.8	.6	2.4	7	12	.1		26	280	.02	.01	.1	1
84	Vegetables, lamb, cereal: [5]																	
	Jar and approx. contents:																	
a	Junior food, net wt., 7½ oz	1 jar	213	87.0	124	4.7	4.3	16.4	49	79	1.5		315	4,690	.06	.11	1.5	2
b	Strained food, net wt., 4½ oz	1 jar	128	87.0	74	2.8	2.6	9.9	29	47	.9		189	2,820	.04	.06	.9	1
c	Ounce (approx. 1¾–2 tbsp.)	1 oz	28	87.0	16	.6	.6	2.2	7	10	.2		42	620	.01	.01	.2	Trace
85	Vegetables, liver, cereal: [5]																	
	Jar and approx. contents:																	
a	Junior food, net wt., 7½ oz	1 jar	213	87.8	100	6.6	.9	16.6	36	121	5.8		345	10,010	.09	.79	3.4	6
b	Strained food, net wt., 4½ oz	1 jar	128	87.8	60	4.0	.5	10.0	22	73	3.5		207	6,020	.05	.47	2.0	4
c	Ounce (approx. 1¾–2 tbsp.)	1 oz	28	87.8	13	.9	.1	2.2	5	16	.8		46	1,330	.01	.10	.5	1
86	Vegetables, liver, bacon, cereal: [5]																	

(A)	(B)			(C)	(D)	(E)	(F)	(G)	(H)	(I)	(J)	(K)	(L)	(M)	(N)	(O)	(P)	(Q)
	Jar and approx. contents:																	
a	Junior food, net wt., 7½ oz	1 jar	213	87.2	121	5.1	4.0	16.0	23	89	5.5		279	9,800	0.06	0.70	2.8	4
b	Strained food, net wt., 4½ oz	1 jar	128	87.2	73	3.1	2.4	9.6	14	54	3.3		168	5,890	.04	.42	1.7	3
c	Ounce (approx. 1¾–2 tbsp.)	1 oz	28	87.2	16	.7	.5	2.1	3	12	.7		37	1,300	.01	.09	.4	1
87	Vegetables, turkey, cereal:[5]																	
	Jar and approx. contents:																	
a	Junior food, net wt., 7½ oz	1 jar	213	88.9	94	4.5	1.7	15.3	47	55	.6		98	850	.02	.06	.9	2
b	Strained food, net wt., 4½ oz	1 jar	128	88.9	56	2.7	1.0	9.2	28	33	.4		59	510	.01	.04	.5	1
c	Ounce (approx. 1¾–2 tbsp.)	1 oz	28	88.9	12	.6	.2	2.0	6	7	.1		13	110	Trace	.01	.1	Trace
	Meat or poultry (approx. 6–8% protein), strained and junior:											[29]						
88	Beef with vegetables:																	
a	Jar, net wt., 4½ oz	1 jar	128	81.6	111	9.5	4.7	7.7	17	108	1.5		145	1,410	.09	.22	2.0	3
b	Ounce (approx. 1¾–2 tbsp.)	1 oz	28	81.6	25	2.1	1.0	1.7	4	24	.3		32	310	.02	.05	.5	1
89	Chicken with vegetables:																	
a	Jar, net wt., 4½ oz	1 jar	128	79.6	128	9.5	5.9	9.2	28	109	1.2		91	1,280	.12	.19	2.0	3
b	Ounce (approx. 1¾–2 tbsp.)	1 oz	28	79.6	28	2.1	1.3	2.0	6	24	.3		20	280	.03	.04	.5	1
90	Turkey with vegetables:																	
a	Jar, net wt., 4½ oz	1 jar	128	81.3	110	8.6	4.1	9.7	49	81	.8		156	1,280	.17	.17	2.3	3
b	Ounce (approx. 1¾–2 tbsp.)	1 oz	28	81.3	24	1.9	.9	2.2	11	18	.2		35	280	.04	.04	.5	1
91	Veal with vegetables:																	
a	Jar, net wt., 4½ oz	1 jar	128	85.0	81	9.1	2.0	6.5	14	91	1.0		122	1,020	.10	.19	2.6	3
b	Ounce (approx. 1¾–2 tbsp.)	1 oz	28	85.0	18	2.0	.5	1.4	3	20	.2		27	230	.02	.04	.6	1
	Fruits and fruit products (with or without thickening), canned:																	
92	Applesauce:																	
	Jar and approx. contents:																	
a	Junior food, net wt., 7¾ oz	1 jar	220	80.8	158	.4	.4	40.9	9	15	.9	13	141	90	.02	.04	.2	Trace
b	Strained food, net wt., 4¾ oz	1 jar	135	80.8	97	.3	.3	25.1	5	9	.5	8	86	50	.01	.03	.1	Trace
c	Ounce (approx. 1¾–2 tbsp.)	1 oz	28	80.8	20	.1	.1	5.3	1	2	.1	2	18	10	Trace	.01	Trace	Trace
93	Applesauce and apricots:																	
	Jar and approx. contents:																	
a	Junior food, net wt., 7¾ oz	1 jar	220	76.7	189	.7	.2	49.7	9	31	.7	([30])	231	1,320	.02	.04	.2	4
b	Strained food, net wt., 4¾ oz	1 jar	135	76.7	116	.4	.1	30.5	5	19	.4	([30])	142	810	.01	.03	.1	3
c	Ounce (approx. 1¾–2 tbsp.)	1 oz	28	76.7	24	.1	Trace	6.4	1	4	.1	([30])	30	170	Trace	.01	Trace	1
94	Bananas (with tapioca or cornstarch, added ascorbic acid), strained:																	
a	Jar, net wt., 4¾ oz	1 jar	135	77.5	113	.5	.3	29.2	18	14	.3	([30])	159	90	.03	.03	.3	47
b	Ounce (approx. 1¾–2 tbsp.)	1 oz	28	77.5	24	.1	.1	6.1	4	3	.1	([30])	33	20	.01	.01	.1	10
95	Bananas and pineapple (with tapioca or cornstarch):																	
	Jar and approx. contents:																	
a	Junior food, net wt., 7¾ oz	1 jar	220	78.5	176	.9	.2	45.5	44	26	.4	130	158	70	.02	.02	.2	4
b	Strained food, net wt., 4¾ oz	1 jar	135	78.5	108	.5	.1	27.9	27	16	.3	80	97	40	.01	.01	.1	3
c	Ounce (approx. 1¾–2 tbsp.)	1 oz	28	78.5	23	.1	Trace	5.9	6	3	.1	17	20	10	Trace	Trace	Trace	1
96	Fruit dessert with tapioca (apricot, pineapple, and/or orange):																	
	Jar and approx. contents:																	
a	Junior food, net wt., 7¾ oz	1 jar	220	77.6	185	.7	.7	47.3	33	20	.9	117	161	990	.04	.02	.4	9
b	Strained food, net wt., 4¾ oz	1 jar	135	77.6	113	.4	.4	29.0	20	12	.5	72	99	610	.03	.01	.3	5
c	Ounce (approx. 1¾–2 tbsp.)	1 oz	28	77.6	24	.1	.1	6.1	4	3	.1	15	21	130	.01	Trace	.1	1
97	Peaches:																	
	Jar and approx. contents:																	
a	Junior food, net wt., 7¾ oz	1 jar	220	78.1	178	1.3	.4	45.5	13	31	.7	([30])	176	1,100	.02	.04	1.5	7
b	Strained food, net wt., 4¾ oz	1 jar	135	78.1	109	.8	.3	27.9	8	19	.4	([30])	108	680	.01	.03	.9	4
c	Ounce (approx. 1¾–2 tbsp.)	1 oz	28	78.1	23	.2	.1	5.9	2	4	.1	([30])	23	140	Trace	.01	.2	1
98	Pears:																	
	Jar and approx. contents:																	
a	Junior food, net wt., 7¾ oz	1 jar	220	82.2	145	.7	.2	37.6	15	18	.4	9	136	70	.04	.04	.4	4
b	Strained food, net wt., 4¾ oz	1 jar	135	82.2	89	.4	.1	23.1	9	11	.3	5	84	40	.03	.03	.3	3
c	Ounce (approx. 1¾–2 tbsp.)	1 oz	28	82.2	19	.1	Trace	4.8	2	2	.1	1	18	10	.01	.01	.1	1
99	Pears and pineapple:																	
	Jar and approx. contents:																	
a	Junior food, net wt., 7¾ oz	1 jar	220	81.5	152	.9	.4	38.7	15	26	.4	([30])	158	40	.07	.04	.4	4
b	Strained food, net wt., 4¾ oz	1 jar	135	81.5	93	.5	.3	23.8	9	16	.3	([30])	97	30	.04	.03	.3	3
c	Ounce (approx. 1¾–2 tbsp.)	1 oz	28	81.5	20	.1	.1	5.0	2	3	.1	([30])	20	10	.01	.01	.1	1
100	Plums with tapioca:																	
	Jar and approx. contents:																	
a	Junior food, net wt., 7¾ oz	1 jar	220	74.8	207	.9	.4	53.5	11	26	.9	84	97	550	.02	.04	.4	4
b	Strained food, net wt., 4¾ oz	1 jar	135	74.8	127	.5	.3	32.8	7	16	.5	51	59	340	.01	.03	.3	3
c	Ounce (approx. 1¾–2 tbsp.)	1 oz	28	74.8	27	.1	.1	6.9	1	3	.1	11	12	70	Trace	.01	.1	1

[5] Most of phosphorus in nuts, legumes, and outer layers of cereal grains is present as phytic acid. See also Appendix D, section on Minerals and Oxalic Acid

[28] Common-size jar listed for strained and junior foods is applicable to items in this group. Nutritive values for other sizes of jars may be calculated from values given for 1 oz.

[29] For further information, see Appendix A, section on Baby Foods, p. 262.

[30] Value varies widely with brand and processing procedures. For further information, see Appendix A, section on Baby Foods, p. 262.

TABLE 1.—*Nutritive values for household measures and market units of foods*—Continued

[Item numbers correspond to those in table 1 of Handbook No. 8, revised 1963. Values in parentheses denote imputed values usually from another form of the food or from a similar food. Zeros in parentheses indicate that amount of a constituent, if present, is probably too small to be measured. Dashes (—) denote lack of reliable data for a constituent believed to be present in a measurable amount. Calculated values, as those based on a recipe, are not in parentheses]

Item No. (A)		Food, approximate measures, units, and weight (edible part unless footnotes indicate otherwise) (B)			Water (C)	Food energy (D)	Protein (E)	Fat (F)	Carbohydrate (G)	Calcium (H)	Phosphorus (I)	Iron (J)	Sodium (K)	Potassium (L)	Vitamin A value (M)	Thiamin (N)	Riboflavin (O)	Niacin (P)	Ascorbic acid (Q)
				Grams	Percent	Calories	Grams	Grams	Grams	Milligrams	Milligrams	Milligrams	Milligrams	Milligrams	International units	Milligrams	Milligrams	Milligrams	Milligrams
		Baby foods [23]—Continued																	
		Fruits and fruit products (with or without thickening), canned—Continued																	
101		Prunes with tapioca:																	
		Jar and approx. contents:																	
	a	Junior food, net wt., 7¾ oz	1 jar	220	76.7	189	0.7	0.4	49.3	15	46	2.0	73	264	880	0.04	0.13	0.9	9
	b	Strained food, net wt., 4¾ oz	1 jar	135	76.7	116	.4	.3	30.2	9	28	1.2	45	162	540	.03	.08	.5	5
	c	Ounce (approx. 1¾–2 tbsp.)	1 oz	28	76.7	24	.1	.1	6.4	2	6	.3	9	34	110	.01	.02	.1	1
		Meat, poultry, eggs, canned:																	
		Beef:																	
102		Strained:																	
	a	Jar, net wt., 3½ oz	1 jar	100	80.3	99	14.7	4.0	(0)	8	127	2.0		183	—	.01	.16	3.5	0
	b	Ounce (approx. 1¾–2 tbsp.)	1 oz	28	80.3	28	4.2	1.1	(0)	2	36	.6		52	—	Trace	.05	1.0	0
103		Junior:																	
	a	Jar, net wt., 3½ oz	1 jar	100	75.6	118	19.3	3.9	(0)	8	163	2.5		242	—	.02	.20	4.3	0
	b	Ounce (approx. 1¾–2 tbsp.)	1 oz	28	75.6	33	5.5	1.1	(0)	2	46	.7		69	—	.01	.06	1.2	0
104		Beef heart (beef with beef heart), strained:																	
	a	Jar, net wt., 3½ oz	1 jar	100	81.1	93	13.5	3.8	.4	5	155	3.7		—	—	.06	.62	3.6	0
	b	Ounce (approx. 1¾–2 tbsp.)	1 oz	28	81.1	26	3.8	1.1	.1	1	44	1.0		—	—	.02	.18	1.0	0
105		Chicken, strained and junior:																	
	a	Jar, net wt., 3½ oz	1 jar	100	77.2	127	13.7	7.6	(0)	—	129	1.9		96	—	.02	.16	3.5	0
	b	Ounce (approx. 1¾–2 tbsp.)	1 oz	28	77.2	36	3.9	2.2	(0)	—	37	.5		27	—	.01	.05	1.0	0
106		Egg yolks, strained:																	
	a	Jar, net wt., 3½ oz	1 jar	94	70.0	197	9.4	17.3	.2	76	241	2.8		55	1,790	.11	.21	Trace	Trace
	b	Ounce (approx. 1¾–2 tbsp.)	1 oz	28	70.0	60	2.8	5.2	.1	23	73	.9		17	540	.03	.06	Trace	Trace
107		Egg yolks with ham or bacon, strained:																	
	a	Jar, net wt., 3⅓ oz	1 jar	94	70.3	196	9.4	17.0	.3	67	174	2.6		77	1,790	.09	.22	.5	—
	b	Ounce (approx. 1¾–2 tbsp.)	1 oz	28	70.3	59	2.8	5.1	.1	20	52	.8		23	540	.03	.07	.1	—
		Lamb:																	
108		Strained:																	
	a	Jar, net wt., 3½ oz	1 jar	100	79.3	107	14.6	4.9	(0)	9	124	2.1		181	—	.02	.17	3.3	—
	b	Ounce (approx. 1¾–2 tbsp.)	1 oz	28	79.3	30	4.1	1.4	(0)	3	35	.6		51	—	.01	.05	.9	—
109		Junior:																	
	a	Jar, net wt., 3½ oz	1 jar	100	76.0	121	17.5	5.1	(0)	13	156	2.7		228	—	.02	.21	4.1	—
	b	Ounce (approx. 1¾–2 tbsp.)	1 oz	28	76.0	34	5.0	1.4	(0)	4	44	.8		65	—	.01	.06	1.2	—
110		Liver, strained:																	
	a	Jar, net wt., 3½ oz	1 jar	100	79.7	97	14.1	3.4	1.5	6	182	5.6	[illegible]	202	24,000	.05	2.00	7.6	10
	b	Ounce (approx. 1¾–2 tbsp.)	1 oz	28	79.7	27	4.0	1.0	.4	2	52	1.6		57	6,800	.01	.57	2.2	3
111		Liver and bacon, strained	1 oz	28	77.0	35	3.9	1.9	.4	2	45	1.2		54	6,240	.01	.56	2.2	2
		Pork:																	
112		Strained:																	
	a	Jar, net wt., 3½ oz	1 jar	100	77.7	118	15.4	5.8	(0)	8	130	1.5		178	—	.19	.20	2.7	—
	b	Ounce (approx. 1¾–2 tbsp.)	1 oz	28	77.7	33	4.4	1.6	(0)	2	37	.4		50	—	.05	.06	.8	—
113		Junior:																	
	a	Jar, net wt., 3½ oz	1 jar	100	74.3	134	18.6	6.0	(0)	8	144	1.2		210	—	.23	.23	2.8	—
	b	Ounce (approx. 1¾–2 tbsp.)	1 oz	28	74.3	38	5.3	1.7	(0)	2	41	.3		60	—	.07	.07	.8	—
		Veal:																	
114		Strained:																	
	a	Jar, net wt., 3½ oz	1 jar	100	80.7	91	15.5	2.7	(0)	10	145	1.7		214	—	.03	.20	4.3	—
	b	Ounce (approx. 1¾–2 tbsp.)	1 oz	28	80.7	26	4.4	.8	(0)	3	41	.5		61	—	.01	.06	1.2	—
115		Junior:																	
	a	Jar, net wt., 3½ oz	1 jar	100	76.9	107	18.8	3.0	(0)	8	157	1.6		206	—	.03	.22	6.0	—
	b	Ounce (approx. 1¾–2 tbsp.)	1 oz	28	76.9	30	5.3	.9	(0)	2	45	.5		58	—	.01	.06	1.7	—
		Vegetables, canned:																	
116		Beans, green:																	
		Jar and approx. contents:																	
	a	Junior food, net wt., 7½ oz	1 jar	213	92.5	47	3.0	.2	10.9	70	53	2.3		198	850	.04	.13	.6	6
	b	Strained food, net wt., 4½ oz	1 jar	128	92.5	28	1.8	.1	6.5	42	32	1.4		119	510	.03	.08	.4	4
	c	Ounce (approx. 1¾–2 tbsp.)	1 oz	28	92.5	6	.4	Trace	1.4	9	7	.3		26	110	.01	.02	.1	1
117		Beets, strained:																	
	a	Jar, net wt., 4½ oz	1 jar	128	89.2	47	1.8	.1	10.6	23	35	.9		292	30	.03	.04	.1	4
	b	Ounce (approx. 1¾–2 tbsp.)	1 oz	28	89.2	10	.4	Trace	2.4	5	8	.2		65	10	.01	.01	Trace	1

(A)	(B)			(C)	(D)	(E)	(F)	(G)	(H)	(I)	(J)	(K)	(L)	(M)	(N)	(O)	(P)	(Q)
118	Carrots:																	
	Jar and approx. contents:																	
a	Junior food, net wt., 7½ oz	1 jar	213	91.5	62	1.5	0.2	14.5	49	45	1.1		386	27,690	0.04	0.06	0.9	6
b	Strained food, net wt., 4½ oz	1 jar	128	91.5	37	.9	.1	8.7	29	27	.6		232	16,640	.03	.04	.5	4
c	Ounce (approx. 1¾–2 tbsp.)	1 oz	28	91.5	8	.2	Trace	1.9	7	6	.1		51	3,690	.01	.01	.1	1
119	Mixed vegetables, including vegetable soup:																	
	Jar and approx. contents:																	
a	Junior food, net wt., 7½ oz	1 jar	213	88.5	79	3.4	.6	18.1	47	77	1.9		362	10,010	.11	.09	1.3	4
b	Strained food, net wt., 4½ oz	1 jar	128	88.5	47	2.0	.4	10.9	28	46	1.2		218	6,020	.06	.05	.8	3
c	Ounce (approx. 1¾–2 tbsp.)	1 oz	28	88.5	10	.5	.1	2.4	6	10	.3		48	1,330	.01	.01	.2	1
120	Peas, strained:[5]																	
a	Jar, net wt., 4½ oz	1 jar	128	85.5	69	5.4	.3	11.9	14	81	1.5		128	640	.10	.12	1.5	13
b	Ounce (approx. 1¾–2 tbsp.)	1 oz	28	85.5	15	1.2	.1	2.6	3	18	.3		28	140	.02	.03	.3	3
121	Spinach, creamed:																	
	Jar and approx. contents:																	
a	Junior food, net wt., 7½ oz	1 jar	213	88.1	92	4.9	1.5	16.0	136	134	1.3	[26]	302	10,650	.04	.28	.6	13
b	Strained food, net wt., 4½ oz	1 jar	128	88.1	55	2.9	.9	9.6	82	81	.8		182	6,400	.03	.17	.4	8
c	Ounce (approx. 1¾–2 tbsp.)	1 oz	28	88.1	12	.7	.2	2.1	18	18	.2		40	1,420	.01	.04	.1	2
122	Squash:																	
	Jar and approx. contents:																	
a	Junior food, net wt., 7½ oz	1 jar	213	92.1	53	1.5	.2	13.2	51	36	.9		294	5,110	.04	.09	.6	17
b	Strained food, net wt., 4½ oz	1 jar	128	92.1	32	.9	.1	7.9	31	22	.5		177	3,070	.03	.05	.4	10
c	Ounce (approx. 1¾–2 tbsp.)	1 oz	28	92.1	7	.2	Trace	1.8	7	5	.1		39	680	.01	.01	.1	2
123	Sweetpotatoes:																	
	Jar and approx. contents:																	
a	Junior food, net wt., 7¾ oz	1 jar	220	82.3	147	2.2	.4	34.1	35	75	.9		396	10,780	.09	.07	.9	18
b	Strained food, net wt., 4¾ oz	1 jar	135	82.3	90	1.4	.3	20.9	22	46	.5		243	6,620	.05	.04	.5	11
c	Ounce (approx. 1¾–2 tbsp.)	1 oz	28	82.3	19	.3	.1	4.4	5	10	.1		51	1,390	.01	.01	.1	2
124	Tomato soup, strained	1 oz	28	93.4	15	.5	Trace	3.8	7	15	.1		85	280	.01	.03	.2	1
	Bacon, cured:																	
125	Raw:																	
a	Slab (refuse: rind, 6%)[1]	1 lb	454	19.3	2,836	35.8	295.5	4.3	55	461	5.1	2,900	554	(0)	1.54	.47	7.7	—
b	Sliced	1 lb	454	19.3	3,016	38.1	314.3	4.5	59	490	5.4	3,084	590	(0)	1.63	.50	8.2	—
126	Cooked (broiled or fried), drained:																	
a	Slab, yield from 1 lb., raw (item 125a)	4.8 oz	136	8.1	807	35.8	70.7	4.3	19	305	4.5	1,389	321	(0)	.69	.46	7.1	—
	Sliced:																	
b	Yield from 1 lb., raw (item 125b)	5.1 oz	145	8.1	860	38.1	75.4	4.5	20	325	4.8	1,480	342	(0)	.74	.49	7.5	—
c	Slice, thick (approx. 12 slices per pound, raw)	2 slices	24	8.1	143	6.4	12.5	.8	3	54	.8	245	57	(0)	.12	.08	1.2	—
d	Slice, medium (approx. 20 slices per pound, raw).	2 slices	15	8.1	86	3.8	7.8	.5	2	34	.5	153	35	(0)	.08	.05	.8	—
e	Slice, thin (approx. 28 slices per pound, raw)	2 slices	10	8.1	61	2.7	5.2	.3	1	22	.3	102	24	(0)	.05	.03	.5	—
	Canned:																	
127	Can, net wt., 16 oz. (1 lb.); 17–18 slices	1 can or 1 lb	454	16.7	3,107	38.6	324.3	4.5	68	417	6.4	[21] (3,084)	[21] (590)	(0)	1.04	.45	6.8	—
	Bacon, Canadian style:																	
128	Unheated:																	
a	Package, net wt., 6 oz. (6 slices, 3⅜-in. diam., ³⁄₁₆ in. thick).	1 pkg	170	61.7	367	34.0	24.5	.5	20	306	5.1	3,215	666	(0)	1.41	.37	8.0	—
b	Pound	1 lb	454	61.7	980	90.7	65.3	1.4	54	816	13.6	8,578	1,778	(0)	3.76	1.00	21.3	—
129	Cooked (broiled or fried), drained:																	
a	Yield from 6 oz., raw (item 128a)	6 slices	126	49.9	349	34.0	22.1	.4	20	275	5.1	3,215	544	(0)	1.16	.21	6.3	—
b	Yield from 1 lb., raw (item 128b)	¾ lb. (approx.)	336	49.9	921	90.7	58.8	1.0	54	732	13.6	8,578	1,452	(0)	3.09	.57	16.8	—
c	Slice (dimensions of uncooked slice, 3⅜-in. diam., ³⁄₁₆ in. thick).	1 slice	21	49.9	58	5.7	3.7	.1	3	46	.9	537	91	(0)	.19	.04	1.1	—
d	Pound	1 lb	454	49.9	1,256	125.2	79.4	1.4	86	989	18.6	11,589	1,960	(0)	4.17	.77	22.7	—
	Baking powders for home use:[22,23]																	
	Sodium aluminum sulfate:																	
130	With monocalcium phosphate monohydrate:																	
a	Tablespoon	1 tbsp	11.0	1.6	14	Trace	Trace	3.4	213	319	—	1,205	17	(0)	(0)	(0)	(0)	(0)
b	Teaspoon	1 tsp	3.0	1.6	4	Trace	Trace	.9	58	87	—	329	5	(0)	(0)	(0)	(0)	(0)
131	With monocalcium phosphate monohydrate and calcium carbonate:																	
a	Tablespoon	1 tbsp	11.0	1.0	9	Trace	Trace	2.1	636	160	—	1,278	—	(0)	(0)	(0)	(0)	(0)
b	Teaspoon	1 tsp	3.0	1.0	2	Trace	Trace	.6	173	44	—	349	—	(0)	(0)	(0)	(0)	(0)
132	With monocalcium phosphate monohydrate and calcium sulfate:																	
a	Tablespoon	1 tbsp	10.5	1.3	11	Trace	Trace	2.6	664	164	—	1,050	—	(0)	(0)	(0)	(0)	(0)
b	Teaspoon	1 tsp	2.9	1.3	3	Trace	Trace	.7	183	45	—	290	—	(0)	(0)	(0)	(0)	(0)

[1] Measure and weight apply to food as it is described with inedible part or parts (refuse) included.

[5] Most of phosphorus in nuts, legumes, and outer layers of cereal grains is present as phytic acid. See also Appendix D, section on Minerals and Oxalic Acid

[25] Common-size jar listed for strained and junior foods is applicable to items in this group. Nutritive values for other sizes of jars may be calculated from values given for 1 oz.

[26] For further information, see Appendix A, section on Baby Foods, p. 262.

[21] Values for raw bacon (item 125b).

[22] List of ingredients on label indicates type of baking powder. Values for energy and proximate constituents are based on starch content.

[23] According to unpublished data, weight of 1 tsp. of baking powder is not equivalent to one-third weight of 1 tbsp. For example, 1 tsp. of tartrate baking powder (item 134) weighs 2.8 g., but weight of 1 tbsp. (9.5 g.) divided by 3 gives a heavier weight of 3.2 g.

TABLE 1.—*Nutritive values for household measures and market units of foods*—Continued

[Item numbers correspond to those in table 1 of Handbook No. 8, revised 1963. Values in parentheses denote imputed values usually from another form of the food or from a similar food. Zeros in parentheses indicate that amount of a constituent, if present, is probably too small to be measured. Dashes (—) denote lack of reliable data for a constituent believed to be present in a measurable amount. Calculated values, as those based on a recipe, are not in parentheses]

Item No.	Food, approximate measures, units, and weight (edible part unless footnotes indicate otherwise)			Values for edible part of foods														
				Water	Food energy	Protein	Fat	Carbohydrate	Calcium	Phosphorus	Iron	Sodium	Potassium	Vitamin A value	Thiamin	Riboflavin	Niacin	Ascorbic acid
(A)	(B)			(C)	(D)	(E)	(F)	(G)	(H)	(I)	(J)	(K)	(L)	(M)	(N)	(O)	(P)	(Q)
			Grams	*Percent*	*Calories*	*Grams*	*Grams*	*Grams*	*Milligrams*	*Milligrams*	*Milligrams*	*Milligrams*	*Milligrams*	*International units*	*Milligrams*	*Milligrams*	*Milligrams*	*Milligrams*
	Baking powders for home use [32] [33]—Continued																	
133	Straight phosphate:																	
a	Tablespoon	1 tbsp	12.5	1.6	15	Trace	Trace	3.7	785	1,180	—	1,028	21	(0)	(0)	(0)	(0)	(0)
b	Teaspoon	1 tsp	3.8	1.6	5	Trace	Trace	1.1	239	359	—	312	6	(0)	(0)	(0)	(0)	(0)
	Tartrate:																	
134	Cream of tartar with tartaric acid:																	
a	Tablespoon	1 tbsp	9.5	1.0	7	Trace	Trace	1.8	0	0	0	694	361	(0)	(0)	(0)	(0)	(0)
b	Teaspoon	1 tsp	2.8	1.0	2	Trace	Trace	.5	0	0	0	204	106	(0)	(0)	(0)	(0)	(0)
	Special low-sodium preparations:																	
135	Commercial powder:																	
a	Tablespoon	1 tbsp	13.5	2.2	23	Trace	Trace	5.6	650	987	—	[34] 1	1,478	(0)	(0)	(0)	(0)	(0)
b	Teaspoon	1 tsp	4.3	2.2	7	Trace	Trace	1.8	207	314	—	[34] Trace	471	(0)	(0)	(0)	(0)	(0)
136	Noncommercial formula [35]	1 tsp	(3)	1.1	2	Trace	Trace	.6	—	—	—	—	622	(0)	(0)	(0)	(0)	(0)
140	**Bamboo shoots**, raw, cut into pieces of 1-in. length	1 lb. or approx. 3 cups.	454	91.0	122	11.8	1.4	23.6	59	268	2.3	—	2,418	90	.68	.32	2.7	18
	Bananas:																	
	Raw:																	
141	Common:																	
	Whole (refuse: skin, 32%): [1] [36]																	
	Regular pack:																	
a	Large, 9¾ in. long,[37] 1⁷⁄₁₆-in. diam	1 banana	200	75.7	116	1.5	.3	30.2	11	35	1.0	1	503	260	.07	.08	1.0	14
b	Medium, 8¾ in. long,[37] 1¹³⁄₃₂-in. diam	1 banana	175	75.7	101	1.3	.2	26.4	10	31	.8	1	440	230	.06	.07	.8	12
c	Small, 7¾ in. long,[37] 1¹¹⁄₃₂-in. diam	1 banana	140	75.7	81	1.0	.2	21.1	8	25	.7	1	352	180	.05	.06	.7	10
	Institutional single-finger pack:																	
d	Petite (size or count, 150 per box of wt., approx. 45–50 lb.; 6–7¼ in. long, 1¹¹⁄₃₂-in. diam.).[38]	1 banana	150	75.7	87	1.1	.2	22.6	8	27	.7	1	377	190	.05	.06	.7	10
e	Sliced	1 cup	150	75.7	128	1.7	.3	33.3	12	39	1.1	2	555	290	.08	.09	1.1	15
f	Mashed	1 cup	225	75.7	191	2.5	.5	50.0	18	58	1.6	2	833	430	.11	.14	1.6	23
g	Pound	1 lb	454	75.7	386	5.0	.9	100.7	36	118	3.2	5	1,678	860	.23	.27	3.2	45
142	Red:																	
a	Whole, 7¼ in. long,[37] 1¹⁷⁄₃₂-in. diam. (refuse: skin, 32%).[1]	1 banana	193	74.4	118	1.6	.3	30.7	13	24	1.0	1	485	520	.07	.05	.8	(13)
b	Sliced	1 cup	150	74.4	135	1.8	.3	35.1	15	27	1.2	2	555	600	.08	.06	.9	(15)
c	Pound	1 lb	454	74.4	408	5.4	.9	106.1	45	82	3.6	5	1,678	1,810	.23	.18	2.7	(45)
143	Dehydrated or banana flakes:																	
a	Cup	1 cup	100	3	340	4.4	.8	88.6	32	104	2.8	4	1,477	760	.18	.24	2.8	7
b	Tablespoon	1 tbsp	6.2	3	21	.3	Trace	5.5	2	6	.2	Trace	92	50	.01	.01	.2	Trace
c	Ounce	1 oz	28	3	96	1.2	.2	25.1	9	29	.8	1	419	220	.05	.07	.8	2
	Bananas, baking type. See Plantain (item 1634).																	
	Barbados-cherry. See Acerola (item 3).																	
144	**Barbecue sauce**	1 cup	250	80.9	228	3.8	17.3	20.0	53	50	2.0	2,038	435	900	.03	.03	.8	13
	Barley, pearled:																	
145	Light	1 cup	200	11.1	698	16.4	2.0	157.6	32	378	4.0	6	320	(0)	.24	.10	6.2	(0)
146	Pot or Scotch	1 cup	200	10.8	696	19.2	2.2	154.4	68	580	5.4	—	592	(0)	.42	.14	7.4	(0)
149	**Bass, black sea,** baked, stuffed:[39]																	
a	Yield from 1 lb., raw fillets, 3¾ oz. of stuffing; 2 fillets with ⅔ cup of stuffing; 8½ in. long, 4½ in. wide, 1½ in. thick.[40]	15½ oz	430	52.9	1,114	69.7	67.9	49.0	—	—	—	—	—	—	—	—	—	—
b	Piece, 3½ in. long, 4½ in. wide, 1½ in. thick;[40] approx. ⅓ cup of stuffing.	1 piece	205	52.9	531	33.2	32.4	23.4	—	—	—	—	—	—	—	—	—	—
c	Pound	1 lb	454	52.9	1,175	73.5	71.7	51.7	—	—	—	—	—	—	—	—	—	—
d	Ounce	1 oz	28	52.9	73	4.6	4.5	3.2	—	—	—	—	—	—	—	—	—	—
152	**Bass, striped,** ovenfried:[41]																	
a	Yield from 1 lb., raw fillets	16⅞ oz	480	60.8	941	103.2	40.8	32.2	—	—	—	—	—	—	—	—	—	—
b	Fillet, 8¾ in. long, 4½ in. wide, ⅝ in. thick[40]	1 fillet	200	60.8	392	43.0	17.0	13.4	—	—	—	—	—	—	—	—	—	—
c	Pound	1 lb	454	60.8	889	97.5	38.6	30.4	—	—	—	—	—	—	—	—	—	—
d	Ounce	1 oz	28	60.8	56	6.1	2.4	1.9	—	—	—	—	—	—	—	—	—	—
	Beans, broad. See Broadbeans (items 481–482).																	

(A)	(B)			(C)	(D)	(E)	(F)	(G)	(H)	(I)	(J)	(K)	(L)	(M)	(N)	(O)	(P)	(Q)
	Beans, common, mature seeds, dry:[5]																	
	White:																	
154	Raw:																	
a	All varieties	1 lb	454	10.9	1,542	101.2	7.3	278.1	653	1,928	35.4	86	5,425	0	2.95	1.00	10.9	—
b	Great Northern	1 cup	180	10.9	612	40.1	2.9	110.3	259	765	14.0	34	2,153	0	1.17	.40	4.3	—
c	Pea (navy)	1 cup	205	10.9	697	45.7	3.3	125.7	295	871	16.0	39	2,452	0	1.33	.45	4.9	—
155	Cooked, Great Northern or navy (no residual cooking liquid):[42]																	
	Cup:																	
a	Great Northern	1 cup	180	69.0	212	14.0	1.1	38.2	90	266	4.9	[43] 13	749	0	.25	.13	1.3	0
b	Pea (navy)	1 cup	190	69.0	224	14.8	1.1	40.3	95	281	5.1	[43] 13	790	0	.27	.13	1.3	0
c	Pound	1 lb	454	69.0	535	35.4	2.7	96.2	227	671	12.2	[43] 32	1,887	0	.64	.32	3.2	0
	Canned, solids and liquids:																	
156	With pork and tomato sauce:																	
	Can and approx. contents:																	
a	Size, 307 × 409[14] (No. 2); net wt., 20 oz. (1 lb. 4 oz.).	1 can	567	70.7	692	34.6	14.7	107.7	306	522	10.2	2,625	1,191	740	.45	.17	3.4	11
b	Size, 404 × 700[14] (No. 3 Cylinder); net wt., 51 oz. (3 lb. 3 oz.).	1 can	1,446	70.7	1,764	88.2	37.6	274.7	781	1,330	26.0	6,695	3,037	1,880	1.16	.43	8.7	29
c	Size, 603 × 700[14] (No. 10); net wt., 110 oz. (6 lb. 14 oz.).	1 can	3,118	70.7	3,804	190.2	81.1	592.4	1,684	2,869	56.1	14,436	6,548	4,050	2.49	.94	18.7	62
d	Cup	1 cup	255	70.7	311	15.6	6.6	48.5	138	235	4.6	1,181	536	330	.20	.08	1.5	5
e	Pound	1 lb	454	70.7	553	27.7	11.8	86.2	245	417	8.2	2,100	953	590	.36	.14	2.7	9
157	With pork and sweet sauce:																	
	Can and approx. contents:																	
a	Size, 307 × 409[14] (No. 2); net wt., 20 oz. (1 lb. 4 oz.).	1 can	567	66.4	851	35.2	26.6	119.6	357	646	13.0	2,155	—	—	.34	.23	2.8	—
b	Size, 404 × 700[14] (No. 3 Cylinder); net wt., 51 oz. (3 lb. 3 oz.).	1 can	1,446	66.4	2,169	89.7	68.0	305.1	911	1,648	33.3	5,495	—	—	.87	.58	7.2	—
c	Size, 603 × 700[14] (No. 10); net wt., 110 oz. (6 lb. 14 oz.).	1 can	3,118	66.4	4,677	193.3	146.5	657.9	1,964	3,555	71.7	11,848	—	—	1.87	1.25	15.6	—
d	Cup	1 cup	255	66.4	383	15.8	12.0	53.8	161	291	5.9	969	—	—	.15	.10	1.3	—
e	Pound	1 lb	454	66.4	680	28.1	21.3	95.7	286	517	10.4	1,724	—	—	.27	.18	2.3	—
158	Without pork:																	
	Can and approx. contents:																	
a	Size, 307 × 409[14] (No. 2); net wt., 20 oz. (1 lb. 4 oz.).	1 can	567	68.5	680	35.7	2.8	130.4	386	686	11.3	1,916	1,520	340	.40	.23	3.4	11
b	Size, 404 × 700[14] (No. 3 Cylinder); net wt., 51 oz. (3 lb. 3 oz.).	1 can	1,446	68.5	1,735	91.1	7.2	332.6	983	1,750	28.9	4,887	3,875	870	1.01	.58	8.7	29
c	Size, 603 × 700[14] (No. 10); net wt., 110 oz. (6 lb. 14 oz.).	1 can	3,118	68.5	3,742	196.4	15.6	717.1	2,120	3,773	62.4	10,539	8,356	1,870	2.18	1.25	18.7	62
d	Cup	1 cup	255	68.5	306	16.1	1.3	58.7	173	309	5.1	862	683	150	.18	.10	1.5	5
e	Pound	1 lb	454	68.5	544	28.6	2.3	104.3	308	549	9.1	1,533	1,216	270	.32	.18	2.7	9
	Red, kidney:																	
159	Raw:																	
a	Cup	1 cup	185	10.4	635	41.6	2.8	114.5	204	751	12.8	19	1,820	40	.94	.37	4.3	—
b	Pound	1 lb	454	10.4	1,556	102.1	6.8	280.8	499	1,842	31.3	45	4,463	90	2.31	.91	10.4	—
160	Cooked (no residual cooking liquid):[42]																	
a	Cup	1 cup	185	69.0	218	14.4	.9	39.6	70	259	4.4	[43] 6	629	10	.20	.11	1.3	—
b	Pound	1 lb	454	69.0	535	35.4	2.3	97.1	172	635	10.9	[43] 14	1,542	30	.50	.27	3.2	—
161	Canned, solids and liquid:																	
	Can and approx. contents:																	
a	Size, 307 × 409[14] (No. 2); net wt., 20 oz. (1 lb. 4 oz.).	1 can	567	76.0	510	32.3	2.3	93.0	164	618	10.2	[43] 17	1,497	30	.28	.23	3.4	—
b	Size, 404 × 700[14] (No. 3 Cylinder); net wt., 51 oz. (3 lb. 3 oz.).	1 can	1,446	76.0	1,301	82.4	5.8	237.1	419	1,576	26.0	[43] 43	3,817	70	.72	.58	8.7	—
c	Size, 603 × 700[14] (No. 10); net wt., 108 oz. (6 lb. 12 oz.).	1 can	3,062	76.0	2,756	174.5	12.2	502.2	888	3,338	55.1	[43] 92	8,084	150	1.53	1.22	18.4	—
d	Cup	1 cup	255	76.0	230	14.5	1.0	41.8	74	278	4.6	[43] 8	673	10	.13	.10	1.5	—
e	Pound	1 lb	454	76.0	408	25.9	1.8	74.4	132	494	8.2	[43] 14	1,198	20	.23	.18	2.7	—

[1] Measure and weight apply to food as it is described with inedible part or parts (refuse) included.

[5] Most of phosphorus in nuts, legumes, and outer layers of cereal grains is present as phytic acid. See also Appendix D, section on Minerals and Oxalic Acid

[14] Dimensions of can: 1st dimension represents diameter; 2d dimension, height of can. 1st or left-hand digit in each dimension gives number of whole inches; next 2 digits give additional fraction of dimension expressed as 16th of an inch.

[32] List of ingredients on label indicates type of baking powder. Values for energy and proximate constituents are based on starch content.

[33] According to unpublished data, weight of 1 tsp. of baking powder is not equivalent to one-third weight of 1 tbsp. For example, 1 tsp. of tartrate baking powder (item 134) weighs 2.8 g., but weight of 1 tbsp. (9.5 g.) divided by 3 gives a heavier weight of 3.2 g.

[34] Value based on single brand.

[35] Values are based on the following formula in "Planning Low-Sodium Meals," Newton Health Dept., Newton, Mass., 1951, as cited in National Academy of Sciences-National Research Council Publication No. 325 "Sodium-Restricted Diets," p. 20, 1954, Washington, D.C.: Potassium bitartrate (cream of tartar) 42.7%, potassium bicarbonate 30.3%, cornstarch 21.3%, tartaric acid 5.7%.

[36] Percent refuse, dimensions, and weight vary widely. For further information, see Appendix B, section on Bananas

[37] Length as measured along outer curvature, from tip to base of pedicel.

[38] Minimum and maximum length, measured as straight-line distance from end of cut pedicel to tip of finger.

[39] Prepared with bacon, butter or margarine, onion, celery, and bread cubes.

[40] Width at widest part; thickness at thickest part.

[41] Prepared with milk, breadcrumbs, butter or margarine, and salt.

[42] For proportion of ingredients used and ratio of cooked to dry legume, see ARS 62-13 (7), section on Legumes, Dry, p. 7, and table 21, p. 25.

[43] Value for product without added salt.

TABLE 1.—*Nutritive values for household measures and market units of foods*—Continued

[Item numbers correspond to those in table 1 of Handbook No. 8, revised 1963. Values in parentheses denote imputed values usually from another form of the food or from a similar food. Zeros in parentheses indicate that amount of a constituent, if present, is probably too small to be measured. Dashes (—) denote lack of reliable data for a constituent believed to be present in a measurable amount. Calculated values, as those based on a recipe, are not in parentheses]

Item No.	Food, approximate measures, units, and weight (edible part unless footnotes indicate otherwise)			Values for edible part of foods: Water	Food energy	Protein	Fat	Carbohydrate	Calcium	Phosphorus	Iron	Sodium	Potassium	Vitamin A value	Thiamin	Riboflavin	Niacin	Ascorbic acid
(A)	(B)			(C)	(D)	(E)	(F)	(G)	(H)	(I)	(J)	(K)	(L)	(M)	(N)	(O)	(P)	(Q)
			Grams	Percent	Calories	Grams	Grams	Grams	Milligrams	Milligrams	Milligrams	Milligrams	Milligrams	International units	Milligrams	Milligrams	Milligrams	Milligrams
	Beans, common, mature seeds, dry [5]—Continued																	
	Pinto, calico, red Mexican:																	
162	Raw:																	
a	All varieties	1 lb	454	8.3	1,583	103.9	5.4	288.9	612	2,073	29.0	45	4,463	—	3.81	0.95	10.0	—
b	Pinto	1 cup	190	8.3	663	43.5	2.3	121.0	257	868	12.2	19	1,870	—	1.60	.40	4.2	—
	Other, including black, brown, Bayo:																	
163	Raw:																	
a	Cup	1 cup	(200)	11.2	678	44.6	3.0	122.4	270	840	15.8	50	2,076	60	1.10	.40	4.4	—
b	Pound	1 lb	454	11.2	1,538	101.2	6.8	277.6	612	1,905	35.8	113	4,708	140	2.49	.91	10.0	—
	Beans, hyacinth. See Hyacinth-beans (items 1137–1138).																	
	Beans, lima: [5]																	
	Immature seeds:																	
164	Raw:																	
a	Cup	1 cup	155	67.5	191	13.0	.8	34.3	81	220	4.3	3	1,008	450	.37	.19	2.2	45
b	Pound	1 lb	454	67.5	558	38.1	2.3	100.2	236	644	12.7	9	2,948	1,320	1.09	.54	6.4	132
165	Cooked (boiled), drained:																	
a	Cup	1 cup	170	71.1	189	12.9	.9	33.7	80	206	4.3	[20] 2	717	480	.31	.17	2.2	29
b	Pound	1 lb	454	71.1	503	34.5	2.3	89.8	213	549	11.3	[20] 5	1,914	1,270	.82	.45	5.9	77
	Canned:																	
	Regular pack:																	
166	Solids and liquid:																	
	Can and approx. contents:																	
a	Size, 211 × 304 [14] (8Z Tall, Buffet); net wt., 8½ oz.	1 can	241	80.8	171	9.9	.7	32.3	[44] 63	161	5.8	[21] 569	535	310	.10	.10	1.2	17
b	Size, 303 × 406 [14] (No. 303); net wt., 16 oz. (1 lb.).	1 can	454	80.8	322	18.6	1.4	60.8	[44] 118	304	10.0	[21] 1,070	1,007	590	.18	.18	2.3	32
c	Size, 603 × 700 [14] (No. 10); net wt., 105 oz. (6 lb. 9 oz.).	1 can	2,977	80.8	2,114	122.1	8.9	398.9	[44] 774	1,995	71.4	[21] 7,026	6,609	3,870	1.18	1.19	14.9	208
d	Cup	1 cup	248	80.8	176	10.2	.7	33.2	[44] 64	166	6.0	[21] 585	551	320	.10	.10	1.2	17
167	Drained solids:																	
	Can and approx. drained contents:																	
a	Size, 211 × 304 [14] (8Z Tall, Buffet); wt., 5½ oz.	1 can	156	74.7	150	8.4	.5	28.5	[44] 44	109	3.7	[21] 368	346	300	.05	.08	.8	9
b	Size, 303 × 406 [14] (No. 303); wt., 11 oz	1 can	312	74.7	300	16.8	.9	57.1	[44] 87	218	7.5	[21] 736	693	590	.09	.16	1.6	19
c	Size, 603 × 700 [14] (No. 10); wt., 72 oz. (4 lb. 8 oz.).	1 can	2,041	74.7	1,959	110.2	6.1	373.5	[44] 571	1,429	49.0	[21] 4,817	4,531	3,880	.61	1.02	10.2	122
d	Cup	1 cup	170	74.7	163	9.2	.5	31.1	[44] 48	119	4.1	[21] 401	377	320	.05	.09	.9	10
e	Pound	1 lb	454	74.7	435	24.5	1.4	83.0	[44] 127	318	10.9	[21] 1,070	1,007	860	.14	.23	2.3	27
168	Drained liquid:																	
a	Pound	1 lb	454	93.3	91	5.9	Trace	17.7	[44] 100	272	10.4	[21] 1,070	1,007	Trace	.18	.14	2.7	45
b	Ounce	1 oz	28	93.3	6	.4	Trace	1.1	[44] 6	17	.7	[21] 67	63	Trace	.01	.01	.2	3
	Special dietary pack (low sodium):																	
169	Solids and liquid:																	
	Can and approx. contents:																	
a	Size, 303 × 406 [14] (No. 303); net wt., 16 oz. (1 lb.).	1 can	454	81.7	318	20.0	1.4	58.5	[44] 118	304	10.9	18	1,007	590	.18	.18	2.3	32
b	Size, 603 × 700 [14] (No. 10); net wt., 105 oz. (6 lb. 9 oz.).	1 can	2,977	81.7	2,084	131.0	8.9	384.0	[44] 774	1,995	71.4	119	6,609	3,870	1.19	1.19	14.9	208
c	Cup	1 cup	248	81.7	174	10.9	.7	32.0	[44] 64	166	6.0	10	551	320	.10	.10	1.2	17
170	Drained solids:																	
	Can and approx. drained contents:																	
a	Size, 303 × 406 [14] (No. 303); wt., 11 oz.	1 can	312	75.6	296	18.1	.9	55.2	[44] 87	218	7.5	12	693	590	.09	.16	1.6	19
b	Size, 603 × 700 [14] (No. 10); wt., 72 oz. (4 lb. 8 oz.).	1 can	2,041	75.6	1,939	118.4	6.1	361.3	[44] 571	1,429	49.0	82	4,531	3,880	.61	1.02	10.2	122
c	Cup	1 cup	170	75.6	162	9.9	.5	30.1	[44] 48	119	4.1	7	377	320	.05	.09	.9	10
d	Pound	1 lb	454	75.6	431	26.3	1.4	80.3	[44] 127	318	10.9	18	1,007	860	.14	.23	2.3	27
171	Drained liquid:																	
a	Pound	1 lb	454	94.4	86	6.4	Trace	15.9	[44] 100	272	10.4	18	1,007	Trace	.18	.14	2.7	45
b	Ounce	1 oz	28	94.4	5	.4	Trace	1.0	[44] 6	17	.7	1	63	Trace	.01	.01	.2	3

(A)	(B)			(C)	(D)	(E)	(F)	(G)	(H)	(I)	(J)	(K)	(L)	(M)	(N)	(O)	(P)	(Q)
	Frozen:																	
	Thick-seeded types, commonly called Fordhooks:																	
172	Not thawed:																	
a	Container, net wt., 10 oz	1 container	284	72.7	290	17.6	0.3	55.4	65	273	5.4	[45] 366	1,392	650	0.28	0.17	3.4	62
b	Cup	1 cup	160	72.7	163	9.9	.2	31.2	37	154	3.0	[45] 206	784	370	.16	.10	1.9	35
c	Pound	1 lb	454	72.7	463	28.1	.5	88.5	104	435	8.6	[45] 585	2,223	1,040	.45	.27	5.4	100
173	Cooked (boiled), drained:																	
a	Yield from 10 oz., frozen lima beans	1¾ cups	295	73.5	283	17.1	.3	54.3	59	257	5.0	[45] 285	1,211	650	.21	.15	3.0	47
b	Yield from 1 lb., frozen lima beans	2¾ cups	470	73.5	452	27.3	.5	86.7	94	409	7.7	[45] 456	2,002	1,040	.33	.24	4.7	75
c	Cup	1 cup	170	73.5	168	10.2	.2	32.5	34	153	2.9	[45] 172	724	390	.12	.09	1.7	29
d	Pound	1 lb	454	73.5	449	27.2	.5	86.6	91	408	7.7	[45] 458	1,932	1,040	.32	.23	4.5	77
	Thin-seeded types, commonly called baby limas:																	
174	Not thawed:																	
a	Container, net wt., 10 oz	1 container	284	67.8	346	21.6	.6	65.3	108	372	8.0	[45] 417	1,244	620	.28	.17	3.4	54
b	Cup	1 cup	165	67.8	201	12.5	.3	38.0	63	216	4.6	[45] 243	723	360	.17	.10	2.0	31
c	Pound	1 lb	454	67.8	553	34.5	.9	104.3	172	594	12.7	[45] 667	1,987	1,000	.45	.27	5.4	86
175	Cooked (boiled), drained:																	
a	Yield from 10 oz., frozen lima beans	1¾ cups	315	68.8	339	21.2	.6	64.0	98	357	7.5	[45] 367	1,120	620	.24	.15	3.2	35
b	Yield from 1 lb., frozen lima beans	2¾ cups	495	68.8	541	33.8	.9	102.2	157	570	11.9	[45] 587	1,788	1,000	.38	.24	5.1	56
c	Cup	1 cup	180	68.8	212	13.3	.4	40.1	63	227	4.7	[45] 232	709	400	.16	.09	2.2	22
d	Pound	1 lb	454	68.8	535	33.6	.9	101.2	159	572	11.8	[45] 585	1,787	1,000	.41	.23	5.4	54
	Mature seeds, dry:																	
176	Raw:																	
	Cup:																	
a	Large seeded (Fordhooks)	1 cup	180	10.3	621	36.7	2.9	115.2	130	693	14.0	7	2,752	Trace	.86	.31	3.4	—
b	Small seeded (baby limas)	1 cup	190	10.3	656	38.8	3.0	121.6	137	732	14.8	8	2,905	Trace	.91	.32	3.6	—
c	Pound	1 lb	454	10.3	1,565	92.5	7.3	290.3	327	1,746	35.4	18	6,936	Trace	2.18	.77	8.6	—
177	Cooked (no residual cooking liquid): [42]																	
a	Cup	1 cup	190	64.1	262	15.6	1.1	48.6	55	293	5.9	[43] 4	1,163	—	.25	.11	1.3	—
b	Pound	1 lb	454	64.1	626	37.2	2.7	116.1	132	699	14.1	[43] 9	2,776	—	.59	.27	3.2	—
178	Bean flour, lima: [5]																	
a	Sifted, spooned into cup	1 cup	126	10.5	432	27.1	1.8	79.4	—	—	—	—	—	(0)	—	—	—	(0)
b	Pound	1 lb	454	10.5	1,556	97.5	6.4	285.8	—	—	—	—	—	(0)	—	—	—	(0)
	Beans, mung: [5]																	
179	Mature seeds, dry, raw:																	
a	Cup	1 cup	210	10.7	714	50.8	2.7	126.6	248	714	16.2	13	2,159	170	.80	.44	5.5	—
b	Pound	1 lb	454	10.7	1,542	109.8	5.9	273.5	535	1,542	34.9	27	4,663	360	1.72	.95	11.8	—
	Sprouted seeds:																	
180	Uncooked:																	
a	Cup	1 cup	105	88.8	37	4.0	.2	6.9	20	67	1.4	5	234	20	.14	.14	.8	20
b	Pound	1 lb	454	88.8	159	17.2	.9	29.9	86	290	5.9	23	1,012	90	.59	.59	3.6	86
181	Cooked (boiled), drained:																	
a	Cup	1 cup	125	91.0	35	4.0	.3	6.5	21	60	1.1	[20] 5	195	30	.11	.13	.9	8
b	Pound	1 lb	454	91.0	127	14.5	.9	23.6	77	218	4.1	[20] 18	708	90	.41	.45	3.2	27
	Beans, snap:																	
	Green:																	
182	Raw, pods broken into 1- to 2-in. lengths:																	
a	Cup	1 cup	110	90.1	35	2.1	.2	7.8	62	48	.9	8	267	660	.09	.12	.6	21
b	Pound (yields about 3⅜ cups cooked beans)	1 lb	454	90.1	145	8.6	.9	32.2	254	200	3.6	32	1,102	2,720	.36	.50	2.3	86
	Cooked (boiled), drained, cooked in—																	
183	Small amount of water, short time:																	
a	Cup, cuts and French style	1 cup	125	92.4	31	2.0	.3	6.8	63	46	.8	[20] 5	189	680	.09	.11	.6	15
b	Pound	1 lb	454	92.4	113	7.3	.9	24.5	227	168	2.7	[20] 18	685	2,450	.32	.41	2.3	54
184	Large amount of water, long time:																	
a	Cup, cuts and French style	1 cup	(125)	92.4	31	2.0	.3	6.8	63	46	.8	[20] 5	189	680	.08	.10	.4	13
b	Pound	1 lb	454	92.4	113	7.3	.9	24.5	227	168	2.7	[20] 18	685	2,450	.27	.36	1.4	45
	Canned:																	
	Regular pack:																	
185	Solids and liquid:																	
	Can and approx. contents:																	
a	Size, 211 × 304 [14] (8Z Tall, Buffet); net wt., 8 oz.	1 can	227	93.5	41	2.3	.2	9.5	77	48	2.7	[21] 536	216	660	.07	.09	.7	9

[5] Most of phosphorus in nuts, legumes, and outer layers of cereal grains is present as phytic acid. See also Appendix D, section on Minerals and Oxalic Acid

[14] Dimensions of can: 1st dimension represents diameter; 2d dimension, height of can. 1st or left-hand digit in each dimension gives number of whole inches; next 2 digits give additional fraction of dimension expressed as 16th of an inch.

[20] Value is for unsalted product. If salt is used, increase value by 236 mg. per 100 g. of vegetable—an estimated figure based on typical amount of salt (0.6%) in canned vegetables. See also Appendix C, section on Cooked Vegetables

[21] Estimated value based on addition of salt in amount of 0.6% of finished product.

[42] For proportion of ingredients used and ratio of cooked to dry legume, see ARS 62-13 (7), section on Legumes, Dry, p. 7, and table 21, p. 25.

[43] Value for product without added salt.

[44] Federal standards provide for addition of certain calcium salts as firming agents. If used, these salts may add calcium not to exceed 26 mg. per 100 g. of finished product. For total can contents, value for item 166a would be 125 mg.; for item 166b, 236 mg.; for item 166c, 1,548 mg.; for item 166d, 129 mg. Data not available to give change in calcium value for drained solids and drained liquid.

[45] Value based on average weighted in accordance with commercial practice in freezing vegetables. Wide range in sodium content occurs. For cooked vegetables, value also represents no additional salting. If salt is moderately added, increase value by 236 mg. per 100 g. of vegetable—an estimated figure based on typical amount of salt (0.6%) in canned vegetables. See also Appendix C, section on Cooked Vegetables, and section on Frozen Fruits and Vegetables

TABLE 1.—*Nutritive values for household measures and market units of foods*—Continued

[Item numbers correspond to those in table 1 of Handbook No. 8, revised 1963. Values in parentheses denote imputed values usually from another form of the food or from a similar food. Zeros in parentheses indicate that amount of a constituent, if present, is probably too small to be measured. Dashes (—) denote lack of reliable data for a constituent believed to be present in a measurable amount. Calculated values, as those based on a recipe, are not in parentheses]

Item No.	Food, approximate measures, units, and weight (edible part unless footnotes indicate otherwise)			Values for edible part of foods														
				Water	Food energy	Protein	Fat	Carbohydrate	Calcium	Phosphorus	Iron	Sodium	Potassium	Vitamin A value	Thiamin	Riboflavin	Niacin	Ascorbic acid
(A)	(B)			(C)	(D)	(E)	(F)	(G)	(H)	(I)	(J)	(K)	(L)	(M)	(N)	(O)	(P)	(Q)
			Grams	*Percent*	*Calories*	*Grams*	*Grams*	*Grams*	*Milligrams*	*Milligrams*	*Milligrams*	*Milligrams*	*Milligrams*	*International units*	*Milligrams*	*Milligrams*	*Milligrams*	*Milligrams*
	Beans, snap—Continued																	
	Green—Continued																	
	Canned—Continued																	
	Regular pack—Continued																	
	Solids and liquid—Continued																	
	Can and approx. contents—Continued																	
b	Size, 303 × 406[14] (No. 303); net wt., 15½ oz.	1 can	439	93.5	79	4.4	0.4	18.4	149	92	5.3	[21] 1,036	417	1,270	0.13	0.18	1.3	18
c	Size, 603 × 700[14] (No. 10); net wt., 101 oz. (6 lb. 5 oz.).	1 can	2,863	93.5	515	28.6	2.9	120.2	973	601	34.4	[21] 6,757	2,720	8,300	.86	1.15	8.6	115
d	Cup	1 cup	239	93.5	43	2.4	.2	10.0	81	50	2.9	[21] 564	227	690	.07	.10	.7	10
e	Pound	1 lb	454	93.5	82	4.5	.5	19.1	154	95	5.4	[21] 1,070	431	1,320	.14	.18	1.4	18
186	Drained solids:																	
	Can and approx. drained contents:																	
	Size, 211 × 304[14] (8Z Tall, Buffet):																	
a	Cuts less than 1½ in. and short cuts (less than ¾ in.); wt., 4½ oz.[46]	1 can	128	91.9	31	1.8	.3	6.7	58	32	1.9	[21] 302	122	600	.04	.06	.4	5
b	Slices (cut lengthwise or French style); wt., 4⅛ oz.[47]	1 can	117	91.9	28	1.6	.2	6.1	53	29	1.8	[21] 276	111	550	.04	.06	.4	5
	Size, 303 × 406[14] (No. 303):																	
c	Cuts less than 1½ in. and short cuts (less than ¾ in.); wt., 9¼ oz.[46]	1 can	262	91.9	63	3.7	.5	13.6	118	66	3.9	[21] 618	249	1,230	.08	.13	.8	10
d	Slices (cut lengthwise or French style); wt., 8¾ oz.[47]	1 can	248	91.9	60	3.5	.5	12.9	112	62	3.7	[21] 585	236	1,170	.07	.12	.7	10
	Size, 603 × 700[14] (No. 10):																	
e	Cuts less than 1½ in. and short cuts (less than ¾ in.); wt., 63 oz. (3 lb. 15 oz.).[46]	1 can	1,786	91.9	429	25.0	3.6	92.9	804	447	26.8	[21] 4,215	1,697	8,390	.54	.89	5.4	71
f	Slices (cut lengthwise or French style); wt., 59 oz. (3 lb. 11 oz.).	1 can	1,673	91.9	402	23.4	3.3	87.0	753	418	25.1	[21] 3,948	1,589	7,860	.50	.84	5.0	67
	Cup:																	
g	Cuts less than 1½ in. and short cuts (less than ¾ in.).	1 cup	135	91.9	32	1.9	.3	7.0	61	34	2.0	[21] 319	128	630	.04	.07	.4	5
h	Slices (cut lengthwise or French style)	1 cup	130	91.9	31	1.8	.3	6.8	59	33	2.0	[21] 307	124	610	.04	.07	.4	5
i	Pound	1 lb	454	91.9	109	6.4	.9	23.6	204	113	6.8	[21] 1,070	431	2,130	.14	.23	1.4	18
187	Drained liquid:																	
a	Pound	1 lb	454	95.9	45	1.8	.5	10.9	68	64	4.1	[21] 1,070	431	Trace	.14	.14	1.4	18
b	Ounce	1 oz	28	95.9	3	.1	Trace	.7	4	4	.3	[21] 67	27	Trace	.01	.01	.1	1
	Special dietary pack (low sodium):																	
188	Solids and liquid:																	
	Can and approx. contents:																	
a	Size, 303 × 406[14] (No. 303); net wt., 15½ oz.	1 can	439	94.8	70	4.8	.4	15.8	149	92	5.3	9	417	1,270	.13	.18	1.3	18
b	Size, 603 × 700[14] (No. 10); net wt., 101 oz. (6 lb. 5 oz.).	1 can	2,863	94.8	458	31.5	2.9	103.1	973	601	34.4	57	2,720	8,300	.86	1.15	8.6	115
c	Cup	1 cup	239	94.8	38	2.6	.2	8.6	81	50	2.9	5	227	690	.07	.10	.7	10
d	Pound	1 lb	454	94.8	73	5.0	.5	16.3	154	95	5.4	9	431	1,320	.14	.18	1.4	18
189	Drained solids:																	
	Can and approx. drained contents; cuts less than 1½ in. and short cuts (less than ¾ in.):																	
a	Size, 303 × 406[14] (No. 303); wt., 9¼ oz.[46]	1 can	262	93.2	58	3.9	.3	12.6	118	66	3.9	5	249	1,230	.08	.13	.8	10
b	Size, 603 × 700[14] (No. 10); wt., 63 oz. (3 lb. 15 oz.).[46]	1 can	1,786	93.2	393	26.8	1.8	85.7	804	447	26.8	36	1,697	8,390	.54	.89	5.4	71
c	Cup, cuts less than 1½ in. and short cuts (less than ¾ in.).	1 cup	135	93.2	30	2.0	.1	6.5	61	34	2.0	3	128	630	.04	.07	.4	5
d	Pound	1 lb	454	93.2	100	6.8	.5	21.8	204	113	6.8	9	431	2,130	.14	.23	1.4	18
190	Drained liquid:																	
a	Pound	1 lb	454	97.3	36	1.8	.5	8.2	68	64	4.1	9	431	Trace	.14	.14	1.4	18

(A)	(B)			(C)	(D)	(E)	(F)	(G)	(H)	(I)	(J)	(K)	(L)	(M)	(N)	(O)	(P)	(Q)
b	Ounce	1 oz	28	97.3	2	0.1	Trace	0.5	4	4	0.3	1	27	Trace	0.01	0.01	0.1	1
	Frozen:																	
	Cut:																	
191	Not thawed:																	
a	Container, net wt., 9 oz	1 container	255	91.7	66	4.3	0.3	15.3	107	84	2.0	3	426	1,480	.18	.26	1.0	23
b	Container, net wt., 10 oz	1 container	284	91.7	74	4.8	.3	17.0	119	94	2.3	3	474	1,650	.20	.28	1.1	26
c	Cup[48]	1 cup	125	91.7	33	2.1	.1	7.5	53	41	1.0	1	209	730	.09	.13	.5	11
d	Pound	1 lb	454	91.7	118	7.7	.5	27.2	191	150	3.6	5	758	2,630	.32	.45	1.8	41
192	Cooked (boiled), drained:																	
a	Yield from 9 oz., frozen beans	1¾ cups	235	92.1	59	3.8	.2	13.4	94	75	1.6	[20] 2	357	1,360	.16	.21	.9	12
b	Yield from 10 oz., frozen beans	1⅞ cups	260	92.1	65	4.2	.3	14.8	104	83	1.8	[20] 3	395	1,510	.18	.23	1.0	13
c	Yield from 1 lb., frozen beans	3⅛ cups	420	92.1	105	6.7	.4	23.9	168	134	2.9	[20] 4	638	2,440	.29	.38	1.7	21
d	Cup	1 cup	135	92.1	34	2.2	.1	7.7	54	43	.9	[20] 1	205	780	.09	.12	.5	7
e	Pound	1 lb	454	92.1	113	7.3	.5	25.9	181	145	3.2	[20] 5	689	2,630	.32	.41	1.8	23
	French style:																	
193	Not thawed:																	
a	Container, net wt., 9 oz	1 container	255	91.6	69	4.3	.3	15.6	102	82	2.3	5	390	1,350	.18	.23	1.0	26
b	Container, net wt., 10 oz	1 container	284	91.6	77	4.8	.3	17.3	114	91	2.6	6	435	1,510	.20	.26	1.1	28
c	Cup[48]	1 cup	100	91.6	27	1.7	.1	6.1	40	32	.9	2	153	530	.07	.09	.4	10
d	Pound	1 lb	454	91.6	122	7.7	.5	27.7	181	145	4.1	9	694	2,400	.32	.41	1.8	45
194	Cooked (boiled), drained:																	
a	Yield from 9 oz., frozen beans	1¾ cups	225	91.9	59	3.6	.2	13.5	86	68	2.0	[20] 5	306	1,190	.14	.18	.7	16
b	Yield from 10 oz., frozen beans	1⅞ cups	250	91.9	65	4.0	.3	15.0	95	75	2.3	[20] 5	340	1,330	.15	.20	.8	18
c	Cup	1 cup	130	91.9	34	2.1	.1	7.8	49	39	1.2	[20] 3	177	690	.08	.10	.4	9
d	Pound	1 lb	454	91.9	118	7.3	.5	27.2	172	136	4.1	[20] 9	617	2,400	.27	.36	1.4	32
	Yellow or wax:																	
195	Raw, pods broken into 1- to 2-in. lengths:																	
a	Cup	1 cup	(110)	91.4	30	1.9	.2	6.6	62	47	.9	8	267	280	.09	.12	.6	22
b	Pound	1 lb	454	91.4	122	7.7	.9	27.2	254	195	3.6	32	1,102	1,130	.36	.50	2.3	91
196	Cooked (boiled), drained:																	
a	Cup	1 cup	(125)	93.4	28	1.8	.3	5.6	63	46	.8	[20] 4	189	290	.09	.11	.6	16
b	Pound	1 lb	454	93.4	100	6.4	.9	20.9	227	168	2.7	[20] 14	685	1,040	.32	.41	2.3	59
	Canned:																	
	Regular pack:																	
197	Solids and liquid:																	
	Can and approx. contents:																	
a	Size, 211 × 304[14] (8Z Tall, Buffet); net wt., 8 oz.	1 can	227	93.7	43	2.3	.5	9.5	77	48	2.7	[21] 536	216	140	.07	.09	.7	11
b	Size, 303 × 406[14] (No. 303); net wt., 15½ oz.	1 can	439	93.7	83	4.4	.9	18.4	149	92	5.3	[21] 1,036	417	260	.13	.18	1.3	22
c	Size, 603 × 700[14] (No. 10); net wt., 101 oz. (6 lb. 5 oz.).	1 can	2,863	93.7	544	28.6	5.7	120.2	973	601	34.4	[21] 6,757	2,720	1,720	.86	1.15	8.6	143
d	Cup	1 cup	239	93.7	45	2.4	.5	10.0	81	50	2.9	[21] 564	227	140	.07	.10	.7	12
e	Pound	1 lb	454	93.7	86	4.5	.9	19.1	154	95	5.4	[21] 1,070	431	270	.14	.18	1.4	23
198	Drained solids:																	
	Can and approx. drained contents:																	
	Size, 211 × 304[14] (8Z Tall, Buffet):																	
a	Cuts less than 1½ in. and short cuts (less than ¾ in.); wt., 4½ oz.[46]	1 can	128	92.2	31	1.8	.4	6.7	58	32	1.9	[21] 302	122	130	.04	.06	.4	6
b	Slices (cut lengthwise or French style); wt., 4⅛ oz.[47]	1 can	117	92.2	28	1.6	.4	6.1	53	29	1.8	[21] 276	111	120	.04	.06	.4	6
	Size, 303 × 406[14] (No. 303):																	
c	Cuts less than 1½ in. and short cuts (less than ¾ in.); wt., 9¼ oz.[46]	1 can	262	92.2	63	3.7	.8	13.6	118	66	3.9	[21] 618	249	260	.08	.13	.8	13
d	Slices (cut lengthwise or French style); wt., 8¾ oz.[47]	1 can	248	92.2	60	3.5	.7	12.9	112	62	3.7	[21] 585	236	250	.07	.12	.7	12
	Size, 603 × 700[14] (No. 10):																	
e	Cuts less than 1½ in. and short cuts (less than ¾ in.); wt., 63 oz. (3 lb. 15 oz.).[46]	1 can	1,786	92.2	429	25.0	5.4	92.9	804	447	26.8	[21] 4,215	1,697	1,700	.54	.89	5.4	89
f	Slices (cut lengthwise or French style); wt., 59 oz. (3 lb. 11 oz.).	1 can	1,673	92.2	402	23.4	5.0	87.0	753	418	25.1	[21] 3,948	1,589	1,670	.50	.84	5.0	84
	Cup:																	
g	Cuts less than 1½ in. and short cuts (less than ¾ in.).	1 cup	135	92.2	32	1.9	.4	7.0	61	34	2.0	[21] 319	128	140	.04	.07	.4	7
h	Slices (cut lengthwise or French style)	1 cup	130	92.2	31	1.8	.4	6.8	59	33	2.0	[21] 307	124	130	.04	.07	.4	7
i	Pound	1 lb	454	92.2	109	6.4	1.4	23.6	204	113	6.8	[21] 1,070	431	450	.14	.23	1.4	23
199	Drained liquid:																	
a	Pound	1 lb	454	96.1	50	1.8	.5	11.3	68	64	4.1	[21] 1,070	431	Trace	.14	.14	1.4	23
b	Ounce	1 oz	28	96.1	3	.1	Trace	.7	4	4	.3	[21] 67	27	Trace	.01	.01	.1	1

[14] Dimensions of can: 1st dimension represents diameter; 2d dimension, height of can. 1st or left-hand digit in each dimension gives number of whole inches; next 2 digits give additional fraction of dimension expressed as 16th of an inch.

[20] Value is for unsalted product. If salt is used, increase value by 236 mg. per 100 g. of vegetable—an estimated figure based on typical amount of salt (0.6%) in canned vegetables. See also Appendix C, section on Cooked Vegetables

[21] Estimated value based on addition of salt in amount of 0.6% of finished product.

[46] Also applies to mixed cuts of lengths varying from ¾ to 2 in.

[47] Also applies to cuts 1½ in. and longer.

[48] Measurement applies to thawed product. See also Appendix C, section on Frozen Fruits and Vegetables

TABLE 1.—*Nutritive values for household measures and market units of foods*—Continued

[Item numbers correspond to those in table 1 of Handbook No. 8, revised 1963. Values in parentheses denote imputed values usually from another form of the food or from a similar food. Zeros in parentheses indicate that amount of a constituent, if present, is probably too small to be measured. Dashes (—) denote lack of reliable data for a constituent believed to be present in a measurable amount. Calculated values, as those based on a recipe, are not in parentheses]

Item No.	Food, approximate measures, units, and weight (edible part unless footnotes indicate otherwise)			Values for edible part of foods: Water	Food energy	Protein	Fat	Carbohydrate	Calcium	Phosphorus	Iron	Sodium	Potassium	Vitamin A value	Thiamin	Riboflavin	Niacin	Ascorbic acid
(A)	(B)			(C)	(D)	(E)	(F)	(G)	(H)	(I)	(J)	(K)	(L)	(M)	(N)	(O)	(P)	(Q)
			Grams	*Percent*	*Calories*	*Grams*	*Grams*	*Grams*	*Milligrams*	*Milligrams*	*Milligrams*	*Milligrams*	*Milligrams*	*International units*	*Milligrams*	*Milligrams*	*Milligrams*	*Milligrams*
	Beans, snap—Continued																	
	Yellow or wax—Continued																	
	Canned—Continued																	
	Special dietary pack (low sodium):																	
200	Solids and liquid:																	
	Can and approx. contents:																	
a	Size, 303 × 406 [14] (No. 303); net wt., 15½ oz.	1 can	439	95.2	66	4.0	0.4	14.9	(149)	(92)	(5.3)	9	417	(260)	(0.13)	(0.18)	(1.3)	(22)
b	Size, 603 × 700 [14] (No. 10); net wt., 101 oz. (6 lb. 5 oz.).	1 can	2,863	95.2	429	25.8	2.9	97.3	(973)	(601)	(34.4)	57	2,720	(1,720)	(.86)	(1.15)	(8.6)	(143)
c	Cup	1 cup	239	95.2	36	2.2	.2	8.1	(81)	(50)	(2.9)	5	227	(140)	(.07)	(.10)	(.7)	(12)
d	Pound	1 lb	454	95.2	68	4.1	.5	15.4	(154)	(95)	(5.4)	9	431	(270)	(.14)	(.18)	(1.4)	(23)
201	Drained solids:																	
	Can and approx. drained contents; cuts less than 1½ in. and short cuts (less than ¾ in.):																	
a	Size, 303 × 406 [14] (No. 303); wt., 9¼ oz. [46]	1 can	262	93.6	55	3.1	.3	12.3	(118)	(66)	(3.9)	5	249	(260)	(.08)	(.13)	(.8)	(13)
b	Size, 603 × 700 [14] (No. 10); wt., 63 oz. (3 lb. 15 oz.). [46]	1 can	1,786	93.6	375	21.4	1.8	83.9	(804)	(447)	(26.8)	36	1,697	(1,790)	(.54)	(.89)	(5.4)	(89)
c	Cup, cuts less than 1½ in. and short cuts (less than ¾ in.).	1 cup	135	93.6	28	1.6	.1	6.3	(61)	(34)	(2.0)	3	128	(140)	(.04)	(.07)	(.4)	(7)
d	Pound	1 lb	454	93.6	95	5.4	.5	21.3	(204)	(113)	(6.8)	9	431	(450)	(.14)	(.23)	(1.4)	(23)
202	Drained liquid:																	
a	Pound	1 lb	454	97.7	32	1.8	.5	6.4	(68)	(64)	(4.1)	9	431	Trace	(.14)	(.14)	(1.4)	(23)
b	Ounce	1 oz	28	97.7	2	.1	Trace	.4	(4)	(4)	(.3)	1	27	Trace	(.01)	(.01)	(.1)	(1)
	Frozen, cut:																	
203	Not thawed:																	
a	Container, net wt., 9 oz	1 container	255	91.1	71	4.6	.3	16.6	92	82	2.0	3	459	260	.20	.23	1.3	31
b	Cup [48]	1 cup	125	91.1	35	2.3	.1	8.1	45	40	1.0	1	225	130	.10	.11	.6	15
c	Pound	1 lb	454	91.1	127	8.2	.5	29.5	163	145	3.6	5	816	450	.36	.41	2.3	54
204	Cooked (boiled), drained:																	
a	Yield from 9 oz., frozen beans	1¾ cups	235	91.5	63	4.0	.2	14.6	82	73	1.6	[20] 2	385	240	.16	.19	.9	14
b	Yield from 1 lb., frozen beans	3⅛ cups	420	91.5	113	7.1	.4	26.0	147	130	2.9	[20] 4	689	420	.29	.34	1.7	25
c	Cup	1 cup	135	91.5	36	2.3	.1	8.4	47	42	.9	[20] 1	221	140	.09	.11	.5	8
d	Pound	1 lb	454	91.5	122	7.7	.5	28.1	159	141	3.2	[20] 5	744	450	.32	.36	1.8	27
	Bean sprouts. See Beans, mung (items 180–181) and Soybeans (items 2143–2144).																	
205	**Beans and frankfurters** (sliced), canned: [5]																	
	Can and approx. contents:																	
a	Size, 211 × 300 [14] (8Z Short); net wt., 8 oz	1 can	227	70.7	327	17.3	16.1	28.6	84	270	4.3	1,224	595	300	.16	.14	3.0	Trace
b	Size, 300 × 407 [14] (No. 300); net wt., 15½ oz	1 can	439	70.7	632	33.4	31.2	55.3	162	522	8.3	2,366	1,150	570	.31	.26	5.7	Trace
c	Cup	1 cup	255	70.7	367	19.4	18.1	32.1	94	303	4.8	1,374	668	330	.18	.15	3.3	Trace
d	Pound	1 lb	454	70.7	653	34.5	32.2	57.2	168	540	8.6	2,445	1,188	590	.32	.27	5.9	Trace
206	**Beaver,** cooked (roasted):																	
a	3 ounces	3 oz	85	56.2	211	24.8	11.6	0	—	—	—	—	—	—	.07	.32	—	—
b	Pound	1 lb	454	56.2	1,125	132.5	62.1	0	—	—	—	—	—	—	.36	1.72	—	—
207	**Beechnuts:** [5]																	
a	In shell (refuse: shells, 39%) [1]	1 lb	454	6.6	1,572	53.7	138.4	56.2	—	—	—	—	—	—	—	—	—	—
b	Shelled	1 lb	454	6.6	2,576	88.0	226.8	92.1	—	—	—	—	—	—	—	—	—	—
	Beef, trimmed to retail basis: [49]																	
	Boneless chuck and chuck cuts:																	
	Boneless beef for stew:																	
	Lean with fat:																	
218	Raw (82% lean, 18% fat)	1 lb	454	60.8	1,166	84.8	88.9	0	50	853	12.7	297	1,357	180	.36	.75	20.4	—
219	Cooked (braised or stewed), drained (81% lean, 19% fat):																	
a	Yield from 1 lb., raw beef (item 218)	10.7 oz	304	49.4	994	79.0	72.7	0	33	426	10.0	138	632	180	.15	.61	12.2	—
b	Cup, chopped or diced pieces (not packed)	1 cup	140	49.4	458	36.4	33.5	0	15	196	4.6	64	291	60	.07	.28	5.6	—
c	Pound	1 lb	454	49.4	1,483	117.9	108.4	0	50	635	15.0	206	943	200	.22	.91	18.1	—

(A)	(B)			(C)	(D)	(E)	(F)	(G)	(H)	(I)	(J)	(K)	(L)	(M)	(N)	(O)	(P)	(Q)
	Lean, trimmed of separable fat:																	
220	Raw	1 lb	454	70.3	717	96.6	33.6	0	54	971	14.5	338	1,546	70	0.42	0.86	23.2	—
221	Cooked (braised or stewed), drained:																	
a	Yield from 1 lb., raw beef (item 220)	10.7 oz	304	59.7	651	91.2	28.9	0	40	486	11.6	160	730	50	.17	.70	14.0	—
b	Cup, chopped or diced pieces (not packed)	1 cup	140	59.7	300	42.0	13.3	0	18	224	5.3	74	336	20	.08	.32	6.4	—
c	Pound	1 lb	454	59.7	971	136.1	43.1	0	59	726	17.2	238	1,089	80	.25	1.04	20.9	—
	Chuck rib roasts or chuck rib steaks (blade or flat-bone cuts):																	
	Choice grade:																	
223	Raw, lean with fat:																	
a	With bone (59% lean, 25% fat) (refuse: bone, 16%).[1]	1 lb	454	51.7	1,349	62.1	120.4	0	34	567	9.2	217	994	240	.27	.56	14.9	—
b	Without bone (70% lean, 30% fat)	1 lb	454	51.7	1,597	73.5	142.4	0	41	671	10.9	257	1,176	280	.32	.66	17.6	—
224	Cooked (braised), drained:																	
	Lean with fat (69% lean, 31% fat):																	
a	Yield from 1 lb., raw beef with bone (item 223a).	9 oz	255	40.3	1,089	57.1	93.6	0	26	281	7.4	100	457	180	.11	.43	8.9	—
b	Yield from 1 lb., raw beef without bone (item 223b).	10.7 oz	304	40.3	1,298	68.1	111.6	0	30	334	8.8	119	545	210	.13	.52	10.6	—
	Cup (not packed):																	
c	Chopped or diced	1 cup	140	40.3	598	31.4	51.4	0	14	154	4.1	55	251	100	.06	.24	4.9	—
d	Ground	1 cup	110	40.3	470	24.6	40.4	0	11	121	3.2	43	197	80	.05	.19	3.9	—
e	Pound	1 lb	454	40.3	1,937	101.6	166.5	0	45	499	13.2	178	813	310	.19	.77	15.9	—
f	Piece, approx. 4⅛ in. long, 2¼ in. wide, ½ in. thick; wt., 3 oz. (steaks); or 2 pieces, 4⅛ in. long, 2¼ in. wide, ¼ in. thick; wt., 1½ oz. each (roasts).	1 or 2 pieces or 3 oz.	85	40.3	363	19.0	31.2	0	9	94	2.5	33	152	60	.04	.14	3.0	—
226	Lean, trimmed of separable fat:																	
a	Yield from 1 lb., raw beef with bone (item 223a).	6.2 oz	176	56.5	438	50.9	24.5	0	23	252	6.5	89	407	40	.09	.39	7.9	—
b	Yield from 1 lb., raw beef without bone (item 223b).	7.4 oz	210	56.5	523	60.7	29.2	0	27	300	7.8	106	486	50	.11	.46	9.5	—
	Cup (not packed):																	
c	Chopped or diced	1 cup	140	56.5	349	40.5	19.5	0	18	200	5.2	71	324	40	.07	.31	6.3	—
d	Ground	1 cup	110	56.5	274	31.8	15.3	0	14	157	4.1	56	254	30	.06	.24	5.0	—
e	Pound	1 lb	454	56.5	1,129	131.1	63.1	0	59	649	16.8	229	1,049	110	.24	1.00	20.4	—
f	Piece, approx. 4⅛ in. long, 2¼ in. wide, ½ in. thick; wt., 3 oz. (steaks); or 2 pieces, 4⅛ in. long, 2¼ in. wide, ¼ in. thick; wt., 1½ oz. each (roasts).	1 or 2 pieces or 3 oz.	85	56.5	212	24.6	11.8	0	11	122	3.1	43	197	20	.05	.19	3.8	—
	Good grade:																	
228	Raw, lean with fat:																	
a	With bone (62% lean, 22% fat) (refuse: bone, 16%).[1]	1 lb	454	56.3	1,153	66.6	96.3	0	38	617	9.9	233	1,066	190	.29	.59	16.0	—
b	Without bone (74% lean, 26% fat)	1 lb	454	56.3	1,374	79.4	114.8	0	45	735	11.8	278	1,270	230	.34	.71	19.1	—
	Cooked (braised), drained:																	
229	Lean with fat (73% lean, 27% fat):																	
a	Yield from 1 lb., raw beef with bone (item 228a).	9 oz	255	44.8	961	61.7	77.3	0	26	309	7.9	108	494	150	.11	.48	9.7	—
b	Yield from 1 lb., raw beef without bone (item 228b).	10.7 oz	304	44.8	1,146	73.6	92.1	0	30	368	9.4	129	589	170	.14	.58	11.6	—
	Cup (not packed):																	
c	Chopped or diced	1 cup	140	44.8	528	33.9	42.4	0	14	169	4.3	59	271	80	.06	.27	5.3	—
d	Ground	1 cup	110	44.8	415	26.6	33.3	0	11	133	3.4	47	213	60	.05	.21	4.2	—
e	Pound	1 lb	454	44.8	1,170	109.8	137.4	0	45	549	14.1	192	878	260	.20	.86	17.2	—
f	Piece, approx. 4⅛ in. long, 2¼ in. wide, ½ in. thick; wt., 3 oz. (steaks); or 2 pieces, 4⅛ in. long, 2¼ in. wide, ¼ in. thick; wt., 1½ oz. each (roasts).	1 or 2 pieces or 3 oz.	85	44.8	320	20.6	25.8	0	9	103	2.6	36	165	50	.04	.16	3.2	—
231	Lean, trimmed of separable fat:																	
a	Yield from 1 lb., raw beef with bone (item 228a).	6.6 oz	186	59.2	407	55.4	19.0	0	24	273	7.1	97	443	30	.10	.43	8.6	—
b	Yield from 1 lb., raw beef without bone (item 228b).	7.8 oz	222	59.2	486	66.2	22.6	0	29	326	8.4	116	530	40	.12	.51	10.2	—

[1] Measure and weight apply to food as it is described with inedible part or parts (refuse) included.

[5] Most of phosphorus in nuts, legumes, and outer layers of cereal grains is present as phytic acid. See also Appendix D, section on Minerals and Oxalic Acid

[14] Dimensions of can: 1st dimension represents diameter; 2d dimension, height of can. 1st or left-hand digit in each dimension gives number of whole inches; next 2 digits give additional fraction of dimension expressed as 16th of an inch.

[30] Value is for unsalted product. If salt is used, increase value by 236 mg. per 100 g. of vegetable—an estimated figure based on typical amount of salt (0.6%) in canned vegetables. See also Appendix C, section on Cooked Vegetables

[44] Also applies to mixed cuts of lengths varying from ¾ to 2 in.

[43] Measurement applies to thawed product. See also Appendix C, section on Frozen Fruits and Vegetables

[49] For further information about items and basis of vitamin and mineral values, see Appendix B, section on Foods Measured in Pieces, Slices, and Other Units and Appendix C, section on Meats

Values for cooked items apply to products prepared without added salt or other seasoning.

TABLE 1.—*Nutritive values for household measures and market units of foods*—Continued

[Item numbers correspond to those in table 1 of Handbook No. 8, revised 1963. Values in parentheses denote imputed values usually from another form of the food or from a similar food. Zeros in parentheses indicate that amount of a constituent, if present, is probably too small to be measured. Dashes (—) denote lack of reliable data for a constituent believed to be present in a measurable amount. Calculated values, as those based on a recipe, are not in parentheses]

Item No. (A)	Food, approximate measures, units, and weight (edible part unless footnotes indicate otherwise) (B)			Water (C)	Food energy (D)	Protein (E)	Fat (F)	Carbohydrate (G)	Calcium (H)	Phosphorus (I)	Iron (J)	Sodium (K)	Potassium (L)	Vitamin A value (M)	Thiamin (N)	Riboflavin (O)	Niacin (P)	Ascorbic acid (Q)
			Grams	Percent	Calories	Grams	Grams	Grams	Milligrams	Milligrams	Milligrams	Milligrams	Milligrams	International units	Milligrams	Milligrams	Milligrams	Milligrams
	Beef, trimmed to retail basis [49]—Continued																	
	Boneless chuck and chuck cuts—Continued																	
	Chuck rib roasts or chuck rib steaks (blade or flat-bone cuts)—Continued																	
	Good grade—Continued																	
	Cooked (braised), drained—Continued																	
	Lean, trimmed of separable fat—Continued																	
	Cup (not packed):																	
c	Chopped or diced	1 cup	140	59.2	307	41.7	14.3	0	18	206	5.3	73	334	30	0.08	0.32	6.4	—
d	Ground	1 cup	110	59.2	241	32.8	11.2	0	14	162	4.2	57	262	20	.06	.25	5.1	—
e	Pound	1 lb	454	59.2	993	135.2	46.3	0	59	667	17.2	237	1,082	80	.24	1.04	20.9	—
f	Piece, approx. 4⅛ in. long, 2¼ in. wide, ½ in. thick; wt., 3 oz. (steaks); or 2 pieces, 4⅛ in. long, 2¼ in. wide, ¼ in. thick; wt., 1½ oz. each (roasts).	1 or 2 pieces or 3 oz.	85	59.2	186	25.3	8.7	0	11	125	3.2	44	202	20	.05	.20	3.9	—
	Chuck roasts or chuck steaks (arm and round-bone cuts):																	
	Choice grade:																	
233	Raw, lean with fat:																	
a	With bone (77% lean, 12% fat) (refuse: bone, 11%).[1]	1 lb	454	64.2	905	78.8	62.9	0	49	731	11.8	276	1,261	130	.34	.70	18.9	—
b	Without bone (86% lean, 14% fat)	1 lb	454	64.2	1,012	88.0	70.3	0	54	816	13.2	308	1,408	140	.38	.78	21.1	—
	Cooked (braised), drained:																	
234	Lean with fat (85% lean, 15% fat):																	
a	Yield from 1 lb., raw beef with bone (item 233a).	9½ oz	270	53.0	780	73.2	51.8	0	32	362	9.2	128	586	90	.14	.57	11.8	—
b	Yield from 1 lb., raw beef without bone (item 233b).	10.7 oz	304	53.0	879	82.4	58.4	0	36	407	10.3	144	659	110	.15	.64	12.8	—
	Cup (not packed):																	
c	Chopped or diced	1 cup	140	53.0	405	37.9	26.9	0	17	188	4.8	66	303	50	.07	.29	5.9	—
d	Ground	1 cup	110	53.0	318	29.8	21.1	0	13	147	3.7	52	238	40	.06	.23	4.6	—
e	Pound	1 lb	454	53.0	1,311	122.9	87.1	0	54	608	15.4	215	983	160	.23	.95	19.1	—
f	Piece, approx. 2½ in. long, 2½ in. wide, ¾ in. thick.	1 piece or 3 oz	85	53.0	246	23.0	16.3	0	10	114	2.9	40	184	30	.04	.18	3.6	—
236	Lean, trimmed of separable fat:																	
a	Yield from 1 lb., raw beef with bone (item 233a).	8.1 oz	230	61.7	444	70.2	16.1	0	32	345	8.7	123	562	30	.13	.53	10.6	—
b	Yield from 1 lb., raw beef without bone (item 233b).	9.1 oz	258	61.7	498	78.7	18.1	0	36	387	9.8	138	630	30	.14	.59	11.9	—
	Cup (not packed):																	
c	Chopped or diced	1 cup	140	61.7	270	42.7	9.8	0	20	210	5.3	75	342	20	.08	.32	6.4	—
d	Ground	1 cup	110	61.7	212	33.6	7.7	0	15	165	4.2	59	269	10	.06	.25	5.1	—
e	Pound	1 lb	454	61.7	875	138.3	31.8	0	64	680	17.2	242	1,106	50	.25	1.04	20.9	—
f	Piece, approx. 2½ in. long, 2½ in. wide, ¾ in. thick.	1 piece or 3 oz	85	61.7	164	25.9	6.0	0	12	128	3.2	45	207	10	.05	.20	3.9	—
	Good grade:																	
238	Raw, lean with fat:																	
a	With bone (79% lean, 10% fat) (refuse: bone, 11%).[1]	1 lb	454	67.3	768	81.7	46.7	0	48	756	12.5	286	1,307	90	.35	.72	19.5	—
b	Without bone (89% lean, 11% fat)	1 lb	454	67.3	866	92.1	52.6	0	54	853	14.1	322	1,474	100	.39	.82	22.0	—
	Cooked (braised), drained:																	
239	Lean with fat (88% lean, 12% fat):																	
a	Yield from 1 lb., raw beef with bone (item 238a).	9½ oz	270	56.3	683	76.7	39.4	0	35	378	10.0	134	614	70	.14	.57	11.6	—
b	Yield from 1 lb., raw beef without bone (item 238b).	10.7 oz	304	56.3	769	86.3	44.4	0	40	426	11.2	151	690	80	.16	.64	13.1	—
	Cup (not packed):																	
c	Chopped or diced	1 cup	140	56.3	354	39.8	20.4	0	18	196	5.2	70	318	40	.07	.29	6.0	—
d	Ground	1 cup	110	56.3	278	31.2	16.1	0	14	154	4.1	55	250	30	.06	.23	4.7	—

(A)	(B)			(C)	(D)	(E)	(F)	(G)	(H)	(I)	(J)	(K)	(L)	(M)	(N)	(O)	(P)	(Q)
e	Pound	1 lb	454	56.3	1,148	128.8	66.2	0	59	635	16.8	225	1,030	120	0.24	0.95	19.5	—
f	Piece, approx. 2½ in. long, 2½ in. wide, ¾ in. thick.	1 piece or 3 oz	85	56.3	215	24.1	12.4	0	11	119	3.1	42	193	20	.04	.18	3.7	—
241	Lean, trimmed of separable fat:																	
a	Yield from 1 lb., raw beef with bone (item 238a).	8.4 oz	238	63.1	426	73.5	12.4	0	33	359	9.3	129	588	20	.13	.55	11.2	—
b	Yield from 1 lb., raw beef without bone (item 238b).	9.4 oz	267	63.1	478	82.5	13.9	0	37	403	10.4	144	660	20	.15	.61	12.5	—
	Cup (not packed):																	
c	Chopped or diced	1 cup	140	63.1	251	43.3	7.3	0	20	211	5.5	76	346	10	.08	.32	6.6	—
d	Ground	1 cup	110	63.1	197	34.0	5.7	0	15	166	4.3	60	212	10	.06	.25	5.2	—
e	Pound	1 lb	454	63.1	812	140.2	23.6	0	64	685	17.7	245	1,122	40	.25	1.04	21.3	—
f	Piece, approx. 2½ in. long, 2½ in. wide, ¾ in. thick.	1 piece or 3 oz	85	63.1	152	26.3	4.4	0	12	128	3.3	46	210	10	.05	.20	4.0	—
	Flank steak, whole or cut pieces such as flank steak fillets, London broil; choice grade:																	
243	Raw (100% lean)	1 lb	454	71.7	653	98.0	25.9	0	59	912	14.5	343	1,568	50	.42	.87	23.5	—
244	Cooked (braised), drained (100% lean):																	
a	Yield from 1 lb., raw beef (item 243)	10.7 oz	304	61.4	596	92.7	22.2	0	43	456	11.6	162	742	40	.17	.70	14.0	—
b	Pound	1 lb	454	61.4	889	138.3	33.1	0	64	680	17.2	242	1,106	50	.25	1.04	20.9	—
c	Piece, approx. 2½ in. long, 2½ in. wide, ¾ in. thick.	1 piece or 3 oz	85	61.4	167	25.9	6.2	0	12	128	3.2	45	207	10	.05	.20	3.9	—
	Loin or short loin:																	
	Porterhouse steak, choice grade:																	
257	Raw, lean with fat and bone (57% lean, 33% fat) (refuse: bone, 9%).[1]	1 lb	454	48.3	1,603	60.8	148.8	0	33	559	9.0	213	973	300	.26	.55	14.6	—
	Cooked (broiled):																	
258	Lean with fat (57% lean, 43% fat):																	
a	Yield from 1 lb., raw beef with bone (item 257).	10.6 oz	301	37.2	1,400	59.3	127.0	0	27	506	7.8	145	664	220	.17	.48	12.6	—
b	Pound	1 lb	454	37.2	2,109	89.4	191.4	0	41	762	11.8	219	1,001	340	.26	.73	19.1	—
260	Lean, trimmed of separable fat:																	
a	Yield from 1 lb., raw beef with bone (item 257).	6.1 oz	172	57.9	385	51.9	18.1	0	21	416	6.4	127	581	30	.14	.40	10.1	—
b	Pound	1 lb	454	57.9	1,016	137.0	47.6	0	54	1,098	16.8	336	1,534	70	.37	1.04	26.8	—
	T-bone steak, choice grade:																	
267	Raw, lean with fat and bone (55% lean, 34% fat) (refuse: bone, 11%).[1]	1 lb	454	47.5	1,596	59.1	149.1	0	32	543	8.8	207	946	300	.25	.53	14.2	—
	Cooked (broiled):																	
268	Lean with fat (56% lean, 44% fat):																	
a	Yield from 1 lb., raw beef with bone (item 267).	10.4 oz	295	36.4	1,395	57.5	127.4	0	24	490	7.7	141	644	220	.17	.47	12.1	—
b	Pound	1 lb	454	36.4	2,146	88.5	196.0	0	36	753	11.8	217	991	340	.25	.73	18.6	—
270	Lean, trimmed of separable fat:																	
a	Yield from 1 lb., raw beef with bone (item 267).	5.8 oz	165	57.9	368	50.2	17.0	0	20	401	6.1	123	562	30	.13	.38	9.7	—
b	Pound	1 lb	454	57.9	1,012	137.9	46.7	0	54	1,102	16.8	338	1,544	70	.37	1.04	26.8	—
	Club steak, choice grade:																	
277	Raw, lean with fat:																	
a	With bone (54% lean, 30% fat) (refuse: bone, 16%).[1]	1 lb	454	49.1	1,443	58.9	132.1	0	34	539	8.7	206	942	260	.25	.52	14.1	—
b	Without bone (64% lean, 36% fat)	1 lb	454	49.1	1,724	70.3	157.9	0	41	644	10.4	246	1,125	310	.30	.63	16.9	—
	Cooked (broiled):																	
278	Lean with fat (58% lean, 42% fat):																	
a	Yield from 1 lb., raw beef with bone (item 277a).	9.8 oz	278	37.9	1,262	57.3	112.9	0	25	487	7.5	140	642	200	.16	.47	12.0	—
b	Yield from 1 lb., raw beef without bone (item 277b).	11.7 oz	331	37.9	1,503	68.2	134.4	0	30	579	8.9	167	764	240	.20	.56	14.2	—
c	Pound	1 lb	454	37.9	2,059	93.4	184.2	0	41	794	12.2	229	1,046	320	.27	.77	19.5	—
280	Lean, trimmed of separable fat:																	
a	Yield from 1 lb., raw beef with bone (item 277a).	5.7 oz	161	56.0	393	47.7	20.9	0	19	383	5.8	117	534	40	.13	.37	9.3	—
b	Yield from 1 lb., raw beef without bone (item 277b).	6.8 oz	192	56.0	468	56.8	25.0	0	23	457	6.9	139	636	40	.15	.44	11.1	—
c	Pound	1 lb	454	56.0	1,107	134.3	59.0	0	54	1,080	16.3	329	1,504	100	.36	1.04	26.3	—
	Loin end or sirloin:																	
	Wedge- and round-bone sirloin steak, choice grade:																	
287	Raw, lean with fat:																	
a	With bone (68% lean, 25% fat) (refuse: bone, 7%).[1]	1 lb	454	55.7	1,316	71.1	112.3	0	42	652	10.5	249	1,138	220	.30	.63	17.1	—
b	Without bone (73% lean, 27% fat)	1 lb	454	55.7	1,420	76.7	121.1	0	45	703	11.3	268	1,227	240	.33	.68	18.4	—

[1] Measure and weight apply to food as it is described with inedible part or parts (refuse) included.

** For further information about items and basis of vitamin and mineral values, see Appendix B, section on Foods Measured in Pieces, Slices, and Other Units and Appendix C, section on Meats

Values for cooked items apply to products prepared without added salt or other seasoning.

TABLE 1.—*Nutritive values for household measures and market units of foods*—Continued

[Item numbers correspond to those in table 1 of Handbook No. 8, revised 1963. Values in parentheses denote imputed values usually from another form of the food or from a similar food. Zeros in parentheses indicate that amount of a constituent, if present, is probably too small to be measured. Dashes (—) denote lack of reliable data for a constituent believed to be present in a measurable amount. Calculated values, as those based on a recipe, are not in parentheses]

Item No. (A)	Food, approximate measures, units, and weight (edible part unless footnotes indicate otherwise) (B)			Water (C)	Food energy (D)	Protein (E)	Fat (F)	Carbohydrate (G)	Calcium (H)	Phosphorus (I)	Iron (J)	Sodium (K)	Potassium (L)	Vitamin A value (M)	Thiamin (N)	Riboflavin (O)	Niacin (P)	Ascorbic acid (Q)
				Values for edible part of foods														
			Grams	Percent	Calories	Grams	Grams	Grams	Milligrams	Milligrams	Milligrams	Milligrams	Milligrams	International units	Milligrams	Milligrams	Milligrams	Milligrams
	Beef, trimmed to retail basis[40]—Continued																	
	Loin end or sirloin—Continued																	
	Wedge- and round-bone sirloin steak, choice grade—Continued																	
	Cooked (broiled):																	
288	Lean with fat (66% lean, 34% fat):																	
a	Yield from 1 lb., raw beef with bone (item 287a).	10.9 oz	308	43.9	1,192	70.8	98.6	0	31	588	8.9	173	793	170	0.20	0.55	14.5	—
b	Yield from 1 lb., raw beef without bone (item 287b).	11.7 oz	331	43.9	1,281	76.1	105.9	0	33	632	9.6	186	852	180	.21	.60	15.6	—
c	Pound	1 lb	454	43.9	1,755	104.3	145.2	0	45	866	13.2	256	1,168	240	.29	.82	21.3	—
d	Piece, approx. 3½ in. long, 2 in. wide, ¾ in. thick.	1 piece or 3 oz	85	43.9	329	19.6	27.2	0	9	162	2.5	48	220	50	.05	.15	4.0	—
290	Lean, trimmed of separable fat:																	
a	Yield from 1 lb., raw beef with bone (item 287a).	7.2 oz	203	58.7	420	65.4	15.6	0	26	530	7.9	160	732	20	.18	.51	13.0	—
b	Yield from 1 lb., raw beef without bone (item 287b).	7.7 oz	218	58.7	451	70.2	16.8	0	28	569	8.5	172	786	30	.19	.55	14.0	—
c	Pound	1 lb	454	58.7	939	146.1	34.9	0	59	1,184	17.7	358	1,636	50	.39	1.13	29.0	—
d	Piece, approx. 3½ in. long, 2 in. wide, ¾ in. thick.	1 piece or 3 oz	85	58.7	176	27.4	6.5	0	11	222	3.3	67	307	10	.07	.21	5.4	—
	Double-bone (flat-bone) sirloin steak, choice grade:																	
	Raw, lean with fat:																	
297 a	With bone (59% lean, 23% fat) (refuse: bone, 18%).[1]	1 lb	454	53.7	1,240	61.1	108.4	0	34	562	9.3	214	978	220	.26	.54	14.7	—
b	Without bone (72% lean, 28% fat)	1 lb	454	53.7	1,510	74.4	132.0	0	41	685	11.3	260	1,190	260	.32	.66	17.9	—
	Cooked (broiled):																	
298	Lean with fat (66% lean, 34% fat):																	
a	Yield from 1 lb., raw beef with bone (item 297a).	9.6 oz	272	42.1	1,110	60.4	94.4	0	27	506	7.9	148	676	160	.17	.49	12.5	—
b	Yield from 1 lb., raw beef without bone (item 297b).	11.7 oz	331	42.1	1,350	73.5	114.9	0	33	616	9.6	180	823	200	.21	.60	15.2	—
c	Pound	1 lb	454	42.1	1,851	100.7	157.4	0	45	844	13.2	247	1,128	270	.28	.82	20.9	—
d	Piece, approx. 2½ in. long, 2½ in. wide, ¾ in. thick.	1 piece or 3 oz	85	42.1	347	18.9	29.5	0	9	158	2.5	46	212	50	.05	.15	3.9	—
300	Lean, trimmed of separable fat:																	
a	Yield from 1 lb., raw beef with bone (item 297a).	6.3 oz	179	58.5	387	54.8	17.0	0	21	437	6.6	134	614	30	.15	.41	10.7	—
b	Yield from 1 lb., raw beef without bone (item 297b).	7.7 oz	218	58.5	471	66.7	20.7	0	26	532	8.1	163	747	30	.18	.50	13.1	—
c	Pound	1 lb	454	58.5	980	138.8	43.1	0	54	1,107	16.8	340	1,555	70	.37	1.04	27.2	—
d	Piece, approx. 2½ in. long, 2½ in. wide, ¾ in. thick.	1 piece or 3 oz	85	58.5	184	26.0	8.1	0	10	207	3.1	64	291	10	.07	.20	5.1	—
	Hipbone (pinbone) sirloin steak, choice grade:																	
	Raw, lean with fat:																	
307 a	With bone (51% lean, 33% fat) (refuse: bone, 15%).[1]	1 lb	454	46.0	1,585	55.8	149.3	0	31	508	8.5	195	893	300	.24	.50	13.3	—
b	Without bone (61% lean, 39% fat)	1 lb	454	46.0	1,869	65.8	176.0	0	36	599	10.0	230	1,053	350	.28	.59	15.7	—
	Cooked (broiled):																	
308	Lean with fat (55% lean, 45% fat):																	
a	Yield from 1 lb., raw beef with bone (item 307a).	9.9 oz	281	35.1	1,368	53.7	126.2	0	25	458	7.0	132	601	220	.15	.45	11.2	—
b	Yield from 1 lb., raw beef without bone (item 307b).	11.7 oz	331	35.1	1,612	63.2	148.6	0	30	540	8.3	155	708	260	.18	.53	13.2	—
c	Pound	1 lb	454	35.1	2,209	86.6	203.7	0	41	739	11.3	212	970	360	.25	.73	18.1	—
d	Piece, approx. 2½ in. long, 2½ in. wide, ¾ in. thick.	1 piece or 3 oz	85	35.1	414	16.2	38.2	0	8	139	2.1	40	181	70	.05	.14	3.4	—
310	Lean, trimmed of separable fat:																	
a	Yield from 1 lb., raw beef with bone (item 307a).	5½ oz	155	56.3	372	46.2	19.4	0	19	370	5.6	113	517	30	.12	.36	9.0	—

(A)	(B)			(C)	(D)	(E)	(F)	(G)	(H)	(I)	(J)	(K)	(L)	(M)	(N)	(O)	(P)	(Q)
b	Yield from 1 lb., raw beef without bone (item 307b).	6.4 oz	182	56.3	437	54.2	22.8	0	22	435	6.6	133	607	40	0.15	0.42	10.6	—
c	Pound	1 lb	454	56.3	1,089	135.2	56.7	0	54	1,084	16.3	331	1,514	100	.36	1.04	26.3	—
d	Piece, approx. 2½ in. long, 2½ in. wide, ¾ in. thick.	1 piece or 3 oz	85	56.3	204	25.3	10.6	0	10	203	3.1	62	283	20	.07	.20	4.9	—
	Plate beef:																	
	Raw, lean with fat:																	
322 a	With bone (54% lean, 33% fat) (refuse: bone, 13%).[1]	1 lb	454	51.3	1,413	63.9	126.6	0	36	583	9.5	224	1,022	250	.27	.57	15.3	—
b	Without bone (62% lean, 38% fat)	1 lb	454	51.3	1,615	73.0	144.7	0	41	667	10.9	256	1,168	290	.31	.65	17.5	—
	Cooked (simmered), drained:																	
	Lean with fat:																	
323 a	Yield from 1 lb., raw beef with bone (item 322a).	9.3 oz	264	39.9	1,140	58.9	98.5	0	24	290	7.7	103	471	190	.11	.45	9.0	—
b	Yield from 1 lb., raw beef without bone (item 322b).	10.7 oz	304	39.9	1,313	67.8	113.4	0	27	334	8.8	119	542	220	.12	.52	10.3	—
c	Pound	1 lb	454	39.9	1,960	101.2	169.2	0	41	499	13.2	177	810	320	.19	.77	15.4	—
	Lean, trimmed of separable fat:																	
325 a	Yield from 1 lb., raw beef with bone (item 322a).	5.7 oz	161	61.1	320	48.8	12.4	0	21	240	6.1	85	390	20	.09	.37	7.4	—
b	Yield from 1 lb., raw beef without bone (item 322b).	6½ oz	185	61.1	368	56.1	14.2	0	24	276	7.0	98	449	20	.10	.43	8.5	—
c	Pound	1 lb	454	61.1	903	137.4	34.9	0	59	676	17.2	240	1,099	60	.25	1.04	20.9	—
	Rib roast, choice grade:																	
	Raw, lean with fat:																	
327 a	With bone (59% lean, 33% fat) (refuse: bone, 8%).[1]	1 lb	454	47.2	1,673	61.8	156.1	0	38	630	9.2	216	989	310	.27	.55	14.8	—
b	Without bone (64% lean, 36% fat)	1 lb	454	47.2	1,819	67.1	169.6	0	41	685	10.0	235	1,074	340	.29	.60	16.1	—
	Cooked (roasted):																	
	Lean with fat (64% lean, 36% fat):																	
328 a	Yield from 1 lb., raw beef with bone (item 327a).	10¾ oz	305	40.0	1,342	60.7	120.2	0	27	567	7.9	149	680	230	.16	.46	11.0	—
b	Yield from 1 lb., raw beef without bone (item 327b).	11.7 oz	331	40.0	1,456	65.9	130.4	0	30	616	8.6	161	738	250	.18	.50	11.9	—
	Cup (not packed):																	
c	Chopped or diced	1 cup	140	40.0	616	27.9	55.2	0	13	260	3.6	68	312	110	.07	.21	5.0	—
d	Ground	1 cup	110	40.0	484	21.9	43.3	0	10	205	2.9	54	245	80	.06	.17	4.0	—
e	Pound	1 lb	454	40.0	1,996	90.3	178.7	0	41	844	11.8	221	1,011	350	.24	.68	16.3	—
f	Piece, approx. 4⅛ in. long, 2¼ in. wide, ¼ in. thick; wt., 1½ oz.	2 pieces or 3 oz	85	40.0	374	16.9	33.5	0	8	158	2.2	41	189	70	.05	.13	3.1	—
	Lean, trimmed of separable fat:																	
330 a	Yield from 1 lb., raw beef with bone (item 327a).	6.9 oz	195	57.2	470	55.0	26.1	0	23	499	7.0	135	616	50	.14	.41	9.9	—
b	Yield from 1 lb., raw beef without bone (item 327b).	7½ oz	212	57.2	511	59.8	28.4	0	25	543	7.6	147	670	50	.15	.45	10.8	—
	Cup (not packed):																	
c	Chopped or diced	1 cup	140	57.2	337	39.5	18.8	0	17	358	5.0	97	442	30	.10	.29	7.1	—
d	Ground	1 cup	110	57.2	265	31.0	14.7	0	13	282	4.0	76	347	30	.08	.23	5.6	—
e	Pound	1 lb	454	57.2	1,093	127.9	60.8	0	54	1,161	16.3	313	1,432	110	.33	.95	23.1	—
f	Piece, approx. 4⅛ in. long, 2¼ in. wide, ¼ in. thick; wt., 1½ oz.	2 pieces or 3 oz	85	57.2	205	24.0	11.4	0	10	218	3.1	59	269	20	.06	.18	4.3	—
	Round steak:																	
	Raw, lean with fat:																	
352 a	With bone (86% lean, 11% fat) (refuse: bone, 3%).[1]	1 lb	454	66.6	863	88.5	53.9	0	53	890	13.1	310	1,416	110	.38	.79	21.3	—
b	Without bone (89% lean, 11% fat)	1 lb	454	66.6	894	91.6	55.8	0	54	921	13.6	321	1,466	110	.39	.82	22.0	—
	Cooked (braised, broiled, or sauteed):																	
	Lean with fat (81% lean, 19% fat):																	
353 a	Yield from 1 lb., raw beef with bone (item 352a).	10.7 oz	304	54.7	793	86.9	46.8	0	36	760	10.6	213	973	80	.24	.67	17.0	—
b	Yield from 1 lb., raw beef without bone (item 352b).	11.1 oz	314	54.7	820	89.8	48.8	0	38	785	11.0	220	1,006	80	.25	.69	17.6	—
c	Pound	1 lb	454	54.7	1,184	129.7	69.9	0	54	1,134	15.9	318	1,453	120	.35	1.00	25.4	—
d	Piece, approx. 4⅛ in. long, 2¼ in. wide, ½ in. thick.	1 piece or 3 oz	85	54.7	222	24.3	13.1	0	10	213	3.0	60	272	20	.07	.19	4.8	—
	Lean, trimmed of separable fat:																	
355 a	Yield from 1 lb., raw beef with bone (item 352a).	9.2 oz	260	61.2	491	81.4	15.9	0	34	697	9.6	199	912	20	.22	.62	15.6	—
b	Yield from 1 lb., raw beef without bone (item 352b).	9½ oz	268	61.2	507	83.9	16.3	0	35	718	9.9	206	940	20	.22	.64	16.1	—
c	Pound	1 lb	454	61.2	857	142.0	27.7	0	59	1,216	16.8	348	1,590	40	.38	1.09	27.2	—
d	Piece, approx. 4⅛ in. long, 2¼ in. wide, ½ in. thick.	1 piece or 3 oz	85	61.2	161	26.6	5.2	0	11	228	3.1	65	298	10	.07	.20	5.1	—

[1] Measure and weight apply to food as it is described with inedible part or parts (refuse) included.

[a] For further information about items and basis of vitamin and mineral values, see Appendix B, section on Foods Measured in Pieces, Slices, and Other Units and Appendix C, section on Meats

Values for cooked items apply to products prepared without added salt or other seasoning.

TABLE 1.—*Nutritive values for household measures and market units of foods*—Continued

[Item numbers correspond to those in table 1 of Handbook No. 8, revised 1963. Values in parentheses denote imputed values usually from another form of the food or from a similar food. Zeros in parentheses indicate that amount of a constituent, if present, is probably too small to be measured. Dashes (—) denote lack of reliable data for a constituent believed to be present in a measurable amount. Calculated values, as those based on a recipe, are not in parentheses]

Item No. (A)	Food, approximate measures, units, and weight (edible part unless footnotes indicate otherwise) (B)			Water (C)	Food energy (D)	Protein (E)	Fat (F)	Carbohydrate (G)	Calcium (H)	Phosphorus (I)	Iron (J)	Sodium (K)	Potassium (L)	Vitamin A value (M)	Thiamin (N)	Riboflavin (O)	Niacin (P)	Ascorbic acid (Q)
			Grams	*Percent*	*Calories*	*Grams*	*Grams*	*Grams*	*Milligrams*	*Milligrams*	*Milligrams*	*Milligrams*	*Milligrams*	*International units*	*Milligrams*	*Milligrams*	*Milligrams*	*Milligrams*
	Beef, trimmed to retail basis[49]—Continued																	
	Rump roast:																	
	Choice grade:																	
357	Raw, lean with fat:																	
a	With bone (63% lean, 22% fat) (refuse: bone, 15%).[1]	1 lb	454	56.5	1,167	67.0	97.4	0	39	616	10.0	235	1,072	190	0.29	0.60	16.1	—
b	Without bone (75% lean, 25% fat)	1 lb	454	56.5	1,374	78.9	114.8	0	45	726	11.8	276	1,262	230	.34	.70	19.0	—
	Cooked (roasted):																	
358	Lean with fat (75% lean, 25% fat):																	
a	Yield from 1 lb., raw beef with bone (item 357a).	9.9 oz	281	48.1	975	66.3	76.7	0			8.7	162	743	140	.17	.51	12.1	—
b	Yield from 1 lb., raw beef without bone (item 357b).	11.7 oz	331	48.1	1,149	78.1	90.4	0	33	652	10.3	191	875	170	.21	.60	14.2	—
	Cup (not packed):																	
c	Chopped or diced	1 cup	140	48.1	486	33.0	38.2	0	14	276	4.3	81	370	70	.09	.25	6.0	—
d	Ground	1 cup	110	48.1	382	26.0	30.0	0	11	217	3.4	64	291	60	.07	.20	4.7	—
e	Pound	1 lb	454	48.1	1,574	107.0	123.8	0	45	894	14.1	262	1,198	230	.28	.82	19.5	—
f	Piece, approx. 4⅛ in. long, 2¼ in. wide, ¼ in. thick; wt., 1½ oz.	2 pieces or 3 oz	85	48.1	295	20.1	23.2	0	9	167	2.6	49	225	40	.05	.15	3.7	—
360	Lean, trimmed of separable fat:																	
a	Yield from 1 lb., raw beef with bone (item 357a).	7.4 oz	211	60.4	439	61.4	19.6	0	25	513	7.8	150	688	30	.16	.46	11.0	—
b	Yield from 1 lb., raw beef without bone (item 357b).	8.8 oz	248	60.4	516	72.2	23.1	0	30	603	9.2	177	809	40	.19	.55	12.9	—
	Cup (not packed):																	
c	Chopped or diced	1 cup	140	60.4	291	40.7	13.0	0	17	340	5.2	100	456	20	.11	.31	7.3	—
d	Ground	1 cup	110	60.4	229	32.0	10.2	0	13	267	4.1	78	358	20	.08	.24	5.7	—
e	Pound	1 lb	454	60.4	943	132.0	42.2	0	54	1,102	16.8	323	1,478	70	.34	1.00	23.6	—
f	Piece, approx. 4⅛ in. long, 2¼ in. wide, ¼ in. thick; wt., 1½ oz.	2 pieces or 3 oz	85	60.4	177	24.7	7.9	0	10	207	3.1	61	277	10	.06	.19	4.4	—
	Good grade:																	
362	Raw, lean with fat:																	
a	With bone (64% lean, 20% fat) (refuse: bone, 16%).[1]	1 lb	454	59.4	1,037	70.1	81.9	0	42	643	10.3	245	1,122	160	.30	.62	16.8	—
b	Without bone (76% lean, 24% fat)	1 lb	454	59.4	1,229	83.0	97.1	0	50	762	12.2	291	1,328	200	.36	.73	19.9	—
	Cooked (roasted):																	
363	Lean with fat (76% lean, 24% fat):																	
a	Yield from 1 lb., raw beef with bone (item 362a).	9.8 oz	278	50.7	881	69.2	65.1	0	31	575	8.6	170	775	120	.18	.53	12.5	—
b	Yield from 1 lb., raw beef without bone (item 362b).	11.7 oz	331	50.7	1,049	82.4	77.5	0	36	685	10.3	202	923	150	.22	.63	14.9	—
	Cup (not packed):																	
c	Chopped or diced	1 cup	140	50.7	444	34.9	32.8	0	15	290	4.3	86	391	60	.09	.27	6.3	—
d	Ground	1 cup	110	50.7	349	27.4	25.7	0	12	228	3.4	67	307	50	.07	.21	5.0	—
e	Pound	1 lb	454	50.7	1,438	112.9	106.1	0	50	939	14.1	277	1,264	200	.29	.86	20.4	—
f	Piece, approx. 4⅛ in. long, 2¼ in. wide, ¼ in. thick; wt., 1½ oz.	2 pieces or 3 oz	85	50.7	269	21.2	19.9	0	9	176	2.6	52	237	40	.06	.16	3.8	—
365	Lean, trimmed of separable fat:																	
a	Yield from 1 lb., raw beef with bone (item 362a).	7.4 oz	211	62.0	401	62.5	15.0	0	27	523	7.8	153	700	20	.16	.46	11.2	—
b	Yield from 1 lb., raw beef without bone (item 362b).	8.9 oz	252	62.0	479	74.6	17.9	0	33	625	9.3	183	836	30	.19	.55	13.4	—
	Cup (not packed):																	
c	Chopped or diced	1 cup	140	62.0	266	41.4	9.9	0	18	347	5.2	101	464	20	.11	.31	7.4	—
d	Ground	1 cup	110	62.0	209	32.6	7.8	0	14	273	4.1	80	365	10	.08	.24	5.8	—
e	Pound	1 lb	454	62.0	862	134.3	32.2	0	59	1,125	16.8	329	1,504	50	.34	1.00	24.0	—
f	Piece, approx. 4⅛ in. long, 2¼ in. wide, ¼ in. thick; wt., 1½ oz.	2 pieces or 3 oz	85	62.0	162	25.2	6.0	0	11	211	3.1	62	282	10	.06	.19	4.5	—
	Ground beef:																	
	Lean with 10% fat:																	
367	Raw:																	
a	Pound (shaped into four 4-oz. patties (item	1 lb	454	68.3	812	93.9	45.4	0	54	871	14.1	329	1,502	90	.40	.83	22.5	—

(A)	(B)			(C)	(D)	(E)	(F)	(G)	(H)	(I)	(J)	(K)	(L)	(M)	(N)	(O)	(P)	(Q)
	367b) or five 3.2-oz. patties (item 367c)).																	
b	Patty, wt., 4 oz	1 patty	113	68.3	202	23.4	11.3	0	14	217	3.5	82	374	20	0.10	0.21	5.6	—
c	Patty, wt., 3.2 oz	1 patty	91	68.3	163	18.8	9.1	0	11	175	2.8	66	301	20	.08	.17	4.5	—
d	Cup, packed	1 cup	226	68.3	405	46.8	22.6	0	27	434	7.0	164	749	50	.20	.42	11.2	—
368	Cooked (well done, oven-broiled, pan-broiled, or sauteed):																	
a	Yield from 1 lb., raw ground beef (item 367a), four 3-oz. patties (item 368c), or five 2.4-oz. patties (item 368d).	12 oz	340	60.0	745	93.2	38.4	0	41	782	11.9	228	1,044	70	.32	.78	20.4	—
b	Pound	1 lb	454	60.0	993	124.3	51.3	0	54	1,043	15.9	305	1,392	90	.43	1.04	27.2	—
c	Patty, approx. 3-in. diam., ⅝ in. thick; wt., 3 oz.	1 patty or 3 oz.	85	60.0	186	23.3	9.6	0	10	196	3.0	57	261	20	.08	.20	5.1	—
d	Patty, approx. 3-in. diam., ½ in. thick; wt., 2.4 oz.	1 patty	68	60.0	149	18.6	7.7	0	8	156	2.4	46	208	10	.06	.16	4.1	—
	Lean with 21% fat:																	
369	Raw:																	
a	Pound (shaped into four 4-oz. patties (item 369b) or five 3.2-oz. patties (item 369c)).	1 lb	454	60.2	1,216	81.2	96.2	0	45	708	12.2	284	1,299	160	.35	.72	19.5	—
b	Patty, wt., 4 oz	1 patty	113	60.2	303	20.2	24.0	0	11	176	3.1	71	323	40	.09	.18	4.9	—
c	Patty, wt., 3.2 oz	1 patty	91	60.2	244	16.3	19.3	0	9	142	2.5	57	261	30	.07	.14	3.9	—
d	Cup, packed	1 cup	226	60.2	606	40.5	47.9	0	23	353	6.1	142	648	80	.17	.36	9.7	—
370	Cooked (oven-broiled, pan-broiled, or sauteed):[50]																	
a	Yield from 1 lb., raw ground beef (item 369a), four 2.9-oz. patties (item 370c), or five 2.3-oz. patties (item 370d).	11½ oz	326	54.2	932	78.9	66.2	0	36	632	10.4	193	884	120	.28	.68	17.6	—
b	Pound	1 lb	454	54.2	1,297	109.8	92.1	0	50	880	14.5	269	1,230	170	.39	.95	24.5	—
c	Patty, approx. 3-in. diam., ⅝ in. thick; wt., 2.9 oz.	1 patty or 2.9 oz.	82	54.2	235	19.8	16.6	0	9	159	2.6	49	221	30	.07	.17	4.4	—
d	Patty, approx. 3-in. diam., ½ in. thick; wt., 2.3 oz.	1 patty	65	54.2	186	15.7	13.2	0	7	126	2.1	38	176	20	.06	.14	3.5	—
	Beef and vegetable stew:																	
371	Cooked (home recipe, with lean beef chuck):[51]																	
a	Cup	1 cup	245	82.4	218	15.7	10.5	15.2	29	184	2.9	[52] 91	613	2,400	.15	.17	4.7	17
b	Pound	1 lb	454	82.4	404	29.0	19.5	28.1	54	340	5.4	[52] 168	1,134	4,450	.27	.32	8.6	32
372	Canned:																	
	Container and approx. contents:																	
a	Can, net wt., 15 oz	1 can	425	82.5	336	24.7	13.2	30.2	51	191	3.8	1,747	740	4,120	.13	.21	4.3	13
b	Can, net wt., 24 oz. (1 lb. 8 oz.)	1 can	680	82.5	537	39.4	21.1	48.3	82	306	6.1	2,795	1,183	6,600	.20	.34	6.8	20
c	Can, net wt., 50 oz. (3 lb. 2 oz.)	1 can	1,418	82.5	1,120	82.2	44.0	100.7	170	638	12.8	5,828	2,467	13,750	.43	.71	14.2	43
d	Cup	1 cup	245	82.5	194	14.2	7.6	17.4	29	110	2.2	1,007	426	2,380	.07	.12	2.5	7
e	Pound	1 lb	454	82.5	358	26.3	14.1	32.2	54	204	4.1	1,864	789	4,400	.14	.23	4.5	14
	Beef, corned, boneless:[49]																	
374	Uncooked	1 lb	454	54.2	1,329	71.7	113.4	0	41	567	10.9	5,897	272	—	.14	.68	7.7	0
375	Cooked:																	
a	Yield from 1 lb., uncooked (item 374)	10.7 oz	304	43.9	1,131	69.6	92.4	0	27	283	8.8	2,867	182	—	.06	.55	4.6	0
b	Pound	1 lb	454	43.9	1,687	103.9	137.9	0	41	422	13.2	4,277	272	—	.09	.82	6.8	0
377	Canned:																	
	Can, approx. contents, and slice cut from piece:																	
a	Can, net wt., 12 oz.; piece, approx. 3¼ in. long, 3 in. wide, 2 in. high.	1 can	340	59.3	734	86.0	40.8	0	68	360	14.6	—	—	—	.07	.82	11.6	0
b	Slice, approx. 3 × 2 × ⅜ in.; ⅛ of piece (item 377a).	1 slice	40	59.3	86	10.1	4.8	0	8	42	1.7	—	—	—	.01	.10	1.4	0
c	Pound	1 lb	454	59.3	980	114.8	54.4	0	91	481	19.5	—	—	—	.09	1.09	15.4	0
379	Canned corned-beef hash (with potato):																	
	Container and approx. contents:																	
a	Can, net wt., 15½ oz	1 can	439	67.4	795	38.6	49.6	47.0	57	294	8.8	2,371	878	—	.04	.40	9.2	—
b	Can, net wt., 24 oz. (1 lb. 8 oz.)	1 can	680	67.4	1,231	59.8	76.8	72.8	88	456	13.6	3,672	1,360	—	.07	.61	14.3	—
c	Cup	1 cup	220	67.4	398	19.4	24.9	23.5	29	147	4.4	1,188	440	—	.02	.20	4.6	—
d	Pound	1 lb	454	67.4	821	39.9	51.3	48.5	59	304	9.1	2,449	907	—	.05	.41	9.5	—
	Beef, dried, chipped:																	
380	Uncooked:																	
	Container and approx. contents:																	
a	Glass jar, net wt., 2½ oz	1 jar	71	47.7	144	24.4	4.5	0	14	287	3.6	3,053	142	—	(.05)	(.23)	(2.7)	0
b	Glass jar, net wt., 5 oz	1 jar	142	47.7	288	48.7	8.9	0	28	574	7.2	6,106	284	—	(.10)	(.45)	(5.4)	0
c	Pound	1 lb	454	47.7	921	155.6	28.6	0	91	1,833	23.1	19,505	907	—	(.32)	(1.45)	(17.2)	0
d	Ounce	1 oz	28	47.7	58	9.7	1.8	0	6	115	1.4	1,219	57	—	(.02)	(.09)	(1.1)	0
381	Cooked, creamed:[51]																	
a	Cup	1 cup	245	72.0	377	20.1	25.2	17.4	257	348	2.0	1,754	375	880	.15	.47	1.5	1
b	Pound	1 lb	454	72.0	699	37.2	46.7	32.2	476	685	3.6	3,248	694	1,630	.27	.86	2.7	2

[1] Measure and weight apply to food as it is described with inedible part or parts (refuse) included.

[49] For further information about items and basis of vitamin and mineral values, see Appendix B, section on Foods Measured in Pieces, Slices, and Other Units and Appendix C, section on Meats

Values for cooked items apply to products prepared without added salt or other seasoning.

[50] Measures and nutritive values represent meat probably cooked to between rare- and medium-done stage. For values of meat cooked to well-done stage, see Appendix A, table 3, p. 264.

[51] For information on ingredients used in preparation, see ARS 62-13 (7), table 22, p. 26.

[52] Applies to product prepared without added salt. With salt, approx. value for 100 g. of stew is 119 mg.; for 1 cup (item 371a), 292 mg.; for 1 lb. (item 371b), 540 mg.

TABLE 1.—*Nutritive values for household measures and market units of foods*—Continued

[Item numbers correspond to those in table 1 of Handbook No. 8, revised 1963. Values in parentheses denote imputed values usually from another form of the food or from a similar food. Zeros in parentheses indicate that amount of a constituent, if present, is probably too small to be measured. Dashes (—) denote lack of reliable data for a constituent believed to be present in a measurable amount. Calculated values, as those based on a recipe, are not in parentheses]

Item No.	Food, approximate measures, units, and weight (edible part unless footnotes indicate otherwise)			Water	Food energy	Protein	Fat	Carbohydrate	Calcium	Phosphorus	Iron	Sodium	Potassium	Vitamin A value	Thiamin	Riboflavin	Niacin	Ascorbic acid
(A)	(B)			(C)	(D)	(E)	(F)	(G)	(H)	(I)	(J)	(K)	(L)	(M)	(N)	(O)	(P)	(Q)
			Grams	*Percent*	*Calories*	*Grams*	*Grams*	*Grams*	*Milli-grams*	*Milli-grams*	*Milli-grams*	*Milli-grams*	*Milli-grams*	*Interna-tional units*	*Milli-grams*	*Milli-grams*	*Milli-grams*	*Milli-grams*
	Beef, potted. See Sausage, cold cuts, and luncheon meats (item 2008).																	
	Beef potpie:																	
382	Home prepared, baked: [53]																	
a	Pie, whole (9-in. diam.)	1 pie	[54]630	55.1	1,550	63.6	91.4	118.4	88	447	11.3	1,789	1,002	5,170	0.69	0.76	12.6	19
b	Piece, ⅓ of pie (item 382a)	1 piece	210	55.1	517	21.2	30.5	39.5	29	149	3.8	596	334	1,720	.23	.25	4.2	6
c	Pound	1 lb	454	55.1	1,116	45.8	65.8	85.3	64	322	8.2	1,288	721	3,720	.50	.54	9.1	14
	Beer. See Beverages (item 394).																	
	Beets, common, red:																	
384	Raw, peeled:																	
a	Diced	1 cup	135	87.3	58	2.2	.1	13.4	22	45	.9	81	452	30	.04	.07	.5	14
b	Whole or diced	1 lb	454	87.3	195	7.3	.5	44.9	73	150	3.2	272	1,520	90	.14	.23	1.8	45
385	Cooked (boiled), drained, peeled:																	
a	Whole beets, 2-in. diam	2 beets	100	90.9	32	1.1	.1	7.2	14	23	.5	[20]43	208	20	.03	.04	.3	6
b	Diced or sliced	1 cup	170	90.9	54	1.9	.2	12.2	24	39	.9	[20]73	354	30	.05	.07	.5	10
c	Pound (approx. 2⅔ cups diced or sliced)	1 lb	454	90.9	145	5.0	.5	32.7	64	104	2.3	[20]195	943	90	.14	.18	1.4	27
	Canned:																	
	Regular pack:																	
386	Solids and liquid:																	
	Can and approx. contents:																	
a	Size, 303 × 406 [14] (No. 303); net wt., 16 oz. (1 lb.).	1 can	454	90.3	154	4.1	.5	35.8	64	77	2.7	[21]1,070	758	50	.05	.09	.5	14
b	Size, 603 × 700 [14] (No. 10); net wt., 104 oz. (6 lb. 8 oz.).	1 can	2,948	90.3	1,002	26.5	2.9	232.9	413	501	17.7	[21]6,957	4,923	290	.29	.59	2.9	88
c	Cup	1 cup	246	90.3	84	2.2	.2	19.4	34	42	1.5	[21]581	411	20	.02	.05	.2	7
387	Drained solids:																	
	Can and approx. drained contents:																	
	Size, 303 × 406 [14] (No. 303):																	
a	Diced and sliced (small slices); wt., 10¼–10½ oz.	1 can	294	89.3	109	2.9	.3	25.9	56	53	2.1	[21]694	491	60	.03	.09	.3	9
b	Whole beets, small and tiny (count 18–35); wt., 10.9 oz.	1 can	308	89.3	114	3.1	.3	27.1	59	55	2.2	[21]727	514	60	.03	.09	.3	9
	Size, 603 × 700 [14] (No. 10):																	
c	Diced; wt., 72 oz. (4 lb. 8 oz.)	1 can	2,041	89.3	755	20.4	2.0	179.6	388	367	14.3	[21]4,817	3,408	410	.20	.61	2.0	61
d	Sliced (large and medium slices) or whole beets (medium and small, count, 50–125); wt., 68 oz. (4 lb. 4 oz.).	1 can	1,928	89.3	713	19.3	1.9	169.7	366	347	13.5	[21]4,550	3,220	390	.19	.58	1.9	58
	Cup:																	
e	Diced or sliced	1 cup	170	89.3	63	1.7	.2	15.0	32	31	1.2	[21]401	284	30	.02	.05	.2	5
f	Whole beets, small	1 cup	160	89.3	59	1.6	.2	14.1	30	29	1.1	[21]378	267	30	.02	.05	.2	5
g	Pound	1 lb	454	89.3	168	4.5	.5	39.9	86	82	3.2	[21]1,070	758	90	.05	.14	.5	14
388	Drained liquid:																	
a	Pound	1 lb	454	92.2	118	3.6	Trace	28.1	23	68	1.8	[21]1,070	758	Trace	.05	.09	.5	14
b	Ounce	1 oz	28	92.2	7	.2	Trace	1.8	1	4	.1	[21]67	47	Trace	Trace	.01	Trace	1
	Special dietary pack (low sodium):																	
389	Solids and liquid:																	
	Can and approx. contents:																	
a	Size, 303 × 406 [14] (No. 303); net wt., 16 oz. (1 lb.).	1 can	454	90.8	145	4.1	Trace	35.4	64	77	2.7	209	758	50	.05	.09	.5	14
b	Size, 603 × 700 [14] (No. 10); net wt., 104 oz. (6 lb. 8 oz.).	1 can	2,948	90.8	943	26.5	Trace	229.9	413	501	17.7	1,356	4,923	290	.29	.59	2.9	88
c	Cup	1 cup	246	90.8	79	2.2	Trace	19.2	34	42	1.5	113	411	20	.02	.05	.2	7
390	Drained solids:																	
	Can and approx. drained contents:																	
a	Size, 303 × 406 [14] (No. 303), diced and sliced; wt., 10¼–10½ oz.	1 can	294	89.8	109	2.6	.3	25.6	56	53	2.1	135	491	60	.03	.09	.3	9
b	Size, 603 × 700 [14] (No. 10), sliced (large and medium slices) or whole beets	1 can	1,928	89.8	713	17.4	1.9	167.7	366	347	13.5	887	3,220	390	.19	.58	1.9	58

(A)	(B)			(C)	(D)	(E)	(F)	(G)	(H)	(I)	(J)	(K)	(L)	(M)	(N)	(O)	(P)	(Q)
	(medium and small, count, 50–125); wt., 68 oz. (4 lb. 4 oz.).																	
	Cup:																	
c	Diced or sliced	1 cup	170	89.8	63	1.5	0.2	14.8	32	31	1.2	78	284	30	0.02	0.05	0.2	5
d	Whole beets, small	1 cup	160	89.8	59	1.4	.2	13.9	30	29	1.1	74	267	30	.02	.05	.2	5
e	Pound	1 lb	454	89.8	168	4.1	.5	39.5	86	82	3.2	209	758	90	.05	.14	.5	14
391	Drained liquid:																	
a	Pound	1 lb	454	92.8	113	3.6	Trace	26.8	23	68	1.8	209	758	Trace	.05	.09	.5	14
b	Ounce	1 oz	28	92.8	7	.2	Trace	1.7	1	4	.1	13	47	Trace	Trace	.01	Trace	1
	Beet greens, common, edible leaves and stems:[55]																	
392	Raw	1 lb	454	90.9	109	10.0	1.4	20.9	540	181	15.0	590	2,586	27,670	.45	1.00	1.8	136
393	Cooked (boiled), drained:																	
a	Cup	1 cup	145	93.6	26	2.5	.3	4.8	144	36	2.8	[20] 110	481	7,400	.10	.22	.4	22
b	Pound	1 lb	454	93.6	82	7.7	.9	15.0	449	113	8.6	[20] 345	1,506	23,130	.32	.68	1.4	68
	Beverages, alcoholic and carbonated nonalcoholic:																	
	Alcoholic:																	
394	Beer (4.5 alcohol by volume; 3.6% by weight):																	
a	Can or bottle (12 fl. oz.)	1 container	360	92.1	[56] 151	1.1	0	13.7	18	108	Trace	25	90	—	.01	.11	2.2	—
b	Cup (8 fl. oz.)	1 cup	240	92.1	[56] 101	.7	0	9.1	12	72	Trace	17	60	—	.01	.07	1.4	—
c	Fluid ounce	1 fl. oz	30	92.1	[56] 13	.1	0	1.1	2	9	Trace	2	8	—	Trace	.01	.2	—
	Gin, rum, vodka, whisky:																	
395	80-proof (33.4% alcohol by weight):																	
a	Jigger (1½ fl. oz. or 44 ml.)	1 jigger	42	66.6	[56] 97	—	—	Trace	—	—	—	Trace	1	—	—	—	—	—
b	Fluid ounce (29.6 ml.)	1 fl. oz	28	66.6	[56] 65	—	—	Trace	—	—	—	Trace	1	—	—	—	—	—
396	86-proof (36.0% alcohol by weight):																	
a	Jigger (1½ fl. oz. or 44 ml.)	1 jigger	42	64.0	[56] 105	—	—	Trace	—	—	—	Trace	1	—	—	—	—	—
b	Fluid ounce (29.6 ml.)	1 fl. oz	28	64.0	[56] 70	—	—	Trace	—	—	—	Trace	1	—	—	—	—	—
397	90-proof (37.9% alcohol by weight):																	
a	Jigger (1½ fl. oz. or 44 ml.)	1 jigger	42	62.1	[56] 110	—	—	Trace	—	—	—	Trace	1	—	—	—	—	—
b	Fluid ounce (29.6 ml.)	1 fl. oz	28	62.1	[56] 74	—	—	Trace	—	—	—	Trace	1	—	—	—	—	—
398	94-proof (39.7% alcohol by weight):																	
a	Jigger (1½ fl. oz. or 44 ml.)	1 jigger	42	60.3	[56] 116	—	—	Trace	—	—	—	Trace	1	—	—	—	—	—
b	Fluid ounce (29.6 ml.)	1 fl. oz	28	60.3	[56] 77	—	—	Trace	—	—	—	Trace	1	—	—	—	—	—
399	100-proof (42.5% alcohol by weight):																	
a	Jigger (1½ fl. oz. or 44 ml.)	1 jigger	42	57.5	[56] 124	—	—	Trace	—	—	—	Trace	1	—	—	—	—	—
b	Fluid ounce (29.6 ml.)	1 fl. oz	28	57.5	[56] 83	—	—	Trace	—	—	—	Trace	1	—	—	—	—	—
	Wines:																	
400	Dessert (18.8% alcohol by volume; 15.3% by weight):[57]																	
a	Wine glass (serving portion, 3½ fl. oz. or 103 ml.).	1 glass	103	76.7	[56] 141	.1	0	7.9	8	—	—	4	77	—	.01	.02	.2	—
b	Sherry glass (serving portion, 2 fl. oz. or 59 ml.).	1 glass	59	76.7	[56] 81	.1	0	4.5	5	—	—	2	44	—	.01	.01	.1	—
c	Fluid ounce (29.6 ml.)	1 fl. oz	30	76.7	[56] 41	Trace	0	2.3	2	—	—	1	23	—	Trace	.01	.1	—
401	Table (12.2% alcohol by volume; 9.9% by weight):[58]																	
a	Wine glass (serving portion 3½ fl. oz. or 103 ml.).	1 glass	102	85.6	[56] 87	.1	0	4.3	9	10	.4	5	94	—	Trace	.01	.1	—
b	Fluid ounce (29.6 ml.)	1 fl. oz	29	85.6	[56] 25	Trace	0	1.2	3	3	.1	1	27	—	Trace	Trace	Trace	—
	Carbonated, nonalcoholic:																	
	Carbonated waters:																	
402	Sweetened (quinine sodas):																	
a	Bottle (12 fl. oz.)	1 bottle	366	92	113	(0)	(0)	29.3	—	—	—	—	—	(0)	(0)	(0)	(0)	(0)
b	Fluid ounce	1 fl. oz	30.5	92	9	(0)	(0)	2.4	—	—	—	—	—	(0)	(0)	(0)	(0)	(0)
403	Unsweetened (club sodas):																	
a	Bottle (12 fl. oz.)	1 container	355	100	0	(0)	(0)	0	—	—	—	—	—	(0)	(0)	(0)	(0)	(0)
b	Fluid ounce	1 fl. oz	29.6	100	0	(0)	(0)	0	—	—	—	—	—	(0)	(0)	(0)	(0)	(0)
404	Cola type:																	
a	Bottle or can (12 fl. oz.)	1 container	369	90	144	(0)	(0)	36.9	—	—	—	—	—	(0)	(0)	(0)	(0)	(0)
b	Fluid ounce	1 fl. oz	30.8	90	12	(0)	(0)	3.1	—	—	—	—	—	(0)	(0)	(0)	(0)	(0)

[14] Dimensions of can: 1st dimension represents diameter; 2d dimension, height of can. 1st or left-hand digit in each dimension gives number of whole inches; next 2 digits give additional fraction of dimension expressed as 16th of an inch.

[20] Value is for unsalted product. If salt is used, increase value by 236 mg. per 100 g. of vegetable—an estimated figure based on typical amount of salt (0.6%) in canned vegetables. See also Appendix C, section on Cooked Vegetables

[21] Estimated value based on addition of salt in amount of 0.6% of finished product.

[53] For information on ingredients used in crust and in filling and for proportion of crust to filling for pies, see ARS 62–13 (7), tables 23 and 24, p. 31, and table 25, p. 32.

[54] Yield of formula used to calculate nutritive values in Agr. Handb. No. 8, rev. 1963.

[55] Oxalic acid present may combine with calcium and magnesium to form insoluble compounds. For further information, see Appendix D, section on Minerals and Oxalic Acid

[56] Caloric value includes total potential calories calculated from alcohol using factor 6.93 per gram applied to alcoholic content by weight. Factors (calories per gram) applied to protein and carbohydrate in wines were 3.36 and 3.92, respectively; in beer, 3.87 and 4.12.

[57] This group includes wines containing more than 15% alcohol (by vol.), such as apple, muscatel, sherries, port, and Tokay; also aperitif wines and vermouths.

[58] This group includes wines containing less than 15% alcohol (by vol.), such as barbera, burgundy, cabernet, chablis, champagnes, chianti, claret, Rhine wines, rosé, and sauternes. Cherry, peach, berry, and varietal wines usually fall in this class, though some may have alcoholic content high enough to be classified with dessert wines.

TABLE 1.—*Nutritive values for household measures and market units of foods*—Continued

[Item numbers correspond to those in table 1 of Handbook No. 8, revised 1963. Values in parentheses denote imputed values usually from another form of the food or from a similar food. Zeros in parentheses indicate that amount of a constituent, if present, is probably too small to be measured. Dashes (—) denote lack of reliable data for a constituent believed to be present in a measurable amount. Calculated values, as those based on a recipe, are not in parentheses]

Item No.		Food, approximate measures, units, and weight (edible part unless footnotes indicate otherwise)			Water	Food energy	Protein	Fat	Carbohydrate	Calcium	Phosphorus	Iron	Sodium	Potassium	Vitamin A value	Thiamin	Riboflavin	Niacin	Ascorbic acid
					Values for edible part of foods														
(A)		(B)			(C)	(D)	(E)	(F)	(G)	(H)	(I)	(J)	(K)	(L)	(M)	(N)	(O)	(P)	(Q)
				Grams	*Percent*	*Calories*	*Grams*	*Grams*	*Grams*	*Milligrams*	*Milligrams*	*Milligrams*	*Milligrams*	*Milligrams*	*International units*	*Milligrams*	*Milligrams*	*Milligrams*	*Milligrams*
		Beverages, alcoholic and carbonated nonalcoholic—Continued																	
		Carbonated, nonalcoholic—Continued																	
405		Cream sodas:																	
	a	Bottle or can (12 fl. oz.)	1 container	371	89	160	(0)	(0)	40.8	—	—	—	—	—	(0)	(0)	(0)	(0)	(0)
	b	Fluid ounce	1 fl. oz	30.9	89	13	(0)	(0)	3.4	—	—	—	—	—	(0)	(0)	(0)	(0)	(0)
406		Fruit-flavored sodas (citrus, cherry, grape, strawberry, Tom Collins mixer, other) (10–13% sugar):																	
	a	Bottle or can (12 fl. oz.)	1 container	372	88	171	(0)	(0)	44.6	—	—	—	—	—	(0)	(0)	(0)	(0)	(0)
	b	Fluid ounce	1 fl. oz	31.0	88	14	(0)	(0)	3.7	—	—	—	—	—	(0)	(0)	(0)	(0)	(0)
407		Ginger ale, pale dry and golden:																	
	a	Bottle or can (12 fl. oz.)	1 container	366	92	113	(0)	(0)	29.3	—	—	—	—	—	(0)	(0)	(0)	(0)	(0)
	b	Fluid ounce	1 fl. oz	30.5	92	9	(0)	(0)	2.4	—	—	—	—	—	(0)	(0)	(0)	(0)	(0)
408		Root beer:																	
	a	Bottle or can (12 fl. oz.)	1 container	370	89.5	152	(0)	(0)	38.9	—	—	—	—	—	(0)	(0)	(0)	(0)	(0)
	b	Fluid ounce	1 fl. oz	30.8	89.5	13	(0)	(0)	3.2	—	—	—	—	—	(0)	(0)	(0)	(0)	(0)
409		Special dietary drinks with artificial sweetener (less than 1 Cal. per ounce):[59]																	
	a	Bottle or can (12 fl. oz.)	1 container	355	100	—	(0)	(0)	—	—	—	—	—	—	(0)	(0)	(0)	(0)	(0)
	b	Fluid ounce	1 fl. oz	29.6	100	—	(0)	(0)	—	—	—	—	—	—	(0)	(0)	(0)	(0)	(0)
		Biscuits, baking powder, baked from home recipe, made with[60]—																	
410		Enriched flour:[61]																	
	a	Biscuit, 2-in. diam., 1¼ in. high (yield from approx. ⅛ cup of dough).	1 biscuit	28	27.4	103	2.1	4.8	12.8	34	49	0.4	175	33	Trace	.06	.06	.5	Trace
	b	Pound	1 lb	454	27.4	1,674	33.6	77.1	207.7	549	794	7.3	2,840	531	Trace	.95	.95	8.2	1
411		Unenriched flour:[61]																	
	a	Biscuit, 2-in. diam., 1¼ in. high (yield from approx. ⅛ cup of dough).	1 biscuit	28	27.4	102	2.1	4.8	12.8	34	49	.1	175	33	Trace	.01	.03	.1	Trace
	b	Pound	1 lb	454	27.4	1,674	33.6	77.1	207.7	549	794	2.3	2,840	531	Trace	.18	.45	2.3	1
412		Self-rising flour, enriched:																	
	a	Biscuit, 2-in. diam., 1¼ in. high (yield from approx. ⅛ cup of dough).	1 biscuit	28	26.8	104	2.0	4.9	12.9	[62] 59	[62] 89	.5	[62] 185	18	Trace	.06	.06	.6	Trace
	b	Pound	1 lb	454	26.8	1,687	32.2	78.9	208.7	[63] 948	[63] 1,438	7.7	[63] 2,994	290	Trace	1.00	1.00	9.5	1
		Biscuit mix with enriched flour and biscuits baked from mix:																	
415		Mix, dry form:																	
		Cup:																	
		Not packed:																	
	a	Spooned into cup or premeasured 1-cup packet.	1 cup or 1 packet.	120	7.5	509	9.2	15.1	82.4	32	318	[64] 3.7	1,560	96	Trace	[64] .53	[64] .31	[64] 3.6	Trace
	b	Poured from container into cup	1 cup	128	7.5	543	9.9	16.1	87.9	35	339	[65] 4.0	1,664	102	Trace	[65] .56	[65] .33	[65] 3.8	Trace
	c	Packed	1 cup	160	7.5	678	12.3	20.2	109.9	43	424	[66] 5.0	2,080	128	Trace	[66] .70	[66] .42	[66] 4.8	Trace
	d	Pound	1 lb	454	7.5	1,923	34.9	57.2	311.6	122	1,202	[67] 14.1	5,897	363	Trace	[67] 2.00	[67] 1.18	[67] 13.6	Trace
416		Biscuits made with milk:[68]																	
	a	Biscuit, 2-in. diam., 1¼ in. high (yield from approx. ⅛ cup of dough).	1 biscuit	28	28.5	91	2.0	2.6	14.6	19	65	[69] .6	272	32	Trace	[69] .08	[69] .07	[69] .6	Trace
	b	Pound	1 lb	454	28.5	1,474	32.2	42.2	237.2	308	1,052	[70] 10.4	4,414	526	Trace	[70] 1.22	[70] 1.18	[70] 9.1	1
417		**Blackberries,** including dewberries, boysenberries, and youngberries, raw.	1 cup	144	84.5	84	1.7	1.3	18.6	46	27	1.3	1	245	290	.04	.06	.6	30
		Blackberries, canned, solids and liquid:																	
418		Water pack without artificial sweetener:																	
	a	Cup	1 cup	244	89.3	98	2.0	1.5	22.0	54	32	1.5	2	281	340	.05	.05	.5	17
	b	Pound	1 lb	454	89.3	181	3.6	2.7	40.8	100	59	2.7	5	522	640	.09	.09	.9	32
421		Sirup pack, heavy:																	
		Can and approx. contents:																	
	a	Size, 303 × 406[14] (No. 303); net wt., 16 oz. (1 lb.).	1 can or 1 lb	454	76.1	413	3.6	2.7	100.7	95	54	2.7	5	494	590	.05	.09	.9	32
	b	Cup	1 cup	256	76.1	233	2.0	1.5	56.8	54	31	1.5	3	279	330	.03	.05	.5	18
		Blackberries, frozen. See Boysenberries (items 436–437).																	

(A)	(B)			(C)	(D)	(E)	(F)	(G)	(H)	(I)	(J)	(K)	(L)	(M)	(N)	(O)	(P)	(Q)
423	**Blackberry juice,** canned, unsweetened	1 cup	245	99.9	91	0.7	1.5	19.1	29	29	(2.2)	(2)	(417)	—	(0.05)	(0.07)	(0.7)	(25)
	Blackeye peas. See Cowpeas (items 896–904).																	
	Blancmange. See Puddings (item 1824).																	
	Blueberries:																	
424	Raw:																	
a	Container, net contents, 1 pt.[71]	1 container	410	83.2	254	2.9	2.1	62.7	62	53	4.1	4	332	410	(.12)	(.25)	(2.1)	57
b	Cup	1 cup	145	83.2	90	1.0	.7	22.2	22	19	1.5	1	117	150	(.04)	(.09)	(.7)	20
c	Pound	1 lb	454	83.2	281	3.2	2.3	69.4	68	59	4.5	5	367	450	(.14)	(.27)	(2.3)	64
	Frozen, not thawed:																	
427	Unsweetened:																	
a	Container, net wt., 10 oz	1 container	284	85.0	156	2.0	1.4	38.6	28	37	2.3	3	230	200	.09	.17	1.4	20
b	Cup[48]	1 cup	165	85.0	91	1.2	.8	22.4	17	21	1.3	2	134	120	.05	.10	.8	12
c	Pound	1 lb	454	85.0	249	3.2	2.3	61.7	45	59	3.6	5	367	320	.14	.27	2.3	32
428	Sweetened with nutritive sweetener:																	
a	Container, net wt., 10 oz	1 container	284	72.3	298	1.7	.9	75.3	17	31	1.1	3	187	90	.11	.14	1.1	23
b	Cup[48]	1 cup	230	72.3	242	1.4	.7	61.0	14	25	.9	2	152	70	.09	.12	.9	18
c	Pound	1 lb	454	72.3	476	2.7	1.4	120.2	27	50	1.8	5	299	140	.18	.23	1.8	36
	Bluefish, cooked:																	
430	Baked or broiled with butter or margarine:																	
a	Yield from 1 lb., raw fillets	12⅞ oz	365	68.0	580	95.6	19.0	0	106	1,048	2.6	[43] 380	—	180	.40	.37	6.9	—
b	Fillet, 7¾ in. long, 3⅞ in. wide, ⅜ in. thick[40]	1 fillet	155	68.0	246	40.6	8.1	0	45	445	1.1	[43] 161	—	80	.17	.16	2.9	—
c	Pound	1 lb	454	68.0	721	118.8	23.6	0	132	1,302	3.2	[43] 472	—	230	.50	.45	8.6	—
d	Ounce	1 oz	28	68.0	45	7.4	1.5	0	8	81	.2	[43] 29	—	10	.03	.03	.5	—
431	Fried:[72]																	
a	Yield from 1 lb., raw fillets	13¾ oz	385	60.8	789	87.4	37.7	18.1	135	989	3.5	[43] 562	—	—	.42	.42	6.9	—
b	Fillet, 8⅛ in. long, 3¼ in. wide, ¾ in. thick[40]	1 fillet	195	60.8	400	44.3	19.1	9.2	68	501	1.8	[43] 285	—	—	.21	.21	3.5	—
c	Pound	1 lb	454	60.8	930	103.0	44.5	21.3	159	1,166	4.1	[43] 662	—	—	.50	.50	8.2	—
d	Ounce	1 oz	28	60.8	58	6.4	2.8	1.3	10	73	.3	[43] 41	—	—	.03	.03	.5	—
	Bockwurst. See Sausage, cold cuts, and luncheon meats (item 1981).																	
	Bologna. See Sausage, cold cuts, and luncheon meats (items 1982–1985).[5]																	
433	**Boston brown bread,** canned:[5]																	
a	Can, net wt., 16 oz. (1 lb.); roll, 5¼ in. long, 3¼-in. diam.	1 can or 1 lb	454	45.0	957	24.9	5.9	206.8	408	726	8.6	1,139	1,325	[73] 0	.50	.27	5.4	0
b	Piece, 3¼-in. diam., ½ in. thick; approx. 1/10 of roll.	1 piece	45	45.0	95	2.5	.6	20.5	41	72	.9	113	131	[73] 0	.05	.03	.5	0
434	**Bouillon cubes or powder (instant):**																	
	Cubes:																	
a	Size, approx. ½ in	1 cube	4	4	5	.8	.1	.2	—	—	—	960	4	—	—	—	—	—
	Powder (instant):																	
	Container and approx. contents:																	
b	Jar, net wt., 2¾ oz	1 jar	78	4	94	15.6	2.3	3.9	—	—	—	18,720	78	—	—	—	—	—
c	Packet (approx. 2½ tsp.)	1 packet	5	4	6	1.0	.2	.3	—	—	—	1,200	5	—	—	—	—	—
d	Teaspoon	1 tsp	2	4	2	.4	.1	.1	—	—	—	480	2	—	—	—	—	—
e	Pound	1 lb	454	4	544	90.7	13.6	22.7	—	—	—	108,864	454	—	—	—	—	—
f	Ounce	1 oz	28	4	34	5.7	.9	1.4	—	—	—	6,804	28	—	—	—	—	—
	Boysenberries:																	
435	Canned, water pack, solids and liquid, without artificial sweetener:																	
a	Cup	1 cup	244	89.8	88	1.7	.2	22.2	(46)	(46)	(2.9)	2	207	320	(.02)	(.24)	(1.7)	17
b	Pound	1 lb	454	89.8	163	3.2	.5	41.3	(86)	(86)	(5.4)	5	386	590	(.05)	(.45)	(3.2)	32

[5] Most of phosphorus in nuts, legumes, and outer layers of cereal grains is present as phytic acid. See also Appendix D, section on Minerals and Oxalic Acid

[14] Dimensions of can: 1st dimension represents diameter; 2d dimension, height of can. 1st or left-hand digit in each dimension gives number of whole inches; next 2 digits give additional fraction of dimension expressed as 16th of an inch.

[40] Width at widest part; thickness at thickest part.

[43] Value for product without added salt.

[48] Measurement applies to thawed product. See also Appendix C, section on Frozen Fruits and Vegetables

[59] Applies to product sweetened only with nonnutritive sweeteners and not to products sweetened with nonnutritive sweeteners in combination with nutritive sweeteners.

[60] For information on ingredients used, see ARS 62–13 (7), table 4, p. 10.

[61] Values are based on biscuits made with baking powder (item 130) and cooking fats (item 999).

[62] Based on use of self-rising flour (item 2445) containing anhydrous monocalcium phosphate. With flour containing leavening ingredients (sodium acid pyrophosphate in combination with either monocalcium phosphate or calcium carbonate) as noted in footnote 393 for item 2445, approx. values are calcium 35 mg., phosphorus 102 mg., sodium 231 mg.

[63] Based on use of self-rising flour (item 2445) containing anhydrous monocalcium phosphate. With flour containing leavening ingredients (sodium acid pyrophosphate in combination with either monocalcium phosphate or calcium carbonate) as noted in footnote 393 for item 2445, approx. values are calcium 562 mg., phosphorus 1,647 mg., sodium 3,747 mg.

[64] With unenriched flour, approx. values are iron 0.7 mg., thiamin 0.06 mg., riboflavin 0.06 mg., niacin 0.8 mg.

[65] With unenriched flour, approx. values are iron 0.8 mg., thiamin 0.06 mg., riboflavin 0.06 mg., niacin 0.9 mg.

[66] With unenriched flour, approx. values are iron 1.0 mg., thiamin 0.08 mg., riboflavin 0.08 mg., niacin 1.1 mg.

[67] With unenriched flour, approx. values are iron 2.7 mg., thiamin 0.23 mg., riboflavin 0.23 mg., niacin 3.2 mg.

[68] For proportion of mix and added ingredients used, see ARS 62–13 (7), table 5, p. 12.

[69] With unenriched flour, approx. values are iron 0.1 mg., thiamin 0.01 mg., riboflavin 0.03 mg., niacin 0.1 mg.

[70] With unenriched flour, approx. values are iron 2.3 mg., thiamin 0.18 mg., riboflavin 0.45 mg., niacin 2.3 mg.

[71] Represents container as customarily filled to volume greater than declared net contents. See also Appendix B, section on Berries, p. 273.

[72] Dipped in egg, milk or water, and breadcrumbs.

[73] Applies to product made with white cornmeal. With yellow cornmeal, value for 1 can or 1 lb. is 320 I.U.; for 1 piece, 30 I.U.

TABLE 1.—*Nutritive values for household measures and market units of foods*—Continued

[Item numbers correspond to those in table 1 of Handbook No. 8, revised 1963. Values in parentheses denote imputed values usually from another form of the food or from a similar food. Zeros in parentheses indicate that amount of a constituent, if present, is probably too small to be measured. Dashes (—) denote lack of reliable data for a constituent believed to be present in a measurable amount. Calculated values, as those based on a recipe, are not in parentheses]

Item No.	Food, approximate measures, units, and weight (edible part unless footnotes indicate otherwise)			Water	Food energy	Protein	Fat	Carbohydrate	Calcium	Phosphorus	Iron	Sodium	Potassium	Vitamin A value	Thiamin	Riboflavin	Niacin	Ascorbic acid
(A)	(B)			(C)	(D)	(E)	(F)	(G)	(H)	(I)	(J)	(K)	(L)	(M)	(N)	(O)	(P)	(Q)
			Grams	*Percent*	*Calories*	*Grams*	*Grams*	*Grams*	*Milligrams*	*Milligrams*	*Milligrams*	*Milligrams*	*Milligrams*	*International units*	*Milligrams*	*Milligrams*	*Milligrams*	*Milligrams*
	Boysenberries—Continued																	
	Frozen, not thawed:																	
436	Unsweetened:																	
a	Container, net wt., 10 oz	1 container	284	86.8	136	3.4	0.9	32.4	71	68	4.5	3	435	(480)	0.06	0.37	2.8	37
b	Cup	1 cup	126	86.8	60	1.5	.4	14.4	32	30	2.0	1	193	(210)	.03	.16	1.3	16
c	Pound	1 lb	454	86.8	218	5.4	1.4	51.7	113	109	7.3	5	694	(770)	.09	.59	4.5	59
437	Sweetened with nutritive sweetener:																	
a	Container, net wt., 10 oz	1 container	284	74.3	273	2.3	.9	69.3	48	48	1.7	3	298	(400)	.06	.28	1.7	23
b	Cup	1 cup	143	74.3	137	1.1	.4	34.9	24	24	.9	1	150	(200)	.03	.14	.9	11
c	Pound	1 lb	454	74.3	435	3.6	1.4	110.7	77	77	2.7	5	476	(640)	.09	.45	2.7	36
	Bran: [5, 74]																	
439	Added sugar, salt, malt extract, vitamins	1 cup	60	3.6	144	7.6	1.8	44.6	[75] 50	[75] 598	[75] 5.8	[73] 493	[75] 466	[75] 2,820	([76])	([77])	([78])	([79])
440	Added sugar, salt, defatted wheat germ, vitamins	1 cup	75	3.0	179	8.1	1.4	59.1	55	[80] 536	.6	368	[80] 355	[81] 3,530	[82] .87	[82] 1.06	[82] 8.7	[81] 26
441	**Bran flakes** (40% bran), added sugar, salt, iron, vitamins. [5, 74]	1 cup	35	3.0	106	3.6	.6	28.2	[83] 19	[83] 125	[83] 12.4	[83] 207	[83] 137	[81] 1,650	[82] .41	[82] .49	[83] 4.1	[81] 12
442	**Bran flakes with raisins**, added sugar, salt, iron, vitamins. [5, 74]	1 cup	50	7.3	144	4.2	.7	39.7	28	[83] 146	[83] 17.7	[83] 212	[83] 154	[81] 2,350	[82] .58	[82] .71	[83] 5.8	[81] 18
	Braunschweiger. See Sausage, cold cuts, and luncheon meats (item 1986).																	
443	**Brazil nuts:** [5]																	
	In shell (refuse: shells, 52%): [1]																	
a	Cup (approx. 13½ large nuts, diam. greater than 73/64 in.).	1 cup	122	4.6	383	8.4	39.2	6.4	109	406	2.0	1	419	Trace	.56	.07	.9	—
b	Pound (approx. 45 extra large nuts, diam. greater than 78/64 in.: 50 large, diam. greater than 73/64 in.: 57 medium, diam. greater than 59/64 in.; yields approx. 1½ cups, large shelled nuts).	1 lb	454	4.6	1,424	31.1	145.6	23.7	405	1,509	7.4	2	1,557	Trace	2.09	.26	3.5	—
c	Ounce (approx. 3 extra large or large nuts or 3½ medium).	1 oz. or 3–3½ nuts.	28	4.6	89	1.9	9.1	1.5	25	94	.5	Trace	97	Trace	.13	.02	.2	—
	Shelled:																	
d	Cup (approx. 32 large kernels)	1 cup	140	4.6	916	20.0	93.7	15.3	260	970	4.8	1	1,001	Trace	1.34	.17	2.2	—
e	Pound (approx. 94 extra large, 103 large, or 133 medium kernels; yield from approx. 2.1 lb., in shell).	1 lb	454	4.6	2,967	64.9	303.5	49.4	844	3,143	15.4	5	3,243	Trace	4.35	.54	7.3	—
f	Ounce (approx. 6 extra large or large kernels or 8 medium).	1 oz. or 6–8 kernels.	28	4.6	185	4.1	19.0	3.1	53	196	1.0	Trace	203	Trace	.27	.03	.5	—
	Breads: [36]																	
	Cracked-wheat bread: [5, 84]																	
444	Fresh:																	
a	Loaf, net wt., 16 oz. (1 lb.); approx. 18 slices (item 444b).	1 loaf or 1 lb	454	34.9	1,193	39.5	10.0	236.3	399	581	5.0	2,400	608	Trace	.53	.41	5.9	Trace
b	Slice, 4 in. wide, 4¼ in. high, 9/16 in. thick; 1/18 of loaf.	1 slice	25	34.9	66	2.2	.6	13.0	22	32	.3	132	34	Trace	.03	.02	.3	Trace
445	Toasted slices:																	
a	Yield from 1-lb. loaf	18 slices	381	22.5	1,193	39.5	10.0	236.3	399	581	5.0	2,400	608	Trace	.42	.41	5.9	Trace
b	Piece	1 slice	21	22.5	66	2.2	.6	13.0	22	32	.3	132	34	Trace	(.03)	.02	.3	Trace
c	Pound	1 lb	454	22.5	1,420	47.2	11.8	281.2	476	689	5.9	2,858	726	Trace	.50	.50	6.8	Trace
446	French or vienna bread and rolls, enriched:																	
	Bread:																	
a	Loaf, net wt., 16 oz. (1 lb.)	1 loaf or 1 lb	454	30.6	1,315	41.3	13.6	251.3	195	386	10.0	2,631	408	Trace	1.27	1.00	11.3	Trace
	Slice:																	
	French:																	
b	Piece, 5 in. wide, 2½ in. high, 1 in. thick	1 slice	35	30.6	102	3.2	1.1	19.4	15	30	.8	203	32	Trace	.10	.08	.9	Trace
c	Piece, 2½ in. wide, 2 in. high, ½ in. thick	1 slice	15	30.6	44	1.4	.5	8.3	6	13	.3	87	14	Trace	.04	.03	.4	Trace
	Vienna:																	
d	Piece, 4¾ in. wide, 4 in. high, ½ in. thick	1 slice	25	30.6	73	2.3	.8	13.9	11	21	.6	145	23	Trace	.07	.06	.6	Trace
e	Roll, hoagie, or submarine, 11½ in. long, 3 in. wide, 2½ in. thick.	1 roll	135	30.6	392	12.3	4.1	74.8	58	115	3.0	783	122	Trace	.38	.30	3.4	Trace
448	French or vienna bread and rolls, unenriched:																	
	Bread:																	

(A)		(B)			(C)	(D)	(E)	(F)	(G)	(H)	(I)	(J)	(K)	(L)	(M)	(N)	(O)	(P)	(Q)
	a	Loaf, net wt., 16 oz. (1 lb.)	1 loaf or 1 lb	454	30.6	1,315	41.3	13.6	251.3	195	386	3.2	2,631	408	Trace	0.36	0.36	3.6	Trace
		Slice:																	
		French:																	
	b	Piece, 5 in. wide, 2½ in. high, 1 in. thick	1 slice	35	30.6	102	3.2	1.1	19.4	15	30	.2	203	32	Trace	.03	.03	.3	Trace
	c	Piece, 2½ in. wide, 2 in. high, ½ in. thick	1 slice	15	30.6	44	1.4	.5	8.3	6	13	.1	87	14	Trace	.01	.01	.1	Trace
		Vienna:																	
	d	Piece, 4¾ in. wide, 4 in. high, ½ in. thick	1 slice	25	30.6	73	2.3	.8	13.9	11	21	.2	145	23	Trace	.02	.02	.2	Trace
	e	Roll, hoagie, or submarine, 11½ in. long, 3 in. wide, 2½ in. thick.	1 roll	135	30.6	392	12.3	4.1	74.8	58	115	.9	783	122	Trace	.11	.11	1.1	Trace
		Italian bread:																	
450		Enriched:																	
	a	Loaf, net wt., 16 oz. (1 lb.)	1 loaf or 1 lb	454	31.8	1,252	41.3	3.6	255.8	77	349	10.0	2,654	336	(0)	1.32	.91	11.8	(0)
	b	Slice, 4½ in. wide, 3¼ in. high, ¾ in. thick, or 7¼ in. wide. 3⅞ in. high, 7/16 in. thick.	1 slice	30	31.8	83	2.7	.2	16.9	5	23	.7	176	22	(0)	.09	.06	.8	(0)
	c	Slice, 3¼ in. wide, 2½ in. high, ½ in. thick	1 slice	10	31.8	28	.9	.1	5.6	2	8	.2	59	7	(0)	.03	.02	.3	(0)
451		Unenriched:																	
	a	Loaf, net wt., 16 oz. (1 lb.)	1 loaf or 1 lb	454	31.8	1,252	41.3	3.6	255.8	77	349	3.2	2,654	336	(0)	.41	.27	3.6	(0)
	b	Slice, 4½ in. wide, 3¼ in. high, ¾ in. thick, or 7¼ in. wide. 3⅞ in. high, 7/16 in. thick.	1 slice	30	31.8	83	2.7	.2	16.9	5	23	.2	176	22	(0)	.03	.02	.2	(0)
	c	Slice, 3¼ in. wide, 2½ in. high, ½ in. thick	1 slice	10	31.8	28	.9	.1	5.6	2	8	.1	59	7	(0)	.01	.01	.1	(0)
		Raisin bread: [84]																	
452		Fresh:																	
	a	Loaf, net wt., 16 oz. (1 lb.); approx. 18 slices (item 452b).	1 loaf or 1 lb	454	35.3	1,188	29.9	12.7	243.1	322	395	5.9	1,656	1,057	Trace	.23	.41	3.2	Trace
	b	Slice, 3¾ in. wide, 3⅝ in. high, ½ in. thick; 1/18 of loaf.	1 slice	25	35.3	66	1.7	.7	13.4	18	22	.3	91	58	Trace	.01	.02	.2	Trace
453		Toasted slices:																	
	a	Yield from 1-lb. loaf	18 slices	376	22.0	1,188	29.9	12.7	243.1	322	395	5.9	1,656	1,057	Trace	.19	.41	3.2	Trace
	b	Piece	1 slice	21	22.0	66	1.7	.7	13.4	18	22	.3	91	58	Trace	(.01)	.02	.2	Trace
	c	Pound	1 lb	454	22.0	1,433	36.3	15.4	293.0	390	476	7.3	1,996	1,275	Trace	.23	.50	3.6	Trace
		Rye bread: [5]																	
		American (⅔ wheat flour, ⅓ rye flour):																	
454		Fresh:																	
		Regular size:																	
	a	Loaf, net wt., 16 oz. (1 lb.)	1 loaf or 1 lb	454	35.5	1,102	41.3	5.0	236.3	340	667	7.3	2,527	658	(0)	.82	.32	6.4	(0)
	b	Slice, 4¾ in. wide, 3¾ in. high, 7/16 in. thick.	1 slice	25	35.5	61	2.3	.3	13.0	19	37	.4	139	36	(0)	.05	.02	.4	(0)
		Snack size:																	
	c	Loaf, net wt., 8 oz	1 loaf	227	35.5	552	20.7	2.5	118.3	170	334	3.6	1,264	329	(0)	.41	.16	3.2	(0)
	d	Slice, 2½ in. wide, 2 in. high, ¼ in. thick	1 slice	7	35.5	17	.6	.1	3.6	5	10	.1	39	10	(0)	.01	Trace	.1	(0)
455		Toasted slices (regular size):																	
	a	Piece	1 slice	22	25.0	61	2.3	.3	13.0	19	37	.4	139	36	(0)	.04	.02	.4	(0)
	b	Pound	1 lb	454	25.0	1,279	48.1	5.9	274.4	395	776	8.6	2,939	767	(0)	.77	.36	7.3	(0)
456		Pumpernickel:																	
		Regular size:																	
	a	Loaf, net wt., 16 oz. (1 lb.)	1 loaf or 1 lb	454	34.0	1,116	41.3	5.4	240.9	381	1,039	10.9	2,581	2,059	(0)	1.04	.64	5.4	(0)
	b	Slice, 5 in. wide, 4 in. high, ⅜ in. thick	1 slice	32	34.0	79	2.9	.4	17.0	27	73	.8	182	145	(0)	.07	.04	.4	(0)
		Snack size:																	
	c	Loaf, net wt., 8 oz	1 loaf	227	34.0	558	20.7	2.7	120.5	191	520	5.4	1,292	1,031	(0)	.52	.32	2.7	(0)
	d	Slice, 2½ in. wide, 2 in. high, ¼ in. thick	1 slice	7	34.0	17	.6	.1	3.7	6	16	.2	40	32	(0)	.02	.01	.1	(0)
		Salt-rising bread, unenriched: [84]																	
457		Fresh:																	
	a	Loaf, net wt., 16 oz. (1 lb.); approx. 19 slices (item 457b).	1 loaf or 1 lb	454	36.5	1,211	35.8	10.9	236.8	104	313	2.7	1,202	304	50	.20	.23	2.7	Trace
	b	Slice, 4⅛ in. wide, 4½ in. high, 7/16 in. thick; 1/19 of loaf.	1 slice	24	36.5	64	1.9	.6	12.5	6	17	.1	64	16	Trace	.01	.01	.1	Trace
458		Toasted slices:																	
	a	Yield from 1-lb. loaf	19 slices	408	29.4	1,211	35.8	10.9	236.8	104	313	2.7	1,202	304	50	.16	.23	2.7	Trace

[1] Measure and weight apply to food as it is described with inedible part or parts (refuse) included.

[5] Most of phosphorus in nuts, legumes, and outer layers of cereal grains is present as phytic acid. See also Appendix D, section on Minerals and Oxalic Acid

[39] For further information, see Appendix B, section on Breads and Appendix C, section on Enriched Foods and Standards of Enrichment and section on Breads

[74] Weight per cup based on method of pouring product from container into measuring cup to overflow and leveling with straight edge. Revised values for minerals and vitamins apply to products on the market in 1972.

[75] Based on revised value per 100 g. of product. Value used for calcium is 84 mg.; for phosphorus, 997 mg.; for iron, 9.7 mg.; for sodium, 822 mg.; for potassium, 776 mg.; for vitamin A, 4,700 I.U. for product with added vitamin A. Without added vitamin A, value is (0).

[76] With added thiamin, values range from 1.16 to 3.53 mg. per 100 g.; 0.70–2.12 mg. per cup.

[77] With added riboflavin, values range from 1.41 to 4.23 mg. per 100 g.; 0.85–2.54 mg. per cup.

[78] With added niacin, values range from 11.6 to 35.3 mg. per 100 g.; 7.0–21.2 mg. per cup.

[79] With added ascorbic acid, values range from 35 to 106 mg. per 100 g.; 21–64 mg. per cup.

[80] Based on revised value per 100 g. of product. Value used for phosphorus is 714 mg.; for potassium, 473 mg.

[81] Basis of revised value for 100 g. of product with added vitamin A is 4,700 I.U.; with added ascorbic acid, 35 mg.

[82] Basis of revised value for 100 g. of product with added thiamin is 1.16 mg.; with added riboflavin, 1.41 mg.; with added niacin, 11.6 mg.

[83] Based on revised value per 100 g. of product. Values used for item 441 are calcium 53 mg., phosphorus 357 mg., iron 35.3 mg., sodium 590 mg., potassium 390 mg. Values used for item 442 are phosphorus 291 mg., iron 35.3 mg., sodium 423 mg., potassium 307 mg.

[84] Count per loaf, both fresh and toasted, includes end slices. Dimensions of slice are for center slice.

TABLE 1.—*Nutritive values for household measures and market units of foods*—Continued

[Item numbers correspond to those in table 1 of Handbook No. 8. revised 1963. Values in parentheses denote imputed values usually from another form of the food or from a similar food. Zeros in parentheses indicate that amount of a constituent, if present, is probably too small to be measured. Dashes (—) denote lack of reliable data for a constituent believed to be present in a measurable amount. Calculated values, as those based on a recipe, are not in parentheses]

Item No.	Food, approximate measures, units, and weight (edible part unless footnotes indicate otherwise)			Water	Food energy	Protein	Fat	Carbohydrate	Calcium	Phosphorus	Iron	Sodium	Potassium	Vitamin A value	Thiamin	Riboflavin	Niacin	Ascorbic acid
				Values for edible part of foods														
(A)	(B)			(C)	(D)	(E)	(F)	(G)	(H)	(I)	(J)	(K)	(L)	(M)	(N)	(O)	(P)	(Q)
			Grams	*Percent*	*Calories*	*Grams*	*Grams*	*Grams*	*Milligrams*	*Milligrams*	*Milligrams*	*Milligrams*	*Milligrams*	*International units*	*Milligrams*	*Milligrams*	*Milligrams*	*Milligrams*
	Breads[26]—Continued																	
	Salt-rising bread, unenriched[84]—Continued																	
	Toasted slices—Continued																	
b	Piece	1 slice	22	29.4	64	1.9	0.6	12.5	6	17	0.1	64	16	Trace	(0.01)	0.01	0.1	Trace
c	Pound	1 lb	454	29.4	1,347	39.9	12.2	263.1	118	349	3.2	1,334	336	50	.17	.23	2.7	Trace
	White bread, enriched, soft-crumb type (made by continuous mix or conventional method):[84 85]																	
461	Fresh:																	
a	Loaf, net wt., 24 oz. (1 lb. 8 oz.); approx. 24 regular slices (item 461b) or 28 thin slices (sandwich type) (item 461c).	1 loaf	680	35.6	1,836	59.2	21.8	343.4	571	660	17.0	3,448	714	Trace	1.70	1.43	16.3	Trace
	Slice:																	
b	Regular, 4⅜ in. wide, 4 in. high, 9/16 in. thick; 1/24 of loaf.	1 slice	28	35.6	76	2.4	.9	14.1	24	27	.7	142	29	Trace	.07	.06	.7	Trace
c	Thin (sandwich type), 4 in. wide, 3⅞ in. high, ½ in. thick; 1/28 of loaf.	1 slice	24	35.6	65	2.1	.8	12.1	20	23	.6	122	25	Trace	.06	.05	.6	Trace
d	Loaf, net wt., 16 oz. (1 lb.); approx. 18 regular slices (item 461e) or 22 thin slices (item 461f).	1 loaf or 1 lb	454	35.6	1,225	39.5	14.5	229.1	381	440	11.3	2,300	476	Trace	1.13	.95	10.9	Trace
	Slice:																	
e	Regular, 4 in. wide, 4¼ in. high, 9/16 in. thick; 1/18 of loaf.	1 slice	25	35.6	68	2.2	.8	12.6	21	24	.6	127	26	Trace	.06	.05	.6	Trace
f	Thin, 4 in. wide, 4 in. high, 7/16 in. thick; 1/22 of loaf.	1 slice	20	35.6	54	1.7	.6	10.1	17	19	.5	101	21	Trace	.05	.04	.5	Trace
g	Cubes	1 cup	30	35.6	81	2.6	1.0	15.2	25	29	.8	152	32	Trace	.08	.06	.7	Trace
h	Crumbs	1 cup	45	35.6	122	3.9	1.4	22.7	38	44	1.1	228	47	Trace	.11	.09	1.1	Trace
462	Toasted slices:																	
	From 1½-lb. loaf:																	
a	Yield from loaf	24 regular or 28 thin slices.	585	25.1	1,836	59.2	21.8	343.4	571	660	17.0	3,448	714	Trace	1.35	1.43	16.3	Trace
b	Slice, regular	1 slice	24	25.1	76	2.4	.9	14.1	24	27	.7	142	29	Trace	.06	.06	.7	Trace
c	Slice, thin (sandwich type)	1 slice	21	25.1	65	2.1	.8	12.1	20	23	.6	122	25	Trace	.05	.05	.6	Trace
	From 1-lb. loaf:																	
d	Yield from loaf	18 regular or 22 thin slices.	390	25.1	1,225	39.5	14.5	229.1	381	440	11.3	2,300	476	Trace	.90	.95	10.9	Trace
e	Slice, regular	1 slice	22	25.1	68	2.2	.8	12.6	21	24	6	127	26	Trace	.05	.05	.6	Trace
f	Slice, thin (sandwich type)	1 slice	17	25.1	54	1.7	.6	10.1	17	19	.5	101	21	Trace	.04	.04	.5	Trace
g	Pound	1 lb	454	25.1	1,424	45.8	16.8	266.7	445	513	13.2	2,676	553	Trace	1.04	1.09	12.7	Trace
	White bread, enriched, firm-crumb type (made by conventional method):[84 85]																	
463	Fresh:																	
a	Loaf, net wt., 32 oz. (2 lb.); approx. 34 thin slices (item 463b).	1 loaf or 2 lb	907	35.0	2,494	81.6	34.5	455.3	871	925	22.7	4,490	1,097	Trace	2.45	1.81	21.8	Trace
b	Slice, 3⅝ in. wide, 4¼ in. high, 7/16 in. thick; 1/34 of loaf.	1 slice	27	35.0	74	2.4	1.0	13.6	26	28	.7	134	33	Trace	.07	.05	.6	Trace
c	Loaf, net wt., 16 oz. (1 lb.); approx. 20 thin slices (item 463d) or 31 slices (item 463e).	1 loaf or 1 lb	454	35.0	1,247	40.8	17.2	227.7	435	463	11.3	2,245	549	Trace	1.22	.91	10.9	Trace
d	Slice, 3¾ in. wide, 4 in. high, 7/16 in. thick; 1/20 of loaf.	1 slice	23	35.0	63	2.1	.9	11.5	22	23	.6	114	28	Trace	.06	.05	.6	Trace
e	Slice, 3¾ in. wide, 4 in. high, ¼ in. thick; 1/30 of loaf.	1 slice	15	35.0	41	1.4	.6	7.5	14	15	.4	74	18	Trace	.04	.03	.4	Trace
f	Cubes	1 cup	30	35.0	83	2.7	1.1	15.1	29	31	.8	149	36	Trace	.08	.06	.7	Trace
g	Crumbs	1 cup	45	35.0	124	4.1	1.7	22.6	43	46	1.1	223	54	Trace	.12	.09	1.1	Trace
464	Toasted slices:																	
	From 2-lb. loaf:																	
a	Yield from loaf	34 slices	780	24.4	2,494	81.6	34.5	455.3	871	925	22.7	4,490	1,097	Trace	1.95	1.81	21.8	Trace
b	Slice	1 slice	23	24.4	74	2.4	1.0	13.6	26	28	.7	134	33	Trace	.06	.05	.6	Trace
	From 1-lb. loaf (20 slices):																	
c	Yield from loaf	20 slices	390	24.4	1,247	40.8	17.2	227.7	435	463	11.3	2,245	549	Trace	.98	.91	10.9	Trace
d	Slice	1 slice	20	24.4	63	2.1	.9	11.5	22	23	.6	114	28	Trace	.05	.05	.6	Trace
	White bread, unenriched, soft-crumb type (made by continuous mix or conventional method):[84 85]																	

(A)	(B)			(C)	(D)	(E)	(F)	(G)	(H)	(I)	(J)	(K)	(L)	(M)	(N)	(O)	(P)	(Q)
467	Fresh:																	
a	Loaf, net wt., 24 oz. (1 lb. 8 oz.); approx. 24 regular slices (item 467b) or 28 thin slices (sandwich type) (item 467c).	1 loaf	680	35.6	1,836	59.2	21.8	343.4	571	660	4.8	3,448	714	Trace	0.46	0.58	7.5	Trace
	Slice:																	
b	Regular, 4⅜ in. wide, 4 in. high, $\frac{9}{16}$ in. thick; $\frac{1}{24}$ of loaf.	1 slice	28	35.6	76	2.4	.9	14.1	24	27	.2	142	29	Trace	.02	.03	.3	Trace
c	Thin (sandwich type), 4 in. wide, 3⅞ in. high, ½ in. thick; $\frac{1}{28}$ of loaf.	1 slice	24	35.6	65	2.1	.8	12.1	20	23	.2	122	25	Trace	.02	.02	.3	Trace
d	Loaf, net wt., 16 oz. (1 lb.); approx. 18 regular slices (item 467e) or 22 thin slices (item 467f).	1 loaf or 1 lb	454	35.6	1,225	39.5	14.5	229.1	381	440	3.2	2,300	476	Trace	.31	.39	5.0	Trace
	Slice:																	
e	Regular, 4 in. wide, 4¼ in. high, $\frac{9}{16}$ in. thick; $\frac{1}{18}$ of loaf.	1 slice	25	35.6	68	2.2	.8	12.6	21	24	.2	127	26	Trace	.02	.02	.3	Trace
f	Thin, 4 in. wide, 4 in. high, $\frac{7}{16}$ in. thick; $\frac{1}{22}$ of loaf.	1 slice	20	35.6	54	1.7	.6	10.1	17	19	.1	101	21	Trace	.01	.02	.2	Trace
g	Cubes	1 cup	30	35.6	81	2.6	1.0	15.2	25	29	.2	152	32	Trace	.02	.03	.3	Trace
h	Crumbs	1 cup	45	35.6	122	3.9	1.4	22.7	38	44	.3	228	47	Trace	.03	.04	.5	Trace
468	Toasted slices:																	
	From 1½-lb. loaf:																	
a	Yield from loaf	24 regular or 28 thin slices.	585	25.1	1,836	59.2	21.8	343.4	571	660	4.8	3,448	714	Trace	.37	.58	7.5	Trace
b	Slice, regular	1 slice	24	25.1	76	2.4	.9	14.1	24	27	.2	142	29	Trace	(.02)	.02	.3	Trace
c	Slice, thin (sandwich type)	1 slice	21	25.1	65	2.1	.8	12.1	20	23	.2	122	25	Trace	(.02)	.02	.3	Trace
	From 1-lb. loaf:																	
d	Yield from loaf	18 regular or 22 thin slices.	390	25.1	1,225	39.5	14.5	229.1	381	440	3.2	2,300	476	Trace	.25	.39	5.0	Trace
e	Slice, regular	1 slice	22	25.1	68	2.2	.8	12.6	21	24	.2	127	26	Trace	(.02)	.02	.3	Trace
f	Slice, thin (sandwich type)	1 slice	17	25.1	54	1.7	.6	10.1	17	19	.1	101	21	Trace	.01	.02	.2	Trace
g	Pound	1 lb	454	25.1	1,424	45.8	16.8	266.7	445	513	3.6	2,676	553	Trace	.29	.45	5.9	Trace
	White bread, unenriched, firm-crumb type (made by conventional method):[34,35]																	
469	Fresh:																	
a	Loaf, net wt., 32 oz. (2 lb.); approx. 34 thin slices (item 469b).	1 loaf or 2 lb	907	35.0	2,494	81.6	34.5	455.3	871	925	6.3	4,490	1,097	Trace	.64	1.17	8.2	Trace
b	Slice, 3⅝ in. wide, 4¼ in. high, $\frac{7}{16}$ in. thick; $\frac{1}{34}$ of loaf.	1 slice	27	35.0	74	2.4	1.0	13.6	26	28	.2	134	33	Trace	.02	.03	.2	Trace
c	Loaf, net wt., 16 oz. (1 lb.); approx. 20 thin slices (item 469d).	1 loaf or 1 lb	454	35.0	1,247	40.8	17.2	227.7	435	463	3.2	2,245	549	Trace	.32	.59	4.1	Trace
d	Slice, 3¾ in. wide, 4 in. high, $\frac{7}{16}$ in. thick; $\frac{1}{20}$ of loaf.	1 slice	23	35.0	63	2.1	.9	11.5	22	23	.2	114	28	Trace	.02	.03	.2	Trace
e	Cubes	1 cup	30	35.0	83	2.7	1.1	15.1	29	31	.2	149	36	Trace	.02	.04	.3	Trace
f	Crumbs	1 cup	45	35.0	124	4.1	1.7	22.6	43	46	.3	223	54	Trace	.03	.06	.4	Trace
470	Toasted slices:																	
	From 2-lb. loaf:																	
a	Yield from loaf	34 slices	780	24.4	2,494	81.6	34.5	455.3	871	925	6.3	4,490	1,097	Trace	.51	1.17	8.2	Trace
b	Slice	1 slice	23	24.4	74	2.4	1.0	13.6	26	28	.2	134	33	Trace	(.02)	.03	.2	Trace
	From 1-lb. loaf:																	
c	Yield from loaf	20 slices	390	24.4	1,247	40.8	17.2	227.7	435	463	3.2	2,245	549	Trace	.26	.59	4.1	Trace
d	Slice	1 slice	20	24.4	63	2.1	.9	11.5	22	23	.2	114	28	Trace	(.02)	.03	.2	Trace
	Whole-wheat bread, firm-crumb type:[5,34,35]																	
471	Fresh:																	
a	Loaf, net wt., 16 oz. (1 lb.); rounded top, approx. 18 slices; flat top or sandwich style, approx. 20 slices.	1 loaf or 1 lb	454	36.4	1,102	47.6	13.6	216.4	449	1,034	13.6	2,390	1,238	Trace	1.17	.54	12.7	Trace
b	Slice, rounded top, 4 in. wide, 4 in. high, $\frac{7}{16}$ in. thick; $\frac{1}{18}$ of loaf.	1 slice	25	36.4	61	2.6	.8	11.9	25	57	.8	132	68	Trace	.06	.03	.7	Trace
c	Slice, flat top or sandwich style, 3⅞ in. wide, 3⅝ in. high, $\frac{7}{16}$ in. thick; $\frac{1}{20}$ of loaf.	1 slice	23	36.4	56	2.4	.7	11.0	23	52	.7	121	63	Trace	.06	.03	.6	Trace
472	Toasted slices:																	
a	Yield from 1-lb. loaf	18 or 20 slices	381	24.3	1,102	47.6	13.6	216.4	449	1,034	13.6	2,390	1,238	Trace	.93	.54	12.7	Trace
b	Piece, rounded top	1 slice	21	24.3	61	2.6	.8	11.9	25	57	.8	132	68	Trace	.05	.03	.7	Trace
c	Piece, flat top or sandwich style	1 slice	19	24.3	56	2.4	.7	11.0	23	52	.7	121	63	Trace	.05	.03	.6	Trace
d	Pound	1 lb	454	24.3	1,311	56.7	16.3	257.2	535	1,229	16.3	2,844	1,474	Trace	1.11	.68	15.4	Trace
	Whole-wheat bread, soft-crumb type:[5,34,35]																	

[5] Most of phosphorus in nuts, legumes, and outer layers of cereal grains is present as phytic acid. See also Appendix D, section on Minerals and Oxalic Acid

[26] For further information, see Appendix B, section on Breads and Appendix C, section on Enriched Foods and Standards of Enrichment and section on Breads

[34] Count per loaf, both fresh and toasted, includes end slices. Dimensions of slice are for center slice.

[35] For definition of terms "soft-crumb" and "firm-crumb," see Appendix B, section on Breads

TABLE 1.—*Nutritive values for household measures and market units of foods*—Continued

[Item numbers correspond to those in table 1 of Handbook No. 8, revised 1963. Values in parentheses denote imputed values usually from another form of the food or from a similar food. Zeros in parentheses indicate that amount of a constituent, if present, is probably too small to be measured. Dashes (—) denote lack of reliable data for a constituent believed to be present in a measurable amount. Calculated values, as those based on a recipe, are not in parentheses]

Item No.	Food, approximate measures, units, and weight (edible part unless footnotes indicate otherwise)			Values for edible part of foods: Water	Food energy	Protein	Fat	Carbohydrate	Calcium	Phosphorus	Iron	Sodium	Potassium	Vitamin A value	Thiamin	Riboflavin	Niacin	Ascorbic acid
(A)	(B)			(C)	(D)	(E)	(F)	(G)	(H)	(I)	(J)	(K)	(L)	(M)	(N)	(O)	(P)	(Q)
			Grams	*Percent*	*Calories*	*Grams*	*Grams*	*Grams*	*Milligrams*	*Milligrams*	*Milligrams*	*Milligrams*	*Milligrams*	*International units*	*Milligrams*	*Milligrams*	*Milligrams*	*Milligrams*
	Breads[26]—Continued																	
	Whole-wheat bread, soft-crumb type[6, 54, 85]—Continued																	
473	Fresh:																	
a	Loaf, net wt., 16 oz. (1 lb.); approx. 16 slices (item 473b).	1 loaf or 1 lb	454	36.4	1,093	41.3	11.8	223.6	381	1,152	13.6	2,404	1,161	Trace	1.37	0.45	12.7	Trace
b	Slice, 4⅛ in. wide, 3⅝ in. high, 9/16 in. thick; 1/16 of loaf.	1 slice	28	36.4	67	2.6	.7	13.8	24	71	.8	148	72	Trace	.09	.03	.8	Trace
474	Toasted slices:																	
a	Yield from 1-lb. loaf	16 slices	381	24.3	1,093	41.3	11.8	223.6	381	1,152	13.6	2,404	1,161	Trace	1.10	.45	12.7	Trace
b	Piece	1 slice	24	24.3	67	2.6	.7	13.8	24	71	.8	148	72	Trace	.07	.03	.8	Trace
c	Pound	1 lb	454	24.3	1,302	49.0	14.1	266.3	454	1,370	16.3	2,862	1,383	Trace	1.31	.54	15.0	Trace
	See also Biscuits; Boston brown bread; Cornbread; Muffins; Rolls; Salt sticks.																	
475	**Breadcrumbs, dry, grated (enriched)**	1 cup	100	6.5	392	12.6	4.6	73.4	122	141	3.6	736	152	Trace	.22	.30	3.5	Trace
	Breadcrumbs and cubes, soft. See White bread (items 461g, 461h, 463f, 463g, 467g, 467h, 469e, 469f).																	
476	**Bread pudding** with raisins (made with enriched bread).[12, 13]	1 cup	265	58.6	496	14.8	16.2	75.3	289	302	2.9	533	570	800	.16	.50	1.3	3
	Bread sticks. See Salt sticks, regular type (item 1965).																	
	Bread stuffing mix and stuffings prepared from mix:																	
477	Mix, dry form:																	
a	Package, net wt., 8 oz	1 pkg	227	6.3	842	29.3	8.6	164.3	281	429	7.3	3,021	390	Trace	.50	.59	7.3	Trace
	Cup:																	
b	Coarse crumbs	1 cup	70	6.3	260	9.0	2.7	50.7	87	132	2.2	932	120	Trace	.15	.18	2.2	Trace
c	Cubes	1 cup	30	6.3	111	3.9	1.1	21.7	37	57	1.0	399	52	Trace	.07	.08	1.0	Trace
	Stuffing:																	
478	Dry, crumbly; prepared with water, table fat:																	
a	Cup	1 cup	140	33.2	501	9.1	30.5	49.8	92	136	2.2	1,254	126	910	.13	.17	2.1	Trace
b	Pound	1 lb	454	33.2	1,624	29.5	98.9	161.5	299	440	7.3	4,064	408	2,950	.41	.54	6.8	Trace
479	Moist; prepared with water, egg, table fat:																	
a	Cup	1 cup	200	61.4	416	8.8	25.6	39.4	80	132	2.0	1,008	116	840	.10	.18	1.6	Trace
b	Pound	1 lb	454	61.4	943	20.0	58.1	89.4	181	299	4.5	2,286	263	1,910	.23	.41	3.6	Trace
	Breakfast cereals. See Corn, Oats, Rice, Wheat, also Bran, Farina.																	
	Broadbeans, raw:[5]																	
481	Immature seeds	1 lb	454	72.3	476	38.1	1.8	80.7	122	712	10.0	18	2,136	1,000	1.27	.77	7.3	136
482	Mature seeds, dry	1 lb	454	11.9	1,533	113.9	7.7	264.0	463	1,774	32.2	—	—	320	2.27	1.36	11.3	—
	Broccoli, stalks (head or bud clusters, stem and leaves):																	
483	Raw, 1 lb. (2 large, 3 medium, or 4 small stalks)	1 lb	454	89.1	145	16.3	1.4	26.8	467	354	5.0	68	1,733	11,340	.45	1.04	4.1	513
484	Cooked (boiled), drained:																	
	Stalks, whole:																	
a	Large	1 stalk	280	91.3	73	8.7	.8	12.6	246	174	2.2	[30] 28	748	7,000	.25	.56	2.2	252
b	Medium	1 stalk	180	91.3	47	5.6	.5	8.1	158	112	1.4	[30] 18	481	4,500	.16	.36	1.4	162
c	Small	1 stalk	140	91.3	36	4.3	.4	6.3	123	87	1.1	[30] 14	374	3,500	.13	.28	1.1	126
d	Stalks, cut into ½-in. pieces	1 cup	155	91.3	40	4.8	.5	7.0	136	96	1.2	[30] 16	414	3,880	.14	.31	1.2	140
e	Stalks, whole or cut	1 lb	454	91.3	118	14.1	1.4	20.4	399	281	3.6	[30] 45	1,211	11,340	.41	.91	3.6	408
	Frozen:																	
	Chopped:																	
485	Not thawed:																	
a	Container, net wt., 10 oz	1 container	284	90.6	82	9.1	.9	14.8	165	168	2.0	48	684	7,380	.20	.37	1.7	199
b	Pound	1 lb	454	90.6	132	14.5	1.4	23.6	263	268	3.2	77	1,093	11,790	.32	.59	2.7	318
486	Cooked (boiled), drained:																	
a	Yield from 10 oz., frozen broccoli	1⅜ cups	250	91.6	65	7.3	.8	11.5	135	140	1.8	[30] 38	530	6,500	.15	.30	1.3	143
b	Yield from 1 lb., frozen broccoli	2⅛ cups	400	91.6	104	11.6	1.2	18.4	216	224	2.8	[30] 60	848	10,400	.24	.48	2.0	228
c	Cup	1 cup	185	91.6	48	5.4	.6	8.5	100	104	1.3	[30] 28	392	4,810	.11	.22	.9	105
d	Pound	1 lb	454	91.6	118	13.2	1.4	20.9	245	254	3.2	[30] 68	962	11,790	.27	.54	2.3	259
	Spears (or stalks):																	
487	Not thawed:																	

(A)	(B)			(C)	(D)	(E)	(F)	(G)	(H)	(I)	(J)	(K)	(L)	(M)	(N)	(O)	(P)	(Q)
a	Container, net wt., 10 oz	1 container	284	90.7	80	9.4	0.6	14.5	122	170	2.0	37	693	5.400	0.20	0.37	1.7	222
b	Pound	1 lb	454	90.7	127	15.0	.9	23.1	195	272	3.2	59	1,107	8,620	.32	.59	2.7	354
488	Cooked (boiled), drained:																	
a	Yield from 10 oz., frozen broccoli	7–9 spears	250	91.4	65	7.8	.5	11.8	103	145	1.8	[20] 30	550	4,750	.15	.28	1.3	183
b	Yield from 1 lb., frozen broccoli	11–14 spears	400	91.4	104	12.4	.8	18.8	164	232	2.8	[20] 48	880	7,600	.24	.44	2.0	292
c	Pound	1 lb	454	91.4	118	14.1	.9	21.3	186	263	3.2	[20] 54	998	8,620	.27	.50	2.3	331
d	Spear or stalk (4½–5 in. long)	1 stalk	30	91.4	8	.9	.1	1.4	12	17	.2	[20] 4	66	570	.02	.03	.2	22
	Brown betty. See Apple brown betty (item 25).																	
	Brownies. See Cookies (items 813–814).																	
	Brussels sprouts:																	
489	Raw, 1 lb. (about 24 sprouts, 1¼- to 1½-in. diam.)	1 lb	454	85.2	204	22.2	1.8	37.6	163	363	6.8	64	1,769	2,490	.45	.73	4.1	463
490	Cooked (boiled), drained:																	
a	Cup (7–8 sprouts, 1¼- to 1½-in. diam.)	1 cup	155	88.2	56	6.5	.6	9.9	50	112	1.7	[20] 16	423	810	.12	.22	1.2	135
b	Sprouts (1¼- to 1½-in. diam.)	4 sprouts	84	88.2	30	3.5	.3	5.4	27	60	.9	[20] 8	229	440	.07	.12	.7	73
c	Pound (about 21 sprouts, 1¼- to 1½-in. diam.)	1 lb	454	88.2	163	19.1	1.8	29.0	145	327	5.0	[20] 45	1,238	2,360	.36	.64	3.6	395
	Frozen:																	
491	Not thawed:																	
a	Container, net wt., 10 oz	1 container	284	88.4	102	9.4	.6	20.7	62	176	2.6	45	932	1,620	.28	.31	1.7	247
b	Pound	1 lb	454	88.4	163	15.0	.9	33.1	100	281	4.1	73	1,488	2,590	.45	.50	2.7	395
492	Cooked (boiled), drained:																	
a	Yield (approx.) from 10 oz., frozen sprouts	1¾–1⅞ cups	285	89.3	94	9.1	.6	18.5	60	174	2.3	[20] 40	841	1,620	.23	.29	1.7	231
b	Yield (approx.) from 1 lb., frozen sprouts	2⅞–3 cups	455	89.3	150	14.6	.9	29.6	96	278	3.6	[20] 64	1,342	2,590	.36	.46	2.7	369
c	Cup	1 cup	155	89.3	51	5.0	.3	10.1	33	95	1.2	[20] 22	457	880	.12	.16	.9	126
	Buckwheat flour: [5, 86]																	
494	Dark, sifted	1 cup	98	12	326	11.5	2.5	70.6	32	340	2.7	—	—	(0)	.57	.15	2.8	(0)
495	Light, sifted	1 cup	98	12	340	6.3	1.2	77.9	11	86	1.0	—	314	(0)	.08	(.04)	(.4)	(0)
	Buckwheat pancake mix and pancakes baked from mix. See Pancakes (items 1461–1462).																	
	Bulgur (parboiled wheat):																	
	Dry, commercial, made from—																	
497	Club wheat	1 cup	175	9	628	15.2	2.5	139.1	53	558	8.2	—	459	(0)	.53	.18	7.4	(0)
498	Hard red winter wheat	1 cup	170	10	602	19.0	2.6	128.7	49	575	6.3	—	389	(0)	.48	.24	7.7	(0)
499	White wheat	1 cup	155	(9)	553	16.0	1.9	121.1	56	465	(7.3)	—	481	(0)	.47	(.16)	(6.5)	(0)
	Canned, made from hard red winter wheat:																	
500	Unseasoned [87]	1 cup	135	56.0	227	8.4	.9	47.3	27	270	1.8	809	117	(0)	.07	.04	3.2	(0)
501	Seasoned [88]	1 cup	135	56.0	246	8.4	4.5	44.3	27	263	1.9	621	151	(0)	.08	.05	4.1	(0)
	Bullock's-heart. See Custard-apple (item 949).																	
	Burbot:																	
503	Raw, whole (refuse: head, tail, fins, entrails, bones, skin, 85%).[1]	1 lb	454	81.1	56	11.8	.6	0	—	129	—	—	—	—	.27	.10	1.0	—
504	Cooked (fried):																	
a	Pound	1 lb	454	60.5	—	167.8	—	0	—	—	—	—	—	—	2.45	1.04	16.8	—
b	Ounce	1 oz	28	60.5	—	10.5	—	0	—	—	—	—	—	—	.15	.07	1.0	—
	Burghul. See Bulgur (items 497–501).																	
505	**Butter:** [89]																	
	Regular type (1 brick or 4 sticks per pound):																	
a	Stick, net wt., 4 oz. (approx. ½ cup)	1 stick	113.4	15.5	812	.7	91.9	.5	23	18	0	1,119	26	3,750	—	—	—	0
b	Cup (approx. ½ brick or 2 sticks of item 505a)	1 cup	227	15.5	1,625	1.4	183.9	.9	45	36	0	2,240	52	7,500	—	—	—	0
c	Tablespoon (approx. ⅛ of stick (item 505a))	1 tbsp	14.2	15.5	102	.1	11.5	.1	3	2	0	140	3	470	—	—	—	0
d	Teaspoon (approx. 1/24 of stick (item 505a))	1 tsp	4.7	15.5	34	Trace	3.8	Trace	1	1	0	46	1	160	—	—	—	0
e	Pat (1 in. square, ⅓ in. high; 90 per pound) [90]	1 pat	5.0	15.5	36	Trace	4.1	Trace	1	1	0	49	1	170	—	—	—	0
f	Cubic inch	1 cu. in	14.7	15.5	105	.1	11.9	.1	3	2	0	145	3	490	—	—	—	0
	Whipped type [91] (6 sticks or two 8-oz. containers [92] per pound):																	
g	Stick, net wt., 2⅔ oz. (approx. ½ cup)	1 stick	75.6	15.5	541	.5	61.2	.3	15	12	0	746	17	2,500	—	—	—	0
h	Cup (approx. 2 sticks of item 505g or ⅔ of 8-oz. container).	1 cup	151	15.5	1,081	.9	122.3	.6	30	24	0	1,490	35	5,000	—	—	—	0

[1] Measure and weight apply to food as it is described with inedible part or parts (refuse) included.

[5] Most of phosphorus in nuts, legumes, and outer layers of cereal grains is present as phytic acid. See also Appendix D, section on Minerals and Oxalic Acid

[12] Cup measure made on product after it had cooled. See also Appendix B, section on Home-Prepared Foods

[13] For information on ingredients used, see ARS 62–13 (7), table 18, pp. 22–23.

[20] Value is for unsalted product. If salt is used, increase value by 236 mg. per 100 g. of vegetable—an estimated figure based on typical amount of salt (0.6%) in canned vegetables. See also Appendix C, section on Cooked Vegetables

[26] For further information, see Appendix B, section on Breads, p and Appendix C, section on Enriched Foods and Standards of Enrichment and section on Breads

[84] Count per loaf, both fresh and toasted, includes end slices. Dimensions of slice are for center slice.

[85] For definition of terms "soft-crumb" and "firm-crumb," see Appendix B, section on Breads

[86] Sifted once, spooned lightly into measuring cup until it was overflowing, then leveled with straight edge.

[87] Processed, partially debranned, whole-kernel wheat with salt added.

[88] Processed, partially debranned, whole-kernel wheat with chicken fat, chicken stock base, dehydrated onion flakes, salt, monosodium glutamate, and herbs.

[89] Nutritive values apply to salted butter. Unsalted butter contains approximately less than 10 mg. of either sodium or potassium per 100 g. Value for vitamin A is year-round average.

[90] Although count per pound and weight given represent most common size pat of butter used in institutions and restaurants, dimensions may vary from those shown. Count per pound and typical dimensions of other sizes of butter pats frequently used are—

Count per pound	Weight per pat (Grams)	Length (Inches)	Width (Inches)	Height (Inches)
27	16.8	2	1⅔	⅓
60	7.6	1¼	1¼	⅓
72	6.3	1¼	1	⅓
108	4.2	1	⅞	⅓

[91] Description and weights shown for whipped butter, except pat (item 505k), apply to butter that has been stirred or whipped until its volume has been increased approx. 50%; for pat, 100%.

[92] Nutritive values shown for 8-oz. container (227 g.) of whipped butter are same as those shown for 1 cup of regular butter (item 505b).

TABLE 1.—*Nutritive values for household measures and market units of foods*—Continued

[Item numbers correspond to those in table 1 of Handbook No. 8, revised 1963. Values in parentheses denote imputed values usually from another form of the food or from a similar food. Zeros in parentheses indicate that amount of a constituent, if present, is probably too small to be measured. Dashes (—) denote lack of reliable data for a constituent believed to be present in a measurable amount. Calculated values, as those based on a recipe, are not in parentheses]

Item No.	Food, approximate measures, units, and weight (edible part unless footnotes indicate otherwise)			Values for edible part of foods														
				Water	Food energy	Protein	Fat	Carbohydrate	Calcium	Phosphorus	Iron	Sodium	Potassium	Vitamin A value	Thiamin	Riboflavin	Niacin	Ascorbic acid
(A)	(B)			(C)	(D)	(E)	(F)	(G)	(H)	(I)	(J)	(K)	(L)	(M)	(N)	(O)	(P)	(Q)
			Grams	*Percent*	*Calories*	*Grams*	*Grams*	*Grams*	*Milligrams*	*Milligrams*	*Milligrams*	*Milligrams*	*Milligrams*	*International units*	*Milligrams*	*Milligrams*	*Milligrams*	*Milligrams*
	Butter [89]—Continued																	
	Whipped type [91] (6 sticks or two 8-oz. containers [92] per pound)—Continued																	
i	Tablespoon (approx. 1/8 of stick (item 505g))	1 tbsp	9.4	15.5	67	0.1	7.6	Trace	2	2	0	93	2	310	—	—	—	0
j	Teaspoon (approx. 1/24 of stick (item 505g))	1 tsp	3.2	15.5	23	Trace	2.6	Trace	1	1	0	32	1	100	—	—	—	0
k	Pat (1¼ in. square, ⅓ in. high; 120 per pound)	1 pat	3.8	15.5	27	Trace	3.1	Trace	1	1	0	38	1	130	—	—	—	0
l	Regular and whipped types	1 lb	454	15.5	3,248	2.7	367.4	1.8	91	73	0	4,477	104	15,000	—	—	—	0
	Buttermilk:																	
509	Fluid, cultured (made from skim milk):																	
a	Quart	1 qt	980	90.5	353	35.3	1.0	50.0	1,186	931	.4	1,274	1,372	40	0.39	1.76	1.0	10
b	Cup	1 cup	245	90.5	88	8.8	.2	12.5	296	233	.1	319	343	10	.10	.44	.2	2
c	Pound	1 lb	454	90.5	163	16.3	.5	23.1	549	431	.2	590	635	20	.18	.82	.5	5
510	Dried:																	
a	Package, net wt., 16 oz. (1 lb.)	1 pkg. or 1 lb	454	2.8	1,755	155.6	24.0	226.8	5,661	4,400	2.7	2,300	7,285	1,000	1.18	7.80	4.1	—
b	Cup	1 cup	120	2.8	464	41.2	6.4	60.0	1,498	1,164	.7	608	1,927	260	.31	2.06	1.1	—
c	Tablespoon	1 tbsp	6.5	2.8	25	2.2	.3	3.3	81	63	Trace	33	104	10	.02	.11	.1	—
511	**Butternuts:** [5]																	
a	In shell (refuse: shells, 86%) [1]	1 lb	454	3.8	399	15.0	38.9	5.3	—	—	4.3	—	—	—	—	—	—	—
b	Shelled	1 lb	454	3.8	2,853	107.5	277.6	38.1	—	—	30.8	—	—	—	—	—	—	—
	Cabbage:																	
	Common varieties (Danish, domestic, pointed types):																	
512	Raw:																	
a	Ground	1 cup	150	92.4	36	2.0	.3	8.1	74	44	.6	30	350	200	.08	.08	.5	[93] 71
b	Shredded coarsely or sliced	1 cup	70	92.4	17	.9	.1	3.8	34	20	.3	14	163	90	.04	.04	.2	[93] 33
c	Shredded finely or chopped	1 cup	90	92.4	22	1.2	.2	4.9	44	26	.4	18	210	120	.05	.05	.3	[93] 42
d	Pound	1 lb	454	92.4	109	5.9	.9	24.5	222	132	1.8	91	1,057	590	.23	.23	1.4	213
	Cooked (boiled until tender), drained:																	
513	Shredded, cooked in small amount of water:																	
a	Cup	1 cup	145	93.9	29	1.6	.3	6.2	64	29	.4	[30] 20	236	190	.06	.06	.4	48
b	Pound	1 lb	454	93.9	91	5.0	.9	19.5	200	91	1.4	[30] 64	739	590	.18	.18	1.4	150
514	Wedges, cooked in large amount of water:																	
a	Cup	1 cup	170	94.3	31	1.7	.3	6.8	71	29	.5	[30] 22	257	200	.03	.03	.2	41
b	Pound	1 lb	454	94.3	82	4.5	.9	18.1	191	77	1.4	[30] 59	685	540	.09	.09	.5	109
515	Dehydrated	1 oz	28	4.0	87	3.5	.5	20.9	115	81	1.1	54	626	370	[94] .13	.11	.9	[94] 60
516	Red, raw:																	
a	Shredded coarsely or sliced	1 cup	70	90.2	22	1.4	.1	4.8	29	25	.6	18	188	30	.06	.04	.3	[93] 43
b	Shredded finely or chopped	1 cup	90	90.2	28	1.8	.2	6.2	38	32	.7	23	241	40	.08	.05	.4	[93] 55
c	Pound	1 lb	454	90.2	141	9.1	.9	31.3	191	159	3.6	118	1,216	180	.41	.27	1.8	277
517	Savoy, raw:																	
a	Cup, shredded coarsely or sliced	1 cup	70	92.0	17	1.7	.1	3.2	47	38	.6	15	188	140	.04	.06	.2	[93] 39
b	Pound	1 lb	454	92.0	109	10.9	.9	20.9	304	245	4.1	100	1,220	910	.23	.36	1.4	249
518	**Cabbage, Chinese** (also called celery cabbage or petsai), compact heading type, raw:																	
a	Cup, 1-in. pieces	1 cup	75	95.0	11	.9	.1	2.3	32	30	.5	17	190	110	.04	.03	.5	[93] 19
b	Pound	1 lb	454	95.0	64	5.4	.5	13.6	195	181	2.7	104	1,148	680	.23	.18	2.7	113
	Cabbage, spoon (also called white mustard cabbage or pakchoy), nonheading green leaf type, leaves and stems:																	
519	Raw:																	
a	Cup, 1-in. pieces	1 cup	70	94.3	11	1.1	.1	2.0	116	31	.6	18	214	2,170	.04	.07	.6	[93] 18
b	Pound	1 lb	454	94.3	73	7.3	.9	13.2	748	200	3.6	118	1,388	14,060	.23	.45	3.6	113
520	Cooked (boiled), drained:																	
a	Cup, 1-in. pieces	1 cup	170	95.2	24	2.4	.3	4.1	252	56	1.0	[30] 31	364	5,270	.07	.14	1.2	26
b	Pound	1 lb	454	95.2	64	6.4	.9	10.9	671	150	2.7	[30] 82	971	14,060	.18	.36	3.2	68
	Cabbage salad. See Coleslaw (items 801–804).																	
	Cakes and cupcakes:																	
	Baked from home recipes: [95] [96]																	
521	Angelfood, tube cake (baked in tube pan):																	
	Cake, 9¾-in. diam., [97] 4 in. high:																	
a	Whole (vol., 247 cu. in.)	1 cake	[98] 716	31.5	1,926	50.8	1.4	431.0	64	158	1.4	2,026	630	0	.07	1.00	1.4	0
b	Piece (2½-in. arc; vol., 20.6 cu. in.; 1/12 of cake).	1 piece	60	31.5	161	4.3	.1	36.1	5	13	.1	170	53	0	.01	.08	.1	0

(A)	(B)		(C)	(D)	(E)	(F)	(G)	(H)	(I)	(J)	(K)	(L)	(M)	(N)	(O)	(P)	(Q)
c	Piece (1⅞-in. arc; vol., 15.4 cu. in.; 1/16 of cake).	1 piece	45	31.5	121	3.2	0.1	27.1	4	10	0.1	127	40	0	Trace	0.06	0.1	0
	Cake, 8½-in. diam.,[97] 3½ in. high:																	
d	Whole (vol., 164 cu. in.)	1 cake	[99] 472	31.5	1,270	33.5	.9	284.1	42	104	.9	1,336	415	0	0.05	.66	.9	0
e	Piece (2¼-in. arc; vol., 13.7 cu. in.; 1/12 of cake).	1 piece	39	31.5	105	2.8	.1	23.5	4	9	.1	110	34	0	Trace	.05	.1	0
f	Piece (1⅝-in. arc; vol., 10.2 cu. in.; 1/16 of cake).	1 piece	30	31.5	81	2.1	.1	18.1	3	7	.1	85	26	0	Trace	.04	.1	0
g	Cube (1 cu. in.)[100]	1 cube	2.9	31.5	8	.2	Trace	1.7	Trace	1	Trace	8	3	0	Trace	Trace	Trace	0
522	Boston cream pie, 8-in. diam., 3⅓ in. high (2-layer cake with custard filling and powdered sugar topping):																	
a	Whole (vol., 166 cu. in.)	1 cake	[99] 825	34.5	2,492	41.3	77.6	411.7	553	833	4.1	1,535	734	1,730	.25	.91	1.7	2
b	Piece (3⅛-in. arc; vol., 20.8 cu. in.; ⅛ of cake).	1 piece	103	34.5	311	5.2	9.7	51.4	69	104	.5	192	92	220	.03	.11	.2	Trace
c	Piece (2⅛-in. arc; vol., 13.8 cu. in.; 1/12 of cake).	1 piece	69	34.5	208	3.5	6.5	34.4	46	70	.3	128	61	140	.02	.08	.1	Trace
d	Cube (1 cu. in.)	1 cube	5.0	34.5	15	.3	.5	2.5	3	5	Trace	9	4	10	Trace	.01	Trace	Trace
	Caramel:																	
523	Without icing:																	
a	Cake, 2-layer, 9-in. diam.,[97] 3 in. high (vol., 180 cu. in.).	1 cake	[99] 864	23.0	3,326	38.9	149.5	464.0	674	916	11.2	2,635	588	1,560	.17	.69	1.7	1
b	Cake, 2-layer, 8-in. diam.,[97] 3 in. high (vol., 142 cu. in.).	1 cake	[99] 680	23.0	2,618	30.6	117.6	365.2	530	721	8.8	2,074	462	1,220	.14	.54	1.4	1
c	Cube (1 cu. in.)[100]	1 cube	4.8	23.0	18	.2	.8	2.6	4	5	.1	15	3	10	Trace	Trace	Trace	Trace
524	With caramel icing[101] (dimensions of items apply to uniced cake; volume in cubic inches to iced cake):																	
	Cake, 2-layer, 9-in. diam.,[97] 3 in. high:																	
a	Whole (vol., 197 cu. in.)	1 cake	[99] 1,261	20.9	4,779	46.7	186.6	745.3	1,059	1,198	18.9	3,178	807	2,520	.25	.88	1.3	1
b	Piece (2⅜-in. arc; vol., 16.4 cu. in.; 1/12 of cake).	1 piece	105	20.9	398	3.9	15.5	62.1	88	100	1.6	265	67	210	.02	.07	.1	Trace
c	Piece (1¾-in. arc; vol., 12.3 cu. in.; 1/16 of cake).	1 piece	79	20.9	299	2.9	11.7	46.7	66	75	1.2	199	51	160	.02	.06	.1	Trace
	Cake, 2-layer, 8-in. diam.,[97] 3 in. high:																	
d	Whole (vol., 156 cu. in.)	1 cake	[99] 1,000	20.9	3,790	37.0	148.0	591.0	840	950	15.0	2,520	640	2,000	.20	.70	1.0	1
e	Piece (2⅛-in. arc; vol., 13.0 cu. in.; 1/12 of cake).	1 piece	83	20.9	315	3.1	12.3	49.1	70	79	1.2	209	53	170	.02	.06	.1	Trace
f	Piece (1⅝-in. arc; vol., 9.8 cu. in.; 1/16 of cake).	1 piece	62	20.9	235	2.3	9.2	36.6	52	59	.9	156	40	120	.01	.04	.1	Trace
g	Cube (1 cu. in.)[100]	1 cube	6.4	20.9	24	.2	.9	3.8	5	6	.1	16	4	10	Trace	Trace	Trace	Trace
	Chocolate (devil's food):[98]																	
525	Without icing:																	
a	Cake, 2-layer, 9-in. diam.,[97] 3 in. high (vol., 180 cu. in.).	1 cake	[99] 890	24.6	3,257	42.7	153.1	462.8	659	1,219	8.0	2,617	1,246	1,340	.18	.89	1.8	1
b	Cake, 2-layer, 8-in. diam.,[97] 3 in. high (vol., 142 cu. in.).	1 cake	[99] 700	24.6	2,562	33.6	120.4	364.0	518	959	6.3	2,058	980	1,050	.14	.70	1.4	1
	Cake, sheet:																	
c	Piece (3 × 3 × 2 in.; vol., 18.0 cu. in.)	1 piece	88	24.6	322	4.2	15.1	45.8	65	121	.8	259	123	130	.02	.09	.2	Trace
d	Piece (2 × 2 × 2 in.; vol., 8.0 cu. in.)	1 piece	39	24.6	143	1.9	6.7	20.3	29	53	.4	115	55	60	.01	.04	.1	Trace
e	Cube (1 cu. in.)[100]	1 cube	4.9	24.6	18	.2	.8	2.5	4	7	Trace	14	7	10	Trace	Trace	Trace	Trace
f	Cupcake, 2¾-in. diam.[97]	1 cupcake	33	24.6	121	1.6	5.7	17.2	24	45	.3	97	46	50	.01	.03	.1	Trace
g	Cupcake, 2½-in. diam.[97]	1 cupcake	25	24.6	92	1.2	4.3	13.0	19	34	.2	74	35	40	.01	.03	.1	Trace
526	With chocolate icing (dimensions of items apply to uniced cake; volume in cubic inches to iced cake):																	

[1] Measure and weight apply to food as it is described with inedible part or parts (refuse) included.

[8] Most of phosphorus in nuts, legumes, and outer layers of cereal grains is present as phytic acid. See also Appendix D, section on Minerals and Oxalic Acid

[80] Value is for unsalted product. If salt is used, increase value by 236 mg. per 100 g. of vegetable—an estimated figure based on typical amount of salt (0.6%) in canned vegetables. See also Appendix C, section on Cooked Vegetables

[88] Oxalic acid present may combine with calcium and magnesium to form insoluble compounds. For further information, see Appendix D, section on Minerals and Oxalic Acid

[90] Nutritive values apply to salted butter. Unsalted butter contains approximately less than 10 mg. of either sodium or potassium per 100 g. Value for vitamin A is year-round average.

[91] Description and weights shown for whipped butter, except pat (item 505k), apply to butter that has been stirred or whipped until its volume has been increased approx. 50%; for pat, 100%.

[92] Nutritive values shown for 8-oz. container (227 g.) of whipped butter are same as those shown for 1 cup of regular butter (item 505b).

[93] Value does not allow for losses that might occur from cutting, chopping, or shredding. See also Appendix C, section on Cut Forms of Raw Fruits and Vegetables; Capping of Strawberries

[94] Applies to unsulfited product. For sulfited product, values for 1 oz. are thiamin 0.03 mg., ascorbic acid 85 mg.

[95] Unenriched cake flour used unless otherwise specified. Values for cakes that contain baking powder and/or fat are based on use of baking powder (item 130) and cooking fats (item 999). For sodium and potassium values of cakes made with sodium-free baking powder and no salt, and for vitamin A values of cakes made with butter or margarine fortified with vitamin A, see Appendix C, section on Cakes

[96] For information on ingredients used in cakes, cake icings, and fillings and also proportion of cake to icing or filling, see ARS 62–13 (7), table 7, pp. 13–15, table 9, p. 16, and table 11, p. 17.

[97] Diameter of cake at top. For more complete information on dimensions and on calculation of volume in cubic inches, see Appendix B, section on Cakes

[98] For basis of this cake, see Appendix B, section on Cakes

[99] Yield of baked cake from formula used to calculate nutritive values in Agr. Handb. No. 8, rev. 1963. See also, Appendix B, section on Cakes,

[100] Weight per cubic inch applies to layer, loaf, sheet, or tube cake but not to cupcakes. For cupcakes, see Appendix B, section on Cakes,

[101] See Appendix B, section on Cakes for information about amount of icing used for this cake.

TABLE 1.—*Nutritive values for household measures and market units of foods*—Continued

[Item numbers correspond to those in table 1 of Handbook No. 8, revised 1963. Values in parentheses denote imputed values usually from another form of the food or from a similar food. Zeros in parentheses indicate that amount of a constituent, if present, is probably too small to be measured. Dashes (—) denote lack of reliable data for a constituent believed to be present in a measurable amount. Calculated values, as those based on a recipe, are not in parentheses]

Item No.	Food, approximate measures, units, and weight (edible part unless footnotes indicate otherwise)			Values for edible part of foods: Water	Food energy	Protein	Fat	Carbohydrate	Calcium	Phosphorus	Iron	Sodium	Potassium	Vitamin A value	Thiamin	Riboflavin	Niacin	Ascorbic acid
(A)	(B)			(C)	(D)	(E)	(F)	(G)	(H)	(I)	(J)	(K)	(L)	(M)	(N)	(O)	(P)	(Q)
			Grams	*Percent*	*Calories*	*Grams*	*Grams*	*Grams*	*Milligrams*	*Milligrams*	*Milligrams*	*Milligrams*	*Milligrams*	*International units*	*Milligrams*	*Milligrams*	*Milligrams*	*Milligrams*
	Cakes and cupcakes—Continued																	
	Baked from home recipes [95] [96]—Continued																	
	Chocolate (devil's food) [55]—Continued																	
	With chocolate icing (dimensions of items apply to uniced cake: volume in cubic inches to iced cake)—Continued																	
	Cake, 2-layer, 9-in. diam.,[97] 3 in. high:																	
a	Whole (vol., 196 cu. in.)	1 cake	[98] 1,193	22.0	4,402	53.7	195.7	665.7	835	1,563	11.9	2,804	1,837	1,910	0.24	1.19	2.4	2
b	Piece (2⅜-in. arc; vol., 16.3 cu. in.; 1/12 of cake).	1 piece	99	22.0	365	4.5	16.2	55.2	69	130	1.0	233	152	160	.02	.10	.2	Trace
c	Piece (1¾-in. arc; vol., 12.2 cu. in.; 1/16 of cake).	1 piece	75	22.0	277	3.4	12.3	41.9	53	98	.8	176	116	120	.02	.08	.2	Trace
	Cake, 2-layer, 8-in. diam.,[97] 3 in. high:																	
d	Whole (vol., 155 cu. in.)	1 cake	[98] 938	22.0	3,461	42.2	153.8	523.4	657	1,229	9.4	2,204	1,445	1,500	.19	.94	1.9	2
e	Piece (2⅛-in. arc; vol., 12.9 cu. in.; 1/12 of cake).	1 piece	78	22.0	288	3.5	12.8	43.5	55	102	.8	183	120	120	.02	.08	.2	Trace
f	Piece (1⅝-in. arc; vol., 9.7 cu. in.; 1/16 of cake).	1 piece	59	22.0	218	2.7	9.7	32.9	41	77	.6	139	91	90	.01	.06	.1	Trace
	Cake, sheet:																	
g	Piece (3 × 3 × 2 in.; vol., 19.6 cu. in.)	1 piece	120	22.0	443	5.4	19.7	67.0	84	157	1.2	282	185	190	.02	.12	.2	Trace
h	Piece (2 × 2 × 2 in.; vol., 8.7 cu. in.)	1 piece	53	22.0	196	2.4	8.7	29.6	37	69	.5	125	82	80	.01	.05	.1	Trace
i	Cube (1 cu. in.) [100]	1 cube	6.1	22.0	23	.3	1.0	3.4	4	8	.1	14	9	10	Trace	.01	Trace	Trace
j	Cupcake, 2¾-in. diam.[97]	1 cupcake	44	22.0	162	2.0	7.2	24.6	31	58	.4	103	68	70	.01	.04	.1	Trace
k	Cupcake, 2½-in. diam.[97]	1 cupcake	34	22.0	125	1.5	5.6	19.0	24	45	.3	80	52	50	.01	.03	.1	Trace
527	With uncooked white icing (dimensions of items apply to uniced cake; volume in cubic inches to iced cake):																	
	Cake, 2-layer, 9-in. diam.,[97] 3 in. high:																	
a	Whole (vol., 193 cu. in.)	1 cake	[98] 1,180	21.3	4,354	44.8	172.3	698.6	696	1,251	8.3	2,761	1,298	2,120	.24	.94	2.4	2
b	Piece (2⅜-in. arc; vol., 16.1 cu. in.; 1/12 of cake).	1 piece	98	21.3	362	3.7	14.3	58.0	58	104	.1	229	108	180	.02	.08	.2	Trace
c	Piece (1¾-in. arc; vol., 12.1 cu. in.; 1/16 of cake).	1 piece	74	21.3	273	2.8	10.8	43.8	44	78	.5	173	81	130	.01	.06	.1	Trace
	Cake, 2-layer, 8-in. diam.,[97] 3 in. high:																	
d	Whole (vol., 152 cu. in.)	1 cake	[98] 928	21.3	3,424	35.3	135.5	549.4	548	984	6.5	2,172	1,021	1,670	.19	.74	1.9	2
e	Piece (2¼-in. arc; vol., 12.7 cu. in.; 1/12 of cake).	1 piece	77	21.3	284	2.9	11.2	45.6	45	82	.5	180	85	140	.02	.06	.2	Trace
f	Piece (1⅝-in. arc; vol., 9.5 cu. in.; 1/16 of cake).	1 piece	58	21.3	214	2.2	8.5	34.3	34	61	.4	136	64	100	.01	.05	.1	Trace
	Cake, sheet:																	
g	Piece (3 × 3 × 2 in.; vol., 19.3 cu. in.)	1 piece	118	21.3	435	4.5	17.2	69.9	70	125	.8	270	130	210	.02	.09	.2	Trace
h	Piece (2 × 2 × 2 in.; vol., 8.6 cu. in.)	1 piece	52	21.3	192	2.0	7.6	30.8	31	55	.4	122	57	90	.01	.04	.1	Trace
i	Cube (1 cu. in.) [100]	1 cube	6.1	21.3	23	.2	.9	3.6	4	6	Trace	14	7	10	Trace	Trace	Trace	Trace
j	Cupcake, 2¾-in. diam.[97]	1 cupcake	44	21.3	162	1.7	6.4	26.0	26	47	.3	103	48	80	.01	.04	.1	Trace
k	Cupcake, 2½-in. diam.[97]	1 cupcake	33	21.3	122	1.3	4.8	19.5	19	35	.2	77	36	60	.01	.03	.1	Trace
	Cottage pudding; made with enriched flour (8 × 8 × 1½ in.):																	
528	Without sauce:																	
a	Whole (vol., 96 cu. in.)	1 cake	[98] 436	26.6	1,500	27.9	49.3	236.7	392	501	6.1	1,304	384	610	.65	.74	5.2	1
b	Piece (2¾ × 4 × 1½ in.; vol., 16.0 cu. in.; 1/6 of cake).	1 piece	73	26.6	251	4.7	8.2	39.6	66	84	1.0	218	64	100	.11	.12	.9	Trace
c	Piece (2 × 4 × 1½ in.; vol., 12.0 cu. in.; 1/8 of cake).	1 piece	54	26.6	186	3.5	6.1	29.3	49	62	.8	161	48	80	.08	.09	.6	Trace
d	Cube (1 cu. in.)	1 cube	4.5	26.6	15	.3	.5	2.4	4	5	.1	13	4	10	.01	.01	.1	Trace
529	With chocolate sauce:[58]																	
a	Piece (dimensions and volume of item 528b) with 1⅓ tbsp. of sauce.	1 piece	99	27.9	315	5.2	8.7	56.1	70	108	1.4	231	139	100	.12	.14	1.0	Trace
b	Piece (dimensions and volume of item 528c) with 1 tbsp. of sauce.	1 piece	74	27.9	235	3.9	6.5	42.0	53	81	1.0	172	104	70	.09	.10	.7	Trace
530	With fruit sauce (strawberry):																	
a	Piece (dimensions and volume of item 528b) with 1⅓ tbsp. of sauce.	1 piece	94	36.6	274	4.8	8.3	45.5	69	87	1.1	219	87	110	.11	.14	1.0	11

(A)	(B)			(C)	(D)	(E)	(F)	(G)	(H)	(I)	(J)	(K)	(L)	(M)	(N)	(O)	(P)	(Q)
b	Piece (dimensions and volume of item 528c) with 1 tbsp. of sauce.	1 piece	70	36.6	204	3.6	6.2	33.9	51	65	0.8	163	65	80	0.08	0.11	0.8	8
	Fruitcake; made with enriched flour:																	
531	Dark:[102]																	
	Loaf, 1 lb. (7½ × 2 × 1½ in.):																	
a	Whole (vol., 22.5 cu. in.)	1 loaf or 1 lb	454	18.1	1,719	21.8	69.4	270.8	327	513	11.8	717	2,250	540	.59	.64	3.6	2
b	Slice (¼ × 2 × 1½ in.; vol., 0.8 cu. in.; 1/30 of loaf).	1 slice	15	18.1	57	.7	2.3	9.0	11	17	.4	24	74	20	.02	.02	.1	Trace
	Tube cake, 3 lb. (7-in. diam.,[97] 2¼ in. high):																	
c	Whole (vol., 77 cu. in.)	1 cake	1,361	18.1	5,158	65.3	208.2	812.5	980	1,538	35.4	2,150	6,751	1,620	1.77	1.91	10.9	5
d	Wedge (⅔-in. arc; vol., 2.4 cu. in.; 1/32 of cake).	1 wedge	43	18.1	163	2.1	6.6	25.7	31	49	1.1	68	213	50	.06	.06	.3	Trace
532	Light:[103]																	
	Loaf, 1 lb. (7½ × 2 × 1½ in.):																	
a	Whole (vol., 22.5 cu. in.)	1 loaf or 1 lb	454	18.7	1,765	27.2	74.8	260.4	308	522	7.3	875	1,057	320	.45	.50	3.2	Trace
b	Slice (¼ × 2 × 1½ in.; vol., 0.8 cu. in.; 1/30 of loaf).	1 slice	15	18.7	58	.9	2.5	8.6	10	17	.2	29	35	10	.02	.02	.1	Trace
	Tube cake, 3 lb. (7-in. diam.,[97] 2¼ in. high):																	
c	Whole (vol., 77 cu. in.)	1 cake	1,361	18.7	5,294	81.7	224.6	781.2	925	1,565	21.8	2,627	3,171	960	1.36	1.50	9.5	1
d	Wedge (⅔-in. arc; vol., 2.4 cu. in.; 1/32 of cake).	1 wedge	43	18.7	167	2.6	7.1	24.7	29	49	.7	83	100	30	.04	.05	.3	Trace
533	Gingerbread; made with enriched flour (9 × 9 × 2 in.):																	
a	Whole (vol., 162 cu. in.)	1 cake	[99] 1,055	30.8	3,344	40.1	112.9	548.6	717	686	24.3	2,500	4,790	950	1.27	1.16	9.5	0
b	Piece (3 × 3 × 2 in.; vol., 18.0 cu. in.; ⅑ of cake).	1 piece	117	30.8	371	4.4	12.5	60.8	80	76	2.7	277	531	110	.14	.13	1.1	0
c	Cube (1 cu. in.)[100]	1 cube	6.5	30.8	21	.2	.7	3.4	4	4	.1	15	30	10	.01	.01	.1	0
	Plain cake or cupcake:																	
534	Without icing:																	
	Cake, sheet (9 × 9 × 2 in.):																	
a	Whole (vol., 162 cu. in.)	1 cake	[99] 777	24.5	2,828	35.0	108.0	434.3	497	793	3.1	2,331	614	1,320	.16	.70	1.6	2
b	Piece (3 × 3 × 2 in.; vol., 18.0 cu. in.; ⅑ of cake).	1 piece	86	24.5	313	3.9	12.0	48.1	55	88	.3	258	68	150	.02	.08	.2	Trace
c	Cube (1 cu. in.)[100]	1 cube	4.8	24.5	17	.2	.7	2.7	3	5	Trace	14	4	10	Trace	Trace	Trace	Trace
d	Cupcake, 2¾-in. diam.[97]	1 cupcake	33	24.5	120	1.5	4.6	18.4	21	34	.1	99	26	60	.01	.03	.1	Trace
e	Cupcake, 2½-in. diam.[97]	1 cupcake	25	24.5	91	1.1	3.5	14.0	16	26	.1	75	20	40	.01	.02	.1	Trace
535	With chocolate icing[55] (dimensions of items apply to uniced cake; volume in cubic inches to iced cake):																	
	Cake, sheet (9 × 9 × 2 in.):																	
a	Whole (vol., 179 cu. in.)	1 cake	[99] 1,109	21.4	4,081	46.6	154.2	658.7	699	1,153	6.7	2,540	1,264	2,000	.22	1.00	2.2	2
b	Piece (3 × 3 × 2 in.; vol., 19.9 cu. in.; ⅑ of cake).	1 piece	123	21.4	453	5.2	17.1	73.1	77	128	.7	282	140	220	.02	.11	.2	Trace
c	Cube (1 cu. in.)[100]	1 cube	6.2	21.4	23	.3	.9	3.7	4	6	Trace	14	7	10	Trace	.01	Trace	Trace
d	Cupcake, 2¾-in. diam.[97]	1 cupcake	47	21.4	173	2.0	6.5	27.9	30	49	.3	108	54	80	.01	.04	.1	Trace
e	Cupcake, 2½-in. diam.[97]	1 cupcake	36	21.4	132	1.5	5.0	21.4	23	37	.2	82	41	60	.01	.03	.1	Trace
536	With boiled white icing (dimensions of items apply to uniced cake; volume in cubic inches to iced cake):																	
	Cake, sheet (9 × 9 × 2 in.):																	
a	Whole (vol., 200 cu. in.)	1 cake	[99] 1,028	22.9	3,619	39.1	107.9	635.3	504	792	3.1	2,693	658	1,340	.21	.72	2.1	2
b	Piece (3 × 3 × 2 in.; vol., 22.2 cu. in.; ⅑ of cake).	1 piece	114	22.9	401	4.3	12.0	70.5	56	88	.3	299	73	150	.02	.08	.2	Trace
c	Cube (1 cu. in.)[100]	1 cube	5.1	22.9	18	.2	.5	3.2	2	4	Trace	13	3	10	Trace	Trace	Trace	Trace
d	Cupcake, 2¾-in. diam.[97]	1 cupcake	44	22.9	155	1.7	4.6	27.2	22	34	.1	115	28	60	.01	.03	.1	Trace
e	Cupcake, 2½-in. diam.[97]	1 cupcake	33	22.9	116	1.3	3.5	20.4	16	25	.1	86	21	40	.01	.02	.1	Trace
537	With uncooked white icing (dimensions of items apply to uniced cake; volume in cubic inches to iced cake):																	
	Cake, sheet (9 × 9 × 2 in.):																	
a	Whole (vol., 176 cu. in.)	1 cake	[99] 1,096	20.6	4,022	37.3	129.3	693.8	548	822	3.3	2,488	669	2,190	.22	.77	1.1	2
b	Piece (3 × 3 × 2 in.; vol., 19.6 cu. in.; ⅑ of cake).	1 piece	121	20.6	444	4.1	14.3	76.6	61	91	.4	275	74	240	.02	.08	.1	Trace

[55] Oxalic acid present may combine with calcium and magnesium to form insoluble compounds. For further information, see Appendix D, section on Minerals and Oxalic Acid

[96] Unenriched cake flour used unless otherwise specified. Values for cakes that contain baking powder and/or fat are based on use of baking powder (item 130) and cooking fats (item 999). For sodium and potassium values of cakes made with sodium-free baking powder and no salt, and for vitamin A values of cakes made with butter or margarine fortified with vitamin A, see Appendix C, section on Cakes

[96] For information on ingredients used in cakes, cake icings, and fillings and also proportion of cake to icing or filling, see ARS 62-13 (7), table 7, pp. 13–15, table 9, p. 16, and table 11, p. 17.

[97] Diameter of cake at top. For more complete information on dimensions and on calculation of volume in cubic inches, see Appendix B, section on Cakes

[98] For basis of this cake, see Appendix B, section on Cakes

[99] Yield of baked cake from formula used to calculate nutritive values in Agr. Handb. No. 8, rev. 1963. See also, Appendix B, section on Cakes

[100] Weight per cubic inch applies to layer, loaf, sheet, or tube cake but not to cupcakes. For cupcakes, see Appendix B, section on Cakes

[102] Yield of baked cake from formula used to calculate nutritive values in Agr. Handb. No. 8, rev. 1963, was 2,904 g. (6.40 lb.).

[103] Yield of baked cake from formula used to calculate nutritive values in Agr. Handb. No. 8, rev. 1963, was 1,247 g. (2.75 lb.).

TABLE 1.—*Nutritive values for household measures and market units of foods*—Continued

[Item numbers correspond to those in table 1 of Handbook No. 8, revised 1963. Values in parentheses denote imputed values usually from another form of the food or from a similar food. Zeros in parentheses indicate that amount of a constituent, if present, is probably too small to be measured. Dashes (—) denote lack of reliable data for a constituent believed to be present in a measurable amount. Calculated values, as those based on a recipe, are not in parentheses]

Item No. (A)	Food, approximate measures, units, and weight (edible part unless footnotes indicate otherwise) (B)			Water (C)	Food energy (D)	Protein (E)	Fat (F)	Carbohydrate (G)	Calcium (H)	Phosphorus (I)	Iron (J)	Sodium (K)	Potassium (L)	Vitamin A value (M)	Thiamin (N)	Riboflavin (O)	Niacin (P)	Ascorbic acid (Q)
				Values for edible part of foods														
			Grams	Percent	Calories	Grams	Grams	Grams	Milligrams	Milligrams	Milligrams	Milligrams	Milligrams	International units	Milligrams	Milligrams	Milligrams	Milligrams
	Cakes and cupcakes—Continued																	
	Baked from home recipes [95, 96]—Continued																	
	Plain cake or cupcake—Continued																	
	With uncooked white icing (dimensions of items apply to uniced cake; volume in cubic inches to iced cake)—Continued																	
	Cake, sheet (9 × 9 × 2 in.)—Continued																	
c	Cube (1 cu. in.) [100]	1 cube	6.2	20.6	23	0.2	0.7	3.9	3	5	Trace	14	4	10	Trace	Trace	Trace	Trace
d	Cupcake, 2¾-in. diam. [97]	1 cupcake	47	20.6	172	1.6	5.5	29.8	24	35	0.1	107	29	90	0.01	0.03	Trace	Trace
e	Cupcake, 2½-in. diam. [97]	1 cupcake	35	20.6	128	1.2	4.1	22.2	18	26	.1	79	21	70	.01	.02	Trace	Trace
538	Pound:																	
	Old fashioned: [104]																	
a	Yield of cake from recipe	3.4 lb	[99] 1,541	17.2	7,289	87.8	454.6	724.3	324	1,217	12.3	1,695	925	4,310	.46	1.39	3.1	0
	Loaf (8½ × 3½ × 3 in.; ⅓ yield of recipe):																	
b	Whole (vol., 89 cu. in.)	1 loaf	514	17.2	2,431	29.3	151.6	241.6	108	406	4.1	565	308	1,440	.15	.46	1.0	0
c	Slice (3½ × 3 × ½ in.; ¹⁄₁₇ of loaf)	1 slice	30	17.2	142	1.7	8.9	14.1	6	24	.2	33	18	80	.01	.03	.1	0
d	Cube (1 cu. in.) [100]	1 cube	5.8	17.2	27	.3	1.7	2.7	1	5	Trace	6	3	20	Trace	.01	Trace	0
539	Modified:																	
	Loaf (8½ × 3½ × 3 in.):																	
a	Whole (vol., 89 cu. in.)	1 loaf	[99] 500	19.4	2,055	32.0	93.5	273.5	200	520	4.0	890	390	1,450	.20	.55	1.0	Trace
b	Slice (3½ × 3 × ½ in.; vol., 5.2 cu. in.; ¹⁄₁₇ of loaf).	1 slice	29	19.4	119	1.9	5.4	15.9	12	30	.2	52	23	80	.01	.03	.1	Trace
c	Cube (1 cu. in.) [100]	1 cube	5.6	19.4	23	.4	1.0	3.1	2	6	Trace	10	4	20	Trace	.01	Trace	Trace
540	Sponge:																	
	Tube cake, 9¾-in. diam., [97] 4 in. high:																	
a	Whole (vol., 247 cu. in.)	1 cake	[99] 790	31.8	2,346	60.0	45.0	427.4	237	885	9.5	1,319	687	3,560	.40	1.11	1.6	Trace
b	Piece (2½-in. arc; vol., 20.6 cu. in.; ¹⁄₁₂ of cake).	1 piece	66	31.8	196	5.0	3.8	35.7	20	74	.8	110	57	300	.03	.09	.1	Trace
c	Piece (1⅞-in. arc; vol., 15.4 cu. in.; ¹⁄₁₆ of cake).	1 piece	49	31.8	146	3.7	2.8	26.5	15	55	.6	82	43	220	.02	.07	.1	Trace
	Tube cake, 8½-in. diam., [97] 3½ in. high:																	
d	Whole (vol., 164 cu. in.)	1 cake	[99] 524	31.8	1,556	39.8	29.9	283.5	157	587	6.3	875	456	2,360	.26	.73	1.0	Trace
e	Piece (2¼-in. arc; vol., 13.7 cu. in.; ¹⁄₁₂ of cake).	1 piece	44	31.8	131	3.3	2.5	23.8	13	49	.5	73	38	200	.02	.06	.1	Trace
f	Piece (1⅝-in. arc; vol., 10.2 cu. in.; ¹⁄₁₆ of cake).	1 piece	33	31.8	98	2.5	1.9	17.9	10	37	.4	55	29	150	.02	.05	.1	Trace
g	Cube (1 cu. in.) [100]	1 cube	3.2	31.8	10	.2	.2	1.7	1	4	Trace	5	3	10	Trace	Trace	Trace	Trace
	White:																	
541	Without icing:																	
a	Cake, 2-layer, 9-in. diam., [97] 3 in. high (vol., 180 cu. in.).	1 cake	[99] 846	24.2	3,173	38.9	135.4	456.8	533	770	1.7	2,733	643	250	.08	.68	1.7	1
b	Cake, 2-layer, 8-in. diam., [97] 3 in. high (vol., 142 cu. in.).	1 cake	[99] 664	24.2	2,490	30.5	106.2	358.6	418	604	1.3	2,145	505	200	.07	.53	1.3	1
c	Cube (1 cu. in.) [100]	1 cube	4.7	24.2	18	.2	.8	2.5	3	4	Trace	15	4	Trace	Trace	Trace	Trace	Trace
542	With coconut icing (dimensions of items apply to uniced cake; volume in cubic inches to iced cake):																	
	Cake, 2-layer, 9-in. diam., [97] 3 in. high:																	
a	Whole (vol., 214 cu. in.)	1 cake	[99] 1,244	21.3	4,615	46.0	165.5	755.1	560	896	3.7	3,197	1,319	250	.12	.87	2.5	1
b	Piece (2⅜-in. arc; vol., 17.8 cu. in.; ¹⁄₁₂ of cake).	1 piece	104	21.3	386	3.8	13.8	63.1	47	75	.3	267	110	20	.01	.07	.2	Trace
c	Piece (1¾-in. arc; vol., 13.4 cu. in.; ¹⁄₁₆ of cake).	1 piece	78	21.3	289	2.9	10.4	47.3	35	56	.2	200	83	20	.01	.05	.2	Trace
	Cake, 2-layer, 8-in. diam., [97] 3 in. high:																	
d	Whole (vol., 169 cu. in.)	1 cake	[99] 977	21.3	3,625	36.1	129.9	593.0	440	703	2.9	2,511	1,036	200	.10	.68	2.0	Trace
e	Piece (2⅛-in. arc; vol., 14.1 cu. in.; ¹⁄₁₂ of cake).	1 piece	81	21.3	301	3.0	10.8	49.2	36	58	.2	208	86	20	.01	.06	.2	Trace
f	Piece (1⅝-in. arc; vol., 10.6 cu. in.; ¹⁄₁₆ of cake).	1 piece	61	21.3	226	2.3	8.1	37.0	27	44	.2	157	65	10	.01	.04	.1	Trace
g	Cube (1 cu. in.) [100]	1 cube	5.8	21.3	22	.2	.8	3.5	3	4	Trace	15	6	Trace	Trace	Trace	Trace	Trace
543	With uncooked white icing (dimensions of																	

(A)	(B)			(C)	(D)	(E)	(F)	(G)	(H)	(I)	(J)	(K)	(L)	(M)	(N)	(O)	(P)	(Q)
	items apply to uniced cake; volume in cubic inches to iced cake):																	
	Cake, 2-layer, 9-in. diam.,[97] 3 in. high:																	
a	Whole (vol., 198 cu. in.)	1 cake	[98] 1,252	20.0	4,695	41.3	161.5	787.5	601	814	1.3	2,930	726	1,380	0.13	0.75	1.3	2
b	Piece (2⅜-in. arc; vol., 16.5 cu. in.; 1/12 of cake).	1 piece	104	20.0	390	3.4	13.4	65.4	50	68	.1	243	60	110	.01	.06	.1	Trace
c	Piece (1¾-in. arc; vol., 12.4 cu. in.; 1/16 of cake).	1 piece	78	20.0	293	2.6	10.1	49.1	37	51	.1	183	45	90	.01	.05	.1	Trace
	Cake, 2-layer, 8-in. diam.,[97] 3 in. high:																	
d	Whole (vol., 156 cu. in.)	1 cake	[99] 983	20.0	3,686	32.4	126.8	618.3	472	639	1.0	2,300	570	1,080	.10	.59	1.0	1
e	Piece (2⅛-in. arc; vol., 13.0 cu. in.; 1/12 of cake).	1 piece	82	20.0	308	2.7	10.6	51.6	39	53	.1	192	48	90	.01	.05	.1	Trace
f	Piece (1⅝-in. arc; vol., 9.8 cu. in.; 1/16 of cake).	1 piece	61	20.0	229	2.0	7.9	38.4	29	40	.1	143	35	70	.01	.04	.1	Trace
g	Cube (1 cu. in.)[100]	1 cube	6.3	20.0	24	.2	.8	4.0	3	4	Trace	15	4	10	Trace	Trace	Trace	Trace
	Yellow:																	
544	Without icing:																	
a	Cake, 2-layer, 9-in. diam.,[97] 3 in. high (vol., 180 cu. in.).	1 cake	[98] 870	23.5	3,158	39.2	110.5	506.3	618	974	3.5	2,245	679	1,310	.17	.70	1.7	2
b	Cake, 2-layer, 8-in. diam.,[97] 3 in. high (vol., 142 cu. in.).	1 cake	[98] 682	23.5	2,476	30.7	86.6	396.9	484	764	2.7	1,760	532	1,020	.14	.55	1.4	Trace
c	Cube (1 cu. in.)[100]	1 cube	4.8	23.5	17	.2	.6	2.8	3	5	Trace	12	4	10	Trace	Trace	Trace	Trace
545	With caramel icing[101] (dimensions of items apply to uniced cake; volume in cubic inches to iced cake):																	
	Cake, 2-layer, 9-in. diam.,[97] 3 in. high:																	
a	Whole (vol., 198 cu. in.)	1 cake	[98] 1,296	21.8	4,692	51.8	151.6	794.4	998	1,335	9.1	2,929	946	2,200	.26	1.04	2.6	2
b	Piece (2⅜-in. arc; vol., 16.5 cu. in.; 1/12 of cake).	1 piece	108	21.8	391	4.3	12.6	66.2	83	111	.8	244	79	180	.02	.09	.2	Trace
c	Piece (1¾-in. arc; vol., 12.4 cu. in.; 1/16 of cake).	1 piece	81	21.8	293	3.2	9.5	49.7	62	83	.6	183	59	140	.02	.06	.2	Trace
	Cake, 2-layer, 8-in. diam.,[97] 3 in. high:																	
d	Whole (vol., 156 cu. in.)	1 cake	[98] 1,016	21.8	3,678	40.6	118.9	622.8	782	1,046	7.1	2,296	742	1,730	.20	.81	2.0	2
e	Piece (2⅛-in. arc; vol., 13.0 cu. in.; 1/12 of cake).	1 piece	85	21.8	308	3.4	9.9	52.1	65	88	.6	192	62	140	.02	.07	.2	Trace
f	Piece (1⅝-in. arc; vol., 9.8 cu. in.; 1/16 of cake).	1 piece	64	21.8	232	2.6	7.5	39.2	49	66	.4	145	47	110	.01	.05	.1	Trace
g	Cube (1 cu. in.)[100]	1 cube	6.5	21.8	24	.3	.8	4.0	5	7	Trace	15	5	10	Trace	.01	Trace	Trace
546	With chocolate icing[55] (dimensions of items apply to uniced cake; volume in cubic inches to iced cake):																	
	Cake, 2-layer, 9-in. diam.,[97] 3 in. high:																	
a	Whole (vol., 197 cu. in.)	1 cake	[98] 1,203	21.2	4,391	50.5	156.4	726.6	818	1,347	7.2	2,502	1,299	1,920	.24	.96	2.4	2
b	Piece (2⅜-in. arc; vol., 16.4 cu. in.; 1/12 of cake).	1 piece	100	21.2	365	4.2	13.0	60.4	68	112	.6	208	108	160	.02	.08	.2	Trace
c	Piece (1¾-in. arc; vol., 12.3 cu. in.; 1/16 of cake).	1 piece	75	21.2	274	3.2	9.8	45.3	51	84	.5	156	81	120	.02	.06	.2	Trace
	Cake, 2-layer, 8-in. diam.,[97] 3 in. high:																	
d	Whole (vol., 155 cu. in.)	1 cake	[98] 943	21.2	3,442	39.6	122.6	569.6	641	1,056	5.7	1,961	1,018	1,510	.19	.75	1.9	2
e	Piece (2⅛-in. arc; vol., 12.9 cu. in.; 1/12 of cake).	1 piece	79	21.2	288	3.3	10.3	47.7	54	88	.5	164	85	130	.02	.06	.2	Trace
f	Piece (1⅝-in. arc; vol., 9.7 cu. in.; 1/16 of cake).	1 piece	59	21.2	215	2.5	7.7	35.6	40	66	.4	123	64	90	.01	.05	.1	Trace
g	Cube (1 cu. in.)[100]	1 cube	6.1	21.2	22	.3	.8	3.7	4	7	Trace	13	7	10	Trace	Trace	Trace	Trace
	Frozen, commercial, devil's food;[55] net wt., 18 oz. (1 lb. 2 oz.):																	
547	With chocolate icing:																	
	Cake, 1-layer (approx. 7½-in. diam., 1¾ in. high):																	
a	Whole (vol., 77 cu. in.)	1 cake	510	21.0	1,938	21.9	89.8	283.6	275	469	4.1	2,142	607	2,190	.10	.41	1.0	1
b	Piece (4-in. arc; vol., 12.8 cu. in.; ⅙ of cake).	1 piece	85	21.0	323	3.7	15.0	47.3	46	78	.7	357	101	370	.02	.07	.2	Trace
c	Cube (1 cu. in.)	1 cube	6.6	21.0	25	.3	1.2	3.7	4	6	.1	28	8	30	Trace	.01	Trace	Trace

[55] Oxalic acid present may combine with calcium and magnesium to form insoluble compounds. For further information, see Appendix D, section on Minerals and Oxalic Acid

[95] Unenriched cake flour used unless otherwise specified. Values for cakes that contain baking powder and/or fat are based on use of baking powder (item 130) and cooking fats (item 999). For sodium and potassium values of cakes made with sodium-free baking powder and no salt, and for vitamin A values of cakes made with butter or margarine fortified with vitamin A, see Appendix C, section on Cakes

[96] For information on ingredients used in cakes, cake icings, and fillings and also proportion of cake to icing or filling, see ARS 62-13 (7), table 7, pp. 13–15, table 9, p. 16, and table 11, p. 17.

[97] Diameter of cake at top. For more complete information on dimensions and on calculation of volume in cubic inches, see Appendix B, section on Cakes

[98] For basis of this size cake, see Appendix B, section on Cakes

[99] Yield of baked cake from formula used to calculate nutritive values in Agr. Handb. No. 8, rev. 1963. See also, Appendix B, section on Cakes

[100] Weight per cubic inch applies to layer, loaf, sheet, or tube cake but not to cupcakes. For cupcakes, see Appendix B, section on Cakes

[101] See Appendix B, section on Cakes for information about amount of icing used for this cake.

[104] Formula for this product deviates from true old-fashioned pound cake in containing higher proportion of fat by weight. For nutritive values of product containing 1 lb. each of flour, sugar, eggs, and cooking fat, see Appendix A, table 3, p. 264.

TABLE 1.—*Nutritive values for household measures and market units of foods*—Continued

[Item numbers correspond to those in table 1 of Handbook No. 8, revised 1963. Values in parentheses denote imputed values usually from another form of the food or from a similar food. Zeros in parentheses indicate that amount of a constituent, if present, is probably too small to be measured. Dashes (—) denote lack of reliable data for a constituent believed to be present in a measurable amount. Calculated values, as those based on a recipe, are not in parentheses]

Item No. (A)	Food, approximate measures, units, and weight (edible part unless footnotes indicate otherwise) (B)			Water (C)	Food energy (D)	Protein (E)	Fat (F)	Carbohydrate (G)	Calcium (H)	Phosphorus (I)	Iron (J)	Sodium (K)	Potassium (L)	Vitamin A value (M)	Thiamin (N)	Riboflavin (O)	Niacin (P)	Ascorbic acid (Q)
			Grams	*Percent*	*Calories*	*Grams*	*Grams*	*Grams*	*Milligrams*	*Milligrams*	*Milligrams*	*Milligrams*	*Milligrams*	*International units*	*Milligrams*	*Milligrams*	*Milligrams*	*Milligrams*
	Cakes and cupcakes—Continued																	
	Frozen, commercial, devil's food;[35] net wt., 18 oz. (1 lb.2 oz.)—Continued																	
548	With whipped-cream filling, chocolate icing:																	
	Cake, 2-layer (approx. 7¼-in. diam., 2 in. high):																	
a	Whole (vol., 84 cu. in.)	1 cake	510	29.7	1,892	17.9	111.7	223.4	408	622	3.1	969	576	1,380	0.10	0.41	1.0	1
b	Piece (3¾-in. arc; vol., 14.0 cu. in.; ⅙ of cake).	1 piece	85	29.7	315	3.0	18.6	37.2	68	104	.5	162	96	230	.02	.07	.2	Trace
c	Cube (1 cu. in.)	1 cube	6.1	29.7	23	.2	1.3	2.7	5	7	Trace	12	7	20	Trace	Trace	Trace	Trace
	Prepared and baked from mixes:[108]																	
550	Angelfood; made with water, flavoring (tube cake, 9¾-in. diam.,[97] 4⅜ in. high):																	
a	Whole (vol., 276 cu. in.)	1 cake	635	34.0	1,645	36.2	1.3	377.2	603	756	1.9	927	381	0	.03	.70	.6	0
b	Piece, 1/12 of cake (vol., 23.0 cu. in.; 2½-in. arc).	1 piece	53	34.0	137	3.0	.1	31.5	50	63	.2	77	32	0	Trace	.06	.1	0
c	Piece, 1/16 of cake (vol., 17.2 cu. in.; 1⅞-in. arc).	1 piece	40	34.0	104	2.3	.1	23.8	38	48	.1	58	24	0	Trace	.04	Trace	0
d	Cube (1 cu. in.)[100]	1 cube	2.3	34.0	6	.1	Trace	1.4	2	3	Trace	3	1	0	Trace	Trace	Trace	0
552	Chocolate malt; made with eggs, water (uniced 2-layer cake, 9-in. diam.,[97] 2⅝ in. high or 8-in. diam.,[97] 3⅜ in. high; vol., 156 cu. in.; wt., 747 g.), with uncooked white icing:																	
a	Whole (vol., 170 cu. in.)	1 cake	1,066	19.8	3,688	36.2	92.7	710.0	672	1,770	7.5	3,390	853	2,030	.32	.75	2.1	1
b	Piece, 1/12 of cake (vol., 14.2 cu. in.; 2⅜-in. arc of 9-in.-diam. cake or 2⅛-in. arc of 8-in.-diam. cake).	1 piece	89	19.8	308	3.0	7.7	59.3	56	148	.6	283	71	170	.03	.06	.2	Trace
c	Piece, 1/16 of cake (vol., 10.6 cu. in.; 1¾-in. arc of 9-in.-diam. cake or 1⅝-in. arc of 8-in.-diam. cake).	1 piece	67	19.8	232	2.3	5.8	44.6	42	111	.5	213	54	130	.02	.05	.1	Trace
d	Cube (1 cu. in.)[100]	1 cube	6.3	19.8	22	.2	.5	4.2	4	10	Trace	20	5	10	Trace	Trace	Trace	Trace
554	Coffeecake, with enriched flour; made with egg, milk:																	
a	Whole (7¾ × 5⅝ × 1¼ in.; vol., 55 cu. in.)	1 cake	430	30.0	1,385	27.1	41.3	225.3	262	748	[108] 6.9	1,853	469	690	[108] .77	[108] .69	[108] 6.0	1
b	Piece, ¼ of cake (vol., 13.8 cu. in.; 3⅞ × 2¾ × 1¼ in.).	1 piece	108	30.0	348	6.8	10.4	56.6	66	188	1.7	465	118	170	.19	.17	1.5	Trace
c	Piece, ⅙ of cake (vol., 9.2 cu. in.; 2⅝ × 2¾ × 1¼ in.).	1 piece	72	30.0	232	4.5	6.9	37.7	44	125	1.2	310	78	120	.13	.12	1.0	Trace
d	Cube (1 cu. in.)	1 cube	7.8	30.0	25	.5	.7	4.1	5	14	.1	34	9	10	.01	.01	.1	Trace
	Cupcakes; made with egg, milk:																	
556	Without icing:																	
a	Cupcakes (yield from 11¾ oz. of mix), 12 of 2¾-in. diam. or 16 of 2½-in. diam.	12 or 16 cupcakes.	400	25.6	1,400	19.6	48.0	223.2	644	940	2.0	1,812	336	600	.16	.44	.8	1
b	Cupcake, 2¾-in. diam.[97]	1 cupcake	33	25.6	116	1.6	4.0	18.4	53	78	.2	149	28	50	.01	.04	.1	Trace
c	Cupcake, 2½-in. diam.[97]	1 cupcake	25	25.6	88	1.2	3.0	14.0	40	59	.1	113	21	40	.01	.03	.1	Trace
557	With chocolate icing:[98]																	
a	Cupcakes (yield from 11¾ oz. of mix, with 6 oz. or ⅝ cup of cooked icing), 12 of 2¾-in. diam. or 16 of 2½-in. diam.	12 or 16 cupcakes.	570	22.2	2,041	25.7	71.8	337.4	741	1,123	4.6	1,910	667	970	.23	.63	1.1	1
b	Cupcake, 2¾-in. diam.[97]	1 cupcake	48	22.2	172	2.2	6.0	28.4	62	95	.4	161	56	80	.02	.05	.1	Trace
c	Cupcake, 2½-in. diam.[97]	1 cupcake	36	22.2	129	1.6	4.5	21.8	47	71	.3	121	42	60	.01	.04	.1	Trace
559	Devil's food; made with eggs, water (uniced 2-layer cake, 9-in. diam.,[97] 2⅞ in. high or 8-in. diam.,[97] 3¾ in. high; vol., 175 cu. in.; wt., 786 g.), with chocolate icing:[98]																	
a	Whole (vol., 192 cu. in.)	1 cake	1,107	23.6	3,753	48.7	136.2	645.4	653	1,162	8.9	2,900	1,439	1,660	.33	.89	3.3	1
b	Piece, 1/12 of cake (vol., 16.0 cu. in.; 2⅜-in. arc of 9-in.-diam. cake or 2⅛-in. arc of 8-in.-diam. cake).	1 piece	92	23.6	312	4.0	11.3	53.6	54	97	.7	241	120	140	.03	.07	.3	Trace
c	Piece, 1/16 of cake (vol., 12.0 cu. in.; 1¾-in. arc of 9-in.-diam. cake or 1⅝-in. arc of 8-in.-diam. cake).	1 piece	69	23.6	234	3.0	8.5	40.2	41	72	.6	181	90	100	.02	.06	.2	Trace

(A)	(B)			(C)	(D)	(E)	(F)	(G)	(H)	(I)	(J)	(K)	(L)	(M)	(N)	(O)	(P)	(Q)
d	Cube (1 cu. in.) [100]	1 cube	5.8	23.6	20	0.3	0.7	3.4	3	6	Trace	15	8	10	Trace	Trace	Trace	Trace
e	Cupcake, 2¾-in. diam. [97]	1 cupcake	46	23.6	156	2.0	5.7	26.8	27	48	0.4	121	60	70	0.01	0.04	0.1	Trace
f	Cupcake, 2½-in. diam. [97]	1 cupcake	35	23.6	119	1.5	4.3	20.4	21	37	.3	92	46	50	.01	.03	.1	Trace
561	Gingerbread; made with water:																	
a	Whole (8¼ × 8¼ × 1⅜ in.; vol., 94 cu. in.)	1 cake	570	37.0	1,573	17.7	38.8	291.3	513	570	9.1	1,733	1,562	Trace	.17	.51	4.6	Trace
b	Piece, ⅑ of cake (2¾ × 2¾ × 1⅜ in.; vol., 10.4 cu. in.).	1 piece	63	37.0	174	2.0	4.3	32.2	57	63	1.0	192	173	Trace	.02	.06	.5	Trace
c	Cube (1 cu. in.) [100]	1 cube	6.1	37.0	17	.2	.4	3.1	5	6	.1	19	17	Trace	Trace	.01	Trace	Trace
563	Honey spice; made with eggs, water (uniced 2-layer cake, 9-in. diam.,[97] 2¾ in. high or 8-in. diam.,[97] 3⅝ in. high; vol., 169 cu. in.; wt., 810 g.), with caramel icing: [101]																	
a	Whole (vol., 187 cu. in.)	1 cake	1,235	22.7	4,347	50.6	133.4	752.1	877	2,384	9.9	3,026	1,013	1,980	.25	1.11	2.5	2
b	Piece, 1/12 of cake (vol., 15.6 cu. in.; 2⅜-in. arc of 9-in.-diam. cake or 2⅛-in. arc of 8-in.-diam. cake).	1 piece	103	22.7	363	4.2	11.1	62.7	73	199	.8	252	84	160	.02	.09	.2	Trace
c	Piece, 1/16 of cake (vol., 11.7 cu. in.; 1¾-in. arc of 9-in.-diam. cake or 1⅝-in. arc of 8-in.-diam. cake).	1 piece	77	22.7	271	3.2	8.3	46.9	55	149	.6	189	63	120	.02	.07	.2	Trace
d	Cube (1 cu. in.) [100]	1 cube	6.6	22.7	23	.3	.7	4.0	5	13	.1	16	5	10	Trace	.01	Trace	Trace
565	Marble; made with eggs, water (uniced 2-layer cake, 9-in. diam.,[97] 2¾ in. high or 8-in. diam.,[97] 3½ in. high; vol., 167 cu. in.; wt., 794 g.), with boiled white icing:																	
a	Whole (vol., 206 cu. in.)	1 cake	1,045	23.6	3,459	46.0	90.9	647.9	815	1,787	8.4	2,707	1,275	940	.21	.84	2.1	1
b	Piece, 1/12 of cake (vol., 17.2 cu. in.; 2⅜-in. arc of 9-in.-diam. cake or 2⅛-in. arc of 8-in.-diam. cake).	1 piece	87	23.6	288	3.8	7.6	53.9	68	149	.7	225	106	80	.02	.07	.2	Trace
c	Piece, 1/16 of cake (vol., 12.9 cu. in.; 1¾-in. arc of 9-in.-diam. cake or 1⅝-in. arc of 8-in.-diam. cake).	1 piece	65	23.6	215	2.9	5.7	40.3	51	111	.5	168	79	60	.01	.05	.1	Trace
d	Cube (1 cu. in.) [100]	1 cube	5.1	23.6	17	.2	.4	3.2	4	9	Trace	13	6	Trace	Trace	Trace	Trace	Trace
567	White; made with egg whites, water (uniced 2-layer cake, 9-in. diam.,[97] 2⅝ in. high or 8-in. diam.,[97] 3⅜ in. high; vol., 160 cu. in.; wt., 785 g.), with chocolate icing: [88]																	
a	Whole (vol., 179 cu. in.)	1 cake	1,140	21.1	4,001	44.5	122.0	715.9	1,129	2,041	5.7	2,588	1,322	680	.23	.91	2.3	2
b	Piece, 1/12 of cake (vol., 14.9 cu. in.; 2⅜-in. arc of 9-in.-diam. cake or 2⅛-in. arc of 8-in.-diam. cake).	1 piece	95	21.1	333	3.7	10.2	59.7	94	170	.5	216	110	60	.02	.08	.2	Trace
c	Piece, 1/16 of cake (vol., 11.2 cu. in.; 1¾-in. arc of 9-in.-diam. cake or 1⅝-in. arc of 8-in.-diam. cake).	1 piece	71	21.1	249	2.8	7.6	44.6	70	127	.4	161	82	40	.01	.06	.1	Trace
d	Cube (1 cu. in.) [100]	1 cube	6.4	21.1	22	.2	.7	4.0	6	11	Trace	15	7	Trace	Trace	.01	Trace	Trace
569	Yellow; made with eggs, water (uniced 2-layer cake, 9-in. diam.,[97] 2⅞ in. high or 8-in. diam.,[97] 3⅝ in. high; vol., 172 cu. in.; wt., 790 g.), with chocolate icing: [88]																	
a	Whole (vol., 189 cu. in.)	1 cake	1,108	25.6	3,734	45.4	125.2	638.2	1,008	2,017	6.6	2,515	1,208	1,550	.22	.89	2.2	2
b	Piece, 1/12 of cake (vol., 15.8 cu. in.; 2⅜-in. arc of 9-in.-diam. cake or 2⅛-in. arc of 8-in.-diam. cake).	1 piece	92	25.6	310	3.8	10.4	53.0	84	167	.6	209	100	130	.02	.07	.2	Trace
c	Piece, 1/16 of cake (vol., 11.8 cu. in.; 1¾-in. arc of 9-in.-diam. cake or 1⅝-in. arc of 8-in.-diam. cake).	1 piece	69	25.6	233	2.8	7.8	39.7	63	126	.4	157	75	100	.01	.06	.1	Trace
d	Cube (1 cu. in.) [100]	1 cube	5.9	25.6	20	.2	.7	3.4	5	11	Trace	13	6	10	Trace	Trace	Trace	Trace
e	Cupcake, 2¾-in. diam. [97]	1 cupcake	46	25.6	155	1.9	5.2	26.5	42	84	.3	104	50	60	.01	.04	.1	Trace
f	Cupcake, 2½-in. diam. [97]	1 cupcake	35	25.6	118	1.4	4.0	20.2	32	64	.2	79	38	50	.01	.03	.1	Trace
	Cake icings prepared from home recipes: [107]																	
570	Caramel:																	
a	Yield from recipe (7½ oz.) [108, 109]	⅝ cup	213	14.1	767	2.8	14.3	162.9	217	134	4.3	177	111	600	.02	.13	Trace	1
b	Cup	1 cup	340	14.1	1,224	4.4	22.8	260.1	347	214	6.8	282	177	950	.03	.20	Trace	1

[88] Oxalic acid present may combine with calcium and magnesium to form insoluble compounds. For further information, see Appendix D, section on Minerals and Oxalic Acid

[97] Diameter of cake at top. For more complete information on dimensions and on calculation of volume in cubic inches, see Appendix B, section on Cakes

[100] Weight per cubic inch applies to layer, loaf, sheet, or tube cake but not to cupcakes. For cupcakes, see Appendix B, section on Cakes,

[101] See Appendix B, section on Cakes for information about amount of icing used for this cake.

[105] For information on ingredients added to cake mixes in preparation of cakes, ingredients used in cake icings, and proportion of cake to icing or filling, see ARS 62–13 (7), tables 8 and 9, p. 16, and table 11, p. 17. Measures and proportions of ingredients added to cake mixes in table 8 are typical for products available in 1960.

[106] With unenriched flour, approx. values for weight of whole cake are iron 2.6 mg., thiamin 0.22 mg., riboflavin 0.47 mg., niacin 2.6 mg.

[107] For information on ingredients used in cake icings, see ARS 62–13 (7), table 9, p. 16.

[108] Formula used to calculate nutritive values shown in Agr. Handb. No. 8, rev. 1963.

[109] This recipe doubled is adequate for 2-layer cake of 9-in. diam.; 1½ recipe for 2-layer cake of 8-in. diam.

TABLE 1.—*Nutritive values for household measures and market units of foods*—Continued

[Item numbers correspond to those in table 1 of Handbook No. 8, revised 1963. Values in parentheses denote imputed values usually from another form of the food or from a similar food. Zeros in parentheses indicate that amount of a constituent, if present, is probably too small to be measured. Dashes (—) denote lack of reliable data for a constituent believed to be present in a measurable amount. Calculated values, as those based on a recipe, are not in parentheses]

Item No. (A)	Food, approximate measures, units, and weight (edible part unless footnotes indicate otherwise) (B)			Water (C)	Food energy (D)	Protein (E)	Fat (F)	Carbohydrate (G)	Calcium (H)	Phosphorus (I)	Iron (J)	Sodium (K)	Potassium (L)	Vitamin A value (M)	Thiamin (N)	Riboflavin (O)	Niacin (P)	Ascorbic acid (Q)
			Grams	Percent	Calories	Grams	Grams	Grams	Milligrams	Milligrams	Milligrams	Milligrams	Milligrams	International units	Milligrams	Milligrams	Milligrams	Milligrams
	Cake icings prepared from home recipes [107]—Continued																	
571	Chocolate: [58]																	
a	Yield from recipe (11¾ oz.) [108]	1¼ cups	333	14.3	1,252	10.7	46.3	224.4	200	370	4.0	203	649	700	0.07	0.33	0.7	1
b	Cup	1 cup	275	14.3	1,034	8.8	38.2	185.4	165	305	3.3	168	536	580	.06	.28	.6	1
572	Coconut:																	
a	Yield from recipe (11 oz.) [108]	1⅞ cups	312	15.0	1,136	5.9	24.0	233.7	19	94	1.6	368	521	0	.03	.12	.6	0
b	Cup	1 cup	166	15.0	604	3.2	12.8	124.3	10	50	.8	196	277	0	.02	.07	.3	0
	White:																	
573	Uncooked:																	
	Yield from recipe (11¼ oz.) [108]	1 cup	319	11.1	1,199	1.6	21.1	260.3	48	38	Trace	156	57	860	Trace	.06	Trace	Trace
574	Boiled:																	
a	Yield from recipe (8⅞ oz.) [108]	2⅔ cups	252	17.9	796	3.5	0	202.4	5	5	Trace	360	45	0	Trace	.08	Trace	0
b	Cup	1 cup	94	17.9	297	1.3	0	75.5	2	2	Trace	134	17	0	Trace	.03	Trace	0
	Cake icings prepared from mixes: [110]																	
576	Chocolate fudge	1 cup	310	15.3	1,172	6.8	44.6	207.7	50	205	3.1	484	195	840	.03	.12	.6	0
	Creamy fudge (contains nonfat dry milk):																	
578	Made with water	1 cup	245	15.1	831	6.9	15.9	182.8	96	218	2.7	568	238	Trace	.05	.20	.7	Trace
579	Made with water, table fat	1 cup	(245)	15.1	938	6.4	37.2	161.5	91	198	2.5	786	218	960	.05	.17	.7	Trace
	Candied fruits. See Cherries, Citron, Ginger root, Grapefruit peel, Lemon peel, Orange peel, Pineapple.																	
	Candy:																	
580	Butterscotch	1 oz	28	1.5	113	Trace	1.0	26.9	5	2	.4	19	1	40	0	Trace	Trace	0
	Candy corn. See Fondant (items 602a, 602f).																	
	Caramels:																	
581	Plain or chocolate	1 oz	28	7.6	113	1.1	2.9	21.7	42	35	.4	64	54	Trace	.01	.05	.1	Trace
582	Plain or chocolate with nuts [5, 58]	1 oz	28	7.1	121	1.3	4.6	20.0	40	39	.4	58	66	10	.03	.05	.1	Trace
583	Chocolate-flavored roll:																	
a	Large (approx. 4⅜ in. long with oval cross section ⅝ × ½ in.), marked for 7 sections.	1 roll	32	5.6	127	.7	2.6	26.5	22	38	.6	63	39	Trace	.01	.02	Trace	Trace
b	Medium (approx. 2½ in. long, ⅝-in. diam.)	1 roll	8	5.6	32	.2	.7	6.6	5	10	.1	16	10	Trace	Trace	.01	Trace	Trace
c	Medium (approx. 1⅛ in. long, ½-in. diam.)	1 roll	7	5.6	28	.2	.6	5.8	5	8	.1	14	9	Trace	Trace	Trace	Trace	Trace
d	Small, bite size (approx. 1½ in. long, ⅜-in. diam.).	1 roll	5	5.6	20	.1	.4	4.1	3	6	.1	10	6	Trace	Trace	Trace	Trace	Trace
e	Ounce (approx. 6 sections of 1 large roll (item 583a), 3½ medium rolls (item 583b), 4 medium rolls (item 583c), or 6 small rolls (item 583d)).	1 oz	28	5.6	112	.6	2.3	23.4	19	34	.5	56	35	Trace	.01	.02	Trace	Trace
	Chocolate: [58]																	
584	Bittersweet	1 oz	28	1.8	135	2.2	11.3	13.3	16	81	1.4	1	174	10	.01	.05	.3	0
585	Semisweet:																	
a	Small pieces (approx. 60 per oz.)	1 cup or one 6-oz. pkg.	170	1.1	862	7.1	60.7	96.9	51	255	4.4	3	553	30	.02	.14	.9	0
b	Ounce	1 oz	28	1.1	144	1.2	10.1	16.2	9	43	.7	1	92	10	Trace	.02	.1	Trace
586	Sweet	1 oz	28	.9	150	1.2	10.0	16.4	27	40	.4	9	76	Trace	.01	.04	.1	Trace
	Chocolate, milk: [58]																	
587	Plain	1 oz	28	.9	147	2.2	9.2	16.1	65	65	.3	27	109	80	.02	.10	.1	Trace
588	With almonds [5]	1 oz	28	1.5	151	2.6	10.1	14.5	65	77	.5	23	125	70	.02	.12	.2	Trace
589	With peanuts [5]	1 oz	28	1.0	154	4.0	10.8	12.6	49	83	.4	19	138	50	.07	.07	1.4	Trace
	Chocolate coated: [58]																	
590	Almonds: [5]																	
a	Cup (single nuts)	1 cup	165	2.0	939	20.3	72.1	65.3	335	566	4.6	97	901	Trace	.20	.87	2.8	Trace
b	Ounce, single nuts (approx. 6–8) or clusters	1 oz	28	2.0	161	3.5	12.4	11.2	58	97	.8	17	155	Trace	.03	.15	.5	Trace
591	Chocolate fudge	1 oz	28	6.2	122	1.1	4.5	20.7	29	31	.4	65	55	Trace	.01	.04	.1	0
592	Chocolate fudge with nuts [5]	1 oz	28	6.0	128	1.4	5.9	19.1	29	39	.4	58	62	Trace	.02	.04	.1	Trace
593	Coconut center	1 oz	28	6.6	124	.8	5.0	20.4	14	22	.3	56	47	0	.01	.02	.1	0
594	Fondant:																	
	Mints, round:																	
a	Large (approx. 2½-in. diam., ⅜ in. thick)	1 mint	35	5.8	144	.6	3.7	28.4	20	19	.4	65	32	Trace	.01	.02	Trace	Trace
b	Small (approx. 1⅜-in. diam., ⅜ in. thick)	1 mint	11	5.8	45	.2	1.2	8.9	6	6	.1	20	10	Trace	Trace	.01	Trace	Trace
c	Miniature (approx. ¾-in. diam., ⅜ in. thick)	1 mint	2.4	5.8	10	Trace	.3	1.9	1	1	Trace	4	2	Trace	Trace	Trace	Trace	Trace

(A)	(B)			(C)	(D)	(E)	(F)	(G)	(H)	(I)	(J)	(K)	(L)	(M)	(N)	(O)	(P)	(Q)
	All chocolate-coated fondant:[111]																	
d	Ounce (approx. ⅞ of 1 large mint (item 594a), 2½ small mints (item 594b), or 12 miniature mints (item 594c)).	1 oz	28	5.8	116	0.5	3.0	23.0	16	15	0.3	52	26	Trace	0.01	0.02	Trace	Trace
595	Fudge, caramel, and peanuts[5]	1 oz	28	8.3	123	2.2	5.1	18.2	51	53	.4	58	85	Trace	.05	.06	0.5	Trace
596	Fudge, peanuts,[5] and caramel	1 oz	28	7.0	130	2.7	6.5	16.6	36	54	.3	36	63	Trace	.07	.04	1.0	Trace
597	Honeycombed hard candy with peanut butter[5]	1 oz	28	1.7	131	1.9	5.5	20.0	23	38	.5	46	64	Trace	.01	.03	.8	Trace
598	Nougat and caramel	1 oz	28	7.7	118	1.1	3.9	20.6	36	35	.5	49	60	10	.02	.05	.1	Trace
599	Peanuts:[5]																	
a	Cup (single nuts)	1 cup	170	1.0	954	27.9	70.2	66.5	197	507	2.6	102	857	Trace	.63	.31	12.6	Trace
b	Ounce, single nuts (approx. 8–16) or clusters (approx. 2).	1 oz	28	1.0	159	4.6	11.7	11.1	33	84	.4	17	143	Trace	.10	.05	2.1	Trace
600	Raisins:																	
a	Cup (single raisins)	1 cup	190	4.8	808	10.3	32.5	134.0	289	331	4.8	122	1,146	290	.15	.40	.8	Trace
b	Ounce, single raisins (approx. 50 small or 18–28 large) or clusters.	1 oz	28	4.8	120	1.5	4.8	20.0	43	49	.7	18	171	40	.02	.06	.1	Trace
601	Vanilla creams	1 oz	28	7.5	123	1.1	4.8	19.9	36	31	.2	52	50	Trace	.01	.02	Trace	Trace
602	Fondant:																	
	Candy corn (pieces approx. ⅞ in. long, ½ in. wide, ¼ in. thick):																	
a	Cup (approx. 143 pieces)	1 cup	200	7.6	728	.2	4.0	179.2	28	12	2.2	424	10	0	Trace	Trace	Trace	0
	Mints, uncoated:																	
b	Piece, round (approx. 1½-in. diam., ½ in. thick)	1 piece	8.8	7.6	32	Trace	.2	7.9	1	1	.1	19	Trace	0	Trace	Trace	Trace	0
c	Piece, square (approx. ⅝ in. long, ⅝ in. wide, ⅜ in. high).	10 pieces	17.6	7.6	64	Trace	.4	15.8	2	1	.2	37	1	0	Trace	Trace	Trace	0
d	Piece, rectangular (approx. ½ in. long, ⅜ in. wide, ⅜ in. high).	10 pieces	7.3	7.6	27	Trace	.1	6.5	1	Trace	.1	15	Trace	0	Trace	Trace	Trace	0
e	Cup (approx. 63 square pieces (item 602c) or 150 rectangular pieces (item 602d)).	1 cup	110	7.6	400	.1	2.2	98.6	15	7	1.2	233	6	0	Trace	Trace	Trace	0
	All uncoated fondant:[112]																	
f	Ounce. Approx. number of pieces: Candy corn 20, mints, round (item 602b) 3, square (item 602c) 16, rectangular (item 602d) 39.	1 oz	28	7.6	103	Trace	.6	25.4	4	2	.3	60	1	0	Trace	Trace	Trace	0
	Fudge:																	
603	Chocolate:[88]																	
a	Ounce	1 oz	28	8.2	113	.8	3.5	21.3	22	24	.3	54	42	Trace	.01	.03	.1	Trace
b	Cubic inch	1 cu. in	21	8.2	84	.6	2.6	15.8	16	18	.2	40	31	Trace	Trace	.02	Trace	Trace
604	Chocolate with nuts:[5,88]																	
a	Ounce	1 oz	28	7.8	121	1.1	4.9	19.6	22	32	.3	48	50	Trace	.01	.03	.1	Trace
b	Cubic inch	1 cu. in	21	7.8	89	.8	3.7	14.5	17	24	.3	36	37	Trace	.01	.02	.1	Trace
605	Vanilla:																	
a	Ounce	1 oz	28	10.0	113	.9	3.1	21.2	32	24	.1	59	36	Trace	.01	.04	Trace	Trace
b	Cubic inch	1 cu. in	21	10.0	84	.6	2.3	15.7	24	17	.1	44	27	Trace	Trace	.03	Trace	Trace
606	Vanilla with nuts:[5,88]																	
a	Ounce	1 oz	28	9.4	120	1.2	4.6	19.5	31	32	.2	53	32	Trace	.01	.04	Trace	Trace
b	Cubic inch	1 cu. in	21	9.4	89	.9	3.4	14.4	23	24	.2	39	24	Trace	.01	.03	Trace	Trace
607	Gum drops, starch jelly pieces	1 oz	28	11.7	98	Trace	.2	24.8	2	Trace	.1	10	1	0	0	Trace	Trace	0
608	Hard	1 oz	28	1.4	109	0	.3	27.6	6	2	.5	9	1	0	0	0	0	0
609	Jellybeans (approx. ¾ in. long, ½ in. wide):																	
a	Cup (approx. 75 jellybeans)	1 cup	220	6.3	807	Trace	1.1	204.8	26	9	2.4	26	2	0	0	Trace	Trace	0
b	Ounce (approx. 10 jellybeans)	1 oz	28	6.3	104	Trace	.1	26.4	3	1	.3	3	Trace	0	0	Trace	Trace	0
610	Marshmallows, plain:																	
	Large:																	
a	Regular type (approx. 1⅛-in. diam., ¾ in. high; 63 per pound).	1 marshmallow	7.2	17.3	23	.1	Trace	5.8	1	Trace	.1	3	Trace	0	0	Trace	Trace	0
b	Soft type (approx. 1⅛-in. diam., 1⅛ in. high; 76 per pound).	1 marshmallow	6.0	17.3	19	.1	Trace	4.8	1	Trace	.1	2	Trace	0	0	Trace	Trace	0
	Miniature or recipe size (approx. ½-in. diam., ½ in. high):																	
c	Cup, no packing	1 cup	46	17.3	147	.9	Trace	37.0	8	3	.7	18	3	0	0	Trace	Trace	0
d	Cup, packed	1 cup	56	17.3	179	1.1	Trace	45.0	10	3	.9	22	3	0	0	Trace	Trace	0
	All sizes:																	
e	Ounce	1 oz	28	17.3	90	.6	Trace	22.8	5	2	.5	11	2	0	0	Trace	Trace	0
	Mints, coated. See Chocolate-coated fondant (items 594a–594d).																	

[5] Most of phosphorus in nuts, legumes, and outer layers of cereal grains is present as phytic acid. See also Appendix D, section on Minerals and Oxalic Acid

[88] Oxalic acid present may combine with calcium and magnesium to form insoluble compounds. For further information, see Appendix D, section on Minerals and Oxalic Acid

[107] For information on ingredients used in cake icings, see ARS 62–13 (7), table 9, p. 16.

[108] Formula used to calculate nutritive values shown in Agr. Handb. No. 8, rev. 1963.

[110] For information on ingredients added to mixes for preparation, see ARS 62–13 (7), table 10, p. 17.

[111] Unit and nutritive values apply also to other types of chocolate-coated fondant than mints.

[112] Unit and nutritive values apply also to other types of uncoated fondant than those shown here.

TABLE 1.—*Nutritive values for household measures and market units of foods*—Continued

[Item numbers correspond to those in table 1 of Handbook No. 8, revised 1963. Values in parentheses denote imputed values usually from another form of the food or from a similar food. Zeros in parentheses indicate that amount of a constituent, if present, is probably too small to be measured. Dashes (—) denote lack of reliable data for a constituent believed to be present in a measurable amount. Calculated values, as those based on a recipe, are not in parentheses]

Item No.	Food, approximate measures, units, and weight (edible part unless footnotes indicate otherwise)			Water	Food energy	Protein	Fat	Carbohydrate	Calcium	Phosphorus	Iron	Sodium	Potassium	Vitamin A value	Thiamin	Riboflavin	Niacin	Ascorbic acid
				Values for edible part of foods														
(A)	(B)			(C)	(D)	(E)	(F)	(G)	(H)	(I)	(J)	(K)	(L)	(M)	(N)	(O)	(P)	(Q)
			Grams	*Percent*	*Calories*	*Grams*	*Grams*	*Grams*	*Milligrams*	*Milligrams*	*Milligrams*	*Milligrams*	*Milligrams*	*International units*	*Milligrams*	*Milligrams*	*Milligrams*	*Milligrams*
	Candy—Continued																	
	Mints, uncoated. See Fondant (items 602b–602f).																	
611	Peanut bars [5,55]	1 oz	28	1.5	146	5.0	9.1	13.4	12	77	0.5	3	127	0	0.12	0.02	2.7	0
612	Peanut brittle (no added salt or soda) [5,55]	1 oz	28	2.0	119	1.6	2.9	23.0	10	27	.7	9	43	0	.05	.01	1.0	0
	Sugar coated:																	
613	Almonds (approx. 1 in. long, ⅝ in. wide): [5]																	
a	Cup	1 cup	195	2.3	889	15.2	36.3	136.9	195	324	3.7	39	497	0	.10	.53	2.0	0
b	Ounce (approx. 8 almonds)	1 oz	28	2.3	129	2.2	5.3	19.9	28	47	.5	6	72	0	.01	.08	.3	0
614	Chocolate disks (approx. ½-in. diam.): [55]																	
a	Cup	1 cup	197	1.2	918	10.2	38.8	143.2	266	276	2.6	142	493	200	.12	.39	.6	Trace
b	Ounce (approx. 31 disks)	1 oz	28	1.2	132	1.5	5.6	20.6	38	40	.4	20	71	30	.02	.06	.1	Trace
	Cantaloups. See Muskmelons (item 1358).																	
	Cape-gooseberries. See Groundcherries (item 1092).																	
	Capicola. See Sausage, cold cuts, and luncheon meats (item 1989).																	
615	**Carambola,** raw (refuse: skin and seeds, 19%). [1]	1 carambola	70	90.4	20	.4	.3	4.5	2	10	.9	1	109	680	.02	.01	.2	20
616	**Carissa** (natalplum), raw:																	
a	Whole (refuse: skin and seeds, 14%) [1]	1 carissa	23	80.8	14	.1	.3	3.2	—	—	—	—	—	10	.01	.01	Trace	8
b	Slices (⅛ in. thick)	1 cup	150	80.8	105	.8	2.0	24.0	—	—	—	—	—	60	.06	.09	.3	57
617	**Carob flour** (St. Johnsbread):																	
a	Cup	1 cup	140	11.2	252	6.3	2.0	113.0	493	113	—	—	—	—	—	—	—	—
b	Tablespoon	1 tbsp	8	11.2	14	.4	.1	6.5	28	6	—	—	—	—	—	—	—	—
	Carrots: [55]																	
619	Raw:																	
	Whole, prepackaged without tops (refuse: crowns, tips, scrapings, 11%): [1]																	
a	Package, declared net wt., 16 oz. (1 lb.); avg. wt., 20 oz. (1¼ lb.); approx. 7 carrots (item 619b).	1 pkg	567	88.2	212	5.6	1.0	48.9	187	182	3.5	237	1,721	[113] 55,510	.30	.25	3.0	40
b	Carrot, approx. 1⅛-in. diam., 7½ in. long; wt., 2⅞ oz.	1 carrot	81	88.2	30	.8	.1	7.0	27	26	.5	34	246	[113] 7,930	.04	.04	.4	6
	Cut forms:																	
c	Strip, ¼–⅜ in. wide, 2½–3 in. long	6–8 strips or 1 oz.	28	88.2	12	.3	.1	2.7	10	10	.2	13	97	[113] 3,120	.02	.01	.2	2
d	Grated or shredded	1 cup	110	88.2	46	1.2	.2	10.7	41	40	.8	52	375	[113] 12,100	.07	.06	.7	9
e	Pound	1 lb	454	88.2	191	5.0	.9	44.0	168	163	3.2	213	1,547	[113] 49,900	.27	.23	2.7	36
620	Cooked (boiled), drained:																	
	Cup:																	
a	Sliced (crosswise), ¼–½ in. thick	1 cup	155	91.2	48	1.4	.3	11.0	51	48	.9	[20] 51	344	[113] 16,280	.08	.08	.8	9
b	Diced (¼- to ½-in. cubes)	1 cup	145	91.2	45	1.3	.3	10.3	48	45	.9	[20] 48	322	[113] 15,230	.07	.07	.7	9
c	Pound (approx. 3 cups, sliced, or 3⅛ cups, diced)	1 lb	454	91.2	141	4.1	.9	32.2	150	141	2.7	[20] 150	1,007	[113] 47,630	.23	.23	2.3	27
	Canned:																	
	Regular pack:																	
621	Solids and liquid:																	
	Container and approx. contents:																	
a	Can, size 303 × 406 [14] (No. 303), or glass jar, size 16 oz.; net wt., 16 oz. (1 lb.).	1 container or 1 lb.	454	91.8	127	2.7	.9	29.5	[114] 113	91	3.2	[21] 1,070	544	[113] 45,360	.09	.09	1.8	9
b	Can, size 603 × 700 [14] (No. 10); net wt., 104 oz. (6 lb. 8 oz.).	1 container	2,948	91.8	825	17.7	5.9	191.6	[114] 737	590	20.6	[21] 6,957	3,538	[113] 294,800	.59	.59	11.8	59
c	Cup	1 cup	246	91.8	69	1.5	.5	16.0	[114] 62	49	1.7	[21] 581	295	[113] 24,600	.05	.05	1.0	5
622	Drained solids:																	
	Container and approx. drained contents:																	
	Can, size 303 × 406 [14] (No. 303), or glass jar, size 16 oz.:																	
a	Whole; wt., 9¾ oz. (approx. 15 carrots (item 622h)).	1 container	276	91.2	83	2.2	.8	18.5	[114] 83	61	1.9	[21] 651	331	[113] 41,400	.06	.08	1.1	6
b	Sliced (crosswise slices, ¼–½ in. thick, diam. less than 1½ in.); wt., 10 oz.	1 container	284	91.2	85	2.3	.9	19.0	[114] 85	62	2.0	[21] 670	341	[113] 42,600	.06	.09	1.1	6
c	Diced (¼-in. cubes); wt., 10½ oz	1 container	298	91.2	89	2.4	.9	20.0	[114] 89	66	2.1	[21] 703	358	[113] 44,700	.06	.09	1.2	6
	Can, size 603 × 700 [14] (No. 10):																	

(A)	(B)			(C)	(D)	(E)	(F)	(G)	(H)	(I)	(J)	(K)	(L)	(M)	(N)	(O)	(P)	(Q)
d	Whole or sliced (crosswise slices, ¼–½ in. thick; diam. less than 1½ in.); wt., 69 oz. (4 lb. 5 oz.).	1 container	1,956	91.2	587	15.6	5.9	131.1	[114] 587	430	13.7	[21] 4,616	2,347	[113] 293,400	0.39	0.59	7.8	39
e	Diced (¼-in. cubes); wt., 72 oz. (4 lb. 8 oz.).	1 container	2,041	91.2	612	16.3	6.1	136.7	[114] 612	449	14.3	[21] 4,817	2,449	[113] 306,150	.41	.61	8.2	41
	Cup:																	
f	Sliced	1 cup	155	91.2	47	1.2	.5	10.4	[114] 47	34	1.1	[21] 366	186	[113] 23,250	.03	.05	.6	3
g	Diced	1 cup	145	91.2	44	1.2	.4	9.7	[114] 44	32	1.0	[21] 342	174	[113] 21,750	.03	.04	.6	3
h	Carrot, approx. 2 in. long, ¾-in. diam	3 carrots	55	91.2	17	.4	.2	3.7	[114] 17	12	.4	[21] 130	66	[113] 8,250	.01	.02	.2	1
i	Pound	1 lb	454	91.2	136	3.6	1.4	30.4	[114] 136	100	3.2	[21] 1,070	544	[113] 68,040	.09	.14	1.8	9
j	Ounce	1 oz	28	91.2	9	.2	.1	1.9	[114] 9	6	.2	[21] 67	34	[113] 4,250	.01	.01	.1	1
623	Drained liquid:																	
a	Pound	1 lb	454	93.3	100	1.8	0	24.9	[114] 64	68	3.6	[21] 1,070	544	Trace	.09	.09	1.8	9
b	Ounce	1 oz	28	93.3	6	.1	0	1.6	[114] 4	4	.2	[21] 67	34	Trace	.01	.01	.1	1
	Special dietary pack (low sodium):																	
624	Solids and liquid:																	
	Container and approx. contents:																	
a	Can, size 303 × 406 [14] (No. 303), or glass jar, size 16 oz.; net wt., 16 oz. (1 lb.).	1 container or 1 lb.	454	93.7	100	3.2	.5	22.7	[114] 113	91	3.2	177	544	[113] 45,360	.09	.09	1.8	9
b	Can, size 603 × 700 [14] (No. 10); net wt., 104 oz. (6 lb. 8 oz.).	1 container	2,948	93.7	649	20.6	2.9	147.4	[114] 737	590	20.6	1,150	3,538	[113] 294,800	.59	.59	11.8	59
c	Cup	1 cup	246	93.7	54	1.7	.2	12.3	[114] 62	49	1.7	96	295	[113] 24,600	.05	.05	1.0	5
625	Drained solids (slices, ¼–½ in. thick, diam. less than 1½ in.):																	
	Container and approx. drained contents:																	
a	Can, size 303 × 406 [14] (No. 303), or glass jar, size 16 oz.; wt., 10 oz.	1 container	284	93.0	71	2.3	.3	15.9	[114] 85	62	2.0	111	341	[113] 42,600	.06	.09	1.1	6
b	Can, size 603 × 700 [14] (No. 10); wt., 69 oz. (4 lb. 5 oz.).	1 container	1,956	93.0	489	15.6	2.0	109.5	[114] 587	430	13.7	763	2,347	[113] 293,400	.39	.59	7.8	39
c	Cup	1 cup	155	93.0	39	1.2	.2	8.7	[114] 47	34	1.1	60	186	[113] 23,250	.03	.05	.6	3
d	Pound	1 lb	454	93.0	113	3.6	.5	25.4	[114] 136	100	3.2	177	544	[113] 68,040	.09	.14	1.8	9
e	Ounce	1 oz	28	93.0	7	.2	Trace	1.6	[114] 9	6	.2	11	34	[113] 4,250	.01	.01	.1	1
626	Drained liquid:																	
a	Pound	1 lb	454	95.2	73	1.8	0	18.1	[114] 64	68	3.6	177	544	Trace	.09	.09	1.8	9
b	Ounce	1 oz	28	95.2	5	.1	0	1.1	[114] 4	4	.2	11	34	Trace	.01	.01	.1	1
627	Dehydrated:																	
a	Pound	1 lb	454	4	1,547	29.9	5.9	367.9	1,161	1,061	27.2	1,216	8,818	453,600	1.41	1.36	13.6	68
b	Ounce	1 oz	28	4	97	1.9	.4	23.0	73	66	1.7	76	551	28,350	.09	.09	.9	4
	Casaba melon. See Muskmelons (item 1359).																	
628	**Cashew nuts,**[8] roasted in oil:																	
a	Cup, whole kernels	1 cup	140	5.2	785	24.1	64.0	41.0	53	522	5.3	[115] 21	650	140	.60	.35	2.5	—
b	Pound (approx. 200–240 large kernels, 260–320 medium, or 350–500 small).	1 lb	454	5.2	2,545	78.0	207.3	132.9	172	1,692	17.2	[115] 68	2,105	450	1.95	1.13	8.2	—
c	Ounce (approx. 14 large kernels, 18 medium, or 26 small).	1 oz	28	5.2	159	4.9	13.0	8.3	11	106	1.1	[115] 4	132	30	.12	.07	.5	—
	Catsup. See Tomato catsup (item 2286).																	
	Cauliflower:																	
630	Raw:																	
a	Head, 6- to 7-in. diam.; wt., 1.9 lb	1 head	860	91.0	232	23.2	1.7	44.7	215	482	9.5	112	2,537	520	.95	.86	6.0	671
	Flowerbuds:																	
b	Whole	1 cup	100	91.0	27	2.7	.2	5.2	25	56	1.1	13	295	60	.11	.10	.7	78
c	Sliced	1 cup	85	91.0	23	2.3	.2	4.4	21	48	.9	11	251	50	.09	.09	.6	66
d	Chopped	1 cup	115	91.0	31	3.1	.2	6.0	29	64	1.3	15	339	70	.13	.12	.8	90
e	Pound	1 lb	454	91.0	122	12.2	.9	23.6	113	254	5.0	59	1,338	270	.50	.45	3.2	354
631	Cooked (boiled), drained:																	
a	Cup	1 cup	125	92.8	28	2.9	.3	5.1	26	53	.9	[20] 11	258	80	.11	.10	.8	69
b	Pound	1 lb	454	92.8	100	10.4	.9	18.6	95	191	3.2	[20] 41	934	270	.41	.36	2.7	249
	Frozen:																	
632	Not thawed:																	
a	Container, net wt., 10 oz	1 container	284	92.9	62	5.7	.6	12.2	54	119	1.7	31	639	90	.17	.17	1.4	159
b	Pound	1 lb	454	92.9	100	9.1	.9	19.5	86	191	2.7	50	1,021	140	.27	.27	2.3	254

[1] Measure and weight apply to food as it is described with inedible part or parts (refuse) included.

[8] Most of phosphorus in nuts, legumes, and outer layers of cereal grains is present as phytic acid. See also Appendix D, section on Minerals and Oxalic Acid

[14] Dimensions of can: 1st dimension represents diameter; 2d dimension, height of can. 1st or left-hand digit in each dimension gives number of whole inches; next 2 digits give additional fraction of dimension expressed as 16th of an inch.

[20] Value is for unsalted product. If salt is used, increase value by 236 mg. per 100 g. of vegetable—an estimated figure based on typical amount of salt (0.6%) in canned vegetables. See also Appendix C, section on Cooked Vegetables

[21] Estimated value based on addition of salt in amount of 0.6% of finished product.

[86] Oxalic acid present may combine with calcium and magnesium to form insoluble compounds. For further information, see Appendix D, section on Minerals and Oxalic Acid

[113] Based on average for carrots marketed as fresh vegetable. For further information on variation in vitamin A values of raw and processed forms, see Appendix C, section on Carrots

[114] Federal standards provide for addition of certain calcium salts as firming agents. If used, these salts may add calcium not to exceed 36 mg. per 100 g. of finished product. Value for item 621a would be 271 mg.; for item 621b, 1,798 mg.; for item 621c, 150 mg. Data not available to give change in calcium value for drained solids and drained liquid.

[115] Applies to unsalted nuts. For salted nuts, value for 1 cup of kernels (item 628a) is approx. 280 mg.; for 1 lb., 907 mg.; for 1 oz., 57 mg.

TABLE 1.—*Nutritive values for household measures and market units of foods*—Continued

[Item numbers correspond to those in table 1 of Handbook No. 8, revised 1963. Values in parentheses denote imputed values usually from another form of the food or from a similar food. Zeros in parentheses indicate that amount of a constituent, if present, is probably too small to be measured. Dashes (—) denote lack of reliable data for a constituent believed to be present in a measurable amount. Calculated values, as those based on a recipe, are not in parentheses]

Item No.	Food, approximate measures, units, and weight (edible part unless footnotes indicate otherwise)			Values for edible part of foods														
				Water	Food energy	Protein	Fat	Carbohydrate	Calcium	Phosphorus	Iron	Sodium	Potassium	Vitamin A value	Thiamin	Riboflavin	Niacin	Ascorbic acid
(A)	(B)			(C)	(D)	(E)	(F)	(G)	(H)	(I)	(J)	(K)	(L)	(M)	(N)	(O)	(P)	(Q)
			Grams	*Percent*	*Calories*	*Grams*	*Grams*	*Grams*	*Milligrams*	*Milligrams*	*Milligrams*	*Milligrams*	*Milligrams*	*International units*	*Milligrams*	*Milligrams*	*Milligrams*	*Milligrams*
	Cauliflower—Continued																	
	Frozen—Continued																	
633	Cooked (boiled), drained:																	
a	Yield from 10 oz., frozen cauliflower	1½ cups	270	94.0	49	5.1	0.5	8.9	46	103	1.4	[20] 27	559	80	0.11	0.14	1.1	111
b	Yield from 1 lb., frozen cauliflower	2.4 cups	430	94.0	77	8.2	.9	14.2	73	163	2.2	[20] 43	890	130	.17	.22	1.7	176
c	Cup (approx. 7 flowerets)	1 cup	180	94.0	32	3.4	.4	5.9	31	68	.9	[20] 18	373	50	.07	.09	.7	74
d	Pound (approx. 2½ cups)	1 lb	454	94.0	82	8.6	.9	15.0	77	172	2.3	[20] 45	939	140	.18	.23	1.8	186
	Caviar, sturgeon:																	
634	Granular:																	
a	Tablespoon	1 tbsp	16	46.0	42	4.3	2.4	.5	44	57	1.9	352	29	—	—	—	—	—
b	Ounce	1 oz	28	46.0	74	7.6	4.3	.9	78	101	3.3	624	51	—	—	—	—	—
635	Pressed:																	
a	Tablespoon	1 tbsp	17	36.0	54	5.8	2.8	.8	—	—	—	—	—	—	—	—	—	—
b	Ounce	1 oz	28	36.0	90	9.8	4.7	1.4	—	—	—	—	—	—	—	—	—	—
	Celery, green (Pascal type):																	
637	Raw:																	
a	Bunch, prepackaged with stalks trimmed of leaves (refuse: root end and trimmings, 11%); [1] 15¾ in. long, 11-in. cir. (at widest part); wt., 2 lb.; approx. 14 stalks.	1 bunch or 2 lb	907	94.1	137	7.3	.8	31.5	315	226	2.4	1,017	2,753	[116] 2,180	.24	.24	2.4	73
	Stalk:																	
b	Large outer, 8 in. long, approx. 1½ in. wide at root end.	1 stalk	40	94.1	7	.4	Trace	1.6	16	11	.1	50	136	[116] 110	.01	.01	.1	4
c	Small inner, 5 in. long, ¾ in. wide	3 stalks	50	94.1	9	.5	.1	2.0	20	14	.2	63	171	[116] 140	.02	.02	.2	5
d	Chopped or diced pieces	1 cup	120	94.1	20	1.1	.1	4.7	47	34	.4	151	409	[116] 320	.04	.04	.4	11
e	Pound	1 lb	454	94.1	77	4.1	.5	17.7	177	127	1.4	572	1,547	[116] 1,220	.14	.14	1.4	41
f	Ounce	1 oz	28	94.1	5	.3	Trace	1.1	11	8	.1	36	97	[116] 80	.01	.01	.1	8
638	Cooked:																	
a	Cup, diced pieces	1 cup	150	95.3	21	1.2	.2	4.7	47	33	.3	[20] 132	359	[116] 390	.03	.05	.5	9
b	Pound (approx. 3 cups, diced pieces (item 638a))	1 lb	454	95.3	64	3.6	.5	14.1	141	100	.9	[20] 399	1,084	[116] 1,180	.09	.14	1.4	27
	Cereals, breakfast. See Corn, Oats, Rice, Wheat, also Bran, Farina.																	
	Cervelat. See Sausage, cold cuts and luncheon meats (items 1990, 2021).																	
	Chard, Swiss: [55]																	
639	Raw	1 lb	454	91.1	113	10.9	1.4	20.9	399	177	14.5	667	2,495	29,480	.27	.77	2.3	145
640	Cooked (boiled), drained:																	
a	Leaves and stalks	1 cup	145	93.7	26	2.6	.3	4.8	106	35	2.6	[20] 125	465	7,830	.06	.16	.6	23
b	Leaves	1 cup	175	93.7	32	3.2	.4	5.8	128	42	3.2	[20] 151	562	9,450	.07	.19	.7	28
c	Pound	1 lb	454	93.7	82	8.2	.9	15.0	331	109	8.2	[20] 390	1,456	24,490	.18	.50	1.8	73
641	**Charlotte russe,** with ladyfingers, whipped-cream filling: [18]																	
a	Yield from recipe [108] (approx. 24 ladyfingers (item 822); 2 cups of filling).	6 servings	685	45.5	1,959	40.4	100.0	229.5	315	623	4.8	295	438	5,070	.21	.69	.7	2
b	Serving, ⅙ of recipe (item 641a) (approx. 4 ladyfingers (item 822); ⅓ cup of filling).	1 serving	114	45.5	326	6.7	16.6	38.2	52	104	.8	49	73	840	.03	.11	.1	Trace
	Cheeses, natural and processed; cheese foods; cheese spreads:																	
	Natural cheeses:																	
643	Blue or Roquefort type:																	
	Prepackaged cut pieces:																	
a	Package, net wt., 4 oz. (rectangular piece, approx. 2¾ × 2½ × 1 in., or triangular piece, 4⅝ × 3⅝ × 3⅝ in.; 1⅛ in. thick).	1 pkg	113	40	416	24.3	34.5	2.3	356	383	(.6)	—	—	(1,400)	.03	.69	1.4	(0)
b	Package, net wt., 3 oz. (sector, approx. 2¾-in. arc, 3½-in. radius, 1 in. high).	1 pkg	85	40	313	18.3	25.9	1.7	268	288	(.4)	—	—	(1,050)	.03	.52	1.0	(0)
	Cup (cheese crumbled):																	
c	Not packed	1 cup	135	40	497	29.0	41.2	2.7	425	458	(.7)	—	—	(1,670)	.04	.82	1.6	(0)
d	Packed	1 cup	249	40	916	53.5	75.9	5.0	784	844	(1.2)	—	—	(3,090)	.07	1.52	3.0	(0)
e	Pound	1 lb	454	40	1,669	97.5	138.3	9.1	1,429	1,538	(2.3)	—	—	(5,620)	.14	2.77	5.4	(0)
f	Ounce	1 oz	28	40	104	6.1	8.6	.6	89	96	(.1)	—	—	(350)	.01	.17	.3	(0)
g	Cubic inch	1 cu. in	[117] 17.3	40	64	3.7	5.3	.3	54	59	(.1)	—	—	(210)	Trace	.11	.2	(0)

(A)	(B)			(C)	(D)	(E)	(F)	(G)	(H)	(I)	(J)	(K)	(L)	(M)	(N)	(O)	(P)	(Q)
644	Brick:																	
	Prepackaged forms:																	
	Cut piece:																	
	Package, approx. contents, and slice cut from piece:																	
a	Package, net wt., 10 oz.; rectangular piece, 4½ × 2¾ × 1⅝ in.	1 pkg	284	41.0	1,051	63.0	86.6	5.4	2,073	1,292	(2.6)	—	—	(3,520)	—	1.28	0.3	(0)
b	Slice, approx. 2¾ × 1⅝ × ¼ in.; 1/18 of piece (item 644a).	1 slice	16	41.0	59	3.6	4.9	.3	117	73	(.1)	—	—	(200)	—	.07	Trace	(0)
	Slice, approx. 7⅛ × 3¾ × 3/32 in.; wt., 1½ oz.:																	
c	Package, net wt., 8 oz.; 5 slices	1 pkg	227	41.0	840	50.4	69.2	4.8	1,657	1,033	(2.0)	—	—	(2,810)	—	1.02	.2	(0)
d	Slice	1 slice	45	41.0	167	10.0	13.7	.9	329	205	(.4)	—	—	(560)	—	.20	Trace	(0)
e	Pound	1 lb	454	41.0	1,678	100.7	138.3	8.6	3,311	2,064	(4.1)	—	—	(5,620)	—	2.04	.5	(0)
f	Ounce	1 oz	28	41.0	105	6.3	8.6	.5	207	129	(.3)	—	—	(350)	—	.13	Trace	(0)
g	Cubic inch	1 cu. in	[117] 17.2	41.0	64	3.8	5.2	.3	126	78	(.2)	—	—	(210)	—	.08	Trace	(0)
645	Camembert (domestic):																	
	Prepackaged triangular piece, approx. 2¼ × 2⅛ × 2⅛ in., 1⅛ in. high; net wt., 1⅓ oz.:																	
a	Package, net wt., 4 oz.; 3 pieces	1 pkg	113	52.2	338	19.8	27.9	2.0	119	208	.6	—	125	(1,140)	0.05	.85	.9	(0)
b	Piece	1 piece	38	52.2	114	6.7	9.4	.7	40	70	.2	—	42	(380)	.02	.29	.3	(0)
c	Cup	1 cup	246	52.2	736	43.1	60.8	4.4	258	453	1.2	—	278	(2,480)	.10	1.85	2.0	(0)
d	Pound	1 lb	454	52.2	1,356	79.4	112.0	8.2	476	835	2.3	—	508	(4,5[illegible])	.18	3.40	3.6	(0)
e	Ounce	1 oz	28	52.2	85	5.0	7.0	.5	30	52	.1	—	31	(290)	.01	.21	.2	(0)
f	Cubic inch	1 cu. in	[117] 17.1	52.2	51	3.0	4.2	.3	18	31	.1	—	19	(170)	.01	.13	.1	(0)
646	Cheddar (domestic type):																	
	Prepackaged forms:																	
	Cut pieces:																	
	Package, approx. contents, and slice cut from piece:																	
a	Package, net wt., 12 oz.; cylindrical piece (Longhorn style), approx. 2⅝-in. diam., 3⅝ in. high.	1 pkg	340	37	1,353	85.0	109.5	7.1	2,550	1,625	3.4	2,380	279	(4,450)	.10	1.56	.3	(0)
b	Slice, approx. 2⅝-in. diam., ¼ in. thick; 1/14 of piece (item 646a).	1 slice	24	37	96	6.0	7.7	.5	180	115	.2	168	20	(310)	.01	.11	Trace	(0)
c	Package, net wt., 10 oz.; rectangular piece, approx. 5⅝ × 1⅝ × 1¾ in.	1 pkg	284	37	1,130	71.0	91.4	6.0	2,130	1,358	2.8	1,988	233	(3,720)	.09	1.31	.3	(0)
d	Slice, approx. 1¾ × 1⅝ × ¼ in.; 1/22 of piece (item 646c).	1 slice	13	37	52	3.3	4.2	.3	98	62	.1	91	11	(170)	Trace	.06	Trace	(0)
e	Package, net wt., 8 oz.; wedge, approx. 3⅞ × 1¾ in., 3½ in. high.	1 pkg	227	37	903	56.8	73.1	4.8	1,703	1,085	2.3	1,589	186	(2,970)	.07	1.04	.2	(0)
	Slices:																	
	Round (midget Longhorn style), approx. 3¼-in. diam., ⅛ in. thick; wt., ¾ oz.:																	
f	Package, net wt., 6 oz.; 8 slices	1 pkg	170	37	677	42.5	54.7	3.6	1,275	813	1.7	1,190	139	(2,230)	.05	.78	.2	(0)
g	Slice	1 slice	21	37	84	5.3	6.8	.4	158	100	.2	147	17	(280)	.01	.10	Trace	(0)
	Semicircular (Longhorn style), approx. 5⅝ in. long, 3½ in. wide at center, ⅛ in. thick; wt., 1¼ oz.:																	
h	Package, net wt., 10 oz.; 8 slices	1 pkg	284	37	1,130	71.0	91.4	6.0	2,130	1,358	2.8	1,988	233	(3,720)	.09	1.31	.3	(0)
i	Slice	1 slice	35	37	139	8.8	11.3	.7	263	167	.4	245	29	(460)	.01	.16	Trace	(0)
	Rectangular, approx. 6⅞ × 3⅞ × 3/32 in.; wt., 1½ oz.:																	
j	Package, net wt., 8 oz.; 5 slices	1 pkg	227	37	903	56.8	73.1	4.8	1,703	1,085	2.3	1,589	186	(2,970)	.07	1.04	.2	(0)
k	Slice	1 slice	45	37	179	11.3	14.5	.9	338	215	.5	315	37	(590)	0.1	.21	Trace	(0)
	Squares, approx. ⅞ × ¾ × ½ in.:[118]																	
l	Package, net wt., 6 oz. (30 squares)	1 pkg	170	37	677	42.5	54.7	3.6	1,275	813	1.7	1,190	139	(2,230)	.05	.78	.2	(0)
m	Cup (approx. 26 squares)[119]	1 cup	140	37	557	35.0	45.1	2.9	1,050	669	1.4	980	115	(1,830)	.04	.64	.1	(0)
n	Shredded form, 1 cup (approx. 1 pkg.; net wt., 4 oz.).	1 cup or 1 pkg.	113	37	450	28.3	36.4	2.4	848	540	1.1	791	93	(1,480)	.03	.52	.1	(0)
o	Pound	1 lb	454	37	1,805	113.4	146.1	9.5	3,402	2,168	4.5	3,175	372	(5,940)	.14	2.09	.5	(0)
p	Ounce	1 oz	28	37	113	7.1	9.1	.6	213	136	.3	198	23	(370)	.01	.13	Trace	(0)
q	Cubic inch	1 cu. in	[117] 17.2	37	68	4.3	5.5	.4	129	82	.2	120	14	(230)	.01	.08	Trace	(0)

[1] Measure and weight apply to food as it is described with inedible part or parts (refuse) included.

[11] For information on ingredients used, see ARS 62-13 (7), table 18, pp. 22-23.

[20] Value is for unsalted product. If salt is used, increase value by 236 mg. per 100 g. of vegetable—an estimated figure based on typical amount of salt (0.6%) in canned vegetables. See also Appendix C, section on Cooked Vegetables

[55] Oxalic acid present may combine with calcium and magnesium to form insoluble compounds. For further information, see Appendix D, section on Minerals and Oxalic Acid

[108] Formula used to calculate nutritive values shown in Agr. Handb. No. 8, rev. 1963.

[116] Value for green varieties based on 270 I.U. per 100 g. of raw celery (item 637) and 260 I.U. per 100 g. of cooked celery (item 638).

[117] Based on specific gravity.

[118] Term "cubed" used on retail package.

[119] Weight per cup and nutritive values also apply to 1 cup of diced cheese (pieces approx. ¼ size of these squares).

TABLE 1.—*Nutritive values for household measures and market units of foods*—Continued

[Item numbers correspond to those in table 1 of Handbook No. 8, revised 1963. Values in parentheses denote imputed values usually from another form of the food or from a similar food. Zeros in parentheses indicate that amount of a constituent, if present, is probably too small to be measured. Dashes (—) denote lack of reliable data for a constituent believed to be present in a measurable amount. Calculated values, as those based on a recipe, are not in parentheses]

Item No.	Food, approximate measures, units, and weight (edible part unless footnotes indicate otherwise)			Values for edible part of foods														
				Water	Food energy	Protein	Fat	Carbohydrate	Calcium	Phosphorus	Iron	Sodium	Potassium	Vitamin A value	Thiamin	Riboflavin	Niacin	Ascorbic acid
(A)	(B)			(C)	(D)	(E)	(F)	(G)	(H)	(I)	(J)	(K)	(L)	(M)	(N)	(O)	(P)	(Q)
			Grams	*Percent*	*Calories*	*Grams*	*Grams*	*Grams*	*Milligrams*	*Milligrams*	*Milligrams*	*Milligrams*	*Milligrams*	*International units*	*Milligrams*	*Milligrams*	*Milligrams*	*Milligrams*
	Cheeses, natural and processed; cheese foods; cheese spreads—Continued																	
	Natural cheeses—Continued																	
647	Cottage cheese (cottage cheese dry curd with creaming mixture; 4.2% milk fat), large or small curd:																	
	Prepackaged container:																	
a	Net wt., 32 oz. (2 lb.)	1 container	907	78.3	961	123.4	38.1	26.3	853	1,379	2.7	2,077	771	(1,540)	0.27	2.27	0.9	(0)
b	Net wt., 12 oz	1 container	340	78.3	360	46.2	14.3	9.9	320	517	1.0	779	289	(580)	.10	.85	.3	(0)
	Cup (cheese spooned into cup):																	
	Not packed:																	
c	Large curd	1 cup	225	78.3	239	30.6	9.5	6.5	212	342	.7	515	191	(380)	.07	.56	.2	(0)
d	Small curd	1 cup	210	78.3	223	28.6	8.8	6.1	197	319	.6	481	179	(360)	.06	.53	.2	(0)
e	Packed (large or small curd)	1 cup	245	78.3	260	33.3	10.3	7.1	230	372	.7	561	208	(420)	.07	.61	.2	(0)
f	Pound	1 lb	454	78.3	481	61.7	19.1	13.2	426	689	1.4	1,039	386	(770)	.14	1.13	.5	(0)
g	Ounce	1 oz	28	78.3	30	3.9	1.2	.8	27	43	.1	65	24	(50)	.01	.07	Trace	(0)
648	Cottage cheese dry curd (without creaming mixture; 0.3% milk fat):																	
a	Prepackaged container, net wt., 12 oz	1 container	340	79.0	292	57.8	1.0	9.2	306	595	1.4	986	245	(30)	.10	.95	(.3)	(0)
	Cup:																	
b	Not packed	1 cup	145	79.0	125	24.7	.4	3.9	131	254	.6	421	104	(10)	.04	.41	(.1)	(0)
c	Packed	1 cup	200	79.0	172	34.0	.6	5.4	180	350	.8	580	144	(20)	.06	.56	(.2)	(0)
d	Pound	1 lb	454	79.0	390	77.1	1.4	12.2	408	794	1.8	1,315	327	(50)	.14	1.27	(.5)	(0)
e	Ounce	1 oz	28	79.0	24	4.8	.1	.8	26	50	.1	82	20	(Trace)	.01	.08	(Trace)	(0)
649	Cream:																	
	Regular:																	
	Prepackaged rectangular piece:																	
a	Package, net wt., 8 oz.; approx. 4⅝ × 2¾ × 1¼ in.	1 pkg	227	51	849	18.2	85.6	4.8	141	216	.5	568	168	(3,500)	(.05)	.54	.2	(0)
b	Package, net wt., 3 oz.; approx. 2⅞ × 2 × ⅞ in.	1 pkg	85	51	318	6.8	32.0	1.8	53	81	.2	213	63	(1,310)	(.02)	.20	.1	(0)
c	Cup	1 cup	232	51	868	18.6	87.5	4.9	144	220	.5	580	172	(3,570)	(.05)	.56	.2	(0)
d	Tablespoon	1 tbsp	14	51	52	1.1	5.3	.3	9	13	Trace	35	10	(220)	(Trace)	.03	Trace	(0)
e	Cubic inch	1 cu. in	[137] 16.1	51	60	1.3	6.1	.3	10	15	Trace	40	12	(250)	(Trace)	.04	Trace	(0)
	Whipped:[130]																	
f	Prepackaged container, net wt., 4 oz. (approx. ¾ cup).	1 container	113	51	423	9.0	42.6	2.4	70	107	.2	283	84	(1,740)	(.02)	.27	.1	(0)
g	Cup	1 cup	155	51	580	12.4	58.4	3.3	96	147	.3	388	115	(2,390)	(.03)	.37	.2	(0)
h	Tablespoon	1 tbsp	10	51	37	.8	3.8	.2	6	10	Trace	25	7	(150)	(Trace)	.02	Trace	(0)
	Regular and whipped:																	
i	Pound	1 lb	454	51	1,696	36.3	171.0	9.5	281	431	.9	1,134	336	(6,990)	(.09)	1.09	.5	(0)
j	Ounce	1 oz	28	51	106	2.3	10.7	.6	18	27	.1	71	21	(440)	(.01)	.07	Trace	(0)
650	Limburger:																	
	Prepackaged piece:																	
	Package, approx. contents, and slice cut from piece:																	
a	Package, net wt., 7 oz.; rectangular piece, 3⅜ × 1⅞ × 1⅞ in.	1 pkg	198	45	683	42.0	55.4	4.4	1,168	778	1.2	—	—	(2,260)	.16	.99	.4	(0)
b	Slice, approx. 1⅞ × 1⅞ × ⅛ in.; 1⁄27 of piece (item 650a).	1 slice	7	45	24	1.5	2.0	.2	41	28	Trace	—	—	(80)	.01	.04	Trace	(0)
c	Pound	1 lb	454	45	1,565	96.2	127.0	10.0	2,676	1,783	2.7	—	—	(5,170)	.36	2.27	.9	(0)
d	Ounce	1 oz	28	45	98	6.0	7.9	.6	167	111	.2	—	—	(320)	.02	.14	.1	(0)
e	Cubic inch	1 cu. in	18.0	45	62	3.8	5.0	.4	106	71	.1	—	—	(210)	.01	.09	Trace	(0)
651	Parmesan:																	
	Prepackaged forms:																	
	Cut piece:																	
a	Package, net wt., 5 oz.; wedge, approx. 4¼ × 3¼ in., 1 in. high.	1 pkg	142	30	558	51.1	36.9	4.1	1,619	1,109	.6	1,042	212	(1,510)	.03	1.04	.3	(0)
b	Pound	1 lb	454	30	1,783	163.3	117.9	13.2	5,171	3,543	1.8	3,329	676	(4,810)	.09	3.31	.9	(0)
c	Ounce	1 oz	28	30	111	10.2	7.4	.8	323	221	.1	208	42	(300)	.01	.21	.1	(0)
	Shredded:[131]																	
	Cup:																	

(A)	(B)			(C)	(D)	(E)	(F)	(G)	(H)	(I)	(J)	(K)	(L)	(M)	(N)	(O)	(P)	(Q)
d	Not packed	1 cup	80	25	338	30.9	22.3	2.4	977	670	0.3	629	128	(910)	0.02	0.62	0.2	(0)
e	Packed	1 cup	110	25	464	42.5	30.7	3.3	1,343	921	.4	865	176	(1,250)	.02	.86	.2	(0)
f	Tablespoon	1 tbsp	5	25	21	1.9	1.4	.2	61	42	Trace	39	8	(60)	Trace	.04	Trace	(0)
g	Pound	1 lb	454	25	1,914	175.1	126.6	13.6	5,538	3,797	1.8	3,565	726	(5,170)	.09	3.54	.9	(0)
h	Ounce	1 oz	28	25	120	10.9	7.9	.9	346	237	.1	223	45	(320)	.01	.22	.1	(0)
	Grated: [121]																	
	Cup:																	
i	Not packed	1 cup	100	17	467	42.7	30.8	3.5	1,352	926	.5	870	177	(1,260)	.02	.87	.2	(0)
j	Packed	1 cup	140	17	654	59.8	43.1	4.9	1,893	1,296	.7	1,218	248	(1,760)	.03	1.22	.3	(0)
k	Tablespoon	1 tbsp	5	17	23	2.1	1.5	.2	68	46	Trace	44	9	(60)	Trace	.04	Trace	(0)
l	Pound	1 lb	454	17	2,118	193.7	139.7	15.9	6,133	4,200	2.3	3,946	803	(5,720)	.09	3.95	.9	(0)
m	Ounce	1 oz	28	17	132	12.1	8.7	1.0	383	263	.1	247	50	(360)	.01	.25	.1	(0)
652	Swiss (domestic):																	
	Prepackaged forms:																	
	Cut piece:																	
	Package, approx. contents, and slice cut from piece:																	
a	Package, net wt., 12 oz.; rectangular piece, approx. 6 × 2 × 2 in.	1 pkg	340	39	1,258	93.5	95.2	5.8	3,145	1,914	3.1	2,414	354	(3,880)	.03	(1.36)	(.3)	(0)
b	Slice, 2 × 2 × ¼ in.; 1/24 of piece (item 652a).	1 slice	14	39	52	3.9	3.9	.2	130	79	.1	99	15	(160)	Trace	(.06)	(Trace)	(0)
	Slice, rectangular, approx. 7½–7¾ × 4 × 1/16 in.; wt., 1¼ oz.: [122]																	
c	Package, net wt., 8 oz.; approx. 7 slices	1 pkg	227	39	840	62.4	63.6	3.9	2,100	1,278	2.0	1,612	236	(2,590)	.02	(.91)	(.2)	(0)
d	Slice	1 slice	35	39	130	9.6	9.8	.6	324	197	.3	249	36	(400)	Trace	(.14)	(Trace)	(0)
e	Pound	1 lb	454	39	1,678	124.7	127.0	7.7	4,196	2,554	4.1	3,221	472	(5,170)	.05	(1.81)	(.5)	(0)
f	Ounce	1 oz	28	39	105	7.8	7.9	.5	262	160	.3	201	29	(320)	Trace	(.11)	(Trace)	(0)
g	Cubic inch [123]	1 cu. in	15.0	39	56	4.1	4.2	.3	139	84	.1	107	16	(170)	Trace	(.06)	(Trace)	(0)
	Pasteurized processed cheese:																	
653	American:																	
	Prepackaged forms:																	
	Loaves (rectangular pieces):																	
	Package, approx. contents, and slice cut from loaf:																	
a	Package, net wt., 32 oz. (2 lb.); rectangular piece, approx. 8½ × 2¾ × 2¼ in.	1 pkg	907	40	3,356	210.4	272.1	17.2	6,322	[124] 6,993	8.2	[124] 10,304	726	(11,070)	.18	3.72	.2	(0)
b	Slice, approx. 2¾ × 2¼ × ¼ in.; 1/34 of loaf (item 653a).	1 slice	27	40	100	6.3	8.1	.5	188	[124] 208	.2	[124] 307	22	(330)	.01	.11	Trace	(0)
c	Package, net wt., 16 oz. (1 lb.); rectangular piece, approx. 6 × 2½ × 1¾ in.	1 pkg. or 1 lb.[125]	454	40	1,678	105.2	136.1	8.6	3,162	[124] 3,497	4.1	[124] 5,153	363	(5,530)	.09	1.86	.1	(0)
d	Slice, approx. 2½ × 1¾ × ¼ in.; 1/24 of loaf (item 653c).	1 slice	19	40	70	4.4	5.7	.4	132	[124] 146	.2	[124] 216	15	(230)	Trace	.08	Trace	(0)
e	Package, net wt., 8 oz. (rectangular piece, approx. 4¼ × 2⅛ × 1½ in.).	1 pkg	227	40	840	52.7	68.1	4.3	1,582	[124] 1,750	2.0	[124] 2,579	182	(2,770)	.05	.93	Trace	(0)
f	Slice, approx. 2⅛ × 1½ × ¼ in.; 1/17 of loaf (item 653e).	1 slice	13	40	48	3.0	3.9	.2	91	[124] 100	.1	[124] 148	10	(160)	Trace	.05	Trace	(0)
	Cup:																	
g	Packed into cup	1 cup	255	40	944	59.2	76.5	4.8	1,777	[124] 1,966	2.3	[124] 2,897	204	(3,110)	.05	1.05	Trace	(0)
h	Diced, not packed	1 cup	140	40	518	32.5	42.0	2.7	976	[124] 1,079	1.3	[124] 1,590	112	(1,710)	.03	.57	Trace	(0)
i	Shredded, not packed	1 cup	113	40	418	26.2	33.9	2.1	788	[124] 871	1.0	[124] 1,284	90	(1,380)	.02	.46	Trace	(0)
	Slices:																	
	Package and approx. contents:																	
j	Package, net wt., 48 oz. (3 lb.) (approx. 6¾ × 3½ × 3 in.; 24 slices marked for cutting into 48 sandwich-size slices (see item 653m) or 72 burger-size slices (see item 653o), or 32 slices marked for cutting into 64 sandwich-size slices (see item 653n) or 96 burger-size slices (see item 653p)).	1 pkg	1,361	40	5,036	315.8	408.3	25.9	9,486	[124] 10,493	12.2	[124] 15,461	1,089	(16,600)	.27	5.58	.3	(0)
k	Package, net wt., 8 oz. (approx. 3½ × 3¾ × 1 in.; 8 sandwich-size slices (see item 653m)).	1 pkg	227	40	840	52.7	68.1	4.3	1,582	[124] 1,750	2.0	[124] 2,579	182	(2,770)	.05	.93	Trace	(0)

[117] Based on specific gravity.

[120] Description and weights shown for whipped cream cheese apply to cream cheese that has been stirred or whipped until its volume has been increased 50%.

[121] Nutritive values shown for Parmesan cheese in Agr. Handb. No. 8, rev. 1963, do not apply to shredded and grated forms. For these forms, nutritive values shown in this publication are based on data for 100 g. of cheese shown in Appendix A, table 3, p. 264.

[122] Dimensions and weights of slices varied considerably within package as well as between packages of different brands.

[123] Weight per cubic inch will vary with size and number of eyes. Weight given applies to cheese with eyes of size commonly found in retail market. Weight per cubic inch of portions of cheese without eyes is 17.8 g.

[124] Values for phosphorus and sodium are based on use of 1.5% anhydrous disodium phosphate as emulsifying agent. If emulsifying agent does not contain either phosphorus or sodium, calculate content of these 2 nutrients from these amounts per 100 g.: Phosphorus 444 mg., sodium 650 mg.

[125] Use also for 1 lb. of other form or forms listed for this item.

TABLE 1.—*Nutritive values for household measures and market units of foods*—Continued

[Item numbers correspond to those in table 1 of Handbook No. 8, revised 1963. Values in parentheses denote imputed values usually from another form of the food or from a similar food. Zeros in parentheses indicate that amount of a constituent, if present, is probably too small to be measured. Dashes (—) denote lack of reliable data for a constituent believed to be present in a measurable amount. Calculated values, as those based on a recipe, are not in parentheses]

Item No.	Food, approximate measures, units, and weight (edible part unless footnotes indicate otherwise)			Water	Food energy	Protein	Fat	Carbohydrate	Calcium	Phosphorus	Iron	Sodium	Potassium	Vitamin A value	Thiamin	Riboflavin	Niacin	Ascorbic acid
				Values for edible part of foods														
(A)	(B)			(C)	(D)	(E)	(F)	(G)	(H)	(I)	(J)	(K)	(L)	(M)	(N)	(O)	(P)	(Q)
			Grams	*Percent*	*Calories*	*Grams*	*Grams*	*Grams*	*Milli-grams*	*Milli-grams*	*Milli-grams*	*Milli-grams*	*Milli-grams*	*Interna-tional units*	*Milli-grams*	*Milli-grams*	*Milli-grams*	*Milli-grams*
	Cheeses, natural and processed; cheese foods; cheese spreads—Continued																	
	Pasteurized processed cheese—Continued																	
	American—Continued																	
	Prepackaged forms—Continued																	
	Slices—Continued																	
	Package and approx. contents—Continued																	
l	Package, net wt., 6 oz. (approx. 3½ × 3⅜ × ¾ in.; 8 sandwich-size slices (see item 653n)).	1 pkg	170	40	629	39.4	51.0	3.2	1,185	[134] 1,311	1.5	[134] 1,931	136	(2,070)	0.03	0.70	Trace	(0)
	Slice, approx. dimensions and weight:																	
	Sandwich size:																	
m	Slice, approx. 3½ × 3⅜ × ⅛ in.; wt., 1 oz.; ⅙ of pkg. (item 653j) or ⅛ of pkg. (item 653k).	1 slice or 1 oz.[136]	28	40	105	6.6	8.5	.5	198	[134] 219	.3	[134] 322	23	(350)	.01	.12	Trace	(0)
n	Slice, approx. 3½ × 3⅜ × ³⁄₃₂ in.; wt., ¾ oz.; ¹⁄₁₆ of pkg. (item 653j) or ⅛ of pkg. (item 653l).	1 slice	21	40	78	4.9	6.3	.4	146	[134] 162	.2	[134] 239	17	(260)	Trace	.09	Trace	(0)
	Burger size:																	
o	Slice, approx. 3½ × 2¼ × ⅛ in.; wt., ⅔ oz.; ¹⁄₁₂ of pkg. (item 653j).	1 slice	19	40	70	4.4	5.7	.4	132	[134] 146	.2	[134] 216	15	(230)	Trace	.08	Trace	(0)
p	Slice, approx. 3½ × 2¼ × ³⁄₃₂ in.; wt., ½ oz.; ¹⁄₁₆ of pkg. (item 653j).	1 slice	14	40	52	3.2	4.2	.3	98	[134] 108	.1	[134] 159	11	(170)	Trace	.06	Trace	(0)
q	Cubic inch	1 cu. in	[117] 17.5	40	65	4.1	5.3	.3	122	[134] 135	.2	[134] 199	14	(210)	Trace	.07	Trace	(0)
654	Pimiento (American):																	
	Prepackaged sandwich-size slices:																	
	Size, approx. 3½ × 3⅜ × ⅛ in.; wt., 1 oz.:																	
a	Package, net wt., 8 oz.; 8 slices	1 pkg	227	40	842	52.2	68.6	4.1	—	—	—	—	—	—	—	—	—	—
b	Slice	1 slice or 1 oz.	28	40	105	6.5	8.6	.5	—	—	—	—	—	—	—	—	—	—
	Size, approx. 3½ × 3⅜ × ³⁄₃₂ in.; wt., ¾ oz.:																	
c	Package, net wt., 12 oz.; 16 slices	1 pkg	340	40	1,261	78.2	102.7	6.1	—	—	—	—	—	—	—	—	—	—
d	Slice	1 slice	21	40	78	4.8	6.8	.4	—	—	—	—	—	—	—	—	—	—
e	Pound	1 lb	454	40	1,683	104.8	137.0	8.2	—	—	—	—	—	—	—	—	—	—
f	Cubic inch	1 cu. in	17.5	40	65	4.0	5.3	.3	—	—	—	—	—	—	—	—	—	—
655	Swiss:																	
	Prepackaged sandwich-size slices:																	
	Size, approx. 3½ × 3⅜ × ⅛ in.; wt., 1 oz.:																	
a	Package, net wt., 8 oz.; 8 slices	1 pkg	227	40	806	59.9	61.1	3.6	2,013	[137] 1,968	(2.0)	[137] 2,649	227	(2,500)	(.02)	.91	0.2	(0)
b	Slice	1 slice or 1 oz.	28	40	101	7.5	7.6	.5	251	[137] 246	(.3)	[137] 331	28	(310)	(Trace)	.11	Trace	(0)
	Size, approx. 3½ × 3⅜ × ³⁄₃₂ in.; wt., ¾ oz.:																	
c	Package, net wt., 12 oz.; 16 slices	1 pkg	340	40	1,207	89.8	91.5	5.4	3,016	[137] 2,948	(3.1)	[137] 3,968	340	(3,740)	(.03)	1.36	.3	(0)
d	Slice	1 slice	21	40	75	5.5	5.6	.3	186	[137] 182	(.2)	[137] 245	21	(230)	(Trace)	.08	Trace	(0)
e	Pound	1 lb	454	40	1,610	119.8	122.0	7.3	4,023	[137] 3,933	(4.1)	[137] 5,294	454	(4,990)	(.05)	1.81	.5	(0)
f	Cubic inch	1 cu. in	[117] 17.9	40	64	4.7	4.8	.3	159	[137] 155	(.2)	[137] 209	18	(200)	(Trace)	.07	Trace	(0)
656	**Pasteurized process cheese food, American:**																	
	Prepackaged forms:																	
	Cut piece:																	
a	Package, net wt., 6 oz. (roll, approx. 4⅝ in. long, 1½-in. diam.).	1 pkg	170	43.2	549	33.7	40.8	12.1	969	[138] 1,282	(1.4)	[138] —	—	(1,670)	(.03)	.99	.3	(0)
b	Slice, approx. 1½-in. diam., ¼ in. thick; ¹⁄₁₈ of roll (item 656a).	1 slice	9	43.2	29	1.8	2.2	.6	51	[138] 68	(.1)	[138] —	—	(90)	(Trace)	.05	Trace	(0)
c	Tablespoon	1 tbsp	14	43.2	45	2.8	3.4	1.0	80	[138] 106	(.1)	[138] —	—	(140)	(Trace)	.08	Trace	(0)
	Slices, sandwich size:																	
	Size, approx. 3½ × 3⅜ × ⅛ in.; wt., 1 oz.:																	
d	Package, net wt., 8 oz.; 8 slices	1 pkg	227	43.2	733	44.9	54.5	16.1	1,294	[138] 1,712	(1.8)	[138] —	—	(2,220)	(.05)	1.32	.5	(0)
e	Slice	1 slice or 1 oz.	28	43.2	92	5.6	6.8	2.0	162	[138] 214	(.2)	[138] —	—	(280)	(.01)	.16	.1	(0)
	Size, approx. 3½ × 3⅜ × ³⁄₃₂ in.; wt., ¾ oz.:																	
f	Package, net wt., 12 oz.; 16 slices	1 pkg	340	43.2	1,098	67.3	81.6	24.1	1,938	[138] 2,564	(2.7)	[138] —	—	(3,330)	(.07)	1.97	.7	(0)
g	Slice	1 slice	21	43.2	68	4.2	5.0	1.5	120	[138] 158	(.2)	[138] —	—	(210)	(Trace)	.12	Trace	(0)
h	Pound	1 lb	454	43.2	1,465	89.8	108.9	32.2	2,586	[138] 3,420	(3.6)	[138] —	—	(4,450)	(.09)	2.63	.9	(0)
i	Cubic inch	1 cu. in	17.5	43.2	57	3.5	4.2	1.2	100	[138] 132	(.1)	[138] —	—	(170)	(Trace)	.10	Trace	(0)
657	**Pasteurized process cheese spread, American:**																	
	Prepackaged forms:																	

(A)	(B)			(C)	(D)	(E)	(F)	(G)	(H)	(I)	(J)	(K)	(L)	(M)	(N)	(O)	(P)	(Q)
	Loaves (rectangular pieces):																	
	Package, approx. contents, and slice cut from loaf:																	
a	Package, net wt., 32 oz. (2 lb.); rectangular piece, approx. 8½ × 2¾ × 2¼ in.	1 pkg	907	48.6	2,612	145.1	194.1	74.4	5,125	[129] 7,936	(5.4)	[129] 14,739	2,177	(7,890)	0.09	4.90	0.9	(0)
b	Slice, approx. 2¾ × 2¼ × ¼ in.; 1/34 of loaf (item 657a).	1 slice	27	48.6	78	4.3	5.8	2.2	153	[129] 236	(.2)	[129] 439	65	(230)	Trace	.15	Trace	(0)
c	Package, net wt., 16 oz. (1 lb.); rectangular piece, approx. 6 × 2½ × 1¾ in.	1 pkg. or 1 lb	454	48.6	1,306	72.6	97.1	37.2	2,563	[129] 3,969	(2.7)	[129] 7,371	1,089	(3,950)	.05	2.45	.5	(0)
d	Slice, approx. 2½ × 1¾ × ¼ in.; 1/24 of loaf (item 657c).	1 slice	19	48.6	55	3.0	4.1	1.6	107	[129] 166	(.1)	[129] 309	46	(170)	Trace	.10	Trace	(0)
e	Package, net wt., 8 oz.; rectangular piece, approx. 4¼ × 2⅛ × 1½ in.	1 pkg	227	48.6	654	36.3	48.6	18.6	1,283	[129] 1,986	(1.4)	[129] 3,689	545	(1,970)	.02	1.23	.2	(0)
f	Slice, approx. 2⅛ × 1½ × ¼ in.; 1/17 of loaf (item 657e).	1 slice	13	48.6	37	2.1	2.8	1.1	73	[129] 114	(.1)	[129] 211	31	(110)	Trace	.07	Trace	(0)
	Cup:																	
g	Packed into cup	1 cup	255	48.6	734	40.8	54.6	20.9	1,441	[129] 2,231	(1.5)	[129] 4,144	612	(2,220)	.03	1.38	.3	(0)
h	Diced, not packed	1 cup	140	48.6	403	22.4	30.0	11.5	791	[129] 1,225	(.8)	[129] 2,275	336	(1,220)	.01	.76	.1	(0)
i	Shredded, packed	1 cup	113	48.6	325	18.1	24.2	9.3	638	[129] 989	(.7)	[129] 1,836	271	(980)	.01	.61	.1	(0)
j	Tablespoon	1 tbsp	14	48.6	40	2.2	3.0	1.1	79	[129] 123	(.1)	[129] 228	34	(120)	Trace	.08	Trace	(0)
k	Cubic inch	1 cu. in	17.5	48.6	50	2.8	3.7	1.4	99	[129] 153	(.1)	[129] 284	42	(150)	Trace	.09	Trace	(0)
	Packed in glass jars and pressurized can:																	
l	Jar, net wt., 5 oz.[130] [131]	1 jar	142	48.6	409	22.7	30.4	11.6	802	[129] 1,243	(.9)	[129] 2,308	341	(1,240)	.01	.77	.1	(0)
m	Can (pressurized), net wt., 4¾ oz.[131]	1 can	135	48.6	389	21.6	28.9	11.1	763	[129] 1,181	(.8)	[129] 2,194	324	(1,170)	.01	.73	.1	(0)
n	Ounce	1 oz	28	48.6	82	4.5	6.1	2.3	160	[129] 248	(.2)	[129] 461	68	(250)	Trace	.15	Trace	(0)
659	Cheese souffle, from home recipe:[51]																	
a	Whole (yield from recipe[108]), 7⅜ × 7⅜[132] × 1⅜ in. (baked in 8-in. square pan) or 6½-in. diam.,[132] 2 in. high (baked in 7-in.-diam.[133] casserole).	1 souffle	440	65.0	959	43.6	75.2	27.3	884	858	4.4	1,602	532	3,520	.22	1.06	.9	Trace
b	Portion, 3 11/16 × 3 11/16[132] × 1⅜ in. (baked in 8-in. square pan) or 5⅛-in. arc,[133] 3¼ × 3¼ in.,[133] 2 in. high (baked in 7-in.-diam.[133] casserole); ¼ of souffle (item 659a).	1 portion	110	65.0	240	10.9	18.8	6.8	221	215	1.1	400	133	880	.06	.26	.2	Trace
c	Cup (collapsed souffle)[56]	1 cup	95	65.0	207	9.4	16.2	5.9	191	185	1.0	346	115	760	.05	.23	.2	Trace
d	Pound	1 lb	454	65.0	989	44.9	77.6	28.1	912	885	4.5	1,651	549	3,630	.23	1.09	.9	Trace
e	Ounce	1 oz	28	65.0	62	2.8	4.8	1.8	57	55	.3	103	34	230	.01	.07	.1	Trace
660	Cheese straws, 5 in. long, ⅜ in. wide, ⅜ in. high	10 pieces	60	21.7	272	6.7	17.9	20.7	155	124	.4	433	38	230	.01	.10	.2	0
661	Cherimoya, raw, 5-in. diam., 3⅞ in. high (refuse: skin and seeds, 42%).[1]	1 fruit	842	73.5	459	6.3	2.0	117.2	112	195	2.4	—	—	50	.49	.54	6.3	44
	Cherries:																	
	Raw:																	
662	Sour, red:																	
	Whole (refuse: pits and stems, 10%):[1]																	
a	Container, net contents, 1 qt.[71]	1 container	785	83.7	410	8.5	2.1	101.0	155	134	2.8	14	1,349	7,070	.35	.42	2.8	71
b	Cup	1 cup	114	83.7	60	1.2	.3	14.7	23	19	.4	2	196	1,030	.05	.06	.4	10
c	Pound	1 lb	454	83.7	237	4.9	1.2	58.4	90	78	1.6	8	780	4,080	.20	.24	1.6	41
	Without pits and stems:																	
d	Cup	1 cup	155	83.7	90	1.9	.5	22.2	34	29	.6	3	296	1,550	.08	.09	.6	16
e	Pound	1 lb	454	83.7	263	5.4	1.4	64.9	100	86	1.8	9	866	4,540	.23	.27	1.8	45
663	Sweet:																	
	Whole (refuse: pits and stems, 10%):[1]																	
a	Cup	1 cup	130	80.4	82	1.5	.4	20.4	26	22	.5	2	223	130	.06	.07	.5	12
b	10 cherries	10 cherries	75	80.4	47	.9	.2	11.7	15	13	.3	1	129	70	.03	.04	.3	7
c	Pound	1 lb	454	80.4	286	5.3	1.2	71.0	90	78	1.6	8	780	450	.20	.24	1.6	41
	Without pits and stems:																	
d	Cup	1 cup	145	80.4	102	1.9	.4	25.2	32	28	.6	3	277	160	.07	.09	.6	15
e	Pound	1 lb	454	80.4	318	5.9	1.4	78.9	100	86	1.8	9	866	500	.23	.27	1.8	45

[1] Measure and weight apply to food as it is described with inedible part or parts (refuse) included.

[50] For further information, see Appendix B, section on Home-Prepared Foods

[51] For information on ingredients used in preparation, see ARS 62–13 (7), table 22, p. 26.

[56] Oxalic acid present may combine with calcium and magnesium to form insoluble compounds. For further information, see Appendix D, section on Minerals and Oxalic Acid

[71] Represents container as customarily filled to volume greater than declared net contents. See also Appendix B, section on Berries

[108] Formula used to calculate nutritive values shown in Agr. Handb. No. 8, rev. 1963.

[117] Based on specific gravity.

[124] Values for phosphorus and sodium are based on use of 1.5% anhydrous disodium phosphate as emulsifying agent. If emulsifying agent does not contain either phosphorus or sodium, calculate content of these 2 nutrients from these amounts per 100 g.: Phosphorus 444 mg., sodium 650 mg.

[126] Use also for 1 oz. of other form or forms listed for this item.

[127] Values for phosphorus and sodium are based on use of 1.5% anhydrous disodium phosphate as emulsifying agent. If emulsifying agent does not contain either phosphorus or sodium, calculate content of these 2 nutrients from these amounts per 100 g.: Phosphorus 540 mg., sodium 681 mg.

[128] Values for phosphorus and sodium are based on use of 1.5% anhydrous disodium phosphate as emulsifying agent. If emulsifying agent does not contain either phosphorus or sodium, calculate content of these 2 nutrients from these amounts per 100 g.: Phosphorus 427 mg., sodium—.

[129] Values for phosphorus and sodium are based on use of 1.5% anhydrous disodium phosphate as emulsifying agent. If emulsifying agent does not contain either phosphorus or sodium, calculate content of these 2 nutrients from these amounts per 100 g.: Phosphorus 548 mg., sodium 1,139 mg.

[130] Available also in 1-lb. and 8-oz. jars. For values of these sizes, use items 657c and 657e.

[131] For 1 cup, use item 657g; for 1 tbsp., item 657j.

[132] Measured at top.

TABLE 1.—*Nutritive values for household measures and market units of foods*—Continued

[Item numbers correspond to those in table 1 of Handbook No. 8, revised 1963. Values in parentheses denote imputed values usually from another form of the food or from a similar food. Zeros in parentheses indicate that amount of a constituent, if present, is probably too small to be measured. Dashes (—) denote lack of reliable data for a constituent believed to be present in a measurable amount. Calculated values, as those based on a recipe, are not in parentheses]

Item No.	Food, approximate measures, units, and weight (edible part unless footnotes indicate otherwise)			Values for edible part of foods														
				Water	Food energy	Protein	Fat	Carbohydrate	Calcium	Phosphorus	Iron	Sodium	Potassium	Vitamin A value	Thiamin	Riboflavin	Niacin	Ascorbic acid
(A)	(B)			(C)	(D)	(E)	(F)	(G)	(H)	(I)	(J)	(K)	(L)	(M)	(N)	(O)	(P)	(Q)
			Grams	*Percent*	*Calories*	*Grams*	*Grams*	*Grams*	*Milligrams*	*Milligrams*	*Milligrams*	*Milligrams*	*Milligrams*	*International units*	*Milligrams*	*Milligrams*	*Milligrams*	*Milligrams*
	Cherries—Continued																	
664	Candied, whole:																	
a	Container, net wt., 4 oz. (approx. ¾ cup)	1 container	113	12.0	383	0.6	0.2	98.0	—	—	—	—	—	—	—	—	—	—
b	10 cherries	10 cherries	35	12.0	119	.2	.1	30.3	—	—	—	—	—	—	—	—	—	—
c	Ounce	1 oz	28	12.0	96	.1	.1	24.6	—	—	—	—	—	—	—	—	—	—
	Canned, solids and liquid:																	
665	Sour (tart), red, water pack, pitted style:																	
	Can and approx. contents:																	
a	Size, 303 × 406 [14] (No. 303); net wt., 16 oz. (1 lb.); approx. 1¾ cups of drained solids and 9½ tbsp. of drained liquid.	1 can or 1 lb	454	88.0	195	3.6	.9	48.5	68	59	1.4	9	590	3,080	0.14	0.09	0.9	23
b	Size, 603 × 700 [14] (No. 10); net wt., 103 oz. (6 lb. 7 oz.); approx. 11¼ cups of drained solids and 3¾ cups of drained liquid.	1 can	2,920	88.0	1,256	23.4	5.8	312.4	438	380	8.8	58	3,796	19,860	.88	.58	5.8	146
c	Cup	1 cup	244	88.0	105	2.0	.5	26.1	37	32	.7	5	317	1,660	.07	.05	.5	12
	Sweet:																	
669	Water pack, without artificial sweetener; light or dark cherries, unpitted style (refuse: pits, 8%): [1]																	
a	Cup	1 cup	270	86.6	119	2.2	.5	29.6	37	32	.7	2	323	150	.05	.05	.5	7
b	Pound	1 lb	454	86.6	200	3.8	.8	49.7	63	54	1.3	4	542	250	.08	.08	.8	13
671	Sirup pack, heavy:																	
	Unpitted style (refuse: pits, 8%): [1]																	
	Can and approx. contents:																	
a	Size, 211 × 304 [14] (8Z Tall, Buffet); net wt., 8¾ oz.; light cherries (approx. ¾ cup of drained solids and 5 tbsp. drained liquid).	1 can	248	78.0	185	2.1	.5	46.8	34	30	.7	2	288	140	.05	.05	.5	7
b	Size, 303 × 406 [14] (No. 303); net wt., 16 oz. (1 lb.); light or dark cherries (approx. 1⅛ cups of drained solids and 9 tbsp. of drained liquid).	1 can or 1 lb	454	78.0	338	3.8	.8	85.5	63	54	1.3	4	526	250	.08	.08	.8	13
c	Size, 603 × 700 [14] (No. 10); net wt., 108 oz. (6 lb. 12 oz.); light or dark cherries (approx. 9 cups of drained solids and 3⅜ cups of drained liquid).	1 can	3,062	78.0	2,282	25.4	5.6	577.5	423	366	8.5	28	3,549	1,690	.56	.56	5.6	85
d	Cup	1 cup	279	78.0	208	2.3	.5	52.6	39	33	.8	3	323	150	.05	.05	.5	8
	Pitted style:																	
	Can and approx. contents:																	
e	Size, 303 × 406 [14] (No. 303); net wt., 16 oz. (1 lb.); light or dark cherries (approx. 1⅛ cups of drained solids and 9⅝ tbsp. of drained liquid).	1 can or 1 lb	454	78.0	367	4.1	.9	93.0	68	59	1.4	5	572	270	.09	.09	.9	14
f	Cup	1 cup	257	78.0	208	2.3	.5	52.7	39	33	.8	3	324	150	05	.05	.5	8
	Frozen, not thawed:																	
	Sour, red:																	
673	Unsweetened	1 lb	454	84.9	249	4.5	1.8	60.8	59	100	3.2	9	853	4,540	.18	.32	1.4	23
674	Sweetened with nutritive sweetener	1 lb	454	70.6	508	4.5	1.8	126.1	54	68	2.3	9	590	2,180	.14	.27	1.4	27
	Chestnuts: [8]																	
677	Fresh:																	
	In shell, approx. 1½-in. diam.; wt., 9 g.; (refuse: shells, 19%): [1]																	
a	Cup	1 cup	120	52.5	189	2.8	1.5	40.9	26	86	1.7	6	441	—	.21	.21	.6	—
b	Pound (approx. 3¾ cups or 50 nuts; yields approx. 13 oz. or 2⅓ cups, shelled nuts).	1 lb	454	52.5	713	10.7	5.5	154.7	99	323	6.2	22	1,668	—	.81	.81	2.2	—
c	10 nuts	10 nuts	90	52.5	141	2.1	1.1	30.7	20	64	1.2	4	331	—	.16	.16	.4	—
	Shelled:																	
d	Cup	1 cup	160	52.5	310	4.6	2.4	67.4	43	141	2.7	10	726	—	.35	.35	1.0	—

(A)	(B)			(C)	(D)	(E)	(F)	(G)	(H)	(I)	(J)	(K)	(L)	(M)	(N)	(O)	(P)	(Q)
e	Pound (yield from approx. 1¼ lb., nuts in shell).	1 lb	454	52.5	880	13.2	6.8	191.0	122	399	7.7	27	2,059	—	1.00	1.00	2.7	—
680	**Chewing gum** (candy-coated pieces, approx. ¾ × ½ × ¼ in.):																	
a	Package, 12 pieces	1 pkg	20	3.5	63	—	—	19.0	—	—	—	—	—	—	(0)	(0)	(0)	(0)
b	Piece	1 piece	1.7	3.5	5	—	—	1.6	—	—	—	—	—	—	(0)	(0)	(0)	(0)
	Chicken, cooked:																	
	All classes, roasted:																	
682	Light meat without skin:																	
	Cup (not packed):																	
a	Chopped or diced	1 cup	140	63.8	232	44.2	4.8	0	15	371	1.8	90	575	80	.06	.14	16.2	—
b	Ground	1 cup	110	63.8	183	34.8	3.7	0	12	292	1.4	70	452	70	.04	.11	12.8	—
c	Pound (approx. 3¼ cups, chopped or diced; 4⅛ cups, ground; or 18 pieces).	1 lb	454	63.8	753	143.3	15.4	0	50	1,202	5.9	290	1,864	270	.18	.45	52.6	—
d	Piece, approx. 2½ in. long, 1⅞ in. wide, ¼ in. thick.	2 pieces	50	63.8	83	15.8	1.7	0	6	133	.7	32	206	30	.02	.05	5.8	—
684	Dark meat without skin:																	
	Cup (not packed):																	
a	Chopped or diced	1 cup	140	64.4	246	39.2	8.8	0	18	321	2.4	120	449	210	.10	.32	7.8	—
b	Ground	1 cup	110	64.4	194	30.8	6.9	0	14	252	1.9	95	353	170	.08	.25	6.2	—
c	Pound (approx. 3¼ cups, chopped or diced; 4⅛ cups, ground; or 45 pieces).	1 lb	454	64.4	798	127.0	28.6	0	59	1,039	7.7	390	1,456	680	.32	1.04	25.4	—
d	Piece, approx. 1⅞ in. long, 1 in. wide, ¼ in. thick.	4 pieces	40	64.4	70	11.2	2.5	0	5	92	.7	34	128	60	.03	.09	2.2	—
685	**Broilers**, ready-to-cook, broiled, flesh only:																	
a	Yield from 1 lb., ready-to-cook broilers	7.1 oz	201	71.0	273	47.8	7.6	0	18	404	3.4	133	551	180	.10	.38	17.7	—
b	Pound	1 lb	454	71.0	617	108.0	17.2	0	41	912	7.7	299	1,243	410	.23	.86	39.9	—
c	Half broiler (wt., raw, ready-to-cook, 1¾ lb.; wt., cooked, 10.4 oz.; refuse: bones and skin, 40%).[1]	½ broiler	294	71.0	240	42.0	6.7	0	16	355	3.0	116	483	160	.09	.34	15.5	—
	Fryers, ready-to-cook, fried:																	
687	Flesh, skin, giblets:																	
a	Yield from 1 lb., ready-to-cook fryers	8 oz	227	53.3	565	69.7	26.8	6.6	30	577	5.2	—	—	1,860	.16	1.29	20.7	—
b	Pound	1 lb	454	53.3	1,129	139.3	53.5	13.2	59	1,152	10.4	—	—	3,720	.32	2.59	41.3	—
c	Whole fryer (wt., raw, ready-to-cook, with giblets, 2½ lb.; wt., cooked, 1⅔ lb.; refuse: bones, 24%).[1]	1 fryer	750	53.3	1,419	175.0	67.3	16.5	74	1,448	13.1	—	—	4,670	.40	3.25	51.9	—
701	Light meat without skin:																	
a	Pound (approx. 18 pieces)	1 lb	454	59.5	894	145.6	27.7	5.0	54	1,270	5.9	308	1,969	230	.23	1.13	58.5	—
b	Piece, approx. 2½ in. long, 1⅞ in. wide, ¼ in. thick.	2 pieces	50	59.5	99	16.1	3.1	.6	6	140	.7	34	217	30	.03	.13	6.5	—
703	Dark meat without skin:																	
a	Pound (approx. 45 pieces)	1 lb	454	57.5	998	137.9	42.2	6.8	64	1,066	8.2	399	1,497	590	.32	2.04	30.8	—
b	Piece, approx. 1⅞ in. long, 1 in. wide, ¼ in. thick.	4 pieces	40	57.5	88	12.2	3.7	.6	6	94	.7	35	132	50	.03	.18	2.7	—
	Cut-up parts from 2½-lb. ready-to-cook fryer, fried:																	
705	Back (refuse: bones, 33%):[1]																	
a	Pound (approx. 7½ backs)	1 lb	454	40.5	1,055	91.2	64.4	20.7	46	796	8.2	—	—	1,190	.21	1.52	20.7	—
b	Piece	1 back	60	40.5	139	12.1	8.5	2.7	6	105	1.1	—	—	160	.03	.20	2.7	—
707	Breast without ribs (refuse: bones, 16%):[1]																	
a	Pound (approx. 4.8 breast halves)	1 lb	454	58.4	773	123.8	24.4	5.7	46	1,052	6.5	—	—	340	.19	.84	56.0	—
b	Piece	½ breast	[133] 94	58.4	160	25.7	5.1	1.2	9	218	1.3	—	—	70	.04	.17	11.6	—
709	Drumstick (refuse: bones, 33%):[1]																	
a	Pound (approx. 8 drumsticks)	1 lb	454	55.0	714	99.1	31.0	3.0	46	717	7.0	—	—	430	.21	1.22	21.6	—
b	Piece	1 drumstick	56	55.0	88	12.2	3.8	.4	6	89	.9	—	—	50	.03	.15	2.7	—
711	Neck (refuse: bones, 27%):[1]																	
a	Pound (approx. 7½ necks)	1 lb	454	50.2	957	88.4	57.6	14.9	40	775	8.9	—	—	1,160	.30	1.36	18.9	—
b	Piece	1 neck	60	50.2	127	11.7	7.6	2.0	5	102	1.2	—	—	150	.04	.18	2.5	—
713	Rib section (refuse: bones, 31%):[1]																	
a	Pound (approx. 22½ rib section halves)	1 lb	454	45.7	933	98.6	48.2	18.5	41	911	6.3	—	—	660	.16	1.47	29.4	—
b	Piece	½ rib section	20	45.7	41	4.3	2.1	.8	2	40	.3	—	—	30	.01	.06	1.3	—
715	Thigh (refuse: bones, 21%):[1]																	
a	Pound (approx. 7 thighs)	1 lb	454	55.8	849	104.3	40.8	9.0	47	846	8.2	—	—	720	.21	1.72	24.4	—
b	Piece	1 thigh	'65	55.8	122	15.0	5.9	1.3	7	121	1.2	—	—	100	.03	.25	3.5	—
717	Wing (refuse: bones, 39%):[1]																	
a	Pound (approx. 9 wings)	1 lb	454	52.6	742	80.2	41.0	7.5	28	653	5.5	—	—	690	.14	.72	18.8	—
b	Piece	1 wing	50	52.6	82	8.8	4.5	.8	3	72	.6	—	—	80	.02	.08	2.1	—

[1] Measure and weight apply to food as it is described with inedible part or parts (refuse) included.

[5] Most of phosphorus in nuts, legumes, and outer layers of cereal grains is present as phytic acid. See also Appendix D, section on Minerals and Oxalic Acid

[14] Dimensions of can: 1st dimension represents diameter; 2d dimension, height of can. 1st or left-hand digit in each dimension gives number of whole inches; next 2 digits give additional fraction of dimension expressed as 16th of an inch.

[133] Refers to ½ breast portion of 2½-lb. chicken.

TABLE 1.—*Nutritive values for household measures and market units of foods*—Continued

[Item numbers correspond to those in table 1 of Handbook No. 8, revised 1963. Values in parentheses denote imputed values usually from another form of the food or from a similar food. Zeros in parentheses indicate that amount of a constituent, if present, is probably too small to be measured. Dashes (—) denote lack of reliable data for a constituent believed to be present in a measurable amount. Calculated values, as those based on a recipe, are not in parentheses]

Item No.	Food, approximate measures, units, and weight (edible part unless footnotes indicate otherwise)			Values for edible part of foods														
				Water	Food energy	Protein	Fat	Carbohydrate	Calcium	Phosphorus	Iron	Sodium	Potassium	Vitamin A value	Thiamin	Riboflavin	Niacin	Ascorbic acid
(A)	(B)			(C)	(D)	(E)	(F)	(G)	(H)	(I)	(J)	(K)	(L)	(M)	(N)	(O)	(P)	(Q)
			Grams	Percent	Calories	Grams	Grams	Grams	Milligrams	Milligrams	Milligrams	Milligrams	Milligrams	International units	Milligrams	Milligrams	Milligrams	Milligrams
	Chicken, cooked—Continued																	
	Roasters, roasted:																	
721	**Flesh, skin, giblets:**																	
a	Yield from 1 lb., ready-to-cook roasters	8.4 oz	238	57.5	576	64.7	33.3	0	29	576	4.8	—	—	1,880	0.19	0.60	19.3	—
b	Pound	1 lb	454	57.5	1,098	123.4	63.5	0	54	1,098	9.1	—	—	3,580	.36	1.13	36.7	—
728	Light meat without skin:																	
	Cup (not packed):																	
a	Chopped or diced	1 cup	140	61.3	255	45.2	6.9	0	15	381	1.8	92	591	150	.11	.14	16.5	—
b	Ground	1 cup	110	61.3	200	35.5	5.4	0	12	299	1.4	73	464	120	.09	.11	13.0	—
c	Pound (approx. 3¼ cups, chopped or diced; 4⅛ cups, ground; or 18 pieces).	1 lb	454	61.3	826	146.5	22.2	0	50	1,234	5.9	299	1,914	500	.36	.45	53.5	—
d	Piece, approx. 2½ in. long, 1⅞ in. wide, ¼ in. thick.	2 pieces	50	61.3	91	16.2	2.5	0	6	136	.7	33	211	60	.04	.05	5.9	—
730	Dark meat without skin:																	
	Cup (not packed):																	
a	Chopped or diced	1 cup	140	62.7	258	41.0	9.1	0	20	329	2.5	123	462	220	.17	.27	7.4	—
b	Ground	1 cup	110	62.7	202	32.2	7.2	0	15	259	2.0	97	363	180	.13	.21	5.8	—
c	Pound (approx. 3¼ cups, chopped or diced; 4⅛ cups, ground; or 45 pieces).	1 lb	454	62.7	835	132.9	29.5	0	64	1,066	8.2	399	1,497	730	.54	.86	24.0	—
d	Piece, approx. 1⅞ in. long, 1 in. wide, ¼ in. thick.	4 pieces	40	62.7	74	11.7	2.6	0	6	94	.7	35	132	60	.05	.08	2.1	—
	Hens and cocks, stewed: [134]																	
734	Flesh, skin, giblets:																	
a	Yield from 1 lb., ready-to-cook hens or cocks	8 oz	227	50.8	708	59.5	50.4	0	25	309	4.1	—	—	2,250	.09	.52	19.5	—
b	Pound	1 lb	454	50.8	1,415	118.8	100.7	0	50	617	8.2	—	—	4,490	.18	1.04	39.0	—
738	Flesh only:																	
	Cup (not packed):																	
a	Chopped or diced	1 cup	140	60.4	291	42.0	12.5	0	17	209	2.1	77	381	350	.06	.21	13.4	—
b	Ground	1 cup	110	60.4	229	33.0	9.8	0	13	164	1.7	61	299	280	.04	.17	10.6	—
c	Pound (approx. 3¼ cups, chopped or diced; or 4⅛ cups, ground).	1 lb	454	60.4	943	136.1	40.4	0	54	676	6.8	249	1,234	1,130	.18	.68	43.5	—
741	Light meat without skin:																	
	Cup (not packed):																	
a	Chopped or diced	1 cup	140	62.1	252	45.1	6.6	0	15	224	1.8	67	428	180	.04	.13	15.4	—
b	Ground	1 cup	110	62.1	198	35.4	5.2	0	12	176	1.4	53	337	140	.03	.10	12.1	—
c	Pound (approx. 3¼ cups, chopped or diced; 4⅛ cups, ground; or 18 pieces).	1 lb	454	62.1	816	146.1	21.3	0	50	726	5.9	218	1,388	590	.14	.41	49.9	—
d	Piece, approx. 2½ in. long, 1⅞ in. wide, ¼ in. thick.	2 pieces	50	62.1	90	16.1	2.4	0	6	80	.7	24	153	70	.02	.05	5.5	—
743	Dark meat without skin:																	
	Cup (not packed):																	
a	Chopped or diced	1 cup	140	61.1	290	39.9	13.3	0	18	193	2.5	90	335	380	.08	.28	11.6	—
b	Ground	1 cup	110	61.1	228	31.4	10.5	0	14	152	2.0	70	263	300	.07	.22	9.1	—
c	Pound (approx. 3¼ cups, chopped or diced; 4⅛ cups, ground; or 45 pieces).	1 lb	454	61.1	939	129.3	43.1	0	59	626	8.2	290	1,084	1,220	.27	.91	37.6	—
d	Piece, approx. 1⅞ in. long, 1 in. wide, ¼ in. thick.	4 pieces	40	61.1	83	11.4	3.8	0	5	55	.7	26	96	110	.02	.08	3.3	—
747	**Chicken, canned,** meat only, boned:																	
a	Can, net wt., 5½ oz. (solid pack)	1 can	156	65.2	309	33.9	18.3	0	33	385	2.3	—	215	360	.06	.19	6.9	6
b	Cup	1 cup	205	65.2	406	44.5	24.0	0	43	506	3.1	—	283	470	.08	.25	9.0	8
c	Pound	1 lb	454	65.2	898	98.4	53.1	0	95	1,120	6.8	—	626	1,040	.18	.54	20.0	18
	Chicken, potted. See Sausage, cold cuts, and luncheon meats (item 2008).																	
748	**Chicken a la king,** cooked, from home recipe: [illegible]																	
a	Cup	1 cup	245	68.2	468	27.4	34.3	12.3	127	358	2.5	760	404	1,130	.10	.42	5.4	12
b	Pound	1 lb	454	68.2	866	50.8	63.5	22.7	236	662	4.5	1,406	748	2,090	.18	.77	10.0	23
749	**Chicken fricassee,** cooked, from home recipe: [illegible]																	
a	Cup	1 cup	240	71.3	386	36.7	22.3	7.7	14	271	2.2	370	336	170	.05	.17	5.8	—
b	Pound	1 lb	454	71.3	730	69.4	42.2	14.5	27	513	4.1	699	635	320	.09	.32	10.9	—
	Chicken potpie:																	
750	Home prepared, baked: [illegible]																	
a	Pie, whole (9-in. diam.)	1 pie	[illegible] 698	56.6	1,640	70.5	94.2	127.7	209	698	9.1	1,787	1,033	9,280	.77	.77	12.6	14

(A)		(B)			(C)	(D)	(E)	(F)	(G)	(H)	(I)	(J)	(K)	(L)	(M)	(N)	(O)	(P)	(Q)
	b	Piece, ⅙ of pie (item 750a)	1 piece	232	56.6	545	23.4	31.3	42.5	70	232	3.0	594	343	3,090	0.26	0.26	4.2	5
	c	Pound	1 lb	454	56.6	1,066	45.8	61.2	83.0	136	454	5.9	1,161	671	6,030	.50	.50	8.2	9
752		Chicken and noodles, cooked, from home recipe:[51]																	
	a	Cup	1 cup	240	71.1	367	22.3	18.5	25.7	26	247	2.2	600	149	430	.05	.17	4.3	Trace
	b	Pound	1 lb	454	71.1	694	42.2	34.9	48.5	50	467	4.1	1,134	281	820	.09	.32	8.2	Trace
753		Chickpeas or garbanzos, mature seeds, dry, raw:[6]																	
	a	Cup	1 cup	200	10.7	720	41.0	9.6	122.0	300	662	13.8	52	1,594	100	.62	.30	4.0	—
	b	Pound	1 lb	454	10.7	1,633	93.0	21.8	276.7	680	1,501	31.3	118	3,615	230	1.41	.68	9.1	—
754		Chicory, Witloof (also called French or Belgian endive), bleached head (forced), raw:[135]																	
	a	Head, 5–7 in. long (refuse: root base and core, 11%).[1]	1 head	60	95.1	8	.5	.1	1.7	10	11	.3	4	97	Trace	—	—	—	—
	b	Cup, chopped ½-in. pieces	1 cup	90	95.1	14	.9	.1	2.9	16	19	.5	6	164	Trace	—	—	—	—
	c	Pound	1 lb	454	95.1	68	4.5	.5	14.5	82	95	2.3	32	826	Trace	—	—	—	—
756		Chili con carne, with beans, canned:																	
		Can and approx. contents:																	
	a	Size, 300 × 407[14] (No. 300); net wt., 15–15½ oz.	1 can	430	72.4	572	32.3	26.2	52.5	138	542	7.3	2,283	1,002	260	.18	.30	5.6	—
	b	Size, 603 × 700[14] (No. 10); net wt., 108 oz. (6 lb. 12 oz.).	1 can	3,062	72.4	4,072	229.7	186.8	373.6	980	3,858	52.1	16,259	7,134	1,840	.92	2.14	39.8	—
	c	Cup	1 cup	255	72.4	339	19.1	15.6	31.1	82	321	4.3	1,354	594	150	.08	.18	3.3	—
	d	Pound	1 lb	454	72.4	603	34.0	27.7	55.3	145	572	7.7	2,409	1,057	270	.14	.32	5.9	—
		Chili powder. See Peppers (item 1544).																	
		Chili sauce. See Peppers (items 1539, 1542) and Tomatoes (item 2287).																	
758		Chives, raw (chopped, ⅛-in. pieces):																	
	a	Tablespoon	1 tbsp	3	91.3	1	.1	Trace	.2	2	1	.1	—	8	170	Trace	Trace	Trace	2
	b	Teaspoon	1 tsp	1	91.3	Trace	Trace	Trace	.1	1	Trace	Trace	—	3	60	Trace	Trace	Trace	1
		Chocolate:																	
759		Bitter or baking:[55 136]																	
	a	Cup, grated	1 cup	132	2.3	667	14.1	70.0	38.1	103	507	8.8	5	1,096	80	.07	.32	2.0	0
	b	Ounce	1 oz	28	2.3	143	3.0	15.0	8.2	22	109	1.9	1	235	20	.01	.07	.4	0
		Bittersweet. See Candy (item 584).																	
		Chocolate sirup (or topping):																	
760		Thin type (chocolate flavored):																	
	a	Pound (12-fl. oz. can)	1 lb. or 1 can	454	31.6	1,111	10.4	9.1	284.4	77	417	7.3	236	1,279	Trace	.09	.82	1.8	0
	b	Cup	1 cup	300	31.6	735	6.9	6.0	188.1	51	276	4.8	156	846	Trace	.06	.21	1.2	0
	c	Fluid ounce	1 fl. oz. or 2 tbsp.	37.5	31.6	92	.9	.8	23.5	6	35	.6	20	106	Trace	.01	.03	.2	0
761		Fudge type:																	
	a	Pound (12-fl. oz. can)	1 lb. or 1 can	454	25.4	1,497	23.1	62.1	244.9	576	721	5.9	404	1,288	680	.18	1.00	1.8	Trace
	b	Cup	1 cup	300	25.4	990	15.3	41.1	162.0	381	477	3.9	267	852	450	.12	.66	1.2	Trace
	c	Fluid ounce (2 tbsp.)	1 fl. oz. or 2 tbsp.	37.5	25.4	124	1.9	5.1	20.3	48	60	.5	33	107	60	.02	.08	.2	Trace
		Chop suey with meat (without noodles):																	
762		Cooked, from home recipe:[51]																	
	a	Cup	1 cup	250	75.4	300	26.0	17.0	12.8	60	248	4.8	1,053	425	600	.28	.38	5.0	33
	b	Pound	1 lb	454	75.4	544	47.2	30.8	23.1	109	449	8.6	1,910	771	1,090	.50	.68	9.1	59
		Chow mein, chicken (without noodles):																	
764		Cooked, from home recipe:[51]																	
	a	Cup	1 cup	250	78.0	255	31.0	10.0	10.0	58	293	2.5	718	473	280	.08	.23	4.3	10
	b	Pound	1 lb	454	78.0	463	56.2	18.1	18.1	104	531	4.5	1,302	857	500	.14	.41	7.7	18
765		Canned:																	
	a	Can, net wt., 16 oz. (1 lb.)	1 can or 1 lb	454	88.8	172	11.8	.5	32.2	82	154	2.3	1,315	758	270	.09	.18	1.8	23
	b	Cup	1 cup	250	88.8	95	6.5	.3	17.8	45	85	1.3	725	418	150	.05	.10	1.0	13
		Cider, pasteurized. See Applejuice (items 27d–27g).																	
767		Citron, candied	1 oz	28	18.0	89	.1	.1	22.7	24	7	.2	82	34	—	—	—	—	—
		Clams, raw, meat only:																	
769		Soft:																	
	a	Gallon (large, 300 or less; medium, 300–500; small, 500 or more).	1 gal. or 8 lb	3,630	80.8	2,977	508.2	69.0	47.2	—	6,643	123.4	1,307	8,531	—	—	—	—	—
	b	Quart (large, 75 or less; medium, 75–125; small, 125 or more).	1 qt. or 2 lb	907	80.8	744	127.0	17.2	11.8	—	1,660	30.8	327	2,131	—	—	—	—	—
	c	Pint (large, 38 or less; medium, 38–62; small, 62 or more).	1 pt. or 1 lb	454	80.8	372	63.5	8.6	5.9	—	830	15.4	163	1,066	—	—	—	—	—

[1] Measure and weight apply to food as it is described with inedible part or parts (refuse) included.

[6] Most of phosphorus in nuts, legumes, and outer layers of cereal grains is present as phytic acid. See also Appendix D, section on Minerals and Oxalic Acid

[14] Dimensions of can: 1st dimension represents diameter; 2d dimension, height of can. 1st or left-hand digit in each dimension gives number of whole inches; next 2 digits give additional fraction of dimension expressed as 16th of an inch.

[51] For information on ingredients used in preparation, see ARS 62–13 (7), table 22, p. 26.

[53] For information on ingredients used in crust and in filling and for proportion of crust to filling for pies, see ARS 62–13 (7), tables 23 and 24, p. 31, and table 25, p. 32.

[54] Yield of formula used to calculate nutritive values in Agr. Handb. No. 8, rev. 1963.

[55] Oxalic acid present may combine with calcium and magnesium to form insoluble compounds. For further information, see Appendix D, section on Minerals and Oxalic Acid

[134] Cock chickens are generally used in canner packs.

[135] Chicory and endive have often been confused with each other. For further description of these products, see Appendix C, section on Chicory and Endive

[136] Contains nonprotein nitrogen. This is omitted from protein value but included in total carbohydrate figure and caloric value. See also Appendix D, section on Protein and Nonprotein Nitrogen and section on Carbohydrate

TABLE 1.—*Nutritive values for household measures and market units of foods*—Continued

[Item numbers correspond to those in table 1 of Handbook No. 8, revised 1963. Values in parentheses denote imputed values usually from another form of the food or from a similar food. Zeros in parentheses indicate that amount of a constituent, if present, is probably too small to be measured. Dashes (—) denote lack of reliable data for a constituent believed to be present in a measurable amount. Calculated values, as those based on a recipe, are not in parentheses]

Item No. (A)	Food, approximate measures, units, and weight (edible part unless footnotes indicate otherwise) (B)			Water (C)	Food energy (D)	Protein (E)	Fat (F)	Carbohydrate (G)	Calcium (H)	Phosphorus (I)	Iron (J)	Sodium (K)	Potassium (L)	Vitamin A value (M)	Thiamin (N)	Riboflavin (O)	Niacin (P)	Ascorbic acid (Q)
			Grams	*Percent*	*Calories*	*Grams*	*Grams*	*Grams*	*Milligrams*	*Milligrams*	*Milligrams*	*Milligrams*	*Milligrams*	*International units*	*Milligrams*	*Milligrams*	*Milligrams*	*Milligrams*
	Clams, raw, meat only—Continued																	
771	Hard or round:																	
a	Gallon (chowders, 110 or less; mediums, 110–175; cherrystones,[137] 175–250; little necks,[137] 250 or more).	1 gal. or 8 lb	3,630	79.8	2,904	402.9	32.7	214.2	2,505	5,481	272.3	7,442	11,289	—	—	—	—	—
b	Quart (chowders, 28 or less; mediums, 28–44; cherrystones,[137] 44–62; little necks,[137] 62 or more).	1 qt. or 2 lb	907	79.8	726	100.7	8.2	53.5	626	1,370	68.0	1,859	2,821	—	—	—	—	—
c	Pint (chowders, 14 or less; mediums, 14–22; cherrystones,[137] 22–31; little necks,[137] 31 or more).	1 pt. or 1 lb	454	79.8	363	50.3	4.1	26.8	313	685	34.0	930	1,411	—	—	—	—	—
d	Clams (4 cherrystones or 5 little necks) [137]	4 or 5 clams	70	79.8	56	7.8	.6	4.1	48	106	5.3	144	218	—	—	—	—	—
773	Hard, soft, unspecified:																	
a	Gallon	1 gal. or 8 lb	3,630	81.7	2,759	457.4	58.1	72.6	2,505	5,881	221.4	4,356	6,570	3,630	3.63	6.53	47.2	363
b	Quart	1 qt. or 2 lb	907	81.7	689	114.3	14.5	18.1	626	1,469	55.3	1,088	1,642	910	.91	1.63	11.8	91
c	Pint	1 pt. or 1 lb	454	81.7	345	57.2	7.3	9.1	313	735	27.7	544	821	450	.45	.82	5.9	45
	Clams, canned (unspecified as to kind):																	
774	Solids and liquid:																	
	Can and approx. contents:																	
a	Size, 211 × 300[14] (8Z Short), chopped; 307 × 202,[14] minced; 201.25 × 401.25,[14] whole; net wt., 7½–8 oz.	1 can	220	86.3	114	17.4	1.5	6.2	121	301	9.0	—	308	—	.02	.24	2.2	—
b	Pound	1 lb	454	86.3	236	35.8	3.2	12.7	249	621	18.6	—	635	—	.05	.50	4.5	—
775	Drained solids:																	
	Can and approx. drained contents:																	
a	Size, 211 × 300[14] (8Z Short), chopped; 307 × 202,[14] minced; 201.25 × 401.25,[14] whole; wt., 3.9–4.2 oz.	1 can	114	77.0	112	18.0	2.9	2.2	—	—	—	—	—	—	—	—	—	—
b	Cup (chopped or minced)	1 cup	160	77.0	157	25.3	4.0	3.0	—	—	—	—	—	—	—	—	—	—
c	Pound	1 lb	454	77.0	445	71.7	11.3	8.6	—	—	—	—	—	—	—	—	—	—
776	Liquor, bouillon, or nectar:																	
	Container and approx. contents:																	
a	Bottle, net contents, 8 fl. oz.; yield, approx. 1 cup.	1 bottle or 1 cup.	240	93.6	46	5.5	.2	5.0	—	—	—	—	—	—	—	—	—	—
b	Can, size 211 × 414[14] (12Z, No. 211 Cylinder); net contents, 12 fl. oz.; yield, approx. 1½ cups.	1 can	360	93.6	68	8.3	.4	7.6	—	—	—	—	—	—	—	—	—	—
c	Fluid ounce	1 fl. oz	30	93.6	6	.7	Trace	.6	—	—	—	—	—	—	—	—	—	—
777	**Clam fritters** (2-in. diam., 1¾ in. thick) [138]	1 fritter	40	40.3	124	4.6	6.0	12.4	30	78	1.4	[43] —	59	—	.01	.05	.4	—
	Cocoa and chocolate-flavored beverage powders: [139 140]																	
778	Cocoa powder with nonfat dry milk [141]	1 oz. or approx. 4 heaping tsp.	28	1.9	102	5.3	.8	20.1	167	155	.5	149	227	10	.04	.21	.2	1
779	Cocoa powder without milk	1 oz. or approx. 4 heaping tsp.	28	1.3	98	1.1	.6	25.3	9	48	.6	76	142	—	.01	.03	.1	0
	Cocoa, dry powder: [136]																	
	Medium fat:																	
	High medium fat:																	
783	Plain:																	
a	Cup	1 cup	86	4.1	228	14.9	16.3	44.3	106	558	9.2	5	1,309	20	.09	.40	2.1	0
b	Tablespoon	1 tbsp	5.4	4.1	14	.9	1.0	2.8	7	35	.6	Trace	82	Trace	.01	.02	.1	0
c	Ounce (approx. 5¼ tbsp.)	1 oz	28	4.1	75	4.9	5.4	14.6	35	184	3.0	2	431	5	.03	.13	.7	0
784	Processed with alkali:																	
a	Cup	1 cup	86	4.1	224	14.9	16.3	41.7	106	558	9.2	617	560	20	.09	.40	2.1	0
b	Tablespoon	1 tbsp	5.4	4.1	14	.9	1.0	2.6	7	35	.6	39	35	Trace	.01	.02	.1	0
c	Ounce (approx. 5¼ tbsp.)	1 oz	28	4.1	74	4.9	5.4	13.7	35	184	3.0	203	185	5	.03	.13	.7	0
	Low medium fat:																	
785	Plain:																	
a	Cup	1 cup	86	5.2	189	16.5	10.9	46.3	131	590	9.2	5	1,309	20	.09	.40	2.1	0
b	Tablespoon	1 tbsp	5.4	5.2	12	1.0	.7	2.9	8	37	.6	Trace	82	Trace	.01	.02	.1	0

(A)		(B)	[illegible]	[illegible]	(C)	(D)	(E)	(F)	(G)	(H)	(I)	(J)	(K)	(L)	(M)	(N)	(O)	(P)	(Q)
	c	Ounce (approx. 5¼ tbsp.)	1 oz	28	5.2	62	5.4	3.6	15.3	43	194	3.0	2	431	5	0.03	0.13	0.7	0
786		Processed with alkali:																	
	a	Cup	1 cup	86	5.2	185	16.5	10.9	43.2	131	590	9.2	617	560	20	.09	.40	2.1	0
	b	Tablespoon	1 tbsp	5.4	5.2	12	1.0	.7	2.7	8	37	.6	39	35	Trace	.01	.02	.1	0
	c	Ounce (approx. 5¼ tbsp.)	1 oz	28	5.2	61	5.4	3.6	14.2	43	194	3.0	203	185	5	.03	.13	.7	0
788		**Coconut cream** (liquid expressed from grated coconut meat):																	
	a	Cup	1 cup	240	54.1	802	10.6	77.3	19.9	36	302	4.3	10	778	0	.05	.02	1.2	2
	b	Tablespoon	1 tbsp	15	54.1	50	.7	4.8	1.2	2	19	.3	1	49	0	Trace	Trace	.1	Trace
		Coconut meat: [5]																	
789		Fresh:																	
	a	In shell (refuse: shell, brown skin, water, 48%),[1] approx. 4⅝-in. diam., 4⅞ in. high; wt., 1⅔ lb.; yield of shredded or grated coconut, approx. 5 cups, not packed (item 789c) or 3 cups, packed (item 789d).	1 coconut	763	50.9	1,373	13.9	140.1	37.3	52	377	6.7	91	1,016	0	.20	.08	2.0	12
		Meat only:																	
	b	Piece, approx. 2 × 2 × ½ in	1 piece	45	50.9	156	1.6	15.9	4.2	6	43	.8	10	115	0	.02	.01	.2	1
		Shredded or grated, spooned into cup:																	
	c	Not packed	1 cup	80	50.9	277	2.8	28.2	7.5	10	76	1.4	18	205	0	.04	.02	.4	2
	d	Packed	1 cup	130	50.9	450	4.6	45.9	12.2	17	124	2.2	30	333	0	.07	.03	.7	4
	e	Pound	1 lb	454	50.9	1,569	15.9	160.1	42.6	59	431	7.7	104	1,161	0	.23	.09	2.3	14
790		Dried, unsweetened (desiccated)	1 lb	454	3.5	3,003	32.7	294.4	104.3	118	848	15.0	—	2,667	0	.27	.18	2.7	0
792		**Coconut milk** (liquid expressed from mixture of grated coconut meat and coconut water).	1 cup	240	65.7	605	7.7	59.8	12.5	38	240	3.8	—	—	0	.07	Trace	1.9	5
793		**Coconut water** (liquid from coconuts)	1 cup	240	94.2	53	.7	.5	11.3	48	31	.7	60	353	0	Trace	Trace	.2	5
		Cod:																	
795		Cooked (broiled), with butter or margarine:																	
	a	Steak, 5½ in. long (with ends doubled back), 4 in. wide, 1¼ in. thick[40] (dimensions of uncooked steak); (refuse: bones, 12%).[1]	1 steak	235	64.6	352	58.9	11.0	0	64	567	2.1	[43] 227	842	370	.17	.23	6.2	[illegible]
	b	Fillet, 5 in. long, 2½ in. wide, ⅞ in. thick[40] (dimensions of uncooked fillet).	1 fillet	65	64.6	111	18.5	3.4	0	20	178	.7	[43] 72	265	120	.05	.07	2.0	—
	c	Pound	1 lb	454	64.6	771	129.3	24.0	0	141	1,243	4.5	[43] 499	1,846	820	.36	.50	13.6	—
	d	Ounce	1 oz	28	64.6	48	8.1	1.5	0	9	78	.3	[43] 31	115	50	.02	.03	.9	—
796		Canned, drained solids:																	
	a	Drained contents from can, size 211 × 400[14] (No. 1 Picnic), of net wt., 11 oz.; drained wt., 8½ oz. (4 pieces, 3½ in. long, 2 in. wide, ⅝ in. thick[40]).	1 can	240	78.6	204	46.1	.7	0	—	—	—	—	—	—	—	.19	—	—
	b	Cup (flaked)	1 cup	140	78.6	119	26.9	.4	0	—	—	—	—	—	—	—	.11	—	—
	c	Pound	1 lb	454	78.6	386	87.1	1.4	0	—	—	—	—	—	—	—	.36	—	—
797		Dehydrated, lightly salted:																	
	a	Cup (shredded)	1 cup	42	12.3	158	34.4	1.2	0	—	374	1.5	3,402	67	0	.03	.19	4.6	—
	b	Ounce	1 oz	28	12.3	106	23.2	.8	0	—	253	1.0	2,296	45	0	.02	.13	3.1	—
798		Dried, salted:																	
	a	Piece, approx. 5½ in. long, 1½ in. wide, ½ in. thick.[40]	1 piece	80	52.4	104	23.2	.6	0	180	—	—	—	—	—	—	—	—	—
	b	Pound	1 lb	454	52.4	590	131.5	3.2	0	1,021	—	—	—	—	—	—	—	—	—
	c	Ounce	1 oz	28	52.4	37	8.2	.2	0	64	—	—	—	—	—	—	—	—	—
		Codfish cakes. See Fishcakes (items 1010–1011).																	
		Coffee, instant, water-soluble solids:[136 142]																	
799		Dry powder:																	
		Regular and freeze-dried:																	
	a	Pound (yields approx. 227 cups of beverage (item 800b)).	1 lb	454	2.6	585	Trace	Trace	(158.8)	812	1,737	25.4	327	14,769	0	0	.95	138.8	0
	b	Ounce (yields approx. 14 cups of beverage (item 800b)).	1 oz	28	2.6	37	Trace	Trace	(9.9)	51	109	1.6	20	923	0	0	.06	8.7	0
		Cup:																	
	c	Regular (yields approx. 27 cups of beverage (item 800b)).	1 cup	55	2.6	71	Trace	Trace	(19.3)	98	211	3.1	40	1,791	0	0	.12	16.8	0
	d	Freeze-dried (yields approx. 35 cups of beverage (item 800b)).	1 cup	70	2.6	90	Trace	Trace	(24.5)	125	268	3.9	50	2,279	0	0	.15	21.4	0

[1] Measure and weight apply to food as it is described with inedible part or parts (refuse) included.

[5] Most of phosphorus in nuts, legumes, and outer layers of cereal grains is present as phytic acid. See also Appendix D, section on Minerals and Oxalic Acid

[14] Dimensions of can: 1st dimension represents diameter; 2d dimension, height of can. 1st or left-hand digit in each dimension gives number of whole inches; next 2 digits give additional fraction of dimension expressed as 16th of an inch.

[40] Width at widest part; thickness at thickest part.

[43] Value for product without added salt.

[136] Contains nonprotein nitrogen. This is omitted from protein value but included in total carbohydrate figure and caloric value. See also Appendix D, section on Protein and Nonprotein Nitrogen and section on Carbohydrate

[137] Commonly eaten raw.

[138] Prepared with flour, baking powder, butter or margarine, and egg.

[139] Values apply to products without added vitamins or minerals. For products with added vitamins and minerals, values vary with brand. This information is given on label.

[140] Heaping teaspoon refers to ordinary teaspoon rather than to standard measuring teaspoon.

[141] Some products currently on market may contain approximately ½ protein and calcium values shown here.

[142] Contains caffeine. For dry powder (item 799), amount present in 1 cup may range from 1,650 to 2,000 mg. (regular), 2,100–2,800 mg. (freeze-dried); in 1 tbsp. may range from 75 to 100 mg. (regular), 105–140 mg. (freeze-dried); in 1 tsp. may range from 24 to 32 mg. (regular), 27–36 mg. (freeze-dried). For beverage (item 800), amount in 1 cup may range from 63 to 81 mg.; in 1 fl. oz., 10–14 mg.

TABLE 1.—*Nutritive values for household measures and market units of foods*—Continued

[Item numbers correspond to those in table 1 of Handbook No. 8, revised 1963. Values in parentheses denote imputed values usually from another form of the food or from a similar food. Zeros in parentheses indicate that amount of a constituent, if present, is probably too small to be measured. Dashes (—) denote lack of reliable data for a constituent believed to be present in a measurable amount. Calculated values, as those based on a recipe, are not in parentheses]

Item No.	Food, approximate measures, units, and weight (edible part unless footnotes indicate otherwise)			Values for edible part of foods														
				Water	Food energy	Protein	Fat	Carbohydrate	Calcium	Phosphorus	Iron	Sodium	Potassium	Vitamin A value	Thiamin	Riboflavin	Niacin	Ascorbic acid
(A)	(B)			(C)	(D)	(E)	(F)	(G)	(H)	(I)	(J)	(K)	(L)	(M)	(N)	(O)	(P)	(Q)
			Grams	*Percent*	*Calories*	*Grams*	*Grams*	*Grams*	*Milligrams*	*Milligrams*	*Milligrams*	*Milligrams*	*Milligrams*	*International units*	*Milligrams*	*Milligrams*	*Milligrams*	*Milligrams*
	Coffee, instant, water-soluble solids [136, 142]—Continued																	
	Dry powder—Continued																	
	Regular and freeze-dried—Continued																	
	Tablespoon:																	
e	Regular (yields approx. 1¼ cups of beverage (item 800b)).	1 tbsp	2.5	2.6	3	Trace	Trace	(0.9)	4	10	0.1	2	81	0	0	0.01	0.8	0
f	Freeze-dried (yields approx. 1¾ cups of beverage (item 800b)).	1 tbsp	3.5	2.6	5	Trace	Trace	(1.2)	6	13	.2	3	114	0	0	.01	1.1	0
	Teaspoon:																	
g	Regular	1 tsp	.8	2.6	1	Trace	Trace	(.3)	1	3	Trace	1	26	0	0	Trace	.2	0
h	Freeze-dried	1 tsp	.9	2.6	1	Trace	Trace	(.3)	2	3	.1	1	29	0	0	Trace	.3	0
800	Beverage (prepared with 2 g. of dry powder to 6 fl. oz. of water):																	
a	Gallon (approx. 21⅓ cups of beverage (item 800b)).	1 gal	3,840	98.1	38	Trace	Trace	Trace	77	154	3.8	38	1,382	0	0	.08	11.5	0
b	Cup (6 fl. oz.)	1 cup	180	98.1	2	Trace	Trace	Trace	4	7	.2	2	65	0	0	Trace	.5	0
c	Fluid ounce	1 fl. oz	30.0	98.1	Trace	Trace	Trace	Trace	1	1	Trace	Trace	11	0	0	Trace	.1	0
	Cola or coke. See Beverages (item 404).																	
	Coleslaw, [143, 144] made with [61]—																	
801	French dressing (homemade)	1 cup	120	80.6	155	1.3	14.8	6.1	50	30	.5	157	236	130	.05	.05	.4	35
802	French dressing (commercial)	1 cup	120	82.6	114	1.4	8.8	9.1	50	31	.5	322	246	130	.05	.05	.4	35
803	Mayonnaise	1 cup	120	79.0	173	1.6	16.8	5.8	53	35	.5	144	239	190	.06	.06	.4	35
804	Salad dressing (mayonnaise type)	1 cup	120	82.9	119	1.4	9.5	8.5	52	34	.5	149	230	180	.06	.06	.4	35
	Collards: [55]																	
	Raw:																	
805	Leaves without stems:																	
a	Prepackaged container, net wt., 20 oz. (1 lb. 4 oz.).	1 container	567	85.3	255	27.2	4.5	42.5	1,418	465	8.5	—	2,552	52,730	.91	1.76	9.6	862
b	Pound	1 lb	454	85.3	204	21.8	3.6	34.0	1,134	372	6.8	—	2,041	42,180	.73	1.41	7.7	689
806	Leaves including stems	1 lb	454	86.9	181	16.3	3.2	32.7	921	286	4.5	195	1,819	29,480	.91	(1.41)	(7.7)	417
	Cooked (boiled), drained:																	
	Leaves without stems, cooked in—																	
807	Small amount of water:																	
a	Cup	1 cup	190	89.6	63	6.8	1.3	9.7	357	99	1.5	[20] —	498	14,820	.21	.38	2.3	144
b	Pound	1 lb	454	89.6	150	16.3	3.2	23.1	853	236	3.6	[20] —	1,188	35,380	.50	.91	5.4	345
808	Large amount of water:																	
a	Cup	1 cup	190	90.2	59	6.5	1.3	9.1	336	91	1.5	[20] —	462	14,820	.13	.27	2.1	97
b	Pound	1 lb	454	90.2	141	15.4	3.2	21.8	803	218	3.6	[20] —	1,102	35,380	.32	.64	5.0	231
	Leaves including stems, cooked in—																	
809	Small amount of water:																	
a	Cup	1 cup	145	90.8	42	3.9	.9	7.1	220	57	.9	[20] 36	339	7,830	.20	.29	1.7	67
b	Pound	1 lb	454	90.8	132	12.2	2.7	22.2	689	177	2.7	[20] 113	1,061	24,490	.64	.91	5.4	209
	Frozen, chopped:																	
810	Not thawed:																	
a	Container, net wt., 10 oz	1 container	284	89.7	91	8.8	1.1	16.5	542	151	3.1	51	736	19,310	.20	.45	2.0	193
b	Pound	1 lb	454	89.7	145	14.1	1.8	26.3	866	240	5.0	82	1,175	30,840	.32	.73	3.2	308
811	Cooked (boiled), drained:																	
a	Yield from 10 oz., frozen collards	1½ cups	250	90.2	75	7.3	1.0	14.0	440	128	2.5	[20] 40	590	17,000	.15	.35	1.5	83
b	Yield from 1 lb., frozen collards	2⅓ cups	400	90.2	120	11.6	1.6	22.4	704	204	4.0	[20] 64	944	27,200	.24	.56	2.4	132
c	Cup	1 cup	170	90.2	51	4.9	.7	9.5	299	87	1.7	[20] 27	401	11,560	.10	.24	1.0	56
d	Pound (yield from approx. 1⅛ lb., frozen collards).	1 lb	454	90.2	136	13.2	1.8	25.4	798	231	4.5	[20] 73	1,070	30,840	.27	.64	2.7	150
	Cookies: [145]																	
812	Assorted (sandwich type, shortbread, sugar wafers, butter flavored, chocolate chip, coconut bars, etc.):																	
a	Package, net wt., 11 oz. (approx. 36 cookies)	1 pkg	312	2.6	1,498	15.9	63.0	221.5	115	509	2.2	1,139	209	250	.09	.16	1.2	Trace
b	Pound (approx. 52 cookies)	1 lb	454	2.6	2,177	23.1	91.6	322.1	168	739	3.2	1,656	304	360	.14	.23	1.8	Trace
	Brownies with nuts: [5, 55]																	
813	Baked from home recipe, [146] enriched flour; rectangular piece, 3 × 1 × ⅞ in., or square piece, 1¾ × 1¾ × ⅞ in.	1 brownie	20	9.8	97	1.3	6.3	10.2	8	30	.4	50	38	40	.04	.02	.1	Trace
814	Frozen, with chocolate icing, commercial:																	

(A)	(B)			(C)	(D)	(E)	(F)	(G)	(H)	(I)	(J)	(K)	(L)	(M)	(N)	(O)	(P)	(Q)
a	Container, net wt., 13 oz. (rectangular piece, 7½ × 5¼ × ⅞ in.).[147]	1 container	368	12.5	1,542	18.0	75.8	223.4	147	460	[148] 5.5	736	659	810	[148] 0.83	[148] 0.29	[148] 1.1	1
b	Brownie, 1½ × 1¾ × ⅞ in.; 1/15 of container (item 814a).	1 brownie	24.5	12.5	103	1.2	5.0	14.9	10	31	[149] .4	49	44	50	[149] .02	[149] .02	[149] .1	Trace
815	Butter, thin, rich (butter-flavored cookies), 2- to 2⅛-in. diam., ¼ in. thick:																	
a	Package, net wt., 8 oz. (approx. 45 cookies)	1 pkg	227	4.5	1,037	13.8	38.4	160.9	286	213	1.1	949	136	1,480	.07	.14	.9	0
b	Cooky	10 cookies	50	4.5	229	3.1	8.5	35.5	63	47	.3	209	30	330	.02	.03	.2	0
c	Pound (approx. 90 cookies)	1 lb	454	4.5	2,073	27.7	76.7	321.6	572	426	2.3	1,896	272	2,950	.14	.27	1.8	0
	Chocolate chip:[55]																	
817	Baked from home recipe,[146] enriched flour; cooky, 2⅓-in. diam.	4 cookies	40	3.0	206	2.2	12.0	24.0	14	40	.8	139	47	40	.04	.04	.4	Trace
818	Commercial type:																	
	Cooky, 2¼-in. diam., ⅜ in. thick:																	
a	Package, net wt., 14½ oz. (approx. 39 cookies).	1 pkg	411	2.7	1,936	22.2	86.3	286.5	160	469	7.4	1,648	551	490	.16	.29	1.6	Trace
b	Cooky	10 cookies	105	2.7	495	5.7	22.1	73.2	41	120	1.9	421	141	130	.04	.07	.4	Trace
	Cooky, 1¾-in. diam., ½ in. thick:																	
c	Package, net wt., 7¾ oz. (approx. 30 cookies).	1 pkg	220	2.7	1,036	11.9	46.2	153.3	86	251	4.0	882	295	260	.09	.15	.9	Trace
d	Cooky	10 cookies	73	2.7	344	3.9	15.3	50.9	28	83	1.3	293	98	90	.03	.05	.3	Trace
	Cooky, 1¾-in. diam., ⅜ in. thick:																	
e	Package, net wt., 15 oz. (approx. 80 cookies)	1 pkg	425	2.7	2,002	23.0	89.3	296.2	166	485	7.7	1,704	570	510	.17	.30	1.7	Trace
f	Cooky	10 cookies	53	2.7	250	2.9	11.1	36.9	21	60	1.0	213	71	60	.02	.04	.2	Trace
g	Pound (approx. 48 cookies (item 818b), 62 cookies (item 818d), or 86 cookies (item 818f)).	1 lb	454	2.7	2,136	24.5	95.3	316.2	177	517	8.2	1,819	608	540	.18	.32	1.8	Trace
819	Coconut bars, 2⅝ × 1⅝ × ⅜ in. or 3 × 1¼ × ¼ in.:																	
a	Cooky	10 cookies	90	3.8	445	5.6	22.1	57.5	65	108	1.3	133	205	140	.04	.05	.4	0
b	Pound (approx. 50 cookies)	1 lb	454	3.8	2,241	28.1	111.1	289.9	327	544	6.4	671	1,034	730	.18	.27	1.8	0
820	Fig bars (square, 1⅝ × 1⅝ × ⅜ in., or rectangular, 1½ × 1¾ × ½ in.):																	
a	Package, net wt., 16 oz. (1 lb.); approx. 32 cookies.	1 pkg. or 1 lb	454	13.6	1,624	17.7	25.4	342.0	354	272	4.5	1,143	898	500	.18	.32	1.4	Trace
b	Cooky	4 cookies	56	13.6	200	2.2	3.1	42.2	44	34	.6	141	111	60	.02	.04	.2	Trace
821	Gingersnaps, 2-in. diam., ¼ in. thick:																	
a	Package, net wt., 16 oz. (1 lb.); approx. 65 cookies.	1 pkg. or 1 lb	454	3.1	1,905	24.9	40.4	362.0	331	213	10.4	2,590	2,096	320	.18	.27	1.8	Trace
b	Cooky	10 cookies	70	3.1	294	3.9	6.2	55.9	51	33	1.6	400	323	50	.03	.04	.3	Trace
822	Ladyfingers, 3¼ × 1⅜ × 1⅛ in. (dimensions before split lengthwise):																	
a	Package, net wt., 3 oz. (approx. 8 ladyfingers split lengthwise).	1 pkg	85	19.2	306	6.6	6.6	54.8	35	139	1.3	60	60	550	.05	.12	.2	0
b	Ladyfinger	4 ladyfingers	44	19.2	158	3.4	3.4	28.4	18	72	.7	31	31	290	.03	.06	.1	0
c	Pound (approx. 41 ladyfingers)	1 lb	454	19.2	1,633	35.4	35.4	292.6	186	744	6.8	322	322	2,950	.27	.64	.9	0
823	Macaroons, 2¾-in. diam., ¼ in. thick:																	
a	Package, net wt., 11 oz. (approx. 16 cookies)	1 pkg	312	4.4	1,482	16.5	72.4	206.2	84	259	2.8	106	1,445	0	.12	.47	1.9	0
b	Cooky	2 cookies	38	4.4	181	2.0	8.8	25.1	10	32	.3	13	176	0	.02	.06	.2	0
c	Pound (approx. 24 cookies)	1 lb	454	4.4	2,155	24.0	105.2	299.8	122	376	4.1	154	2,100	0	.18	.68	2.7	0
824	Marshmallow (plain cooky with marshmallow topping, coconut- or chocolate-coated):																	
	Cooky, coconut-coated, 2⅛-in. diam., 1⅛ in. thick:																	
a	Package, net wt., 7½ oz. (approx. 12 cookies)	1 pkg	213	9.8	871	8.5	28.1	154.0	45	121	1.1	445	194	550	.04	.13	.4	Trace
b	Cooky	4 cookies	72	9.8	294	2.9	9.5	52.1	15	41	.4	150	66	190	.01	.04	.1	Trace
	Cooky, chocolate-coated, 1¾-in. diam., ¾ in. thick:																	
c	Package, net wt., 8 oz. (approx. 18 cookies)	1 pkg	227	9.8	928	9.1	30.0	164.1	48	129	1.1	474	207	590	.05	.14	.5	Trace
d	Cooky	4 cookies	52	9.8	213	2.1	6.9	37.6	11	30	.3	109	47	140	.01	.03	.1	Trace

[5] Most of phosphorus in nuts, legumes, and outer layers of cereal grains is present as phytic acid. See also Appendix D, section on Minerals and Oxalic Acid

[30] Value is for unsalted product. If salt is used, increase value by 236 mg. per 100 g. of vegetable—an estimated figure based on typical amount of salt (0.6%) in canned vegetables. See also Appendix C, section on Cooked Vegetables

[51] For information on ingredients used in preparation, see ARS 62–13 (7), table 22, p. 26.

[55] Oxalic acid present may combine with calcium and magnesium to form insoluble compounds. For further information, see Appendix D, section on Minerals and Oxalic Acid

[136] Contains nonprotein nitrogen. This is omitted from protein value but included in total carbohydrate figure and caloric value. See also Appendix D, section on Protein and Nonprotein Nitrogen and section on Carbohydrate

[142] Contains caffeine. For dry powder (item 799), amount present in 1 cup may range from 1,650 to 2,000 mg. (regular), 2,100–2,800 mg. (freeze-dried); in 1 tbsp. may range from 75 to 100 mg. (regular), 105–140 mg. (freeze-dried); in 1 tsp. may range from 24 to 32 mg. (regular), 27–36 mg. (freeze-dried). For beverage (item 800), amount in 1 cup may range from 63 to 81 mg.; in 1 fl. oz., 10–14 mg.

[143] Values are for product immediately after preparation. Values for energy and fat are reduced if dressing drains from slaw and is not served.

[144] Weights per cup based on coleslaw made with finely shredded or chopped cabbage.

[145] Products are commercial unless otherwise specified.

[146] For information on ingredients used, see ARS 62–13 (7), table 12, p. 17.

[147] Length and width at middle of piece.

[148] Based on product made with unenriched flour. With enriched flour, approx. values are iron 5.9 mg., thiamin 0.44 mg., riboflavin 0.37 mg., niacin 1.8 mg.

[149] Based on product made with unenriched flour. With enriched flour, approx. values are iron 0.4 mg., thiamin 0.03 mg., riboflavin 0.02 mg., niacin 0.1 mg.

TABLE 1.—*Nutritive values for household measures and market units of foods*—Continued

[Item numbers correspond to those in table 1 of Handbook No. 8, revised 1963. Values in parentheses denote imputed values usually from another form of the food or from a similar food. Zeros in parentheses indicate that amount of a constituent, if present, is probably too small to be measured. Dashes (—) denote lack of reliable data for a constituent believed to be present in a measurable amount. Calculated values, as those based on a recipe, are not in parentheses]

Item No.	Food, approximate measures, units, and weight (edible part unless footnotes indicate otherwise)			Water	Food energy	Protein	Fat	Carbohydrate	Calcium	Phosphorus	Iron	Sodium	Potassium	Vitamin A value	Thiamin	Riboflavin	Niacin	Ascorbic acid
(A)	(B)			(C)	(D)	(E)	(F)	(G)	(H)	(I)	(J)	(K)	(L)	(M)	(N)	(O)	(P)	(Q)
			Grams	*Percent*	*Calories*	*Grams*	*Grams*	*Grams*	*Milligrams*	*Milligrams*	*Milligrams*	*Milligrams*	*Milligrams*	*International units*	*Milligrams*	*Milligrams*	*Milligrams*	*Milligrams*
	Cookies [145]—Continued																	
	Marshmallow (plain cooky with marshmallow topping, coconut- or chocolate-coated)—Continued																	
e	Pound (approx. 25 cookies (item 824b) or 35 cookies (item 824d)).	1 lb	454	9.8	1,855	18.1	59.9	328.0	95	259	2.3	948	413	1,180	0.09	0.27	0.9	1
825	Molasses:																	
a	Cooky, 3⅝-in. diam., ¾ in. thick	1 cooky	32.5	4.0	137	2.1	3.4	24.7	17	27	.7	125	45	30	.01	.02	.2	0
b	Pound (approx. 14 cookies)	1 lb	454	4.0	1,914	29.0	48.1	344.7	231	376	9.5	1,751	626	360	.18	.27	3.2	0
826	Oatmeal with raisins, 2⅝-in. diam., ¼ in. thick:																	
a	Package, net wt., 14 oz. (approx. 30 cookies)	1 pkg	397	2.8	1,790	24.6	61.1	291.8	83	405	11.5	643	1,469	200	.44	.32	2.0	1
b	Cooky	4 cookies	52	2.8	235	3.2	8.0	38.2	11	53	1.5	84	192	30	.06	.04	.3	Trace
c	Pound (approx. 35 cookies)	1 lb	454	2.8	2,046	28.1	69.9	333.4	95	463	13.2	735	1,678	230	.50	.36	2.3	1
827	Peanut (sandwich-type cookies or sugar wafers, with peanut filling): [5, 88]																	
	Sandwich type:																	
a	Package, net wt., 10 oz. (approx. 23 cookies (item 827b)).	1 pkg	284	2.3	1,343	28.4	54.2	190.3	119	329	2.6	491	497	570	.20	.23	8.0	Trace
b	Cooky, 1¾-in. diam., ½ in. thick; 37 per pound.	4 cookies	49	2.3	232	4.9	9.4	32.8	21	57	.4	85	86	100	.03	.04	1.4	Trace
	Sugar wafer type:																	
c	Package, net wt., 6¾ oz. (3 rectangular pieces, 8¾ × 2¾ × ⅜ in.; each marked for cutting into 10 cookies).	1 pkg	191	2.3	903	19.1	36.5	128.0	80	222	1.7	330	334	380	.13	.15	5.3	Trace
d	Package, net wt., 9 oz. (4 rectangular pieces, 8¾ × 2¾ × ⅜ in.; each marked for cutting into 10 cookies).	1 pkg	255	2.3	1,206	25.5	48.7	170.9	107	296	2.3	441	446	510	.18	.20	7.1	Trace
e	Cooky, 1¾ × 1⅜ × ⅜ in. (1/30 of pkg. (item 827c) or 1/40 of pkg. (item 827d)); 65 cookies per pound.	10 cookies	70	2.3	331	7.0	13.4	46.9	29	81	.6	121	123	140	.05	.06	2.0	Trace
f	Sandwich type or sugar wafer type	1 lb	454	2.3	2,146	45.4	86.6	303.9	191	526	4.1	785	794	910	.32	.36	12.7	Trace
828	Raisin (biscuit type):																	
a	Package, net wt., 7½ oz. (3 rectangular pieces, 10⅛ × 2¼ × ¼ in.; each marked for cutting into 4 or 5 cookies).	1 pkg	213	8.2	807	9.4	11.3	172.1	151	334	4.5	111	579	450	.09	.17	1.3	1
b	Cooky, 2¼ × 2½ × ¼ in.; 1/12 of pkg. (item 828a).	4 cookies	71	8.2	269	3.1	3.8	57.4	50	111	1.5	37	193	150	.03	.06	.4	Trace
c	Cooky, 2¼ × 2 × ¼ in.; 1/15 of pkg. (item 828a).	4 cookies	57	8.2	216	2.5	3.0	46.1	40	89	1.2	30	155	120	.02	.05	.3	Trace
d	Pound (approx. 25½ cookies (item 828b) or 32 cookies (item 828c)).	1 lb	454	8.2	1,719	20.0	24.0	366.5	322	712	9.5	236	1,234	950	.18	.36	2.7	1
829	Sandwich type (chocolate [88] or vanilla):																	
a	Package, net wt., 16 oz. (1 lb.); approx. 31 cookies (item 829b) or 45 cookies (item 829c).	1 pkg. or 1 lb.	454	2.2	2,245	21.8	102.1	314.3	118	1,093	3.2	2,191	172	0	.18	.18	2.3	0
	Cooky:																	
b	Oval, cross section, 3⅛ × 1¼ in., ⅜ in. thick	4 cookies	60	2.2	297	2.9	13.5	41.6	16	145	.4	290	23	0	.02	.02	.3	0
c	Round, 1¾-in. diam., ⅜ in. thick	4 cookies	40	2.2	198	1.9	9.0	27.7	10	96	.3	193	15	0	.02	.02	.2	0
830	Shortbread, 1⅝ × 1⅝ × ¼ in.:																	
a	Package, net wt., 10¼ oz. (approx. 40 cookies)	1 pkg	291	3.0	1,449	21.0	67.2	189.4	204	454	1.5	175	192	230	.12	.15	1.5	0
b	Cooky	10 cookies	75	3.0	374	5.4	17.3	48.8	53	117	.4	45	50	60	.03	.04	.4	0
c	Pound (approx. 60 cookies)	1 lb	454	3.0	2,259	32.7	104.8	295.3	318	708	2.3	272	299	360	.18	.23	2.3	0
831	Sugar, soft, thick, with enriched flour, home recipe; [148] cooky, 2¼-in. diam., ¼ in. thick.	10 cookies	80	7.9	355	4.8	13.4	54.4	62	82	1.1	254	61	90	.13	.13	1.0	Trace
832	Sugar wafers:																	
	Cooky, 3½ × 1 × ½ in.:																	
a	Package, net wt., 13¼ oz. (approx. 40 cookies)	1 pkg	376	1.4	1,824	18.4	72.9	276.0	135	301	1.1	711	226	530	.04	.15	1.9	0
b	Cooky	10 cookies	95	1.4	461	4.7	18.4	69.7	34	76	.3	180	57	130	.01	.04	.5	0
	Cooky, 2½ × ¾ × ¼ in.:																	
c	Package, net wt., 8½ oz. (approx. 69 cookies)	1 pkg	241	1.4	1,169	11.8	46.8	176.9	87	193	.7	455	145	340	.02	.10	1.2	0
d	Cooky	10 cookies	35	1.4	170	1.7	6.8	25.7	13	28	.1	66	21	50	Trace	.01	.2	0
e	Cooky, 3½ × 1½ × ¼ in. [150]	10 cookies	70	1.4	340	3.4	13.6	51.4	25	56	.2	132	42	100	.01	.03	.4	0
f	Cooky, 1¾ × 1½ × ¾ in. [150]	10 cookies	90	1.4	437	4.4	17.5	66.1	32	72	.3	170	54	130	.01	.04	.5	0

(A)	(B)		(C)	(D)	(E)	(F)	(G)	(H)	(I)	(J)	(K)	(L)	(M)	(N)	(O)	(P)	(Q)
	cookies (item 832d)).																
833	Vanilla wafers:																
	Regular:																
	Whole:																
a	Package, net wt., 12 oz. (approx. 85 cookies (item 833b) or 113 cookies (item 833c)).	1 pkg	340	2.8	1,571	18.4	54.7	253.0	139	214	1.4	857	245	440	0.07	0.24	1.0	0
b	Cooky, 1¾-in. diam., ¼ in. thick; 113 per pound.	10 cookies	40	2.8	185	2.2	6.4	29.8	16	25	.2	101	29	50	.01	.03	.1	0
c	Cooky, 1⅝-in. diam., ¼ in. thick; 151 per pound.	10 cookies	30	2.8	139	1.6	4.8	22.3	12	19	.1	76	22	40	.01	.02	.1	0
d	Crumbled	1 cup	80	2.8	370	4.3	12.9	59.5	33	50	.3	202	58	100	.02	.06	.2	0
	Brown edge, 2¾-in. diam., ¼ in. thick; 78 per pound:																
e	Package, net wt., 10 oz. (approx. 49 cookies)	1 pkg	284	2.8	1,312	15.3	45.7	211.3	116	179	1.1	716	204	370	.06	.20	.9	0
f	Cooky	10 cookies	58	2.8	268	3.1	9.3	43.2	24	37	.2	146	42	80	.01	.04	.2	0
	Biscuit type, rectangular piece, 2¼ × 1½ × ¼ in.; 96 per pound:																
g	Package, net wt., 11 oz. (approx. 66 cookies)	1 pkg	312	2.8	1,441	16.8	50.2	232.1	128	197	1.2	786	225	410	.06	.22	.9	0
h	Cooky	10 cookies	47	2.8	217	2.5	7.6	35.0	19	30	.2	118	34	60	.01	.03	.1	0
i	Regular, brown edge, biscuit type	1 lb	454	2.8	2,096	24.5	73.0	337.5	186	286	1.8	1,143	327	590	.09	.32	1.4	0
	Cookies, prepared and baked from mixes:[151]																
837	Brownies, with enriched flour, made with incomplete mix, egg, water, nuts; rectangular piece, 3 × 1 × ⅞ in., or square piece, 1¾ × 1¾ × ⅞ in.[5 55]	1 brownie	20	10.7	86	1.0	4.0	12.6	9	27	.4	33	34	20	.03	.02	.1	Trace
839	Plain, with unenriched flour, made with egg, water; cooky, 1⅝-in. diam., ⅜ in. thick.	10 cookies	56	4.5	276	2.7	13.6	36.4	49	91	.3	194	24	70	.01	.03	.2	0
	Cooking oil. See Oils (item 1401).																
	Cooky dough, plain, chilled in roll:																
841	Unbaked; container, net wt., 18 oz. (1 lb. 2 oz.); roll, 10½ in. long, 1¾-in. diam.	1 roll	510	13.6	2,290	17.9	115.3	299.9	168	337	1.5	2,530	224	360	.10	.15	1.0	0
842	Baked; cooky, 2½-in. diam., ¼ in. thick; 1/40 of roll (item 841).	4 cookies	48	4.5	238	1.9	12.0	31.2	17	35	.1	263	23	30	.01	.01	.1	0
	Corn, sweet:[5 152]																
844	Raw, white and yellow, husked (refuse: cob, 45%).[1]	1 lb	454	72.7	240	8.7	2.5	55.1	7	277	1.7	Trace	699	[153] 1,000	.37	.30	4.2	30
	Cooked (boiled), drained, white and yellow:																
845	Kernels, cut off cob before cooking:																
a	Cup	1 cup	165	76.5	137	5.3	1.7	31.0	5	147	1.0	[20] Trace	272	[153] 660	.18	.17	2.1	12
b	Pound	1 lb	454	76.5	376	14.5	4.5	85.3	14	404	2.7	[20] Trace	748	[153] 1,810	.50	.45	5.9	32
846	Kernels, cooked on cob (refuse: cob, 45%):[1]																
a	Ear, 5 in. long, 1¾-in. diam	1 ear	140	74.1	70	2.5	.8	16.2	2	69	.5	[20] Trace	151	[153] 310	.09	.08	1.1	7
b	Pound	1 lb	454	74.1	227	8.2	2.5	52.4	7	222	1.5	[20] Trace	489	[153] 1,000	.30	.25	3.5	22
	Canned:																
	Regular pack:																
	Cream style, white and yellow:																
847	Solids and liquid:																
	Can and approx. contents:																
a	Size, 211 × 304[14] (8Z Tall, Buffet); net wt., 8¾ oz.	1 can	248	76.3	203	5.2	1.5	49.6	7	139	1.5	[21] 585	(241)	[153] 820	.07	.12	2.5	12
b	Size, 303 × 406[14] (No. 303); net wt., 17 oz. (1 lb. 1 oz.).	1 can	482	76.3	395	10.1	2.9	96.4	14	270	2.9	[21] 1,138	(468)	[153] 1,590	.14	.24	4.8	24
c	Size, 603 × 700[14] (No. 10); net wt., 106 oz. (6 lb. 10 oz.).	1 can	3,005	76.3	2,464	63.1	18.0	601.0	90	1,683	18.0	[21] 7,092	(2,915)	[153] 9,920	.90	1.50	30.1	150
d	Cup	1 cup	256	76.3	210	5.4	1.5	51.2	8	143	1.5	[21] 604	(248)	[153] 840	.08	.13	2.6	13
e	Pound	1 lb	454	76.3	372	9.5	2.7	90.7	14	254	2.7	[21] 1,070	(440)	[153] 1,500	.14	.23	4.5	23
	Whole kernel:																
	Vacuum pack, yellow:																
848	Solids and liquid:																
	Can and approx. contents:																
a	Size, 211 × 304[14] (8Z Tall, Buffet); net wt., 7 oz.	1 can	198	75.5	164	5.0	1.0	40.6	6	145	1.0	[21] 467	(192)	690	(.06)	(.12)	(2.2)	10

[1] Measure and weight apply to food as it is described with inedible part or parts (refuse) included.

[5] Most of phosphorus in nuts, legumes, and outer layers of cereal grains is present as phytic acid. See also Appendix D, section on Minerals and Oxalic Acid

[14] Dimensions of can: 1st dimension represents diameter; 2d dimension, height of can. 1st or left-hand digit in each dimension gives number of whole inches; next 2 digits give additional fraction of dimension expressed as 16th of an inch.

[20] Value is for unsalted product. If salt is used, increase value by 236 mg. per 100 g. of vegetable—an estimated figure based on typical amount of salt (0.6%) in canned vegetables. See also Appendix C, section on Cooked Vegetables

[21] Estimated value based on addition of salt in amount of 0.6% of finished product.

[55] Oxalic acid present may combine with calcium and magnesium to form insoluble compounds. For further information, see Appendix D, section on Minerals and Oxalic Acid

[145] Products are commercial unless otherwise specified.

[146] For information on ingredients used, see ARS 62–13 (7), table 12, p. 17.

[150] Size sometimes found in boxes of assorted cookies.

[151] For information on ingredients used, see ARS 62–13 (7), table 13, p. 18.

[152] Proximate composition and energy value vary with maturity and variety. Values shown here are based on averages derived from data available on maturity for varieties of commercial importance. For further information, see Appendix C, section on Corn, Sweet

[153] Based on yellow varieties; white varieties contain only trace of cryptoxanthin and carotenes, the pigments in corn that have biological activity.

TABLE 1.—*Nutritive values for household measures and market units of foods*—Continued

[Item numbers correspond to those in table 1 of Handbook No. 8, revised 1963. Values in parentheses denote imputed values usually from another form of the food or from a similar food. Zeros in parentheses indicate that amount of a constituent, if present, is probably too small to be measured. Dashes (—) denote lack of reliable data for a constituent believed to be present in a measurable amount. Calculated values, as those based on a recipe, are not in parentheses]

Item No. (A)	Food, approximate measures, units, and weight (edible part unless footnotes indicate otherwise) (B)		Weight	Water (C)	Food energy (D)	Protein (E)	Fat (F)	Carbohydrate (G)	Calcium (H)	Phosphorus (I)	Iron (J)	Sodium (K)	Potassium (L)	Vitamin A value (M)	Thiamin (N)	Riboflavin (O)	Niacin (P)	Ascorbic acid (Q)
			Grams	Percent	Calories	Grams	Grams	Grams	Milligrams	Milligrams	Milligrams	Milligrams	Milligrams	International units	Milligrams	Milligrams	Milligrams	Milligrams
	Corn, sweet [5, 152]—Continued																	
	Canned—Continued																	
	Regular pack—Continued																	
	Whole kernel—Continued																	
	Vacuum pack, yellow—Continued																	
	Solids and liquid—Continued																	
	Can and approx. contents—Continued																	
b	Size, 307 × 306 [14] (12Z Vacuum, No. 2 Vacuum); net wt., 12 oz.	1 can	340	75.5	282	8.5	1.7	69.7	10	248	1.7	[21] 802	(330)	1,190	(0.10)	(0.20)	(3.7)	17
c	Size, 603 × 600 [14] (No. 10 Vacuum); net wt., 75 oz. (4 lb. 11 oz.).	1 can	2,126	75.5	1,765	53.2	10.6	435.8	64	1,552	10.6	[21] 5,017	(2,062)	7,440	(.64)	(1.28)	(23.4)	106
d	Cup	1 cup	210	75.5	174	5.3	1.1	43.1	6	153	1.1	[21] 496	(204)	740	(.06)	(.13)	(2.3)	11
e	Pound	1 lb	454	75.5	376	11.3	2.3	93.0	14	331	2.3	[21] 1,070	(440)	1,590	(.14)	(.27)	(5.0)	23
	Wet pack, white and yellow:																	
849	Solids and liquid:																	
	Can and approx. contents:																	
a	Size, 211 × 304 [14] (8Z Tall, Buffet); net wt., 8¾ oz.	1 can	248	80.9	164	4.7	1.5	38.9	10	119	1.0	[21] 585	241	[153] 670	.07	.12	2.2	12
b	Size, 303 × 406 [14] (No. 303); net wt., 17 oz. (1 lb. 1 oz.).	1 can	482	80.9	318	9.2	2.9	75.7	19	231	1.9	[21] 1,138	468	[153] 1,300	.14	.24	4.3	24
c	Size, 603 × 700 [14] (No. 10); net wt., 106 oz. (6 lb. 10 oz.).	1 can	3,005	80.9	1,983	57.1	18.0	471.8	120	1,443	12.0	[21] 7,092	2,915	[153] 8,110	.90	1.50	27.0	150
d	Cup	1 cup	256	80.9	169	4.9	1.5	40.2	10	123	1.0	[21] 604	248	[153] 690	.08	.13	2.3	13
e	Pound	1 lb	454	80.9	299	8.6	2.7	71.2	18	218	1.8	[21] 1,070	440	[153] 1,220	.14	.23	4.1	23
850	Drained solids:																	
	Can and approx. drained contents:																	
a	Size, 211 × 304 [14] (8Z Tall, Buffet); wt., 5¼ oz.	1 can	149	75.9	125	3.9	1.2	29.5	7	73	.7	[21] 352	145	[153] 520	.04	.07	1.3	6
b	Size, 303 × 406 [14] (No. 303); wt., 10½ oz.	1 can	298	75.9	250	7.7	2.4	59.0	15	146	1.5	[21] 703	289	[153] 1,040	.09	.15	2.7	12
c	Size, 603 × 700 [14] (No. 10); wt., 70 oz. (4 lb. 6 oz.).	1 can	1,984	75.9	1,667	51.6	15.9	392.8	99	972	9.9	[21] 4,682	1,924	[153] 6,940	.60	.99	17.9	79
d	Cup	1 cup	165	75.9	139	4.3	1.3	32.7	8	81	.8	[21] 389	160	[153] 580	.05	.08	1.5	7
e	Pound	1 lb	454	75.9	381	11.8	3.6	89.8	23	222	2.3	[21] 1,070	440	[153] 1,590	.14	.23	4.1	18
851	Drained liquid:																	
a	Pound	1 lb	454	91.7	118	2.3	Trace	31.3	14	204	1.4	[21] 1,070	440	Trace	.14	.18	4.1	32
b	Ounce	1 oz	28	91.7	7	.1	Trace	2.0	1	13	.1	[21] 67	27	Trace	.01	.01	.3	2
	Special dietary pack (low sodium):																	
	Cream style, white and yellow:																	
852	Solids and liquid:																	
	Can and approx. contents:																	
a	Size, 211 × 304 [14] (8Z Tall, Buffet); net wt., 8¾ oz.	1 can	248	77.3	203	6.4	2.7	45.9	7	139	1.5	5	(241)	[153] 670	.07	.12	2.5	12
b	Size, 303 × 406 [14] (No. 303); net wt., 17 oz. (1 lb. 1 oz.).	1 can	482	77.3	395	12.5	5.3	89.2	14	270	2.9	10	(468)	[153] 1,300	.14	.24	4.8	24
c	Cup	1 cup	256	77.3	210	6.7	2.8	47.4	8	143	1.5	5	(248)	[153] 690	.08	.13	2.6	13
d	Pound	1 lb	454	77.3	372	11.8	5.0	83.9	14	254	2.7	9	(440)	[153] 1,220	.14	.23	4.5	23
	Whole kernel, wet pack, white and yellow:																	
853	Solids and liquid:																	
	Can and approx. contents:																	
a	Size, 211 × 304 [14] (8Z Tall, Buffet); net wt., 8¾ oz.	1 can	248	83.6	141	4.7	1.2	33.7	10	119	1.0	5	241	[153] 670	.07	.12	2.2	12
b	Size, 303 × 406 [14] (No. 303); net wt., 17 oz. (1 lb. 1 oz.).	1 can	482	83.6	275	9.2	2.4	65.6	19	231	1.9	10	468	[153] 1,300	.14	.24	4.3	24
c	Size, 603 × 700 [14] (No. 10); net wt., 106 oz. (6 lb. 10 oz.).	1 can	3,005	83.6	1,713	57.1	15.0	408.7	120	1,442	12.0	60	2,915	[153] 8,110	.90	1.50	27.0	150
d	Cup	1 cup	256	83.6	146	4.9	1.3	34.8	10	123	1.0	5	248	[153] 690	.08	.13	2.3	13
e	Pound	1 lb	454	83.6	259	8.6	2.3	61.7	18	218	1.8	9	440	[153] 1,220	.14	.23	4.1	23
854	Drained solids:																	
	Can and approx. drained contents:																	
a	Size, 211 × 304 [14] (8Z Tall, Buffet); wt., 5¼ oz.	1 can	149	78.4	118	3.7	1.0	26.8	7	73	.7	3	145	[153] 520	.04	.07	1.3	6

(A)	(B)			(C)	(D)	(E)	(F)	(G)	(H)	(I)	(J)	(K)	(L)	(M)	(N)	(O)	(P)	(Q)
b	Size, 303 × 406 [14] (No. 303); wt., 10½ oz.	1 can	298	78.4	226	7.5	2.1	53.6	15	146	1.5	6	289	[153] 1,040	0.09	0.15	2.7	12
c	Size, 603 × 700 [14] (No. 10); wt., 70 oz. (4 lb. 6 oz.).	1 can	1,984	78.4	1,508	49.6	13.9	357.4	99	972	9.9	40	1,924	[153] 6,940	.60	.99	17.9	79
d	Cup	1 cup	165	78.4	152	4.1	1.2	29.7	8	81	.8	3	160	[153] 580	.05	.08	1.5	7
e	Pound	1 lb	454	78.4	345	11.3	3.2	81.6	23	222	2.3	9	440	[153] 1,590	.14	.23	4.1	18
855	Drained liquid:																	
a	Pound	1 lb	454	94.8	77	2.3	Trace	19.5	14	204	1.4	9	440	Trace	.14	.18	4.1	32
b	Ounce	1 oz	28	94.8	5	.1	Trace	1.2	1	13	.1	1	27	Trace	.01	.01	.3	2
	Frozen:																	
	Kernels, cut off cob:																	
856	Not thawed:																	
a	Container, net wt., 10 oz	1 container	284	76.2	233	8.8	1.4	55.9	9	222	2.3	3	574	[153] (990)	.31	.20	4.5	23
b	Cup	1 cup	165	76.2	135	5.1	.8	32.5	5	129	1.3	2	333	[153] (580)	.18	.12	2.6	13
c	Pound	1 lb	454	76.2	372	14.1	2.3	89.4	14	354	3.6	5	916	[153] (1,590)	.50	.32	7.3	36
857	Cooked (boiled), drained:																	
a	Yield from 10 oz., frozen corn	1⅔ cups	275	77.2	217	8.3	1.4	51.7	8	201	2.2	[20] 3	506	[153] (960)	.25	.17	4.1	14
b	Yield from 1 lb., frozen corn	2⅔ cups	440	77.2	348	13.2	2.2	82.7	13	321	3.5	[20] 4	810	[153] (1,540)	.40	.26	6.6	22
c	Cup	1 cup	165	77.2	130	5.0	.8	31.0	5	120	1.3	[20] 2	304	[153] (580)	.15	.10	2.5	8
d	Pound	1 lb	454	77.2	358	13.6	2.3	85.3	14	331	3.6	[20] 5	835	[153] (1,590)	.41	.27	6.8	23
	Kernels, on cob (refuse: cob, 45%): [1]																	
858	Not thawed:																	
	Natural length ear, 5 in. long; wt., approx. 8 oz.:																	
a	Container of 4 ears	4 ears	908	72.1	489	18.0	5.0	112.9	15	509	4.0	5	1,268	[153] (1,750)	.85	.45	9.5	50
b	Container of 6 ears	6 ears	1,362	72.1	734	27.0	7.5	169.3	22	764	6.0	7	1,903	[153] (2,620)	1.27	.67	14.2	75
c	Ear	1 ear	227	72.1	122	4.5	1.2	28.2	4	127	1.0	1	317	[153] (440)	.21	.11	2.4	12
d	Ear trimmed to length of approx. 3½ in.; wt., 4 oz.	1 ear	113	72.1	61	2.2	.6	14.1	2	63	.5	1	158	[153] (220)	.11	.06	1.2	6
e	Pound	1 lb	454	72.1	245	9.0	2.5	56.4	7	254	2.0	2	634	[153] (870)	.42	.22	4.7	25
859	Cooked (boiled), drained:																	
	Natural length ear, 5 in. long:																	
a	Yield from 4 ears (item 858a)	4 ears	917	73.2	474	17.7	5.0	109.0	15	484	4.0	[20] 5	1,165	[153] (1,750)	.71	.40	8.6	35
b	Yield from 6 ears (item 858b)	6 ears	1,376	73.2	711	26.5	7.5	163.5	22	727	6.0	[20] 7	1,748	[153] (2,620)	1.06	.61	12.9	53
c	Yield from 1 ear (item 858c)	1 ear	229	73.2	118	4.4	1.2	27.2	4	121	1.0	[20] 1	291	[153] (440)	.18	.10	2.1	9
d	Yield from ear trimmed to length of approx. 3½ in. (item 858d).	1 ear	114	73.2	59	2.2	.6	13.5	2	60	.5	[20] 1	145	[153] (220)	.09	.05	1.1	4
e	Pound (approx. yield from 1 lb., frozen corn).	1 lb	454	73.2	235	8.7	2.5	53.9	7	240	2.0	[20] 2	576	[153] (870)	.35	.20	4.2	17
860	**Corn flour:** [5, 154]																	
a	Cup	1 cup	117	12	431	9.1	3.0	89.9	7	(92)	2.1	(1)	—	[153] 400	.23	.07	1.6	(0)
b	Pound	1 lb	454	12	1,669	35.4	11.8	348.4	27	(744)	8.2	(5)	—	[153] 1,540	.91	.27	6.4	(0)
861	**Corn fritters** (2-in. diam., 1½ in. thick): [5, 81]																	
a	Yield from recipe [108]	17¾ fritters	622	29.1	2,345	48.5	133.7	246.9	398	964	10.6	2,967	827	[155] 2,490	1.00	1.24	10.0	12
b	Fritter	1 fritter	35	29.1	132	2.7	7.5	13.9	22	54	.6	167	47	[155] 140	.06	.07	.6	1
	Corn grits, degermed: [5, 156]																	
	Enriched:																	
862	Dry form:																	
a	Cup	1 cup	160	12	579	13.9	1.3	125.0	6	117	[157] 4.6	2	128	[153] 700	[157] .70	[157] .42	[157] 5.6	(0)
b	Pound	1 lb	454	12	1,642	39.5	3.6	354.3	18	331	[157] 13.0	5	363	[153] 2,000	[157] 2.0	[157] 1.2	[157] 16.0	(0)
863	Cooked:																	
a	Cup	1 cup	245	87.1	125	2.9	.2	27.0	2	25	[157] .7	[158] 502	27	[153] 150	[157] .10	[157] .07	[157] 1.0	(0)
b	Pound	1 lb	454	87.1	231	5.4	.5	49.9	5	45	[157] 1.4	[158] 930	50	[153] 270	[157] .18	[157] .14	[157] 1.8	(0)
	Unenriched:																	
864	Dry form:																	
a	Cup	1 cup	160	12	579	13.9	1.3	125.0	6	117	1.6	2	128	[153] 700	.21	.06	1.9	(0)
b	Pound	1 lb	454	12	1,642	39.5	3.6	354.3	18	331	4.5	5	363	[153] 2,000	.59	.18	5.4	(0)

[1] Measure and weight apply to food as it is described with inedible part or parts (refuse) included.

[5] Most of phosphorus in nuts, legumes, and outer layers of cereal grains is present as phytic acid. See also Appendix D, section on Minerals and Oxalic Acid

[14] Dimensions of can: 1st dimension represents diameter; 2d dimension, height of can. 1st or left-hand digit in each dimension gives number of whole inches; next 2 digits give additional fraction of dimension expressed as 16th of an inch.

[20] Value is for unsalted product. If salt is used, increase value by 236 mg. per 100 g. of vegetable—an estimated figure based on typical amount of salt (0.6%) in canned vegetables. See also Appendix C, section on Cooked Vegetables

[80] Estimated value based on addition of salt in amount of 0.6% of finished product.

[81] For information on ingredients used in preparation, see ARS 62-13 (7), table 22, p. 26.

[108] Formula used to calculate nutritive values shown in Agr. Handb. No. 8, rev. 1963.

[152] Proximate composition and energy value vary with maturity and variety. Values shown here are based on average derived from data available on maturity for varieties of commercial importance. For further information, see Appendix C, section on Corn, Sweet

[153] Based on yellow varieties; white varieties contain only trace of cryptoxanthin and carotenes, the pigments in corn that have biological activity.

[154] Weight per cup is based on method of pouring product from container into measuring cup with as little fall as possible, then leveling with straight edge. For corn flour, see Appendix B, section on Nonliquid Foods and section on Cornmeals and Related Products

[155] Based on fritters made with yellow sweet corn; with white corn, value is 1,430 I.U. for yield from recipe (item 861a); 80 I.U. for 1 fritter (item 861b).

[156] For dry form of cereal, weight per cup is based on method of pouring cereal from container into measuring cup with as little fall as possible, then leveling with straight edge. See also Appendix B, section on Nonliquid Foods and section on Breakfast-Type Cereals

For cooked cereal, weight per cup represents hot cereal immediately after cooking and is based on specific proportion of cereal and water in cooked product. See ARS 62-13 (7), section on Alimentary Pastes and Other Cereal Products, pp. 6-7, and table 3, p. 9.

[157] Based on product with minimum level of enrichment. See also Appendix C, section on Enriched Foods and Standards of Enrichment

[158] Based on value of 205 mg. per 100 g. for product cooked with salt added as specified by manufacturers. If cooked without added salt, value is negligible.

TABLE 1.—*Nutritive values for household measures and market units of foods*—Continued

[Item numbers correspond to those in table 1 of Handbook No. 8, revised 1963. Values in parentheses denote imputed values usually from another form of the food or from a similar food. Zeros in parentheses indicate that amount of a constituent, if present, is probably too small to be measured. Dashes (—) denote lack of reliable data for a constituent believed to be present in a measurable amount. Calculated values, as those based on a recipe, are not in parentheses]

Item No. (A)	Food, approximate measures, units, and weight (edible part unless footnotes indicate otherwise) (B)			Water (C)	Food energy (D)	Protein (E)	Fat (F)	Carbohydrate (G)	Calcium (H)	Phosphorus (I)	Iron (J)	Sodium (K)	Potassium (L)	Vitamin A value (M)	Thiamin (N)	Riboflavin (O)	Niacin (P)	Ascorbic acid (Q)
			Grams	*Percent*	*Calories*	*Grams*	*Grams*	*Grams*	*Milligrams*	*Milligrams*	*Milligrams*	*Milligrams*	*Milligrams*	*International units*	*Milligrams*	*Milligrams*	*Milligrams*	*Milligrams*
	Corn grits, degermed [5] [156]—Continued																	
	Unenriched—Continued																	
865	Cooked:																	
a	Cup	1 cup	245	87.1	125	2.9	0.2	27.0	2	25	0.2	[158] 502	27	[153] 150	0.05	0.02	0.5	(0)
b	Pound	1 lb	454	87.1	231	5.4	.5	49.9	5	45	.5	[158] 930	50	[153] 270	.09	.05	.9	(0)
	Corn muffins. See Muffins, corn (items 1347–1348) and Muffin mix, corn, and muffins and cornbread baked from mix (item 1350).																	
	Corn oil. See Oils (items 1401a, 1401b, 1401f, 1401h, 1401j).																	
	Corn products used mainly as ready-to-eat breakfast cereals: [5] [74]																	
	Corn flakes:																	
866	Plain, added sugar, salt, iron, vitamins:																	
a	Flakes	1 cup	25	3.8	97	2.0	.1	21.3	([159])	[160] 9	[160] .6	251	30	[81] 1,180	[82] .29	[82] .35	[82] 2.9	[81] 9
b	Crumbs	1 cup	85	3.8	328	6.7	.3	72.5	([159])	[160] 29	[160] 1.9	854	102	[81] 4,000	[82] .99	[82] 1.20	[82] 9.9	[81] 30
867	Sugar coated, added salt, iron, vitamins	1 cup	40	2.2	154	1.8	.1	36.5	[161] 1	10	[161] 1.0	[161] 267	[161] 27	[81] 1,880	[82] .46	[82] .56	[82] 4.6	[81] 14
	Corn, puffed:																	
868	Plain, added sugar, salt, iron, vitamins	1 cup	20	3.6	80	1.6	.8	16.2	4	18	[162] 2.3	[163] 233	—	[81] 940	[82] .23	[82] .28	[82] 2.3	[81] 7
	Presweetened, added salt, iron, vitamins:																	
869	Without added flavor	1 cup	30	5.0	114	1.2	.1	26.9	3	8	[164] .8	90	[164] 23	[81] 1,410	[82] .35	[82] .42	[82] 3.5	[81] 11
870	Cocoa flavored	1 cup	30	2.1	117	1.9	.7	26.0	6	27	[162] 3.5	255	—	[165] (0)	[82] .35	[82] .42	[82] 3.5	[166] 11
871	Fruit flavored	1 cup	30	2.1	119	1.7	.8	26.2	9	21	[162] 3.5	[167] 228	—	[81] 1,410	[82] .35	[82] .42	[82] 3.5	[81] 11
872	Corn, shredded, added sugar, salt, iron, thiamin, niacin.	1 cup	25	3.0	97	1.8	.1	21.7	1	10	.6	[168] 269	—	(0)	.11	.05	.5	(0)
875	**Corn pudding:** [5] [51]																	
a	Yield from recipe [108]	3 cups	740	76.7	770	29.6	34.8	96.2	488	622	3.7	3,226	1,251	1,920	.22	.96	3.0	15
b	Cup	1 cup	245	76.7	255	9.8	11.5	31.9	162	206	1.2	1,068	414	640	.07	.32	1.0	5
	Corn sirup. See Sirup, table blends (item 2051).																	
	Cornbread, baked from home recipe: [5]																	
	Cornbread, southern style, made with [60]—																	
876	Whole-ground cornmeal:																	
a	Whole (7½ × 7½ × 1½ in.; vol., 84.4 cu. in.)	1 cornbread	[54] 703	53.9	1,455	52.0	50.6	204.6	844	1,483	7.7	4,415	1,104	[169] 1,050	.91	1.34	4.2	7
b	Piece (2½ × 2½ × 1½ in.; vol., 9.4 cu. in.; ⅑ of cornbread).	1 piece	78	53.9	161	5.8	5.6	22.7	94	165	.9	490	122	[169] 120	.10	.15	.5	1
c	Cube (1 cu. in.)	1 cube	8.3	53.9	17	.6	.6	2.4	10	18	.1	52	13	[169] 10	.01	.02	Trace	Trace
877	Degermed cornmeal, enriched:																	
a	Whole (7½ × 7½ × 1⅝ in.; vol., 91.4 cu. in.)	1 cornbread	[54] 747	50.2	1,673	53.0	44.8	259.2	814	1,165	[170] 10.5	4,415	1,173	[169] 1,120	[170] 1.27	[170] 1.79	[170] 8.2	7
b	Piece (2½ × 2½ × 1⅝ in.; vol., 10.2 cu. in.; ⅑ of cornbread).	1 piece	83	50.2	186	5.9	5.0	28.8	90	129	[171] 1.2	491	130	[169] 120	[171] .14	[171] .20	[171] .9	1
c	Cube (1 cu. in.)	1 cube	8.2	50.2	18	.6	.5	2.8	9	13	[172] .1	48	13	[169] 10	[172] .01	[172] .02	[172] .1	Trace
879	Corn pone, made with white whole-ground cornmeal, baked (9-in. diam., 28.3-in. cir., ¾ in. high): [60]																	
a	Pone, whole	1 pone	[54] 485	51.8	989	21.8	25.7	175.6	301	791	5.8	1,921	296	Trace	.73	.24	4.4	0
b	Sector, 3½-in. arc; ⅛ of pone	1 sector	60	51.8	122	2.7	3.2	21.7	37	98	.7	238	37	Trace	.09	.03	.5	0
880	Spoonbread, made with white whole-ground cornmeal: [60]																	
a	Yield from recipe [108]	2⅔ cups	645	63.0	1,258	43.2	73.5	109.0	619	1,058	6.5	3,109	851	1,870	.58	1.16	2.6	3
b	Cup	1 cup	240	63.0	468	16.1	27.4	40.6	230	394	2.4	1,157	317	700	.22	.43	1.0	1
	See also Muffins, corn (items 1347–1348).																	
882	**Cornbread baked from mix.** See Muffin mix, corn, and muffins and cornbread baked from mix (items 1349–1350).																	
	Cornmeal, white or yellow: [5] [156]																	
883	Whole ground, unbolted, dry	1 cup	122	12	433	11.2	4.8	89.9	24	312	2.9	(1)	(346)	[153] 620	.46	.13	2.4	(0)
884	Bolted (nearly whole grain), dry	1 cup	122	12	442	11.0	4.1	90.9	(21)	(272)	2.2	(1)	(303)	[153] 590	.37	.10	2.3	(0)
	Degermed, enriched:																	
885	Dry form	1 cup	138	12	502	10.9	1.7	108.2	8	137	[157] 4.0	1	166	[153] 610	[157] .61	[157] .36	[157] 4.8	(0)
886	Cooked	1 cup	240	87.7	120	2.6	.5	25.7	2	34	[157] 1.0	[173] 264	38	[153] 140	[157] .14	[157] .10	[157] 1.2	(0)
	Degermed, unenriched:																	
887	Dry form	1 cup	138	12	502	10.9	1.7	108.2	8	137	1.5	1	166	[153] 610	.19	.07	1.4	(0)

(A)	(B)			(C)	(D)	(E)	(F)	(G)	(H)	(I)	(J)	(K)	(L)	(M)	(N)	(O)	(P)	(Q)
888	Cooked	1 cup	240	87.7	120	2.6	0.5	25.7	2	34	0.5	[173] 264	38	[153] 140	0.05	0.02	0.2	(0)
	Self-rising:[174]																	
	Whole ground:																	
889	With soft wheat flour added	1 cup	134	11.3	465	11.5	3.9	96.3	403	836	[175] 2.1	1,849	[176] 284	[153] 510	[175] .34	[175] .09	[175] 2.3	(0)
890	Without wheat flour added	1 cup	134	11.3	465	11.4	4.3	95.9	402	859	[175] 2.3	1,849	[176] 314	[153] 600	[175] .38	[175] .11	[175] 2.4	(0)
	Degermed:																	
891	With soft wheat flour added	1 cup	141	11.3	491	10.9	1.6	105.9	412	739	[177] 1.4	1,946	[176] 154	[153] 490	[177] .17	[177] .07	[177] 1.4	(0)
892	Without wheat flour added	1 cup	141	11.3	491	10.6	1.6	106.2	409	739	[177] 1.4	1,946	[176] 159	[153] 590	[177] .18	[177] .07	[177] 1.3	(0)
894	**Cornstarch**, stirred:																	
a	Cup, lightly filled	1 cup	128	12	463	.4	Trace	112.1	(0)	(0)	(0)	Trace	Trace	(0)	(0)	(0)	(0)	(0)
b	Tablespoon, not packed	1 tbsp	8	12	29	Trace	Trace	7.0	(0)	(0)	(0)	Trace	Trace	(0)	(0)	(0)	(0)	(0)
	Cottage cheese and Cottage cheese dry curd. See Cheeses (items 647–648).																	
	Cottage pudding. See Cakes (items 528–530).																	
	Cottonseed oil. See Oils (items 1401f, 1401h, 1401j).																	
	Cowpeas, including blackeye peas:[5]																	
	Immature seeds:																	
896	Raw:																	
a	Cup (blackeye peas)	1 cup	145	66.8	184	13.1	1.2	31.6	39	249	3.3	3	784	540	.62	.19	2.3	42
b	Pound	1 lb	454	66.8	576	40.8	3.6	98.9	122	780	10.4	9	2,454	1,680	1.95	.59	7.3	132
897	Cooked (boiled), drained:																	
a	Cup (blackeye peas)	1 cup	165	71.8	178	13.4	1.3	29.9	40	241	3.5	[20] 2	625	580	.50	.18	2.3	28
b	Pound	1 lb	454	71.8	490	36.7	3.6	82.1	109	662	9.5	[20] 5	1,719	1,590	1.36	.50	6.4	77
898	Canned, solids and liquid (blackeye peas):																	
	Can and approx. contents:																	
a	Size, 303 × 406[14] (No. 303); net wt., 16 oz. (1 lb.).	1 can or 1 lb	454	81.0	318	22.7	1.4	56.2	82	508	6.8	[21] 1,070	1,597	270	.41	.23	2.3	14
b	Cup	1 cup	255	81.0	179	12.8	.8	31.6	46	286	3.8	[21] 602	898	150	.23	.13	1.3	8
	Frozen (blackeye peas):																	
899	Not thawed:																	
a	Container, net wt., 10 oz	1 container	284	65.8	372	25.6	1.1	67.0	80	508	8.8	[45] 142	1,099	480	1.28	.34	4.0	37
b	Cup	1 cup	160	65.8	210	14.4	.6	37.8	45	286	5.0	[45] 80	619	270	.72	.19	2.2	21
c	Pound	1 lb	454	65.8	594	40.8	1.8	107.0	127	812	14.1	[45] 227	1,755	770	2.04	.54	6.4	59
900	Cooked (boiled), drained:																	
a	Yield from 10 oz., frozen blackeye peas	1½ cups (approx.).	260	66.1	338	23.1	1.0	61.1	65	437	7.3	[45] 101	876	440	1.04	.29	3.6	23
b	Yield from 1 lb., frozen blackeye peas	2½ cups	420	66.1	546	37.4	1.7	98.7	105	706	11.8	[45] 164	1,415	710	1.68	.46	5.9	38
c	Cup	1 cup	170	66.1	221	15.1	.7	40.0	43	286	4.8	[45] 66	573	290	.68	.19	2.4	15
d	Pound (yield from approx. 17 oz., frozen blackeye peas).	1 lb	454	66.1	590	40.4	1.8	106.6	113	762	12.7	[45] 177	1,529	770	1.81	.50	6.4	41
	Young pods, with seeds:																	
901	Raw	1 lb	454	86.0	200	15.0	1.4	43.1	295	295	4.5	18	975	7,260	.68	.64	5.4	150
902	Cooked (boiled), drained	1 lb	454	89.5	154	11.8	1.4	31.8	249	222	3.2	[20] 14	889	6,350	.41	.41	3.6	77

[5] Most of phosphorus in nuts, legumes, and outer layers of cereal grains is present as phytic acid. See also Appendix D, section on Minerals and Oxalic Acid

[14] Dimensions of can: 1st dimension represents diameter; 2d dimension, height of can. 1st or left-hand digit in each dimension gives number of whole inches; next 2 digits give additional fraction of dimension expressed as 16th of an inch.

[20] Value is for unsalted product. If salt is used, increase value by 236 mg. per 100 g. of vegetable—an estimated figure based on typical amount of salt (0.6%) in canned vegetables. See also Appendix C, section on Cooked Vegetables

[21] Estimated value based on addition of salt in amount of 0.6% of finished product.

[45] Value based on average weighted in accordance with commercial practice in freezing vegetables. Wide range in sodium content occurs. For cooked vegetables, value also represents no additional salting. If salt is moderately added, increase value by 236 mg. per 100 g. of vegetable—an estimated figure based on typical amount of salt (0.6%) in canned vegetables. See also Appendix C, section on Cooked Vegetables and section on Frozen Fruits and Vegetables

[51] For information on ingredients used in preparation, see ARS 62–13 (7), table 22, p. 26.

[54] Yield of formula used to calculate nutritive values in Agr. Handb. No. 8, rev. 1963.

[60] For information on ingredients used, see ARS 62–13 (7), table 4, p. 10.

[74] Weight per cup based on method of pouring product from container into measuring cup to overflow and leveling with straight edge. Revised values for minerals and vitamins apply to products on the market in 1972.

[81] Basis of revised value for 100 g. of product with added vitamin A is 4,700 I.U.; with added ascorbic acid, 35 mg.

[82] Basis of revised value for 100 g. of product with added thiamin is 1.16 mg.; with added riboflavin, 1.41 mg.; with added niacin, 11.6 mg.

[108] Formula used to calculate nutritive values shown in Agr. Handb. No. 8, rev. 1963.

[153] Based on yellow varieties; white varieties contain only trace of cryptoxanthin and carotenes, the pigments in corn that have biological activity.

[156] For dry form of cereal, weight per cup is based on method of pouring cereal from container into measuring cup with as little fall as possible, then leveling with straight edge. See also Appendix B, section on Nonliquid Foods and section on Breakfast-Type Cereals

For cooked cereal, weight per cup represents hot cereal immediately after cooking and is based on specific proportion of cereal and water in cooked product. See ARS 62–13 (7), section on Alimentary Pastes and Other Cereal Products, pp. 6–7, and table 3, p. 9.

[157] Based on product with minimum level of enrichment. See also Appendix C, section on Enriched Foods and Standards of Enrichment

[158] Based on value of 205 mg. per 100 g. for product cooked with salt added as specified by manufacturers. If cooked without added salt, value is negligible.

[159] Values range from 3 to 26 mg. per 100 g. of product, less than 1 to 7 mg. per cup of flakes, and less than 3 to 22 mg. per cup of crumbs.

[160] Based on revised value per 100 g. of product. Value used for phosphorus is 34 mg.; for iron 2.2 mg.

[161] Based on revised value per 100 g. of product. Value used for calcium is 3 mg., for iron 2.5 mg., for sodium 668 mg., for potassium 67 mg.

[162] Based on revised value of 11.7 mg. per 100 g. of product.

[163] Based on revised value of 1,164 mg. per 100 g. of product.

[164] Based on revised value per 100 g. of product. Value used for iron is 2.5 mg.; for potassium 78 mg.

[165] Product does not contain added vitamin A.

[166] Based on revised value of 35 mg. per 100 g. of product.

[167] Based on revised value of 760 mg. per 100 g. of product.

[168] Based on revised value of 1,076 mg. per 100 g. of product.

[169] Based on cornbread made with white cornmeal. For cornbread made with yellow cornmeal, values for item 876 are 2,180 I.U. for whole cornbread, 240 I.U. for 1 piece (1/9 of cornbread), 30 I.U. for 1 cu. in.; values for item 877 are 2,320 I.U. for whole cornbread, 260 I.U. for 1 piece (1/9 of cornbread), 30 I.U. for 1 cu. in.

[170] For cornbread made with unenriched degermed cornmeal, values are iron 5.2 mg., thiamin 0.52 mg., riboflavin 1.27 mg., niacin 3.0 mg.

[171] For cornbread made with unenriched degermed cornmeal, values are iron 0.6 mg., thiamin 0.06 mg., riboflavin 0.14 mg., niacin 0.3 mg.

[172] For cornbread made with unenriched degermed cornmeal, values are iron 0.1 mg., thiamin 0.01 mg., riboflavin 0.01 mg., niacin trace.

[173] Based on value of 110 mg. per 100 g. for product cooked with salt added as specified by manufacturers. If cooked without added salt, value is negligible.

[174] Much of self-rising cornmeal on the market is enriched. For further information, especially on calcium content, see Appendix C, section on Enriched Foods and Standards of Enrichment

[175] Value applies to unenriched product. For enriched product, minimum values per cup are iron 3.9 mg., thiamin 0.59 mg., riboflavin 0.35 mg., niacin 4.7 mg.

[176] Amount of potassium contributed by cornmeal and flour. Small quantities of additional potassium may be provided by other ingredients.

[177] Value applies to unenriched product. For enriched product, minimum values per cup are iron 4.1 mg., thiamin 0.62 mg., riboflavin 0.37 mg., niacin 4.9 mg.

TABLE 1.—*Nutritive values for household measures and market units of foods*—Continued

[Item numbers correspond to those in table 1 of Handbook No. 8, revised 1963. Values in parentheses denote imputed values usually from another form of the food or from a similar food. Zeros in parentheses indicate that amount of a constituent, if present, is probably too small to be measured. Dashes (—) denote lack of reliable data for a constituent believed to be present in a measurable amount. Calculated values, as those based on a recipe, are not in parentheses]

Item No. (A)	Food, approximate measures, units, and weight (edible part unless footnotes indicate otherwise) (B)			Water (C)	Food energy (D)	Protein (E)	Fat (F)	Carbohydrate (G)	Calcium (H)	Phosphorus (I)	Iron (J)	Sodium (K)	Potassium (L)	Vitamin A value (M)	Thiamin (N)	Riboflavin (O)	Niacin (P)	Ascorbic acid (Q)
			Grams	Percent	Calories	Grams	Grams	Grams	Milligrams	Milligrams	Milligrams	Milligrams	Milligrams	International units	Milligrams	Milligrams	Milligrams	Milligrams
	Cowpeas, including blackeye peas [5]—Continued																	
	Mature seeds, dry:																	
903	Raw:																	
a	Cup (blackeye peas)	1 cup	170	10.5	583	38.8	2.6	104.9	126	724	9.9	60	1,741	50	1.79	0.36	3.7	—
b	Pound	1 lb	454	10.5	1,556	103.4	6.8	279.9	336	1,932	26.3	159	4,645	140	4.76	.95	10.0	—
904	Cooked: [43]																	
a	Cup	1 cup	250	80.0	190	12.8	.8	34.5	43	238	3.3	[43] 20	573	30	.40	.10	1.0	—
b	Pound	1 lb	454	80.0	345	23.1	1.4	62.6	77	431	5.9	[43] 36	1,039	50	.73	.18	1.8	—
	Crab, including blue, Dungeness, rock, king:																	
905	Cooked (steamed):																	
	Cup:																	
	Not packed:																	
a	Pieces of crabmeat	1 cup	155	78.5	144	26.8	2.9	.8	67	271	1.2	[43] —	—	3,360	.25	.12	4.3	8
b	Flaked crabmeat	1 cup	125	78.5	116	21.6	2.4	.6	54	219	1.0	[43] —	—	2,710	.20	.10	3.5	2
c	Packed (pieces or flaked meat)	1 cup	210	78.5	195	36.3	4.0	1.1	90	368	1.7	[43] —	—	4,560	.34	.17	5.9	4
d	Pound	1 lb	454	78.5	422	78.5	8.6	2.3	195	794	3.6	[43] —	—	9,840	.73	.36	12.7	9
906	Crab, canned, drained solids:																	
	Drained contents from can, size 307 × 113 [14] (No. ½), of net wt., 6½ oz.; drained wt., 4⅖ oz.:																	
a	Blue crab (claw or white)	1 can	125	77.2	126	21.8	3.1	1.4	56	228	1.0	1,250	138	—	.10	.10	2.4	—
	Drained contents from can, size 307 × 200.25 [14] (No. ½ Flat), of net wt., 7½ oz.; drained wt., 6⅓ oz.:																	
b	King crab	1 can	180	77.2	182	31.3	4.5	2.0	81	328	1.4	1,800	198	—	.14	.14	3.4	—
	Cup:																	
	Not packed:																	
c	Claw	1 cup	115	77.2	116	20.0	2.9	1.3	52	209	.9	1,150	127	—	.09	.09	2.2	—
d	White or king	1 cup	135	77.2	136	23.5	3.4	1.5	61	246	1.1	1,350	149	—	.11	.11	2.6	—
e	Packed (claw; white or king)	1 cup	160	77.2	162	27.8	4.0	1.8	72	291	1.3	1,600	176	—	.13	.13	3.0	—
f	Pound	1 lb	454	77.2	458	78.9	11.3	5.0	204	826	3.6	4,536	499	—	.36	.36	8.6	—
907	Crab, deviled: [178]																	
a	Cup	1 cup	240	63.3	451	27.4	22.6	31.9	113	329	2.9	[43] 2,081	398	—	.19	.26	3.6	14
b	Pound	1 lb	454	63.3	853	51.7	42.6	60.3	213	621	5.4	[43] 3,933	753	—	.36	.50	6.8	27
908	Crab, imperial: [179]																	
a	Cup	1 cup	220	71.9	323	32.1	16.7	8.6	132	365	2.0	[43] 1,602	288	—	.13	.26	2.4	11
b	Pound	1 lb	454	71.9	667	66.2	34.5	17.7	272	753	4.1	[43] 3,302	594	—	.27	.54	5.0	23
	Crackers:																	
910	Animal (approx. 175 per pound):																	
a	Package, net wt., 2 oz. (approx. 22 crackers)	1 pkg	57	3.0	245	3.8	5.4	45.5	30	65	.3	173	54	70	.02	.06	.2	Trace
b	Cracker	10 crackers	26	3.0	112	1.7	2.4	20.8	14	30	.1	79	25	30	.01	.03	.1	Trace
c	Pound	1 lb	454	3.0	1,946	29.9	42.6	362.4	236	517	2.3	1,374	431	590	.18	.45	1.4	Trace
911	Butter:																	
	Whole:																	
	Round, 1⅞-in. diam., 3/16 in. thick (approx. 138 per pound):																	
	Package:																	
a	Net wt., 16 oz. (1 lb.) (loose pack)	1 pkg. or 1 lb.	454	4.6	2,077	31.8	80.7	305.3	671	1,179	2.7	4,953	513	1,000	.05	.18	4.5	(0)
b	Net wt., 10–12 oz. (3 inner packs)	1 pkg	312	4.6	1,429	21.8	55.5	210.0	462	811	1.9	3,407	353	690	.03	.12	3.1	(0)
c	Cracker	10 crackers	33	4.6	151	2.3	5.9	22.2	49	86	.2	360	37	70	Trace	.01	.3	(0)
	Rectangular, 2½ in. long, 1⅜ in. wide, ⅛ in. thick (approx. 120 per pound):																	
d	Package, net wt., 11½ oz	1 pkg	326	4.6	1,493	22.8	58.0	219.4	482	848	2.0	3,560	368	720	.03	.13	3.3	(0)
e	Cracker	10 crackers	38	4.6	174	2.7	6.8	25.6	56	99	.2	415	43	80	Trace	.02	.4	(0)
f	Crumbed (finely crushed, spooned into cup without packing; approx. 24 round crackers or 21 rectangular).	1 cup	80	4.6	366	5.6	14.2	53.8	118	208	.5	874	90	180	.01	.03	.8	(0)
g	Whole or crumbed	1 lb	454	4.6	2,077	31.8	80.7	305.3	671	1,179	2.7	4,953	513	1,000	.05	.18	4.5	(0)
912	Cheese:																	
	Whole:																	
	Cut into various shapes (hexagon, clover, etc.),																	

(A)	(B)			(C)	(D)	(E)	(F)	(G)	(H)	(I)	(J)	(K)	(L)	(M)	(N)	(O)	(P)	(Q)
	1⅞-in. diam. at widest cross section, 5/16 in. thick (approx. 145 per pound):																	
a	Package, net wt., 8½ oz	1 pkg	241	3.9	1,154	27.0	51.3	145.6	810	745	2.2	2,504	263	870	0.02	0.24	1.9	(0)
b	Cracker	10 crackers	31.3	3.9	150	3.5	6.7	18.9	105	97	.3	325	34	110	Trace	.03	.3	(0)
	Rectangular sticks, 1⅝ in. long, ¼ in. thick (approx. 500 per pound):																	
	Package:																	
c	Net wt., 11 oz	1 pkg	312	3.9	1,494	34.9	66.5	188.4	1,048	964	2.8	3,242	340	1,120	.03	.31	2.5	(0)
d	Net wt., 2¼ oz	1 pkg	64	3.9	307	7.2	13.6	38.7	215	198	.6	665	70	230	.01	.06	.5	(0)
e	Cracker	10 crackers	9.1	3.9	44	1.0	1.9	5.5	31	28	.1	95	10	30	Trace	.01	.1	(0)
	Round, 1⅞-in. diam., 3/16 in. thick (approx. 132 per pound):																	
f	Package, net wt., 8 oz	1 pkg	227	3.9	1,087	25.4	48.4	137.1	763	701	2.0	2,359	247	820	.02	.23	1.8	(0)
g	Cracker	10 crackers	34.4	3.9	165	3.9	7.3	20.8	116	106	.3	357	37	120	Trace	.03	.3	(0)
	Square, 1 in., ⅛ in. thick (approx. 420 per pound):																	
	Package:																	
h	Net wt., 10 oz	1 pkg	284	3.9	1,360	31.8	60.5	171.5	954	878	2.6	2,951	310	1,020	.03	.28	2.3	(0)
i	Net wt., 6¼ oz	1 pkg	177	3.9	848	19.8	37.7	106.9	595	547	1.6	1,839	193	640	.02	.18	1.4	(0)
j	Net wt., 2 oz	1 pkg	57	3.9	273	6.4	12.1	34.4	192	176	.5	592	62	210	.01	.06	.5	(0)
k	Cracker	10 crackers	10.8	3.9	52	1.2	2.3	6.5	36	33	.1	112	12	40	Trace	.01	.1	(0)
l	Crumbed (finely crushed, spooned into cup without packing; approx. 93 rectangular sticks, 25 round crackers, or 79 squares (1 in.)).	1 cup	85	3.9	407	9.5	18.1	51.3	286	263	.8	883	93	310	.01	.09	.7	(0)
m	Whole or crumbed	1 lb	454	3.9	2,173	50.8	96.6	274.0	1,524	1,402	4.1	4,713	494	1,630	.05	.45	3.6	(0)
	Graham:																	
913	Chocolate coated:[180]																	
a	Cracker, 2½ in. long, 2 in. wide, ¼ in. thick	1 cracker	13	1.9	62	.7	3.1	8.8	15	27	.3	53	42	10	.01	.04	.2	(0)
b	Pound	1 lb	454	1.9	2,155	23.1	106.6	308.0	513	925	11.8	1,846	1,452	270	.32	1.27	5.4	(0)
914	Plain:																	
	Whole, rectangular piece, approx. 5 in. long, 2½ in. wide, 3/16 in. thick (approx. 32 per pound), marked for division into 2 pieces, 2½ in. square, 3/16 in. thick (approx. 64 per pound), or into 4 small rectangular pieces, 2½ in. long, 1¼ in. wide, 3/16 in. thick (approx. 132 per pound):																	
a	Package, net wt., 16 oz. (1 lb.)	1 pkg. or 1 lb.	454	6.4	1,742	36.3	42.6	332.5	181	676	6.8	3,039	1,742	(0)	.18	.95	6.8	(0)
b	Cracker, 1 large rectangular piece, 2 squares (2½ in.), or 4 small rectangular pieces.	1 or 2 or 4 pieces.	14.2	6.4	55	1.1	1.3	10.4	6	21	.2	95	55	(0)	.01	.03	.2	(0)
	Crumbed (finely crushed, spooned into cup):																	
c	Not packed (approx. 6 large rectangular crackers (item 914b)).	1 cup	85	6.4	326	6.8	8.0	62.3	34	127	1.3	570	326	(0)	.03	.18	1.3	(0)
d	Packed (approx. 7½ large rectangular crackers (item 914b)).	1 cup	105	6.4	403	8.4	9.9	77.0	42	156	1.6	704	403	(0)	.04	.22	1.6	(0)
915	Sugar honey:																	
	Whole, rectangular piece, approx. 5 in. long, 2½ in. wide, 3/16 in. thick (approx. 32 per pound), marked for division into 2 pieces, 2½ in. square, 3/16 in. thick (approx. 64 per pound), or into 4 small rectangular pieces, 2½ in. long, 1¼ in. wide, 3/16 in. thick (approx. 132 per pound):																	
a	Package, net wt., 16 oz. (1 lb.)	1 pkg. or 1 lb.	454	3.3	1,864	30.4	51.7	346.6	399	1,492	7.3	2,286	1,225	—	.01	[181].68	4.5	(0)
b	Cracker, 1 large rectangular piece, 2 squares (2½ in.), or 4 small rectangular pieces.	1, 2, or 4 pieces	14.2	3.3	58	1.0	1.6	10.8	12	47	.2	72	38	—	Trace	[181].02	.1	(0)
	Crumbed (finely crushed, spooned into cup):																	
c	Not packed (approx. 6 large rectangular crackers (item 915b)).	1 cup	85	3.3	349	5.7	9.7	64.9	75	280	1.4	428	230	—	.03	[181].13	.9	(0)
d	Packed (approx. 7½ large rectangular crackers (item 915b)).	1 cup	105	3.3	432	7.0	12.0	80.2	92	345	1.7	529	284	—	.03	[181].16	1.1	(0)
916	Saltines, 1⅞ in. square, ⅛ in. thick (approx. 160 per pound):																	
	Whole:																	
	Package:																	
a	Net wt., 16 oz. (1 lb.)	1 pkg. or 1 lb.[182]	454	4.3	1,964	40.8	54.4	324.3	[183]95	408	[183]5.4	(4,990)	(544)	(0)	[183].05	[183].18	[183]4.5	(0)

[8] Most of phosphorus in nuts, legumes, and outer layers of cereal grains is present as phytic acid. See also Appendix D, section on Minerals and Oxalic Acid

[14] Dimensions of can: 1st dimension represents diameter; 2d dimension, height of can. 1st or left-hand digit in each dimension gives number of whole inches; next 2 digits give additional fraction of dimension expressed as 16th of an inch.

[43] For proportion of ingredients used and ratio of cooked to dry legume, see ARS 62-13 (7), section on Legumes, Dry, p. 7, and table 21, p. 25.

[48] Value for product without added salt.

[178] Prepared with bread cubes, butter or margarine, parsley, eggs, lemon juice, and catsup.

[179] Prepared with butter or margarine, flour, milk, onion, green pepper, eggs, and lemon juice.

[180] Count per pound and dimensions vary considerably.

[181] Based on corrected value of 0.15 mg. per 100 g.

[182] Use also for 1 lb. of crumbed crackers.

[183] Based on product made with unenriched flour.

TABLE 1.—*Nutritive values for household measures and market units of foods*—Continued

[Item numbers correspond to those in table 1 of Handbook No. 8, revised 1963. Values in parentheses denote imputed values usually from another form of the food or from a similar food. Zeros in parentheses indicate that amount of a constituent, if present, is probably too small to be measured. Dashes (—) denote lack of reliable data for a constituent believed to be present in a measurable amount. Calculated values, as those based on a recipe, are not in parentheses]

Item No.	Food, approximate measures, units, and weight (edible part unless footnotes indicate otherwise)			Water	Food energy	Protein	Fat	Carbohydrate	Calcium	Phosphorus	Iron	Sodium	Potassium	Vitamin A value	Thiamin	Riboflavin	Niacin	Ascorbic acid
(A)	(B)			(C)	(D)	(E)	(F)	(G)	(H)	(I)	(J)	(K)	(L)	(M)	(N)	(O)	(P)	(Q)
			Grams	*Percent*	*Calories*	*Grams*	*Grams*	*Grams*	*Milligrams*	*Milligrams*	*Milligrams*	*Milligrams*	*Milligrams*	*International units*	*Milligrams*	*Milligrams*	*Milligrams*	*Milligrams*
	Crackers—Continued																	
	Saltines, 1⅞ in. square, ⅛ in. thick (approx. 160 per pound)—Continued																	
	Whole—Continued																	
	Package—Continued																	
b	Net wt., 7–7¼ oz	1 pkg	202	4.3	875	18.2	24.2	144.4	[183] 42	182	[183] 2.4	(2,222)	(242)	(0)	[183] 0.02	[183] 0.08	[183] 2.0	(0)
c	Cracker	10 crackers	28.4	4.3	123	2.6	3.4	20.3	[183] 6	26	[183] .3	(312)	(34)	(0)	[183] Trace	[183] .01	[183] .3	(0)
d	Packet (4 crackers)	1 packet	11	4.3	48	1.0	1.3	8.0	[183] 2	10	[183] .1	(123)	(13)	(0)	[183] Trace	[183] Trace	[183] .1	(0)
e	Crumbed (finely crushed, spooned into cup without packing; approx. 24½ crackers).	1 cup	70	4.3	303	6.3	8.4	50.1	[183] 15	63	[183] .8	(770)	(84)	(0)	[183] .01	[183] .03	[183] .7	(0)
917	Sandwich type, cheese-peanut butter, 1⅝ in. square, ⅜ in. thick, or round, 1⅝-in. diam., ⅜ in. thick:																	
a	Package, net wt., 6 oz., 4 packets (item 917b)	1 pkg	170	2.4	835	25.8	40.6	95.4	95	304	1.0	1,686	384	70	.05	.12	6.0	(0)
b	Packet, net wt., 1½ oz., 6 sandwiches	1 packet	42	2.4	209	6.5	10.2	23.8	24	76	.3	422	96	20	.01	.03	1.5	(0)
c	Packet, net wt., 1 oz., 4 sandwiches	1 packet or 1 oz.	28	2.4	139	4.3	6.8	15.9	16	51	.2	281	64	10	.01	.02	1.0	(0)
d	Pound	1 lb	454	2.4	2,227	68.9	108.4	254.5	254	812	2.7	4,500	1,025	180	.14	.32	15.9	(0)
918	Soda:																	
	Whole:																	
	Biscuit, 2⅜ in. × 2⅛ in., ¼ in. thick (approx. 90 per pound):																	
a	Package, net wt., 3½ oz	1 pkg	99	4.0	435	9.1	13.0	69.9	[183] 22	88	[183] 1.5	1,089	119	(0)	[183] .01	[183] .05	[183] 1.0	(0)
b	Biscuit	10 biscuits	50.4	4.0	221	4.6	6.6	35.6	[183] 11	45	[183] .8	554	60	(0)	[183] .01	[183] .03	[183] .5	(0)
	Regular, 1⅞ in. square, ⅛ in. thick (approx. 160 per pound):																	
c	Package, net wt., 16 oz. (1 lb.)	1 pkg. or 1 lb.[184]	454	4.0	1,991	41.7	59.4	320.2	[183] 100	404	[183] 6.8	4,990	544	(0)	[183] .05	[183] .23	[183] 4.5	(0)
d	Cracker	10 crackers	28.4	4.0	125	2.6	3.7	20.1	[183] 6	25	[183] .4	312	34	(0)	[183] Trace	[183] .01	[183] .3	(0)
	Soup or oyster (hexagon shaped, ½-in. sides, 3⁄16–7⁄16 in. thick, 530–600 per pound; round, ⅞-in. diam. 7⁄16 in. thick, approx. 650 per pound):																	
	Package:																	
e	Net wt., 16 oz. (1 lb.) (hexagon shaped or round).	1 pkg. or 1 lb.	454	4.0	1,991	41.7	59.4	320.2	[183] 100	404	[183] 6.8	4,990	544	(0)	[183] .05	[183] .23	[183] 4.5	(0)
f	Net wt., 5 oz. (hexagon shaped)	1 pkg	142	4.0	623	13.1	18.6	100.3	[183] 31	126	[183] 2.1	1,562	170	(0)	[183] .01	[183] .07	[183] 1.4	(0)
g	Cup	1 cup	45	4.0	198	4.1	5.9	31.8	[183] 10	40	[183] .7	495	54	(0)	[183] Trace	[183] .02	[183] .5	(0)
h	Cracker	10 crackers	7.5	4.0	33	.7	1.0	5.3	[183] 2	7	[183] .1	83	9	(0)	[183] Trace	[183] Trace	[183] .1	(0)
i	Crumbed (approx. 14 biscuits, 25 square crackers, or 1½ cups of oyster crackers).	1 cup	70	4.0	307	6.4	9.2	49.4	[183] 15	62	[183] 1.1	770	84	(0)	[183] .01	[183] .04	[183] .7	(0)
	Cranberries:																	
920	Raw:																	
a	Package, net wt., 16 oz. (1 lb.) (refuse: stems and damaged berries, 4%);[1] yields approx. 4½ cups, whole, or 4 cups, chopped, cranberries.	1 pkg. or 1 lb.	454	87.9	200	1.7	3.0	47.0	61	44	2.2	9	357	170	.13	.09	.4	48
	Cup:																	
b	Whole	1 cup	95	87.9	44	.4	.7	10.3	13	10	.5	2	78	40	.03	.02	.1	10
c	Chopped	1 cup	110	87.9	51	.4	.8	11.9	15	11	.6	2	90	45	.03	.02	.1	12
922	**Cranberry juice cocktail**, bottled (approx. 33% cranberry juice), sweetened with nutritive sweetener:																	
	Container and approx. contents:																	
a	Bottle, net contents, 16 fl. oz. (1 pt.)	1 bottle or 1 pt.	506	83.2	329	.5	.5	83.5	25	15	1.5	5	51	Trace	.05	.05	.2	[185] 81
b	Bottle, net contents, 32 fl. oz. (1 qt.)	1 bottle or 1 qt.	1,012	83.2	658	1.0	1.0	167.0	50	30	3.0	10	101	Trace	.10	.10	.3	[185] 162
c	Cup	1 cup	253	83.2	164	.3	.3	41.7	13	8	.8	3	25	Trace	.03	.03	.1	[185] 40
d	Glass (6 fl. oz.)	1 glass	190	83.2	124	.2	.2	31.4	10	6	.6	2	19	Trace	.02	.02	.1	[185] 30
e	Fluid ounce	1 fl. oz	31.6	83.2	21	Trace	Trace	5.2	2	1	.1	Trace	3	Trace	Trace	Trace	Trace	[185] 5
923	**Cranberry sauce**, sweetened with nutritive sweetener:																	
	Canned, strained:																	
	Can and approx. contents:																	
a	Can, size 300 × 407[14] (No. 300); net wt., 16 oz. (1 lb.).	1 can or 1 lb.	454	62.1	662	.5	.9	170.1	27	18	.9	5	136	90	.05	.05	.2	9

(A)	(B)			(C)	(D)	(E)	(F)	(G)	(H)	(I)	(J)	(K)	(L)	(M)	(N)	(O)	(P)	(Q)
b	Can, size 603 × 700[14] (No. 10); net wt., 117 oz. (7 lb. 5 oz.).	1 can	3,317	62.1	4,843	3.3	6.6	1,243.9	199	133	6.6	33	995	660	0.33	0.33	1.3	66
c	Cup	1 cup	277	62.1	404	.3	.6	103.9	17	11	.6	3	83	60	.03	.03	.1	6
d	Packet, net wt., ½ oz	1 packet	14	62.1	20	Trace	Trace	5.3	1	1	Trace	Trace	4	Trace	Trace	Trace	Trace	Trace
924	Home prepared, unstrained[136]	1 cup	277	53.9	493	.6	.8	126.0	19	14	.6	3	105	60	.03	.03	.3	6
925	Cranberry-orange relish, uncooked[136]	1 cup	275	53.6	490	1.1	1.1	124.9	52	22	1.1	3	198	190	.08	.06	.3	50
	Cream, fluid:																	
928	Half-and-half (cream and milk; 11.7% fat):																	
a	Cup	1 cup	242	79.7	324	7.7	28.3	11.1	261	206	.1	111	312	1,160	.07	.39	.1	2
b	Tablespoon	1 tbsp	15	79.7	20	.5	1.8	.7	16	13	Trace	7	19	70	Trace	.02	Trace	Trace
929	Light, coffee, or table (20.6% fat):																	
a	Cup	1 cup	240	71.5	506	7.2	49.4	10.3	245	192	.1	103	293	2,020	.07	.36	.1	2
b	Tablespoon	1 tbsp	15	71.5	32	.5	3.1	.6	15	12	Trace	6	18	130	Trace	.02	Trace	Trace
930	Light whipping or whipping (31.3% fat):																	
a	Cup	1 cup or approx. 2 cups whipped.	239	62.1	717	6.0	74.8	8.6	203	160	.1	86	244	3,060	.05	.29	.1	2
b	Tablespoon	1 tbsp	15	62.1	45	.4	4.7	.5	13	10	Trace	5	15	190	Trace	.02	Trace	Trace
931	Heavy or heavy whipping (37.6% fat):																	
a	Cup	1 cup or approx. 2 cups whipped.	238	56.6	838	5.2	89.5	7.4	179	140	.1	76	212	3,670	.05	.26	.1	2
b	Tablespoon	1 tbsp	15	56.6	53	.3	5.6	.5	11	9	Trace	5	13	230	Trace	.02	Trace	Trace
934	Cream puffs with custard filling (approx. 3½-in. diam., 2 in. high).[12]	1 cream puff	130	58.3	303	8.5	18.1	26.7	105	148	.9	108	157	460	.05	.22	.1	Trace
	Cress, garden:[137]																	
935	Raw	1 lb	454	89.4	145	11.8	3.2	24.9	367	345	5.9	64	2,749	42,180	.36	1.18	4.5	313
	Cooked (boiled), drained, cooked in—																	
936	Small amount of water, short time:																	
a	Cup	1 cup	135	92.5	31	2.6	.8	5.1	82	65	1.1	[20] 11	477	10,400	.08	.22	1.1	46
b	Pound	1 lb	454	92.5	104	8.6	2.7	17.2	277	218	3.6	[20] 36	1,601	34,930	.27	.73	3.6	154
937	Large amount of water, long time:																	
a	Cup	1 cup	135	92.9	30	2.4	.8	4.9	78	59	.9	[20] 11	443	9,450	.05	.20	.9	31
b	Pound	1 lb	454	92.9	100	8.2	2.7	16.3	263	200	3.2	[20] 36	1,488	31,750	.18	.68	3.2	104
	Cucumbers, raw:																	
942	Not pared:																	
	Whole (refuse: ends, 3%):[1]																	
a	Large, 2⅛-in. diam.,[138] 8¼ in. long (approx. 1½ per pound).	1 cucumber	310	95.1	45	2.7	.3	10.2	75	81	3.3	18	481	750	.09	.12	.6	33
b	Small, 1¾-in. diam.,[138] 6⅜ in. long (approx. 2⅔ per pound).	1 cucumber	175	95.1	25	1.5	.2	5.8	42	46	1.9	10	272	420	.05	.07	.3	19
	Sliced (⅛ in. thick):																	
c	Cup	1 cup	105	95.1	16	.9	.1	3.6	26	28	1.2	6	168	260	03	.04	.2	12
d	Slices (6 from large cucumber (item 942a) or 8 from small cucumber (item 942b); wt., approx. 1 oz.).	6 large or 8 small slices, or 1 oz.	28	95.1	4	.3	Trace	1.0	7	8	.3	2	45	70	01	.01	.1	3
e	Whole (ends removed) and slices	1 lb	454	95.1	68	4.1	.5	15.4	113	122	5.0	27	726	1,130	.14	.18	.9	50
943	Pared:[139]																	
	Whole (dimensions of cucumber before paring):																	
a	Large, 2⅛-in. diam.,[138] 8¼ in. long	1 cucumber	280	95.7	39	1.7	.3	9.0	48	50	.8	17	448	Trace	.08	.11	.6	31
b	Small, 1¾-in. diam.,[138] 6⅜ in. long	1 cucumber	158	95.7	22	.9	.2	5.1	27	28	.5	9	253	Trace	.05	.06	.3	17
	Sliced (⅛ in. thick):																	
c	Cup	1 cup	140	95.7	20	.8	.1	4.5	24	25	.4	8	224	Trace	.04	.06	.3	15
d	Slices (6½ from large cucumber (item 943a) or 9 from small cucumber (item 943b); wt., approx. 1 oz.).	6½ large or 9 small slices, or 1 oz.[130]	28	95.7	4	.2	Trace	.9	5	5	.1	2	45	Trace	.01	.01	.1	3
e	Diced	1 cup	145	95.7	20	.9	.1	4.6	25	26	.4	9	232	Trace	.04	.06	.3	16
f	Pound	1 lb	454	95.7	64	2.7	.5	14.5	77	82	1.4	27	726	Trace	.14	.18	.9	50
	Cucumber pickles. See Pickles (items 1558–1561).																	
947	Cusk, steamed:																	
a	Pound	1 lb	454	74.3	481	106.1	3.2	0	122	1,284	4.5	[43] 336	1,751	—	.14	.45	12.2	—
b	Ounce	1 oz	28	74.3	30	6.6	.2	0	8	80	.3	[43] 21	109	—	.01	.03	.8	—

[1] Measure and weight apply to food as it is described with inedible part or parts (refuse) included.

[12] For information on ingredients used, see ARS 62–13 (7), table 18, pp. 22–23.

[14] Dimensions of can: 1st dimension represents diameter; 2d dimension, height of can. 1st or left-hand digit in each dimension gives number of whole inches; next 2 digits give additional fraction of dimension expressed as 16th of an inch.

[20] Value is for unsalted product. If salt is used, increase value by 236 mg. per 100 g. of vegetable—an estimated figure based on typical amount of salt (0.6%) in canned vegetables. See also Appendix C, section on Cooked Vegetables

[43] Value for product without added salt.

[130] Use also for 1 oz. of other form or forms listed for this item.

[133] Based on product made with unenriched flour.

[134] Use also for 1 lb. of biscuit-type crackers or 1 lb. of crumbed crackers.

[135] Value listed is based on product with label stating 30 mg. per 6-fl. oz. serving.

[136] For information on ingredients used, see ARS 62–13 (7), table 26, p. 32.

[137] Refers to cultivated plant *Lepedium sativum*. Owing to its habit of getting out of bounds and growing wild, it is sometimes called fieldcress. Other native wild species of *Lepidium*, such as *L. virginicum*, are sometimes eaten but are not available on the market.

[138] Diameter at widest part.

[139] Split-knife peeler used.

TABLE 1.—*Nutritive values for household measures and market units of foods*—Continued

[Item numbers correspond to those in table 1 of Handbook No. 8, revised 1963. Values in parentheses denote imputed values usually from another form of the food or from a similar food. Zeros in parentheses indicate that amount of a constituent, if present, is probably too small to be measured. Dashes (—) denote lack of reliable data for a constituent believed to be present in a measurable amount. Calculated values, as those based on a recipe, are not in parentheses]

Item No.	Food, approximate measures, units, and weight (edible part unless footnotes indicate otherwise)			Water	Food energy	Protein	Fat	Carbohydrate	Calcium	Phosphorus	Iron	Sodium	Potassium	Vitamin A value	Thiamin	Riboflavin	Niacin	Ascorbic acid
(A)	(B)			(C)	(D)	(E)	(F)	(G)	(H)	(I)	(J)	(K)	(L)	(M)	(N)	(O)	(P)	(Q)
			Grams	Percent	Calories	Grams	Grams	Grams	Milligrams	Milligrams	Milligrams	Milligrams	Milligrams	International units	Milligrams	Milligrams	Milligrams	Milligrams
948	**Custard, baked** [12 13]	1 cup	265	77.2	305	14.3	14.6	29.4	297	310	1.1	209	387	930	0.11	0.50	0.3	1
	Custard, frozen. See Ice cream (items 1139, 1141).																	
949	**Custard-apple,** bullock's-heart, raw (refuse: skin and seeds, 42%).[1]	1 lb	454	71.5	266	4.5	1.6	66.3	71	53	2.1	—	—	Trace	.21	.26	1.3	58
	Dandelion greens:																	
950	Raw	1 lb	454	85.6	204	12.2	3.2	41.7	848	299	14.1	345	1,801	63,500	.86	1.18	—	159
951	Cooked (boiled), drained:																	
a	Cup, greens not pressed down (approx. ½ cup, greens pressed down).	1 cup	105	89.8	35	2.1	.6	6.7	147	44	1.9	[20] 46	244	12,290	.14	.17	—	19
b	Pound	1 lb	454	89.8	150	9.1	2.7	29.0	635	191	8.2	[20] 200	1,052	53,070	.59	.73	—	82
	Danish pastry. See Rolls and buns (item 1899).																	
952	**Dates, moisturized or hydrated:**																	
	Whole:																	
	With pits (refuse: pits, 13%):[1]																	
a	Container, net wt., 12 oz	1 container	340	22.5	810	6.5	1.5	215.6	175	186	8.9	3	1,917	150	.27	.30	6.5	0
b	10 dates	10 dates	92	22.5	219	1.8	.4	58.3	47	50	2.4	1	518	40	.07	.08	1.8	0
c	Pound	1 lb	454	22.5	1,081	8.7	2.0	287.7	233	249	11.8	4	2,557	200	.36	.39	8.7	0
	Without pits:																	
d	Container, net wt., 8 oz	1 container	227	22.5	622	5.0	1.1	165.5	134	143	6.8	2	1,471	110	.20	.23	5.0	0
e	Container, net wt., 10 oz	1 container	284	22.5	778	6.2	1.4	207.0	168	179	8.5	3	1,840	140	.26	.28	6.2	0
f	Container, net wt., 16 oz. (1 lb.)	1 container or 1 lb.	454	22.5	1,243	10.0	2.3	330.7	268	286	13.6	5	2,939	230	.41	.45	10.0	0
g	10 dates	10 dates	80	22.5	219	1.8	.4	58.3	47	50	2.4	1	518	40	.07	.08	1.8	0
h	Chopped	1 cup	178	22.5	488	3.9	.9	129.8	105	112	5.3	2	1,153	90	.16	.18	3.9	0
	Deviled ham. See Sausage, cold cuts, and luncheon meats (item 1993).																	
	Dewberries. See Blackberries (item 417).																	
	Doughnuts:																	
957	Cake type, plain:																	
a	3⅝-in. diam., 1¼ in. high; wt., approx. 2 oz	1 doughnut	58	23.7	227	2.7	10.8	29.8	23	110	[190] .8	291	52	50	[190] .09	[190] .09	[190] .7	Trace
b	3¼-in. diam., 1 in. high; wt., approx. 1½ oz	1 doughnut	42	23.7	164	1.9	7.8	21.6	17	80	[191] .6	210	38	30	[191] .07	[191] .07	[191] .5	Trace
c	2½-in. diam., 1 in. high; wt., approx. ⅞ oz	1 doughnut	25	23.7	98	1.2	4.7	12.9	10	48	[192] .4	125	23	20	[192] .04	[192] .04	[192] .3	Trace
d	1½-in. diam., ¾ in. high; wt., approx. ½ oz	1 doughnut	14	23.7	55	.6	2.6	7.2	6	27	[193] .2	70	13	10	[193] .02	[193] .02	[193] .2	Trace
958	Yeast leavened, plain, 3¾-in. diam., 1¼ in. high; wt., approx. 1½ oz.[194]	1 doughnut	42	28.3	176	2.7	11.3	16.0	16	32	[195] .6	99	34	30	[195] .07	[195] .07	[195] .6	0
965	**Eclairs** with custard filling and chocolate icing (approx. 5 in. long, 2 in. wide, 1¾ in. high).[13]	1 eclair	100	56.2	239	6.2	13.6	23.2	80	112	.7	82	122	340	.04	.16	.1	Trace
	Eggs:																	
	Chicken:																	
	Raw:																	
968	Whole, fresh:																	
	Egg:																	
a	Extra large, 27 oz. per dozen[196] (refuse: shell, 10%).[1]	1 egg	64	73.7	94	7.4	6.6	.5	31	118	1.3	70	74	680	.06	.17	Trace	0
b	Large, 24 oz. per dozen[196] (refuse: shell, 12%).[1]	1 egg	57	73.7	82	6.5	5.8	.5	27	103	1.2	61	65	590	.05	.15	Trace	0
c	Medium, 21 oz. per dozen[196] (refuse: shell, 12%).[1]	1 egg	50	73.7	72	5.7	5.1	.4	24	90	1.0	54	57	520	.05	.13	Trace	0
d	Cup (approx. 4¼ extra large eggs, 4⅞ large, or 5½ medium).	1 cup	243	73.7	396	31.3	27.9	2.2	131	498	5.6	296	313	2,870	.26	.72	.1	0
e	Pound (approx. 8 extra large eggs, 9 large, or 10 medium).	1 lb	454	73.7	739	58.5	52.2	4.1	245	930	10.4	553	585	5,350	.48	1.35	.3	0
969	Whites, fresh:																	
	Egg white of—																	
a	Extra large egg	1 white	38	87.6	19	4.1	Trace	.3	3	6	Trace	55	53	0	Trace	.10	Trace	0
b	Large egg	1 white	33	87.6	17	3.6	Trace	.3	3	5	Trace	48	46	0	Trace	.09	Trace	0
c	Medium egg	1 white	29	87.6	15	3.2	Trace	.2	3	4	Trace	42	40	0	Trace	.08	Trace	0
d	Cup (egg whites of approx. 6.4 extra large eggs, 7.4 large, or 8.4 medium).	1 cup	243	87.6	124	26.5	.1	1.9	22	36	.2	355	338	0	.01	.66	.2	0
e	Pound (egg whites of approx. 12 extra large eggs, 13.7 large, or 15.6 medium).	1 lb	454	87.6	231	49.4	.1	3.6	41	68	.5	662	631	0	.02	1.23	.5	0

(A)	(B)			(C)	(D)	(E)	(F)	(G)	(H)	(I)	(J)	(K)	(L)	(M)	(N)	(O)	(P)	(Q)
970	Yolks, fresh: [197]																	
	Egg yolk of—																	
a	Extra large egg	1 yolk	19	51.1	66	3.0	5.8	0.1	27	108	1.0	10	19	650	0.04	0.08	Trace	0
b	Large egg	1 yolk	17	51.1	59	2.7	5.2	.1	24	97	.9	9	17	580	.04	.07	Trace	0
c	Medium egg	1 yolk	15	51.1	52	2.4	4.6	.1	21	85	.8	8	15	510	.03	.07	Trace	0
d	Cup (egg yolks of approx. 12.8 extra large eggs, 14.3 large, or 16.2 medium).	1 cup	243	51.1	846	38.9	74.4	1.5	343	1,383	13.4	126	238	8,260	.54	1.07	0.1	0
e	Pound (egg yolks of approx. 24 extra large eggs, 26.7 large, or 30.2 medium).	1 lb	454	51.1	1,579	72.6	138.8	2.7	640	2,581	24.9	236	445	15,420	1.02	2.00	.2	0
	Cooked:																	
973	Fried: [51]																	
	Egg, prepared using—																	
a	Extra large egg	1 egg	52	67.7	112	7.2	8.9	.2	31	115	1.2	176	73	740	.05	.16	Trace	0
b	Large egg	1 egg	46	67.7	99	6.3	7.9	.1	28	102	1.1	155	64	650	.05	.14	Trace	0
c	Medium egg	1 egg	40	67.7	86	5.5	6.9	.1	24	89	1.0	135	56	570	.04	.12	Trace	0
d	Pound (yield from approx. 8¾ extra large eggs, 10 large, or 11⅓ medium).	1 lb	454	67.7	980	62.6	78.0	1.4	272	1,007	10.9	1,533	635	6,440	.45	1.36	.3	0
974	Hard cooked:																	
	Egg, prepared using—																	
a	Extra large egg (refuse: shell, 10%) [1]	1 egg	64	73.7	94	7.4	6.6	.5	31	118	1.3	70	74	680	.05	.16	Trace	0
b	Large egg (refuse: shell, 12%) [1]	1 egg	57	73.7	82	6.5	5.8	.5	27	103	1.2	61	65	590	.04	.14	Trace	0
c	Medium egg (refuse: shell, 12%) [1]	1 egg	50	73.7	72	5.7	5.1	.4	24	90	1.0	54	57	520	.04	.12	Trace	0
d	Cup, chopped (approx. 2.4 extra large eggs, 2.7 large, or 3 medium).	1 cup	136	73.7	222	17.5	15.6	1.2	73	279	3.1	166	175	1,600	.12	.38	.1	0
e	Pound (whole, approx. 8 extra large eggs, 9 large, or 10 medium; chopped, approx. 3⅓ cups).	1 lb	454	73.7	739	58.5	52.2	4.1	245	930	10.4	553	585	5,350	.41	1.27	.3	0
975	Omelet.[51] Use scrambled eggs (items 977a, 977b, 977c, 977e).[198]																	
976	Poached: [51]																	
	Egg, prepared using —																	
a	Extra large egg	1 egg	57	73.3	94	7.4	6.6	.5	31	118	1.3	154	74	680	.05	.14	Trace	0
b	Large egg	1 egg	50	73.3	82	6.5	5.8	.5	27	103	1.2	136	65	590	.04	.13	Trace	0
c	Medium egg	1 egg	44	73.3	72	5.7	5.1	.4	24	90	1.0	119	57	520	.04	.11	Trace	0
d	Pound (approx. 8 extra large eggs, 9 large, or 10 medium).	1 lb	454	73.3	739	58.5	52.2	3.6	249	930	10.4	1,229	585	5,350	.36	1.13	.3	0
977	Scrambled: [51]																	
	Prepared using—																	
a	Extra large egg	1 egg	73	72.1	126	8.2	9.4	1.8	58	138	1.2	188	107	790	.06	.20	Trace	0
b	Large egg	1 egg	64	72.1	111	7.2	8.3	1.5	51	121	1.1	164	93	690	.05	.18	Trace	0
c	Medium egg	1 egg	56	72.1	97	6.3	7.2	1.3	45	106	1.0	144	82	600	.04	.16	Trace	0
d	Cup (yield from approx. 3 extra large eggs, 3.4 large, or 3.8 medium).	1 cup	220	72.1	381	24.6	28.4	5.3	176	416	3.7	565	321	2,380	.18	.62	.2	0
e	Pound (yield from approx. 6.2 extra large eggs, 7 large, or 7.8 medium).	1 lb	454	72.1	785	50.8	58.5	10.9	363	857	7.7	1,166	662	4,900	.36	1.27	.3	0
983	Duck, whole, fresh, raw:																	
a	Egg (refuse: shell, 12%) [1]	1 egg	80	70.4	134	9.4	10.2	.5	39	137	2.0	(86)	(91)	870	.13	(.21)	.1	0
b	Pound (approx. 6½ eggs (item 983a))	1 lb	454	70.4	866	60.3	65.8	3.2	254	885	12.7	(553)	(585)	5,580	.82	(1.36)	.5	0
984	Goose, whole, fresh, raw:																	
a	Egg (refuse: shell, 13%) [1]	1 egg	165	70.4	266	20.0	19.1	1.9	—	—	—	—	—	—	—	—	—	—
b	Pound (approx. 3⅛ eggs (item 984a))	1 lb	454	70.4	839	63.1	60.3	5.9	—	—	—	—	—	—	—	—	—	—
985	Turkey, whole, fresh, raw:																	
a	Egg (refuse: shell, 12%) [1]	1 egg	90	72.6	135	10.4	9.3	1.3	—	—	—	—	—	—	—	—	Trace	—
b	Pound (approx. 5.7 eggs (item 985a))	1 lb	454	72.6	771	59.4	53.5	7.7	—	—	—	—	—	—	—	—	.1	—
987	**Eggplant**, cooked (boiled), drained:																	
a	Cup, diced	1 cup	200	94.3	38	2.0	.4	8.2	22	42	1.2	[20] 2	300	20	.10	.08	1.0	6
b	Pound	1 lb	454	94.3	86	4.5	.9	18.6	50	95	2.7	[20] 5	680	50	.23	.18	2.3	14
989	**Endive** (curly endive and escarole), raw: [135]																	
a	Cup, cut or broken into small pieces	1 cup	50	93.1	10	.9	.1	2.1	41	27	.9	7	147	1,650	.04	.07	.3	5
b	Pound	1 lb	454	93.1	91	7.7	.5	18.6	367	245	7.7	64	1,334	14,970	.32	.64	2.3	45

[1] Measure and weight apply to food as it is described with inedible part or parts (refuse) included.

[12] Cup measure made on product after it had cooled. See also Appendix B, section on Home-Prepared Foods

[13] For information on ingredients used, see ARS 62-13 (7), table 18, pp. 22-23.

[20] Value is for unsalted product. If salt is used, increase value by 236 mg. per 100 g. of vegetable—an estimated figure based on typical amount of salt (0.6%) in canned vegetables. See also Appendix C, section on Cooked Vegetables

[51] For information on ingredients used in preparation, see ARS 62-13 (7), table 22, p. 26.

[135] Chicory and endive have often been confused with each other. For further description of these products, see Appendix C, section on Chicory and Endive

[190] Based on product made with enriched flour. With unenriched flour, approx. values are iron 0.3 mg., thiamin 0.02 mg., riboflavin 0.04 mg., niacin 0.2 mg.

[191] Based on product made with enriched flour. With unenriched flour, approx. values are iron 0.2 mg., thiamin 0.01 mg., riboflavin 0.03 mg., niacin 0.1 mg.

[192] Based on product made with enriched flour. With unenriched flour, approx. values are iron 0.1 mg., thiamin 0.01 mg., riboflavin 0.02 mg., niacin 0.1 mg.

[193] Based on product made with enriched flour. With unenriched flour, approx. values are iron 0.1 mg., thiamin trace, riboflavin 0.01 mg., niacin trace.

[194] For nutritive values of glazed doughnuts made with enriched flour, see Appendix A, table 3, p. 264.

[195] Based on product made with enriched flour. With unenriched flour, approx. values per doughnut are iron 0.3 mg., thiamin 0.02 mg., riboflavin 0.03 mg., niacin 0.2 mg.

[196] Represents minimum weight per dozen required by Federal regulations governing weight classes of shell eggs (*13*). For minimum weights to use for weight classes, see Appendix B, section on Eggs

[197] Fresh yolks include small proportion of white.

[198] In Agr. Handb. No. 8, rev. 1963, nutritive values shown for 100 g. of omelet are same as those shown for 100 g. of scrambled eggs.

TABLE 1.—*Nutritive values for household measures and market units of foods*—Continued

[Item numbers correspond to those in table 1 of Handbook No. 8, revised 1963. Values in parentheses denote imputed values usually from another form of the food or from a similar food. Zeros in parentheses indicate that amount of a constituent, if present, is probably too small to be measured. Dashes (—) denote lack of reliable data for a constituent believed to be present in a measurable amount. Calculated values, as those based on a recipe, are not in parentheses]

Item No. (A)	Food, approximate measures, units, and weight (edible part unless footnotes indicate otherwise) (B)			Water (C)	Food energy (D)	Protein (E)	Fat (F)	Carbohydrate (G)	Calcium (H)	Phosphorus (I)	Iron (J)	Sodium (K)	Potassium (L)	Vitamin A value (M)	Thiamin (N)	Riboflavin (O)	Niacin (P)	Ascorbic acid (Q)
			Grams	Percent	Calories	Grams	Grams	Grams	Milligrams	Milligrams	Milligrams	Milligrams	Milligrams	International units	Milligrams	Milligrams	Milligrams	Milligrams
	Escarole, raw. See Endive (item 989).																	
	Farina:[156]																	
	Enriched:																	
	Regular (about 15 min. cooking time):																	
991	Dry form	1 cup	180	10.3	668	20.5	1.6	138.6	45	193	([200])	4	149	(0)	[157] 0.79	[157] 0.47	[157] 6.3	(0)
992	Cooked	1 cup	245	89.5	103	3.2	.2	21.3	10	29	([200])	353	22	(0)	[157].10	[157].07	[157] 1.0	(0)
	Quick cooking (about 2–5 min. cooking time):																	
993	Dry form	1 cup	180	10.3	652	20.5	1.6	134.8	900	[199] 1,010	([200])	[201] 450	149	(0)	[157].79	[157].47	[157] 6.3	(0)
994	Cooked	1 cup	245	89.0	105	3.2	.2	21.8	147	[199] 162	([200])	[202] 466	25	(0)	[157].12	[157].07	[157] 1.0	(0)
	Instant cooking (about ½ min. cooking time):																	
995	Dry form	1 cup	190	10.3	688	21.7	1.7	142.3	950	752	([203])	13	158	(0)	[157].84	[157].49	[157] 6.7	(0)
996	Cooked	1 cup	245	85.9	135	4.2	.2	27.9	189	147	([203])	461	32	(0)	[157].17	[157].10	[157] 1.2	(0)
	Unenriched, regular (about 15 min. cooking time):																	
997	Dry form	1 cup	180	10.3	668	20.5	1.6	138.6	45	193	2.7	4	149	(0)	.11	.18	1.3	(0)
998	Cooked	1 cup	245	89.5	103	3.2	.2	21.3	10	29	.5	353	22	(0)	.02	.02	.2	(0)
999	**Fats**, cooking (vegetable fat, mixed fat shortenings):[204]																	
	Container and approx. contents:																	
a	Can, net wt., 16 oz. (1 lb.)	1 can or 1 lb.	454	0	4,010	0	453.6	0	0	0	0	0	0	—	0	0	0	0
b	Can, net wt., 48 oz. (3 lb.)	1 can	1,361	0	12,031	0	1,361.0	0	0	0	0	0	0	—	0	0	0	0
c	Cup	1 cup	200	0	1,768	0	200.0	0	0	0	0	0	0	—	0	0	0	0
d	Tablespoon	1 tbsp	12.5	0	111	0	12.5	0	0	0	0	0	0	—	0	0	0	0
	Figs:																	
1001	Raw:																	
	Whole:																	
a	Large, 2½-in. diam. (approx. 7 per pound)	1 fig	65	77.5	52	.8	.2	13.2	23	14	.4	1	126	50	.04	.03	.3	1
b	Medium, 2¼-in. diam. (approx. 9 per pound)	1 fig	50	77.5	40	.6	.2	10.2	18	11	.3	1	97	40	.03	.03	.2	1
c	Small, 1½-in. diam. (approx. 11 per pound)	1 fig	40	77.5	32	.5	.1	8.1	14	9	.2	1	78	30	.02	.02	.2	1
	Canned, solids and liquid; whole style:																	
1003	Water pack, without artificial sweetener:																	
	Can and approx. contents:																	
a	Size, 303 × 406[14] (No. 303); net wt., 16 oz. (1 lb.); 12–20 figs and approx. 9½ tbsp. of drained liquid.	1 can or 1 lb.	454	86.6	218	2.3	.9	56.2	64	64	1.8	9	703	140	.14	.14	.9	5
b	Cup	1 cup	248	86.6	119	1.2	.5	30.8	35	35	1.0	5	384	70	.07	.07	.5	2
c	Figs with drained liquid	3 figs; 1¾ tbsp. liquid.	80	86.6	38	.4	.2	9.9	11	11	.3	2	124	20	.02	.02	.2	1
1005	Sirup pack, heavy:																	
	Can and approx. contents:																	
a	Size, 211 × 304[14] (8Z Tall, Buffet); net wt., 8¾ oz.; 6–12 figs and approx. 5 tbsp. of drained liquid.	1 can	248	77.2	208	1.2	.5	54.1	32	32	1.0	5	370	70	.07	.07	.5	2
b	Size, 303 × 406[14] (No. 303); net wt., 17 oz. (1 lb. 1 oz.); 12–20 figs and approx. 10 tbsp. of drained liquid.	1 can	482	77.2	405	2.4	1.0	105.1	63	63	1.9	10	718	140	.14	.14	1.0	5
c	Cup	1 cup	259	77.2	218	1.3	.5	56.5	34	34	1.0	5	386	80	.08	.08	.5	3
d	Pound	1 lb	454	77.2	381	2.3	.9	98.9	59	59	1.8	9	676	140	.14	.14	.9	5
e	Figs with drained liquid	3 figs; 1¾ tbsp. liquid.	85	77.2	71	.4	.2	18.5	11	11	.3	2	127	30	.03	.03	.2	1
1008	**Filberts** (hazelnuts):[5]																	
	In shell (refuse: shells, 54%):[1]																	
a	Pound (yields approx. 7⅓ oz., shelled nuts)	1 lb	454	5.8	1,323	26.3	130.2	34.9	436	703	7.1	4	1,469	—	.96	—	1.9	Trace
b	10 nuts	10 nuts	30	5.8	87	1.7	8.6	2.3	29	47	.5	Trace	97	—	.06	—	.1	Trace
	Shelled:																	
c	Whole	1 cup	135	5.8	856	17.0	84.2	22.5	282	455	4.6	3	950	—	.62	—	1.2	Trace
	Chopped:																	
d	Cup	1 cup	115	5.8	729	14.5	71.8	19.2	240	388	3.9	2	810	—	.53	—	1.0	Trace
e	Tablespoon	1 tbsp	7	5.8	44	.9	4.4	1.2	15	24	.2	Trace	49	—	.03	—	.1	Trace
f	Ground	1 cup	75	5.8	476	9.5	46.8	12.5	157	253	2.6	2	528	—	.35	—	.7	Trace
g	Pound (yield from approx. 2¼ lb., in shell)	1 lb	454	5.8	2,876	57.2	283.0	75.8	948	1,529	15.4	9	3,193	—	2.09	—	4.1	Trace

(A)	(B)		(C)	(D)	(E)	(F)	(G)	(H)	(I)	(J)	(K)	(L)	(M)	(N)	(O)	(P)	(Q)
h	Ounce (approx. 20 nuts)	1 oz	28	5.8	180	3.6	17.7	4.7	59	96	1.0	1	200	—	0.13	—	0.3	Trace
	Fish. See individual kinds; Cod, etc.																	
	Fishcakes, cooked:																	
1010	Fried: [205]																	
	Regular or bite size:																	
a	Cake, regular size, 3-in. diam., ⅝ in. thick, or 2½-in. diam., ⅞ in. thick; bite size, 1¼-in. diam., ⅝ in. thick.	1 regular-size cake or 5 bite-size cakes.	60	66.0	103	8.8	4.8	5.6	—	—	—	—	—	—	—	—	—	—
b	All sizes	1 lb	454	66.0	780	66.7	36.3	42.2	—	—	—	—	—	—	—	—	—	—
1011	Frozen:																	
	Regular or bite size:																	
a	Cake, regular size, 3-in. diam., ⅝ in. thick, or 2½-in. diam., ⅞ in. thick; bite size, 1¼-in. diam., ⅝ in. thick.	1 regular-size cake or 5 bite-size cakes.	60	52.9	162	5.5	10.7	10.3	—	—	—	—	—	—	—	—	—	—
b	All sizes	1 lb	454	52.9	1,225	41.7	81.2	78.0	—	—	—	—	—	—	—	—	—	—
1012	**Fish flakes,** canned, solids and liquid:																	
	Can and approx. contents:																	
a	Size, 307 × 113 [14] (No. ½); net wt., 7 oz	1 can	198	72.1	220	48.9	1.2	0	97	459	1.6	—	—	—	—	—	—	—
b	Cup	1 cup	165	72.1	183	40.8	1.0	0	81	383	1.3	—	—	—	—	—	—	—
c	Pound	1 lb	454	72.1	503	112.0	2.7	0	222	1,052	3.6	—	—	—	—	—	—	—
1016	**Fish loaf,** cooked, 8¾ × 4⅛ × 2½ in.: [206]																	
a	Whole	1 loaf	1,215	72.2	1,507	171.3	45.0	88.7	—	—	—	—	—	—	—	—	—	—
b	Slice, 4⅛ × 2½ × 1 in.; ⅛ of loaf	1 slice	150	72.2	186	21.2	5.6	11.0	—	—	—	—	—	—	—	—	—	—
c	Pound	1 lb	454	72.2	562	64.0	16.8	33.1	—	—	—	—	—	—	—	—	—	—
1017	**Fish sticks,** breaded, cooked, frozen, 4 × 1 × ½ in.; wt., 1 oz.:																	
	Container and approx. contents:																	
a	Container, net wt., 16 oz. (1 lb.); approx. 16 fish sticks.	1 container or 1 lb.	454	65.8	798	75.3	40.4	29.5	50	758	1.8	—	—	0	.18	0.32	7.3	—
b	Container, net wt., 8 oz.; approx. 8 fish sticks	1 container	227	65.8	400	37.7	20.2	14.8	25	379	.9	—	—	0	.09	.16	3.6	—
c	Fish stick	1 fish stick or 1 oz.	28	65.8	50	4.7	2.5	1.8	3	47	.1	—	—	0	.01	.02	.5	—
1019	**Flounder,** baked with butter or margarine:																	
a	Fillet, 8¼ in. long, 2¾ in. wide, ¼ in. thick [40]	1 fillet	100	58.1	202	30.0	8.2	0	23	344	1.4	[43] 237	587	—	.07	.08	2.5	2
b	Fillet, 6 in. long, 2½ in. wide, ¼ in. thick [40]	1 fillet	57	58.1	115	17.1	4.7	0	13	196	.8	[43] 135	335	—	.04	.05	1.4	1
c	Pound	1 lb	454	58.1	916	136.1	37.2	0	104	1,560	6.4	[43] 1,075	2,663	—	.32	.36	11.3	9
d	Ounce	1 oz	28	58.1	57	8.5	2.3	0	7	98	.4	[43] 67	166	—	.02	.02	.7	1
	Flour. See Corn, Rye, Soybean, Wheat.																	
	Frankfurters. See Sausage, cold cuts, and luncheon meats (items 1994–2000).																	
	Frostings. See Cake icings prepared from home recipes (items 570–574) and Cake icings prepared from mixes (items 576, 578–579).																	
	Frozen custard. See Ice cream (items 1139, 1141).																	
	Fruit cocktail, canned, solids and liquid:																	
1021	Water pack, without artificial sweetener:																	
	Can and approx. contents:																	
a	Size, 211 × 304 [14] (8Z Tall, Buffet); net wt., 8 oz.	1 can	227	89.6	84	.9	.2	22.0	20	30	.9	11	381	340	.05	.02	1.1	5
b	Size, 303 × 406 [14] (No. 303); net wt., 16 oz. (1 lb.).	1 can or 1 lb.	454	89.6	168	1.8	.5	44.0	41	59	1.8	23	762	680	.09	.05	2.3	9
c	Cup	1 cup	245	89.6	91	1.0	.2	23.8	22	32	1.0	12	412	370	.05	.02	1.2	5
1023	Sirup pack, heavy:																	
	Can and approx. contents:																	
a	Size, 303 × 406 [14] (No. 303); net wt., 17 oz. (1 lb. 1 oz.).	1 can	482	79.6	366	1.9	.5	95.0	43	58	1.9	24	776	670	.10	.05	1.9	10

[1] Measure and weight apply to food as it is described with inedible part or parts (refuse) included.

[5] Most of phosphorus in nuts, legumes, and outer layers of cereal grains is present as phytic acid. See also Appendix D, section on Minerals and Oxalic Acid

[14] Dimensions of can: 1st dimension represents diameter; 2d dimension, height of can. 1st or left-hand digit in each dimension gives number of whole inches; next 2 digits give additional fraction of dimension expressed as 16th of an inch.

[40] Width at widest part; thickness at thickest part.

[43] Value for product without added salt.

[156] For dry form of cereal, weight per cup is based on method of pouring cereal from container into measuring cup with as little fall as possible, then leveling with straight edge. See also Appendix B, section on Nonliquid Foods and section on Breakfast-Type Cereals

For cooked cereal, weight per cup represents hot cereal immediately after cooking and is based on specific proportion of cereal and water in cooked product. See ARS 62–13 (7), section on Alimentary Pastes and Other Cereal Products, pp. 6–7, and table 3, p. 9.

[157] Based on product with minimum level of enrichment. See also Appendix C, section on Enriched Foods and Standards of Enrichment

[199] Applies to product containing disodium phosphate. Without disodium phosphate, values per 100 g. are 396 mg. for dry form (item 993), 46 mg., cooked (item 994); values per cup are 713 mg. for dry form (item 993), 113 mg., cooked (item 994). Values for cooked form are about the same whether salt is or is not added during cooking.

[200] If label claim for dry form (items 991, 993) is 12.0 mg. per ounce, equivalent to approx. 42.4 mg. per 100 g. and corresponding to 5 mg. per 100 g., cooked; values per cup are 76.3 mg. for dry form (items 991, 993) and 12.3 mg., cooked (items 992, 994). If label claim for dry form of quick-cooking farina is approx. 0.8 mg. per ounce and based on minimum level of enrichment, equivalent to 2.9 mg. per 100 g. and corresponding to 0.3 mg. per 100 g., cooked (item 994); values per cup are 5.2 mg. for dry form (item 993) and 0.7 mg., cooked (item 994).

[201] Applies to product containing disodium phosphate. Without disodium phosphate, value is 7 mg. per 100 g., 13 mg. per cup.

[202] Applies to product containing disodium phosphate, cooked with salt added as specified by manufacturers, and is based on revised value of 190 mg. per 100 g. Without disodium phosphate and cooked with salt added, value is 162 mg. per 100 g., 397 mg. per cup. If cooked without added salt, value for product with disodium phosphate is 29 mg. per 100 g., 71 mg. per cup; without disodium phosphate, 1 mg. per 100 g., 2 mg. per cup.

[203] Based on label claim of 12.0 mg. per ounce for dry form, equivalent to 42.4 mg. per 100 g. and corresponding to 6.4 mg. per 100 g., cooked; values per cup are 80.6 mg. for dry form (item 995) and 15.7 mg. for cooked form (item 996).

[204] Weights of volume measures do not apply to whipped type.

[205] Prepared with canned flaked fish, potato, and egg.

[206] Prepared with canned flaked fish, bread cubes, eggs, tomatoes, onion, and butter or margarine.

TABLE 1.—*Nutritive values for household measures and market units of foods*—Continued

[Item numbers correspond to those in table 1 of Handbook No. 8, revised 1963. Values in parentheses denote imputed values usually from another form of the food or from a similar food. Zeros in parentheses indicate that amount of a constituent, if present, is probably too small to be measured. Dashes (—) denote lack of reliable data for a constituent believed to be present in a measurable amount. Calculated values, as those based on a recipe, are not in parentheses]

Item No.	Food, approximate measures, units, and weight (edible part unless footnotes indicate otherwise)			Water	Food energy	Protein	Fat	Carbohydrate	Calcium	Phosphorus	Iron	Sodium	Potassium	Vitamin A value	Thiamin	Riboflavin	Niacin	Ascorbic acid
				Values for edible part of foods														
(A)	(B)			(C)	(D)	(E)	(F)	(G)	(H)	(I)	(J)	(K)	(L)	(M)	(N)	(O)	(P)	(Q)
			Grams	*Percent*	*Calories*	*Grams*	*Grams*	*Grams*	*Milligrams*	*Milligrams*	*Milligrams*	*Milligrams*	*Milligrams*	*International units*	*Milligrams*	*Milligrams*	*Milligrams*	*Milligrams*
	Fruit cocktail, canned, solids and liquid—Continued																	
	Sirup pack, heavy—Continued																	
	Can and approx. contents—Continued																	
b	Size, 401 × 411 [14] (No. 2½); net wt., 30 oz. (1 lb. 14 oz.).	1 can	851	79.6	647	3.4	0.9	167.6	77	102	3.4	43	1,370	1,190	0.17	0.09	3.4	17
c	Size, 603 × 700 [14] (No. 10); net wt., 108 oz. (6 lb. 12 oz.).	1 can	3,062	79.6	2,327	12.2	3.1	603.2	276	367	12.2	153	4,930	4,290	.61	.31	12.2	61
d	Cup	1 cup	255	79.6	194	1.0	.3	50.2	23	31	1.0	13	411	360	.05	.08	1.0	5
e	Pound	1 lb	454	79.6	345	1.8	.5	89.4	41	54	1.8	23	730	640	.09	.05	1.8	9
	Fruit salad, canned, solids and liquid:																	
1025	Water pack, without artificial sweetener:																	
	Can and approx. contents:																	
a	Size, 211 × 304 [14] (8Z Tall, Buffet); net wt., 8 oz.	1 can	227	90.1	79	.9	.2	20.7	18	25	.7	2	316	1,070	.02	.07	1.4	7
b	Size, 303 × 406 [14] (No. 303); net wt., 16 oz. (1 lb.).	1 can or 1 lb.	454	90.1	159	1.8	.5	41.3	36	50	1.4	5	631	2,130	.05	.14	2.7	14
c	Cup	1 cup	245	90.1	86	1.0	.2	22.3	20	27	.7	2	341	1,150	.02	.07	1.5	7
1027	Sirup pack, heavy:																	
	Can and approx. contents:																	
a	Size, 211 × 304 [14] (8Z Tall, Buffet); net wt., 8¾ oz.	1 can	248	80.0	186	.7	.2	48.1	20	27	.7	2	332	1,120	.02	.07	1.5	5
b	Size, 303 × 406 [14] (No. 303); net wt., 17 oz. (1 lb. 1 oz.).	1 can	482	80.0	362	1.4	.5	93.5	39	53	1.4	5	646	2,170	.05	.14	2.9	10
c	Size, 603 × 700 [14] (No. 10); net wt., 108 oz. (6 lb. 12 oz.).	1 can	3,062	80.0	2,297	9.2	3.1	594.0	245	337	9.2	31	4,103	13,780	.31	.92	18.4	61
d	Cup	1 cup	255	80.0	191	.8	.3	49.5	20	28	.8	3	342	1,150	.03	.08	1.5	5
e	Pound	1 lb	454	80.0	340	1.4	.5	88.0	36	50	1.4	5	608	2,040	.05	.14	2.7	9
	Garbanzos. See Chickpeas (item 753).																	
1029	**Garlic,** cloves, raw (clove, approx. 1¼ × ⅝ × ⅜ in.).	1 clove	3	61.3	4	.2	Trace	.9	1	6	Trace	1	16	Trace	.01	Trace	Trace	Trace
1030	**Gelatin, dry:**																	
	Prepackaged forms:																	
	Envelope (wt., 7 g.):																	
	Package and approx. contents:																	
a	Size, net wt., 8 oz. (32 envelopes)	1 pkg	227	13.0	760	194.3	.2	0	—	—	—	—	—	—	—	—	—	—
b	Size, net wt., 1 oz. (4 envelopes)	1 pkg. or 1 oz.[120]	28	13.0	95	24.3	Trace	0	—	—	—	—	—	—	—	—	—	—
c	Envelope	1 envelope	7	13.0	23	6.0	Trace	0	—	—	—	—	—	—	—	—	—	—
	Capsule (wt., 10 grains):																	
d	Bottle, approx. 50 capsules	1 bottle	32	13.0	107	27.4	Trace	0	—	—	—	—	—	—	—	—	—	—
e	Capsule	1 capsule	.6	13.0	2	.5	Trace	0	—	—	—	—	—	—	—	—	—	—
	Gelatin dessert powder and desserts made from dessert powder:																	
1031	Dessert powder:																	
a	Package, net wt., 6 oz	1 pkg	170	1.6	631	16.0	0	149.6	—	—	—	541	—	—	—	—	—	—
b	Package, net wt., 3 oz	1 pkg	85	1.6	315	8.0	0	74.8	—	—	—	270	—	—	—	—	—	—
c	Pound	1 lb	454	1.6	1,683	42.6	0	399.2	—	—	—	1,442	—	—	—	—	—	—
d	Ounce	1 oz	28	1.6	105	2.7	0	24.9	—	—	—	90	—	—	—	—	—	—
	Desserts made with water: [207]																	
1032	Plain:																	
a	Yield from 3-oz. pkg	2¼ cups (approx.).	540	84.2	315	8.0	0	74.8	—	—	—	270	—	—	—	—	—	—
b	Cup	1 cup	240	84.2	142	3.6	0	33.8	—	—	—	122	—	—	—	—	—	—
1033	With fruit added:																	
a	Yield from 3-oz. pkg., 1 cup of sliced bananas, and 1 cup of grapes.	3½ cups (approx.).	840	81.8	563	10.9	.8	137.8	—	—	—	286	—	—	—	—	—	25
b	Cup	1 cup	240	81.8	161	3.1	.2	39.4	—	—	—	82	—	—	—	—	—	7
	Gin. See Beverages (items 395–399).																	
	Ginger ale. See Beverages (item 407).																	
	Gingerbread. See Cakes (item 533) and Cake mixes (item 561).																	
1034	**Ginger root, crystallized** (candied):																	
a	Pound	1 lb	454	12.0	1,542	1.4	.9	395.1	—	—	—	—	—	—	—	—	—	—

(A)	(B)		(C)	(D)	(E)	(F)	(G)	(H)	(I)	(J)	(K)	(L)	(M)	(N)	(O)	(P)	(Q)
b	Ounce	1 oz	28	12.0	96	0.1	0.1	24.7	—	—	—	—	—	—	—	—	—	—
1035	**Ginger root, fresh** (refuse: scrapings, 7%)[1]	1 lb	454	87.0	207	5.9	4.2	40.1	97	152	8.9	25	1,114	40	0.08	0.17	3.0	17
	Gizzard:																	
	Chicken, all classes:																	
1036	Raw	1 lb	454	75.0	513	91.2	12.2	3.2	45	476	13.2	295	1,089	—	.14	.91	20.4	—
1037	Cooked (simmered):																	
a	Yield from 1 lb., raw	11⅞ oz	336	68.0	497	90.7	11.1	2.4	30	239	10.4	192	709	—	.07	.71	17.1	—
b	Cup, chopped or diced pieces	1 cup	145	68.0	215	39.2	4.8	1.0	13	103	4.5	83	306	—	.03	.30	7.4	—
c	Pound	1 lb	454	68.0	671	122.5	15.0	3.2	41	322	14.1	259	957	—	.09	.95	23.1	—
1038	Goose, raw	1 lb	454	73.0	631	97.1	24.0	0	—	—	—	—	—	—	—	—	—	—
	Turkey, all classes:																	
1039	Raw	1 lb	454	70.3	712	92.1	33.1	5.0	—	—	—	263	771	—	.23	.59	22.7	—
1040	Cooked (simmered):																	
a	Yield from 1 lb., raw	11⅞ oz	336	62.7	659	90.0	28.9	3.7	—	—	—	171	501	—	.10	.47	19.5	—
b	Cup, chopped or diced pieces	1 cup	145	62.7	284	38.9	12.5	1.6	—	—	—	74	216	—	.04	.20	8.4	—
c	Pound	1 lb	454	62.7	889	121.6	39.0	5.0	—	—	—	231	676	—	.14	.64	26.3	—
	Gluten flour. See Wheat flours (item 2444).																	
	Goat milk. See Milk, goat (item 1335).																	
	Goose, domesticated, cooked (roasted):																	
1042	Total edible (flesh, skin, giblets):																	
a	Yield from 1-lb. ready-to-cook goose	8½ oz	240	39.1	1,022	56.9	86.4	0	(26)	(576)	(5.0)	—	—	—	(.19)	(.58)	(19.4)	—
b	Pound	1 lb	454	39.1	1,932	107.5	163.3	0	(50)	(1,089)	(9.5)	—	—	—	(.36)	(1.09)	(36.7)	—
1046	Flesh only:																	
a	Pound (approx. 13⅓ pieces (item 1046))	1 lb	454	54.8	1,057	153.8	44.5	0	(64)	(1,256)	(7.7)	562	2,744	—	(.50)	(.73)	(42.2)	—
b	Piece, approx. 3½ in. long, 3 in. wide, ¼ in. thick.	2½ pieces or 3 oz.	85	54.8	198	28.8	8.3	0	(12)	(235)	(1.4)	105	514	—	(.09)	(.14)	(7.9)	—
1048	**Gooseberries, raw**[208]	1 cup	150	88.9	59	1.2	.3	14.6	27	23	.8	2	233	440	—	—	—	50
1052	**Granadilla, purple (passion fruit),** raw (refuse: shell, 48%).[1]	1 fruit	35	75.1	16	.4	.1	3.9	2	12	.3	5	63	130	Trace	.02	.3	5
	Grapefruit and grapefruit juice:																	
	Raw:																	
	Grapefruit used for pulp, served whole, halved, as sections, or as cut-up fruit:																	
	Pink, red, white:																	
1053	All varieties:[209]																	
a	Whole fruit,[210] 3⁹⁄₁₆-in. diam. (refuse: peel, seeds, core, membranes around sections, handling loss, 51%).[1]	1 grapefruit	400	88.4	80	1.0	.2	20.8	31	31	.8	2	265	160	.08	.04	.4	[211] 74
b	Halved fruit, 3⁹⁄₁₆-in. diam., served with peel (refuse: peel, part of core, membranes between sections, 47%).[1] [212]	½ grapefruit	184	88.4	40	.5	.1	10.3	16	16	.4	1	132	80	.04	.02	.2	[211] 37
c	Sections (approx. yield from 1 grapefruit, 3⁹⁄₁₆-in. diam.).	1 cup	200	88.4	82	1.0	.2	21.2	32	32	.8	2	270	160	.08	.04	.4	[211] 76
d	Sections, with juice (2 tbsp. per cup)	1 cup	230	88.4	94	1.2	.2	24.4	37	37	.9	2	311	180	.09	.05	.5	[211] 87
e	Cut-up fruit, bite-size pieces (see item 1054e for additional description of size pieces), spooned into cup without packing.	1 cup	(175)	88.4	72	.9	.2	18.6	28	28	.7	2	236	140	.07	.04	.4	[211] 67
1054	California and Arizona (Marsh Seedless):																	
a	Whole fruit,[210] 3¾-in. diam., size 40[213] (refuse: peel, seeds, membranes around sections, handling loss, 57%).[1]	1 grapefruit	400	87.5	76	.9	.2	19.8	55	34	.7	2	232	20	.07	.03	.3	[211] 69
b	Halved fruit, 3¾-in. diam., served with peel (refuse: peel and membranes between sections, 57%).[1]	½ grapefruit	200	87.5	38	.4	.1	9.9	28	17	.3	1	116	10	.03	.02	.2	[211] 34
c	Sections	1 cup	190	87.5	84	1.0	.2	21.9	61	38	.8	2	257	20	.08	.04	.4	[211] 76
d	Sections, with juice (2 tbsp. per cup)	1 cup	220	87.5	97	1.1	.2	25.3	70	44	.9	2	297	20	.09	.04	.4	[211] 88
e	Cut-up fruit, bite-size pieces (prepared by cutting pared fruit into 10–12 sectors and each sector into 5–6 pieces, approx. ½- to ¾-in. lengths), spooned into cup without packing.	1 cup	175	87.5	77	.9	.2	20.1	56	35	.7	2	236	20	.07	.04	.4	[211] 70

[1] Measure and weight apply to food as it is described with inedible part or parts (refuse) included.

[14] Dimensions of can: 1st dimension represents diameter; 2d dimension, height of can. 1st or left-hand digit in each dimension gives number of whole inches; next 2 digits give additional fraction of dimension expressed as 16th of an inch.

[138] Use also for 1 oz. of other form or forms listed for this item.

[207] For proportion of mix and added ingredients, see ARS 62–13 (7), table 19, p. 24.

[208] Production of gooseberries is restricted by Federal or State regulations that prohibit shipments of plants to certain designated States and areas within some States. Regulations have been enacted to prevent further spread of white pine blister rust inasmuch as these plants are alternate hosts of this disease.

[209] This item should be used when data are needed to represent countrywide and year-round use of grapefruit marketed as fresh fruit.

[210] See Appendix B, section on Citrus Fruits for explanation of basis for sizes and weights shown for whole citrus fruits.

[211] Value weighted by monthly and total season shipments for marketing as fresh fruit.

[212] Refuse and weight apply to halved fruit after removal of 8% refuse (seeds and part of core) in preparation for serving.

[213] Size refers to count of fruit in ⁷⁄₁₀-bushel container with net weight of approx. 35 lb.

TABLE 1.—*Nutritive values for household measures and market units of foods*—Continued

[Item numbers correspond to those in table 1 of Handbook No. 8, revised 1963. Values in parentheses denote imputed values usually from another form of the food or from a similar food. Zeros in parentheses indicate that amount of a constituent, if present, is probably too small to be measured. Dashes (—) denote lack of reliable data for a constituent believed to be present in a measurable amount. Calculated values, as those based on a recipe, are not in parentheses]

Item No.	Food, approximate measures, units, and weight (edible part unless footnotes indicate otherwise)			Water	Food energy	Protein	Fat	Carbohydrate	Calcium	Phosphorus	Iron	Sodium	Potassium	Vitamin A value	Thiamin	Riboflavin	Niacin	Ascorbic acid
(A)	(B)			(C)	(D)	(E)	(F)	(G)	(H)	(I)	(J)	(K)	(L)	(M)	(N)	(O)	(P)	(Q)
			Grams	Percent	Calories	Grams	Grams	Grams	Milligrams	Milligrams	Milligrams	Milligrams	Milligrams	International units	Milligrams	Milligrams	Milligrams	Milligrams
	Grapefruit and grapefruit juice—Continued																	
	Raw—Continued																	
	Grapefruit used for pulp, served whole, halved, as sections, or as cut-up fruit—Continued																	
	Pink, red, white—Continued																	
1055	Florida, all varieties:																	
a	Whole fruit,[210] 3⁹⁄₁₆-in. diam., size 48[214] (refuse: peel, seeds, core, membranes) around sections, handling loss, 50%).[1]	1 grapefruit	400	89.1	76	1.0	0.2	19.8	30	30	0.8	2	270	160	0.08	0.04	0.4	[211] 74
b	Halved fruit, 3⁹⁄₁₆-in. diam., served with peel (refuse: peel, part of core, membranes between sections, 46%).[1 212]	½ grapefruit	184	89.1	38	.5	.1	9.8	15	15	.4	1	134	80	.04	.02	.2	[211] 37
c	Sections	1 cup	200	89.1	76	1.0	.2	19.8	30	30	.8	2	270	160	.08	.04	.4	[211] 74
d	Sections, with juice (2 tbsp. per cup)	1 cup	230	89.1	87	1.2	.2	22.8	35	35	.9	2	311	180	.09	.05	.5	[211] 85
e	Cut-up fruit, bite-size pieces (see item 1054e for additional description of size pieces), spooned into cup without packing.	1 cup	(175)	89.1	67	.9	.2	17.3	26	26	.7	2	236	140	.07	.04	.4	[211] 65
1056	Texas, all varieties:																	
a	Whole fruit,[210] 3⅜-in. diam., size 48[215] (refuse: peel, seeds, core, membranes around sections, handling loss, 50%).[1]	1 grapefruit	380	87.7	82	1.0	.2	21.5	29	29	.8	2	257	[216] 20	.08	.04	.4	72
b	Halved fruit, 3⅜-in. diam., served with peel (refuse: peel, part of core, membranes between sections, 46%).[1 212]	½ grapefruit	175	87.7	41	.5	.1	10.7	14	14	.4	1	128	[217] 10	.04	.02	.2	36
c	Sections	1 cup	200	87.7	86	1.0	.2	22.6	30	30	.8	2	270	[218] 20	.08	.04	.4	76
d	Sections, with juice (2 tbsp. per cup)	1 cup	230	87.7	99	1.2	.2	26.0	35	35	.9	2	311	[219] 20	.09	.05	.5	87
e	Cut-up fruit, bite-size pieces (see item 1054e for additional description of size pieces), spooned into cup without packing.	1 cup	(175)	87.7	75	.9	.2	19.8	26	26	.7	2	236	[220] 20	.07	.04	.4	67
	Pink and red:																	
1057	Seeded (including Foster Pink):																	
	Whole fruit[210] (refuse: peel, seeds, core, membranes around sections, handling loss, 52%):[1]																	
a	Large, 4⅜-in. diam., size 27[214]	1 grapefruit	714	88.6	137	1.7	.3	35.6	55	55	1.4	3	463	1,510	.14	.07	.7	[211] 134
b	Medium, 4³⁄₁₆-in. diam., size 32[214]	1 grapefruit	602	88.6	116	1.4	.3	30.1	46	46	1.2	3	390	1,270	.12	.06	.6	[211] 113
c	Small, 3¹⁵⁄₁₆-in. diam., size 36[214]	1 grapefruit	536	88.6	103	1.3	.3	26.8	41	41	1.0	3	347	1,130	.10	.05	.5	[211] 100
	Halved fruit served with peel (refuse: peel, part of core, membranes between sections, 48%):[1 212]																	
d	Large, 4⅜-in. diam	½ grapefruit	328	88.6	68	.9	.2	17.7	27	27	.7	2	230	750	.07	.03	.3	[211] 67
e	Medium, 4³⁄₁₆-in. diam	½ grapefruit	277	88.6	58	.7	.1	15.0	23	23	.6	1	194	630	.06	.03	.3	[211] 56
f	Small, 3¹⁵⁄₁₆-in. diam	½ grapefruit	246	88.6	51	.6	.1	13.3	20	20	.5	1	173	560	.05	.03	.3	[211] 50
g	Sections	1 cup	200	88.6	80	1.0	.2	20.8	32	32	.8	2	270	880	.08	.04	.4	[211] 78
h	Sections, with juice (2 tbsp. per cup)	1 cup	230	88.6	92	1.2	.2	23.9	37	37	.9	2	311	1,010	.09	.05	.5	[211] 90
i	Cut-up fruit, bite-size pieces (see item 1054e for additional description of size pieces), spooned into cup without packing.	1 cup	(175)	88.6	70	.9	.2	18.2	28	28	.7	2	236	770	.07	.04	.4	[211] 68
1058	Seedless (including Pink Marsh, Redblush):																	
	Whole fruit[210] (refuse: peel, seeds, membranes around sections, handling loss, 49%):[1]																	
a	Large, 3¹⁵⁄₁₆-in. diam., size 36[214]	1 grapefruit	536	88.6	109	1.4	.3	28.4	44	44	1.1	3	369	1,200	.11	.05	.5	[211] 98
b	Medium, 3¾-in. diam., size 40[214]	1 grapefruit	482	88.6	98	1.2	.2	25.6	39	39	1.0	2	332	1,080	.10	.05	.5	[211] 88
c	Small, 3⁹⁄₁₆-in. diam., size 48[214]	1 grapefruit	402	88.6	82	1.0	.2	21.3	33	33	.8	2	277	900	.08	.04	.4	[211] 74
	Halved fruit served with peel (refuse: peel, membranes between sections, 49%):[1]																	
d	Large, 3¹⁵⁄₁₆-in. diam	½ grapefruit	268	88.6	55	.7	.1	14.2	22	22	.5	1	185	600	.05	.03	.3	[211] 49
e	Medium, 3¾-in. diam	½ grapefruit	241	[illegible]	[illegible]	[illegible]	[illegible]	[illegible]	[illegible]	[illegible]	[illegible]	[illegible]	[illegible]	[illegible]	[illegible]	[illegible]	[illegible]	[illegible]

(A)	(B)			(C)	(D)	(E)	(F)	(G)	(H)	(I)	(J)	(K)	(L)	(M)	(N)	(O)	(P)	(Q)
f	Small, 3⁹⁄₁₆-in. diam	½ grapefruit	201	88.6	41	0.5	0.1	10.7	16	16	0.4	1	138	450	0.04	0.02	0.2	[211] 37
g	Sections	1 cup	200	88.6	80	1.0	.2	20.8	32	32	.8	2	270	880	.08	.04	.4	[211] 72
h	Sections, with juice (2 tbsp. per cup)	1 cup	230	88.6	92	1.2	.2	23.9	37	37	.9	2	311	1,010	.09	.05	.5	[211] 83
i	Cut-up fruit, bite-size pieces (see item 1054e for additional description of size pieces), spooned into cup without packing.	1 cup	(175)	88.6	70	.9	.2	18.2	28	28	.7	2	236	770	.07	.04	.4	[211] 63
	White:																	
1059	Seeded (Duncan, other varieties):																	
	Whole fruit [210] (refuse: peel, seeds, core, membranes around sections, handling loss, 55%): [1]																	
a	Large, 4⅜-in. diam., size 27 [214]	1 grapefruit	714	88.2	132	1.6	.3	34.7	51	51	1.3	3	434	30	.13	.06	.6	[211] 122
b	Medium, 4³⁄₁₆-in. diam., size 32 [214]	1 grapefruit	602	88.2	111	1.4	.3	29.3	43	43	1.1	3	366	30	.11	.05	.5	[211] 103
c	Small, 3¹⁵⁄₁₆-in. diam., size 36 [214]	1 grapefruit	536	88.2	99	1.2	.2	26.0	39	39	1.0	2	326	20	.10	.05	.5	[211] 92
	Halved fruit served with peel (refuse: peel, part of core, membranes between sections, 51%): [1] [212]																	
d	Large, 4⅜-in. diam	½ grapefruit	328	88.2	66	.8	.2	17.4	26	26	.6	2	217	20	.06	.03	.3	[211] 61
e	Medium, 4³⁄₁₆-in. diam	½ grapefruit	277	88.2	56	.7	.1	14.7	22	22	.5	1	183	10	.05	.03	.3	[211] 52
f	Small, 3⁵⁄₁₆-in. diam	½ grapefruit	246	88.2	49	.6	.1	13.0	19	19	.5	1	163	10	.05	.02	.2	[211] 46
g	Sections	1 cup	200	88.2	82	1.0	.2	21.6	32	32	.8	2	270	20	.08	.04	.4	[211] 76
h	Sections, with juice (2 tbsp. per cup)	1 cup	230	88.2	94	1.2	.2	24.8	37	37	.9	2	311	20	.09	.05	.5	[211] 87
i	Cut-up fruit, bite-size pieces (see item 1054e for additional description of size pieces), spooned into cup without packing.	1 cup	(175)	88.2	72	.9	.2	18.9	28	28	.7	2	236	20	.07	.04	.4	[211] 67
1060	Seedless (Marsh seedless):																	
	Whole fruit [210] (refuse: peel, seeds, membranes around sections, handling loss, 51%): [1]																	
a	Large, 3¹⁵⁄₁₆-in. diam., size 36 [214]	1 grapefruit	536	88.9	102	1.3	.3	26.5	42	42	1.1	3	355	30	.11	.05	.5	[211] 97
b	Medium, 3¾-in. diam., size 40 [214]	1 grapefruit	482	88.9	92	1.2	.2	23.9	38	38	.9	2	319	20	.09	.05	.5	[211] 87
c	Small, 3⁹⁄₁₆-in. diam., size 48 [214]	1 grapefruit	402	88.9	77	1.0	.2	19.9	32	32	.8	2	266	20	.08	.04	.4	[211] 73
	Halved fruit served with peel (refuse: peel and membranes between sections, 51%): [1]																	
d	Large, 3¹⁵⁄₁₆-in. diam	½ grapefruit	268	88.9	51	.7	.1	13.3	21	21	.5	1	177	10	.05	.03	.3	[211] 49
e	Medium, 3¾-in. diam	½ grapefruit	241	88.9	46	.6	.1	11.9	19	19	.5	1	159	10	.05	.02	.2	[211] 44
f	Small, 3⁹⁄₁₆-in. diam	½ grapefruit	201	88.9	38	.5	.1	9.9	16	16	.4	1	133	10	.04	.02	.2	[211] 36
g	Sections	1 cup	200	88.9	78	1.0	.2	20.2	32	32	.8	2	270	20	.08	.04	.4	[211] 74
h	Sections, with juice (2 tbsp. per cup)	1 cup	230	88.9	90	1.2	.2	23.2	37	37	.9	2	311	20	.09	.05	.5	[211] 85
i	Cut-up fruit, bite-size pieces (see item 1054e for additional description of size pieces), spooned into cup without packing.	1 cup	(175)	88.9	68	.9	.2	17.7	28	28	.7	2	236	20	.07	.04	.4	[211] 65
	Grapefruit juice and grapefruit used for juice:																	
	Pink, red, white:																	
1061	All varieties:																	
a	Juice	1 cup	246	90.0	96	1.2	.2	22.6	22	37	.5	2	399	200	.10	.05	.5	[211] 93
b	Whole fruit used for juice, [210] 3⁹⁄₁₆-in. diam. (refuse: peel, seeds, core, membranes, handling loss, 51%); [1] yield of juice, approx. 196 g. (¾–⅞ cup).	1 grapefruit	400	90.0	76	1.0	.2	18.0	18	29	.4	2	318	160	.08	.04	.4	[211] 74
1062	California and Arizona (Marsh Seedless):																	
a	Juice	1 cup	247	89.0	104	1.0	.2	25.2	22	37	.5	2	400	20	.10	.05	.5	[211] 99
b	Whole fruit used for juice, [210] 3¾-in. diam., size 40 [213] (refuse: peel, seeds, membranes, handling loss, 57%); [1] yield of juice, approx. 172 g. (⅔ cup).	1 grapefruit	400	89.0	72	.7	.2	17.5	15	26	.3	2	279	20	.07	.03	.3	[211] 69
1063	Florida, all varieties:																	
a	Juice	1 cup	246	90.4	91	1.2	.2	21.6	22	37	.5	2	399	200	.10	.05	.5	[211] 91

[1] Measure and weight apply to food as it is described with inedible part or parts (refuse) included.

[210] See Appendix B, section on Citrus Fruits for explanation of basis for sizes and weights shown for whole citrus fruits.

[211] Value weighted by monthly and total season shipments for marketing as fresh fruit.

[212] Refuse and weight apply to halved fruit after removal of 8% refuse (seeds and part of core) in preparation for serving.

[213] Size refers to count of fruit in ⁷⁄₁₀-bushel container with net weight of approx. 35 lb.

[214] Size refers to count of fruit in ⅘-bushel container with net weight of approx. 42½ lb.

[215] Size refers to count of fruit in ⁷⁄₁₀-bushel container with net weight of approx. 40 lb. If shipped in 1⅗-bushel container with net weight approx. 80 lb., count for same size fruit is 96.

[216] Value applies to white-fleshed varieties. For pink- and red-fleshed varieties, value would be 840 I.U.

[217] Value applies to white-fleshed varieties. For pink- and red-fleshed varieties, value would be 420 I.U.

[218] Value applies to white-fleshed varieties. For pink- and red-fleshed varieties, value would be 880 I.U.

[219] Value applies to white-fleshed varieties. For pink- and red-fleshed varieties, value would be 1,010 I.U.

[220] Value applies to white-fleshed varieties. For pink- and red-fleshed varieties, value would be 770 I.U.

TABLE 1.—*Nutritive values for household measures and market units of foods*—Continued

[Item numbers correspond to those in table 1 of Handbook No. 8, revised 1963. Values in parentheses denote imputed values usually from another form of the food or from a similar food. Zeros in parentheses indicate that amount of a constituent, if present, is probably too small to be measured. Dashes (—) denote lack of reliable data for a constituent believed to be present in a measurable amount. Calculated values, as those based on a recipe, are not in parentheses]

Item No.	Food, approximate measures, units, and weight (edible part unless footnotes indicate otherwise)			Water	Food energy	Protein	Fat	Carbohydrate	Calcium	Phosphorus	Iron	Sodium	Potassium	Vitamin A value	Thiamin	Riboflavin	Niacin	Ascorbic acid
				Values for edible part of foods														
(A)	(B)			(C)	(D)	(E)	(F)	(G)	(H)	(I)	(J)	(K)	(L)	(M)	(N)	(O)	(P)	(Q)
			Grams	*Percent*	*Calories*	*Grams*	*Grams*	*Grams*	*Milligrams*	*Milligrams*	*Milligrams*	*Milligrams*	*Milligrams*	*International units*	*Milligrams*	*Milligrams*	*Milligrams*	*Milligrams*
	Grapefruit and grapefruit juice—Continued																	
	Raw—Continued																	
	Grapefruit juice and grapefruit used for juice—Continued																	
	Pink, red, white—Continued																	
	Florida, all varieties—Continued																	
b	Whole fruit used for juice,[210] 3⁹⁄₁₆-in. diam., size 48 [214] (refuse: peel, seeds, core, membranes, handling loss, 50%);[1] yield of juice, approx. 200 g. (¾–⅞ cup).	1 grapefruit	400	90.4	74	1.0	0.2	17.6	18	40	0.4	2	324	160	0.08	0.04	0.4	[211] 74
1064	Texas, all varieties:																	
a	Juice	1 cup	247	89.2	104	1.2	.2	24.7	22	37	.5	2	400	[221] 20	.10	.05	.5	94
b	Whole fruit used for juice,[210] 3⅜-in. diam., size 48 [215] (refuse: peel, seeds, core, membranes, handling loss, 50%);[1] yield of juice, approx. 190 g. (¾ cup).	1 grapefruit	380	89.2	80	1.0	.2	19.0	17	29	.4	2	308	[222] 20	.08	.04	.4	72
	Pink and red:																	
1065	Seeded (including Foster Pink):																	
a	Juice	1 cup	246	90.0	93	1.2	.2	22.4	22	37	.5	2	399	1,080	.10	.05	.5	[211] 96
	Whole fruit used for juice [210] (refuse: peel, seeds, core, membranes, handling loss, 52%):[1]																	
b	Large, 4⅜-in. diam., size 27;[214] yield of juice, approx. 343 g. (approx. 1⅜ cups).	1 grapefruit	714	90.0	130	1.7	.3	31.2	31	51	.7	3	555	1,510	.14	.07	.7	[211] 134
c	Medium, 4³⁄₁₆-in. diam., size 32;[214] yield of juice, approx. 289 g. (approx. 1⅙ cup).	1 grapefruit	602	90.0	110	1.4	.3	26.3	26	43	.6	3	468	1,270	.12	.06	.6	[211] 113
d	Small, 3¹⁵⁄₁₆-in. diam., size 36;[214] yield of juice, approx. 257 g. (approx. 1 cup).	1 grapefruit	536	90.0	98	1.3	.3	23.4	23	39	.5	3	417	1,130	.10	.05	.5	[211] 100
1066	Seedless (including Pink Marsh, Redblush):																	
a	Juice	1 cup	246	90.0	96	1.0	.2	22.9	22	37	.5	2	399	1,080	.10	.05	.5	[211] 89
	Whole fruit used for juice [210] (refuse: peel, seeds, membranes, handling loss, 49%):[1]																	
b	Large, 3¹⁵⁄₁₆-in. diam., size 36;[214] yield of juice, approx. 273 g. (approx. 1⅛ cups).	1 grapefruit	536	90.0	107	1.1	.3	25.4	25	41	.5	3	443	1,200	.11	.05	.5	[211] 98
c	Medium, 3¾-in. diam., size 40;[214] yield of juice, approx. 246 g. (1 cup).	1 grapefruit	482	90.0	96	1.0	.2	22.9	22	37	.5	2	398	1,080	.10	.05	.5	[211] 88
d	Small. 3⁹⁄₁₆-in. diam., size 48;[214] yield of juice, approx. 205 g. (approx. ⅞ cup).	1 grapefruit	402	90.0	80	.8	.2	19.1	18	31	.4	2	332	900	.08	.04	.4	[211] 74
	White:																	
1067	Seeded (Duncan, other varieties):																	
a	Juice	1 cup	246	89.6	98	1.2	.2	23.4	22	37	.5	2	399	20	.10	.05	.5	[211] 93
	Whole fruit used for juice [210] (refuse: peel, seeds, core, membranes, handling loss, 55%):[1]																	
b	Large, 4⅜-in. diam., size 27;[214] yield of juice approx. 321 g. (approx. 1⅓ cups).	1 grapefruit	714	89.6	129	1.6	.3	30.5	29	48	.6	3	521	30	.13	.06	.6	[211] 122
c	Medium, 4³⁄₁₆-in. diam., size 32;[214] yield of juice, approx. 271 g. (approx. 1⅛ cups).	1 grapefruit	602	89.6	108	1.4	.3	25.7	24	41	.5	3	439	30	.11	.05	.5	[211] 103
d	Small, 3¹⁵⁄₁₆-in. diam., size 36;[214] yield of juice, approx. 241 g. (approx. 1 cup).	1 grapefruit	536	89.6	96	1.2	.2	22.9	22	36	.5	2	391	20	.10	.05	.5	[211] 92
1068	Seedless (Marsh Seedless):																	
a	Juice	1 cup	246	90.2	93	1.2	.2	22.1	22	37	.5	2	399	20	.10	.05	.5	[211] 91
	Whole fruit used for juice [210] (refuse: peel,																	

(A)	(B)		(C)	(D)	(E)	(F)	(G)	(H)	(I)	(J)	(K)	(L)	(M)	(N)	(O)	(P)	(Q)
	seed, membranes, handling loss, 51%):[1]																
b	Large, 3⁹⁄₁₆-in. diam., size 36;[214] yield of juice, approx. 263 g. (1–1⅛ cups).	1 grapefruit	536	90.2	100	1.3	0.8	23.6	24	39	0.5	3	425	30	0.11	0.05	0.5	[211] 97
c	Medium, 3¾-in. diam., size 40;[214] yield of juice, approx. 236 g. (approx. 1 cup).	1 grapefruit	482	90.2	90	1.2	.2	21.3	21	35	.5	2	383	20	.09	.05	.5	[211] 87
d	Small, 3⁹⁄₁₆-in. diam., size 48;[214] yield of juice, approx. 197 g. (¾–⅞ cup).	1 grapefruit	402	90.2	75	1.0	.2	17.7	18	30	.4	2	319	20	.08	.04	.4	[211] 78
	Canned:																
	Sections, solids and liquid:																
1069	Water pack, without artificial sweetener	1 cup	244	91.3	73	1.5	.2	18.5	[223] 32	34	.7	10	351	20	.07	.05	.5	78
1070	Sirup pack:																
	Can and approx. contents:																
a	Size, 211 × 304[14] (8Z Tall, Buffet); net wt., 8½ oz.	1 can	241	81.1	169	1.4	.2	42.9	[223] 31	34	.7	2	325	20	.07	.05	.5	72
b	Size, 303 × 406[14] (No. 303); net wt., 16 oz. (1 lb.).	1 can or 1 lb.	454	81.1	318	2.7	.5	80.7	[223] 59	64	1.4	5	612	50	.14	.09	.9	136
c	Size, 404 × 700[14] (46Z, No. 3 Cylinder); net wt., 50 oz. (3 lb. 2 oz.).	1 can	1,418	81.1	993	8.5	1.4	252.4	[223] 184	199	4.3	14	1,914	140	.43	.28	2.8	425
d	Cup	1 cup	254	81.1	178	1.5	.3	45.2	[223] 33	36	.8	3	343	30	.08	.05	.5	76
	Juice:																
1071	Unsweetened:																
	Can and approx. contents:																
a	Size, 202 × 314[14] (6½Z); net contents, 6 fl. oz.	1 can	185	89.2	76	.9	.2	18.1	15	26	.7	2	300	20	.06	.04	.4	63
b	Size, 404 × 700[14] (46Z, No. 3 Cylinder); net contents, 46 fl. oz. (1 qt. 14 fl. oz.).	1 can	1,419	89.2	582	7.1	1.4	139.1	114	199	5.7	14	2,299	140	.43	.28	2.8	482
c	Cup	1 cup	247	89.2	101	1.2	.2	24.2	20	35	1.0	2	400	20	.07	.05	.5	84
d	Fluid ounce	1 fl. oz	30.9	89.2	13	.2	Trace	3.0	2	4	.1	Trace	50	Trace	.01	.01	.1	11
1072	Sweetened with nutritive sweetener:																
	Can and approx. contents:																
a	Size, 202 × 314[14] (6½Z); net contents, 6 fl. oz.	1 can	187	86.2	99	.9	.2	23.9	15	26	.7	2	303	20	.06	.04	.4	58
b	Size, 404 × 700[14] (46Z, No. 3 Cylinder); net contents, 46 fl. oz. (1 qt. 14 fl. oz.).	1 can	1,436	86.2	761	7.2	1.4	183.8	115	201	5.7	14	2,326	140	.43	.29	2.9	445
c	Cup	1 cup	250	86.2	133	1.3	.3	32.0	20	35	1.0	3	405	30	.08	.05	.5	78
d	Fluid ounce	1 fl. oz	31.2	86.2	17	.2	Trace	4.0	2	4	.1	Trace	51	Trace	.01	.01	.1	10
	Frozen concentrated juice:																
	Unsweetened (38° Brix):																
1073	Undiluted:																
	Can and approx. contents:																
a	6 fl. oz. (yields 3 cups diluted juice weighing 740 g.).	1 can	207	62	300	3.9	.8	71.6	70	124	.8	8	1,250	60	.29	.12	1.4	286
b	12 fl. oz. (yields 1½ qt. diluted juice weighing 1,480 g.).	1 can	415	62	602	7.9	1.7	143.6	141	249	1.7	17	2,507	120	.58	.25	2.8	573
c	32 fl. oz. (1 qt.) (yields 1 gal. diluted juice weighing 3,944 g.).	1 can	1,105	62	1,602	21.0	4.4	382.3	376	663	4.4	44	6,674	330	1.55	.66	7.4	1,525
1074	Diluted with 3 parts water by volume:																
a	Quart	1 qt	987	89.3	405	4.9	1.0	96.7	99	168	1.0	10	1,678	80	.39	.17	1.9	385
b	Cup	1 cup	247	89.3	101	1.2	.2	24.2	25	42	.2	2	420	20	.10	.04	.5	96
c	Glass (6 fl. oz.)	1 glass	185	89.3	76	.9	.2	18.1	19	31	.2	2	315	20	.07	.03	.4	72
	Sweetened with nutritive sweetener (43° Brix):																
1075	Undiluted:																
	Can and approx. contents:																
a	6 fl. oz. (yields 3 cups diluted juice weighing 744 g.).	1 can	212	57	350	3.4	.6	85.2	59	106	.6	6	1,077	50	.25	.11	1.2	246
b	12 fl. oz. (yields 1½ qt. diluted juice weighing 1,488 g.).	1 can	424	57	700	6.8	1.3	170.4	119	212	1.3	13	2,154	100	.50	.21	2.4	492
c	32 fl. oz. (1 qt.) (yields 1 gal. diluted juice weighing 3,969 g.).	1 can	1,130	57	1,865	18.1	3.4	454.3	316	565	3.4	34	5,740	280	1.31	.57	6.3	1,311
1076	Diluted with 3 parts water by volume:																
a	Quart	1 qt	992	87.8	466	4.0	1.0	113.1	79	139	1.0	10	1,428	70	.33	.14	1.6	327
b	Cup	1 cup	248	87.8	117	1.0	.2	28.3	20	35	.2	2	357	20	.08	.03	.4	82
c	Glass (6 fl. oz.)	1 glass	186	87.8	87	.7	.2	21.2	15	26	.2	2	268	10	.06	.02	.3	61

[1] Measure and weight apply to food as it is described with inedible part or parts (refuse) included.

[14] Dimensions of can: 1st dimension represents diameter; 2d dimension, height of can. 1st or left-hand digit in each dimension gives number of whole inches; next 2 digits give additional fraction of dimension expressed as 16th of an inch.

[210] See Appendix B, section on Citrus Fruits for explanation of basis for sizes and weights shown for whole citrus fruits.

[211] Value weighted by monthly and total season shipments for marketing as fresh fruit.

[214] Size refers to count of fruit in ⅘-bushel container with net weight of approx. 42½ lb.

[215] Size refers to count of fruit in 7⁄10-bushel container with net weight of approx. 40 lb. If shipped in 1⅗-bushel container with net weight approx. 80 lb., count for same size fruit is 96.

[221] Value applies to white-fleshed varieties. For pink- and red-fleshed varieties, value would be 1,090 I.U.

[222] Value applies to white-fleshed varieties. For pink- and red-fleshed varieties, value would be 840 I.U.

[223] Federal standards provide for addition of certain calcium salts as firming agents. If used, these salts may add calcium not to exceed 35 mg. per 100 g. of finished product. Value for item 1069 would be 117 mg.; for item 1070a, 116 mg.; for item 1070b, 218 mg.; for item 1070c, 681 mg.; for item 1070d, 122 mg.

TABLE 1.—*Nutritive values for household measures and market units of foods*—Continued

[Item numbers correspond to those in table 1 of Handbook No. 8, revised 1963. Values in parentheses denote imputed values usually from another form of the food or from a similar food. Zeros in parentheses indicate that amount of a constituent, if present, is probably too small to be measured. Dashes (—) denote lack of reliable data for a constituent believed to be present in a measurable amount. Calculated values, as those based on a recipe, are not in parentheses]

Item No. (A)		Food, approximate measures, units, and weight (edible part unless footnotes indicate otherwise) (B)			Water (C)	Food energy (D)	Protein (E)	Fat (F)	Carbohydrate (G)	Calcium (H)	Phosphorus (I)	Iron (J)	Sodium (K)	Potassium (L)	Vitamin A value (M)	Thiamin (N)	Riboflavin (O)	Niacin (P)	Ascorbic acid (Q)
					Values for edible part of foods														
				Grams	*Percent*	*Calories*	*Grams*	*Grams*	*Grams*	*Milligrams*	*Milligrams*	*Milligrams*	*Milligrams*	*Milligrams*	*International units*	*Milligrams*	*Milligrams*	*Milligrams*	*Milligrams*
		Grapefruit and grapefruit juice—Continued																	
		Dehydrated (crystals):																	
1077		Dry form:																	
	a	Ounce	1 oz	28	1.0	107	1.4	0.3	25.6	25	44	0.3	3	446	20	0.10	0.05	0.5	99
	b	Pound (yields approx. 1 gal. of juice)	1 lb	454	1.0	1,715	21.8	4.5	409.6	395	703	4.5	45	7,131	360	1.63	.73	7.7	1,588
1078		Prepared with water (1 lb. of crystals yields approx. 1 gal. of juice).	1 cup	247	89.5	99	1.2	.2	23.7	22	40	.2	2	412	20	.10	.05	.5	91
		Grapefruit juice and orange juice blended:																	
		Canned:																	
1079		Unsweetened:																	
		Can and approx. contents:																	
	a	Size, 202 × 314 [14] (6½Z); net contents, 6 fl. oz.	1 can	185	88.7	80	1.1	.4	18.7	19	28	.6	2	340	190	.09	.04	.4	63
	b	Size, 404 × 700 [14] (46Z, No. 3 Cylinder); net contents, 46 fl. oz. (1 qt. 14 fl. oz.).	1 can	1,422	88.7	611	8.5	2.8	143.6	142	213	4.3	14	2,616	1,420	.71	.28	2.8	483
	c	Cup	1 cup	247	88.7	106	1.5	.5	24.9	25	37	.7	2	454	250	.12	.05	.5	84
	d	Fluid ounce	1 fl. oz	30.9	88.7	13	.2	.1	3.1	3	5	.1	Trace	57	30	.02	.01	.1	11
1080		Sweetened with nutritive sweetener:																	
		Can and approx. contents:																	
	a	Size, 202 × 314 [14] (6½Z); net contents, 6 fl. oz.	1 can	186	86.9	93	.9	.2	22.7	19	28	.6	2	340	190	.09	.04	.4	63
	b	Size, 404 × 700 [14] (46Z, No. 3 Cylinder); net contents, 46 fl. oz. (1 qt. 14 fl. oz.).	1 can	1,432	86.9	716	7.2	1.4	174.7	142	213	4.3	14	2,616	1,420	.71	.28	2.8	483
	c	Cup	1 cup	249	86.9	125	1.2	.2	30.4	25	37	.7	2	454	250	.12	.05	.5	84
	d	Fluid ounce	1 fl. oz	31.1	86.9	16	.2	Trace	3.8	3	5	.1	Trace	57	30	.02	.01	.1	11
		Frozen concentrated juice, unsweetened:																	
1081		Undiluted:																	
		Can and approx. contents:																	
	a	6 fl. oz. (yields 3 cups diluted juice weighing 742 g.).	1 can	210	59.1	330	4.4	1.1	77.9	61	99	.8	4	1,308	800	.48	.06	2.3	302
	b	12 fl. oz. (yields 1½ qt. diluted juice weighing 1,484 g.).	1 can	420	59.1	659	8.8	2.1	155.8	122	197	1.7	8	2,617	1,600	.97	.13	4.6	605
	c	32 fl. oz. (1 qt.) (yields 1 gal. diluted juice weighing 3,958 g.).	1 can	1,120	59.1	1,758	23.5	5.6	415.5	325	526	4.5	22	6,978	4,260	2.58	.34	12.3	1,613
1082		Diluted with 3 parts water by volume:																	
	a	Quart	1 qt	992	88.4	436	6.0	1.0	104.2	79	129	1.0	Trace	1,756	1,090	.60	.10	3.0	407
	b	Cup	1 cup	248	88.4	109	1.5	.2	26.0	20	32	.2	Trace	439	270	.15	.02	.7	102
	c	Glass (6 fl. oz.)	1 glass	185	88.4	81	1.1	.2	19.4	15	24	.2	Trace	327	200	.11	.02	.6	76
1083		**Grapefruit peel,** candied	1 oz	28	17.4	90	.1	.1	22.9	—	—	—	—	—	—	—	—	—	—
		Grapes:																	
		Raw:																	
1084		American type (slip skin) as Concord, Delaware, Niagara, Catawba, Scuppernong, whole (refuse: seeds and skins, 34%): [1]																	
	a	Fruit, ¾-in. diam., ¾ in. high	10 grapes	40	81.6	18	.3	.3	4.1	4	3	.1	1	42	30	(.01)	(.01)	(.1)	1
	b	Cup (approx. 38 grapes)	1 cup	153	81.6	70	1.3	1.0	15.9	16	12	.4	3	160	100	(.05)	(.03)	(.3)	4
	c	Pound (approx. 3 cups)	1 lb	454	81.6	207	3.9	3.0	47.0	48	36	1.2	9	473	300	(.15)	(.09)	(.9)	12
1085		European type (adherent skin) as Thompson Seedless, Emperor, Flame Tokay, Ribier, Malaga, Muscat:																	
		Whole:																	
		Seedless types:																	
	a	Fruit, ⅝-in. diam., ⅞ in. high	10 grapes	50	81.4	34	.3	.2	8.7	6	10	.2	2	87	(50)	.03	.02	.2	2
	b	Cup	1 cup	160	81.4	107	1.0	.5	27.7	19	32	.6	5	277	(160)	.08	.05	.5	6
		Seeded types (refuse: seeds, 5%): [1]																	
		Fruit:																	
	c	Tokay and Emperor varieties, ¾-in. diam., ⅞ in. high.	10 grapes	60	81.4	38	.3	.2	9.9	7	11	.2	2	99	(60)	.03	.02	.2	2
	d	Ribier, ⅞-in. diam., ⅞ in. high	10 grapes	70	81.4	45	.4	.2	11.5	8	13	.3	2	115	(70)	.03	.02	.2	3
	e	Cup	1 cup	160	81.4	102	.9	.5	26.3	18	30	.6	5	263	(150)	.08	.05	.5	6
	f	Halves, all varieties [284]	1 cup	175	81.4	117	1.1	.5	30.3	21	35	.7	5	303	(180)	.09	.05	.5	7

(A)	(B)			(C)	(D)	(E)	(F)	(G)	(H)	(I)	(J)	(K)	(L)	(M)	(N)	(O)	(P)	(Q)
g	Pound, seedless types and halves of all varieties.	1 lb	454	81.4	304	2.7	1.4	78.5	54	91	1.8	14	785	(450)	0.23	0.14	1.4	18
	Canned:																	
	Thompson Seedless, solids and liquid:																	
1086	Water pack, without artificial sweetener:																	
a	Cup	1 cup	245	85.5	125	1.2	.2	33.3	20	32	.7	10	270	170	.10	.02	.5	5
b	Pound	1 lb	454	85.5	231	2.3	.5	61.7	36	59	1.4	18	499	320	.18	.05	.9	9
1087	Sirup pack, heavy:																	
	Can and approx. contents:																	
a	Size, 211 × 304 [14] (8Z Tall, Buffet); net wt., 8¾ oz.	1 can	248	79.1	191	1.2	.2	49.6	20	32	.7	10	260	170	.10	.02	.5	5
b	Cup	1 cup	256	79.1	197	1.3	.3	51.2	20	33	.8	10	269	180	.10	.03	.5	5
c	Pound	1 lb	454	79.1	349	2.3	.5	90.7	36	59	1.4	18	476	320	.18	.05	.9	9
	Grapejuice:																	
1088	Canned or bottled:																	
	Container and approx. contents:																	
a	Bottle, net contents, 4 fl. oz	1 bottle	127	82.9	84	.3	Trace	21.1	14	15	.4	3	147	—	.05	.03	.3	[15] Trace
b	Bottle, net contents, 24 fl. oz. (1pt. 8 fl. oz.)	1 bottle	760	82.9	502	1.5	Trace	126.2	84	91	2.3	15	882	—	.30	.15	1.5	[15] Trace
c	Bottle, net contents, 40 fl. oz. (1 qt. 8 fl. oz.)	1 bottle	1,266	82.9	836	2.5	Trace	210.2	139	152	3.8	25	1,469	—	.51	.25	2.5	[15] Trace
d	Cup	1 cup	253	82.9	167	.5	Trace	42.0	28	30	.8	5	293	—	.10	.05	.5	[15] Trace
e	Glass (6 fl. oz.)	1 glass	190	82.9	125	.4	Trace	31.5	21	23	.6	4	220	—	.08	.04	.4	[15] Trace
f	Fluid ounce	1 fl. oz	31.6	82.9	21	.1	Trace	5.2	3	4	.1	1	37	—	.01	.01	.1	[15] Trace
	Frozen concentrate, sweetened with nutritive sweetener:																	
1089	Undiluted:																	
	Can and approx. contents:																	
a	6 fl. oz. (yields 3 cups diluted juice weighing 748 g.).	1 can	216	52.8	395	1.3	Trace	100.0	22	32	.9	6	255	40	.13	.22	1.5	[225] 32
b	12 fl. oz. (yields 6 cups diluted juice weighing 1,497 g.).	1 can	432	52.8	791	2.6	Trace	200.0	43	65	1.7	13	510	80	.26	.43	3.0	[225] 65
c	Fluid ounce	1 fl. oz	36.0	52.8	66	.2	Trace	16.7	4	5	.1	1	42	10	.02	.04	.3	[225] 5
1090	Diluted with 3 parts water by volume:																	
a	Quart	1 qt	998	86.4	529	2.0	Trace	132.7	30	40	1.0	10	339	50	.20	.30	2.0	[226] 40
b	Cup	1 cup	250	86.4	133	.5	Trace	33.3	8	10	.3	3	85	10	.05	.08	.5	[226] 10
c	Glass (6 fl. oz.)	1 glass	187	86.4	99	.4	Trace	24.9	6	7	.2	2	64	10	.04	.06	.4	[226] 7
1091	**Grape drink,** canned (approx. 30% grapejuice): [227]																	
	Can and approx. contents:																	
a	Size, 307 × 710; [14] net contents, 32 fl. oz. (1 qt.). [228]	1 can or 1 qt	1,000	86.0	540	1.0	Trace	138.0	30	40	1.0	10	350	—	2.00	2.40	1.0	—
b	Size, 404 × 700 [14] (46Z, No. 3 Cylinder); net contents, 46 fl. oz. (1 qt. 14 fl. oz.).	1 can	1,437	86.0	776	1.4	Trace	198.3	43	57	1.4	14	503	—	.14	.14	1.4	230
c	Cup	1 cup	250	86.0	135	.3	Trace	34.5	8	10	.3	3	88	—	.03	.03	.3	40
d	Glass (6 fl. oz.)	1 glass	187	86.0	101	.2	Trace	25.8	6	7	.2	2	65	—	.02	.02	.2	30
e	Fluid ounce	1 fl. oz	31.3	86.0	17	Trace	Trace	4.3	1	1	Trace	Trace	11	—	Trace	Trace	Trace	5
	Griddlecakes. See Pancakes (items 1453–1455, 1457–1458, 1460–1462).																	
	Grits. See Corn grits (items 862–865).																	
1092	**Groundcherries** (poha or cape-gooseberries), raw, without husks:																	
a	Cup	1 cup	140	85.4	74	2.7	1.0	15.7	13	56	1.4	—	—	1,010	.15	.06	3.9	15
b	Pound	1 lb	454	85.4	240	8.6	3.2	50.8	41	181	4.5	—	—	3,270	.50	.18	12.7	50
1100	**Haddock,** fried (panfried or ovenfried): [73]																	
a	Yield from 1 lb., raw fillets	12⅘ oz	362	66.3	597	71.0	23.2	21.0	145	894	4.3	[43] 641	1,260	—	.14	.25	11.6	7
b	Fillet, 6⅜ in. long, 2½ in. wide, ⅝ in. thick, or 2¾ in. long, 2½ in. wide, ⅞ in. thick. [40]	1 fillet	110	66.3	182	21.6	7.0	6.4	44	272	1.3	[43] 195	383	—	.04	.08	3.5	2
c	Pound	1 lb	454	66.3	748	88.9	29.0	26.3	181	1,120	5.4	[43] 803	1,579	—	.18	.32	14.5	9
d	Ounce	1 oz	28	66.3	47	5.6	1.8	1.6	11	70	.3	[43] 50	99	—	.01	.02	.9	1

[1] Measure and weight apply to food as it is described with inedible part or parts (refuse) included.

[14] Dimensions of can: 1st dimension represents diameter; 2d dimension, height of can. 1st or left-hand digit in each dimension gives number of whole inches; next 2 digits give additional fraction of dimension expressed as 16th of an inch.

[15] Applies to product without added ascorbic acid. For value of product with added ascorbic acid, refer to label.

[40] Width at widest part; thickness at thickest part.

[43] Value for product without added salt.

[73] Dipped in egg, milk or water, and breadcrumbs.

[224] Seeds removed from seeded types.

[225] Applies to product without added ascorbic acid. With added ascorbic acid, based on claim that 8 fl. oz. of reconstituted juice contain 30 mg. of ascorbic acid, value for 6-fl. oz. can (item 1089a) is 90 mg.; for 12-fl. oz. can (item 1089b), 180 mg.; for 1 fl. oz. (item 1089c), 15 mg.

[226] Applies to product without added ascorbic acid. With added ascorbic acid, based on claim that 8 fl. oz. of reconstituted juice contain 30 mg. of ascorbic acid, value for 1 qt. (item 1090a) is 120 mg.; for 1 cup (item 1090b), 30 mg.; for 1 glass (6 fl. oz.) (item 1090c), 22 mg.

[227] Ascorbic acid may be added as preservative or as nutrient. Excepting item 1091a, ascorbic acid value listed is based on product with label stating 30 mg. per 6-fl. oz. serving. If label claim is 30 mg. for 8-fl. oz. serving, value would be 172 mg. for item 1091b, 30 mg. for item 1091c, 22 mg. for item 1091d, 4 mg. for item 1091e. Sometimes product is enriched with thiamin and riboflavin but not with ascorbic acid. For this product, thiamin and riboflavin values, respectively, would be 2.87 and 3.45 mg. for item 1091b, 0.50 and 0.60 mg. for item 1091c, 0.37 and 0.45 mg. for item 1091d, 0.06 and 0.08 mg. for item 1091e. Ascorbic acid values would be trace for these items.

[228] Can size and nutritive values apply to product fortified with thiamin and riboflavin but not with ascorbic acid.

TABLE 1.—*Nutritive values for household measures and market units of foods*—Continued

[Item numbers correspond to those in table 1 of Handbook No. 8, revised 1963. Values in parentheses denote imputed values usually from another form of the food or from a similar food. Zeros in parentheses indicate that amount of a constituent, if present, is probably too small to be measured. Dashes (—) denote lack of reliable data for a constituent believed to be present in a measurable amount. Calculated values, as those based on a recipe, are not in parentheses]

Item No.	Food, approximate measures, units, and weight (edible part unless footnotes indicate otherwise)			Water	Food energy	Protein	Fat	Carbohydrate	Calcium	Phosphorus	Iron	Sodium	Potassium	Vitamin A value	Thiamin	Riboflavin	Niacin	Ascorbic acid
(A)	(B)			(C)	(D)	(E)	(F)	(G)	(H)	(I)	(J)	(K)	(L)	(M)	(N)	(O)	(P)	(Q)
			Grams	*Percent*	*Calories*	*Grams*	*Grams*	*Grams*	*Milligrams*	*Milligrams*	*Milligrams*	*Milligrams*	*Milligrams*	*International units*	*Milligrams*	*Milligrams*	*Milligrams*	*Milligrams*
1104	**Halibut, Atlantic and Pacific,** broiled with butter or margarine:																	
a	Yield from 1 lb., raw fillets	12⅞ oz	365	66.6	624	92.0	25.6	0	58	905	2.9	[43] 489	1,916	2,480	0.18	0.26	30.3	—
b	Fillet (quadrangular piece, 6½ in. long, 2–2¾ in. wide, ⅝ in. thick) or lengthwise-cut steak with skin and bones removed (quadrangular piece, 2¾–6 in. long, 3⅜ in. wide, ⅜–⅝ in. thick).[40] [229]	1 fillet or 1 steak.	125	66.6	214	31.5	8.8	0	20	310	1.0	[43] 168	656	850	.06	.09	10.4	—
c	Pound	1 lb	454	66.6	776	114.3	31.8	0	73	1,125	8.6	[43] 608	2,381	3,080	.23	.82	37.6	—
d	Ounce	1 oz	28	66.6	48	7.1	2.0	0	5	70	.2	[43] 38	149	190	.01	.02	2.4	—
	Ham. See Pork (items 1698–1699, 1701, 1766–1769, 1771, 1783) and Sausage (items 2005–2006).																	
	Hamburger. See Beef (items 367–370).																	
1108	**Ham croquette** (panfried);[51] 1-in. diam., 3 in. long:																	
a	Yield from recipe[108]	9 croquettes	595	54.0	1,493	97.0	89.8	69.6	411	952	12.5	2,035	494	1,550	1.67	1.31	14.9	Trace
b	Croquette	1 croquette	65	54.0	163	10.6	9.8	7.6	45	104	1.4	222	54	170	.18	.14	1.6	Trace
c	Pound (approx. 7 croquettes)	1 lb	454	54.0	1,139	73.9	68.5	53.1	313	726	9.5	1,551	376	1,180	1.27	1.00	11.3	Trace
	Hazelnuts. See Filberts (item 1008).																	
	Headcheese. See Sausage, cold cuts, and luncheon meats (item 2001).																	
	Heart:																	
1111	Beef, lean, cooked (braised):																	
a	Cup, chopped or diced pieces	1 cup	145	61.3	273	45.4	8.3	1.0	9	262	8.6	[43] 151	336	40	.36	1.77	11.0	1
b	Pound	1 lb	454	61.3	853	142.0	25.9	3.2	27	821	26.8	[43] 472	1,052	140	1.13	5.53	34.5	5
c	Ounce	1 oz	28	61.3	53	8.9	1.6	.2	2	51	1.7	[43] 29	66	10	.07	.35	2.2	Trace
1115	Calf, cooked (braised):																	
a	Cup, chopped or diced pieces	1 cup	145	60.3	302	40.3	13.2	2.6	6	215	6.4	[43] 164	363	60	.42	2.09	11.7	Trace
b	Pound	1 lb	454	60.3	943	126.1	41.3	8.2	18	671	20.0	[43] 513	1,134	180	1.32	6.53	36.7	Trace
c	Ounce	1 oz	28	60.3	59	7.9	2.6	.5	1	42	1.2	[43] 32	71	10	.08	.41	2.3	Trace
1117	Chicken, cooked (simmered):																	
a	Cup, chopped or diced pieces	1 cup	145	66.7	251	36.7	10.4	.1	6	155	5.2	[43] 100	203	(40)	.09	1.33	7.7	6
b	Pound	1 lb	454	66.7	785	114.8	32.7	.5	18	485	16.3	[43] 313	635	(140)	.27	4.17	24.0	18
c	Ounce	1 oz	28	66.7	49	7.2	2.0	Trace	1	30	1.0	[43] 20	40	(10)	.02	.26	1.5	1
1119	Hog, cooked (braised):																	
a	Cup, chopped or diced pieces	1 cup	145	61.0	283	44.7	10.0	.4	6	175	7.1	[43] 94	186	60	.29	2.49	9.7	1
b	Pound	1 lb	454	61.0	885	139.7	31.3	1.4	18	549	22.2	[43] 295	581	180	.91	7.80	30.4	5
c	Ounce	1 oz	28	61.0	55	8.7	2.0	.1	1	34	1.4	[43] 18	36	10	.06	.49	1.9	Trace
1121	Lamb, cooked (braised):																	
a	Cup, chopped or diced pieces	1 cup	145	54.1	377	42.8	20.9	1.5	20	335	—	[43] —	—	150	.30	1.49	9.3	Trace
b	Pound	1 lb	454	54.1	1,179	133.8	65.3	4.5	64	1,048	—	[43] —	—	450	.95	4.67	29.0	Trace
c	Ounce	1 oz	28	54.1	74	8.4	4.1	.3	4	65	—	[43] —	—	30	.06	.29	1.8	Trace
1123	Turkey, all classes, cooked (simmered):																	
a	Cup, chopped or diced pieces	1 cup	145	63.2	313	32.8	19.1	.3	—	—	—	[43] 88	306	(40)	.36	1.42	8.3	(6)
b	Pound	1 lb	454	63.2	980	102.5	59.9	.9	—	—	—	[43] 277	957	(140)	1.13	4.45	25.9	(18)
c	Ounce	1 oz	28	63.2	61	6.4	3.7	.1	—	—	—	[43] 17	60	(10)	.07	.28	1.6	(1)
	Herring:																	
	Canned, solids and liquid:																	
1126	Plain:																	
	Can and approx. contents:																	
a	Size, 300 × 407[14] (No. 300); net wt., 15 oz.; drained solids, 10⅜ oz. (approx. 4 pieces, 3½ in. long, 2 in. wide, ¾ in. thick;[40] wt., 2.7 oz.); drained liquid, 4⅝ oz.	1 can	425	62.9	884	84.6	57.8	0	625	1,262	7.7	—	—	—	—	.77	—	—
b	Pound	1 lb	454	62.9	943	90.3	61.7	0	667	1,347	8.2	—	—	—	—	.82	—	—
1127	In tomato sauce:																	
a	Herring, 4¾ in. long, 1⅛ in. wide, ⅝ in. thick;[40] wt., 1⅓ oz.; 1 tbsp. sauce, wt., ⅝ oz.	1 herring with 1 tbsp. sauce.	55	66.7	97	8.7	5.8	2.0	—	134	—	—	—	—	—	.06	1.9	—
b	Pound	1 lb	454	66.7	798	71.7	47.6	16.8	—	1,102	—	—	—	—	—	.50	15.9	—

(A)	(B)			(C)	(D)	(E)	(F)	(G)	(H)	(I)	(J)	(K)	(L)	(M)	(N)	(O)	(P)	(Q)
1128	Pickled:																	
a	Bismarck herring, 7 in. long, 1½ in. wide, ½ in. thick.[40]	1 herring	50	59.4	112	10.2	7.6	0	—	—	—	—	—	—	—	—	—	—
	Marinated pieces, ⅝ in. long, ¾ in. wide, ¼ in. thick to 3⅝ in. long, ¾ in. wide, ½ in. thick;[40] wt., 3–22 g.:																	
b	Piece, 1¾ in. long, ⅞ in. wide, ½ in. thick	1 piece	15	59.4	33	3.1	2.3	0	—	—	—	—	—	—	—	—	—	—
c	Pound	1 lb	454	59.4	1,012	92.5	68.5	0	—	—	—	—	—	—	—	—	—	—
d	Ounce	1 oz	28	59.4	63	5.8	4.3	0	—	—	—	—	—	—	—	—	—	—
1132	Smoked, kippered, canned, drained solids:																	
a	Drained contents from can of net wt., 3¼ oz. (2 fillets (item 1132d) or 4 fillets (item 1132e)).	1 can	80	61.0	169	17.8	10.3	0	53	203	1.1	—	—	20	—	0.22	2.6	—
b	Drained contents from can of net wt., 8 oz. (3 fillets (item 1132c)).	1 can	195	61.0	411	43.3	25.2	0	129	495	2.7	—	—	60	—	.55	6.4	—
c	Fillet, 7 in. long, 2¼ in. wide, ¼ in. thick[40]	1 fillet	65	61.0	137	14.4	8.4	0	43	165	.9	—	—	20	—	.18	2.1	—
d	Fillet, 4⅝ in. long, 1¾ in. wide, ¼ in. thick[40]	1 fillet	40	61.0	84	8.9	5.2	0	26	102	.6	—	—	10	—	.11	1.3	—
e	Fillet, 2⅝ in. long, 1⅝ in. wide, ¼ in. thick[40]	1 fillet	20	61.0	42	4.4	2.6	0	13	51	.3	—	—	10	—	.06	.7	—
f	Pound	1 lb	454	61.0	957	100.7	58.5	0	299	1,152	6.4	—	—	140	—	1.27	15.0	—
	Hominy grits, dry. See Corn grits (items 862–865).																	
1134	**Honey, strained or extracted:**																	
a	Container, net wt., 16 oz. (1 lb.)	1 lb	454	17.2	1,379	1.4	0	373.8	23	27	2.3	23	231	0	0.02	.18	1.4	5
b	Packet (½ oz., approx. 2 tsp.)	1 packet or ½ oz.	14	17.2	43	Trace	0	11.5	1	1	.1	1	7	0	Trace	.01	Trace	Trace
c	Cup	1 cup	339	17.2	1,031	1.0	0	279.0	17	20	1.7	17	173	0	.02	.14	1.0	3
d	Tablespoon	1 tbsp	21	17.2	64	.1	0	17.3	1	1	.1	1	11	0	Trace	.01	.1	Trace
	Honeydew melon. See Muskmelons (item 1360).																	
	Horseradish:																	
1135	Raw (refuse: parings, 27%)[1]	1 lb	454	74.6	288	10.6	1.0	89.4	464	212	4.6	26	1,867	—	.23	—	—	268
1136	Prepared:																	
a	Tablespoon	1 tbsp	15	87.1	6	.2	Trace	1.4	9	5	.1	14	44	—	—	—	—	—
b	Teaspoon	1 tsp	5	87.1	2	.1	Trace	.5	3	2	Trace	5	15	—	—	—	—	—
	Hyacinth-beans, raw:																	
1137	Young pods, cut ½-in. pieces	1 cup	90	88.8	32	2.5	.3	6.6	51	48	.9	2	257	520	.08	.10	.8	18
1138	Mature seeds, dry[5]	1 lb	454	11.8	1,533	100.7	6.8	276.7	331	1,896	23.1	—	—	—	2.81	.82	9.5	—
	Ice cream and frozen custard, plain (commercial):[230]																	
1139	Regular (approx. 10% fat):																	
	Hardened:																	
	Prepackaged container and approx. contents:																	
a	Container, net contents, ½ gal	½ gal	1,064	63.2	2,054	47.9	112.8	221.3	1,553	1,224	.5	[43] 670	1,926	4,680	.43	2.23	1.1	11
b	Container, net contents, 1 qt. (solid pack or 8 precut slices[231]).	1 qt. or 8 slices.	532	63.2	1,027	23.9	56.4	110.7	777	612	.3	[43] 335	963	2,340	.21	1.12	.5	5
c	Slice (4 fl. oz., ⅛ qt.)[231]	1 slice	66	63.2	127	3.0	7.0	13.7	96	76	Trace	[43] 42	119	290	.03	.14	.1	1
d	Cup (8 fl. oz.)	1 cup	133	63.2	257	6.0	14.1	27.7	194	153	.1	[43] 84	241	590	.05	.28	.1	1
e	Soft serve (frozen custard)	1 cup	173	63.2	334	7.8	18.3	36.0	253	199	.1	[43] 109	313	760	.07	.36	.2	2
1141	Rich (approx. 16% fat), hardened.																	
a	Prepackaged container, net contents, ½ gal	½ gal	1,188	62.8	2,637	30.9	191.3	213.8	927	725	.2	[43] 392	1,129	7,840	.24	1.31	1.2	12
b	Cup (8 fl. oz.)	1 cup	148	62.8	329	3.8	23.8	26.6	115	90	Trace	[43] 49	141	980	.03	.16	.1	1
1143	**Ice milk (5.1% fat):**																	
	Hardened:																	
a	Container, net contents, ½ gal	½ gal	1,048	66.7	1,593	50.3	53.4	234.8	1,635	1,300	1.0	[43] 713	2,044	2,200	.52	2.31	1.0	10
b	Cup (8 fl. oz.)	1 cup	131	66.7	199	6.3	6.7	29.3	204	162	.1	[43] 89	255	280	.07	.29	.1	1
c	Soft serve, cup (8 fl. oz.)	1 cup	175	66.7	266	8.4	8.9	39.2	273	217	.2	[43] 119	341	370	.09	.39	.2	2
1144	**Ices, water, lime**	1 cup	193	66.9	[232] 247	.8	Trace	62.9	Trace	Trace	Trace	Trace	6	Trace	Trace	Trace	Trace	2
	Icings. See Cake icings prepared from home recipes (items 570–574) and Cake icings prepared from mixes (items 576, 578–579).																	
1148	**Jams and preserves, sweetened with regular amount of nutritive sweetener:**																	
	Container and approx. contents:																	
a	Glass or jar, net wt., 10 oz	1 glass or jar	284	29	772	1.7	.3	198.8	57	26	2.8	34	250	30	.03	.09	.6	[233] 6
b	Glass or jar, net wt., 12 oz	1 glass or jar	340	29	925	2.0	.3	238.0	68	31	3.4	41	299	30	.03	.10	.7	[233] 7
c	Jar, net wt., 32 oz. (2 lb.); preserves	1 jar	907	29	2,467	5.4	.9	634.9	181	82	9.1	109	798	90	.09	.27	1.8	[233] 18
d	Packet, net wt., ½ oz. (approx. ⅔ tbsp.)	1 packet	14	29	38	.1	Trace	9.8	3	1	.1	2	12	Trace	Trace	Trace	Trace	[233] Trace
e	Tablespoon	1 tbsp	20	29	54	.1	Trace	14.0	4	2	.2	2	18	Trace	Trace	.01	Trace	[233] Trace

[1] Measure and weight apply to food as it is described with inedible part or parts (refuse) included.
[5] Most of phosphorus in nuts, legumes, and outer layers of cereal grains is present as phytic acid. See also Appendix D, section on Minerals and Oxalic Acid
[14] Dimensions of can: 1st dimension represents diameter; 2d dimension, height of can. 1st or left-hand digit in each dimension gives number of whole inches; next 2 digits give additional fraction of dimension expressed as 16th of an inch.
[40] Width at widest part; thickness at thickest part.
[43] Value for product without added salt.
[51] For information on ingredients used in preparation, see ARS 62–13 (7), table 22, p. 26.
[106] Formula used to calculate nutritive values shown in Agr. Handb. No. 8, rev. 1963.
[229] Weight of steak with skin and bones, approx. 146 g.
[230] Commercial products. Frozen custard must contain egg yolk, which contributes slightly more vitamin A value than is present in ice creams made with milk products only.
[231] Precut slices do not apply to frozen custard.
[232] Based on corrected value of 128 Cal. per 100 g.
[233] For red cherry or strawberry jam and preserves, value would be 43 mg. for 10-oz. jar, 51 mg. for 12-oz. jar, 136 mg. for 2-lb. jar, 2 mg. for ½-oz. packet, 3 mg. for 1 tbsp.

TABLE 1.—*Nutritive values for household measures and market units of foods*—Continued

[Item numbers correspond to those in table 1 of Handbook No. 8, revised 1963. Values in parentheses denote imputed values usually from another form of the food or from a similar food. Zeros in parentheses indicate that amount of a constituent, if present, is probably too small to be measured. Dashes (—) denote lack of reliable data for a constituent believed to be present in a measurable amount. Calculated values, as those based on a recipe, are not in parentheses]

Item No.	Food, approximate measures, units, and weight (edible part unless footnotes indicate otherwise)			Water	Food energy	Protein	Fat	Carbohydrate	Calcium	Phosphorus	Iron	Sodium	Potassium	Vitamin A value	Thiamin	Riboflavin	Niacin	Ascorbic acid
(A)	(B)			(C)	(D)	(E)	(F)	(G)	(H)	(I)	(J)	(K)	(L)	(M)	(N)	(O)	(P)	(Q)
			Grams	*Percent*	*Calories*	*Grams*	*Grams*	*Grams*	*Milligrams*	*Milligrams*	*Milligrams*	*Milligrams*	*Milligrams*	*International units*	*Milligrams*	*Milligrams*	*Milligrams*	*Milligrams*
1149	**Jellies, sweetened with regular amount of nutritive sweetener:**																	
	Container and approx. contents:																	
a	Glass or jar, net wt., 10 oz	1 glass or jar	284	29	775	0.3	0.3	200.5	60	20	4.3	48	213	30	0.03	0.09	0.6	[234] 11
b	Jar, net wt., 32 oz. (2 lb.)	1 jar	907	29	2,476	.9	.9	640.3	190	63	13.6	154	680	90	.09	.27	1.8	[234] 36
c	Packet, net wt., ½ oz. (approx. ¾ tbsp.)	1 packet	14	29	38	Trace	Trace	9.9	3	1	.2	2	11	Trace	Trace	Trace	Trace	[234] 1
d	Cup	1 cup	300	29	819	.3	.3	211.8	63	21	4.5	51	225	30	.03	.09	.6	[234] 12
e	Tablespoon	1 tbsp	18	29	49	Trace	Trace	12.7	4	1	.3	3	14	Trace	Trace	.01	Trace	[234] 1
	Kale, leaves without stems, midribs: [58]																	
1153	Raw	1 lb	454	82.7	240	(27.2)	(3.6)	40.8	1,129	422	12.2	(340)	(1,715)	45,360	.73	1.18	9.5	844
1155	Cooked (boiled), drained:																	
a	Cup	1 cup	110	87.8	43	(5.0)	(.8)	6.7	206	64	1.8	[20] (47)	(243)	9,130	.11	.20	1.8	102
b	Pound	1 lb	454	87.8	177	(20.4)	(3.2)	27.7	848	263	7.3	[20] (195)	(1,002)	37,650	.45	.82	7.3	422
	Frozen (leaf kale):																	
1157	Not thawed:																	
a	Container, net wt., 10 oz	1 container	284	90.0	91	9.1	1.4	15.6	381	142	3.1	74	684	23,290	.23	.51	2.3	182
b	Pound	1 lb	454	90.0	145	14.5	2.3	24.9	608	227	5.0	118	1,093	37,200	.36	.82	3.6	290
1158	Cooked (boiled), drained:																	
a	Yield from 10 oz., frozen kale	1⅔ cups	218	90.5	68	6.5	1.1	11.8	264	105	2.2	[20] 46	421	17,880	.13	.33	1.5	83
b	Yield from 1 lb., frozen kale	2⅔ cups	350	90.5	109	10.5	1.8	18.9	424	168	3.5	[20] 74	676	28,700	.21	.53	2.5	133
c	Cup	1 cup	130	90.5	40	3.9	.7	7.0	157	62	1.3	[20] 27	251	10,660	.08	.20	.9	49
d	Pound (yield from 1.3 lb., frozen kale)	1 lb	454	90.5	141	13.6	2.3	24.5	549	218	4.5	[20] 95	875	37,200	.27	.68	3.2	172
1160	**Kidney, beef, cooked (braised):**																	
a	Cup, slices approx. ¼ in. thick or pieces approx. ½ × ½ × ¼ in.	1 cup	140	53.0	353	46.2	16.8	1.1	25	342	18.3	[43] 354	454	1,610	.71	6.75	15.0	—
b	Pound	1 lb	454	53.0	1,143	149.7	54.4	3.6	82	1,107	59.4	[43] 1,148	1,470	5,220	2.31	21.86	48.5	—
	Knockwurst. See Sausage, cold cuts, and luncheon meats (item 2002).																	
	Kohlrabi, thickened bulb-like stems:																	
1165	Raw, diced	1 cup	140	90.3	41	2.8	.1	9.2	57	71	.1	11	521	30	.08	.06	.4	92
1166	Cooked (boiled), drained:																	
a	Cup, diced	1 cup	165	92.2	40	2.8	.2	8.7	54	68	.5	[20] 10	429	30	.10	.05	.3	71
b	Pound	1 lb	454	92.2	109	7.7	.5	24.0	150	186	1.4	[20] 27	1,179	90	.27	.14	.9	195
1167	**Kumquats,** raw, medium size (refuse: seeds, 7%)[1]	1 kumquat	20	81.3	12	.2	Trace	3.2	12	4	.1	1	44	110	.01	.02	—	7
	Ladyfingers. See Cookies (item 822).																	
	Lamb, retail cuts: [49]																	
	Leg:																	
1184	**Raw, lean with fat:**																	
a	With bone (70% lean, 14% fat) (refuse: bone, 16%).[1]	1 lb	454	64.8	845	67.7	61.7	0	38	617	5.3	237	1,083	—	.61	.84	19.6	—
b	Without bone (83% lean, 17% fat)	1 lb	454	64.8	1,007	80.7	73.5	0	45	735	6.4	282	1,291	—	.72	1.00	23.4	—
	Cooked (roasted):																	
1185	Lean with fat (83% lean, 17% fat):																	
a	Yield from 1 lb., raw lamb with bone (item 1184a).	9.4 oz	267	54.0	745	67.6	50.5	0	29	555	4.5	106	757	—	.40	.72	14.7	—
b	Yield from 1 lb., raw lamb without bone (item 1184b).	11.2 oz	318	54.0	887	80.5	60.1	0	35	661	5.4	197	902	—	.48	.86	17.5	—
c	Cup, chopped or diced pieces (not packed)	1 cup	140	54.0	391	35.4	26.5	0	15	291	2.4	87	396	—	.21	.38	7.7	—
d	Pound	1 lb	454	54.0	1,266	114.8	85.7	0	50	943	7.7	281	1,286	—	.68	1.22	24.9	—
e	Piece, approx. 4⅛ in. long, 2¼ in. wide, ¼ in. thick; wt., 1½ oz.	2 pieces or 3 oz.	85	54.0	237	21.5	16.1	0	9	177	1.4	53	241	—	.13	.23	4.7	—
1187	Lean, trimmed of separable fat:																	
a	Yield from 1 lb., raw lamb with bone (item 1184a).	7.8 oz	221	62.2	411	63.4	15.5	0	29	526	4.9	155	710	—	.35	.66	13.7	—
b	Yield from 1 lb., raw lamb without bone (item 1184b).	9.3 oz	264	62.2	491	75.8	18.5	0	34	628	5.8	186	849	—	.42	.79	16.4	—
c	Cup, chopped or diced pieces (not packed)	1 cup	140	62.2	260	40.2	9.8	0	18	333	3.1	98	450	—	.22	.42	8.7	—
d	Pound	1 lb	454	62.2	844	130.2	31.8	0	59	1,080	10.0	319	1,458	—	.73	1.36	28.1	—
e	Piece, approx. 4⅛ in. long, 2¼ in. wide, ¼ in. thick; wt., 1½ oz.	2 pieces or 3 oz.	85	62.2	158	24.4	6.0	0	11	202	1.9	60	273	—	.14	.26	5.3	—

(A)	(B)			(C)	(D)	(E)	(F)	(G)	(H)	(I)	(J)	(K)	(L)	(M)	(N)	(O)	(P)	(Q)
	Loin chops:																	
1199	Raw (62% lean, 24% fat) (refuse: bone, 14%)[1]	1 lb	454	57.7	1,146	63.7	97.0	0	35	567	4.7	223	1,019	—	0.57	0.79	18.5	—
	Cooked (broiled):																	
1200	Lean with fat (66% lean, 34% fat):																	
a	Yield from 1 lb., raw chops with bone (item 1199).	10.1 oz	285	47.0	1,023	62.7	83.8	0	26	490	3.7	154	702	—	.34	.66	14.3	—
	Yield from 1 chop, raw with bone; ⅓ or ¼ of item 1199:																	
b	Cut 3 per pound	3.4 oz	95	47.0	341	20.9	27.9	0	9	163	1.2	51	234	—	.11	.22	4.8	—
c	Cut 4 per pound	2.5 oz	71	47.0	255	15.6	20.9	0	6	122	.9	38	175	—	.09	.16	3.6	—
d	Pound	1 lb	454	47.0	1,628	99.8	133.4	0	41	780	5.9	245	1,118	—	.54	1.04	22.7	—
1202	Lean, trimmed of separable fat:																	
a	Yield from 1 lb., raw chops with bone (item 1199).	6.9 oz	196	62.1	368	55.3	14.7	0	24	429	3.9	135	619	—	.29	.55	12.0	—
	Yield from 1 chop, raw with bone; ⅓ or ¼ of item 1199:																	
b	Cut 3 per pound	2.3 oz	65	62.1	122	18.3	4.9	0	8	142	1.3	45	205	—	.10	.18	4.0	—
c	Cut 4 per pound	1.7 oz	49	62.1	92	13.8	3.7	0	6	107	1.0	34	155	—	.07	.14	3.0	—
d	Pound	1 lb	454	62.1	853	127.9	34.0	0	54	993	9.1	313	1,432	—	.68	1.27	27.7	—
	Rib chops:																	
1214	Raw (54% lean, 26% fat) (refuse: bone, 20%)[1]	1 lb	454	53.4	1,229	54.7	110.2	0	33	478	3.6	191	875	—	.49	.68	15.8	—
	Cooked (broiled):																	
1215	Lean with fat (62% lean, 38% fat):																	
a	Yield from 1 lb., raw chops with bone (item 1214).	9.5 oz	268	42.9	1,091	53.9	95.4	0	24	418	2.9	132	604	—	.32	.56	12.3	—
	Yield from 1 chop, raw with bone; ⅓ or ¼ of item 1214:																	
b	Cut 3 per pound	3.1 oz	89	42.9	362	17.9	31.7	0	8	139	1.0	44	200	—	.11	.19	4.1	—
c	Cut 4 per pound	2.4 oz	67	42.9	273	13.5	23.9	0	6	105	.7	33	151	—	.08	.14	3.1	—
d	Pound	1 lb	454	42.9	1,846	91.2	161.5	0	41	708	5.0	223	1,021	—	.54	.95	20.9	—
1217	Lean, trimmed of separable fat:																	
a	Yield from 1 lb., raw chops with bone (item 1214).	6 oz	171	60.3	361	46.5	18.0	0	19	363	3.2	114	521	—	.26	.46	10.1	—
	Yield from 1 chop, raw with bone; ⅓ or ¼ of item 1214:																	
b	Cut 3 per pound	2 oz	57	60.3	120	15.5	6.0	0	6	121	1.1	38	174	—	.09	.15	3.4	—
c	Cut 4 per pound	1½ oz	43	60.3	91	11.7	4.5	0	5	91	.8	29	131	—	.06	.12	2.5	—
d	Pound	1 lb	454	60.3	957	123.4	47.6	0	50	962	8.6	302	1,382	—	.68	1.22	26.8	—
	Shoulder:																	
1229	Raw, lean with fat:																	
a	With bone (63% lean, 22% fat) (refuse: bone, 15%).[1]	1 lb	454	59.6	1,082	58.9	92.0	0	35	516	3.9	206	942	—	.53	.73	17.1	—
b	Without bone (74% lean, 26% fat)	1 lb	454	59.6	1,275	69.4	108.4	0	41	608	4.5	243	1,110	—	.62	.86	20.1	—
	Cooked (roasted):																	
1230	Lean with fat (74% lean, 26% fat):																	
a	Yield from 1 lb., raw lamb with bone (item 1229a).	9½ oz	270	49.6	913	58.6	73.4	0	27	464	3.2	144	656	—	.35	.62	12.7	—
b	Yield from 1 lb., raw lamb without bone (item 1229b).	11.2 oz	318	49.6	1,075	69.0	86.5	0	32	547	3.8	169	773	—	.41	.73	14.9	—
c	Cup, chopped or diced pieces (not packed)	1 cup	140	49.6	473	30.4	38.1	0	14	241	1.7	74	340	—	.18	.32	6.6	—
d	Pound	1 lb	454	49.6	1,533	98.4	123.4	0	45	780	5.4	241	1,102	—	.59	1.04	21.3	—
e	Piece, approx. 2½ in. long, 2½ in. wide, ¼ in. thick; wt., 1 oz.	3 pieces or 3 oz.	85	49.6	287	18.4	23.1	0	9	146	1.0	45	206	—	.11	.20	4.0	—
1232	Lean, trimmed of separable fat:																	
a	Yield from 1 lb., raw lamb with bone (item 1229a).	7 oz	200	61.4	410	53.6	20.0	0	24	438	3.8	131	600	—	.30	.56	11.4	—
b	Yield from 1 lb., raw lamb without bone (item 1229b).	8.3 oz	235	61.4	482	63.0	23.5	0	28	515	4.5	154	706	—	.35	.66	13.4	—
c	Cup, chopped or diced pieces (not packed)	1 cup	140	61.4	287	37.5	14.0	0	17	307	2.7	92	420	—	.21	.39	8.0	—
d	Pound	1 lb	454	61.4	930	121.6	45.4	0	54	993	8.6	298	1,362	—	.68	1.27	25.9	—
e	Piece, approx. 2½ in. long, 2½ in. wide, ¼ in. thick; wt., 1 oz.	3 pieces or 3 oz.	85	61.4	174	22.8	8.5	0	10	186	1.6	56	255	—	.13	.24	4.8	—
1241	**Lard:**																	
a	Pound	1 lb	454	0	4,091	0	453.6	0	0	0	0	0	0	0	0	0	0	0
b	Cup	1 cup	205	0	1,849	0	205.0	0	0	0	0	0	0	0	0	0	0	0
c	Tablespoon	1 tbsp	13	0	117	0	13.0	0	0	0	0	0	0	0	0	0	0	0

[1] Measure and weight apply to food as it is described with inedible part or parts (refuse) included.

[29] Value is for unsalted product. If salt is used, increase value by 236 mg. per 100 g. of vegetable—an estimated figure based on typical amount of salt (0.6%) in canned vegetables. See also Appendix C, section on Cooked Vegetables

[41] Value for product without added salt.

[49] For further information about items and basis of vitamin and mineral values, see Appendix B, section on Foods Measured in Pieces, Slices, and Other Units and Appendix C, section on Meats Values for cooked items apply to products prepared without added salt or other seasoning.

[55] Oxalic acid present may combine with calcium and magnesium to form insoluble compounds. For further information, see Appendix D, section on Minerals and Oxalic Acid

[234] For guava jelly, value would be 114 mg. for 10-oz. jar, 7 mg. for 1 tbsp.

TABLE 1.—*Nutritive values for household measures and market units of foods*—Continued

[Item numbers correspond to those in table 1 of Handbook No. 8, revised 1963. Values in parentheses denote imputed values usually from another form of the food or from a similar food. Zeros in parentheses indicate that amount of a constituent, if present, is probably too small to be measured. Dashes (—) denote lack of reliable data for a constituent believed to be present in a measurable amount. Calculated values, as those based on a recipe, are not in parentheses]

Item No.	Food, approximate measures, units, and weight (edible part unless footnotes indicate otherwise)			Water	Food energy	Protein	Fat	Carbohydrate	Calcium	Phosphorus	Iron	Sodium	Potassium	Vitamin A value	Thiamin	Riboflavin	Niacin	Ascorbic acid
(A)	(B)			(C)	(D)	(E)	(F)	(G)	(H)	(I)	(J)	(K)	(L)	(M)	(N)	(O)	(P)	(Q)
			Grams	*Percent*	*Calories*	*Grams*	*Grams*	*Grams*	*Milligrams*	*Milligrams*	*Milligrams*	*Milligrams*	*Milligrams*	*International units*	*Milligrams*	*Milligrams*	*Milligrams*	*Milligrams*
	Lemons, raw; portion used:																	
1243	Pulp (peeled fruit):																	
	Whole fruit [210] (refuse: peel and seeds, 33%): [1]																	
	Large:																	
a	2⅝-in. diam., size 115 [235]	1 lemon	158	90.1	29	1.2	0.3	8.7	28	17	0.6	2	146	20	0.04	0.02	0.1	[236] 56
b	2¼-in. diam., size 140 [235]	1 lemon	130	90.1	24	1.0	.3	7.1	23	14	.5	2	120	20	.03	.02	.1	[236] 46
c	Medium, 2⅛-in. diam., size 165 [235]	1 lemon	110	90.1	20	.8	.2	6.0	19	12	.4	1	102	10	.03	.01	.1	[236] 39
d	Slice, "cartwheel," 3/16 in. thick, with peel (refuse: peel, 32%); [1] 9–11 slices in fruit of medium to large sizes.	1 slice [237]	10	90.1	2	.1	Trace	.5	2	1	Trace	Trace	9	Trace	Trace	Trace	Trace	[236] 4
	Wedges, with peel (refuse: peel, 32%), [1] prepared from—																	
	Large fruit, 2⅝-in. diam., size 115: [235]																	
e	Wedge, approx. 1⅞-in. arc; ¼ of fruit	1 wedge	40	90.1	7	.3	.1	2.2	7	4	.2	1	38	10	.01	.01	Trace	[236] 14
f	Wedge, approx. 1¼-in. arc; ⅙ of fruit	1 wedge	26	90.1	5	.2	.1	1.5	5	3	.1	Trace	24	Trace	.01	Trace	Trace	[236] 9
	Medium fruit, 2⅛-in. diam., size 165: [235]																	
g	Wedge, 1⅝-in. arc; ¼ of fruit	1 wedge	28	90.1	5	.2	.1	1.6	5	3	.1	Trace	26	Trace	.01	Trace	Trace	[236] 10
h	Wedge, 1⅛-in. arc; ⅙ of fruit	1 wedge	18	90.1	3	.1	Trace	1.0	3	2	.1	Trace	17	Trace	Trace	Trace	Trace	[236] 6
1244	Fruit, including peel [210] (refuse: seeds, 1%): [1]																	
	Large:																	
a	2⅝-in. diam., size 115 [235]	1 lemon	158	87.4	[238] 31	1.9	.5	16.7	95	28	1.1	5	227	50	.08	.06	.3	120
b	2¼-in. diam., size 140 [235]	1 lemon	130	87.4	[238] 26	1.5	.4	13.8	79	19	.9	4	187	40	.06	.05	.3	99
c	Medium, 2⅛-in. diam., size 165 [235]	1 lemon	110	87.4	[238] 22	1.3	.3	11.7	66	16	.8	3	158	30	.05	.04	.2	84
1245	**Lemon juice, raw:**																	
a	Cup	1 cup	244	91.0	61	1.2	.5	19.5	17	24	.5	2	344	50	.07	.02	.2	112
b	Tablespoon	1 tbsp	15.2	91.0	4	.1	Trace	1.2	1	2	Trace	Trace	21	Trace	Trace	Trace	Trace	7
c	Yield from 1 lb. of lemons (approx. range, ⅝–⅞ cup of juice).	¾ cup (approx. avg.).	195	91.0	49	1.0	.4	15.6	14	20	.4	2	275	40	.06	.02	.2	90
1246	**Lemon juice, canned, unsweetened:**																	
	Can and approx. contents:																	
a	Size, 202 × 314 [14] (6½Z); net contents, 6 fl. oz	1 can	183	91.6	42	.7	.2	13.9	13	18	.4	2	258	40	.05	.02	.2	77
b	Cup	1 cup	244	91.6	56	1.0	.2	18.5	17	24	.5	2	344	50	.07	.02	.2	102
c	Tablespoon	1 tbsp	15.2	91.6	3	.1	Trace	1.2	1	2	Trace	Trace	21	Trace	Trace	Trace	Trace	6
d	Fluid ounce	1 fl. oz	30.6	91.6	7	.1	Trace	2.3	2	3	.1	Trace	43	10	.01	Trace	Trace	13
	Lemon juice, frozen, unsweetened:																	
1247	Single-strength juice:																	
a	6 fluid ounces	1 can	183	92.0	40	.7	.4	13.2	13	16	.5	2	258	40	.05	.02	.2	81
b	Tablespoon	1 tbsp	15.2	92.0	3	.1	Trace	1.1	1	1	Trace	Trace	21	Trace	Trace	Trace	Trace	7
1248	Concentrate (42° Brix)	1 lb	454	58.0	526	10.4	4.1	169.6	150	218	4.1	23	2,985	360	.64	.27	1.4	1,043
	Lemon peel:																	
1249	Raw, grated (medium grating):																	
a	Tablespoon	1 tbsp	6	81.6	([239])	.1	Trace	1.0	8	1	Trace	Trace	10	Trace	Trace	Trace	Trace	8
b	Teaspoon	1 tsp	2	81.6	([239])	Trace	Trace	.3	3	Trace	Trace	Trace	3	Trace	Trace	Trace	Trace	3
1250	Candied	1 oz	28	17.4	90	.1	.1	22.9	—	—	—	—	—	—	—	—	—	—
	Lemonade concentrate, frozen:																	
1251	Undiluted:																	
	Can and approx. contents:																	
a	6 fl. oz. (yields 1 qt. diluted juice weighing 990 g.).	1 can	219	48.5	427	.4	.2	111.9	9	13	.4	4	153	40	.05	.06	.7	66
b	12 fl. oz. (yields 2 qt. diluted juice weighing 1,980 g.).	1 can	440	48.5	858	.9	.4	224.8	18	26	.9	9	308	80	.10	.12	1.3	132
c	32 fl. oz. (1 qt.) (yields 5⅓ qt. diluted juice weighing 5,291 g.).	1 can	1,173	48.5	2,287	2.3	1.2	599.4	47	70	2.3	23	821	200	.26	.30	3.5	352
1252	Diluted with 4⅓ parts water by volume:																	
a	Quart	1 qt	990	88.5	427	.4	.2	111.9	9	13	.4	4	153	40	.05	.06	.7	66
b	Cup	1 cup	248	88.5	107	.1	Trace	28.3	2	3	.1	1	40	10	.01	.02	.2	17
c	Glass (6 fl. oz.)	1 glass	185	88.5	81	.1	Trace	21.1	2	2	.1	1	30	10	.01	.01	.1	13
	Lentils, mature seeds, dry: [5]																	
	Whole:																	
1253	Raw	1 cup	190	11.1	646	46.9	2.1	114.2	150	716	12.9	57	1,501	110	.70	.42	3.8	—

(A)	(B)		(C)	(D)	(E)	(F)	(G)	(H)	(I)	(J)	(K)	(L)	(M)	(N)	(O)	(P)	(Q)
1254	Cooked	1 cup	200	72.0	212	15.6	Trace	38.6	50	238	4.2	[48] —	498	40	0.14	0.12	1.2	0
1255	Split, without seedcoat, raw	1 cup	190	10.4	656	46.9	1.7	117.4	87	494	12.9	—	—	110	.70	.42	3.8	—
	Lettuce, raw:																	
1256	Butterhead varieties such as Boston types and Bibb:																	
a	Whole, head approx. 5-in. diam. (refuse: outer leaves and core, 26%).[1]	1 head	220	95.1	23	2.0	.3	4.1	57	42	3.3	15	430	1,580	.10	.10	.5	18
b	Leaves, 1 large (outer leaf), 2 medium (inner leaves), or 3 small (large heart leaves).	1 large, 2 medium, or 3 small leaves.	15	95.1	2	.2	Trace	.4	5	4	.3	1	40	150	.01	.01	Trace	1
c	Chopped or shredded pieces	1 cup	55	95.1	8	.7	.1	1.4	19	14	1.1	5	145	530	.08	.08	.2	[86] 4
d	Pound	1 lb	454	95.1	64	5.4	.9	11.3	159	118	9.1	41	1,198	4,400	.27	.27	1.4	36
1257	Cos, or romaine, such as Dark Green and White Paris:																	
a	Chopped or shredded pieces	1 cup	55	94.0	10	.7	.2	1.9	37	14	.8	5	145	1,050	.03	.04	.2	[86] 10
b	Pound	1 lb	454	94.0	82	5.9	1.4	15.9	308	113	6.4	41	1,198	8,620	.23	.36	1.8	82
1258	Crisphead varieties such as Iceberg, New York, Great Lakes strains:																	
	Whole, prepackaged trimmed head, approx. 6-in. diam.; wt., 1¼ lb.:																	
a	Good quality (refuse: core, 5%)[1]	1 head	567	95.5	70	4.8	.5	15.6	108	118	2.7	48	943	1,780	.32	.32	1.6	32
b	Fair quality (refuse: coarse leaves and core, 26%).[1]	1 head	567	95.5	55	3.8	.4	12.2	84	92	2.1	38	734	1,380	.25	.25	1.3	25
c	Portion of leaf, 5 × 4½ in. (dimensions with edges curled up).	1 piece	20	95.5	3	.2	Trace	.6	4	4	.1	2	35	70	.01	.01	.1	1
	Cut up:																	
	Wedge, approx. ¼ of head:																	
d	From good-quality head	1 wedge	135	95.5	18	1.2	.1	3.9	27	30	.7	12	236	450	.08	.08	.4	[86] 8
e	From fair-quality head	1 wedge	105	95.5	14	.9	.1	3.0	21	23	.5	9	184	350	.06	.06	.3	[86] 6
	Wedge, approx. ⅛ of head:																	
f	From good-quality head	1 wedge	90	95.5	12	.8	.1	2.6	18	20	.5	8	158	300	.05	.05	.3	[86] 5
g	From fair-quality head	1 wedge	70	95.5	9	.6	.1	2.0	14	15	.4	6	123	230	.04	.04	.2	[86] 4
h	Chunks, small	1 cup	75	95.5	10	.7	.1	2.2	15	17	.4	7	131	250	.05	.05	.2	[86] 5
i	Chopped or shredded pieces	1 cup	55	95.5	7	.5	.1	1.6	11	12	.3	5	96	180	.03	.03	.2	[86] 3
j	Pound	1 lb	454	95.5	59	4.1	.5	13.2	91	100	2.3	41	794	1,500	.27	.27	1.4	27
1259	Looseleaf or bunching varieties such as Grand Rapids, Salad Bowl, Simpson:																	
a	Chopped or shredded pieces	1 cup	55	94.0	10	.7	.2	1.9	37	14	.8	5	145	1,050	.03	.04	.2	[86] 10
b	Pound	1 lb	454	94.0	82	5.9	1.4	15.9	308	113	6.4	41	1,198	8,620	.23	.36	1.8	82
	Lima beans. See Beans, lima (items 164–177).																	
1260	Limes,[210] acid type, raw, pulp from fruit of 2-in. diam. (refuse: peel and seeds, 16%).[1]	1 lime	80	89.3	19	.5	.1	6.4	22	12	.4	1	69	10	.02	.01	.1	25
1261	Limejuice, raw; and limes used for juice:																	
	Juice:																	
a	Cup	1 cup	246	90.3	64	.7	.2	22.1	22	27	.5	2	256	20	.05	.02	.2	79
b	Tablespoon	1 tbsp	15.4	90.3	4	Trace	Trace	1.4	1	2	Trace	Trace	16	Trace	Trace	Trace	Trace	5
	Whole fruit used for juice[210] (refuse: peel, seeds, membranes, 52%):[1]																	
c	Large, 2⅛-in. diam.; yield of juice, approx. 46 g. (3 tbsp.).	1 lime	95	90.3	12	.1	Trace	4.1	4	5	.1	Trace	47	Trace	.01	Trace	Trace	15
d	Medium, 2-in. diam.; yield of juice, approx. 38 g. (2½ tbsp.).	1 lime	80	90.3	10	.1	Trace	3.5	3	4	.1	Trace	40	Trace	.01	Trace	Trace	12
e	Small, 1⅞-in. diam.; yield of juice, approx. 34 g. (2¼ tbsp.).	1 lime	70	90.3	9	.1	Trace	3.0	3	4	.1	Trace	35	Trace	.01	Trace	Trace	11
1262	Limejuice, canned unsweetened:																	
a	Cup	1 cup	246	90.3	64	.7	.2	22.1	22	27	.5	2	256	20	.05	.02	.2	52
b	Tablespoon	1 tbsp	15.4	90.3	4	Trace	Trace	1.4	1	2	Trace	Trace	16	Trace	Trace	Trace	Trace	3
c	Fluid ounce	1 fl. oz	30.7	90.3	8	.1	Trace	2.8	3	3	.1	Trace	32	Trace	.01	Trace	Trace	6
	Limeade concentrate, frozen:																	
1263	Undiluted:																	
	Can and approx. contents:																	
a	6 fl. oz. (yields 1 qt. diluted juice weighing 989 g.).	1 can	218	50.0	408	.4	.2	107.9	11	13	.2	Trace	129	Trace	.02	.02	.2	26
b	12 fl. oz. (yields 2 qt. diluted juice weighing 1,977 g.).	1 can	437	50.0	817	.9	.4	216.3	22	26	.4	Trace	258	Trace	.04	.04	.4	52

[1] Measure and weight apply to food as it is described with inedible part or parts (refuse) included.

[8] Most of phosphorus in nuts, legumes, and outer layers of cereal grains is present as phytic acid. See also Appendix D, section on Minerals and Oxalic Acid

[14] Dimensions of can: 1st dimension represents diameter; 2d dimension, height of can. 1st or left-hand digit in each dimension gives number of whole inches; next 2 digits give additional fraction of dimension expressed as 16th of an inch.

[48] Value for product without added salt.

[86] Value does not allow for losses that might occur from cutting, chopping, or shredding. See also Appendix C, section on Cut Forms of Raw Fruits and Vegetables; Capping of Strawberries

[210] See Appendix B, section on Citrus Fruits for explanation of basis for sizes and weights shown for whole citrus fruits.

[235] Size refers to count of fruit in 7/10-bushel container with net weight of approx. 40 lb.

[236] Applies to lemons marketed in summer.

[237] Average-size slice from medium and large fruits in the retail market. Average weights of slices cut from fruits of these sizes range from about 9 to 10.5 g.

[238] Based on pulp. There is no basis for assessing caloric value of peel or effect that inclusion of peel may have on digestibility of product.

[239] Value cannot be calculated inasmuch as digestibility of peel is not known.

TABLE 1.—*Nutritive values for household measures and market units of foods*—Continued

[Item numbers correspond to those in table 1 of Handbook No. 8, revised 1963. Values in parentheses denote imputed values usually from another form of the food or from a similar food. Zeros in parentheses indicate that amount of a constituent, if present, is probably too small to be measured. Dashes (—) denote lack of reliable data for a constituent believed to be present in a measurable amount. Calculated values, as those based on a recipe, are not in parentheses]

Item No.	Food, approximate measures, units, and weight (edible part unless footnotes indicate otherwise)			Water	Food energy	Protein	Fat	Carbohydrate	Calcium	Phosphorus	Iron	Sodium	Potassium	Vitamin A value	Thiamin	Riboflavin	Niacin	Ascorbic acid
(A)	(B)			(C)	(D)	(E)	(F)	(G)	(H)	(I)	(J)	(K)	(L)	(M)	(N)	(O)	(P)	(Q)
			Grams	*Percent*	*Calories*	*Grams*	*Grams*	*Grams*	*Milligrams*	*Milligrams*	*Milligrams*	*Milligrams*	*Milligrams*	*International units*	*Milligrams*	*Milligrams*	*Milligrams*	*Milligrams*
	Limeade concentrate, frozen—Continued																	
	Undiluted—Continued																	
	Can and approx. contents—Continued																	
c	32 fl. oz. (1 qt.) (yields 5⅓ qt. diluted juice weighing 5,283 g.).	1 can	1,165	50.0	2,179	2.3	1.2	576.7	58	70	1.2	Trace	687	Trace	0.12	0.12	1.2	140
1264	Diluted with 4⅓ parts water by volume:																	
a	Quart	1 qt	989	88.9	408	.4	.2	107.9	11	13	.2	Trace	129	Trace	.02	.02	.2	26
b	Cup	1 cup	247	88.9	102	.1	Trace	27.0	3	3	Trace	Trace	32	Trace	Trace	Trace	Trace	6
c	Glass (6 fl. oz.)	1 glass	185	88.9	76	.1	Trace	20.4	2	2	Trace	Trace	24	Trace	Trace	Trace	Trace	4
	Liver:																	
1267	Beef, cooked (fried):																	
a	Slice, approx. 6½ in. long, 2⅜ in. wide,[240] ⅜ in. thick; wt., 3 oz.	1 slice	85	56.0	195	22.4	9.0	4.5	9	405	7.5	[43] 156	323	[241] 45,390	.22	3.56	14.0	23
b	Pound (approx. 5⅓ slices (item 1267a))	1 lb	454	56.0	1,039	119.8	48.1	24.0	50	2,159	39.9	[43] 835	1,724	[241] 242,220	1.18	19.01	74.8	122
1269	Calf, cooked (fried):																	
a	Slice, approx. 6½ in. long, 2⅜ in. wide,[240] ⅜ in. thick; wt., 3 oz.	1 slice	85	51.4	222	25.1	11.2	3.4	11	456	12.1	[43] 100	385	[241] 27,800	.20	3.54	14.0	31
b	Pound (approx. 5⅓ slices (item 1269a))	1 lb	454	51.4	1,184	133.8	59.9	18.1	59	2,436	64.4	[43] 535	2,055	[241] 148,330	1.09	18.92	74.8	168
1271	Chicken, all classes, cooked (simmered):																	
a	Whole, approx. 2 in. long, 2 in. wide, ⅝ in. thick	1 liver	25	65.0	41	6.6	1.1	.8	3	40	2.1	[43] 15	38	[241] 3,080	.04	.67	2.9	4
b	Chopped	1 cup	140	65.0	231	37.1	6.2	4.3	15	223	11.9	[43] 85	211	[241] 17,220	.24	3.77	16.4	22
c	Pound (whole, approx. 18 livers (item 1271a), chopped, approx. 3¼ cups).	1 lb	454	65.0	748	120.2	20.0	14.1	50	721	38.6	[43] 277	685	[241] 55,790	.77	12.20	53.1	73
1274	Hog, cooked (fried):																	
a	Slice, approx. 6½ in. long, 2⅜ in. wide,[240] ⅜ in. thick; wt., 3 oz.	1 slice	85	54.0	205	25.4	9.8	2.1	13	458	24.7	[43] 94	336	[241] 12,670	.29	3.71	19.0	19
b	Pound (approx. 5⅓ slices (item 1274a))	1 lb	454	54.0	1,093	135.6	52.2	11.3	68	2,445	132.0	[43] 503	1,792	[241] 67,590	1.54	19.78	101.2	100
1276	Lamb, cooked (broiled):																	
a	Slice, approx. 3½ in. long, 2 in. wide,[240] ⅜ in. thick; wt., 1.6 oz.	1 slice	45	50.4	117	14.5	5.6	1.3	7	257	8.1	[43] 38	149	[241] 33,530	.22	2.30	11.2	16
b	Pound (approx. 10 slices (item 1276a))	1 lb	454	50.4	1,184	146.5	56.2	12.7	73	2,595	81.2	[43] 386	1,501	[241] 337,930	2.22	23.18	112.9	163
1278	Turkey, all classes, cooked (simmered):																	
	Whole:																	
a	From 20- to 25-lb. turkey	1 liver	122	63.3	212	34.0	5.9	3.8	—	—	—	[43] 67	172	[241] 21,350	.20	2.55	17.4	—
b	From 17-lb. turkey	1 liver	110	63.3	191	30.7	5.3	3.4	—	—	—	[43] 61	155	[241] 19,250	.18	2.30	15.7	—
c	From 12- to 13-lb. turkey	1 liver	75	63.3	131	20.9	3.6	2.3	—	—	—	[43] 41	106	[241] 13,130	.12	1.57	10.7	—
d	Chopped	1 cup	140	63.3	244	39.1	6.7	4.3	—	—	—	[43] 77	197	[241] 24,500	.22	2.93	20.0	—
e	Pound (whole, approx. number of livers: 3.7 of item 1278a, 4⅛ of item 1278b, or 6 of item 1278c; chopped, approx. 3¼ cups).	1 lb	454	63.3	789	126.6	21.8	14.1	—	—	—	[43] 249	640	[241] 79,380	.73	9.48	64.9	—
	Liver paste. See Pâté de foie gras (item 1478).																	
	Liver sausage or liverwurst. See Sausage, cold cuts, and luncheon meats (items 2003–2004).																	
1280	**Lobster, northern,** cooked:																	
a	Cup (½-in. cubes or bite-size pieces, ¾ × ¾ × ½ in.).	1 cup	145	76.8	138	27.1	2.2	.4	94	278	1.2	305	261	—	.15	.10	—	—
b	Pound	1 lb	454	76.8	431	84.8	6.8	1.4	295	871	3.6	953	816	—	.45	.32	—	—
1281	**Lobster Newburg** [242]	1 cup	250	64.0	485	46.3	26.5	12.8	218	480	2.3	[43] 573	428	—	.18	.28	—	—
1282	**Lobster salad** [243] (approx. ½ cup of salad; wt., 4 oz.; with tomato wedges, wt., 5⅓ oz.).	1 salad	260	80.3	286	26.3	16.6	6.0	94	247	2.3	[43] 322	686	—	.23	.21	—	47
	Lobster paste. See Shrimp or lobster paste, canned (item 2047).																	
	Loganberries:																	
1283	Raw:																	
a	Cup	1 cup	144	83.0	89	1.4	.9	21.5	50	24	1.7	(1)	245	(290)	(.04)	(.06)	(.6)	35
b	Pound	1 lb	454	83.0	281	4.5	2.7	67.6	159	77	5.4	(5)	771	(910)	(.14)	(.18)	(1.8)	109
1291	**Loquats,** raw (refuse: seeds, 23%) [1]	10 fruits	160	86.5	59	.5	.2	15.3	25	44	.5	—	429	830	—	—	—	1
	Luncheon meat. See Sausage, cold cuts, and luncheon meats (items 2005–2006).																	
1295	**Lychees,** raw (refuse: thin shell and seeds, 40%) [1]	10 fruits	150	81.9	58	.8	.3	14.8	7	38	.4	3	153	—	—	.05	—	38

(A)	(B)		(C)	(D)	(E)	(F)	(G)	(H)	(I)	(J)	(K)	(L)	(M)	(N)	(O)	(P)	(Q)
	Macaroni:																
	Enriched:																
1298	Dry form:																
a	Package, net wt., 16 oz. (1 lb.)	1 pkg. or 1 lb.	454	10.4	1,674	56.7	5.4	341.1	122	735	[157] 13.0	9	894	(0)	[157] 4.0	[157] 1.7	[157] 27.0	(0)
b	Package, net wt., 8 oz	1 pkg	227	10.4	838	28.4	2.7	170.7	61	368	[157] 6.5	5	447	(0)	[157] 2.0	[157] .85	[157] 13.5	(0)
1299	Cooked, firm stage: [244]																
a	Yield from 1 lb. of macaroni, dry form	8⅘ cups	1,140	64.1	1,674	56.7	5.4	341.1	122	735	[157] 13.0	[245] 9	894	(0)	[157] 2.05	[157] 1.14	[157] 16.0	(0)
b	Yield from 8 oz. of macaroni, dry form	4⅖ cups	570	64.1	838	28.4	2.7	170.7	61	368	[157] 6.5	[245] 5	447	(0)	[157] 1.03	[157] .57	[157] 8.0	(0)
c	Cup, hot macaroni [246] (cut lengths, elbows, shells).	1 cup	130	64.1	192	6.5	.7	39.1	14	85	[157] 1.4	[245] 1	103	(0)	[157] .23	[157] .13	[157] 1.8	(0)
d	Pound (yield from approx. 6½ oz. of macaroni, dry form).	1 lb	454	64.1	671	22.7	2.3	136.5	50	295	[157] 5.0	[245] 5	358	(0)	[157] .82	[157] .45	[157] 6.4	(0)
1300	Cooked, tender stage: [244]																
a	Yield from 1 lb. of macaroni, dry form	10⅔ cups (hot) or 14 cups (cold).[246]	1,480	73.0	1,674	56.7	5.4	341.1	122	735	[157] 13.0	[245] 9	894	(0)	[157] 2.07	[157] 1.18	[157] 16.3	(0)
b	Yield from 8 oz. of macaroni, dry form	5.3 cups (hot) or 7 cups (cold).[246]	740	73.0	838	28.4	2.7	170.7	61	368	[157] 6.5	[245] 5	447	(0)	[157] 1.04	[157] .59	[157] 8.1	(0)
	Cup (cut lengths, elbows, shells): [246]																
c	Hot macaroni	1 cup	140	73.0	155	4.8	.6	32.2	11	70	[157] 1.3	[245] 1	85	(0)	[157] .20	[157] .11	[157] 1.5	(0)
d	Cold macaroni	1 cup	105	73.0	117	3.6	.4	24.2	8	53	[157] .9	[245] 1	64	(0)	[157] .15	[157] .08	[157] 1.2	(0)
e	Pound (yield from approx. 5 oz. of macaroni, dry form).	1 lb	454	73.0	503	15.4	1.8	104.3	36	227	[157] 4.1	[245] 5	277	(0)	[157] .64	[157] .36	[157] 5.0	(0)
	Unenriched:																
1301	Dry form:																
a	Package, net wt., 16 oz. (1 lb.)	1 pkg. or 1 lb.	454	10.4	1,674	56.7	5.4	341.1	122	735	5.9	9	894	(0)	.41	.27	7.7	(0)
b	Package, net wt., 8 oz	1 pkg	227	10.4	838	28.4	2.7	170.7	61	368	3.0	5	447	(0)	.20	.14	3.9	(0)
1302	Cooked, firm stage: [244]																
a	Yield from 1 lb. of macaroni, dry form	8⅘ cups	1,140	64.1	1,674	56.7	5.4	341.1	122	735	5.9	[245] 9	894	(0)	.23	.23	4.6	(0)
b	Yield from 8 oz. of macaroni, dry form	4⅖ cups	570	64.1	838	28.4	2.7	170.7	61	368	3.0	[245] 5	447	(0)	.11	.11	2.3	(0)
c	Cup, hot macaroni [246] (cut lengths, elbows, shells).	1 cup	130	64.1	192	6.5	.7	39.1	14	85	.7	[245] 1	103	(0)	.03	.03	.5	(0)
d	Pound (yield from approx. 6½ oz. of macaroni, dry form).	1 lb	454	64.1	671	22.7	2.3	136.5	50	295	2.3	[245] 5	358	(0)	.09	.09	1.8	(0)
1303	Cooked, tender stage: [244]																
a	Yield from 1 lb. of macaroni, dry form	10⅔ cups (hot) or 14 cups (cold).[246]	1,480	73.0	1,674	56.7	5.4	341.1	122	735	5.9	[245] 9	894	(0)	.15	.15	4.4	(0)
b	Yield from 8 oz. of macaroni, dry form	5.3 cups (hot) or 7 cups (cold).[246]	740	73.0	838	28.4	2.7	170.7	61	368	3.0	[245] 5	447	(0)	.07	.07	2.2	(0)
	Cup (cut lengths, elbows, shells): [246]																
c	Hot macaroni	1 cup	140	73.0	155	4.8	.6	32.2	11	70	.6	[245] 1	85	(0)	.01	.01	.4	(0)
d	Cold macaroni	1 cup	105	73.0	117	3.6	.4	24.2	8	53	.4	[245] 1	64	(0)	.01	.01	.3	(0)
e	Pound (yield from approx. 5 oz. of macaroni, dry form).	1 lb	454	73.0	503	15.4	1.8	104.3	36	277	1.8	[245] 5	277	(0)	.05	.05	1.4	(0)
	Macaroni (enriched) and cheese:																
1304	Baked, made from home recipe: [51]																
a	Yield from recipe [108]	7 cups	1,400	58.2	3,010	117.6	155.4	281.4	2,534	2,254	12.6	7,602	1,680	6,020	1.40	2.80	12.6	4
b	Cup (served hot)	1 cup	200	58.2	430	16.8	22.2	40.2	362	322	1.8	1,086	240	860	.20	.40	1.8	Trace
c	Pound	1 lb	454	58.2	975	38.1	50.3	91.2	821	730	4.1	2,463	544	1,950	.45	.91	4.1	1
1305	Canned:																
	Can and approx. contents:																
a	Size, 300 × 407 [14] (No. 300); net wt., 15–15¼ oz.; approx. 1¾ cups.	1 can	430	80.2	409	16.8	17.2	46.0	357	327	1.7	1,307	249	470	.22	.43	1.7	Trace
b	Size, 404 × 700 [14] (No. 3 Cylinder); net wt., 50 oz. (3 lb. 2 oz.); approx. 6 cups.	1 can	1,418	80.2	1,347	55.3	56.7	151.7	1,177	1,078	5.7	4,311	822	1,560	.71	1.42	5.7	1
c	Cup	1 cup	240	80.2	228	9.4	9.6	25.7	199	182	1.0	730	139	260	.12	.24	1.0	Trace
d	Pound	1 lb	454	80.2	431	17.7	18.1	48.5	376	345	1.8	1,379	263	500	.23	.45	1.8	Trace

[1] Measure and weight apply to food as it is described with inedible part or parts (refuse) included.

[14] Dimensions of can: 1st dimension represents diameter; 2d dimension, height of can. 1st or left-hand digit in each dimension gives number of whole inches; next 2 digits give additional fraction of dimension expressed as 16th of an inch.

[43] Value for product without added salt.

[51] For information on ingredients used in preparation, see ARS 62–13 (7), table 22, p. 26.

[108] Formula used to calculate nutritive values shown in Agr. Handb. No. 8, rev. 1963.

[157] Based on product with minimum level of enrichment. See also Appendix C, section on Enriched Foods and Standards of Enrichment

[240] Width at widest part.

[241] Values vary widely in all kinds of liver.

[242] Prepared with butter or margarine, egg yolks, sherry, and cream.

[243] Prepared with onion, sweet pickle, celery, eggs, and salad dressing (mayonnaise type); served with tomato wedges.

[244] Unless indicated otherwise, weight per cup applies to product immediately after cooking and is based on specific proportion of alimentary paste and water in cooked product. For further information, see Appendix B, section on Home-Prepared Foods and ARS 62–13 (7), section on Alimentary Pastes and Other Cereal Products, pp. 6–7, and table 3, p. 9.

[245] Value applies to product cooked in unsalted water.

[246] Hot macaroni applies to product measured immediately after cooking; cold macaroni to product measured after it had cooled. See also Appendix B, section on Home-Prepared Foods

TABLE 1.—*Nutritive values for household measures and market units of foods*—Continued

[Item numbers correspond to those in table 1 of Handbook No. 8, revised 1963. Values in parentheses denote imputed values usually from another form of the food or from a similar food. Zeros in parentheses indicate that amount of a constituent, if present, is probably too small to be measured. Dashes (—) denote lack of reliable data for a constituent believed to be present in a measurable amount. Calculated values, as those based on a recipe, are not in parentheses]

Item No.	Food, approximate measures, units, and weight (edible part unless footnotes indicate otherwise)			Water	Food energy	Protein	Fat	Carbohydrate	Calcium	Phosphorus	Iron	Sodium	Potassium	Vitamin A value	Thiamin	Riboflavin	Niacin	Ascorbic acid
				Values for edible part of foods														
(A)	(B)			(C)	(D)	(E)	(F)	(G)	(H)	(I)	(J)	(K)	(L)	(M)	(N)	(O)	(P)	(Q)
			Grams	*Percent*	*Calories*	*Grams*	*Grams*	*Grams*	*Milligrams*	*Milligrams*	*Milligrams*	*Milligrams*	*Milligrams*	*International units*	*Milligrams*	*Milligrams*	*Milligrams*	*Milligrams*
1308	**Mackerel, Atlantic,** broiled with butter or margarine:																	
a	Yield from 1 lb., raw fillets	12⅞ oz	365	61.6	861	79.6	57.7	0	22	1,022	4.4	[43]—	—	(1,930)	0.55	0.99	27.7	—
b	Fillet, 8½ in. long, 2½ in. wide, ½ in. thick [40] (dimensions of uncooked fillet).	1 fillet	105	61.6	248	22.9	16.6	0	6	294	1.3	[43]—	—	(560)	.16	.28	8.0	—
c	Pound	1 lb	454	61.6	1,070	98.9	71.7	0	27	1,270	5.4	[43]—	—	(2,400)	.68	1.22	34.5	—
d	Ounce	1 oz	28	61.6	67	6.2	4.5	0	2	79	.3	[43]—	—	(150)	.04	.08	2.2	—
1310	**Mackerel, Pacific,** canned, solids and liquid: [347]																	
	Can and approx. contents:																	
a	Size, 300 × 407 [14] (No. 300); net wt., 15 oz.; drained solids, 12¾ oz. (approx. 3⅔ pieces, 4 in. long, 1½ in. wide, 1 in. thick, [40] or approx. 1.9 cups, pieces flaked); drained liquid, 2¼ oz.	1 can	425	66.4	765	89.7	42.5	0	1,105	1,224	9.4	—	—	180	.18	1.40	37.4	—
b	Pound	1 lb	454	66.4	816	95.7	45.4	0	1,179	1,306	10.0	—	—	140	.14	1.50	39.9	—
1311	**Mackerel, salted:**																	
a	Fillet, 7¾ in. long, 2½ in. wide, ½ in. thick [40]	1 fillet	112	43.0	342	20.7	28.1	0	—	—	—	—	—	—	—	—	—	—
b	Pound	1 lb	454	43.0	1,383	83.9	113.9	0	—	—	—	—	—	—	—	—	—	—
c	Ounce	1 oz	28	43.0	86	5.2	7.1	0	—	—	—	—	—	—	—	—	—	—
1313	**Malt,** dry	1 oz	28	5.2	104	.37	.5	21.9	—	—	1.1	—	—	—	.14	.09	2.6	—
1314	**Malt extract,** dried	1 oz	28	3.2	104	1.7	Trace	25.3	14	83	2.5	23	65	—	.10	.13	2.8	—
1315	**Mamey** (mammee apple), raw (refuse: skin and seeds, 38%). [1]	1 fruit	1,410	86.2	446	4.4	4.4	109.3	96	96	6.1	181	411	2,010	.17	.35	3.5	122
	Mandarin oranges. See Tangerines (item 2262).																	
1316	**Mangos,** raw:																	
a	Whole (refuse: seeds and skin, 23%) [1]	1 fruit	300	81.7	152	1.6	.9	38.8	23	30	.9	16	487	11,090	.12	.12	2.5	81
b	Diced or sliced	1 cup	165	81.7	109	1.2	.7	27.7	17	21	.7	12	312	7,920	.08	.08	1.8	58
c	Pound	1 lb	454	81.7	299	3.2	1.8	76.2	45	59	1.8	32	857	21,770	.23	.23	5.0	159
1317	**Margarine:** [348]																	
	Regular type (1 brick or 4 sticks per pound):																	
a	Stick, net wt., 4 oz. (approx. ½ cup)	1 stick	113.4	15.5	816	.7	91.9	.5	23	18	0	1,119	26	3,750	—	—	—	0
b	Cup (approx. ½ brick or 2 sticks of item 1317a)	1 cup	227	15.5	1,634	1.4	183.9	.9	45	36	0	2,240	52	7,500	—	—	—	0
c	Tablespoon (approx. ⅛ of stick (item 1317a))	1 tbsp	14.2	15.5	102	.1	11.5	.1	3	2	0	140	3	470	—	—	—	0
d	Teaspoon (approx. 1/24 of stick (item 1317a))	1 tsp	4.7	15.5	34	Trace	3.8	Trace	1	1	0	46	1	160	—	—	—	0
e	Pat (1 in. square, ⅓ in. high; 90 per pound)	1 pat	5.0	15.5	36	Trace	4.1	Trace	1	1	0	49	1	170	—	—	—	0
f	Cubic inch	1 cu. in	14.7	15.5	106	.1	11.9	.1	3	2	0	145	3	490	—	—	—	0
	Soft type (two 8-oz. containers per pound). See items 1317b, 1317c, 1317d. [349]																	
	Whipped type [350] (6 sticks or two 8-oz. containers [351] per pound):																	
g	Stick, net wt., 2⅔ oz. (approx. ½ cup)	1 stick	75.6	15.5	544	.5	61.2	.3	15	12	0	746	17	2,500	—	—	—	0
h	Cup (approx. 2 sticks of item 1317g or ⅔ of 8-oz. container).	1 cup	151	15.5	1,087	.9	122.3	.6	30	24	0	1,490	35	5,000	—	—	—	0
i	Tablespoon (approx. ⅛ of stick (item 1317g))	1 tbsp	9.4	15.5	68	.1	7.6	Trace	2	2	0	93	2	310	—	—	—	0
j	Teaspoon (approx. 1/24 of stick (item 1317g))	1 tsp	3.2	15.5	23	Trace	2.6	Trace	1	1	0	32	1	100	—	—	—	0
k	Pat (1¼ in. square, ⅓ in. high; 120 per pound)	1 pat	3.8	15.5	27	Trace	3.1	Trace	1	1	0	38	1	130	—	—	—	0
l	Regular, soft and whipped types	1 lb	454	15.5	3,266	2.7	367.4	1.8	91	73	0	4,477	104	15,000	—	—	—	0
1318	**Marmalade,** citrus, sweetened with regular amount of nutritive sweetener:																	
	Container and approx. contents:																	
a	Jar, net wt., 12 oz	1 jar	340	29.0	874	1.7	.3	238.3	119	31	2.0	48	112	—	.07	.07	.3	20
b	Packet, net wt., ½ oz. (approx. ¾ tbsp.)	1 packet	14	29.0	36	.1	Trace	9.8	5	1	.1	2	5	—	Trace	Trace	Trace	1
c	Tablespoon	1 tbsp	20	29.0	51	.1	Trace	14.0	7	2	.1	3	7	—	Trace	Trace	Trace	1
d	Pound	1 lb	454	29.0	1,166	2.3	.5	318.0	159	41	2.7	64	150	—	.09	.09	.5	27
	Matai. See Waterchestnut, Chinese (item 2422).																	
	Mayonnaise. See Salad dressings (item 1938).																	
	Meat loaf. See Sausage, cold cuts, and luncheon meats (item 2007).																	
	Meat. See Beef, Lamb, Pork, Veal.																	
	Mellorine. See Appendix C, p. 283.																	
	Melons. See Muskmelons (items 1358–1361) and Watermelon (item 2424).																	

(A)	(B)			(C)	(D)	(E)	(F)	(G)	(H)	(I)	(J)	(K)	(L)	(M)	(N)	(O)	(P)	(Q)
	Milk, cow:																	
	Fluid (pasteurized and raw):																	
1320	Whole, 3.5% fat:[252]																	
a	Quart	1 qt	976	87.4	634	34.2	34.2	47.8	1,152	908	0.4	488	1,405	[253] 1,410	0.29	1.66	1.0	10
b	Cup	1 cup	244	87.4	159	8.5	8.5	12.0	288	227	.1	122	351	[253] 350	.07	.41	.2	2
1322	Skim:																	
a	Quart	1 qt	980	90.5	353	35.3	1.0	50.0	1,186	931	.4	510	1,421	[253] 40	.34	1.76	.7	10
b	Cup	1 cup	245	90.5	88	8.8	.2	12.5	296	233	.1	127	355	[253] 10	.09	.44	.2	2
1323	Low fat with 2% nonfat milk solids added:																	
a	Quart	1 qt	984	87.0	581	41.3	19.7	59.0	1,407	1,102	.5	600	1,722	[253] 810	.40	2.07	.9	10
b	Cup	1 cup	246	87.0	145	10.3	4.9	14.8	352	276	.1	150	431	[253] 200	.10	.52	.2	2
	Half-and-half (cream and milk). See Cream (item 928).																	
	Canned:																	
1324	Evaporated (unsweetened):																	
a	Cup	1 cup	252	73.8	345	17.6	19.9	24.4	635	517	.3	297	764	[253] 810	.10	.86	.5	3
b	Fluid ounce	1 fl. oz	31.5	73.8	43	2.2	2.5	3.1	79	65	Trace	37	95	[253] 100	.01	.11	.1	Trace
1325	Condensed (sweetened):																	
a	Cup	1 cup	306	27.1	982	24.8	26.6	166.2	802	630	.3	343	961	1,100	.24	1.16	.6	3
b	Fluid ounce	1 fl. oz	38.2	27.1	123	3.1	3.3	20.7	100	79	Trace	43	120	140	.03	.15	.1	Trace
	Dry:[154]																	
1326	Whole:																	
a	Regular	1 cup	128	2.0	643	33.8	35.2	48.9	1,164	906	.6	518	1,702	1,450	.37	1.87	.9	8
	Instant:																	
b	Low-density type (proportions for use: 4¼ oz. of milk to 3¾ cups of water to yield 1 qt.).	1 cup	70	2.0	351	18.5	19.3	26.7	636	496	.4	284	931	790	.20	1.02	.5	4
c	High-density type (proportions for use: ¼ cup of milk to 1 cup of water).	1 cup	105	2.0	527	27.7	28.9	40.1	954	743	.5	425	1.397	1,190	.30	1.53	.7	6
d	Regular and instant	1 lb	454	2.0	2,277	119.8	124.7	173.3	4,123	3,211	2.3	1,837	6,033	5,130	1.32	6.62	3.2	27
1327	Nonfat, regular:																	
a	Cup	1 cup	120	3.0	436	43.1	1.0	62.8	1,570	1,219	.7	638	2,094	[254] 40	.42	(2.16)	1.1	8
b	Pound	1 lb	454	3.0	1,647	162.8	3.6	237.2	5,933	4,609	2.7	2,413	7,915	[254] 140	1.59	(8.16)	4.1	32
1328	Nonfat, instant:																	
a	Envelope, wt., 3.2 oz.[255]	1 envelope	91	4.0	327	32.6	.6	47.0	1,177	915	.5	479	1,570	[254] 30	.32	1.62	.8	6
	Cup:																	
b	Low-density type (3.2 oz.[255] equals approx. 1⅓ cups).	1 cup	68	4.0	244	24.3	.5	35.1	879	683	.4	358	1,173	[254] 20	.24	1.21	.6	5
c	High-density type (3.2 oz.[255] equals approx. ⅞ cup).	1 cup	104	4.0	373	37.2	.7	53.7	1,345	1,045	.6	547	1,794	[254] 30	.36	1.85	.9	7
d	Pound	1 lb	454	4.0	1,628	162.4	3.2	234.1	5,865	4,559	2.7	2,386	7,825	[254] 140	1.59	8.07	4.1	32
	Malted:																	
1329	Dry powder[256]	1 oz. or approx. 3 heaping tsp.	28	2.6	116	4.2	2.4	20.1	82	108	.6	125	204	290	.09	.15	.1	(0)
1330	Beverage[186 257]	1 cup	235	78.2	244	11.0	10.3	27.5	317	287	.7	214	470	590	.14	.49	.2	2
	Chocolate drink, fluid, commercial (approx. 90% milk):																	
1331	Made with skim milk (2% butterfat added):																	
a	Quart	1 qt	1,000	82.8	760	33.0	23.0	109.0	1,080	910	2.0	460	1,420	840	.40	1.60	1.0	10
b	Cup	1 cup	250	82.8	190	8.3	5.8	27.3	270	228	.5	115	355	210	.10	.40	.3	3
1332	Made with whole 3.5% fat milk:																	
a	Quart	1 qt	1,000	81.5	850	34.0	34.0	110.0	1,110	940	2.0	470	1,460	1,300	.30	1.60	1.0	10
b	Cup	1 cup	250	81.5	213	8.5	8.5	27.5	278	235	.5	118	365	330	.08	.40	.3	3

[1] Measure and weight apply to food as it is described with inedible part or parts (refuse) included.

[14] Dimensions of can: 1st dimension represents diameter; 2d dimension, height of can. 1st or left-hand digit in each dimension gives number of whole inches; next 2 digits give additional fraction of dimension expressed as 16th of an inch.

[40] Width at widest part; thickness at thickest part.

[43] Value for product without added salt.

[154] Weight per cup is based on method of pouring product from container into measuring cup with as little fall as possible, then leveling with straight edge. For corn flour, see Appendix B, section on Nonliquid Foods and section on Cornmeals and Related Products

[186] For information on ingredients used, see ARS 62–13 (7), table 26, p. 32.

[247] Vitamin values based on data for drained solids.

[248] Nutritive values apply to salted margarine. Unsalted margarine contains less than 10 mg. per 100 g. of either sodium or potassium. Vitamin A value based on minimum required to meet Federal specifications for margarine with vitamin A added; namely, 15,000 I.U. of vitamin A per pound.

[249] For 1 cup (approx. 8-oz. container), 1 tbsp., and 1 tsp. of soft-type margarine, weights and nutritive values shown for corresponding volumes of regular margarine (items 1317b, 1317c, and 1317d, respectively) are applicable.

[250] Description and weights shown for whipped margarine, except pat (item 1317k), apply to margarine that has been stirred or whipped until its volume has been increased approx. 50%; for pat, 100%.

[251] Nutritive values for 8-oz. container (227 g.) of whipped margarine are same as shown for 1 cup of regular margarine (item 1317b).

[252] Minimum Federal standards for fat have been proposed (23) as 3¼%. Minimum standards for fat in different States vary considerably, and commercial milks may range slightly above required minimums. Selection of values to be used in dietary calculations may need to be based on information at local level.

[253] Value applies to product without added vitamin A. Standards of identity have been proposed (23) that would require addition of vitamin A to skim milk and low-fat milk (items 1322, 1323) at level of 2,000 I.U. per quart (about 500 I.U. per cup) and would permit optional addition of vitamin A to evaporated milk (item 1324) at level of 125 I.U. per fluid ounce (about 1,000 I.U. per cup).

[254] Value applies to unfortified product. Based on minimum level of enrichment, value for fortified product is 2,650 I.U. for item 1327a, 10,000 I.U. for item 1327b, 2,000 I.U. for item 1328a, 1,500 I.U. for item 1328b, 2,290 I.U. for item 1328c, 10,000 I.U. for item 1328d.

[255] Amount by weight specified by manufacturers to add to 3¾ cups of water to yield 1 qt. of liquid skim milk. For amount to use by volume (spoon, cup, or similar measure), follow package directions.

[256] Values are based on unfortified products.

[257] Prepared with malted milk powder and whole milk.

TABLE 1.—*Nutritive values for household measures and market units of foods*—Continued

[Item numbers correspond to those in table 1 of Handbook No. 8, revised 1963. Values in parentheses denote imputed values usually from another form of the food or from a similar food. Zeros in parentheses indicate that amount of a constituent, if present, is probably too small to be measured. Dashes (—) denote lack of reliable data for a constituent believed to be present in a measurable amount. Calculated values, as those based on a recipe, are not in parentheses]

Item No.	Food, approximate measures, units, and weight (edible part unless footnotes indicate otherwise)			Water	Food energy	Protein	Fat	Carbohydrate	Calcium	Phosphorus	Iron	Sodium	Potassium	Vitamin A value	Thiamin	Riboflavin	Niacin	Ascorbic acid
				Values for edible part of foods														
(A)	(B)			(C)	(D)	(E)	(F)	(G)	(H)	(I)	(J)	(K)	(L)	(M)	(N)	(O)	(P)	(Q)
			Grams	*Percent*	*Calories*	*Grams*	*Grams*	*Grams*	*Milligrams*	*Milligrams*	*Milligrams*	*Milligrams*	*Milligrams*	*International units*	*Milligrams*	*Milligrams*	*Milligrams*	*Milligrams*
	Milk, cow—Continued																	
	Chocolate beverages, homemade: [196]																	
1333	Hot chocolate	1 cup	250	80.5	238	8.8	12.5	26.0	260	235	0.5	120	370	360	0.08	0.40	0.3	3
1334	Hot cocoa	1 cup	250	79.0	243	9.5	11.5	27.3	295	283	1.0	128	363	400	.10	.45	.5	8
	Buttermilk. See Buttermilk (items 509–510).																	
1335	**Milk, goat, fluid:**																	
a	Quart	1 qt	976	87.5	654	31.2	39.0	44.9	1,250	1,035	1.0	332	1,757	(1,560)	.39	1.07	2.9	10
b	Cup	1 cup	244	87.5	163	7.8	9.8	11.2	315	259	.2	83	439	(390)	.10	.27	.7	2
1336	**Milk, human,** U.S. samples	1 fl. oz	30.8	85.2	24	.3	1.2	2.9	10	4	Trace	5	16	70	Trace	.01	.1	2
1337	**Milk, reindeer**	1 cup	248	64.1	580	26.8	48.6	10.2	630	491	.2	389	394	—	—	—	—	—
	Mixed vegetables, frozen. See Vegetables, mixed, frozen (items 2403–2404).																	
	Molasses, cane:																	
1339	First extraction or light:																	
a	Bottle, net contents, 12 fl. oz	1 bottle	493	24	1,242	—	—	[258] 320.5	813	222	21.2	74	4,521	—	.35	.30	1.0	—
b	Cup	1 cup	328	24	827	—	—	[258] 213.2	541	148	14.1	49	3,008	—	.23	.20	.7	—
c	Tablespoon	1 tbsp	20	24	50	—	—	[258] 13.0	33	9	.9	3	183	—	.01	.01	Trace	—
d	Fluid ounce	1 fl. oz	41	24	103	—	—	[258] 26.7	68	18	1.8	6	376	—	.03	.02	.1	—
1340	Second extraction or medium:																	
a	Bottle, net contents, 12 fl. oz	1 bottle	493	24	1,144	—	—	[258] 295.8	1,430	340	29.6	182	5,241	—	—	.59	5.9	—
b	Cup	1 cup	328	24	761	—	—	[258] 196.8	951	226	19.7	121	3,487	—	—	.39	3.9	—
c	Tablespoon	1 tbsp	20	24	46	—	—	[258] 12.0	58	14	1.2	7	213	—	—	.02	.2	—
d	Fluid ounce	1 fl. oz	41	24	95	—	—	[258] 24.6	119	28	2.5	15	436	—	—	.05	.5	—
1341	Third extraction or blackstrap:																	
a	Bottle, net contents, 12 fl. oz	1 bottle	493	24	1,050	—	—	[258] 271.2	3,372	414	79.4	473	14,430	—	.54	.94	9.9	—
b	Cup	1 cup	328	24	699	—	—	[258] 180.4	2,244	276	52.8	315	9,601	—	.36	.62	6.6	—
c	Tablespoon	1 tbsp	20	24	43	—	—	[258] 11.0	137	17	3.2	19	585	—	.02	.04	.4	—
d	Fluid ounce	1 fl. oz	41	24	87	—	—	[258] 22.6	280	34	6.6	39	1,200	—	.05	.08	.8	—
1342	Barbados:																	
a	Cup	1 cup	328	24	889	—	—	[258] 229.6	804	164	—	—	—	—	.20	.66	—	—
b	Tablespoon	1 tbsp	20	24	54	—	—	[258] 14.0	49	10	—	—	—	—	.01	.04	—	—
c	Fluid ounce	1 fl. oz	41	24	111	—	—	[258] 28.7	100	21	—	—	—	—	.02	.08	—	—
	Mortadella. See Sausage, cold cuts, and luncheon meats (item 2010).																	
	Muffins, baked from home recipes: [60]																	
	Plain, made with—																	
1343	Enriched flour:																	
a	Yield from recipe [108]	12 muffins	485	38.0	1,426	37.8	49.0	205.2	504	732	7.8	2,139	606	490	.82	1.12	6.8	2
b	Muffin (3-in. diam. at top, 2-in. diam. at bottom, 1½ in. high; yield from approx. 3 tbsp. of batter).	1 muffin	40	38.0	118	3.1	4.0	16.9	42	60	.6	176	50	40	.07	.09	.6	Trace
c	Pound	1 lb	454	38.0	1,334	35.4	45.8	191.9	472	685	7.3	2,000	567	450	.77	1.04	6.4	2
1344	Unenriched flour:																	
a	Yield from recipe [108]	12 muffins	485	38.0	1,426	37.8	49.0	205.2	504	732	2.9	2,139	606	490	.19	.68	1.9	2
b	Muffin (3-in. diam. at top, 2-in. diam. at bottom, 1½ in. high; yield from approx. 3 tbsp. of batter).	1 muffin	40	38.0	118	3.1	4.0	16.9	42	60	.2	176	50	40	.02	.06	.2	Trace
c	Pound	1 lb	454	38.0	1,334	35.4	45.8	191.9	472	685	2.7	2,000	567	450	.18	.64	1.8	2
	Other, made with enriched flour:																	
1345	Blueberry:																	
a	Yield from recipe [108]	8 muffins	315	39.0	885	23.0	29.3	132.0	265	416	5.0	1,991	362	690	.50	.63	3.8	3
b	Muffin (2⅜-in. diam. at top, 2-in. diam. at bottom, 1½ in. high; yield from approx. 3 tbsp. of batter).	1 muffin	40	39.0	112	2.9	3.7	16.8	34	53	.6	253	46	90	.06	.08	.5	Trace
c	Pound	1 lb	454	39.0	1,275	33.1	42.2	190.1	381	599	7.3	2,867	522	1,000	.73	.91	5.4	5
1346	Bran:																	
a	Yield from recipe [108]	7½ muffins	295	35.1	770	22.7	28.9	127.1	419	1,195	10.9	1,322	1,271	680	.41	.71	11.8	1
b	Muffin (2⅝-in. diam. at top, 2-in. diam. at bottom, 1⅜ in. high; yield from approx. ¼ cup of batter).	1 muffin	40	35.1	104	3.1	3.9	17.2	57	162	1.5	179	172	90	.06	.10	1.6	Trace
c	Pound	1 lb	454	35.1	1,184	34.9	44.5	195.5	644	1,837	16.8	2,032	1,955	1,040	.64	1.09	18.1	1

(A)	(B)		(C)	(D)	(E)	(F)	(G)	(H)	(I)	(J)	(K)	(L)	(M)	(N)	(O)	(P)	(Q)
	Corn, made with—																
1347	Enriched degermed cornmeal:																
a	Yield from recipe [108]	13 muffins	520	32.7	1,633	36.9	52.5	250.1	546	879	8.8	2,501	702	1,560	1.04	1.20	8.3	2
b	Muffin (2⅜-in. diam. at top, 2-in. diam. at bottom, 1½ in. high; yield from approx. ¼ cup of batter).	1 muffin	40	32.7	126	2.8	4.0	19.2	42	68	.7	192	54	120	.08	.09	.6	Trace
c	Pound	1 lb	454	32.7	1,424	32.2	45.8	218.2	476	767	7.7	2,182	612	1,360	.91	1.04	7.3	1
1348	Whole-ground cornmeal:																
a	Yield from recipe [108]	12½ muffins	500	37.8	1,440	36.0	51.5	212.5	560	1,080	7.0	2,475	660	1,550	.85	.85	5.0	2
b	Muffin (2⅜-in. diam. at top, 2-in. diam. at bottom, 1½ in. high; yield from approx. ¼ cup of batter).	1 muffin	40	37.8	115	2.9	4.1	17.0	45	86	.6	198	53	120	.07	.07	.4	Trace
c	Pound	1 lb	454	37.8	1,306	32.7	46.7	192.8	508	980	6.4	2,245	599	1,410	.77	.77	4.5	1
	Muffin mix, corn, and muffins and cornbread baked from mix: [259]																
1349	Mix, dry form, with enriched flour:																
a	Package, net wt., 12 oz	1 pkg	340	7.8	1,418	21.1	39.1	244.1	1,020	1,608	6.1	2,244	258	510	.82	.54	7.1	0
	Cup:																
b	Not packed	1 cup	130	7.8	542	8.1	15.0	93.3	390	615	2.3	858	99	200	.31	.21	2.7	0
c	Packed	1 cup	170	7.8	709	10.5	19.6	122.1	510	804	3.1	1,122	129	260	.41	.27	3.6	0
d	Pound	1 lb	454	7.8	1,892	28.1	52.2	325.7	1,361	2,146	8.2	2,994	345	680	1.09	.73	9.5	0
1350	Muffins and cornbread; made with egg and milk: [68]																
	Muffin, 2⅜-in. diam. at top, 2-in. diam. at bottom, 1½ in. high:																
a	Yield from 12 oz. of mix (item 1349a)	12 muffins	490	30.4	1,588	33.8	51.9	245.0	1,181	1,862	7.4	2,347	539	1,180	.88	.93	6.9	1
b	Muffin (yield from approx. ¼ cup of batter)	1 muffin	40	30.4	130	2.8	4.2	20.0	96	152	.6	192	44	100	.07	.08	.6	Trace
	Cornbread, 7½ × 7½ × 1⅜ in.:																
c	Whole (vol., 77.3 cu. in.; yield from 12 oz. of mix (item 1349a)).	1 cornbread	500	30.4	1,620	34.5	53.0	250.0	1,205	1,900	7.5	2,395	550	1,200	.90	.95	7.0	1
d	Piece (2½ × 2½ × 1⅜ in.; vol., 8.6 cu. in.; ⅑ of cornbread).	1 piece	55	30.4	178	3.8	5.8	27.5	133	209	.8	263	61	130	.10	.10	.8	Trace
e	Cube (1 cu. in.)	1 cube	6.5	30.4	21	.4	.7	3.3	16	25	.1	31	7	20	.01	.01	.1	Trace
f	Pound	1 lb	454	30.4	1,470	31.3	48.1	226.8	1,093	1,724	6.8	2,173	499	1,090	.82	.86	6.4	1
	Mushrooms: [136]																
1354	*Agaricus campestris*, cultivated commercially, raw:																
a	Cup, slices, chopped or diced pieces	1 cup	70	90.4	20	1.9	.2	3.1	4	81	.6	11	290	Trace	.07	.32	2.9	2
b	Pound	1 lb	454	90.4	127	12.2	1.4	20.0	27	526	3.6	68	1,878	Trace	.45	2.09	19.1	14
1356	Other edible species, raw:																
a	Cup, slices, chopped or diced pieces	1 cup	70	89.1	25	1.3	.4	4.6	9	68	1.0	7	263	Trace	.07	.23	4.8	2
b	Pound	1 lb	454	89.1	159	8.6	2.7	29.5	59	440	6.4	45	1,701	Trace	.45	1.50	30.8	14
	Muskmelons:																
	Raw:																
1358	Cantaloups with orange-colored flesh:																
a	Whole, 5-in. diam.; wt., approx. 2⅓ lb. (refuse: rind and cavity contents, 50%).[1]	1 melon	1,060	91.2	159	3.7	.5	39.8	74	85	2.1	64	1,330	18,020	.21	.16	3.2	175
b	Half, 5-in. diam., served with rind (refuse: rind, 43%).[1]	½ melon	477	91.2	82	1.9	.3	20.4	38	44	1.1	33	682	9,240	.11	.08	1.6	[93] 90
c	Cubed or diced pieces; melon balls (approx. 20 per cup).	1 cup	160	91.2	48	1.1	.2	12.0	22	26	.6	19	402	5,440	.06	.05	1.0	[93] 53
d	Pound	1 lb	454	91.2	136	3.2	.5	34.0	64	73	1.8	54	1,139	15,420	.18	.14	2.7	150
1359	Casaba (Golden Beauty):																
a	Whole, 6½-in. diam., 7¾ in. long; wt., approx. 6 lb. (refuse: rind and cavity contents, 50%).[1]	1 melon	2,722	91.5	367	16.3	Trace	88.5	(191)	(218)	(5.4)	(163)	(3,416)	410	(.54)	(.41)	(8.2)	177
b	Wedge, 7¾ in. long, 2 in. wide at center; ⅒ of melon (item 1359a); served with rind (refuse: rind, 43%).[1]	1 wedge	245	91.5	38	1.7	Trace	9.1	(20)	(22)	(.6)	(17)	(351)	40	(.06)	(.04)	(.8)	[93] 18
c	Cubed or diced pieces; melon balls (approx. 20 per cup).	1 cup	170	91.5	46	2.0	Trace	11.1	(24)	(27)	(.7)	(20)	(427)	50	(.07)	(.05)	(1.0)	[93] 22
d	Pound	1 lb	454	91.5	122	5.4	Trace	29.5	(64)	(73)	(1.8)	(54)	(1,139)	140	(.18)	(.14)	(2.7)	59
1360	Honeydew:																
a	Whole, 6½-in. diam., 7 in. long; wt., approx. 5¼ lb. (refuse: rind and cavity contents, 37%).[1]	1 melon	2,380	90.6	495	12.0	4.5	115.5	210	240	6.0	180	3,763	600	.60	.45	9.0	345

[1] Measure and weight apply to food as it is described with inedible part or parts (refuse) included.

[66] For information on ingredients used, see ARS 62–13 (7), table 4, p. 10.

[68] For proportion of mix and added ingredients used, see ARS 62–13 (7), table 5, p. 12.

[93] Value does not allow for losses that might occur from cutting, chopping, or shredding. See also Appendix C, section on Cut Forms of Raw Fruits and Vegetables; Capping of Strawberries

[108] Formula used to calculate nutritive values shown in Agr. Handb. No. 8, rev. 1963.

[136] Contains nonprotein nitrogen. This is omitted from protein value but included in total carbohydrate figure and caloric value. See also Appendix D, section on Protein and Nonprotein Nitrogen and section on Carbohydrate

[196] For information on ingredients used, see ARS 62–13 (7), table 26, p. 32.

[258] Value for total sugars.

[259] Contains yellow degermed cornmeal. Weight of 1 cup of mix, not packed (item 1349b), will vary with degree of lumping in product. Weight per cup shown is based on product with all lumps broken up and filled by pouring.

TABLE 1.—*Nutritive values for household measures and market units of foods*—Continued

[Item numbers correspond to those in table 1 of Handbook No. 8, revised 1963. Values in parentheses denote imputed values usually from another form of the food or from a similar food. Zeros in parentheses indicate that amount of a constituent, if present, is probably too small to be measured. Dashes (—) denote lack of reliable data for a constituent believed to be present in a measurable amount. Calculated values, as those based on a recipe, are not in parentheses]

Item No. (A)		Food, approximate measures, units, and weight (edible part unless footnotes indicate otherwise) (B)			Water (C)	Food energy (D)	Protein (E)	Fat (F)	Carbohydrate (G)	Calcium (H)	Phosphorus (I)	Iron (J)	Sodium (K)	Potassium (L)	Vitamin A value (M)	Thiamin (N)	Riboflavin (O)	Niacin (P)	Ascorbic acid (Q)
					Values for edible part of foods														
				Grams	Percent	Calories	Grams	Grams	Grams	Milligrams	Milligrams	Milligrams	Milligrams	Milligrams	International units	Milligrams	Milligrams	Milligrams	Milligrams
		Muskmelons—Continued																	
		Raw—Continued																	
		Honeydew—Continued																	
	b	Wedge, 7 in. long, 2 in. wide at center; 1/10 of melon (item 1360a); served with rind (refuse: rind, 84%).[1]	1 wedge	226	90.6	49	1.2	0.4	11.5	21	24	0.6	18	374	60	0.06	0.04	0.9	[93] 34
	c	Cubed or diced pieces; melon balls (approx. 20 per cup).	1 cup	170	90.6	56	1.4	.5	13.1	24	27	.7	20	427	70	.07	.05	1.0	[93] 39
	d	Pound	1 lb	454	90.6	150	3.6	1.4	34.9	64	73	1.8	54	1,139	180	.18	.14	2.7	104
		Frozen:																	
1361		Melon balls (cantaloup and Honeydew) in sirup, not thawed:																	
	a	Container, net wt., 12 oz	1 container	340	83.2	211	2.0	.3	53.4	34	41	1.0	31	639	5,240	.10	.07	1.7	54
	b	Cup [46]	1 cup	230	83.2	143	1.4	.2	36.1	23	28	.7	21	432	3,540	.07	.05	1.2	37
	c	Pound	1 lb	454	83.2	281	2.7	.5	71.2	45	54	1.4	41	853	6,990	.14	.09	2.3	73
		Mustard greens:																	
1366		Raw	1 lb	454	89.5	141	13.6	2.3	25.4	830	227	13.6	145	1,710	31,750	.50	1.00	3.6	440
1367		Cooked (boiled), drained:																	
	a	Cup, leaves without stems, midribs	1 cup	140	92.6	32	3.1	.6	5.6	193	45	2.5	[20] 25	308	8,120	.11	.20	.8	67
	b	Pound	1 lb	454	92.6	104	10.0	1.8	18.1	626	145	8.2	[20] 82	998	26,310	.36	.64	2.7	218
		Frozen, chopped:																	
1368		Not thawed:																	
	a	Container, net wt., 10 oz	1 container	284	93.5	57	6.5	1.1	9.1	327	128	4.5	34	557	17,040	.11	.34	1.1	97
	b	Pound	1 lb	454	93.5	91	10.4	1.8	14.5	522	204	7.3	54	889	27,220	.18	.54	1.8	154
1369		Cooked (boiled), drained:																	
	a	Yield from 10 oz., frozen mustard greens	1.4 cups	212	93.8	42	4.7	.8	6.6	220	91	3.2	[20] 21	333	12,720	.06	.21	.8	42
	b	Yield from 1 lb., frozen mustard greens	2¼ cups	340	93.8	68	7.5	1.4	10.5	354	146	5.1	[20] 34	534	20,400	.10	.34	1.4	68
	c	Cup	1 cup	150	93.8	30	3.3	.6	4.7	156	65	2.3	[20] 15	236	9,000	.05	.15	.6	30
	d	Pound (yield from 1⅓ lb., frozen mustard greens).	1 lb	454	93.8	91	10.0	1.8	14.1	472	195	6.8	[20] 45	712	27,220	.14	.45	1.8	91
		Mustard spinach (tendergreen):																	
1370		Raw	1 lb	454	92.2	100	10.0	1.4	17.7	953	127	6.8	—	—	44,910	—	—	—	590
1371		Cooked (boiled), drained:																	
	a	Cup	1 cup	(180)	94.5	29	3.1	.4	5.0	284	32	1.4	[20] —	—	14,760	—	—	—	117
	b	Pound	1 lb	454	94.5	73	7.7	.9	12.7	717	82	3.6	[20] —	—	37,200	—	—	—	295
		Mustard, prepared:																	
1372		Brown:																	
	a	Cup	1 cup	250	78.1	228	14.8	15.8	13.3	310	335	4.5	3,268	325	—	—	—	—	—
	b	Teaspoon, individual serving pouch, or cup	1 tsp., pouch, or cup.	5	78.1	5	.3	.3	.3	6	7	.1	65	7	—	—	—	—	—
1373		Yellow:																	
	a	Cup	1 cup	250	80.2	188	11.8	11.0	16.0	210	183	5.0	3,130	325	—	—	—	—	—
	b	Teaspoon, individual serving pouch, or cup	1 tsp., pouch, or cup.	5	80.2	4	.2	.2	.3	4	4	.1	63	7	—	—	—	—	—
1374		Nectarines, raw, 2½-in. diam. (refuse: pits, 8%)[1]	1 nectarine	150	81.8	88	.8	Trace	23.6	6	33	.7	8	406	2,280	—	—	—	18
		New Zealand spinach: [58]																	
1375		Raw	1 lb	454	92.6	86	10.0	1.4	14.1	263	209	11.8	721	3,606	19,500	.18	.77	2.7	136
1376		Cooked (boiled), drained:																	
	a	Cup	1 cup	(180)	94.8	23	3.1	.4	3.8	86	50	2.7	[20] 166	833	6,480	.05	.18	.9	25
	b	Pound	1 lb	454	94.8	59	7.7	.9	9.5	218	127	6.8	[20] 417	2,100	16,330	.14	.45	2.3	64
		Noodles, egg noodles:																	
		Enriched:																	
1377		Dry form:																	
	a	Package, net wt., 16 oz. (1 lb.)	1 pkg. or 1 lb	454	9.8	1,760	58.1	20.9	326.6	141	830	[187] 13.0	23	617	1,000	[187] 4.0	[187] 1.7	[187] 27.0	(0)
	b	Package, net wt., 8 oz	1 pkg	227	9.8	881	29.1	10.4	163.4	70	415	[187] 6.5	11	309	500	[187] 2.0	[187] .85	[187] 13.5	(0)
1378		Cooked: [244]																	
	a	Yield from 1 lb. of noodles, dry form	8⅘ cups	1,410	70.8	1,760	58.1	20.9	326.6	141	830	[187] 13.0	[245] 23	617	1,000	[187] 1.97	[187] 1.13	[187] 16.9	(0)
	b	Yield from 8 oz. of noodles, dry form	4⅖ cups	705	70.8	881	29.1	10.4	163.4	70	415	[187] 6.5	[245] 11	309	500	[187] .99	[187] .56	[187] 8.5	(0)
	c	Cup	1 cup	160	70.8	200	6.6	2.4	37.3	16	94	[187] 1.4	[245] 3	70	110	[187] .22	[187] .13	[187] 1.9	(0)
	d	Pound (yield from approx. 5⅛ oz. of noodles, dry form).	1 lb	454	70.8	567	18.6	6.8	105.7	45	268	[187] 4.1	[245] 9	200	320	[187] .64	[187] .36	[187] 5.4	(0)

(A)	(B)		(C)	(D)	(E)	(F)	(G)	(H)	(I)	(J)	(K)	(L)	(M)	(N)	(O)	(P)	(Q)
	Unenriched:																
1379	Dry form:																
a	Package, net wt., 16 oz. (1 lb.)	1 pkg. or 1 lb	454	9.8	1,760	58.1	20.9	326.6	141	830	8.6	23	617	1,000	0.77	0.41	9.5	(0)
b	Package, net wt., 8 oz	1 pkg	227	9.8	881	29.1	10.4	163.4	70	415	4.3	11	309	500	.39	.20	4.8	(0)
1380	Cooked:[344]																
a	Yield from 1 lb. of noodles, dry form	8⅘ cups	1,410	70.8	1,760	58.1	20.9	326.6	141	830	8.6	[345] 23	617	1,000	.42	.28	5.6	(0)
b	Yield from 8 oz. of noodles, dry form	4⅖ cups	705	70.8	881	29.1	10.4	163.4	70	415	4.3	[345] 11	309	500	.21	.14	2.8	(0)
c	Cup	1 cup	160	70.8	200	6.6	2.4	37.3	16	94	1.0	[345] 3	70	110	.05	.03	.6	(0)
d	Pound (yield from approx. 5⅛ oz. of noodles, dry form).	1 lb	454	70.8	567	18.6	6.8	105.7	45	268	2.7	[345] 9	200	320	.14	.09	1.8	(0)
1381	Noodles, chow mein, canned:																
a	Can, net wt., 5 oz	1 can	142	1.1	694	18.7	33.4	82.4	—	—	—	—	—	—	—	—	—	—
b	Can, net wt., 3 oz	1 can	85	1.1	416	11.2	20.0	49.3	—	—	—	—	—	—	—	—	—	—
c	Cup	1 cup	45	1.1	220	5.9	10.6	26.1	—	—	—	—	—	—	—	—	—	—
	Nuts. See individual kinds.																
	Oat products used mainly as hot breakfast cereals:[5] [360]																
	Oat flakes, maple-flavored, instant-cooking (about 1 min. cooking time):																
1384	Dry form	1 cup	95	7.4	365	13.9	4.0	68.7	48	342	3.3	1	—	(0)	.33	—	—	(0)
1385	Cooked	1 cup	240	83.0	166	6.2	1.9	31.2	24	156	1.4	[361] 257	—	(0)	.14	—	—	(0)
	Oat granules, maple-flavored, regular (about 3 min. cooking time):																
1386	Dry form	1 cup	105	7.0	402	15.5	4.2	76.1	63	420	4.0	1	—	(0)	.42	—	—	(0)
1387	Cooked	1 cup	245	85.2	147	5.6	1.5	27.9	25	154	1.5	[361] 176	—	(0)	.15	—	—	(0)
	Oat and wheat cereal:																
1388	Dry form	1 cup	95	10.0	346	14.0	4.8	64.9	50	402	3.7	2	—	(0)	.47	.17	2.5	(0)
1389	Cooked	1 cup	245	83.6	159	6.4	2.2	29.6	27	184	1.7	[361] 412	—	(0)	.22	.07	1.2	(0)
	Oatmeal or rolled oats, regular (5 min. or longer cooking time) and instant-cooking (about 1 min. cooking time):																
1390	Dry form[362]	1 cup	80	8.3	312	11.4	5.9	54.6	42	324	3.6	2	282	(0)	.48	.11	.8	(0)
1391	Cooked	1 cup	240	86.5	132	4.8	2.4	23.3	22	137	1.4	[361] 523	146	(0)	.19	.05	.2	(0)
	Oat products used mainly as ready-to-eat breakfast cereals:[5] [74]																
1392	Oats, shredded, added protein, sugar, salt, minerals, vitamins.	1 cup	45	3.9	171	8.5	.9	32.4	119	143	2.4	275	—	(0)	1.59	1.90	15.9	(0)
1393	Oats, puffed, added sugar, salt, minerals, vitamins	1 cup	25	3.4	99	3.0	1.4	18.8	44	102	[182] 2.9	317	—	[81] 1,180	[82] .29	[82] .35	[82] 2.9	[81] 9
1394	Oats (with corn), puffed, added salt, minerals, vitamins, sugar-covered.	1 cup	35	1.9	139	2.3	1.2	30.0	[363] (63)	[363] (144)	([363])	206	—	[81] 1,650	[82] .41	[82] .49	[82] 4.1	[81] 12
	Ocean perch, Atlantic (redfish):																
1397	Cooked, fried:[73]																
a	Pound	1 lb	454	59.0	1,030	86.2	60.3	30.8	150	1,025	5.9	[41] 694	1,288	—	.45	.50	8.2	—
b	Ounce	1 oz	28	59.0	64	5.4	3.8	1.9	9	64	.4	[41] 43	81	—	.03	.03	.5	—
1398	Frozen, breaded, fried, reheated (fillet, 6¾ in. long, 1¾ in. wide, ⅝ in. thick;[40] wt., 3.2 oz.):[364]																
a	Yield from container, net wt., 16 oz. (1 lb.)[364] (5 fillets).	15½ oz	440	43.2	1,404	83.2	83.2	72.6	—	—	—	—	—	—	—	—	—	—
b	Fillet	1 fillet	88	43.2	281	16.6	16.6	14.5	—	—	—	—	—	—	—	—	—	—
c	Pound	1 lb	454	43.2	1,447	85.7	85.7	74.8	—	—	—	—	—	—	—	—	—	—
1401	Oils, salad or cooking:																
	Container and approx. contents:																

[1] Measure and weight apply to food as it is described with inedible part or parts (refuse) included.

[5] Most of phosphorus in nuts, legumes, and outer layers of cereal grains is present as phytic acid. See also Appendix D, section on Minerals and Oxalic Acid

[30] Value is for unsalted product. If salt is used, increase value by 236 mg. per 100 g. of vegetable—an estimated figure based on typical amount of salt (0.6%) in canned vegetables. See also Appendix C, section on Cooked Vegetables

[40] Width at widest part; thickness at thickest part.

[41] Value for product without added salt.

[42] Measurement applies to thawed product. See also Appendix C, section on Frozen Fruits and Vegetables

[58] Oxalic acid present may combine with calcium and magnesium to form insoluble compounds. For further information, see Appendix D, section on Minerals and Oxalic Acid

[73] Dipped in egg, milk or water, and breadcrumbs.

[74] Weight per cup based on method of pouring product from container into measuring cup to overflow and leveling with straight edge. Revised values for minerals and vitamins apply to products on the market in 1972.

[81] Basis of revised value for 100 g. of product with added vitamin A is 4,700 I.U.; with added ascorbic acid, 35 mg.

[82] Basis of revised value for 100 g. of product with added thiamin is 1.16 mg.; with added riboflavin, 1.41 mg.; with added niacin, 11.6 mg.

[98] Value does not allow for losses that might occur from cutting, chopping, or shredding. See also Appendix C, section on Cut Forms of Raw Fruits and Vegetables; Capping of Strawberries

[137] Based on product with minimum level of enrichment. See also Appendix C, section on Enriched Foods and Standards of Enrichment

[182] Based on revised value of 11.7 mg. per 100 g. of product.

[344] Unless indicated otherwise, weight per cup applies to product immediately after cooking and is based on specific proportion of alimentary paste and water in cooked product. For further information, see Appendix B, section on Home-Prepared Foods and ARS 62–13 (7), section on Alimentary Pastes and Other Cereal Products, pp. 6–7, and table 3, p. 9.

[345] Value applies to product cooked in unsalted water.

[360] For dry form of cereal, weight per cup is based on method of pouring cereal from container into measuring cup with as little fall as possible, then leveling with straight edge. See also Appendix B, section on Nonliquid Foods and section on Breakfast-Type Cereals For cooked cereal, weight per cup represents hot cereal immediately after cooking and is based on specific proportion of cereal and water in cooked product. See ARS 62–13 (7), section on Alimentary Pastes and Other Cereal Products, pp. 6–7, and table 3, p. 9. For item 1386, physical structure has changed to enable shorter cooking time, weight per cup (as shown) of dry form is less, volume of water used for cooking reduced to 2½ cups, but proportions of ingredients used, proportion of weight of cooked cereal, and ratio of weights—cooked to dried—as shown in table 3 of ARS 62–13 still apply.

[361] Applies to product cooked with salt added as specified by manufacturers. If cooked without added salt, value is negligible.

[362] If cereal is spooned into cup with packing, weight per cup would be increased by as much as 20 g. per cup.

[363] Based on revised value per 100 g. of product with added mineral. Value used for calcium is (180) mg.; for phosphorus, (410) mg. Values for iron range from 2.5 to 11.7 mg. per 100 g.; 0.9–4.1 mg. per cup. Without added calcium, value should be based on 26 mg. per 100 g.; without added phosphorus, 159 mg.

[364] Dimensions, net weight, or weight before reheating.

TABLE 1.—*Nutritive values for household measures and market units of foods*—Continued

[Item numbers correspond to those in table 1 of Handbook No. 8. revised 1963. Values in parentheses denote imputed values usually from another form of the food or from a similar food. Zeros in parentheses indicate that amount of a constituent, if present, is probably too small to be measured. Dashes (—) denote lack of reliable data for a constituent believed to be present in a measurable amount. Calculated values, as those based on a recipe, are not in parentheses]

Item No. (A)	Food, approximate measures, units, and weight (edible part unless footnotes indicate otherwise) (B)			Water (C)	Food energy (D)	Protein (E)	Fat (F)	Carbohydrate (G)	Calcium (H)	Phosphorus (I)	Iron (J)	Sodium (K)	Potassium (L)	Vitamin A value (M)	Thiamin (N)	Riboflavin (O)	Niacin (P)	Ascorbic acid (Q)
			Grams	Percent	Calories	Grams	Grams	Grams	Milligrams	Milligrams	Milligrams	Milligrams	Milligrams	International units	Milligrams	Milligrams	Milligrams	Milligrams
	Oils, salad or cooking—Continued																	
	Container and approx. contents—Continued																	
	Corn, safflower, soybean oils, soybean-cottonseed oil blend: [265]																	
a	Bottle, net contents, 16 fl. oz. (1 pt.)	1 bottle or 1 pt.	436	0	3,854	0	436.0	0	0	0	0	0	0	—	0	0	0	0
b	Bottle, net contents, 24 fl. oz. (1 pt. 8 fl. oz.)	1 bottle	654	0	5,781	0	654.0	0	0	0	0	0	0	—	0	0	0	0
	Olive oil:																	
c	Bottle, net contents, 4 fl. oz	1 bottle	108	0	955	0	108.0	0	0	0	0	0	0	—	0	0	0	0
d	Bottle or can, net contents, 16 fl. oz. (1 pt.)	1 container or 1 pt.	432	0	3,819	0	432.0	0	0	0	0	0	0	—	0	0	0	0
	Peanut oil:																	
e	Bottle, net contents, 24 fl. oz. (1 pt. 8 fl. oz.)	1 bottle	648	0	5,728	0	648.0	0	0	0	0	0	0	—	0	0	0	0
	Quart:																	
f	Corn, cottonseed, safflower, sesame, soybean oils, soybean-cottonseed oil blend.	1 qt	872	0	7,708	0	872.0	0	0	0	0	0	0	—	0	0	0	0
g	Olive or peanut oil	1 qt	864	0	7,638	0	864.0	0	0	0	0	0	0	—	0	0	0	0
	Cup:																	
h	Corn, cottonseed, safflower, sesame, soybean oils, soybean-cottonseed oil blend.	1 cup	218	0	1,927	0	218.0	0	0	0	0	0	0	—	0	0	0	0
i	Olive or peanut oil	1 cup	216	0	1,909	0	216.0	0	0	0	0	0	0	—	0	0	0	0
	Tablespoon:																	
j	Corn, cottonseed, safflower, sesame, soybean oils, soybean-cottonseed oil blend.	1 tbsp	13.6	0	120	0	13.6	0	0	0	0	0	0	—	0	0	0	0
k	Olive or peanut oil	1 tbsp	13.5	0	119	0	13.5	0	0	0	0	0	0	—	0	0	0	0
	Okra: [55]																	
1402	Raw:																	
a	Cup, crosscut slices	1 cup	100	88.9	36	2.4	.3	7.6	92	51	.6	3	249	520	(.17)	(.21)	(1.0)	31
b	Pound	1 lb	454	88.9	163	10.9	1.4	34.5	417	231	2.7	14	1,129	2,360	(.77)	(.95)	(4.5)	141
1403	Cooked (boiled), drained:																	
a	Pod, 3 in. long, ⅝-in. diam	10 pods	106	91.1	31	2.1	.3	6.4	98	43	.5	[20] 2	184	520	(.14)	(.19)	(1.0)	21
b	Cup, crosscut slices	1 cup	160	91.1	46	3.2	.5	9.6	147	66	.8	[20] 3	278	780	(.21)	(.29)	(1.4)	32
c	Pound	1 lb	454	91.1	132	9.1	1.4	27.2	417	186	2.3	[20] 9	789	2,220	(.59)	(.82)	(4.1)	91
1404	Frozen, cuts and pods:																	
	Not thawed:																	
a	Container, net wt., 10 oz	1 container	284	87.9	111	6.5	.3	25.6	267	145	1.7	6	622	1,360	.48	.60	2.8	45
b	Pound	1 lb	454	87.9	177	10.4	.5	40.8	426	231	2.7	9	993	2,180	.77	.95	4.5	73
1405	Cooked (boiled), drained:																	
a	Yield from 10 oz., frozen okra	9 oz	255	88.3	97	5.6	.3	22.4	240	110	1.3	[20] 5	418	1,220	.36	.43	2.6	31
b	Yield from 1 lb., frozen okra	14⅖ oz	408	88.3	155	9.0	.4	35.9	384	175	2.0	[20] 8	669	1,960	.57	.69	4.1	49
c	Cup, cuts	1 cup	185	88.3	70	4.1	.2	16.3	174	80	.9	[20] 4	303	890	.26	.31	1.9	22
d	Pound	1 lb	454	88.3	172	10.0	.5	39.9	426	195	2.3	[20] 9	744	2,180	.64	.77	4.5	54
	Oleomargarine. See Margarine (item 1317).																	
	Olives, pickled; canned or bottled: [266]																	
1406	Green:																	
	Whole (refuse: pits, 16%): [1]																	
a	Small, select, or standard, approx. 10/16-in. diam., 13/16 in. long; 135 per pound.	10 olives	34	78.2	33	.4	3.6	.4	17	5	.5	686	16	90	—	—	—	—
b	Large, approx. 12/16-in. diam., 15/16 in. long; 98 per pound.	10 olives	46	78.2	45	.5	4.9	.5	24	7	.6	926	21	120	—	—	—	—
c	Giant, approx. 14/16-in. diam., 12/16 in. long; 53–64 per pound.	10 olives	78	78.2	76	.9	8.3	.9	40	11	1.0	1,572	36	200	—	—	—	—
d	Pound, pitted	1 lb	454	78.2	526	6.4	57.6	5.9	277	77	7.3	10,886	249	1,360	—	—	—	—
	Ripe:																	
1407	Ascolano:																	
	Whole (refuse: pits, 14%): [1]																	
a	Extra large, approx. 12/16-in. diam., 1 in. long; 82 per pound.	10 olives	55	80.0	61	.5	6.5	1.2	40	8	.8	385	16	30	Trace	Trace	—	—
b	Mammoth, approx. 13/16-in. diam., 1 1/16 in. long; 70 per pound.	10 olives	65	80.0	72	.6	7.7	1.5	47	9	.9	454	19	30	Trace	Trace	—	—
c	Giant, approx. 13/16-in. diam., 12/16 in. long; 53–60 per pound.	10 olives	80	80.0	89	.8	9.5	1.8	58	11	1.1	559	23	40	Trace	Trace	—	—

(A)	(B)			(C)	(D)	(E)	(F)	(G)	(H)	(I)	(J)	(K)	(L)	(M)	(N)	(O)	(P)	(Q)
d	Jumbo, approx. 15/16-in. diam., 1 3/16 in. long; 46–50 per pound.	10 olives	95	80.0	105	0.9	11.3	2.1	69	13	1.3	664	28	50	Trace	Trace	—	—
e	Sliced	1 cup	135	80.0	174	1.5	18.6	3.5	113	22	2.2	1,098	46	80	Trace	Trace	—	—
f	Pound, pitted	1 lb	454	80.0	585	5.0	62.6	11.8	381	73	7.3	3,688	154	270	Trace	Trace	—	—
1408	Manzanillo:																	
	Whole (refuse: pits, 14%):[1]																	
a	Small, approx. 10/16-in. diam., 13/16 in. long; 135 per pound.	10 olives	34	80.0	38	.3	4.0	.8	25	5	.5	237	10	20	Trace	Trace	—	—
b	Medium, approx. 11/16-in. diam., 14/16 in. long; 113 per pound.	10 olives	40	80.0	44	.4	4.7	.9	29	6	.6	280	12	20	Trace	Trace	—	—
c	Large, approx. 12/16-in. diam., 15/16 in. long; 98 per pound.	10 olives	46	80.0	51	.4	5.5	1.0	33	6	.6	322	13	20	Trace	Trace	—	—
d	Extra large, approx. 12/16-in. diam., 1 in. long; 82 per pound.	10 olives	55	80.0	61	.5	6.5	1.2	40	8	.8	385	16	30	Trace	Trace	—	—
e	Sliced	1 cup	135	80.0	174	1.5	18.6	3.5	113	22	2.2	1,098	46	80	Trace	Trace	—	—
f	Pound, pitted	1 lb	454	80.0	585	5.0	62.6	11.8	381	73	7.3	3,688	154	270	Trace	Trace	—	—
1409	Mission:																	
	Whole (refuse: pits, 14%):[1]																	
a	Small, approx. 10/16-in. diam., 13/16 in. long; 135 per pound.	10 olives	34	73.0	54	.4	5.9	.9	31	5	.5	219	8	20	Trace	Trace	—	—
b	Medium, approx. 11/16-in. diam., 14/16 in. long; 113 per pound.	10 olives	40	73.0	63	.4	6.9	1.1	36	6	.6	258	9	20	Trace	Trace	—	—
c	Large, approx. 12/16-in. diam., 15/16 in. long; 98 per pound.	10 olives	46	73.0	73	.5	8.0	1.3	42	7	.7	297	11	30	Trace	Trace	—	—
d	Extra large, approx. 12/16-in. diam., 15/16 in. long; 82 per pound.	10 olives	55	73.0	87	.6	9.5	1.5	50	8	.8	355	13	30	Trace	Trace	—	—
e	Sliced	1 cup	135	73.0	248	1.6	27.1	4.3	143	23	2.3	1,013	36	90	Trace	Trace	—	—
f	Pound, pitted	1 lb	454	73.0	835	5.4	91.2	14.5	481	77	7.7	3,402	122	320	Trace	Trace	—	—
1410	Sevillano:																	
	Whole (refuse: pits, 14%):[1]																	
a	Giant, approx. 13/16-in. diam., 1 2/16 in. long; 53–60 per pound.	10 olives	80	84.4	64	.8	6.5	1.9	51	14	1.1	570	30	40	Trace	Trace	—	—
b	Jumbo, approx. 15/16-in. diam., 1 3/16 in. long; 46–50 per pound.	10 olives	95	84.4	76	.9	7.8	2.2	60	16	1.3	676	36	50	Trace	Trace	—	—
c	Colossal, approx. 1-in. diam., 1 4/16 in. long; 36–40 per pound.	10 olives	119	84.4	95	1.1	9.7	2.8	76	20	1.6	847	45	60	Trace	Trace	—	—
d	Supercolossal, approx. 1 1/16-in. diam., 1 6/16 in. long; 32 per pound.	10 olives	142	84.4	114	1.3	11.6	3.3	90	24	2.0	1,011	54	70	Trace	Trace	—	—
e	Sliced	1 cup	135	84.4	126	1.5	12.8	3.6	100	27	2.2	1,118	59	80	Trace	Trace	—	—
f	Pound, pitted	1 lb	454	84.4	422	5.0	43.1	12.2	336	91	7.3	3,756	200	270	Trace	Trace	—	—
1411	Ripe, salt cured, oil coated, Greek style:																	
	Whole (refuse: pits, 20%):[1]																	
a	Medium, 188 per pound	10 olives	24	43.8	65	.4	6.9	1.7	—	6	—	631	—	—	—	—	—	—
b	Extra large, 137 per pound	10 olives	33	43.8	89	.6	9.5	2.3	—	8	—	868	—	—	—	—	—	—
c	Pound, pitted	1 lb	454	43.8	1,533	10.0	162.4	39.5	—	132	—	14,914	-	—	—	—	—	—
	Olive oil. See Oils (items 1401c, 1401d, 1401g, 1401i, 1401k).																	
	Omelet. See Eggs, omelet (item 975).																	
	Onions, mature (dry):																	
1412	Raw:																	
	Cup:																	
a	Chopped	1 cup	170	89.1	65	2.6	.2	14.8	46	61	.9	17	267	[267] 70	0.05	0.07	0.3	17
b	Grated or ground	1 cup	235	89.1	89	3.5	.2	20.4	63	85	1.2	24	369	[267] 90	.07	.09	.5	24
c	Sliced	1 cup	115	89.1	44	1.7	.1	10.0	31	41	.6	12	181	[267] 50	.03	.05	.2	12
d	Tablespoon, chopped or minced	1 tbsp	10	89.1	4	.2	Trace	.9	3	4	.1	1	16	[267] Trace	Trace	Trace	Trace	1
e	Pound	1 lb	454	89.1	172	6.8	.5	39.5	122	163	2.3	45	712	[267] 180	.14	.18	.9	45
1413	Cooked (boiled), drained:																	
a	Cup, whole or sliced	1 cup	210	91.8	61	2.5	.2	13.7	50	61	.8	[20] 15	231	[267] 80	.06	.06	.4	15
b	Pound	1 lb	454	91.8	132	5.4	.5	29.5	109	132	1.8	[20] 32	499	[267] 180	.14	.14	.9	32
	Onions, young green (bunching varieties), **raw:**																	
1415	Bulb and entire top:																	
a	Cup, chopped or sliced	1 cup	100	89.4	36	1.5	.2	8.2	51	39	1.0	5	231	(2,000)	.05	.05	.4	32
b	Tablespoon, chopped	1 tbsp	6	89.4	2	.1	Trace	.5	3	2	.1	Trace	14	(120)	Trace	Trace	Trace	2
c	Pound	1 lb	454	89.4	163	6.8	.9	37.2	231	177	4.5	23	1,048	(9,070)	.23	.23	1.8	145

[1] Measure and weight apply to food as it is described with inedible part or parts (refuse) included.

[20] Value is for unsalted product. If salt is used, increase value by 236 mg. per 100 g. of vegetable—an estimated figure based on typical amount of salt (0.6%) in canned vegetables. See also Appendix C, section on Cooked Vegetables.

[25] Oxalic acid present may combine with calcium and magnesium to form insoluble compounds. For further information, see Appendix D, section on Minerals and Oxalic Acid.

[265] Other common container sizes available are 38 fl. oz. (1 qt. 6 fl. oz.), 48 fl. oz. (1 qt. 1 pt.), 128 fl. oz. (1 gal.).

[266] See Appendix B, section on Olives and Pickles for basis of dimensions and counts per pound shown for sizes of whole olives and for sources of information on other commercial sizes.

[267] Value based on yellow-fleshed varieties; white-fleshed varieties contain only trace.

TABLE 1.—*Nutritive values for household measures and market units of foods*—Continued

[Item numbers correspond to those in table 1 of Handbook No. 8, revised 1963. Values in parentheses denote imputed values usually from another form of the food or from a similar food. Zeros in parentheses indicate that amount of a constituent, if present, is probably too small to be measured. Dashes (—) denote lack of reliable data for a constituent believed to be present in a measurable amount. Calculated values, as those based on a recipe, are not in parentheses]

Item No. (A)		Food, approximate measures, units, and weight (edible part unless footnotes indicate otherwise) (B)			Water (C)	Food energy (D)	Protein (E)	Fat (F)	Carbohydrate (G)	Calcium (H)	Phosphorus (I)	Iron (J)	Sodium (K)	Potassium (L)	Vitamin A value (M)	Thiamin (N)	Riboflavin (O)	Niacin (P)	Ascorbic acid (Q)
				Grams	Percent	Calories	Grams	Grams	Grams	Milligrams	Milligrams	Milligrams	Milligrams	Milligrams	International units	Milligrams	Milligrams	Milligrams	Milligrams
		Onions, young green (bunching varieties), raw—Continued																	
1416		Bulb and white portion of top:																	
	a	Onions, 2 medium (4⅛ in. long, ⅝-in. diam.) or 6 small (3 in. long, ⅜-in. diam.).	2 medium or 6 small onions.	30	87.6	14	0.3	0.1	3.2	12	12	0.2	2	69	Trace	0.02	0.01	0.1	8
	b	Cup, chopped or sliced	1 cup	100	87.6	45	1.1	.2	10.5	40	39	.6	5	231	Trace	.05	.04	.4	25
	c	Tablespoon, chopped	1 tbsp	6	87.6	3	.1	Trace	.6	2	2	Trace	Trace	14	Trace	Trace	Trace	Trace	2
	d	Pound	1 lb	454	87.6	204	5.0	.9	47.6	181	177	2.7	23	1,048	Trace	.23	.18	1.8	113
1417		Tops only (green portion):																	
	a	Cup, chopped	1 cup	100	91.8	27	1.6	.4	5.5	56	39	2.2	5	231	4,000	.07	.10	.6	51
	b	Tablespoon, chopped	1 tbsp	6	91.8	2	.1	Trace	.3	3	2	.1	Trace	14	240	Trace	.01	Trace	3
	c	Pound	1 lb	454	91.8	122	7.3	1.8	24.9	254	177	10.0	23	1,048	18,140	.32	.45	2.7	231
		Oranges, raw, used for peeled fruit served whole, sectioned, or as cut-up fruit:																	
1420		All commercial varieties:[265]																	
	a	Whole fruit,[210] 2⅝-in. diam. (refuse: peel and seeds, 27%);[1] (weighted estimate or size and weight based on varieties and quantities marketed).	1 orange	180	86.0	64	1.3	.3	16.0	54	26	.5	1	263	260	.13	.05	.5	[269] (66)
	b	Sections without membranes	1 cup	180	86.0	88	1.8	.4	22.0	74	36	.7	2	360	360	.18	.07	.7	[269] (90)
		Cut-up fruit:																	
	c	Bite-size pieces	1 cup	165	86.0	81	1.7	.3	20.1	68	33	.7	2	330	330	.17	.07	.7	[269] (83)
	d	Diced, small pieces	1 cup	210	86.0	103	2.1	.4	25.6	86	42	.8	2	420	420	.21	.08	.8	[269] (105)
		California:																	
1421		Navels (winter oranges):																	
		Whole fruit[210] (refuse: peel and navel formation, 32%):[1]																	
	a	Large, 3 1/16-in. diam., size 72[233]	1 orange	252	85.4	87	2.2	.2	21.8	69	38	.7	2	333	(340)	.17	.07	.7	[269] (105)
	b	Medium, 2⅞-in. diam., size 88[235]	1 orange	206	85.4	71	1.8	.1	17.8	56	31	.6	1	272	(280)	.14	.06	.6	[269] (85)
	c	Small, 2⅜-in. diam., size 138[235]	1 orange	131	85.4	45	1.2	.1	11.3	36	20	.4	1	173	(180)	.09	.04	.4	[269] (54)
		Sections (from medium fruit) spooned into cup without packing:																	
	d	With membranes	1 cup	150	85.4	77	2.0	.2	19.1	60	33	.6	2	291	(300)	.15	.06	.6	[269] (92)
	e	Without membranes	1 cup	165	85.4	84	2.1	.2	21.0	66	36	.7	2	320	(330)	.17	.07	.7	[269] (101)
		Cut-up fruit:																	
		Bite-size pieces, approx. ½- to ⅝-in. lengths (prepared from medium fruit cut into 8 sectors with 3 crosswise cuts of each sector; spooned into cup without packing), using—																	
	f	Peeled fruit with membranes	1 cup	150	85.4	77	2.0	.2	19.1	60	33	.6	2	291	(300)	.15	.06	.6	[269] (92)
	g	Pared fruit without membranes	1 cup	160	85.4	82	2.1	.2	20.3	64	35	.6	2	310	(320)	.16	.06	.6	[269] (98)
	h	Diced, small pieces	1 cup	210	85.4	107	2.7	.2	26.7	84	46	.8	2	407	(420)	.21	.08	.8	[269] (128)
		Slices, "cartwheel," ¼ in. thick, without peel:[270]																	
	i	2½-in. diam	1 slice	21	85.4	11	.3	Trace	2.7	8	5	.1	Trace	41	(40)	.02	.01	.1	[269] (13)
	j	2¼-in. diam	1 slice	18	85.4	9	.2	Trace	2.8	7	4	.1	Trace	35	(40)	.02	.01	.1	[269] (11)
		Wedges, served with peel (from medium orange, 2⅞-in. diam., size 88[235]) (refuse: peel and navel formation, 32%):[1]																	
	k	2¼-in. arc; ¼ of fruit	1 wedge	52	85.4	18	.5	Trace	4.5	14	8	.1	Trace	69	(70)	.04	.01	.1	[269] (22)
	l	1½-in. arc; ⅙ of fruit	1 wedge	34	85.4	12	.3	Trace	2.9	9	5	.1	Trace	45	(50)	.02	.01	.1	[269] (14)
1422		Valencias (summer oranges):																	
		Whole fruit[210] (refuse: peel and seeds, 25%):[1]																	
	a	Large, 3 1/16-in. diam., size 72[235]	1 orange	252	85.6	96	2.3	.6	23.4	76	42	1.5	2	359	(380)	.19	.08	.8	[269] (93)
	b	Medium, 2⅝-in. diam., size 113[235]	1 orange	161	86.5	62	1.4	.4	15.0	48	27	1.0	1	230	(240)	.12	.05	.5	[269] (59)
	c	Small, 2⅜-in. diam., size 138[235]	1 orange	131	85.6	50	1.2	.3	12.2	39	22	.8	1	187	(200)	.10	.04	.4	[269] (48)
	d	Sections without membranes (from medium fruit), spooned into cup without packing.	1 cup	180	85.6	92	2.2	.5	22.3	72	40	1.4	2	342	(360)	.18	.07	.7	[269] (88)
		Cut-up fruit:																	
		Bite-size pieces, approx. ½- to ⅝-in. lengths (prepared from medium fruit cut into 8																	

(A)		(B)		(C)	(D)	(E)	(F)	(G)	(H)	(I)	(J)	(K)	(L)	(M)	(N)	(O)	(P)	(Q)
		sectors with 3 crosswise cuts of each sector; spooned into cup without packing), using—																
	e	Peeled fruit with membranes	1 cup	155	85.6	79	1.9	0.5	19.2	62	34	1.2	2	295	(310)	0.16	0.06	0.6	[269] (76)
	f	Pared fruit without membranes	1 cup	165	85.6	84	2.0	.5	20.5	66	36	1.3	2	314	(330)	.17	.07	.7	[269] (81)
	g	Diced, small pieces	1 cup	210	85.6	107	2.5	.6	26.0	84	46	1.7	2	399	(420)	.21	.08	.8	[269] (103)
		Slices, "cartwheel," ¼ in. thick, without peel:[270]																
	h	2⅝-in. diam	1 slice	20	85.6	10	.2	.1	2.5	8	4	.2	Trace	38	(40)	.02	.01	.1	[269] (10)
	i	2-in. diam	1 slice	15	85.6	8	.2	Trace	1.9	6	3	.1	Trace	29	(30)	.02	.01	.1	[269] (7)
		Wedges, served with peel (from medium orange, 2⅝-in. diam., size 113[266]) (refuse: peel and seeds, 25%):[1]																
	j	2⅙-in. arc; ¼ of fruit	1 wedge	40	85.6	15	.4	.1	3.7	12	7	.2	Trace	57	(60)	.03	.01	.1	[269] (15)
	k	1⅝-in. arc; ⅙ of fruit	1 wedge	27	85.6	10	.2	.1	2.5	8	4	.2	Trace	39	(40)	.02	.01	.1	[269] (10)
		Florida:																
1423		All commercial varieties:																
		Whole fruit[210] (refuse: peel and seeds, 26%):[1]																
	a	Average size, 2⅝-in. diam. (weighted estimate of size and weight based on varieties and quantities marketed).[271]	1 orange	190	86.4	66	1.0	(.3)	16.9	60	24	.3	1	(290)	(280)	.14	.06	.6	[269] (63)
	b	Large, 2¹⁵⁄₁₆-in. diam., size 80[272]	1 orange	255	86.4	89	1.3	(.4)	22.6	81	32	.4	2	(389)	(380)	.19	.08	.8	[269] (85)
	c	Medium, 2¹¹⁄₁₆-in. diam., size 100[272]	1 orange	204	86.4	71	1.1	(.3)	18.1	65	26	.3	2	(311)	(300)	.15	.06	.6	[269] (68)
	d	Small, 2½-in. diam., size 125[272]	1 orange	163	86.4	57	.8	(.2)	14.5	52	21	.2	1	(248)	(240)	.12	.05	.5	[269] (54)
	e	Sections without membranes (from medium size fruit).	1 cup	185	86.4	87	1.3	(.4)	22.2	80	31	.4	2	(381)	(370)	.19	.07	.7	[269] (83)
		Cut-up fruit:																
	f	Bite-size pieces, approx. ½- to ⅝-in. lengths (prepared from medium fruit cut into 8 sectors with 3 crosswise cuts of each sector; spooned into cup without packing).	1 cup	(165)	86.4	78	1.2	(.3)	19.8	71	28	.3	2	(340)	(330)	.17	.07	.7	[269] (74)
	g	Diced, small pieces	1 cup	210	86.4	99	1.5	(.4)	25.2	90	36	.4	2	(433)	(420)	.21	.08	.8	[269] (95)
		Slices, "cartwheel," ¼ in. thick, without peel:																
	h	2½-in. diam	1 slice	21	86.4	10	.1	(Trace)	2.5	9	4	Trace	Trace	(43)	(40)	.02	.01	.1	[269] (9)
	i	2-in. diam	1 slice	15	86.4	7	.1	(Trace)	1.8	6	3	Trace	Trace	(31)	(30)	.02	.01	.1	[269] (7)
		Wedges, served with peel (from medium orange, 2¹¹⁄₁₆-in. diam., size 100[272]) (refuse: peel and seeds, 26%):[1]																
	j	2⅛-in. arc; ¼ of fruit	1 wedge	51	86.4	18	.3	(.1)	4.5	16	6	.1	Trace	(78)	(80)	.04	.02	.2	[269] (17)
	k	1⅝-in. arc; ⅙ of fruit	1 wedge	34	86.4	12	.2	(.1)	3.0	11	4	.1	Trace	(52)	(50)	.03	.01	.1	[269] (11)
1424		**Oranges, raw, used with peel** (California Valencias):																
	a	Whole fruit,[210] medium, 2⅝-in. diam. (refuse: seeds, 1%).[1]	1 orange	161	82.3	[267] 64	2.1	.5	24.7	112	35	1.3	3	312	400	.16	.08	.8	113
	b	Cut-up fruit, chopped in small pieces	1 cup	170	82.3	[267] 68	2.2	.5	26.4	119	37	1.4	3	333	430	.17	.09	.9	121
		Orange juice, raw, and oranges used for juice:																
1425		All commercial varieties:[268]																
	a	Juice	1 cup	248	88.3	112	1.7	.5	25.8	27	42	.5	2	496	500	.22	.07	1.0	[269] 124
	b	Whole fruit used for juice,[210] 2⅝-in. diam. (estimated—see item 1420a) (refuse: peel, membranes, seeds, handling loss, 52%);[1] yield of juice, approx. 86 g. (⅓ cup).	1 orange	180	88.3	39	.6	.2	9.0	10	15	.2	1	173	170	.08	.03	.3	[269] 43
		California:																
1426		Navels (winter oranges):																
	a	Juice	1 cup	249	87.2	120	2.5	.2	28.1	27	45	.5	2	483	500	.22	.07	1.0	[269] 152
		Whole fruit used for juice[210] (refuse: peel, membranes, seeds, handling loss, 59%):[1]																
	b	Large, 3³⁄₁₆-in. diam., size 72;[266] yield of juice, approx. 103 g. (⅜ cup).	1 orange	252	87.2	50	1.0	.1	11.7	11	19	.2	1	200	210	.09	.03	.4	[269] 63
	c	Medium, 2⅞-in. diam., size 88;[266] yield of juice, approx. 84 g. (⅓ cup).	1 orange	206	87.2	41	.8	.1	9.5	9	15	.2	1	164	170	.08	.03	.3	[269] 52
	d	Small, 2⅝-in. diam., size 138;[266] yield of juice, approx. 54 g. (⅙–¼ cup).	1 orange	131	87.2	26	.5	.1	6.1	6	10	.1	1	104	110	.05	.02	.2	[269] 33

[1] Measure and weight apply to food as it is described with inedible part or parts (refuse) included.

[210] See Appendix B, section on Citrus Fruits for explanation of basis for sizes and weights shown for whole citrus fruits.

[266] Size refers to count of fruit in ⁷⁄₁₀-bushel container with net weight of approx. 40 lb.

[267] Based on pulp. There is no basis for assessing caloric value of peel or effect that inclusion of peel may have on digestibility of product.

[268] This item should be used when data are needed to represent countrywide and year-round use of oranges marketed as fresh fruit.

[269] Value weighted by monthly and total season shipments for marketing as fresh fruit. See also Appendix C, section on Citrus Fruits

[270] Medium-size fruits (113's and 88's) yield from 5 to 9 slices with average weights per slice ranging from 13 to 21 g.

[271] This item should be used when data are needed to represent year-round use of Florida oranges marketed as fresh fruit.

[272] Size refers to count of fruit in ⅘-bushel container with net weight of approx. 45 lb.

TABLE 1.—*Nutritive values for household measures and market units of foods*—Continued

[Item numbers correspond to those in table 1 of Handbook No. 8, revised 1963. Values in parentheses denote imputed values usually from another form of the food or from a similar food. Zeros in parentheses indicate that amount of a constituent, if present, is probably too small to be measured. Dashes (—) denote lack of reliable data for a constituent believed to be present in a measurable amount. Calculated values, as those based on a recipe, are not in parentheses]

Item No.	Food, approximate measures, units, and weight (edible part unless footnotes indicate otherwise)			Water	Food energy	Protein	Fat	Carbohydrate	Calcium	Phosphorus	Iron	Sodium	Potassium	Vitamin A value	Thiamin	Riboflavin	Niacin	Ascorbic acid
				Values for edible part of foods														
(A)	(B)			(C)	(D)	(E)	(F)	(G)	(H)	(I)	(J)	(K)	(L)	(M)	(N)	(O)	(P)	(Q)
			Grams	*Percent*	*Calories*	*Grams*	*Grams*	*Grams*	*Milligrams*	*Milligrams*	*Milligrams*	*Milligrams*	*Milligrams*	*International units*	*Milligrams*	*Milligrams*	*Milligrams*	*Milligrams*
	Orange juice, raw, and oranges used for juice—Continued																	
	California—Continued																	
1427	Valencias (summer oranges):																	
a	Juice	1 cup	248	87.8	117	2.5	0.7	26.0	27	47	0.7	2	471	500	0.22	0.07	1.0	[269] 122
	Whole fruit used for juice [210] (refuse: peel, membranes, seeds, handling loss, 51%): [1]																	
b	Large, 3⅟16-in. diam., size 72; [266] yield of juice, approx. 123 g. (½ cup).	1 orange	252	87.8	58	1.2	.4	13.0	14	23	.4	1	235	250	.11	.04	.5	[269] 61
c	Medium, 2⅝-in. diam., size 113; [266] yield of juice, approx. 79 g. (⅓ cup).	1 orange	161	87.8	37	.8	.2	8.3	9	15	.2	1	150	160	.07	.02	.3	[269] 39
d	Small, 2⅜-in. diam., size 138; [266] yield of juice, approx. 64 g. (¼ cup).	1 orange	131	87.8	30	.6	.2	6.7	7	12	.2	1	122	130	.06	.02	.3	[269] 31
	Florida:																	
1428	All commercial varieties:																	
a	Juice	1 cup	247	88.8	106	1.5	.5	24.7	25	40	.5	2	509	490	.22	.07	1.0	[269] 111
b	Whole fruit used for juice, [210] 2⅝-in. diam. (estimated—see item 1423a) (refuse: peel, membranes, seeds, handling loss, 50%); [1] yield of juice, approx. 95 g. (⅜ cup).	1 orange	190	88.8	41	.6	.2	9.5	10	15	.2	1	196	190	.09	.03	.4	[269] 43
1429	Early and midseason (Hamlin, Parson Brown, Pineapple):																	
a	Juice	1 cup	246	89.6	98	1.2	.5	22.9	25	37	.5	2	512	490	.22	.07	1.0	[269] 125
	Whole fruit used for juice [210] (refuse: peel, membranes, seeds, handling loss, 52%): [1]																	
b	Large, 2¹⁵⁄₁₆-in. diam., size 80; [272] yield of juice, approx. 122 g. (½ cup).	1 orange	255	89.6	49	.6	.2	11.4	12	18	.2	1	255	240	.11	.04	.5	[269] 62
c	Medium, 2¹¹⁄₁₆-in. diam., size 100; [272] yield of juice, approx. 98 g. (⅜ cup).	1 orange	204	89.6	39	.5	.2	9.1	10	15	.2	1	204	200	.09	.03	.4	[269] 50
d	Small, 2½-in. diam., size 125; [272] yield of juice, approx. 78 g. (⅓ cup).	1 orange	163	89.6	31	.4	.2	7.3	8	12	.2	1	163	160	.07	.02	.3	[269] 40
1430	Late season (Valencias):																	
a	Juice	1 cup	248	88.3	112	1.5	.5	26.0	25	45	.5	2	503	500	.22	.07	1.0	[269] 92
	Whole fruit used for juice [210] (refuse: peel, membranes, seeds, handling loss, 48%): [1]																	
b	Large, 2¹⁵⁄₁₆-in. diam., size 80; [272] yield of juice, approx. 133 g. (½ cup).	1 orange	255	88.3	60	.8	.3	13.9	13	24	.3	1	269	270	.12	.04	.5	[269] 49
c	Medium, 2¹¹⁄₁₆-in. diam., size 100; [272] yield of juice, approx. 106 g. (⅜–½ cup).	1 orange	204	88.3	48	.6	.2	11.1	11	19	.2	1	215	210	.10	.03	.4	[269] 39
d	Small, 2½-in. diam., size 125; [272] yield of juice, approx. 85 g. (⅓ cup).	1 orange	163	88.3	38	.5	.2	8.9	8	15	.2	1	172	170	.08	.03	.3	[269] 31
1431	Temple: [273]																	
a	Juice	1 cup	248	88.0	134	(1.2)	(.5)	32.0	(25)	42	.5	2	—	(500)	.22	.07	1.0	[269] 124
	Whole fruit used for juice [210] (refuse: peel, membranes, seeds, handling loss, 48%): [1]																	
b	Large, 3⅛-in. diam., size 66; [273] yield of juice, approx. 161 g. (⅝–⅔ cup).	1 orange	309	88.0	87	(.8)	(.3)	20.7	(16)	27	.3	2	—	(320)	.14	.05	.6	[269] 80
c	Medium, 2⅞-in. diam., sizes 80–100; [273] yield of juice, approx. 120 g. (½ cup).	1 orange	230	88.0	65	(.6)	(.2)	15.4	(12)	20	.2	1	—	(240)	.11	.04	.5	[269] 60
d	Small, 2⁹⁄₁₆-in. diam., size 120; [273] yield of juice, approx. 88 g. (⅓–⅜ cup).	1 orange	170	88.0	48	(.4)	(.2)	11.4	(9)	15	.2	1	—	(180)	.08	.03	.4	[269] 44
	Orange juice, canned: [274]																	
1432	Unsweetened:																	
	Can and approx. contents:																	
a	Size, 202 × 314 [14] (6½Z); net contents, 6 fl. oz.	1 can	186	87.4	89	1.5	.4	20.8	19	33	.7	2	370	370	.13	.04	.6	74
b	Size, 404 × 700 [14] (46Z, No. 3 Cylinder); net contents, 46 fl. oz. (1 qt. 14 fl. oz.).	1 can	1,429	87.4	686	11.4	2.9	160.0	143	257	5.7	14	2,844	2,860	1.00	.29	4.3	572
c	Cup	1 cup	249	87.4	120	2.0	.5	27.9	25	45	1.0	2	496	500	.17	.05	.7	100
d	Fluid ounce	1 fl. oz	31.1	87.4	15	.2	.1	3.5	3	6	.1	Trace	62	60	.02	.01	.1	12
1433	Sweetened with nutritive sweetener:																	
	Can and approx. contents:																	
a	Size, 202 × 314 [14] (6½Z); net contents, 6 fl. oz.	1 can	187	86.5	97	1.3	.4	22.8	(19)	33	.7	2	(370)	370	.13	.04	.6	74

(A)	(B)		(C)	(D)	(E)	(F)	(G)	(H)	(I)	(J)	(K)	(L)	(M)	(N)	(O)	(P)	(Q)
b	Size, 404 × 700 [14] (46Z, No. 3 Cylinder); net contents, 46 fl. oz. (1 qt. 14 fl. oz.).	1 can	1,434	86.5	746	10.0	2.9	174.9	(143)	257	5.7	14	(2,844)	2,860	1.00	0.29	4.3	572
c	Cup	1 cup	250	86.5	130	1.8	.5	30.5	(25)	45	1.0	2	(496)	500	.17	.05	.7	100
d	Fluid ounce	1 fl. oz	31.2	86.5	16	.2	.1	3.8	(3)	6	.1	Trace	(62)	60	.02	.01	.1	12
	Orange juice concentrate, canned, unsweetened: [275]																	
1434	Undiluted:																	
	Can and approx. contents:																	
a	Size, 603 × 700 [14] (No. 10); net contents, 96 fl. oz. (3 qt.).	1 can	3,625	42.0	8,084	148.6	47.1	1,837.9	1,849	3,118	47.1	181	34,148	34,800	14.14	4.35	61.6	8,301
b	Fluid ounce	1 fl. oz	37.8	42.0	84	1.5	.5	19.2	19	33	.5	2	356	360	.15	.05	.6	87
1435	Diluted with 5 parts water by volume:																	
a	Cup	1 cup	248	88.2	114	2.0	.7	25.5	25	45	.7	2	476	500	.20	.05	.7	117
b	Fluid ounce	1 fl. oz	31.0	88.2	14	.2	.1	3.2	3	6	.1	Trace	60	60	.02	.01	.1	15
	Orange juice concentrate, frozen, unsweetened: [274] [276]																	
1436	Undiluted:																	
	Can and approx. contents:																	
a	6 fl. oz. (yields 3 cups diluted juice weighing 746 g.).	1 can	213	55.2	362	5.3	.4	86.7	75	126	.9	4	1,500	1,620	.68	.11	2.8	360
b	12 fl. oz. (yields 1½ qt. diluted juice weighing 1,492 g.).	1 can	427	55.2	726	10.7	.9	173.8	149	252	1.7	9	3,006	3,240	1.37	.21	5.6	722
c	32 fl. oz. (1 qt.) (yields 1 gal. diluted juice weighing 3,978 g.).	1 can	1,139	55.2	1,936	28.5	2.3	463.6	399	672	4.6	23	8,019	8,640	3.64	.57	14.8	1,925
1437	Diluted with 3 parts water by volume:																	
a	Quart	1 qt	995	87.2	488	7.0	1.0	115.4	100	169	1.0	10	2,010	2,160	.92	.14	3.7	478
b	Cup	1 cup	249	87.2	122	1.7	.2	28.9	25	42	.2	2	503	540	.23	.03	.9	120
c	Glass (6 fl. oz.)	1 glass	187	87.2	92	1.3	.2	21.7	19	32	.2	2	378	410	.17	.03	.7	90
	Orange juice, dehydrated (crystals):																	
1438	Dry form:																	
a	Ounce	1 oz	28	1.0	108	1.4	.5	25.2	24	38	.5	2	490	480	.19	.06	.8	102
b	Pound (yields approx. 1 gal. of juice)	1 lb	454	1.0	1,724	22.7	7.7	403.3	381	608	7.7	36	7,838	7,620	3.04	.95	13.2	1,628
1439	Prepared with water (1 lb. of crystals yields approx. 1 gal. of juice).	1 cup	248	88.0	114	1.5	.5	26.8	25	40	.5	2	518	500	.20	.07	1.0	109
	Orange peel:																	
1440	Raw, grated (medium-size grating):																	
a	Tablespoon	1 tbsp	6	72.5	([239])	.1	Trace	1.5	10	1	Trace	Trace	13	30	.01	.01	.1	8
b	Teaspoon	1 tsp	2	72.5	([239])	Trace	Trace	.5	3	Trace	Trace	Trace	4	10	Trace	Trace	Trace	3
c	Ounce	1 oz	28	72.5	([239])	.4	.1	7.1	46	6	.2	1	60	120	.03	.03	.3	39
1441	Candied:																	
a	Ounce	1 oz	28	17.4	90	.1	.1	22.9	—	—	—	—	—	—	—	—	—	—
b	Pound	1 lb	454	17.4	1,433	1.8	1.4	365.6	—	—	—	—	—	—	—	—	—	—
	Orange-cranberry relish. See Cranberry-orange relish (item 925).																	
1442	**Orange juice and apricot juice drink,** canned (approx. 40% fruit juices):																	
a	Can, size 404 × 700 [14] (46Z, No. 3 Cylinder); net contents, 46 fl. oz. (1 qt. 14 fl. oz.).	1 can	1,434	86.7	717	4.3	1.4	182.1	72	115	1.4	Trace	1,348	8,320	.29	.14	2.9	([277])
b	Cup	1 cup	249	86.7	125	.7	.2	31.6	12	20	.2	Trace	234	1,440	.05	.02	.5	([277])
c	Glass (6 fl. oz.)	1 glass	187	86.7	94	.6	.2	23.7	9	15	.2	Trace	176	1,080	.04	.02	.4	([277])
d	Fluid ounce	1 fl. oz	31.2	86.7	16	.1	Trace	4.0	2	2	Trace	Trace	29	180	.01	Trace	.1	([277])
	Oysterplant. See Salsify (item 1962).																	
	Oysters:																	
	Raw (chilled), meat only:																	
1443	Eastern:																	
	Can and approx. drained contents:																	
a	Can (net contents, 12 fl. oz.[278]), drained wt., 12 oz.; approx. 18–27 Selects (medium) or 27–44 Standards (small).	18–27 Select or 27–44 Standard oysters.	340	84.6	224	28.6	6.1	11.6	320	486	18.7	248	411	1,050	.48	.61	8.5	—
b	Cup, approx. 13–19 Selects (medium) or 19–31 Standards (small).	1 cup	240	84.6	158	20.2	4.3	8.2	226	343	13.2	175	290	740	.34	.43	6.0	—

[1] Measure and weight apply to food as it is described with inedible part or parts (refuse) included.

[14] Dimensions of can: 1st dimension represents diameter; 2d dimension, height of can. 1st or left-hand digit in each dimension gives number of whole inches; next 2 digits give additional fraction of dimension expressed as 16th of an inch.

[210] See Appendix B, section on Citrus Fruits for explanation of basis for sizes and weights shown for whole citrus fruits.

[235] Size refers to count of fruit in 7/10-bushel container with net weight of approx. 40 lb.

[239] Value cannot be calculated inasmuch as digestibility of peel is not known.

[269] Value weighted by monthly and total season shipments for marketing as fresh fruit. See also Appendix C, section on Citrus Fruits

[272] Size refers to count of fruit in 4/5-bushel container with net weight of approx. 45 lb.

[273] Temple orange is botanically a tangor, which is a hybrid of sweet orange and tangerine. For practical purposes, since it is marketed as an orange, it has been classified with oranges in table.

[274] For retail market, prepared mainly from Florida oranges.

[275] Approximately two-thirds of canned concentrate, which is packed largely for institutional use, is prepared from California Valencias; remainder from Florida oranges.

[276] Weights and nutritive values apply to concentrate with 44.8% of orange juice soluble solids (by weight) to meet minimum requirement stated in Florida State Grades (Regulation No. 105–1.19) effective October 1965 (4). Values in Agr. Handb. No. 8, rev. 1963, apply to concentrate with 41.8% of soluble solids, the minimum percent required when Handbook No. 8 was published. Based on the new regulation, values for 100 g. of concentrate and diluted juice are shown in Appendix A, table 3, p. 264.

[277] Ascorbic acid may be added as preservative or as nutrient. For value of product, refer to label.

[278] Oysters of other sizes are available in 12-fl. oz. can.

TABLE 1.—*Nutritive values for household measures and market units of foods*—Continued

[Item numbers correspond to those in table 1 of Handbook No. 8, revised 1963. Values in parentheses denote imputed values usually from another form of the food or from a similar food. Zeros in parentheses indicate that amount of a constituent, if present, is probably too small to be measured. Dashes (—) denote lack of reliable data for a constituent believed to be present in a measurable amount. Calculated values, as those based on a recipe, are not in parentheses]

Item No. (A)		Food, approximate measures, units, and weight (edible part unless footnotes indicate otherwise) (B)			Water (C)	Food energy (D)	Protein (E)	Fat (F)	Carbohydrate (G)	Calcium (H)	Phosphorus (I)	Iron (J)	Sodium (K)	Potassium (L)	Vitamin A value (M)	Thiamin (N)	Riboflavin (O)	Niacin (P)	Ascorbic acid (Q)
				Grams	Percent	Calories	Grams	Grams	Grams	Milligrams	Milligrams	Milligrams	Milligrams	Milligrams	International units	Milligrams	Milligrams	Milligrams	Milligrams
		Oysters—Continued																	
		Raw—Continued																	
		Eastern—Continued																	
	c	Pound, approx. 19 or less Counts (extra large); 19–25 Extra Selects (large); 25–36 Selects (medium); 36–59 Standards (small); or over 59, Very Small.	1 lb	454	84.6	299	38.1	8.2	15.4	426	649	24.9	331	549	1,410	0.64	0.82	11.3	—
	d	Ounce, approx. 2 Selects (medium) or 3 Standards (small).	1 oz	28	84.6	19	2.4	.5	1.0	27	41	1.6	21	34	90	.04	.05	.7	—
1444		Pacific and Western (Olympia):																	
		Pacific:																	
		Can and approx. drained contents:																	
	a	Can (net contents, 12 fl. oz.[278]), drained wt., 12 oz.; approx. 6–9 Medium or 9–13 Small.	6–9 Medium or 9–13 Small oysters.	340	79.1	309	36.0	7.5	21.8	289	520	24.5	—	—	—	.41	—	4.4	102
	b	Cup, approx. 4–6 Medium or 6–9 Small	1 cup	240	79.1	218	25.4	5.3	15.4	204	367	17.3	—	—	—	.29	—	3.1	72
		Pacific and Western (Olympia):																	
	c	Pound (Pacific, 8 or less Large, 8–11 Medium, 12–17 Small, over 17 Extra Small; Western (Olympia), 275–300).	1 lb	454	79.1	413	48.1	10.0	29.0	386	694	32.7	—	—	—	.54	—	5.9	136
1445		Cooked (fried):[73]																	
	a	Oyster, Select (medium), approx. 1¾ in. long, 1 in. wide (yield from raw oyster, approx. 3 in. long, 1½ in. wide; wt., 14 g.).	4 Select oysters.	45	54.7	108	3.9	6.3	8.4	68	108	3.6	[43] 93	91	200	.08	.13	1.4	—
	b	Ounce, approx. 2½ Select oysters	1 oz	28	54.7	68	2.4	3.9	5.3	43	68	2.3	[43] 58	58	120	.05	.08	.9	—
1447		Frozen, solids and liquid:																	
	a	Can, net contents, 12 fl. oz	1 can	360	87.4	—	22.0	—	—	—	—	—	1,368	756	1,120	.50	.65	9.0	—
	b	Pound	1 lb	454	87.4	—	27.7	—	—	—	—	—	1,724	953	1,410	.64	.82	11.3	—
		Oyster stew, home-prepared:[81]																	
1451		1 part oysters to 2 parts milk by volume (approx. 6 medium oysters per cup).[279]	1 cup	240	82.0	233	12.5	15.4	10.8	274	266	4.6	814	319	820	.14	.43	2.2	—
1452		1 part oysters to 3 parts milk by volume (approx. 4 medium oysters per cup).[279]	1 cup	240	83.7	206	11.8	12.7	11.3	281	262	3.4	487	331	670	.14	.43	1.7	—
		Pancakes, baked from home recipe,[80] made with—																	
1453		Enriched flour:																	
	a	Cake, 6-in. diam., ½ in. thick (yield from approx. 7 tbsp. of batter).	1 cake	73	50.1	169	5.2	5.1	24.9	74	101	.9	310	90	90	.12	.16	.9	Trace
	b	Cake, 4-in. diam., ⅜ in. thick (yield from approx. 2–2½ tbsp. of batter).	1 cake	27	50.1	62	1.9	1.9	9.2	27	38	.4	115	33	30	.05	.06	.4	Trace
	c	Pound	1 lb	454	50,1	1,048	32.2	31.8	154.7	458	631	5.9	1,928	558	540	.77	1.00	5.9	2
1454		Unenriched flour:																	
	a	Cake, 6-in. diam., ½ in. thick (yield from approx. 7 tbsp. of batter).	1 cake	73	50.1	169	5.2	5.1	24.9	74	101	.4	310	90	90	.04	.10	.3	Trace
	b	Cake, 4-in. diam., ⅜ in. thick (yield from approx. 2–2½ tbsp. of batter).	1 cake	27	50.1	62	1.9	1.9	9.2	27	38	.2	115	33	30	.01	.04	.1	Trace
	c	Pound	1 lb	454	50.1	1,048	32.2	31.8	154.7	458	631	2.7	1,928	558	540	.23	.64	1.8	2
		Pancake and waffle mixes and pancakes baked from mixes:[68]																	
		Plain and buttermilk:																	
1455		Mix (pancake and waffle), with enriched flour, dry form; poured or spooned into cup:																	
	a	Not packed	1 cup	135	8.3	481	11.6	2.4	102.2	608	797	4.2	1,935	219	0	.59	.46	3.9	0
	b	Packed	1 cup	147	8.3	523	12.6	2.6	111.3	662	867	4.6	2,107	238	0	.65	.50	4.3	0
1457		Pancakes, made with egg, milk:																	
	a	Cake, 6-in. diam., ½ in. thick (yield from approx. 7 tbsp. of batter).	1 cake	73	50.6	164	5.3	5.3	23.7	157	190	.9	412	112	180	.11	.18	.6	Trace
	b	Cake, 4-in. diam., ⅜ in. thick (yield from approx. 2–2⅓ tbsp. of batter).	1 cake	27	50.6	61	1.9	2.0	8.7	58	70	.3	152	42	70	.04	.06	.2	Trace
	c	Pound	1 lb	454	50.6	1,021	32.7	33.1	147.0	975	1,179	5.4	2,558	699	1,130	.68	1.09	3.6	2
1458		Mix (pancake and waffle), with unenriched flour, poured or spooned into cup:																	
	a	Not packed	1 cup	135	8.3	481	11.6	2.4	102.2	608	797	1.9	1,935	219	0	.16	.11	1.5	0

(A)		(B)			(C)	(D)	(E)	(F)	(G)	(H)	(I)	(J)	(K)	(L)	(M)	(N)	(O)	(P)	(Q)
	b	Packed	1 cup	147	8.3	523	12.6	2.6	111.3	662	867	2.1	2,107	238	0	0.18	0.12	1.6	0
1460		Pancakes, made with egg, milk:																	
	a	Cake, 6-in. diam., ½ in. thick (yield from approx. 7 tbsp. of batter).	1 cake	73	50.6	164	5.3	5.3	23.7	157	190	.5	412	112	180	.04	.12	.3	Trace
	b	Cake, 4-in. diam., ⅜ in. thick (yield from approx. 2–2½ tbsp. of batter).	1 cake	27	50.6	61	1.9	2.0	8.7	58	70	.2	152	42	70	.02	.05	.1	Trace
	c	Pound	1 lb	454	50.6	1,021	32.7	33.1	147.0	975	1,179	3.2	2,558	669	1,130	.27	.77	1.8	2
		Buckwheat and other cereal flours:																	
1461		Mix, dry form; poured or spooned into cup:																	
	a	Not packed	1 cup	130	11.2	426	13.7	2.5	91.4	606	1,074	4.0	1,734	619	Trace	.47	.16	2.9	0
	b	Packed	1 cup	135	11.2	443	14.2	2.6	94.9	629	1,115	4.2	1,801	643	Trace	.49	.16	3.0	0
1462		Pancakes, made with egg, milk:																	
	a	Cake, 6-in. diam., ½ in. thick (yield from approx. 7 tbsp. of batter).	1 cake	73	57.9	146	5.0	6.6	17.4	161	246	.9	339	179	170	.09	.12	.5	Trace
	b	Cake, 4-in. diam., ⅜ in. thick (yield from approx. 2–2½ tbsp. of batter).	1 cake	27	57.9	54	1.8	2.5	6.4	59	91	.4	125	66	60	.03	.04	.2	Trace
	c	Pound	1 lb	454	57.9	907	30.8	41.3	108.0	998	1,529	5.9	1,111	2,105	1,040	.54	.73	3.2	2
1470		**Papaws,** common, North American type, raw:																	
	a	Whole, 2-in. diam., 3¾ in. long (refuse: rind and seeds, 25%).[1]	1 papaw	130	76.6	83	5.1	.9	16.4	—	—	—	—	—	—	—	—	—	—
	b	Mashed	1 cup	250	76.6	213	13.0	2.3	42.0	—	—	—	—	—	—	—	—	—	—
1471		**Papayas,** raw:																	
	a	Whole, medium fruit, 3½-in. diam., 5⅛ in. high; wt., approx. 1 lb. (refuse: skin and seeds, 33%).[1]	1 papaya or 1 lb.	454	88.7	119	1.8	.3	30.4	61	49	.9	9	711	5,320	.12	.12	.9	170
	b	Cubed (½-in. pieces)	1 cup	140	88.7	55	.8	.1	14.0	28	22	.4	4	328	2,450	.06	.06	.4	78
	c	Mashed	1 cup	230	88.7	90	1.4	.2	23.0	46	37	.7	7	538	4,030	.09	.09	.7	129
	d	Pound	1 lb	454	88.7	177	2.7	.5	45.4	91	73	1.4	14	1,061	7,940	.18	.18	1.4	254
1472		**Parsley,** common garden (plain) and curled-leaf varieties, raw:																	
		Chopped:																	
	a	Cup	1 cup	60	85.1	26	2.2	.4	5.1	122	38	3.7	27	436	5,100	.07	.16	.7	103
	b	Tablespoon	1 tbsp	3.5	85.1	2	.1	Trace	.3	7	2	.2	2	25	300	Trace	.01	Trace	6
	c	Pound	1 lb	454	85.1	200	16.3	2.7	38.6	921	286	28.1	204	3,298	38,560	.54	1.18	5.4	780
	d	Sprig, approx. 2½ in. long	10 sprigs	10	85.1	4	.4	.1	.9	20	6	.6	5	73	850	.01	.03	.1	17
		Parsnips:[65]																	
1473		Raw, prepackaged without tops (refuse: parings, 15%);[1] package, net wt., 16 oz. (1 lb.).	1 pkg. or 1 lb	454	79.1	293	6.6	1.9	67.5	193	297	2.7	46	2,086	120	.31	.35	.8	[280] 62
1474		Cooked (boiled), drained:																	
		Whole:																	
	a	Large parsnip, 9 in. long, 2¼-in. diam	1 parsnip	160	82.2	106	2.4	.8	23.8	72	99	1.0	[80] 13	606	50	.11	.13	.2	16
	b	Small parsnip, 6 in. long, 1⅛-in. diam	1 parsnip	35	82.2	23	.5	.2	5.2	16	22	.2	[80] 3	133	10	.02	.03	Trace	4
	c	Diced or 2-in. lengths	1 cup	155	82.2	102	2.3	.8	23.1	70	96	.9	[80] 12	587	50	.11	.12	.2	16
	d	Mashed	1 cup	210	82.2	139	3.2	1.1	31.3	95	130	1.3	[80] 17	796	60	.15	.17	.2	21
	e	Pound (approx. 3 cups, diced or 2-in. lengths; 2⅛ cups, mashed).	1 lb	454	82.2	299	6.8	2.3	67.6	204	281	2.7	[80] 36	1,719	140	.32	.36	.5	45
		Passion fruit. See Granadilla (item 1052).																	
1475		**Pastina,** egg, enriched, dry form	1 cup	170	10.4	651	21.9	7.0	122.1	60	330	[157] 4.9	9	—	370	[157] 1.50	[157] .65	[157] 10.2	(0)
		Pastry shell, plain. See Piecrust (items 1597–1600).																	
1478		**Pâté de foie gras,** canned:																	
	a	Tablespoon	1 tbsp	13	37.0	60	1.5	5.7	.6	—	—	—	—	—	—	.01	.04	.3	—
	b	Teaspoon	1 tsp	4	37.0	18	.5	1.8	.2	—	—	—	—	—	—	Trace	.01	.1	—
		Peaches:																	
1479		Raw:																	
		Whole:																	
		Peeled (refuse: thin skin and pits, 13%):[1]																	
	a	Fruit, 2¾-in. diam. (approx. 2½ per pound)	1 peach	175	89.1	58	.9	.2	14.8	14	29	.8	2	308	[281] 2,030	.03	.08	1.5	11
	b	Fruit, 2½-in. diam. (approx. 4 per pound)	1 peach	115	89.1	38	.6	.1	9.7	9	19	.5	1	202	[281] 1,330	.02	.05	1.0	7
	c	Pound	1 lb	454	89.1	150	2.4	.4	38.3	36	75	2.0	4	797	[281] 5,250	.08	.20	3.9	28
		Pared (refuse: parings with some adherent flesh and pits, 24%):[1]																	
	d	Fruit, 2¾-in. diam. (approx. 2½ per pound)	1 peach	175	89.1	51	.8	.1	12.9	12	25	.7	1	269	[281] 1,770	.03	.07	1.3	.9
	e	Fruit, 2½-in. diam. (approx. 4 per pound)	1 peach	115	89.1	33	.5	.1	8.5	8	17	.4	1	177	[281] 1,160	.02	.04	.9	6

[1] Measure and weight apply to food as it is described with inedible part or parts (refuse) included.

[80] Value is for unsalted product. If salt is used, increase value by 236 mg. per 100 g. of vegetable—an estimated figure based on typical amount of salt (0.6%) in canned vegetables. See also Appendix C, section on Cooked Vegetables

[43] Value for product without added salt.

[51] For information on ingredients used in preparation, see ARS 62-13 (7), table 22, p. 26.

[65] Oxalic acid present may combine with calcium and magnesium to form insoluble compounds. For further information, see Appendix D, section on Minerals and Oxalic Acid

[60] For information on ingredients used, see ARS 62-13 (7), table 4, p. 10.

[68] For proportion of mix and added ingredients used, see ARS 62-13 (7), table 5, p. 12.

[72] Dipped in egg, milk or water, and breadcrumbs.

[157] Based on product with minimum level of enrichment. See also Appendix C, section on Enriched Foods and Standards of Enrichment

[278] Oysters of other sizes are available in 12-fl. oz. can.

[279] Contains added salt and butter or margarine.

[280] Year-round average. Value for parsnips in fall within 3 months of harvest is about 93 mg. per pound and drops to less than half this value if storage exceeds 6 months.

[281] Based on value of 1,330 I.U. per 100 g. for yellow-fleshed varieties; for white-fleshed varieties, value is about 50 I.U. per 100 g.

TABLE 1.—*Nutritive values for household measures and market units of foods*—Continued

[Item numbers correspond to those in table 1 of Handbook No. 8, revised 1963. Values in parentheses denote imputed values usually from another form of the food or from a similar food. Zeros in parentheses indicate that amount of a constituent, if present, is probably too small to be measured. Dashes (—) denote lack of reliable data for a constituent believed to be present in a measurable amount. Calculated values, as those based on a recipe, are not in parentheses]

Item No. (A)	Food, approximate measures, units, and weight (edible part unless footnotes indicate otherwise) (B)			Water (C)	Food energy (D)	Protein (E)	Fat (F)	Carbohydrate (G)	Calcium (H)	Phosphorus (I)	Iron (J)	Sodium (K)	Potassium (L)	Vitamin A value (M)	Thiamin (N)	Riboflavin (O)	Niacin (P)	Ascorbic acid (Q)
									Values for edible part of foods									
			Grams	*Percent*	*Calories*	*Grams*	*Grams*	*Grams*	*Milligrams*	*Milligrams*	*Milligrams*	*Milligrams*	*Milligrams*	*International units*	*Milligrams*	*Milligrams*	*Milligrams*	*Milligrams*
	Peaches—Continued																	
	Raw—Continued																	
	Whole—Continued																	
	Pared (refuse: parings with some adherent flesh and pits, 24%)[1]—Continued																	
f	Pound	1 lb	454	89.1	131	2.1	0.3	33.4	31	65	1.7	3	696	[281] 4,580	0.07	0.17	3.4	24
g	Sliced	1 cup	170	89.1	65	1.0	.2	16.5	15	32	.9	2	343	[281] 2,260	.03	.09	1.7	12
h	Diced	1 cup	185	89.1	70	1.1	.2	17.9	17	35	.9	2	374	[281] 2,460	.04	.09	1.9	13
i	Pound	1 lb	454	89.1	172	2.7	.5	44.0	41	86	2.3	5	916	[281] 6,030	.09	.23	4.5	32
	Canned, solids and liquid:																	
1480	Water pack, without artificial sweetener, clingstone peaches:																	
	Can, approx. contents and peach half served with liquid (halved style):																	
a	Size, 211 × 304[14] (8Z Tall, Buffet); net wt., 8 oz.; halved style.	1 can	227	91.1	70	.9	.2	18.4	9	30	.7	5	311	1,020	.02	.07	1.4	7
b	Size, 603 × 700[14] (No. 10); net wt., 103 oz. (6 lb. 7 oz.); halved and sliced styles (30–35 or 35–40 halves and approx. 4 cups of drained liquid; approx. 8½ cups of drained slices and 4 cups of drained liquid).	1 can	2,920	91.1	905	11.7	2.9	236.5	117	380	8.8	58	4,000	13,140	.29	.88	17.5	88
	Peach half with drained liquid:																	
c	Count, 30–35	1 half; 2 tbsp. liquid.	91	91.1	28	.4	.1	7.4	4	12	.3	2	125	410	.01	.03	.5	3
d	Count, 35–40	1 half; 1⅔ tbsp. liquid.	77	91.1	24	.3	.1	6.2	3	10	.2	2	105	350	.01	.02	.5	2
e	Cup, halved or sliced styles	1 cup	244	91.1	76	1.0	.2	19.8	10	32	.7	5	334	1,100	.02	.07	1.5	7
f	Pound	1 lb	454	91.1	141	1.8	.5	36.7	18	59	1.4	9	621	2,040	.05	.14	2.7	14
1483	Sirup pack, heavy:																	
	Can, approx. contents and peach half served with liquid (halved style):																	
a	Size, 211 × 304[14] (8Z Tall, Buffet); net wt., 8¾ oz.; sliced style of clingstone and freestone peaches (approx. ¾ cup of drained slices and 5½ tbsp. drained liquid).	1 can	248	79.1	193	1.0	.2	49.8	10	30	.7	5	322	1,070	.02	.05	1.5	7
b	Size, 303 × 406[14] (No. 303); net wt., 16 oz. (1 lb.); halved and sliced styles of clingstone and freestone peaches (5–8 halves, 2⅜-in. diam.,[282] 2–2¼ in. long,[283] and approx. 10 tbsp. of drained liquid; approx. 1¼ cups of drained slices and 10 tbsp. of drained liquid).	1 can or 1 lb	454	79.1	354	1.8	.5	91.2	18	54	1.4	9	590	1,950	.05	.09	2.7	14
c	Peach half with drained liquid	1 half; 1⅔ tbsp. liquid.	76	79.1	59	.3	.1	15.3	3	9	.2	2	99	330	.01	.02	.5	2
d	Size, 401 × 411[14] (No. 2½); net wt., 29 oz. (1 lb. 13 oz.); halved and sliced styles of clingstone and freestone peaches, or chunk style of freestone peaches (7 halves, 2⅝-in. diam.,[282] 2⅜ in. long,[283] and approx. 1¼ cups of drained liquid; approx. 2¼ cups of drained slices or chunks and approx. 18 tbsp. of drained liquid).	1 can	822	79.1	641	3.3	.8	165.2	33	99	2.5	16	1,069	3,530	.08	.16	4.9	25
e	Peach half with drained liquid	1 half; 2⅔ tbsp. liquid.	117	79.1	91	.5	.1	23.5	5	14	.4	2	152	500	.01	.02	.7	4
f	Size, 603 × 700[14] (No. 10); net wt., 108 oz. (6 lb. 12 oz.); halves and sliced styles of clingstone peaches (25–30, 30–35, 35–40 peach halves and approx. 4¼ cups of drained liquid; approx. 8½ cups of drained slices and 4¼ cups of drained liquid).	1 can	3,062	79.1	2,388	12.2	3.1	615.5	122	367	9.2	61	3,981	13,170	.31	.61	18.4	92

(A)	(B)			(C)	(D)	(E)	(F)	(G)	(H)	(I)	(J)	(K)	(L)	(M)	(N)	(O)	(P)	(Q)
	Peach half with drained liquid:																	
g	Count, 25–30	1 half; 2½ tbsp. liquid.	109	79.1	85	0.4	0.1	21.9	4	13	0.3	2	142	470	0.01	0.02	0.7	3
h	Count, 30–35	1 half; 2⅛ tbsp. liquid.	96	79.1	75	.4	.1	19.3	4	12	.3	2	125	410	.01	.02	.6	3
i	Count, 35–40	1 half; 1¾ tbsp. liquid.	81	79.1	63	.3	.1	16.3	3	10	.2	2	105	350	.01	.02	.5	2
j	Cup, halved, sliced, or chunk styles	1 cup	256	79.1	200	1.0	.3	51.5	10	31	.8	5	333	1,100	.03	.05	1.5	8
	Dehydrated, sulfured, nugget type, and pieces:																	
1485	Uncooked:																	
a	Cup	1 cup	100	3.0	340	4.8	(.9)	88.0	(62)	(151)	3.5	(21)	(1,229)	(5,000)	Trace	.10	7.8	14
b	Pound	1 lb	454	3.0	1,542	21.8	(4.1)	399.2	(281)	(685)	15.9	(95)	(5,575)	(22,680)	.01	.45	35.4	64
1486	Cooked, fruit and liquid, with added sugar:[9]																	
a	Cup	1 cup	290	66.6	351	3.2	(.6)	90.8	(44)	(104)	2.3	(15)	(847)	(2,580)	Trace	.06	4.9	6
b	Pound	1 lb	454	66.6	549	5.0	(.9)	142.0	(68)	(163)	3.6	(23)	(1,325)	(4,040)	Trace	.09	7.7	9
	Dried, sulfured (halves):																	
1487	Uncooked:																	
a	Container, net wt., 11–12 oz	1 container	326	25.0	854	10.1	2.3	222.7	156	381	19.6	52	3,097	12,710	.03	.62	17.3	59
b	Cup[10]	1 cup	160	25.0	419	5.0	1.1	109.3	77	187	9.6	26	1,520	6,240	.02	.30	8.5	29
c	Pound (approx. 31 large or 35 medium halves)	1 lb	454	25.0	1,188	14.1	3.2	309.8	218	531	27.2	73	4,309	17,690	.05	.86	24.0	82
	10 halves:																	
d	Large	10 halves	145	25.0	380	4.5	1.0	99.0	70	170	8.7	23	1,378	5,660	.01	.28	7.7	26
e	Medium	10 halves	130	25.0	341	4.0	.9	88.8	62	152	7.8	21	1,235	5,070	.01	.25	6.9	23
	Cooked, fruit and liquid:[9]																	
1488	Without added sugar:																	
a	Cup	1 cup	(250)	76.5	205	2.5	.5	53.5	38	93	4.8	13	743	3,050	.01	.15	3.8	5
b	Pound	1 lb	454	76.5	372	4.5	.9	97.1	68	168	8.6	23	1,347	5,530	.01	.27	6.8	9
1489	With added sugar:																	
a	Cup	1 cup	(270)	67.3	321	2.4	.5	83.2	35	86	4.3	11	705	2,890	.01	.14	3.8	5
b	Pound	1 lb	454	67.3	540	4.1	.9	139.7	59	145	7.3	18	1,184	4,850	.01	.23	6.4	9
1490	Frozen, sliced, sweetened with nutritive sweetener, not thawed:																	
a	Container, net wt., 10 oz	1 container	284	76.5	250	1.1	.3	64.2	11	37	1.4	6	352	1,850	.03	.11	2.0	[284] 114
b	Cup[48]	1 cup	250	76.5	220	1.0	.3	56.5	10	33	1.3	5	310	1,630	.03	.10	1.8	[284] 100
c	Pound	1 lb	454	76.5	399	1.8	.5	102.5	18	59	2.3	9	562	2,950	.05	.18	3.2	[284] 181
1491	**Peach nectar**, canned (approx. 40% fruit):																	
	Can and approx. contents:																	
a	Size, 202 × 308[14] (6Z); net contents, 5½ fl. oz	1 can	171	87.2	82	.3	Trace	21.2	7	19	.3	2	133	740	.02	.03	.7	[15] Trace
b	Size, 211 × 414[14] (12Z, No. 211 Cylinder); net contents, 12 fl. oz.	1 can	373	87.2	179	.7	Trace	46.3	15	41	.7	4	291	1,600	.04	.07	1.5	[15] Trace
c	Cup	1 cup	249	87.2	120	.5	Trace	30.9	10	27	.5	2	194	1,070	.02	.05	1.0	[15] Trace
d	Glass (6 fl. oz.)	1 glass	187	87.2	90	.4	Trace	23.2	7	21	.4	2	146	800	.02	.04	.7	[15] Trace
e	Fluid ounce	1 fl. oz	31.1	87.2	15	.1	Trace	3.9	1	3	.1	Trace	24	130	Trace	.01	.1	[15] Trace
	Peanuts:[5, 55]																	
1495	Roasted in shell (with skins):																	
	Whole (refuse: shells, 33%):[1]																	
a	Pound (yields approx. 10.7 oz., shelled nuts)	1 lb	454	1.8	1,769	79.6	148.0	62.6	219	1,237	6.7	15	2,130	—	.97	.40	52.0	0
b	10 nuts (jumbo)	10 nuts	27	1.8	105	4.7	8.8	3.7	13	74	.4	1	127	—	.06	.02	3.1	0
	Shelled, chopped form:																	
c	Cup	1 cup	144	1.8	838	37.7	70.1	29.7	104	586	3.2	7	1,009	—	.46	.19	24.6	0
d	Tablespoon	1 tbsp	9	1.8	52	2.4	4.4	1.9	6	37	.2	Trace	63	—	.03	.01	1.5	0
1496	Roasted, salted (Spanish and Virginia types):																	
a	Cup, whole, halves, chopped form	1 cup	144	1.6	842	37.4	71.7	27.1	107	577	3.0	602	971	—	.46	.19	24.8	0
b	Whole nuts, approx. 20 Spanish type or 10 Virginia type; or 1 tbsp. of chopped form.	10 or 20 whole nuts or 1 tbsp., chopped.	9	1.6	53	2.3	4.5	1.7	7	36	.2	38	61	—	.03	.01	1.5	0
c	Pound	1 lb	454	1.6	2,654	117.9	225.9	85.3	336	1,819	9.5	1,896	3,057	—	1.45	.59	78.0	0
d	Ounce	1 oz	28	1.6	166	7.4	14.1	5.3	21	114	.6	119	191	—	.09	.04	4.9	0
1499	**Peanut butter** made with moderate amounts of added fat, nutritive sweetener, salt:[5]																	

[1] Measure and weight apply to food as it is described with inedible part or parts (refuse) included.

[5] Most of phosphorus in nuts, legumes, and outer layers of cereal grains is present as phytic acid. See also Appendix D, section on Minerals and Oxalic Acid

[9] For information on proportion of fruit, sugar, and water used, see ARS 62–13 (7), section on Fruits, Dried and Dehydrated, p. 7, and table 20, p. 24.

[10] Separated pieces when stuck together.

[14] Dimensions of can: 1st dimension represents diameter; 2d dimension, height of can. 1st or left-hand digit in each dimension gives number of whole inches; next 2 digits give additional fraction of dimension expressed as 16th of an inch.

[15] Applies to product without added ascorbic acid. For value of product with added ascorbic acid, refer to label.

[48] Measurement applies to thawed product. See also Appendix C, section on Frozen Fruits and Vegetables

[55] Oxalic acid present may combine with calcium and magnesium to form insoluble compounds. For further information, see Appendix D, section on Minerals and Oxalic Acid

[281] Based on value of 1,330 I.U. per 100 g. for yellow-fleshed varieties; for white-fleshed varieties, value is about 50 I.U. per 100 g.

[282] Greatest dimension taken at right angles to line running from stem to blossom end.

[283] Length as measured in straight line from stem to blossom end.

[284] Based on average value of 40 mg. per 100 g. weighted in accordance with commercial freezing practices. For products without added ascorbic acid, value is about 31 mg. for 10-oz. container, 28 mg. for 1 cup, 50 mg. for 1 lb.; for those with added ascorbic acid, value is 116 mg. for 10-oz. container, 103 mg. for 1 cup, 186 mg. for 1 lb. See also Appendix C, section on Frozen Fruits and Vegetables

TABLE 1.—*Nutritive values for household measures and market units of foods*—Continued

[Item numbers correspond to those in table 1 of Handbook No. 8, revised 1963. Values in parentheses denote imputed values usually from another form of the food or from a similar food. Zeros in parentheses indicate that amount of a constituent, if present, is probably too small to be measured. Dashes (—) denote lack of reliable data for a constituent believed to be present in a measurable amount. Calculated values, as those based on a recipe, are not in parentheses]

Item No. (A)	Food, approximate measures, units, and weight (edible part unless footnotes indicate otherwise) (B)			Water (C)	Food energy (D)	Protein (E)	Fat (F)	Carbohydrate (G)	Calcium (H)	Phosphorus (I)	Iron (J)	Sodium (K)	Potassium (L)	Vitamin A value (M)	Thiamin (N)	Riboflavin (O)	Niacin (P)	Ascorbic acid (Q)
			Grams	*Percent*	*Calories*	*Grams*	*Grams*	*Grams*	*Milligrams*	*Milligrams*	*Milligrams*	*Milligrams*	*Milligrams*	*International units*	*Milligrams*	*Milligrams*	*Milligrams*	*Milligrams*
	Peanut butter made with moderate amounts of added fat, nutritive sweetener, salt [5]—Continued																	
	Container and approx. contents:																	
a	Can, size 603 × 700 [14] No. 10); net wt., 110 oz. (6 lb. 14 oz.).	1 can	3,118	1.7	18,365	785.7	1,577.7	586.2	1,840	11,848	59.2	18,864	19,550	—	3.74	3.74	458.3	0
	Glass jar:																	
b	Size, 12 oz.; net wt., 12 oz	1 jar	340	1.7	2,003	85.7	172.0	63.9	201	1,292	6.5	2,057	2,132	—	.41	.41	50.0	0
c	Size, 18 oz.; net wt., 18 oz. (1 lb. 2 oz.)	1 jar	510	1.7	3,004	128.5	258.1	95.9	301	1,938	9.7	3,086	3,198	—	.61	.61	75.0	0
d	Size, 28 oz.; net wt., 28 oz. (1 lb. 12 oz.)	1 jar	794	1.7	4,677	200.1	401.8	149.3	468	3,017	15.1	4,804	4,978	—	.95	.95	116.7	0
e	Cup	1 cup	258	1.7	1,520	65.0	130.5	48.5	152	980	4.9	1,561	1,618	—	.31	.31	37.9	0
f	Tablespoon	1 tbsp	16	1.7	94	4.0	8.1	3.0	9	61	.3	97	100	—	.02	.02	2.4	0
g	Pound	1 lb	454	1.7	2,672	114.3	229.5	85.3	268	1,724	8.6	2,744	2,844	—	.54	.54	66.7	0
1501	**Peanut flour, defatted** [6]	1 cup	60	7.3	223	28.7	5.5	18.9	62	432	2.1	5	712	—	.45	.13	16.7	0
	Peanut oil. See Oils (items 1401e, 1401g, 1401i, 1401k).																	
	Pears:																	
1502	Raw, including skin:																	
	Whole (refuse: stem and core, 9%): [1]																	
a	Bartletts, 2½-in. diam., 3½ in. high (approx. 2½ per pound).	1 pear	180	83.2	100	1.1	.7	25.1	13	18	.5	3	213	30	.03	.07	.2	7
b	Boscs, 2½-in. diam., 3½ in. high (approx. 3 per pound).	1 pear	155	83.2	86	1.0	.6	21.6	11	16	.4	3	183	30	.03	.06	.1	6
c	D'Anjous, 3-in. diam., 3½ in. high (approx. 2 per pound).	1 pear	220	83.2	122	1.4	.8	30.6	16	22	.6	4	260	40	.04	.08	.2	8
d	Sliced or cubed	1 cup	165	83.2	101	1.2	.7	25.2	13	18	.5	3	215	30	.03	.07	.2	7
e	Pound	1 lb	454	83.2	277	3.2	1.8	69.4	36	50	1.4	9	590	90	.09	.18	.5	18
	Canned, solids and liquid:																	
1504	Water pack, without artificial sweetener:																	
	Can, approx. contents and pear half served with liquid:																	
a	Size, 211 × 304 [14] (8Z Tall, Buffet); net wt., 8 oz.; halved style (5 pears, 2-in. diam.,[282] 2⅛ in. long,[283] and approx. 5 tbsp. of drained liquid).	1 can	227	91.1	73	.5	.5	18.8	11	16	.5	2	200	10	.02	.05	.2	2
b	Pear half with drained liquid	1 half; 1 tbsp. liquid.	45	91.1	14	.1	.1	3.7	2	3	.1	Trace	40	Trace	Trace	.01	Trace	Trace
c	Size, 603 × 700 [14] (No. 10); net wt., 103 oz. (6 lb. 7 oz.); halved style (30–35 pear halves, 2¼-in. diam.,[282] 2½ in. long,[283] or 35–40 pear halves, 2⅛-in. diam.,[282] 2½ in. long,[283] and approx. 4 cups of drained liquid).	1 can	2,920	91.1	934	5.8	5.8	242.4	146	204	5.8	29	2,570	120	.29	.58	2.9	29
	Pear half with drained liquid:																	
d	Count 30–35	1 half; 2 tbsp. liquid.	91	91.1	29	.2	.2	7.6	5	6	.2	1	80	Trace	.01	.02	.1	1
e	Count 35–40	1 half; 1⅔ tbsp. liquid.	77	91.1	25	.2	.2	6.4	4	5	.2	1	68	Trace	.01	.02	.1	1
f	Cup	1 cup	244	91.1	78	.5	.5	20.3	12	17	.5	2	215	10	.02	.05	.2	2
g	Pound	1 lb	454	91.1	145	.9	.9	37.6	23	32	.9	5	399	20	.05	.09	.5	5
1507	Sirup pack, heavy:																	
	Can, approx. contents and pear half served with liquid (halved style):																	
a	Size, 211 × 304 [14] (8Z Tall, Buffet); net wt., 8½ oz.; halved and sliced styles (5 pear halves, 2-in. diam.,[282] 2⅛ in. long,[283] and approx. 5 tbsp. of drained liquid; approx. ⅝ cup of drained slices and 5 tbsp. of drained liquid).	1 can	241	79.8	183	.5	.5	47.2	12	17	.5	2	202	10	.02	.05	.2	2
b	Pear half with drained liquid	1 half; 1 tbsp. liquid.	48	79.8	36	.1	.1	9.4	2	3	.1	Trace	40	Trace	Trace	.01	Trace	Trace
c	Size, 303 × 406 [14] (No. 303); net wt., 16 oz. (1 lb.); halved and sliced styles (5–8	1 can or 1 lb	454	79.8	345	.9	.9	88.9	23	32	.9	5	381	20	.05	.09	.5	5

(A)		(B)		(C)	(D)	(E)	(F)	(G)	(H)	(I)	(J)	(K)	(L)	(M)	(N)	(O)	(P)	(Q)
		halves, 2⅛-in. diam.,[282] 2⅝ in. long,[283] approx. 10 tbsp. of drained liquid; approx. 1⅓ cups of drained slices and 10 tbsp. of drained liquid).																
	d	Pear half with drained liquid	1 half; 1⅝ tbsp. liquid.	76	79.8	58	0.2	0.2	14.9	4	5	0.2	1	64	Trace	0.01	0.02	0.1	1
	e	Size, 401 × 411[14] (No. 2½); net wt., 29 oz. (1 lb. 13 oz.); halved style (6–9 halves,[285] 2½-in. diam.,[282] 2⅞ in. long,[283] and approx. 18 tbsp. of drained liquid).	1 can	822	79.8	625	1.6	1.6	161.1	41	58	1.6	8	690	80	.08	.16	.8	8
	f	Pear half with drained liquid	1 half; 2¼ tbsp. liquid.	108	79.8	78	.2	.2	20.2	5	7	.2	1	87	Trace	.01	.02	.1	1
	g	Size, 603 × 700[14] (No. 10); net wt., 106 oz. (6 lb. 10 oz.); halved style[286] (25–30 pear halves, 2⅝-in. diam.,[282] 2⅝ in. long,[283] or 30–35 pear halves, 2¼-in. diam.,[282] 2½ in. long,[283] or 35–40 pear halves, 2⅛-in. diam.,[282] 2½ in. long,[283] and approx. 4⅛ cups of drained liquid).	1 can	3,005	79.8	2,284	6.0	6.0	589.0	150	210	6.0	30	2,524	120	.30	.60	3.0	30
		Pear half with drained liquid:																
	h	Count 25–30	1 half; 2⅓ tbsp. liquid.	107	79.8	81	.2	.2	21.0	5	7	.2	1	90	Trace	.01	.02	.1	1
	i	Count 30–35	1 half; 2 tbsp. liquid.	94	79.8	71	.2	.2	18.4	5	7	.2	1	79	Trace	.01	.02	.1	1
	j	Count 35–40	1 half; 1¾ tbsp. liquid.	79	79.8	60	.2	.2	15.5	4	6	.2	1	66	Trace	.01	.02	.1	1
	k	Cup	1 cup	255	79.8	194	.5	.5	50.0	13	18	.5	3	214	10	.03	.05	.3	3
		Dried, sulfured (halves):																
1509		Uncooked:																
	a	Cup[10]	1 cup	180	26.0	482	5.6	3.2	121.1	63	86	2.3	13	1,031	130	.02	.32	1.1	13
	b	Pound (approx. 26 halves)	1 lb	454	26.0	1,216	14.1	8.2	305.3	159	218	5.9	32	2,599	320	.05	.82	2.7	32
	c	10 halves	10 halves	175	26.0	469	5.4	3.2	117.8	61	84	2.3	12	1,003	120	.02	.32	1.1	12
		Cooked, fruit and liquid:[9]																
1510		Without added sugar:																
	a	Cup	1 cup	255	65.2	321	3.8	2.0	80.8	41	59	1.5	8	686	80	.01	.20	.8	5
	b	Pound	1 lb	454	65.2	572	6.8	3.6	143.8	73	104	2.7	14	1,220	140	.02	.36	1.4	9
1511		With added sugar:																
	a	Cup	1 cup	280	59.1	423	3.6	2.2	106.4	42	56	1.7	8	683	80	.01	.20	.6	6
	b	Pound	1 lb	454	59.1	685	5.9	3.6	172.4	68	91	2.7	14	1,107	140	.01	.32	.9	9
1512		Pear nectar, canned (approx. 40% fruit):																
		Can and approx. contents:																
	a	Size, 202 × 308[14] (6Z); net contents, 5½ fl. oz	1 can	172	86.2	89	.5	.3	22.7	5	9	.2	2	67	Trace	Trace	.03	Trace	[15] Trace
	b	Size, 211 × 414[14] (12Z, No. 211 Cylinder); net contents, 12 fl. oz.	1 can	375	86.2	195	1.1	.8	49.5	11	19	.4	4	146	Trace	Trace	.08	Trace	[15] Trace
	c	Cup	1 cup	250	86.2	130	.8	.5	33.0	8	13	.3	3	98	Trace	Trace	.05	Trace	[15] Trace
	d	Glass (6 fl. oz.)	1 glass	187	86.2	97	.6	.4	24.7	6	9	.2	2	73	Trace	Trace	.04	Trace	[15] Trace
	e	Fluid ounce	1 fl. oz	31.2	86.2	16	.1	.1	4.1	1	2	Trace	Trace	12	Trace	Trace	.01	Trace	[15] Trace
		Peas, green, immature:[5]																
1515		Raw:																
	a	Cup	1 cup	145	78.0	122	9.1	.6	20.9	38	168	2.8	3	458	930	.51	.20	4.2	39
	b	Pound (yields approx. 2⅔ cups, cooked peas)	1 lb	454	78.0	381	28.6	1.8	65.3	118	526	8.6	9	1,433	2,900	1.59	.64	13.2	122
1516		Cooked (boiled), drained:																
	a	Cup	1 cup	160	81.5	114	8.6	.6	19.4	37	158	2.9	[20] 2	314	860	.45	.18	3.7	32
	b	Pound (yield from approx. 2¾ lb., peas in pod, or from 1 1/16 lb., shelled peas).	1 lb	454	81.5	322	24.5	1.8	54.9	104	449	8.2	[20] 5	889	2,450	1.27	.50	10.4	91
		Canned:																
		Alaska (Early or June peas):																
		Regular pack:																
1517		Solids and liquid:																
		Container and approx. contents:																
	a	Can, size 211 × 304[14] (8Z Tall, Buffet); net wt., 8½ oz.	1 can	241	82.6	159	8.4	.7	30.1	48	159	4.1	[21] 569	231	1,080	.22	.12	2.2	22

[1] Measure and weight apply to food as it is described with inedible part or parts (refuse) included.

[5] Most of phosphorus in nuts, legumes, and outer layers of cereal grains is present as phytic acid. See also Appendix D, section on Minerals and Oxalic Acid

[9] For information on proportion of fruit, sugar, and water used, see ARS 62–13 (7), section on Fruits, Dried and Dehydrated, p. 7, and table 20, p. 24.

[10] Separated pieces when stuck together.

[14] Dimensions of can: 1st dimension represents diameter; 2d dimension, height of can. 1st or left-hand digit in each dimension gives number of whole inches; next 2 digits give additional fraction of dimension expressed as 16th of an inch.

[15] Applies to product without added ascorbic acid. For value of product with added ascorbic acid, refer to label.

[20] Value is for unsalted product. If salt is used, increase value by 236 mg. per 100 g. of vegetable—an estimated figure based on typical amount of salt (0.6%) in canned vegetables. See also Appendix C, section on Cooked Vegetables

[21] Estimated value based on addition of salt in amount of 0.6% of finished product.

[282] Greatest dimension taken at right angles to line running from stem to blossom end.

[283] Length as measured in straight line from stem to blossom end.

[285] Counts of 9–10 and 11–12 may also be available.

[286] Counts of 20–25, 40–45, 45–50, 50–60, and 60–70 may also be available.

TABLE 1.—*Nutritive values for household measures and market units of foods*—Continued

[Item numbers correspond to those in table 1 of Handbook No. 8, revised 1963. Values in parentheses denote imputed values usually from another form of the food or from a similar food. Zeros in parentheses indicate that amount of a constituent, if present, is probably too small to be measured. Dashes (—) denote lack of reliable data for a constituent believed to be present in a measurable amount. Calculated values, as those based on a recipe, are not in parentheses]

Item No.	Food, approximate measures, units, and weight (edible part unless footnotes indicate otherwise)			Water	Food energy	Protein	Fat	Carbohydrate	Calcium	Phosphorus	Iron	Sodium	Potassium	Vitamin A value	Thiamin	Riboflavin	Niacin	Ascorbic acid
(A)	(B)			(C)	(D)	(E)	(F)	(G)	(H)	(I)	(J)	(K)	(L)	(M)	(N)	(O)	(P)	(Q)
			Grams	Percent	Calories	Grams	Grams	Grams	Milligrams	Milligrams	Milligrams	Milligrams	Milligrams	International units	Milligrams	Milligrams	Milligrams	Milligrams
	Peas, green, immature [5]—Continued																	
	Canned—Continued																	
	Alaska (Early or June peas)—Continued																	
	Regular pack—Continued																	
	Solids and liquid—Continued																	
	Container and approx. contents—Continued																	
b	Can, size 303 × 406 [14] (No. 303), or glass jar, size 16 oz.; net wt., 17 oz. (1 lb. 1 oz.).	1 can or jar	482	82.6	318	16.9	1.4	60.3	96	318	8.2	[21] 1,138	463	2,170	0.43	0.24	4.3	43
c	Can, size 603 × 700 [14] (No. 10); net wt., 105 oz. (6 lb. 9 oz.) to 106 oz. (6 lb. 10 oz.).	1 can	2,991	82.6	1,974	104.7	9.0	373.9	598	1,974	50.8	[21] 7,059	2,871	13,460	2.69	1.50	26.9	269
d	Cup	1 cup	249	82.6	164	8.7	.7	31.1	50	164	4.2	[21] 588	239	1,120	.22	.12	2.2	22
e	Pound	1 lb	454	82.6	299	15.9	1.4	56.7	91	299	7.7	[21] 1,070	435	2,040	.41	.23	4.1	41
1518	Drained solids:																	
	Container and approx. drained contents:																	
a	Can, size 211 × 304 [14] (8Z Tall, Buffet); wt., 5½ oz.	1 can	157	77.0	138	7.4	.6	26.4	41	119	3.0	[21] 371	151	1,080	.14	.09	1.3	13
b	Can, size 303 × 406 [14] (No. 303), or glass jar, size 16 oz.; wt., 11 oz.	1 can or jar	313	77.0	275	14.7	1.3	52.6	81	238	5.9	[21] 739	300	2,160	.28	.19	2.5	25
c	Can, size 603 × 700 [14] (No. 10); wt., 70 oz. (4 lb. 6 oz.).	1 can	1,984	77.0	1,746	93.2	7.9	333.3	516	1,508	37.7	[21] 4,682	1,905	13,690	1.79	1.19	15.9	159
d	Cup	1 cup	170	77.0	150	8.0	.7	28.6	44	129	3.2	[21] 401	163	1,170	.15	.10	1.4	14
e	Pound	1 lb	454	77.0	399	21.3	1.8	76.2	118	345	8.6	[21] 1,070	435	3,130	.41	.27	3.6	36
1519	Drained liquid:																	
a	Pound	1 lb	454	92.3	118	5.9	Trace	23.6	45	218	5.9	[21] 1,070	435	Trace	.45	.18	4.5	45
b	Ounce	1 oz	28	92.3	7	.4	Trace	1.5	3	14	.4	[21] 67	27	Trace	.03	.01	.3	3
	Special dietary pack (low sodium):																	
1520	Solids and liquid:																	
	Container and approx. contents:																	
a	Can, size 211 × 304 [14] (8Z Tall, Buffet); net wt., 8½ oz.	1 can	241	85.9	133	8.7	.7	23.6	48	159	4.1	7	231	1,080	.22	.12	2.2	22
b	Can, size 303 × 406 [14] (No. 303), or glass jar, size 16 oz.; net wt., 17 oz. (1 lb. 1 oz.).	1 can or jar	482	85.9	265	17.4	1.4	47.2	96	318	8.2	14	463	2,170	.43	.24	4.3	43
c	Can, size 603 × 700 [14] (No. 10); net wt., 105 oz. (6 lb. 9 oz.) to 106 oz. (6 lb. 10 oz.).	1 can	2,991	85.9	1,645	107.7	9.0	293.1	598	1,974	50.8	90	2,871	13,460	2.69	1.50	26.9	269
d	Cup	1 cup	249	85.9	137	9.0	.7	24.4	50	164	4.2	7	239	1,120	.22	.12	2.2	22
e	Pound	1 lb	454	85.9	249	16.3	1.4	44.5	91	299	7.7	14	435	2,040	.41	.23	4.1	41
1521	Drained solids:																	
	Container and approx. drained contents:																	
a	Can, size 211 × 304 [14] (8Z Tall, Buffet); wt., 5½ oz.	1 can	157	80.1	122	7.5	.6	22.5	41	119	3.0	5	151	1,080	.14	.09	1.3	13
b	Can, size 303 × 406 [14] (No. 303), or glass jar, size 16 oz.; wt., 11 oz.	1 can or jar	313	80.1	244	15.0	1.3	44.8	81	238	5.9	9	300	2,160	.28	.19	2.5	25
c	Can, size 603 × 700 [14] (No. 10); wt., 70 oz. (4 lb. 6 oz.).	1 can	1,984	80.1	1,548	95.2	7.9	283.7	516	1,508	37.7	60	1,905	13,690	1.79	1.19	15.9	159
d	Cup	1 cup	170	80.1	133	8.2	.7	24.3	44	129	3.2	5	163	1,170	.15	.10	1.4	14
e	Pound	1 lb	454	80.1	354	21.8	1.8	64.9	118	345	8.6	14	435	3,130	.41	.27	3.6	36
1522	Drained liquid:																	
a	Pound	1 lb	454	94.1	100	6.4	Trace	18.6	45	218	5.9	14	435	Trace	.45	.18	4.5	45
b	Ounce	1 oz	28	94.1	6	.4	Trace	1.2	3	14	.4	1	27	Trace	.03	.01	.3	3
	Sweet (sweet wrinkled peas, sugar peas):																	
	Regular pack:																	
1523	Solids and liquid:																	
	Container and approx. contents:																	
a	Can, size 211 × 304 [14] (8Z Tall, Buffet); net wt., 8½ oz.	1 can	241	84.8	137	8.2	.7	25.1	46	140	3.6	[21] 569	231	1,080	.27	.14	2.4	22
b	Can, size 303 × 406 [14] (No. 303), or glass jar, size 16 oz.; net wt., 17 oz. (1 lb. 1 oz).	1 can or jar	482	84.8	275	16.4	1.4	50.1	92	280	7.2	[21] 1,138	463	2,170	.53	.29	4.8	43

(A)	(B)			(C)	(D)	(E)	(F)	(G)	(H)	(I)	(J)	(K)	(L)	(M)	(N)	(O)	(P)	(Q)
c	Can, size 603 × 700[14] (No. 10); net wt., 105 oz. (6 lb. 9 oz.) to 106 oz. (6 lb. 10 oz.).	1 can	2,991	84.8	1,705	101.7	9.0	311.1	568	1,735	44.9	[21] 7,059	2,871	13,460	3.29	1.79	29.9	269
d	Cup	1 cup	249	84.8	142	8.5	.7	25.9	47	144	3.7	[21] 588	239	1,120	.27	.15	2.5	22
e	Pound	1 lb	454	84.8	259	15.4	1.4	47.2	86	263	6.8	[21] 1,070	435	2,040	.50	.27	4.5	41
1524	Drained solids:																	
	Container and approx. drained contents:																	
a	Can, size 211 × 304[14] (8Z Tall, Buffet); wt., 5½ oz.	1 can	157	79.0	126	7.2	.6	23.6	39	105	2.7	[21] 371	151	1,080	.17	.09	1.6	13
b	Can, size 303 × 406[14] (No. 303), or glass jar, size 16 oz.; wt., 11 oz.	1 can or jar	313	79.0	250	14.4	1.3	47.0	78	210	5.3	[21] 739	300	2,160	.34	.19	3.1	25
c	Can, size 603 × 700[14] (No. 10); wt., 70 oz. (4 lb. 6 oz.).	1 can	1,984	79.0	1,587	91.3	7.9	297.6	496	1,329	33.7	[21] 4,682	1,905	13,690	2.18	1.19	19.8	159
d	Cup	1 cup	170	79.0	136	7.8	.7	25.5	43	114	2.9	[21] 401	163	1,170	.19	.10	1.7	14
e	Pound	1 lb	454	79.0	363	20.9	1.8	68.0	113	304	7.7	[21] 1,070	435	3,130	.50	.27	4.5	36
1525	Drained liquid:																	
a	Pound	1 lb	454	93.3	100	5.9	Trace	19.5	41	191	5.0	[21] 1,070	435	Trace	.54	.23	5.0	45
b	Ounce	1 oz	28	93.3	6	.4	Trace	1.2	3	12	.3	[21] 67	27	Trace	.03	.01	.3	3
	Special dietary pack (low sodium):																	
1526	Solids and liquid:																	
	Container and approx. contents:																	
a	Can, size 211 × 304[14] (8Z Tall, Buffet); net wt., 8½ oz.	1 can	241	87.8	113	8.0	.7	19.8	46	140	3.6	7	231	1,080	.27	.14	2.4	22
b	Can, size 303 × 406[14] (No. 303), or glass jar, size 16 oz.; net wt., 17 oz. (1 lb. 1 oz).	1 can or jar	482	87.8	227	15.9	1.4	39.5	92	280	7.2	14	463	2,170	.53	.29	4.8	43
c	Can, size 603 × 700[14] (No. 10); net wt., 105 oz. (6 lb. 9 oz.) to 106 oz. (6 lb. 10 oz.).	1 can	2,991	87.8	1,406	98.7	9.0	245.3	568	1,735	44.9	90	2,871	13,460	3.29	1.79	29.9	269
d	Cup	1 cup	249	87.8	117	8.2	.7	20.4	47	144	3.7	7	239	1,120	.27	.15	2.5	22
e	Pound	1 lb	454	87.8	213	15.0	1.4	37.2	86	263	6.8	14	435	2,040	.50	.27	4.5	41
1527	Drained solids:																	
	Container and approx. drained contents:																	
a	Can, size 211 × 304[14] (8Z Tall, Buffet); wt., 5½ oz.	1 can	157	81.8	113	6.9	.6	20.4	39	105	2.7	5	151	1,080	.17	.09	1.6	13
b	Can, size 303 × 406[14] (No. 303), or glass jar, size 16 oz.; wt., 11 oz.	1 can or jar	313	81.8	225	13.8	1.3	40.7	78	210	5.3	9	300	2,160	.34	.19	3.1	25
c	Can, size 603 × 700[14] (No. 10); wt., 70 oz. (4 lb. 6 oz.).	1 can	1,984	81.8	1,428	87.3	7.9	257.9	496	1,329	33.7	60	1,905	13,690	2.18	1.19	19.8	159
d	Cup	1 cup	170	81.8	122	7.5	.7	22.1	43	114	2.9	5	163	1,170	.19	.10	1.7	14
e	Pound	1 lb	454	81.8	327	20.0	1.8	59.0	113	304	7.7	14	435	3,130	.50	.27	4.5	36
1528	Drained liquid:																	
a	Pound	1 lb	454	94.9	82	5.9	Trace	15.4	41	191	5.0	14	435	Trace	.54	.23	5.0	45
b	Ounce	1 oz	28	94.9	5	.4	Trace	1.0	3	12	.3	1	27	Trace	.03	.01	.3	3
	Frozen:																	
1529	Not thawed:																	
a	Container, net wt., 10 oz	1 container	284	80.7	207	15.3	.9	36.4	57	256	5.7	[45] 366	426	1,930	.91	.28	5.7	54
b	Cup	1 cup	145	80.7	106	7.8	.4	18.6	29	131	2.9	[45] 187	218	990	.46	.15	2.9	28
c	Pound	1 lb	454	80.7	331	24.5	1.4	58.1	91	408	9.1	[45] 585	680	3,080	1.45	.45	9.1	86
1530	Cooked (boiled), drained:																	
a	Yield from 1 lb., frozen peas	2½ cups	404	82.1	275	20.6	1.2	47.7	77	347	7.7	[45] 465	545	2,420	1.09	.36	6.9	53
b	Yield from 10 oz., frozen peas	1⅗ cups	253	82.1	172	12.9	.8	29.9	48	218	4.8	[45] 291	342	1,520	.68	.23	4.3	33
c	Cup	1 cup	160	82.1	109	8.2	.5	18.9	30	138	3.0	[45] 184	216	960	.43	.14	2.7	21
d	Pound (yield from approx. 1 lb. 2 oz., frozen peas).	1 lb	454	82.1	308	23.1	1.4	53.5	86	390	8.6	[45] 522	612	2,720	1.22	.41	7.7	59
	Peas, mature seeds, dry:																	
	Whole:																	
1531	Raw:																	
a	Cup	1 cup	(200)	11.7	680	48.2	2.6	120.6	128	680	10.2	70	2,010	240	1.48	.58	6.0	—
b	Pound	1 lb	454	11.7	1,542	109.3	5.9	273.5	290	1,542	23.1	159	4,559	540	3.36	1.32	13.6	—
	Split without seedcoat:																	
1532	Raw:																	
a	Cup	1 cup	200	9.3	696	48.4	2.0	125.4	66	536	10.2	80	1,790	240	1.48	.58	6.0	—
b	Pound	1 lb	454	9.3	1,579	109.8	4.5	284.4	150	1,216	23.1	181	4,060	540	3.36	1.32	13.6	—
1533	Cooked:[43]																	

[5] Most of phosphorus in nuts, legumes, and outer layers of cereal grains is present as phytic acid. See also Appendix D, section on Minerals and Oxalic Acid

[14] Dimensions of can: 1st dimension represents diameter; 2d dimension, height of can. 1st or left-hand digit in each dimension gives number of whole inches; next 2 digits give additional fraction of dimension expressed as 16th of an inch.

[21] Estimated value based on addition of salt in amount of 0.6% of finished product.

[43] For proportion of ingredients used and ratio of cooked to dry legume, see ARS 62-13 (7), section on Legumes, Dry, p. 7, and table 21, p. 25.

[45] Value based on average weighted in accordance with commercial practice in freezing vegetables. Wide range in sodium content occurs. For cooked vegetables, value also represents no additional salting. If salt is moderately added, increase value by 236 mg. per 100 g. of vegetable—an estimated figure based on typical amount of salt (0.6%) in canned vegetables. See also Appendix C, section on Cooked Vegetables and section on Frozen Fruits and Vegetables

TABLE 1.—*Nutritive values for household measures and market units of foods*—Continued

[Item numbers correspond to those in table 1 of Handbook No. 8, revised 1963. Values in parentheses denote imputed values usually from another form of the food or from a similar food. Zeros in parentheses indicate that amount of a constituent, if present, is probably too small to be measured. Dashes (—) denote lack of reliable data for a constituent believed to be present in a measurable amount. Calculated values, as those based on a recipe, are not in parentheses]

Item No.	Food, approximate measures, units, and weight (edible part unless footnotes indicate otherwise)			Values for edible part of foods														
				Water	Food energy	Protein	Fat	Carbohydrate	Calcium	Phosphorus	Iron	Sodium	Potassium	Vitamin A value	Thiamin	Riboflavin	Niacin	Ascorbic acid
(A)	(B)			(C)	(D)	(E)	(F)	(G)	(H)	(I)	(J)	(K)	(L)	(M)	(N)	(O)	(P)	(Q)
			Grams	*Percent*	*Calories*	*Grams*	*Grams*	*Grams*	*Milligrams*	*Milligrams*	*Milligrams*	*Milligrams*	*Milligrams*	*International units*	*Milligrams*	*Milligrams*	*Milligrams*	*Milligrams*
	Peas, mature seeds, dry—Continued																	
	Split without seedcoat—Continued																	
	Cooked [42]—Continued																	
a	Cup	1 cup	200	70.0	230	16.0	0.6	41.6	22	178	3.4	[43] 26	592	80	0.30	0.18	1.8	—
b	Pound	1 lb	454	70.0	522	36.3	1.4	94.3	50	404	7.7	[43] 59	1,343	180	.68	.41	4.1	—
	Peas and carrots, frozen: [5]																	
1534	Not thawed:																	
a	Container, net wt., 10 oz	1 container	284	85.4	156	9.4	.9	29.5	74	168	3.4	[45] 261	486	26,410	.57	.20	3.7	28
b	Cup	1 cup	140	85.4	77	4.6	.4	14.6	36	83	1.7	[45] 129	239	13,020	.28	.10	1.8	14
c	Pound	1 lb	454	85.4	249	15.0	1.4	47.2	118	268	5.4	[45] 417	776	42,180	.91	.32	5.9	45
1535	Cooked (boiled), drained:																	
a	Yield from 1 lb., frozen peas and carrots	2¾ cups	445	85.8	236	14.2	1.3	44.9	111	254	4.9	[45] 374	699	41,390	.85	.31	5.8	36
b	Yield from 10 oz., frozen peas and carrots	1¾ cups	278	85.8	147	8.9	.8	28.1	70	158	3.1	[45] 234	436	25,850	.53	.19	3.6	22
c	Cup	1 cup	160	85.8	85	5.1	.5	16.2	40	91	1.8	[45] 134	251	14,880	.30	.11	2.1	13
d	Pound (yield from approx. 1 lb. ⅓ oz., frozen peas and carrots).	1 lb	454	85.8	240	14.5	1.4	45.8	113	259	5.0	[45] 381	712	42,180	.86	.32	5.9	36
1536	**Pecans:** [5, 56]																	
	In shell (refuse: shells, 47%): [1]																	
	Size and approx. count per pound:																	
a	Oversize (55 or less per pound)	10 nuts	82	3.4	299	4.0	31.0	6.4	32	126	1.0	Trace	262	60	.37	.06	.4	1
b	Extra large (56–63 per pound)	10 nuts	76	3.4	277	3.7	28.7	5.9	29	116	1.0	Trace	243	50	.35	.05	.4	1
c	Large (64–77 per pound)	10 nuts	65	3.4	236	3.2	24.5	5.0	25	99	.8	Trace	207	40	.30	.04	.3	1
d	Pound (yields approx. 8.5 oz., shelled nuts)	1 lb	454	3.4	1,652	22.1	171.2	35.1	175	695	5.8	Trace	1,450	310	2.07	.31	2.2	5
	Shelled:																	
	Halves:																	
	Size and approx. count per pound:																	
e	Mammoth (250 or less per pound)	10 nuts	18	3.4	124	1.7	12.8	2.6	13	52	.4	Trace	109	20	.15	.02	.2	Trace
f	Jumbo (301–350 per pound)	10 nuts	14	3.4	96	1.3	10.0	2.0	10	40	.3	Trace	84	20	.12	.02	.1	Trace
g	Large (451–550 per pound)	10 nuts	9	3.4	62	.8	6.4	1.3	7	26	.2	Trace	54	10	.08	.01	.1	Trace
h	Cup	1 cup	108	3.4	742	9.9	76.9	15.8	79	312	2.6	Trace	651	140	.93	.14	1.0	2
	Chopped or pieces:																	
i	Cup	1 cup	118	3.4	811	10.9	84.0	17.2	86	341	2.8	Trace	712	150	1.01	.15	1.1	2
j	Tablespoon	1 tbsp	7.5	3.4	52	.7	5.3	1.1	5	22	.2	Trace	45	10	.06	.01	.1	Trace
k	Ground	1 cup	95	3.4	653	8.7	67.6	13.9	69	275	2.3	Trace	573	120	.82	.12	.9	2
l	Pound (yield from approx. 1.9 lb., in shell)	1 lb	454	3.4	3,116	41.7	323.0	66.2	331	1,311	10.9	Trace	2,735	590	3.90	.59	4.1	9
m	Ounce	1 oz	28	3.4	195	2.6	20.2	4.1	21	82	.7	Trace	171	40	.24	.04	.3	1
	Peppers, hot, chili:																	
	Immature, green:																	
1539	Canned, chili sauce	1 cup	245	93.9	49	1.7	.2	12.3	12	34	1.0	—	—	1,490	.07	.07	1.7	167
	Mature, red:																	
1542	Canned, chili sauce	1 cup	245	94.1	51	2.2	1.5	9.6	22	39	1.2	—	—	23,500	.02	.22	1.5	74
1544	Dried, chili powder with added seasoning	1 tsp	2	8.5	7	.3	.2	1.1	5	4	.3	31	20	1,300	Trace	.02	.2	Trace
	Peppers, sweet, garden varieties:																	
	Immature, green:																	
1545	Raw:																	
	Whole (refuse: stem end, seeds, core, 18%): [1]																	
a	Fancy grade, 3¾ in. long, 3-in. diam. (approx. 2¼ per pound).	1 pepper	200	93.4	36	2.0	.3	7.9	15	36	1.1	21	349	690	.13	.13	.8	210
b	No. 1 grade, 2¾ in. long, 2½-in. diam. (approx. 5 per pound).	1 pepper	90	93.4	16	.9	.1	3.5	7	16	.5	10	157	310	.06	.06	.4	94
c	Cut into strips	1 cup	100	93.4	22	1.2	.2	4.8	9	22	.7	13	213	420	.08	.08	.5	128
d	Sliced	1 cup	80	93.4	18	1.0	.2	3.8	7	18	.6	10	170	340	.06	.06	.4	102
e	Chopped or diced	1 cup	150	93.4	33	1.8	.3	7.2	14	33	1.1	20	320	630	.12	.12	.8	192
f	Pound	1 lb	454	93.4	100	5.4	.9	21.8	41	100	3.2	59	966	1,910	.36	.36	2.3	581
g	Ring, 3-in. diam., ¼ in. thick	1 ring	10	93.4	2	.1	Trace	.5	1	2	.1	1	21	40	.01	.01	.1	13
	Cooked:																	
1546	Boiled, drained:																	
a	Pepper, Fancy grade	1 pepper	160	94.7	29	1.6	.3	6.1	15	26	.8	14	238	690	.10	.11	.7	154
b	Pepper, No. 1 grade	1 pepper	73	94.7	13	.7	.1	2.8	7	12	.4	7	109	310	.05	.05	(.4)	70
c	Strips	1 cup	135	94.7	24	1.4	.3	5.1	12	22	.7	12	201	570	.08	.09	.6	130
d	Pound	1 lb	454	94.7	82	4.5	.9	17.2	41	73	2.3	41	676	1,910	.27	.32	2.3	435

(A)	(B)			(C)	(D)	(E)	(F)	(G)	(H)	(I)	(J)	(K)	(L)	(M)	(N)	(O)	(P)	(Q)
1547	Stuffed with beef and crumbs (pepper, 2¾ in. long, 2½-in. diam.,[337] with 1⅛ cups of stuffing).[51]	1 stuffed pepper.	185	63.1	315	24.1	10.2	31.1	78	224	3.9	581	477	520	0.17	0.81	4.6	74
1548	Mature, red, raw:																	
	Whole (refuse: stem end, seeds, core, 18%):[1]																	
a	Fancy grade, 3¾ in. long, 3-in. diam. (approx. 2¼ per pound).	1 pepper	200	90.7	51	2.8	.5	11.6	21	49	1.0	—	—	7,300	(.13)	(.13)	(.8)	335
b	No. 1 grade, 2¾ in. long, 2½-in. diam. (approx. 5 per pound).	1 pepper	90	90.7	23	1.0	.2	5.2	10	22	.4	—	—	3,280	(.06)	(.06)	(.4)	151
c	Cut into strips	1 cup	100	90.7	31	1.4	.3	7.1	13	30	.6	—	—	4,450	(.08)	(.08)	(.5)	204
d	Sliced	1 cup	80	90.7	25	1.1	.2	5.7	10	24	.5	—	—	3,560	(.06)	(.06)	(.4)	163
e	Chopped or diced	1 cup	150	90.7	47	2.1	.5	10.7	20	45	.9	—	—	6,680	(.12)	(.12)	(.8)	306
f	Pound	1 lb	454	90.7	141	6.4	1.4	32.2	59	136	2.7	—	—	20,190	(.36)	(.36)	(2.3)	925
g	Ring, 3-in. diam., ¼ in. thick	1 ring	10	90.7	3	.1	Trace	.7	1	3	.1	—	—	450	(.01)	(.01)	(.1)	20
	Persimmons, raw:																	
1551	Japanese, or kaki, 2½-in. diam., 3 in. high, variety without seeds (refuse: calyx and skin, 16%).[1]	1 persimmon	200	78.6	129	1.2	.7	33.1	10	44	.5	10	292	4,550	.05	.03	.2	18
1552	Native (refuse: seeds and calyx, 18%)[1]	1 persimmon	30	64.4	31	.2	.1	8.2	7	6	.6	Trace	76	—	—	—	—	16
	Pickles:																	
	Cucumber:																	
1558	Dill:																	
	Whole:																	
a	Large, approx. 4 in. long, 1¾-in. diam	1 pickle	135	93.3	15	.9	.3	3.0	35	28	1.4	1,928	270	140	Trace	.03	Trace	8
b	Medium, approx. 3¾ in. long, 1¼-in. diam	1 pickle	65	93.3	7	.5	.1	1.4	17	14	.7	928	130	70	Trace	.01	Trace	4
c	Sliced lengthwise with triangular shaped cross section (spears or sticks); piece, approx. 6 in. long with radii of cross section, approx. ½–¾ in.	1 pickle	30	93.3	3	.2	.1	.7	8	6	.3	428	60	30	Trace	.01	Trace	2
	Sliced crosswise; piece, 1½-in. diam., ¼ in. thick:																	
d	Cup (approx. 23 slices)	1 cup	155	93.3	17	1.1	.3	3.4	40	33	1.6	2,213	310	160	Trace	.03	Trace	9
e	Slice	2 slices	13	93.3	1	.1	Trace	.3	3	3	.1	186	26	10	Trace	Trace	Trace	1
1559	Fresh, sweetened with nutritive sweetener (bread-and-butter); crosscut slice, 1½-in. diam., ¼ in. thick:																	
a	Cup (approx. 23 slices)	1 cup	170	78.7	124	1.5	.3	30.4	54	46	3.1	1,144	—	240	Trace	.05	Trace	15
b	Slice	2 slices	15	78.7	11	.1	Trace	2.7	5	4	.3	101	—	20	Trace	Trace	Trace	1
1560	Sour:																	
	Whole:																	
a	Large, 4 in. long, 1¾-in. diam	1 pickle	135	94.8	14	.7	.3	2.7	23	20	4.3	1,827	—	140	Trace	.03	Trace	9
b	Medium, 3¾ in. long, 1¼-in. diam	1 pickle	65	94.8	7	.3	.1	1.3	11	10	2.1	879	—	70	Trace	.01	Trace	5
1561	Sweet (sweetened with nutritive sweetener):																	
	Whole:																	
	Gherkins:																	
a	Large, approx. 3 in. long, 1-in. diam	1 pickle	35	60.7	51	.2	.1	12.8	4	6	.4	—	—	30	Trace	.01	Trace	2
b	Small, approx. 2½ in. long, ¾-in. diam	1 pickle	15	60.7	22	.1	.1	5.5	2	2	.2	—	—	10	Trace	Trace	Trace	1
c	Midgut, approx. 2⅛ in. long, ⅜-in. diam	1 pickle	6	60.7	9	Trace	Trace	2.2	1	1	.1	—	—	10	Trace	Trace	Trace	Trace
d	Sliced lengthwise with triangular shaped cross section; piece, approx. 4½ in. long with radii of cross section, approx. ¾ in.	1 pickle	20	60.7	29	.1	.1	7.3	2	3	.2	—	—	20	Trace	Trace	Trace	1
e	Chopped, approx. ¼-in. cubes	1 cup	160	60.7	234	1.1	.6	58.4	19	26	1.9	—	—	140	Trace	.08	Trace	10
	Chowchow or mustard pickles (cucumber with added cauliflower, onion, mustard):																	
1562	Sour	1 cup	240	87.6	70	3.4	3.1	9.8	77	127	6.2	3,211	—	—	—	—	—	—
1563	Sweet	1 cup	245	68.9	284	3.7	2.2	66.2	56	54	3.7	1,291	—	—	—	—	—	—
1565	Relish, finely cut or chopped, sweet:																	
a	Cup	1 cup	245	63.0	338	1.2	1.5	83.3	49	34	2.0	1,744	—	—	—	—	—	—
b	Tablespoon	1 tbsp	15	63.0	21	.1	.1	5.1	3	2	.1	107	—	—	—	—	—	—
c	Packet (approx. ⅜ tbsp.)	1 packet	10	63.0	14	.1	.1	3.4	2	1	.1	71	—	—	—	—	—	—
	Pies:																	
	Baked, piecrust made with unenriched flour (9-in. diam., 28.3-in. cir.):[338, 339]																	

[1] Measure and weight apply to food as it is described with inedible part or parts (refuse) included.

[5] Most of phosphorus in nuts, legumes, and outer layers of cereal grains is present as phytic acid. See also Appendix D, section on Minerals and Oxalic Acid

[43] For proportion of ingredients used and ratio of cooked to dry legume, see ARS 62–13 (7), section on Legumes, Dry, p. 7, and table 21, p. 25.

[44] Value for product without added salt.

[45] Value based on average weighted in accordance with commercial practice in freezing vegetables. Wide range in sodium content occurs. For cooked vegetables, value also represents no additional salting. If salt is moderately added, increase value by 236 mg. per 100 g. of vegetable—an estimated figure based on typical amount of salt (0.6%) in canned vegetables. See also Appendix C, section on Cooked Vegetables, and section on Frozen Fruits and Vegetables

[51] For information on ingredients used in preparation, see ARS 62–13 (7), table 22, p. 26.

[53] Oxalic acid present may combine with calcium and magnesium to form insoluble compounds. For further information, see Appendix D, section on Minerals and Oxalic Acid

[337] Dimensions of raw pepper.

[338] For information on ingredients used in fillings and for proportions of crust and filling used for these pies, see ARS 62–13 (7), table 15, pp. 19–20, and table 16, p. 21. For information on sodium values, see Appendix C, section on Pies

[339] If piecrust is made with enriched flour, increase values for nutrients in milligrams per 100 g. of pie by following amounts:

	Iron	*Thiamin*	*Riboflavin*	*Niacin*
1-crust pie	0.3	0.03	0.03	0.3
2-crust pie	.4	.06	.04	.5

These basic units may be applied to various weights of volume measures shown here.

TABLE 1.—*Nutritive values for household measures and market units of foods*—Continued

[Item numbers correspond to those in table 1 of Handbook No. 8, revised 1963. Values in parentheses denote imputed values usually from another form of the food or from a similar food. Zeros in parentheses indicate that amount of a constituent, if present, is probably too small to be measured. Dashes (—) denote lack of reliable data for a constituent believed to be present in a measurable amount. Calculated values, as those based on a recipe, are not in parentheses]

Item No.	Food, approximate measures, units, and weight (edible part unless footnotes indicate otherwise)			Values for edible part of foods														
				Water	Food energy	Protein	Fat	Carbohydrate	Calcium	Phosphorus	Iron	Sodium	Potassium	Vitamin A value	Thiamin	Riboflavin	Niacin	Ascorbic acid
(A)	(B)			(C)	(D)	(E)	(F)	(G)	(H)	(I)	(J)	(K)	(L)	(M)	(N)	(O)	(P)	(Q)
			Grams	*Percent*	*Calories*	*Grams*	*Grams*	*Grams*	*Milligrams*	*Milligrams*	*Milligrams*	*Milligrams*	*Milligrams*	*International units*	*Milligrams*	*Milligrams*	*Milligrams*	*Milligrams*
	Pies—Continued																	
	Baked, piecrust made with unenriched flour (9-in. diam., 28.3-in. cir.) [288, 289]—Continued																	
1566	Apple:																	
a	Pie, whole	1 pie	[54] 945	47.6	2,419	20.8	104.9	360.0	76	208	2.8	2,844	756	280	0.19	0.19	3.8	9
b	Sector, 4¾-in. arc; ⅙ of pie	1 sector	158	47.6	404	3.5	17.5	60.2	13	35	.5	476	126	50	.03	.03	.6	2
c	Sector, 3½-in. arc; ⅛ of pie	1 sector	118	47.6	302	2.6	13.1	45.0	9	26	.4	355	94	40	.02	.02	.5	1
d	Sector, 1-in. arc	1 sector	33.4	47.6	86	.7	3.7	12.7	3	7	.1	101	27	10	.01	.01	.1	Trace
1567	Banana custard:																	
a	Pie, whole	1 pie	[54] 910	54.4	2,011	41.0	84.6	279.4	601	746	4.6	1,765	1,847	2,280	.36	1.18	2.7	9
b	Sector, 4¾-in. arc; ⅙ of pie	1 sector	152	54.4	336	6.8	14.1	46.7	100	125	.8	295	309	380	.06	.20	.5	2
c	Sector, 3½-in. arc; ⅛ of pie	1 sector	114	54.4	252	5.1	10.6	35.0	75	93	.6	221	231	290	.05	.15	.3	1
d	Sector, 1-in. arc	1 sector	32.2	54.4	71	1.4	3.0	9.9	21	26	.2	62	65	80	.01	.04	.1	Trace
1568	Blackberry:																	
a	Pie, whole	1 pie	[54] 945	51.0	2,296	24.6	104.0	325.1	180	246	4.7	2,533	945	850	.19	.19	2.8	38
b	Sector, 4¾-in. arc; ⅙ of pie	1 sector	158	51.0	384	4.1	17.4	54.4	30	41	.8	423	158	140	.03	.03	.5	6
c	Sector, 3½-in. arc; ⅛ of pie	1 sector	118	51.0	287	3.1	13.0	40.6	22	31	.6	316	118	110	.02	.02	.4	5
d	Sector, 1-in. arc	1 sector	33.4	51.0	81	.9	3.7	11.5	6	9	.2	90	33	30	.01	.01	.1	1
1569	Blueberry:																	
a	Pie, whole	1 pie	[54] 945	51.0	2,287	22.7	102.1	329.8	104	217	5.7	2,533	614	280	.19	.19	2.8	28
b	Sector, 4¾-in. arc; ⅙ of pie	1 sector	158	51.0	382	3.8	17.1	55.1	17	36	.9	423	103	50	.03	.03	.5	5
c	Sector, 3½-in. arc; ⅛ of pie	1 sector	118	51.0	286	2.8	12.7	41.2	13	27	.7	316	77	40	.02	.02	.4	4
d	Sector, 1-in. arc	1 sector	33.4	51.0	81	.8	3.6	11.7	4	8	.2	90	22	10	.01	.01	.1	1
	Boston cream. See Cakes (item 522).																	
1570	Butterscotch:																	
a	Pie, whole	1 pie	[54] 910	45.1	2,430	40.0	100.1	348.5	683	737	8.2	1,947	865	2,370	.27	.91	1.8	Trace
b	Sector, 4¾-in. arc; ⅙ of pie	1 sector	152	45.1	406	6.7	16.7	58.2	114	123	1.4	325	144	400	.05	.15	.3	Trace
c	Sector, 3½-in. arc; ⅛ of pie	1 sector	114	45.1	304	5.0	12.5	43.7	86	92	1.0	244	108	300	.03	.11	.2	Trace
d	Sector, 1-in. arc	1 sector	32.2	45.1	86	1.4	3.5	12.3	24	26	.3	69	31	80	.01	.03	.1	Trace
1571	Cherry:																	
a	Pie, whole	1 pie	[54] 945	46.6	2,466	24.6	106.8	362.9	132	236	2.8	2,873	992	4,160	.19	.19	4.7	Trace
b	Sector, 4¾-in. arc; ⅙ of pie	1 sector	158	46.6	412	4.1	17.9	60.7	22	40	.5	480	166	690	.03	.03	.8	Trace
c	Sector, 3½-in. arc; ⅛ of pie	1 sector	118	46.6	308	3.1	13.3	45.3	17	30	.4	359	124	520	.02	.02	.6	Trace
d	Sector, 1-in. arc	1 sector	33.4	46.6	87	.9	3.8	12.8	5	8	.1	102	35	150	.01	.01	.2	Trace
1572	Chocolate chiffon:																	
a	Pie, whole	1 pie	[54] 648	33.0	2,125	44.1	99.1	283.2	156	629	7.8	1,633	713	2,010	.19	.65	1.3	0
b	Sector, 4¾-in. arc; ⅙ of pie	1 sector	108	33.0	354	7.3	16.5	47.2	26	105	1.3	272	119	330	.03	.11	.2	0
c	Sector, 3½-in. arc; ⅛ of pie	1 sector	81	33.0	266	5.5	12.4	35.4	19	79	1.0	204	89	250	.02	.08	.2	0
d	Sector, 1-in. arc	1 sector	22.9	33.0	75	1.6	3.5	10.0	5	22	.3	58	25	70	.01	.02	Trace	0
1573	Chocolate meringue:																	
a	Pie, whole	1 pie	[54] 910	48.4	2,293	43.7	109.2	304.9	628	892	6.4	2,330	1,265	1,730	.27	1.09	1.8	Trace
b	Sector, 4¾-in. arc; ⅙ of pie	1 sector	152	48.4	383	7.3	18.2	50.9	105	149	1.1	389	211	290	.05	.18	.3	Trace
c	Sector, 3½-in. arc; ⅛ of pie	1 sector	114	48.4	287	5.5	13.7	38.2	79	112	.8	292	158	220	.03	.14	.2	Trace
d	Sector, 1-in. arc	1 sector	32.2	48.4	81	1.5	3.9	10.8	22	32	.2	82	45	60	.01	.04	.1	Trace
1574	Coconut custard:																	
a	Pie, whole	1 pie	[54] 910	55.4	2,139	54.6	113.8	226.6	855	1,056	6.4	2,248	1,483	2,090	.55	1.73	2.7	0
b	Sector, 4¾-in. arc; ⅙ of pie	1 sector	152	55.4	357	9.1	19.0	37.8	143	176	1.1	375	248	350	.09	.29	.5	0
c	Sector, 3½-in. arc; ⅛ of pie	1 sector	114	55.4	268	6.8	14.3	28.4	107	132	.8	282	186	260	.07	.22	.3	0
d	Sector, 1-in. arc	1 sector	32.2	55.4	76	1.9	4.0	8.0	30	37	.2	80	52	70	.02	.06	.1	0
1575	Custard:																	
a	Pie, whole	1 pie	[54] 910	58.1	1,984	55.5	101.0	212.9	874	1,028	5.5	2,612	1,247	2,090	.46	1.46	2.7	0
b	Sector, 4¾-in. arc; ⅙ of pie	1 sector	152	58.1	331	9.3	16.9	35.6	146	172	.9	436	208	350	.08	.24	.5	0
c	Sector, 3½-in. arc; ⅛ of pie	1 sector	114	58.1	249	7.0	12.7	26.7	109	129	.7	327	156	260	.06	.18	.3	0
d	Sector, 1-in. arc	1 sector	32.2	58.1	70	2.0	3.6	7.5	31	36	.2	92	44	70	.02	.05	.1	0
1576	Lemon chiffon:																	
a	Pie, whole	1 pie	[54] 648	35.6	2,028	45.4	81.6	283.8	149	538	5.8	1,691	525	1,100	.19	.52	1.3	19
b	Sector, 4¾-in. arc; ⅙ of pie	1 sector	108	35.6	338	7.6	13.6	47.3	25	90	1.0	282	87	180	.03	.09	.2	3
c	Sector, 3½-in. arc; ⅛ of pie	1 sector	81	35.6	254	5.7	10.2	35.5	19	67	.7	211	66	140	.02	.06	.2	2
d	Sector, 1-in. arc	1 sector	22.9	35.6	72	1.6	2.9	10.0	5	19	.2	60	19	40	.01	.02	Trace	1
1577	Lemon meringue:																	
a	Pie, whole	1 pie	[54] 840	47.4	2,142	31.1	85.7	316.7	118	412	4.2	2,369	420	1,430	.25	.67	1.7	25
b	Sector, 4¾-in. arc; ⅙ of pie	1 sector	140	47.4	357	5.2	14.3	52.8	20	69	.7	395	70	240	.04	.11	.3	4

(A)	(B)			(C)	(D)	(E)	(F)	(G)	(H)	(I)	(J)	(K)	(L)	(M)	(N)	(O)	(P)	(Q)
c	Sector, 3⅛-in. arc; ⅛ of pie	1 sector	105	47.4	268	3.9	10.7	39.6	15	51	0.5	296	53	180	0.03	0.08	0.2	3
d	Sector, 1-in. arc	1 sector	29.7	47.4	76	1.1	3.0	11.2	4	15	.1	84	15	50	.01	.02	.1	1
1578	Mince:																	
a	Pie, whole	1 pie	[54] 945	43.0	2,561	23.6	108.7	389.3	265	359	9.5	4,234	1,682	20	.66	.38	3.8	9
b	Sector, 4¾-in. arc; ⅙ of pie	1 sector	158	43.0	428	4.0	18.2	65.1	44	60	1.6	708	281	Trace	.11	.06	.6	2
c	Sector, 3½-in. arc; ⅛ of pie	1 sector	118	43.0	320	3.0	13.6	48.6	33	45	1.2	529	210	Trace	.08	.05	.5	1
d	Sector, 1-in. arc	1 sector	33.4	43.0	91	.8	3.8	13.8	9	13	.3	150	59	Trace	.02	.01	.1	Trace
1579	Peach:																	
a	Pie, whole	1 pie	[54] 945	47.5	2,410	23.6	101.1	361.0	95	274	4.7	2,533	1,408	6,900	.19	.38	6.6	28
b	Sector, 4¾-in. arc; ⅙ of pie	1 sector	158	47.5	403	4.0	16.9	60.4	16	46	.8	423	235	1,150	.03	.06	1.1	5
c	Sector, 3½-in. arc; ⅛ of pie	1 sector	118	47.5	301	3.0	12.6	45.1	12	34	.6	316	176	860	.02	.05	.8	4
d	Sector, 1-in. arc	1 sector	33.4	47.5	85	.8	3.6	12.8	3	10	.2	90	50	240	.01	.01	.2	1
1580	Pecan:																	
a	Pie, whole	1 pie	[54] 825	19.5	3,449	42.1	188.9	423.2	388	850	23.1	1,823	1,015	1,320	1.32	.58	2.5	Trace
b	Sector, 4¾-in. arc; ⅙ of pie	1 sector	138	19.5	577	7.0	31.6	70.8	65	142	3.9	305	170	220	.22	.10	.4	Trace
c	Sector, 3½-in. arc; ⅛ of pie	1 sector	103	19.5	431	5.3	23.6	52.8	48	106	2.9	228	127	160	.16	.07	.3	Trace
d	Sector, 1-in. arc	1 sector	29.2	19.5	122	1.5	6.7	15.0	14	30	.8	65	36	50	.05	.02	.1	Trace
1581	Pineapple:																	
a	Pie, whole	1 pie	[54] 945	48.0	2,391	20.8	101.1	360.0	123	198	4.7	2,561	680	190	.38	.19	3.8	9
b	Sector, 4¾-in. arc; ⅙ of pie	1 sector	158	48.0	400	3.5	16.9	60.2	21	33	.8	428	114	30	.06	.03	.6	2
c	Sector, 3½-in. arc; ⅛ of pie	1 sector	118	48.0	299	2.6	12.6	45.0	15	25	.6	320	85	20	.05	.02	.5	1
d	Sector, 1-in. arc	1 sector	33.4	48.0	85	.7	3.6	12.7	4	7	.2	91	24	10	.01	.01	.1	Trace
1582	Pineapple chiffon:																	
a	Pie, whole	1 pie	[54] 648	41.1	1,866	42.8	78.4	253.4	156	492	5.8	1,659	635	2,270	.26	.58	2.6	6
b	Sector, 4¾-in. arc; ⅙ of pie	1 sector	108	41.1	311	7.1	13.1	42.2	26	82	1.0	276	106	380	.04	.10	.4	1
c	Sector, 3½-in. arc; ⅛ of pie	1 sector	81	41.1	233	5.3	9.8	31.7	19	62	.7	207	79	280	.03	.07	.3	1
d	Sector, 1-in. arc	1 sector	22.9	41.1	66	1.5	2.8	9.0	5	17	.2	59	22	80	.01	.02	.1	Trace
1583	Pineapple custard:																	
a	Pie, whole	1 pie	[54] 910	54.3	2,002	36.4	79.2	292.1	455	592	3.6	1,693	883	1,640	.36	.82	3.6	9
b	Sector, 4¾-in. arc; ⅙ of pie	1 sector	152	54.3	334	6.1	13.2	48.8	76	99	.6	283	147	270	.06	.14	.6	2
c	Sector, 3½-in. arc; ⅛ of pie	1 sector	114	54.3	251	4.6	9.9	36.6	57	74	.5	212	111	210	.05	.10	.5	1
d	Sector, 1-in. arc	1 sector	32.2	54.3	71	1.3	2.8	10.3	16	21	.1	60	31	60	.01	.03	.1	Trace
1584	Pumpkin:																	
a	Pie, whole	1 pie	[54] 910	59.2	1,920	36.4	101.9	223.0	464	628	4.6	1,947	1,456	22,480	.27	.91	4.6	Trace
b	Sector, 4¾-in. arc; ⅙ of pie	1 sector	152	59.2	321	6.1	17.0	37.2	78	105	.8	325	243	3,750	.05	.15	.8	Trace
c	Sector, 3½-in. arc; ⅛ of pie	1 sector	114	59.2	241	4.6	12.8	27.9	58	79	.6	244	182	2,810	.03	.11	.6	Trace
d	Sector, 1-in. arc	1 sector	32.2	59.2	68	1.3	3.6	7.9	16	22	.2	69	52	800	.01	.03	.2	Trace
1585	Raisin:																	
a	Pie, whole	1 pie	[54] 945	42.5	2,552	24.6	101.1	406.4	170	378	8.5	2,693	1,814	50	.28	.28	2.8	9
b	Sector, 4¾-in. arc; ⅙ of pie	1 sector	158	42.5	427	4.1	16.9	67.9	28	63	1.4	450	303	10	.05	.05	.5	2
c	Sector, 3½-in. arc; ⅛ of pie	1 sector	118	42.5	319	3.1	12.6	50.7	21	47	1.1	336	227	10	.04	.04	.4	1
d	Sector, 1-in. arc	1 sector	33.4	42.5	90	.9	3.6	14.4	6	13	.3	95	64	Trace	.01	.01	.1	Trace
1586	Rhubarb:																	
a	Pie, whole	1 pie	[54] 945	47.4	2,391	23.6	101.1	361.0	605	246	6.6	2,552	1,503	470	.19	.38	2.8	28
b	Sector, 4¾-in. arc; ⅙ of pie	1 sector	158	47.4	400	4.0	16.9	60.4	101	41	1.1	427	251	80	.03	.06	.5	5
c	Sector, 3½-in. arc; ⅛ of pie	1 sector	118	47.4	299	3.0	12.6	45.1	76	31	.8	319	188	60	.02	.05	.4	4
d	Sector, 1-in. arc	1 sector	33.4	47.4	85	.8	3.6	12.8	21	9	.2	90	53	20	.01	.01	.1	1
1587	Strawberry:																	
a	Pie, whole	1 pie	[54] 742	58.4	1,469	14.1	58.6	229.3	119	186	5.2	1,439	890	300	.15	.30	3.0	186
b	Sector, 4¾-in. arc; ⅙ of pie	1 sector	124	58.4	246	2.4	9.8	38.3	20	31	.9	241	149	50	.02	.05	.5	31
c	Sector, 3½-in. arc; ⅛ of pie	1 sector	93	58.4	184	1.8	7.3	28.7	15	23	.7	180	112	40	.02	.04	.4	23
d	Sector, 1-in. arc	1 sector	26.2	58.4	52	.5	2.1	8.1	4	7	.2	51	31	10	.01	.01	.1	7
1588	Sweetpotato:																	
a	Pie, whole	1 pie	[54] 910	59.3	1,938	41.0	102.8	215.7	628	764	4.6	1,984	1,483	21,840	.46	1.09	2.7	36
b	Sector, 4¾-in. arc; ⅙ of pie	1 sector	152	59.3	324	6.8	17.2	36.0	105	128	.8	331	248	3,640	.08	.18	.5	6
c	Sector, 3½-in. arc; ⅛ of pie	1 sector	114	59.3	243	5.1	12.9	27.0	79	96	.6	249	186	2,730	.06	.14	.3	5
d	Sector, 1-in. arc	1 sector	32.2	59.3	69	1.4	3.6	7.6	22	27	.2	70	52	770	.02	.04	.1	1
	Frozen in unbaked form (8-in. diam., 25.1-in. cir.; net wt., 20 oz. (1 lb. 4 oz.) to 26 oz. (1 lb. 10 oz.): [26]																	
	Apple:																	
1589	Unbaked pie, whole	1 pie	660	56.3	1.386	10.6	54.8	219.1	46	112	1.3	[26] 1,168	396	90	.11	.09	1.0	9
1590	Baked:																	
a	Pie, whole	1 pie	550	47.3	1.386	10.6	54.8	219.1	46	112	1.3	[26] 1,168	396	70	.09	.08	.9	6

[26] For further information, see Appendix B, section on Frozen Pies for size of pie, and Appendix C, section on Pies for sodium content.

[54] Yield of formula used to calculate nutritive values in Agr. Handb. No. 8, rev. 1963.

[288] For information on ingredients used in fillings and for proportions of crust and filling used for these pies, see ARS 62–13 (7), table 15, pp. 19–20, and table 16, p. 21. For information on sodium values, see Appendix C, section on Pies

[289] If piercrust is made with enriched flour, increase values for nutrients in milligrams per 100 g. of pie by following amounts:

	Iron	*Thiamin*	*Riboflavin*	*Niacin*
1-crust pie	0.3	0.03	0.03	0.3
2-crust pie	.4	.06	.04	.5

These basic units may be applied to various weights of volume measures shown here.

TABLE 1.—*Nutritive values for household measures and market units of foods*—Continued

[Item numbers correspond to those in table 1 of Handbook No. 8, revised 1963. Values in parentheses denote imputed values usually from another form of the food or from a similar food. Zeros in parentheses indicate that amount of a constituent, if present, is probably too small to be measured. Dashes (—) denote lack of reliable data for a constituent believed to be present in a measurable amount. Calculated values, as those based on a recipe, are not in parentheses]

Item No. (A)	Food, approximate measures, units, and weight (edible part unless footnotes indicate otherwise) (B)			Water (C)	Food energy (D)	Protein (E)	Fat (F)	Carbohydrate (G)	Calcium (H)	Phosphorus (I)	Iron (J)	Sodium (K)	Potassium (L)	Vitamin A value (M)	Thiamin (N)	Riboflavin (O)	Niacin (P)	Ascorbic acid (Q)
			Grams	*Percent*	*Calories*	*Grams*	*Grams*	*Grams*	*Milligrams*	*Milligrams*	*Milligrams*	*Milligrams*	*Milligrams*	*International units*	*Milligrams*	*Milligrams*	*Milligrams*	*Milligrams*
	Pies—Continued																	
	Frozen in unbaked form (8-in. diam., 25.1-in. cir.; net wt., 20 oz. (1 lb. 4 oz.) to 26 oz. (1 lb. 10 oz.) [28]—Continued																	
	Apple—Continued																	
	Baked—Continued																	
b	Sector, 4⅛-in. arc; ⅙ of pie	1 sector	92	47.3	231	1.8	9.1	36.5	8	19	0.2	[96] 195	66	10	0.01	0.01	0.2	1
c	Sector, 3⅛-in. arc; ⅛ of pie	1 sector	69	47.3	173	1.3	6.9	27.4	6	14	.2	[96] 146	50	10	.01	.01	.1	1
d	Sector, 1-in. arc	1 sector	21.9	47.3	55	.4	2.2	8.7	2	4	.1	[96] 47	16	Trace	Trace	Trace	Trace	Trace
	Cherry:																	
1591	Unbaked pie, whole	1 pie	660	47.8	1,690	12.5	70.0	257.4	73	139	1.3	[96] 1,333	475	1,850	.12	.11	1.4	14
1592	Baked:																	
a	Pie, whole	1 pie	580	40.6	1,690	12.5	70.0	257.4	73	139	1.3	[96] 1,333	475	1,670	.10	.10	1.3	10
b	Sector, 4⅛-in. arc; ⅙ of pie	1 sector	97	40.6	282	2.1	11.7	42.9	12	23	.2	[96] 222	79	280	.02	.02	.2	2
c	Sector, 3⅛-in. arc; ⅛ of pie	1 sector	73	40.6	211	1.6	8.8	32.2	9	17	.2	[96] 167	59	210	.01	.01	.2	1
d	Sector, 1-in. arc	1 sector	23.1	40.6	67	.5	2.8	10.3	3	5	.1	[96] 53	19	70	Trace	Trace	Trace	Trace
1594	Coconut custard, baked:																	
a	Pie, whole	1 pie	600	51.2	1,494	36.0	72.0	177.0	570	690	3.6	[96] 1,512	1,032	960	.24	.96	1.2	Trace
b	Sector, 4⅛-in. arc; ⅙ of pie	1 sector	100	51.2	249	6.0	12.0	29.5	95	115	.6	[96] 252	172	160	.04	.16	.2	Trace
c	Sector, 3⅛-in. arc; ⅛ of pie	1 sector	75	51.2	187	4.5	9.0	22.1	71	86	.5	[96] 189	129	120	.03	.12	.2	Trace
d	Sector, 1-in. arc	1 sector	23.9	51.2	60	1.4	2.9	7.1	23	27	.1	[96] 60	41	40	.01	.04	Trace	Trace
	Prepared from mix (filling and piecrust), baked:																	
1596	Coconut custard pie (filling made with mix, egg yolks, milk), 8-in. diam., 25.1-in. cir.: [290]																	
a	Pie, whole	1 pie	797	57.6	1,618	34.3	63.0	231.9	741	821	3.2	1,873	1,227	1,670	.24	1.12	1.6	Trace
b	Sector, 4⅛-in. arc; ⅙ of pie	1 sector	133	57.6	270	5.7	10.5	38.7	124	137	.5	313	205	280	.04	.19	.3	Trace
c	Sector, 3⅛-in. arc; ⅛ of pie	1 sector	100	57.6	203	4.3	7.9	29.1	93	103	.4	235	154	210	.03	.14	.2	Trace
d	Sector, 1-in. arc	1 sector	31.8	57.6	65	1.4	2.5	9.3	30	33	.1	75	49	70	.01	.04	.1	Trace
	Piecrust or plain pastry, made with [291]—																	
	Enriched flour:																	
1597	Unbaked	1 pie shell	194	20.9	900	11.1	60.1	79.0	25	91	3.1	1,102	89	0	.47	.27	3.7	0
1598	Baked	1 pie shell	180	14.9	900	11.0	60.1	78.8	25	90	3.1	1,100	89	0	.36	.25	3.2	0
	Unenriched flour:																	
1599	Unbaked	1 pie shell	194	20.9	900	11.1	60.1	79.0	25	91	.8	1,102	89	0	.06	.06	1.0	0
1600	Baked	1 pie shell	180	14.9	900	11.0	60.1	78.8	25	90	.9	1,100	89	0	.05	.05	.9	0
	Piecrust mix (including stick form) and piecrust baked from mix:																	
1601	Mix, dry form:																	
a	Package, 10 oz	1 pkg	284	8.6	1,482	20.4	92.9	140.6	131	273	1.4	1,968	179	0	.11	.11	2.0	0
	Cup:																	
b	Not packed	1 cup	120	8.6	626	8.6	39.2	59.4	55	115	.6	832	76	0	.05	.05	.8	0
c	Packed	1 cup	195	8.6	1,018	14.0	63.8	96.5	90	187	1.0	1,351	123	0	.08	.08	1.4	0
1602	Piecrust, prepared with water, baked (yield from 10-oz. pkg. (item 1601a)).	11.3 oz	320	18.7	1,485	20.5	93.1	140.8	131	272	1.3	2,602	179	0	.10	.10	1.6	0
1605	Pigs' feet, pickled	2 oz	57	66.9	113	9.5	8.4	0	—	—	—	—	—	—	—	—	—	—
1610	Pimientos, canned, solids and liquid:																	
	Container and approx. contents:																	
a	Can, size 211 × 200 [14] (4Z Pimiento), or glass jar, size 4Z; net wt., 4 oz.	1 can or jar	113	92.4	31	1.0	.6	6.6	[292] 8	19	1.7	—	—	2,600	.02	.07	.5	107
b	Can, size 603 × 700 [14] (No. 10); net wt., 109 oz. (6 lb. 13 oz.).	1 can	3,090	92.4	834	27.8	15.5	179.2	[292] 216	525	46.4	—	—	71,070	.62	1.85	12.4	2,936
c	Glass jar, size 2Z; net wt., 2 oz	1 jar	57	92.4	15	.5	.3	3.3	[292] 4	10	.9	—	—	1,310	.01	.03	.2	54
d	Pound	1 lb	454	92.4	122	4.1	2.3	26.3	[292] 32	77	6.8	—	—	10,430	.09	.27	1.8	431
	Pineapple:																	
1611	Raw:																	
a	Cup, diced pieces	1 cup	155	85.3	81	.6	.3	21.2	26	12	.8	2	226	110	.14	.05	.3	26
b	Pound (approx. 3 cups, diced pieces or 5½ slices)	1 lb	454	85.3	236	1.8	.9	62.1	77	36	2.3	5	662	320	.41	.14	.9	77
c	Slice, approx. 3½-in. diam., ¾ in. thick	1 slice	84	85.3	44	.3	.2	11.5	14	7	.4	1	123	60	.08	.03	.2	14
1612	Candied:																	
	Prepackaged slices (2¼-in. diam., ¾ in. thick) and chunks (¾ in. long, [293] ½ in. thick; length of outside arc, ¾ in.):																	

(A)	(B)		(C)	(D)	(E)	(F)	(G)	(H)	(I)	(J)	(K)	(L)	(M)	(N)	(O)	(P)	(Q)
	Container and approx. contents:																
a	Net wt., 4 oz.; 2 slices or approx. ½ cup of chunks (27 chunks).	1 container	113	18.0	357	0.9	0.5	90.4	—	—	—	—	—	—	—	—	—
b	Net wt., 8 oz.; 4 slices, or 1 cup of chunks, packed, or 1⅛ cups, not packed (55 chunks).	1 container	227	18.0	717	1.8	.9	181.6	—	—	—	—	—	—	—	—	—
c	Ounce	1 oz	28	18.0	90	.2	.1	22.7	—	—	—	—	—	—	—	—	—
	Canned, solids and liquid:																
1618	Water pack, without artificial sweetener (small tidbits, 1¼ in. long,[293] ½ in. thick; length of outside arc, ½ in.):																
a	Cup	1 cup	246	89.1	96	.7	.2	25.1	30	12	0.7	2	244	120	0.20	0.05	0.5	17
b	Pound	1 lb	454	89.1	177	1.4	.5	46.3	54	23	1.4	5	449	230	.36	.09	.9	32
	Sirup pack:																
1616	Heavy:																
	Can and approx. contents:																
a	Size, 307 × 208[14] (No. 1 Flat); net wt., 8¼ oz.; sliced and crushed styles (4 medium slices and approx. 5 tbsp. drained liquid or 1 cup (scant) of crushed pineapple).	1 can	234	79.9	178	.7	.2	45.4	26	12	.7	2	225	120	.19	.05	.5	16
b	Size, 211 × 414[14] (No. 211 Cylinder); net wt., 13¼ oz.; chunk, tidbit, and crushed styles (approx. 1½ cups of solids and liquid, or approx. 1⅛ cups of drained chunks, or small tidbits and 8 tbsp. of drained liquid).	1 can	376	79.9	278	1.1	.4	72.9	41	19	1.1	4	361	190	.30	.08	.8	26
c	Size, 307 × 409[14] (No. 2); net wt., 20 oz. (1 lb. 4 oz.); sliced, chunk, tidbit, and crushed styles (approx. 2¼ cups of solids and liquid, chunk, tidbit, crushed styles, or 10 medium slices and approx. 12 tbsp. of drained liquid, or 2 cups of drained chunks or small tidbits and approx. 12 tbsp. of drained liquid).	1 can	567	79.9	420	1.7	.6	110.0	62	28	1.7	6	544	280	.45	.11	1.1	40
d	Size, 401 × 411[14] (No. 2½); net wt., 29½ oz. (1 lb. 13½ oz.); sliced style (8 large slices and approx. 18 tbsp. of drained liquid).	1 can	836	79.9	619	2.5	.8	162.2	420	.67	.17	1.7	59	92	42	2.5	8	808
e	Cup, chunk, tidbit, crushed styles	1 cup	255	79.9	189	.8	.3	49.5	28	13	.8	3	245	130	.20	.05	.5	18
	Fruit (slices, chunks, tidbits) with drained liquid:																
f	Large slice (3½-in. diam., 7/16 in. thick; diam. of core hole, 1¼–1⅜ in.), or 8 chunks (approx. ⅞ in. long,[293] ⅞ in. thick; length of outside arc, ⅞ in.), or 17 small tidbits (approx. 1¼ in. long,[293] ½ in. thick; length of outside arc, ½ in.); with 2¼ tbsp. of drained liquid.	1 slice, 8 chunks, or 17 small tidbits; 2¼ tbsp. liquid.	105	79.9	78	.3	.1	20.4	12	5	.3	1	101	50	.08	.02	.2	7
g	Medium slice (3-in. diam., 5/16 in. thick; diam. of core hole, 1–1⅜ in.), or 4 chunks (approx. ⅞ in. long,[293] ⅞ in. thick; length of outside arc, ⅞ in.), or 9 small tidbits (1¼ in. long,[293] ½ in. thick; length of outside arc, ½ in.); with 1¼ tbsp. of drained liquid.	1 slice, 4 chunks, or 9 small tidbits; 1¼ tbsp. liquid.	58	79.9	43	.2	.1	11.3	6	3	.2	1	56	30	.05	.01	.1	4
h	Pound	1 lb	454	79.9	336	1.4	.5	88.0	50	23	1.4	5	435	230	.36	.09	.9	32
1617	Extra heavy:																
	Can and approx. contents:																
a	Size, 211 × 304[14] (8Z Tall, Buffet); net wt., 8¾ oz.; crushed style, approx. 1 cup (scant).	1 can	248	75.9	223	.7	.2	58.0	27	12	.7	2	233	100	.20	.05	.5	15
b	Size, 307 × 409[14] (No. 2); net wt., 20½ oz. (1 lb. 4½ oz.); sliced style (10 medium slices and approx. 13 tbsp. of drained liquid).	1 can	581	75.9	523	1.7	.6	136.0	64	29	1.7	6	546	230	.46	.12	1.2	35

[14] Dimensions of can: 1st dimension represents diameter; 2d dimension, height of can. 1st or left-hand digit in each dimension gives number of whole inches; next 2 digits give additional fraction of dimension expressed as 16th of an inch.

[289] For further information, see Appendix B, section on Frozen Pies, for size of pie, and Appendix C, section on Pies for sodium content.

[290] For information on ingredients added to mix and proportion of crust to filling, see ARS 62-13 (7), table 17, p. 21.

[291] For information on ingredients used, see ARS 62-13 (7), table 14, p. 18.

[292] Federal standards provide for addition of certain calcium salts as firming agents; if used, these salts may add calcium not to exceed 26 mg. per 100 g. of finished product.

[293] Length as measured along radius from inside arc to outside arc.

TABLE 1.—*Nutritive values for household measures and market units of foods*—Continued

[Item numbers correspond to those in table 1 of Handbook No. 8, revised 1963. Values in parentheses denote imputed values usually from another form of the food or from a similar food. Zeros in parentheses indicate that amount of a constituent, if present, is probably too small to be measured. Dashes (—) denote lack of reliable data for a constituent believed to be present in a measurable amount. Calculated values, as those based on a recipe, are not in parentheses]

Item No.	Food, approximate measures, units, and weight (edible part unless footnotes indicate otherwise)			Values for edible part of foods														
				Water	Food energy	Protein	Fat	Carbohydrate	Calcium	Phosphorus	Iron	Sodium	Potassium	Vitamin A value	Thiamin	Riboflavin	Niacin	Ascorbic acid
(A)	(B)			(C)	(D)	(E)	(F)	(G)	(H)	(I)	(J)	(K)	(L)	(M)	(N)	(O)	(P)	(Q)
			Grams	*Percent*	*Calories*	*Grams*	*Grams*	*Grams*	*Milligrams*	*Milligrams*	*Milligrams*	*Milligrams*	*Milligrams*	*International units*	*Milligrams*	*Milligrams*	*Milligrams*	*Milligrams*
	Pineapple—Continued																	
	Canned, solids and liquid—Continued																	
	Sirup pack—Continued																	
	Extra heavy—Continued																	
	Can and approx. contents—Continued																	
c	Size, 401 × 411 [14] (No. 2½); net wt., 30 oz. (1 lb. 14 oz.); sliced and chunk styles (8 large slices and approx. 19 tbsp. of drained liquid; approx. 3¼ cups of solids and liquid, chunk style).	1 can		851	75.9	766	2.6	0.9	199.1	94	43	2.6	9	800	340	0.68	0.17	1.7	51
d	Cup, chunk or crushed styles	1 cup		260	75.9	234	.8	.3	60.8	29	13	.8	3	244	100	.21	.05	.5	16
	Fruit (slices, chunks) with drained liquid:																	
e	Large slice (3½-in. diam., 7/16 in. thick; diam. of core hole, 1¼–1⅜ in.) or 8 chunks (approx. ⅞ in. long, [298] ⅞ in. thick; length of outside arc, ⅞ in.); with 2⅓ tbsp. of drained liquid.	1 slice or 8 chunks; 2⅓ tbsp. liquid.		105	75.9	95	.3	.1	24.6	12	5	.3	1	99	40	.08	.02	.2	6
f	Medium slice (3-in. diam., 5/16 in. thick; diam. of core hole, 1–1⅜ in.) or 4 chunks (approx. ⅞ in. long, [298] ⅞ in. thick; length of outside arc, ⅞ in.); with 1¼ tbsp. of drained liquid.	1 slice or 4 chunks; 1¼ tbsp. liquid.		58	75.9	52	.2	.1	13.6	6	3	.2	1	55	20	.05	.01	.1	8
g	Pound	1 lb		454	75.9	408	1.4	.5	106.1	50	23	1.4	5	426	180	.36	.09	.9	27
1618	Frozen chunks, sweetened with nutritive sweetener, not thawed:																	
	Can and approx. contents:																	
a	Size, 211 × 414 [14] (12Z, No. 211 Cylinder); net wt., 13½ oz.	1 can		383	77.1	326	1.5	.4	85.0	34	15	1.5	8	383	110	.38	.11	1.1	31
b	Size, 603 × 700 [14] (No. 10); net wt., 104 oz. (6 lb. 8 oz.).	1 can		2,948	77.1	2,506	11.8	2.9	654.5	265	118	11.8	59	2,948	880	2.95	.88	8.8	236
c	Cup [48]	1 cup		245	77.1	208	1.0	.2	54.4	22	10	1.0	5	245	70	.25	.07	.7	20
d	Pound	1 lb		454	77.1	386	1.8	.5	100.7	41	18	1.8	9	454	140	.45	.14	1.4	36
	Pineapple juice:																	
1619	Canned, unsweetened:																	
	Can and approx. contents:																	
a	Size, 202 × 314 [14] (6½Z); net contents, 6 fl. oz. or 1 glass (6 fl. oz.).	1 can or 1 glass		188	85.6	103	.8	.2	25.4	28	17	.6	2	280	90	.09	.04	.4	[294] 17
b	Size, 211 × 414 [14] (12Z, No. 211 Cylinder); net contents, 12 fl. oz.	1 can		376	85.6	207	1.5	.4	50.8	56	34	1.1	4	560	190	.19	.08	.8	[294] 34
c	Size, 307 × 409 [14] (No. 2); net contents, 18 fl. oz. (1 pt. 2 fl. oz.).	1 can		563	85.6	310	2.3	.6	76.0	84	51	1.7	6	839	280	.28	.11	1.1	[294] 51
d	Size, 404 × 700 [14] (46Z, No. 3 Cylinder); net contents, 46 fl. oz. (1 qt. 14 fl. oz.).	1 can		1,440	85.6	792	5.8	1.4	194.4	216	130	4.3	14	2,146	720	.72	.29	2.9	[294] 130
e	Size, 603 × 700 [14] (No. 10); net contents, 98 fl. oz. (3 qt. 2 oz.).	1 can		3,067	85.6	1,687	12.3	3.1	414.0	460	276	9.2	31	4,570	1,530	1.53	.61	6.1	[294] 276
f	Cup	1 cup		250	85.6	138	1.0	.3	33.8	38	23	.8	3	373	130	.13	.05	.5	[294] 23
g	Fluid ounce	1 fl. oz		31.3	85.6	17	.1	Trace	4.2	5	3	.1	Trace	47	20	.02	.01	.1	[294] 3
	Frozen concentrate, unsweetened:																	
1620	Undiluted:																	
a	Can, net contents, 6 fl. oz. (yields 3 cups diluted juice weighing 748 g.).	1 can		216	53.1	387	2.8	.2	95.7	84	60	1.9	6	1,020	110	.50	.13	1.9	[295] 91
b	Fluid ounce	1 fl. oz		35.9	53.1	64	.5	Trace	15.9	14	10	.3	1	169	20	.08	.02	.3	[295] 15
1621	Diluted with 3 parts water by volume:																	
a	Cup	1 cup		250	86.5	130	1.0	.1	32.0	28	20	.8	3	340	30	.18	.05	.5	[296] 30
b	Glass (6 fl. oz.)	1 glass		187	86.5	97	.7	.1	23.9	21	15	.6	2	254	20	.13	.04	.4	[296] 22
c	Fluid ounce	1 fl. oz		31.2	86.5	16	.1	Trace	4.0	3	2	.1	Trace	42	Trace	.02	.01	.1	[296] 4
1622	**Pineapple juice and grapefruit juice drink,** canned (approx. 50% fruit juices):																	
	Can and approx. contents:																	
a	Size, 202 × 314 [14] (6½Z); net contents, 6 fl. oz. or 1 glass (6 fl. oz.).	1 can or 1 glass		187	86.0	101	.4	.1	25.4	9	9	.4	Trace	116	20	.04	.02	.2	([277])

(A)	(B)			(C)	(D)	(E)	(F)	(G)	(H)	(I)	(J)	(K)	(L)	(M)	(N)	(O)	(P)	(Q)
b	Size, 404 × 700 [14] (46Z, No. 3 Cylinder); net contents, 46 fl. oz. (1 qt. 14 fl. oz.).	1 can	1,438	86.0	777	2.9	0.6	195.6	72	72	2.9	Trace	892	140	0.29	0.14	1.4	([277])
c	Cup	1 cup	250	86.0	135	.5	.1	34.0	13	13	.5	Trace	155	30	.05	.03	.3	([277])
d	Fluid ounce	1 fl. oz	31.3	86.0	17	.1	Trace	4.3	2	2	.1	Trace	19	Trace	.01	Trace	Trace	([277])
1623	**Pineapple juice and orange juice drink, canned (approx. 40% fruit juices):**																	
	Can and approx. contents:																	
a	Size, 404 × 700 [14] (46Z, No. 3 Cylinder); net contents, 46 fl. oz. (1 qt. 14 fl. oz.).	1 can	1,438	86.0	777	2.9	1.4	194.1	72	86	2.9	Trace	1,007	720	.29	.14	1.4	([277])
b	Cup	1 cup	250	86.0	135	.5	.3	33.8	13	15	.5	Trace	175	130	.05	.03	.3	([277])
c	Glass (6 fl. oz.)	1 glass	187	86.0	101	.4	.2	25.2	9	11	.4	Trace	131	90	.04	.02	.2	([277])
d	Fluid ounce	1 fl. oz	31.3	86.0	17	.1	Trace	4.2	2	2	.1	Trace	22	20	.01	Trace	Trace	([277])
	Pinenuts: [5]																	
1624	Pignolias, shelled	1 oz	28	5.6	156	8.8	13.4	3.3	—	—	—	—	—	—	.18	—	—	—
1625	Piñon:																	
a	In shell (refuse: shells, 42%) [1]	1 lb	454	3.1	1,671	34.2	159.2	53.9	32	1,589	13.7	—	—	80	3.37	.61	11.8	Trace
b	Shelled	1 oz	28	3.1	180	3.7	17.2	5.8	3	171	1.5	—	—	10	.36	.07	1.3	Trace
1626	**Pistachionuts:** [5]																	
a	In shell (refuse: shells, 50%) [1]	1 lb	454	5.3	1,347	43.8	121.8	43.1	297	1,134	16.6	—	2,204	520	1.52	—	3.2	0
b	Shelled	1 lb	454	5.3	2,694	87.5	243.6	86.2	594	2,268	33.1	—	4,409	1,040	3.04	—	6.4	0
1627	**Pitanga** (Surinam-cherry), **raw:**																	
a	Whole (refuse: stems, blossom ends, seeds, 19%) [1]	2 fruits	12	85.8	5	.1	Trace	1.2	1	1	Trace	—	—	150	Trace	Trace	Trace	3
b	Pitted	1 cup	170	85.8	87	1.4	.7	21.3	15	19	.3	—	—	2,550	.05	.07	.5	51
	Pizza: [297]																	
	From home recipe, baked (in 14-in. diam. pan): [53]																	
1628	With cheese topping:																	
a	Whole, 13¾-in. diam., 43.2-in. cir	1 pizza	[54] 520	48.3	1,227	62.4	43.2	147.2	1,149	1,014	5.2	3,650	676	3,280	.31	1.04	5.2	42
b	Sector, 5⅓-in. arc; ⅛ of pizza	1 sector	65	48.3	153	7.8	5.4	18.4	144	127	.7	456	85	410	.04	.13	.7	5
c	Sector, 1-in. arc	1 sector	12.0	48.3	28	1.4	1.0	3.4	27	23	.1	84	16	80	.01	.02	.1	1
d	Pound	1 lb	454	48.3	1,070	54.4	37.6	128.4	1,002	885	4.5	3,184	590	2,860	.27	.91	4.5	36
1629	With sausage topping: [298]																	
a	Whole, 13¾-in. diam., 43.2-in. cir	1 pizza	[54] 535	50.6	1,252	41.7	49.8	158.4	91	492	6.4	3,900	899	3,000	.48	.64	8.0	48
b	Sector, 5⅓-in. arc; ⅛ of pizza	1 sector	67	50.6	157	5.2	6.2	19.8	11	62	.8	488	113	380	.06	.08	1.0	6
c	Sector, 1-in. arc	1 sector	12.4	50.6	29	1.0	1.2	3.7	2	11	.1	90	21	70	.01	.01	.2	1
d	Pound	1 lb	454	50.6	1,061	35.4	42.2	134.3	77	417	5.4	3,307	762	2,540	.41	.54	6.8	41
	Chilled, with cheese, commercial:																	
1630	Partially baked:																	
a	Container, net wt., 20 oz.; 12-in.-diam. pizza, ¼ in. thick; cir., 37.7 in.	1 pizza	567	53.3	1,179	44.2	32.9	175.2	686	714	4.0	3,050	533	2,380	.34	.79	5.1	34
b	Pound	1 lb	454	53.3	943	35.4	26.3	140.2	549	572	3.2	2,440	426	1,910	.27	.64	4.1	27
1631	Baked:																	
a	Yield from 12-in.-diam. pizza, cir., 37.7 in. (item 1630a).	17 oz	482	45.1	1,179	44.2	32.9	175.2	686	714	4.0	3,050	533	1,880	.29	.77	4.8	29
b	Sector, 4¾-in. arc; ⅛ of pizza [299]	1 sector	60	45.1	147	5.5	4.1	21.9	86	89	.5	380	67	230	.04	.10	.6	4
c	Sector, 1-in. arc [299]	1 sector	12.8	45.1	31	1.2	.9	4.6	18	19	.1	81	14	50	.01	.02	.1	1
d	Yield from 1 lb., chilled, partially baked pizza (item 1630b).	13.6 oz	386	45.1	943	35.4	26.3	140.2	549	572	3.2	2,440	426	1,510	.23	.62	3.9	23
e	Pound	1 lb	454	45.1	1,111	41.7	30.8	164.7	649	671	4.1	2,871	503	1,770	.27	.73	4.5	27
	Frozen, with cheese, commercial:																	
1632	Partially baked:																	
a	Container, net wt., 15 oz.; 10-in.-diam. pizza, ¼ in. thick; cir., 31.4 in.	1 pizza	425	48.9	973	37.8	28.1	140.7	621	621	3.8	2,571	455	1,910	.26	.68	3.8	21
b	Container, net wt., 11 oz.; four 5¼-in.-diam. pizzas, ⅛ in. thick; cir., 16½ in.	4 pizzas	312	48.9	714	27.8	20.6	103.3	456	456	2.8	1,888	334	1,400	.19	.50	2.8	16
c	Pound	1 lb	454	48.9	1,039	40.4	29.9	150.1	662	662	4.1	2,744	485	2,040	.27	.73	4.1	23
1633	Baked:																	
a	Yield from 10-in.-diam. pizza, cir., 31.4 in. (item 1632a).	14 oz	398	45.3	973	37.8	28.1	140.7	621	621	3.8	2,571	455	1,750	.24	.68	3.8	21

[1] Measure and weight apply to food as it is described with inedible part or parts (refuse) included.

[5] Most of phosphorus in nuts, legumes, and outer layers of cereal grains is present as phytic acid. See also Appendix D, section on Minerals and Oxalic Acid

[14] Dimensions of can: 1st dimension represents diameter; 2d dimension, height of can. 1st or left-hand digit in each dimension gives number of whole inches; next 2 digits give additional fraction of dimension expressed as 16th of an inch.

[46] Measurement applies to thawed product. See also Appendix C, section on Frozen Fruits and Vegetables

[53] For information on ingredients used in crust and in filling and for proportion of crust to filling for pies, see ARS 62–13 (7), tables 23 and 24, p. 31, and table 25, p. 32.

[54] Yield of formula used to calculate nutritive values in Agr. Handb. No. 8, rev. 1963.

[277] Ascorbic acid may be added as preservative or as nutrient. For value of product, refer to label.

[293] Length as measured along radius from inside arc to outside arc.

[294] Applies to product without added ascorbic acid. With added ascorbic acid, based on claim that 4 fl. oz. contain 30 mg. of ascorbic acid, value for 6-fl. oz. can or glass (item 1619a) is 45 mg.; for 12-fl. oz. can (item 1619b), 90 mg.; for 18-fl. oz. can (item 1619c), 135 mg.; for 46-fl. oz. can (item 1619d), 345 mg.; for 98-fl. oz. can (item 1619e), 735 mg.; for 1 cup (item 1619f), 60 mg.; for 1 fl. oz. (item 1619g), 7.5 mg. Brands differ in amount added.

[295] Applies to product without added ascorbic acid. With added ascorbic acid, based on claim that 4 fl. oz. of reconstituted juice contain 30 mg. of ascorbic acid, value for 6-fl. oz. can (1620a) is 180 mg.; for 1 fl. oz. (item 1620b), 30 mg.

[296] Applies to product without added ascorbic acid. With added ascorbic acid, based on claim that 4 fl. oz. of reconstituted juice contain 30 mg. of ascorbic acid, value for 1 cup (item 1621a) is 60 mg.; for 1 glass (6 fl. oz.) (item 1621b), 45 mg.; for 1 fl. oz. (item 1621c), 7.5 mg.

[297] Values are based on products made with unenriched flour. With enriched flour, increase values per 100 g. of product as follows: Iron 0.8 mg., thiamin 0.12 mg., riboflavin 0.08 mg., niacin, 0.9 mg.

[298] Measures, their weights, and nutritive values apply to product that does not contain cheese. For nutritive values of product with cheese, made with unenriched flour, see Appendix A, table 3, p. 264.

[299] Based on dimensions of partially baked product.

TABLE 1.—*Nutritive values for household measures and market units of foods*—Continued

[Item numbers correspond to those in table 1 of Handbook No. 8, revised 1963. Values in parentheses denote imputed values usually from another form of the food or from a similar food. Zeros in parentheses indicate that amount of a constituent, if present, is probably too small to be measured. Dashes (—) denote lack of reliable data for a constituent believed to be present in a measurable amount. Calculated values, as those based on a recipe, are not in parentheses]

Item No. (A)	Food, approximate measures, units, and weight (edible part unless footnotes indicate otherwise) (B)			Water (C)	Food energy (D)	Protein (E)	Fat (F)	Carbohydrate (G)	Calcium (H)	Phosphorus (I)	Iron (J)	Sodium (K)	Potassium (L)	Vitamin A value (M)	Thiamin (N)	Riboflavin (O)	Niacin (P)	Ascorbic acid (Q)
			Grams	Percent	Calories	Grams	Grams	Grams	Milligrams	Milligrams	Milligrams	Milligrams	Milligrams	International units	Milligrams	Milligrams	Milligrams	Milligrams
	Pizza [297]—Continued																	
	Frozen, with cheese, commercial—Continued																	
	Baked—Continued																	
	Yield from 10-in. diam. pizza, cir., 31.4 in. (item 1632a)—Continued																	
b	Sector, 4½-in. arc; ⅐ of pizza [298]	1 sector	57	45.3	139	5.4	4.0	20.1	89	89	0.5	367	65	250	0.03	0.10	0.6	3
c	Sector, 1-in. arc [299]	1 sector	12.7	45.3	31	1.2	.9	4.5	20	20	.1	82	14	60	.01	.02	.1	1
d	Yield from four 5¼-in.-diam. pizzas, cir., 16½ in. (item 1632b).	10.3 oz. or 4 pizzas.	292	45.3	714	27.8	20.6	103.3	456	456	2.8	1,888	334	1,280	.18	.50	2.8	16
e	Pizza	1 pizza	73	45.3	179	6.9	5.2	25.8	114	114	.7	472	83	320	.04	.12	.7	4
f	Yield from 1 lb., frozen, partially baked pizza (item 1632c).	15 oz	424	45.3	1,039	40.4	29.9	150.1	662	662	4.1	2,744	485	1,870	.25	.72	4.1	23
g	Pound	1 lb	454	45.3	1,111	43.1	32.2	160.6	708	708	4.1	2,935	517	2,000	.27	.77	4.5	27
1634	Plantain (baking banana), raw:																	
a	Whole, 11 in. long,[87] 1⅞-in. diam. (refuse: skin, 28%).[1 300]	1 banana	365	66.4	313	2.9	1.1	82.0	18	79	1.8	13	1,012	—	.16	.11	1.6	37
b	Pound	1 lb	454	66.4	540	5.0	1.8	141.5	32	136	3.2	23	1,746	([301])	.27	.18	2.7	64
	Plums:																	
	Raw:																	
1639	Damson:																	
	Whole (refuse: pits and clinging pulp, 9%):[1]																	
a	Cup	1 cup	145	81.1	87	.7	Trace	23.5	24	22	.7	3	395	(400)	11	.04	.7	—
b	Fruit, 1-in. diam	10 plums	110	81.1	66	.5	Trace	17.8	18	17	.5	2	299	(300)	.08	.03	.5	—
c	Pound	1 lb	454	81.1	272	2.1	Trace	73.5	74	70	2.1	8	1,234	(1,240)	.33	.12	2.1	—
	Pitted:																	
d	Cup, halves	1 cup	170	81.1	112	.9	Trace	30.3	31	29	.9	3	508	(510)	.14	.05	.9	—
e	Pound	1 lb	454	81.1	299	2.3	Trace	80.7	82	77	2.3	9	1,356	(1,360)	.36	.14	2.3	—
1640	Japanese and hybrid:																	
	Whole (refuse: pits, 6%):[1]																	
a	Fruit, 2⅛-in. diam	1 plum	70	86.6	32	.3	.1	8.1	8	12	.3	1	112	160	.02	.02	.3	4
b	Pound	1 lb	454	86.6	205	2.1	.9	52.4	51	77	2.1	4	725	1,070	.13	.13	2.1	26
	Pitted:																	
	Cup:																	
c	Halves	1 cup	185	86.6	89	.9	.4	22.8	22	33	.9	2	315	460	.06	.06	.9	11
d	Slices or diced pieces	1 cup	165	86.6	79	.8	.3	20.3	20	30	.8	2	281	410	.05	.05	.8	10
e	Pound	1 lb	454	86.6	218	2.3	.9	55.8	54	82	2.3	5	771	1,130	.14	.14	2.3	27
1641	Prune type:																	
	Whole (refuse: pits, 6%):[1]																	
a	Fruit, 1½-in. diam	1 plum	30	78.7	21	.2	.1	5.6	3	5	.1	Trace	48	[302] 80	.01	.01	.1	1
b	Pound	1 lb	454	78.7	320	3.4	.9	84.0	51	77	2.1	4	725	[302] 1,280	.13	.13	2.1	17
	Pitted:																	
c	Halves	1 cup	165	78.7	124	1.3	.3	32.5	20	30	.8	2	281	[302] 500	.05	.05	.8	7
d	Pound	1 lb	454	78.7	340	3.6	.9	89.4	54	82	2.3	5	771	[302] 1,360	.14	.14	2.3	18
	Canned, solids and liquid; purple (Italian prunes), whole, unpitted style (refuse: pits, 5%):[1]																	
1643	Water pack, without artificial sweetener:																	
	Can and approx. contents:																	
a	Size, 303 × 406 [14] (No. 303); net wt., 16 oz. (1 lb.); approx. 10–14 plums and 9 tbsp. of drained liquid.	1 can or 1 lb	454	86.8	198	1.7	.9	51.3	39	43	4.3	9	638	5,390	.09	.09	1.7	9
b	Cup	1 cup	262	86.8	114	1.0	.5	29.6	22	25	2.5	5	368	3,110	.05	.05	1.0	5
c	Fruit with drained liquid	3 plums; 2 tbsp. liquid.	100	86.8	44	.4	.2	11.3	9	10	1.0	2	141	1,190	.02	.02	.4	2
1645	Sirup pack, heavy:																	
	Can and approx. contents:																	
a	Size, 303 × 406 [14] (No. 303); net wt., 16¾–17 oz. (1 lb. ¾ oz. to 1 lb. 1 oz.); approx. 10–14 plums and 9¾ tbsp. of drained liquid.	1 can	478	77.4	377	1.8	.5	98.1	41	45	4.1	5	645	5,490	.09	.09	1.8	9
b	Size, 401 × 411 [14] (No. 2½); net wt., 30 oz. (1 lb. 14 oz.); approx. 12–20 plums and 17 tbsp. of drained liquid.	1 can	851	77.4	671	3.2	.8	174.6	73	81	7.3	8	1,148	9,780	.16	.16	3.2	16

(A)	(B)			(C)	(D)	(E)	(F)	(G)	(H)	(I)	(J)	(K)	(L)	(M)	(N)	(O)	(P)	(Q)
c	Cup	1 cup	272	77.4	214	1.0	0.3	57.8	23	26	2.3	3	367	3,130	0.05	0.05	1.0	5
d	Pound	1 lb	454	77.4	358	1.7	.4	93.1	39	43	3.9	4	612	5,210	.09	.09	1.7	9
e	Fruit with drained liquid	3 plums; 2¾ tbsp. liquid.	140	77.4	110	.5	.1	28.7	12	13	1.2	1	189	1,610	.03	.03	.5	3
	Poha. See Groundcherries (item 1092).																	
1648	**Pokeberry** (poke) shoots, cooked (boiled), drained	1 cup	165	92.9	33	3.8	.7	5.1	87	54	2.0	[20]—	—	14,360	.12	.41	1.8	135
1650	**Pollock**, cooked, creamed:[303]																	
a	Cup	1 cup	250	74.7	320	34.8	14.8	10.0	—	—	—	[43]278	595	—	.08	.33	1.8	Trace
b	Pound	1 lb	454	74.7	581	63.1	26.8	18.1	—	—	—	[43]503	1,080	—	.14	.59	3.2	Trace
1651	**Pomegranate**, raw, 3⅜-in. diam., 2¾ in. high (refuse: skin and seeds, 44%).[1]	1 pomegranate	275	82.3	97	.8	.5	25.3	5	12	.5	5	399	Trace	.05	.05	.5	6
	Popcorn:[5]																	
1653	Unpopped	1 cup	205	9.8	742	24.4	9.6	147.8	(21)	(541)	(5.1)	(6)	—	—	(.80)	(.23)	(4.3)	(0)
	Popped (commercial):																	
1654	Plain, large kernel[304]	1 cup	6	4.0	23	.8	.3	4.6	(1)	(17)	(.2)	(Trace)	—	—	—	(.01)	(.1)	(0)
1655	Oil and salt added, large kernel[304]	1 cup	9	3.1	41	.9	2.0	5.3	1	19	.2	175	—	—	—	.01	.2	0
1656	Sugar coated	1 cup	35	4.0	134	2.1	1.2	29.9	2	47	.5	[43]Trace	—	—	—	.02	.4	0
1657	**Popovers**, baked (home recipe[60] with enriched flour), 2¾-in. diam. at top, 2-in. diam. at bottom, height at center, 4 in.; yield from approx. ¼ cup batter.	1 popover	40	54.9	90	3.5	3.7	10.3	38	56	[306].6	88	60	130	[306].06	[306].10	[306].4	Trace
	Pork, fresh, retail cuts:[49]																	
	Ham:																	
1698	Raw, lean with fat:																	
a	With bone and skin (63% lean, 22% fat) (refuse: bone and skin, 15%).[1]	1 lb	454	56.5	1,188	61.3	102.6	0	35	686	9.3	215	981	(0)	2.98	.72	16.0	—
b	Without bone and skin (74% lean, 26% fat)	1 lb	454	56.5	1,397	72.1	120.7	0	41	807	10.9	252	1,154	(0)	3.51	.84	18.8	—
	Cooked (baked or roasted):																	
1699	Lean with fat (74% lean, 26% fat):																	
a	Yield from 1 lb., raw ham with bone and skin (item 1698a).	9.2 oz	262	45.5	980	60.8	80.2	0	26	618	7.9	148	675	(0)	1.34	.60	12.1	—
b	Yield from 1 lb., raw ham without bone and skin (item 1698b).	10.9 oz	308	45.5	1,152	70.8	94.2	0	31	727	9.2	178	798	(0)	1.57	.71	14.2	—
	Cup (not packed):																	
c	Chopped or diced	1 cup	140	45.5	524	32.2	42.8	0	14	330	4.2	79	361	(0)	.71	.32	6.4	—
d	Ground	1 cup	110	45.5	411	25.3	33.7	0	11	260	3.3	62	283	(0)	.56	.25	5.1	—
e	Pound	1 lb	454	45.5	1,696	104.3	138.8	0	45	1,070	13.6	256	1,168	(0)	2.31	1.04	20.9	—
f	Piece, approx. 4⅛ in. long, 2¼ in. wide, ¼ in. thick; wt., 1½ oz.	2 pieces or 3 oz.	85	45.5	318	19.6	26.0	0	9	201	2.6	48	220	(0)	.43	.20	3.9	—
1701	Lean, trimmed of separable fat:																	
a	Yield from 1 lb., raw ham with bone and skin (item 1698a).	6.8 oz	194	58.9	421	57.6	19.4	0	25	598	7.4	141	645	(0)	1.24	.56	11.1	—
b	Yield from 1 lb., raw ham without bone and skin (item 1698b).	8.1 oz	228	58.9	495	67.7	22.8	0	30	702	8.7	166	758	(0)	1.46	.66	13.0	—
	Cup (not packed):																	
c	Chopped or diced	1 cup	140	58.9	304	41.6	14.0	0	18	431	5.3	102	466	(0)	.90	.41	8.0	—
d	Ground	1 cup	110	58.9	239	32.7	11.0	0	14	339	4.2	80	366	(0)	.70	.32	6.3	—
e	Pound	1 lb	454	58.9	984	134.7	45.4	0	59	1,397	17.2	330	1,509	(0)	2.90	1.32	25.9	—
f	Piece, approx. 4⅛ in. long, 2¼ in. wide, ¼ in. thick; wt., 1½ oz.	2 pieces or 3 oz.	85	58.9	184	25.2	8.5	0	11	262	3.2	62	282	(0)	.54	.25	4.8	—
	Loin and loin chops:																	
1715	Raw, lean with fat:																	
a	With bone (63% lean, 16% fat) (refuse: bone, 21%).[1]	1 lb	454	57.2	1,065	61.1	89.0	0	36	690	9.3	214	978	(0)	2.97	.71	15.9	—
b	Without bone (80% lean, 20% fat)	1 lb	454	57.2	1,352	77.6	112.9	0	45	875	11.8	272	1,242	(0)	3.76	.90	20.1	—
	Cooked:																	
	Lean with fat:																	
1716	Baked or roasted loin roast (80% lean, 20% fat):																	
a	Yield from 1 lb., raw loin with bone (item 1715a).	8.6 oz	244	45.8	883	59.8	69.5	0	27	625	7.8	147	670	(0)	2.24	.63	13.7	—

[1] Measure and weight apply to food as it is described with inedible part or parts (refuse) included.

[5] Most of phosphorus in nuts, legumes, and outer layers of cereal grains is present as phytic acid. See also Appendix D, section on Minerals and Oxalic Acid

[14] Dimensions of can: 1st dimension represents diameter; 2d dimension, height of can. 1st or left-hand digit in each dimension gives number of whole inches; next 2 digits give additional fraction of dimension expressed as 16th of an inch.

[20] Value is for unsalted product. If salt is used, increase value by 236 mg. per 100 g. of vegetable—an estimated figure based on typical amount of salt (0.6%) in canned vegetables. See also Appendix C, section on Cooked Vegetables

[37] Length as measured along outer curvature, from tip to base of pedicel.

[43] Value for product without added salt.

[49] For further information about items and basis of vitamin and mineral values, see Appendix B, section on Foods Measured in Pieces, Slices, and Other Units and Appendix C, section on Meats Values for cooked items apply to products prepared without added salt or other seasoning.

[60] For information on ingredients used, see ARS 62-13 (7), table 4, p. 10.

[297] Values are based on products made with unenriched flour. With enriched flour, increase values per 100 g. of product as follows: iron 0.8 mg., thiamin 0.12 mg., riboflavin 0.08 mg., niacin 0.9 mg.

[299] Based on dimensions of partially baked product.

[300] Dimensions and weight apply to Horn variety—common cooking variety. These measurements vary widely. See also Appendix B, section on Bananas

[301] Values for 1 lb. edible portion range from 50 I.U. for white-fleshed varieties to as much as 5,440 I.U. for those with deep-yellow flesh.

[302] Value applies to all prune-type plums except Italian and Imperial prunes. For these, value for 1 fruit is 380 I.U.; for 1 lb. of fruit with pits, 5,700 I.U.; for 1 cup of halves, 2,200 I.U.; for 1 lb. of pitted fruit, 6,100 I.U.

[303] Prepared with flour, butter or margarine, and milk.

[304] Smaller kernels may weigh as much as 6 g. more per cup.

[306] With unenriched flour approx. values for 1 popover are iron 0.4 mg., thiamin 0.02 mg., riboflavin 0.08 mg., niacin 0.1 mg.

TABLE 1.—*Nutritive values for household measures and market units of foods*—Continued

Item numbers correspond to those in table 1 of Handbook No. 8, revised 1963. Values in parentheses denote imputed values usually from another form of the food or from a similar food. Zeros in parentheses indicate that amount of a constituent, if present, is probably too small to be measured. Dashes (—) denote lack of reliable data for a constituent believed to be present in a measurable amount. Calculated values, as those based on a recipe, are not in parentheses]

Item No.	Food, approximate measures, units, and weight (edible part unless footnotes indicate otherwise)			Water	Food energy	Protein	Fat	Carbohydrate	Calcium	Phosphorus	Iron	Sodium	Potassium	Vitamin A value	Thiamin	Riboflavin	Niacin	Ascorbic acid
				Values for edible part of foods														
(A)	(B)			(C)	(D)	(E)	(F)	(G)	(H)	(I)	(J)	(K)	(L)	(M)	(N)	(O)	(P)	(Q)
			Grams	*Percent*	*Calories*	*Grams*	*Grams*	*Grams*	*Milligrams*	*Milligrams*	*Milligrams*	*Milligrams*	*Milligrams*	*International units*	*Milligrams*	*Milligrams*	*Milligrams*	*Milligrams*
	Pork, fresh, retail cuts [40]—Continued																	
	Loin and loin chops—Continued																	
	Cooked—Continued																	
	Lean with fat—Continued																	
	Baked or roasted loin roast (80% lean, 20% fat)—Continued																	
b	Yield from 1 lb., raw loin without bone (item 1715b).	10.9 oz	308	45.8	1,115	75.5	87.8	0	34	788	9.9	185	846	(0)	2.83	0.80	17.2	—
c	Cup, chopped or diced pieces (not packed)	1 cup	140	45.8	507	34.3	39.9	0	15	358	4.5	84	384	(0)	1.29	.36	7.8	—
d	Pound	1 lb	454	45.8	1,642	111.1	129.3	0	50	1,161	14.5	272	1,244	(0)	4.17	1.18	25.4	—
e	Piece, approx. 2½ in. long, 2½ in. wide, ¾ in. thick; wt., 3 oz.	1 piece or 3 oz	85	45.8	308	20.8	24.2	0	9	218	2.7	51	233	(0)	.78	.22	4.8	—
1717	Broiled loin chops (72% lean, 28% fat):																	
a	Yield from 1 lb., raw chops with bone (item 1715a).	8.2 oz	233	42.3	911	57.6	73.9	0	28	624	7.9	141	645	(0)	2.24	.65	13.5	—
b	Yield from 1 lb., raw chops without bone (item 1715b).	10.4 oz	295	42.3	1,153	72.9	93.5	0	35	791	10.0	179	816	(0)	2.83	.83	17.1	—
	Yield from 1 chop, raw with bone; ⅓ or ¼ of item 1715a:																	
c	Cut 3 per pound	2.7 oz	78	42.3	305	19.3	24.7	0	9	209	2.7	47	216	(0)	.75	.22	4.5	—
d	Cut 4 per pound	2 oz	58	42.3	227	14.3	18.4	0	7	155	2.0	35	160	(0)	.56	.16	3.4	—
	Lean, trimmed of separable fat:																	
1719	Baked or roasted loin roast:																	
a	Yield from 1 lb., raw loin with bone (item 1715a).	6.9 oz	195	55.0	495	57.3	27.7	0	25	605	7.4	140	642	(0)	2.11	.60	12.7	—
b	Yield from 1 lb., raw loin without bone (item 1715b).	8.7 oz	247	55.0	627	72.6	35.1	0	32	766	9.4	178	813	(0)	2.67	.77	16.1	—
c	Cup, chopped or diced pieces (not packed)	1 cup	140	55.0	356	41.2	19.9	0	18	434	5.3	101	461	(0)	1.51	.43	9.1	—
d	Pound	1 lb	454	55.0	1,152	133.4	64.4	0	59	1,406	17.2	327	1,494	(0)	4.90	1.41	29.5	—
e	Piece, approx 2½ in. long, 2½ in. wide, ¾ in. thick; wt., 3 oz.	1 piece or 3 oz	85	55.0	216	25.0	12.1	0	11	264	3.2	61	280	(0)	.92	.26	5.5	—
1720	Broiled loin chops:																	
a	Yield from 1 lb., raw chops with bone (item 1715a).	5.9 oz	168	52.6	454	51.4	25.9	0	22	544	6.6	126	576	(0)	1.90	.55	11.4	—
b	Yield from 1 lb., raw chops without bone (item 1715b).	7½ oz	212	52.6	572	64.9	32.6	0	28	687	8.3	159	727	(0)	2.40	.70	14.4	—
	Yield from 1 chop, raw with bone; ⅓ or ¼ of item 1715a:																	
c	Cut 3 per pound	2 oz	56	52.6	151	17.1	8.6	0	7	181	2.2	42	192	(0)	.63	.18	3.8	—
d	Cut 4 per pound	1½ oz	42	52.6	113	12.9	6.5	0	5	136	1.6	32	144	(0)	.47	.14	2.9	—
	Shoulder cuts (Boston butt and picnic):																	
	Boston butt:																	
1734	Raw, lean with fat:																	
a	With bone and skin (74% lean, 20% fat) (refuse: bone and skin, 6%).[1]	1 lb	454	59.3	1,220	65.9	104.1	0	38	735	9.8	231	1,054	(0)	3.20	.77	17.1	—
b	Without bone and skin (79% lean, 21% fat)	1 lb	454	59.3	1,302	70.3	111.1	0	41	785	10.4	246	1,125	(0)	3.42	.82	18.3	—
	Cooked (roasted):																	
1735	Lean with fat (79% lean, 21% fat):																	
a	Yield from 1 lb., raw meat with bone and skin (item 1734a).	10.2 oz	290	48.1	1,024	65.3	82.7	0	29	664	8.4	160	731	(0)	1.45	.67	12.8	—
b	Yield from 1 lb., raw meat without bone and skin (item 1734b).	10.9 oz	308	48.1	1,087	69.3	87.8	0	31	705	8.9	170	776	(0)	1.54	.71	13.6	—
	Cup (not packed):																	
c	Chopped or diced	1 cup	140	48.1	494	31.5	39.9	0	14	321	4.1	77	353	(0)	.70	.32	6.2	—
d	Ground	1 cup	110	48.1	388	24.8	31.4	0	11	252	3.2	61	278	(0)	.55	.25	4.8	—
e	Pound	1 lb	454	48.1	1,601	102.1	129.3	0	45	1,039	13.2	250	1,144	(0)	2.27	1.04	20.0	—
f	Piece, approx. 2½ in. long, 2½ in. wide, ¼ in. thick; wt., 1 oz.	3 pieces or 3 oz.	85	48.1	300	19.1	24.2	0	9	195	2.5	47	214	(0)	.43	.20	3.7	—
1737	Lean, trimmed of separable fat:																	
a	Yield from 1 lb., raw meat with bone and skin (item 1734a).	8.1 oz	229	57.5	559	61.8	32.7	0	27	634	7.8	151	692	(0)	1.35	.62	11.9	—
b	Yield from 1 lb., raw meat without bone and skin (item 1734b).	8.6 oz	244	57.5	595	65.9	34.9	0	29	676	8.3	161	738	(0)	1.44	.66	12.7	—

(A)	(B)			(C)	(D)	(E)	(F)	(G)	(H)	(I)	(J)	(K)	(L)	(M)	(N)	(O)	(P)	(Q)
c	Chopped or diced	1 cup	140	57.5	342	37.8	20.0	0	17	388	4.8	93	423	(0)	0.83	0.38	7.3	—
d	Ground	1 cup	110	57.5	268	29.7	15.7	0	13	305	3.7	73	333	(0)	.65	.30	5.7	—
e	Pound	1 lb	454	57.5	1,107	122.5	64.9	0	54	1,256	15.4	300	1,372	(0)	2.68	1.22	23.6	—
f	Piece, approx. 2½ in. long, 2½ in. wide, ¼ in. thick; wt., 1 oz.	3 pieces or 3 oz.	85	57.5	207	23.0	12.2	0	10	235	2.9	56	258	(0)	.50	.23	4.4	—
	Picnic:																	
1749	Raw, lean with fat:																	
a	With bone and skin (61% lean, 22% fat) (refuse: bone and skin, 18%).[1]	1 lb	454	58.9	1,083	59.0	92.2	0	34	664	9.0	207	944	(0)	2.87	.69	15.4	—
b	Without bone and skin (74% lean, 26% fat)	1 lb	454	58.9	1,315	71.7	112.0	0	41	807	10.9	251	1,147	(0)	3.49	.84	18.6	—
	Cooked (simmered):																	
1750	Lean with fat (74% lean, 26% fat):																	
a	Yield from 1 lb., raw meat with bone and skin (item 1749a).	8.4 oz	238	45.7	890	55.2	72.6	0	24	331	7.1	97	442	(0)	1.29	.60	11.4	—
b	Yield from 1 lb., raw meat without bone and skin (item 1749b).	10.2 oz	290	45.7	1,085	67.3	88.5	0	29	403	8.7	118	538	(0)	1.57	.73	13.9	—
c	Cup, chopped or diced pieces (not packed)	1 cup	140	45.7	524	32.5	42.7	0	14	195	4.2	57	260	(0)	.76	.35	6.7	—
d	Pound	1 lb	454	45.7	1,696	105.2	138.3	0	45	631	13.6	184	842	(0)	2.45	1.13	21.8	—
e	Piece, approx. 2½ in. long, 2½ in. wide, ¼ in. thick; wt., 1 oz.	3 pieces or 3 oz.	85	45.7	318	19.7	25.9	0	9	118	2.6	34	158	(0)	.46	.21	4.1	—
1752	Lean, trimmed of separable fat:																	
a	Yield from 1 lb., raw meat with bone and skin (item 1749a).	6.2 oz	176	60.3	373	51.0	17.2	0	21	310	6.3	89	408	(0)	1.16	.53	10.4	—
b	Yield from 1 lb., raw meat without bone and skin (item 1749b).	7.6 oz	215	60.3	456	62.4	21.1	0	26	378	7.7	109	499	(0)	1.42	.65	12.7	—
c	Cup, chopped or diced pieces (not packed)	1 cup	140	60.3	297	40.6	13.7	0	17	246	5.0	71	325	(0)	.92	.42	8.3	—
d	Pound	1 lb	454	60.3	962	131.5	44.5	0	54	798	16.3	230	1,052	(0)	2.99	1.36	26.8	—
e	Piece, approx. 2½ in. long, 2½ in. wide, ¼ in. thick; wt., 1 oz.	3 pieces or 3 oz.	85	60.3	180	24.7	8.3	0	10	150	3.1	43	198	(0)	.56	.26	5.0	—
	Spareribs:																	
1761	Raw, lean meat with fat and bone (refuse: bone, 40%).[1]	1 lb	454	51.8	976	39.2	89.7	0	22	432	5.9	137	627	(0)	1.91	.46	10.2	—
1762	Cooked (braised), lean meat with fat:																	
a	Yield from 1 lb., raw spareribs (item 1761)	6.3 oz	180	39.7	792	37.4	70.0	0	16	218	4.7	65	299	(0)	.77	.38	6.1	—
b	Pound	1 lb	454	39.7	1,996	94.3	176.5	0	41	549	11.8	165	754	(0)	1.95	.95	15.4	—
	Pork, cured: [**]																	
	Dry, long cure, country style:																	
	Ham, unbaked:																	
1766	Medium fatness, lean meat with fat, bone, skin (refuse: bone and skin, 13%).[1]	1 lb	454	42	1,535	66.7	138	1.2	—	—	—	3,415	1,067	(0)	—	—	—	—
1767	Relatively lean, lean meat with fat, bone, skin (refuse: bone and skin, 14%).[1]	1 lb	454	49	1,209	76.1	98	1.2	—	—	—	3,896	1,218	(0)	—	—	—	—
	Light cure, commercial:																	
	Ham:																	
1768	Unbaked, lean with fat:																	
a	With bone and skin (65% lean, 21% fat) (refuse: bone and skin, 14%).[1]	1 lb	454	56.5	1,100	68.3	89.7	0	39	632	10.1	3,497	1,093	(0)	2.82	.76	16.0	—
b	Without bone and skin (76% lean, 24% fat)	1 lb	454	56.5	1,279	79.4	104.3	0	45	735	11.8	4,065	1,270	(0)	3.28	.88	18.6	—
	Baked or roasted:																	
1769	Lean with fat (84% lean, 16% fat):																	
a	Yield from 1 lb., unbaked ham with bone and skin (item 1768a).	11.3 oz	320	53.6	925	66.9	70.7	0	29	550	8.3	2,395	749	(0)	1.50	.58	11.5	—
b	Yield from 1 lb., unbaked ham without bone and skin (item 1768b).	13.1 oz	372	53.6	1,075	77.7	82.2	0	33	640	9.7	2,782	870	(0)	1.75	.67	13.4	—
	Cup (not packed):																	
c	Chopped or diced	1 cup	140	53.6	405	29.3	30.9	0	13	241	3.6	1,049	328	(0)	.66	.25	5.0	—
d	Ground	1 cup	110	53.6	318	23.0	24.3	0	10	189	2.9	823	258	(0)	.52	.20	4.0	—
e	Pound	1 lb	454	53.6	1,311	94.8	100.2	0	41	780	11.8	3,394	1,062	(0)	2.13	.82	16.3	—
f	Piece, approx. 4⅛ in. long, 2¼ in. wide, ¼ in. thick; wt., 1½ oz.	2 pieces or 3 oz.	85	53.6	246	17.8	18.8	0	8	146	2.2	637	199	(0)	.40	.15	3.1	—
1771	Lean, trimmed of separable fat:																	
a	Yield from 1 lb., unbaked ham with bone and skin (item 1768a).	8.7 oz	246	61.9	460	62.2	21.6	0	27	492	7.9	2,227	697	(0)	1.43	.57	11.1	—
b	Yield from 1 lb., unbaked ham without bone and skin (item 1768b).	10.2 oz	288	61.9	539	72.9	25.3	0	32	576	9.2	2,610	816	(0)	1.67	.66	13.0	—
	Cup (not packed):																	
c	Chopped or diced	1 cup	140	61.9	262	35.4	12.3	0	15	280	4.5	1,267	396	(0)	.81	.32	6.3	—
d	Ground	1 cup	110	61.9	206	27.8	9.7	0	12	220	3.5	995	311	(0)	.64	.25	5.0	—
e	Pound	1 lb	454	61.9	848	114.8	39.9	0	50	907	14.5	4,110	1,286	(0)	2.63	1.04	20.4	—
f	Piece, approx. 4⅛ in. long, 2¼ in. wide, ¼ in. thick; wt., 1½ oz.	2 pieces or 3 oz.	85	61.9	159	21.5	7.5	0	9	170	2.7	770	241	(0)	.49	.20	3.8	—

[1] Measure and weight apply to food as it is described with inedible part or parts (refuse) included.

[**] For further information about items and basis of vitamin and mineral values, see Appendix B, section on Foods Measured in Pieces, Slices, and Other Units and Appendix C, section on Meats. Values for cooked items apply to products prepared without added salt or other seasoning.

TABLE 1.—*Nutritive values for household measures and market units of foods*—Continued

[Item numbers correspond to those in table 1 of Handbook No. 8, revised 1963. Values in parentheses denote imputed values usually from another form of the food or from a similar food. Zeros in parentheses indicate that amount of a constituent, if present, is probably too small to be measured. Dashes (—) denote lack of reliable data for a constituent believed to be present in a measurable amount. Calculated values, as those based on a recipe, are not in parentheses]

Item No.	Food, approximate measures, units, and weight (edible part unless footnotes indicate otherwise)			Water	Food energy	Protein	Fat	Carbohydrate	Calcium	Phosphorus	Iron	Sodium	Potassium	Vitamin A value	Thiamin	Riboflavin	Niacin	Ascorbic acid
(A)	(B)			(C)	(D)	(E)	(F)	(G)	(H)	(I)	(J)	(K)	(L)	(M)	(N)	(O)	(P)	(Q)
			Grams	*Percent*	*Calories*	*Grams*	*Grams*	*Grams*	*Milligrams*	*Milligrams*	*Milligrams*	*Milligrams*	*Milligrams*	*International units*	*Milligrams*	*Milligrams*	*Milligrams*	*Milligrams*
	Pork, cured[40]—Continued																	
	Light cure, commercial—Continued																	
	Shoulder cuts (Boston butt and picnic):																	
	Boston butt:																	
1773	Unbaked, lean with fat:																	
a	With bone and skin (70% lean, 23% fat) (refuse: bone and skin, 7%).[1]	1 lb	454	55.7	1,227	72.5	101.7	0	42	641	11.0	3,712	1,160	(0)	2.99	0.81	17.0	—
b	Without bone and skin (75% lean, 25% fat).	1 lb	454	55.7	1,320	78.0	109.3	0	45	689	11.8	3,994	1,248	(0)	3.22	.87	18.2	—
	Baked or roasted:																	
1774	Lean with fat (83% lean, 17% fat):																	
a	Yield from 1 lb., unbaked meat with bone and skin (item 1773a).	11 oz	312	47.7	1,030	71.4	80.2	0	81	577	9.4	2,556	800	(0)	1.65	.66	12.8	—
b	Yield from 1 lb., unbaked meat without bone and skin (item 1773b).	11.8 oz	336	47.7	1,109	76.9	86.4	0	84	622	10.1	2,753	861	(0)	1.78	.71	13.8	—
	Cup (not packed):																	
c	Chopped or diced	1 cup	140	47.7	462	32.1	36.0	0	14	259	4.2	1,149	360	(0)	.74	.29	5.7	—
d	Ground	1 cup	110	47.7	363	25.2	28.3	0	11	204	3.3	902	282	(0)	.58	.23	4.5	—
e	Pound	1 lb	454	47.7	1,497	103.9	116.6	0	45	839	13.6	3,720	1,164	(0)	2.40	.95	18.6	—
f	Piece, approx. 2½ in. long, 2½ in. wide, ¼ in. thick; wt., 1 oz.	3 pieces or 3 oz.	85	47.7	281	19.5	21.8	0	9	157	2.6	698	218	(0)	.45	.18	3.5	—
1776	Lean, trimmed of separable fat:																	
a	Yield from 1 lb., unbaked meat with bone and skin (item 1773a).	9.1 oz	259	53.9	629	72.0	35.7	0	81	565	9.3	2,578	806	(0)	1.66	.65	13.0	—
b	Yield from 1 lb., unbaked meat without bone and skin (item 1773b).	9.8 oz	279	53.9	678	77.6	38.5	0	88	608	10.0	2,778	869	(0)	1.79	.70	14.0	—
	Cup (not packed):																	
c	Chopped or diced	1 cup	140	53.9	340	38.9	19.3	0	17	305	5.0	1,398	436	(0)	.90	.35	7.0	—
d	Ground	1 cup	110	53.9	267	30.6	15.2	0	13	240	4.0	1,095	343	(0)	.70	.28	5.5	—
e	Pound	1 lb	454	53.9	1,102	126.1	62.6	0	54	989	16.3	4,514	1,412	(0)	2.90	1.18	22.7	—
f	Piece, approx. 2½ in. long, 2½ in. wide, ¼ in. thick; wt., 1 oz.	3 pieces or 3 oz.	85	53.9	207	23.6	11.7	0	10	185	3.1	845	264	(0)	.54	.21	4.3	—
	Picnic:																	
1778	Unbaked, lean with fat:																	
a	With bone and skin (57% lean, 25% fat) (refuse: bone and skin, 18%).[1]	1 lb	454	56.7	1,060	62.5	87.8	0	37	558	9.3	3,200	1,000	(0)	2.58	.69	14.6	—
b	Without bone and skin (70% lean, 30% fat).	1 lb	454	56.7	1,298	76.2	107.0	0	45	680	11.3	3,901	1,219	(0)	3.15	.84	17.8	—
	Baked or roasted:																	
1779	Lean with fat (82% lean, 18% fat):																	
a	Yield from 1 lb., unbaked meat with bone and skin (item 1778a).	9.7 oz	275	48.8	888	61.6	69.3	0	28	501	8.0	2,205	690	(0)	1.43	.55	11.0	—
b	Yield from 1 lb., unbaked meat without bone and skin (item 1778b).	11.8 oz	336	48.8	1,085	75.3	84.7	0	34	612	9.7	2,696	843	(0)	1.75	.67	13.4	—
	Cup (not packed):																	
c	Chopped or diced	1 cup	140	48.8	452	31.4	35.3	0	14	255	4.1	1,124	352	(0)	.73	.28	5.6	—
d	Ground	1 cup	110	48.8	355	24.6	27.7	0	11	200	3.2	881	276	(0)	.57	.22	4.4	—
e	Pound	1 lb	454	48.8	1,465	101.6	114.3	0	45	826	13.2	3,637	1,138	(0)	2.36	.91	18.1	—
f	Piece, approx. 2½ in. long, 2½ in. wide, ¼ in. thick; wt., 1 oz.	3 pieces or 3 oz.	85	48.8	275	19.0	21.4	0	9	155	2.5	680	213	(0)	.44	.17	3.4	—
1781	Lean, trimmed of separable fat:																	
a	Yield from 1 lb., unbaked meat with bone and skin (item 1778a).	6.8 oz	192	57.2	405	54.5	19.0	0	25	422	7.1	1,951	610	(0)	1.25	.50	9.6	—
b	Yield from 1 lb., unbaked meat without bone and skin (item 1778b).	8.3 oz	235	57.2	496	66.7	23.3	0	31	517	8.7	2,388	747	(0)	1.53	.61	11.8	—
	Cup (not packed):																	
c	Chopped or diced	1 cup	140	57.2	295	39.8	13.9	0	18	308	5.2	1,425	446	(0)	.91	.36	7.0	—
d	Ground	1 cup	110	57.2	232	31.2	10.9	0	14	242	4.1	1,117	349	(0)	.72	.29	5.5	—
e	Pound	1 lb	454	57.2	957	128.8	44.9	0	59	998	16.8	4,611	1,443	(0)	2.95	1.18	22.7	—
f	Piece, approx. 2½ in. long, 2½ in. wide, ¼ in. thick; wt., 1 oz.	3 pieces or 3 oz.	85	57.2	179	24.1	8.4	0	11	187	3.1	863	270	(0)	.55	.22	4.3	—

(A)	(B)			(C)	(D)	(E)	(F)	(G)	(H)	(I)	(J)	(K)	(L)	(M)	(N)	(O)	(P)	(Q)
	Pork, cured, canned:																	
	Ham:																	
1783	Total can contents:																	
a	Can, net wt., 16 oz. (1 lb.)	1 can or 1 lb	454	65.0	875	83.0	55.8	4.1	50	708	12.2	(4,250)	(1,328)	(0)	2.40	0.86	17.2	—
b	Can, net wt., 48 oz. (3 lb.)	1 can	1,361	65.0	2,627	249.1	167.4	12.2	150	2,123	36.7	(12,754)	(3,986)	(0)	7.21	2.59	51.7	—
c	Can, net wt., 128 oz. (8 lb.)	1 can	3,629	65.0	7,004	664.1	446.4	32.7	399	5,661	98.0	(34,002)	(10,626)	(0)	19.23	6.90	137.9	—
	Pork, cured. See also Bacon (items 125–129).																	
	Pork sausage. See Sausage, cold cuts, and luncheon meats (items 2013–2016).																	
	Potatoes: [55]																	
1785	Raw:																	
	With skin:																	
	Pared by mechanical methods (refuse: parings and trimmings, 25%): [1]																	
	Potato:																	
a	Long type, 2⅓-in. diam., 4¾ in. long	1 potato	250	79.8	143	3.9	.2	32.1	13	99	1.1	6	763	Trace	.19	.08	2.8	[306] 38
b	Round type, 2½-in. diam. (medium size, approx. 3 per pound).	1 potato	150	79.8	86	2.4	.1	19.2	8	60	.7	3	458	Trace	.11	.05	1.7	[306] 23
c	Pound	1 lb	454	79.8	259	7.1	.3	58.2	24	180	2.0	10	1,385	Trace	.34	.14	5.1	[306] 68
	Pared with split-knife peeler (refuse: parings and trimmings, 10%): [1]																	
	Potato:																	
d	Long type, 2⅓-in. diam., 4¾ in. long	1 potato	250	79.8	171	4.7	.2	38.5	16	119	1.4	7	916	Trace	.23	.09	3.4	[306] 45
e	Round type, 2½-in. diam. (medium size, approx. 3 per pound).	1 potato	150	79.8	103	2.8	.1	23.1	9	72	.8	4	549	Trace	.14	.05	2.0	[306] 27
f	Pound	1 lb	454	79.8	310	8.6	.4	69.8	29	216	2.4	12	1,661	Trace	.41	.16	6.1	[306] 82
	Without skin:																	
g	Chopped, diced, or sliced	1 cup	150	79.8	114	3.2	.2	25.7	11	80	.9	5	611	Trace	.15	.06	2.3	[306] 30
h	Pound	1 lb	454	79.8	345	9.5	.5	77.6	32	240	2.7	14	1,846	Trace	.45	.18	6.8	[306] 91
	Cooked:																	
1786	Baked in skin (refuse: skins and adhering potato, 23%): [1]																	
a	Potato, long type, 2⅓-in. diam., 4¾ in. long (dimensions of uncooked potato).	1 potato	202	75.1	145	4.0	.2	32.8	14	101	1.1	[20] 6	782	Trace	.15	.07	2.7	[306] 31
b	Pound	1 lb	454	75.1	325	9.1	.3	73.7	31	227	2.4	[20] 14	1,757	Trace	.34	.15	6.1	[306] 69
1787	Boiled in skin:																	
	Whole (refuse: skins and eyes, 9%); [1] (dimensions apply to uncooked potato):																	
a	Potato, long type, 2⅓-in. diam., 4¾ in. long	1 potato	250	79.8	173	4.8	.2	38.9	16	121	1.4	[20] 7	926	Trace	.20	.09	3.4	[306] 36
b	Potato, round type, 2½-in. diam. (medium size).	1 potato	150	79.8	104	2.9	.1	23.3	10	72	.8	[20] 4	556	Trace	.12	.05	2.0	[306] 22
c	Pound	1 lb	454	79.8	314	8.7	.4	70.6	29	219	2.5	[20] 12	1,680	Trace	.37	.17	6.2	[306] 66
d	Diced or sliced	1 cup	155	79.8	118	3.3	.2	26.5	11	82	.9	[20] 5	631	Trace	.14	.06	2.3	[306] 25
e	Pound	1 lb	454	79.8	345	9.5	.5	77.6	32	240	2.7	[20] 14	1,846	Trace	.41	.18	6.8	[306] 73
1788	Boiled, pared before cooking:																	
	Whole (dimensions apply to uncooked potato):																	
	Pared by mechanical methods:																	
a	Long type, 2⅓-in. diam., 4¾ in. long	1 potato	188	82.8	122	3.6	.2	27.3	11	79	.9	[20] 4	536	Trace	.17	.07	2.3	[306] 30
b	Round type, 2½-in. diam. (medium size)	1 potato	112	82.8	73	2.1	.1	16.2	7	47	.6	[20] 2	319	Trace	.10	(.05)	1.3	[306] 18
	Pared by split-knife peeler:																	
c	Long type, 2⅓-in. diam., 4¾ in. long	1 potato	225	82.8	146	4.3	.2	32.6	14	95	1.1	[20] 5	641	Trace	.20	.08	2.7	[306] 36
d	Round type, 2½-in. diam. (medium size)	1 potato	135	82.8	88	2.6	.1	19.6	8	57	.7	[20] 3	385	Trace	.12	(.05)	1.6	[306] 22
e	Diced or sliced	1 cup	155	82.8	101	2.9	.2	22.5	9	65	.8	[20] 3	442	Trace	.14	.05	1.9	[306] 25
f	Pound	1 lb	454	82.8	295	8.6	.5	65.8	27	191	2.3	[20] 9	1,293	Trace	.41	.14	5.4	[306] 78
1789	French fried: [307]																	
	Strips:																	
a	Length, over 3½ in. to 4 in	10 strips	78	44.7	214	3.4	10.3	28.1	12	87	1.0	[20] 5	665	Trace	.10	.06	2.4	[306] 16
b	Length, over 2 in. to 3½ in	10 strips	50	44.7	137	2.2	6.6	18.0	8	56	.7	[20] 3	427	Trace	.07	.04	1.6	[306] 11
c	Length, 1–2 in	10 strips	35	44.7	96	1.5	4.6	12.6	5	39	.5	[20] 2	299	Trace	.05	.03	1.1	[306] 7
d	Pound	1 lb	454	44.7	1,243	19.5	59.9	163.3	68	508	5.9	[20] 27	3,869	Trace	.59	.36	14.1	[306] 95
1790	Fried from raw: [307]																	
a	Cup	1 cup	170	46.9	456	6.8	24.1	55.4	26	172	1.9	379	1,318	Trace	.20	.12	4.8	[306] 32
b	Pound	1 lb	454	46.9	1,216	18.1	64.4	147.9	68	458	5.0	1,012	3,515	Trace	.54	.32	12.7	[306] 86

[1] Measure and weight apply to food as it is described with inedible part or parts (refuse) included.

[20] Value is for unsalted product. If salt is used, increase value by 236 mg. per 100 g. of vegetable—an estimated figure based on typical amount of salt (0.6%) in canned vegetables. See also Appendix C, section on Cooked Vegetables

[40] For further information about items and basis of vitamin and mineral values, see Appendix B, section on Foods Measured in Pieces, Slices, and Other Units and Appendix C, section on Meats

Values for cooked items apply to products prepared without added salt or other seasoning.

[55] Oxalic acid present may combine with calcium and magnesium to form insoluble compounds. For further information, see Appendix D, section on Minerals and Oxalic Acid

[306] Based on year-round average of 20 mg. per 100 g. For recently dug potatoes, apply basis of 26 mg. per 100 g.; after 3 months' storage, 13 mg. per 100 g.; after 6 months', 9 mg. per 100 g. See also Appendix C, section on Potatoes Values for cooked potatoes (items 1786 to 1795) are derived from raw potatoes with year-round average value of 20 mg. per 100 g.

[307] For information on ingredients used in preparation, see ARS 62–13 (7), table 22, p. 26. Number of potatoes to use in potato dishes may differ from number given in ARS 62–13 if sizes of potatoes shown in present publication are used.

TABLE 1.—*Nutritive values for household measures and market units of foods*—Continued

[Item numbers correspond to those in table 1 of Handbook No. 8, revised 1963. Values in parentheses denote imputed values usually from another form of the food or from a similar food. Zeros in parentheses indicate that amount of a constituent, if present, is probably too small to be measured. Dashes (—) denote lack of reliable data for a constituent believed to be present in a measurable amount. Calculated values, as those based on a recipe, are not in parentheses]

Item No.	Food, approximate measures, units, and weight (edible part unless footnotes indicate otherwise)			Water	Food energy	Protein	Fat	Carbohydrate	Calcium	Phosphorus	Iron	Sodium	Potassium	Vitamin A value	Thiamin	Riboflavin	Niacin	Ascorbic acid
(A)	(B)			(C)	(D)	(E)	(F)	(G)	(H)	(I)	(J)	(K)	(L)	(M)	(N)	(O)	(P)	(Q)
			Grams	Percent	Calories	Grams	Grams	Grams	Milligrams	Milligrams	Milligrams	Milligrams	Milligrams	International units	Milligrams	Milligrams	Milligrams	Milligrams
	Potatoes [55]—Continued																	
	Cooked—Continued																	
1791	Hashed brown after holding overnight: [307]																	
a	Cup	1 cup	155	54.2	355	4.8	18.1	45.1	19	122	1.4	446	736	Trace	0.12	0.08	3.3	[306] 14
b	Pound	1 lb	454	54.2	1,039	14.1	53.1	132.0	54	358	4.1	1,306	2,155	Trace	.36	.23	9.5	[306] 41
1792	Mashed, milk added: [307]																	
a	Cup	1 cup	210	82.8	137	4.4	1.5	27.3	50	103	.8	632	548	40	.17	.11	2.1	[306] 21
b	Pound	1 lb	454	82.8	295	9.5	3.2	59.0	109	222	1.8	1,365	1,184	90	.36	.23	4.5	[306] 45
1793	Mashed, milk and table fat added: [307]																	
a	Cup	1 cup	210	79.8	197	4.4	9.0	25.8	50	101	.8	695	525	360	.17	.11	2.1	[306] 19
b	Pound	1 lb	454	79.8	426	9.5	19.5	55.8	109	218	1.8	1,501	1,134	770	.36	.23	4.5	[306] 41
	Scalloped and au gratin: [307]																	
1794	With cheese:																	
a	Cup	1 cup	245	71.1	355	13.0	19.4	33.3	311	299	1.2	1,095	750	780	.15	.29	2.2	[306] 25
b	Pound	1 lb	454	71.1	658	24.0	35.8	61.7	576	553	2.3	2,028	1,388	1,450	.27	.54	4.1	[306] 45
1795	Without cheese:																	
a	Cup	1 cup	245	76.7	255	7.4	9.6	36.0	132	181	1.0	870	801	390	.15	.22	2.5	[306] 27
b	Pound	1 lb	454	76.7	472	13.6	17.7	66.7	245	336	1.8	1,610	1,483	730	.27	.41	4.5	[306] 50
	Dehydrated mashed: [308]																	
	Flakes without milk:																	
1797	Dry form:																	
a	Cup	1 cup	45	5.2	164	3.2	.3	37.8	[309] 16	(78)	.8	40	(720)	Trace	.10	.03	2.4	14
b	Pound	1 lb	454	5.2	1,651	32.7	2.7	381.0	[309] 159	(785)	7.7	404	(7,258)	Trace	1.04	.27	24.5	145
1798	Prepared, water, milk, table fat, salt added:																	
a	Cup	1 cup	210	79.3	195	4.0	6.7	30.5	[309] 65	99	.6	485	601	270	.08	.08	1.9	11
b	Pound	1 lb	454	79.3	422	8.6	14.5	65.8	[309] 141	213	1.4	1,048	1,297	590	.18	.18	4.1	23
	Granules without milk:																	
1799	Dry form:																	
a	Cup	1 cup	200	7.1	704	16.6	1.2	160.8	[309] 88	406	4.8	168	(3,200)	Trace	.32	.22	9.8	38
b	Pound	1 lb	454	7.1	1,597	37.6	2.7	364.7	[309] 200	921	10.9	381	(7,258)	Trace	.73	.50	22.2	86
1800	Prepared, water, milk, table fat, salt added:																	
a	Cup	1 cup	210	78.6	202	4.2	7.6	30.2	[309] 67	109	1.1	538	609	230	.08	.11	1.5	6
b	Pound	1 lb	454	78.6	435	9.1	16.3	65.3	[309] 145	236	2.3	1,161	1,315	500	.18	.23	3.2	14
	Granules with milk:																	
1801	Dry form:																	
a	Cup	1 cup	200	6.3	716	21.8	2.2	155.4	[309] 284	474	7.0	164	3,696	120	.38	.60	8.4	32
b	Pound	1 lb	454	6.3	1,624	49.4	5.0	352.4	[309] 644	1,075	15.9	372	8,383	270	.86	1.36	19.1	73
1802	Prepared, water, milk, table fat, salt added:																	
a	Cup	1 cup	210	81.4	166	4.2	4.6	27.5	[309] 65	92	1.3	491	704	190	.06	.11	1.7	6
b	Pound	1 lb	454	81.4	358	9.1	10.0	59.4	[309] 141	200	2.7	1,061	1,520	410	.14	.23	3.6	14
	Frozen:																	
	Diced, shredded, or crinkle cut for hashed browning:																	
1803	Not thawed:																	
a	Container, net wt., 12 oz	1 container	340	81.0	248	4.1	Trace	59.2	34	102	2.4	27	578	Trace	.24	.03	2.0	31
b	Container, net wt., 32 oz. (2 lb.)	1 container	907	81.0	662	10.9	Trace	157.8	91	272	6.3	73	1,542	Trace	.63	.09	5.4	82
	Cup:																	
c	Crinkle cut	1 cup	110	81.0	80	1.3	Trace	19.1	11	33	.8	9	187	Trace	.08	.01	.7	10
d	Diced and shredded	1 cup	140	81.0	102	1.7	Trace	24.4	14	42	1.0	11	238	Trace	.10	.01	.8	13
e	Pound	1 lb	454	81.0	331	5.4	Trace	78.9	45	136	3.2	36	771	Trace	.32	.05	2.7	41
1804	Cooked (hashed brown): [307]																	
a	Yield from 12 oz., frozen hashed brown potatoes.	1⅓ cups	205	56.1	459	4.1	23.6	59.5	37	103	2.5	613	580	Trace	.14	.04	2.1	16
b	Yield from 2 lb. frozen hashed brown potatoes.	3½ cups	545	56.1	1,221	10.9	62.7	158.1	98	273	6.5	1,630	1,542	Trace	.38	.11	5.5	44
c	Cup	1 cup	155	56.1	347	3.1	17.8	45.0	28	78	1.9	463	439	Trace	.11	.03	1.6	12
d	Pound	1 lb	454	56.1	1,016	9.1	52.2	131.5	82	227	5.4	1,356	1,284	Trace	.32	.09	4.5	36
	French fried (straight-cut and crinkle-cut strips, with cross section, approx. ½ × ½ in.): [310]																	
1805	Not thawed:																	
	Container:																	

(A)	(B)			(C)	(D)	(E)	(F)	(G)	(H)	(I)	(J)	(K)	(L)	(M)	(N)	(O)	(P)	(Q)
a	Net wt., 9 oz	1 container	255	63.5	434	7.1	16.6	66.6	18	171	3.6	[20] 8	1,290	Trace	0.36	0.05	5.4	51
b	Net wt., 16 oz. (1 lb.)	1 container or 1 lb.	454	63.5	771	12.7	29.5	118.4	32	304	6.4	[20] 14	2,295	Trace	.64	.09	9.5	91
c	Net wt., 32 oz. (2 lb.)	1 container	907	63.5	1,542	25.4	59.0	236.7	63	608	12.7	[20] 27	4,589	Trace	1.27	.18	19.0	181
	Strips:																	
d	Length, over 3½ in. to 4 in	10 strips	100	63.5	170	2.8	6.5	26.1	7	67	1.4	[20] 3	506	Trace	.14	.02	2.1	20
e	Length, over 2 in. to 3½ in	10 strips	65	63.5	111	1.8	4.2	17.0	5	44	.9	[20] 2	329	Trace	.09	.01	1.4	13
f	Length, 1–2 in	10 strips	45	63.5	77	1.3	2.9	11.7	3	30	.6	[20] 1	228	Trace	.06	.01	.9	9
1806	Ovenheated:																	
	Yield from—																	
a	9 oz., frozen french-fried potatoes	7 oz	198	52.9	434	7.1	16.6	66.6	18	171	3.6	[20] 8	1,290	Trace	.28	.04	5.1	42
b	16 oz. (1 lb.), frozen french-fried potatoes	12⅖ oz	352	52.9	771	12.7	29.5	118.4	32	304	6.4	[20] 14	2,295	Trace	.49	.07	9.2	74
c	32 oz. (2 lb.), frozen french-fried potatoes	24⅘ oz	704	52.9	1,542	25.4	59.0	236.7	63	608	12.7	[20] 27	4,589	Trace	.99	.14	18.3	148
	Strips (dimensions before heating):																	
d	Length, over 3½ in. to 4 in	10 strips	78	52.9	172	2.8	6.6	26.3	7	67	1.4	[20] 3	509	Trace	.11	.02	2.0	16
e	Length, over 2 in. to 3½ in	10 strips	50	52.9	110	1.8	4.2	16.9	5	43	.9	[20] 2	326	Trace	.07	.01	1.3	11
f	Length, 1–2 in	10 strips	35	52.9	77	1.3	2.9	11.8	3	30	.6	[20] 1	228	Trace	.05	.01	.9	7
g	Pound	1 lb	454	52.9	998	16.3	38.1	152.9	41	390	8.2	[20] 18	2,957	Trace	.64	.09	11.8	95
1809	**Potato chips** (smooth and corrugated surface):																	
a	Chips, $^2/_{32}$–$^3/_{32}$ in. thick with oval cross section, 1¾ × 2½ in.	10 chips	20	1.8	114	1.1	8.0	10.0	8	28	.4	[311] —	226	Trace	.04	.01	1.0	3
b	Pound	1 lb	454	1.8	2,576	24.0	180.5	226.8	181	631	8.2	[311] —	5,126	Trace	.95	.32	21.8	73
c	Ounce	1 oz	28	1.8	161	1.5	11.3	14.2	11	39	.5	[311] —	320	Trace	.06	.02	1.4	5
	Potato salad, from home recipe, made with [307]—																	
1811	Cooked salad dressing, seasonings:																	
a	Cup	1 cup	250	76.0	248	6.8	7.0	40.8	80	160	1.5	1,320	798	350	.20	.18	2.8	28
b	Pound	1 lb	454	76.0	449	12.2	12.7	73.9	145	290	2.7	2,395	1,447	640	.36	.32	5.0	50
1812	Mayonnaise and french dressing, hard-cooked eggs, seasonings:																	
a	Cup	1 cup	250	72.4	363	7.5	23.0	33.5	48	158	2.0	1,200	740	450	.18	.15	2.3	28
b	Pound	1 lb	454	72.4	658	13.6	41.7	60.8	86	286	3.6	2,177	1,343	820	.32	.27	4.1	50
1813	**Potato sticks**, ¾–2¾ in. long with cross section, ⅛ × ⅛ in.:																	
a	Cup	1 cup	35	1.5	190	2.2	12.7	17.8	15	49	.6	[311] —	46	Trace	.07	.02	1.7	14
b	Pound	1 lb	454	1.5	2,468	29.0	165.1	230.4	200	631	8.2	[311] —	5,126	Trace	.95	.32	21.8	181
c	Ounce	1 oz	28	1.5	154	1.8	10.3	14.4	12	39	.5	[311] —	320	Trace	.06	.02	1.4	11
1814	**Pretzels:**																	
	Package:																	
a	Net wt., 11 oz. (3 rings (item 1814h) or logs (item 1814j)).	1 pkg	312	4.5	1,217	30.6	14.0	236.8	69	409	4.7	[312] 5,242	406	(0)	.06	.09	2.2	(0)
b	Net wt., 10 oz. (1 ring (item 1814g), thins (item 1814i), rods (item 1814k), or sticks (items 1814l–1814m)).	1 pkg	284	4.5	1,108	27.8	12.8	215.6	62	372	4.3	[312] 4,771	369	(0)	.06	.09	2.0	(0)
c	Net wt., 8 oz. (eight 1-oz. packets of sticks (item 1814l)).	1 pkg	227	4.5	885	22.2	10.2	172.3	50	297	3.4	[312] 3,814	295	(0)	.05	.07	1.6	(0)
d	Packet (approx. 45 sticks)	1 packet or 1 oz.	28	4.5	111	2.8	1.3	21.5	6	37	.4	[312] 476	37	(0)	.01	.01	.2	(0)
e	Net wt., 7½ oz. (dutch pretzels) (item 1814f)	1 pkg	213	4.5	831	20.9	9.6	161.7	47	279	3.2	[312] 3,578	277	(0)	.04	.06	1.5	(0)
	Pretzels:																	
	Twisted types: [313]																	
f	Dutch, 2¾ × 2⅝ × ⅝ in	1 pretzel	16	4.5	62	1.6	.7	12.1	4	21	.2	[312] 269	21	(0)	Trace	Trace	.1	(0)
	Rings:																	
g	1 ring (piece, 1½-in. diam. with 1-in.-diam. hole; cross section of ring, ¼ in.).	10 pretzels	20	4.5	78	2.0	.9	15.2	4	26	.3	[312] 336	26	(0)	Trace	.01	.1	(0)
h	3 rings, 1⅞ × 1¾ × ¼ in	10 pretzels	30	4.5	117	2.9	1.4	22.8	7	39	.5	[312] 504	39	(0)	.01	.01	.2	(0)
i	Thins, 3¼ × 2¼ × ¼ in	10 pretzels	60	4.5	234	5.9	2.7	45.5	13	79	.9	[312] 1,008	78	(0)	.01	.02	.4	(0)
	Extruded types:																	
j	Logs, 3 in. long, ½-in. diam	10 pretzels	50	4.5	195	4.9	2.3	38.0	11	66	.8	[312] 840	65	(0)	.01	.02	.4	(0)
k	Rods, 7½–7¾ in. long, ½-in. diam	1 pretzel	14	4.5	55	1.4	.6	10.6	3	18	.2	[312] 235	18	(0)	Trace	Trace	.1	(0)
	Sticks:																	
l	Piece, 3⅛ in. long, approx. ⅛-in. diam	10 pretzels	6	4.5	23	.6	.3	4.6	1	8	.1	[312] 101	8	(0)	Trace	Trace	Trace	(0)

[20] Value is for unsalted product. If salt is used, increase value by 236 mg. per 100 g. of vegetable—an estimated figure based on typical amount of salt (0.6%) in canned vegetables. See also Appendix C, section on Cooked Vegetables

[56] Oxalic acid present may combine with calcium and magnesium to form insoluble compounds. For further information, see Appendix D, section on Minerals and Oxalic Acid

[306] Based on year-round average of 20 mg. per 100 g. For recently dug potatoes, apply basis of 26 mg. per 100 g.; after 3 months' storage, 13 mg. per 100 g.; after 6 months', 9 mg. per 100 g. See also Appendix C, section on Potatoes Values for cooked potatoes (items 1786 to 1795) are derived from raw potatoes with year-round average value of 20 mg. per 100 g.

[307] For information on ingredients used in preparation, see ARS 62–13 (7), table 22, p. 26. Number of potatoes to use in potato dishes may differ from number given in ARS 62–13 if sizes of potatoes shown in present publication are used.

[308] Nutritive values apply to products without added vitamins and minerals. Ascorbic acid values vary widely. See also Appendix C, section on Potatoes

[309] Federal standards provide for addition of calcium stearoyl-2-lactylate as conditioning agent. If used, this salt may add about 26 mg. of calcium per 100 g. of dehydrated product (items 1797, 1799, 1801). Calcium values for mashed potatoes prepared from these items would also be increased by about 4 mg. per 100 g. of product.

[310] Nutritive values do not apply to other styles of frozen french-fried potatoes, such as shoestring, slices, dices, and rissole.

[311] Sodium content is variable and may be as high as 1,000 mg. per 100 g.

[312] Sodium content is variable. For example, very thin pretzel sticks contain about twice the average amount listed.

[313] Except for 1-ring pretzels, dimensions apply to perimeter of pretzel.

TABLE 1.—*Nutritive values for household measures and market units of foods*—Continued

[Item numbers correspond to those in table 1 of Handbook No. 8, revised 1963. Values in parentheses denote imputed values usually from another form of the food or from a similar food. Zeros in parentheses indicate that amount of a constituent, if present, is probably too small to be measured. Dashes (—) denote lack of reliable data for a constituent believed to be present in a measurable amount. Calculated values, as those based on a recipe, are not in parentheses]

Item No. (A)	Food, approximate measures, units, and weight (edible part unless footnotes indicate otherwise) (B)			Water (C)	Food energy (D)	Protein (E)	Fat (F)	Carbohydrate (G)	Calcium (H)	Phosphorus (I)	Iron (J)	Sodium (K)	Potassium (L)	Vitamin A value (M)	Thiamin (N)	Riboflavin (O)	Niacin (P)	Ascorbic acid (Q)
				Values for edible part of foods														
			Grams	*Percent*	*Calories*	*Grams*	*Grams*	*Grams*	*Milli-grams*	*Milli-grams*	*Milli-grams*	*Milli-grams*	*Milli-grams*	*Interna-tional units*	*Milli-grams*	*Milli-grams*	*Milli-grams*	*Milli-grams*
	Pretzels—Continued																	
	Pretzels—Continued																	
	Extruded types—Continued																	
	Sticks—Continued																	
m	Piece, 2¼ in. long, approx. ⅛-in. diam	10 pretzels	8	4.5	12	0.3	0.1	2.3	1	4	Trace	[312] 50	4	(0)	Trace	Trace	Trace	(0)
n	Pound	1 lb	454	4.5	1,769	44.5	20.4	344.3	100	594	6.8	[312] 7,620	590	(0)	0.09	0.14	3.2	(0)
	Prunes:																	
	Dehydrated, nugget type and pieces:																	
1816	Uncooked:																	
a	Cup	1 cup	100	2.5	344	3.3	.5	91.3	90	107	4.4	11	940	2,170	.12	.22	2.1	4
b	Pound	1 lb	454	2.5	1,560	15.0	2.3	414.1	408	485	20.0	50	4,264	9,840	.54	1.00	9.5	18
1817	Cooked, fruit and liquid with added sugar:[9]																	
a	Cup	1 cup	(280)	50.7	504	3.4	.6	131.9	87	104	4.2	11	921	2,130	.08	.20	2.0	3
b	Pound	1 lb	454	50.7	816	5.4	.9	213.6	141	168	6.8	18	1,492	3,450	.14	.32	3.2	5
	Dried, "softenized":																	
1818	Uncooked:																	
	Whole:																	
	With pits:																	
	Extra large size (average: not more than 43 per pound) (refuse: pits, 12%):[1]																	
a	Container, net wt., 16 oz. (1 lb.)	1 container or 1 lb.	454	28.0	1,018	8.4	2.4	269.1	204	315	15.6	32	2,770	6,390	.36	.68	6.4	12
b	10 prunes	10 prunes	122	28.0	274	2.3	.6	72.4	55	85	4.2	9	745	1,720	.10	.18	1.7	3
	Large size (average: not more than 53 per pound) (refuse: pits, 13%):[1]																	
c	Container, net wt., 16 oz. (1 lb.)	1 container or 1 lb.	454	28.0	1,006	8.3	2.4	266.0	201	312	15.4	32	2,739	6,310	.36	.67	6.3	12
d	10 prunes	10 prunes	97	28.0	215	1.8	.5	56.9	43	67	3.3	7	586	1,350	.08	.14	1.4	3
	Medium size (average: not more than 67 per pound) (refuse: pits, 14%):[1]																	
e	Container, net wt., 32 oz. (2 lb.)	1 container	907	28.0	1,989	16.4	4.7	525.7	398	616	30.4	62	5,413	12,480	.70	1.33	12.5	23
f	10 prunes	10 prunes	75	28.0	164	1.4	.4	43.5	33	51	2.5	5	448	1,030	.06	.11	1.0	2
g	Pound	1 lb	454	28.0	995	8.2	2.3	262.9	199	308	15.2	31	2,707	6,240	.35	.66	6.2	12
h	All sizes (refuse: pits, 13%)[1]	1 cup	185	28.0	411	3.4	1.0	108.5	82	127	6.3	13	1,117	2,580	.14	.27	2.6	5
	Without pits:																	
i	Container, net wt., 12 oz	1 container	340	28.0	867	7.1	2.0	229.2	173	269	13.3	27	2,360	5,440	.31	.58	5.4	10
j	Cup[10]	1 cup	180	28.0	459	3.8	1.1	121.3	92	142	7.0	14	1,249	2,880	.16	.31	2.9	5
k	10 prunes	10 prunes	102	28.0	260	2.1	.6	68.7	52	81	4.0	8	708	1,630	.09	.17	1.6	3
l	Pound	1 lb	454	28.0	1,157	9.5	2.7	305.7	231	358	17.7	36	3,148	7,260	.41	.77	7.3	14
	Chopped or ground:																	
m	Cup, not packed	1 cup	160	28.0	408	3.4	1.0	107.8	82	126	6.2	13	1,110	2,560	.14	.27	2.6	5
n	Cup, packed	1 cup	260	28.0	663	5.5	1.6	175.2	133	205	10.1	21	1,804	4,160	.23	.44	4.2	8
	Cooked, fruit and liquid (refuse: pits, 15%):[1,9]																	
1819	Without added sugar (served cold):																	
a	Cup	1 cup	250	66.4	253	2.1	.6	66.7	51	79	3.8	9	695	1,590	.07	.15	1.5	2
b	Pound	1 lb	454	66.4	459	3.9	1.2	121.1	93	143	6.9	15	1,261	2,890	.13	.27	2.7	4
1820	With added sugar (served cold):																	
a	Cup	1 cup	280	53.2	409	1.9	.5	107.3	45	71	3.6	7	624	1,430	.06	.14	1.4	2
b	Pound	1 lb	454	53.2	663	3.1	.8	173.9	73	116	5.8	12	1,010	2,310	.11	.23	2.3	4
1821	**Prune juice**, canned or bottled:																	
	Container and approx. contents:																	
a	Bottle, net contents, 4 fl. oz	1 bottle	128	80	99	.5	.1	24.3	18	26	5.2	3	301	—	.01	.01	.5	[314] 3
b	Bottle, net contents, 32 fl. oz. (1 qt.)	1 bottle or 1 qt.	1,025	80	789	4.1	1.0	194.8	144	205	42.0	21	2,409	—	.10	.10	4.1	[314] 21
c	Bottle, net contents, 40 fl. oz. (1 qt. 8 fl. oz.)	1 bottle	1,281	80	986	5.1	1.3	243.4	179	256	52.5	26	3,010	—	.13	.13	5.1	[314] 26
d	Cup	1 cup	256	80	197	1.0	.3	48.6	36	51	10.5	5	602	—	.03	.03	1.0	[314] 5
e	Glass (6 fl. oz.)	1 glass	192	80	148	.8	.2	36.5	27	38	7.9	4	451	—	.02	.02	.8	[314] 4
1822	**Prune whip**, baked:[13]																	
a	Served hot[315]	1 cup	90	57.3	140	4.0	.2	33.2	20	30	1.2	148	261	410	.02	.13	.5	2
b	Served cold[13]	1 cup	130	57.3	208	5.7	.3	48.0	29	43	1.7	218	377	600	.03	.18	.7	3
	Puddings with starch base, prepared from home recipe:[13,315]																	

(A)		(B)			(C)	(D)	(E)	(F)	(G)	(H)	(I)	(J)	(K)	(L)	(M)	(N)	(O)	(P)	(Q)
1823		Chocolate	1 cup	260	65.8	385	8.1	12.2	66.8	250	255	1.3	146	445	390	0.05	0.36	0.3	1
1824		Vanilla (blancmange)	1 cup	255	76.0	283	8.9	9.9	40.5	298	232	Trace	166	352	410	.08	.41	.3	2
		Puddings, other. See individual kinds; Bread, etc.																	
		Pudding mixes and puddings made from mixes:																	
		With starch base:																	
1825		Mix, chocolate, regular, dry form:																	
	a	Package, net wt., 6 oz	1 pkg	170	1.7	614	5.1	3.6	155.6	34	160	2.7	760	162	Trace	.08	.12	.7	0
	b	Package, net wt., 4 oz	1 pkg	113	1.7	408	3.4	2.4	103.4	23	106	1.8	505	107	Trace	.02	.08	.5	0
	c	Ounce	1 oz	28	1.7	102	.9	.6	25.9	6	27	.5	127	27	Trace	.01	.02	.1	0
1826		Pudding made with milk, cooked: [307, 315]																	
	a	Yield from 4 oz. of mix and 2 cups of milk	2¼ cups (approx.).	583	70.0	723	19.8	17.5	132.9	595	554	1.7	752	793	760	.12	.87	.6	8
	b	Cup	1 cup	260	70.0	322	8.8	7.8	59.3	265	247	.8	335	354	340	.05	.39	.3	2
1827		Mix, chocolate, instant, dry form:																	
	a	Package, net wt., 6¾ oz	1 pkg	191	.7	682	5.9	3.1	173.4	468	168	3.8	772	162	Trace	.02	.11	.6	0
	b	Package, net wt., 4½ oz	1 pkg	128	.7	457	4.0	2.0	116.2	314	113	2.6	517	109	Trace	.01	.08	.4	0
	c	Ounce	1 oz	28	.7	101	.9	.5	25.7	69	25	.6	115	24	Trace	Trace	.02	.1	0
1828		Pudding made with milk, without cooking:																	
	a	Yield from 4½ oz. of mix and 2 cups of milk	2⅓ cups (approx.).	616	68.7	770	18.5	15.4	150.3	887	561	3.1	764	795	800	.18	.92	.6	5
	b	Cup	1 cup	260	68.7	325	7.8	6.5	63.4	374	237	1.3	322	335	340	.08	.39	.3	2
1832		**Pumpkin, canned:** [316]																	
		Can and approx. contents:																	
	a	Size, 303 × 406 [14] (No. 303); net wt., 16 oz. (1 lb.).	1 can or 1 lb	454	90.2	150	4.5	1.4	35.8	113	118	1.8	[317] 9	1,089	29,030	.14	.23	2.7	23
	b	Size, 401 × 411 [14] (No. 2½); net wt., 29 oz. (1 lb. 13 oz.).	1 can	822	90.2	271	8.2	2.5	64.9	206	214	3.3	[317] 16	1,973	52,610	.25	.41	4.9	41
	c	Size, 603 × 700 [14] (No. 10); net wt., 106 oz. (6 lb. 10 oz.).	1 can	3,005	90.2	992	30.1	9.0	237.4	751	781	12.0	[317] 60	7,212	192,320	.90	1.50	18.0	150
	d	Cup	1 cup	245	90.2	81	2.5	.7	19.4	61	64	1.0	[317] 5	588	15,680	.07	.12	1.5	12
1833		**Pumpkin and squash seed kernels,** dry, hulled:																	
	a	Cup	1 cup	140	4.4	774	40.6	65.4	21.0	71	1,602	15.7	—	—	100	.34	.27	3.4	—
	b	Pound	1 lb	454	4.4	2,508	131.5	211.8	68.0	231	5,189	50.8	—	—	320	1.09	.86	10.9	—
1841		**Rabbit, domesticated,** flesh only, cooked (stewed):																	
	a	Yield from 1 lb., ready-to-cook rabbit	8.6 oz	245	59.8	529	71.8	24.7	0	51	635	3.7	100	902	—	.12	.17	27.7	—
		Cup:																	
	b	Chopped or diced	1 cup	140	59.8	302	41.0	14.1	0	29	363	2.1	57	515	—	.07	.10	15.8	—
	c	Ground	1 cup	110	59.8	238	32.2	11.1	0	23	285	1.7	45	405	—	.06	.08	12.4	—
	d	Pound	1 lb	454	59.8	980	132.9	45.8	0	95	1,175	6.8	186	1,669	—	.23	.32	51.3	—
1844		**Radishes,** common, raw:																	
		Whole, prepackaged without tops (round, red type); (refuse: stem ends, rootlets, trimmings, 10%): [1]																	
	a	Package, net wt., 6 oz	1 pkg	170	94.5	26	1.5	.2	5.5	46	47	1.5	28	493	20	.05	.05	.5	40
		Radish:																	
	b	Large (over 1- to 1¼-in. diam.)	10 radishes	90	94.5	14	.8	.1	2.9	24	25	.8	15	261	10	.02	.02	.2	21
	c	Medium (¾- to 1-in. diam.)	10 radishes	50	94.5	8	.5	Trace	1.6	14	14	.5	8	145	Trace	.01	.01	.1	12
	d	Sliced	1 cup	115	94.5	20	1.2	.1	4.1	35	36	1.2	21	370	10	.03	.03	.3	30
	e	Pound	1 lb	454	94.5	77	4.5	.5	16.3	136	141	4.5	82	1,461	50	.14	.14	1.4	118
		Raisins, natural (unbleached), seedless type: [318]																	
1846		Uncooked:																	
		Whole:																	
	a	Package, net wt., 15 oz. (approx. 3 cups, not packed (item 1846d), or 2½ cups, packed (item 1846e)).	1 pkg	425	18.0	1,228	10.6	.9	329.0	264	429	14.9	115	3,243	90	.47	.34	2.1	4
	b	Package, net wt., 1½ oz. (approx. ⅓ cup, not packed (item 1846d)).	1 pkg	43	18.0	124	1.1	.1	33.3	27	43	1.5	12	328	10	.05	.03	.2	Trace
	c	Package, net wt., ½ oz. (approx. 1½ tbsp.)	1 pkg	14	18.0	40	.4	Trace	10.8	9	14	.5	4	107	Trace	.02	.01	.1	Trace
		Cup: [10]																	
	d	Not packed	1 cup	145	18.0	419	3.6	.3	112.2	90	146	5.1	39	1,106	30	.16	.12	.7	1
	e	Packed	1 cup	165	18.0	477	4.1	.3	127.7	102	167	5.8	45	1,259	30	.18	.13	.8	2
	f	Tablespoon	1 tbsp	9	18.0	26	.2	Trace	7.0	6	9	.3	2	69	Trace	.01	.01	Trace	Trace

[1] Measure and weight apply to food as it is described with inedible part or parts (refuse) included.

[9] For information on proportion of fruit, sugar, and water used, see ARS 62–13 (7), section on Fruits, Dried and Dehydrated, p. 7, and table 20, p. 24.

[10] Separated pieces when stuck together.

[12] Cup measure made on product after it had cooled. See also Appendix B, section on Home-Prepared Foods

[13] For information on ingredients used, see ARS 62–13 (7), table 18, pp. 22–23.

[14] Dimensions of can: 1st dimension represents diameter; 2d dimension, height of can. 1st or left-hand digit in each dimension gives number of whole inches; next 2 digits give additional fraction of dimension expressed as 16th of an inch.

[307] For proportion of mix and added ingredients, see ARS 62–13 (7), table 19, p. 24.

[312] Sodium content is variable. For example, very thin pretzel sticks contain about twice the average amount listed.

[314] Applies to product without added ascorbic acid. With added ascorbic acid, based on claim that 6 fl. oz. contain 30 mg. of ascorbic acid, value for 4-fl. oz. can (item 1821a) is 20 mg.; for 32-fl. oz. can (item 1821b), 160 mg.; for 40-fl. oz. can (item 1821c), 200 mg.; for 1 cup (item 1821d), 40 mg.; for 6-fl. oz. glass (item 1821e), 30 mg.

[315] Cup measure made on product immediately after cooking. See also Appendix B, section on Home-Prepared Foods

[316] May be mixture of pumpkin and winter squash.

[317] Applies to product without added salt. If salt is added, value for sodium estimated on basis of 236 mg. per 100 g. is 1,070 mg. for 1-lb. can, 1,940 mg. for 29-oz. can, 7,092 mg. for 106-oz. can, 578 mg. for 1 cup.

[318] Prepared mainly from Thompson Seedless grapes.

TABLE 1.—*Nutritive values for household measures and market units of foods*—Continued

[Item numbers correspond to those in table 1 of Handbook No. 8, revised 1963. Values in parentheses denote imputed values usually from another form of the food or from a similar food. Zeros in parentheses indicate that amount of a constituent, if present, is probably too small to be measured. Dashes (—) denote lack of reliable data for a constituent believed to be present in a measurable amount. Calculated values, as those based on a recipe, are not in parentheses]

Item No. (A)	Food, approximate measures, units, and weight (edible part unless footnotes indicate otherwise) (B)			Water (C)	Food energy (D)	Protein (E)	Fat (F)	Carbohydrate (G)	Calcium (H)	Phosphorus (I)	Iron (J)	Sodium (K)	Potassium (L)	Vitamin A value (M)	Thiamin (N)	Riboflavin (O)	Niacin (P)	Ascorbic acid (Q)
			Grams	Percent	Calories	Grams	Grams	Grams	Milligrams	Milligrams	Milligrams	Milligrams	Milligrams	International units	Milligrams	Milligrams	Milligrams	Milligrams
	Raisins, natural (unbleached), seedless type [318]—Continued																	
	Uncooked—Continued																	
	Chopped:																	
g	Cup, not packed	1 cup	135	18.0	390	3.4	0.3	104.5	84	136	4.7	36	1,030	30	0.15	0.11	0.7	1
h	Cup, packed	1 cup	190	18.0	549	4.8	.4	147.1	118	192	6.7	51	1,450	40	.21	.15	1.0	2
	Ground:																	
i	Cup, not packed	1 cup	200	18.0	578	5.0	.4	154.8	124	202	7.0	54	1,526	40	.22	.16	1.0	2
j	Cup, packed	1 cup	270	18.0	780	6.8	.5	209.0	167	273	9.5	73	2,060	50	.30	.22	1.4	3
k	Pound (whole raisins, approx. 3⅛ cups, not packed (item 1846d), or 2¾ cups, packed (item 1846e)).	1 lb	454	18.0	1,311	11.3	.9	351.1	281	458	15.9	122	3,461	90	.50	.36	2.3	5
l	Ounce	1 oz	28	18.0	82	.7	.1	21.9	18	29	1.0	8	216	10	.03	.02	.1	Trace
1847	Cooked, fruit (seedless raisins) and liquid, added sugar. [9]	1 cup	295	41.4	628	3.5	.3	166.4	86	139	4.7	38	1,047	30	.12	.09	.6	Trace
	Raspberries:																	
	Raw:																	
1848	Black:																	
a	Cup	1 cup	134	80.8	98	2.0	1.9	21.0	40	29	1.2	1	267	Trace	(.04)	(.12)	(1.2)	24
b	Pound	1 lb	454	80.8	331	6.8	6.4	71.2	136	100	4.1	5	903	Trace	(.14)	(.41)	(4.1)	82
1849	Red:																	
a	Container, net contents, 1 pt. [71]	1 container	325	84.2	185	3.9	1.6	44.2	72	72	2.9	3	546	420	.10	.29	2.9	81
b	Cup	1 cup	123	84.2	70	1.5	.6	16.7	27	27	1.1	1	207	160	.04	.11	1.1	31
c	Pound	1 lb	454	84.2	259	5.4	2.3	61.7	100	100	4.1	5	762	590	.14	.41	4.1	113
	Canned, water pack, solids and liquid, without artificial sweetener:																	
1851	Red:																	
a	Cup	1 cup	243	90.1	85	1.7	.2	21.4	36	36	1.5	2	277	220	.02	.10	1.2	22
b	Pound	1 lb	454	90.1	159	3.2	.5	39.9	68	68	2.7	5	517	410	.05	.18	2.3	41
1852	Frozen, red, sweetened with nutritive sweetener, not thawed:																	
a	Container, net wt., 10 oz	1 container	284	74.3	278	2.0	.6	69.9	37	48	1.7	3	284	(200)	.06	.17	1.7	60
b	Cup [48]	1 cup	250	74.3	245	1.8	.5	61.5	33	43	1.5	3	250	(180)	.05	.15	1.5	53
	Redfish. See Ocean perch, Atlantic (items 1397–1398).																	
	Rennin products:																	
1859	Tablet (salts, starch, rennin enzyme), ⅝-in. diam., ¼-in. thick; wt., 0.9 g.:																	
a	Package, net wt., 0.35 oz. (12 tablets)	1 pkg	11	9.0	12	Trace	.1	2.7	386	22	—	2,453	—	0	0	0	0	0
b	Tablet	1 tablet	.9	9.0	1	Trace	Trace	.2	32	2	—	201	—	0	0	0	0	0
1860	Dessert, home-prepared with tablet: [13]																	
a	Yield from recipe [108]	2⅛ cups (approx.).	545	81.1	485	16.9	19.1	63.2	605	452	Trace	447	687	760	.16	.82	.5	5
b	Cup [315]	1 cup	255	81.1	227	7.9	8.9	29.6	283	212	Trace	209	321	360	.08	.38	.3	3
	Dessert mixes and desserts prepared from mixes:																	
	Chocolate:																	
1861	Mix, dry form:																	
a	Package, net wt., 2 oz	1 pkg	57	1.0	221	1.6	1.9	52.2	95	74	—	40	—	—	—	—	—	—
b	Tablespoon	1 tbsp	9	1.0	35	.3	.3	8.2	15	12	—	6	—	—	—	—	—	—
1862	Dessert made with milk: [307]																	
a	Yield from 2 oz. of mix and 2 cups of milk	2⅛ cups (approx.).	545	77.9	556	18.5	20.7	76.8	665	523	Trace	283	681	760	.16	.82	.5	5
b	Cup [315]	1 cup	255	77.9	260	8.7	9.7	36.0	311	245	Trace	133	319	360	.08	.38	.3	3
	Other flavors (vanilla, caramel, fruit flavorings):																	
1863	Mix, dry form:																	
a	Package, net wt., 1½ oz	1 pkg	43	.4	165	Trace	Trace	42.6	[319] 50	[319] 39	—	3	—	—	—	—	—	—
b	Tablespoon	1 tbsp	10	.4	38	Trace	Trace	9.9	[320] 12	[320] 9	—	1	—	—	—	—	—	—
1864	Dessert made with milk: [307]																	
a	Yield from 1½ oz. of mix and 2 cups of milk	2⅛ cups (approx.).	530	79.7	504	17.0	19.1	67.8	[321] 620	[321] 488	Trace	244	678	800	.16	.85	.5	5
b	Cup [315]	1 cup	250	79.7	238	8.0	9.0	32.0	[322] 293	[322] 230	Trace	115	320	380	.08	.40	.3	3
	Rhubarb: [55]																	

(A)		(B)		(C)	(D)	(E)	(F)	(G)	(H)	(I)	(J)	(K)	(L)	(M)	(N)	(O)	(P)	(Q)
1865		Raw:																
	a	With full tops (freshly harvested), (refuse: ends and full leaves, 55%).[1]	1 lb	454	94.8	33	1.2	0.2	7.6	196	37	1.6	4	512	200	(0.06)	(0.14)	(0.6)	18
	b	Well trimmed (refuse: ends and trimmings, 14%).[1]	1 lb	454	94.8	62	2.3	.4	14.4	374	70	3.1	8	979	390	(.12)	(.27)	(1.2)	35
	c	Diced	1 cup	122	94.8	20	.7	.1	4.5	117	22	1.0	2	306	120	(.04)	(.09)	(.4)	11
1866		Cooked, added sugar[13]	1 cup	270	62.8	381	1.4	.3	97.2	211	41	1.6	5	548	220	(.05)	(.14)	(.8)	16
		Frozen, sweetened:																
1867		Not thawed:																
	a	Package, net wt., 10 oz	1 pkg	284	80.1	213	1.7	.6	52.5	264	40	2.3	11	599	230	.06	.14	.6	23
	b	Pound	1 lb	454	80.1	340	2.7	.9	83.9	422	64	3.6	18	957	360	.09	.23	.9	36
1868		Cooked, added sugar:[13]																
	a	Yield from 10 oz., frozen rhubarb	1¼ cups (approx.).	340	62.6	486	1.7	.7	123.1	265	41	2.4	10	598	240	.07	.14	.7	20
	b	Yield from 1 lb., frozen rhubarb	2 cups (approx.).	544	62.6	778	2.7	1.1	196.9	424	65	3.8	16	957	380	.11	.22	1.1	33
	c	Cup	1 cup	270	62.6	386	1.4	.5	97.7	211	32	1.9	8	475	190	.05	.11	.5	16
		Rice:[5]																
		Brown:																
1869		Raw:																
		Cup:																
	a	Long grain	1 cup	185	12.0	666	13.9	3.5	143.2	59	409	3.0	17	396	(0)	.63	.09	8.7	(0)
	b	Short grain	1 cup	200	12.0	720	15.0	3.8	154.8	64	442	3.2	18	428	(0)	.68	.10	9.4	(0)
	c	Pound	1 lb	454	12.0	1,633	34.0	8.6	351.1	145	1,002	7.3	41	971	(0)	1.54	.23	21.3	(0)
1870		Cooked, long grain:[323]																
		Cup:																
	a	Hot rice[315]	1 cup	195	70.3	232	4.9	1.2	49.7	23	142	1.0	[261]550	137	(0)	.18	.04	2.7	(0)
	b	Cold rice[12]	1 cup	145	70.3	173	3.6	.9	37.0	17	106	.7	[261]409	102	(0)	.13	.03	2.0	(0)
	c	Pound	1 lb	454	70.3	540	11.3	2.7	115.7	54	331	2.3	[261]1,279	318	(0)	.41	.09	6.4	(0)
		White (fully milled or polished):																
		Enriched:																
		Common commercial varieties:																
1871		Raw:																
		Cup:																
	a	Long grain	1 cup	185	12.0	672	12.4	.7	148.7	44	174	[324]5.4	9	170	(0)	[324].81	[325].06	[324]6.5	(0)
	b	Medium grain	1 cup	195	12.0	708	13.1	.8	156.8	47	183	[324]5.7	10	179	(0)	[324].86	[325].06	[324]6.8	(0)
	c	Short grain	1 cup	200	12.0	726	13.4	.8	160.8	48	188	[324]5.8	10	184	(0)	[324].88	[325].06	[324]7.0	(0)
	d	Pound	1 lb	454	12.0	1,647	30.4	1.8	364.7	109	426	[324]13.0	23	417	(0)	[324]2.0	[325].14	[324]16.0	(0)
1872		Cooked (moist, soft stage), long grain:[326]																
		Cup:																
	a	Hot rice[315]	1 cup	205	72.6	223	4.1	.2	49.6	21	57	[324]1.8	[261]767	57	(0)	[324].23	[325].02	[324]2.1	(0)
	b	Cold rice[12]	1 cup	145	72.6	158	2.9	.1	35.1	15	41	[324]1.3	[261]542	41	(0)	[324].16	[325].01	[324]1.5	(0)
	c	Pound	1 lb	454	72.6	494	9.1	.5	109.8	45	127	[324]4.1	[261]1,696	127	(0)	[324].50	[325].05	[324]4.5	(0)
		Parboiled, long grain, regular:																
1873		Dry form:																
	a	Cup	1 cup	185	10.3	683	13.7	.6	150.4	111	370	[324]5.4	17	278	(0)	[324].81	[325].07	[324]6.5	(0)
	b	Pound	1 lb	454	10.3	1,674	33.6	1.4	368.8	272	907	[324]13.0	41	680	(0)	[324]2.0	[325].18	[324]16.0	(0)
1874		Cooked:[323]																
		Cup:																
	a	Hot rice[315]	1 cup	175	73.4	186	3.7	.2	40.8	33	100	[324]1.4	[261]627	75	(0)	[324].19	[325].02	[324]2.1	(0)
	b	Cold rice[12]	1 cup	145	73.4	154	3.0	.1	33.8	28	83	[324]1.2	[261]519	62	(0)	[324].16	[325].01	[324]1.7	(0)
	c	Pound	1 lb	454	73.4	481	9.5	.5	105.7	86	259	[324]3.6	[261]1,624	195	(0)	[324].50	[325].05	[324]5.4	(0)
		Precooked (instant), long grain:[327]																

[1] Measure and weight apply to food as it is described with inedible part or parts (refuse) included.

[5] Most of phosphorus in nuts, legumes, and outer layers of cereal grains is present as phytic acid. See also Appendix D, section on Minerals and Oxalic Acid

[9] For information on proportion of fruit, sugar, and water used, see ARS 62-13 (7), section on Fruits, Dried and Dehydrated, p. 7, and table 20, p. 24.

[12] Cup measure made on product after it had cooled. See also Appendix B, section on Home-Prepared Foods

[13] For information on ingredients used, see ARS 62-13 (7), table 18, pp. 22-23.

[48] Measurement applies to thawed product. See also Appendix C, section on Frozen Fruits and Vegetables

[55] Oxalic acid present may combine with calcium and magnesium to form insoluble compounds. For further information, see Appendix D, section on Minerals and Oxalic Acid

[71] Represents container as customarily filled to volume greater than declared net contents. See also Appendix B, section on Berries

[108] Formula used to calculate nutritive values shown in Agr. Handb. No. 8, rev. 1963.

[207] For proportion of mix and added ingredients, see ARS 62-13 (7), table 19, p. 24.

[261] Applies to product cooked with salt added as specified by manufacturers. If cooked without added salt, value is negligible.

[315] Cup measure made on product immediately after cooking. See also Appendix B, section on Home-Prepared Foods

[318] Prepared mainly from Thompson Seedless grapes.

[319] For raspberry- and strawberry-flavored mixes and desserts prepared from them, values are calcium 73 mg., phosphorus trace.

[320] For raspberry- and strawberry-flavored mixes and desserts prepared from them, values are calcium 17 mg., phosphorus trace.

[321] For raspberry- and strawberry-flavored mixes and desserts prepared from them, values are calcium 641 mg., phosphorus 445 mg.

[322] For raspberry- and strawberry-flavored mixes and desserts prepared from them, values are calcium 296 mg., phosphorus 206 mg.

[323] For proportion of ingredients used and ratio of cooked cereal to dry product, see ARS 62-13 (7), section on Alimentary Pastes and Other Cereal Products, pp. 6-7, and table 3, p. 9.

[324] Values for iron, thiamin, and niacin are based on minimum levels of enrichment specified in standards of identity; values for riboflavin, on value for unenriched rice. See also Appendix C, section on Enriched Foods and Standards of Enrichment

[325] Standards of identity for enrichment of rice with riboflavin are still pending. Values when shown are for unenriched rice. They are based on following amounts per 100 g.: Item 1871, 0.03 mg.; item 1872, 0.01 mg.; item 1873, 0.04 mg.; item 1874, 0.01 mg. No data are available to show values for items 1875 and 1876.

[326] Based on long-grain type with ratio of cooked cereal to dry product of 3.3:1. See ARS 62-13 (7), section on Alimentary Pastes and Other Cereal Products, pp. 6-7, and table 3, p. 9.

[327] Weights and nutrient content per cup of both dry and ready-to-serve forms apply to product with directions on package to combine equal volumes of rice and boiling water, allow to stand 5 minutes, and fluff with fork. Measures for 1 cup of hot rice apply to product immediately after preparation; for cold rice, after rice had cooled. See also Appendix B, section on Home-Prepared Foods

TABLE 1.—*Nutritive values for household measures and market units of foods*—Continued

[Item numbers correspond to those in table 1 of Handbook No. 8, revised 1963. Values in parentheses denote imputed values usually from another form of the food or from a similar food. Zeros in parentheses indicate that amount of a constituent, if present, is probably too small to be measured. Dashes (—) denote lack of reliable data for a constituent believed to be present in a measurable amount. Calculated values, as those based on a recipe, are not in parentheses]

Item No.		Food, approximate measures, units, and weight (edible part unless footnotes indicate otherwise)			Water	Food energy	Protein	Fat	Carbohydrate	Calcium	Phosphorus	Iron	Sodium	Potassium	Vitamin A value	Thiamin	Riboflavin	Niacin	Ascorbic acid
(A)		(B)			(C)	(D)	(E)	(F)	(G)	(H)	(I)	(J)	(K)	(L)	(M)	(N)	(O)	(P)	(Q)
				Grams	Percent	Calories	Grams	Grams	Grams	Milligrams	Milligrams	Milligrams	Milligrams	Milligrams	International units	Milligrams	Milligrams	Milligrams	Milligrams
		Rice[5]—Continued																	
		White (fully milled or polished)—Continued																	
		Enriched—Continued																	
		Precooked (instant), long grain[327]—Continued																	
1875		Dry form:																	
	a	Cup	1 cup	95	9.6	355	7.1	0.2	78.4	5	62	[334] 2.8	1	—	(0)	[334] 0.42	([335])	[334] 3.3	(0)
	b	Pound	1 lb	454	9.6	1,696	34.0	.9	374.2	23	295	[334] 13.0	5	—	(0)	[334] 2.0	([335])	[334] 16.0	(0)
1876		Ready-to-serve, fluffed:[328]																	
		Cup:																	
	a	Hot rice	1 cup	165	72.9	180	3.6	Trace	39.9	5	31	[334] 1.3	[361] 450	—	(0)	[334] .21	([335])	[334] 1.7	(0)
	b	Cold rice	1 cup	130	72.9	142	2.9	Trace	31.5	4	25	[334] 1.0	[361] 355	—	(0)	[334] .17	([335])	[334] 1.3	(0)
	c	Pound	1 lb	454	72.9	494	10.0	Trace	109.8	14	86	[334] 3.6	[361] 1,238	—	(0)	[334] .59	([335])	[334] 4.5	(0)
		Unenriched:																	
		Common commercial varieties:																	
1877		Raw:																	
		Cup:																	
	a	Long grain	1 cup	185	12.0	672	12.4	.7	148.7	44	174	1.5	9	170	(0)	.13	0.06	3.0	(0)
	b	Medium grain	1 cup	195	12.0	708	13.1	.8	156.8	47	183	1.6	10	179	(0)	.14	.06	3.1	(0)
	c	Short grain	1 cup	200	12.0	726	13.4	.8	160.8	48	188	1.6	10	184	(0)	.14	.06	3.2	(0)
	d	Pound	1 lb	454	12.0	1,647	30.4	1.8	364.7	109	426	3.6	23	417	(0)	.32	.14	7.3	(0)
1878		Cooked (moist, soft stage), long grain:[326]																	
		Cup:																	
	a	Hot rice[316]	1 cup	205	72.6	223	4.1	.2	49.6	21	57	.4	[361] 767	57	(0)	.04	.02	.8	(0)
	b	Cold rice[13]	1 cup	145	72.6	158	2.9	.1	35.1	15	41	.3	[361] 542	41	(0)	.03	.01	.6	(0)
	c	Pound	1 lb	454	72.6	494	9.1	.5	109.8	45	127	.9	[361] 1,696	127	(0)	.09	.05	1.8	(0)
1881		**Rice polish:**[5]																	
	a	Stirred, spooned into cup	1 cup	105	9.8	278	12.7	13.4	60.6	72	1,161	16.9	Trace	750	(0)	1.93	.19	29.6	(0)
	b	Pound	1 lb	454	9.8	1,202	54.9	58.1	261.7	313	5,017	73.0	Trace	3,239	(0)	8.35	.82	127.9	(0)
		Rice products used mainly as hot breakfast cereals:[5 156]																	
		Rice, granulated, added nutrients:																	
1882		Dry form:																	
	a	Cup	1 cup	170	7.4	651	10.2	.5	146.0	15	163	9.2	—	—	(0)	.71	.19	9.9	(0)
	b	Pound	1 lb	454	7.4	1,737	27.2	1.4	389.6	41	435	24.5	—	—	(0)	1.91	.50	26.3	(0)
1883		Cooked:																	
	a	Cup	1 cup	245	87.5	123	2.0	Trace	27.4	5	32	1.7	[361] 431	Trace	(0)	.15	.02	2.0	(0)
	b	Pound	1 lb	454	87.5	227	3.6	Trace	50.8	9	59	3.2	[361] 798	Trace	(0)	.27	.05	3.6	(0)
		Rice products used mainly as ready-to-eat breakfast cereals:[5 74]																	
1884		Rice, ovenpopped, added sugar, salt, iron, vitamins	1 cup	30	3.2	117	1.8	.1	26.3	[328] 6	[328] 28	[328] .8	[328] 283	[328] 29	[81] 1,410	[83] .35	[83] .42	[83] 3.5	[81] 11
1885		Rice, puffed, without salt and sugar; added iron, thiamin, niacin.	1 cup	15	3.7	60	.9	.1	13.4	3	14	.3	Trace	15	(0)	.07	.01	.7	(0)
		Rice, presweetened:																	
1886		Ovenpopped, added salt, iron, vitamins	1 cup	45	1.8	175	1.9	.3	40.8	[329] 16	33	[329] .9	318	—	[81] 2,120	[83] .52	[83] .63	[83] 5.2	[81] 16
1887		Puffed, added honey or cocoa, salt, fat, iron, vitamins.	1 cup	35	2.4	140	1.6	1.4	30.3	[330] 7	29	[330] 1.2	[330] 148	[330] 33	[330] 1,650	[83] .41	[83] .49	[83] 4.1	[166] 12
1888		Rice, shredded, added sugar, salt, iron, thiamin, niacin.	1 cup	25	3.0	98	1.3	.1	22.2	4	24	.5	[330] 229	—	(0)	.10	[330] .02	1.8	(0)
		Rice, with protein concentrate, mainly—																	
1889		Wheat gluten and casein; added sugar, salt, minerals, vitamins; minute flakes.	1 cup	85	3.0	325	34.0	.2	46.6	135	270	15.0	[331] 332	[331] 90	[331] 1,800	[331] 1.50	1.79	15.0	45
1890		Wheat gluten; added sugar, salt, iron, vitamins	1 cup	20	2.5	77	4.0	.1	14.9	[331] 7	[331] 32	[331] 2.3	[331] 142	[331] 30	[331] 940	[83] .23	[83] .28	[83] 2.3	7
1891		**Rice pudding** with raisins[5 11 13]	1 cup	265	65.8	387	9.5	8.2	70.8	260	249	1.1	188	469	290	.08	.37	.5	Trace
1893		**Rockfish,** ovensteamed:[332]																	
	a	Yield from 1 lb., raw fillets	13 oz	370	75.4	396	67.0	9.3	7.0	—	—	—	[43] 252	1,650	—	.19	.44	—	4
	b	Fillet, 7 in. long, 3⅜ in. wide, ⅝ in. thick[40]	1 fillet	115	75.4	123	20.8	2.9	2.2	—	—	—	[43] 78	513	—	.06	.14	—	1
	c	Pound	1 lb	454	75.4	485	82.1	11.3	8.6	—	—	—	[43] 308	2,023	—	.23	.54	—	5
	d	Ounce	1 oz	28	75.4	30	5.1	.7	.5	—	—	—	[43] 19	126	—	.01	.03	—	Trace
1897		**Roe,** herring, canned, solids and liquid:																	
		Can and approx. contents:																	
	a	Size, 211 × 304[14] (8Z Tall, Buffet); net wt., 8 oz.	1 can	227	72.4	268	48.8	6.4	.7	34	785	2.7	—	—	—	—	—	—	5
	b	Size, 300 × 407[14] (No. 300); net wt., 15 oz	1 can	425	72.4	502	91.4	11.9	1.3	64	1,471	5.1	—	—	—	—	—	—	9
	c	**Pound**	1 lb	454	72.4	535	97.5	12.7	1.4	68	1,569	5.4	—	—	—	—	—	—	[illegible]

(A)	(B)		(C)	(D)	(E)	(F)	(G)	(H)	(I)	(J)	(K)	(L)	(M)	(N)	(O)	(P)	(Q)
	Rolls and buns:																
1898	**Baked from home recipe, made with milk and enriched flour:** [69]																
a	Roll (cloverleaf, 2½-in. diam., 2 in. high; yield from 40 g. of dough).	1 roll	35	26.1	119	2.9	3.0	19.6	16	36	[338] 0.7	98	41	30	[333] 0.09	[333] 0.09	[333] 0.8	Trace
b	Pound (approx. 13 rolls (item 1898a))	1 lb	454	26.1	1,538	37.2	39.5	254.5	213	463	[334] 9.5	1,266	531	360	[334] 1.13	[334] 1.18	[334] 10.4	Trace
	Commercial: [38]																
	Ready-to-serve:																
1899	Danish pastry (plain without fruit or nuts):																
	Prepackaged ring:																
	Package, approx. contents and piece cut from ring:																
a	Package, net wt., 12 oz. (round piece, approx. 8-in. diam. with 2-in.-diam. hole; cir., 25¼ in.; or ring, 3 in. wide, 1⅛ in. high).	1 pkg	340	22.0	1,435	25.2	79.9	155.0	170	371	3.1	1,244	381	1,050	.24	.51	2.7	Trace
b	Cut piece, approx. 3⅛-in. arc; ⅛ of pkg. (item 1899a).	1 piece	42	22.0	179	3.1	10.0	19.4	21	46	.4	156	48	130	.03	.06	.3	Trace
c	Package, net wt., 5 oz. (round piece, approx. 7-in. diam. with 4-in.-diam. hole; cir., 22¼ in.; or ring, 1½ in. wide, ⅞ in. high).	1 pkg	142	22.0	599	10.5	33.4	64.8	71	155	1.3	520	159	440	.10	.21	1.1	Trace
d	Cut piece, approx. 5½-in. arc; ¼ of pkg. (item 1899c).	1 piece	35	22.0	150	2.6	8.3	16.2	18	39	.3	130	40	110	.02	.05	.3	Trace
e	Rectangular piece, approx. 6½ in. long, 2¾ in. wide, ¾ in. high.	1 pastry	75	22.0	317	5.6	17.6	34.2	38	82	.7	275	84	230	.05	.11	.6	Trace
f	Round piece, approx. 4¼-in. diam., 1 in. high	1 pastry	65	22.0	274	4.8	15.3	29.6	33	71	.6	238	73	200	.04	.10	.5	Trace
g	Pound	1 lb	454	22.0	1,914	33.6	106.6	206.8	227	494	4.1	1,660	508	1,410	.32	.68	3.6	Trace
h	Ounce	1 oz	28	22.0	120	2.1	6.7	12.9	14	31	.3	104	32	90	.02	.04	.2	Trace
	Hard rolls:																
1900	Enriched:																
a	Roll (round, or kaiser, 3¾-in. diam., 2 in. high; rectangular, 4¾ × 2¾ × 2½ in.).	1 roll	50	25.4	156	4.9	1.6	29.8	24	46	1.2	313	49	Trace	.13	.12	1.4	Trace
b	Roll (rectangular, 3¾ × 2½ × 1¾ in.)	1 roll	25	25.4	78	2.5	.8	14.9	12	23	.6	156	24	Trace	.07	.06	.7	Trace
c	Pound (approx. 9 rolls (item 1900a) or 18 rolls (item 1900b)).	1 lb	454	25.4	1,415	44.5	14.5	269.9	213	417	10.4	2,835	440	Trace	1.18	1.04	12.2	Trace
1901	Unenriched:																
a	Roll (round, or kaiser, 3¾-in. diam., 2 in. high; rectangular, 4¾ × 2¾ × 2½ in.).	1 roll	50	25.4	156	4.9	1.6	29.8	24	46	.4	313	49	Trace	.03	.05	.4	Trace
b	Roll (rectangular, 3¾ × 2½ × 1¾ in.)	1 roll	25	25.4	78	2.5	.8	14.9	12	23	.2	156	24	Trace	.01	.02	.2	Trace
c	Pound (approx. 9 rolls (item 1901a) or 18 rolls (item 1901b)).	1 lb	454	25.4	1,415	44.5	14.5	269.9	213	417	3.6	2,835	440	Trace	.23	.41	3.6	Trace

[5] Most of phosphorus in nuts, legumes, and outer layers of cereal grains is present as phytic acid. See also Appendix D, section on Minerals and Oxalic Acid

[12] **Cup measure made on product after it had cooled. See also Appendix B, section on Home-Prepared Foods**

[13] For information on ingredients used, see ARS 62–13 (7), table 18, pp. 22–23.

[14] Dimensions of can: 1st dimension represents diameter; 2d dimension, height of can. 1st or left-hand digit in each dimension gives number of whole inches; next 2 digits give additional fraction of dimension expressed as 16th of an inch.

[38] For further information, see Appendix C, section on Enriched Foods and Standards of Enrichment

[40] Width at widest part; thickness at thickest part.

[42] Value for product without added salt.

[69] For information on ingredients used, see ARS 62–13 (7), table 4, p. 10.

[74] Weight per cup based on method of pouring product from container into measuring cup to overflow and leveling with straight edge. Revised values for minerals and vitamins apply to products on the market in 1972.

[81] Basis of revised value for 100 g. of product with added vitamin A is 4,700 I.U.; with added ascorbic acid, 35 mg.

[82] Basis of revised value for 100 g. of product with added thiamin is 1.16 mg.; with added riboflavin, 1.41 mg.; with added niacin, 11.6 mg.

[186] For dry form of cereal, weight per cup is based on method of pouring cereal from container into measuring cup with as little fall as possible, then leveling with straight edge. See also Appendix B, section on Nonliquid Foods and section on Breakfast-Type Cereals

For cooked cereal, weight per cup represents hot cereal immediately after cooking and is based on specific proportion of cereal and water in cooked product. See ARS 62–13 (7), section on Alimentary Pastes and Other Cereal Products, pp. 6–7, and table 3, p. 9.

[188] Based on revised value of 35 mg. per 100 g. of product.

[261] Applies to product cooked with salt added as specified by manufacturers. If cooked without added salt, value is negligible.

[315] Cup measure made on product immediately after cooking. See also Appendix B, section on Home-Prepared Foods

[323] For proportion of ingredients used and ratio of cooked cereal to dry product, see ARS 62–13 (7), section on Alimentary Pastes and Other Cereal Products, pp. 6–7, and table 3, p. 9.

[324] Values for iron, thiamin, and niacin are based on minimum levels of enrichment specified in standards of identity; values for riboflavin, on value for unenriched rice. See also Appendix C, section on Enriched Foods and Standards of Enrichment

[325] Standards of identity for enrichment of rice with riboflavin are still pending. Values when shown are for unenriched rice. They are based on following amounts per 100 g.: Item 1871, 0.03 mg.; item 1872, 0.01 mg.; item 1873, 0.04 mg.; item 1874, 0.01 mg. No data are available to show values for items 1875 and 1876.

[326] Based on long-grain type with ratio of cooked cereal to dry product of 3.3:1. See ARS 62–13 (7), section on Alimentary Pastes and Other Cereal Products, pp. 6–7, and table 3, p. 9.

[327] Weights and nutrient content per cup of both dry and ready-to-serve forms apply to product with directions on package to combine equal volumes of rice and boiling water, allow to stand 5 minutes, and fluff with fork. Measures for 1 cup of hot rice apply to product immediately after preparation; for cold rice, after rice had cooled. See also Appendix B, section on Home-Prepared Foods

[328] Based on revised value per 100 g. of product. Value used for calcium is 19 mg., for phosphorus 92 mg., for iron 2.5 mg., for sodium 942 mg., for potassium 95 mg.

[329] Based on revised value per 100 g. of product. Value used for calcium is 35 mg., for iron 1.9 mg.

[330] Based on revised value per 100 g. of product. Values used for item 1887 are calcium 20 mg., iron 3.5 mg., sodium 422 mg., potassium 94 mg., vitamin A 4,700 I.U. for product with added vitamin A. Without added vitamin A, value is (0). Values used for item 1888 are sodium 917 mg., riboflavin 0.07 mg.

[331] Based on revised value per 100 g. of product. Values used for item 1889 are sodium 390 mg., potassium 106 mg., vitamin A 2,120 I.U., thiamin 1.76 mg. Values used for item 1890 are calcium 35 mg., phosphorus 159 mg., iron 11.7 mg., sodium 710 mg., potassium 152 mg., vitamin A 4,700 I.U.

[332] Prepared with onion.

[333] With unenriched flour, approx. values are iron 0.3 mg., thiamin 0.02 mg., riboflavin 0.05 mg., niacin 0.3 mg.

[334] With unenriched flour, approx. values are iron 3.6 mg., thiamin 0.27 mg., riboflavin 0.64 mg., niacin 3.6 mg.

TABLE 1.—*Nutritive values for household measures and market units of foods*—Continued

[Item numbers correspond to those in table 1 of Handbook No. 8, revised 1963. Values in parentheses denote imputed values usually from another form of the food or from a similar food. Zeros in parentheses indicate that amount of a constituent, if present, is probably too small to be measured. Dashes (—) denote lack of reliable data for a constituent believed to be present in a measurable amount. Calculated values, as those based on a recipe, are not in parentheses]

Item No. (A)	Food, approximate measures, units, and weight (edible part unless footnotes indicate otherwise) (B)			Values for edible part of foods: Water (C)	Food energy (D)	Protein (E)	Fat (F)	Carbohydrate (G)	Calcium (H)	Phosphorus (I)	Iron (J)	Sodium (K)	Potassium (L)	Vitamin A value (M)	Thiamin (N)	Riboflavin (O)	Niacin (P)	Ascorbic acid (Q)
			Grams	*Percent*	*Calories*	*Grams*	*Grams*	*Grams*	*Milligrams*	*Milligrams*	*Milligrams*	*Milligrams*	*Milligrams*	*International units*	*Milligrams*	*Milligrams*	*Milligrams*	*Milligrams*
	Rolls and buns—Continued																	
	Commercial [36]—Continued																	
	Ready-to-serve—Continued																	
	Hoagie or submarine roll. See French or vienna bread and rolls, enriched and unenriched (items 446e, 448e).																	
	Plain (soft rolls or buns):																	
1902	Enriched:																	
a	Cloverleaf (round, 2 or 3 pull-apart sections, 2½-in. diam., 2 in. high); pan or dinner (2 in. square, 2 in. high).	1 roll	28	31.4	83	2.3	1.6	14.8	21	24	0.5	142	27	Trace	0.08	0.05	0.6	Trace
	Frankfurter (hotdog) and hamburger (sandwich):																	
b	Package, net wt., 11⅓ oz.; 8 rolls	1 pkg	325	31.4	969	26.7	18.2	172.3	241	276	6.2	1,645	309	Trace	.91	.59	7.2	Trace
c	Roll or bun (frankfurter, 6 in. long, 2 in. wide, 1½ in. high; hamburger, 3½-in. diam., 1½ in. high).	1 roll or bun	40	31.4	119	3.3	2.2	21.2	30	34	.8	202	38	Trace	.11	.07	.9	Trace
d	Pound (approx. 16 cloverleaf or pan rolls (item 1902a) or approx. 11 frankfurter or hamburger rolls (item 1902c)).	1 lb	454	31.4	1,352	37.2	25.4	240.4	336	386	8.6	2,295	431	Trace	1.27	.82	10.0	Trace
1903	Unenriched:																	
a	Cloverleaf (round, 2 or 3 pull-apart sections, 2½-in. diam., 2 in. high); pan or dinner (2 in. square, 2 in. high).	1 roll	28	31.4	83	2.3	1.6	14.8	21	24	.2	142	27	Trace	.02	.03	.2	Trace
	Frankfurter (hotdog) and hamburger (sandwich):																	
b	Package, net wt., 11⅓ oz.; 8 rolls	1 pkg	325	31.4	969	26.7	18.2	172.3	241	276	2.3	1,645	309	Trace	.20	.29	2.6	Trace
c	Roll or bun (frankfurter, 6 in. long, 2 in. wide, 1½ in. high; hamburger, 3½-in. diam., 1½ in. high).	1 roll or bun	40	31.4	119	3.3	2.2	21.2	30	34	.3	202	38	Trace	.02	.04	.3	Trace
d	Pound (approx. 16 cloverleaf or pan rolls (item 1903a) or approx. 11 frankfurter or hamburger rolls (item 1903c)).	1 lb	454	31.4	1,352	37.2	25.4	240.4	336	386	3.2	2,295	431	Trace	.27	.41	3.6	Trace
	Partially baked (brown-and-serve):																	
	Enriched:																	
1907	Unbrowned:																	
	Cloverleaf and pan:																	
a	Package, net wt., 12 oz.; 12 rolls	1 pkg	340	33.0	1,017	26.9	23.1	172.0	238	279	6.1	1,649	309	Trace	.81	.70	7.5	Trace
b	Roll (cloverleaf, round, 2 or 3 pull-apart sections, 2½-in. diam., 2 in. high; pan or dinner, 2 in. square, 2 in. high).	1 roll	28	33.0	84	2.2	1.9	14.2	20	23	.5	136	25	Trace	.07	.06	.6	Trace
c	Pound	1 lb	454	33.0	1,356	35.8	30.8	229.5	318	372	8.2	2,200	413	Trace	1.1	.93	10.0	Trace
1908	Browned:																	
a	Yield from 1 lb., unbrowned rolls	14⅔ oz	415	26.9	1,356	35.8	30.8	229.5	318	372	8.2	2,200	413	Trace	1.1	.93	10.0	Trace
b	Yield from 12-oz. pkg. (item 1907a)	12 rolls	310	26.9	1,017	26.9	23.1	172.0	238	279	6.1	1,649	309	Trace	.81	.70	7.5	Trace
c	Roll (item 1907b, browned)	1 roll	26	26.9	84	2.2	1.9	14.2	20	23	.5	136	25	Trace	.07	.06	.6	Trace
d	Pound	1 lb	454	26.9	1,488	39.5	35.4	248.6	349	404	9.1	2,409	454	Trace	1.18	1.02	10.9	Trace
	Unenriched:																	
1909	Unbrowned:																	
	Cloverleaf and pan:																	
a	Package, net wt., 12 oz.; 12 rolls	1 pkg	340	33.0	1,017	26.9	23.1	172.0	238	279	2.4	1,649	309	Trace	.19	.30	2.5	Trace
b	Roll (cloverleaf, round, 2 or 3 pull-apart sections, 2½-in. diam., 2 in. high; pan or dinner, 2 in. square, 2 in. high).	1 roll	28	33.0	84	2.2	1.9	14.2	20	23	.2	136	25	Trace	.02	.02	.2	Trace
c	Pound	1 lb	454	33.0	1,356	35.8	30.8	229.5	318	372	3.2	2,200	413	Trace	.25	.39	3.3	Trace
1910	Browned:																	
a	Yield from 1 lb., unbrowned rolls	14⅔ oz	415	26.9	1,356	35.8	30.8	229.5	318	372	3.2	2,200	413	Trace	.25	.39	3.3	Trace
b	Yield from 12-oz. pkg. (item 1909a)	12 rolls	310	26.9	1,017	26.9	23.1	172.0	238	279	2.4	1,649	309	Trace	.19	.30	2.5	Trace
c	Roll (item 1909b, browned)	1 roll	26	26.9	84	2.2	1.9	14.2	20	23	.2	136	25	Trace	.02	.02	.2	Trace

(A)	(B)			(C)	(D)	(E)	(F)	(G)	(H)	(I)	(J)	(K)	(L)	(M)	(N)	(O)	(P)	(Q)
d	Pound	1 lb	454	26.9	1,488	39.5	35.4	248.6	349	404	3.2	2,409	454	Trace	0.27	0.43	3.6	Trace
	Roll dough and rolls baked from dough:																	
	Enriched:																	
1911	Dough, unraised, frozen:																	
	Parkerhouse rolls:																	
a	Package, net wt., 24 oz. (1 lb. 8 oz.); 24 rolls (item 1911b).	1 pkg	680	38.5	1,822	51.0	34.0	322.3	224	517	12.2	3,087	558	Trace	1.82	1.35	15.0	Trace
b	Roll, 2⅝ in. long, 2 in. wide, 1⅝ in. high	1 roll	28	38.5	75	2.1	1.4	13.3	9	21	.5	127	23	Trace	.07	.06	.6	Trace
c	Pound	1 lb	454	38.5	1,216	34.0	22.7	215.0	150	345	8.0	2,059	372	Trace	1.22	.90	10.0	Trace
1912	Rolls, parkerhouse, baked:																	
a	Yield from 1 lb., frozen dough	13¾ oz	390	28.3	1,216	34.0	22.7	215.0	150	345	8.0	2,059	372	Trace	1.03	.86	9.0	Trace
b	Yield from 24 oz., frozen dough	24 rolls	585	28.3	1,822	51.0	34.0	322.3	224	517	12.2	3,087	558	Trace	1.55	1.29	13.5	Trace
c	Roll (item 1911b, baked)	1 roll	24	28.3	75	2.1	1.4	13.3	9	21	.5	127	23	Trace	.06	(.06)	(.6)	Trace
d	Pound	1 lb	454	28.3	1,411	38.6	24.5	254.0	177	399	9.5	2,395	435	Trace	1.20	1.00	10.5	Trace
	Unenriched:																	
1913	Dough, unraised, frozen:																	
	Parkerhouse rolls:																	
a	Package, net wt., 24 oz. (1 lb. 8 oz.); 24 rolls (item 1913b).	1 pkg	680	38.5	1,822	51.0	34.0	322.3	224	517	6.1	3,087	558	Trace	.57	.61	6.7	Trace
b	Roll, 2⅝ in. long, 2 in. wide, 1⅝ in. high	1 roll	28	38.5	75	2.1	1.4	13.3	9	21	.3	127	23	Trace	.02	.03	.3	Trace
c	Pound	1 lb	454	38.5	1,216	34.0	22.7	215.0	150	345	4.1	2,059	372	Trace	.38	.41	4.4	Trace
1914	Rolls, parkerhouse, baked:																	
a	Yield from 1 lb., frozen dough	13¾ oz	390	28.3	1,216	34.0	22.7	215.0	150	345	4.1	2,059	372	Trace	.32	.39	4.0	Trace
b	Yield from 24 oz., frozen dough	24 rolls	585	28.3	1,822	51.0	34.0	322.3	224	517	6.1	3,087	558	Trace	.49	.58	6.0	Trace
c	Roll (item 1913b, baked)	1 roll	24	28.3	75	2.1	1.4	13.3	9	21	.3	127	23	Trace	(.02)	(.03)	(.3)	Trace
d	Pound	1 lb	454	28.3	1,411	38.6	24.5	254.0	177	399	4.5	2,395	435	Trace	.38	.45	4.6	Trace
1916	**Rolls prepared with roll mix and water, baked:** [68]																	
a	Roll, cloverleaf, 2½-in. diam., 2 in. high	1 roll	35	30.6	105	3.2	1.6	19.1	20	34	[335] .2	110	43	Trace	[335] .02	[335] .04	[335] .2	Trace
b	Pound (approx. 13 rolls (item 1916a))	1 lb	454	30.6	1,356	40.8	20.4	247.2	254	440	[336] 2.7	1,420	558	Trace	[336] .23	[336] .54	[336] 3.2	Trace
	Root beer. See Beverages (item 408).																	
	Rum. See Beverages (items 395–399).																	
1918	**Rusk,** 3⅜-in. diam., ½ in. thick:																	
a	Package, net wt., 4 oz. (13 rusks)	1 pkg	113	4.8	473	15.6	9.8	80.2	23	134	1.5	278	182	260	.09	.25	1.2	Trace
b	Rusk	1 rusk	9	4.8	38	1.2	.8	6.4	2	11	.1	22	14	20	.01	.02	.1	Trace
c	Pound (approx. 50 rusks)	1 lb	454	4.8	1,901	62.6	39.5	322.1	91	540	5.9	1,116	730	1,040	.36	1.00	5.0	Trace
	Rutabagas:																	
1919	Raw, cubed	1 cup	140	87.0	64	1.5	.1	15.4	92	55	.6	7	335	810	.10	.10	1.5	60
1920	Cooked (boiled), drained:																	
	Cup:																	
a	Cubed or sliced	1 cup	170	90.2	60	1.5	.2	13.9	100	53	.5	[20] 7	284	940	.10	.10	1.4	44
b	Mashed	1 cup	240	90.2	84	2.2	.2	19.7	142	74	.7	[20] 10	401	1,320	.14	.14	1.9	62
c	Pound	1 lb	454	90.2	159	4.1	.5	37.2	268	141	1.4	[20] 18	758	2,490	.27	.27	3.6	118
	Rye flours: [6]																	
1922	Light:																	
a	Unsifted, spooned into cup	1 cup	102	11	364	9.6	1.0	79.5	22	189	1.1	(1)	159	(0)	.15	.07	.6	(0)
b	Sifted, spooned into cup	1 cup	88	11	314	8.3	.9	68.6	19	163	1.0	(1)	137	(0)	.13	.06	.5	(0)
1923	Medium, sifted, spooned into cup	1 cup	(88)	11	308	10.0	1.5	65.8	(24)	231	2.3	(1)	179	(0)	.26	.11	2.2	(0)
1924	Dark, spooned into cup	1 cup	128	11	419	20.9	3.3	87.2	69	(686)	5.8	1	1,101	(0)	.78	.28	3.5	(0)
1925	**Rye wafers, whole-grain:**																	
a	Package, net wt., 8 oz. (3 packets of 12 wafers, 3½ in. long, 1⅞ in. wide, ¼ in. thick, marked for breaking into 3 smaller wafers, approx. 1⅞ in. long, 1⅛ in. wide, ¼ in. thick).	1 pkg	227	6.0	781	29.5	2.7	173.2	120	881	8.9	2,002	1,362	(0)	.73	.57	2.7	(0)
b	Wafer, 3½ in. long, 1⅞ in. wide, ¼ in. thick	10 wafers	65	6.0	224	8.5	.8	49.6	34	252	2.5	573	390	(0)	.21	.16	.8	(0)
c	Pound	1 lb	454	6.0	1,560	59.0	5.4	346.1	240	1,760	17.7	4,001	2,722	(0)	1.45	1.13	5.4	(0)
	Safflower oil. See Oils (items 1401a, 1401b, 1401f, 1401h, 1401j).																	
	Salad dressings, commercial: [337]																	
	Blue and Roquefort cheese:																	
1929	Regular:																	
a	Cup	1 cup	245	32.3	1,235	11.8	128.1	18.1	198	181	.5	2,680	91	510	.02	.25	.2	5
b	Tablespoon	1 tbsp	15	32.3	76	.7	7.8	1.1	12	11	Trace	164	6	30	Trace	.02	Trace	Trace

[6] Most of phosphorus in nuts, legumes, and outer layers of cereal grains is present as phytic acid. See also Appendix D, section on Minerals and Oxalic Acid

[20] Value is for unsalted product. If salt is used, increase value by 236 mg. per 100 g. of vegetable—an estimated figure based on typical amount of salt (0.6%) in canned vegetables. See also Appendix C, section on Cooked Vegetables

[36] For further information, see Appendix C, section on Enriched Foods and Standards of Enrichment

[68] For proportion of mix and added ingredients used, see ARS 62-13 (7), table 5, p. 12.

[335] Based on rolls made from mix containing unenriched flour. If rolls are made from mix containing enriched flour, approx. values are iron 0.7 mg., thiamin 0.09 mg., riboflavin 0.09 mg., niacin 0.8 mg.

[336] Based on rolls made from mix containing unenriched flour. If rolls are made from mix containing enriched flour, approx. values are iron 9.1 mg., thiamin 1.13 mg., riboflavin 1.13 mg., niacin 10.0 mg.

[337] Values apply to products containing salt. For those without salt, sodium content is low, ranging from 25 mg. to 110 mg. per cup and less than 2 mg. to 7 mg. per tablespoon; amount usually is indicated on label.

TABLE 1.—*Nutritive values for household measures and market units of foods*—Continued

[Item numbers correspond to those in table 1 of Handbook No. 8, revised 1963. Values in parentheses denote imputed values usually from another form of the food or from a similar food. Zeros in parentheses indicate that amount of a constituent, if present, is probably too small to be measured. Dashes (—) denote lack of reliable data for a constituent believed to be present in a measurable amount. Calculated values, as those based on a recipe, are not in parentheses]

Item No.	Food, approximate measures, units, and weight (edible part unless footnotes indicate otherwise)			Water	Food energy	Protein	Fat	Carbohydrate	Calcium	Phosphorus	Iron	Sodium	Potassium	Vitamin A value	Thiamin	Riboflavin	Niacin	Ascorbic acid
(A)	(B)			(C)	(D)	(E)	(F)	(G)	(H)	(I)	(J)	(K)	(L)	(M)	(N)	(O)	(P)	(Q)
			Grams	Percent	Calories	Grams	Grams	Grams	Milligrams	Milligrams	Milligrams	Milligrams	Milligrams	International units	Milligrams	Milligrams	Milligrams	Milligrams
	Salad dressings, commercial[137]—Continued																	
	Blue and Roquefort cheese—Continued																	
	Special dietary (low calorie):																	
1930	Low fat (approx. 5 Cal. per teaspoon):																	
a	Cup	1 cup	255	83.7	194	7.7	15.0	10.5	163	120	0.3	2,825	87	430	0.01	0.18	0.3	5
b	Tablespoon	1 tbsp	16	83.7	12	.5	.9	.7	10	8	Trace	177	5	30	Trace	.01	Trace	Trace
1931	Low fat (approx. 1 Cal. per teaspoon):																	
a	Cup	1 cup	245	93.1	47	3.4	2.7	3.4	86	59	.2	2,778	71	200	.01	.10	.1	5
b	Tablespoon	1 tbsp	15	93.1	3	.2	.2	.2	5	4	Trace	170	4	10	Trace	.01	Trace	Trace
	French:																	
1932	Regular:																	
a	Cup	1 cup	250	38.8	1,025	1.5	97.3	43.8	28	85	1.0	3,425	198	—	—	—	—	—
b	Tablespoon	1 tbsp	16	38.8	66	.1	6.2	2.8	2	2	.1	219	13	—	—	—	—	—
1933	Special dietary (low calorie), low fat (approx. 5 Cal. per teaspoon):																	
a	Cup	1 cup	260	77.3	250	1.0	11.2	40.6	29	36	1.0	2,046	205	—	—	—	—	—
b	Tablespoon	1 tbsp	16	77.3	15	.1	.7	2.5	2	2	.1	126	13	—	—	—	—	—
	Italian:																	
1936	Regular:																	
a	Cup	1 cup	235	27.5	1,297	.5	141.0	16.2	24	9	.5	4,916	85	Trace	Trace	Trace	Trace	—
b	Tablespoon	1 tbsp	15	27.5	83	Trace	9.0	1.0	2	1	Trace	314	2	Trace	Trace	Trace	Trace	—
1937	Special dietary (low calorie, approx. 2 Cal. per teaspoon):																	
a	Cup	1 cup	240	90.1	120	.5	11.3	6.2	5	12	.5	1,889	36	Trace	Trace	Trace	Trace	—
b	Tablespoon	1 tbsp	15	90.1	8	Trace	.7	.4	Trace	1	Trace	118	2	Trace	Trace	Trace	Trace	—
1938	Mayonnaise:																	
a	Cup	1 cup	220	15.1	1,580	2.4	175.8	4.8	40	62	1.1	1,318	75	620	.04	.09	Trace	—
b	Tablespoon	1 tbsp	14	15.1	101	.2	11.2	.3	3	4	.1	84	5	40	Trace	.01	Trace	—
1939	Russian:																	
a	Cup	1 cup	245	34.5	1,210	3.9	124.5	25.5	47	91	1.5	2,127	385	1,690	.12	.12	1.5	15
b	Tablespoon	1 tbsp	15	34.5	74	.2	7.6	1.6	3	6	.1	130	24	100	.01	.01	.1	1
	Salad dressing (mayonnaise type):																	
1940	Regular:																	
a	Cup	1 cup	235	40.6	1,022	2.4	99.4	33.8	33	61	.5	1,377	21	520	.02	.07	Trace	—
b	Tablespoon	1 tbsp	15	40.6	65	.2	6.3	2.2	2	4	Trace	88	1	30	Trace	Trace	Trace	—
1941	Special dietary (low calorie, approx. 8 Cal. per teaspoon):																	
a	Cup	1 cup	250	80.7	340	2.8	31.8	12.0	45	70	.5	295	23	550	.03	.08	Trace	—
b	Tablespoon	1 tbsp	16	80.7	22	.2	2.0	.8	3	4	Trace	19	1	40	Trace	Trace	Trace	—
	Thousand Island:																	
1942	Regular:																	
a	Cup	1 cup	250	32.0	1,255	2.0	125.5	38.5	28	43	1.5	1,750	283	800	.05	.08	.5	8
b	Tablespoon	1 tbsp	16	32.0	80	.1	8.0	2.5	2	3	.1	112	18	50	Trace	Trace	Trace	Trace
1943	Special dietary (low calorie, approx. 10 Cal. per teaspoon):																	
a	Cup	1 cup	245	68.2	441	2.2	33.6	38.2	27	42	1.5	1,715	277	780	.05	.07	.5	7
b	Tablespoon	1 tbsp	15	68.2	27	.1	2.1	2.3	2	3	.1	105	17	50	Trace	Trace	Trace	Trace
	Salad dressings, made from home recipe:[138]																	
1944	French:																	
a	Cup	1 cup	220	24.2	1,390	.7	154.2	7.9	13	7	.2	1,450	57	—	—	—	—	—
b	Tablespoon	1 tbsp	14	24.2	88	Trace	9.8	.5	1	Trace	Trace	92	4	—	—	—	—	—
1945	Cooked:																	
a	Cup	1 cup	255	68.0	418	11.2	25.2	38.8	227	237	1.5	1,856	296	1,250	.13	.41	.5	Trace
b	Tablespoon	1 tbsp	16	68.0	26	.7	1.6	2.4	14	15	.1	116	19	80	.01	.03	Trace	Trace
	Salad oil. See Oils (item 1401).																	
	Salami. See Sausage, cold cuts, and luncheon meats (items 2017–2018).																	
	Salmon, canned, solids and liquid:																	
1947	Atlantic:																	
	Can and approx. contents:																	
a	Size, 307 × 200.25 [14] (No. ½ Flat); net wt., 7¾ oz.; drained solids, 6¼ oz. (approx. 1 cup); drained liquid, 1½ oz.	1 can	220	64.2	447	47.7	26.8	0	—	—	—	—	—	—	—	—	—	—

(A)	(B)		(C)	(D)	(E)	(F)	(G)	(H)	(I)	(J)	(K)	(L)	(M)	(N)	(O)	(P)	(Q)
b	Size, 301 × 411 [14] (No. 1 Tall); net wt., 16 oz. (1 lb.); drained solids, 13 oz. (2 cups); drained liquid, 3 oz.	1 can or 1 lb --	454	64.2	921	98.4	55.3	0	—	—	—	—	—	—	—	—	—	—
c	Size, 603 × 405; [14] net wt., 64 oz. (4 lb.); drained solids, 52 oz. (3 lb. 4 oz.), 8 cups; drained liquid, 12 oz.	1 can --------	1,814	64.2	3,682	393.6	221.3	0	—	—	—	—	—	—	—	—	—	—
1949	Chinook (king):																	
	Can and approx. contents:																	
a	Size, 307 × 200.25 [14] (No. ½ Flat); net wt., 7¾ oz.; drained solids, 6¼ oz. (approx. 1 cup); drained liquid, 1½ oz.	1 can --------	220	64.4	462	43.1	30.8	0	[338] 339	636	2.0	[339] —	805	510	0.07	0.31	16.1	—
b	Size, 301 × 411 [14] (No. 1 Tall); net wt., 16 oz. (1 lb.); drained solids, 13 oz. (2 cups); drained liquid, 3 oz.	1 can or 1 lb --	454	64.4	953	88.9	63.5	0	[338] 699	1,311	4.1	[339] —	1,660	1,040	.14	.64	33.1	—
c	Size, 603 × 405; [14] net wt., 64 oz. (4 lb.); drained solids, 52 oz. (3 lb. 4 oz.), 8 cups; drained liquid, 12 oz.	1 can --------	1,814	64.4	3,809	355.5	254.0	0	[338] 2,794	5,242	16.3	[339] —	6,639	4,170	.54	2.54	132.4	—
1951	Chum:																	
	Can and approx. contents:																	
a	Size, 307 × 200.25 [14] (No. ½ Flat); net wt., 7¾ oz.; drained solids, 6¼ oz. (approx. 1 cup); drained liquid, 1½ oz.	1 can --------	220	70.8	306	47.3	11.4	0	[338] 548	774	1.5	[339] —	739	130	.04	.85	15.6	—
b	Size, 301 × 411 [14] (No. 1 Tall); net wt., 16 oz. (1 lb.); drained solids, 13 oz. (2 cups); drained liquid, 3 oz.	1 can or 1 lb --	454	70.8	631	97.5	23.6	0	[338] 1,129	1,597	3.2	[339] —	1,524	270	.09	.73	32.2	—
c	Size, 603 × 405; [14] net wt., 64 oz. (4 lb.); drained solids, 52 oz. (3 lb. 4 oz.), 8 cups; drained liquid, 12 oz.	1 can --------	1,814	70.8	2,521	390.0	94.3	0	[338] 4,517	6,385	12.7	[339] —	6,095	1,090	.36	2.90	128.8	—
1953	Coho (silver):																	
	Can and approx. contents:																	
a	Size, 307 × 200.25 [14] (No. ½ Flat); net wt., 7¾ oz.; drained solids, 6¼ oz. (approx. 1 cup); drained liquid, 1½ oz.	1 can --------	220	69.3	337	45.8	15.6	0	[338] 537	634	2.0	[339] 772	746	180	.07	.40	16.3	—
b	Size, 301 × 411 [14] (No. 1 Tall); net wt., 16 oz. (1 lb.); drained solids, 13 oz. (2 cups); drained liquid, 3 oz.	1 can or 1 lb --	454	69.3	694	94.3	32.2	0	[338] 1,107	1,306	4.1	[339] 1,592	1,538	360	.14	.82	33.6	—
c	Size, 603 × 405; [14] net wt., 64 oz. (4 lb.); drained solids, 52 oz. (3 lb. 4 oz.), 8 cups; drained liquid, 12 oz.	1 can --------	1,814	69.3	2,775	377.3	128.8	0	[338] 4,426	5,224	16.3	[339] 6,367	6,149	1,450	.54	3.27	134.2	—
1955	Pink (humpback):																	
	Can and approx. contents:																	
a	Size, 307 × 200.25 [14] (No. ½ Flat); net wt., 7¾ oz.; drained solids, 6¼ oz. (approx. 1 cup); drained liquid, 1½ oz.	1 can --------	220	70.8	310	45.1	13.0	0	[338] 431	629	1.8	[339] 851	794	150	.07	.40	17.6	—
b	Size, 301 × 411 [14] (No. 1 Tall); net wt., 16 oz. (1 lb.); drained solids, 13 oz. (2 cups); drained liquid, 3 oz.	1 can or 1 lb --	454	70.8	640	93.0	26.8	0	[338] 889	1,297	3.6	[339] 1,755	1,637	320	.14	.82	36.3	—
c	Size, 603 × 405; [14] net wt., 64 oz. (4 lb.); drained solids, 52 oz. (3 lb. 4 oz.), 8 cups; drained liquid, 12 oz.	1 can --------	1,814	70.8	2,558	371.9	107.0	0	[338] 3,555	5,188	14.5	[339] 7,020	6,549	1,270	.54	3.27	145.1	—
1957	Sockeye (red):																	
	Can and approx. contents:																	
a	Size, 307 × 200.25 [14] (No. ½ Flat); net wt., 7¾ oz.; drained solids, 6¼ oz. (approx. 1 cup); drained liquid, 1½ oz.	1 can --------	220	67.2	376	44.7	20.5	0	[338] 570	757	2.6	[339] 1,148	757	510	.09	.85	16.1	—
b	Size, 301 × 411 [14] (No. 1 Tall); net wt., 16 oz. (1 lb.); drained solids, 13 oz. (2 cups); drained liquid, 3 oz.	1 can or 1 lb --	454	67.2	776	92.1	42.2	0	[338] 1,175	1,560	5.4	[339] 2,368	1,560	1,040	.18	.73	33.1	—
c	Size, 603 × 405; [14] net wt., 64 oz. (4 lb.); drained solids, 52 oz. (3 lb. 4 oz.), 8 cups; drained liquid, 12 oz.	1 can --------	1,814	67.2	3,102	368.2	168.7	0	[338] 4,698	6,240	21.8	[339] 9,469	6,240	4,170	.73	2.90	132.4	—
1958	**Salmon, broiled or baked with butter or margarine:**																	
	Steak (refuse: bones, 12%): [1]																	
a	Piece, 6¾ in. long, 2½ in. wide, 1 in. thick (dimensions of uncooked steak).	1 steak -------	145	63.4	232	34.5	9.4	0	—	528	1.5	[42] 148	565	200	.20	.08	12.5	—

[1] Measure and weight apply to food as it is described with inedible part or parts (refuse) included.

[14] Dimensions of can: 1st dimension represents diameter; 2d dimension, height of can. 1st or left-hand digit in each dimension gives number of whole inches; next 2 digits give additional fraction of dimension expressed as 16th of an inch.

[42] Value for product without added salt.

[186] For information on ingredients used, see ARS 62–13 (7), table 26, p. 32.

[337] Values apply to products containing salt. For those without salt, sodium content is low, ranging from 25 mg. to 110 mg. per cup and less than 2 mg. to 7 mg. per tablespoon; amount usually is indicated on label.

[338] Based on total contents of can. If bones are discarded or salmon is canned with bones removed, value will be greatly reduced.

[339] For product canned without added salt, values for items 1949, 1951, 1953, and 1957 are approx. 105 mg. for can, net wt., 7¾ oz.; 220 mg. for can, net wt., 1 lb.; 870 mg. for can, net wt., 64 oz. For item 1955, values are 140 mg. for can, net wt., 7¾ oz.; 290 mg. for can, net wt., 1 lb.; 1,160 mg. for can, net wt., 64 oz.

TABLE 1.—*Nutritive values for household measures and market units of foods*—Continued

[Item numbers correspond to those in table 1 of Handbook No. 8, revised 1963. Values in parentheses denote imputed values usually from another form of the food or from a similar food. Zeros in parentheses indicate that amount of a constituent, if present, is probably too small to be measured. Dashes (—) denote lack of reliable data for a constituent believed to be present in a measurable amount. Calculated values, as those based on a recipe, are not in parentheses]

Item No. (A)		Food, approximate measures, units, and weight (edible part unless footnotes indicate otherwise) (B)			Water (C)	Food energy (D)	Protein (E)	Fat (F)	Carbohydrate (G)	Calcium (H)	Phosphorus (I)	Iron (J)	Sodium (K)	Potassium (L)	Vitamin A value (M)	Thiamin (N)	Riboflavin (O)	Niacin (P)	Ascorbic acid (Q)
				Grams	*Percent*	*Calories*	*Grams*	*Grams*	*Grams*	*Milligrams*	*Milligrams*	*Milligrams*	*Milligrams*	*Milligrams*	*International units*	*Milligrams*	*Milligrams*	*Milligrams*	*Milligrams*
		Salmon, broiled or baked with butter or margarine—Continued																	
		Steak (refuse: bones, 12%) [1]—Continued																	
	b	Pound	1 lb	454	63.4	727	107.8	29.5	0	—	1,653	4.8	[43] 463	1,768	640	0.64	0.24	39.1	—
	c	Fillet	1 lb	454	63.4	826	122.5	33.6	0	—	1,878	5.4	[43] 526	2,009	730	.73	.27	44.5	—
	d	Ounce	1 oz	28	63.4	52	7.7	2.1	0	—	117	.3	[43] 33	126	50	.05	.02	2.8	—
1959		**Salmon rice loaf,** 7½ × 7½ × 1½ in.: [340]																	
	a	Whole	1 loaf	1,045	74.4	1,275	125.4	47.0	76.3	—	—	—	—	—	—	—	—	—	—
	b	Piece, 3¾ × 2½ × 1½ in.; ⅙ of loaf	1 piece	174	74.4	212	20.9	7.8	12.7	—	—	—	—	—	—	—	—	—	—
	c	Pound	1 lb	454	74.4	553	54.4	20.4	33.1	—	—	—	—	—	—	—	—	—	—
1960		**Salmon, smoked:**																	
	a	Pound	1 lb	454	58.9	798	98.0	42.2	0	64	1,111	—	—	—	—	—	—	—	—
	b	Ounce	1 oz	28	58.9	50	6.1	2.6	0	4	69	—	—	—	—	—	—	—	—
1962		**Salsify, cooked (boiled), drained:**																	
	a	Cup, cubed	1 cup	135	81.0	([341])	3.5	.8	[19] 20.4	57	72	1.8	[20] —	359	10	.04	.05	.3	9
	b	Pound	1 lb	454	81.0	([341])	11.8	2.7	[19] 68.5	191	240	5.9	[20] —	1,207	50	.14	.18	.9	32
1963		**Salt, table:**																	
	a	Cup	1 cup	290	.2	0	0	0	0	734	—	.3	112,398	12	0	0	0	0	0
	b	Tablespoon	1 tbsp	17	.2	0	0	0	0	43	—	Trace	6,589	1	0	0	0	0	0
	c	Teaspoon	1 tsp	5.5	.2	0	0	0	0	14	—	Trace	2,132	Trace	0	0	0	0	0
		Salt sticks:																	
1965		Regular type (bread sticks without salt coating):																	
	a	Stick, 7¾ in. long, ¾-in. diam	10 sticks	100	5	384	12.0	2.9	75.3	28	99	.9	[342] 700	92	Trace	.06	.07	1.0	Trace
	b	Stick, 4¼ in. long, ½-in. diam	10 sticks	50	5	192	6.0	1.5	37.7	14	50	.5	[342] 350	46	Trace	.03	.04	.5	Trace
1966		Vienna bread type:																	
	a	Stick, 6½ in. long, 1¼ in. wide	1 stick	35	25	106	3.3	1.1	20.3	16	31	.3	548	33	Trace	.02	.03	.3	Trace
		Sandwich spread (with chopped pickle):																	
1967		Regular:																	
	a	Cup	1 cup	245	45.4	929	1.7	88.7	39.0	37	49	1.7	1,534	225	690	.02	.07	Trace	15
	b	Tablespoon	1 tbsp	15	45.4	57	.1	5.4	2.4	2	3	.1	94	14	40	Trace	Trace	Trace	1
1968		Special dietary (low calorie, approx. 5 Cal. per teaspoon).	1 tbsp	(15)	80.2	17	.2	1.4	1.2	2	3	.1	94	14	40	Trace	Trace	Trace	1
		Sardines, Atlantic, canned in oil:																	
1971		Solids and liquid:																	
		Can and approx. contents:																	
	a	Size, 405 × 301 × 014 [343] (No. ¼ Oil); net wt., 3¾ oz.	1 can	106	50.6	330	21.8	25.9	.6	375	460	3.7	541	594	190	.02	.17	4.7	—
	b	Pound	1 lb	454	50.6	1,411	93.4	110.7	2.7	1,606	1,969	15.9	2,313	2,540	820	.09	.73	20.0	—
	c	Ounce	1 oz	28	50.6	88	5.8	6.9	.2	100	123	1.0	145	159	50	.01	.05	1.2	—
1972		Drained solids:																	
		Can and approx. drained contents:																	
	a	Size, 405 × 301 × 014 [343] (No. ¼ Oil); drained wt., 3¼ oz.; 5–20 sardines.	1 can	92	61.8	187	22.1	10.2	—	402	459	2.7	757	543	200	.03	.18	5.0	—
		Sardines, approx. dimensions and count in can of net wt., 3¾ oz.:																	
	b	Fish, 3½ in. long, 1½ in. wide, ⅜ in. thick; [40] 5 per can.	1 fish	20	61.8	41	4.8	2.2	—	87	100	.6	165	118	40	.01	.04	1.1	—
	c	Fish, 3 in. long, 1 in. wide, ½ in. thick; [40] 8 per can.	1 fish	12	61.8	24	2.9	1.3	—	52	60	.3	99	71	30	Trace	.02	6	—
	d	Fish, 2⅔ in. long, ½ in. wide, ¼ in. thick; [40] 16–20 per can.	1 fish	5	61.8	10	1.2	.6	—	22	25	.1	41	30	10	Trace	.01	.3	—
	e	Pound	1 lb	454	61.8	921	108.9	50.3	—	1,982	2,263	13.2	3,733	2,676	1,000	.14	.91	24.5	—
	f	Ounce	1 oz	28	61.8	58	6.8	3.1	—	124	141	.8	233	167	60	.01	.06	1.5	—
1977		**Sauerkraut,** canned, solids and liquid:																	
		Can and approx. contents:																	
	a	Size, 303 × 406 [14] (No. 303); net wt., 16 oz. (1 lb.).	1 can or 1 lb	454	92.8	82	4.5	.9	18.1	163	82	2.3	[344] 3,388	635	230	.14	.18	.9	64
	b	Size, 603 × 700 [14] (No. 10); net wt., 99 oz. (6 lb. 3 oz.).	1 can	2,807	92.8	505	28.1	5.6	112.3	1,011	505	14.0	[344] 20,968	3,930	1,400	.84	1.12	5.6	393
	c	Cup	1 cup	235	92.8	42	2.4	.5	9.4	85	42	1.2	[344] 1,755	329	120	.07	.09	.5	33
1978		**Sauerkraut juice,** canned:																	
		Can and approx. contents:																	

(A)	(B)			(C)	(D)	(E)	(F)	(G)	(H)	(I)	(J)	(K)	(L)	(M)	(N)	(O)	(P)	(Q)
a	Size, 303 × 406[14] (No. 303); net contents, 15 fl. oz.	1 can	453	94.6	45	3.2	Trace	10.4	168	63	5.0	[344] 3,565	—	—	0.14	0.18	0.9	82
b	Cup	1 cup	242	94.6	24	1.7	Trace	5.6	90	34	2.7	[344] 1,905	—	—	.07	.10	.5	44
	Sausage, cold cuts, and luncheon meats:																	
1980	Blood sausage (blood pudding) and blood and tongue sausage:																	
a	Slice, approx. 2¼-in. diam., ⅛ in. thick (blood sausage).	1 slice	8	46.4	32	1.1	3.0	Trace	—	—	—	—	—	—	—	—	—	—
b	Slice, loaf shape, approx. 5 × 4⅝ × ¹⁄₁₆ in. (blood and tongue sausage).	1 slice	25	46.4	99	3.5	9.2	.1	—	—	—	—	—	—	—	—	—	—
c	Pound	1 lb	454	46.4	1,787	64.0	167.4	1.4	—	—	—	—	—	—	—	—	—	—
d	Ounce	1 oz	28	46.4	112	4.0	10.5	.1	—	—	—	—	—	—	—	—	—	—
1981	Bockwurst:																	
a	Link	1 link	65	61.9	172	7.3	15.4	.4	—	—	—	—	—	—	—	—	—	—
b	Pound, approx. 7 links (item 1981a)	1 lb	454	61.9	1,198	51.3	107.5	2.7	—	—	—	—	—	—	—	—	—	—
	Bologna, including kinds made with and without binders and meat byproducts or variety meats:																	
1982	All samples:																	
	Prepackaged forms:																	
	Chub:																	
	Package, approx. contents and slice cut from piece:																	
a	Package, net wt., 32 oz. (2 lb.); cylindrical piece, approx. 8¾ in. long, 3-in. diam.	1 pkg	907	56.2	2,757	109.7	249.4	10.0	63	1,161	16.3	11,791	2,086	—	1.45	2.00	23.6	—
b	Slice, approx. ⅛ in. thick; ¹⁄₇₀ of piece (item 1982a).	1 slice	13	56.2	40	1.6	3.6	.1	1	17	.2	169	30	—	.02	.03	.3	—
c	Ring, net wt., 12 oz.; piece, approx. 15 in. long, 1⅜-in. diam.	1 ring	340	56.2	1,034	41.1	93.5	3.7	24	435	6.1	4,420	782	—	.54	.75	8.8	—
	Slices (approx. ⅛ in. thick):																	
	Package and approx. contents:																	
d	Package, net wt., 16 oz. (1 lb.); approx. 16 slices (item 1982g) or 20 slices (item 1982h).	1 pkg or 1 lb.[125]	454	56.2	1,379	54.9	124.7	5.0	32	581	8.2	5,897	1,043	—	.73	1.00	11.8	—
e	Package, net wt., 8 oz.; approx. 8 slices (item 1982g) or 10 slices (item 1982h).	1 pkg	227	56.2	690	27.5	62.4	2.5	16	291	4.1	2,951	522	—	.36	.50	5.9	—
f	Package, net wt., 6 oz.; approx. 6 slices (item 1982g) or 8 slices (item 1982h).	1 pkg	170	56.2	517	20.6	46.8	1.9	12	218	3.1	2,210	391	—	.27	.37	4.4	—
	Slice, approx. dimensions and weight:																	
g	Size, approx. 4½-in. diam. (4⅜–4½ in.); wt., 1 oz.	1 slice or 1 oz.[126]	28	56.2	86	3.4	7.8	.3	2	36	.5	369	65	—	.05	.06	.7	—
h	Size, approx. 4-in. diam. (3⅞–4⅛ in.); wt., ¾ oz.	1 slice	22	56.2	67	2.7	6.1	.2	2	28	.4	286	51	—	.04	.05	.6	—
1983	Without binders:																	
	Prepackaged forms:																	
	Chub:																	
	Package, approx. contents and slice cut from piece:																	
a	Package, net wt., 32 oz. (2 lb.); cylindrical piece, approx. 8¾ in. long, 3-in. diam.	1 pkg	907	57.4	2,512	120.6	206.8	33.6	—	—	—	—	—	—	—	—	—	—
b	Slice, approx. ⅛ in. thick; ¹⁄₇₀ of piece (item 1983a).	1 slice	13	57.4	36	1.7	3.0	.5	—	—	—	—	—	—	—	—	—	—
c	Ring, net wt., 12 oz.; piece, approx. 15 in. long, 1⅜-in. diam.	1 ring	340	57.4	942	45.2	77.5	12.6	—	—	—	—	—	—	—	—	—	—
	Slices (approx. ⅛ in. thick):																	
	Package and approx. contents:																	
d	Package, net wt., 16 oz. (1 lb.); approx. 16 slices (item 1983g) or 20 slices (item 1983h).	1 pkg. or 1 lb.[125]	454	57.4	1,256	60.3	103.4	16.8	—	—	—	—	—	—	—	—	—	—

[1] Measure and weight apply to food as it is described with inedible part or parts (refuse) included.

[14] Dimensions of can: 1st dimension represents diameter; 2d dimension, height of can. 1st or left-hand digit in each dimension gives number of whole inches; next 2 digits give additional fraction of dimension expressed as 16th of an inch.

[19] If prepared from freshly harvested sample, large proportion of carbohydrate may be inulin, which is of doubtful availability. If prepared from stored sample, inulin may have been converted to available sugars.

[20] Value is for unsalted product. If salt is used, increase value by 236 mg. per 100 g. of vegetable—an estimated figure based on typical amount of salt (0.6%) in canned vegetables. See also Appendix C, section on Cooked Vegetables.

[40] Width at widest part; thickness at thickest part.

[43] Value for product without added salt.

[125] Use also for 1 lb. of other form or forms listed for this item.

[126] Use also for 1 oz. of other form or forms listed for this item.

[340] Prepared with salmon, rice, water, milk, bread cubes, eggs, parsley, green pepper, and lemon juice.

[341] Values for 1 cup range from 16 Cal. when prepared from freshly harvested salsify to 94 Cal. when prepared from stored salsify; corresponding range for 1 lb. is from 54 to 318 Cal.

[342] Based on value of approx. 700 mg. per 100 g. for product without salt coating. Sodium value of 1,674 mg. per 100 g. shown in Agr. Handb. No. 8, rev. 1963, represents product with salt coating.

[343] Dimensions of can: 1st dimension represents length, 2d dimension, width; 3d dimension, height of can. 1st or left-hand digit in each dimension gives number of whole inches; next 2 digits give additional fraction of dimension expressed as 16th of an inch.

[344] Values for sauerkraut and sauerkraut juice are based on salt contents of 1.9 and 2.0%, respectively, in finished products. Amounts in some samples may vary significantly from this estimate.

TABLE 1.—*Nutritive values for household measures and market units of foods*—Continued

[Item numbers correspond to those in table 1 of Handbook No. 8, revised 1963. Values in parentheses denote imputed values usually from another form of the food or from a similar food. Zeros in parentheses indicate that amount of a constituent, if present, is probably too small to be measured. Dashes (—) denote lack of reliable data for a constituent believed to be present in a measurable amount. Calculated values, as those based on a recipe, are not in parentheses]

Item No. (A)	Food, approximate measures, units, and weight (edible part unless footnotes indicate otherwise) (B)			Water (C)	Food energy (D)	Protein (E)	Fat (F)	Carbohydrate (G)	Calcium (H)	Phosphorus (I)	Iron (J)	Sodium (K)	Potassium (L)	Vitamin A value (M)	Thiamin (N)	Riboflavin (O)	Niacin (P)	Ascorbic acid (Q)
			Grams	Percent	Calories	Grams	Grams	Grams	Milligrams	Milligrams	Milligrams	Milligrams	Milligrams	International units	Milligrams	Milligrams	Milligrams	Milligrams
	Sausage, cold cuts, and luncheon meats—Continued																	
	Bologna, including kinds made with and without binders and meat byproducts or variety meats—Continued																	
	Without binders—Continued																	
	Prepackaged forms—Continued																	
	Slices (approx. ⅛ in. thick)—Continued																	
	Package and approx. contents—Continued																	
e	Package, net wt., 8 oz.; approx. 8 slices (item 1983g) or 10 slices (item 1983h).	1 pkg	227	57.4	629	30.2	51.8	8.4	—	—	—	—	—	—	—	—	—	—
f	Package, net wt., 6 oz.; approx. 6 slices (item 1983g) or 8 slices (item 1983h).	1 pkg	170	57.4	471	22.6	38.8	6.3	—	—	—	—	—	—	—	—	—	—
	Slice, approx. dimensions and weight:																	
g	Size, approx. 4½-in. diam. (4⅜–4½ in.); wt., 1 oz.	1 slice or 1 oz.[136]	28	57.4	79	3.8	6.5	1.0	—	—	—	—	—	—	—	—	—	—
h	Size, approx. 4-in. diam. (3⅞–4⅛ in.); wt., ¾ oz.	1 slice	22	57.4	61	2.9	5.0	.8	—	—	—	—	—	—	—	—	—	—
1984	With nonfat dry milk.[346]																	
1985	With cereal:																	
	Prepackaged forms:																	
	Chub:																	
	Package, approx. contents and slice cut from piece:																	
a	Package, net wt., 32 oz. (2 lb.); cylindrical piece, approx. 8¾ in. long, 3-in. diam.	1 pkg	907	57.9	2,376	128.8	186.8	35.4	—	—	—	—	—	—	—	—	—	—
b	Slice, approx. ⅛ in. thick; 1/70 of piece (item 1985a).	1 slice	13	57.9	34	1.8	2.7	.5	—	—	—	—	—	—	—	—	—	—
c	Ring, net wt., 12 oz.; piece, approx. 15 in. long, 1⅜-in. diam.	1 ring	340	57.9	891	48.3	70.0	13.3	—	—	—	—	—	—	—	—	—	—
	Slices (approx. ⅛ in. thick):																	
	Package and approx. contents:																	
d	Package, net wt., 16 oz. (1 lb.); approx. 16 slices (item 1985g) or 20 slices (item 1985h).	1 pkg. or 1 lb.[136]	454	57.9	1,188	64.4	93.4	17.7	—	—	—	—	—	—	—	—	—	—
e	Package, net wt., 8 oz.; approx. 8 slices (item 1985g) or 10 slices (item 1985h).	1 pkg	227	57.9	595	32.2	46.8	8.9	—	—	—	—	—	—	—	—	—	—
f	Package, net wt., 6 oz.; approx. 6 slices (item 1985g) or 8 slices (item 1985h).	1 pkg	170	57.9	445	24.1	35.0	6.6	—	—	—	—	—	—	—	—	—	—
	Slice, approx. dimensions and weight:																	
g	Size, approx. 4½-in. diam. (4⅜–4½ in.); wt., 1 oz.	1 slice or 1 oz.[136]	28	57.9	74	4.0	5.8	1.1	—	—	—	—	—	—	—	—	—	—
h	Size, approx. 4-in. diam. (3⅞–4⅛ in.); wt., ¾ oz.	1 slice	22	57.9	58	3.1	4.5	.9	—	—	—	—	—	—	—	—	—	—
1986	Braunschweiger (smoked liverwurst):																	
	Prepackaged forms:																	
	Roll:																	
	Package, approx. contents and slice cut from piece:																	
a	Package, net wt., 16 oz. (1 lb.); roll, approx. 6½ in. long, 2½-in. diam.[346]	1 pkg. or 1 lb	454	52.6	1,447	67.1	124.3	10.4	45	1,111	26.8	—	—	29,620	0.77	6.53	37.2	—
b	Slice, approx. 2½-in. diam., ¼ in. thick; 1/25 of roll (item 1986a).	1 slice	18	52.6	57	2.7	4.9	.4	2	44	1.1	—	—	1,180	.03	.26	1.5	—
c	Package, net wt., 8 oz.; roll, approx. 5½ in. long, 2-in. diam.[346]	1 pkg	227	52.6	724	33.6	62.2	5.2	23	556	13.4	—	—	14,820	.39	3.27	18.6	—
d	Slice, approx. 2-in. diam., ¼ in. thick; 1/22 of roll (item 1986c).	1 slice	10	52.6	32	1.5	2.7	.2	1	25	.6	—	—	650	.02	.14	.8	—
	Slice, approx. 3⅛-in. diam., ¼ in. thick; wt., 1 oz.:																	
e	Package, net wt., 6 oz.; 6 slices	1 pkg	170	52.6	542	25.2	46.6	3.9	17	417	10.0	—	—	11,100	.29	2.45	13.9	—

(A)	(B)		(C)	(D)	(E)	(F)	(G)	(H)	(I)	(J)	(K)	(L)	(M)	(N)	(O)	(P)	(Q)
f	Slice	1 slice or 1 oz	28	52.6	90	4.2	7.8	0.7	3	69	1.7	—	—	1,850	0.05	0.41	2.3	—
	Brown-and-serve sausage:																	
1987	Before browning:																	
	Prepackaged patties or links:																	
	Package and approx. contents:																	
a	Package, net wt., 8 oz.; approx. 8–9 patties (item 1987b) or 10–11 links (item 1987c).	1 pkg	227	45.3	892	30.6	81.7	6.1	—	—	—	—	—	—	—	—	—	—
b	Patty, oval piece, approx. 2⅜ × 1⅞ in., ½ in. thick.	1 patty or 1 oz.[196]	28	45.3	111	3.8	10.2	.8	—	—	—	—	—	—	—	—	—	—
c	Link, approx. 3⅞ in. long, ⅝-in. diam	1 link	21	45.3	83	2.8	7.6	.6	—	—	—	—	—	—	—	—	—	—
d	Pound	1 lb	454	45.3	1,783	61.2	163.3	12.2	—	—	—	—	—	—	—	—	—	—
1988	Browned:																	
a	Yield from 8-oz. pkg. (item 1987a)	8–9 patties or 10–11 links.	180	39.9	760	29.7	68.0	5.0	—	—	—	—	—	—	—	—	—	—
b	Yield from 1 patty (item 1987b)	1 patty	23	39.9	97	3.8	8.7	.6	—	—	—	—	—	—	—	—	—	—
c	Yield from 1 link (item 1987c)	1 link	17	39.9	72	2.8	6.4	.5	—	—	—	—	—	—	—	—	—	—
d	Pound	1 lb	454	39.9	1,914	74.8	171.5	12.7	—	—	—	—	—	—	—	—	—	—
1989	Capicola or Capacola:																	
	Prepackaged square slice, approx. 4¼ × 4¼ in., 1/16 in. thick; wt., ¾ oz.:																	
a	Package, net wt., 4½ oz.; approx. 6 slices	1 pkg	128	26.2	639	25.9	58.6	0	—	—	—	—	—	—	—	—	—	—
b	Slice	1 slice[347]	21	26.2	105	4.2	9.6	0	—	—	—	—	—	—	—	—	—	—
c	Pound, approx. 21½ slices (item 1989b)	1 lb	454	26.2	2,263	91.6	207.7	0	—	—	—	—	—	—	—	—	—	—
d	Ounce	1 oz	28	26.2	141	5.7	13.0	0	—	—	—	—	—	—	—	—	—	—
	Cervelat:																	
1990	Dry:																	
	Prepackaged roll:																	
	Package, approx. contents and slice cut from roll:																	
a	Package, net wt., 5⅓ oz.; roll, approx. 6 in. long, 1½-in. diam.	1 pkg	150	29.4	677	36.9	56.4	2.6	21	441	4.1	—	—	(0)	.41	.35	8.3	—
b	Slice, approx. 1½-in. diam., ⅛ in. thick; 1/50 of roll (item 1990a).	4 slices	12	29.4	54	3.0	4.5	.2	2	35	.3	—	—	(0)	.03	.03	.7	—
c	Pound	1 lb	454	29.4	2,046	111.6	170.6	7.7	64	1,334	12.2	—	—	(0)	1.22	1.04	24.9	—
d	Ounce (approx. 9½ slices (item 1990b))	1 oz	28	29.4	128	7.0	10.7	.5	4	83	.8	—	—	(0)	.08	.07	1.6	—
1991	Soft. See Thuringer cervelat (summer sausage) (item 2021).																	
1992	Country-style sausage	1 lb	454	49.9	1,565	68.5	141.1	0	41	762	10.4	—	—	—	1.00	.86	14.1	—
1993	Deviled ham, canned:																	
	Container and approx. contents:																	
a	Can, net wt., 2¼ oz	1 can	64	50.5	225	8.9	20.7	0	5	59	1.3	—	—	(0)	.09	.06	1.0	—
b	Can, net wt., 3 oz	1 can	85	50.5	298	11.8	27.5	0	7	78	1.8	—	—	(0)	.12	.09	1.4	—
c	Can, net wt., 4½ oz	1 can	128	50.5	449	17.8	41.3	0	10	118	2.7	—	—	(0)	.18	.13	2.0	—
d	Cup	1 cup	225	50.5	790	31.3	72.7	0	18	207	4.7	—	—	(0)	.32	.23	3.6	—
e	Tablespoon	1 tbsp	13	50.5	46	1.8	4.2	0	1	12	.3	—	—	(0)	.02	.01	.2	—
f	Pound	1 lb	454	50.5	1,592	63.1	146.5	0	36	417	9.5	—	—	(0)	.64	.45	7.3	—
g	Ounce	1 oz	28	50.5	100	3.9	9.2	0	2	26	.6	—	—	(0)	.04	.03	.5	—
	Frankfurters (franks, furters, hotdogs, wieners), including kinds made with and without binders and meat byproducts or variety meats:																	
	Chilled or refrigerated:																	
1994	All samples:																	
	Prepackaged frankfurters:																	
	Package and approx. contents:																	
a	Package, net wt., 16 oz. (1 lb.); approx. 8 frankfurters (item 1994b) or 10 frankfurters (item 1994c).	1 pkg. or 1 lb	454	55.6	1,402	56.7	125.2	8.2	32	603	8.6	4,990	998	—	.73	.91	12.2	—
	Frankfurter, approx. dimensions and weight:																	
b	Size, approx. 5 in. long, ⅞-in. diam.; wt., 2 oz.	1 frankfurter	57	55.6	176	7.1	15.7	1.0	4	76	1.1	627	125	—	.09	.11	1.5	—
c	Size, approx. 5 in. long, ¾-in. diam.; wt., 1⅗ oz.	1 frankfurter	45	55.6	139	5.6	12.4	.8	3	60	.9	495	99	—	.07	.09	1.2	—
1995	Without binders:																	
	Not smoked:																	
	Prepackaged frankfurters:																	

[195] Use also for 1 lb. of other form or forms listed for this item.
[196] Use also for 1 oz. of other form or forms listed for this item.
[345] For bologna made with nonfat dry milk, use weights of volume measures and protein values shown for all meat bologna. Values for other nutrients may be different, but data are lacking on amounts present.
[346] Cut pieces of this approx. diam. also marketed in other lengths and weights. Weight and nutritive values shown for slices (items 1986b, 1986d) also apply to ¼-in. slices cut from those pieces.
[347] Weight and nutritive values also apply to round slice, approx. 4¾-in. diam., 1/16 in. thick.

TABLE 1.—*Nutritive values for household measures and market units of foods*—Continued

[Item numbers correspond to those in table 1 of Handbook No. 8, revised 1963. Values in parentheses denote imputed values usually from another form of the food or from a similar food. Zeros in parentheses indicate that amount of a constituent, if present, is probably too small to be measured. Dashes (—) denote lack of reliable data for a constituent believed to be present in a measurable amount. Calculated values, as those based on a recipe, are not in parentheses]

Item No.	Food, approximate measures, units, and weight (edible part unless footnotes indicate otherwise)			Values for edible part of foods															
				Water	Food energy	Protein	Fat	Carbohydrate	Calcium	Phosphorus	Iron	Sodium	Potassium	Vitamin A value	Thiamin	Riboflavin	Niacin	Ascorbic acid
(A)	(B)			(C)	(D)	(E)	(F)	(G)	(H)	(I)	(J)	(K)	(L)	(M)	(N)	(O)	(P)	(Q)
			Grams	*Percent*	*Calories*	*Grams*	*Grams*	*Grams*	*Milligrams*	*Milligrams*	*Milligrams*	*Milligrams*	*Milligrams*	*International units*	*Milligrams*	*Milligrams*	*Milligrams*	*Milligrams*
	Sausage, cold cuts, and luncheon meats—Continued																	
	Frankfurters (franks, furters, hotdogs, wieners), including kinds made with and without binders and meat byproducts or variety meats—Continued																	
	Chilled or refrigerated—Continued																	
	Without binders—Continued																	
	Not smoked—Continued																	
	Prepackaged frankfurters—Continued																	
	Package and approx. contents:																	
a	Package, net wt., 16 oz. (1 lb.); approx. 8 frankfurters (item 1995c) or 10 frankfurters (item 1995d).	1 pkg. or 1 lb	454	56.5	1,343	59.4	115.7	11.3	—	—	—	—	—	—	—	—	—	—
b	Package, net wt., 5½ oz.; approx. 16 frankfurters (item 1995e).	1 pkg	156	56.5	462	20.4	39.8	3.9	—	—	—	—	—	—	—	—	—	—
	Frankfurter, approx. dimensions and weight:																	
c	Size, approx. 5 in. long, ⅞-in. diam.; wt., 2 oz.	1 frankfurter	57	56.5	169	7.5	14.5	1.4	—	—	—	—	—	—	—	—	—	—
d	Size, approx. 5 in. long, ¾-in. diam.; wt., 1⅗ oz.	1 frankfurter	45	56.5	133	5.9	11.5	1.1	—	—	—	—	—	—	—	—	—	—
e	Size, approx. 1¾ in. long, ½-in. diam.; wt., ⅓ oz.	1 frankfurter	10	56.5	30	1.3	2.6	.3	—	—	—	—	—	—	—	—	—	—
	Half smoked:																	
	Prepackaged frankfurters:																	
	Package and approx. contents:																	
f	Package, net wt., 11 oz.; approx. 5 frankfurters (item 1995g).	1 pkg	312	56.5	924	40.9	79.6	7.8	—	—	—	—	—	—	—	—	—	—
g	Frankfurter, approx. 5 in. long, 1-in. diam.; wt., 2⅕ oz.	1 frankfurter	62	56.5	184	8.1	15.8	1.6	—	—	—	—	—	—	—	—	—	—
	Smoked:																	
	Prepackaged frankfurters:																	
	Package and approx. contents:																	
h	Package, net wt., 12 oz.; approx. 8 frankfurters (item 1995j) or 10 frankfurters (item 1995k).	1 pkg	340	56.5	1,006	44.5	86.7	8.5	—	—	—	—	—	—	—	—	—	—
i	Package, net wt., 5 oz.; approx. 16 frankfurters (item 1995l).	1 pkg	142	56.5	420	18.6	36.2	3.6	—	—	—	—	—	—	—	—	—	—
	Frankfurter, approx. dimensions and weight:																	
j	Size, approx. 4¾ in. long, ¾-in. diam.; wt., 1½ oz.	1 frankfurter	42	56.5	124	5.5	10.7	1.1	—	—	—	—	—	—	—	—	—	—
k	Size, approx. 4½ in. long, ¾-in. diam.; wt., 1⅕ oz.	1 frankfurter	34	56.5	101	4.5	8.7	.9	—	—	—	—	—	—	—	—	—	—
l	Size, approx. 1¾ in. long, ⅝-in. diam.; wt., ⅓ oz.	1 frankfurter	9	56.5	27	1.2	2.3	.2	—	—	—	—	—	—	—	—	—	—
1996	With nonfat dry milk:																	
	Prepackaged frankfurters:																	
	Package and approx. contents:																	
a	Package, net wt., 16 oz. (1 lb.); approx. 8 frankfurters (item 1996b) or 10 frankfurters (item 1996c).	1 pkg. or 1 lb	454	54.2	1,361	59.4	116.1	15.4	—	—	—	—	—	—	—	—	—	—
	Frankfurter, approx. dimensions and weight:																	
b	Size, approx. 5 in. long, ⅞-in. diam.; wt., 2 oz.	1 frankfurter	57	54.2	171	7.5	14.6	1.9	—	—	—	—	—	—	—	—	—	—
c	Size, approx. 5 in. long, ¾-in. diam.; wt., 1⅗ oz.	1 frankfurter	45	54.2	135	5.9	11.5	1.5	—	—	—	—	—	—	—	—	—	—
1997	With cereal:																	
	Prepackaged frankfurters:																	
	Package and approx. contents:																	
a	Package, net wt., 16 oz. (1 lb.); approx. 8 frankfurters (item 1997b) or 10	1 pkg. or 1 lb	454	61.7	1,125	65.3	93.4	.9	—	—	—	—	—	—	—	—	—	—

(A)	(B)			(C)	(D)	(E)	(F)	(G)	(H)	(I)	(J)	(K)	(L)	(M)	(N)	(O)	(P)	(Q)
	frankfurters (item 1997c).																	
	Frankfurter, approx. dimensions and weight:																	
b	Size, approx. 5 in. long, ⅞-in. diam.; wt., 2 oz.	1 frankfurter	57	61.7	141	8.2	11.7	0.1	—	—	—	—	—	—	—	—	—	—
c	Size, approx. 5 in. long, ¾-in. diam.; wt., 1⅝ oz.	1 frankfurter	45	61.7	112	6.5	9.3	.1	—	—	—	—	—	—	—	—	—	—
1998	With nonfat dry milk and cereal:																	
	Prepackaged frankfurters:																	
	Package and approx. contents:																	
a	Package, net wt., 16 oz. (1 lb.); approx. 8 frankfurters (item 1998b) or 10 frankfurters (item 1998c).	1 pkg. or 1 lb	454	50.5	—	64.4	98.4	—	—	—	—	—	—	—	—	—	—	—
	Frankfurter, approx. dimensions and weight:																	
b	Size, approx. 5 in. long, ⅞-in. diam.; wt., 2 oz.	1 frankfurter	57	50.5	—	8.1	12.4	—	—	—	—	—	—	—	—	—	—	—
c	Size, approx. 5 in. long, ¾-in. diam.; wt., 1⅝ oz.	1 frankfurter	45	50.5	—	6.4	9.8	—	—	—	—	—	—	—	—	—	—	—
1999	Cooked (reheated), all samples:																	
a	Yield from 1 lb., raw (item 1994a)	15.7 oz	445	57.3	1,353	55.2	121.0	7.1	22	454	6.7	—	—	—	0.67	0.89	11.1	—
b	Yield from 1 frankfurter (item 1994b)	1 frankfurter	56	57.3	170	6.9	15.2	.9	3	57	.8	—	—	—	.08	.11	1.4	—
c	Yield from 1 frankfurter (item 1994c)	1 frankfurter	44	57.3	134	5.5	12.0	.7	2	45	.7	—	—	—	.07	.09	1.1	—
d	Pound	1 lb	454	57.3	1,379	56.2	123.4	7.3	23	463	6.8	—	—	—	.68	.91	11.3	—
2000	Canned:																	
a	Drained contents (7 frankfurters (item 2000b)) from can; net wt., 12 oz.[348]	7 frankfurters	340	66.0	751	45.6	61.5	.7	31	493	7.5	—	—	—	.10	.41	8.2	—
b	Frankfurter, approx. 4⅞ in. long, ⅞-in. diam.; wt., 1.7 oz.	1 frankfurter	48	66.0	106	6.4	8.7	.1	4	70	1.1	—	—	—	.01	.06	1.2	—
c	Pound	1 lb	454	66.0	1,002	60.8	82.1	.9	41	658	10.0	—	—	—	.14	.54	10.9	—
2001	Headcheese:																	
	Prepackaged square slice, approx. 4 × 4 in., $^{3}/_{32}$ in. thick; wt., 1 oz.:																	
a	Package, net wt., 8 oz.; approx. 8 slices	1 pkg	227	58.8	608	35.2	49.9	2.3	20	393	5.2	—	—	(0)	.09	.23	2.0	—
b	Slice	1 slice or 1 oz	28	58.8	76	4.4	4.4	6.2	3	49	.7	—	—	(0)	.01	.03	.3	—
c	Pound	1 lb	454	58.8	1,216	70.3	99.8	4.5	41	785	10.4	—	—	(0)	.18	.45	4.1	—
2002	Knockwurst:																	
	Prepackaged link, approx. 4 in. long, 1⅛-in. diam.; wt., 2.4 oz.:																	
a	Package, net wt., 12 oz.; approx. 5 links	1 pkg	340	57.6	945	47.9	78.9	7.5	27	524	7.1	—	—	—	(.58)	(.71)	(8.8)	—
b	Link	1 link	68	57.6	189	9.6	15.8	1.5	5	105	1.4	—	—	—	(.12)	(.14)	(1.8)	—
c	Pound	1 lb	454	57.6	1,261	64.0	105.2	10.0	36	699	9.5	—	—	—	(.77)	(.95)	(11.8)	—
	Liverwurst:																	
2003	Fresh (not smoked)	1 lb	454	53.9	1,393	73.5	116.1	8.2	41	1,080	24.5	—	—	28,800	.91	5.90	25.9	—
2004	Smoked. See Sausage, cold cuts, and luncheon meats (item 1986).																	
	Luncheon meat:																	
2005	Boiled ham:																	
	Prepackaged slices:																	
	Package and approx. contents:																	
a	Package, net wt., 8 oz.; approx. 8 slices (item 2005c).	1 pkg	227	59.1	531	34.1	38.6	0	25	377	6.4	—	—	(0)	1.00	.34	5.9	—
b	Package, net wt., 6 oz.; approx. 8 slices (item 2005d).	1 pkg	170	59.1	398	32.3	28.9	0	19	282	4.8	—	—	(0)	.75	.26	4.4	—
	Slice, approx. dimensions and weight:																	
c	Rectangular, approx. 6¼ × 4 × $^{1}/_{16}$ in.; wt., 1 oz.	1 slice or 1 oz	28	59.1	66	5.4	4.8	0	3	47	.8	—	—	(0)	.12	.04	.7	—
d	Square, approx. 4¼ × 4¼ × $^{1}/_{16}$ in.; wt., ¾ oz.	1 slice	21	59.1	49	4.0	3.6	0	2	35	.6	—	—	(0)	.09	.03	.5	—
e	Pound	1 lb	454	59.1	1,061	86.2	77.1	0	50	753	12.7	—	—	(0)	2.00	.68	11.8	—
2006	Pork, cured ham or shoulder, chopped, spiced or unspiced, canned:																	
	Can, approx. contents, and slice cut from piece:																	
a	Can, net wt., 12 oz.; rectangular piece, approx. 3½ in. long, 2 in. wide, 3 in. high.	1 can	340	54.9	1,000	51.0	84.7	4.4	31	367	7.5	4,196	755	(0)	1.05	.71	10.2	—
b	Can, net wt., 7 oz.; rectangular piece, approx. 3½ in. long, 2 in. wide, 1¾ in. high.	1 can	198	54.9	582	29.7	49.3	2.6	18	214	4.4	2,443	440	(0)	.61	.42	5.9	—
c	Slice, approx. 3 × 2 × ½ in.; ⅙ of piece (item 2006a) or ⅓ of piece (item 2006b).	1 slice	60	54.9	176	9.0	14.9	.8	5	65	1.3	740	133	(0)	.19	.13	1.8	—
d	Pound	1 lb	454	54.9	1,334	68.0	112.9	5.9	41	490	10.0	5,597	1,007	(0)	1.41	.95	13.6	—
e	Ounce	1 oz	28	54.9	83	4.3	7.1	.4	3	31	.6	350	63	(0)	.09	.06	.9	—

[348] Net weight given on can represents drained solids only.

Table 1.—*Nutritive values for household measures and market units of foods*—Continued

[Item numbers correspond to those in table 1 of Handbook No. 8, revised 1963. Values in parentheses denote imputed values usually from another form of the food or from a similar food. Zeros in parentheses indicate that amount of a constituent, if present, is probably too small to be measured. Dashes (—) denote lack of reliable data for a constituent believed to be present in a measurable amount. Calculated values, as those based on a recipe, are not in parentheses]

Item No. (A)	Food, approximate measures, units, and weight (edible part unless footnotes indicate otherwise) (B)			Water (C)	Food energy (D)	Protein (E)	Fat (F)	Carbohydrate (G)	Calcium (H)	Phosphorus (I)	Iron (J)	Sodium (K)	Potassium (L)	Vitamin A value (M)	Thiamin (N)	Riboflavin (O)	Niacin (P)	Ascorbic acid (Q)
			Grams	Percent	Calories	Grams	Grams	Grams	Milligrams	Milligrams	Milligrams	Milligrams	Milligrams	International units	Milligrams	Milligrams	Milligrams	Milligrams
	Sausage, cold cuts, and luncheon meats—Continued																	
2007	Meat loaf	1 lb	454	64.1	907	72.1	59.9	15.0	41	807	8.2	—	—	—	0.59	1.00	11.3	—
2008	Meat, potted (includes potted beef, chicken, turkey):																	
	Container and approx. contents:																	
a	Can, net wt., 3–3¼ oz.[340]	1 can	90	60.7	223	15.8	17.3	0	—	—	—	—	—	—	.03	.20	1.1	—
b	Can, net wt., 5½ oz.[340]	1 can	156	60.7	387	27.3	30.0	0	—	—	—	—	—	—	.05	.34	1.9	—
c	Cup	1 cup	225	60.7	558	39.4	43.2	0	—	—	—	—	—	—	.07	.50	2.7	—
d	Tablespoon	1 tbsp	13	60.7	32	2.3	2.5	0	—	—	—	—	—	—	Trace	.03	.2	—
e	Pound	1 lb	454	60.7	1,125	79.4	87.1	0	—	—	—	—	—	—	.14	1.00	5.4	—
f	Ounce	1 oz	28	60.7	70	5.0	5.4	0	—	—	—	—	—	—	.01	.06	.3	—
2009	Minced ham	1 lb	454	61.7	1,034	62.1	76.7	20.0	36	404	9.5	—	—	(0)	1.68	1.00	15.4	—
2010	Mortadella:																	
a	Slice, approx. 4⅞-in. diam., 3/32 in. thick	1 slice	25	48.9	79	5.1	6.3	.2	3	60	.8	—	—	—	—	—	—	—
b	Pound	1 lb	454	48.9	1,429	92.5	113.4	2.7	54	1,080	14.1	—	—	—	—	—	—	—
c	Ounce	1 oz	28	48.9	89	5.8	7.1	.2	3	67	.9	—	—	—	—	—	—	—
2011	Polish sausage:																	
	Prepackaged links:																	
	Package and approx. contents:																	
a	Package, net wt., 16 oz. (1 lb.); approx. 2 sausages (item 2011b) or 6 sausages (item 2011c).	1 pkg. or 1 lb	454	53.7	1,879	71.2	117.0	5.4	41	798	10.9	—	—	(0)	1.54	86	14.1	—
	Sausage, approx. dimensions and weight:																	
b	Size, approx. 10 in. long, 1¼-in. diam.; wt., 8 oz.	1 sausage	227	53.7	690	35.6	58.6	2.7	20	400	5.4	—	—	(0)	.77	.43	7.0	—
c	Size, approx. 5⅜ in. long, 1-in. diam.; wt., 2.7 oz.	1 sausage	76	53.7	231	11.9	19.6	.9	7	134	1.8	—	—	(0)	.26	.14	2.4	—
	Pork sausage:																	
2013	Raw:																	
	Prepackaged roll, brick, rope form, links, or patties:																	
	Package and approx. contents:																	
a	Package, net wt., 16 oz. (1 lb.) (roll, approx. 5⅞ in. long, 2¼-in. diam., or 5⅝ in. long, 2½-in. diam.; brick, approx. 5⅛ × 3 × 1⅞ in.; rope form, approx. 20 in. long, 1¼-in. diam.; 16 links (item 2013e)).	1 pkg. or 1 lb.[196]	454	38.1	2,259	42.6	230.4	Trace	23	417	6.4	3,357	635	(0)	1.95	.77	10.4	—
b	Package, net wt., 8 oz. (approx. 4 patties (item 2013d) or 8 links (item 2013e)).	1 pkg	227	38.1	1,130	21.3	115.3	Trace	11	209	3.2	1,680	318	(0)	.98	.39	5.2	—
	Sausage, approx. dimensions and weight:																	
c	Piece, approx. 3 in. long, 1¼-in. diam.; wt., 2.4 oz.; 3/20 of rope form (see item 2013a).	1 piece	68	38.1	339	6.4	34.5	Trace	3	63	1.0	503	95	(0)	.29	.12	1.6	—
d	Patty, approx. 3⅞-in. diam., ¼ in. thick; wt., 2 oz.	1 patty	57	38.1	284	5.4	29.0	Trace	3	52	.8	422	80	(0)	.25	.10	1.3	—
e	Link, approx. 4 in. long, ⅞-in. diam.; wt., 1 oz.	1 link or 1 oz.[196]	28	38.1	141	2.7	14.4	Trace	1	26	.4	210	40	(0)	.12	.05	.7	—
2014	Cooked:																	
a	Yield from 1 lb., raw (item 2013a)	7½ oz	213	34.8	1,014	38.6	94.1	Trace	15	345	5.1	2,041	573	(0)	1.68	.72	7.9	—
b	Yield from 8 oz., raw (item 2013b)	3.8 oz	107	34.8	509	19.4	47.3	Trace	7	173	2.6	1,025	288	(0)	.85	.36	4.0	—
c	Piece (dimensions of uncooked piece (item 2013c)).	1 piece	32	34.8	152	5.8	14.1	Trace	2	52	.8	307	86	(0)	.25	.11	1.2	—
d	Patty, (dimensions of uncooked patty (item 2013d)).	1 patty	27	34.8	129	4.9	11.9	Trace	2	44	.6	259	73	(0)	.21	.09	1.0	—
e	Link (dimensions of uncooked link (item 2013e)).	1 link	13	34.8	62	2.4	5.7	Trace	1	21	.3	125	35	(0)	.10	.04	.5	—
	Canned:																	
2015	Solids and liquid:																	
a	Can, net wt., 8 oz.; approx. 14 sausage links (item 2016a).	1 can	227	42.1	942	31.3	87.2	5.4	18	341	4.8	—	—	(0)	.48	.43	7.5	—

(A)	(B)			(C)	(D)	(E)	(F)	(G)	(H)	(I)	(J)	(K)	(L)	(M)	(N)	(O)	(P)	(Q)
b	Pound	1 lb	454	42.1	1,882	62.6	174.2	10.9	36	680	9.5	—	—	(0)	0.86	0.86	15.0	—
c	Ounce	1 oz	28	42.1	118	3.9	10.9	.7	2	43	.6	—	—	(0)	.05	.05	.9	—
2016	Drained solids:																	
a	Drained contents from can (item 2015a), 14 sausage links, wt., 5.7 oz.	14 sausages	162	43.2	617	29.6	53.1	3.1	18	340	4.5	—	—	—	—	—	—	—
b	Link (approx. 3 in. long, ½-in. diam.; 1/14 of item 2016a).	1 link	12	43.2	46	2.2	3.9	.2	1	25	.3	—	—	—	—	—	—	—
c	Pound	1 lb	454	43.2	1,728	83.0	148.8	8.6	50	953	12.7	—	—	—	—	—	—	—
d	Ounce	1 oz	28	43.2	108	5.2	9.3	.5	3	60	.8	—	—	—	—	—	—	—
	Pork sausage, link, smoked. See Sausage, country-style (item 1992).																	
	Salami:																	
2017	Dry:																	
	Prepackaged forms:																	
	Roll:																	
	Package, approx. contents, and slice cut from roll:																	
a	Package, net wt., 8¼ oz. (roll, approx. 6⅝ in. long, 1¾-in. diam.).	1 pkg	234	29.8	1,053	55.7	89.2	2.8	33	662	8.4	—	—	—	.87	.59	12.4	—
b	Slice, approx. 1¾-in. diam., ⅛ in. thick; 1/47 of pkg. (item 2017a).	1 slice	5	29.8	23	1.2	1.9	.1	1	14	.2	—	—	—	.02	.01	.3	—
	Slice, approx. 3⅛-in. diam., 1/16 in. thick, or 2¾-in. diam., 3/32 in. thick; wt., ⅓ oz.:																	
c	Package, net wt., 4 oz. (approx. 12 slices (item 2017d)).	1 pkg	113	29.8	509	26.9	43.1	1.4	16	320	4.1	—	—	—	.42	.28	6.0	—
d	Slice	1 slice	10	29.8	45	2.4	3.8	.1	1	28	.4	—	—	—	.04	.03	.5	—
e	Pound	1 lb	454	29.8	2,041	108.0	172.8	5.4	64	1,284	16.3	—	—	—	1.68	1.13	24.0	—
f	Ounce	1 oz	28	29.8	128	6.7	10.8	.3	4	80	1.0	—	—	—	.10	.07	1.5	—
2018	Cooked:																	
	Prepackaged slices, approx. ⅛ in. thick:																	
	Package and approx. contents:																	
a	Package, net wt., 16 oz. (1 lb.); approx. 16 slices (item 2018c) or 20 slices (item 2018d).	1 pkg. or 1 lb	454	51.0	1,411	79.4	116.1	6.4	45	907	11.8	—	—	—	1.13	1.09	18.6	—
b	Package, net wt., 8 oz.; approx. 8 slices (item 2018c) or 10 slices (item 2018d).	1 pkg	227	51.0	706	39.7	58.1	3.2	23	454	5.9	—	—	—	.57	.54	9.3	—
	Slice, approx. dimensions and weight:																	
c	Size, approx. 4½-in. diam. (4¼–4½ in.); wt., 1 oz.	1 slice or 1 oz	28	51.0	88	5.0	7.3	.4	3	57	.7	—	—	—	.07	.07	1.2	—
d	Size, approx. 4-in. diam. (3⅞–4⅛ in.); wt., ¾ oz.	1 slice	22	51.0	68	3.9	5.6	.3	2	44	.6	—	—	—	.06	.05	.9	—
2019	Scrapple:																	
	Prepackaged loaf:																	
	Package, approx. contents, and slice cut from loaf:																	
a	Package, net wt., 16 oz. (1 lb.); rectangular piece, approx. 4½ × 2¾ × 2⅛ in.	1 pkg. or 1 lb	454	61.3	975	39.9	61.7	66.2	23	290	5.4	—	—	—	.86	.41	8.2	—
b	Slice, approx. 2¾ × 2⅛ × ¼ in.; 1/18 of loaf (item 2019a).	1 slice	25	61.3	54	2.2	3.4	3.7	1	16	.3	—	—	—	.05	.02	.5	—
c	Ounce	1 oz	28	61.3	61	2.5	3.9	4.1	1	18	.3	—	—	—	.05	.08	.5	—
2020	Souse:																	
	Prepackaged slice, square, approx. 3⅞ × 3⅞ in., ⅛ in. thick; wt., 1 oz.:																	
a	Package, net wt., 6 oz.; approx. 6 slices	1 pkg	170	70.3	308	22.1	22.8	2.0	—	—	—	—	—	(0)	—	—	—	—
b	Slice	1 slice or 1 oz	28	70.3	51	3.7	3.8	.3	—	—	—	—	—	(0)	—	—	—	—
c	Pound	1 lb	454	70.3	821	59.0	60.8	5.4	—	—	—	—	—	(0)	—	—	—	—
2021	Thuringer cervelat (summer sausage):[350]																	
	Prepackaged slices:																	
	Package and approx. contents:																	
a	Package, net wt., 8 oz.; approx. 8 slices (item 2021c) or 10 slices (item 2021d).	1 pkg	227	48.5	697	42.2	55.6	3.6	25	486	6.4	—	—	—	.25	.59	9.5	—
b	Package, net wt., 4 oz.; approx. 15 slices (item 2021e).	1 pkg	113	48.5	347	21.0	27.7	1.8	12	242	3.2	—	—	—	.12	.29	4.7	—
	Slice, approx. dimensions and weight:																	
c	Size, approx. 4⅜-in. diam., ⅛ in. thick; wt., 1 oz.	1 slice or 1 oz	28	48.5	87	5.3	6.9	.5	3	61	.8	—	—	—	.03	.07	1.2	—
d	Size, approx. 4⅛-in. diam., ⅛ in. thick; wt., ¾ oz.	1 slice	22	48.5	68	4.1	5.4	.4	2	47	.6	—	—	—	.02	.06	.9	—

[135] Use also for 1 lb. of other form or forms listed for this item.
[136] Use also for 1 oz. of other form or forms listed for this item.

[349] Based on can size information obtained for potted beef.
[350] Term "summer sausage" as used here applies to soft cervelat.

TABLE 1.—*Nutritive values for household measures and market units of foods*—Continued

[Item numbers correspond to those in table 1 of Handbook No. 8, revised 1963. Values in parentheses denote imputed values usually from another form of the food or from a similar food. Zeros in parentheses indicate that amount of a constituent, if present, is probably too small to be measured. Dashes (—) denote lack of reliable data for a constituent believed to be present in a measurable amount. Calculated values, as those based on a recipe, are not in parentheses]

Item No. (A)	Food, approximate measures, units, and weight (edible part unless footnotes indicate otherwise) (B)			Values for edible part of foods														
				Water (C)	Food energy (D)	Protein (E)	Fat (F)	Carbohydrate (G)	Calcium (H)	Phosphorus (I)	Iron (J)	Sodium (K)	Potassium (L)	Vitamin A value (M)	Thiamin (N)	Riboflavin (O)	Niacin (P)	Ascorbic acid (Q)
			Grams	*Percent*	*Calories*	*Grams*	*Grams*	*Grams*	*Milligrams*	*Milligrams*	*Milligrams*	*Milligrams*	*Milligrams*	*International units*	*Milligrams*	*Milligrams*	*Milligrams*	*Milligrams*
	Sausage cold cuts, and luncheon meats—Continued																	
	Thuringer cervelat (summer sausage) [350]—Continued																	
	Prepackaged slices—Continued																	
	Slice, approx. dimensions and weight—Continued																	
e	Size, approx. 2⅞-in. diam., 1/16 in. thick; wt., ¼ oz.	1 slice	7.5	48.5	23	1.4	1.8	0.1	1	16	0.2	—	—	—	0.01	0.02	0.3	—
f	Pound (approx. 16 slices (item 2021c), 20 slices (item 2021d), or 60 slices (item 2021e)).	1 lb	454	48.5	1,393	84.4	111.1	7.3	50	971	12.7	—	—	—	.50	1.18	19.1	—
2022	Vienna sausage, canned:																	
a	Drained contents from can, net wt., 4 oz. (water pack); or from can, net wt., 5 oz. (broth pack); [351] 7 sausages (item 2022b), wt., 4 oz.	7 sausages	113	63.0	271	15.8	22.4	.3	9	173	2.4	—	—	—	.09	.15	2.9	—
b	Sausage, approx. 2 in. long, ⅞-in. diam	1 sausage	16	63.0	38	2.2	3.2	Trace	1	24	.3	—	—	—	.01	.02	.4	—
	Scallops, bay and sea:																	
2024	Cooked (steamed)	1 lb	454	73.1	508	105.2	6.4	—	522	1,533	13.6	[43] 1,202	2,159	—	—	—	—	—
2025	Frozen, breaded, fried, reheated (sea scallops):																	
	Random pack (pieces, ⅞ in. long, ⅞ in. wide, ⅝ in. thick to 2¼ in. long, 1⅝ in. wide, ⅞ in. thick; [353] wt., 5–20 g.): [353]																	
a	Yield from container, net wt., 7 oz. [354] (15–20 scallops).	6⅔ oz	189	60.2	367	34.0	15.9	19.8	—	—	—	—	—	—	—	—	—	—
b	Yield from container, net wt., 12 oz. [354] (30–35 scallops).	11⅖ oz	324	60.2	629	58.3	27.2	34.0	—	—	—	—	—	—	—	—	—	—
c	Scallop	1 scallop	10	60.2	19	1.8	.8	1.1	—	—	—	—	—	—	—	—	—	—
	Uniform pack (counts of 10–15, 15–20, 20–25, 25–30, 30–35 per pound):																	
d	Yield from container, net wt., 80 oz. (5 lb.) [354 355]	76⅕ oz	2,160	60.2	4,190	388.8	181.4	226.8	—	—	—	—	—	—	—	—	—	—
	Scallop:																	
e	Size, 15–20 per pound	1 scallop	25	60.2	49	4.5	2.1	2.6	—	—	—	—	—	—	—	—	—	—
f	Size, 25–30 per pound	1 scallop	15	60.2	29	2.7	1.3	1.6	—	—	—	—	—	—	—	—	—	—
	Random and uniform pack:																	
g	Yield from 1 lb., frozen, breaded, fried scallops	15¼ oz	432	60.2	838	77.8	36.3	45.4	—	—	—	—	—	—	—	—	—	—
h	Pound	1 lb	454	60.2	880	81.6	38.1	47.6	—	—	—	—	—	—	—	—	—	—
	Scrapple. See Sausage, cold cuts, and luncheon meats (item 2019).																	
	Sesame oil. See Oils (items 1401f, 1401h, 1401j).																	
2033	**Sesame seeds, dry, hulled, decorticated:**																	
a	Cup	1 cup	150	5.5	873	27.3	80.1	26.4	165	888	3.6	—	—	—	.27	.20	8.1	0
b	Tablespoon	1 tbsp	8	5.5	47	1.5	4.3	1.4	9	47	.2	—	—	—	.01	.01	.4	0
2035	**Shad, baked:** [356]																	
a	Yield from 1 lb., raw fillets	12⅞ oz	365	64.0	734	84.7	41.2	0	88	1,142	2.2	[43] 288	1,376	110	.47	.95	31.4	—
b	Pound	1 lb	454	64.0	912	105.2	51.3	0	109	1,420	2.7	[43] 358	1,710	140	.59	1.18	39.0	—
c	Ounce	1 oz	28	64.0	57	6.6	3.2	0	7	89	.2	[43] 22	107	10	.04	.07	2.4	—
2039	**Shallot** bulbs, raw, chopped	1 tbsp	10	79.8	7	.3	Trace	1.7	4	6	.1	1	33	Trace	.01	Trace	Trace	1
2041	**Sherbet, orange:**																	
a	Prepackaged container, net contents, ½ gal	½ gal	1,542	67.0	2,066	13.9	18.5	474.9	247	200	.3	154	339	930	.15	.46	.3	81
b	Cup (8 fl. oz.)	1 cup	193	67.0	259	1.7	2.3	59.4	31	25	Trace	19	42	120	.02	.06	Trace	4
	Shortbread. See Cookies (item 830).																	
	Shrimp:																	
2043	Cooked (french fried): [357]																	
a	Pound	1 lb	454	56.9	1,021	92.1	49.0	45.4	327	866	9.1	[43] 844	1,039	—	.18	.36	12.2	—
b	Ounce	1 oz	28	56.9	64	5.8	3.1	2.8	20	54	.6	[43] 53	65	—	.01	.02	.8	—
	Canned:																	
2045	Drained solids of wet pack:																	
	Can and approx. drained contents:																	
a	Size, 307 × 113; [14] wt., 4½ oz. [358] (approx. 1 cup; 22 large shrimp (item 2045b), 40 medium (item 2045c), or 76 small (item 2045d)).	1 can or 1 cup	128	70.4	148	31.0	1.4	.9	147	337	4.0	—	156	80	.01	.04	2.8	—
	Shrimp:																	

(A)	(B)			(C)	(D)	(E)	(F)	(G)	(H)	(I)	(J)	(K)	(L)	(M)	(N)	(O)	(P)	(Q)
b	Large, approx. 3¼ in. long [359]	10 shrimp	58	70.4	67	14.0	0.6	0.4	67	153	1.8	—	71	30	Trace	0.02	1.0	—
c	Medium, approx. 2½ in. long [359]	10 shrimp	32	70.4	37	7.7	.4	.2	37	84	1.0	—	39	20	Trace	.01	.6	—
d	Small, approx. 2 in. long [359]	10 shrimp	17	70.4	20	4.1	.2	.1	20	45	.5	—	21	10	Trace	.01	.3	—
e	Pound	1 lb	454	70.4	526	109.8	5.0	3.2	522	1,193	14.1	—	553	270	0.05	.14	8.2	—
f	Ounce	1 oz	28	70.4	33	6.9	.3	.2	33	75	.9	—	35	20	Trace	.01	.5	—
2047	Shrimp or lobster paste, canned	1 tsp	7	61.3	13	1.5	.7	.1	—	—	—	—	—	—	—	.02	—	—
	Sirups:																	
2049	Maple:																	
a	Bottle, net contents, 12 fl. oz	1 bottle	472	33	1,189	—	—	306.8	491	38	5.7	47	831	—	—	—	—	0
b	Half gallon	½ gal	2,519	33	6,348	—	—	1,637.4	2,620	202	30.2	252	4,433	—	—	—	—	0
c	Cup	1 cup	315	33	794	—	—	204.8	328	25	3.8	32	554	—	—	—	—	0
d	Tablespoon	1 tbsp	19.7	33	50	—	—	12.8	20	2	.2	2	35	—	—	—	—	0
2050	Sorghum:																	
a	Cup	1 cup	330	23	848	—	—	224.4	568	83	41.3	—	—	—	—	.33	.3	—
b	Tablespoon	1 tbsp	20.6	23	53	—	—	14.0	35	5	2.6	—	—	—	—	.02	Trace	—
c	Pound (approx. 11 fl. oz.)	1 lb	454	23	1,166	—	—	308.4	780	113	56.7	—	—	—	—	.45	.5	—
	Table blends:																	
2051	Chiefly corn, light and dark:																	
	Container and approx. contents:																	
a	Bottle, net contents, 16 fl. oz. (1 pt.)	1 bottle or 1 pt.	657	24	1,905	0	0	492.8	302	105	26.9	[360] 447	26	0	0	0	0	0
b	Bottle, net contents, 32 fl. oz. (1 qt.)	1 bottle or 1 qt.	1,313	24	3,808	0	0	984.8	604	210	53.8	[360] 893	53	0	0	0	0	0
c	Can, net wt., 68 oz. (4 lb. 4 oz.)	1 can	1,928	24	5,591	0	0	1,446.0	887	308	79.0	[360] 1,311	77	0	0	0	0	0
d	Cup	1 cup	328	24	951	0	0	246.0	151	52	13.4	[360] 223	13	0	0	0	0	0
e	Tablespoon	1 tbsp	20.5	24	59	0	0	15.4	9	3	.8	[360] 14	1	0	0	0	0	0
f	Pound (approx. 11 oz.)	1 lb	454	24	1,315	0	0	340.2	209	73	18.6	[360] 308	18	0	0	0	0	0
2052	Cane and maple:																	
	Container and approx. contents:																	
a	Bottle, net contents, 12 fl. oz	1 bottle	472	33	1,189	0	0	306.8	76	5	Trace	9	123	0	0	0	0	0
b	Bottle, net contents, 24 fl. oz. (1 pt. 8 fl. oz.)	1 bottle	945	33	2,381	0	0	614.3	151	9	Trace	19	246	0	0	0	0	0
c	Cup	1 cup	315	33	794	0	0	204.8	50	3	Trace	6	82	0	0	0	0	0
d	Tablespoon	1 tbsp	19.7	33	50	0	0	12.8	3	Trace	Trace	Trace	5	0	0	0	0	0
	Soft drinks. See Beverages (items 402–409).																	
	Soups, commercial:																	
	Canned:																	
	Asparagus, cream of:																	
2059	Condensed:																	
	Can and approx. contents:																	
a	Size, 211 × 400 [14] (No. 1 Picnic); net wt., 10½ oz.	1 can	298	85.8	161	6.0	4.2	25.0	66	92	1.8	2,444	298	750	.09	.21	1.8	—
b	Cup	1 cup	245	85.8	132	4.9	3.4	20.6	54	76	1.5	2,009	245	610	.07	.17	1.5	—
c	Ounce	1 oz	28	85.8	15	.6	.4	2.4	6	9	.2	232	28	70	.01	.02	.2	—
2060	Prepared with equal volume of water	1 cup	240	92.9	65	2.4	1.7	10.1	26	38	.7	984	120	310	.05	.10	.7	—
2061	Prepared with equal volume of milk	1 cup	245	86.4	147	6.9	5.9	16.7	176	157	.7	1,068	301	490	.07	.29	.7	Trace
	Bean with pork:																	
2062	Condensed:																	
	Can and approx. contents:																	
a	Size, 211 × 400 [14] (No. 1 Picnic); net wt., 11½ oz.	1 can	326	68.9	437	20.9	15.0	56.4	163	329	5.9	2,628	1,030	1,700	.36	.20	2.6	7
	Size, 404 × 700 [14] (No. 3 Cylinder):																	
b	Net wt., 51 oz. (3 lb. 3 oz.)	1 can	1,446	68.9	1,938	92.5	66.5	250.2	723	1,460	26.0	11,655	4,569	7,520	1.59	.87	11.6	29
c	Net wt., 54 oz. (3 lb. 6 oz.)	1 can	1,531	68.9	2,052	98.0	70.4	264.9	766	1,546	27.6	12,340	4,838	7,960	1.68	.92	12.2	31
d	Cup	1 cup	265	68.9	355	17.0	12.2	45.8	133	268	4.8	2,136	837	1,380	.29	.16	2.1	5
e	Ounce	1 oz	28	68.9	38	1.8	1.3	4.9	14	29	.5	229	90	150	.03	.02	.2	1
2063	Prepared with equal volume of water	1 cup	250	84.4	168	8.0	5.8	21.8	63	128	2.3	1,008	395	650	.13	.08	1.0	3
	Beef broth, bouillon, consomme:																	
2064	Condensed:																	
	Can and approx. contents:																	
a	Size, 211 × 400 [14] (No. 1 Picnic); net wt., 10½ oz.	1 can	298	91.6	77	12.5	0	6.6	Trace	77	1.2	1,943	322	Trace	Trace	.06	3.0	—
b	Size, 404 × 700 [14] [361] (No. 3 Cylinder); net wt., 49 oz. (3 lb. 1 oz.) to 50 oz. (3 lb. 2 oz.).	1 can	1,404	91.6	365	59.0	0	30.9	Trace	365	5.6	9,154	1,516	Trace	Trace	.28	14.0	—

[14] Dimensions of can: 1st dimension represents diameter; 2d dimension, height of can. 1st or left-hand digit in each dimension gives number of whole inches; next 2 digits give additional fraction of dimension expressed as 16th of an inch.

[43] Value for product without added salt.

[350] Term "summer sausage" as used here applied to soft cervelat.

[351] For water pack, net weight given on can represents solids only (sausage); for broth pack, total can contents (sausage and broth).

[352] Dimensions of fish before reheating; width and thickness of fish at center.

[353] Random pack applies to product on retail market and uniform pack to product for use in restaurants and institutions.

[354] Net weight of container before reheating scallops.

[355] Number per container will depend on size in terms of count per pound.

[356] Prepared with butter or margarine and bacon slices.

[357] Dipped in egg, breadcrumbs, and flour or in batter.

[358] Also represents declared net weight of can.

[359] Length as measured along outer curvature.

[360] Applies to product with added salt.

[361] Based on information from 2 leading manufacturers of soup, can size and net weight apply to beef consomme but not to beef broth or bouillon.

TABLE 1.—*Nutritive values for household measures and market units of foods*—Continued

[Item numbers correspond to those in table 1 of Handbook No. 8, revised 1963. Values in parentheses denote imputed values usually from another form of the food or from a similar food. Zeros in parentheses indicate that amount of a constituent, if present, is probably too small to be measured. Dashes (—) denote lack of reliable data for a constituent believed to be present in a measurable amount. Calculated values, as those based on a recipe, are not in parentheses]

Item No. (A)	Food, approximate measures, units, and weight (edible part unless footnotes indicate otherwise) (B)			Water (C)	Food energy (D)	Protein (E)	Fat (F)	Carbohydrate (G)	Calcium (H)	Phosphorus (I)	Iron (J)	Sodium (K)	Potassium (L)	Vitamin A value (M)	Thiamin (N)	Riboflavin (O)	Niacin (P)	Ascorbic acid (Q)
			Grams	*Percent*	*Calories*	*Grams*	*Grams*	*Grams*	*Milligrams*	*Milligrams*	*Milligrams*	*Milligrams*	*Milligrams*	*International units*	*Milligrams*	*Milligrams*	*Milligrams*	*Milligrams*
	Soups, commercial—Continued																	
	Canned—Continued																	
	Beef broth, bouillon, consomme—Continued																	
	Condensed—Continued																	
c	Cup	1 cup	245	91.6	64	10.3	0	5.4	Trace	64	1.0	1,597	265	Trace	Trace	0.05	2.5	—
d	Ounce	1 oz	28	91.6	7	1.2	0	.6	Trace	7	.1	185	31	Trace	Trace	.01	.3	—
2065	Prepared with equal volume of water	1 cup	240	95.8	31	5.0	0	2.6	Trace	31	.5	782	130	Trace	Trace	.02	1.2	—
	Beef noodle:																	
2066	Condensed:																	
	Can and approx. contents:																	
a	Size, 211 × 400 [14] (No. 1 Picnic); net wt., 10½ oz.	1 can	298	86.4	170	9.5	6.6	17.3	18	119	2.1	2,277	191	150	0.12	.15	2.7	3
b	Size, 404 × 700 [14] (No. 3 Cylinder); net wt., 51 oz. (3 lb. 3 oz.).	1 can	1,446	86.4	824	46.3	31.8	83.9	87	578	10.1	11,047	925	720	.58	.72	13.0	14
c	Cup	1 cup	245	86.4	140	7.8	5.4	14.2	15	98	1.7	1,872	157	120	.10	.12	2.2	2
d	Ounce	1 oz	28	86.4	16	.9	.6	1.6	2	11	.2	217	18	10	.01	.01	.3	Trace
2067	Prepared with equal volume of water	1 cup	240	93.2	67	3.8	2.6	7.0	7	48	1.0	917	77	50	.05	.07	1.0	Trace
	Celery, cream of:																	
2068	Condensed:																	
	Can and approx. contents:																	
a	Size, 211 × 400 [14] (No. 1 Picnic); net wt., 10½ oz.	1 can	298	84.6	215	4.2	12.5	22.1	119	89	1.5	2,372	268	510	.03	.12	1.2	3
b	Size, 404 × 700 [14] (No. 3 Cylinder); net wt., 50 oz. (3 lb. 2 oz.).	1 can	1,418	84.6	1,021	19.9	59.6	104.9	567	425	7.1	11,287	1,276	2,410	.14	.57	5.7	14
c	Cup	1 cup	245	84.6	176	3.4	10.3	18.1	98	74	1.2	1,950	221	420	.02	.10	1.0	2
d	Ounce	1 oz	28	84.6	20	.4	1.2	2.1	11	9	.1	226	26	50	Trace	.01	.1	Trace
2069	Prepared with equal volume of water	1 cup	240	92.3	86	1.7	5.0	8.9	48	36	.5	955	108	190	.02	.05	Trace	Trace
2070	Prepared with equal volume of milk	1 cup	245	85.8	169	6.4	9.3	15.2	198	154	.7	1,039	289	390	.05	.27	.7	2
	Chicken consomme:																	
2071	Condensed:																	
	Can and approx. contents:																	
a	Size, 211 × 400 [14] (No. 1 Picnic); net wt., 10½ oz.	1 can	298	93.7	54	8.3	.3	4.5	30	176	3.0	1,794	—	—	—	—	—	—
b	Size, 404 × 700 [14] (No. 3 Cylinder); net wt., 49 oz. (3 lb. 1 oz.).	1 can	1,389	93.7	250	38.9	1.4	20.8	139	820	13.9	8,362	—	—	—	—	—	—
c	Cup	1 cup	245	93.7	44	6.9	.2	3.7	25	145	2.5	1,475	—	—	—	—	—	—
d	Ounce	1 oz	28	93.7	5	.8	Trace	.4	3	17	.3	171	—	—	—	—	—	—
2072	Prepared with equal volume of water	1 cup	240	96.8	22	3.4	Trace	1.9	12	72	1.2	722	—	—	—	—	—	—
	Chicken, cream of:																	
2073	Condensed:																	
	Can and approx. contents:																	
a	Size, 211 × 400 [14] (No. 1 Picnic); net wt., 10½ oz.	1 can	298	83.8	235	7.2	14.3	20.0	57	86	1.2	2,411	197	1,040	.03	.12	1.5	Trace
b	Size, 404 × 700 [14] (No. 3 Cylinder); net wt., 50 oz. (3 lb. 2 oz.).	1 can	1,418	83.8	1,120	34.0	68.1	95.0	269	411	5.7	11,472	936	4,960	.14	.57	7.1	Trace
c	Cup	1 cup	245	83.8	194	5.9	11.8	16.4	47	71	1.0	1,982	162	860	.02	.10	1.2	Trace
d	Ounce	1 oz	28	83.8	22	.7	1.4	1.9	5	8	.1	229	19	100	Trace	.01	.1	Trace
2074	Prepared with equal volume of water	1 cup	240	91.9	94	2.9	5.8	7.9	24	34	.5	970	79	410	.02	.05	.5	Trace
2075	Prepared with equal volume of milk	1 cup	245	85.4	179	7.4	10.3	14.5	172	152	.5	1,054	260	610	.05	.27	.7	2
	Chicken gumbo:																	
2076	Condensed:																	
	Can and approx. contents:																	
a	Size, 211 × 400 [14] (No. 1 Picnic); net wt., 10½ oz.	1 can	298	87.6	137	7.7	3.9	18.2	48	63	1.5	2,360	265	540	.06	.09	3.3	12
b	Size, 404 × 700 [14] (No. 3 Cylinder); net wt., 50 oz. (3 lb. 2 oz.).	1 can	1,418	87.6	652	36.9	18.4	86.5	227	298	7.1	11,231	1,262	2,550	.28	.43	15.6	57
c	Cup	1 cup	245	87.6	113	6.4	3.2	14.9	39	51	1.2	1,940	218	440	.05	.07	2.7	10
d	Ounce	1 oz	28	87.6	13	.7	.4	1.7	5	6	.1	225	25	50	.01	.01	.3	1
2077	Prepared with equal volume of water	1 cup	240	93.8	55	3.1	1.4	7.4	19	24	.5	950	108	220	.02	.05	1.2	5
	Chicken noodle:																	
2078	Condensed:																	
	Can and approx. contents:																	

(A)	(B)			(C)	(D)	(E)	(F)	(G)	(H)	(I)	(J)	(K)	(L)	(M)	(N)	(O)	(P)	(Q)
a	Size, 211 × 400 [14] (No. 1 Picnic); net wt., 10½ oz.	1 can	298	86.6	158	8.3	4.8	19.7	21	89	1.2	2,432	137	90	0.30	0.06	2.1	Trace
b	Size, 404 × 700 [14] (No. 3 Cylinder); net wt., 51 oz. (3 lb. 3 oz.).	1 can	1,446	86.6	766	40.5	23.1	95.4	101	434	5.8	11,799	665	430	.14	.29	10.1	Trace
c	Cup	1 cup	245	86.6	130	6.9	3.9	16.2	17	74	1.0	1,999	113	70	.02	.05	1.7	Trace
d	Ounce	1 oz	28	86.6	15	.8	.5	1.9	2	9	.1	231	13	10	Trace	.01	.2	Trace
2079	Prepared with equal volume of water	1 cup	240	93.3	62	3.4	1.9	7.9	10	36	.5	979	55	50	.02	.02	.7	Trace
	Chicken with rice:																	
2080	Condensed:																	
	Can and approx. contents:																	
a	Size, 211 × 400 [14] (No. 1 Picnic); net wt., 10½ oz.	1 can	298	89.6	116	7.7	3.0	14.0	21	63	.9	2,277	244	390	Trace	.06	1.8	—
b	Size, 404 × 700 [14] (No. 3 Cylinder); net wt., 51 oz. (3 lb. 3 oz.).	1 can	1,446	89.6	564	37.6	14.5	68.0	101	304	4.8	11,047	1,186	1,880	Trace	.29	8.7	—
c	Cup	1 cup	245	89.6	96	6.4	2.5	11.5	17	51	.7	1,872	201	320	Trace	.05	1.5	—
d	Ounce	1 oz	28	89.6	11	.7	.3	1.3	2	6	.1	217	23	40	Trace	.01	.2	—
2081	Prepared with equal volume of water	1 cup	240	94.8	48	3.1	1.2	5.8	7	24	.2	917	98	140	Trace	.02	.7	—
	Chicken vegetable:																	
2082	Condensed:																	
	Can and approx. contents:																	
a	Size, 211 × 400 [14] (No. 1 Picnic); net wt., 10½–10¾ oz.	1 can	302	84.5	187	10.8	6.0	28.3	45	100	1.5	2,552	242	5,440	.06	.09	2.7	—
b	Size, 404 × 700 [14] (No. 3 Cylinder); net wt., 50 oz. (3 lb. 2 oz.) to 51 oz. (3 lb. 3 oz.).	1 can	1,432	84.5	888	48.7	28.6	110.8	215	473	7.2	12,100	1,146	25,780	.29	.48	12.9	—
c	Cup	1 cup	250	84.5	155	8.5	5.0	19.3	88	83	1.3	2,118	200	4,500	.05	.08	2.3	—
d	Ounce	1 oz	28	84.5	18	1.0	.6	2.2	4	9	.1	240	23	510	.01	.01	.3	—
2083	Prepared with equal volume of water	1 cup	245	92.2	76	4.2	2.5	9.6	17	39	.5	1,034	98	2,160	.02	.05	1.0	—
	Clam chowder, Manhattan type (with tomatoes, without milk):																	
2084	Condensed:																	
	Can and approx. contents:																	
a	Size, 211 × 400 [14] (No. 1 Picnic); net wt., 10¾ oz.	1 can	305	83.7	201	5.5	6.4	30.5	88	116	2.7	2,336	458	2,170	.06	.06	2.7	—
b	Size, 404 × 700 [14] (No. 3 Cylinder); net wt., 51 oz. (3 lb. 3 oz.) to 52 oz. (3 lb. 4 oz.).	1 can	1,460	83.7	964	26.3	30.7	146.0	423	555	13.1	11,184	2,190	10,370	.29	.29	13.1	—
c	Cup	1 cup	250	83.7	165	4.5	5.3	25.0	73	95	2.3	1,915	375	1,780	.05	.05	2.3	—
d	Ounce	1 oz	28	83.7	19	.5	.6	2.8	8	11	.3	217	43	200	.01	.01	.3	—
2085	Prepared with equal volume of water	1 cup	245	91.9	81	2.2	2.5	12.3	34	47	1.0	938	184	880	.02	.02	1.0	—
	Minestrone:																	
2086	Condensed:																	
	Can and approx. contents:																	
a	Size, 211 × 400 [14] (No. 1 Picnic); net wt., 10¾ oz.	1 can	305	79.0	265	12.2	8.5	35.4	92	149	2.1	2,480	778	5,800	.18	.15	2.7	—
b	Size, 404 × 700 [14] (No. 3 Cylinder); net wt., 50 oz. (3 lb. 2 oz.) to 51 oz. (3 lb. 3 oz.).	1 can	1,432	79.0	1,246	57.3	40.1	166.1	430	702	10.0	11,642	3,652	27,210	.86	.72	12.9	—
c	Cup	1 cup	250	79.0	218	10.0	7.0	29.0	75	123	1.8	2,033	638	4,750	.15	.13	2.3	—
d	Ounce	1 oz	28	79.0	25	1.1	.8	3.3	9	14	.2	230	72	540	.02	.01	.3	—
2087	Prepared with equal volume of water	1 cup	245	89.5	105	4.9	3.4	14.2	37	59	1.0	995	314	2,350	.07	.05	1.0	—
	Mushroom, cream of:																	
2088	Condensed:																	
	Can and approx. contents:																	
a	Size, 211 × 400 [14] (No. 1 Picnic); net wt., 10½ oz.	1 can	298	79.3	331	5.7	23.8	25.0	101	128	.9	2,369	244	180	.03	.30	1.8	Trace
b	Size, 404 × 700 [14] (No. 3 Cylinder); net wt., 50 oz. (3 lb. 2 oz.) to 51 oz. (3 lb. 3 oz.).	1 can	1,432	79.3	1,590	27.2	114.6	120.3	487	616	4.3	11,384	1,174	860	.14	1.43	8.6	Trace
c	Cup	1 cup	245	79.3	272	4.7	19.6	20.6	83	105	.7	1,948	201	150	.02	.25	1.5	Trace
d	Ounce	1 oz	28	79.3	31	.5	2.3	2.4	10	12	.1	225	23	20	Trace	.03	.2	Trace
2089	Prepared with equal volume of water	1 cup	240	89.6	134	2.4	9.6	10.1	41	50	.5	955	98	70	.02	.12	.7	Trace
2090	Prepared with equal volume of milk	1 cup	245	83.2	216	6.9	14.2	16.2	191	169	.5	1,039	279	250	.05	.34	.7	1
	Onion:																	
2091	Condensed:																	
	Can and approx. contents:																	
a	Size, 211 × 400 [14] (No. 1 Picnic); net wt., 10½ oz.	1 can	298	86.9	161	13.1	6.3	12.8	69	69	1.2	2,608	256	Trace	Trace	.06	Trace	—
b	Cup	1 cup	245	86.9	132	10.8	5.1	10.5	56	56	1.0	2,144	211	Trace	Trace	.05	Trace	—
c	Ounce	1 oz	28	86.9	15	1.2	.6	1.2	7	7	.1	248	24	Trace	Trace	.01	Trace	—
2092	Prepared with equal volume of water	1 cup	240	93.4	65	5.3	2.4	5.3	29	26	.5	1,051	103	Trace	Trace	.02	Trace	—

[14] Dimensions of can: 1st dimension represents diameter; 2d dimension, height of can, 1st or left-hand digit in each dimension gives number of whole inches; next 2 digits give additional fraction of dimension expressed as 16th of an inch.

TABLE 1.—*Nutritive values for household measures and market units of foods*—Continued

[Item numbers correspond to those in table 1 of Handbook No. 8, revised 1963. Values in parentheses denote imputed values usually from another form of the food or from a similar food. Zeros in parentheses indicate that amount of a constituent, if present, is probably too small to be measured. Dashes (—) denote lack of reliable data for a constituent believed to be present in a measurable amount. Calculated values, as those based on a recipe, are not in parentheses]

Item No.	Food, approximate measures, units, and weight (edible part unless footnotes indicate otherwise)			Values for edible part of foods														
				Water	Food energy	Protein	Fat	Carbohydrate	Calcium	Phosphorus	Iron	Sodium	Potassium	Vitamin A value	Thiamin	Riboflavin	Niacin	Ascorbic acid
(A)	(B)			(C)	(D)	(E)	(F)	(G)	(H)	(I)	(J)	(K)	(L)	(M)	(N)	(O)	(P)	(Q)
			Grams	*Percent*	*Calories*	*Grams*	*Grams*	*Grams*	*Milligrams*	*Milligrams*	*Milligrams*	*Milligrams*	*Milligrams*	*International units*	*Milligrams*	*Milligrams*	*Milligrams*	*Milligrams*
	Soups, commercial—Continued																	
	Canned—Continued																	
	Pea, green:																	
2093	Condensed:																	
	Can and approx. contents:																	
a	Size, 211 × 400 [14] (No. 1 Picnic); net wt., 11–11¼ oz.	1 can	316	72.8	335	14.5	5.7	58.1	114	288	2.2	2,319	506	880	0.13	0.16	2.8	19
b	Size, 404 × 700 [14] (No. 3 Cylinder); net wt., 52 oz. (3 lb. 4 oz.).	1 can	1,474	72.8	1,562	67.8	26.5	271.2	531	1,341	10.3	10,819	2,358	4,130	.59	.74	13.3	88
c	Cup	1 cup	255	72.8	270	11.7	4.6	46.9	92	232	1.8	1,872	408	710	.10	.13	2.3	15
d	Ounce	1 oz	28	72.8	30	1.3	.5	5.2	10	26	.2	208	45	80	.01	.01	.3	2
2094	Prepared with equal volume of water	1 cup	245	86.4	130	5.6	2.2	22.5	44	113	1.0	899	196	340	.05	.05	1.0	7
2095	Prepared with equal volume of milk	1 cup	250	79.9	213	10.5	6.5	29.3	198	235	1.0	983	383	530	.10	.28	1.3	10
	Pea, split:																	
2096	Condensed:																	
	Can and approx. contents:																	
a	Size, 211 × 400 [14] (No. 1 Picnic); net wt., 11¼ oz.	1 can	319	70.7	376	22.3	8.3	54.2	80	389	3.5	2,447	702	1,150	.64	.38	3.5	3
b	Size, 404 × 700 [14] (No. 3 Cylinder); net wt., 51 oz. (3 lb. 3 oz.).	1 can	1,446	70.7	1,706	101.2	37.6	245.8	362	1,764	15.9	11,091	3,181	5,210	2.89	1.74	15.9	12
c	Cup	1 cup	255	70.7	301	17.9	6.6	43.4	64	311	2.8	1,956	561	920	.51	.31	2.8	2
d	Ounce	1 oz	28	70.7	33	2.0	.7	4.8	7	35	.3	217	62	100	.06	.03	.3	Trace
2097	Prepared with equal volume of water	1 cup	245	85.4	145	8.6	3.2	20.6	29	149	1.5	941	270	440	.25	.15	1.5	1
	Tomato:																	
2098	Condensed:																	
	Can and approx. contents:																	
a	Size, 211 × 400 [14] (No. 1 Picnic); net wt., 10¾ oz.	1 can	305	81.0	220	4.9	6.4	38.7	34	82	1.8	2,416	573	2,470	.15	.09	2.7	31
b	Size, 404 × 700 [14] (No. 3 Cylinder); net wt., 51 oz. (3 lb. 3 oz.).	1 can	1,446	81.0	1,041	23.1	30.4	183.6	159	390	8.7	11,452	2,718	11,710	.72	.43	13.0	145
c	Cup	1 cup	250	81.0	180	4.0	5.3	31.8	28	68	1.5	1,980	470	2,030	.13	.08	2.3	25
d	Ounce	1 oz	28	81.0	20	.5	.6	3.6	3	8	.2	225	53	230	.01	.01	.3	3
2099	Prepared with equal volume of water	1 cup	245	90.5	88	2.0	2.5	15.7	15	34	.7	970	230	1,000	.05	.05	1.2	12
2100	Prepared with equal volume of milk	1 cup	250	84.0	173	6.5	7.0	22.5	168	155	.8	1,055	418	1,200	.10	.25	1.3	15
	Turkey noodle:																	
2101	Condensed:																	
	Can and approx. contents:																	
a	Size, 211 × 400 [14] (No. 1 Picnic); net wt., 10½ oz.	1 can	298	84.6	194	10.7	7.2	20.9	36	107	1.5	2,479	191	480	.12	.12	3.0	Trace
b	Size, 404 × 700 [14] (No. 3 Cylinder); net wt., 50 oz. (3 lb. 2 oz.).	1 can	1,418	84.6	922	51.0	34.0	99.3	170	510	7.1	11,798	908	2,270	.57	.57	14.2	Trace
c	Cup	1 cup	245	84.6	159	8.8	5.9	17.2	29	88	1.2	2,038	157	390	.10	.10	2.5	Trace
d	Ounce	1 oz	28	84.6	18	1.0	.7	2.0	3	10	.1	236	18	50	.01	.01	.3	Trace
2102	Prepared with equal volume of water	1 cup	240	92.3	79	4.3	2.9	8.4	14	43	.7	998	77	190	.05	.05	1.2	Trace
	Vegetable beef:																	
2103	Condensed:																	
	Can and approx. contents:																	
a	Size, 211 × 400 [14] (No. 1 Picnic); net wt., 10¾ oz.	1 can	305	83.8	198	12.8	5.5	24.1	31	119	1.8	2,605	400	6,710	.09	.12	2.4	—
	Size, 404 × 700 [14] (No. 3 Cylinder):																	
b	Net wt., 50 oz. (3 lb. 2 oz.)	1 can	1,418	83.8	922	59.6	25.5	112.0	142	553	8.5	12,110	1,858	31,200	.43	.57	11.3	—
c	Net wt., 52 oz. (3 lb. 4 oz.)	1 can	1,474	83.8	958	61.9	26.5	116.4	147	575	8.8	12,588	1,931	32,430	.44	.59	11.8	—
d	Cup	1 cup	250	83.8	163	10.5	4.5	19.8	25	98	1.5	2,135	328	5,500	.08	.10	2.0	—
e	Ounce	1 oz	28	83.8	18	1.2	.5	2.2	3	11	.2	242	37	620	.01	.01	.2	—
2104	Prepared with equal volume of water	1 cup	245	91.9	78	5.1	2.2	9.6	12	49	.7	1,046	162	2,700	.05	.05	1.0	—
	Vegetable with beef broth:																	
2105	Condensed:																	
	Can and approx. contents:																	
a	Size, 211 × 400 [14] (No. 1 Picnic); net wt., 10¾ oz.	1 can	305	83.4	195	6.7	4.3	33.6	49	98	2.1	2,105	598	7,630	.09	.06	3.1	—

(A)	(B)			(C)	(D)	(E)	(F)	(G)	(H)	(I)	(J)	(K)	(L)	(M)	(N)	(O)	(P)	(Q)
b	Size, 404 × 700 [14] (No. 3 Cylinder); net wt., 51 oz. (3 lb. 3 oz.) to 52 oz. (3 lb. 4 oz.).	1 can	1,460	83.4	934	32.1	20.4	160.6	234	467	10.2	10,074	2,862	36.500	0.44	0.29	14.6	—
c	Cup	1 cup	250	83.4	160	5.5	3.5	27.5	40	80	1.8	1,725	490	6,250	.08	.05	2.5	—
d	Ounce	1 oz	28	83.4	18	.6	.4	3.1	5	9	.2	196	56	710	.01	.01	.3	—
2106	Prepared with equal volume of water	1 cup	245	91.7	78	2.7	1.7	13.5	20	39	.7	845	240	3,190	.05	.02	1.2	—
	Vegetarian vegetable:																	
2107	Condensed:																	
	Can and approx. contents:																	
a	Size, 211 × 400 [14] (No. 1 Picnic); net wt., 10¾ oz.	1 can	305	83.7	195	5.5	5.2	32.3	49	98	2.4	2,086	427	7,020	.09	.09	2.1	—
b	Size, 404 × 700 [14] (No. 3 Cylinder); net wt., 51 oz. (3 lb. 3 oz.).	1 can	1,446	83.7	925	26.0	24.6	153.3	231	463	11.6	9,891	2,024	33,260	.43	.43	10.1	—
c	Cup	1 cup	250	83.7	160	4.5	4.3	26.5	40	80	2.0	1,710	350	5,750	.08	.08	1.8	—
d	Ounce	1 oz	28	83.7	18	.5	.5	3.0	5	9	.2	194	40	650	.01	.01	.2	—
2108	Prepared with equal volume of water	1 cup	245	91.8	78	2.2	2.0	13.2	20	39	1.0	838	172	2,940	.05	.05	1.0	—
	Dehydrated: [362]																	
	Beef noodle:																	
2109	Mix, dry form (2-oz. pkg.)	1 pkg	57	6.1	221	7.8	4.2	37.2	27	84	1.1	1,350	131	70	.30	.16	2.3	2
2110	Prepared with 2 oz. of mix in 3 cups water	1 cup	240	93.1	67	2.4	1.2	11.5	10	26	.5	420	41	20	.10	.05	.7	Trace
	Chicken noodle:																	
2111	Mix, dry form (2-oz. pkg.)	1 pkg	57	5.7	218	8.3	5.7	33.1	34	82	1.4	2,438	83	190	.30	.15	2.4	3
2112	Prepared with 2 oz. of mix in 4 cups water	1 cup	240	94.7	53	1.9	1.4	7.7	7	19	.2	578	19	50	.07	.05	.5	Trace
	Chicken rice:																	
2113	Mix, dry form (1½-oz. pkg.)	1 pkg	43	9.8	152	3.9	2.9	27.0	19	30	.3	1,876	31	Trace	.02	.01	.5	—
2114	Prepared with 1½ oz. of mix in 3 cups water	1 cup	240	94.9	48	1.2	1.0	8.4	7	10	Trace	622	10	Trace	Trace	Trace	.2	—
	Onion:																	
2115	Mix, dry form (1½-oz. pkg.)	1 pkg	43	2.8	150	6.0	4.6	23.2	42	49	.6	2,871	238	30	.05	.03	.3	6
2116	Prepared with 1½ oz. of mix in 4 cups water	1 cup	240	95.8	36	1.4	1.2	5.5	10	12	.2	689	58	Trace	Trace	Trace	Trace	2
	Pea, green:																	
2117	Mix, dry form (4-oz. pkg.)	1 pkg	113	3.1	409	25.3	4.6	69.6	68	354	6.1	2,667	988	140	.50	.52	4.6	1
2118	Prepared with 4 oz. [363] of mix in 3 cups water	1 cup	245	86.7	123	7.6	1.5	20.6	20	105	2.0	796	294	50	.15	.15	1.5	Trace
	Tomato vegetable with noodles:																	
2119	Mix, dry form (2½-oz. pkg.)	1 pkg	71	3.7	247	6.2	5.7	44.5	33	80	1.4	4,357	123	1,700	.21	.13	1.8	18
2120	Prepared with 2½ oz. of mix in 4 cups water	1 cup	240	92.5	65	1.4	1.4	12.2	7	19	.2	1,025	29	480	.05	.02	.5	5
2134	Soursop, raw:																	
a	Cup, pureed	1 cup	225	81.7	146	2.3	.7	36.7	32	61	1.4	32	596	20	.16	.11	2.0	45
b	Pound	1 lb	454	81.7	295	4.5	1.4	73.9	64	122	2.7	64	1,202	50	.32	.23	4.1	91
	Souse. See Sausage, cold cuts, and luncheon meats (item 2020).																	
	Soybeans: [5]																	
	Mature seeds, dry:																	
2139	Raw:																	
a	Cup	1 cup	210	10.0	846	71.6	37.2	70.4	475	1,163	17.6	11	3,522	170	2.31	.65	4.6	—
b	Pound	1 lb	454	10.0	1,828	154.7	80.3	152.0	1,025	2,513	38.1	23	7,607	360	4.99	1.41	10.0	—
2140	Cooked: [42]																	
a	Cup	1 cup	180	71.0	234	19.8	10.3	19.4	131	322	4.9	[43] 4	972	50	.38	.16	1.1	0
b	Pound	1 lb	454	71.0	590	49.9	25.9	49.0	331	812	12.2	[43] 9	2,449	140	.95	.41	2.7	0
	Sprouted seeds:																	
2143	Raw:																	
a	Cup	1 cup	105	86.3	48	6.5	1.5	5.6	50	70	1.1	—	—	80	.24	.21	.8	14
b	Pound	1 lb	454	86.3	209	28.1	6.4	24.0	218	304	4.5	—	—	360	1.04	.91	3.6	59
2144	Cooked (boiled), drained:																	
a	Cup	1 cup	125	89.0	48	6.6	1.8	4.6	54	63	.9	—	—	100	.20	.19	.9	5
b	Pound	1 lb	454	89.0	172	24.0	6.4	16.8	195	227	3.2	—	—	360	.73	.68	3.2	18
2145	Soybean curd (tofu): [5]																	
a	Piece (2½ × 2¾ × 1 in.)	1 piece	120	84.8	86	9.4	5.0	2.9	154	151	2.3	8	50	0	.07	.04	.1	0
b	Pound	1 lb	454	84.8	327	35.4	19.1	10.9	581	572	8.6	32	191	0	.27	.14	.5	0
	Soybean flours: [5]																	
2146	Full fat:																	
	Cup:																	
a	Not stirred	1 cup	85	8.0	358	31.2	17.3	25.8	169	474	7.1	1	1,411	90	.72	.26	1.8	0
b	Stirred	1 cup	70	8.0	295	25.7	14.2	21.3	139	391	5.9	1	1,162	80	.60	.22	1.5	0
c	Pound	1 lb	454	8.0	1,910	166.5	92.1	137.9	903	2,531	38.1	5	7,530	500	3.86	1.41	9.5	0
2148	Low fat:																	
a	Cup, stirred	1 cup	88	8.0	313	38.2	5.9	32.2	231	558	8.0	1	1,636	70	.73	.32	2.3	0
b	Pound	1 lb	454	8.0	1,615	196.9	30.4	166.0	1,193	2,876	41.3	5	8,432	360	3.76	1.63	11.8	0

[5] Most of phosphorus in nuts, legumes, and outer layers of cereal grains is present as phytic acid. See also Appendix D, section on Minerals and Oxalic Acid, p. 284.

[14] Dimensions of can: 1st dimension represents diameter; 2d dimension, height of can. 1st or left-hand digit in each dimension gives number of whole inches; next 2 digits give additional fraction of dimension expressed as 16th of an inch.

[42] For proportion of ingredients used and ratio of cooked to dry legume, see ARS 62–13 (7), section on Legumes, Dry, p. 7, and table 21, p. 25.

[43] Value for product without added salt.

[362] Weight of packages of dehydrated soup mixes may vary as much as ¼ oz. However, this variation in weight would result in only negligible differences in composition of soups in ready-to-serve form.

[363] Nutritive values shown for item 2118 on pp. 58 and 113 of Agr. Handb. No. 8, rev. 1963, were based on soup prepared with 4 oz. of mix in 3 cups of water.

TABLE 1.—*Nutritive values for household measures and market units of foods*—Continued

[Item numbers correspond to those in table 1 of Handbook No. 8, revised 1963. Values in parentheses denote imputed values usually from another form of the food or from a similar food. Zeros in parentheses indicate that amount of a constituent, if present, is probably too small to be measured. Dashes (—) denote lack of reliable data for a constituent believed to be present in a measurable amount. Calculated values, as those based on a recipe, are not in parentheses]

Item No. (A)		Food, approximate measures, units, and weight (edible part unless footnotes indicate otherwise) (B)			Water (C)	Food energy (D)	Protein (E)	Fat (F)	Carbohydrate (G)	Calcium (H)	Phosphorus (I)	Iron (J)	Sodium (K)	Potassium (L)	Vitamin A value (M)	Thiamin (N)	Riboflavin (O)	Niacin (P)	Ascorbic acid (Q)
				Grams	*Percent*	*Calories*	*Grams*	*Grams*	*Grams*	*Milligrams*	*Milligrams*	*Milligrams*	*Milligrams*	*Milligrams*	*International units*	*Milligrams*	*Milligrams*	*Milligrams*	*Milligrams*
		Soybean flours[5]—Continued																	
2149		Defatted:																	
	a	Cup, stirred	1 cup	100	8.0	326	47.0	0.9	38.1	265	655	11.1	1	1,820	40	1.09	0.34	2.6	0
	b	Pound	1 lb	454	8.0	1,479	213.2	4.1	172.8	1,202	2,971	50.3	5	8,256	180	4.94	1.54	11.8	0
		Soybean oil and Soybean-cottonseed oil blend. See Oils (items 1401a, 1401b, 1401f, 1401h, 1401j).																	
2156		**Soy sauce:**																	
	a	Cup	1 cup	290	62.8	197	16.2	3.8	27.6	238	302	13.9	21,243	1,061	0	.06	.73	1.2	0
	b	Tablespoon	1 tbsp	18	62.8	12	1.0	.2	1.7	15	19	.9	1,319	66	0	Trace	.05	.1	0
	c	Fluid ounce	1 fl. oz	36.4	62.8	25	2.0	.5	3.5	30	38	1.7	2,666	133	0	.01	.09	.1	0
		Spaghetti (regular, thin, vermicelli):																	
		Enriched:																	
2157		Dry form:																	
	a	Package, net wt., 16 oz. (1 lb.)	1 pkg. or 1 lb	454	10.4	1,674	56.7	5.4	341.1	122	735	[157] 13.0	9	894	(0)	[157] 4.0	[157] 1.7	[157] 27.0	(0)
	b	Package, net wt., 8 oz	1 pkg	227	10.4	838	28.4	2.7	170.7	61	368	[157] 6.5	5	447	(0)	[157] 2.0	[157] .85	[157] 13.5	(0)
2158		Cooked, firm stage, "al dente":[344]																	
	a	Yield from 1 lb. of spaghetti, dry form	8⅔ cups	1,140	64.1	1,674	56.7	5.4	341.1	122	735	[157] 13.0	[345] 9	894	(0)	[157] 2.05	[157] 1.14	[157] 16.0	(0)
	b	Yield from 8 oz. of spaghetti, dry form	4⅓ cups	570	64.1	838	28.4	2.7	170.7	61	368	[157] 6.5	[345] 5	447	(0)	[157] 1.03	[157] .57	[157] 8.0	(0)
	c	Cup	1 cup	130	64.1	192	6.5	.7	39.1	14	85	[157] 1.4	[345] 1	103	(0)	[157] .23	[157] .13	[157] 1.8	(0)
	d	Pound (yield from approx. 6½ oz. of spaghetti, dry form).	1 lb	454	64.1	671	22.7	2.3	136.5	50	295	[157] 5.0	[345] 5	358	(0)	[157] .82	[157] .45	[157] 6.4	(0)
2159		Cooked, tender stage:[344]																	
	a	Yield from 1 lb. of spaghetti, dry form	10⅝ cups	1,480	73.0	1,674	56.7	5.4	341.1	122	735	[157] 13.0	[345] 9	894	(0)	[157] 2.07	[157] 1.18	[157] 16.3	(0)
	b	Yield from 8 oz. of spaghetti, dry form	5.3 cups	740	73.0	838	28.4	2.7	170.7	61	368	[157] 6.5	[345] 5	447	(0)	[157] 1.04	[157] .59	[157] 8.1	(0)
	c	Cup	1 cup	140	73.0	155	4.8	.6	32.2	11	70	[157] 1.3	[345] 1	85	(0)	[157] .20	[157] .11	[157] 1.5	(0)
	d	Pound (yield from approx. 5 oz. of spaghetti, dry form).	1 lb	454	73.0	508	15.4	1.8	104.8	36	227	[157] 4.1	[345] 5	277	(0)	[157] .64	[157] .36	[157] 5.0	(0)
		Unenriched:																	
2160		Dry form:																	
	a	Package, net wt., 16 oz. (1 lb.)	1 pkg. or 1 lb	454	10.4	1,674	56.7	5.4	341.1	122	735	5.9	9	894	(0)	.41	.27	7.7	(0)
	b	Package, net wt., 8 oz	1 pkg	227	10.4	838	28.4	2.7	170.7	61	368	3.0	5	447	(0)	.20	.14	3.9	(0)
2161		Cooked, firm stage, "al dente":[344]																	
	a	Yield from 1 lb. of spaghetti, dry form	8⅔ cups	1,140	64.1	1,674	56.7	5.4	341.1	122	735	5.9	[345] 9	894	(0)	.28	.28	4.6	(0)
	b	Yield from 8 oz. of spaghetti, dry form	4⅓ cups	570	64.1	838	28.4	2.7	170.7	61	368	3.0	[345] 5	447	(0)	.11	.11	2.3	(0)
	c	Cup	1 cup	130	64.1	192	6.5	.7	39.1	14	85	.7	[345] 1	103	(0)	.03	.03	.5	(0)
	d	Pound (yield from approx. 6½ oz. of spaghetti, dry form).	1 lb	454	64.1	671	22.7	2.3	136.5	50	295	2.3	[345] 5	358	(0)	.09	.09	1.8	(0)
2162		Cooked, tender stage:[344]																	
	a	Yield from 1 lb. of spaghetti, dry form	10⅝ cups	1,480	73.0	1,674	56.7	5.4	341.1	122	735	5.9	[345] 9	894	(0)	.15	.15	4.4	(0)
	b	Yield from 8 oz. of spaghetti, dry form	5.3 cups	740	73.0	838	28.4	2.7	170.7	61	368	3.0	[345] 5	447	(0)	.07	.07	2.2	(0)
	c	Cup	1 cup	140	73.0	155	4.8	.6	32.2	11	70	.6	[345] 1	85	(0)	.01	.01	.4	(0)
	d	Pound (yield from approx. 5 oz. of spaghetti, dry form).	1 lb	454	73.0	508	15.4	1.8	104.8	36	227	1.8	[345] 5	277	(0)	.05	.05	1.4	(0)
		Spaghetti (enriched) in tomato sauce with cheese:																	
2163		Cooked, from home recipe:[81]																	
	a	Yield from recipe[166]	8⅓ cups	2,095	77.0	2,179	73.3	73.3	310.1	670	1,131	18.9	(8,003)	3,415	9,010	2.10	1.47	18.9	105
	b	Cup	1 cup	250	77.0	260	8.8	8.8	37.0	80	135	2.3	(955)	408	1,080	.25	.18	2.3	13
	c	Pound	1 lb	454	77.0	472	15.9	15.9	67.1	145	245	4.1	(1,733)	739	1,950	.45	.32	4.1	23
2164		Canned (regular or ring-shaped spaghetti):																	
		Can and approx. contents:																	
	a	Size, 300 × 407[14] (No. 300); net wt., 15¼ oz.; approx. 1¾ cups.	1 can	432	80.1	328	9.5	2.6	66.5	69	151	4.8	1,650	523	1,600	.60	.48	7.8	17
	b	Size, 307 × 512[14] (No. 2 Cylinder); net wt., 26 oz. (1 lb. 10 oz.) to 26½ oz. (1 lb. 10½ oz.); approx. 3 cups.	1 can	744	80.1	565	16.4	4.5	114.6	119	260	8.2	2,842	900	2,750	1.04	.82	13.4	30
	c	Size, 404 × 700[14] (No. 3 Cylinder); net wt., 51 oz. (3 lb. 3 oz.); approx. 5¾ cups regular spaghetti.	1 can	1,446	80.1	1,099	31.8	8.7	222.7	231	506	15.9	5,524	1,750	5,350	2.02	1.59	26.0	58
	d	Cup	1 cup	250	80.1	190	5.5	1.5	38.5	40	88	2.8	955	303	930	.35	.28	4.5	10
	e	Pound	1 lb	454	80.1	345	10.0	2.7	69.9	73	159	5.0	1,733	549	1,680	.64	.50	8.2	18

(A)	(B)			(C)	(D)	(E)	(F)	(G)	(H)	(I)	(J)	(K)	(L)	(M)	(N)	(O)	(P)	(Q)
	Spaghetti (enriched) with meatballs and tomato sauce:																	
2165	Cooked, from home recipe:[51]																	
a	Yield from recipe[106] (either 7 cups of meatballs[364] in tomato sauce or 13 cups of mixture of spaghetti, meatballs,[364] tomato sauce; 2 oz. Parmesan cheese as topping).	7 lb. 1½ oz	3,220	70.0	4,315	241.5	151.3	502.3	1,610	3,059	48.3	13,105	8,630	20,610	3.22	3.86	51.5	290
b	Cup (mixture of spaghetti, meatballs, tomato sauce, cheese).	1 cup	248	70.0	332	18.6	11.7	38.7	124	236	3.7	1,009	665	1,590	.25	.30	4.0	22
c	Pound	1 lb	454	70.0	608	34.0	21.3	70.8	227	431	6.8	1,846	1,216	2,900	.45	.54	7.8	41
d	Portion, ⅙ of yield (item 2165a) (either 1⅛ cups of spaghetti cooked to firm stage and 1½ cups of meatballs[364] in tomato sauce or 2⅛ cups of mixture of spaghetti, meatballs,[364] tomato sauce; 2 tbsp. grated Parmesan cheese as topping).	1 portion	537	70.0	720	40.3	25.2	83.8	269	510	8.1	2,186	1,439	3,440	.54	.64	8.6	48
2166	Canned (regular or ring-shaped spaghetti):																	
	Can and approx. contents:																	
a	Size, 300 × 407[14] (No. 300); net wt., 15 oz.; approx. 1¾ cups; with regular spaghetti, 4–6 meatballs, 1- to 1½-in. diam.; with ring-shaped spaghetti, 18 meatballs, ¾-in. diam.	1 can	425	78.0	438	20.8	17.4	48.5	89	191	5.5	2,074	417	1,700	.26	.30	3.8	9
b	Cup	1 cup	250	78.0	258	12.8	10.8	28.5	58	118	3.8	1,220	245	1,000	.15	.18	2.8	5
c	Pound	1 lb	454	78.0	467	22.2	18.6	51.7	95	204	5.9	2,214	445	1,810	.27	.32	4.1	9
2168	**Spanish rice, cooked from home recipe:**[5, 51]																	
a	Yield from recipe[106]	2½ cups	607	78.5	528	10.9	10.3	100.8	85	237	3.6	1,918	1,402	4,010	.24	.18	4.2	91
b	Cup	1 cup	245	78.5	213	4.4	4.2	40.7	34	96	1.5	774	566	1,620	.10	.07	1.7	37
	Spinach:[55]																	
2169	Raw:																	
	Prepackaged (good quality):																	
a	Container, net wt., 10 oz	1 container	284	90.7	74	9.1	.9	12.2	264	145	8.8	202	1,335	23,000	.28	.57	1.7	145
b	Container, net wt., 20 oz. (1 lb. 4 oz.)	1 container	567	90.7	147	18.1	1.7	24.4	527	289	17.6	403	2,665	45,930	.57	1.13	3.4	289
c	Cup (chopped spinach)	1 cup	55	90.7	14	1.8	.2	2.4	51	28	1.7	39	259	4,460	.06	.11	.3	28
d	Pound	1 lb	454	90.7	118	14.5	1.4	19.5	422	231	14.1	322	2,132	36,740	.45	.91	2.7	231
2170	Cooked (boiled), drained:																	
a	Cup, leaves	1 cup	180	92.0	41	5.4	.5	6.5	167	68	4.0	[20] 90	583	14,580	.13	.25	.9	50
b	Pound	1 lb	454	92.0	104	13.6	1.4	16.8	422	172	10.0	[20] 227	1,470	36,740	.32	.64	2.3	127
	Canned, whole leaf, cut leaf or sliced, chopped:																	
	Regular pack:																	
2171	Solids and liquid:																	
	Can and approx. contents:																	
a	Size, 211 × 304[14] (8Z Tall, Buffet); net wt., 7¾ oz.	1 can	220	93.0	42	4.4	.9	6.6	187	57	4.6	[21] 519	550	12,100	.04	.22	.7	81
b	Size, 303 × 406[14] (No. 303); net wt., 15 oz.	1 can	425	93.0	81	8.5	1.7	12.8	361	111	8.9	[21] 1,003	1,063	23,380	.09	.43	1.3	60
c	Size, 401 × 411[14] (No. 2½); net wt., 27 oz. (1 lb. 11 oz.).	1 can	765	93.0	145	15.3	3.1	23.0	650	199	16.1	[21] 1,805	1,913	42,080	.15	.77	2.3	107
d	Size, 603 × 700[14] (No. 10); net wt., 98 oz. (6 lb. 2 oz.).	1 can	2,778	93.0	528	55.6	11.1	83.3	2,361	722	58.3	[21] 6,556	6,945	152,790	.56	2.78	8.3	389
e	Cup	1 cup	232	93.0	44	4.6	.9	7.0	197	60	4.9	[21] 548	580	12,760	.05	.23	.7	32
f	Pound	1 lb	454	93.0	86	9.1	1.8	13.6	386	118	9.5	[21] 1,070	1,134	24,950	.09	.45	1.4	64
2172	Drained solids:																	
	Can and approx. drained contents:																	
a	Size, 211 × 304[14] (8Z Tall, Buffet); wt., 5¼ oz.	1 can	149	91.4	36	4.0	.9	5.4	176	39	3.9	[21] 352	373	11,920	.03	.18	.4	21
b	Size, 303 × 406[14] (No. 303); wt., 10¼ oz.	1 can	291	91.4	70	7.9	1.7	10.5	343	76	7.6	[21] 687	728	23,280	.06	.35	.9	41
c	Size, 401 × 411[14] (No. 2½); wt., 18⅔ oz. (1 lb. 2⅔ oz.).	1 can	529	91.4	127	14.3	3.2	19.0	624	138	13.8	[21] 1,248	1,323	42,320	.11	.63	1.6	74
d	Size, 603 × 700[14] (No. 10); wt., 58½ oz. (3 lb. 10½ oz.).	1 can	1,658	91.4	398	44.8	9.9	59.7	1,956	431	43.1	[21] 3,913	4,145	132,640	.33	1.99	5.0	232
e	Cup	1 cup	205	91.4	49	5.5	1.2	7.4	242	53	5.3	[21] 484	513	16,400	.04	.25	.6	29
f	Pound	1 lb	454	91.4	109	12.2	2.7	16.3	535	118	11.8	[21] 1,070	1,134	36,290	.09	.54	1.4	64

[5] Most of phosphorus in nuts, legumes, and outer layers of cereal grains is present as phytic acid. See also Appendix D, section on Minerals and Oxalic Acid

[14] Dimensions of can: 1st dimension represents diameter; 2d dimension, height of can. 1st or left-hand digit in each dimension gives number of whole inches; next 2 digits give additional fraction of dimension expressed as 16th of an inch.

[20] Value is for unsalted product. If salt is used, increase value by 236 mg. per 100 g. of vegetable—an estimated figure based on typical amount of salt (0.6%) in canned vegetables. See also Appendix C, section on Cooked Vegetables

[21] Estimated value based on addition of salt in amount of 0.6% of finished product.

[51] For information on ingredients used in preparation, see ARS 62–13 (7), table 22, p. 26.

[55] Oxalic acid present may combine with calcium and magnesium to form insoluble compounds. For further information, see Appendix D, section on Minerals and Oxalic Acid

[106] Formula used to calculate nutritive values shown in Agr. Handb. No. 8, rev. 1963.

[157] Based on product with minimum level of enrichment. See also Appendix C, section on Enriched Foods and Standards of Enrichment

[344] Unless indicated otherwise, weight per cup applies to product immediately after cooking and is based on specific proportion of alimentary paste and water in cooked product. For further information, see Appendix B, section on Home-Prepared Foods and ARS 62–13 (7), section on Alimentary Pastes and Other Cereal Products, pp. 6–7, and table 3, p. 9.

[345] Value applies to product cooked in unsalted water.

[364] For yield from recipe (item 2165a), approx. 24 meatballs; for portion (item 2165d), approx. 4 meatballs.

TABLE 1.—*Nutritive values for household measures and market units of foods*—Continued

[Item numbers correspond to those in table 1 of Handbook No. 8, revised 1963. Values in parentheses denote imputed values usually from another form of the food or from a similar food. Zeros in parentheses indicate that amount of a constituent, if present, is probably too small to be measured. Dashes (—) denote lack of reliable data for a constituent believed to be present in a measurable amount. Calculated values, as those based on a recipe, are not in parentheses]

Item No. (A)	Food, approximate measures, units, and weight (edible part unless footnotes indicate otherwise) (B)			Water (C)	Food energy (D)	Protein (E)	Fat (F)	Carbohydrate (G)	Calcium (H)	Phosphorus (I)	Iron (J)	Sodium (K)	Potassium (L)	Vitamin A value (M)	Thiamin (N)	Riboflavin (O)	Niacin (P)	Ascorbic acid (Q)
			Grams	*Percent*	*Calories*	*Grams*	*Grams*	*Grams*	*Milligrams*	*Milligrams*	*Milligrams*	*Milligrams*	*Milligrams*	*International units*	*Milligrams*	*Milligrams*	*Milligrams*	*Milligrams*
	Spinach[55]—Continued																	
	Canned, whole leaf, cut leaf or sliced, chopped—Continued																	
	Regular pack—Continued																	
2173	Drained liquid:																	
a	Pound	1 lb	454	96.8	27	2.3	0	5.9	9	113	4.1	[21] 1,070	1,134	Trace	0.09	0.32	1.4	64
b	Ounce	1 oz	28	96.8	2	.1	0	.4	1	7	.3	[21] 67	71	Trace	.01	.02	.1	4
	Special dietary pack (low sodium):																	
2174	Solids and liquid:																	
	Can and approx. contents:																	
a	Size, 211 × 304[14] (8Z Tall, Buffet); net wt., 7¾ oz.	1 can	220	92.8	46	5.5	.9	7.3	187	57	4.6	75	550	12,100	.04	.22	.7	31
b	Size, 303 × 406[14] (No. 303); net wt., 15 oz.	1 can	425	92.8	89	10.6	1.7	14.0	361	111	8.9	145	1,063	23,380	.09	.48	1.3	60
c	Size, 603 × 700[14] (No. 10); net wt., 98 oz. (6 lb. 2 oz.).	1 can	2,778	92.8	583	69.5	11.1	91.7	2,361	722	58.3	945	6,945	152,790	.56	2.78	8.3	389
d	Cup	1 cup	232	92.8	49	5.8	.9	7.7	197	60	4.9	79	580	12,760	.05	.23	.7	32
e	Pound	1 lb	454	92.8	95	11.3	1.8	15.0	386	118	9.5	154	1,134	24,950	.09	.45	1.4	64
2175	Drained solids:																	
	Can and approx. drained contents:																	
a	Size, 211 × 304[14] (8Z Tall, Buffet); wt., 5¼ oz.	1 can	149	91.3	39	4.8	.7	6.0	176	39	3.9	48	373	11,920	.03	.18	.4	21
b	Size, 303 × 406[14] (No. 303); wt., 10¼ oz	1 can	291	91.3	76	9.3	1.5	11.6	343	76	7.6	93	728	23,280	.06	.35	.9	41
c	Size, 603 × 700[14] (No. 10); wt., 58½ oz. (3 lb. 10½ oz.).	1 can	1,658	91.3	431	53.1	8.3	66.3	1,956	431	43.1	531	4,145	132,640	.33	1.99	5.0	232
d	Cup	1 cup	205	91.3	53	6.6	1.0	8.2	242	53	5.3	66	518	16,400	.04	.25	.6	29
e	Pound	1 lb	454	91.3	118	14.5	2.3	18.1	535	118	11.8	145	1,134	36,290	.09	.54	1.4	64
2176	Drained liquid:																	
a	Pound	1 lb	454	96.7	36	2.3	0	9.1	9	118	4.1	145	1,134	Trace	.09	.32	1.4	64
b	Ounce	1 oz	28	96.7	2	.1	0	.6	1	7	.3	9	71	Trace	.01	.02	.1	4
	Frozen:																	
	Chopped:																	
2177	Not thawed:																	
a	Container, net wt., 10 oz	1 container	284	91.6	68	8.8	.9	10.8	321	128	6.0	162	1,005	22,440	.26	.45	1.4	82
b	Pound	1 lb	454	91.6	109	14.1	1.4	17.2	513	204	9.5	259	1,606	35,880	.41	.73	2.3	132
2178	Cooked (boiled), drained:																	
a	Yield from 10 oz., frozen spinach	1¹⁄₁₆ cups	220	91.9	51	6.6	.7	8.1	249	97	4.6	[30] 114	783	17,380	.15	.33	.9	42
b	Yield from 1 lb., frozen spinach	1.7 cups	350	91.9	81	10.5	1.1	13.0	396	154	7.4	[30] 182	1,166	27,650	.25	.53	1.4	67
c	Cup	1 cup	205	91.9	47	6.2	.6	7.6	232	90	4.3	[30] 107	683	16,200	.14	.31	.8	39
d	Pound (yield from approx. 1.3 lb., frozen spinach).	1 lb	454	91.9	104	13.6	1.4	16.8	513	200	9.5	[30] 236	1,510	35,830	.32	.68	1.8	86
	Leaf:																	
2179	Not thawed:																	
a	Container, net wt., 10 oz	1 container	284	91.3	71	8.5	.9	11.9	298	128	7.1	151	1,098	23,000	.28	.45	1.4	99
b	Pound	1 lb	454	91.3	113	13.6	1.4	16.1	476	204	11.3	240	1,746	36,740	.45	.73	2.3	159
2180	Cooked (boiled), drained:																	
a	Yield from 10 oz., frozen spinach	1⅛ cups (approx.).	220	91.8	53	6.4	.7	8.6	231	97	5.5	[30] 108	796	17,820	.18	.31	1.1	62
b	Yield from 1 lb., frozen spinach	1⅞ cups (approx.).	350	91.8	84	10.2	1.1	13.7	368	154	8.8	[30] 172	1,267	28,350	.28	.49	1.8	98
c	Cup	1 cup	190	91.8	46	5.5	.6	7.4	200	84	4.8	[30] 93	688	15,390	.15	.27	1.0	53
d	Pound (yield from approx. 1.3 lb., frozen spinach).	1 lb	454	91.8	109	13.2	1.4	17.7	476	200	11.3	[30] 222	1,642	36,740	.36	.64	2.3	127
	Spinach, New Zealand. See New Zealand spinach (items 1375–1376).																	
2185	Spot, baked:																	
a	Pound	1 lb	454	53.8	1,338	103.4	99.3	0	—	—	—	[265] 1,415	—	—	—	—	—	—
b	Ounce	1 oz	28	53.8	84	6.5	6.2	0	—	—	—	[265] 88	—	—	—	—	—	—
	Squash:																	
	Summer:																	
	All varieties:																	
2191	Raw:																	
a	Cup, sliced; cubed or diced	1 cup	130	94.0	25	1.4	.1	5.5	36	38	.5	1	263	530	.07	.12	1.3	[30] 29

(A)		(B)			(C)	(D)	(E)	(F)	(G)	(H)	(I)	(J)	(K)	(L)	(M)	(N)	(O)	(P)	(Q)
	b	Pound	1 lb	454	94.0	86	5.0	0.5	19.1	127	132	1.8	5	916	1,860	0.23	0.41	4.5	100
2192		Cooked (boiled), drained:																	
		Cup:																	
	a	Sliced	1 cup	180	95.5	25	1.6	.2	5.6	45	45	.7	[20] 2	254	700	.09	.14	1.4	18
	b	Cubed or diced	1 cup	210	95.5	29	1.9	.2	6.5	53	53	.8	[20] 2	296	820	.11	.17	1.7	21
	c	Mashed	1 cup	240	95.5	34	2.2	.2	7.4	60	60	1.0	[20] 2	338	940	.12	.19	1.9	24
	d	Pound	1 lb	454	95.5	64	4.1	.5	14.1	113	113	1.8	[20] 5	640	1,770	.23	.36	3.6	45
		Crookneck and Straightneck, Yellow:																	
2193		Raw:																	
	a	Cup, sliced; cubed or diced	1 cup	130	93.7	26	1.6	.3	5.6	36	38	.5	1	263	600	.07	.12	1.3	[33] 33
	b	Pound	1 lb	454	93.7	91	5.4	.9	19.5	127	132	1.8	5	916	2,090	.23	.41	4.5	113
2194		Cooked (boiled), drained:																	
		Cup:																	
	a	Sliced	1 cup	180	95.3	27	1.8	.4	5.6	45	45	.7	[20] 2	254	790	.09	.14	1.4	20
	b	Cubed or diced	1 cup	210	95.3	32	2.1	.4	6.5	53	53	.8	[20] 2	296	920	.11	.17	1.7	23
	c	Mashed	1 cup	240	95.3	36	2.4	.5	7.4	60	60	1.0	[20] 2	338	1,060	.12	.19	1.9	26
	d	Pound	1 lb	454	95.3	68	4.5	.9	14.1	113	113	1.8	[20] 5	640	2,000	.23	.36	3.6	50
		Scallop varieties, white and pale green:																	
2195		Raw:																	
	a	Cup, sliced; cubed or diced	1 cup	130	93.3	27	1.2	.1	6.6	36	38	.5	1	263	250	.07	.12	1.3	[33] 23
	b	Pound	1 lb	454	93.3	95	4.1	.5	23.1	127	132	1.8	5	916	860	.23	.41	4.5	82
2196		Cooked (boiled), drained:																	
		Cup:																	
	a	Sliced	1 cup	180	95.0	29	1.3	.2	6.8	45	45	.7	[20] 2	254	320	.09	.14	1.4	14
	b	Cubed or diced	1 cup	210	95.0	34	1.5	.2	8.0	53	53	.8	[20] 2	296	380	.11	.17	1.7	17
	c	Mashed	1 cup	240	95.0	38	1.7	.2	9.1	60	60	1.0	[20] 2	338	430	.12	.19	1.9	19
	d	Pound	1 lb	454	95.0	73	3.2	.5	17.2	113	113	1.8	[20] 5	640	820	.23	.36	3.6	36
		Zucchini and Cocozelle (Italian marrow type), green:																	
2197		Raw:																	
	a	Cup, sliced; cubed or diced	1 cup	130	94.6	22	1.6	.1	4.7	36	38	.5	1	263	[366] 420	.07	.12	1.3	[33] 25
	b	Pound	1 lb	454	94.6	77	5.4	.5	16.3	127	132	1.8	5	916	[366] 1,450	.23	.41	4.5	86
2198		Cooked (boiled), drained:																	
		Cup:																	
	a	Sliced	1 cup	180	96.0	22	1.8	.2	4.5	45	45	.7	[20] 2	254	[366] 540	.09	.14	1.4	16
	b	Cubed or diced	1 cup	210	96.0	25	2.1	.2	5.3	53	53	.8	[20] 2	296	[366] 630	.11	.17	1.7	19
	c	Mashed	1 cup	240	96.0	29	2.4	.2	6.0	60	60	1.0	[20] 2	338	[366] 720	.12	.19	1.9	22
	d	Pound	1 lb	454	96.0	54	4.5	.5	11.3	113	113	1.8	[20] 5	640	[366] 1,360	.23	.36	3.6	41
		Winter:																	
		All varieties, cooked:																	
2200		Baked:																	
	a	Cup, mashed	1 cup	205	81.4	129	3.7	.8	31.6	57	98	1.6	[20] 2	945	[367] 8,610	.10	.27	1.4	27
	b	Pound	1 lb	454	81.4	286	8.2	1.8	69.9	127	218	3.6	[20] 5	2,091	[367] 19,050	.23	.59	3.2	59
2201		Boiled:																	
	a	Cup, mashed	1 cup	245	88.8	93	2.7	.7	22.5	49	78	1.2	[20] 2	632	[367] 8,580	.10	.25	1.0	20
	b	Pound	1 lb	454	88.8	172	5.0	1.4	41.7	91	145	2.3	[20] 5	1,170	[367] 15,880	.18	.45	1.8	36
		Acorn:																	
2202		Raw:																	
	a	Whole, 4-in. diam., 4½ in. high; wt., 1¼ lb. (refuse: cavity contents and rind, 24%).[1]	1 squash	567	86.3	190	6.5	.4	48.3	134	99	3.9	4	1,655	[367] 5,170	.22	.47	2.6	60
		Without cavity contents (refuse: rind, 10%):[1]																	
	b	½ squash	½ squash	244	86.3	97	3.3	.2	24.6	68	51	2.0	2	843	[367] 2,640	.11	.24	1.3	31
	c	Pound	1 lb	454	86.3	180	6.1	.4	45.7	127	94	3.7	4	1,567	[367] 4,900	.20	.45	2.4	57
		Cooked:																	
2203		Baked:																	
	a	½ squash (item 2202b, baked) (refuse: rind, 20%).[1]	½ squash	195	82.9	86	3.0	.2	21.8	61	45	1.7	[20] 2	749	[367] 2,180	.08	.20	1.1	20
	b	Cup, mashed	1 cup	205	82.9	113	3.9	.2	28.7	80	59	2.3	[20] 2	984	[367] 2,870	.10	.27	1.4	27
	c	Pound	1 lb	454	82.9	249	8.6	.5	63.5	177	132	5.0	[20] 5	2,177	[367] 6,350	.23	.59	3.2	59
2204		Boiled:																	
	a	Cup, mashed	1 cup	245	89.7	83	2.9	.2	20.6	69	49	2.0	[20] 2	659	[367] 2,700	.10	.25	1.0	20
	b	Pound	1 lb	454	89.7	154	5.4	.5	38.1	127	91	3.6	[20] 5	1,220	[367] 4,990	.18	.45	1.8	36

[1] Measure and weight apply to food as it is described with inedible part or parts (refuse) included.

[14] Dimensions of can: 1st dimension represents diameter; 2d dimension, height of can. 1st or left-hand digit in each dimension gives number of whole inches; next 2 digits give additional fraction of dimension expressed as 16th of an inch.

[20] Value is for unsalted product. If salt is used, increase value by 236 mg. per 100 g. of vegetable—an estimated figure based on typical amount of salt (0.6%) in canned vegetables. See also Appendix C, section on Cooked Vegetables

[21] Estimated value based on addition of salt in amount of 0.6% of finished product.

[55] Oxalic acid present may combine with calcium and magnesium to form insoluble compounds. For further information, see Appendix D, section on Minerals and Oxalic Acid

[33] Value does not allow for losses that might occur from cutting, chopping, or shredding. See also Appendix C, section on Cut Forms of Raw Fruits and Vegetables; Capping of Strawberries

[365] Based on fish with salt added in cooking.

[366] Applies to squash including skin; flesh has no appreciable vitamin A value.

[367] Value based on freshly harvested squash. Carotenoid content increases during storage, amount of increase varying according to variety and conditions of storage. More information is needed on relative contents of individual carotenoids and their rates of increase under usual storage conditions before a suitable vitamin A value can be derived for stored product.

TABLE 1.—*Nutritive values for household measures and market units of foods*—Continued

[Item numbers correspond to those in table 1 of Handbook No. 8, revised 1963. Values in parentheses denote imputed values usually from another form of the food or from a similar food. Zeros in parentheses indicate that amount of a constituent, if present, is probably too small to be measured. Dashes (—) denote lack of reliable data for a constituent believed to be present in a measurable amount. Calculated values, as those based on a recipe, are not in parentheses]

Item No. (A)		Food, approximate measures, units, and weight (edible part unless footnotes indicate otherwise) (B)			Water (C)	Food energy (D)	Protein (E)	Fat (F)	Carbohydrate (G)	Calcium (H)	Phosphorus (I)	Iron (J)	Sodium (K)	Potassium (L)	Vitamin A value (M)	Thiamin (N)	Riboflavin (O)	Niacin (P)	Ascorbic acid (Q)
				Grams	*Percent*	*Calories*	*Grams*	*Grams*	*Grams*	*Milligrams*	*Milligrams*	*Milligrams*	*Milligrams*	*Milligrams*	*International units*	*Milligrams*	*Milligrams*	*Milligrams*	*Milligrams*
		Squash—Continued																	
		Winter—Continued																	
		Butternut, cooked:																	
2206		Baked:																	
	a	Cup, mashed	1 cup	205	79.6	139	3.7	0.2	35.9	82	148	2.1	[20] 2	1,248	[367] 13,120	0.10	0.27	1.4	16
	b	Pound	1 lb	454	79.6	308	8.2	.5	79.4	181	327	4.5	[20] 5	2,762	[367] 29,030	.23	.59	3.2	36
2207		Boiled:																	
	a	Cup, mashed	1 cup	245	87.8	100	2.7	.2	25.5	71	120	1.7	[20] 2	835	[367] 13,230	.10	.25	1.0	12
	b	Pound	1 lb	454	87.8	186	5.0	.5	47.2	132	222	3.2	[20] 5	1,547	[367] 24,490	.18	.45	1.8	23
		Hubbard, cooked:																	
2209		Baked:																	
	a	Cup, mashed	1 cup	205	85.1	103	3.7	.8	24.0	49	80	1.6	[20] 2	556	[367] 9,840	.10	.27	1.4	21
	b	Pound	1 lb	454	85.1	227	8.2	1.8	53.1	109	177	3.6	[20] 5	1,229	[367] 21,770	.23	.59	3.2	45
2210		Boiled:																	
		Cup:																	
	a	Cubed or diced	1 cup	235	91.1	71	2.6	.7	16.2	40	61	1.2	[20] 2	357	[367] 9,640	.09	.24	.9	14
	b	Mashed	1 cup	245	91.1	74	2.7	.7	16.9	42	64	1.2	[20] 2	372	[367] 10,050	.10	.25	1.0	15
	c	Pound	1 lb	454	91.1	136	5.0	1.4	31.3	77	118	2.3	[20] 5	689	[367] 18,600	.18	.45	1.8	27
		Squash, winter, frozen:																	
2213		Not thawed:																	
	a	Container, net wt., 12 oz	1 container	340	88.8	129	4.1	1.0	31.3	85	109	3.4	3	704	13,260	.10	.24	1.7	34
	b	Pound	1 lb	454	88.8	172	5.4	1.4	41.7	113	145	4.5	5	939	17,690	.14	.32	2.3	45
2214		Cooked (heated):																	
	a	Cup	1 cup	240	88.8	91	2.9	.7	22.1	60	77	2.4	[20] 2	497	9,360	.07	.17	1.2	19
	b	Pound	1 lb	454	88.8	172	5.4	1.4	41.7	113	145	4.5	[20] 5	939	17,690	.14	.32	2.3	36
		Starch. See Cornstarch (item 894).																	
		St. Johnsbread. See Carob flour (item 617).																	
		Strawberries:																	
2217		Raw:																	
		Container, net contents, 1 pt.:[71]																	
	a	Good quality (refuse: caps and stems, 4%)[1]	1 container	340	89.9	121	2.3	1.6	27.4	69	69	3.3	3	535	200	.10	.28	2.0	[368] 193
	b	Fair quality (refuse: caps, stems, green and damaged berries, 13%).[1]	1 container	340	89.9	109	2.1	1.5	24.8	62	62	3.0	3	485	180	.09	.21	1.8	[368] 175
		Container, net contents, 1 qt.:[71]																	
	c	Good quality (refuse: caps and stems, 4%)[1]	1 container	680	89.9	242	4.6	3.3	54.8	137	137	6.5	7	1,071	390	.20	.46	3.9	[368] 385
	d	Fair quality (refuse: caps, stems, green and damaged berries, 13%).[1]	1 container	680	89.9	219	4.1	3.0	49.7	124	124	5.9	6	970	350	.18	.41	3.5	[368] 349
	e	Cup, whole berries	1 cup	149	89.9	55	1.0	.7	12.5	31	31	1.5	1	244	90	.04	.10	.9	[368] 88
	f	Pound	1 lb	454	89.9	168	3.2	2.3	38.1	95	95	4.5	5	744	270	.14	.32	2.7	[368] 268
2218		Canned, water pack, solids and liquid, without artificial sweetener:																	
	a	Cup	1 cup	242	93.7	53	1.0	.2	13.6	34	34	1.7	2	269	100	.02	.07	1.0	48
	b	Pound	1 lb	454	93.7	100	1.8	.5	25.4	64	64	3.2	5	503	180	.05	.14	1.8	91
		Frozen, sweetened with nutritive sweetener, not thawed:																	
2219		Sliced:																	
	a	Container, net wt., 10 oz	1 container	284	71.3	310	1.4	.6	79.0	40	48	2.0	3	318	90	.06	.17	1.4	151
	b	Container, net wt., 16 oz. (1 lb.)	1 container or 1 lb.	454	71.3	494	2.3	.9	126.1	64	77	3.2	5	508	140	.09	.27	2.3	240
	c	Cup[48]	1 cup	255	71.3	278	1.3	.5	70.9	36	43	1.8	3	286	80	.05	.15	1.3	135
2220		Whole:																	
	a	Container, net wt., 16 oz. (1 lb.)	1 container or 1 lb.	454	75.7	417	1.8	.9	106.6	59	73	2.7	5	472	140	.09	.27	2.3	249
	b	Cup[48]	1 cup	255	75.7	235	1.0	.5	59.9	33	41	1.5	3	265	80	.05	.15	1.3	140
		Sturgeon:																	
2222		Cooked, steamed:																	
	a	Pound	1 lb	454	67.5	726	115.2	25.9	0	181	1,193	9.1	[43] 490	1,066	—	—	—	—	—
	b	Ounce	1 oz	28	67.5	45	7.2	1.6	0	11	75	.6	[43] 31	67	—	—	—	—	—
2223		Smoked:																	
	a	Pound	1 lb	454	63.7	676	141.5	8.2	0	—	—	—	—	—	—	—	—	—	—
	b	Ounce	1 oz	28	63.7	42	8.8	.5	0	—	—	—	—	—	—	—	—	—	—

(A)	(B)			(C)	(D)	(E)	(F)	(G)	(H)	(I)	(J)	(K)	(L)	(M)	(N)	(O)	(P)	(Q)
	Succotash (corn and lima beans), frozen:[5]																	
2224	Not thawed:																	
a	Container, net wt., 10 oz	1 container	284	73.0	275	12.2	1.1	61.1	40	253	3.1	[45] 128	775	(850)	0.31	0.17	4.3	26
b	Cup	1 cup	155	73.0	150	6.7	.6	33.3	22	138	1.7	[45] 70	423	(470)	.17	.09	2.3	14
c	Pound	1 lb	454	73.0	440	19.5	1.8	97.5	64	404	5.0	[45] 204	1,238	(1,360)	.50	.27	6.8	41
2225	Cooked (boiled), drained:																	
a	Cup	1 cup	170	74.1	158	7.1	.7	34.9	22	145	1.7	[45] 65	418	(510)	.15	.09	2.2	10
b	Pound	1 lb	454	74.1	422	19.1	1.8	93.0	59	386	4.5	[45] 172	1,116	(1,360)	.41	.23	5.9	27
	Sugars:																	
	Beet or cane:																	
2229	Brown, spooned into cup:																	
a	Without packing	1 cup	145	2.1	541	0	0	139.8	123	28	4.9	44	499	0	.01	.04	.3	0
b	With packing[369]	1 cup	220	2.1	821	0	0	212.1	187	42	7.5	66	757	0	.02	.07	.4	0
2230	Granulated:																	
a	Cup	1 cup	200	.5	770	0	0	199.0	0	0	.2	2	6	0	0	0	0	0
b	Tablespoon	1 tbsp	12	.5	46	0	0	11.9	0	0	Trace	Trace	Trace	0	0	0	0	0
c	Teaspoon	1 tsp	4	.5	15	0	0	4.0	0	0	Trace	Trace	Trace	0	0	0	0	0
d	Lump (rectangular tablet, 1⅛ × ¾ × 5/16 in.; or two ½-in. cubes).	1 tablet or 2 cubes.	5	.5	19	0	0	5.0	0	0	Trace	Trace	Trace	0	0	0	0	0
e	Packet, wt., 5–7 g	1 packet	6	.5	23	0	0	6.0	0	0	Trace	Trace	Trace	0	0	0	0	0
2231	Powdered (10X or confectioners):																	
	Unsifted, spooned into cup:																	
a	Cup	1 cup	120	.5	462	0	0	119.4	0	0	.1	1	4	0	0	0	0	0
b	Tablespoon	1 tbsp	8	.5	31	0	0	8.0	0	0	Trace	Trace	Trace	0	0	0	0	0
c	Sifted, spooned into cup	1 cup	100	.5	385	0	0	99.5	0	0	.1	1	3	0	0	0	0	0
2234	Maple (piece, approx. 1¾ × 1¼ × ½ in.; wt., approx. 1 oz.).	1 piece or 1 oz.	28	8	99	—	—	25.5	41	3	.4	4	69	—	—	—	—	—
2235	**Sugar-apples** (sweetsop), raw, pulp	1 cup	250	73.3	235	4.5	.8	59.3	55	103	1.5	28	688	30	.25	.35	2.5	85
2236	**Sunflower seed kernels,** dry:[370]																	
	In hull (refuse: hulls, 46%):[1]																	
a	Pound (yields approx. 1⅔ cups hulled seeds)	1 lb	454	4.8	1,371	58.8	115.8	48.7	294	2,050	17.4	73	2,253	120	4.80	.56	13.2	—
b	Cup (yields approx. ⅓ cup hulled seeds)	1 cup	85	4.8	257	11.0	21.7	9.1	55	384	3.3	14	422	20	.90	.11	2.5	—
	Hulled:																	
c	Container, net wt., 16 oz. (1 lb.)	1 lb	454	4.8	2,540	108.9	214.6	90.3	544	3,797	32.2	136	4,173	230	8.89	1.04	24.5	—
d	Cup	1 cup	145	4.8	812	34.8	68.6	28.9	174	1,214	10.3	44	1,334	70	2.84	.33	7.8	—
	Surinam-cherry. See Pitanga (item 1627).																	
	Sweetbreads (thymus), cooked (braised):																	
2241	Beef (yearlings)	3 oz	85	49.6	272	22.0	19.7	0	—	309	—	[43] 99	368	—	—	—	—	—
2243	Calf	3 oz	85	62.7	143	27.7	2.7	0	—	—	—	[43] —	—	—	.05	.14	2.5	—
2245	Lamb	3 oz	85	64.6	149	23.9	5.2	0	—	173	—	[43] —	—	—	—	—	—	—
	Sweetpotatoes:[55]																	
	Raw:																	
2246	All commercial varieties:																	
	With skin:																	
	Pared by mechanical methods (refuse: parings and trimmings, 28%):[1]																	
a	Potato, 5 in. long, 2-in. diam	1 potato	180	70.6	148	2.2	.5	34.1	41	61	.9	13	315	11,400	.13	.08	.8	27
b	Pound	1 lb	454	70.6	372	5.6	1.3	85.9	105	154	2.3	33	794	28,740	.33	.20	2.0	69
	Pared with split-knife peeler (refuse: parings and trimmings, 10%):[1]																	
c	Potato, 5 in. long, 2-in. diam	1 potato	180	70.6	185	2.8	.6	42.6	52	76	1.1	16	394	14,260	.16	.10	1.0	34
d	Pound	1 lb	454	70.6	465	6.9	1.6	107.4	131	192	2.9	41	992	35,920	.41	.24	2.4	86
e	Without skin	1 lb	454	70.6	517	7.7	1.8	119.3	145	213	3.2	45	1,102	39,920	.45	.27	2.7	95
2247	Firm fleshed[371] (Jersey types):																	
	With skin:																	
	Pared by mechanical methods (refuse: parings and trimmings, 28%):[1]																	
a	Potato, 5 in. long, 2-in. diam	1 potato	180	74.0	132	2.3	.9	29.2	41	61	.9	13	315	[372] 11,920	.13	.08	.8	30
b	Pound	1 lb	454	74.0	333	5.9	2.3	73.5	105	154	2.3	33	794	[372] 30,050	.33	.20	2.0	75

[1] Measure and weight apply to food as it is described with inedible part or parts (refuse) included.

[5] Most of phosphorus in nuts, legumes, and outer layers of cereal grains is present as phytic acid. See also Appendix D, section on Minerals and Oxalic Acid

[39] Value is for unsalted product. If salt is used, increase value by 236 mg. per 100 g. of vegetable—an estimated figure based on typical amount of salt (0.6%) in canned vegetables. See also Appendix C, section on Cooked Vegetables

[43] Value for product without added salt.

[45] Value based on average weighted in accordance with commercial practice in freezing vegetables. Wide range in sodium content occurs. For cooked vegetables, value also represents no additional salting. If salt is moderately added, increase value by 236 mg. per 100 g. of vegetable—an estimated figure based on typical amount of salt (0.6%) in canned vegetables. See also Appendix C, section on Cooked Vegetables and section on Frozen Fruits and Vegetables

[48] Measurement applies to thawed product. See also Appendix C, section on Frozen Fruits and Vegetables

[55] Oxalic acid present may combine with calcium and magnesium to form insoluble compounds. For further information, see Appendix D, section on Minerals and Oxalic Acid

[71] Represents container as customarily filled to volume greater than declared net contents. See also Appendix B, section on Berries

[367] Value based on freshly harvested squash. Carotenoid content increases during storage, amount of increase varying according to variety and conditions of storage. More information is needed on relative contents of individual carotenoids and their rates of increase under usual storage conditions before a suitable vitamin A value can be derived for stored product.

[368] Value does not allow for losses that might occur from capping. See also Appendix C, section on Cut Forms of Raw Fruits and Vegetables; Capping of Strawberries

[369] Packed tight enough for sugar to hold shape of cup after being turned out.

[370] Data do not apply to product salted in shell.

[371] Term refers to flesh of cooked product.

[372] Based on value of 9,200 I.U. per 100 g., an average derived to represent firm-fleshed varieties of commercial importance. For varieties having deep-orange flesh, use value of about 10,000 I.U. per 100 g.; for light-yellow, about 600 I.U. per 100 g.

TABLE 1.—*Nutritive values for household measures and market units of foods*—Continued

[Item numbers correspond to those in table 1 of Handbook No. 8, revised 1963. Values in parentheses denote imputed values usually from another form of the food or from a similar food. Zeros in parentheses indicate that amount of a constituent, if present, is probably too small to be measured. Dashes (—) denote lack of reliable data for a constituent believed to be present in a measurable amount. Calculated values, as those based on a recipe, are not in parentheses]

Item No.		Food, approximate measures, units, and weight (edible part unless footnotes indicate otherwise)			Values for edible part of foods														
					Water	Food energy	Protein	Fat	Carbohydrate	Calcium	Phosphorus	Iron	Sodium	Potassium	Vitamin A value	Thiamin	Riboflavin	Niacin	Ascorbic acid
(A)		(B)			(C)	(D)	(E)	(F)	(G)	(H)	(I)	(J)	(K)	(L)	(M)	(N)	(O)	(P)	(Q)
				Grams	*Percent*	*Calories*	*Grams*	*Grams*	*Grams*	*Milligrams*	*Milligrams*	*Milligrams*	*Milligrams*	*Milligrams*	*International units*	*Milligrams*	*Milligrams*	*Milligrams*	*Milligrams*
		Sweetpotatoes [53]—Continued																	
		Raw—Continued																	
		Firm fleshed [371] (Jersey types)—Continued																	
		With skin—Continued																	
		Pared with split-knife peeler (refuse: parings and trimmings, 10%): [1]																	
	c	Potato, 5 in. long, 2-in. diam	1 potato	180	74.0	165	2.9	1.1	36.5	52	76	1.1	16	394	[372] 14,900	0.16	0.10	1.0	37
	d	Pound	1 lb	454	74.0	416	7.3	2.9	91.8	131	192	2.9	41	992	[372] 37,550	.41	.24	2.4	94
	e	Without skin	1 lb	454	74.0	463	8.2	3.2	102.1	145	213	3.2	45	1,102	[372] 41,730	.45	.27	2.7	104
2248		Soft fleshed [371] (mainly Porto Rico variety):																	
		With skin:																	
		Pared by mechanical methods (refuse: parings and trimmings, 28%): [1]																	
	a	Potato, 5 in. long, 2-in. diam	1 potato	180	69.7	152	2.2	.4	35.4	41	61	.9	13	315	[373] 11,280	.13	.08	.8	26
	b	Pound	1 lb	454	69.7	382	5.6	1.0	89.2	105	154	2.3	33	794	[373] 28,410	.33	.20	2.0	65
		Pared with split-knife peeler (refuse: parings and trimmings, 10%): [1]																	
	c	Potato, 5 in. long, 2-in. diam	1 potato	180	69.7	190	2.8	.5	44.2	52	76	1.1	16	394	[373] 14,090	.16	.10	1.0	32
	d	Pound	1 lb	454	69.7	478	6.9	1.2	111.4	131	192	2.9	41	992	[373] 35,510	.41	.24	2.4	82
	e	Without skin	1 lb	454	69.7	531	7.7	1.4	123.8	145	213	3.2	45	1,102	[373] 39,460	.45	.27	2.7	91
		Cooked, all:																	
2249		Baked in skin (refuse: skin, 22%): [1]																	
	a	Potato, 5 in. long, 2-in. diam. (dimensions before cooking).	1 potato	146	63.7	161	2.4	.6	37.0	46	66	1.0	[30] 14	342	9,230	.10	.08	.8	25
	b	Pound	1 lb	454	63.7	499	7.4	1.8	115.0	142	205	3.2	[30] 42	1,061	28,660	.32	.25	2.5	78
2250		Boiled in skin:																	
		Whole (refuse: skins, 16%): [1]																	
	a	Potato, 5 in. long, 2-in. diam. (dimensions before cooking).	1 potato	180	70.6	172	2.6	.6	39.8	48	71	1.1	[30] 15	367	11,940	.14	.09	.9	26
	b	Pound	1 lb	454	70.6	434	6.5	1.5	100.2	122	179	2.7	[30] 38	926	30,100	.34	.23	2.3	65
	c	Mashed	1 cup	255	70.6	291	4.3	1.0	67.1	82	120	1.8	[30] 26	620	20,150	.23	.15	1.5	43
	d	Pound (without skins)	1 lb	454	70.6	517	7.7	1.8	119.3	145	213	3.2	[30] 45	1,102	35,830	.41	.27	2.7	77
2251		Candied: [61]																	
		Piece, 2½ in. long, 2-in. diam. (dimensions before cooking), prepared using ½ of—																	
	a	Potato peeled by mechanical methods	1 piece	85	60.0	143	1.1	2.8	29.1	31	37	.8	36	162	5,360	.05	.03	.3	9
	b	Potato peeled with split-knife peeler	1 piece	105	60.0	176	1.4	3.5	35.9	39	45	.9	44	200	6,620	.06	.04	.4	11
	c	Pound	1 lb	454	60.0	762	5.9	15.0	155.1	168	195	4.1	191	862	28,580	.27	.18	1.8	45
		Canned:																	
		Liquid pack, solids and liquid:																	
2252		Regular pack in sirup:																	
		Can and approx. contents:																	
	a	Size, 404 × 307 [14] (No. 3 Vacuum, No. 3 Squat); net wt., 22 oz. (1 lb. 6 oz.) to 23 oz. (1 lb. 7 oz.).	1 can	638	70.7	727	6.4	1.3	175.5	83	185	4.5	306	(766)	31,900	.19	.19	3.8	51
	b	Size, 603 × 700 [14] (No. 10); net wt., 102 oz. (6 lb. 6 oz.).	1 can	2,892	70.7	3,297	28.9	5.8	795.3	376	839	20.2	1,388	(3,470)	144,600	.87	.87	17.4	231
	c	Pound	1 lb	454	70.7	517	4.5	.9	124.7	59	132	3.2	218	(544)	22,680	.14	.14	2.7	36
2254		Vacuum or solid pack:																	
		Can and approx. contents (regular pack):																	
	a	Size, 404 × 307 [14] (No. 3 Vacuum, No. 3 Squat); net wt., 17 oz. (1 lb. 1 oz.) to 18 oz. (1 lb. 2 oz.).	1 can	496	71.9	536	9.9	1.0	123.5	124	203	4.0	238	992	38,690	.25	.20	3.0	69
	b	Piece, approx. 2¾ in. long, 1-in. diam	1 piece	40	71.9	43	.8	.1	10.0	10	16	.3	19	80	3,120	.02	.02	.2	6
		Cup:																	
	c	Pieces	1 cup	200	71.9	216	4.0	.4	49.8	50	82	1.6	96	400	15,600	.10	.08	1.2	28
	d	Mashed	1 cup	255	71.9	275	5.1	.5	63.5	64	105	2.0	122	510	19,890	.13	.10	1.5	36
	e	Pound	1 lb	454	71.9	490	9.1	.9	112.9	113	186	3.6	218	907	35,380	.23	.18	2.7	64
		Dehydrated flakes:																	
2255		Dry form	1 cup	120	2.8	455	5.0	.7	108.0	72	96	2.6	217	674	[374] 56,400	.07	.16	1.6	54
2256		Prepared with water:																	
	a	Cup	1 cup	255	75.7	242	2.6	.3	57.6	38	51	1.5	115	357	[374] 30,600	.05	.08	.8	28

(A)	(B)		(C)	(D)	(E)	(F)	(G)	(H)	(I)	(J)	(K)	(L)	(M)	(N)	(O)	(P)	(Q)
b	Pound	1 lb	454	75.7	431	4.5	0.5	102.5	68	91	2.7	204	635	[374] 54,430	0.09	0.14	1.4	50
	Sweetsop. See Sugar-apples (item 2235).																	
	Swiss chard. See Chard, Swiss (items 639–640).																	
2258	**Swordfish,** broiled with butter or margarine (refuse: skin, 6%):[1]																	
a	Yield from 1 lb., raw	10.1 oz	305	64.6	499	80.3	17.2	0	77	788	3.7	[43] —	—	5,880	.11	.14	31.3	—
b	Piece, 4½ in. long, 2⅛ in. wide, ⅞ in. thick	1 piece	145	64.6	237	38.2	8.2	0	37	375	1.8	[43] —	—	2,790	.05	.07	14.9	—
c	Pound	1 lb	454	64.6	742	119.4	25.6	0	115	1,173	5.5	[43] —	—	8,740	.17	.21	46.5	—
d	Ounce	1 oz	28	64.6	46	7.4	1.6	0	7	73	.3	[43] —	—	550	.01	.01	2.9	—
2261	**Tangelo juice, raw, and tangelos used for juice:**[375]																	
	Juice:																	
a	Cup	1 cup	247	89.4	101	1.2	(.2)	24.0	—	—	—	—	—	—	—	—	—	67
	Fruit used for juice[210] (refuse: peel, membranes, seeds, 44%):[1]																	
b	Large, 2¾-in. diam., size 100[273]	1 tangelo	204	89.4	47	.6	(.1)	11.1	—	—	—	—	—	—	—	—	—	31
c	Medium, 2⁹⁄₁₆-in. diam., size 120[273]	1 tangelo	170	89.4	39	.5	(.1)	9.2	—	—	—	—	—	—	—	—	—	26
d	Small, 2¼-in. diam., size 168[273]	1 tangelo	122	89.4	28	.3	(.1)	6.6	—	—	—	—	—	—	—	—	—	18
2262	**Tangerines, raw** (Dancy variety):																	
	Whole fruit[210] (refuse: peel and seeds, 26%):[1]																	
a	Large, 2½-in. diam., size 150[273]	1 tangerine	136	87	46	.8	.2	11.7	40	18	.4	2	127	420	.06	.02	.1	31
b	Medium, 2⅜-in. diam., size 176[273]	1 tangerine	116	87	39	.7	.2	10.0	34	15	.3	2	108	360	.05	.02	.1	27
c	Small, 2¼-in. diam., size 210[273]	1 tangerine	97	87	33	.6	.1	8.3	29	13	.3	1	90	300	.04	.01	.1	22
d	Sections, without membranes	1 cup	195	87	90	1.6	.4	22.6	78	35	.8	4	246	820	.12	.04	.2	60
	Tangerine juice:																	
2263	Raw (Dancy variety)	1 cup	247	88.9	106	1.2	.5	24.9	44	35	.5	2	440	1,040	.15	.05	.2	77
	Canned:																	
2264	Unsweetened:																	
	Can and approx. contents:																	
a	Size, 202 × 314[14] (6½Z); net contents, 6 fl. oz.	1 can	185	88.8	80	.9	.4	18.9	33	26	.4	2	329	780	(.11)	(.04)	(.2)	41
b	Size, 404 × 700[14] (46Z, No. 3 Cylinder); net contents, 46 fl. oz. (1 qt. 14 fl. oz.).	1 can	1,421	88.8	611	7.1	2.8	144.9	256	199	2.8	14	2,529	5,970	(.85)	(.28)	(1.4)	313
c	Cup	1 cup	247	88.8	106	1.2	.5	25.2	44	35	.5	2	440	1,040	(.15)	(.05)	(.2)	54
d	Fluid ounce	1 fl. oz	30.9	88.8	13	.2	.1	3.2	6	4	.1	Trace	55	130	(.02)	(.01)	(Trace)	7
2265	Sweetened with nutritive sweetener:																	
	Can and approx. contents:																	
a	Size, 202 × 314[14] (6½Z); net contents, 6 fl. oz.	1 can	187	87.0	94	.9	.4	22.4	33	26	.4	2	329	780	(.11)	(.04)	(.2)	41
b	Size, 404 × 700[14] (46Z, No. 3 Cylinder); net contents, 46 fl. oz. (1 qt. 14 fl. oz.).	1 can	1,431	87.0	716	7.2	2.9	171.7	256	199	2.8	14	2,529	5,970	(.85)	(.28)	(1.4)	313
c	Cup	1 cup	249	87.0	125	1.2	.5	29.9	44	35	.5	2	440	1,040	(.15)	(.05)	(.2)	54
d	Fluid ounce	1 fl. oz	31.1	87.0	16	.2	.1	3.7	6	4	.1	Trace	55	130	(.02)	(.01)	(Trace)	7
	Frozen concentrate, unsweetened:																	
2266	Undiluted:																	
	Can and approx. contents:																	
a	6 fl. oz. (yields 3 cups diluted juice weighing 743 g.).	1 can	211	58	342	3.6	(1.5)	80.8	131	101	1.5	4	1,293	3,070	.43	.12	.9	203
b	12 fl. oz. (yields 1½ qt. diluted juice weighing 1,486 g.).	1 can	422	58	684	7.2	(3.0)	161.6	262	203	3.0	8	2,587	6,140	.86	.24	1.9	405
c	32 fl. oz. (1 qt.) (yields 1 gal. diluted juice weighing 3,964 g.).	1 can	1,125	58	1,823	19.1	(7.9)	430.9	698	540	7.9	23	6,896	16,380	2.28	.62	5.1	1,080
2267	Diluted with 3 parts water by volume:																	
a	Quart	1 qt	992	88.1	456	5.0	(2.0)	107.1	179	139	2.0	10	1,726	4,090	.58	.16	1.3	268
b	Cup	1 cup	248	88.1	114	1.2	(.5)	26.8	45	35	.5	2	432	1,020	.14	.04	.3	67
c	Glass (6 fl. oz.)	1 glass	186	88.1	86	.9	(.4)	20.1	33	26	.4	2	324	770	.11	.03	.2	50
2268	**Tapioca,** dry (pearl and granulated quick-cooking):																	
a	Package, net wt., 8 oz. (approx. 1½ cups)	1 pkg	227	12.6	799	1.4	.5	196.1	23	41	.9	7	41	(0)	(0)	(0)	(0)	(0)
b	Cup[376]	1 cup	152	12.6	535	.9	.3	131.3	15	27	.6	5	27	(0)	(0)	(0)	(0)	(0)
c	Tablespoon	1 tbsp	8.4	12.6	30	.1	Trace	7.3	1	2	Trace	Trace	2	(0)	(0)	(0)	(0)	(0)

[1] Measure and weight apply to food as it is described with inedible part or parts (refuse) included.

[14] Dimensions of can: 1st dimension represents diameter; 2d dimension, height of can. 1st or left-hand digit in each dimension gives number of whole inches; next 2 digits give additional fraction of dimension expressed as 16th of an inch.

[30] Value is for unsalted product. If salt is used, increase value by 236 mg. per 100 g. of vegetable—an estimated figure based on typical amount of salt (0.6%) in canned vegetables. See also Appendix C, section on Cooked Vegetables

[43] Value for product without added salt.

[51] For information on ingredients used in preparation, see ARS 62-13 (7), table 22, p. 26.

[35] Oxalic acid present may combine with calcium and magnesium to form insoluble compounds. For further information, see Appendix D, section on Minerals and Oxalic Acid

[210] See Appendix B, section on Citrus Fruits for explanation of basis for sizes and weights shown for whole citrus fruits.

[273] Size refers to count of fruit in ⅘-bushel container with net weight of approx. 45 lb.

[371] Term refers to flesh of cooked product.

[372] Based on value of 9,200 I.U. per 100 g., an average derived to represent firm-fleshed varieties of commercial importance. For varieties having deep-orange flesh, use value of about 10,000 I.U. per 100 g.; for light-yellow, about 600 I.U. per 100 g.

[373] Based on value of 8,700 I.U. per 100 g. derived to represent soft-fleshed varieties of commercial importance. Values range from 8,000 to more than 20,000 I.U. per 100 g.

[374] Value varies widely; it is related to variety of sweetpotato. For dehydrated form (item 2255), basis of value shown is 47,000 I.U. per 100 g.; for product prepared for serving (item 2256), 12,000 I.U. per 100 g. Value for dehydrated form may range from 21,000 to 72,000 I.U. per 100 g.; for product prepared for serving, 5,000–18,000 I.U. per 100 g.

[375] Tangelo is a hybrid of grapefruit and tangerine with the scientific name *Citrus paradisi* × *Citrus reticulata*.

[376] Granulated type was stirred to lighten, spooned into cup to overflow, and leveled with straight edge.

TABLE 1.—*Nutritive values for household measures and market units of foods*—Continued

[Item numbers correspond to those in table 1 of Handbook No. 8, revised 1963. Values in parentheses denote imputed values usually from another form of the food or from a similar food. Zeros in parentheses indicate that amount of a constituent, if present, is probably too small to be measured. Dashes (—) denote lack of reliable data for a constituent believed to be present in a measurable amount. Calculated values, as those based on a recipe, are not in parentheses]

Item No.	Food, approximate measures, units, and weight (edible part unless footnotes indicate otherwise)			Water	Food energy	Protein	Fat	Carbohydrate	Calcium	Phosphorus	Iron	Sodium	Potassium	Vitamin A value	Thiamin	Riboflavin	Niacin	Ascorbic acid
				Values for edible part of foods														
(A)	(B)			(C)	(D)	(E)	(F)	(G)	(H)	(I)	(J)	(K)	(L)	(M)	(N)	(O)	(P)	(Q)
			Grams	*Percent*	*Calories*	*Grams*	*Grams*	*Grams*	*Milligrams*	*Milligrams*	*Milligrams*	*Milligrams*	*Milligrams*	*International units*	*Milligrams*	*Milligrams*	*Milligrams*	*Milligrams*
	Tapioca desserts: [12, 13]																	
2269	Apple tapioca	1 cup	250	70.1	293	0.5	0.3	73.5	8	10	0.5	128	65	30	Trace	Trace	Trace	Trace
2270	Tapioca cream pudding	1 cup	165	71.8	221	8.3	8.4	28.2	173	180	.7	257	223	480	0.07	0.30	0.2	2
	Tartar sauce:																	
2273	Regular:																	
a	Cup	1 cup	230	34.4	1,221	3.2	132.9	9.7	41	74	2.1	1,626	179	510	.02	.07	Trace	2
b	Tablespoon	1 tbsp	14	34.4	74	.2	8.1	.6	3	4	.1	99	11	30	Trace	Trace	Trace	Trace
2274	Special dietary (low calorie, approx. 10 Cal. per teaspoon).	1 tbsp	14	68.1	31	.1	3.1	.9	3	4	.1	99	11	30	Trace	Trace	Trace	Trace
	Tendergreen. See Mustard spinach (items 1370–1371).																	
	Thuringer. See Sausage, cold cuts, and luncheon meats (item 2021).																	
2280	**Tilefish,** baked:																	
a	Pound	1 lb	454	71.6	626	111.1	16.8	0	—	—	—	—	—	—	—	—	—	—
b	Ounce	1 oz	28	71.6	39	6.9	1.0	0	—	—	—	—	—	—	—	—	—	—
2281	**Tomatoes, green,** raw (refuse: cores and stem ends, 9%).[1]	1 lb	454	93.0	99	5.0	.8	21.1	54	111	2.1	12	1,007	1,110	.25	.17	2.1	83
	Tomatoes, ripe:																	
2282	Raw:																	
	Not peeled (refuse: cores and stem ends, 9%):																	
	Prepackaged:																	
	Container and approx. contents:																	
a	Package, declared net wt., 12 oz. (avg. wt., approx. 14 oz.[377]); 3 tomatoes (item 2282b) or 4 tomatoes (item 2282c).[1]	1 pkg	400	93.5	80	4.0	.7	17.1	47	98	1.8	11	888	3,280	.22	.15	2.5	[378] 84
	Tomato (approx. dimensions and wt.):[1]																	
b	Size, approx. 2⅗-in. diam.; wt., 4¾ oz. (3 per package (item 2282a)).	1 tomato	135	93.5	27	1.4	.2	5.8	16	33	.6	4	300	1,110	.07	.05	.9	[378] 28
c	Size, approx. 2⅜-in. diam.; wt., 3½ oz. (4 per package (item 2282a)).	1 tomato	100	93.5	20	1.0	.2	4.3	12	25	.5	3	222	820	.05	.04	.6	[378] 21
	Bulk:[1]																	
d	Tomato, approx. 3-in. diam., 2⅛ in. high; wt., 7 oz.	1 tomato	200	93.5	40	2.0	.4	8.6	24	49	.9	5	444	1,640	.11	.07	1.3	[378] 42
e	Prepackaged and bulk[1]	1 lb	454	93.5	91	4.5	.8	19.4	54	111	2.1	12	1,007	3,720	.25	.17	2.9	[378] 95
	Peeled (refuse: skins, cores, stem ends, trimmings, 12%):																	
f	Yield of package (item 2282a)	1 pkg	352	93.5	77	3.9	.7	16.5	46	95	1.8	11	859	3,170	.21	.14	2.5	[378] 81
	Tomato:[1]																	
g	Size, approx. 2⅗-in. diam. (see item 2282b)	1 tomato	135	93.5	26	1.3	.2	5.6	15	32	.6	4	290	1,070	.07	.05	.8	[378] 27
h	Size, approx. 2⅜-in. diam. (see item 2282c)	1 tomato	100	93.5	19	1.0	.2	4.1	11	24	.4	3	215	790	.05	.04	.6	[378] 20
i	Size, approx. 3-in. diam. (see item 2282d)	1 tomato	200	93.5	39	1.9	.4	8.3	23	48	.9	5	429	1,580	.11	.07	1.2	[378] 40
j	Pound[1]	1 lb	454	93.5	88	4.4	.8	18.8	52	108	2.0	12	974	3,590	.24	.16	2.8	[378] 92
2283	Cooked (boiled)	1 cup	241	92.4	63	3.1	.5	13.3	36	77	1.4	[20] 10	692	2,410	.17	.12	1.9	58
	Canned, solids and liquid:																	
2284	Regular pack:																	
	Can and approx. contents:																	
a	Size, 303 × 406[14] (No. 303); net wt., 16 oz. (1 lb.).	1 can or 1 lb	454	93.7	95	4.5	.9	19.5	[379] 27	86	2.3	590	984	4,080	.23	.14	3.2	77
b	Size, 401 × 411[14] (No. 2½); net wt., 28 oz. (1 lb. 12 oz.).	1 can	794	93.7	167	7.9	1.6	34.1	[379] 48	151	4.0	1,032	1,723	7,150	.40	.24	5.6	135
c	Size, 603 × 700[14] (No. 10); net wt., 102 oz. (6 lb. 6 oz.).	1 can	2,892	93.7	607	28.9	5.8	124.4	[379] 174	549	14.5	3,760	6,276	26,030	1.45	.87	20.2	492
d	Cup	1 cup	241	93.7	51	2.4	.5	10.4	[379] 14	46	1.2	313	523	2,170	.12	.07	1.7	41
2285	Special dietary pack (low sodium):																	
	Can and approx. contents:																	
a	Size, 303 × 406[14] (No. 303); net wt., 16 oz. (1 lb.).	1 can or 1 lb	454	94.1	91	4.5	.9	19.1	[379] 27	86	2.3	14	984	4,080	.23	.14	3.2	77
b	Size, 603 × 700[14] (No. 10); net wt., 102 oz. (6 lb. 6 oz.).	1 can or 1 lb	2,892	94.1	578	28.9	5.8	121.5	[379] 174	549	14.5	87	6,276	26,030	1.45	.87	20.2	492

(A)	(B)		(C)	(D)	(E)	(F)	(G)	(H)	(I)	(J)	(K)	(L)	(M)	(N)	(O)	(P)	(Q)
c	Cup	1 cup	241	94.1	48	2.4	0.5	10.1	[379] 14	46	1.2	7	523	2,170	0.12	0.07	1.7	41
2286	**Tomato catsup,** canned or bottled:																	
	Container and approx. contents:																	
a	Bottle, net wt., 12 oz	1 bottle	340	68.6	360	6.8	1.4	86.4	75	170	2.7	[380] 3,543	1,234	4,760	.31	.24	5.4	51
b	Bottle, net wt., 14 oz	1 bottle	397	68.6	421	7.9	1.6	100.8	87	199	3.2	[380] 4,137	1,441	5,560	.36	.28	6.4	60
c	Bottle, net wt., 20 oz. (1 lb. 4 oz.)	1 bottle	567	68.6	601	11.3	2.3	144.0	125	284	4.5	[380] 5,908	2,058	7,940	.51	.40	9.1	85
d	Can, size 603 × 700 [14] (No. 10); net wt., 115 oz. (7 lb. 3 oz.).	1 can	3,260	68.6	3,456	65.2	13.0	828.0	717	1,630	26.1	[380] 33,969	11,834	45,640	2.93	2.28	52.2	489
e	Packet, net wt., ½ oz	1 packet	14	68.6	15	.3	.1	3.6	3	7	.1	[380] 146	51	200	.01	.01	.2	2
f	Cup	1 cup	273	68.6	289	5.5	1.1	69.3	60	137	2.2	[380] 2,845	991	3,820	.25	.19	4.4	41
g	Tablespoon	1 tbsp	15	68.6	16	.3	.1	3.8	3	8	.1	[380] 156	54	210	.01	.01	.2	2
h	Pound	1 lb	454	68.6	481	9.1	1.8	115.2	100	227	3.6	[380] 4,727	1,647	6,350	.41	.32	7.3	68
2287	**Tomato chili sauce,** bottled:																	
	Container and approx. contents:																	
a	Bottle, net wt., 12 oz	1 bottle	340	68.0	354	8.5	1.0	84.3	68	177	(2.7)	[380] 4,549	(1,258)	(4,760)	(.31)	(.24)	(5.4)	(54)
b	Can, size 603 × 700 [14] (No. 10); net wt., 114 oz. (7 lb. 2 oz.).	1 can	3,232	68.0	3,361	80.8	9.7	801.5	646	1,681	(25.9)	[380] 43,244	(11,958)	(45,250)	(2.91)	(2.26)	(51.7)	(517)
c	Cup	1 cup	273	68.0	284	6.8	.8	67.7	55	142	(2.2)	[380] 3,653	(1,010)	(3,820)	(.25)	(.19)	(4.4)	(44)
d	Tablespoon	1 tbsp	15	68.0	16	.4	Trace	3.7	3	8	(.1)	[380] 201	(56)	(210)	(.01)	(.01)	(.2)	(2)
e	Pound	1 lb	454	68.0	472	11.3	1.4	112.5	91	236	(3.6)	[380] 6,069	(1,678)	(6,350)	(.41)	(.32)	(7.3)	(73)
	Tomato juice:																	
	Canned or bottled:																	
2288	Regular pack:																	
	Container and approx. contents:																	
a	Bottle, net contents, 32 fl. oz. (1 qt.)	1 bottle or 1 qt.	972	93.6	185	8.7	1.0	41.8	68	175	8.7	1,944	2,206	7,780	.49	.29	7.8	156
	Can:																	
b	Size, 202 × 308 [14] (6Z); net contents, 5½ fl. oz.	1 can	167	93.6	32	1.5	.2	7.2	12	30	1.5	334	379	1,340	.08	.05	1.3	27
c	Size, 404 × 700 [14] (46Z, No. 3 Cylinder); net contents, 46 fl. oz. (1 qt. 14 fl. oz.).	1 can	1,398	93.6	266	12.6	1.4	60.1	98	252	12.6	2,796	3,173	11,180	.70	.42	11.2	224
d	Cup	1 cup	243	93.6	46	2.2	.2	10.4	17	44	2.2	486	552	1,940	.12	.07	1.9	39
e	Glass (6 fl. oz.)	1 glass	182	93.6	35	1.6	.2	7.8	13	33	1.6	364	413	1,460	.09	.05	1.5	29
f	Fluid ounce	1 fl. oz	30.4	93.6	6	.3	Trace	1.3	2	5	.3	61	69	240	.02	.01	.2	5
2289	Special dietary pack (low sodium):																	
	Can and approx. contents:																	
a	Size, 211 × 414 [14] (12Z, No. 211 Cylinder); net contents, 12 fl. oz.	1 can	363	94.2	69	2.9	.4	15.6	25	65	3.3	11	824	2,900	.18	.11	2.5	58
b	Size, 307 × 409 [14] (No. 2); net contents, 18 fl. oz. (1 pt. 2 fl. oz.).	1 can	545	94.2	104	4.4	.5	23.4	38	98	4.9	16	1,237	4,360	.27	.16	3.8	87
c	Cup	1 cup	242	94.2	46	1.9	.2	10.4	17	44	2.2	7	549	1,940	.12	.07	1.7	39
d	Glass (6 fl. oz.)	1 glass	182	94.2	35	1.5	.2	7.8	13	33	1.6	5	413	1,460	.09	.05	1.3	29
e	Fluid ounce	1 fl. oz	30.3	94.2	6	.2	Trace	1.3	2	5	.3	1	69	240	.02	.01	.2	5
	Dehydrated (crystals):																	
2292	Dry form:																	
a	Ounce	1 oz	28	1.0	86	3.3	.6	19.3	24	79	2.2	(1,115)	997	3,710	.15	.11	3.8	68
b	Pound (yields approx. 1¾ gal. of juice)	1 lb	454	1.0	1,374	52.6	10.0	309.4	386	1,266	35.4	(17,845)	15,958	59,420	2.36	1.81	61.2	1,084
2293	Prepared with water (1 lb. of crystals yields approx. 1¾ gal. of juice).	1 cup	243	93.5	49	1.9	.2	10.9	15	44	1.2	(627)	561	2,090	.07	.07	2.2	39
2294	**Tomato juice cocktail,** canned or bottled:																	
	Container and approx. contents:																	
a	Bottle, net contents, 26 fl. oz. (1 pt. 10 fl. oz.)	1 bottle	788	93.0	165	5.5	.8	39.4	79	142	7.1	1,576	1,741	6,300	.39	.16	4.7	126
b	Cup	1 cup	243	93.0	51	1.7	.2	12.2	24	44	2.2	486	537	1,940	.12	.05	1.5	39
c	Glass (6 fl. oz.)	1 glass	182	93.0	38	1.3	.2	9.1	18	33	1.6	364	402	1,460	.09	.04	1.1	29
d	Fluid ounce	1 fl. oz	30.3	93.0	6	.2	Trace	1.5	3	5	.3	61	67	240	.02	.01	.2	5
2295	**Tomato paste,** canned:																	
	Can and approx. contents:																	
a	Size, 202 × 306; [14] net wt., 6 oz	1 can	170	75.0	139	5.8	.7	31.6	46	119	6.0	[381] 65	1,510	5,610	.34	.20	5.3	83
b	Size, 603 × 700 [14] (No. 10); net wt., 111 oz. (6 lb. 15 oz.).	1 can	3,147	75.0	2,581	107.0	12.6	585.3	850	2,203	110.1	[381] 1,196	27,945	103,850	6.29	3.78	97.6	1,542
c	Cup	1 cup	262	75.0	215	8.9	1.0	48.7	71	183	9.2	[381] 100	2,237	8,650	.52	.31	8.1	128
d	Pound	1 lb	454	75.0	372	15.4	1.8	84.4	122	318	15.9	[381] 172	4,028	14,970	.91	.54	14.1	222

[1] Measure and weight apply to food as it is described with inedible part or parts (refuse) included.

[12] Cup measure made on product after it had cooled. See also Appendix B, section on Home-Prepared Foods

[13] For information on ingredients used, see ARS 62–13 (7), table 18, pp. 22–23.

[14] Dimensions of can: 1st dimension represents diameter; 2d dimension, height of can. 1st or left-hand digit in each dimension gives number of whole inches; next 2 digits give additional fraction of dimension expressed as 16th of an inch.

[20] Value is for unsalted product. If salt is used, increase value by 236 mg. per 100 g. of vegetable—an estimated figure based on typical am'unt of salt (0.6%) in canned vegetables. See also Appendix C, section on Cooked Vegetables

[377] Actual net weight exceeds declared net weight. For further information, see Appendix B, section on Tomatoes

[378] Based on year-round average of 23 mg. per 100 g. Samples marketed from November through May average 10 mg. per 100 g.; from June through October, around 26 mg.

[379] Federal standards provide for addition of certain calcium salts as firming agents. If used for whole tomatoes, these salts may add calcium not to exceed 26 mg. per 100 g. of finished product; for cut forms (dices, slices, wedges), 100 mg.

[380] Applies to regular pack. For volume measures that apply to special dietary pack (low sodium), values for 12-oz. bottle (items 2286a, 2287a) range from 17 to 119 mg.; for No. 10 can (item 2286d), from 163 to 1,141 mg.; for No. 10 can (item 2287b), from 162 to 1,131 mg.; for 1 cup (items 2286f, 2287c), from 14 to 96 mg.; for 1 tbsp. (items 2286g, 2287d), from 1 to 5 mg.; for 1 lb. (items 2286h, 2287e), from 23 to 159 mg.

[381] Applies to more usual product with no salt added. If salt is added, sodium content is about 1,343 mg. for 6-oz. can (item 2295a); 24,861 mg. for No. 10 can (item 2295b); 2,070 mg. for 1 cup (item 2295c); 3,583 mg. for 1 lb. (item 2295d).

TABLE 1.—*Nutritive values for household measures and market units of foods*—Continued

[Item numbers correspond to those in table 1 of Handbook No. 8, revised 1963. Values in parentheses denote imputed values usually from another form of the food or from a similar food. Zeros in parentheses indicate that amount of a constituent, if present, is probably too small to be measured. Dashes (—) denote lack of reliable data for a constituent believed to be present in a measurable amount. Calculated values, as those based on a recipe, are not in parentheses]

Item No. (A)	Food, approximate measures, units, and weight (edible part unless footnotes indicate otherwise) (B)			Water (C)	Food energy (D)	Protein (E)	Fat (F)	Carbohydrate (G)	Calcium (H)	Phosphorus (I)	Iron (J)	Sodium (K)	Potassium (L)	Vitamin A value (M)	Thiamin (N)	Riboflavin (O)	Niacin (P)	Ascorbic acid (Q)
			Grams	*Percent*	*Calories*	*Grams*	*Grams*	*Grams*	*Milligrams*	*Milligrams*	*Milligrams*	*Milligrams*	*Milligrams*	*International units*	*Milligrams*	*Milligrams*	*Milligrams*	*Milligrams*
2296	**Tomato puree,** canned:																	
	Regular pack:																	
	Can and approx. contents:																	
a	Size, 401 × 411 [14] (No. 2½); net wt., 29 oz. (1 lb. 13 oz.).	1 can	822	87.0	321	14.0	1.6	73.2	107	279	14.0	3,280	3,502	13,150	0.74	0.41	11.5	271
b	Size, 603 × 700 [14] (No. 10); net wt., 106 oz. (61 lb. 10 oz.).	1 can	3,005	87.0	1,172	51.1	6.0	267.4	391	1,022	51.1	11,990	12,801	48,080	2.70	1.50	42.1	992
c	Pound	1 lb	454	87.0	177	7.7	.9	40.4	59	154	7.7	1,810	1,932	7,260	.41	.23	6.4	150
2297	Special dietary pack (low sodium)	1 lb	454	88.0	177	7.7	.9	40.4	59	154	7.7	27	1,932	7,260	.41	.23	6.4	150
	Tongue:																	
2302	Beef, medium-fat, cooked (braised):																	
a	Slice, approx. 3 in. long, 2 in. wide, ⅛ in. thick	1 slice	20	60.8	49	4.3	3.3	.1	1	23	.4	[43] 12	33	—	.01	.06	.7	—
b	Pound (approx. 22⅔ slices (item 2302a))	1 lb	454	60.8	1,107	97.5	75.8	1.8	32	531	10.0	[43] 277	744	—	.23	1.32	15.9	—
2306	Calf, cooked (braised):																	
a	Slice, approx. 3 in. long, 2 in. wide, ⅛ in. thick	1 slice	20	68.5	32	4.8	1.2	.2	—	—	—	[43] —	—	—	—	—	—	—
b	Pound (approx. 22⅔ slices (item 2306a))	1 lb	454	68.5	726	108.4	27.2	4.5	—	—	—	[43] —	—	—	—	—	—	—
2308	Hog, cooked (braised):																	
a	Slice, approx. 3 in. long, 2 in. wide, ⅛ in. thick	1 slice	20	59.4	51	4.4	3.5	.1	5	24	.3	[43] —	—	—	.01	(.06)	(.7)	—
b	Pound (approx. 22⅔ slices (item 2308a))	1 lb	454	59.4	1,148	99.8	78.9	2.3	118	540	6.4	[43] —	—	—	.32	(1.32)	(15.9)	—
2310	Lamb, cooked (braised):																	
a	Slice, approx. 3 in. long, 2 in. wide, ⅛ in. thick	1 slice	20	60.2	51	4.1	3.6	.1	—	20	—	[43] —	—	—	—	—	—	—
b	Pound (approx. 22⅔ slices (item 2310a))	1 lb	454	60.2	1,152	93.0	82.6	2.3	—	463	—	[43] —	—	—	—	—	—	—
2312	Sheep, cooked (braised):																	
a	Slice, approx. 3 in. long, 2 in. wide, ⅛ in. thick	1 slice	20	51.6	65	4.0	5.1	.5	—	—	.7	[43] —	—	—	—	—	—	—
b	Pound (approx. 22⅔ slices (item 2310a))	1 lb	454	51.6	1,465	89.8	114.8	10.9	—	—	15.4	[43] —	—	—	—	—	—	—
	Tuna:																	
	Canned: [382]																	
	In oil:																	
2323	Solids and liquid:																	
	Can and approx. contents:																	
	Size, 307 × 113 [14] (No. ½):																	
a	Solid pack, net wt., 7 oz	1 can	198	52.6	570	47.9	40.6	0	12	582	2.2	1,584	596	180	.08	.18	20.0	—
b	Chunk style, net wt., 6½ oz	1 can	184	52.6	530	44.5	37.7	0	11	541	2.0	1,472	554	170	.07	.17	18.6	—
c	Flake or grated style, net wt., 6–6¼ oz.	1 can	174	52.6	501	42.1	35.7	0	10	512	1.9	1,392	524	160	.07	.16	17.6	—
	Size, 303 × 212 [14] (Family):																	
d	Chunk style, net wt., 9¼ oz	1 can	262	52.6	755	63.4	53.7	0	16	770	2.9	2,096	789	240	.10	.24	26.5	—
	Size, 401 × 205½ [14] (No. 1):																	
e	Solid pack, net wt., 13 oz	1 can	369	52.6	1,063	89.3	75.6	0	22	1,085	4.1	2,952	1,111	330	.15	.33	37.3	—
	Size, 603 × 408: [14]																	
f	Solid pack, net wt., 64 oz. (4 lb.)	1 can	1,814	52.6	5,224	439.0	371.9	0	109	5,333	20.0	14,512	5,460	1,630	.73	1.63	183.2	—
g	Chunk style, net wt., 60 oz. (3 lb. 12 oz.)	1 can	1,701	52.6	4,899	411.6	348.7	0	102	5,001	18.7	13,608	5,120	1,530	.68	1.53	171.8	—
h	Pound (all styles)	1 lb	454	52.6	1,306	109.8	93.0	0	27	1,334	5.0	3,629	1,365	410	.18	.41	45.8	—
2324	Drained solids:																	
	Can and approx. drained contents:																	
	Size, 307 × 113 [14] (No. ½):																	
a	Solid pack, wt., 6 oz	1 can	169	60.6	333	48.7	13.9	0	(14)	395	3.2	—	—	140	.08	.20	20.1	—
b	Chunk style, wt., 5½ oz	1 can	157	60.6	309	45.2	12.9	0	(13)	367	3.0	—	—	130	.08	.19	18.7	—
	Size, 303 × 212 [14] (Family):																	
c	Chunk style, wt., 7.9 oz	1 can	223	60.6	439	64.2	18.3	0	(18)	522	4.2	—	—	180	.11	.27	26.5	—
	Size, 401 × 205½ [14] (No. 1):																	
d	Solid pack, wt., 11 oz	1 can	313	60.6	617	90.1	25.7	0	(25)	732	5.9	—	—	250	.16	.38	37.2	—
	Size, 603 × 408: [14]																	
e	Solid pack, wt., 54 oz. (3 lb. 6 oz.)	1 can	1,542	60.6	3,038	444.1	126.4	0	(123)	3,608	29.3	—	—	1,230	.77	1.85	183.5	—
f	Chunk style, wt., 51 oz. (3 lb. 3 oz.)	1 can	1,446	60.6	2,849	416.4	118.6	0	(116)	3,384	27.5	—	—	1,160	.72	1.74	172.1	—
	Cup:																	
g	Solid pack and chunk style	1 cup	160	60.6	315	46.1	13.1	0	(13)	374	3.0	—	—	130	.08	.19	19.0	—
h	Pound (solid pack and chunk style)	1 lb	454	60.6	894	130.6	37.2	0	(36)	1,061	8.6	—	—	360	.23	.54	54.0	—
	In water:																	
2325	Solids and liquid:																	

(A)		(B)			(C)	(D)	(E)	(F)	(G)	(H)	(I)	(J)	(K)	(L)	(M)	(N)	(O)	(P)	(Q)
		Can and approx. contents:																	
		Size, 211 × 109 [14] (No. ¼):																	
	a	Solid pack, net wt., 3½ oz	1 can	99	70.0	126	27.7	0.8	0	16	188	1.6	[383] 41	276	—	—	0.10	13.2	—
	b	Chunk style, net wt., 3¼ oz	1 can	92	70.0	117	25.8	.7	0	15	175	1.5	[383] 38	257	—	—	.09	12.2	—
		Size, 307 × 113 [14] (No. ½):																	
	c	Solid pack, net wt., 7 oz	1 can	198	70.0	251	55.4	1.6	0	32	376	3.2	[383] 81	552	—	—	.20	26.8	—
	d	Chunk style, net wt., 6½ oz	1 can	184	70.0	234	51.5	1.5	0	29	350	2.9	[383] 75	513	—	—	.18	24.5	—
		Size, 401 × 205½ [14] (No. 1):																	
	e	Solid pack, net wt., 13 oz	1 can	369	70.0	469	103.3	3.0	0	59	701	5.9	[383] 151	1,030	—	—	.37	49.1	—
		Size, 603 × 408: [14]																	
	f	Solid pack, net wt., 66½ oz. (4 lb. 2½ oz.)	1 can	1,885	70.0	2,394	527.8	15.1	0	302	3,582	30.2	[383] 773	5,259	—	—	1.89	250.7	—
	g	Pound (all styles)	1 lb	454	70.0	576	127.0	3.6	0	73	862	7.3	[383] 186	1,266	—	—	.45	60.3	—
2326		**Tuna salad:** [384]																	
	a	Cup	1 cup	205	69.8	349	29.9	21.5	7.2	41	291	2.7	[42] —	—	590	0.08	.23	10.3	2
	b	Pound	1 lb	454	69.8	771	66.2	47.6	15.9	91	644	5.9	[42] —	—	1,320	.18	.50	22.7	5
		Turkey, cooked:																	
		All classes, roasted:																	
2328		Total edible (flesh, skin, giblets):																	
	a	Yield from 1 lb., ready-to-cook turkey	8.6 oz	245	55.4	644	66.2	40.2	0	—	—	—	—	—	—	—	—	—	—
	b	Pound	1 lb	454	55.4	1,193	122.5	74.4	0	—	—	—	—	—	—	—	—	—	—
2331		Flesh only: [385]																	
		Cup (not packed):																	
	a	Chopped or diced	1 cup	140	61.2	266	44.1	8.5	0	11	351	2.5	182	514	—	.07	.25	10.8	—
	b	Ground	1 cup	110	61.2	209	34.7	6.7	0	9	276	2.0	143	404	—	.06	.20	8.5	—
	c	Pound (approx. 3¼ cups, chopped or diced; 4⅛ cups, ground; or 5⅓ pieces, white meat, with 10⅔ pieces, dark meat).	1 lb	454	61.2	862	142.9	27.7	0	36	1,139	8.2	590	1,665	—	.23	.82	34.9	—
	d	Pieces (1 slice of white meat, 4 in. long, 2 in. wide, ¼ in. thick; wt., 1½ oz.; with 2 slices of dark meat, 2½ in. long, 1⅝ in. wide, ¼ in. thick; wt., ¾ oz. each).	3 pieces or 3 oz.	85	61.2	162	26.8	5.2	0	7	213	1.5	111	312	—	.04	.15	6.5	—
2335		Light meat without skin:																	
		Cup (not packed):																	
	a	Chopped or diced	1 cup	140	62.1	246	46.1	5.5	0	—	—	1.7	115	575	—	.07	.20	15.5	—
	b	Ground	1 cup	110	62.1	194	36.2	4.3	0	—	—	1.3	90	452	—	.06	.15	12.2	—
	c	Pound (approx. 3¼ cups, chopped or diced; 4⅛ cups, ground; or 10⅔ pieces).	1 lb	454	62.1	798	149.2	17.7	0	—	—	5.4	372	1,864	—	.23	.64	50.3	—
	d	Piece, approx. 4 in. long, 2 in. wide, ¼ in. thick; wt., 1½ oz.	2 pieces or 3 oz.	85	62.1	150	28.0	3.3	0	—	—	1.0	70	349	—	.04	.12	9.4	—
2337		Dark meat without skin:																	
		Cup (not packed):																	
	a	Chopped or diced	1 cup	140	60.5	284	42.0	11.0	0	—	—	3.2	139	557	—	.06	.32	5.9	—
	b	Ground	1 cup	110	60.5	223	33.0	9.1	0	—	—	2.5	109	438	—	.04	.25	4.6	—
	c	Pound (approx. 3¼ cups, chopped or diced; 4⅛ cups, ground; or 21⅓ pieces).	1 lb	454	60.5	921	136.1	37.6	0	—	—	10.4	449	1,805	—	.18	1.04	19.1	—
	d	Piece, approx. 2½ in. long, 1⅝ in. wide, ¼ in. thick; wt., ¾ oz.	4 pieces or 3 oz.	85	60.5	173	25.5	7.1	0	—	—	2.0	84	338	—	.03	.20	3.6	—
2339		**Turkey giblets** (some gizzard fat), simmered:																	
	a	Cup, chopped or diced	1 cup	145	61.0	338	29.9	22.3	2.3	—	—	—	—	—	—	—	3.94	—	—
	b	Pound	1 lb	454	61.0	1,057	93.4	69.9	7.3	—	—	—	—	—	—	—	12.34	—	—
2349		**Turkey, canned,** meat only, boned:																	
	a	Can, net wt., 5½ oz. (solid pack)	1 can	156	64.9	315	32.6	19.5	0	16	—	2.2	—	—	200	.03	.22	7.3	—
	b	Cup	1 cup	205	64.9	414	42.8	25.6	0	21	—	2.9	—	—	270	.04	.29	9.6	—
	c	Pound	1 lb	454	64.9	916	94.8	56.7	0	45	—	6.4	—	—	590	.09	.64	21.3	—
		Turkey, potted. See Sausage, cold cuts, and luncheon meats (item 2008).																	
		Turkey potpie:																	
2350		Home prepared, baked: [58]																	
	a	Pie, whole (9-in. diam.)	1 pie	[54] 698	56.2	1,654	72.6	94.2	129.1	188	705	9.8	1,906	1,382	9,280	.77	.91	17.5	14
	b	Piece, ⅓ of pie (item 2350a)	1 piece	232	56.2	550	24.1	31.3	42.9	63	234	3.2	633	459	3,090	.26	.30	5.8	5
	c	Pound	1 lb	454	56.2	1,075	47.2	61.2	83.9	122	458	6.4	1,238	898	6,030	.50	.59	11.3	9

[14] Dimensions of can: 1st dimension represents diameter; 2d dimension, height of can. 1st or left-hand digit in each dimension gives number of whole inches; next 2 digits give additional fraction of dimension expressed as 16th of an inch.

[42] Value for product without added salt.

[58] For information on ingredients used in crust and in filling and for proportion of crust to filling for pies, see ARS 62-13 (7), tables 23 and 24, p. 31, and table 25, p. 32.

[54] Yield of formula used to calculate nutritive values in Agr. Handb. No. 8, rev. 1963.

[382] Several species of fish are marketed as tuna. They are designated "white," "light," or "dark" on basis of their color designation in Munsell units of value. The term "white" is limited to the species *Thunnus germo* (albacore).

[383] Applies to special dietary pack (low sodium). For regular water pack with salt added, based on 1 sample, value would be 866 mg. for can, net wt., 3½ oz.; 805 mg. for can, net wt., 3¼ oz.; 1,733 mg. for can, net wt., 7 oz.; 1,610 mg. for can, net wt., 6½ oz.; 3,229 mg. for can, net wt., 13 oz.; 16,494 mg. for can, net wt., 66½ oz.; 3,939 mg. for 1 lb.

[384] Prepared with tuna, celery, salad dressing (mayonnaise type), pickle, onion, and egg.

[385] Nutritive values based on 50% light meat, 50% dark meat.

TABLE 1.—*Nutritive values for household measures and market units of foods*—Continued

[Item numbers correspond to those in table 1 of Handbook No. 8, revised 1963. Values in parentheses denote imputed values usually from another form of the food or from a similar food. Zeros in parentheses indicate that amount of a constituent, if present, is probably too small to be measured. Dashes (—) denote lack of reliable data for a constituent believed to be present in a measurable amount. Calculated values, as those based on a recipe, are not in parentheses]

Item No. (A)	Food, approximate measures, units, and weight (edible part unless footnotes indicate otherwise) (B)			Water (C)	Food energy (D)	Protein (E)	Fat (F)	Carbohydrate (G)	Calcium (H)	Phosphorus (I)	Iron (J)	Sodium (K)	Potassium (L)	Vitamin A value (M)	Thiamin (N)	Riboflavin (O)	Niacin (P)	Ascorbic acid (Q)
			Grams	*Percent*	*Calories*	*Grams*	*Grams*	*Grams*	*Milligrams*	*Milligrams*	*Milligrams*	*Milligrams*	*Milligrams*	*International units*	*Milligrams*	*Milligrams*	*Milligrams*	*Milligrams*
	Turnips:																	
2352	Raw, cubed or sliced	1 cup	130	91.5	39	1.3	0.3	8.6	51	39	0.7	64	348	Trace	0.05	0.09	0.8	47
2353	Cooked (boiled), drained:																	
	Cup:																	
a	Cubed	1 cup	155	93.6	36	1.2	.3	7.6	54	37	.6	[20] 53	291	Trace	.06	.08	.5	34
b	Mashed	1 cup	230	93.6	53	1.8	.5	11.3	81	55	.9	[20] 78	432	Trace	.09	.12	.7	51
c	Pound	1 lb	454	93.6	104	3.6	.9	22.2	159	109	1.8	[20] 154	853	Trace	.18	.23	1.4	100
	Turnip greens, leaves including stems:																	
2354	Raw	1 lb	454	90.3	127	13.6	1.4	22.7	1,116	263	8.2	—	—	34,470	(.95)	(1.77)	(3.6)	631
	Cooked (boiled), drained, cooked in—																	
2355	Small amount of water, short time:																	
a	Cup	1 cup	145	93.2	29	3.2	.3	5.2	267	54	1.6	[20] —	—	9,140	.22	.35	.9	100
b	Pound	1 lb	454	93.2	91	10.0	.9	16.3	835	168	5.0	[20] —	—	28,580	.68	1.09	2.7	313
2356	Large amount of water, long time:																	
a	Cup	1 cup	(145)	93.5	28	3.2	.3	4.8	252	49	1.5	[20] —	—	8,270	.15	.33	.7	68
b	Pound	1 lb	454	93.5	86	10.0	.9	15.0	789	154	4.5	[20] —	—	25,860	.45	1.04	2.3	213
2357	Canned, solids and liquid:																	
	Can and approx. contents:																	
a	Size, 303 × 406 [14] (No. 303); net wt., 15 oz	1 can	425	93.7	77	6.4	1.3	13.6	425	128	6.8	[21] 1,003	1,033	19,980	.09	.38	2.6	81
b	Size, 603 × 700 [14] (No. 10); net wt., 98 oz. (6 lb. 2 oz.).	1 can	2,778	93.7	500	41.7	8.3	88.9	2,778	833	44.4	[21] 6,556	6,751	130,570	.56	2.50	16.7	528
c	Cup	1 cup	232	93.7	42	3.5	.7	7.4	232	70	3.7	[21] 548	564	10,900	.05	.21	1.4	44
d	Pound	1 lb	454	93.7	82	6.8	1.4	14.5	454	136	7.3	[21] 1,070	1,102	21,320	.09	.41	2.7	86
	Frozen, chopped:																	
2358	Not thawed:																	
a	Container, net wt., 10 oz	1 container	284	92.3	65	7.4	.9	11.4	372	116	4.8	65	534	19,600	.17	.31	1.4	97
b	Pound	1 lb	454	92.3	104	11.8	1.4	18.1	594	186	7.7	104	853	31,300	.27	.50	2.8	154
2359	Cooked (boiled), drained:																	
a	Yield from 10 oz., frozen turnip greens	1⅓ cups	220	92.7	51	5.5	.7	8.6	260	86	3.5	[20] 37	328	15,180	.11	.20	.9	42
b	Yield from 1 lb., frozen turnip greens	2⅛ cups	352	92.7	81	8.8	1.1	13.7	415	137	5.6	[20] 60	524	24,290	.18	.32	1.4	67
c	Cup	1 cup	165	92.7	38	4.1	.5	6.4	195	64	2.6	[20] 28	246	11,390	.08	.15	.7	31
d	Pound (yield from approx. 1.3 lb., frozen turnip greens).	1 lb	454	92.7	104	11.3	1.4	17.7	535	177	7.3	[20] 77	676	31,300	.23	.41	1.8	86
	Veal: [40]																	
	Chuck cuts and boneless veal for stew:																	
2369	Raw, lean with fat:																	
a	With bone (69% lean, 11% fat) (refuse: bone, 20%).[1]	1 lb	454	70	628	70.4	36	0	40	722	10.5	246	1,126	—	.52	.94	23.6	—
b	Without bone (86% lean, 14% fat)	1 lb	454	70	785	88.0	45	0	50	903	13.2	308	1,408	—	.64	1.17	29.5	—
2370	Cooked (braised, pot-roasted, or stewed), drained (85% lean, 15% fat):																	
a	Yield from 1 lb., raw veal with bone (item 2369a).	8.4 oz	240	58.5	564	67.0	30.7	0	29	362	8.4	117	536	—	.22	.70	15.4	—
b	Yield from 1 lb., raw veal without bone (item 2369b).	10.6 oz	299	58.5	703	83.4	38.3	0	36	451	10.5	146	667	—	.27	.87	19.1	—
c	Cup, chopped or diced pieces (not packed)	1 cup	140	58.5	329	39.1	17.9	0	17	211	4.9	68	313	—	.13	.41	9.0	—
d	Pound	1 lb	454	58.5	1,066	126.6	58.1	0	54	685	15.9	222	1,013	—	.41	1.32	29.0	—
e	Piece, approx. 2½ in. long, 2½ in. wide, ¾ in. thick.	1 piece or 3 oz.	85	58.5	200	23.7	10.9	0	10	128	3.0	41	190	—	.08	.25	5.4	—
	Loin cuts:																	
2381	Raw, lean with fat:																	
a	With bone (71% lean, 12% fat) (refuse: bone, 17%).[1]	1 lb	454	69	681	72.3	41	0	41	734	10.9	253	1,157	—	.53	.96	24.2	—
b	Without bone (85% lean, 15% fat)	1 lb	454	69	821	87.1	50	0	50	885	13.2	305	1,394	—	.64	1.16	29.2	—
2382	Cooked (braised or broiled) (77% lean, 23% fat):																	
a	Yield from 1 lb., raw loin with bone (item 2381a).	9.5 oz	269	58.9	629	71.0	36.0	0	30	605	8.6	174	795	—	.19	.67	14.5	—
b	Yield from 1 lb., raw loin without bone (item 2381b).	11.4 oz	324	58.9	758	85.5	43.4	0	36	729	10.4	209	958	—	.23	.81	17.5	—
c	Cup, chopped or diced pieces (not packed)	1 cup	140	58.9	328	37.0	18.8	0	15	315	4.5	91	414	—	.10	.35	7.6	—
d	Pound	1 lb	454	58.9	1,061	119.8	68.0	0	50	1,021	14.5	294	1,342	—	.32	1.13	24.5	—

(A)	(B)			(C)	(D)	(E)	(F)	(G)	(H)	(I)	(J)	(K)	(L)	(M)	(N)	(O)	(P)	(Q)
e	Piece, approx. 2½ in. long, 2½ in. wide, ¾ in. thick.	1 piece or 3 oz.	85	58.9	199	22.4	11.4	0	9	191	2.7	55	251	—	0.06	0.21	4.6	—
	Plate, breast of veal:																	
2385	Raw, lean with fat:																	
a	With bone (58% lean, 21% fat) (refuse: bone, 21%).[1]	1 lb	454	64	828	65.6	61	0	39	652	9.7	230	1,050	—	.48	.87	22.0	—
b	Without bone (74% lean, 26% fat)	1 lb	454	64	1,048	83.0	77	0	50	826	12.2	291	1,328	—	.61	1.10	27.8	—
2386	Cooked (braised or stewed) (73% lean, 27% fat):																	
a	Yield from 1 lb., raw veal with bone (item 2385a).	8.3 oz	237	52.1	718	61.9	50.2	0	28	327	7.8	108	495	—	.12	.57	10.9	—
b	Yield from 1 lb., raw veal without bone (item 2385b).	10.6 oz	299	52.1	906	78.0	63.4	0	36	413	9.9	137	624	—	.15	.72	13.8	—
c	Pound	1 lb	454	52.1	1,374	118.4	96.2	0	54	626	15.0	207	947	—	.23	1.09	20.9	—
	Rib roast:																	
2389	Raw:																	
a	With bone (63% lean, 14% fat) (refuse: bone, 23%).[1]	1 lb	454	66	723	65.7	49	0	38	664	9.8	230	1,051	—	.48	.87	22.0	—
b	Without bone (82% lean, 18% fat)	1 lb	454	66	939	85.3	64	0	50	862	12.7	299	1,365	—	.62	1.13	28.6	—
2390	Cooked (roasted):																	
a	Yield from 1 lb., raw veal with bone (item 2389a).	8½ oz	241	54.6	648	65.6	40.7	0	29	598	8.2	161	735	—	.31	.75	18.8	—
b	Yield from 1 lb., raw veal without bone (item 2389b).	11 oz	313	54.6	842	85.1	52.9	0	38	776	10.6	208	953	—	.41	.97	24.4	—
	Cup (not packed):																	
c	Chopped or diced	1 cup	140	54.6	377	38.1	23.7	0	17	347	4.8	93	427	—	.18	.43	10.9	—
d	Ground	1 cup	110	54.6	296	29.9	18.6	0	13	273	3.7	73	335	—	.14	.34	8.6	—
e	Pound	1 lb	454	54.6	1,220	123.4	76.7	0	54	1,125	15.4	302	1,382	—	.59	1.41	35.4	—
f	Piece, approx. 4⅛ in. long, 2¼ in. wide, ¼ in. thick; wt., 1½ oz.	2 pieces or 3 oz.	85	54.6	229	23.1	14.4	0	10	211	2.9	57	259	—	.11	.26	6.6	—
	Round with rump (roasts and leg cutlets):																	
2393	Raw, lean with fat:																	
a	With bone (67% lean, 10% fat) (refuse: bone, 23%).[1]	1 lb	454	70	573	68.1	31	0	38	699	10.1	238	1,090	—	.50	.90	22.8	—
b	Without bone (87% lean, 13% fat)	1 lb	454	70	744	88.5	41	0	50	907	13.2	310	1,416	—	.64	1.17	29.6	—
2394	Cooked (braised or broiled):																	
a	Yield from 1 lb., raw veal with bone (item 2393a).	8.7 oz	247	60.4	534	66.9	27.4	0	27	571	7.9	164	749	—	.17	.62	13.3	—
b	Yield from 1 lb., raw veal without bone (item 2393b).	11.3 oz	321	60.4	693	87.0	35.6	0	35	742	10.3	213	974	—	.22	.80	17.3	—
c	Cup, chopped or diced pieces (not packed)	1 cup	140	60.4	302	37.9	15.5	0	15	323	4.5	93	424	—	.10	.35	7.6	—
d	Pound	1 lb	454	60.4	980	122.9	50.3	0	50	1,048	14.5	301	1,376	—	.32	1.13	24.5	—
e	Piece, approx. 4⅛ in. long, 2¼ in. wide, ½ in. thick; wt., 3 oz. (cutlets); or 2 pieces, 4⅛ in. long, 2¼ in. wide, ¼ in. thick; wt., 1½ oz. each (roasts).	1 or 2 pieces or 3 oz.	85	60.4	184	23.0	9.4	0	9	196	2.7	56	258	—	.06	.21	4.6	—
2396	**Vegetable juice cocktail, canned:**																	
	Can and approx. contents:																	
a	Size, 202 × 314[14] (6½Z); net contents, 6 fl. oz.; or 1 glass (6 fl. oz.).	1 can or 1 glass.	182	94.1	31	1.6	.2	6.6	22	40	.9	(364)	(402)	1,270	.09	.05	1.5	16
b	Size, 307 × 512[14] (No. 2 Cylinder); net contents, 24 fl. oz. (1 pt. 8 fl. oz.).	1 can	727	94.1	124	6.5	.7	26.2	87	160	3.6	(1,454)	(1,607)	5,090	.36	.22	5.8	65
c	Size, 404 × 700[14] (46Z, No. 3 Cylinder); net contents, 46 fl. oz. (1 qt. 14 fl. oz.).	1 can	1,394	94.1	237	12.5	1.4	50.2	167	307	7.0	(2,788)	(3,081)	9,760	.70	.42	11.2	125
d	Cup	1 cup	242	94.1	41	2.2	.2	8.7	29	53	1.2	(484)	(535)	1,690	.12	.07	1.9	22
e	Fluid ounce	1 fl. oz	30.3	94.1	5	.3	Trace	1.1	4	7	.2	(61)	(67)	210	.02	.01	.2	3
	Vegetables, mixed (carrots, corn, peas, green snap beans, lima beans), frozen:																	
2403	Not thawed:																	
a	Container, net wt., 10 oz	1 container	284	82.1	185	9.4	.9	38.9	74	187	4.0	[45] 168	591	14,200	.37	.20	3.4	26
b	Pound	1 lb	454	82.1	295	15.0	1.4	62.1	118	299	6.4	[45] 268	943	22,680	.59	.32	5.4	41
2404	Cooked (boiled), drained:																	
a	Yield from 10 oz., frozen vegetables	1½ cups	275	82.6	176	8.8	.8	36.9	69	173	3.6	[45] 146	525	13,610	.33	.19	3.0	22
b	Yield from 1 lb., frozen vegetables	2⅖ cups	445	82.6	285	14.2	1.3	59.6	111	280	5.8	[45] 236	850	22,030	.53	.31	4.9	36
c	Cup	1 cup	182	82.6	116	5.8	.5	24.4	46	115	2.4	[45] 96	348	9,010	.22	.13	2.0	15

[1] Measure and weight apply to food as it is described with inedible part or parts (refuse) included.

[14] Dimensions of can: 1st dimension represents diameter; 2d dimension, height of can. 1st or left-hand digit in each dimension gives number of whole inches; next 2 digits give additional fraction of dimension expressed as 16th of an inch.

[20] Value is for unsalted product. If salt is used, increase value by 236 mg. per 100 g. of vegetable—an estimated figure based on typical amount of salt (0.6%) in canned vegetables. See also Appendix C, section on Cooked Vegetables

[21] Estimated value based on addition of salt in amount of 0.6% of finished product.

[45] Value based on average weighted in accordance with commercial practice in freezing vegetables. Wide range in sodium content occurs. For cooked vegetables, value also represents no additional salting. If salt is moderately added, increase value by 236 mg. per 100 g. of vegetable—an estimated figure based on typical amount of salt (0.6%) in canned vegetables. See also Appendix C, section on Cooked Vegetables, p. 281, and section on Frozen Fruits and Vegetables

[46] For further information about items and basis of vitamin and mineral values, see Appendix B, section on Foods Measured in Pieces, Slices, and Other Units and Appendix C, section on Meats Values for cooked items apply to products prepared without added salt or other seasoning.

TABLE 1.—*Nutritive values for household measures and market units of foods*—Continued

[Item numbers correspond to those in table 1 of Handbook No. 8, revised 1963. Values in parentheses denote imputed values usually from another form of the food or from a similar food. Zeros in parentheses indicate that amount of a constituent, if present, is probably too small to be measured. Dashes (—) denote lack of reliable data for a constituent believed to be present in a measurable amount. Calculated values, as those based on a recipe, are not in parentheses]

Item No. (A)	Food, approximate measures, units, and weight (edible part unless footnotes indicate otherwise) (B)			Water (C)	Food energy (D)	Protein (E)	Fat (F)	Carbohydrate (G)	Calcium (H)	Phosphorus (I)	Iron (J)	Sodium (K)	Potassium (L)	Vitamin A value (M)	Thiamin (N)	Riboflavin (O)	Niacin (P)	Ascorbic acid (Q)
			Grams	*Percent*	*Calories*	*Grams*	*Grams*	*Grams*	*Milligrams*	*Milligrams*	*Milligrams*	*Milligrams*	*Milligrams*	*International units*	*Milligrams*	*Milligrams*	*Milligrams*	*Milligrams*
	Vegetables, mixed (carrots, corn, peas, green snap beans, lima beans), frozen—Continued																	
	Cooked (boiled), drained—Continued																	
d	Pound	1 lb	454	82.6	290	14.5	1.4	60.8	113	286	5.9	[65] 240	866	22,450	0.54	0.32	5.0	36
	Vegetable-oyster. See Salsify (item 1962).																	
2405	**Venison, lean meat only, raw**	3 oz	85	74	107	17.9	3.4	0	9	212	—	—	—	—	.20	.41	5.4	—
	Vienna sausage. See Sausage, cold cuts, and luncheon meats (item 2022).																	
	Vinegar:																	
2406	Cider:																	
a	Quart	1 qt	960	93.8	134	Trace	(0)	56.6	(58)	(86)	(5.8)	10	960	—	—	—	—	—
b	Cup	1 cup	240	93.8	34	Trace	(0)	14.2	(14)	(22)	(1.4)	2	240	—	—	—	—	—
c	Tablespoon	1 tbsp	15	93.8	2	Trace	(0)	.9	(1)	(1)	(.1)	Trace	15	—	—	—	—	—
2407	Distilled:																	
a	Quart	1 qt	960	95	115	—	—	48.0	—	—	—	10	144	—	—	—	—	—
b	Cup	1 cup	240	95	29	—	—	12.0	—	—	—	2	36	—	—	—	—	—
c	Tablespoon	1 tbsp	15	95	2	—	—	.8	—	—	—	Trace	2	—	—	—	—	—
	Vodka. See Beverages (items 395–399).																	
	Waffles:																	
	Baked from home recipe, made with [60]—																	
2409	Enriched flour:																	
a	Round, 7-in. diam., ⅝ in. thick (yield from approx. 7 tbsp. of batter).	1 waffle	75	41.4	209	7.0	7.4	28.1	85	130	1.3	356	109	250	.13	.19	1.0	Trace
	Square, 9 × 9 × ⅝ in. (yield from approx. 1⅛ cups of batter):																	
b	Whole	1 waffle	200	41.4	558	18.6	19.6	75.0	226	346	3.4	950	290	660	.34	.50	2.6	1
c	Section, 4½ × 4½ × ⅝ in.; ¼ of item 2409b	1 section	50	41.4	140	4.7	4.9	18.8	57	87	.9	238	73	170	.09	.13	.7	Trace
d	Pound	1 lb	454	41.4	1,266	42.2	44.5	170.1	513	785	7.7	2,155	658	1,500	.77	1.13	5.9	2
2410	Unenriched flour:																	
a	Round, 7-in. diam., ⅝ in. thick (yield from approx. 7 tbsp. of batter).	1 waffle	75	41.4	209	7.0	7.4	28.1	85	130	.7	356	109	250	.04	.14	.3	Trace
	Square, 9 × 9 × ⅝ in. (yield from approx. 1⅛ cups of batter):																	
b	Whole	1 waffle	200	41.4	558	18.6	19.6	75.0	226	346	1.8	950	290	660	.10	.36	.8	1
c	Section, 4½ × 4½ × ⅝ in.; ¼ of item 2410b	1 section	50	41.4	140	4.7	4.9	18.8	57	87	.5	238	73	170	.03	.09	.2	Trace
d	Pound	1 lb	454	41.4	1,266	42.2	44.5	170.1	513	785	4.1	2,155	658	1,500	.23	.82	1.8	2
2411	Frozen, made with enriched flour, prebaked, unheated:																	
	Waffle, 4⅝ × 3¾ × ⅝ in.:																	
a	Container, net wt., 12 oz.; 10 waffles	1 container	340	42.1	860	24.1	21.1	142.8	415	707	[386] 6.1	2,190	537	440	[386] .58	[386] .54	[386] 4.1	Trace
b	Waffle	1 waffle	34	42.1	86	2.4	2.1	14.3	41	71	[387] .6	219	54	40	[387] .06	[387] .05	[387] .4	Trace
	Waffle, 3½ × 2¾ × ⅝ in. or 3¾ × 2¾ × ½ in.; wt., ¾–⅞ oz.:																	
c	Container, net wt., 5 oz.; 6 waffles, 3½ × 2¾ × ⅝ in.	1 container	142	42.1	359	10.1	8.8	59.6	173	295	[388] 2.6	914	224	180	[388] .24	[388] .23	[388] 1.7	Trace
d	Container, net wt., 9 oz.; 12 waffles, 3¾ × 2¾ × ½ in.	1 container	255	42.1	645	18.1	15.8	107.1	311	530	[389] 4.6	1,642	403	330	[389] .43	[389] .41	[389] 3.1	Trace
e	Waffle	1 waffle	22	42.1	56	1.6	1.4	9.2	27	46	[390] .4	142	35	30	[390] .04	[390] .04	[390] .3	Trace
f	Pound	1 lb	454	42.1	1,148	32.2	28.1	190.5	553	943	[391] 8.2	2,921	717	590	[391] .77	[391] .73	[391] 5.4	Trace
	Waffle mixes and waffles baked from mixes:																	
2416	Mix (pancake and waffle), with enriched flour, dry form. See Pancake and waffle mix (item 1455).																	
2417	Waffles, made with egg, milk: [65]																	
a	Round, 7-in. diam., ⅝ in. thick (yield from approx. 7 tbsp. of batter).	1 waffle	75	41.7	206	6.6	8.0	27.2	179	257	1.0	515	146	170	.11	.17	.7	Trace
	Square, 9 × 9 × ⅝ in. (yield from approx. 1⅛ cups of batter):																	
b	Whole	1 waffle	200	41.7	550	17.6	21.2	72.4	478	686	2.6	1,372	390	460	.28	.46	1.8	1
c	Section, 4½ × 4½ × ⅝ in.; ¼ of item 2417b	1 section	50	41.7	138	4.4	5.3	18.1	120	172	.7	343	98	120	.07	.12	.5	Trace
d	Pound	1 lb	454	41.7	1,247	39.9	48.1	164.2	1,084	1,556	5.9	3,112	885	1,040	.64	1.04	4.1	3

(A)		(B)			(C)	(D)	(E)	(F)	(G)	(H)	(I)	(J)	(K)	(L)	(M)	(N)	(O)	(P)	(Q)
2418		Mix (pancake and waffle), with unenriched flour, dry form. See Pancake and waffle mix (item 1458).																	
2419		**Waffles,** made with egg, milk:[68]																	
	a	Round, 7-in. diam., ⅝ in. thick (yield from approx. 7 tbsp. of batter).	1 waffle	75	41.7	206	6.6	8.0	27.2	179	257	0.7	515	146	170	0.06	0.14	0.3	Trace
		Square, 9 × 9 × ⅝ in. (yield from approx. 1⅛ cups of batter):																	
	b	Whole	1 waffle	200	41.7	550	17.6	21.2	72.4	478	686	1.8	1,372	390	460	.16	.38	.8	1
	c	Section, 4½ × 4½ × ⅝ in.; ¼ of item 2419b	1 section	50	41.7	138	4.4	5.3	18.1	120	172	.5	343	98	120	.04	.10	.2	Trace
	d	Pound	1 lb	454	41.7	1,247	39.9	48.1	164.2	1,084	1,556	4.1	3,112	885	1,040	.36	.86	1.8	3
		Walnuts:[5]																	
2420		Black:																	
	a	In shell (refuse: shells, 78%),[1] 1 lb. (yields approx. 3½ oz., shelled nuts).	1 lb	454	3.1	627	20.5	59.2	14.8	Trace	569	6.0	3	459	300	.22	.11	.7	—
		Shelled:																	
		Chopped or broken kernels:																	
	b	Cup	1 cup	125	3.1	785	25.6	74.1	18.5	Trace	713	7.5	4	575	380	.28	.14	.9	—
	c	Tablespoon	1 tbsp	8	3.1	50	1.6	4.7	1.2	Trace	46	.5	Trace	37	20	.02	.01	.1	—
	d	Ground (finely)	1 cup	80	3.1	502	16.4	47.4	11.8	Trace	456	4.8	2	368	240	.18	.09	.6	—
	e	Pound (yield from approx. 4½ lb., in shell)	1 lb	454	3.1	2,849	93.0	269.0	67.1	Trace	2,586	27.2	14	2,087	1,360	1.00	.50	3.2	—
	f	Ounce	1 oz	28	3.1	178	5.8	16.8	4.2	Trace	162	1.7	1	130	90	.06	.03	.2	—
2421		Persian or English:																	
		In shell (refuse: shells, 55%):[1]																	
	a	Pound (yields approx. 7.2 oz., shelled nuts)	1 lb	454	3.5	1,329	30.2	130.6	32.2	202	776	6.3	4	918	60	.67	.27	1.8	4
	b	10 large nuts (approx. 1$\frac{5}{16}$-in. diam.)	10 nuts	110	3.5	322	7.3	31.7	7.8	49	188	1.5	1	223	10	.16	.06	.4	1
		Shelled:																	
	c	Halves, 1 cup (approx. 50)	1 cup	100	3.5	651	14.8	64.0	15.8	99	380	3.1	2	450	30	.33	.13	.9	2
		Chopped pieces or chips:																	
	d	Cup	1 cup	120	3.5	781	17.8	76.8	19.0	119	456	3.7	2	540	40	.40	.16	1.1	2
	e	Tablespoon	1 tbsp	8	3.5	52	1.2	5.1	1.3	8	30	.2	Trace	36	Trace	.03	.01	.1	Trace
	f	Pound (yield from approx. 2¼ lb., in shell)	1 lb	454	3.5	2,953	67.1	290.3	71.7	449	1,724	14.1	9	2,041	140	1.50	.59	4.1	9
	g	Ounce (approx. 14 halves)	1 oz	28	3.5	185	4.2	18.1	4.5	28	108	.9	1	128	10	.09	.04	.3	1
2422		**Waterchestnut,** Chinese (matai, waternut), raw, 1 lb., 20–28 corms, 1¼- to 2-in. diam. (refuse: skin, 23%).[1,5]	1 lb	454	78.3	276	4.9	.7	66.4	14	227	2.1	70	1,747	0	.49	.70	3.5	14
2423		**Watercress,** leaves including stems, raw:																	
	a	Whole, 1 cup (approx. 10 sprigs) or cut (½- to ¾-in. pieces).	1 cup	35	93.3	7	.8	.1	1.1	53	19	.6	18	99	1,720	.03	.06	.3	28
	b	Chopped, finely	1 cup	125	93.3	24	2.8	.4	3.8	189	68	2.1	65	353	6,130	.10	.20	1.1	99
		Water ice. See Ices, water (item 1144).																	
2424		**Watermelon,** raw:																	
	a	Whole, 16 in. long, 10-in. diam.; wt., approx. 32⅔ lb. (refuse: rind, seeds, cutting loss, 54%).[1]	1 melon	14,822	92.6	1,773	34.1	13.6	436.4	477	682	34.1	68	6,818	40,230	2.05	2.05	13.6	477
	b	Piece, $\frac{1}{16}$ of melon (item 2424a) (wedge, 4-in. arc with 8-in. radii, or slice, 10-in. diam., 1 in. thick) (refuse: rind, seeds, cutting loss, 54%).[1]	1 piece	926	92.6	111	2.1	.9	27.3	30	43	2.1	4	426	2,510	.13	.13	.9	30
	c	Diced pieces	1 cup	160	92.6	42	.8	.3	10.2	11	16	.8	2	160	940	.05	.05	.3	11
	d	Pound	1 lb	454	92.6	118	2.3	.9	29.0	32	45	2.3	5	454	2,680	.14	.14	.9	32
2427		**Weakfish,** broiled with butter or margarine:																	
	a	Pound	1 lb	454	61.4	943	111.6	51.7	0	—	—	—	[385]2,540	2,109	—	.45	.36	15.9	—
	b	Ounce	1 oz	28	61.4	59	7.0	3.2	0	—	—	—	[385]159	132	—	.03	.02	1.0	—
2428		**Welsh rarebit**[51]	1 cup	232	70.2	415	18.8	31.6	14.6	582	432	.7	770	320	1,230	.09	.53	.2	Trace
		West Indian cherry. See Acerola (item 3).																	
		Wheat flour:[5]																	
2435		Whole (from hard wheats), stirred, spooned into cup.	1 cup	120	12	400	16.0	2.4	85.2	49	446	4.0	4	444	(0)	.66	.14	5.2	(0)
		Patent (white), plain:																	
		All-purpose or family flour:																	
2439		Enriched:																	
	a	Unsifted, dipped with cup, standard granulation.	1 cup	137	12	499	14.4	1.4	104.3	22	119	[157]4.0	3	130	(0)	[157].60	[157].36	[157]4.8	(0)

[1] Measure and weight apply to food as it is described with inedible part or parts (refuse) included.

[5] Most of phosphorus in nuts, legumes, and outer layers of cereal grains is present as phytic acid. See also Appendix D, section on Minerals and Oxalic Acid

[6] Value based on average weighted in accordance with commercial practice in freezing vegetables. Wide range in sodium content occurs. For cooked vegetables, value also represents no additional salting. If salt is moderately added, increase value by 236 mg. per 100 g. of vegetable—an estimated figure based on typical amount of salt (0.6%) in canned vegetables. See also Appendix C, section on Cooked Vegetables, and section on Frozen Fruits and Vegetables

[51] For information on ingredients used in preparation, see ARS 62–13 (7), table 22, p. 26.

[60] For information on ingredients used, see ARS 62–13 (7), table 4, p. 10.

[68] For proportion of mix and added ingredients used, see ARS 62–13 (7), table 5, p. 12.

[157] Based on product with minimum level of enrichment. See also Appendix C, section on Enriched Foods and Standards of Enrichment

[385] Based on fish with salt added in cooking.

[386] With unenriched flour, approx. values are iron 3.7 mg., thiamin 0.20 mg., riboflavin 0.31 mg., niacin 1.4 mg.

[387] With unenriched flour, approx. values are iron 4.0 mg., thiamin 0.02 mg., riboflavin 0.03 mg., niacin 0.1 mg.

[388] With unenriched flour, approx. values are iron 1.6 mg., thiamin 0.09 mg., riboflavin 0.13 mg., niacin 0.6 mg.

[389] With unenriched flour, approx. values are iron 2.8 mg., thiamin 0.15 mg., riboflavin 0.23 mg., niacin 1.0 mg.

[390] With unenriched flour, approx. values are iron 0.2 mg., thiamin 0.01 mg., riboflavin 0.02 mg., niacin 0.1 mg.

[391] With unenriched flour, approx. values are iron 5.0 mg., thiamin 0.27 mg., riboflavin 0.41 mg., niacin 1.8 mg.

TABLE 1.—*Nutritive values for household measures and market units of foods*—Continued

[Item numbers correspond to those in table 1 of Handbook No. 8, revised 1963. Values in parentheses denote imputed values usually from another form of the food or from a similar food. Zeros in parentheses indicate that amount of a constituent. if present, is probably too small to be measured. Dashes (—) denote lack of reliable data for a constituent believed to be present in a measurable amount. Calculated values, as those based on a recipe, are not in parentheses]

Item No. (A)	Food, approximate measures, units, and weight (edible part unless footnotes indicate otherwise) (B)		Grams	Water (C)	Food energy (D)	Protein (E)	Fat (F)	Carbohydrate (G)	Calcium (H)	Phosphorus (I)	Iron (J)	Sodium (K)	Potassium (L)	Vitamin A value (M)	Thiamin (N)	Riboflavin (O)	Niacin (P)	Ascorbic acid (Q)
			Grams	Percent	Calories	Grams	Grams	Grams	Milligrams	Milligrams	Milligrams	Milligrams	Milligrams	International units	Milligrams	Milligrams	Milligrams	Milligrams
	Wheat flour[5]—Continued																	
	Patent (white), plain—Continued																	
	All-purpose or family flour—Continued																	
	Enriched—Continued																	
b	Unsifted, spooned into cup, standard granulation.	1 cup	125	12	455	13.1	1.3	95.1	20	109	[157] 3.6	3	119	(0)	[157] 0.55	[157] 0.33	[157] 4.4	(0)
c	Unsifted, spooned into cup, instant blending.[393]	1 cup	129	12	470	13.5	1.3	98.2	21	112	[157] 3.7	3	123	(0)	[157] .57	[157] .34	[157] 4.5	(0)
d	Sifted, spooned into cup, standard granulation.	1 cup	115	12	419	12.1	1.2	87.5	18	100	[157] 3.3	2	109	(0)	[157] .51	[157] .30	[157] 4.0	(0)
2440	Unenriched:																	
a	Unsifted, dipped with cup, standard granulation.	1 cup	137	12	499	14.4	1.4	104.3	22	119	1.1	3	130	(0)	.08	.07	1.2	(0)
b	Unsifted, spooned into cup, standard granulation.	1 cup	125	12	455	13.1	1.3	95.1	20	109	1.0	3	119	(0)	.08	.06	1.1	(0)
c	Unsifted, spooned into cup, instant blending.[393]	1 cup	129	12	470	13.5	1.3	98.2	21	112	1.0	3	123	(0)	.08	.06	1.2	(0)
d	Sifted, spooned into cup, standard granulation.	1 cup	115	12	419	12.1	1.2	87.5	18	100	.9	2	109	(0)	.07	.06	1.0	(0)
	Bread flour, standard granulation:																	
2441	Enriched:																	
a	Unsifted, dipped with cup	1 cup	137	12	500	16.2	1.5	102.3	22	130	[157] 4.0	3	130	(0)	[157] .60	[157] .36	[157] 4.8	(0)
b	Sifted, spooned into cup	1 cup	115	12	420	13.6	1.3	85.9	18	109	[157] 3.3	2	109	(0)	[157] .51	[157] .30	[157] 4.0	(0)
2442	Unenriched:																	
a	Unsifted, dipped with cup	1 cup	137	12	500	16.2	1.5	102.3	22	130	1.2	3	130	(0)	.11	.08	1.4	(0)
b	Sifted, spooned into cup	1 cup	115	12	420	13.6	1.3	85.9	18	109	1.0	2	109	(0)	.09	.07	1.2	(0)
2443	Cake or pastry flour:																	
a	Unsifted, dipped with cup	1 cup	118	12	430	8.9	.9	93.7	20	86	.6	2	112	(0)	.04	.04	.8	(0)
b	Unsifted, spooned into cup	1 cup	109	12	397	8.2	.9	86.5	19	80	.5	2	104	(0)	.03	.03	.8	(0)
c	Sifted, spooned into cup	1 cup	96	12	349	7.2	.8	76.2	16	70	.5	2	91	(0)	.03	.03	.7	(0)
2444	Gluten flour (45% gluten, 55% patent flour):																	
a	Unsifted, dipped with cup	1 cup	140	8.5	529	58.0	2.7	66.1	56	196	—	3	84	(0)	—	—	—	(0)
b	Unsifted or sifted, spooned into cup	1 cup	135	8.5	510	55.9	2.6	63.7	54	189	—	3	81	(0)	—	—	—	(0)
2445	Self-rising flour, enriched (anhydrous monocalcium phosphate used as a baking acid):[393]																	
a	Unsifted, spooned into cup	1 cup	125	11.5	440	11.6	1.3	92.8	331	583	[157] 3.6	1,349	[394] —	(0)	[157] .55	[157] .33	[157] 4.4	(0)
b	Sifted, spooned into cup	1 cup	115	11.5	405	10.7	1.2	85.3	305	536	[157] 3.3	1,241	[394] —	(0)	[157] .51	[157] .30	[157] 4.0	(0)
	Wheat, parboiled. See Bulgur (items 497–501).																	
	Wheat products used mainly as hot breakfast cereals:[5, 156]																	
	Wheat, rolled:[396]																	
2448	Dry form	1 cup	85	10.1	289	8.4	1.7	64.8	31	291	2.7	2	323	(0)	.31	.10	3.5	(0)
2449	Cooked	1 cup	240	79.7	180	5.3	1.0	40.6	19	182	1.7	[396] 708	202	(0)	.17	.07	2.2	(0)
	Wheat, whole-meal:																	
2450	Dry form	1 cup	125	10.4	423	16.9	2.5	90.4	56	498	4.6	3	463	(0)	.64	.16	5.9	(0)
2451	Cooked	1 cup	245	87.7	110	4.4	.7	23.0	17	127	1.2	[361] 519	118	(0)	.15	.05	1.5	(0)
	Wheat and malted barley cereal, toasted:																	
	Quick cooking (about 3 min. cooking time):																	
2452	Dry form	1 cup	135	6.4	517	16.2	2.2	106.0	68	473	3.5	1	—	(0)	.46	.08	—	(0)
2453	Cooked	1 cup	245	84.1	159	4.9	.7	32.3	22	145	1.0	[361] 176	Trace	(0)	.12	.02	—	(0)
	Instant cooking (about 1 min. cooking time):																	
2454	Dry form	1 cup	115	6.6	439	16.1	1.8	87.6	46	449	4.7	1	—	(0)	.39	.10	—	(0)
2455	Cooked	1 cup	245	80.0	196	7.4	.7	39.4	22	201	2.2	[361] 250	Trace	(0)	.17	.05	—	(0)
	Also see Farina (items 991–998).																	
	Wheat products used mainly as ready-to-eat breakfast cereals:[5, 74]																	
	Wheat bran. See Bran (items 439–442).																	
2456	Wheat flakes, added sugar, salt, iron, vitamins	1 cup	30	3.5	106	3.1	.5	24.2	12	[397] 83	([397])	310	[397] 81	[81] 1,410	[82] .35	[82] .42	[82] 3.5	[81] 11
2457	Wheat germ, without salt and sugar, toasted	1 tbsp	6	4.2	23	1.8	.7	3.0	3	[398] 70	.5	Trace	57	10	[398] .11	[398] .05	.3	1
	Wheat, puffed:																	
2458	Without salt and sugar; added iron, thiamin, niacin.	1 cup	15	3.4	54	2.3	.2	11.8	4	48	.6	1	51	(0)	.08	.03	1.2	(0)

(A)	(B)		(C)	(D)	(E)	(F)	(G)	(H)	(I)	(J)	(K)	(L)	(M)	(N)	(O)	(P)	(Q)
2459	With sugar or sugar and honey, and salt; added iron and vitamins.	1 cup	35	2.8	132	2.1	0.7	30.9	[399] 7	53	[399] 1.2	56	[399] 61	[399] 1,650	[82] 0.41	[82] 0.49	[82] 4.1	[166] 12
	Wheat, shredded:																
2460	Without sugar, salt, or other added ingredients:																
a	Oblong biscuit (3¾ × 2¼ × 1 in. or 2½ × 2 × 1¼ in.).	1 biscuit	25	6.6	89	2.5	.5	20.0	11	97	.9	1	87	(0)	.06	.03	1.1	(0)
b	Round biscuit (3-in. diam. × 1 in.)	1 biscuit	20	6.6	71	2.0	.4	16.0	9	78	.7	1	70	(0)	.04	.02	.9	(0)
c	Spoon-size biscuit (1 × ⅝ × ⅜ in.)	1 cup or 50 biscuits.	50	6.6	177	5.0	1.0	40.0	22	194	1.8	2	174	(0)	.11	.06	2.2	(0)
d	Biscuits, crumbled	1 cup	35	6.6	124	3.5	.7	28.0	15	136	1.2	1	122	(0)	.08	.04	1.5	(0)
e	Biscuits, finely crushed (3 oblong or 4 round or 1½ cups spoon size).	1 cup	75	6.6	266	7.4	1.5	59.9	32	291	2.6	2	261	(0)	.17	.08	3.3	(0)
2461	With malt, salt, sugar; iron and vitamins added:																
a	Bite-size squares	1 cup	55	3.2	201	5.0	1.6	44.9	21	[400] 176	[401] 19.4	383	[400] 99	[401] 2,590	[401] .64	[401] .78	[401] 6.4	[401] 19
b	Shreds	1 cup	40	3.2	146	3.6	1.2	32.7	16	[400] 128	[401] 14.1	279	[400] 72	[401] 1,880	[401] .46	[401] .56	[401] 4.6	[401] 14
	Wheat and malted barley:																
2462	Flakes, added sugar, salt, iron, vitamins	1 cup	40	3.1	157	3.5	.5	33.7	20	100	[400] 1.4	[400] 226	—	[81] 1,880	[82] .46	[82] .56	[82] 4.6	[81] 14
2463	Granules, without sugar; added salt, iron, vitamins.	1 cup	110	2.9	430	11.0	.7	92.8	58	[402] 233	[402] 3.9	[402] 814	253	[81] 5,170	[82] 1.28	[82] 1.55	[82] 12.8	[81] 39
	Whey:																
2464	Fluid	1 cup	246	93.1	64	2.2	.7	12.5	125	130	.2	—	—	20	.07	.34	.2	—
2465	Dried	1 lb	454	4.5	1,583	58.5	5.0	333.4	2,930	2,672	6.4	—	—	230	2.27	11.39	3.6	—
	Whiskey. See Beverages (items 395–399).																
	Whitefish, lake:																
2466	Raw:																
a	Whole (refuse: head, tail, fins, entrails, bones, skin, 53%).[1]	1 lb	454	71.7	330	40.3	17.5	0	—	576	.9	111	637	4,820	.30	.26	6.4	—
b	Drawn (refuse: head, tail, fins, bones, skin, 49%).[1]	1 lb	454	71.7	359	43.7	19.0	0	—	625	.9	120	692	5,230	.32	.28	6.9	—
c	Flesh only	1 lb	454	71.7	703	85.7	37.2	0	—	1,225	1.8	236	1,356	10,250	.64	.54	13.6	—
2467	Cooked (baked), stuffed[403]	1 oz	28	63.2	61	4.3	4.0	1.6	—	70	.1	[43] 55	82	570	.03	.03	.7	Trace
2468	Smoked	1 lb	454	68.2	703	94.8	33.1	0	100	1,243	—	—	—	—	—	—	—	—
	White sauce:[186]																
2469	Thin	1 cup	250	78.7	303	9.8	21.8	18.0	305	243	.3	878	365	800	.10	.43	.5	2
2470	Medium	1 cup	250	73.3	405	9.8	31.3	22.0	288	233	.5	948	348	1,150	.10	.43	.5	2
2471	Thick	1 cup	250	67.9	495	10.0	39.0	27.5	268	225	.8	998	333	1,430	.13	.40	.8	2
2472	Wildrice, raw	1 cup	160	8.5	565	22.6	1.1	120.5	30	542	6.7	11	352	(0)	.72	1.01	9.9	(0)
	Wine. See Beverages (items 400, 401).																
2474	Yam, tuber, raw (refuse: skin, 14%)[1]	1 lb	454	73.5	394	8.2	.8	90.5	78	209	2.3	—	2,341	Trace	.39	.16	2.0	35
2475	Yambean, tuber, raw (refuse: parings, 10%)[1]	1 lb	454	85.1	225	5.7	.8	52.2	61	73	2.4	—	—	Trace	.16	.12	1.2	82
	Yeast:[136]																
	Bakers:																
2476	Compressed:[404]																
a	Package, net wt., 0.6 oz. (piece, 1¼-in. square, ¾ in. high).	1 pkg	18	71.0	15	(2.2)	.1	2.0	2	71	.9	3	110	Trace	.13	.30	2.0	Trace
b	Ounce	1 oz	28	71.0	24	(3.4)	.1	3.1	4	112	1.4	5	173	Trace	.20	.47	3.2	Trace

[1] Measure and weight apply to food as it is described with inedible part or parts (refuse) included.

[5] Most of phosphorus in nuts, legumes, and outer layers of cereal grains is present as phytic acid. See also Appendix D, section on Minerals and Oxalic Acid

[43] Value for product without added salt.

[74] Weight per cup based on method of pouring product from container into measuring cup to overflow and leveling with straight edge. Revised values for minerals and vitamins apply to products on the market in 1972.

[81] Basis of revised value for 100 g. of product with added vitamin A is 4,700 I.U.; with added ascorbic acid, 35 mg.

[82] Basis of revised value for 100 g. of product with added thiamin is 1.16 mg.; with added riboflavin, 1.41 mg.; with added niacin, 11.6 mg.

[136] Contains nonprotein nitrogen. This is omitted from protein value but included in total carbohydrate figure and caloric value. See also Appendix D, section on Protein and Nonprotein Nitrogen and section on Carbohydrate

[156] For dry form of cereal, weight per cup is based on method of pouring cereal from container into measuring cup with as little fall as possible, then leveling with straight edge. See also Appendix B, section on Nonliquid Foods, p. 267, and section on Breakfast-Type Cereals, p. 269. For cooked cereal, weight per cup represents hot cereal immediately after cooking and is based on specific proportion of cereal and water in cooked product. See ARS 62–13 (7), section on Alimentary Pastes and Other Cereal Products, pp. 6–7, and table 3, p. 9.

[157] Based on product with minimum level of enrichment. See also Appendix C, section on Enriched Foods and Standards of Enrichment

[166] Based on revised value of 35 mg. per 100 g. of product.

[186] For information on ingredients used, see ARS 62–13 (7), table 26, p. 32.

[261] Applies to product cooked with salt added as specified by manufacturers. If cooked without added salt, value is negligible.

[392] Calculation of nutritive values based on assumption that instant-blending flour and flour of standard granulation have same nutritive value differing only in physical structure.

[393] Acid ingredient most commonly used in self-rising flour. When sodium acid pyrophosphate in combination with either anhydrous monocalcium phosphate or calcium carbonate is used, values for item 2445a are calcium 150 mg., phosphorus 675 mg., sodium 1,700 mg.; for item 2445b, calcium 138 mg., phosphorus 621 mg., sodium 1,564 mg.

[394] 90% of potassium value contributed by flour. Small quantities of additional potassium may be provided by other ingredients.

[395] Weight per cup and nutritive values apply to product requiring 5 min. or longer cooking time. For values of instant-cooking type (1-min. cooking), see Appendix A, table 3, p. 264, and Appendix B, section on Breakfast-Type Cereals, p. 269. Nutritive values for 100 g. of the dry form in Agr. Handb. No. 8, rev. 1963, still apply, but those for the cooked form differ as indicated.

[396] Based on revised value of 295 mg. per 100 g. for product cooked with salt added as specified by manufacturers. If cooked without added salt, value is negligible.

[397] Phosphorus and potassium values based on revised value per 100 g. of product. Value used for phosphorus is 276 mg.; for potassium 270 mg. With added iron, values range from 3.5 to 11.7 mg. per 100 g.; 1.1–3.5 mg. per cup.

[398] Based on revised value per 100 g. of product. Value used for phosphorus is 1,164 mg., for thiamin 1.76 mg., for riboflavin 0.78 mg.

[399] Based on revised value per 100 g. of product. Value used for calcium is 19 mg.; for iron, 3.5 mg. for product with added iron. Without added iron, value should be based on 1.1 mg. Value used for potassium is 175 mg.; for vitamin A, 4,700 I.U. for product with added vitamin A. Without added vitamin A, value is (0).

[400] Based on revised value per 100 g. of product. Values used for item 2461 are phosphorus 320 mg. and potassium 180 mg. Values used for item 2462 are iron 3.5 mg. and sodium 564 mg.

[401] Basis of revised value for 100 g. of product with added iron is 35.3 mg.; with added vitamin A, 4,700 I.U.; with added thiamin, 1.16 mg.; with added riboflavin, 1.41 mg.; with added niacin, 11.6 mg.; with added ascorbic acid, 35 mg. For products without these nutrients added, values should be based on these amounts per 100 g. of cereal: Iron 3.5 mg., vitamin A (0), thiamin 0.14 mg., riboflavin 0.21 mg., niacin 5.3 mg., ascorbic acid (0).

[402] Based on revised value per 100 g. of product. Value used for phosphorus is 212 mg., for iron 3.5 mg., for sodium 740 mg.

[403] Prepared with bacon, butter or margarine, onion, celery, and breadcrumbs.

[404] Product is sometimes fortified. For fortified compressed yeast, thiamin value for 1 piece (item 2476a) ranges from 0.5 to 4.5 mg.; for 1 oz. (item 2476b), from 0.7–7.1 mg.; niacin value for 1 piece (item 2476a) ranges from 20.0 to 31.7 mg.; for 1 oz. (item 2476b), from 31.5 to 49.9 mg.

TABLE 1.—*Nutritive values for household measures and market units of foods*—Continued

[Item numbers correspond to those in table 1 of Handbook No. 8. revised 1963. Values in parentheses denote imputed values usually from another form of the food or from a similar food. Zeros in parentheses indicate that amount of a constituent, if present, is probably too small to be measured. Dashes (—) denote lack of reliable data for a constituent believed to be present in a measurable amount. Calculated values, as those based on a recipe, are not in parentheses]

Item No. (A)		Food, approximate measures, units, and weight (edible part unless footnotes indicate otherwise) (B)			Water (C)	Food energy (D)	Protein (E)	Fat (F)	Carbohydrate (G)	Calcium (H)	Phosphorus (I)	Iron (J)	Sodium (K)	Potassium (L)	Vitamin A value (M)	Thiamin (N)	Riboflavin (O)	Niacin (P)	Ascorbic acid (Q)
				Grams	Percent	Calories	Grams	Grams	Grams	Milligrams	Milligrams	Milligrams	Milligrams	Milligrams	International units	Milligrams	Milligrams	Milligrams	Milligrams
		Yeast [136]—Continued																	
		Bakers—Continued																	
2477		**Dry (active):**																	
	a	**Package, net wt., ¼ oz. (scant tablespoon)**	1 pkg	7	5.0	20	(2.6)	0.1	2.7	(3)	(90)	(1.1)	(4)	(140)	Trace	0.16	0.38	2.6	Trace
	b	**Ounce**	1 oz	28	5.0	80	(10.5)	.5	11.0	(12)	(366)	(4.6)	(15)	(566)	Trace	.66	1.53	10.4	Trace
2478		**Brewer's, debittered:**																	
	a	Tablespoon	1 tbsp	8	5.0	23	(3.1)	.1	3.1	[405] 17	140	1.4	10	152	Trace	1.25	.34	3.0	Trace
	b	Ounce	1 oz	28	5.0	80	(11.0)	.3	10.9	[405] 60	497	4.9	34	537	Trace	4.43	1.21	10.7	Trace
2479		Torula	1 oz	28	6.0	79	(10.9)	.3	10.5	[406] 120	486	5.5	4	580	Trace	3.97	1.43	12.6	Trace
		Yogurt:																	
2481		Made from partially skimmed milk:																	
	a	Container, net wt., 8 oz	1 container	226	89.0	113	7.7	3.8	11.8	271	212	.1	115	323	150	.09	.41	.2	2
	b	Cup	1 cup	245	89.0	123	8.3	4.2	12.7	294	230	.1	125	350	170	.10	.44	.2	2
2482		Made from whole milk:																	
	a	Container, net wt., 8 oz	1 container	226	88.0	140	6.8	7.7	11.1	251	197	.1	106	298	320	.07	.36	.2	2
	b	Cup	1 cup	245	88.0	152	7.4	8.3	12.0	272	213	.1	115	323	340	.07	.39	.2	2
		Youngberries. See Blackberries (item 417).																	
2483		**Zwieback:**																	
	a	Package, net wt., 6 oz. (approx. 24 pieces)	1 pkg	170	5.0	719	18.2	15.0	126.3	22	117	1.0	425	255	70	.09	.12	1.5	(0)
	b	Piece, approx. 3½ × 1½ × ½ in	1 piece	7	5.0	30	.7	.6	5.2	1	5	Trace	18	11	Trace	Trace	Trace	.1	(0)
	c	Pound (approx. 65 pieces (item 2483b))	1 lb	454	5.0	1,919	48.5	39.9	337.0	59	313	2.7	1,134	680	180	.23	.32	4.1	(0)

[136] Contains nonprotein nitrogen. This is omitted from protein value but included in total carbohydrate figure and caloric value. See also Appendix D, section on Protein and Nonprotein Nitrogen and section on Carbohydrate

[405] Values for 1 tbsp. (item 2478a) range from 5.6 to 60 mg.; for 1 oz. (item 2478b), from 20 to 215 mg.

[406] Values range from 17 to 284 mg. per ounce.

TABLE 2.—*Fatty acid values for household measures and market units of foods*

[Item and footnote numbers correspond to those in table 1 of this publication. Values in parentheses denote imputed values usually from another form of the food or from a similar food. Dashes (—) denote lack of reliable data for a constituent believed to be present in a measurable amount. Calculated values, as those based on a recipe, are not in parentheses]

Item No.	Food, approximate measures, units, and weight (edible part unless footnotes indicate otherwise)			Principal sources of fat	Amount in edible part of foods			
					Total fat	Total saturated fatty acids	Unsaturated fatty acids: Oleic $C_{18}(-2H)$	Unsaturated fatty acids: Linoleic $C_{18}(-4H)$
(A)	(B)			(C)	(D)	(E)	(F)	(G)
			Grams		*Grams*	*Grams*	*Grams*	*Grams*
	Albacore.[1] See Tuna (items 2323–2324).							
	Almonds:							
8	Dried:							
	In shell (refuse: shells, 60%):[2]							
a	Cup	1 cup	78		16.9	1.4	11.3	3.4
b	Pound	1 lb	454		98.3	7.9	65.9	19.7
c	10 nuts	10 nuts	25		5.4	.4	3.6	1.1
	Shelled:							
d	Whole	1 cup	142		77.0	6.2	51.6	15.4
	Chopped:							
e	Cup	1 cup	130		70.5	5.6	47.2	14.1
f	Tablespoon	1 tbsp	8		4.3	.3	2.9	.9
	Slivered:							
g	Cup, not packed	1 cup	115		62.3	5.0	41.8	12.5
h	Cup, packed	1 cup	135		73.2	5.9	49.0	14.6
i	Sliced (approx. 1/16 in. thick)	1 cup	95		51.5	4.1	34.5	10.3
j	Pound	1 lb	454		245.9	19.7	164.7	49.2
k	Ounce	1 oz	28		15.4	1.2	10.3	3.1
9	Roasted (in oil), salted:							
a	Cup (approx. 120 nuts)	1 cup	157		90.6	7.3	60.7	18.1
b	Pound	1 lb	454		261.7	21.0	175.4	52.3
c	Ounce (approx. 22 nuts)	1 oz	28		16.4	1.3	11.0	3.3
10	**Almond meal,** partially defatted	1 oz	28		5.2	.4	3.5	1.0
25	**Apple brown betty**[3]	1 cup	215	Butter, breadcrumbs	7.5	3.2	2.6	.7
	Avocados, raw:							
64	All commercial varieties:							
a	Whole fruit (refuse: seed and skin, 25%);[4] wt., 10⅔ oz.	1 avocado	302		37.1	7.4	16.7	4.8
b	Halved fruit served with skin (refuse: skin, 10%).[2]	½ avocado	125		18.5	3.7	8.3	2.4
c	Cube (½ in.)	1 cup	150		24.6	4.9	11.1	3.2
d	Puree (mashed or sieved)	1 cup	230		37.7	7.5	17.0	4.9
65	California mainly Fuerte (marketed in midwinter and late winter):							
a	Whole fruit (refuse: seed and skin, 24%);[2] wt., 10 oz.; diam., 3⅛ in.	1 avocado	284		36.7	7.3	16.5	4.8
b	Halved fruit, 3⅛-in. diam., served with skin (refuse: skin, 10%).[2]	½ avocado	120		18.4	3.7	8.3	2.4
c	Cube (½ in.)	1 cup	150		25.5	5.1	11.5	3.3
d	Puree (mashed or sieved)	1 cup	230		39.1	7.8	17.6	5.1

[1] Almost all catch is canned as tuna.
[2] Measure and weight apply to food as it is described with inedible part or parts (refuse) included.
[3] Cup measure made on product after it had cooled. See also Appendix B, section on Home-Prepared Foods
[4] Percent refuse and weight of fruit are weighted according to production, estimated as 90% from California, 10% from Florida.

TABLE 2.—*Fatty acid values for household measures and market units of foods*—Continued

[Item and footnote numbers correspond to those in table 1 of this publication. Values in parentheses denote imputed values usually from another form of the food or from a similar food. Dashes (—) denote lack of reliable data for a constituent believed to be present in a measurable amount. Calculated values, as those based on a recipe, are not in parentheses]

Item No. (A)		Food, approximate measures, units, and weight (edible part unless footnotes indicate otherwise) (B)			Principal sources of fat (C)	Amount in edible part of foods: Total fat (D)	Total saturated fatty acids (E)	Unsaturated fatty acids: Oleic $C_{18}(-2H)$ (F)	Unsaturated fatty acids: Linoleic $C_{18}(-4H)$ (G)
				Grams		*Grams*	*Grams*	*Grams*	*Grams*
		Avocados, raw—Continued							
66		Florida (marketed in late summer and fall):							
	a	Whole fruit (refuse: seed and skin, 33%);[2] wt., 16 oz.; diam., 3⅝ in.	1 avocado	454		33.4	6.7	15.0	4.8
	b	Halved fruit, 3⅝-in. diam., served with skin (refuse: skin, 15%).[2]	½ avocado	180		16.8	3.4	7.6	2.2
	c	Cube (½ in.)	1 cup	150		16.5	3.3	7.4	2.1
	d	Puree (mashed or sieved)	1 cup	230		25.3	5.1	11.4	3.3
		Bacon, cured:							
125		Raw:							
	a	Slab (refuse: rind, 6%)[2]	1 lb	454		295.5	94.6	141.8	26.6
	b	Sliced	1 lb	454		314.3	100.6	150.9	28.3
126		Cooked (broiled or fried), drained:							
	a	Slab, yield from 1 lb., raw (item 125a)	4.8 oz	136		70.7	22.6	33.9	6.4
		Sliced:							
	b	Yield from 1 lb., raw (item 125b)	5.1 oz	145		75.4	24.1	36.2	6.8
	c	Slice, thick (approx. 12 slices per pound, raw).	2 slices	24		12.5	4.0	6.0	1.1
	d	Slice, medium (approx. 20 slices per pound, raw).	2 slices	15		7.8	2.5	3.7	.7
	e	Slice, thin (approx. 28 slices per pound, raw).	2 slices	10		5.2	1.7	2.5	.5
		Canned:							
127		Can, net wt., 16 oz. (1 lb.); 17–18 slices	1 can or 1 lb	454		324.3	103.8	155.7	29.2
		Bacon, Canadian style:							
128		Unheated:							
	a	Package, net wt., 6 oz. (6 slices, 3⅜-in. diam., 3/16 in. thick).	1 pkg	170		24.5	8.8	10.3	2.2
	b	Pound	1 lb	454		65.3	23.5	27.4	5.9
129		Cooked (broiled or fried), drained:							
	a	Yield from 6 oz., raw (item 128a)	6 slices	126		22.1	7.9	9.3	2.0
	b	Yield from 1 lb., raw (item 128b)	¾ lb. (approx.)	336		58.8	21.2	24.7	5.3
	c	Slice (dimensions of uncooked slice, 3⅜-in. diam., 3/16 in. thick).	1 slice	21		3.7	1.3	1.5	.3
	d	Pound	1 lb	454		79.4	28.6	33.3	7.2
144		**Barbecue sauce**	1 cup	250	Corn oil	17.3	1.7	4.8	9.2
		Beans, common, mature seeds, white, dry:							
		Canned, solids and liquid:							
156		With pork and tomato sauce:							
		Can and approx. contents:							
	a	Size, 307 × 409[5] (No. 2); net wt., 20 oz. (1 lb. 4 oz.).	1 can	567	Pork	14.7	5.8	6.2	1.3
	b	Size, 404 × 700[5] (No. 3 Cylinder); net wt., 51 oz. (3 lb. 3 oz.).	1 can	1,446	do	37.6	18.6	15.8	3.3
	c	Size, 603 × 700[5] (No. 10); net wt., 110 oz. (6 lb. 14 oz.).	1 can	3,118	do	81.1	29.3	34.0	7.2

(A)	(B)			(C)	(D)	(E)	(F)	(G)
d	Cup	1 cup	255	Pork	6.6	2.4	2.8	0.6
e	Pound	1 lb	454	do	11.8	4.3	4.9	1.0
157	With pork and sweet sauce:							
	Can and approx. contents:							
a	Size, 307 × 409 [5] (No. 2); net wt., 20 oz. (1 lb. 4 oz.).	1 can	567	do	26.6	9.6	11.2	2.4
b	Size, 404 × 700 [5] (No. 3 Cylinder); net wt., 51 oz. (3 lb. 3 oz.).	1 can	1,446	do	68.0	24.4	28.5	6.1
c	Size, 603 × 700 [5] (No. 10); net wt., 110 oz. (6 lb. 14 oz.).	1 can	3,118	do	146.5	52.7	61.4	13.1
d	Cup	1 cup	255	do	12.0	4.3	5.0	1.1
e	Pound	1 lb	454	do	21.3	7.7	8.9	1.9
207	**Beechnuts:**							
a	In shell (refuse: shells, 39%) [2]	1 lb	454		138.4	11.1	74.7	42.9
b	Shelled	1 lb	454		226.8	18.1	122.5	70.3
	Beef, trimmed to retail basis:							
	Boneless chuck and chuck cuts:							
	Boneless beef for stew:							
	Lean with fat:							
218	Raw (82% lean, 18% fat)	1 lb	454		88.9	42.7	39.1	1.8
219	Cooked (braised or stewed), drained (81% lean, 19% fat):							
a	Yield from 1 lb., raw beef (item 218).	10.7 oz	304		72.7	34.9	32.0	1.5
b	Cup, chopped or diced pieces (not packed).	1 cup	140		33.5	16.1	14.7	.7
c	Pound	1 lb	454		108.4	52.0	47.7	2.2
	Lean, trimmed of separable fat:							
220	Raw	1 lb	454		33.6	16.1	14.8	.7
221	Cooked (braised or stewed), drained:							
a	Yield from 1 lb., raw beef (item 220).	10.7 oz	304		28.9	13.9	12.7	.6
b	Cup, chopped or diced pieces (not packed).	1 cup	140		13.3	6.4	5.9	.3
c	Pound	1 lb	454		43.1	20.7	19.0	.9
	Chuck rib roasts or chuck rib steaks (blade or flat-bone cuts):							
	Choice grade:							
223	Raw, lean with fat:							
a	With bone (59% lean, 25% fat) (refuse: bone, 16%). [2]	1 lb	454		120.4	57.8	53.0	2.4
b	Without bone (70% lean, 30% fat)	1 lb	454		142.4	68.4	62.7	2.8
	Cooked (braised), drained:							
224	Lean with fat (69% lean, 31% fat):							
a	Yield from 1 lb., raw beef with bone (item 223a).	9 oz	255		93.6	44.9	41.2	1.9
b	Yield from 1 lb., raw beef without bone (item 223b).	10.7 oz	304		111.6	53.6	49.1	2.2
	Cup (not packed):							
c	Chopped or diced	1 cup	140		51.4	24.7	22.6	1.0
d	Ground	1 cup	110		40.4	19.4	17.8	.8
e	Pound	1 lb	454		166.5	79.9	73.3	3.3
f	Piece, approx. 4⅛ in. long, 2¼ in. wide, ½ in. thick; wt., 3 oz. (steaks); or 2 pieces, 4⅛ in. long, 2¼ in. wide,	1 or 2 pieces or 3 oz.	85		31.2	15.0	13.7	.6

[2] Measure and weight apply to food as it is described with inedible part or parts (refuse) included.

[5] Dimensions of can: 1st dimension represents diameter; 2d dimension, height of can. 1st or left-hand digit in each dimension gives number of whole inches; next 2 digits give additional fraction of dimension expressed as 16th of an inch.

TABLE 2.—*Fatty acid values for household measures and market units of foods*—Continued

[Item and footnote numbers correspond to those in table 1 of this publication. Values in parentheses denote imputed values usually from another form of the food or from a similar food. Dashes (—) denote lack of reliable data for a constituent believed to be present in a measurable amount. Calculated values, as those based on a recipe, are not in parentheses]

Item No. (A)	Food, approximate measures, units, and weight (edible part unless footnotes indicate otherwise) (B)			Principal sources of fat (C)	Total fat (D)	Total saturated fatty acids (E)	Unsaturated fatty acids: Oleic $C_{18}(-2H)$ (F)	Unsaturated fatty acids: Linoleic $C_{18}(-4H)$ (G)
			Grams		*Grams*	*Grams*	*Grams*	*Grams*
	Beef, trimmed to retail basis—Continued							
	Boneless chuck and chuck cuts—Continued							
	Chuck rib roasts or chuck rib steaks (blade or flat-bone cuts)—Continued							
	Choice grade—Continued							
	Cooked (braised), drained—Continued							
	Lean with fat (69% lean, 31% fat)—Continued							
	¼ in. thick; wt., 1½ oz. each (roasts).							
226	Lean, trimmed of separable fat:							
a	Yield from 1 lb., raw beef with bone (item 223a).	6.2 oz	176		24.5	11.8	10.8	0.5
b	Yield from 1 lb., raw beef without bone (item 223b).	7.4 oz	210		29.2	14.0	12.8	.6
	Cup (not packed):							
c	Chopped or diced	1 cup	140		19.5	9.4	8.6	.4
d	Ground	1 cup	110		15.3	7.3	6.7	.3
e	Pound	1 lb	454		63.1	30.3	27.8	1.3
f	Piece, approx. 4⅛ in. long, 2¼ in. wide, ½ in. thick; wt., 3 oz. (steaks); or 2 pieces, 4⅛ in. long, 2¼ in. wide, ¼ in. thick; wt., 1½ oz. each (roasts).	1 or 2 pieces or 3 oz.	85		11.8	5.7	5.2	.2
	Good grade:							
228	**Raw, lean with fat:**							
a	With bone (62% lean, 22% fat) (refuse: bone, 16%).[2]	1 lb	454		96.3	46.2	42.4	1.9
b	Without bone (74% lean, 26% fat)	1 lb	454		114.8	55.1	50.5	2.3
	Cooked (braised), drained:							
229	Lean with fat (73% lean, 27% fat):							
a	Yield from 1 lb., raw beef with bone (item 228a).	9 oz	255		77.3	37.1	34.0	1.5
b	Yield from 1 lb., raw beef without bone (item 228b).	10.7 oz	304		92.1	44.2	40.5	1.8
	Cup (not packed):							
c	Chopped or diced	1 cup	140		42.4	20.4	18.7	.8
d	Ground	1 cup	110		33.3	16.0	14.7	.7
e	Pound	1 lb	454		137.4	66.0	60.5	2.7
f	Piece, approx. 4⅛ in. long, 2¼ in. wide, ½ in. thick; wt., 3 oz. (steaks); or 2 pieces, 4⅛ in. long, 2¼ in. wide, ¼ in. thick; wt., 1½ oz. each (roasts).	1 or 2 pieces or 3 oz.	85		25.8	12.4	11.4	.5
231	Lean, trimmed of separable fat:							

(A)		(B)		(C)	(D)	(E)	(F)	(G)
	a	Yield from 1 lb., raw beef with bone (item 228a).	6.6 oz	186	19.0	9.1	8.4	0.4
	b	Yield from 1 lb., raw beef without bone (item 228b).	7.8 oz	222	22.6	10.8	9.9	.5
		Cup (not packed):						
	c	Chopped or diced	1 cup	140	14.3	6.9	6.3	.3
	d	Ground	1 cup	110	11.2	5.4	4.9	.2
	e	Pound	1 lb	454	46.3	22.2	20.4	.9
	f	Piece, approx. 4⅛ in. long, 2¼ in. wide, ½ in. thick; wt., 3 oz. (steaks); or 2 pieces, 4⅛ in. long, 2¼ in. wide, ¼ in. thick; wt., 1½ oz. each (roasts).	1 or 2 pieces or 3 oz.	85	8.7	4.2	3.8	.2
		Chuck roasts or chuck steaks (arm and round-bone cuts):						
		Choice grade:						
233		Raw, lean with fat:						
	a	With bone (77% lean, 12% fat) (refuse: bone, 11%).[2]	1 lb	454	62.9	30.2	27.7	1.3
	b	Without bone (86% lean, 14% fat)	1 lb	454	70.3	33.7	30.9	1.4
		Cooked (braised), drained:						
234		Lean with fat (85% lean, 15% fat):						
	a	Yield from 1 lb., raw beef with bone (item 233a).	9½ oz	270	51.8	24.9	22.8	1.0
	b	Yield from 1 lb., raw beef without bone (item 233b).	10.7 oz	304	58.4	28.0	25.7	1.2
		Cup (not packed):						
	c	Chopped or diced	1 cup	140	26.9	12.9	11.8	.5
	d	Ground	1 cup	110	21.1	10.1	9.3	.4
	e	Pound	1 lb	454	87.1	41.8	38.3	1.7
	f	Piece, approx. 2½ in. long, 2½ in. wide, ¾ in. thick.	1 piece or 3 oz	85	16.3	7.8	7.2	.3
236		Lean, trimmed of separable fat:						
	a	Yield from 1 lb., raw beef with bone (item 233a).	8.1 oz	230	16.1	7.7	7.1	.3
	b	Yield from 1 lb., raw beef without bone (item 233b).	9.1 oz	258	18.1	8.7	8.0	.4
		Cup (not packed):						
	c	Chopped or diced	1 cup	140	9.8	4.7	4.3	.2
	d	Ground	1 cup	110	7.7	3.7	3.4	.2
	e	Pound	1 lb	454	31.8	15.3	14.0	.6
	f	Piece, approx. 2½ in. long, 2½ in. wide, ¾ in. thick.	1 piece or 3 oz	85	6.0	2.9	2.6	.1
		Good grade:						
238		Raw, lean wih fat:						
	a	With bone (79% lean, 10% fat) (refuse: bone, 11%).[2]	1 lb	454	46.7	22.4	20.5	.9
	b	Without bone (89% lean, 11% fat)	1 lb	454	52.6	25.2	23.1	1.1
		Cooked (braised), drained:						
239		Lean with fat (88% lean, 12% fat):						
	a	Yield from 1 lb., raw beef with bone (item 238a).	9½ oz	270	39.4	18.9	17.3	.8
	b	Yield from 1 lb., raw beef without bone (item 238b).	10.7 oz	304	44.4	21.3	19.5	.9
		Cup (not packed):						
	c	Chopped or diced	1 cup	140	20.4	9.8	9.0	.4
	d	Ground	1 cup	110	16.1	7.7	7.1	.3
	e	Pound	1 lb	454	66.2	31.8	29.1	1.3

[2] Measure and weight apply to food as it is described with inedible part or parts (refuse) included.

TABLE 2.—*Fatty acid values for household measures and market units of foods*—Continued

[Item and footnote numbers correspond to those in table 1 of this publication. Values in parentheses denote imputed values usually from another form of the food or from a similar food. Dashes (—) denote lack of reliable data for a constituent believed to be present in a measurable amount. Calculated values, as those based on a recipe, are not in parentheses]

Item No. (A)		Food, approximate measures, units, and weight (edible part unless footnotes indicate otherwise) (B)			Principal sources of fat (C)	Amount in edible part of foods: Total fat (D)	Total saturated fatty acids (E)	Unsaturated fatty acids: Oleic $C_{18}(-2H)$ (F)	Unsaturated fatty acids: Linoleic $C_{18}(-4H)$ (G)
				Grams		*Grams*	*Grams*	*Grams*	*Grams*
		Beef, trimmed to retail basis—Continued							
		Boneless chuck and chuck cuts—Continued							
		Chuck roasts or chuck steaks (arm and round-bone cuts)—Continued							
		Good grade—Continued							
		Cooked (braised) drained—Continued							
		Lean with fat (88% lean, 12% fat)—Continued							
	f	Piece, approx. 2½ in. long, 2½ in. wide, ¾ in. thick.	1 piece or 3 oz	85		12.4	6.0	5.5	0.2
241		Lean, trimmed of separable fat:							
	a	Yield from 1 lb., raw beef with bone (item 238a).	8.4 oz	238		12.4	6.0	5.5	.2
	b	Yield from 1 lb., raw beef without bone (item 238b).	9.4 oz	267		13.9	6.7	6.1	.3
		Cup (not packed):							
	c	Chopped or diced	1 cup	140		7.3	3.5	3.2	.1
	d	Ground	1 cup	110		5.7	2.7	2.5	.1
	e	Pound	1 lb	454		23.6	11.3	10.4	.5
	f	Piece, approx. 2½ in. long, 2½ in. wide, ¾ in. thick.	1 piece or 3 oz	85		4.4	2.1	1.9	.1
		Flank steak, whole or cut pieces such as flank steak fillets, London broil; choice grade:							
243		Raw (100% lean)	1 lb	454		25.9	12.4	11.4	.5
244		Cooked (braised), drained (100% lean):							
	a	Yield from 1 lb., raw beef (item 243)	10.7 oz	304		22.2	10.7	9.8	.4
	b	Pound	1 lb	454		33.1	15.9	14.6	.7
	c	Piece, approx. 2½ in. long, 2½ in. wide, ¾ in. thick.	1 piece or 3 oz	85		6.2	3.0	2.7	.1
		Loin or short loin:							
		Porterhouse steak, choice grade:							
257		Raw, lean with fat and bone (57% lean, 33% fat) (refuse: bone, 9%).[2]	1 lb	454		148.8	71.4	65.5	3.0
		Cooked (broiled):							
258		Lean with fat (57% lean, 43% fat):							
	a	Yield from 1 lb., raw beef with bone (item 257).	10.6 oz	301		127.0	61.0	55.9	2.5
	b	Pound	1 lb	454		191.4	91.9	84.2	3.8
260		Lean, trimmed of separable fat:							
	a	Yield from 1 lb., raw beef with bone (item 257).	6.1 oz	172		18.1	8.7	8.0	.4
	b	Pound	1 lb	454		47.6	22.8	20.9	1.0
		T-bone steak, choice grade:							
267		Raw, lean with fat and bone (55% lean, 34% fat) (refuse: bone, 11%).[2]	1 lb	454		149.1	71.6	65.6	3.0
		Cooked (broiled):							
268		Lean with fat (56% lean, 44% fat):							

(A)		(B)		(C)	(D)	(E)	(F)	(G)
	a	Yield from 1 lb., raw beef with bone (item 267).	10.4 oz	295	127.4	61.2	56.1	2.5
	b	Pound	1 lb	454	196.0	94.1	86.2	3.9
270		Lean, trimmed of separable fat:						
	a	Yield from 1 lb., raw beef with bone (item 267).	5.8 oz	165	17.0	8.2	7.5	.3
	b	Pound	1 lb	454	46.7	22.4	20.5	.9
		Club steak, choice grade:						
277		Raw, lean with fat:						
	a	With bone (54% lean, 30% fat) (refuse: bone, 16%).[2]	1 lb	454	132.1	63.4	58.1	2.6
	b	Without bone (64% lean, 36% fat)	1 lb	454	157.9	75.8	69.5	3.2
		Cooked (broiled):						
278		Lean with fat (58% lean, 42% fat):						
	a	Yield from 1 lb., raw beef with bone (item 277a).	9.8 oz	278	112.9	54.2	49.7	2.3
	b	Yield from 1 lb., raw beef without bone (item 277b).	11.7 oz	331	134.4	64.5	59.1	2.7
	c	Pound	1 lb	454	184.2	88.4	81.0	3.7
280		Lean, trimmed of separable fat:						
	a	Yield from 1 lb., raw beef with bone (item 277a).	5.7 oz	161	20.9	10.0	9.2	.4
	b	Yield from 1 lb., raw beef without bone (item 277b).	6.8 oz	192	25.0	12.0	11.0	.5
	c	Pound	1 lb	454	59.0	28.3	26.0	1.2
		Loin end or sirloin:						
		Wedge- and round-bone sirloin steak, choice grade:						
287		Raw, lean with fat:						
	a	With bone (68% lean, 25% fat) (refuse: bone, 7%).[2]	1 lb	454	112.3	53.9	49.4	2.2
	b	Without bone (73% lean, 27% fat)	1 lb	454	121.1	58.1	53.3	2.4
		Cooked (broiled):						
288		Lean with fat (66% lean, 34% fat):						
	a	Yield from 1 lb., raw beef with bone (item 287a).	10.9 oz	308	98.6	47.3	43.4	2.0
	b	Yield from 1 lb., raw beef without bone (item 287b).	11.7 oz	331	105.9	50.8	46.6	2.1
	c	Pound	1 lb	454	145.2	70.0	63.9	2.9
	d	Piece, approx. 2½ in. long, 2½ in. wide, ¾ in. thick.	1 piece or 3 oz	85	27.2	13.1	12.0	.5
290		Lean, trimmed of separable fat:						
	a	Yield from 1 lb., raw beef with bone (item 287a).	7.2 oz	203	15.6	7.5	6.9	.3
	b	Yield from 1 lb., raw beef without bone (item 287b).	7.7 oz	218	16.8	8.1	7.4	.3
	c	Pound	1 lb	454	34.9	16.8	15.4	.7
	d	Piece, approx. 2½ in. long, 2½ in. wide, ¾ in. thick.	1 piece or 3 oz	85	6.5	3.1	2.9	.1
		Double-bone (flat-bone) sirloin steak, choice grade:						
297		Raw, lean with fat:						
	a	With bone (59% lean, 23% fat) (refuse: bone, 18%).[2]	1 lb	454	108.4	52.0	47.7	2.2
	b	Without bone (72% lean, 28% fat)	1 lb	454	132.0	63.4	58.1	2.6
		Cooked (broiled):						
298		Lean with fat (66% lean, 34% fat):						

[2] Measure and weight apply to food as it is described with inedible part or parts (refuse) included.

TABLE 2.—*Fatty acid values for household measures and market units of foods*—Continued

[Item and footnote numbers correspond to those in table 1 of this publication. Values in parentheses denote imputed values usually from another form of the food or from a similar food. Dashes (—) denote lack of reliable data for a constituent believed to be present in a measurable amount. Calculated values, as those based on a recipe, are not in parentheses]

Item No.		Food, approximate measures, units, and weight (edible part unless footnotes indicate otherwise)			Principal sources of fat	Amount in edible part of foods: Total fat	Total saturated fatty acids	Unsaturated fatty acids: Oleic $C_{18}(-2H)$	Linoleic $C_{18}(-4H)$
(A)		(B)			(C)	(D)	(E)	(F)	(G)
				Grams		Grams	Grams	Grams	Grams
		Beef, trimmed to retail basis—Continued							
		Loin end or sirloin—Continued							
		Double-bone (flat-bone) sirloin steak, choice grade—Continued							
		Cooked (broiled)—Continued							
		Lean with fat (66% lean, 34% fat)—Continued							
	a	Yield from 1 lb., raw beef with bone (item 297a).	9.6 oz	272		94.4	45.3	41.5	1.9
	b	Yield from 1 lb., raw beef without bone (item 297b).	11.7 oz	331		114.9	55.2	50.6	2.3
	c	Pound	1 lb	454		157.4	75.6	69.3	3.1
	d	Piece, approx. 2½ in. long, 2½ in. wide, ¾ in. thick.	1 piece or 3 oz	85		29.5	14.2	13.0	.6
300		Lean, trimmed of separable fat:							
	a	Yield from 1 lb., raw beef with bone (item 297a).	6.3 oz	179		17.0	8.2	7.5	.3
	b	Yield from 1 lb., raw beef without bone (item 297b).	7.7 oz	218		20.7	9.9	9.1	.4
	c	Pound	1 lb	454		43.1	20.7	19.0	.9
	d	Piece, approx. 2½ in. long, 2½ in. wide, ¾ in. thick.	1 piece or 3 oz	85		8.1	3.9	3.6	.2
		Hipbone (pinbone) sirloin steak, choice grade:							
307		Raw, lean with fat:							
	a	With bone (51% lean, 33% fat) (refuse: bone, 15%).[2]	1 lb	454		149.3	71.7	65.7	3.0
	b	Without bone (61% lean, 39% fat)	1 lb	454		176.0	84.5	77.4	3.5
		Cooked (broiled):							
308		Lean with fat (55% lean, 45% fat):							
	a	Yield from 1 lb., raw beef with bone (item 307a).	9.9 oz	281		126.2	60.6	55.5	2.5
	b	Yield from 1 lb., raw beef without bone (item 307b).	11.7 oz	331		148.6	71.3	65.4	3.0
	c	Pound	1 lb	454		203.7	97.8	89.6	4.1
	d	Piece, approx. 2½ in. long, 2½ in. wide, ¾ in. thick.	1 piece or 3 oz	85		38.2	18.3	16.8	.8
310		Lean, trimmed of separable fat:							
	a	Yield from 1 lb., raw beef with bone (item 307a).	5½ oz	155		19.4	9.3	8.5	.4
	b	Yield from 1 lb., raw beef without bone (item 307b).	6.4 oz	182		22.8	10.9	10.0	.5
	c	Pound	1 lb	454		56.7	27.2	24.9	1.1
	d	Piece, approx. 2½ in. long, 2½ in. wide, ¾ in. thick.	1 piece or 3 oz	85		10.6	5.1	4.7	.2
		Plate beef:							
322		Raw, lean with fat:							

(A)		(B)		(C)	(D)	(E)	(F)	(G)
	a	With bone (54% lean, 33% fat) (refuse: bone, 13%).[2]	1 lb	454	126.6	60.8	55.7	2.5
	b	Without bone (62% lean, 38% fat)	1 lb	454	144.7	69.5	63.7	2.9
		Cooked (simmered), drained:						
323		Lean with fat:						
	a	Yield from 1 lb., raw beef with bone (item 322a).	9.3 oz	264	98.5	47.3	43.3	2.0
	b	Yield from 1 lb., raw beef without bone (item 322b).	10.7 oz	304	113.4	54.4	49.9	2.3
	c	Pound	1 lb	454	169.2	81.2	74.4	3.4
325		Lean, trimmed of separable fat:						
	a	Yield from 1 lb., raw beef with bone (item 322a).	5.7 oz	161	12.4	6.0	5.5	.2
	b	Yield from 1 lb., raw beef without bone (item 322b).	6½ oz	185	14.2	6.8	6.2	.3
	c	Pound	1 lb	454	34.9	16.8	15.4	.7
		Rib roast, choice grade:						
327		Raw, lean with fat:						
	a	With bone (59% lean, 33% fat) (refuse: bone, 8%).[2]	1 lb	454	156.1	74.9	68.7	3.1
	b	Without bone (64% lean, 36% fat)	1 lb	454	169.6	81.4	74.6	3.4
		Cooked (roasted):						
328		Lean with fat (64% lean, 36% fat):						
	a	Yield from 1 lb., raw beef with bone (item 327a).	10¾ oz	305	120.2	57.7	52.9	2.4
	b	Yield from 1 lb., raw beef without bone (item 327b).	11.7 oz	331	130.4	62.6	57.4	2.6
		Cup (not packed):						
	c	Chopped or diced	1 cup	140	55.2	26.5	24.3	1.1
	d	Ground	1 cup	110	43.3	20.8	19.1	.9
	e	Pound	1 lb	454	178.7	85.8	78.6	3.6
	f	Piece, approx. 4⅛ in. long, 2¼ in. wide, ¼ in. thick; wt., 1½ oz.	2 pieces or 3 oz	85	33.5	16.1	14.7	.7
330		Lean, trimmed of separable fat:						
	a	Yield from 1 lb., raw beef with bone (item 327a).	6.9 oz	195	26.1	12.5	11.5	.5
	b	Yield from 1 lb., raw beef without bone (item 327b).	7½ oz	212	28.4	13.6	12.5	.6
		Cup (not packed):						
	c	Chopped or diced	1 cup	140	18.8	9.0	8.3	.4
	d	Ground	1 cup	110	14.7	7.1	6.5	.3
	e	Pound	1 lb	454	60.8	29.2	26.8	1.2
	f	Piece, approx. 4⅛ in. long, 2¼ in. wide, ¼ in. thick; wt., 1½ oz.	2 pieces or 3 oz	85	11.4	5.5	5.0	.2
		Round steak:						
352		Raw, lean with fat:						
	a	With bone (86% lean, 11% fat) (refuse: bone, 3%).[2]	1 lb	454	53.9	25.9	23.7	1.1
	b	Without bone (89% lean, 11% fat)	1 lb	454	55.8	26.8	24.6	1.1
		Cooked (braised, broiled, or sauteed):						
353		Lean with fat (81% lean, 19% fat):						
	a	Yield from 1 lb., raw beef with bone (item 352a).	10.7 oz	304	46.8	22.5	20.6	.9
	b	Yield from 1 lb., raw beef without bone (item 352b).	11.1 oz	314	48.4	23.2	21.3	1.0
	c	Pound	1 lb	454	69.9	33.6	30.8	1.4
	d	Piece, approx. 4⅛ in. long, 2¼ in. wide, ½ in. thick.	1 piece or 3 oz	85	13.1	6.3	5.8	.3

[2] Measure and weight apply to food as it is described with inedible part or parts (refuse) included.

TABLE 2.—*Fatty acid values for household measures and market units of foods*—Continued

[Item and footnote numbers correspond to those in table 1 of this publication. Values in parentheses denote imputed values usually from another form of the food or from a similar food. Dashes (—) denote lack of reliable data for a constituent believed to be present in a measurable amount. Calculated values, as those based on a recipe, are not in parentheses]

Item No. (A)		Food, approximate measures, units, and weight (edible part unless footnotes indicate otherwise) (B)			Principal sources of fat (C)	Total fat (D)	Total saturated fatty acids (E)	Unsaturated fatty acids: Oleic $C_{18}(-2H)$ (F)	Unsaturated fatty acids: Linoleic $C_{18}(-4H)$ (G)
				Grams		*Grams*	*Grams*	*Grams*	*Grams*
		Beef, trimmed to retail basis—Continued							
		Round steak—Continued							
		Cooked (braised, broiled, or sauteed)—Continued							
355		Lean, trimmed of separable fat:							
	a	Yield from 1 lb., raw beef with bone (item 352a).	9.2 oz	260		15.9	7.6	7.0	0.3
	b	Yield from 1 lb., raw beef without bone (item 352b).	9½ oz	268		16.3	7.8	7.2	.3
	c	Pound	1 lb	454		27.7	13.3	12.2	.6
	d	Piece, approx. 4⅛ in. long, 2¼ in. wide, ½ in. thick.	1 piece or 3 oz	85		5.2	2.5	2.3	.1
		Rump roast:							
		Choice grade:							
357		Raw, lean with fat:							
	a	With bone (63% lean, 22% fat) (refuse: bone, 15%).[2]	1 lb	454		97.4	46.8	42.9	1.9
	b	Without bone (75% lean, 25% fat)	1 lb	454		114.8	55.1	50.5	2.3
		Cooked (roasted):							
358		Lean with fat (75% lean, 25% fat):							
	a	Yield from 1 lb., raw beef with bone (item 357a).	9.9 oz	281		76.7	36.8	33.7	1.5
	b	Yield from 1 lb., raw beef without bone (item 357b).	11.7 oz	331		90.4	43.4	39.8	1.8
		Cup (not packed):							
	c	Chopped or diced	1 cup	140		38.2	18.3	16.8	.8
	d	Ground	1 cup	110		30.0	14.4	13.2	.6
	e	Pound	1 lb	454		123.8	59.4	54.5	2.5
	f	Piece, approx. 4⅛ in. long, 2¼ in. wide, ¼ in. thick; wt., 1½ oz.	2 pieces or 3 oz	85		23.2	11.1	10.2	.5
360		Lean, trimmed of separable fat:							
	a	Yield from 1 lb., raw beef with bone (item 357a).	7.4 oz	211		19.6	9.4	8.6	.4
	b	Yield from 1 lb., raw beef without bone (item 357b).	8.8 oz	248		23.1	11.1	10.2	.5
		Cup (not packed):							
	c	Chopped or diced	1 cup	140		13.0	6.2	5.7	.3
	d	Ground	1 cup	110		10.2	4.9	4.5	.2
	e	Pound	1 lb	454		42.2	20.3	18.6	.8
	f	Piece, approx. 4⅛ in. long, 2¼ in. wide, ¼ in. thick; wt., 1½ oz.	2 pieces or 3 oz	85		7.9	3.8	3.5	.2
		Good grade:							
362		**Raw, lean with fat:**							
	a	With bone (64% lean, 20% fat) (refuse: bone, 16%).[2]	1 lb	454		81.9	39.3	36.0	1.6
	b	Without bone (76% lean, 24% fat)	1 lb	454		97.1	46.6	42.7	1.9
		Cooked (roasted):							
363		**Lean with fat (76% lean, 24% fat):**							

(A)		(B)		(C)	(D)	(E)	(F)	(G)
	a	Yield from 1 lb., raw beef with bone (item 362a).	9.8 oz	278	65.1	31.2	28.6	1.3
	b	Yield from 1 lb., raw beef without bone (item 362b).	11.7 oz	331	77.5	37.2	34.1	1.6
		Cup (not packed):						
	c	Chopped or diced	1 cup	140	32.8	15.7	14.4	.7
	d	Ground	1 cup	110	25.7	12.3	11.3	.5
	e	Pound	1 lb	454	106.1	50.9	46.7	2.1
	f	Piece, approx. 4⅛ in. long, 2¼ in. wide, ¼ in. thick; wt., 1½ oz.	2 pieces or 3 oz	85	19.9	9.6	8.8	.4
365		Lean, trimmed of separable fat:						
	a	Yield from 1 lb., raw beef with bone (item 362a).	7.4 oz	211	15.0	7.2	6.6	.3
	b	Yield from 1 lb., raw beef without bone (item 362b).	8.9 oz	252	17.9	8.6	7.9	.4
		Cup (not packed):						
	c	Chopped or diced	1 cup	140	9.9	4.8	4.4	.2
	d	Ground	1 cup	110	7.8	3.7	3.4	.2
	e	Pound	1 lb	454	32.2	15.5	14.2	.6
	f	Piece, approx. 4⅛ in. long, 2¼ in. wide, ¼ in. thick; wt., 1½ oz.	2 pieces or 3 oz	85	6.0	2.9	2.6	.1
		Ground beef:						
		Lean with 10% fat:						
367		Raw:						
	a	Pound (shaped into four 4-oz. patties (item 367b) or five 3.2-oz. patties (item 367c)).	1 lb	454	45.4	21.8	20.0	.9
	b	Patty, wt., 4 oz	1 patty	113	11.3	5.4	5.0	.2
	c	Patty, wt., 3.2 oz	1 patty	91	9.1	4.4	4.0	.2
	d	Cup, packed	1 cup	226	22.6	10.8	9.9	.5
368		Cooked (well done, oven-broiled, pan-broiled, or sauteed):						
	a	Yield from 1 lb., raw ground beef (item 367a) (four 3-oz. patties (item 368c) or five 2.4-oz. patties (item 368d)).	12 oz	340	38.4	18.4	16.9	.8
	b	Pound	1 lb	454	51.3	24.6	22.6	1.0
	c	Patty, approx. 3-in. diam., ⅝ in. thick; wt., 3 oz.	1 patty or 3 oz	85	9.6	4.6	4.2	.2
	d	Patty, approx. 3-in. diam., ½ in. thick; wt., 2.4 oz.	1 patty	68	7.7	3.7	3.4	.2
		Lean with 21% fat:						
369		Raw:						
	a	Pound (shaped into four 4-oz. patties (item 369b) or five 3.2-oz. patties (item 369c)).	1 lb	454	96.2	46.2	42.3	1.9
	b	Patty, wt., 4 oz	1 patty	113	24.0	11.5	10.6	.5
	c	Patty, wt., 3.2 oz	1 patty	91	19.3	9.3	8.5	.4
	d	Cup, packed	1 cup	226	47.9	23.0	21.1	1.0
370		Cooked (oven-broiled, pan-broiled, or sauteed):[6]						
	a	Yield from 1 lb., raw ground beef (item 369a) (four 2.9-oz. patties (item 370c) or five 2.3-oz. patties (item 370d)).	11½ oz	326	66.2	31.8	29.1	1.3

[2] Measures and weight apply to food as it is described with inedible part or parts (refuse) included.
[6] Measures and fatty acid values represent meat probably cooked to between rare- and medium-done stage. For values of meat cooked to well-done stage, see Appendix A, table 3. p. 264.

TABLE 2.—*Fatty acid values for household measures and market units of foods*—Continued

[Item and footnote numbers correspond to those in table 1 of this publication. Values in parentheses denote imputed values usually from another form of the food or from a similar food. Dashes (—) denote lack of reliable data for a constituent believed to be present in a measurable amount. Calculated values, as those based on a recipe, are not in parentheses]

Item No. (A)		Food, approximate measures, units, and weight (edible part unless footnotes indicate otherwise) (B)			Principal sources of fat (C)	Total fat (D)	Total saturated fatty acids (E)	Unsaturated fatty acids: Oleic $C_{18}(-2H)$ (F)	Unsaturated fatty acids: Linoleic $C_{18}(-4H)$ (G)
				Grams		*Grams*	*Grams*	*Grams*	*Grams*
		Beef, trimmed to retail basis—Continued							
		Ground beef—Continued							
		Lean with 21% fat—Continued							
		Cooked (oven-broiled, pan-broiled, or sauteed) [6]—Continued							
	b	Pound	1 lb	454		92.1	44.2	40.5	1.8
	c	Patty, approx. 3-in. diam., ⅝ in. thick; wt., 2.9 oz.	1 patty or 2.9 oz	82		16.6	8.0	7.3	.3
	d	Patty, approx. 3-in. diam., ½ in. thick; wt., 2.3 oz.	1 patty	65		13.2	6.3	5.8	.3
		Beef and vegetable stew:							
371		Cooked (home recipe, with lean beef chuck):							
	a	Cup	1 cup	245	Beef	10.5	4.9	4.5	.2
	b	Pound	1 lb	454	do	19.5	9.2	8.4	.4
		Beef, corned, boneless:							
374		Uncooked	1 lb	454		113.4	54.4	49.9	2.3
375		Cooked:							
	a	Yield from 1 lb., uncooked (item 374)	10.7 oz	304		92.4	44.4	40.7	1.9
	b	Pound	1 lb	454		137.9	66.2	60.7	2.8
377		Canned:							
		Can, approx. contents, and slice cut from piece:							
	a	Can, net wt., 12 oz.; piece, approx. 3¼ in. long, 3 in. wide, 2 in. high.	1 can	340		40.8	19.6	18.0	.8
	b	Slice, approx. 3 × 2 × ⅜ in.; ⅛ of piece (item 377a).	1 slice	40		4.8	2.3	2.1	.1
	c	Pound	1 lb	454		54.4	26.1	24.0	1.1
379		Canned corned-beef hash (with potato):							
		Container and approx. contents:							
	a	Can, net wt., 15½ oz	1 can	439	Beef	49.6	23.8	21.8	1.0
	b	Can, net wt., 24 oz. (1 lb. 8 oz.)	1 can	680	do	76.8	36.9	33.8	1.6
	c	Cup	1 cup	220	do	24.9	11.9	10.9	.5
	d	Pound	1 lb	454	do	51.3	24.6	22.5	1.0
		Beef, dried, chipped:							
380		Uncooked:							
		Container and approx. contents:							
	a	Glass jar, net wt., 2½ oz	1 jar	71		4.5	2.1	2.0	.1
	b	Glass jar, net wt., 5 oz	1 jar	142		8.9	4.3	3.9	.2
	c	Pound	1 lb	454		28.6	13.7	12.6	.6
381		Cooked, creamed:							
	a	Cup	1 cup	245	Milk, butter, beef	25.2	13.7	8.6	.8
	b	Pound	1 lb	454	do	46.7	25.4	15.8	1.5
		Beef potpie:							
382		Home prepared, baked:							

(A)		(B)			(C)	(D)	(E)	(F)	(G)
	a	Pie, whole (9-in. diam.)	1 pie	[7] 630	Vegetable shortening, beef	91.4	25.3	44.6	17.9
	b	Piece, ⅓ of pie (item 382a)	1 piece	210	do	30.5	8.4	14.9	6.0
	c	Pound	1 lb	454	do	65.8	18.2	32.1	12.9
		Biscuits, baking powder, baked from home recipe, made with—							
410, 411, or 412		Enriched, unenriched, or self-rising flour:							
		Made with lard:							
	a	Biscuit, 2-in. diam., 1¼ in. high	1 biscuit	28	Lard	4.8	1.8	2.2	.5
	b	Pound	1 lb	454	do	77.1	28.8	35.0	8.5
		Made with vegetable shortening:							
	c	Biscuit, 2-in. diam., 1¼ in. high	1 biscuit	28	Vegetable shortening	4.8	1.2	2.3	1.1
	d	Pound	1 lb	454	do	77.1	19.1	38.0	17.4
		Biscuit mix and biscuits baked from mix:							
415		Mix, dry form:							
		Cup:							
		Not packed:							
	a	Spooned into cup or premeasured 1-cup packet.	1 cup or 1 packet	120	do	15.1	3.7	7.4	3.5
	b	Poured from container into cup	1 cup	128	do	16.1	3.9	7.9	3.8
	c	Packed	1 cup	160	do	20.2	4.9	9.8	4.7
	d	Pound	1 lb	454	do	57.2	13.9	27.9	13.3
416		Biscuits made with milk:							
	a	Biscuit, 2-in. diam., 1¼ in. high	1 biscuit	28	do	2.6	.6	1.3	.6
	b	Pound	1 lb	454	do	42.2	10.3	20.5	9.8
		Blancmange. See Puddings (item 1824).							
		Braunschweiger. See Sausage, cold cuts, and luncheon meats (item 1986).							
443		**Brazil nuts:**							
		In shell (refuse: shells, 52%): [2]							
	a	Cup	1 cup	122		39.2	7.8	18.8	10.2
	b	Pound	1 lb	454		145.6	29.1	69.9	37.9
	c	Ounce	1 oz. or 3–3½ nuts	28		9.1	1.8	4.4	2.4
		Shelled:							
	d	Cup	1 cup	140		93.7	18.7	45.0	24.3
	e	Pound	1 lb	454		303.5	60.7	145.7	78.9
	f	Ounce	1 oz. or 6–8 kernels	28		19.0	3.8	9.1	4.9
		Breads:							
		Cracked-wheat bread:							
444		Fresh:							
	a	Loaf, net wt., 16 oz. (1 lb.)	1 loaf or 1 lb	454	Vegetable shortening	10.0	2.1	4.2	3.0
	b	Slice, $\frac{1}{18}$ of loaf	1 slice	25	do	.6	.1	.2	.2
445		Toasted slices:							
	a	Yield from 1-lb. loaf	18 slices	381	do	10.0	2.1	4.2	3.0
	b	Piece	1 slice	21	do	.6	.1	.2	.2
	c	Pound	1 lb	454	do	11.8	2.4	5.0	3.5
446 or 448		French or vienna bread and rolls, enriched or unenriched:							
		Bread:							
	a	Loaf, net wt., 16 oz. (1 lb.)	1 loaf or 1 lb	454	do	13.6	3.0	6.1	3.7
		Slice:							
		French:							
	b	Piece, 5 in. wide, 2½ in. high, 1 in. thick.	1 slice	35	do	1.1	.2	.5	.3

[2] Measure and weight apply to food as it is described with inedible part or parts (refuse) included.

[6] Measures and fatty acid values represent meat probably cooked to between rare- and medium-done stage. For values of meat cooked to well-done stage, see Appendix A, table 3, p. 264.

[7] Yield of formula used to calculate nutritive values in Agr. Handb. No. 8, rev. 1963.

TABLE 2.—*Fatty acid values for household measures and market units of foods*—Continued

[Item and footnote numbers correspond to those in table 1 of this publication. Values in parentheses denote imputed values usually from another form of the food or from a similar food. Dashes (—) denote lack of reliable data for a constituent believed to be present in a measurable amount. Calculated values, as those based on a recipe, are not in parentheses]

Item No. (A)		Food, approximate measures, units, and weight (edible part unless footnotes indicate otherwise) (B)			Principal sources of fat (C)	Amount in edible part of foods: Total fat (D)	Total saturated fatty acids (E)	Unsaturated fatty acids: Oleic $C_{18}(-2H)$ (F)	Unsaturated fatty acids: Linoleic $C_{18}(-4H)$ (G)
				Grams		*Grams*	*Grams*	*Grams*	*Grams*
		Breads—Continued							
		French or vienna bread and rolls, enriched or unenriched—Continued							
		Bread—Continued							
		Slice—Continued							
		French—Continued							
	c	Piece, 2½ in. wide, 2 in. high, ½ in. thick.	1 slice	15	Vegetable shortening	0.5	0.1	0.2	0.1
		Vienna:							
	d	Piece, 4¾ in. wide, 4 in. high, ½ in. thick.	1 slice	25	do	.8	.2	.3	.2
	e	Roll, hoagie or submarine, 11½ in. long, 3 in. wide, 2½ in. thick.	1 roll	135	do	4.1	.9	1.8	1.1
		Raisin bread:							
452		Fresh:							
	a	Loaf, net wt., 16 oz. (1 lb.)	1 loaf or 1 lb	454	do	12.7	2.9	5.9	3.3
	b	Slice, 1/18 of loaf	1 slice	25	do	.7	.2	.3	.2
453		Toasted slices:							
	a	Yield from 1-lb. loaf	18 slices	376	do	12.7	2.9	5.9	3.3
	b	Piece	1 slice	21	do	.7	.2	.3	.2
	c	Pound	1 lb	454	do	15.4	3.6	7.2	3.9
		Salt-rising bread:							
457		Fresh:							
	a	Loaf, net wt., 16 oz. (1 lb.)	1 loaf or 1 lb	454	do	10.9	2.8	4.6	2.8
	b	Slice, 1/19 of loaf	1 slice	24	do	.6	.1	.2	.1
458		Toasted slices:							
	a	Yield from 1-lb. loaf	19 slices	408	do	10.9	2.8	4.6	2.8
	b	Piece	1 slice	22	do	.6	.1	.2	.1
	c	Pound	1 lb	454	do	12.2	3.2	5.1	3.1
		White bread, enriched or unenriched, soft-crumb type (made by continuous mix or conventional method):							
461 or 467		Fresh:							
	a	Loaf, net wt., 24 oz. (1 lb. 8 oz.)	1 loaf	680	do	21.8	5.0	9.9	5.7
		Slice:							
	b	Regular, 1/24 of loaf	1 slice	28	do	.9	.2	.4	.2
	c	Thin (sandwich type), 1/28 of loaf	1 slice	24	do	.8	.2	.4	.2
	d	Loaf, net wt., 16 oz. (1 lb.)	1 loaf or 1 lb	454	do	14.5	3.3	6.6	3.8
		Slice:							
	e	Regular, 1/18 of loaf	1 slice	25	do	.8	.2	.4	.2
	f	Thin, 1/22 of loaf	1 slice	20	do	.6	.1	.3	.2
	g	Cubes	1 cup	30	do	1.0	.2	.4	.3
	h	Crumbs	1 cup	45	do	1.4	.3	.7	.4

(A)		(B)			(C)	(D)	(E)	(F)	(G)
462 or 468		Toasted slices:							
		From 1½-lb. loaf:							
	a	Yield from loaf	24 regular or 28 thin slices.	585	Vegetable shortening	21.8	5.0	9.9	5.7
	b	Slice, regular	1 slice	24	do	.9	.2	.4	.2
	c	Slice, thin (sandwich type)	1 slice	21	do	.8	.2	.4	.2
		From 1-lb. loaf:							
	d	Yield from loaf	18 regular or 22 thin slices.	390	do	14.5	3.3	6.6	3.8
	e	Slice, regular	1 slice	22	do	.8	.2	.4	.2
	f	Slice, thin (sandwich type)	1 slice	17	do	.6	.1	.3	.2
	g	Pound	1 lb	454	do	16.8	3.8	7.7	4.4
		White bread, enriched or unenriched, firm-crumb type (made by conventional method):							
463 or 469		Fresh:							
	a	Loaf, net wt., 32 oz. (2 lb.)	1 loaf or 2 lb	907	do	34.5	7.9	15.8	9.0
	b	Slice, 1/34 of loaf	1 slice	27	do	1.0	.2	.5	.3
	c	Loaf, net wt., 16 oz. (1 lb.)	1 loaf or 1 lb	454	do	17.2	3.9	7.9	4.5
	d	Slice, 1/20 of loaf	1 slice	23	do	.9	.2	.4	.2
	e	Slice, 1/31 of loaf	1 slice	15	do	.6	.1	.3	.1
	f	Cubes	1 cup	30	do	1.1	.3	.5	.3
	g	Crumbs	1 cup	45	do	1.7	.4	.8	.4
464 or 470		Toasted slices:							
		From 2-lb. loaf:							
	a	Yield from loaf	34 slices	780	do	34.5	7.9	15.8	9.0
	b	Slice	1 slice	23	do	1.0	.2	.5	.3
		From 1-lb. loaf (20 slices):							
	c	Yield from loaf	20 slices	390	do	17.2	3.9	7.9	4.5
	d	Slice	1 slice	20	do	.9	.2	.4	.2
		Whole-wheat bread, firm-crumb type:							
471		Fresh:							
	a	Loaf, net wt., 16 oz. (1 lb.)	1 loaf or 1 lb	454	do	13.6	2.7	5.5	4.3
	b	Slice, 1/18 of loaf	1 slice	25	do	.8	.1	.3	.2
	c	Slice, 1/20 of loaf	1 slice	23	do	.7	.1	.3	.2
472		Toasted slices:							
	a	Yield from 1-lb. loaf	18 or 20 slices	381	do	13.6	2.7	5.5	4.3
	b	Slice, 1/18 of loaf	1 slice	21	do	.8	.1	.3	.2
	c	Slice, 1/20 of loaf	1 slice	19	do	.7	.1	.3	.2
	d	Pound	1 lb	454	do	16.3	3.2	6.6	5.2
		Whole-wheat bread, soft-crumb type:							
473		Fresh:							
	a	Loaf, net wt., 16 oz. (1 lb.)	1 loaf or 1 lb	454	do	11.8	2.3	4.8	3.8
	b	Slice, 1/16 of loaf	1 slice	28	do	.7	.1	.3	.2
474		Toasted slices:							
	a	Yield from 1-lb. loaf	16 slices	381	do	11.8	2.3	4.8	3.8
	b	Piece	1 slice	24	do	.7	.1	.3	.2
	c	Pound	1 lb	454	do	14.1	2.8	5.7	4.5
475		**Breadcrumbs, dry, grated**	1 cup	100	do	4.6	1.1	2.1	1.2
		Breadcrumbs and cubes, soft. See White bread (items 461 or 467g, 461 or 467h, 463 or 469f, 463 or 469g).							
476		**Bread pudding with raisins**[3]	1 cup	265	Milk, butter, eggs, breadcrumbs.	16.2	7.7	5.9	1.0

[3] Cup measure made on product after it had cooled. See also **Appendix B**, section on Home-Prepared Foods

TABLE 2.—*Fatty acid values for household measures and market units of foods*—Continued

[Item and footnote numbers correspond to those in table 1 of this publication. Values in parentheses denote imputed values usually from another form of the food or from a similar food. Dashes (—) denote lack of reliable data for a constituent believed to be present in a measurable amount. Calculated values, as those based on a recipe, are not in parentheses]

Item No. (A)		Food, approximate measures, units, and weight (edible part unless footnotes indicate otherwise) (B)			Principal sources of fat (C)	Total fat (D)	Total saturated fatty acids (E)	Unsaturated fatty acids: Oleic $C_{18}(-2H)$ (F)	Unsaturated fatty acids: Linoleic $C_{18}(-4H)$ (G)
				Grams		*Grams*	*Grams*	*Grams*	*Grams*
		Breadsticks. See Salt sticks (item 1965).							
		Bread stuffing mix and stuffings prepared from mix:							
477		Mix, dry form:							
	a	Package, net wt., 8 oz	1 pkg	227	Vegetable shortening	8.6	2.0	3.9	2.2
		Cup:							
	b	Coarse crumbs	1 cup	70	do	2.7	.6	1.2	.7
	c	Cubes	1 cup	30	do	1.1	.3	.5	.3
		Stuffing:							
478		Dry, crumbly; prepared with water, table fat:							
	a	Cup	1 cup	140	Butter, vegetable shortening.	30.5	16.0	10.4	1.5
	b	Pound	1 lb	454	do	98.9	51.7	33.7	4.9
479		Moist; prepared with water, egg, table fat:							
	a	Cup	1 cup	200	Butter, vegetable shortening, egg.	25.6	13.1	8.9	1.3
	b	Pound	1 lb	454	do	58.1	29.7	20.1	2.9
		Brown betty. See Apple brown betty (item 25).							
		Brownies. See Cookies (items 813–814).							
		Buckwheat pancakes. See Pancakes, baked from mixes (item 1462).							
505		**Butter:**							
		Regular type (1 brick or 4 sticks per pound):							
	a	Stick, net wt., 4 oz. (approx. ½ cup)	1 stick	113.4		91.9	50.5	30.3	2.8
	b	Cup (approx. ½ brick or 2 sticks of item 505a).	1 cup	227		183.9	101.1	60.7	5.5
	c	Tablespoon (approx. ⅛ of stick (item 505a)).	1 tbsp	14.2		11.5	6.3	3.8	.3
	d	Pat (1 in. square, ⅓ in. high; 90 per pound).	1 pat	5.0		4.1	2.2	1.3	.1
	e	Cubic inch	1 cu. in	14.7		11.9	6.5	3.9	.4
		Whipped type[8] (6 sticks or two 8-oz. containers[9] per pound):							
	f	Stick, net wt., 2⅔ oz. (approx. ⅓ cup)	1 stick	75.6		61.2	33.7	20.2	1.8
	g	Cup (approx. 2 sticks of item 505f or ⅔ of 8-oz. container).	1 cup	151		122.3	67.3	40.4	3.7
	h	Tablespoon (approx. ⅛ of stick (item 505f)).	1 tbsp	9.4		7.6	4.2	2.5	.2
	i	Pat (1¼ in. square, ⅓ in. high; 120 per pound).	1 pat	3.8		3.1	1.7	1.0	.1
	j	Regular and whipped types	1 lb	454		367.4	202.1	121.3	11.0

(A)		(B)		(C)		(D)	(E)	(F)	(G)
510		**Buttermilk, dried:**							
	a	Package, net wt., 16 oz. (1 lb.)	1 pkg	454		24.0	13.3	7.9	0.7
	b	Cup	1 cup	120		6.4	3.5	2.1	.2
	c	Tablespoon	1 tbsp	6.5		.3	.2	.1	Trace
		Cabbage salad. See Coleslaw (items 801–804).							
		Cakes and cupcakes:							
		Baked from home recipes:							
522		Boston cream pie, 8-in. diam., 3⅓ in. high (2-layer cake with custard filling and powdered sugar topping):							
		Piece (2⅛-in. arc; 1/12 of cake):							
	a	Made with vegetable shortening	1 piece	69	Vegetable shortening, egg, milk.	6.5	2.0	3.0	1.1
	b	Made with butter	1 piece	69	Butter, egg, milk	6.1	3.0	2.1	.3
		Cube (1 cu. in.):							
	c	Made with vegetable shortening	1 cube	5.0	Vegetable shortening, egg, milk.	.5	.1	.2	.1
	d	Made with butter	1 cube	5.0	Butter, egg, milk	.4	.2	.2	Trace
		Caramel:							
523		Without icing:							
		Cake, 2-layer, 9-in. diam., 3 in. high:							
	a	Made with vegetable shortening	1 cake	864	Vegetable shortening, egg, milk.	149.5	40.2	72.7	29.9
	b	Made with butter	1 cake	882	Butter, egg, milk	138.5	72.0	47.4	5.3
		Cube (1 cu. in.):[10]							
	c	Made with vegetable shortening	1 cube	4.8	Vegetable shortening, egg, milk.	.8	.2	.4	.2
	d	Made with butter	1 cube	4.9	Butter, egg, milk	.8	.4	.3	Trace
524		With caramel icing (dimensions of items apply to uniced cake; volume in cubic inches to iced cake):							
		Cake, 2-layer, 9-in. diam., 3 in. high:							
		Piece (1¾-in. arc; 1/16 of cake):							
	a	Made with vegetable shortening	1 piece	79	Vegetable shortening, egg, butter, milk.	11.7	3.5	5.5	2.1
	b	Made with butter	1 piece	80	Butter, egg, milk	10.9	5.7	3.7	.4
		Cube (1 cu. in.):[10]							
	c	Made with vegetable shortening	1 cube	6.4	Vegetable shortening, egg, butter, milk.	.9	.3	.4	.2
	d	Made with butter	1 cube	6.5	Butter, egg, milk	.9	.5	.3	Trace
		Chocolate (devil's food):							
525		Without icing:							
		Cake, sheet:							
		Piece (2 × 2 × 2 in.):							
	a	Made with vegetable shortening	1 piece	39	Vegetable shortening, chocolate, egg, milk.	6.7	2.4	3.0	1.0
	b	Made with butter	1 piece	40	Butter, egg, milk, chocolate.	6.4	3.4	2.2	.2
		Cube (1 cu. in.):[10]							
	c	Made with vegetable shortening	1 cube	4.9	Vegetable shortening, chocolate, egg, milk.	.8	.3	.4	.1
	d	Made with butter	1 cube	5.0	Butter, egg, milk, chocolate.	.8	.4	.3	Trace

[8] Description and weights shown for whipped butter, except pat (item 505l), apply to butter that has been stirred or whipped until its volume has been increased approx. 50%; for pat, 100%.

[9] Fatty acid values for 8-oz. container (227 g.) of whipped butter are same as those shown for 1 cup of regular butter (item 505b).

[10] Weight per cubic inch applies to layer, loaf, sheet, or tube cake but not to cupcakes. For cupcakes, see Appendix B, section on Cakes

TABLE 2.—*Fatty acid values for household measures and market units of foods*—Continued

[Item and footnote numbers correspond to those in table 1 of this publication. Values in parentheses denote imputed values usually from another form of the food or from a similar food. Dashes (—) denote lack of reliable data for a constituent believed to be present in a measurable amount. Calculated values, as those based on a recipe, are not in parentheses]

Item No. (A)		Food, approximate measures, units, and weight (edible part unless footnotes indicate otherwise) (B)		Weight	Principal sources of fat (C)	Total fat (D)	Total saturated fatty acids (E)	Unsaturated fatty acids: Oleic $C_{18}(-2H)$ (F)	Unsaturated fatty acids: Linoleic $C_{18}(-4H)$ (G)
				Grams		*Grams*	*Grams*	*Grams*	*Grams*
		Cakes and cupcakes—Continued							
		Baked from home recipes—Continued							
		Chocolate (devil's food)—Continued							
526		With chocolate icing (dimensions of items apply to uniced cake; volume in cubic inches to iced cake):							
		Cake, 2-layer, 9-in. diam., 3 in. high:							
		Piece (1¾-in. arc; 1/16 of cake):							
	a	Made with vegetable shortening	1 piece	75	Vegetable shortening, chocolate, milk, egg, butter.	12.3	4.9	5.8	1.5
	b	Made with butter	1 piece	75	Butter, chocolate, milk, egg.	11.6	6.2	4.1	.4
		Cube (1 cu. in.): [10]							
	c	Made with vegetable shortening	1 cube	6.1	Vegetable shortening, chocolate, milk, egg, butter.	1.0	.4	.4	.1
	d	Made with butter	1 cube	6.1	Butter, chocolate, milk, egg.	.9	.5	.3	Trace
527		With uncooked white icing (dimensions of items apply to uniced cake; volume in cubic inches to iced cake):							
		Cake, 2-layer, 9-in. diam., 3 in. high:							
		Piece (1¾-in. arc; 1/16 of cake):							
	a	Made with vegetable shortening	1 piece	74	Vegetable shortening, chocolate, egg, butter, cream, milk.	10.8	4.1	4.7	1.5
	b	Made with butter	1 piece	74	Butter, chocolate, egg, cream, milk.	10.1	5.4	3.5	.3
		Cube (1 cu. in.): [10]							
	c	Made with vegetable shortening	1 cube	6.1	Vegetable shortening, chocolate, egg, butter, cream, milk.	.9	.3	.4	.1
	d	Made with butter	1 cube	6.2	Butter, chocolate, egg, cream, milk.	.8	.5	.3	Trace
		Cottage pudding (8 × 8 × 1½ in.):							
528		Without sauce:							
		Piece (2 × 4 × 1½ in.; ⅛ of cake):							
	a	Made with vegetable shortening	1 piece	54	Vegetable shortening, egg, milk.	6.1	1.7	2.9	1.2
	b	Made with butter	1 piece	55	Butter, egg, milk	5.7	2.9	2.0	.3
		Cube (1 cu. in.):							
	c	Made with vegetable shortening	1 cube	4.5	Vegetable shortening, egg, milk.	.5	.1	.2	.1

(A)		(B)			(C)	(D)	(E)	(F)	(G)
	d	Made with butter	1 cube	4.6	Butter, egg, milk	0.5	0.2	0.2	Trace
529		With chocolate sauce:							
	a	Piece, made with vegetable shortening (item 528a) with 1 tbsp. of sauce.	1 piece	74	Vegetable shortening, egg, milk, chocolate.	6.5	2.0	3.0	1.2
	b	Piece, made with butter (item 528b) with 1 tbsp. of sauce.	1 piece	75	Butter, egg, milk, chocolate.	6.2	3.2	2.1	.3
530		With fruit sauce (strawberry):							
	a	Piece, made with vegetable shortening (item 528a) with 1 tbsp. of sauce.	1 piece	70	Vegetable shortening, egg, milk.	6.2	1.7	2.9	1.2
	b	Piece, made with butter (item 528b) with 1 tbsp. of sauce.	1 piece	71	Butter, egg, milk	5.8	2.9	2.0	.3
		Fruitcake:							
531		Dark:							
		Loaf, 1 lb. (7½ × 2 × 1½ in.):							
		Slice (¼ × 2 × 1½ in.; 1/30 of loaf):							
	a	Made with vegetable shortening	1 slice	15	Vegetable shortening, pecans, almonds, egg, cream.	2.3	.5	1.2	.4
	b	Made with butter	1 slice	15	Butter, pecans, almonds, egg, cream.	2.1	.7	1.0	.2
		Tube cake, 3 lb. (7-in. diam., 2¼ in. high):							
		Wedge (⅔-in. arc; 1/32 of cake):							
	c	Made with vegetable shortening	1 wedge	43	Vegetable shortening, pecans, almonds, egg, cream.	6.6	1.4	3.5	1.3
	d	Made with butter	1 wedge	43	Butter, pecans, almonds, egg, cream.	5.9	2.0	2.7	.6
532		Light:							
		Loaf, 1 lb. (7½ × 2 × 1½ in.):							
		Slice (¼ × 2 × 1½ in.; 1/30 of loaf):							
	a	Made with vegetable shortening	1 slice	15	Vegetable shortening, almonds, cream.	2.5	.6	1.3	.5
	b	Made with butter	1 slice	15	Butter, almonds, cream	2.4	.9	1.1	.2
		Tube cake, 3 lb. (7-in. diam., 2¼ in. high):							
		Wedge (⅔-in. arc; 1/32 of cake):							
	c	Made with vegetable shortening	1 wedge	43	Vegetable shortening, almonds, cream.	7.1	1.6	3.8	1.4
	d	Made with butter	1 wedge	43	Butter, almonds, cream	6.8	2.4	3.1	.7
533		Gingerbread (9 × 9 × 2 in.):							
		Piece (3× 3 × 2 in.; 1/9 of cake):							
	a	Made with vegetable shortening	1 piece	117	Vegetable shortening, egg.	12.5	3.2	6.1	2.6
	b	Made with butter	1 piece	119	Butter, egg	11.7	6.0	4.0	.5
		Cube (1 cu. in.):[10]							
	c	Made with vegetable shortening	1 cube	6.5	Vegetable shortening, egg.	.7	.2	.3	.1
	d	Made with butter	1 cube	6.6	Butter, egg	.6	.3	.2	Trace
		Plain cake or cupcake:							
534		Without icing:							
		Cake, sheet (9 × 9 × 2 in.):							
		Piece (3 × 3 × 2 in.; 1/9 of cake):							
	a	Made with vegetable shortening	1 piece	86	Vegetable shortening, egg, milk.	12.0	3.3	5.7	2.3

[10] Weight per cubic inch applies to layer, loaf, sheet, or tube cake but not to cupcakes. For cupcakes, see Appendix B, section on Cakes

TABLE 2.—*Fatty acid values for household measures and market units of foods*—Continued

[Item and footnote numbers correspond to those in table 1 of this publication. Values in parentheses denote imputed values usually from another form of the food or from a similar food. Dashes (—) denote lack of reliable data for a constituent believed to be present in a measurable amount. Calculated values, as those based on a recipe, are not in parentheses]

Item No. (A)		Food, approximate measures, units, and weight (edible part unless footnotes indicate otherwise) (B)		Grams	Principal sources of fat (C)	Total fat (D)	Total saturated fatty acids (E)	Unsaturated fatty acids: Oleic $C_{18}(-2H)$ (F)	Unsaturated fatty acids: Linoleic $C_{18}(-4H)$ (G)
						Grams	Grams	Grams	Grams
		Cakes and cupcakes—Continued							
		Baked from home recipes—Continued							
		Plain cake or cupcake—Continued							
		Without icing—Continued							
		Cake, sheet (9 × 9 × 2 in.)—Continued							
		Piece (3 × 3 × 2 in.; 1/9 of cake)—Continued							
	b	Made with butter	1 piece	87	Butter, egg, milk	11.0	5.7	3.8	0.5
		Cube (1 cu. in.): [10]							
	c	Made with vegetable shortening	1 cube	4.8	Vegetable shortening, egg, milk.	.7	.2	.3	.1
	d	Made with butter	1 cube	4.9	Butter, egg, milk	.6	.3	.2	Trace
535		With chocolate icing (dimensions of items apply to uniced cake; volume in cubic inches to iced cake):							
		Cake, sheet (9 × 9 × 2 in.):							
		Piece (3 × 3 × 2 in.; 1/9 of cake):							
	a	Made with vegetable shortening	1 piece	123	Vegetable shortening, chocolate, milk, butter, egg.	17.1	6.2	7.5	2.5
	b	Made with butter	1 piece	124	Butter, chocolate, milk, egg.	16.2	8.6	5.6	.6
		Cube (1 cu. in.): [10]							
	c	Made with vegetable shortening	1 cube	6.2	Vegetable shortening, chocolate, milk, butter, egg.	.9	.3	.4	.1
	d	Made with butter	1 cube	6.2	Butter, chocolate, milk, egg.	.8	.4	.3	Trace
536		With boiled white icing (dimensions of items apply to uniced cake; volume in cubic inches to iced cake):							
		Cake, sheet (9 × 9 × 2 in.):							
		Piece (3 × 3 × 2 in.; 1/9 of cake):							
	a	Made with vegetable shortening	1 piece	114	Vegetable shortening, egg, milk.	12.0	3.3	5.7	2.3
	b	Made with butter	1 piece	115	Butter, egg, milk	11.2	5.8	3.8	.5
		Cube (1 cu. in.): [10]							
	c	Made with vegetable shortening	1 cube	5.1	Vegetable shortening, egg, milk.	.5	.1	.3	.1
	d	Made with butter	1 cube	5.2	Butter, egg, milk	.5	.3	.2	Trace
537		With uncooked white icing (dimensions of items apply to uniced cake; volume in cubic inches to iced cake):							
		Cake, sheet (9 × 9 × 2 in.):							
		Piece (3 × 3 × 2 in.; 1/9 of cake):							
	a	Made with vegetable shortening	1 piece	121	Vegetable shortening, butter, egg, cream,	14.3	4.6	6.5	2.4

(A)		(B)		(C)		(D)	(E)	(F)	(G)
	b	Made with butter	1 piece	122	Butter, egg, cream, milk	13.4	7.0	4.6	0.5
		Cube (1 cu. in.):[10]							
	c	Made with vegetable shortening	1 cube	6.2	Vegetable shortening, butter, egg, cream, milk.	.7	.2	.3	.1
	d	Made with butter	1 cube	6.2	Butter, egg, cream, milk	.7	.4	.2	Trace
		Pound:							
538		Old fashioned:[11]							
		Loaf (8½ × 3½ × 3 in.):							
		Slice (3½ × 3 × ½ in.; 1/17 of loaf):							
	a	Made with vegetable shortening	1 slice	30	Vegetable shortening, egg.	8.9	2.3	4.4	1.8
	b	Made with butter	1 slice	31	Butter, egg	8.2	4.2	2.8	.3
		Cube (1 cu. in.):[10]							
	c	Made with vegetable shortening	1 cube	5.8	Vegetable shortening, egg.	1.7	.4	.8	.4
	d	Made with butter	1 cube	5.9	Butter, egg	1.6	.8	.5	.1
539		Modified:							
		Loaf (8½ × 3½ × 3 in.):							
		Slice (3½ × 3 × ½ in.; 1/17 of loaf):							
	a	Made with vegetable shortening	1 slice	29	Vegetable shortening, egg, milk.	5.4	1.4	2.6	1.0
	b	Made with butter	1 slice	30	Butter, egg, milk	5.1	2.5	1.8	.2
		Cube (1 cu. in.):[10]							
	c	Made with vegetable shortening	1 cube	5.6	Vegetable shortening, egg, milk.	1.0	.3	.5	.2
	d	Made with butter	1 cube	5.7	Butter, egg, milk	1.0	.5	.3	Trace
540		Sponge:							
		Tube cake, 8½-in. diam., 3½ in. high:							
	a	Piece (1⅝-in. arc; 1/16 of cake)	1 piece	33	Egg	1.9	.6	.8	.1
	b	Cube (1 cu. in.)[10]	1 cube	3.2	do	.2	.1	.1	Trace
		White:							
541		Without icing:							
		Cake, 2-layer, 9-in. diam., 3 in. high:							
	a	Made with vegetable shortening	1 cake	846	Vegetable shortening, milk.	135.4	35.6	66.3	28.8
	b	Made with butter	1 cake	864	Butter, milk	124.4	67.8	41.0	4.5
		Cube (1 cu. in.):[10]							
	c	Made with vegetable shortening	1 cube	4.7	Vegetable shortening, milk.	.8	.2	.4	.2
	d	Made with butter	1 cube	4.8	Butter, milk	.7	.4	.2	Trace
542		With coconut icing (dimensions of items apply to uniced cake; volume in cubic inches to iced cake):							
		Cake, 2-layer, 9-in. diam., 3 in. high:							
		Piece (1¾-in. arc; 1/16 of cake):							
	a	Made with vegetable shortening	1 piece	78	Vegetable shortening, coconut, milk.	10.4	3.9	4.3	1.8
	b	Made with butter	1 piece	79	Butter, coconut, milk	9.7	5.9	2.7	.3
		Cube (1 cu. in.):[10]							
	c	Made with vegetable shortening	1 cube	5.8	Vegetable shortening, coconut, milk.	.8	.3	.3	.1
	d	Made with butter	1 cube	5.9	Butter, coconut, milk	.7	.4	.2	Trace
543		With uncooked white icing (dimensions of items apply to uniced cake; volume in cubic inches to iced cake):							

[10] Weight per cubic inch applies to layer, loaf, sheet, or tube cake but not to cupcakes. For cupcakes, see Appendix B, section on Cakes

[11] Formula for this product deviates from true old-fashioned pound cake in containing higher proportion of fat by weight. For fatty acid values of product containing 1 lb. each of flour, sugar, eggs, and fat, see Appendix A, table 3, p. 264.

TABLE 2.—*Fatty acid values for household measures and market units of foods*—Continued

[Item and footnote numbers correspond to those in table 1 of this publication. Values in parentheses denote imputed values usually from another form of the food or from a similar food. Dashes (—) denote lack of reliable data for a constituent believed to be present in a measurable amount. Calculated values, as those based on a recipe, are not in parentheses]

Item No. (A)	Food, approximate measures, units, and weight (edible part unless footnotes indicate otherwise) (B)			Principal sources of fat (C)	Amount in edible part of foods: Total fat (D)	Total saturated fatty acids (E)	Unsaturated fatty acids: Oleic $C_{18}(-2H)$ (F)	Unsaturated fatty acids: Linoleic $C_{18}(-4H)$ (G)
			Grams		*Grams*	*Grams*	*Grams*	*Grams*
	Cakes and cupcakes—Continued							
	Baked from home recipes—Continued							
	White—Continued							
	With uncooked white icing (dimensions of items apply to uniced cake; volume in cubic inches to iced cake)—Continued							
	Cake, 2-layer, 9-in. diam., 3 in. high:							
	Piece (1¾-in. arc; 1/16 of cake):							
a	Made with vegetable shortening	1 piece	78	Vegetable shortening, butter, cream, milk.	10.1	3.1	4.7	1.9
b	Made with butter	1 piece	80	Butter, cream, milk	9.5	5.2	3.1	.3
	Cube (1 cu. in.): [10]							
c	Made with vegetable shortening	1 cube	6.3	Vegetable shortening, butter, cream, milk.	.8	.3	.4	.2
d	Made with butter	1 cube	6.4	Butter, cream, milk	.8	.4	.3	Trace
	Yellow:							
544	Without icing:							
	Cake, 2-layer, 9-in. diam., 3 in. high:							
a	Made with vegetable shortening	1 cake	870	Vegetable shortening, egg, milk.	110.5	30.7	52.7	21.6
b	Made with butter	1 cake	880	Butter, egg, milk	102.1	52.9	34.7	4.3
	Cube (1 cu. in.): [10]							
c	Made with vegetable shortening	1 cube	4.8	Vegetable shortening, egg, milk.	.6	.2	.3	.1
d	Made with butter	1 cube	4.9	Butter, egg, milk	.6	.3	.2	Trace
545	With caramel icing (dimensions of items apply to uniced cake; volume in cubic inches to iced cake):							
	Cake, 2-layer, 9-in. diam., 3 in. high:							
	Piece (1¾-in. arc; 1/16 of cake):							
a	Made with vegetable shortening	1 piece	81	Vegetable shortening, milk, egg, butter.	9.5	2.9	4.4	1.7
b	Made with butter	1 piece	82	Butter, milk, egg	8.9	4.6	3.0	.4
	Cube (1 cu. in.): [10]							
c	Made with vegetable shortening	1 cube	6.5	Vegetable shortening, milk, egg, butter.	.8	.2	.4	.1
d	Made with butter	1 cube	6.6	Butter, milk, egg	.7	.4	.2	Trace
546	With chocolate icing (dimensions of items apply to uniced cake; volume in cubic inches to iced cake):							
	Cake, 2-layer, 9-in. diam., 3 in. high:							
	Piece (1¾-in. arc; 1/16 of cake):							
a	Made with vegetable shortening	1 piece	75	Vegetable shortening, chocolate, milk, egg, butter.	9.8	3.4	4.3	1.5

(A)		(B)		(C)	(D)	(E)	(F)	(G)
	b	Made with butter	1 piece	76 Butter, chocolate, milk, egg.	9.3	4.9	3.2	0.3
		Cube (1 cu. in.):[10]						
	c	Made with vegetable shortening	1 cube	6.1 Vegetable shortening, chocolate, milk, egg, butter.	.8	.3	.4	.1
	d	Made with butter	1 cube	6.2 Butter, chocolate, milk, egg.	.8	.4	.3	Trace
		Frozen, commercial, devil's food; net wt., 18 oz. (1 lb. 2 oz.):						
547		With chocolate icing (1-layer cake, approx. 7½-in. diam., 1¾ in. high):						
	a	Piece (4-in. arc; ⅛ of cake)	1 piece	85 Butter, chocolate, cream cheese, vegetable shortening, egg, milk.	15.0	7.7	5.4	.7
	b	Cube (1 cu. in.)	1 cube	6.6 do	1.2	.6	.4	.1
548		With whipped-cream filling, chocolate icing (2-layer cake, approx. 7¼-in. diam., 2 in. high):						
	a	Piece (3¾-in. arc; ⅙ of cake)	1 piece	85 Vegetable shortening, cream, chocolate, egg, milk.	18.6	6.2	9.5	1.9
	b	Cube (1 cu. in.)	1 cube	6.1 do	1.3	.4	.7	.1
		Prepared and baked from mixes:						
552		Chocolate malt; made with eggs, water (uniced 2-layer cake, 9-in. diam., 2⅝ in. high or 8-in. diam., 3⅜ in. high), with uncooked white icing:						
	a	Piece (1¾-in. arc of 9-in.-diam. cake or 1⅝-in. arc of 8-in.-diam. cake; ⅟₁₆ of cake).	1 piece	67 Vegetable shortening, butter, egg, cream, cocoa, malted milk.	5.8	2.1	2.5	.8
	b	Cube (1 cu. in.)[10]	1 cube	6.3 do	.5	.2	.2	.1
554		Coffeecake; made with egg, milk (7¾ × 5⅝ × 1¼ in.):						
	a	Piece (2⅝ × 2¾ × 1¼ in.; ⅙ of cake)	1 piece	72 Vegetable shortening, egg, milk.	6.9	2.0	3.2	1.3
	b	Cube (1 cu. in.)	1 cube	7.8 do	.7	.2	.4	.1
		Cupcake; made with egg, milk (2½-in. diam.):						
556		Without icing	1 cupcake	25 do	3.0	.8	1.4	.6
557		With chocolate icing	1 cupcake	36 Vegetable shortening, chocolate, butter, milk, egg.	4.5	1.8	1.9	.5
559		Devil's food; made with eggs, water (uniced 2-layer cake, 9-in. diam., 2⅞ in. high or 8-in. diam., 3¾ in. high), with chocolate icing:						
	a	Piece (1¾-in. arc of 9-in.-diam. cake or 1⅝-in. arc of 8-in.-diam. cake; ⅟₁₆ of cake).	1 piece	69 Vegetable shortening, chocolate, egg, butter, milk.	8.5	3.3	3.6	1.0
	b	Cube (1 cu. in.)[10]	1 cube	5.8 do	.7	.3	.3	.1
561		Gingerbread; made with water (8¼ × 8¼ × 1⅜ in.):						
	a	Piece (2¾ × 2¾ × 1⅜ in.; ⅑ of cake)	1 piece	63 Vegetable shortening	4.3	1.1	2.1	1.0
	b	Cube (1 cu. in.)[10]	1 cube	6.1 do	.4	.1	.2	.1
563		Honey spice; made with eggs, water (uniced 2-layer cake, 9-in. diam., 2¾ in. high or 8-in. diam., 3⅝ in. high), with caramel icing:						

[10] Weight per cubic inch applies to layer, loaf, sheet, or tube cake but not to cupcakes. For cupcakes, see Appendix B, section on Cakes

TABLE 2.—*Fatty acid values for household measures and market units of foods*—Continued

[Item and footnote numbers correspond to those in table 1 of this publication. Values in parentheses denote imputed values usually from another form of the food or from a similar food. Dashes (—) denote lack of reliable data for a constituent believed to be present in a measurable amount. Calculated values, as those based on a recipe, are not in parentheses]

Item No. (A)		Food, approximate measures, units, and weight (edible part unless footnotes indicate otherwise) (B)			Principal sources of fat (C)	Total fat (D)	Total saturated fatty acids (E)	Unsaturated fatty acids: Oleic $C_{18}(-2H)$ (F)	Unsaturated fatty acids: Linoleic $C_{18}(-4H)$ (G)
				Grams		*Grams*	*Grams*	*Grams*	*Grams*
		Cakes and cupcakes—Continued							
		Prepared and baked from mixes—Continued							
		Honey spice; made with eggs, water (uniced 2-layer cake, 9-in. diam., 2¾ in. high or 8-in. diam., 3⅝ in. high), with caramel icing—Continued							
	a	Piece (1¾-in. arc of 9-in.-diam. cake or 1⅝-in. arc of 8-in.-diam. cake; 1/16 of cake).	1 piece	77	Vegetable shortening, egg, butter, milk.	8.3	2.5	3.9	1.5
	b	Cube (1 cu. in.) [10]	1 cube	6.6	do	.7	.2	.3	.1
565		Marble; made with eggs, water (uniced 2-layer cake, 9-in. diam., 2¾ in. high or 8-in. diam., 3½ in. high), with boiled white icing:							
	a	Piece (1¾-in. arc of 9-in.-diam. cake or 1⅝-in. arc of 8-in.-diam. cake; 1/16 of cake).	1 piece	65	Vegetable shortening, egg, cocoa.	5.7	1.6	2.7	1.1
	b	Cube (1 cu. in.) [10]	1 cube	5.1	do	.4	.1	.2	.1
567		White; made with egg whites, water (uniced 2-layer cake, 9-in. diam., 2⅝ in. high or 8-in. diam., 3⅜ in. high), with chocolate icing:							
	a	Piece (1¾-in. arc of 9-in.-diam. cake or 1⅝-in. arc of 8-in.-diam. cake; 1/16 of cake).	1 piece	71	Vegetable shortening, chocolate, butter, milk.	7.6	2.8	3.3	1.1
	b	Cube (1 cu. in.) [10]	1 cube	6.4	do	.7	.3	.3	.1
569		Yellow; made with eggs, water (uniced 2-layer cake, 9-in. diam., 2⅞ in. high or 8-in. diam., 3⅝ in. high), with chocolate icing:							
	a	Piece (1¾-in. arc of 9-in.-diam. cake or 1⅝-in. arc of 8-in.-diam. cake; 1/16 of cake).	1 piece	69	Vegetable shortening, chocolate, egg, butter, milk.	7.8	2.8	3.4	1.1
	b	Cube (1 cu. in.) [10]	1 cube	5.9	do	.7	.2	.3	.1
		Cake icings prepared from home recipes:							
570		Caramel:							
	a	Yield from recipe (7½ oz.) [12,13]	⅝ cup	213	Butter, milk	14.3	7.8	4.7	.4
	b	Cup	1 cup	340	do	22.8	12.5	7.5	.7
571		Chocolate:							
	a	Yield from recipe (11¾ oz.) [12]	1¼ cups	333	Chocolate, butter, milk	46.3	25.8	16.5	1.1
	b	Cup	1 cup	275	do	38.2	21.3	13.6	.9
572		Coconut:							
	a	Yield from recipe (11 oz.) [12]	1⅞ cups	312	Coconut	24.0	20.7	1.7	Trace
	b	Cup	1 cup	166	do	12.8	11.0	.9	Trace

(A)		(B)			(C)	(D)	(E)	(F)	(G)
573		White, uncooked; yield from recipe (11¼ oz.).[12]	1 cup	319	Butter, cream	21.1	11.6	7.0	0.1
		Cake icings prepared from mixes:							
576		Chocolate fudge, made with water, table fat:							
	a	Butter used	1 cup	310	Butter, vegetable shortening, cocoa.	44.6	18.5	18.3	5.2
		Margarine used:							
	b	Regular type	1 cup	310	Margarine, vegetable shortening, cocoa.	44.6	10.9	22.0	10.2
	c	Soft type	1 cup	310	do	44.6	11.1	19.2	12.6
		Creamy fudge (contains nonfat dry milk):							
578		Made with water	1 cup	245	Vegetable shortening, cocoa.	15.9	5.0	7.5	2.8
579		Made with water, table fat:							
	a	Butter used	1 cup	(245)	Butter, vegetable shortening, cocoa.	37.2	17.2	14.3	3.2
		Margarine used:							
	b	Regular type	1 cup	(245)	Margarine, vegetable shortening, cocoa.	37.2	8.6	18.5	8.9
	c	Soft type	1 cup	(245)	do	37.2	8.9	15.2	11.5
		Candy:							
580		Butterscotch	1 oz	28	Butter	1.0	.5	.3	Trace
		Candy corn. See Fondant (items 602a, 602b).							
		Caramels:							
581		Plain or chocolate	1 oz	28	Cacao butter, chocolate (chocolate only).	2.9	1.6	1.1	.1
582		Plain or chocolate, with nuts	1 oz	28	Cacao butter, pecans, chocolate (chocolate only).	4.6	1.6	2.2	.5
583		Chocolate-flavored roll:							
	a	Large (approx. 4⅜ in. long with oval cross section ⅝ × ½ in.); marked for 7 sections.	1 roll	32	Vegetable shortening, chocolate.	2.6	.8	1.3	.5
	b	Medium (approx. 2½ in. long, ⅜-in. diam.).	1 roll	8	do	.7	.2	.3	.1
	c	Medium (approx. 1⅛ in. long, ½-in. diam.).	1 roll	7	do	.6	.2	.3	.1
	d	Small, bite size (approx. 1½ in. long, ⅜-in. diam.).	1 roll	5	do	.4	.1	.2	.1
	e	Ounce (approx. 6 sections of 1 large roll (item 583a), 3½ medium rolls (item 583b), 4 medium rolls (item 583c), or 6 small rolls (item 583d)).	1 oz	28	do	2.3	.7	1.1	.5
		Chocolate:							
584		Bittersweet	1 oz	28	Chocolate, cacao butter	11.3	6.3	4.2	.2
585		Semisweet:							
	a	Small pieces (approx. 60 per ounce)	1 cup or one 6-oz. pkg.	170	do	60.7	34.0	22.5	1.2
	b	Ounce	1 oz	28	do	10.1	5.7	3.7	.2
586		Sweet	1 oz	28	Cacao butter, chocolate	10.0	5.6	3.7	.2
		Chocolate, milk:							
587		Plain	1 oz	28	Cacao butter, chocolate, milk.	9.2	5.1	3.3	.2
588		With almonds	1 oz	28	Cacao butter, almonds, chocolate, milk.	10.1	4.5	4.4	.6
589		With peanuts	1 oz	28	Peanuts, cacao butter, chocolate, milk.	10.8	4.5	4.2	1.5

[10] Weight per cubic inch applies to layer, loaf, sheet, or tube cake but not to cupcakes. For cupcakes, see Appendix B, section on Cakes

[12] Formula used to calculate nutritive values shown in Agr. Handb. No. 8, rev. 1963.

[13] This recipe doubled is adequate for 2-layer cake of 9-in. diam.; 1½ recipe for 2-layer cake of 8-in. diam.

TABLE 2.—*Fatty acid values for household measures and market units of foods*—Continued

[Item and footnote numbers correspond to those in table 1 of this publication. Values in parentheses denote imputed values usually from another form of the food or from a similar food. Dashes (—) denote lack of reliable data for a constituent believed to be present in a measurable amount. Calculated values, as those based on a recipe, are not in parentheses]

Item No.		Food, approximate measures, units, and weight (edible part unless footnotes indicate otherwise)			Principal sources of fat	Amount in edible part of foods: Total fat	Total saturated fatty acids	Unsaturated fatty acids: Oleic $C_{18}(-2H)$	Unsaturated fatty acids: Linoleic $C_{18}(-4H)$
(A)		(B)			(C)	(D)	(E)	(F)	(G)
				Grams		Grams	Grams	Grams	Grams
		Candy—Continued							
		Chocolate coated:							
590		Almonds:							
	a	Cup (single nuts)	1 cup	165	Almonds, vegetable shortening.	72.1	12.2	48.0	9.1
	b	Ounce, single nuts (approx. 6–8) or clusters.	1 oz	28	do	12.4	2.1	8.2	1.6
591		Chocolate fudge	1 oz	28	Vegetable shortening, chocolate.	4.5	1.5	2.5	.3
592		Chocolate fudge, with nuts	1 oz	28	Vegetable shortening, English walnuts, chocolate.	5.9	1.5	2.6	1.4
593		Coconut center	1 oz	28	Vegetable shortening, coconut.	5.0	2.9	1.9	Trace
594		Fondant:							
		Mints, round:							
	a	Large (approx. 2½-in. diam., ⅜ in. thick).	1 mint	35	Vegetable shortening	3.7	1.1	2.4	.2
	b	Small (approx. 1⅜-in. diam., ⅜ in. thick).	1 mint	11	do	1.2	.4	.7	.1
	c	Miniature (approx. ¾-in. diam., ⅜ in. thick).	1 mint	2.4	do	.3	.1	.2	Trace
		All chocolate-coated fondant:							
	d	Ounce (approx. ⅞ of 1 large mint (item 594a), 2½ small mints (item 594b), or 12 miniature mints (item 594c)).	1 oz	28	do	3.0	.9	1.9	.1
595		Fudge, caramel, and peanuts	1 oz	28	Vegetable shortening, peanuts.	5.1	1.4	2.9	.7
596		Fudge, peanuts, and caramel	1 oz	28	do	6.5	1.8	3.5	1.0
597		Honeycombed hard candy with peanut butter.	1 oz	28	Vegetable shortening, peanut butter.	5.5	1.6	3.1	.6
598		Nougat and caramel	1 oz	28	Vegetable shortening	3.9	1.2	2.4	.3
599		Peanuts:							
	a	Cup (single nuts)	1 cup	170	Peanuts, vegetable shortening.	70.2	18.3	36.7	12.2
	b	Ounce, single nuts (approx. 8–16) or clusters (approx. 2).	1 oz	28	do	11.7	3.0	6.1	2.0
600		Raisins:							
	a	Cup (single raisins)	1 cup	190	Cacao butter, chocolate, milk.	32.5	18.1	11.8	.7
	b	Ounce, single raisins (approx. 50 small or 18–28 large) or clusters.	1 oz	28	do	4.8	2.7	1.8	.1
601		Vanilla creams	1 oz	28	Vegetable shortening	4.8	1.4	2.8	.5

(A)		(B)			(C)	(D)	(E)	(F)	(G)
602		Fondant:							
		Candy corn (pieces, approx. ⅞ in. long, ½ in. wide, ¼ in. thick):							
	a	Cup (approx. 143 pieces)	1 cup	200	Vegetable shortening	4.0	1.0	2.0	0.9
	b	Ounce (approx. 20 pieces)	1 oz	28	do	.6	.1	.3	.1
		Fudge:							
603		Chocolate:							
	a	Ounce	1 oz	28	Vegetable shortening, chocolate.	3.5	1.2	1.6	.5
	b	Cubic inch	1 cu. in	21	do	2.6	.9	1.2	.4
604		Chocolate with nuts:							
	a	Ounce	1 oz	28	Vegetable shortening, English walnuts, chocolate.	4.9	1.2	1.7	1.6
	b	Cubic inch	1 cu. in	21	do	3.7	.9	1.3	1.2
605		Vanilla:							
	a	Ounce	1 oz	28	Vegetable shortening	3.1	.8	1.6	.7
	b	Cubic inch	1 cu. in	21	do	2.3	.6	1.2	.5
606		Vanilla with nuts:							
	a	Ounce	1 oz	28	Vegetable shortening, English walnuts.	4.6	.8	1.7	1.7
	b	Cubic inch	1 cu. in	21	do	3.4	.6	1.3	1.3
		Mints, coated. See Chocolate-coated fondant (items 594a–594d).							
611		Peanut bars	1 oz	28	Peanuts	9.1	2.0	3.9	2.6
612		Peanut brittle	1 oz	28	do	2.9	.6	1.3	.9
		Sugar coated:							
613		Almonds (approx. 1 in. long, ⅝ in. wide):							
	a	Cup	1 cup	195	Almonds	36.3	2.9	24.3	7.3
	b	Ounce (approx. 8 almonds)	1 oz	28	do	5.3	.4	3.5	1.1
614		Chocolate disks (approx. ½-in. diam.):							
	a	Cup	1 cup	197	Cacao butter, chocolate, milk.	38.8	21.7	14.0	.8
	b	Ounce (approx. 31 disks)	1 oz	28	do	5.6	3.1	2.0	.1
		Capicola. See Sausage, cold cuts, and luncheon meats (item 1989).							
628		**Cashew nuts,** roasted in oil:							
	a	Cup, whole kernels	1 cup	140		64.0	10.9	44.8	4.5
	b	Pound	1 lb	454		207.3	35.2	145.1	14.5
	c	Ounce (approx. 14 large kernels, 18 medium, or 26 small).	1 oz	28		13.0	2.2	9.1	.9
641		**Charlotte russe,** with ladyfingers, whipped-cream filling:							
	a	Yield from recipe [12] (approx. 24 ladyfingers (item 822); 2 cups of filling).	6 servings	685	Cream, egg	100.0	49.7	35.4	4.1
	b	Serving, ⅙ of recipe (item 641a)	1 serving	114	do	16.6	8.3	5.9	.7
		Cheeses, natural and processed; cheese foods; cheese spreads:							
		Natural cheeses:							
643		Blue or Roquefort type:							
		Prepackaged cut pieces:							
	a	Package, net wt., 4 oz	1 pkg	113		34.5	19.0	11.4	1.0
	b	Package, net wt., 3 oz	1 pkg	85		25.9	14.3	8.6	.8
		Cup (cheese crumbled):							
	c	Not packed	1 cup	135		41.2	22.7	13.6	1.2
	d	Packed	1 cup	249		75.9	41.8	25.0	2.3
	e	Pound	1 lb	454		138.3	76.1	45.6	4.2
	f	Ounce	1 oz	28		8.6	4.8	2.9	.3
	g	Cubic inch	1 cu. in	[14] 17.3		5.3	2.9	1.7	.2

[12] Formula used to calculate nutritive values shown in Agr. Handb. No. 8. rev. 1963.
[14] Based on specific gravity.

TABLE 2.—*Fatty acid values for household measures and market units of foods*—Continued

[Item and footnote numbers correspond to those in table 1 of this publication. Values in parentheses denote imputed values usually from another form of the food or from a similar food. Dashes (—) denote lack of reliable data for a constituent believed to be present in a measurable amount. Calculated values, as those based on a recipe, are not in parentheses]

Item No. (A)		Food, approximate measures, units, and weight (edible part unless footnotes indicate otherwise) (B)			Principal sources of fat (C)	Amount in edible part of foods: Total fat (D)	Total saturated fatty acids (E)	Unsaturated fatty acids: Oleic $C_{18}(-2H)$ (F)	Unsaturated fatty acids: Linoleic $C_{18}(-4H)$ (G)
				Grams		Grams	Grams	Grams	Grams
		Cheeses, natural and processed; cheese foods; cheese spreads—Continued							
		Natural cheeses—Continued							
644		Brick:							
		Prepackaged forms:							
		Cut piece:							
	a	Package, net wt., 10 oz	1 pkg	284		86.6	47.7	28.6	2.6
	b	Slice, 1/18 of piece (item 644a)	1 slice	16		4.9	2.7	1.6	.1
		Slice, wt., 1½ oz.:							
	c	Package, net wt., 8 oz.; 5 slices	1 pkg	227		69.2	38.1	22.8	2.1
	d	Slice	1 slice	45		13.7	7.6	4.5	.4
	e	Pound	1 lb	454		138.3	76.1	45.6	4.2
	f	Ounce	1 oz	28		8.6	4.8	2.9	.3
	g	Cubic inch	1 cu. in	[14] 17.2		5.2	2.9	1.7	.2
645		Camembert (domestic):							
		Prepackaged piece, net wt., 1⅓ oz.:							
	a	Package, net wt., 4 oz.; 3 pieces	1 pkg	113		27.9	15.3	9.2	.8
	b	Piece	1 piece	38		9.4	5.2	3.1	.3
	c	Cup	1 cup	246		60.8	33.4	20.0	1.8
	d	Pound	1 lb	454		112.0	61.6	37.0	3.4
	e	Ounce	1 oz	28		7.0	3.8	2.3	.2
	f	Cubic inch	1 cu. in	[14] 17.1		4.2	2.3	1.4	.1
646		Cheddar (domestic type):							
		Prepackaged forms:							
		Cut pieces:							
	a	Package, net wt., 12 oz	1 pkg	340		109.5	60.2	36.1	3.3
	b	Slice, 1/14 of piece (item 646a)	1 slice	24		7.7	4.3	2.6	.2
	c	Package, net wt., 10 oz	1 pkg	284		91.4	50.3	30.2	2.8
	d	Slice, 1/22 of piece (item 646c)	1 slice	13		4.2	2.3	1.4	.1
	e	Package, net wt., 8 oz	1 pkg	227		73.1	40.2	24.1	2.2
		Slices:							
		Round (midget Longhorn style), wt., ¾ oz.:							
	f	Package, net wt., 6 oz.; 8 slices	1 pkg	170		54.7	30.1	18.1	1.6
	g	Slice	1 slice	21		6.8	3.7	2.2	.2
		Semicircular (Longhorn style), wt., 1¼ oz.:							
	h	Package, net wt., 10 oz.; 8 slices	1 pkg	284		91.4	50.3	30.2	2.8
	i	Slice	1 slice	35		11.3	6.2	3.7	.3
		Rectangular, wt., 1½ oz.:							
	j	Package, net wt., 8 oz.; 5 slices	1 pkg	227		73.1	40.2	24.1	2.2
	k	Slice	1 slice	45		14.5	8.0	4.8	.4
		Squares, approx. ⅞ × ¾ × ½ in.: [15]							
	l	Package, net wt., 6 oz. (30 squares)	1 pkg	170		54.7	30.1	18.1	1.6
	m	Cup (approx. 26 squares) [16]	1 cup	140		45.1	24.8	14.9	1.4

(A)		(B)		(C)	(D)	(E)	(F)	(G)
	n	Shredded form, 1 cup (approx. 1 pkg.; net wt., 4 oz.).	1 cup or 1 pkg	113	36.4	20.0	12.0	1.1
	o	Pound	1 lb	454	146.1	80.3	48.2	4.4
	p	Ounce	1 oz	28	9.1	5.0	3.0	.3
	q	Cubic inch	1 cu. in	[14] 17.2	5.5	3.0	1.8	.2
647		Cottage cheese (cottage cheese dry curd with creaming mixture; 4.2% milk fat), large or small curd:						
		Prepackaged container:						
	a	Net wt., 32 oz. (2 lb.)	1 container	907	38.1	21.0	12.6	1.2
	b	Net wt., 12 oz	1 container	340	14.3	7.9	4.7	.4
		Cup (cheese spooned into cup):						
		Not packed:						
	c	Large curd	1 cup	225	9.5	5.2	3.1	.3
	d	Small curd	1 cup	210	8.8	4.9	2.9	.3
	e	Packed (large or small curd)	1 cup	245	10.3	5.7	3.4	.3
	f	Pound	1 lb	454	19.1	10.5	6.3	.6
	g	Ounce	1 oz	28	1.2	.7	.4	Trace
649		Cream:						
		Regular:						
		Prepackaged rectangular piece:						
	a	Package, net wt., 8 oz	1 pkg	227	85.6	47.1	28.2	2.6
	b	Package, net wt., 3 oz	1 pkg	85	32.0	17.6	10.6	1.0
	c	Cup	1 cup	232	87.5	48.1	28.9	2.6
	d	Tablespoon	1 tbsp	14	5.3	2.9	1.7	.2
	e	Cubic inch	1 cu. in	[14] 16.1	6.1	3.3	2.0	.2
		Whipped: [17]						
	f	Prepackaged container, net wt., 4 oz. (approx. ¾ cup).	1 container	113	42.6	23.4	14.1	1.3
	g	Cup	1 cup	155	58.4	32.1	19.3	1.8
	h	Tablespoon	1 tbsp	10	3.8	2.1	1.2	.1
		Regular and whipped:						
	i	Pound	1 lb	454	171.0	94.1	56.4	5.1
	j	Ounce	1 oz	28	10.7	5.9	3.5	.3
650		Limburger:						
		Prepackaged piece:						
	a	Package, net wt., 7 oz	1 pkg	198	55.4	30.5	18.3	1.7
	b	Slice, 1/27 of piece (item 650a)	1 slice	7	2.0	1.1	.6	.1
	c	Pound	1 lb	454	127.0	69.9	41.9	3.8
	d	Ounce	1 oz	28	7.9	4.4	2.6	.2
	e	Cubic inch	1 cu. in	18.0	5.0	2.8	1.7	.2
651		Parmesan:						
		Prepackaged forms:						
		Cut piece:						
	a	Package, net wt., 5 oz.; wedge	1 pkg	142	36.9	20.3	12.2	1.1
	b	Pound	1 lb	454	117.9	64.9	38.9	3.5
	c	Ounce	1 oz	28	7.4	4.1	2.4	.2
		Shredded: [18]						
		Cup:						
	d	Not packed	1 cup	80	22.3	12.3	7.4	.7
	e	Packed	1 cup	110	30.7	16.9	10.1	.9

[14] Based on specific gravity.
[15] Term "cubed" used on retail package.
[16] Weight per cup and fatty acid values also apply to 1 cup of diced cheese (pieces approx. ¼ size of these squares).
[17] Description and weights shown for whipped cream cheese apply to cream cheese that has been stirred or whipped until its volume has been increased 50%.
[18] Values shown for Parmesan cheese in Agr. Handb. No. 8, rev. 1963, do not apply to shredded and grated forms. For these forms, values shown in this table are based on data for 100 g. of cheese shown in Appendix A, table 3, p. 264.

TABLE 2.—*Fatty acid values for household measures and market units of foods*—Continued

[Item and footnote numbers correspond to those in table 1 of this publication. Values in parentheses denote imputed values usually from another form of the food or from a similar food. Dashes (—) denote lack of reliable data for a constituent believed to be present in a measurable amount. Calculated values, as those based on a recipe, are not in parentheses]

Item No. (A)	Food, approximate measures, units, and weight (edible part unless footnotes indicate otherwise) (B)			Principal sources of fat (C)	Amount in edible part of foods: Total fat (D)	Total saturated fatty acids (E)	Unsaturated fatty acids: Oleic $C_{18}(-2H)$ (F)	Unsaturated fatty acids: Linoleic $C_{18}(-4H)$ (G)
			Grams		*Grams*	*Grams*	*Grams*	*Grams*
	Cheeses, natural and processed; cheese foods; cheese spreads—Continued							
	Natural cheeses—Continued							
	Parmesan—Continued							
	Prepackaged forms—Continued							
	Shredded [18]—Continued							
f	Tablespoon	1 tbsp	5		1.4	0.8	0.5	Trace
g	Pound	1 lb	454		126.6	69.6	41.8	3.8
h	Ounce	1 oz	28		7.9	4.3	2.6	.2
	Grated: [18]							
	Cup:							
i	Not packed	1 cup	110		30.8	16.9	10.2	.9
j	Packed	1 cup	140		43.1	23.7	14.2	1.3
k	Tablespoon	1 tbsp	5		1.5	.8	.5	Trace
l	Pound	1 lb	454		139.7	76.8	46.1	4.2
m	Ounce	1 oz	28		8.7	4.8	2.9	.3
652	Swiss (domestic):							
	Prepackaged forms:							
	Cut piece:							
a	Package, net wt., 12 oz	1 pkg	340		95.2	52.4	31.4	2.9
b	Slice, 1/24 of piece (item 652a)	1 slice	14		3.9	2.2	1.3	.1
	Slice, wt., 1¼ oz.:							
c	Package, net wt., 8 oz.; approx. 7 slices.	1 pkg	227		63.6	35.0	21.0	1.9
d	Slice	1 slice	35		9.8	5.4	3.2	.3
e	Pound	1 lb	454		127.0	69.9	41.9	3.8
f	Ounce	1 oz	28		7.9	4.4	2.6	.2
g	Cubic inch [19]	1 cu. in	15.0		4.2	2.3	1.4	.1
	Pasteurized process cheese:							
653	American:							
	Prepackaged forms:							
	Loaves (rectangular pieces):							
a	Package, net wt., 32 oz. (2 lb.)	1 pkg	907		272.1	149.7	89.8	8.2
b	Slice, 1/34 of loaf (item 653a)	1 slice	27		8.1	4.5	2.7	.2
c	Package, net wt., 16 oz. (1 lb.)	1 pkg. or 1 lb. [20]	454		136.1	74.8	44.9	4.1
d	Slice, 1/24 of loaf (item 653c)	1 slice	19		5.7	3.1	1.9	.2
e	Package, net wt., 8 oz	1 pkg	227		68.1	37.5	22.5	2.0
f	Slice, 1/17 of loaf (item 653e)	1 slice	13		3.9	2.2	1.3	.1
	Cup:							
g	Packed into cup	1 cup	255		76.5	42.1	25.3	2.3
h	Diced, not packed	1 cup	140		42.0	23.1	13.9	1.3
i	Shredded, not packed	1 cup	113		33.9	18.7	11.2	1.0
	Slices:							

(A)		(B)		(C)	(D)	(E)	(F)	(G)
		Large slices marked for cutting into burger- and sandwich-size slices:						
	j	Package, net wt., 48 oz. (3 lb.)	1 pkg	1,361	408.3	224.6	134.7	12.2
	k	Package, net wt., 8 oz	1 pkg	227	68.1	37.5	22.5	2.0
	l	Package, net wt., 6 oz	1 pkg	170	51.0	28.1	16.8	1.5
		Slices cut from these packages:						
		Sandwich size:						
	m	Slice, wt., 1 oz	1 slice or 1 oz.[21]	28	8.5	4.7	2.8	.3
	n	Slice, wt., ¾ oz	1 slice	21	6.3	3.5	2.1	.2
		Burger size:						
	o	Slice, wt., ⅔ oz	1 slice	19	5.7	3.1	1.9	.2
	p	Slice, wt., ½ oz	1 slice	14	4.2	2.3	1.4	.1
	q	Cubic inch	1 cu. in	[14] 17.5	5.3	2.9	1.7	.2
654		Pimiento (American):						
		Prepackaged sandwich-size slices:						
		Slice, wt., 1 oz.:						
	a	Package, net wt., 8 oz.; 8 slices	1 pkg	227	68.6	37.7	22.6	2.1
	b	Slice	1 slice or 1 oz	28	8.6	4.7	2.8	.3
		Slice, wt., ¾ oz.:						
	c	Package, net wt., 12 oz.; 16 slices	1 pkg	340	102.7	56.5	33.9	3.1
	d	Slice	1 slice	21	6.3	3.5	2.1	.2
	e	Pound	1 lb	454	137.0	75.3	45.2	4.1
	f	Cubic inch	1 cu. in	17.5	5.3	2.9	1.7	.2
655		Swiss:						
		Prepackaged sandwich-size slices:						
		Slice, wt., 1 oz.:						
	a	Package, net wt., 8 oz.; 8 slices	1 pkg	227	61.1	33.6	20.2	1.8
	b	Slice	1 slice or 1 oz	28	7.6	4.2	2.5	.2
		Slice, wt., ¾ oz.:						
	c	Package, net wt., 12 oz.; 16 slices	1 pkg	340	91.5	50.3	30.2	2.8
	d	Slice	1 slice	21	5.6	3.1	1.9	.2
	e	Pound	1 lb	454	122.0	67.1	40.3	3.7
	f	Cubic inch	1 cu. in	[14] 17.9	4.8	2.7	1.6	.1
656		**Pasteurized process cheese food, American:**						
		Prepackaged forms:						
		Cut piece:						
	a	Package, net wt., 6 oz. (roll)	1 pkg	170	40.8	22.4	13.5	1.2
	b	Slice, 1/18 of roll (item 656a)	1 slice	9	2.2	1.2	.7	.1
	c	Tablespoon	1 tbsp	14	3.4	1.8	1.1	.1
		Slices, sandwich size:						
		Slice, wt., 1 oz.:						
	d	Package, net wt., 8 oz.; 8 slices	1 pkg	227	54.5	30.0	18.0	1.6
	e	Slice	1 slice or 1 oz	28	6.8	3.7	2.2	.2
		Slice, wt., ¾ oz.:						
	f	Package, net wt., 12 oz.; 16 slices	1 pkg	340	81.6	44.9	26.9	2.4
	g	Slice	1 slice	21	5.0	2.8	1.7	.2
	h	Pound	1 lb	454	108.9	59.9	35.9	3.3
	i	Cubic inch	1 cu. in	17.5	4.2	2.3	1.4	.1

[14] Based on specified gravity.

[18] Values shown for Parmesan cheese in Agr. Handb. No. 8, rev. 1963, do not apply to shredded and grated forms. For these forms, values shown in this table are based on data for 100 g. of cheese shown in Appendix A, table 3, p. 264.

[19] Weight per cubic inch will vary with size and number of eyes. Weight given applies to cheese with eyes of size commonly found in retail market. Weight per cubic inch of portions of cheese without eyes is 17.8 g.

[20] Use also for 1 lb. of other form or forms listed for this item.

[21] Use also for 1 oz. of other form or forms listed for this item.

TABLE 2.—*Fatty acid values for household measures and market units of foods*—Continued

[Item and footnote numbers correspond to those in table 1 of this publication. Values in parentheses denote imputed values usually from another form of the food or from a similar food. Dashes (—) denote lack of reliable data for a constituent believed to be present in a measurable amount. Calculated values, as those based on a recipe, are not in parentheses]

Item No. (A)	Food, approximate measures, units, and weight (edible part unless footnotes indicate otherwise) (B)			Principal sources of fat (C)	Amount in edible part of foods: Total fat (D)	Total saturated fatty acids (E)	Unsaturated fatty acids: Oleic $C_{18}(-2H)$ (F)	Unsaturated fatty acids: Linoleic $C_{18}(-4H)$ (G)
			Grams		*Grams*	*Grams*	*Grams*	*Grams*
	Cheeses, natural and processed; cheese foods; cheese spreads—Continued							
657	**Pasturized process cheese spread, American:**							
	Prepackaged forms:							
	Loaves (rectangular pieces):							
a	Package, net wt., 32 oz. (2 lb.)	1 pkg	907		194.1	106.8	64.0	5.8
b	Slice, 1/34 of loaf (item 657a)	1 slice	27		5.8	3.2	1.9	.2
c	Package, net wt., 16 oz. (1 lb.)	1 pkg. or 1 lb	454		97.1	53.4	32.0	2.9
d	Slice, 1/24 of loaf (item 657c)	1 slice	19		4.1	2.2	1.3	.1
e	Package, net wt., 8 oz	1 pkg	227		48.6	26.7	16.0	1.5
f	Slice, 1/17 of loaf (item 657e)	1 slice	13		2.8	1.5	.9	.1
	Cup:							
g	Packed into cup	1 cup	255		54.6	30.0	18.0	1.6
h	Diced, not packed	1 cup	140		30.0	16.5	9.9	.9
i	Shredded, packed	1 cup	113		24.2	13.3	8.0	.7
j	Tablespoon	1 tbsp	14		3.0	1.6	1.0	.1
k	Cubic inch	1 cu. in	17.5		3.7	2.1	1.2	.1
	Packed in glass jars and pressurized can:							
l	Jar, net wt., 5 oz.[22 23]	1 jar	142		30.4	16.7	10.0	.9
m	Can (pressurized), net wt., 4¾ oz.[23]	1 can	135		28.9	15.9	9.5	.9
n	Ounce	1 oz	28		6.1	3.3	2.0	.2
659	**Cheese souffle**, from home recipe:							
a	Whole (yield from recipe[12]), 7⅞ × 7⅞ × 1⅜ in. (baked in 8-in. square pan), or 6½-in. diam., 2 in. high (baked in 7-in.-diam. casserole).	1 souffle	440	Butter, cheese, egg, milk	75.2	37.9	26.4	2.9
b	Portion, 3¹¹⁄₁₆ × 3¹¹⁄₁₆ × 1⅜ in. (baked in 8-in. square pan), or 5⅛-in. arc, 3¼ × 3¼ in., 2 in. high (baked in 7-in.-diam. casserole); ¼ of souffle (item 659a).	1 portion	110	do	18.8	9.5	6.6	.7
c	Cup (collapsed souffle)	1 cup	95	do	16.2	8.2	5.7	.6
d	Pound	1 lb	454	do	77.6	39.1	27.2	2.9
e	Ounce	1 oz	28	do	4.8	2.4	1.7	.2
660	**Cheese straws**, 5 in. long, ⅜ in. wide, ⅜ in. high:							
a	Made with vegetable shortening	10 pieces	60	Vegetable shortening, cheese.	17.9	6.4	7.8	2.8
b	Made with lard	10 pieces	60	Lard, cheese	17.9	7.9	7.4	1.4
	Chicken, cooked:							
	All classes, roasted:							
682	Light meat without skin:							
	Cup (not packed):							
a	Chopped or diced	1 cup	140		4.8	1.5	1.8	1.0
b	Ground	1 cup	110		3.7	1.2	1.4	.7
c	Pound	1 lb	454		15.4	4.9	5.9	3.1
d	Piece, approx. 2½ in. long, 1⅞ in. wide, ¼ in. thick.	2 pieces	50		1.7	.5	.6	.3

(A)		(B)		(C)		(D)	(E)	(F)	(G)
684		Dark meat without skin:							
		Cup (not packed):							
	a	Chopped or diced	1 cup	140		8.8	2.8	3.3	1.8
	b	Ground	1 cup	110		6.9	2.2	2.6	1.4
	c	Pound	1 lb	454		28.6	9.2	10.8	5.7
	d	Piece, approx. 1⅞ in. long, 1 in. wide, ¼ in. thick.	4 pieces	40		2.5	.8	1.0	.5
685		**Broilers**, ready-to-cook, broiled, flesh only:							
	a	Yield from 1 lb., ready-to-cook broilers	7.1 oz	201		7.6	2.5	2.9	1.5
	b	Pound	1 lb	454		17.2	5.5	6.5	3.4
	c	Half broiler (wt., raw, ready-to-cook, 1¾ lb.; wt., cooked, 10.4 oz.; refuse: bones and skin, 40%).[2]	½ broiler	294		6.7	2.2	2.5	1.3
		Fryers, ready-to-cook, fried:							
687		Flesh, skin, giblets:							
	a	Yield from 1 lb., ready-to-cook fryers	8 oz	227	Vegetable shortening	26.8	8.0	11.3	5.6
	b	Pound	1 lb	454	do	53.5	16.1	22.5	11.2
	c	Whole fryer (wt., raw, ready-to-cook, with giblets, 2½ lb.; wt., cooked, 1⅔ lb.; refuse: bones, 24%).[2]	1 fryer	750	do	67.3	20.2	28.3	14.1
701		Light meat without skin:							
	a	Pound	1 lb	454	do	27.7	7.8	12.8	5.8
	b	Piece, approx. 2½ in. long, 1⅞ in. wide, ¼ in. thick.	2 pieces	50	do	3.1	.9	1.4	.6
703		Dark meat without skin:							
	a	Pound	1 lb	454	do	42.2	12.2	18.1	8.8
	b	Piece, approx. 1⅞ in. long, 1 in. wide, ¼ in. thick.	4 pieces	40	do	3.7	1.1	1.6	.8
		Cut-up parts from 2½-lb. ready-to-cook fryer, fried:							
705		Back (refuse: bones, 33%):[2]							
	a	Pound	1 lb	454	do	64.4	19.3	26.4	13.5
	b	Piece	1 back	60	do	8.5	2.6	3.5	1.8
707		Breast without ribs (refuse: bones, 16%):[2]							
	a	Pound	1 lb	454	do	24.4	7.1	10.5	5.1
	b	Piece	½ breast[24]	94	do	5.1	1.5	2.2	1.1
709		Drumstick (refuse: bones, 33%):[2]							
	a	Pound	1 lb	454	do	31.0	9.0	13.3	6.5
	b	Piece	1 drumstick	56	do	3.8	1.1	1.6	.8
711		Neck (refuse: bones, 27%):[2]							
	a	Pound	1 lb	454	do	57.6	17.8	23.0	11.5
	b	Piece	1 neck	60	do	7.6	2.4	3.0	1.5
713		Rib section (refuse: bones, 31%):[2]							
	a	Pound	1 lb	454	do	48.2	14.0	20.7	10.1
	b	Piece	½ rib section	20	do	2.1	.6	.9	.4
715		Thigh (refuse: bones, 21%):[2]							
	a	Pound	1 lb	454	do	40.8	12.3	16.7	8.6
	b	Piece	1 thigh	65	do	5.9	1.8	2.4	1.2
717		Wing (refuse: bones, 39%):[2]							
	a	Pound	1 lb	454	do	41.0	12.3	17.2	8.6
	b	Piece	1 wing	50	do	4.5	1.4	1.9	.9

[2] Measure and weight apply to food as it is described with inedible part or parts (refuse) included.
[12] Formula used to calculate nutritive values shown in Agr. Handb. No. 8, rev. 1963.
[22] Available also in 1-lb. and 8-oz. jars. For values of these sizes, use items 657c and 657e.
[23] For 1 cup, use item 657g; for 1 tbsp., item 657j.
[24] Refers to ½ breast portion of 2½-lb. chicken.

TABLE 2.—*Fatty acid values for household measures and market units of foods*—Continued

[Item and footnote numbers correspond to those in table 1 of this publication. Values in parentheses denote imputed values usually from another form of the food or from a similar food. Dashes (—) denote lack of reliable data for a constituent believed to be present in a measurable amount. Calculated values, as those based on a recipe, are not in parentheses]

Item No. (A)		Food, approximate measures, units, and weight (edible part unless footnotes indicate otherwise) (B)			Principal sources of fat (C)	Amount in edible part of foods: Total fat (D)	Total saturated fatty acids (E)	Unsaturated fatty acids: Oleic $C_{18}(-2H)$ (F)	Unsaturated fatty acids: Linoleic $C_{18}(-4H)$ (G)
				Grams		*Grams*	*Grams*	*Grams*	*Grams*
		Chicken, cooked—Continued							
		Roasters, roasted:							
721		Flesh, skin, giblets:							
	a	Yield from 1 lb., ready-to-cook roasters	8.4 oz	238		33.3	10.7	12.7	6.7
	b	Pound	1 lb	454		63.5	20.3	24.1	12.7
728		Light meat without skin:							
		Cup (not packed):							
	a	Chopped or diced	1 cup	140		6.9	2.2	2.6	1.4
	b	Ground	1 cup	110		5.4	1.7	2.0	1.1
	c	Pound	1 lb	454		22.2	7.1	8.4	4.4
	d	Piece, approx. 2½ in. long, 1⅞ in. wide, ¼ in. thick.	2 pieces	50		2.5	.8	.9	.5
730		Dark meat without skin:							
		Cup (not packed):							
	a	Chopped or diced	1 cup	140		9.1	2.9	3.5	1.8
	b	Ground	1 cup	110		7.2	2.3	2.7	1.4
	c	Pound	1 lb	454		29.5	9.4	11.2	5.9
	d	Piece, approx. 1⅞ in. long, 1 in. wide, ¼ in. thick.	4 pieces	40		2.6	.8	1.0	.5
		Hens and cocks, stewed:							
734		Flesh, skin, giblets:							
	a	Yield from 1 lb., ready-to-cook hens or cocks.	8 oz	227		50.4	16.1	19.2	10.1
	b	Pound	1 lb	454		100.7	32.2	38.3	20.1
738		Flesh only:							
		Cup (not packed):							
	a	Chopped or diced	1 cup	140		12.5	4.0	4.7	2.5
	b	Ground	1 cup	110		9.8	3.1	3.7	2.0
	c	Pound	1 lb	454		40.4	12.9	15.3	8.1
741		Light meat without skin:							
		Cup (not packed):							
	a	Chopped or diced	1 cup	140		6.6	2.1	2.5	1.3
	b	Ground	1 cup	110		5.2	1.7	2.0	1.0
	c	Pound	1 lb	454		21.3	6.8	8.1	4.3
	d	Piece, approx. 2½ in. long, 1⅞ in. wide, ¼ in. thick.	2 pieces	50		2.4	.8	.9	.5
743		Dark meat without skin:							
		Cup (not packed):							
	a	Chopped or diced	1 cup	140		13.3	4.3	5.1	2.7
	b	Ground	1 cup	110		10.5	3.3	4.0	2.1
	c	Pound	1 lb	454		43.1	13.8	16.4	8.6
	d	Piece, approx. 1⅞ in. long, 1 in. wide, ¼ in. thick.	4 pieces	40		3.8	1.2	1.4	.8
747		**Chicken, canned**, meat only, boned:							
	a	Can, net wt., 5½ oz. (solid pack)	1 can	156		18.3	5.8	6.9	3.7

(A)		(B)		(C)		(D)	(E)	(F)	(G)
	b	Cup	1 cup	205		24.0	7.7	9.1	4.8
	c	Pound	1 lb	454		53.1	17.0	20.2	10.6
748		**Chicken a la king,** cooked, from home recipe:							
	a	Cup	1 cup	245	Chicken, vegetable shortening, cream, egg, milk.	34.3	12.7	14.3	3.3
	b	Pound	1 lb	454	do	63.5	23.5	26.5	6.2
749		**Chicken fricassee,** cooked, from home recipe:							
	a	Cup	1 cup	240	Chicken	22.3	7.2	8.5	4.5
	b	Pound	1 lb	454	do	42.2	13.5	16.0	8.4
		Chicken potpie:							
750		Home prepared, baked:							
	a	Pie, whole (9-in. diam.)	1 pie	[7] 698	Vegetable shortening, cream, chicken, butter.	94.2	32.9	39.3	15.4
	b	Piece, ⅓ of pie (item 750a)	1 piece	232	do	31.3	10.9	13.1	5.1
	c	Pound	1 lb	454	do	61.2	21.4	25.5	10.0
752		**Chicken and noodles,** cooked, from home recipe:							
	a	Cup	1 cup	240	Chicken, egg	18.5	5.9	7.1	3.5
	b	Pound	1 lb	454	do	34.9	11.2	13.4	6.7
753		**Chickpeas** or garbanzos, mature seeds, dry, raw:							
	a	Cup	1 cup	200		9.6	.9	4.8	3.5
	b	Pound	1 lb	454		21.8	2.0	10.9	7.8
756		**Chili con carne,** with beans, canned:							
		Can and approx. contents:							
	a	Size, 300 × 407 [5] (No. 300); net wt., 15–15½ oz.	1 can	430	Beef	26.2	12.6	11.5	.5
	b	Size, 603 × 700 [5] (No. 10); net wt., 108 oz. (6 lb. 12 oz.).	1 can	3,062	do	186.8	89.7	82.1	3.7
	c	Cup	1 cup	255	do	15.6	7.5	6.8	.3
	d	Pound	1 lb	454	do	27.7	13.3	12.2	.5
		Chocolate:							
759		Bitter or baking:							
	a	Cup, grated	1 cup	132		70.0	39.2	25.9	1.4
	b	Ounce	1 oz	28		15.0	8.4	5.6	.3
		Bittersweet. See Candy (item 584).							
		Chocolate sirup (or topping):							
760		Thin type (chocolate flavored):							
	a	Pound (12-fl. oz. can)	1 lb. or 1 can	454		9.1	5.1	3.4	.2
	b	Cup	1 cup	300		6.0	3.4	2.2	.1
	c	Fluid ounce	1 fl. oz. or 2 tbsp	37.5		.8	.4	.3	Trace
761		Fudge type:							
	a	Pound (12-fl. oz. can)	1 lb. or 1 can	454	Chocolate, milk, butter	62.1	34.6	22.2	1.5
	b	Cup	1 cup	300	do	41.1	22.9	14.7	1.0
	c	Fluid ounce (2 tbsp.)	1 fl. oz. or 2 tbsp	37.5	do	5.1	2.9	1.8	.1
		Chop suey with meat (without noodles):							
762		Cooked, from home recipe:							
	a	Cup	1 cup	250	Butter, beef, pork	17.0	8.5	6.2	.7
	b	Pound	1 lb	454	do	30.8	15.5	11.2	1.3
		Chow mein, chicken (without noodles):							
764		Cooked, from home recipe:							
	a	Cup	1 cup	250	Chicken, corn oil, soybeans.	10.0	2.4	3.4	3.1
	b	Pound	1 lb	454	do	18.1	4.4	6.2	5.7

[5] Dimensions of can: 1st dimension represents diameter; 2d dimension, height of can. 1st or left-hand digit in each dimension gives number of whole inches; next 2 digits give aditional fraction of dimension expressed as 16th of an inch.

[7] Yield of formula used to calculate nutritive values in Agr. Handb. No. 8, rev. 1963.

TABLE 2.—*Fatty acid values for household measures and market units of foods*—Continued

[Item and footnote numbers correspond to those in table 1 of this publication. Values in parentheses denote imputed values usually from another form of the food or from a similar food. Dashes (—) denote lack of reliable data for a constituent believed to be present in a measurable amount. Calculated values, as those based on a recipe, are not in parentheses]

Item No. (A)	Food, approximate measures, units, and weight (edible part unless footnotes indicate otherwise) (B)			Principal sources of fat (C)	Amount in edible part of foods: Total fat (D)	Total saturated fatty acids (E)	Unsaturated fatty acids: Oleic $C_{18}(-2H)$ (F)	Unsaturated fatty acids: Linoleic $C_{18}(-4H)$ (G)
			Grams		*Grams*	*Grams*	*Grams*	*Grams*
	Cocoa and chocolate-flavored beverage powders:[25]							
778	Cocoa powder with nonfat dry milk	1 oz. or approx. 4 heaping tsp.	28	Cocoa, milk	0.8	0.5	0.3	Trace
779	Cocoa powder without milk	1 oz. or approx. 4 heaping tsp.	28	Cocoa	.6	.3	.2	Trace
	Cocoa, dry powder:							
	Medium fat:							
	High medium fat:							
783 or 784	Plain or processed with alkali:							
a	Cup	1 cup	86		16.3	9.2	6.0	0.3
b	Tablespoon	1 tbsp	5.4		1.0	.6	.4	Trace
c	Ounce (approx. 5¼ tbsp.)	1 oz	28		5.4	3.0	2.0	.1
	Low medium fat:							
785 or 786	Plain or processed with alkali:							
a	Cup	1 cup	86		10.9	6.1	4.0	.2
b	Tablespoon	1 tbsp	5.4		.7	.4	.3	Trace
c	Ounce (approx. 5¼ tbsp.)	1 oz	28		3.6	2.0	1.3	.1
788	**Coconut cream** (liquid expressed from grated coconut meat):							
a	Cup	1 cup	240		77.3	66.5	5.4	Trace
b	Tablespoon	1 tbsp	15		4.8	4.2	.3	Trace
	Coconut meat:							
789	Fresh:							
a	In shell (refuse: shell, brown skin, water, 48%).[2]	1 coconut	763		140.1	120.5	9.8	Trace
	Meat only:							
b	Piece, approx. 2 × 2 × ½ in	1 piece	45		15.9	13.7	1.1	Trace
	Shredded or grated, spooned into cup:							
c	Not packed	1 cup	80		28.2	24.3	2.0	Trace
d	Packed	1 cup	130		45.9	39.5	3.2	Trace
e	Pound	1 lb	454		160.1	137.7	11.2	Trace
790	Dried, unsweetened (desiccated)	1 lb	454		294.4	253.2	20.6	Trace
792	**Coconut milk** (liquid expressed from mixture of grated coconut meat and coconut water).	1 cup	240		59.8	51.4	4.2	Trace
	Coleslaw,[26 27] made with—							
801	French dressing (homemade):							
a	Made with corn oil	1 cup	120	Corn oil	14.8	1.5	4.1	7.7
b	Made with cottonseed oil	1 cup	120	Cottonseed oil	14.8	3.6	3.1	7.3
802	French dressing (commercial)	1 cup	120	Soybean oil, cottonseed oil, corn oil.	8.8	1.5	1.8	4.5
803	Mayonnaise	1 cup	120	do	16.8	3.0	3.6	8.4
804	Salad dressing (mayonnaise type)	1 cup	120	do	9.5	1.7	2.1	4.6

(A)		(B)		(C)		(D)	(E)	(F)	(G)
		Cookies: [28]							
		Brownies with nuts:							
813		Baked from home recipe; rectangular piece, 3 × 1 × ⅞ in., or square piece, 1¾ × 1¾ × ⅞ in.:							
	a	Made with vegetable shortening	1 brownie	20	Pecans, vegetable shortening, chocolate, egg.	6.3	1.4	3.3	1.1
	b	Made with butter	1 brownie	20	Pecans, butter, chocolate, egg.	6.0	2.0	2.8	.6
814		Frozen, with chocolate icing, commercial:							
	a	Container, net wt., 13 oz. (rectangular piece, 7½ × 5¼ × ⅞ in.)	1 container	368	Pecans, butter, chocolate, vegetable shortening, egg, milk.	75.8	25.6	35.9	8.4
	b	Brownie, 1½ × 1¾ × ⅞ in., 1/15 of container (item 814a).	1 brownie	24.5	do	5.0	1.7	2.4	.6
		Chocolate chip:							
817		Baked from home recipe; cooky, 2⅓-in. diam.:							
	a	Made with vegetable shortening	4 cookies	40	Vegetable shortening, chocolate, walnuts, egg.	12.0	3.4	5.1	2.8
	b	Made with butter	4 cookies	40	Butter, chocolate, walnuts, egg.	11.2	5.3	3.6	1.3
818		Commercial type:							
		Cooky, 2¼-in. diam., ⅜ in. thick:							
	a	Package, net wt., 14½ oz. (approx. 39 cookies).	1 pkg	411	Vegetable shortening, chocolate, walnuts, egg.	86.3	26.2	32.4	21.3
	b	Cooky	10 cookies	105	do	22.1	6.7	8.3	5.4
		Cooky, 1¾-in. diam., ½ in. thick:							
	c	Package, net wt., 7¾ oz. (approx. 30 cookies).	1 pkg	220	do	46.2	14.0	17.3	11.4
	d	Cooky	10 cookies	73	do	15.3	4.7	5.8	3.8
		Cooky, 1¾-in. diam., ⅜ in. thick:							
	e	Package, net wt., 15 oz. (approx. 80 cookies).	1 pkg	425	do	89.3	27.1	33.5	22.0
	f	Cooky	10 cookies	53	do	11.1	3.4	4.2	2.7
	g	Pound (approx. 43 cookies (item 818b), 62 cookies (item 818d), or 86 cookies (item 818f)).	1 lb	454	do	95.3	28.9	35.7	23.5
819		Coconut bars, 2⅜ × 1⅝ × ⅜ in. or 3 × 1¼ × ¼ in.:							
	a	Cooky	10 cookies	90	Vegetable shortening, coconut, egg.	22.1	8.4	8.9	3.6
	b	Pound (approx. 50 cookies)	1 lb	454	do	111.1	42.6	44.7	18.3
820		Fig bars (square, 1⅝ × 1⅝ × ⅜ in., or rectangular, 1½ × 1¾ × ½ in.):							
	a	Package, net wt., 16 oz. (1 lb.); approx. 32 cookies.	1 pkg. or 1 lb	454	Vegetable shortening, egg, milk.	25.4	6.9	12.1	4.9
	b	Cooky	4 cookies	56	do	3.1	.9	1.5	.6
821		Gingersnaps, 2-in. diam., ¼ in. thick:							
	a	Package, net wt., 16 oz. (1 lb.); approx. 65 cookies.	1 pkg. or 1 lb	454	do	40.4	10.6	19.3	8.6
	b	Cooky	10 cookies	70	do	6.2	1.6	3.0	1.3

[2] Measure and weight apply to food as it is described with inedible part or parts (refuse) included.
[25] Heaping teaspoon refers to ordinary teaspoon rather than to standard measuring teaspoon.
[26] Values are for product immediately after preparation. Values for fat and fatty acids are reduced if dressing drains from slaw and is not served.
[27] Weights per cup based on coleslaw made with finely shredded or chopped cabbage.
[28] Products are commercial unless otherwise specified.

TABLE 2.—*Fatty acid values for household measures and market units of foods*—Continued

[Item and footnote numbers correspond to those in table 1 of this publication. Values in parentheses denote imputed values usually from another form of the food or from a similar food. Dashes (—) denote lack of reliable data for a constituent believed to be present in a measurable amount. Calculated values, as those based on a recipe, are not in parentheses]

Item No. (A)		Food, approximate measures, units, and weight (edible part unless footnotes indicate otherwise) (B)			Principal sources of fat (C)	Amount in edible part of foods: Total fat (D)	Total saturated fatty acids (E)	Unsaturated fatty acids: Oleic $C_{18}(-2H)$ (F)	Unsaturated fatty acids: Linoleic $C_{18}(-4H)$ (G)
				Grams		*Grams*	*Grams*	*Grams*	*Grams*
		Cookies [28]—Continued							
822		Ladyfingers, 3¼ × 1⅜ × 1⅛ in. (dimensions before split lengthwise):							
	a	Package, net wt., 3 oz. (approx. 8 ladyfingers split lengthwise).	1 pkg	85	Egg	6.6	2.1	2.9	0.5
	b	Ladyfinger	4 ladyfingers	44	do	3.4	1.1	1.5	.3
	c	Pound (approx. 41 ladyfingers)	1 lb	454	do	35.4	11.1	15.4	2.9
825		Molasses:							
	a	Cooky, 3⅝-in. diam., ¾ in. thick	1 cooky	32.5	Vegetable shortening, egg.	3.4	.9	1.7	.7
	b	Pound (approx. 14 cookies)	1 lb	454	do	48.1	12.1	23.4	10.4
826		Oatmeal with raisins, 2⅝-in. diam., ¼ in. thick:							
	a	Package, net wt., 14 oz. (approx. 30 cookies).	1 pkg	397	Vegetable shortening, oatmeal, egg, milk.	61.1	15.7	29.1	14.1
	b	Cooky	4 cookies	52	do	8.0	2.1	3.8	1.8
	c	Pound (approx. 35 cookies)	1 lb	454	do	69.9	18.0	33.3	16.1
828		Raisin (biscuit type):							
	a	Package, net wt., 7½ oz. (3 rectangular pieces, 10⅛ × 2¼ × ¼ in.; each marked for cutting into 4 or 5 cookies).	1 pkg	213	Vegetable shortening, egg, milk.	11.3	3.1	5.3	2.2
	b	Cooky, 2¼ × 2½ × ¼ in.; 1/12 of pkg. (item 828a).	4 cookies	71	do	3.8	1.0	1.8	.7
	c	Cooky, 2¼ × 2 × ¼ in.; 1/15 of pkg. (item 828a).	4 cookies	57	do	3.0	.8	1.4	.6
	d	Pound (approx. 25½ cookies (item 828b) or 32 cookies (item 828c)).	1 lb	454	do	24.0	6.5	11.3	4.7
829		Sandwich type (chocolate or vanilla):							
	a	Package, net wt., 16 oz. (1 lb.); approx. 31 cookies (item 829b) or 45 cookies (item 829c).	1 pkg. or 1 lb	454	Vegetable shortening, chocolate (chocolate only), egg.	102.1	27.6	49.8	21.1
		Cooky:							
	b	Oval, cross section, 3⅛ × 1¼ in., ⅜ in. thick.	4 cookies	60	do	13.5	3.7	6.6	2.8
	c	Round, 1¾-in. diam., ⅜ in. thick	4 cookies	40	do	9.0	2.4	4.4	1.9
830		Shortbread, 1⅝ × 1⅝ × ¼ in.:							
	a	Package, net wt., 10¼ oz. (approx. 40 cookies).	1 pkg	291	Vegetable shortening, egg.	67.2	16.8	33.2	14.9
	b	Cooky	10 cookies	75	do	17.3	4.3	8.6	3.8
	c	Pound (approx. 60 cookies)	1 lb	454	do	104.8	26.2	51.8	23.2
831		Sugar, soft, thick, home recipe; cooky, 2¼-in. diam., ¼ in. thick:							
	a	Made with vegetable shortening	10 cookies	80	Vegetable shortening, egg, milk.	13.4	3.6	6.5	2.8
	b	Made with butter	10 cookies	80	Butter, egg, milk	12.2	6.4	4.1	.5
832		Sugar wafers:							
		Cooky, 3½ × 1 × ½ in.:							

(A)		(B)			(C)	(D)	(E)	(F)	(G)
	a	Package, net wt., 13¼ oz. (approx. 40 cookies).	1 pkg	376	Vegetable shortening, egg.	72.9	18.5	36.0	15.5
	b	Cooky	10 cookies	95	do	18.4	4.7	9.1	3.9
		Cooky, 2½ × ¾ × ¼ in.:							
	c	Package, net wt., 8½ oz. (approx. 69 cookies).	1 pkg	241	do	46.8	11.8	23.1	10.0
	d	Cooky	10 cookies	35	do	6.8	1.7	3.4	1.5
	e	Cooky, 3½ × 1½ × ¼ in	10 cookies	70	do	13.6	3.4	6.7	2.9
	f	Cooky, 1¾ × 1½ × ¾ in	10 cookies	90	do	17.5	4.4	8.6	3.7
	g	Pound (approx. 48 cookies (item 832b) or 128 cookies (item 832d)).	1 lb	454	do	88.0	22.3	43.5	18.7
		Cookies, prepared and baked from mixes:							
837		Brownies, with enriched flour; made with incomplete mix, egg, water, nuts; rectangular piece, 3 × 1 × ⅞ in., or square piece, 1¾ × 1¾ × ⅞ in.	1 brownie	20	Vegetable shortening, walnuts, cocoa, egg.	4.0	.8	1.5	1.3
839		Plain, with unenriched flour; made with egg, water; cooky, 1⅝-in. diam., ⅜ in. thick.	10 cookies	56	Vegetable shortening, egg.	13.6	3.4	6.7	2.9
		Cooking oil. See Oils (item 1401).							
		Cooky dough, plain, chilled in roll:							
841		Unbaked; container, net wt., 18 oz. (1 lb. 2 oz.); roll, 10½ in. long, 1¾-in. diam.	1 roll	510	do	115.3	28.9	57.2	25.0
842		Baked; cooky, 2½-in. diam., ¼ in. thick; 1/40 of roll (item 841).	4 cookies	48	do	12.0	3.0	6.0	2.6
860		**Corn flour:**[29]							
	a	Cup	1 cup	117		3.0	.3	1.0	1.3
	b	Pound	1 lb	454		11.8	1.3	4.0	5.2
861		**Corn fritters** (2-in. diam., 1½ in. thick):							
	a	Yield from recipe[12]	17¾ fritters	622	Vegetable shortening, egg, milk, butter.	133.7	36.1	64.2	27.0
	b	Fritter	1 fritter	35	do	7.5	2.0	3.6	1.5
		Corn muffins. See Muffins, corn (items 1347–1348), and Muffin mix, corn, and muffins and cornbread baked from mix (item 1350).							
		Corn oil. See Oils (items 1401a–1401e).							
875		**Corn pudding:**							
	a	Yield from recipe[12]	3 cups	740	Milk, vegetable shortening, egg.	34.8	13.0	14.3	2.9
	b	Cup	1 cup	245	do	11.5	4.3	4.7	1.0
		Cornbread, baked from home recipe:							
		Cornbread, southern style, made with—							
876		Whole-ground cornmeal:							
		Made with lard:							
	a	Whole (7½ × 7½ × 1½ in.; vol., 84.4 cu. in.).	1 cornbread	[7]703	Lard, egg	50.6	16.2	21.8	7.9
	b	Piece (2½ × 2½ × 1½ in.; vol., 9.4 cu. in.; ⅑ of cornbread).	1 piece	78	do	5.6	1.8	2.4	.9
		Made with vegetable shortening:[30]							
	c	Whole (7½ × 7½ × 1½ in.; vol., 84.4 cu. in.).	1 cornbread	[7]703	Vegetable shortening, egg.	50.6	12.4	23.1	11.3
	d	Piece (2½ × 2½ × 1½ in.; vol., 9.4 cu. in.; ⅑ of cornbread).	1 piece	78	do	5.6	1.4	2.6	1.3

[7] Yield of formula used to calculate nutritive values in Agr. Handb. No. 8, rev. 1963.
[12] Formula used to calculate nutritive values shown in Agr. Handb. No. 8, rev. 1963.
[28] Products are commercial unless otherwise specified.
[29] Weight per cup is based on method of pouring product from container into measuring cup with as little fall as possible, then leveling with straight edge. For corn flour, see Appendix B, section on Nonliquid Foods and section on Cornmeals and Related Products
[30] Values based on these revised amounts per 100 g. of product: Total saturated fatty acids 1.8 g., oleic acid 3.3 g., linoleic acid 1.6 g.

TABLE 2.—*Fatty acid values for household measures and market units of foods*—Continued

[Item and footnote numbers correspond to those in table 1 of this publication. Values in parentheses denote imputed values usually from another form of the food or from a similar food. Dashes (—) denote lack of reliable data for a constituent believed to be present in a measurable amount. Calculated values, as those based on a recipe, are not in parentheses]

Item No. (A)		Food, approximate measures, units, and weight (edible part unless footnotes indicate otherwise) (B)			Principal sources of fat (C)	Total fat (D)	Total saturated fatty acids (E)	Unsaturated fatty acids: Oleic $C_{18}(-2H)$ (F)	Unsaturated fatty acids: Linoleic $C_{18}(-4H)$ (G)
				Grams		Grams	Grams	Grams	Grams
		Cornbread, baked from home recipe—Continued							
		Cornbread, southern style, made with—Continued							
877		Degermed cornmeal, enriched:							
		Made with lard:							
	a	Whole (7½ × 7½ × 1⅝ in.; vol., 91.4 cu. in.).	1 cornbread	[7] 747	Lard, egg	44.8	15.5	19.9	5.2
	b	Piece (2½ × 2½ × 1⅝ in.; vol., 10.2 cu. in.; ⅑ of cornbread).	1 piece	83	do	5.0	1.7	2.2	.6
		Made with vegetable shortening: [31]							
	c	Whole (7½ × 7½ × 1⅝ in.; vol., 91.4 cu. in.).	1 cornbread	[7] 747	Vegetable shortening, egg.	44.8	11.7	21.1	7.8
	d	Piece (2½ × 2½ × 1⅝ in.; vol., 10.2 cu. in.; ⅑ of cornbread).	1 piece	83	do	5.0	1.3	2.3	.9
879		Corn pone, made with white whole-ground cornmeal, baked (9-in. diam., 28.3-in. cir., ¾ in. high):							
		Made with lard:							
	a	Pone, whole	1 pone	[7] 485	Lard, egg	25.7	7.3	10.8	5.7
	b	Sector, 3½-in. arc; ⅛ of pone	1 sector	60	do	3.2	.9	1.3	.7
		Made with vegetable shortening: [32]							
	c	Pone, whole	1 pone	[7] 485	Vegetable shortening, egg.	25.7	5.1	11.4	7.7
	d	Sector, 3½-in. arc; ⅛ of pone	1 sector	60	do	3.2	.6	1.4	.9
880		Spoonbread, made with white whole-ground cornmeal:							
		Made with lard:							
	a	Yield from recipe [12]	2⅔ cups	645	Lard, egg, milk	73.5	28.2	31.1	7.4
	b	Cup	1 cup	240	do	27.4	10.5	11.6	2.7
		Made with vegetable shortening: [33]							
	c	Yield from recipe [12]	2⅔ cups	645	Vegetable shortening, egg, milk.	73.5	23.3	32.6	11.9
	d	Cup	1 cup	240	do	27.4	8.7	12.1	4.4
		See also Muffins, corn (items 1347–1348).							
882		**Cornbread baked from mix.** See Muffin mix, corn, and muffins and cornbread baked from mix (items 1349–1350).							
		Cornmeal, white or yellow: [34]							
883		Whole ground, unbolted, dry	1 cup	122		4.8	.5	1.6	2.1
884		Bolted (nearly whole grain), dry	1 cup	122		4.1	.5	1.4	1.8
		Self-rising:							
		Whole ground:							
889		With soft wheat flour added	1 cup	134		3.9	.4	1.3	1.7
890		Without wheat flour added	1 cup	134		4.3	.5	1.5	1.9
		Cottage cheese. See item 647.							

(A)		(B)		(C)		(D)	(E)	(F)	(G)
		Cottage pudding. See Cakes (items 528–530).							
		Cottonseed oil. See Oils (items 1401f–1401h).							
		Crackers:							
910		Animal (approx. 175 per pound):							
	a	Package, net wt., 2 oz. (approx. 22 crackers).	1 pkg	57	Vegetable shortening, egg.	5.4	1.4	2.6	1.1
	b	Cracker	10 crackers	26	do	2.4	.6	1.2	.5
	c	Pound	1 lb	454	do	42.6	10.9	20.7	8.8
911		Butter:							
		Whole:							
		Round, 1⅞-in. diam., 3⁄16 in. thick (approx. 138 per pound):							
		Package:							
	a	Net wt., 16 oz. (1 lb.) (loose pack)	1 pkg. or 1 lb	454	Vegetable shortening, butter.	80.7	27.4	35.1	14.0
	b	Net wt., 10–12 oz. (3 inner packs)	1 pkg	312	do	55.5	18.8	24.1	9.6
	c	Cracker	10 crackers	33	do	5.9	2.0	2.6	1.0
		Rectangular, 2½ in. long, 1⅜ in. wide, ⅛ in. thick (approx. 120 per pound):							
	d	Package, net wt., 11½ oz	1 pkg	326	do	58.0	19.7	25.2	10.0
	e	Cracker	10 crackers	38	do	6.8	2.3	2.9	1.2
	f	Crumbed (finely crushed, spooned into cup without packing; approx. 24 round crackers or 21 rectangular).	1 cup	80	do	14.2	4.8	6.2	2.5
	g	Whole or crumbed	1 lb	454	do	80.7	27.4	35.1	14.0
912		Cheese:							
		Whole:							
		Cut into various shapes (hexagon, clover, etc.), 1⅞-in. diam. at widest cross section, 3⁄16 in. thick (approx. 145 per pound):							
	a	Package, net wt., 8½ oz	1 pkg	241	Vegetable shortening, butter, cheese.	51.3	19.9	21.1	7.2
	b	Cracker	10 crackers	31.3	do	6.7	2.6	2.7	.9
		Rectangular sticks, 1⅝ in. long, ¼ in. thick (approx. 500 per pound):							
		Package:							
	c	Net wt., 11 oz	1 pkg	312	do	66.5	25.7	27.3	9.3
	d	Net wt., 2¼ oz	1 pkg	64	do	13.6	5.3	5.6	1.9
	e	Cracker	10 crackers	9.1	do	1.9	.7	.8	.3
		Round, 1⅞-in. diam., 3⁄16 in. thick (approx. 132 per pound):							
	f	Package, net wt., 8 oz	1 pkg	227	do	48.4	18.7	19.9	6.8
	g	Cracker	10 crackers	34.4	do	7.3	2.8	3.0	1.0
		Square, 1 in., ⅛ in. thick (approx. 420 per pound):							
		Package:							
	h	Net wt., 10 oz	1 pkg	284	do	60.5	23.4	24.9	8.5
	i	Net wt., 6¼ oz	1 pkg	177	do	37.7	14.6	15.5	5.3
	j	Net wt., 2 oz	1 pkg	57	do	12.1	4.7	5.0	1.7
	k	Cracker	10 crackers	10.8	do	2.3	.9	.9	.3

[7] Yield of formula used to calculate nutritive values in Agr. Handb. No. 8, rev. 1963.

[12] Formula used to calculate nutritive values shown in Agr. Handb. No. 8, rev. 1963.

[31] Values based on these revised amounts per 100 g. of product: Total saturated fatty acids 1.6 g., oleic acid 2.8 g., linoleic acid 1.1 g.

[32] Values based on these revised amounts per 100 g. of product: Total saturated fatty acids 1.1 g., oleic acid 2.4 g., linoleic acid 1.6 g.

[33] Values based on these revised amounts per 100 g. of product: Total saturated fatty acids 3.6 g., oleic acid 5.1 g., linoleic acid 1.8 g.

[34] For dry form of cereal, weight per cup is based on method of pouring cereal from container into measuring cup with as little fall as possible, then leveling with straight edge. See also Appendix B, section on Nonliquid Foods and section on Breakfast-Type Cereals For cooked cereal, weight per cup represents hot cereal immediately after cooking and is based on specific proportion of cereal and water in cooked product. See ARS 62–13 (7), section on Alimentary Pastes and Other Cereal Products, pp. 6–7, and table 3, p. 9.

TABLE 2.—*Fatty acid values for household measures and market units of foods*—Continued

[Item and footnote numbers correspond to those in table 1 of this publication. Values in parentheses denote imputed values usually from another form of the food or from a similar food. Dashes (—) denote lack of reliable data for a constituent believed to be present in a measurable amount. Calculated values, as those based on a recipe, are not in parentheses]

Item No. (A)		Food, approximate measures, units, and weight (edible part unless footnotes indicate otherwise) (B)			Principal sources of fat (C)	Amount in edible part of foods: Total fat (D)	Total saturated fatty acids (E)	Unsaturated fatty acids: Oleic $C_{18}(-2H)$ (F)	Unsaturated fatty acids: Linoleic $C_{18}(-4H)$ (G)
				Grams		*Grams*	*Grams*	*Grams*	*Grams*
		Crackers—Continued							
		Cheese—Continued							
	l	Crumbed (finely crushed, spooned into cup without packing; approx. 93 rectangular sticks, 25 round crackers, or 79 squares (1 in.)).	1 cup	85	Vegetable shortening, butter, cheese.	18.1	7.0	7.4	2.5
	m	Whole or crumbed	1 lb	454	do	96.6	37.4	39.7	13.5
		Graham:							
913		Chocolate coated:							
	a	Cracker, 2½ in. long, 2 in. wide, ¼ in. thick.	1 cracker	13	Vegetable shortening, chocolate.	3.1	.9	1.9	.2
	b	Pound	1 lb	454	do	106.6	31.9	65.2	6.7
914		Plain:							
		Whole, rectangular piece, approx. 5 in. long, 2½ in. wide, 3/16 in. thick (approx. 32 per pound), marked for division into 2 pieces, 2½ in. square, 3/16 in. thick (approx. 64 per pound), or into 4 small rectangular pieces, 2½ in. long, 1¼ in. wide, 3/16 in. thick (approx. 132 per pound):							
	a	Package, net wt., 16 oz. (1 lb.)	1 pkg. or 1 lb	454	Vegetable shortening	42.6	10.3	20.6	10.2
	b	Cracker, 1 large rectangular piece, 2 squares (2½ in.), or 4 small rectangular pieces.	1, 2, or 4 pieces	14.2	do	1.3	.3	.6	.3
		Crumbed (finely crushed, spooned into cup):							
	c	Not packed (approx. 6 large rectangular crackers (item 914b)).	1 cup	85	do	8.0	1.9	3.9	1.9
	d	Packed (approx. 7½ large rectangular crackers (item 914b)).	1 cup	105	do	9.9	2.4	4.8	2.4
915		Sugar honey:							
		Whole, rectangular piece, approx. 5 in. long, 2½ in. wide, 3/16 in. thick (approx. 32 per pound), marked for division into 2 pieces, 2½ in. square, 3/16 in. thick (approx. 64 per pound), or into 4 small rectangular pieces, 2½ in. long, 1¼ in. wide, 3/16 in. thick (approx. 132 per pound):							
	a	Package, net wt., 16 oz. (1 lb.)	1 pkg. or 1 lb	454	do	51.7	12.5	25.0	12.3

(A)		(B)		(C)		(D)	(E)	(F)	(G)
	b	Cracker, 1 large rectangular piece, 2 squares (2½ in.), or 4 small rectangular pieces.	1, 2, or 4 pieces	14.2	Vegetable shortening	1.6	0.4	0.8	0.4
		Crumbed (finely crushed, spooned into cup):							
	c	Not packed (approx. 6 large rectangular crackers (item 915b)).	1 cup	85	do	9.7	2.3	4.7	2.3
	d	Packed (approx. 7½ large rectangular crackers (item 915b)).	1 cup	105	do	12.0	2.9	5.8	2.8
916		Saltines, 1⅞ in. square, ⅛ in. thick (approx. 160 per pound):							
		Whole:							
		Package:							
	a	Net wt., 16 oz. (1 lb.)	1 pkg. or 1 lb.[85]	454	do	54.4	13.1	26.3	13.0
	b	Net wt., 7–7¼ oz	1 pkg	202	do	24.2	5.8	11.7	5.8
	c	Cracker	10 crackers	28.4	do	3.4	.8	1.6	.8
	d	Packet (4 crackers)	1 packet	11	do	1.3	.3	.6	.3
	e	Crumbed (finely crushed, spooned into cup without packing; approx. 24½ crackers).	1 cup	70	do	8.4	2.0	4.1	2.0
917		Sandwich type, cheese-peanut butter, 1⅝ in. square, ⅜ in. thick or round, 1⅝-in. diam., ⅜ in. thick:							
	a	Package, net wt., 6 oz.; 4 packets (item 917b).	1 pkg	170	Vegetable shortening, peanut butter, cheese.	40.6	10.7	18.7	9.5
	b	Packet, net wt., 1½ oz.; 6 sandwiches	1 packet	42	do	10.2	2.7	4.7	2.4
	c	Packet, net wt., 1 oz.; 4 sandwiches	1 packet or 1 oz	28	do	6.8	1.8	3.1	1.6
	d	Pound	1 lb	454	do	108.4	28.6	49.9	25.4
918		Soda:							
		Whole:							
		Biscuit, 2⅜ in. × 2⅛ in., ¼ in. thick (approx. 90 per pound):							
	a	Package, net wt., 3½ oz	1 pkg	99	Vegetable shortening	13.0	3.1	6.3	3.1
	b	Biscuit	10 biscuits	50.4	do	6.6	1.6	3.2	1.6
		Regular, 1⅞ in. square, ⅛ in. thick (approx. 160 per pound):							
	c	Package, net wt., 16 oz. (1 lb.)	1 pkg. or 1 lb.[86]	454	do	59.4	14.2	28.7	14.2
	d	Cracker	10 crackers	28.4	do	3.7	.9	1.8	.9
		Soup or oyster (hexagon shaped, ½ in. sides, 3/16–7/16 in. thick, 530–600 per pound; round, ⅞-in. diam., 7/16 in. thick, approx. 650 per pound):							
		Package:							
	e	Net wt., 16 oz. (1 lb.) (hexagon shaped or round).	1 pkg. or 1 lb	454	do	59.4	14.2	28.7	14.2
	f	Net wt., 5 oz. (hexagon shaped)	1 pkg	142	do	18.6	4.5	9.0	4.4
	g	Cup	1 cup	45	do	5.9	1.4	2.8	1.4
	h	Cracker	10 crackers	7.5	do	1.0	.2	.5	.2
	i	Crumbed (approx. 14 biscuits, 25 square crackers, or 1½ cups of oyster crackers).	1 cup	70	do	9.2	2.2	4.4	2.2
		Cream, fluid:							
928		Half-and-half (cream and milk; 11.7% fat):							
	a	Cup	1 cup	242		28.3	15.6	9.3	.8
	b	Tablespoon	1 tbsp	15		1.8	1.0	.6	.1

[85] Use also for 1 lb. of crumbed crackers.
[86] Use also for 1 lb. of biscuit-type crackers or 1 lb. of crumbed crackers.

TABLE 2.—*Fatty acid values for household measures and market units of foods*—Continued

[Item and footnote numbers correspond to those in table 1 of this publication. Values in parentheses denote imputed values usually from another form of the food or from a similar food. Dashes (—) denote lack of reliable data for a constituent believed to be present in a measurable amount. Calculated values, as those based on a recipe, are not in parentheses]

Item No. (A)		Food, approximate measures, units, and weight (edible part unless footnotes indicate otherwise) (B)			Principal sources of fat (C)	Total fat (D)	Total saturated fatty acids (E)	Unsaturated fatty acids: Oleic $C_{18}(-2H)$ (F)	Unsaturated fatty acids: Linoleic $C_{18}(-4H)$ (G)
				Grams		*Grams*	*Grams*	*Grams*	*Grams*
		Cream, fluid—Continued							
929		Light, coffee, or table (20.6% fat):							
	a	Cup	1 cup	240		49.4	27.2	16.3	1.5
	b	Tablespoon	1 tbsp	15		3.1	1.7	1.0	.1
930		Light whipping or whipping (31.3% fat):							
	a	Cup	1 cup or approx. 2 cups whipped.	239		74.8	41.2	24.7	2.2
	b	Tablespoon	1 tbsp	15		4.7	2.6	1.5	.1
931		Heavy or heavy whipping (37.6% fat):							
	a	Cup	1 cup or approx. 2 cups whipped.	238		89.5	49.2	29.5	2.7
	b	Tablespoon	1 tbsp	15		5.6	3.1	1.9	.2
934		**Cream puffs** with custard filling	1 cream puff	130	Vegetable shortening, egg, milk.	18.1	5.6	8.3	2.9
948		**Custard, baked** [3]	1 cup	265	Milk, egg	14.6	6.8	5.4	.7
		Custard, frozen. See Ice cream (items 1139, 1141).							
		Danish pastry. See Rolls and buns (item 1899).							
		Deviled ham. See Sausage, cold cuts, and luncheon meats (item 1993).							
		Doughnuts:							
957		Cake type, plain:							
	a	3⅝-in. diam., 1¼ in. high; wt., approx. 2 oz.	1 doughnut	58	Vegetable shortening, egg.	10.8	2.7	5.3	2.3
	b	3¼-in. diam., 1 in. high; wt., approx. 1½ oz.	1 doughnut	42	do	7.8	2.0	3.9	1.7
	c	2½-in. diam., 1 in. high; wt., approx. ⅞ oz.	1 doughnut	25	do	4.7	1.2	2.3	1.0
	d	1½-in. diam., ¾ in. high; wt., approx. ½ oz.	1 doughnut	14	do	2.6	.7	1.3	.5
958		Yeast leavened, plain, 3¾-in. diam., 1¼ in. high; wt., approx. 1½ oz. [37]	1 doughnut	42	do	11.3	2.8	5.6	2.5
965		**Eclairs** with custard filling and chocolate icing	1 eclair	100	Vegetable shortening, egg, milk, chocolate, butter.	13.6	4.4	6.2	2.1
		Eggs:							
		Chicken:							
		Raw:							
968		Whole, fresh:							
		Egg:							
	a	Extra large, 27 oz. per dozen (refuse: shell, 10%). [2]	1 egg	64		6.6	2.1	2.9	.5
	b	Large, 24 oz. per dozen (refuse: shell, 12%). [2]	1 egg	57		5.8	1.8	2.5	.4

(A)		(B)			(C)	(D)	(E)	(F)	(G)
	c	Medium, 21 oz. per dozen (refuse: shell, 12%).[2]	1 egg	50		5.1	1.6	2.2	0.4
	d	Cup	1 cup	243		27.9	8.9	12.3	1.9
	e	Pound	1 lb	454		52.2	16.7	23.0	3.6
970		Yolks, fresh:							
		Egg yolk of—							
	a	Extra large egg	1 yolk	19		5.8	1.9	2.6	.4
	b	Large egg	1 yolk	17		5.2	1.7	2.3	.4
	c	Medium egg	1 yolk	15		4.6	1.5	2.0	.3
	d	Cup	1 cup	243		74.4	23.8	32.7	5.2
	e	Pound	1 lb	454		138.8	44.4	61.1	9.7
		Cooked:							
973		Fried:							
		Egg, prepared using—							
	a	Extra large egg	1 egg	52	Egg, butter	8.9	3.3	3.7	.5
	b	Large egg	1 egg	46	do	7.9	2.9	3.3	.5
	c	Medium egg	1 egg	40	do	6.9	2.5	2.9	.4
	d	Pound	1 lb	454	do	78.0	28.8	32.5	4.8
974		Hard cooked:							
		Egg, prepared using—							
	a	Extra large egg (refuse: shell, 10%).[3]	1 egg	64		6.6	2.1	2.9	.5
	b	Large egg (refuse: shell, 12%)[3]	1 egg	57		5.8	1.8	2.5	.4
	c	Medium egg (refuse: shell, 12%)[3]	1 egg	50		5.1	1.6	2.2	.4
	d	Cup, chopped	1 cup	136		15.6	5.0	6.9	1.1
	e	Pound	1 lb	454		52.2	16.7	23.0	3.6
975		Omelet. Use scrambled eggs (items 977a, 977b, 977c, 977e).							
976		Poached:							
		Egg, prepared using—							
	a	Extra large egg	1 egg	57		6.6	2.1	2.9	.5
	b	Large egg	1 egg	50		5.8	1.8	2.5	.4
	c	Medium egg	1 egg	44		5.1	1.6	2.2	.4
	d	Pound	1 lb	454		52.2	16.7	23.0	3.6
977		Scrambled:							
		Prepared using—							
	a	Extra large egg	1 egg	73	Egg, butter, milk	9.4	3.2	3.6	.5
	b	Large egg	1 egg	64	do	8.3	2.8	3.1	.5
	c	Medium egg	1 egg	56	do	7.2	2.4	2.7	.4
	d	Cup	1 cup	220	do	28.4	9.6	10.7	1.6
	e	Pound	1 lb	454	do	58.5	19.8	22.1	3.2
999		**Fats, cooking** (vegetable fat):[38, 39]							
		Container and approx. contents:							
	a	Can, net wt., 16 oz. (1 lb.)	1 can or 1 lb	454		453.6	113.2	228.6	98.9
	b	Can, net wt., 48 oz. (3 lb.)	1 can	1,361		1,361.0	339.6	685.9	296.7
	c	Cup	1 cup	200		200.0	49.9	100.8	43.6
	d	Tablespoon	1 tbsp	12.5		12.5	3.1	6.3	2.7
1008		**Filberts** (hazelnuts):							
		In shell (refuse: shells, 54%):							
	a	Pound	1 lb	454		130.2	6.5	70.3	20.8
	b	10 nuts	10 nuts	30		8.6	.4	4.7	1.4

[2] Measure and weight apply to food as it is described with inedible part or parts (refuse) included.

[3] Cup measure made on product after it had cooled. See also Appendix B, section on Home-Prepared Foods

[37] For fatty acid values of glazed doughnuts, see Appendix A, table 3, p. 264.

[38] Weights of volume measures do not apply to whipped type.

[39] Fatty acid content based on following revised values for 100 g. of vegetable fat: Total saturated fatty acids 25.0 g., oleic acid 50.4 g., linoleic acid 21.8 g. See also Appendix A, section on Fats, p. 263.

TABLE 2.—*Fatty acid values for household measures and market units of foods*—Continued

[Item and footnote numbers correspond to those in table 1 of this publication. Values in parentheses denote imputed values usually from another form of the food or from a similar food. Dashes (—) denote lack of reliable data for a constituent believed to be present in a measurable amount. Calculated values, as those based on a recipe, are not in parentheses]

Item No. (A)	Food, approximate measures, units, and weight (edible part unless footnotes indicate otherwise) (B)			Principal sources of fat (C)	Amount in edible part of foods: Total fat (D)	Total saturated fatty acids (E)	Unsaturated fatty acids: Oleic $C_{18}(-2H)$ (F)	Unsaturated fatty acids: Linoleic $C_{18}(-4H)$ (G)
			Grams		*Grams*	*Grams*	*Grams*	*Grams*
	Filberts (hazelnuts)—Continued							
	Shelled:							
c	Whole	1 cup	135		84.2	4.2	45.5	13.5
	Chopped:							
d	Cup	1 cup	115		71.8	3.6	38.8	11.5
e	Tablespoon	1 tbsp	7		4.4	.2	2.4	.7
f	Ground	1 cup	75		46.8	2.3	25.3	7.5
g	Pound	1 lb	454		283.0	14.2	152.9	45.3
h	Ounce (approx. 20 nuts)	1 oz	28		17.7	.9	9.6	2.8
	Frostings. See Cake icings prepared from home recipes (items 570–573) and Cake icings prepared from mixes (items 576, 578–579).							
	Frozen custard. See Ice cream (items 1139, 1141).							
	Garbanzos. See Chickpeas (item 753).							
	Gingerbread. See Cakes (item 533) and Cake mixes (item 561).							
	Goat milk. See Milk, goat (item 1335).							
	Griddle cakes. See Pancakes (items 1453 or 1454, 1457 or 1460, 1462).							
	Ham. See Pork (items 1698–1699, 1701, 1766–1769, 1771, 1783) and Sausage (items 2005–2006).							
	Hamburger. See Beef (items 367–370).							
1108	**Ham croquette** (panfried); 1-in. diam., 3 in. long:							
a	Yield from recipe [13]	9 croquettes	595	Butter, ham, vegetable shortening.	89.8	35.6	36.7	9.2
b	Croquette	1 croquette	65	do	9.8	3.9	4.0	1.0
c	Pound	1 lb	454	do	68.5	27.2	27.9	7.0
	Hazelnuts. See Filberts (item 1008).							
	Headcheese. See Sausage, cold cuts, and luncheon meats (item 2001).							
	Herring:							
	Canned, solids and liquid:							
1126	Plain:							
	Can and approx. contents:							
a	Size, 300 × 407 [5] (No. 300); net wt., 15 oz.	1 can	425		57.8	11.0	—	11.0
b	Pound	1 lb	454		61.7	11.7	—	11.7
1127	In tomato sauce:							
a	Herring, 4¾ in. long, 1⅛ in. wide, ⅝ in. thick; wt., 1⅓ oz.; 1 tbsp. sauce, wt., ⅗ oz.	1 herring with 1 tbsp. sauce.	55		5.8	1.1	—	1.1

(A)		(B)		(C)	(D)	(E)	(F)	(G)
	b	Pound	1 lb	454	47.6	9.1	—	9.1
1128		Pickled:						
	a	Bismarck herring, 7 in. long, 1½ in. wide, ½ in. thick.	1 herring	50	7.6	1.4	—	1.4
	b	Marinated piece, 1¾ in. long, ⅞ in. wide, ½ in. thick.	1 piece	15	2.3	.4	—	.4
	c	Pound	1 lb	454	68.5	13.0	—	13.0
1132		Smoked, kippered, canned, drained solids:						
	a	Drained contents from can of net wt., 3¼ oz. (2 fillets (item 1132d) or 4 fillets (item 1132e)).	1 can	80	10.3	2.0	—	2.0
	b	Drained contents from can of net wt., 8 oz. (3 fillets (item 1132c)).	1 can	195	25.2	4.8	—	4.8
	c	Fillet, 7 in. long, 2¼ in. wide, ¼ in. thick	1 fillet	65	8.4	1.6	—	1.6
	d	Fillet, 4⅜ in. long, 1¾ in. wide, ¼ in. thick	1 fillet	40	5.2	1.0	—	1.0
	e	Fillet, 2⅜ in. long, 1⅜ in. wide, ¼ in. thick	1 fillet	20	2.6	.5	—	.5
	f	Pound	1 lb	454	58.5	11.1	—	11.1
		Ice cream and frozen custard, plain (commercial):						
1139		Regular (approx. 10% fat):						
		Hardened:						
		Prepackaged container and approx. contents:						
	a	Container, net contents, ½ gal	½ gal	1,064	112.8	62.0	37.2	3.4
	b	Container, net contents, 1 qt. (solid pack or 8 precut slices [40]).	1 qt. or 8 slices	532	56.4	31.0	18.6	1.7
	c	Slice (4 fl. oz., ⅛ of qt.) [40]	1 slice	66	7.0	3.8	2.3	.2
	d	Cup (8 fl. oz.)	1 cup	133	14.1	7.8	4.7	.4
	e	Soft serve (frozen custard)	1 cup	173	18.3	10.1	6.1	.6
1141		Rich (approx. 16% fat), hardened:						
	a	Prepackaged container, net contents, ½ gal.	½ gal	1,188	191.3	105.8	63.1	5.7
	b	Cup (8 fl. oz.)	1 cup	148	23.8	13.1	7.9	.7
1143		**Ice milk** (5.1% fat):						
		Hardened:						
	a	Container, net contents, ½ gal	½ gal	1,048	53.4	29.3	17.6	1.6
	b	Cup (8 fl. oz.)	1 cup	131	6.7	3.7	2.2	.2
	c	Soft serve, cup (8 fl. oz.)	1 cup	175	8.9	4.9	2.9	.3
		Icings. See Cake icings prepared from home recipes (items 570–573) and Cake icings prepared from mixes (items 576, 578–579).						
		Ladyfingers. See Cookies (item 822).						
		Lamb, retail cuts:						
		Leg:						
1184		Raw, lean with fat:						
	a	With bone (70% lean, 14% fat) (refuse: bone, 16%). [2]	1 lb	454	61.7	34.6	22.2	1.9
	b	Without bone (83% lean, 17% fat)	1 lb	454	73.5	41.2	26.5	2.2
		Cooked (roasted):						
1185		Lean with fat (83% lean, 17% fat):						
	a	Yield from 1 lb., raw lamb with bone (item 1184a).	9.4 oz	267	50.5	28.3	18.2	1.5
	b	Yield from 1 lb., raw lamb without bone (item 1184b).	11.2 oz	318	60.1	33.7	21.6	1.8
	c	Cup, chopped or diced pieces (not packed).	1 cup	140	26.5	14.8	9.5	.8

[2] Measure and weight apply to food as it is described with inedible part or parts (refuse) included.

[5] Dimensions of can: 1st dimension represents diameter; 2d dimension, height of can. 1st or left-hand digit in each dimension gives number of whole inches; next 2 digits give additional fraction of dimension expressed as 16th of an inch.

[13] Formula used to calculate nutritive values shown in Agr. Handb. No. 8, rev. 1963.

[40] Precut slices do not apply to frozen custard.

TABLE 2.—*Fatty acid values for household measures and market units of foods*—Continued

[Item and footnote numbers correspond to those in table 1 of this publication. Values in parentheses denote imputed values usually from another form of the food or from a similar food. Dashes (—) denote lack of reliable data for a constituent believed to be present in a measurable amount. Calculated values, as those based on a recipe, are not in parentheses]

Item No. (A)		Food, approximate measures, units, and weight (edible part unless footnotes indicate otherwise) (B)			Principal sources of fat (C)	Amount in edible part of foods: Total fat (D)	Total saturated fatty acids (E)	Unsaturated fatty acids: Oleic $C_{18}(-2H)$ (F)	Unsaturated fatty acids: Linoleic $C_{18}(-4H)$ (G)
				Grams		*Grams*	*Grams*	*Grams*	*Grams*
		Lamb, retail cuts—Continued							
		Leg—Continued							
		Cooked (roasted)—Continued							
		Lean with fat (83% lean, 17% fat)—Continued							
	d	Pound	1 lb	454		85.7	48.8	30.9	2.6
	e	Piece, approx. 4⅛ in. long, 2¼ in. wide, ¼ in. thick; wt., 1½ oz.	2 pieces or 3 oz	85		16.1	9.0	5.8	.5
1187		Lean, trimmed of separable fat:							
	a	Yield from 1 lb., raw lamb with bone (item 1184a).	7.8 oz	221		15.5	8.7	5.6	.5
	b	Yield from 1 lb., raw lamb without bone (item 1184b).	9.3 oz	264		18.5	10.4	6.7	.6
	c	Cup, chopped or diced pieces (not packed).	1 cup	140		9.8	5.5	3.5	.3
	d	Pound	1 lb	454		31.8	17.8	11.4	1.0
	e	Piece, approx. 4⅛ in. long, 2¼ in. wide, ¼ in. thick; wt., 1½ oz.	2 pieces or 3 oz	85		6.0	3.4	2.2	.2
		Loin chops:							
1199		Raw (62% lean, 24% fat) (refuse: bone, 14%).[2]	1 lb	454		97.0	54.3	34.9	2.9
		Cooked (broiled):							
1200		Lean with fat (66% lean, 34% fat):							
	a	Yield from 1 lb., raw chops with bone (item 1199).	10.1 oz	285		83.8	46.9	30.2	2.5
		Yield from 1 chop, raw with bone; ⅓ or ¼ of item 1199:							
	b	Cut 3 per pound	3.4 oz	95		27.9	15.6	10.0	.8
	c	Cut 4 per pound	2.5 oz	71		20.9	11.7	7.5	.6
	d	Pound	1 lb	454		133.4	74.7	48.0	4.0
1202		Lean, trimmed of separable fat:							
	a	Yield from 1 lb., raw chops with bone (item 1199).	6.9 oz	196		14.7	8.2	5.3	.4
		Yield from 1 chop, raw with bone; ⅓ or ¼ of item 1199:							
	b	Cut 3 per pound	2.3 oz	65		4.9	2.7	1.8	.1
	c	Cut 4 per pound	1.7 oz	49		3.7	2.1	1.3	.1
	d	Pound	1 lb	454		34.0	19.0	12.2	1.0
		Rib chops:							
1214		Raw (54% lean, 26% fat) (refuse: bone, 20%).[2]	1 lb	454		110.2	61.7	39.7	3.3
		Cooked (broiled):							
1215		Lean with fat (62% lean, 38% fat):							
	a	Yield from 1 lb., raw chops with bone	9.5 oz	268		95.4	53.4	34.3	2.9

(A)		(B)			(C)	(D)	(E)	(F)	(G)
		(item 1214).							
		Yield from 1 chop, raw with bone; ⅓ or ¼ of item 1214:							
	b	Cut 3 per pound	3.1 oz	89		31.7	17.8	11.4	1.0
	c	Cut 4 per pound	2.4 oz	67		23.9	13.4	8.6	.7
	d	Pound	1 lb	454		161.5	90.4	58.1	4.8
1217		Lean, trimmed of separable fat:							
	a	Yield from 1 lb., raw chops with bone (item 1214).	6 oz	171		18.0	10.1	6.5	.5
		Yield from 1 chop, raw with bone; ⅓ or ¼ of item 1214:							
	b	Cut 3 per pound	2 oz	57		6.0	3.4	2.2	.2
	c	Cut 4 per pound	1½ oz	43		4.5	2.5	1.6	.1
	d	Pound	1 lb	454		47.6	26.7	17.1	1.4
		Shoulder:							
1229		Raw, lean with fat:							
	a	With bone (63% lean, 22% fat) (refuse: bone, 15%).[2]	1 lb	454		92.0	51.5	33.1	2.8
	b	Without bone (74% lean, 26% fat)	1 lb	454		108.4	60.7	39.0	3.3
		Cooked (roasted):							
1230		Lean with fat (74% lean, 26% fat):							
	a	Yield from 1 lb., raw lamb with bone (item 1229a).	9½ oz	270		73.4	41.1	26.4	2.2
	b	Yield from 1 lb., raw lamb without bone (item 1229b).	11.2 oz	318		86.5	48.4	31.1	2.6
	c	Cup, chopped or diced pieces (not packed).	1 cup	140		38.1	21.3	13.7	1.1
	d	Pound	1 lb	454		123.4	69.1	44.4	3.7
	e	Piece, approx. 2½ in. long, 2½ in. wide, ¼ in. thick; wt., 1 oz.	3 pieces or 3 oz	85		23.1	12.9	8.3	.7
1232		Lean, trimmed of separable fat:							
	a	Yield from 1 lb., raw lamb with bone (item 1229a).	7 oz	200		20.0	11.2	7.2	.6
	b	Yield from 1 lb., raw lamb without bone (item 1229b).	8.3 oz	235		23.5	13.2	8.5	.7
	c	Cup, chopped or diced pieces (not packed).	1 cup	140		14.0	7.8	5.0	.4
	d	Pound	1 lb	454		45.4	25.4	16.3	1.4
	e	Piece, approx. 2½ in. long, 2½ in. wide, ¼ in. thick; wt., 1 oz.	3 pieces or 3 oz	85		8.5	4.8	3.1	.3
1241		**Lard:**							
	a	Pound	1 lb	454		453.6	172.4	208.7	45.4
	b	Cup	1 cup	205		205.0	77.9	94.3	20.5
	c	Tablespoon	1 tbsp	13		13.0	4.9	6.0	1.3
1274		**Liver, hog, cooked (fried):**							
	a	Slice, approx. 6½ in. long, 2⅜ in. wide,[41] ⅜ in. thick; wt., 3 oz.	1 slice	85	Vegetable shortening	9.8	2.9	3.8	1.4
	b	Pound (approx. 5⅓ slices (item 1274a))	1 lb	454	do	52.2	15.3	20.4	7.3
		Luncheon meat. See Sausage, cold cuts, and luncheon meats (items 2005–2006).							
		Macaroni (enriched) and cheese:							
1304		Baked, made from home recipe:							
		Made with butter:							
	a	Yield from recipe[12]	7 cups	1,400	Cheese, butter, milk	155.4	83.3	51.4	6.7
	b	Cup (served hot)	1 cup	200	do	22.2	11.9	7.3	1.0
	c	Pound	1 lb	454	do	50.3	27.0	16.6	2.2

[2] Measure and weight apply to food as it is described with inedible part or parts (refuse) included.
[12] Formula used to calculate nutritive values shown in Agr. Handb. No. 8, rev. 1963.
[41] Width at widest part.

TABLE 2.—*Fatty acid values for household measures and market units of foods*—Continued

[Item and footnote numbers correspond to those in table 1 of this publication. Values in parentheses denote imputed values usually from another form of the food or from a similar food. Dashes (—) denote lack of reliable data for a constituent believed to be present in a measurable amount. Calculated values, as those based on a recipe, are not in parentheses]

Item No. (A)		Food, approximate measures, units, and weight (edible part unless footnotes indicate otherwise) (B)			Principal sources of fat (C)	Amount in edible part of foods: Total fat (D)	Total saturated fatty acids (E)	Unsaturated fatty acids: Oleic $C_{18}(-2H)$ (F)	Unsaturated fatty acids: Linoleic $C_{18}(-4H)$ (G)
				Grams		*Grams*	*Grams*	*Grams*	*Grams*
		Macaroni (enriched) and cheese—Continued							
		Baked, made from home recipe—Continued							
		Made with margarine:							
		Regular type: [43]							
	d	Yield from recipe [13]	7 cups	1,400	Cheese, margarine, milk	155.4	62.8	61.7	20.6
	e	Cup (served hot)	1 cup	200	do	22.2	8.9	8.8	2.9
	f	Pound	1 lb	454	do	50.8	20.2	20.0	6.7
		Soft type: [43]							
	g	Yield from recipe [13]	7 cups	1,400	do	155.4	62.7	53.8	26.9
	h	Cup (served hot)	1 cup	200	do	22.2	9.0	7.7	3.8
	i	Pound	1 lb	454	do	50.8	20.8	17.4	8.7
1305		Canned:							
		Can and approx. contents:							
	a	Size, 300 × 407 [5] (No. 300); net wt., 15–15¼ oz.	1 can	430	Cheese, corn oil, milk	17.2	7.6	5.5	2.6
	b	Size, 404 × 700 [5] (No. 3 Cylinder); net wt., 50 oz. (3 lb. 2 oz.).	1 can	1,418	do	56.7	25.0	18.2	8.5
	c	Cup	1 cup	240	do	9.6	4.2	3.1	1.4
	d	Pound	1 lb	454	do	18.1	8.0	5.8	2.7
1317		Margarine:							
		Regular type (1 brick or 4 sticks per pound): [44]							
	a	Stick, net wt., 4 oz. (approx. ½ cup)	1 stick	113.4		91.9	16.8	47.0	25.2
	b	Cup (approx. ½ brick or 2 sticks of item 1317a).	1 cup	227		183.9	33.6	94.1	50.3
	c	Tablespoon (approx. ⅛ of stick (item 1317a)).	1 tbsp	14.2		11.5	2.1	5.9	3.1
	d	Pound	1 lb	454		367.4	67.2	188.0	100.6
	e	Pat (1 in. square, ⅓ in. high: 90 per pound).	1 pat	5.0		4.1	.7	2.1	1.1
	f	Cubic inch	1 cu. in	14.7		11.9	2.2	6.1	3.3
		Soft type (two 8-oz. containers per pound): [45]							
	g	Cup (one 8-oz. container)	1 cup or 1 container.	227		183.9	35.8	68.3	70.9
	h	Tablespoon	1 tbsp	14.2		11.5	2.2	4.3	4.4
	i	Teaspoon	1 tsp	4.7		3.8	.7	1.4	1.5
	j	Pound	1 lb	454		367.4	70.6	136.4	141.8
		Whipped type (6 sticks or two 8-oz. containers per pound): [44 46 47]							
	k	Stick, net wt., 2⅔ oz. (approx. ½ cup)	1 stick	75.6		61.2	11.2	31.3	16.8
	l	Cup (approx. 2 sticks of item 1317k or ⅔ of 8-oz. container).	1 cup	151		122.3	22.4	62.6	33.5
	m	Tablespoon (approx. ⅛ of stick (item 1317k)).	1 tbsp	9.4		7.6	1.4	3.9	2.1
	n	Pat (1¼ in. square, ⅓ in. high; 120 per pound).	1 pat	3.8		3.1	.6	1.6	.8

(A)		(B)			(C)	(D)	(E)	(F)	(G)
		Mayonnaise. See Salad dressings (item 1938).							
		Mellorine. See Appendix C, p. 283.							
		Milk, cow:							
		Fluid (pasteurized and raw):							
1320		Whole, 3.5% fat:[48]							
	a	Quart	1 qt	976		34.2	18.7	11.3	1.0
	b	Cup	1 cup	244		8.5	4.7	2.8	.2
1323		Low fat with 2% nonfat milk solids added:							
	a	Quart	1 qt	984		19.7	10.8	6.5	.6
	b	Cup	1 cup	246		4.9	2.7	1.6	.1
		Canned:							
1324		Evaporated (unsweetened):							
	a	Cup	1 cup	252		19.9	10.9	6.6	.6
	b	Fluid ounce	1 fl. oz	31.5		2.5	1.4	.8	.1
1325		Condensed (sweetened):							
	a	Cup	1 cup	306		26.6	14.7	8.8	.8
	b	Fluid ounce	1 fl. oz	38.2		3.3	1.8	1.1	.1
		Dry:[29]							
1326		Whole:							
	a	Regular	1 cup	128		35.2	19.4	11.6	1.0
		Instant:							
	b	Low-density type (proportions for use: 4¼ oz. of milk to 3⅔ cups of water to yield 1 qt.).	1 cup	70		19.3	10.6	6.4	.6
	c	High-density type (proportions for use: ¼ cup of milk to 1 cup of water).	1 cup	105		28.9	15.9	9.5	.9
	d	Regular and instant	1 lb	454		124.7	68.6	41.2	3.7
		Chocolate drink, fluid, commercial (approx. 90% milk):							
1331		Made with skim milk (2% butterfat added):							
	a	Quart	1 qt	1,000	Butterfat, cocoa	23.0	12.7	7.7	.7
	b	Cup	1 cup	250	do	5.8	3.2	1.9	.2
1332		Made with whole 3.5%-fat milk:							
	a	Quart	1 qt	1,000	Milk, cocoa	34.0	18.7	11.3	1.0
	b	Cup	1 cup	250	do	8.5	4.7	2.8	.3
		Chocolate beverages, homemade:							
1333		Hot chocolate	1 cup	250	Milk, chocolate	12.5	6.9	4.3	.4
1334		Hot cocoa	1 cup	250	Milk, cocoa	11.5	6.3	3.9	.3
		Buttermilk. See Buttermilk, dried (item 510).							

[5] Dimensions of can: 1st dimension represents diameter; 2d dimension, height of can. 1st or left-hand digit in each dimension gives number of whole inches; next 2 digits give additional fraction of dimension expressed as 16th of an inch.

[19] Formula used to calculate nutritive values shown in Agr. Handb. No. 8, rev. 1963.

[29] Weight per cup is based on method of pouring product from container into measuring cup with as little fall as possible, then leveling with straight edge. For corn flour, see Appendix B, section on Nonliquid Foods and section on Cornmeals and Related Products

[42] Values based on these revised amounts per 100 g. of product: Total saturated fatty acids 4.5 g., oleic acid 4.4 g., linoleic acid 1.5 g.

[43] Values based on these revised amounts per 100 g. of product: Total saturated fatty acids 4.5 g., oleic acid 3.8 g., linoleic acid 1.9 g.

[44] Values based on these revised amounts per 100 g. of product: Total saturated fatty acids 14.8 g., oleic acid 41.4 g., linoleic acid 22.2 g. See also Appendix A, section on Fats, p. 263.

[45] Values based on these revised amounts per 100 g. of product: Total saturated fatty acids 15.6 g., oleic acid 30.1 g., linoleic acid 31.2 g. See also Appendix A, section on Fats, p. 263.

[46] Description and weights shown for whipped margarine, except pat (item 1317n), apply to margarine that has been stirred or whipped until its volume has been increased approx. 50%; for pat, 100%.

[47] Values for 1 lb. are same as for 1 lb. of regular type.

[48] Minimum Federal standards for fat have been proposed (23) as 3¼%. Minimum standards for fat in different States vary considerably, and commercial milks may range slightly above required minimums. Selection of values to be used in dietary calculations may need to be based on information at local level.

TABLE 2.—*Fatty acid values for household measures and market units of foods*—Continued

[Item and footnote numbers correspond to those in table 1 of this publication. Values in parentheses denote imputed values usually from another form of the food or from a similar food. Dashes (—) denote lack of reliable data for a constituent believed to be present in a measurable amount. Calculated values, as those based on a recipe, are not in parentheses]

Item No. (A)		Food, approximate measures, units, and weight (edible part unless footnotes indicate otherwise) (B)			Principal sources of fat (C)	Amount in edible part of foods: Total fat (D)	Total saturated fatty acids (E)	Unsaturated fatty acids: Oleic $C_{18}(-2H)$ (F)	Unsaturated fatty acids: Linoleic $C_{18}(-4H)$ (G)
				Grams		Grams	Grams	Grams	Grams
1335		**Milk, goat,** fluid:							
	a	Quart	1 qt	976		39.0	24.2	9.8	2.0
	b	Cup	1 cup	244		9.8	6.1	2.4	.5
1336		**Milk, human,** U.S. samples	1 fl. oz	30.8		1.2	.6	.4	.1
		Muffins, baked from home recipes:							
1343 or 1344		Plain, made with enriched or unenriched flour:							
	a	Yield from recipe[12]	12 muffins	485	Vegetable shortening, egg.	49.0	12.5	23.7	10.3
	b	Muffin (3-in. diam. at top, 2-in. diam. at bottom, 1½ in. high).	1 muffin	40	do	4.0	1.0	2.0	.8
	c	Pound	1 lb	454	do	45.8	11.7	22.2	9.6
		Other, made with enriched flour:							
1345		Blueberry:							
	a	Yield from recipe[12]	8 muffins	315	Vegetable shortening, egg, milk.	29.3	8.9	13.2	4.9
	b	Muffin (2⅜-in. diam. at top, 2-in. diam. at bottom, 1½ in. high).	1 muffin	40	do	3.7	1.1	1.7	.6
	c	Pound	1 lb	454	do	42.2	12.8	19.0	7.1
1346		Bran:[49]							
	a	Yield from recipe[12]	7½ muffins	295	do	28.9	8.8	12.9	5.2
	b	Muffin (2⅝-in. diam. at top, 2-in. diam. at bottom, 1⅜ in. high).	1 muffin	40	do	3.9	1.2	1.7	.7
	c	Pound	1 lb	454	do	44.5	13.5	19.8	7.9
		Corn, made with—							
1347		Enriched degermed cornmeal:							
		Made with lard:							
	a	Yield from recipe[12]	13 muffins	520	Lard, milk, egg	52.5	20.5	22.5	5.4
	b	Muffin (2⅜-in. diam. at top, 2-in. diam. at bottom, 1½ in. high).	1 muffin	40	do	4.0	1.6	1.7	.4
	c	Pound	1 lb	454	do	45.8	17.9	19.6	4.7
		Made with vegetable shortening:[50]							
	d	Yield from recipe[12]	13 muffins	520	Vegetable shortening, milk, egg.	52.5	15.9	24.0	9.7
	e	Muffin (2⅜-in. diam. at top, 2-in. diam. at bottom, 1½ in. high).	1 muffin	40	do	4.0	1.2	1.8	.7
	f	Pound	1 lb	454	do	45.8	13.8	20.9	8.4
1348		Whole-ground cornmeal:							
		Made with lard:							
	a	Yield from recipe[12]	12½ muffins	500	Lard, milk, egg	51.5	19.1	21.6	6.6
	b	Muffin (2⅜-in. diam. at top, 2-in. diam. at bottom, 1½ in. high).	1 muffin	40	do	4.1	1.5	1.7	.5
	c	Pound	1 lb	454	do	46.7	17.3	19.6	6.0

(A)		(B)			(C)	(D)	(E)	(F)	(G)
		Made with vegetable shortening:[51]							
	d	Yield from recipe[12]	12½ muffins	500	Vegetable shortening, milk, egg.	51.5	15.2	22.7	10.2
	e	Muffin (2⅜-in. diam. at top, 2-in. diam. at bottom, 1½ in. high).	1 muffin	40	do	4.1	1.2	1.8	.8
	f	Pound	1 lb	454	do	46.7	13.7	20.6	9.3
		Muffin mix, corn, muffins and cornbread baked from mix:							
1349		Mix, dry form, with enriched flour:							
	a	Package, net wt., 12 oz	1 pkg	340	Vegetable shortening	39.1	9.1	19.1	9.1
		Cup:							
	b	Not packed	1 cup	130	do	15.0	3.5	7.3	3.5
	c	Packed	1 cup	170	do	19.6	4.6	9.6	4.6
	d	Pound	1 lb	454	do	52.2	12.2	25.5	12.2
1350		Muffins and cornbread; made with egg and milk:							
		Muffins, 2⅜-in. diam. at top, 2-in. diam. at bottom, 1½ in. high:							
	a	Yield from 12 oz. of mix (item 1349a)	12 muffins	490	Vegetable shortening, milk, egg.	51.9	15.0	24.2	9.8
	b	Muffin	1 muffin	40	do	4.2	1.2	2.0	.8
		Cornbread, 7½ × 7½ × 1⅜ in.:							
	c	Whole (yield from 12 oz. of mix (item 1349a)).	1 cornbread	500	do	53.0	15.3	24.7	10.1
	d	Piece (2½ × 2½ × 1⅜ in.; ⅑ of cornbread).	1 piece	55	do	5.8	1.7	2.7	1.1
	e	Cube (1 cu. in.)	1 cube	6.5	do	.7	.2	.3	.1
	f	Pound	1 lb	454	do	48.1	13.9	22.4	9.1
		Noodles, egg noodles, enriched or unenriched:							
1377 or 1379		Dry form:							
	a	Package, net wt., 16 oz. (1 lb.)	1 pkg. or 1 lb	454	Egg	20.9	6.7	9.2	1.5
	b	Package, net wt., 8 oz	1 pkg	227	do	10.4	3.3	4.6	.7
		Nuts. See individual kinds.							
		Oat products used mainly as hot breakfast cereals:[52]							
		Oat flakes, maple-flavored, instant-cooking:							
1384		Dry form	1 cup	95		4.0	.9	1.3	1.6
1385		Cooked	1 cup	240		1.9	.4	.6	.8
		Oat granules, maple-flavored, regular:							
1386		Dry form	1 cup	105		4.2	.9	1.3	1.7
1387		Cooked	1 cup	245		1.5	.3	.5	.6
		Oat and wheat cereal:							
1388		Dry form	1 cup	95		4.8	1.0	1.5	2.0
1389		Cooked	1 cup	245		2.2	.4	.7	.9
		Oatmeal or rolled oats, regular or instant-cooking:							
1390		Dry form[53]	1 cup	80		5.9	1.3	1.9	2.4
1391		Cooked	1 cup	240		2.4	.5	.8	1.0

[12] Formula used to calculate nutritive values shown in Agr. Handb. No. 8, rev. 1963.

[49] Values based on these revised amounts per 100 g. of product: Total saturated fatty acids 3.0 g., oleic acid 4.4 g., linoleic acid 1.8 g.

[50] Values based on these revised amounts per 100 g. of product: Total saturated fatty acids 3.1 g., oleic acid 4.6 g., linoleic acid 1.9 g.

[51] Values based on these revised amounts per 100 g. of product: Total saturated fatty acids 3.0 g., oleic acid 4.5 g., linoleic acid 2.0 g.

[52] For dry form of cereal, weight per cup is based on method of pouring cereal from container into measuring cup with as little fall as possible, then leveling with straight edge. See also Appendix B, section on Nonliquid Foods and section on Breakfast-Type Cereals For cooked cereal, weight per cup represents hot cereal immediately after cooking and is based on specific proportion of cereal and water in cooked product. See ARS 62–13 (7), section on Alimentary Pastes and Other Cereal Products, pp. 6–7, and table 3, p. 9. For item 1386, physical structure has changed to enable shorter cooking time, weight per cup (as shown) of dry form is less, volume of water used for cooking reduced to 2½ cups, but proportions of ingredients used, proportion of weight of cooked cereal, and ratio of weights—cooked to dried—as shown in table 3 of ARS 62–13 still apply.

[53] If cereal is spooned into cup with packing, weight per cup would be increased by as much as 20 g. per cup.

TABLE 2.—*Fatty acid values for household measures and market units of foods*—Continued

[Item and footnote numbers correspond to those in table 1 of this publication. Values in parentheses denote imputed values usually from another form of the food or from a similar food. Dashes (—) denote lack of reliable data for a constituent believed to be present in a measurable amount. Calculated values, as those based on a recipe, are not in parentheses]

Item No. (A)	Food, approximate measures, units, and weight (edible part unless footnotes indicate otherwise) (B)			Principal sources of fat (C)	Amount in edible part of foods: Total fat (D)	Total saturated fatty acids (E)	Unsaturated fatty acids: Oleic $C_{18}(-2H)$ (F)	Linoleic $C_{18}(-4H)$ (G)
			Grams		Grams	Grams	Grams	Grams
	Oat products used mainly as ready-to-eat breakfast cereals:[64]							
1392	Oats, shredded, with protein and other added nutrients.	1 cup	45		0.9	0.2	0.3	0.4
1401	**Oils, salad or cooking:**							
	Corn:							
	Container and approx. contents:							
a	Bottle, net contents, 16 fl. oz. (1 pt.)	1 bottle or 1 pt	436		436.0	43.6	122.1	231.1
b	Bottle, net contents, 24 fl. oz. (1 pt. 8 fl. oz.).	1 bottle	654		654.0	65.4	183.1	346.6
c	Quart	1 qt	872		872.0	87.2	244.2	462.2
d	Cup	1 cup	218		218.0	21.8	61.0	115.5
e	Tablespoon	1 tbsp	13.6		13.6	1.4	3.8	7.2
	Cottonseed:							
f	Quart	1 qt	872		872.0	218.0	183.1	436.0
g	Cup	1 cup	218		218.0	54.5	45.8	109.0
h	Tablespoon	1 tbsp	13.6		13.6	3.4	2.9	6.8
	Olive:							
	Container and approx. contents:							
i	Bottle, net contents, 4 fl. oz	1 bottle	108		108.0	11.9	82.1	7.6
j	Bottle or can, net contents, 16 fl. oz. (1 pt.).	1 container or 1 pt	432		432.0	47.5	328.3	30.2
k	Quart	1 qt	864		864.0	95.0	656.6	60.5
l	Cup	1 cup	216		216.0	23.8	164.2	15.1
m	Tablespoon	1 tbsp	13.5		13.5	1.5	10.3	.9
	Peanut:							
	Container and approx. contents:							
n	Bottle, net contents, 24 fl. oz. (1 pt. 8 fl. oz.).	1 bottle	648		648.0	116.6	304.6	187.9
o	Quart	1 qt	864		864.0	155.5	406.1	250.6
p	Cup	1 cup	216		216.0	38.9	101.5	62.6
q	Tablespoon	1 tbsp	13.5		13.5	2.4	6.3	3.9
	Safflower:							
	Container and approx. contents:							
r	Bottle, net contents, 16 fl. oz. (1 pt.)	1 bottle or 1 pt	436		436.0	34.9	65.4	313.9
s	Bottle, net contents, 24 fl. oz. (1 pt. 8 fl. oz.).	1 bottle	654		654.0	52.3	98.1	470.9
t	Quart	1 qt	872		872.0	69.8	130.8	627.8
u	Cup	1 cup	218		218.0	17.4	32.7	157.0
v	Tablespoon	1 tbsp	13.6		13.6	1.1	2.0	9.8
	Sesame:							
w	Quart	1 qt	872		872.0	122.1	331.4	366.2
x	Cup	1 cup	218		218.0	30.5	82.8	91.6
y	Tablespoon	1 tbsp	13.6		13.6	1.9	5.2	5.7

(A)		(B)		(C)		(D)	(E)	(F)	(G)
		Soybean:							
		Container and approx. contents:							
	z	Bottle, net contents, 16 fl. oz. (1 pt.)	1 bottle or 1 pt	436		436.0	65.4	87.2	226.7
	aa	Bottle, net contents, 24 fl. oz. (1 pt. 8 fl. oz.).	1 bottle	654		654.0	98.1	130.8	340.1
	ab	Quart	1 qt	872		872.0	130.8	174.4	453.4
	ac	Cup	1 cup	218		218.0	32.7	43.6	113.4
	ad	Tablespoon	1 tbsp	13.6		13.6	2.0	2.7	7.1
		Oleomargarine. See Margarine (item 1317).							
		Olives, pickled; canned or bottled:							
1406		Green:							
		Whole (refuse: pits, 16%):[2]							
	a	Small, select, or standard, approx. 10/16-in. diam., 13/16 in. long; 135 per pound.	10 olives	34		3.6	.4	2.8	.3
	b	Large, approx. 12/16-in. diam., 15/16 in. long; 98 per pound.	10 olives	46		4.9	.5	3.7	.3
	c	Giant, approx. 14/16-in. diam., 1 2/16 in. long; 53–64 per pound.	10 olives	78		8.3	.9	6.3	.6
	d	Pound, pitted	1 lb	454		57.6	6.4	43.8	4.0
		Ripe:							
1407		Ascolano:							
		Whole (refuse: pits, 14%):[2]							
	a	Extra large, approx. 12/16-in. diam., 1 in. long; 82 per pound.	10 olives	55		6.5	.7	5.0	.5
	b	Mammoth, approx. 13/16-in. diam., 1 1/16 in. long; 70 per pound.	10 olives	65		7.7	.8	5.9	.5
	c	Giant, approx. 13/16-in. diam., 1 3/16 in. long; 53–60 per pound.	10 olives	80		9.5	1.0	7.2	.7
	d	Jumbo, approx. 15/16-in. diam., 1 3/16 in. long; 46–50 per pound.	10 olives	95		11.3	1.2	8.6	.8
	e	Sliced	1 cup	135		18.6	2.1	14.2	1.3
	f	Pound, pitted	1 lb	454		62.6	6.9	47.6	4.4
1408		Manzanillo:							
		Whole (refuse: pits, 14%):[2]							
	a	Small, approx. 10/16-in. diam., 13/16 in. long; 135 per pound.	10 olives	34		4.0	.4	3.1	.3
	b	Medium, approx. 11/16-in. diam., 14/16 in. long; 113 per pound.	10 olives	40		4.7	.5	3.6	.3
	c	Large, approx. 12/16-in. diam., 15/16 in. long; 98 per pound.	10 olives	46		5.5	.6	4.2	.4
	d	Extra large, approx. 12/16-in. diam., 1 in. long; 82 per pound.	10 olives	55		6.5	.7	5.0	.5
	e	Sliced	1 cup	135		18.6	2.1	14.2	1.3
	f	Pound, pitted	1 lb	454		62.6	6.9	47.6	4.4
1409		Mission:							
		Whole (refuse: pits, 14%):[2]							
	a	Small, approx. 10/16-in. diam., 13/16 in. long; 135 per pound.	10 olives	34		5.9	.6	4.5	.4
	b	Medium, approx. 11/16-in. diam., 14/16 in. long; 113 per pound.	10 olives	40		6.9	.8	5.3	.5
	c	Large, approx. 12/16-in. diam., 15/16 in. long; 98 per pound.	10 olives	46		8.0	.9	6.1	.6
	d	Extra large, approx. 12/16-in. diam., 1 in. long; 82 per pound.	10 olives	55		9.5	1.0	7.2	.7
	e	Sliced	1 cup	135		27.1	3.0	20.6	1.9
	f	Pound, pitted	1 lb	454		91.2	10.0	69.3	6.4

[2] Measure and weight apply to food as it is described with inedible part or parts (refuse) included.
[54] Weight per cup based on method of pouring product from container into measuring cup to overflow and leveling with straight edge.

TABLE 2.—*Fatty acid values for household measures and market units of foods*—Continued

[Item and footnote numbers correspond to those in table 1 of this publication. Values in parentheses denote imputed values usually from another form of the food or from a similar food. Dashes (—) denote lack of reliable data for a constituent believed to be present in a measurable amount. Calculated values, as those based on a recipe, are not in parentheses]

Item No. (A)		Food, approximate measures, units, and weight (edible part unless footnotes indicate otherwise) (B)	Measure	Weight (Grams)	Principal sources of fat (C)	Total fat (D) (Grams)	Total saturated fatty acids (E) (Grams)	Unsaturated fatty acids: Oleic $C_{18}(-2H)$ (F) (Grams)	Unsaturated fatty acids: Linoleic $C_{18}(-4H)$ (G) (Grams)
		Olives, pickled; canned or bottled—Continued							
		Ripe—Continued							
1410		Sevillano:							
		Whole (refuse: pits, 14%):[2]							
	a	Giant, approx. 13/16-in. diam., 12/16 in. long; 53–60 per pound.	10 olives	80		6.5	0.7	5.0	0.5
	b	Jumbo, approx. 15/16-in. diam., 13/16 in. long; 46–50 per pound.	10 olives	95		7.8	.8	5.9	.5
	c	Colossal, approx. 1-in. diam., 14/16 in. long; 36–40 per pound.	10 olives	119		9.7	1.1	7.4	.7
	d	Supercolossal, approx. 11/16-in. diam., 19/16 in. long; 32 per pound.	10 olives	142		11.6	1.3	8.8	.8
	e	Sliced	1 cup	135		12.8	1.4	9.7	.9
	f	Pound, pitted	1 lb	454		43.1	4.7	32.7	3.0
1411		Ripe, salt cured, oil coated, Greek style:							
		Whole (refuse: pits, 20%):[2]							
	a	Medium, 188 per pound	10 olives	24		6.9	.8	5.2	.5
	b	Extra large, 137 per pound	10 olives	33		9.5	1.0	7.2	.7
	c	Pound, pitted	1 lb	454		162.4	17.9	123.4	11.4
		Olive oil. See Oils (items 1401i–1401m).							
		Omelet. See Eggs, omelet (item 975).							
1453 or 1454		**Pancakes**, baked from home recipe, made with enriched or unenriched flour:							
	a	Cake, 6-in. diam., ½ in. thick	1 cake	73	Vegetable shortening, egg.	5.1	1.3	2.5	1.0
	b	Cake, 4-in. diam., ⅜ in. thick	1 cake	27	do	1.9	.5	.9	.4
	c	Pound	1 lb	454	do	31.8	8.2	15.2	6.5
		Pancakes, baked from mixes:							
1457 or 1460		Plain and buttermilk with enriched or unenriched flour; made with egg, milk:							
	a	Cake, 6-in. diam., ½ in. thick	1 cake	73	Vegetable shortening, milk, egg.	5.3	1.9	2.3	.8
	b	Cake, 4-in. diam., ⅜ in. thick	1 cake	27	do	2.0	.7	.8	.3
	c	Pound	1 lb	454	do	33.1	11.7	14.0	4.7
1462		Buckwheat and other cereal flours; made with egg, milk:							
	a	Cake, 6-in. diam., ½ in. thick	1 cake	73	do	6.6	2.2	2.9	1.1
	b	Cake, 4-in. diam., ⅜ in. thick	1 cake	27	do	2.5	.8	1.1	.4
	c	Pound	1 lb	454	do	41.3	13.5	18.1	6.8
1475		**Pastina**, egg, enriched, dry form	1 cup	170	Egg	7.0	2.2	3.1	.5
		Pastry shell, plain. See Piecrust (items 1597–1600).							
		Peanuts:							
1495		Roasted in shell (with skins):							

(A)		(B)			(C)	(D)	(E)	(F)	(G)
		Whole (refuse: shells, 33%):[2]							
	a	Pound	1 lb	454		148.0	32.5	63.6	42.9
	b	10 nuts (jumbo)	10 nuts	27		8.8	1.9	3.8	2.6
		Shelled, chopped form:							
	c	Cup	1 cup	144		70.1	15.4	30.2	20.3
	d	Tablespoon	1 tbsp	9		4.4	1.0	1.9	1.3
1496		Roasted, salted (Spanish and Virginia types):							
	a	Cup, whole, halves, chopped form	1 cup	144		71.7	15.8	30.8	20.8
	b	Whole nuts, approx. 20 Spanish type or 10 Virginia type; or 1 tbsp. of chopped form.	10 or 20 whole nuts or 1 tbsp. chopped.	9		4.5	1.0	1.9	1.3
	c	Pound	1 lb	454		225.9	49.7	97.1	65.5
	d	Ounce	1 oz	28		14.1	3.1	6.1	4.1
1499		**Peanut butter** made with moderate amounts of added fat, nutritive sweetener, salt:							
		Container and approx. contents:							
	a	Can, size 603 × 700[5] (No. 10); net wt., 110 oz. (6 lb. 14 oz.).	1 can	3,118	Peanuts, vegetable shortening.	1,577.7	294.0	745.8	447.7
		Glass jar:							
	b	Size, 12 oz.; net wt., 12 oz	1 jar	340	do	172.0	32.1	81.3	48.8
	c	Size, 18 oz.; net wt., 18 oz. (1 lb. 2 oz.)	1 jar	510	do	258.1	48.1	122.0	73.2
	d	Size, 28 oz.; net wt., 28 oz. (1 lb. 12 oz.)	1 jar	794	do	401.8	74.9	189.9	114.0
	e	Cup	1 cup	258	do	130.5	24.3	61.7	37.1
	f	Tablespoon	1 tbsp	16	do	8.1	1.5	3.8	2.3
1501		**Peanut flour,** defatted	1 cup	60		5.5	1.2	2.4	1.6
		Peanut oil. See Oils (items 1401n–1401q).							
1536		**Pecans:**							
		In shell (refuse: shells, 47%):[2]							
		Size and approx. count per pound:							
	a	Oversize (55 or less per pound)	10 nuts	82		31.0	2.2	19.5	6.2
	b	Extra large (56–63 per pound)	10 nuts	76		28.7	2.0	18.1	5.7
	c	Large (64–77 per pound)	10 nuts	65		24.5	1.7	15.4	4.9
	d	Pound	1 lb	454		171.2	12.0	107.8	34.2
		Shelled:							
		Halves:							
		Size and approx. count per pound:							
	e	Mammoth (250 or less per pound)	10 nuts	18		12.8	.9	8.1	2.6
	f	Jumbo (301–350 per pound)	10 nuts	14		10.0	.7	6.3	2.0
	g	Large (451–550 per pound)	10 nuts	9		6.4	.4	4.0	1.3
	h	Cup	1 cup	108		76.9	5.4	48.4	15.4
		Chopped or pieces:							
	i	Cup	1 cup	118		84.0	5.9	52.9	16.8
	j	Tablespoon	1 tbsp	7.5		5.3	.4	3.4	1.1
	k	Ground	1 cup	95		67.6	4.7	42.6	13.5
	l	Pound	1 lb	454		323.0	22.6	203.5	64.6
	m	Ounce	1 oz	28		20.2	1.4	12.7	4.0
1547		**Peppers, sweet, garden varieties, immature green, cooked, stuffed with beef and crumbs** (pepper, 2¾ in. long, 2½-in. diam., with 1⅛ cups of stuffing).	1 stuffed pepper	185	Beef, butter, bread, milk	10.2	4.8	4.0	.6
		Pies:							
		Baked (9-in. diam., 28.3-in. cir.):[55]							
1566		Apple:							
		Sector, 3½-in. arc; ⅛ of pie:							

[2] Measure and weight apply to food as it is described with inedible part or parts (refuse) included.
[5] Dimensions of can: 1st dimension represents diameter; 2d dimension, height of can. 1st or left-hand digit in each dimension gives number of whole inches; next 2 digits give additional fraction of dimension expressed as 16th of an inch.
[55] For pies containing lard, substitution of fat in formula was made on equal weight basis.

TABLE 2.—*Fatty acid values for household measures and market units of foods*—Continued

[Item and footnote numbers correspond to those in table 1 of this publication. Values in parentheses denote imputed values usually from another form of the food or from a similar food. Dashes (—) denote lack of reliable data for a constituent believed to be present in a measurable amount. Calculated values, as those based on a recipe, are not in parentheses]

Item No.	Food, approximate measures, units, and weight (edible part unless footnotes indicate otherwise)			Principal sources of fat	Amount in edible part of foods: Total fat	Total saturated fatty acids	Unsaturated fatty acids: Oleic $C_{18}(-2H)$	Unsaturated fatty acids: Linoleic $C_{18}(-4H)$
(A)	(B)			(C)	(D)	(E)	(F)	(G)
			Grams		*Grams*	*Grams*	*Grams*	*Grams*
	Pies—Continued							
	Baked (9-in. diam., 28.3-in. cir.) [55]—Continued							
	Apple—Continued							
	Sector, 3½-in. arc; ⅛ of pie—Continued							
a	Made with vegetable shortening	1 sector	118	Vegetable shortening, butter.	13.1	3.4	6.4	2.8
b	Made with lard	1 sector	118	Lard, butter	13.1	5.0	5.9	1.4
	Sector, 1-in. arc:							
c	Made with vegetable shortening	1 sector	33.4	Vegetable shortening, butter.	3.7	1.0	1.8	.8
d	Made with lard	1 sector	33.4	Lard, butter	3.7	1.4	1.7	.4
1567	Banana custard:							
	Sector, 3½-in. arc; ⅛ of pie:							
a	Made with vegetable shortening	1 sector	114	Vegetable shortening, milk, egg.	10.6	3.4	4.8	1.8
b	Made with lard	1 sector	114	Lard, milk, egg	10.6	4.3	4.6	.9
	Sector, 1-in. arc:							
c	Made with vegetable shortening	1 sector	32.2	Vegetable shortening, milk, egg.	3.0	1.0	1.4	.5
d	Made with lard	1 sector	32.2	Lard, milk, egg	3.0	1.2	1.3	.3
1568	Blackberry:							
	Sector, 3½-in. arc; ⅛ of pie:							
a	Made with vegetable shortening	1 sector	118	Vegetable shortening	13.0	3.2	6.5	2.9
b	Made with lard	1 sector	118	Lard	13.0	4.9	5.9	1.4
	Sector, 1-in. arc:							
c	Made with vegetable shortening	1 sector	33.4	Vegetable shortening	3.7	.9	1.8	.8
d	Made with lard	1 sector	33.4	Lard	3.7	1.4	1.7	.4
1569	Blueberry:							
	Sector, 3½-in. arc; ⅛ of pie:							
a	Made with vegetable shortening	1 sector	118	Vegetable shortening	12.7	3.2	6.3	2.9
b	Made with lard	1 sector	118	Lard	12.7	4.8	5.8	1.3
	Sector, 1-in. arc:							
c	Made with vegetable shortening	1 sector	33.4	Vegetable shortening	3.6	.9	1.8	.8
d	Made with lard	1 sector	33.4	Lard	3.6	1.4	1.6	.4
1570	Butterscotch:							
	Sector, 3½-in. arc; ⅛ of pie:							
a	Made with vegetable shortening	1 sector	114	Vegetable shortening, butter, milk, egg.	12.5	4.5	5.4	1.8
b	Made with lard	1 sector	114	Lard, butter, milk, egg	12.5	5.4	5.2	1.0
	Sector, 1-in. arc:							
c	Made with vegetable shortening	1 sector	32.2	Vegetable shortening, butter, milk, egg.	3.5	1.3	1.5	.5
d	Made with lard	1 sector	32.2	Lard, butter, milk, egg	3.5	1.5	1.5	.3
1571	Cherry:							

(A)	(B)		(C)		(D)	(E)	(F)	(G)
a	Made with vegetable shortening	1 sector	118	Vegetable shortening, butter.	13.3	3.5	6.5	2.9
b	Made with lard	1 sector	118	Lard, butter	13.3	5.1	6.0	1.4
	Sector, 1-in. arc:							
c	Made with vegetable shortening	1 sector	33.4	Vegetable shortening, butter.	3.8	1.0	1.8	.8
d	Made with lard	1 sector	33.4	Lard, butter	3.8	1.5	1.7	.4
1572	Chocolate chiffon:							
	Sector, 3½-in. arc; ⅛ of pie:							
a	Made with vegetable shortening	1 sector	81	Vegetable shortening, chocolate, egg.	12.4	4.2	5.7	1.8
b	Made with lard	1 sector	81	Lard, chocolate, egg	12.4	5.1	5.4	1.0
	Sector, 1-in. arc:							
c	Made with vegetable shortening	1 sector	22.9	Vegetable shortening, chocolate, egg.	3.5	1.2	1.6	.5
d	Made with lard	1 sector	22.9	Lard, chocolate, egg	3.5	1.4	1.5	.3
1573	Chocolate meringue:							
	Sector, 3½-in. arc; ⅛ of pie:							
a	Made with vegetable shortening	1 sector	114	Vegetable shortening, chocolate, milk, egg.	13.7	5.1	6.0	1.8
b	Made with lard	1 sector	114	Lard, chocolate, milk, egg	13.7	6.0	5.7	1.0
	Sector, 1-in. arc:							
c	Made with vegetable shortening	1 sector	32.2	Vegetable shortening, chocolate, milk, egg.	3.9	1.4	1.7	.5
d	Made with lard	1 sector	32.2	Lard, chocolate, milk, egg	3.9	1.7	1.6	.3
1574	Coconut custard:							
	Sector, 3½-in. arc; ⅛ of pie:							
a	Made with vegetable shortening	1 sector	114	Vegetable shortening, milk, egg, coconut.	14.3	5.7	5.7	1.8
b	Made with lard	1 sector	114	Lard, milk, egg, coconut	14.3	6.6	5.4	1.0
	Sector, 1-in. arc:							
c	Made with vegetable shortening	1 sector	32.2	Vegetable shortening, milk, egg, coconut.	4.0	1.6	1.6	.5
d	Made with lard	1 sector	32.2	Lard, milk, egg, coconut	4.0	1.9	1.5	.3
1575	Custard:							
	Sector, 3½-in. arc; ⅛ of pie:							
a	Made with vegetable shortening	1 sector	114	Vegetable shortening, milk, egg.	12.7	4.3	5.6	1.8
b	Made with lard	1 sector	114	Lard, milk, egg	12.7	5.2	5.3	1.0
	Sector, 1-in. arc:							
c	Made with vegetable shortening	1 sector	32.2	Vegetable shortening, milk, egg.	3.6	1.2	1.6	.5
d	Made with lard	1 sector	32.2	Lard, milk, egg	3.6	1.5	1.5	.3
1576	Lemon chiffon:							
	Sector, 3½-in. arc; ⅛ of pie:							
a	Made with vegetable shortening	1 sector	81	Vegetable shortening, egg.	10.2	2.7	4.9	1.8
b	Made with lard	1 sector	81	Lard, egg	10.2	3.7	4.6	1.0
	Sector, 1-in. arc:							
c	Made with vegetable shortening	1 sector	22.9	Vegetable shortening, egg.	2.9	.8	1.4	.5
d	Made with lard	1 sector	22.9	Lard, egg	2.9	1.0	1.3	.3
1577	Lemon meringue:							
	Sector, 3½-in. arc; ⅛ of pie:							
a	Made with vegetable shortening	1 sector	105	Vegetable shortening, egg, butter.	10.7	3.2	5.0	1.8
b	Made with lard	1 sector	105	Lard, egg, butter	10.7	4.1	4.7	.9

[a] For pies containing lard, substitution of fat in formula was made on equal weight basis.

TABLE 2.—*Fatty acid values for household measures and market units of foods*—Continued

[Item and footnote numbers correspond to those in table 1 of this publication. Values in parentheses denote imputed values usually from another form of the food or from a similar food. Dashes (—) denote lack of reliable data for a constituent believed to be present in a measurable amount. Calculated values, as those based on a recipe, are not in parentheses]

Item No.		Food, approximate measures, units, and weight (edible part unless footnotes indicate otherwise)			Principal sources of fat	Amount in edible part of foods: Total fat	Total saturated fatty acids	Unsaturated fatty acids: Oleic $C_{18}(-2H)$	Linoleic $C_{18}(-4H)$
(A)		(B)			(C)	(D)	(E)	(F)	(G)
				Grams		*Grams*	*Grams*	*Grams*	*Grams*
		Pies—Continued							
		Baked (9-in. diam., 28.3-in. cir.)[55]—Continued							
		Lemon meringue—Continued							
		Sector, 1-in. arc:							
	c	Made with vegetable shortening	1 sector	29.7	Vegetable shortening, egg, butter.	3.0	0.9	1.4	0.5
	d	Made with lard	1 sector	29.7	Lard, egg, butter	3.0	1.2	1.3	.3
1578		Mince:							
		Sector, 3½-in. arc; ⅛ of pie:							
	a	Made with vegetable shortening	1 sector	118	Vegetable shortening, suet.	13.6	3.6	6.7	2.9
	b	Made with lard	1 sector	118	Lard, suet	13.6	5.2	6.2	1.4
		Sector, 1-in. arc:							
	c	Made with vegetable shortening	1 sector	33.4	Vegetable shortening, suet.	3.8	1.0	1.9	.8
	d	Made with lard	1 sector	33.4	Lard, suet	3.8	1.5	1.8	.4
1579		Peach:							
		Sector, 3½-in. arc; ⅛ of pie:							
	a	Made with vegetable shortening	1 sector	118	Vegetable shortening	12.6	3.1	6.3	2.8
	b	Made with lard	1 sector	118	Lard	12.6	4.7	5.8	1.3
		Sector, 1-in. arc:							
	c	Made with vegetable shortening	1 sector	33.4	Vegetable shortening	3.6	.9	1.8	.8
	d	Made with lard	1 sector	33.4	Lard	3.6	1.3	1.6	.4
1580		Pecan:							
		Sector, 3½-in. arc; ⅛ of pie:							
	a	Made with vegetable shortening	1 sector	103	Pecans, vegetable shortening, egg.	23.6	3.3	13.6	4.7
	b	Made with lard	1 sector	103	Pecans, lard, egg	23.6	4.2	13.3	3.9
		Sector, 1-in. arc:							
	c	Made with vegetable shortening	1 sector	29.2	Pecans, vegetable shortening, egg.	6.7	.9	3.9	1.3
	d	Made with lard	1 sector	29.2	Pecans, lard, egg	6.7	1.2	3.8	1.1
1581		Pineapple:							
		Sector, 3½-in. arc; ⅛ of pie:							
	a	Made with vegetable shortening	1 sector	118	Vegetable shortening	12.6	3.1	6.3	2.8
	b	Made with lard	1 sector	118	Lard	12.6	4.7	5.8	1.3
		Sector, 1-in. arc:							
	c	Made with vegetable shortening	1 sector	33.4	Vegetable shortening	3.6	.9	1.8	.8
	d	Made with lard	1 sector	33.4	Lard	3.6	1.3	1.6	.4
1582		Pineapple chiffon:							
		Sector, 3½-in. arc; ⅛ of pie:							
	a	Made with vegetable shortening	1 sector	81	Vegetable shortening, egg.	9.8	2.6	4.7	1.8
	b	Made with lard	1 sector	81	Lard, egg	9.8	3.5	4.4	.9
		Sector, 1-in. arc:							

(A)		(B)		(C)		(D)	(E)	(F)	(G)
	c	Made with vegetable shortening	1 sector	22.9	Vegetable shortening, egg.	2.8	0.7	1.3	0.5
	d	Made with lard	1 sector	22.9	Lard, egg	2.8	1.0	1.3	.3
1583		Pineapple custard:							
		Sector, 3½-in. arc; ⅛ of pie:							
	a	Made with vegetable shortening	1 sector	114	Vegetable shortening, milk, egg.	9.9	3.0	4.6	1.7
	b	Made with lard	1 sector	114	Lard, milk, egg	9.9	3.9	4.3	.9
		Sector, 1-in. arc:							
	c	Made with vegetable shortening	1 sector	32.2	Vegetable shortening, milk, egg.	2.8	.9	1.3	.5
	d	Made with lard	1 sector	32.2	Lard, milk, egg	2.8	1.1	1.2	.3
1584		Pumpkin:							
		Sector, 3½-in. arc; ⅛ of pie:							
	a	Made with vegetable shortening	1 sector	114	Vegetable shortening, butter, egg, milk.	12.8	4.5	5.6	1.8
	b	Made with lard	1 sector	114	Lard, butter, egg, milk	12.8	5.4	5.3	1.0
		Sector, 1-in. arc:							
	c	Made with vegetable shortening	1 sector	32.2	Vegetable shortening, butter, egg, milk.	3.6	1.3	1.6	.5
	d	Made with lard	1 sector	32.2	Lard, butter, egg, milk	3.6	1.5	1.5	.3
1585		Raisin:							
		Sector, 3½-in. arc; ⅛ of pie:							
	a	Made with vegetable shortening	1 sector	118	Vegetable shortening	12.6	3.1	6.3	2.8
	b	Made with lard	1 sector	118	Lard	12.6	4.7	5.8	1.3
		Sector, 1-in. arc:							
	c	Made with vegetable shortening	1 sector	33.4	Vegetable shortening	3.6	.9	1.8	.8
	d	Made with lard	1 sector	33.4	Lard	3.6	1.3	1.6	.4
1586		Rhubarb:							
		Sector, 3½-in. arc; ⅛ of pie:							
	a	Made with vegetable shortening	1 sector	118	Vegetable shortening	12.6	3.1	6.3	2.8
	b	Made with lard	1 sector	118	Lard	12.6	4.7	5.8	1.3
		Sector, 1-in. arc:							
	c	Made with vegetable shortening	1 sector	33.4	Vegetable shortening	3.6	.9	1.8	.8
	d	Made with lard	1 sector	33.4	Lard	3.6	1.3	1.6	.4
1587		Strawberry:							
		Sector, 3½-in. arc; ⅛ of pie:							
	a	Made with vegetable shortening	1 sector	93	Vegetable shortening	7.3	1.8	3.7	1.7
	b	Made with lard	1 sector	93	Lard	7.3	2.8	3.4	.8
		Sector, 1-in. arc:							
	c	Made with vegetable shortening	1 sector	26.2	Vegetable shortening	2.1	.5	1.0	.5
	d	Made with lard	1 sector	26.2	Lard	2.1	.8	.9	.2
1588		Sweetpotato:							
		Sector, 3½-in. arc; ⅛ of pie:							
	a	Made with vegetable shortening	1 sector	114	Vegetable shortening, butter, milk, egg.	12.9	4.6	5.6	1.9
	b	Made with lard	1 sector	114	Lard, butter, milk, egg	12.9	5.6	5.3	1.0
		Sector, 1-in. arc:							
	c	Made with vegetable shortening	1 sector	32.2	Vegetable shortening, butter, milk, egg.	3.6	1.3	1.6	.5
	d	Made with lard	1 sector	32.2	Lard, butter, milk, egg	3.6	1.6	1.5	.3
		Frozen in unbaked form (8-in. diam., 25.1-in. cir.):							
		Apple:							
1589		Unbaked pie, whole	1 pie	660	Vegetable shortening	54.8	13.6	27.3	12.2
1590		Baked:							
	a	Sector, 4⅛-in. arc; ⅙ of pie	1 sector	92	do	9.1	2.3	4.6	2.0
	b	Sector, 1-in. arc	1 sector	21.9	do	2.2	.5	1.1	.5

[a] For pies containing lard, substitution of fat in formula was made on equal weight basis.

TABLE 2.—*Fatty acid values for household measures and market units of foods*—Continued

[Item and footnote numbers correspond to those in table 1 of this publication. Values in parentheses denote imputed values usually from another form of the food or from a similar food. Dashes (—) denote lack of reliable data for a constituent believed to be present in a measurable amount. Calculated values, as those based on a recipe, are not in parentheses]

Item No. (A)		Food, approximate measures, units, and weight (edible part unless footnotes indicate otherwise) (B)			Principal sources of fat (C)	Total fat (D)	Total saturated fatty acids (E)	Oleic $C_{18}(-2H)$ (F)	Linoleic $C_{18}(-4H)$ (G)
				Grams		*Grams*	*Grams*	*Grams*	*Grams*
		Pies—Continued							
		Frozen in unbaked form (8-in. diam., 25.1-in. cir.)—Continued							
		Cherry:							
1591		Unbaked pie, whole	1 pie	660	Vegetable shortening	70.0	17.4	34.8	15.6
1592		Baked:							
	a	Sector, 4⅛-in. arc; ⅙ of pie	1 sector	97	do	11.7	2.9	5.8	2.6
	b	Sector, 1-in. arc	1 sector	23.1	do	2.8	.7	1.4	.6
1594		Coconut custard, baked:							
	a	Sector, 4⅛-in. arc; ⅙ of pie	1 sector	100	Vegetable shortening, egg, coconut.	12.0	5.0	4.6	1.6
	b	Sector, 1-in. arc	1 sector	23.9	do	2.9	1.2	1.1	.4
		Prepared from mix (filling and piecrust), baked:							
1596		Coconut custard pie (filling made with mix, egg yolks, milk), 8-in. diam., 25.1-in. cir.:							
	a	Sector, 3⅛-in. arc; ⅛ of pie	1 sector	100	Vegetable shortening, milk, coconut, egg.	7.9	3.4	3.9	1.0
	b	Sector, 1-in. arc	1 sector	31.8	do	2.5	1.1	1.2	.3
		Piecrust or plain pastry, made with enriched or unenriched flour:							
1597 or 1599		Unbaked:							
	a	Made with vegetable shortening	1 pie shell	194	Vegetable shortening	60.1	14.9	29.9	13.4
	b	Made with lard	1 pie shell	194	Lard	60.1	22.6	27.5	6.3
1598 or 1600		Baked:							
	a	Made with vegetable shortening	1 pie shell	180	Vegetable shortening	60.1	14.9	29.9	13.4
	b	Made with lard	1 pie shell	180	Lard	60.1	22.6	27.5	6.3
		Piecrust mix (including stick form) and piecrust baked from mix:							
1601		Mix, dry form:							
	a	Package, 10 oz	1 pkg	284	Vegetable shortening	92.9	23.0	46.0	21.0
		Cup:							
	b	Not packed	1 cup	120	do	39.2	9.7	19.4	8.9
	c	Packed	1 cup	195	do	63.8	15.8	31.6	14.4
1602		Piecrust, prepared with water, baked (yield from 10-oz. pkg. (item 1601a)).	11.3 oz	320	do	93.1	23.0	46.1	21.1
1605		**Pigs' feet, pickled**	2 oz	57		8.4	3.0	3.5	.8
1626		**Pistachionuts:**							
	a	In shell (refuse: shells, 50%) [2]	1 lb	454		121.8	12.2	79.2	23.1
	b	Shelled	1 lb	454		243.6	24.4	158.3	46.3
		Pizza:							
		From home recipe, baked (in 14-in.-diam. pan):							
1628		With cheese topping:							

(A)		(B)			(C)	(D)	(E)	(F)	(G)
	a	Whole, 13¾-in. diam., 43.2-in. cir	1 pizza	[7] 520	Cheese, vegetable shortening, olive oil.	43.2	16.9	18.4	4.2
	b	Sector, 5⅓-in. arc; ⅛ of pizza	1 sector	65	do	5.4	2.1	2.3	.5
	c	Sector, 1-in. arc	1 sector	12.0	do	1.0	.4	.4	.1
	d	Pound	1 lb	454	do	37.6	14.7	16.1	3.7
1629		With sausage topping: [56]							
	a	Whole, 13¾-in. diam., 43.2-in. cir	1 pizza	[7] 535	Pork, cheese, vegetable shortening, olive oil.	49.8	14.5	23.2	6.3
	b	Sector, 5⅓-in. arc; ⅛ of pizza	1 sector	67	do	6.2	1.8	2.9	.8
	c	Sector, 1-in. arc	1 sector	12.4	do	1.2	.3	.5	.1
	d	Pound	1 lb	454	do	42.2	12.3	19.7	5.3
		Chilled, with cheese, commercial:							
1630		Partially baked:							
	a	Container, net wt., 20 oz.; 12-in.-diam. pizza, ¼ in. thick; cir., 37.7 in.	1 pizza	567	Cheese, vegetable shortening, olive oil.	32.9	11.6	14.4	4.4
	b	Pound	1 lb	454	do	26.3	9.3	11.5	3.5
1631		Baked:							
	a	Yield from 12-in.-diam. pizza, cir., 37.7 in. (item 1630a).	17 oz	482	do	32.9	11.6	14.4	4.4
	b	Sector, 4¾-in. arc; ⅛ of pizza [57]	1 sector	60	do	4.1	1.4	1.8	.5
	c	Sector, 1-in. arc [57]	1 sector	12.8	do	.9	.3	.4	.1
	d	Yield from 1 lb., chilled, partially baked pizza (item 1630b).	13.6 oz	386	do	26.3	9.3	11.5	3.5
	e	Pound	1 lb	454	do	30.8	10.9	13.5	4.1
		Frozen, with cheese, commercial:							
1632		Partially baked:							
	a	Container, net wt., 15 oz.; 10-in.-diam. pizza, ¼ in. thick; cir., 31.4 in.	1 pizza	425	do	28.1	10.2	12.2	3.5
	b	Container, net wt., 11 oz.; four 5¼-in.-diam. pizzas, ⅛ in. thick; cir., 16½ in.	4 pizzas	312	do	20.6	7.5	9.0	2.6
	c	Pound	1 lb	454	do	29.9	10.8	13.1	3.8
1633		Baked:							
	a	Yield from 10-in.-diam. pizza, cir., 31.4 in. (item 1632a).	14 oz	398	do	28.1	10.2	12.2	3.5
	b	Sector, 4½-in. arc; ⅐ of pizza [57]	1 sector	57	do	4.0	1.5	1.8	.5
	c	Sector, 1-in. arc [57]	1 sector	12.7	do	.9	.3	.4	.1
	d	Yield from four 5¼-in.-diam. pizzas, cir., 16½ in. (item 1632b).	10.3 oz. or 4 pizzas	292	do	20.6	7.5	9.0	2.6
	e	Pizza	1 pizza	73	do	5.2	1.9	2.3	.6
	f	Yield from 1 lb., frozen, partially baked pizza (item 1632c).	15 oz	424	do	29.9	10.8	13.1	3.8
	g	Pound	1 lb	454	do	32.2	11.7	14.1	4.0
		Popcorn:							
1653		Unpopped	1 cup	205		9.6	1.0	2.7	5.1
		Popped (commercial):							
1654		Plain, large kernel [58]	1 cup	6		.3	Trace	.1	.2
1655		Oil and salt added, large kernel: [58]							
	a	Coconut oil added	1 cup	9	Coconut oil	2.0	1.4	.2	.2
	b	Butter added	1 cup	9	Butter	2.0	.9	.6	.2
1656		Sugar coated	1 cup	35	Coconut oil	1.2	.4	.3	.4

[3] Measure and weight apply to food as it is described with inedible part or parts (refuse) included.
[7] Yield of formula used to calculate nutritive values in Agr. Handb. No. 8, rev. 1963.
[56] Measures, their weights, and fatty acid values apply to product that does not contain cheese. For fatty acid values of product with cheese, see Appendix A, table 3, p. 264.
[57] Based on dimensions of partially baked product.
[58] Smaller kernels may weigh as much as 6 g. more per cup.

TABLE 2.—*Fatty acid values for household measures and market units of foods*—Continued

[Item and footnote numbers correspond to those in table 1 of this publication. Values in parentheses denote imputed values usually from another form of the food or from a similar food. Dashes (—) denote lack of reliable data for a constituent believed to be present in a measurable amount. Calculated values, as those based on a recipe, are not in parentheses]

Item No.		Food, approximate measures, units, and weight (edible part unless footnotes indicate otherwise)			Principal sources of fat	Amount in edible part of foods: Total fat	Total saturated fatty acids	Unsaturated fatty acids: Oleic $C_{18}(-2H)$	Linoleic $C_{18}(-4H)$
(A)		(B)			(C)	(D)	(E)	(F)	(G)
				Grams		*Grams*	*Grams*	*Grams*	*Grams*
1657		**Popovers,** baked (home recipe), 2¾-in. diam. at top, 2-in. diam. at bottom, height at center, 4 in.	1 popover	40	Vegetable shortening, egg, milk.	3.7	1.3	1.6	0.5
		Pork, fresh, retail cuts:							
		Ham:							
1698		Raw, lean with fat:							
	a	With bone and skin (63% lean, 22% fat) (refuse: bone and skin, 15%).[2]	1 lb	454		102.6	36.9	43.1	9.2
	b	Without bone and skin (74% lean, 26% fat).	1 lb	454		120.7	43.5	50.7	10.9
		Cooked (baked or roasted):							
1699		Lean with fat (74% lean, 26% fat):							
	a	Yield from 1 lb., raw ham with bone and skin (item 1698a).	9.2 oz	262		80.2	28.9	33.7	7.2
	b	Yield from 1 lb., raw ham without bone and skin (item 1698b).	10.9 oz	308		94.2	33.9	39.6	8.5
		Cup:							
	c	Chopped or diced (not packed)	1 cup	140		42.8	15.4	18.0	3.9
	d	Ground	1 cup	110		33.7	12.1	14.2	3.0
	e	Pound	1 lb	454		138.8	50.0	58.3	12.5
	f	Piece, approx. 4⅛ in. long, 2¼ in. wide, ¼ in. thick; wt., 1½ oz.	2 pieces or 3 oz	85		26.0	9.4	10.9	2.3
1701		Lean, trimmed of separable fat:							
	a	Yield from 1 lb., raw ham with bone and skin (item 1698a).	6.8 oz	194		19.4	7.0	8.1	1.7
	b	Yield from 1 lb., raw ham without bone and skin (item 1698b).	8.1 oz	228		22.8	8.2	9.6	2.1
		Cup:							
	c	Chopped or diced (not packed)	1 cup	140		14.0	5.0	5.9	1.3
	d	Ground	1 cup	110		11.0	4.0	4.6	1.0
	e	Pound	1 lb	454		45.4	16.3	19.1	4.1
	f	Piece, approx. 4⅛ in. long, 2¼ in. wide, ¼ in. thick; wt., 1½ oz.	2 pieces or 3 oz	85		8.5	3.1	3.6	.8
		Loin and loin chops:							
1715		Raw, lean with fat:							
	a	With bone (63% lean, 16% fat) (refuse: bone, 21%).[2]	1 lb	454		89.0	32.0	37.4	8.0
	b	Without bone (80% lean, 20% fat)	1 lb	454		112.9	40.6	47.4	10.2
		Cooked:							
		Lean with fat:							
1716		Baked or roasted loin roast (80% lean, 20% fat):							
	a	Yield from 1 lb., raw loin with bone (item 1715a).	8.6 oz	244		69.5	25.0	29.2	6.3

(A)	(B)		(C)	(D)	(E)	(F)	(G)
b	Yield from 1 lb., raw loin without bone (item 1715b).	10.9 oz	308	87.8	31.6	36.9	7.9
c	Cup, chopped or diced pieces (not packed).	1 cup	140	39.9	14.4	16.8	3.6
d	Pound	1 lb	454	129.3	46.5	54.3	11.6
e	Piece, approx. 2½ in. long, 2½ in. wide, ¾ in. thick; wt., 3 oz.	1 piece or 3 oz	85	24.2	8.7	10.2	2.2
1717	Broiled loin chops (72% lean, 28% fat):						
a	Yield from 1 lb., raw chops with bone (item 1715a).	8.2 oz	233	73.9	26.6	31.0	6.7
b	Yield from 1 lb., raw chops without bone (item 1715b).	10.4 oz	295	93.5	33.7	39.3	8.4
	Yield from 1 chop, raw with bone; ⅓ or ¼ of item 1715a:						
c	Cut 3 per pound	2.7 oz	78	24.7	8.9	10.4	2.2
d	Cut 4 per pound	2 oz	58	18.4	6.6	7.7	1.7
	Lean, trimmed of separable fat:						
1719	Baked or roasted loin roast:						
a	Yield from 1 lb., raw loin with bone (item 1715a).	6.9 oz	195	27.7	10.0	11.6	2.5
b	Yield from 1 lb., raw loin without bone (item 1715b).	8.7 oz	247	35.1	12.6	14.7	3.2
c	Cup, chopped or diced pieces (not packed).	1 cup	140	19.9	7.2	8.4	1.8
d	Pound	1 lb	454	64.4	23.2	27.0	5.8
e	Piece, approx. 2½ in. long, 2½ in. wide, ¾ in. thick; wt., 3 oz.	1 piece or 3 oz	85	12.1	4.4	5.1	1.1
1720	Broiled loin chops:						
a	Yield from 1 lb., raw chops with bone (item 1715a).	5.9 oz	168	25.9	9.3	10.9	2.3
b	Yield from 1 lb., raw chops without bone (item 1715b).	7½ oz	212	32.6	11.7	13.7	2.9
	Yield from 1 chop, raw with bone; ⅓ or ¼ of item 1715a:						
c	Cut 3 per pound	2 oz	56	8.6	3.1	3.6	.8
d	Cut 4 per pound	1½ oz	42	6.5	2.3	2.7	.6
	Shoulder cuts (Boston butt and picnic):						
	Boston butt:						
1734	Raw, lean with fat:						
a	With bone and skin (74% lean, 20% fat) (refuse: bone and skin, 6%).[2]	1 lb	454	104.1	37.5	43.7	9.4
b	Without bone and skin (79% lean, 21% fat).	1 lb	454	111.1	40.0	46.7	10.0
	Cooked (roasted):						
1735	Lean with fat (79% lean, 21% fat):						
a	Yield from 1 lb., raw meat with bone and skin (item 1734a).	10.2 oz	290	82.7	29.8	34.7	7.4
b	Yield from 1 lb., raw meat without bone and skin (item 1734b).	10.9 oz	308	87.8	31.6	36.9	7.9
	Cup:						
c	Chopped or diced (not packed)	1 cup	140	39.9	14.4	16.8	3.6
d	Ground	1 cup	110	31.4	11.3	13.2	2.8
e	Pound	1 lb	454	129.3	46.5	54.3	11.6
f	Piece, approx. 2½ in. long, 2½ in. wide, ¼ in. thick; wt., 1 oz.	3 pieces or 3 oz	85	24.2	8.7	10.2	2.2

[2] Measure and weight apply to food as it is described with inedible part or parts (refuse) included.

TABLE 2.—*Fatty acid values for household measures and market units of foods*—Continued

[Item and footnote numbers correspond to those in table 1 of this publication. Values in parentheses denote imputed values usually from another form of the food or from a similar food. Dashes (—) denote lack of reliable data for a constituent believed to be present in a measurable amount. Calculated values, as those based on a recipe, are not in parentheses]

Item No.		Food, approximate measures, units, and weight (edible part unless footnotes indicate otherwise)			Principal sources of fat	Amount in edible part of foods: Total fat	Total saturated fatty acids	Unsaturated fatty acids: Oleic $C_{18}(-2H)$	Linoleic $C_{18}(-4H)$
(A)		(B)			(C)	(D)	(E)	(F)	(G)
				Grams		*Grams*	*Grams*	*Grams*	*Grams*
		Pork, fresh, retail cuts—Continued							
		Shoulder cuts (Boston butt and picnic)—Continued							
		Boston butt—Continued							
		Cooked (roasted)—Continued							
1737		Lean, trimmed of separable fat:							
	a	Yield from 1 lb., raw meat with bone and skin (item 1734a).	8.1 oz	229		32.7	11.8	13.7	2.9
	b	Yield from 1 lb., raw meat without bone and skin (item 1734b).	8.6 oz	244		34.9	12.6	14.7	3.1
		Cup:							
	c	Chopped or diced (not packed)	1 cup	140		20.0	7.2	8.4	1.8
	d	Ground	1 cup	110		15.7	5.7	6.6	1.4
	e	Pound	1 lb	454		64.9	23.4	27.3	5.8
	f	Piece, approx. 2½ in. long, 2½ in. wide, ¼ in. thick; wt., 1 oz.	3 pieces or 3 oz	85		12.2	4.4	5.1	1.1
		Picnic:							
1749		Raw, lean with fat:							
	a	With bone and skin (61% lean, 22% fat) (refuse: bone and skin, 18%).[2]	1 lb	454		92.2	33.2	38.7	8.3
	b	Without bone and skin (74% lean, 26% fat).	1 lb	454		112.0	40.3	47.0	10.1
		Cooked (simmered):							
1750		Lean with fat (74% lean, 26% fat):							
	a	Yield from 1 lb., raw meat with bone and skin (item 1749a).	8.4 oz	238		72.6	26.1	30.5	6.5
	b	Yield from 1 lb., raw meat without bone and skin (item 1749b).	10.2 oz	290		88.5	31.9	37.2	8.0
	c	Cup, chopped or diced pieces (not packed).	1 cup	140		42.7	15.4	17.9	3.8
	d	Pound	1 lb	454		138.3	49.8	58.1	12.4
	e	Piece, approx. 2½ in. long, 2½ in. wide, ¼ in. thick; wt., 1 oz.	3 pieces or 3 oz	85		25.9	9.3	10.9	2.3
1752		Lean, trimmed of separable fat:							
	a	Yield from 1 lb., raw meat with bone and skin (item 1947a).	6.2 oz	176		17.2	6.2	7.2	1.5
	b	Yield from 1 lb., raw meat without bone and skin (item 1749b).	7.6 oz	215		21.1	7.6	8.9	1.9
	c	Cup, chopped or diced pieces (not packed).	1 cup	140		13.7	4.9	5.8	1.2
	d	Pound	1 lb	454		44.5	16.0	18.7	4.0
	e	Piece, approx. 2½ in. long, 2½ in. wide, ¼ in. thick; wt., 1 oz.	3 pieces or 3 oz	85		8.3	3.0	3.5	.7
		Spareribs:							
1761		Raw, lean meat with fat and bone (refuse: bone, 40%).[2]	1 lb	454		89.7	32.3	37.7	8.1
1762		Cooked (braised), lean meat with fat:							

(A)		(B)		(C)	(D)	(E)	(F)	(G)
	a	Yield from 1 lb., raw spareribs (item 1761).	6.3 oz	180	70.0	25.2	29.4	6.3
	b	Pound	1 lb	454	176.5	63.5	74.1	15.9
		Pork, cured:						
		Dry, long cure, country style:						
		Ham, unbaked:						
1766		Medium fatness, lean meat with fat, bone, skin (refuse: bone and skin, 13%).[2]	1 lb	454	138	49.7	58.0	12.4
1767		Relatively lean, lean meat with fat, bone, skin (refuse: bone and skin, 14%).[2]	1 lb	454	98	35.3	41.2	8.8
		Light cure, commercial:						
		Ham:						
1768		Unbaked, lean with fat:						
	a	With bone and skin (65% lean, 21% fat) (refuse: bone and skin, 14%).[2]	1 lb	454	89.7	32.3	37.7	8.1
	b	Without bone and skin (76% lean, 24% fat).	1 lb	454	104.3	37.5	43.8	9.4
		Baked or roasted:						
1769		Lean with fat (84% lean, 16% fat):						
	a	Yield from 1 lb., unbaked ham with bone and skin (item **1768a**).	11.3 oz	320	70.7	25.5	29.7	6.4
	b	Yield from 1 lb., unbaked ham without bone and skin (item 1768b).	13.1 oz	372	82.2	29.6	34.5	7.4
		Cup (not packed):						
	c	Chopped or diced	1 cup	140	30.9	11.1	13.0	2.8
	d	Ground	1 cup	110	24.3	8.7	10.2	2.2
	e	Pound	1 lb	454	100.2	36.1	42.1	9.0
	f	Piece, approx. 4⅛ in. long, 2¼ in. wide, ¼ in. thick; wt., 1½ oz.	2 pieces or 3 oz	85	18.8	6.8	7.9	1.7
1771		Lean, trimmed of separable fat:						
	a	Yield from 1 lb., unbaked ham with bone and skin (item 1768a).	8.7 oz	246	21.6	7.8	9.1	1.9
	b	Yield from 1 lb., unbaked ham without bone and skin (item 1768b).	10.2 oz	288	25.3	9.1	10.6	2.3
		Cup (not packed):						
	c	Chopped or diced	1 cup	140	12.3	4.4	5.2	1.1
	d	Ground	1 cup	110	9.7	3.5	4.1	.9
	e	Pound	1 lb	454	39.9	14.4	16.8	3.6
	f	Piece, approx. 4⅛ in. long, 2¼ in. wide, ¼ in. thick; wt., 1½ oz.	2 pieces or 3 oz	85	7.5	2.7	3.2	.7
		Shoulder cuts, Boston butt and picnic:						
		Boston butt:						
1773		Unbaked, lean with fat:						
	a	With bone and skin (70% lean, 23% fat) (refuse: bone and skin, 7%).[2]	1 lb	454	101.7	36.6	42.7	9.2
	b	Without bone and skin (75% lean, 25% fat).	1 lb	454	109.3	39.3	45.9	9.8
		Baked or roasted:						
1774		Lean with fat (83% lean, 17% fat):						
	a	Yield from 1 lb., unbaked meat with bone and skin (item 1773a).	11 oz	312	80.2	28.9	33.7	7.2

[2] Measure and weight apply to food as it is described with inedible part or parts (refuse) included.

TABLE 2.—*Fatty acid values for household measures and market units of foods*—Continued

[Item and footnote numbers correspond to those in table 1 of this publication. Values in parentheses denote imputed values usually from another form of the food or from a similar food. Dashes (—) denote lack of reliable data for a constituent believed to be present in a measurable amount. Calculated values, as those based on a recipe, are not in parentheses]

Item No. (A)	Food, approximate measures, units, and weight (edible part unless footnotes indicate otherwise) (B)		Grams	Principal sources of fat (C)	Total fat (D)	Total saturated fatty acids (E)	Unsaturated fatty acids: Oleic $C_{18}(-2H)$ (F)	Unsaturated fatty acids: Linoleic $C_{18}(-4H)$ (G)
					Grams	*Grams*	*Grams*	*Grams*
	Pork, cured—Continued							
	Light cure, commercial—Continued							
	Shoulder cuts, Boston butt and picnic—Continued							
	Boston butt—Continued							
	Baked or roasted—Continued							
	Lean with fat (83% lean, 17% fat)—Continued							
b	Yield from 1 lb., unbaked meat without bone and skin (item 1773b).	11.8 oz	336		86.4	31.1	36.3	7.8
	Cup (not packed):							
c	Chopped or diced	1 cup	140		36.0	13.0	15.1	3.2
d	Ground	1 cup	110		28.3	10.2	11.9	2.5
e	Pound	1 lb	454		116.6	42.0	49.0	10.5
f	Piece, approx. 2½ in. long, 2½ in. wide, ¼ in. thick; wt., 1 oz.	3 pieces or 3 oz	85		21.8	7.8	9.2	2.0
1776	Lean, trimmed of separable fat:							
a	Yield from 1 lb., unbaked meat with bone and skin (item 1773a).	9.1 oz	259		35.7	12.9	15.0	3.2
b	Yield from 1 lb., unbaked meat without bone and skin (item 1773b).	9.8 oz	279		38.5	13.9	16.2	3.5
	Cup (not packed):							
c	Chopped or diced	1 cup	140		19.3	6.9	8.1	1.7
d	Ground	1 cup	110		15.2	5.5	6.4	1.4
e	Pound	1 lb	454		62.6	22.5	26.3	5.6
f	Piece, approx. 2½ in. long, 2½ in. wide, ¼ in. thick; wt., 1 oz.	3 pieces or 3 oz	85		11.7	4.2	4.9	1.1
	Picnic:							
1778	Unbaked, lean with fat:							
a	With bone and skin (57% lean, 25% fat) (refuse: bone and skin, 18%).[2]	1 lb	454		87.8	31.6	36.9	7.9
b	Without bone and skin (70% lean, 30% fat).	1 lb	454		107.0	38.5	44.9	9.6
	Baked or roasted:							
1779	Lean with fat (82% lean, 18% fat):							
a	Yield from 1 lb., unbaked meat with bone and skin (item 1778a).	9.7 oz	275		69.3	24.9	29.1	6.2
b	Yield from 1 lb., unbaked meat without bone and skin (item 1778b).	11.8 oz	336		84.7	30.5	35.6	7.6
	Cup (not packed):							
c	Chopped or diced	1 cup	140		35.3	12.7	14.8	3.2
d	Ground	1 cup	110		27.7	10.0	11.6	2.5
e	Pound	1 lb	454		114.3	41.1	48.0	10.3

(A)	(B)			(C)	(D)	(E)	(F)	(G)
f	Piece, approx. 2½ in. long, 2½ in. wide, ¼ in. thick; wt., 1 oz.	3 pieces or 3 oz	85		21.4	7.7	9.0	1.9
1781	Lean, trimmed of separable fat:							
a	Yield from 1 lb., unbaked meat with bone and skin (item 1778a).	6.8 oz	192		19.0	6.8	8.0	1.7
b	Yield from 1 lb., unbaked meat without bone and skin (item 1778b).	8.3 oz	235		23.3	8.4	9.8	2.1
	Cup (not packed):							
c	Chopped or diced	1 cup	140		13.9	5.0	5.8	1.3
d	Ground	1 cup	110		10.9	3.9	4.6	1.0
e	Pound	1 lb	454		44.9	16.2	18.9	4.0
f	Piece, approx. 2½ in. long, 2½ in. wide, ¼ in. thick; wt., 1 oz.	3 pieces or 3 oz	85		8.4	3.0	3.5	.8
	Pork, cured, canned:							
	Ham:							
1783	Total can contents:							
a	Can, net wt., 16 oz. (1 lb.)	1 can or 1 lb	454		55.8	20.1	23.5	5.0
b	Can, net wt., 48 oz. (3 lb.)	1 can	1,361		167.4	60.3	70.4	15.1
c	Can, net wt., 128 oz. (8 lb.)	1 can	3,629		446.4	160.8	187.6	40.3
	Pork, cured. See also Bacon (items 125–129).							
	Pork sausage. See Sausage, cold cuts, and luncheon meats (items 2013–2016).							
	Potatoes:							
	Cooked:							
1789	French fried:							
	Strips:							
a	Length, over 3½ in. to 4 in	10 strips	78	Cottonseed oil	10.3	2.6	2.2	5.1
b	Length, over 2 in. to 3½ in	10 strips	50	do	6.6	1.7	1.4	3.3
c	Length, 1–2 in	10 strips	35	do	4.6	1.2	1.0	2.3
d	Pound	1 lb	454	do	59.9	15.0	12.6	29.9
1790	Fried from raw:							
a	Cup	1 cup	170	Vegetable shortening	24.1	6.0	12.1	5.3
b	Pound	1 lb	454	do	64.4	16.1	32.2	14.2
1791	Hashed brown after holding overnight:							
a	Cup	1 cup	155	do	18.1	4.5	9.1	4.0
b	Pound	1 lb	454	do	53.1	13.3	26.5	11.7
1793	Mashed, milk and table fat added:							
	Made with butter:							
a	Cup	1 cup	210	Butter, milk	9.0	4.9	2.9	.3
b	Pound	1 lb	454	do	19.5	10.6	6.3	.6
	Made with margarine:							
	Regular type:[59]							
c	Cup	1 cup	210	Margarine, milk	9.0	2.1	4.3	2.1
d	Pound	1 lb	454	do	19.5	4.4	9.3	4.6
	Soft type:[60]							
e	Cup	1 cup	210	do	9.0	2.1	3.2	3.0
f	Pound	1 lb	454	do	19.5	4.6	7.0	6.5
	Scalloped and au gratin:							
1794	With cheese:							
	Made with butter:							
a	Cup	1 cup	245	Cheese, butter, milk	19.4	10.5	6.3	.6
b	Pound	1 lb	454	do	35.8	19.5	11.7	1.1

[3] Measure and weight apply to food as it is described with inedible part or parts (refuse) included.
[59] Values based on these revised amounts per 100 g. of product: Total saturated fatty acids 1.0 g., oleic acid 2.1 g., linoleic acid 1.0 g.
[60] Values based on these revised amounts per 100 g. of product: Total saturated fatty acids 1.0 g., oleic acid 1.5 g., linoleic acid 1.4 g.

TABLE 2.—*Fatty acid values for household measures and market units of foods*—Continued

[Item and footnote numbers correspond to those in table 1 of this publication. Values in parentheses denote imputed values usually from another form of the food or from a similar food. Dashes (—) denote lack of reliable data for a constituent believed to be present in a measurable amount. Calculated values, as those based on a recipe, are not in parentheses]

Item No. (A)	Food, approximate measures, units, and weight (edible part unless footnotes indicate otherwise) (B)			Principal sources of fat (C)	Amount in edible part of foods: Total fat (D)	Total saturated fatty acids (E)	Unsaturated fatty acids: Oleic $C_{18}(-2H)$ (F)	Unsaturated fatty acids: Linoleic $C_{18}(-4H)$ (G)
			Grams		*Grams*	*Grams*	*Grams*	*Grams*
	Potatoes—Continued							
	Cooked—Continued							
	Scalloped and au gratin—Continued							
	With cheese—Continued							
	Made with margarine:							
	Regular type: [61]							
c	Cup	1 cup	245	Cheese, margarine, milk	19.4	7.7	7.7	2.5
d	Pound	1 lb	454	do	35.8	14.3	14.2	4.5
	Soft type: [62]							
e	Cup	1 cup	245	do	19.4	7.8	6.6	3.3
f	Pound	1 lb	454	do	35.8	14.4	12.3	6.1
1795	Without cheese:							
	Made with butter:							
a	Cup	1 cup	245	Butter, milk	9.6	5.2	3.1	.3
b	Pound	1 lb	454	do	17.7	9.6	5.8	.5
	Made with margarine:							
	Regular type: [63]							
c	Cup	1 cup	245	Margarine, milk	9.6	3.1	4.1	1.6
d	Pound	1 lb	454	do	17.7	5.8	7.6	3.0
	Soft type: [64]							
e	Cup	1 cup	245	do	9.6	3.2	3.3	2.3
f	Pound	1 lb	454	do	17.7	5.9	6.2	4.2
	Dehydrated mashed, prepared from—							
1798	Flakes without milk:							
	Water, milk, table fat added:							
	Made with butter:							
a	Cup	1 cup	210	Butter, milk	6.7	3.6	2.1	.2
b	Pound	1 lb	454	do	14.5	7.8	4.6	.4
	Made with margarine:							
	Regular type: [65]							
c	Cup	1 cup	210	Margarine, milk	6.7	1.8	3.0	1.4
d	Pound	1 lb	454	do	14.5	3.9	6.6	3.0
	Soft type: [66]							
e	Cup	1 cup	210	do	6.7	1.8	2.4	1.9
f	Pound	1 lb	454	do	14.5	4.0	5.1	4.2
1800	Granules without milk:							
	Water, milk, table fat added:							
	Made with butter:							
a	Cup	1 cup	210	Butter, milk	7.6	4.1	2.4	.2
b	Pound	1 lb	454	do	16.3	8.8	5.2	.5
	Made with margarine:							
	Regular type: [67]							
c	Cup	1 cup	210	Margarine, milk	7.6	1.9	3.5	1.6
d	Pound	1 lb	454	do	16.3	4.2	7.5	3.5
	Soft type: [68]							
e	Cup	1 cup	210	do	7.6	2.0	2.7	2.3
f	Pound	1 lb	454	do	16.3	4.3	5.8	4.9

(A)		(B)			(C)	(D)	(E)	(F)	(G)
1802		Granules with milk:							
		Water, table fat added:							
		Made with butter:							
	a	Cup	1 cup	210	Butter	4.6	2.4	1.4	0.1
	b	Pound	1 lb	454	do	10.0	5.2	3.1	.3
		Made with margarine:							
		Regular type:[69]							
	c	Cup	1 cup	210	Margarine	4.6	.8	2.2	1.2
	d	Pound	1 lb	454	do	10.0	1.7	4.8	2.6
		Soft type:[70]							
	e	Cup	1 cup	210	do	4.6	.8	1.6	1.7
	f	Pound	1 lb	454	do	10.0	1.8	3.5	3.6
		Frozen:							
1804		Diced, shredded, or crinkle cut for hashed browning, cooked, hashed brown:							
	a	Yield from 12 oz., frozen hashed brown potatoes.	1⅓ cups	205	Cottonseed oil	23.6	5.9	5.0	11.8
	b	Yield from 2 lb., frozen hashed brown potatoes.	3½ cups	545	do	62.7	15.7	13.2	31.3
	c	Cup	1 cup	155	do	17.8	4.5	3.8	8.9
	d	Pound	1 lb	454	do	52.2	13.1	11.0	26.1
		French fried (straight-cut and crinkle-cut strips, with cross section, approx. ½ × ½ in.):[71]							
1805		Not thawed:							
		Container:							
	a	Net wt., 9 oz	1 container	255	do	16.6	4.1	3.5	8.3
	b	Net wt., 16 oz. (1 lb.)	1 container or 1 lb.	454	do	29.5	7.3	6.2	14.7
	c	Net wt., 32 oz. (2 lb.)	1 container	907	do	59.0	14.7	12.3	29.5
		Strips:							
	d	Length, over 3½ in. to 4 in	10 strips	100	do	6.5	1.6	1.4	3.3
	e	Length, over 2 in. to 3½ in	10 strips	65	do	4.2	1.1	.9	2.1
	f	Length, 1–2 in	10 strips	45	do	2.9	.7	.6	1.5
1806		Ovenheated:							
		Yield from—							
	a	9 oz., frozen french-fried potatoes	7 oz	198	do	16.6	4.1	3.5	8.3
	b	16 oz. (1 lb.), frozen french-fried potatoes.	12⅖ oz	352	do	29.5	7.3	6.2	14.7
	c	32 oz. (2 lb.), frozen french-fried potatoes.	24⅘ oz	704	do	59.0	14.7	12.3	29.5
		Strips (dimensions before heating):							
	d	Length, over 3½ in. to 4 in	10 strips	78	do	6.6	1.6	1.4	3.3
	e	Length, over 2 in. to 3½ in	10 strips	50	do	4.2	1.1	.9	2.1
	f	Length, 1–2 in	10 strips	35	do	2.9	.7	.6	1.5
	g	Pound	1 lb	454	do	38.1	9.5	8.0	19.1
1809		**Potato chips** (smooth and corrugated surface):							
	a	Chips, 2⁄32–3⁄32 in. thick with oval cross section, 1¾ × 2½ in.	10 chips	20	do	8.0	2.0	1.7	4.0
	b	Pound	1 lb	454	do	180.5	45.1	37.9	90.3
	c	Ounce	1 oz	28	do	11.3	2.8	2.4	5.6

[61] Values based on these revised amounts per 100 g. of product: Total saturated fatty acids 3.2 g., oleic acid 3.1 g., linoleic acid 1.0 g.
[62] Values based on these revised amounts per 100 g. of product: Total saturated fatty acids 3.2 g., oleic acid 2.7 g., linoleic acid 1.4 g.
[63] Values based on these revised amounts per 100 g. of product: Total saturated fatty acids 1.3 g., oleic acid 1.7 g., linoleic acid 0.7 g.
[64] Values based on these revised amounts per 100 g. of product: Total saturated fatty acids 1.3 g., oleic acid 1.4 g., linoleic acid 0.9 g.
[65] Values based on these revised amounts per 100 g. of product: Total saturated fatty acids 0.9 g., oleic acid 1.4 g., linoleic acid 0.7 g.
[66] Values based on these revised amounts per 100 g. of product: Total saturated fatty acids 0.9 g., oleic acid 1.1 g., linoleic acid 0.9 g.
[67] Values based on these revised amounts per 100 g. of product: Total saturated fatty acids 0.9 g., oleic acid 1.7 g., linoleic acid 0.8 g.
[68] Values based on these revised amounts per 100 g. of product: Total saturated fatty acids 0.9 g., oleic acid 1.3 g., linoleic acid 1.1 g.
[69] Values based on these revised amounts per 100 g. of product: Total saturated fatty acids 0.4 g., oleic acid 1.1 g., linoleic acid 0.6 g.
[70] Values based on these revised amounts per 100 g. of product: Total saturated fatty acids 0.4 g., oleic acid 0.8 g., linoleic acid 0.8 g.
[71] Fatty acid values do not apply to other styles of frozen french-fried potatoes, such as shoestring, slices, dices, and rissole.

TABLE 2.—*Fatty acid values for household measures and market units of foods*—Continued

[Item and footnote numbers correspond to those in table 1 of this publication. Values in parentheses denote imputed values usually from another form of the food or from a similar food. Dashes (—) denote lack of reliable data for a constituent believed to be present in a measurable amount. Calculated values, as those based on a recipe, are not in parentheses]

Item No. (A)		Food, approximate measures, units, and weight (edible part unless footnotes indicate otherwise) (B)		Grams	Principal sources of fat (C)	Total fat (D) Grams	Total saturated fatty acids (E) Grams	Unsaturated fatty acids: Oleic $C_{18}(-2H)$ (F) Grams	Unsaturated fatty acids: Linoleic $C_{18}(-4H)$ (G) Grams
		Potato salad, from home recipe, made with—							
1811		Cooked salad dressing, seasonings:							
		Butter used:							
	a	Cup	1 cup	250	Butter, milk, egg	7.0	3.5	2.4	0.3
	b	Pound	1 lb	454	--do--	12.7	6.4	4.3	.5
		Margarine used:							
		Regular type: [72]							
	c	Cup	1 cup	250	Margarine, milk, egg	7.0	2.0	3.1	1.3
	d	Pound	1 lb	454	--do--	12.7	3.7	5.6	2.3
		Soft type: [73]							
	e	Cup	1 cup	250	--do--	7.0	2.1	2.5	1.7
	f	Pound	1 lb	454	--do--	12.7	3.7	4.6	3.1
1812		Mayonnaise and french dressing, hard-cooked eggs, seasonings:							
	a	Cup	1 cup	250	Soybean oil, cottonseed oil, corn oil, eggs.	23.0	4.5	5.6	10.2
	b	Pound	1 lb	454	--do--	41.7	8.1	10.2	18.5
1813		**Potato sticks,** ¾–2¾ in. long with cross section, ⅛ × ⅛ in.:							
	a	Cup	1 cup	35	Cottonseed oil	12.7	3.2	2.7	6.4
	b	Pound	1 lb	454	--do--	165.1	41.3	34.7	82.6
	c	Ounce	1 oz	28	--do--	10.3	2.6	2.2	5.2
		Puddings with starch base, prepared from home recipe: [74]							
1823		Chocolate	1 cup	260	Milk, cocoa, butter	12.2	6.7	4.6	.3
1824		Vanilla (blancmange)	1 cup	255	Milk	9.9	5.5	3.3	.3
		Puddings, other. See individual kinds; Bread, etc.							
		Pudding mixes and puddings made from mixes:							
		With starch base:							
1825		Mix, chocolate, regular, dry form:							
	a	Package, net wt., 6 oz	1 pkg	170	Cocoa	3.6	2.0	1.3	.1
	b	Package, net wt., 4 oz	1 pkg	113	--do--	2.4	1.3	.9	Trace
	c	Ounce	1 oz	28	--do--	.6	.3	.2	Trace
1826		Pudding made with milk, cooked: [74]							
	a	Yield from 4 oz. of mix and 2 cups of milk.	2¼ cups (approx.)	583	Milk, cocoa	17.5	9.6	5.9	.5
	b	Cup	1 cup	260	--do--	7.8	4.3	2.6	.2
1827		Mix, chocolate, instant, dry form:							
	a	Package, net wt., 6¾ oz	1 pkg	191	Cocoa	3.1	1.7	1.1	.1
	b	Package, net wt., 4½ oz	1 pkg	128	--do--	2.0	1.2	.8	Trace
	c	Ounce	1 oz	28	--do--	.5	.3	.2	Trace
1828		Pudding made with milk without cooking:							

(A)		(B)			(C)	(D)	(E)	(F)	(G)
	a	Yield from 4½ oz. of mix and 2 cups of milk.	2⅓ cups (approx.)	616	Milk, cocoa	15.4	8.5	5.2	0.7
	b	Cup	1 cup	260	do	6.5	3.6	2.2	.3
1833		**Pumpkin and squash seed kernels,** dry, hulled	1 cup	140		65.4	11.8	23.5	27.5
		Rennin products:							
1860		Dessert, home-prepared with tablet:							
	a	Yield of recipe [12]	2⅛ cups (approx.)	545	Milk	19.1	10.5	6.3	.5
	b	Cup [74]	1 cup	255	do	8.9	4.9	3.0	.3
		Dessert mixes and desserts prepared from mixes:							
		Chocolate:							
1861		Mix, dry form:							
	a	Package, net wt., 2 oz	1 pkg	57	Cocoa	1.9	1.1	.7	Trace
	b	Tablespoon	1 tbsp	9	do	.3	.2	.1	Trace
1862		Dessert made with milk:							
	a	Yield from 2 oz. of mix and 2 cups of milk.	2⅛ cups (approx.)	545	Milk, cocoa	20.7	11.4	6.9	.6
	b	Cup [74]	1 cup	255	do	9.7	5.3	3.2	.3
		Other flavors (vanilla, caramel, fruit flavoring):							
1864		Dessert made with milk:							
	a	Yield from 1½ oz. of mix and 2 cups of milk.	2⅛ cups (approx.)	530	Milk	19.1	10.5	6.3	.1
	b	Cup [74]	1 cup	250	do	9.0	5.0	3.0	Trace
1891		**Rice pudding with raisins** [3]	1 cup	265	do	8.2	4.5	2.7	.3
		Rolls and buns:							
1898		Baked from home recipe, made with milk and enriched flour:							
	a	Roll (cloverleaf)	1 roll	35	Vegetable shortening, milk, egg.	3.0	.9	1.4	.6
	b	Pound	1 lb	454	do	39.5	11.2	18.2	7.9
		Commercial:							
		Ready-to-serve:							
1899		Danish pastry (plain, without fruit or nuts):							
		Prepackaged ring:							
		Package and piece cut from ring:							
	a	Package, net wt., 12 oz	1 pkg	340	Vegetable shortening, butter, egg.	79.9	23.7	37.3	14.8
	b	Cut piece, ⅛ of pkg. (item 1899a).	1 piece	42	do	10.0	3.0	4.7	1.8
	c	Package, net wt., 5 oz	1 pkg	142	do	33.4	9.9	15.6	6.2
	d	Cut piece, ¼ of pkg. (item 1899c).	1 piece	35	do	8.3	2.5	3.9	1.5
	e	Rectangular piece	1 pastry	75	do	17.6	5.2	8.2	3.3
	f	Round piece	1 pastry	65	do	15.3	4.5	7.1	2.8
	g	Pound	1 lb	454	do	106.6	31.7	49.8	19.7
	h	Ounce	1 oz	28	do	6.7	2.0	3.1	1.2
		Hard rolls:							
1900 or 1901		Enriched and unenriched:							
	a	Roll (round, or kaiser, 3¾-in. diam., 2 in. high; rectangular, 4¾ × 2¾ × 2½ in.).	1 roll	50	Vegetable shortening	1.6	.4	.7	.4

[3] Cup measure made on product after it had cooled. See also Appendix B, section on Home-Prepared Foods

[12] Formula used to calculate nutritive values shown in Agr. Handb. No. 8, rev. 1963.

[72] Values based on these revised amounts per 100 g. of product: Total saturated fatty acids 0.8 g., oleic acid 1.2 g., linoleic acid 0.5 g.

[73] Values based on these revised amounts per 100 g. of product: Total saturated fatty acids 0.8 g., oleic acid 1.0 g., linoleic acid 0.7 g.

[74] Cup measure made on product immediately after cooking. See also Appendix B, section on Home-Prepared Foods

TABLE 2.—*Fatty acid values for household measures and market units of foods*—Continued

[Item and footnote numbers correspond to those in table 1 of this publication. Values in parentheses denote imputed values usually from another form of the food or from a similar food. Dashes (—) denote lack of reliable data for a constituent believed to be present in a measurable amount. Calculated values, as those based on a recipe, are not in parentheses]

Item No. (A)	Food, approximate measures, units, and weight (edible part unless footnotes indicate otherwise) (B)			Principal sources of fat (C)	Amount in edible part of foods: Total fat (D)	Total saturated fatty acids (E)	Unsaturated fatty acids: Oleic $C_{18}(-2H)$ (F)	Unsaturated fatty acids: Linoleic $C_{18}(-4H)$ (G)
			Grams		*Grams*	*Grams*	*Grams*	*Grams*
	Rolls and buns—Continued							
	Commercial—Continued							
	Ready-to-serve—Continued							
	Hard rolls—Continued							
	Enriched and unenriched—Continued							
b	Roll (rectangular, 3¾ × 2½ × 1¾ in.).	1 roll	25	Vegetable shortening	0.8	0.2	0.4	0.2
c	Pound	1 lb	454	do	14.5	3.2	6.5	3.9
	Hoagie or submarine roll. See French or vienna bread and rolls, enriched or unenriched (item 446 or 448e).							
	Plain (soft rolls or buns):							
1902 or 1903	Enriched or unenriched:							
a	Cloverleaf; pan or dinner	1 roll	28	do	1.6	.4	.7	.4
	Frankfurter (hotdog) and hamburger (sandwich):							
b	Package, net wt., 11½ oz.; 8 rolls	1 pkg	325	do	18.2	4.3	8.7	4.5
c	Roll or bun (frankfurter; hamburger).	1 roll or bun	40	do	2.2	.5	1.1	.5
d	Pound	1 lb	454	do	25.4	6.0	12.1	6.2
	Partially baked (brown-and-serve):							
	Enriched or unenriched:							
1907 or 1909	Unbrowned:							
	Cloverleaf and pan:							
a	Package, net wt., 12 oz.; 12 rolls	1 pkg	340	do	23.1	5.5	11.1	5.5
b	Roll (cloverleaf; pan or dinner)	1 roll	28	do	1.9	.5	.9	.5
c	Pound	1 lb	454	do	30.8	7.4	14.8	7.4
1908 or 1910	Browned:							
a	Yield from 1 lb., unbrowned rolls	14⅔ oz	415	do	30.8	7.4	14.8	7.4
b	Yield from 12-oz. pkg. (item 1907 or 1909a).	12 rolls	310	do	23.1	5.5	11.1	5.5
c	Roll (item 1907 or 1909b, browned)	1 roll	26	do	1.9	.5	.9	.5
d	Pound	1 lb	454	do	35.4	8.5	17.0	8.5
	Roll dough and rolls baked from dough:							
	Enriched or unenriched:							
1911 or 1913	Dough, unraised, frozen:							
	Parkerhouse rolls:							
a	Package, net wt., 24 oz. (1 lb. 8 oz.); 24 rolls (item 1911 or 1913b).	1 pkg	680	do	34.0	8.0	16.1	8.4
b	Roll	1 roll	28	do	1.4	.3	.7	.3
c	Pound	1 lb	454	do	22.7	5.4	10.8	5.6

(A)		(B)			(C)	(D)	(E)	(F)	(G)
1912 or 1914		Rolls, parkerhouse, baked:							
	a	Yield from 1 lb., frozen dough	13¾ oz	390	Vegetable shortening	22.7	5.4	10.8	5.6
	b	Yield from 24 oz., frozen dough	24 rolls	585	do	34.0	8.0	16.1	8.4
	c	Roll (item 1911 or 1913b, baked)	1 roll	24	do	1.4	.3	.7	.3
	d	Pound	1 lb	454	do	24.5	5.8	11.6	6.1
1916		**Rolls prepared with roll mix** and water, baked:							
	a	Roll, cloverleaf, 2½-in. diam., 2 in. high	1 roll	35	do	1.6	.4	.7	.4
	b	Pound (approx. 13 rolls (item 1916a))	1 lb	454	do	20.4	4.9	9.7	4.9
1918		**Rusk,** 3⅜-in. diam., ½ in. thick:							
	a	Package, net wt., 4 oz	1 pkg	113	Vegetable shortening, egg, milk.	9.8	2.9	4.5	1.8
	b	Rusk	1 rusk	9	do	.8	.2	.4	.1
	c	Pound	1 lb	454	do	39.5	11.7	17.9	7.1
		Safflower oil. See Oils (items 1401r–1401v).							
		Salad dressings, commercial:							
		Blue and Roquefort cheese:							
1929		Regular:							
	a	Cup	1 cup	245	Soybean oil, cottonseed oil, corn oil, cheese.	128.1	26.1	28.1	61.5
	b	Tablespoon	1 tbsp	15	do	7.8	1.6	1.7	3.8
1930		Special dietary (low calorie), low fat (approx. 5 Cal. per teaspoon):							
	a	Cup	1 cup	255	Cheese	15.0	8.3	5.0	.5
	b	Tablespoon	1 tbsp	16	do	.9	.5	.3	Trace
		French:							
1932		Regular:							
	a	Cup	1 cup	250	Soybean oil, cottonseed oil, corn oil.	97.3	16.9	20.4	50.6
	b	Tablespoon	1 tbsp	16	do	6.2	1.1	1.3	3.2
1933		Special dietary (low calorie), low fat (approx. 5 Cal. per teaspoon):							
	a	Cup	1 cup	260	do	11.2	2.0	2.3	5.8
	b	Tablespoon	1 tbsp	16	do	.7	.1	.1	.4
		Italian:							
1936		Regular:							
	a	Cup	1 cup	235	do	141.0	24.5	29.6	73.3
	b	Tablespoon	1 tbsp	15	do	9.0	1.6	1.9	4.7
1937		Special dietary (low calorie, approx. 2 Cal. per teaspoon):							
	a	Cup	1 cup	240	do	11.3	2.0	2.4	5.9
	b	Tablespoon	1 tbsp	15	do	.7	.1	.1	.4
1938		Mayonnaise:							
	a	Cup	1 cup	220	Soybean oil, cottonseed oil, corn oil, egg.	175.8	31.3	38.1	88.6
	b	Tablespoon	1 tbsp	14	do	11.2	2.0	2.4	5.6
1939		Russian:							
	a	Cup	1 cup	245	do	124.5	22.1	26.9	62.6
	b	Tablespoon	1 tbsp	15	do	7.6	1.4	1.7	3.8
		Salad dressing (mayonnaise type):							
1940		Regular:							
	a	Cup	1 cup	235	do	99.4	18.0	22.0	49.4
	b	Tablespoon	1 tbsp	15	do	6.3	1.1	1.4	3.2
1941		Special dietary (low calorie, approx. 8 Cal. per teaspoon):							
	a	Cup	1 cup	250	do	31.8	5.8	7.0	15.8
	b	Tablespoon	1 tbsp	16	do	2.0	.4	.4	1.0

TABLE 2.—*Fatty acid values for household measures and market units of foods*—Continued

[Item and footnote numbers correspond to those in table 1 of this publication. Values in parentheses denote imputed values usually from another form of the food or from a similar food. Dashes (—) denote lack of reliable data for a constituent believed to be present in a measurable amount. Calculated values, as those based on a recipe, are not in parentheses]

Item No. (A)		Food, approximate measures, units, and weight (edible part unless footnotes indicate otherwise) (B)			Principal sources of fat (C)	Amount in edible part of foods: Total fat (D)	Total saturated fatty acids (E)	Unsaturated fatty acids: Oleic $C_{18}(-2H)$ (F)	Unsaturated fatty acids: Linoleic $C_{18}(-4H)$ (G)
				Grams		*Grams*	*Grams*	*Grams*	*Grams*
		Salad dressings, commercial—Continued							
		Thousand Island:							
1942		Regular:							
	a	Cup	1 cup	250	Soybean oil, cottonseed oil, corn oil, egg.	125.5	22.2	27.1	63.0
	b	Tablespoon	1 tbsp	16	do	8.0	1.4	1.7	4.0
1943		Special dietary (low calorie, approx. 10 Cal. per teaspoon):							
	a	Cup	1 cup	245	do	33.6	5.9	7.3	16.9
	b	Tablespoon	1 tbsp	15	do	2.1	.4	.4	1.0
		Salad dressings, made from home recipe:							
1944		French:							
		Made with corn oil:							
	a	Cup	1 cup	220	Corn oil	154.2	15.4	43.0	81.6
	b	Tablespoon	1 tbsp	14	do	9.8	1.0	2.7	5.2
		Made with cottonseed oil:							
	c	Cup	1 cup	220	Cottonseed oil	154.2	38.6	32.4	77.1
	d	Tablespoon	1 tbsp	14	do	9.8	2.5	2.1	4.9
1945		Cooked:							
		Made with butter:							
	a	Cup	1 cup	255	Butter, milk, egg	25.2	13.0	8.8	1.0
	b	Tablespoon	1 tbsp	16	do	1.6	.8	.6	.1
		Made with margarine:							
		Regular type:[75]							
	c	Cup	1 cup	255	Margarine, milk, egg	25.2	7.4	11.5	4.6
	d	Tablespoon	1 tbsp	16	do	1.6	.5	.7	.3
		Soft type:[76]							
	e	Cup	1 cup	255	do	25.2	7.6	9.4	6.3
	f	Tablespoon	1 tbsp	16	do	1.6	.5	.6	.4
		Salad oil. See Oils (item 1401).							
		Salmon, canned, solids and liquid:							
1949		Chinook (king):							
		Can and approx. contents:							
	a	Size, 307 × 200.25[5] (No. ½ Flat); net wt., 7¾ oz.	1 can	220		30.8	9.5	9.1	.5
	b	Size, 301 × 411[5] (No. 1 Tall); net wt., 16 oz. (1 lb.).	1 can or 1 lb	454		63.5	19.5	18.7	1.0
	c	Size, 603 × 405;[5] net wt., 64 oz. (4 lb.)	1 can	1,814		254.0	78.0	74.9	4.0
1955		Pink (humpback):							
		Can and approx. contents:							
	a	Size, 307 × 200.25[5] (No. ½ Flat); net wt., 7¾ oz.	1 can	220		13.0	3.4	3.0	.2
	b	Size, 301 × 411[5] (No. 1 Tall); net wt., 16 oz. (1 lb.).	1 can or 1 lb	454		26.8	7.0	6.2	.5
	c	Size, 603 × 405;[5] net wt., 64 oz. (4 lb.)	1 can	1,814		107.0	28.1	24.7	2.0

(A)		(B)			(C)	(D)	(E)	(F)	(G)
		Salt sticks:							
1965		Regular type (bread sticks without salt coating):							
	a	Stick, 7¾ in. long, ¾-in. diam	10 sticks	100	Vegetable shortening	2.9	0.6	1.2	0.9
	b	Stick, 4¼ in. long, ½-in. diam	10 sticks	50	do	1.5	.3	.6	.4
1966		Vienna bread type:							
	a	Stick, 6½ in. long, 1¼ in. wide	1 stick	35	do	1.1	.2	.5	.3
		Sausage, cold cuts, and luncheon meats:							
1986		Braunschweiger (smoked liverwurst):							
		Prepackaged forms:							
		Roll:							
		Package, approx. contents and slice cut from piece:							
	a	Package, net wt., 16 oz. (1 lb.); roll approx. 6½ in. long, 2½-in. diam.[77]	1 pkg. or 1 lb	454	Pork	124.3	44.7	52.2	11.2
	b	Slice, approx. 2½-in. diam., ¼ in. thick; 1/25 of roll (item 1986a).	1 slice	18	do	4.9	1.8	2.1	.4
	c	Package, net wt., 8 oz.; roll approx. 5½ in. long, 2-in. diam.[77]	1 pkg	227	do	62.2	22.4	26.1	5.6
	d	Slice, approx. 2-in. diam., ¼ in. thick; 1/22 of roll (item 1986c).	1 slice	10	do	2.7	1.0	1.2	.2
		Slice, approx. 3⅛-in. diam., ¼ in. thick; wt., 1 oz.:							
	e	Package, net wt., 6 oz.; 6 slices	1 pkg	170	do	46.6	16.8	19.6	4.2
	f	Slice	1 slice or 1 oz	28	do	7.8	2.8	3.3	.7
1989		Capicola or Capacola:							
		Prepackaged square slice, approx. 4¼ × 4¼ in., 1/16 in. thick; wt., ¾ oz.:							
	a	Package, net wt., 4½ oz.; approx. 6 slices	1 pkg	128	do	58.6	21.1	24.6	5.3
	b	Slice	1 slice[78]	21	do	9.6	3.5	4.0	.9
	c	Pound, approx. 21½ slices (item 1989b)	1 lb	454	do	207.7	74.8	87.3	18.7
	d	Ounce	1 oz	28	do	13.0	4.7	5.5	1.2
1992		Country-style sausage	1 lb	454	do.[79]	141.1	50.8	59.2	12.7
1993		Deviled ham, canned:							
		Container and approx. contents:							
	a	Can, net wt., 2¼ oz	1 can	64	Pork	20.7	7.4	8.7	1.9
	b	Can, net wt., 3 oz	1 can	85	do	27.5	9.9	11.5	2.5
	c	Can, net wt., 4½ oz	1 can	128	do	41.3	14.9	17.4	3.7
	d	Cup	1 cup	225	do	72.7	26.2	30.5	6.5
	e	Tablespoon	1 tbsp	13	do	4.2	1.5	1.8	.4
	f	Pound	1 lb	454	do	146.5	52.8	61.6	13.2
	g	Ounce	1 oz	28	do	9.2	3.3	3.8	.8
2001		Headcheese:							
		Prepackaged square slice, approx. 4 × 4 in., 3/32 in. thick; wt., 1 oz.:							
	a	Package, net wt., 8 oz.; approx. 8 slices	1 pkg	227	do	49.9	18.0	21.0	4.5
	b	Slice	1 slice or 1 oz	28	do	6.2	2.2	2.6	.6
	c	Pound	1 lb	454	do	99.8	35.9	41.9	9.0

[5] Dimensions of can: 1st dimension represents diameter; 2d dimension, height of can. 1st or left-hand digit in each dimension gives number of whole inches; next 2 digits give additional fraction of dimension expressed as 16th of an inch.

[75] Values based on these revised amounts per 100 g. of product: Total saturated fatty acids 2.9 g., oleic acid 4.5 g., linoleic acid 1.8 g.

[76] Values based on these revised amounts per 100 g. of product: Total saturated fatty acids 3.0 g., oleic acid 3.7 g., linoleic acid 2.5 g.

[77] Cut pieces of this approx. diam. also marketed in other lengths and weights. Weight and fatty acid values shown for slices (items 1986b, 1986d) also apply to ¼-in. slices cut from those pieces.

[78] Weight and fatty acid values also apply to round slice, approx. 4¾-in. diam., 1/16 in. thick.

[79] Country-style sausage may at times contain some beef. For such products, these fatty acid values do not apply.

TABLE 2.—*Fatty acid values for household measures and market units of foods*—Continued

[Item and footnote numbers correspond to those in table 1 of this publication. Values in parentheses denote imputed values usually from another form of the food or from a similar food. Dashes (—) denote lack of reliable data for a constituent believed to be present in a measurable amount. Calculated values, as those based on a recipe, are not in parentheses]

Item No.		Food, approximate measures, units, and weight (edible part unless footnotes indicate otherwise)			Principal sources of fat	Amount in edible part of foods: Total fat	Total saturated fatty acids	Unsaturated fatty acids: Oleic $C_{18}(-2H)$	Linoleic $C_{18}(-4H)$
(A)		(B)			(C)	(D)	(E)	(F)	(G)
				Grams		Grams	Grams	Grams	Grams
		Sausage, cold cuts, and luncheon meats—Continued							
		Luncheon meat:							
2005		Boiled ham:							
		Prepackaged slices:							
		Package and approx. contents:							
	a	Package, net wt., 8 oz.; approx. 8 slices (item 2005c).	1 pkg	227	Pork	38.6	13.9	16.2	3.5
	b	Package, net wt., 6 oz.; approx. 8 slices (item 2005d).	1 pkg	170	do	28.9	10.4	12.1	2.6
		Slice, approx. dimensions and weight:							
	c	Rectangular, approx. 6¼ × 4 × 1/16 in.; wt., 1 oz.	1 slice or 1 oz	28	do	4.8	1.7	2.0	.4
	d	Square, approx. 4¼ × 4¼ × 1/16 in.; wt., ¾ oz.	1 slice	21	do	3.6	1.3	1.5	.3
	e	Pound	1 lb	454	do	77.1	27.8	32.4	6.9
2006		Pork, cured ham or shoulder, chopped. spiced or unspiced, canned:							
		Can, approx. contents, and slice cut from piece:							
	a	Can, net wt., 12 oz.; rectangular piece, approx. 3½ in. long, 2 in. wide, 3 in. high.	1 piece	340	do	84.7	30.5	38.1	5.9
	b	Can, net wt., 7 oz.; rectangular piece, approx. 3½ in. long, 2 in. wide, 1¾ in. high.	1 can	198	do	49.3	17.7	22.2	3.4
	c	Slice, approx. 3 × 2 × ½ in.; ⅗ of piece (item 2006a) or ⅓ of piece (item 2006b).	1 slice	60	do	14.9	5.4	6.7	1.0
	d	Pound	1 lb	454	do	112.9	40.6	50.8	7.9
	e	Ounce	1 oz	28	do	7.1	2.5	3.2	.5
2009		Minced ham	1 lb	454	do	76.7	27.6	32.2	6.9
		Pork sausage:							
2013		Raw:							
		Prepackaged roll, brick, rope form, links, or patties:							
		Package and approx. contents:							
	a	Package, net wt., 16 oz. (1 lb.) (roll, approx. 5⅞ in. long, 2¼-in. diam. or 5⅜ in. long, 2½-in. diam.; brick, approx. 5⅛ × 3 × 1⅞ in.; rope form, approx. 20 in. long, 1¼-in. diam.; 16 links (item 2013e)).	1 pkg. or 1 lb. [20]	454	do	230.4	83.0	96.8	20.7

(A)		(B)			(C)	(D)	(E)	(F)	(G)
	b	Package, net wt., 8 oz. (approx. 4 patties (item 2013d) or 8 links (item 2013e)).	1 pkg	227	Pork	115.3	41.5	48.4	10.4
		Sausage, approx. dimensions and weight:							
	c	Piece, approx. 3 in. long, 1¼-in. diam.; wt., 2.4 oz.; 3/20 of rope form (see item 2013a).	1 piece	68	do	34.5	12.4	14.5	3.1
	d	Patty, approx. 3⅞-in. diam., ¼ in. thick; wt., 2 oz.	1 patty	57	do	29.0	10.4	12.2	2.6
	e	Link, approx. 4 in. long, ⅞-in. diam.; wt., 1 oz.	1 link or 1 oz.[21]	28	do	14.4	5.2	6.0	1.3
2014		Cooked:							
	a	Yield from 1 lb., raw (item 2013a)	7½ oz	213	do	94.1	33.9	39.5	8.5
	b	Yield from 8 oz., raw (item 2013b)	3.8 oz	107	do	47.3	17.0	19.9	4.3
	c	Piece (dimensions of uncooked piece (item 2013c)).	1 piece	32	do	14.1	5.1	5.9	1.3
	d	Patty (dimensions of uncooked patty (item 2013d)).	1 patty	27	do	11.9	4.3	5.0	1.1
	e	Link (dimensions of uncooked link (item 2013e)).	1 link	13	do	5.7	2.1	2.4	.5
		Canned:							
2015		Solids and liquid:							
	a	Can, net wt., 8 oz.; approx. 14 sausage links (item 2016a).	1 can	227	do	87.2	31.4	36.6	7.9
	b	Pound	1 lb	454	do	174.2	62.7	73.2	15.7
	c	Ounce	1 oz	28	do	10.9	3.9	4.6	1.0
2016		Drained solids:							
	a	Drained contents from can (item 2015a), 14 sausage links; wt., 5.7 oz.	14 sausages	162	do	53.1	19.1	22.3	4.8
	b	Link (approx. 3 in. long, 1½-in. diam.; 1/14 of item 2016a).	1 link	12	do	3.9	1.4	1.7	.4
	c	Pound	1 lb	454	do	148.8	53.6	62.5	13.4
	d	Ounce	1 oz	28	do	9.3	3.3	3.9	.8
		Pork sausage, link, smoked. See Sausage, country-style (item 1992).							
2020		Souse:							
		Prepackaged slice, square, approx. 3⅞ × 3⅞ in., ⅛ in. thick; wt., 1 oz.:							
	a	Package, net wt., 6 oz.; approx. 6 slices	1 pkg	170	do	22.8	8.2	9.6	2.1
	b	Slice	1 slice or 1 oz	28	do	3.8	1.4	1.6	.3
	c	Pound	1 lb	454	do	60.8	21.9	25.5	5.5
		Sesame oil. See Oils (items 1401w–1401y).							
2033		**Sesame seeds,** dry, hulled, decorticated:							
	a	Cup	1 cup	150		80.1	11.2	30.4	33.6
	b	Tablespoon	1 tbsp	8		4.3	.6	1.6	1.8
		Shortbread. See Cookies (item 830).							
		Soups, commercial:							
		Canned:							
		Bean with pork:							
2062		Condensed:							

[20] Use also for 1 lb. of other form or forms listed for this item.
[21] Use also for 1 oz. of other form or forms listed for this item.

TABLE 2.—*Fatty acid values for household measures and market units of foods*—Continued

[Item and footnote numbers correspond to those in table 1 of this publication. Values in parentheses denote imputed values usually from another form of the food or from a similar food. Dashes (—) denote lack of reliable data for a constituent believed to be present in a measurable amount. Calculated values, as those based on a recipe, are not in parentheses]

Item No. (A)	Food, approximate measures, units, and weight (edible part unless footnotes indicate otherwise) (B)			Principal sources of fat (C)	Amount in edible part of foods: Total fat (D)	Total saturated fatty acids (E)	Unsaturated fatty acids: Oleic $C_{18}(-2H)$ (F)	Linoleic $C_{18}(-4H)$ (G)
			Grams		*Grams*	*Grams*	*Grams*	*Grams*
	Soups, commercial—Continued							
	Canned—Continued							
	Bean with pork—Continued							
	Condensed—Continued							
	Can and approx. contents:							
a	Size, 211 × 400 [5] (No. 1 Picnic); net wt., 11½ oz.	1 can	326	Corn oil, pork	15.0	3.3	5.2	5.0
	Size 404 × 700 [5] (No. 3 Cylinder):							
b	Net wt., 51 oz. (3 lb. 3 oz.)	1 can	1,446	do	66.5	14.5	22.9	22.1
c	Net wt., 54 oz. (3 lb. 6 oz.)	1 can	1,531	do	70.4	15.3	24.2	23.4
d	Cup	1 cup	265	do	12.2	2.7	4.2	4.1
e	Ounce	1 oz	28	do	1.3	.3	.5	.4
2063	Prepared with equal volume of water	1 cup	250	do	5.8	1.3	2.0	1.9
	Beef noodle:							
2066	Condensed:							
	Can and approx. contents:							
a	Size, 211 × 400 [5] (No. 1 Picnic); net wt., 10½ oz.	1 can	298	Beef, corn oil, egg	6.6	2.1	2.4	1.5
b	Size, 404 × 700 [5] (No. 3 Cylinder); net wt., 51 oz. (3 lb. 3 oz.).	1 can	1,446	do	31.8	10.0	11.9	7.4
c	Cup	1 cup	245	do	5.4	1.7	2.0	1.3
d	Ounce	1 oz	28	do	.6	.2	.2	.1
2067	Prepared with equal volume of water	1 cup	240	do	2.6	.8	1.0	.6
	Celery, cream of:							
2068	Condensed:							
	Can and approx. contents:							
a	Size, 211 × 400 [5] (No. 1 Picnic); net wt., 10½ oz.	1 can	298	Corn oil, cream	12.5	2.2	3.6	5.5
b	Size, 404 × 700 [5] (No. 3 Cylinder); net wt., 50 oz. (3 lb. 2 oz.).	1 can	1,418	do	59.6	10.6	17.3	26.4
c	Cup	1 cup	245	do	10.3	1.8	3.0	4.6
d	Ounce	1 oz	28	do	1.2	.2	.4	.5
2069	Prepared with equal volume of water	1 cup	240	do	5.0	.9	1.5	2.2
2070	Prepared with equal volume of milk	1 cup	245	Corn oil, milk, cream	9.3	3.1	2.8	2.5
	Chicken, cream of:							
2073	Condensed:							
	Can and approx. contents:							
a	Size, 211 × 400 [5] (No. 1 Picnic); net wt., 10½ oz.	1 can	298	Corn oil, cream, chicken	14.3	2.3	4.2	6.5
b	Size, 404 × 700 [5] (No. 3 Cylinder); net wt., 50 oz. (3 lb. 2 oz.).	1 can	1,418	do	68.1	10.8	19.9	31.1
c	Cup	1 cup	245	do	11.8	1.9	3.4	5.4
d	Ounce	1 oz	28	do	1.4	.2	.4	.6
2074	Prepared with equal volume of water	1 cup	240	do	5.8	.9	1.7	2.6
2075	Prepared with equal volume of milk	1 cup	245	Milk, corn oil, cream, chicken.	10.3	3.5	3.2	2.7

(A)		(B)			(C)	(D)	(E)	(F)	(G)
		Mushroom, cream of:							
2088		Condensed:							
		Can and approx. contents:							
	a	Size, 211 × 400 [5] (No. 1 Picnic); net wt., 10½ oz.	1 can	298	Corn oil, cream	23.8	3.3	6.7	11.5
	b	Size, 404 × 700 [5] (No. 3 Cylinder); net wt., 50 oz. (3 lb. 2 oz.) to 51 oz. (3 lb. 3 oz.).	1 can	1,432	do	114.6	15.9	32.4	55.3
	c	Cup	1 cup	245	do	19.6	2.7	5.5	9.5
	d	Ounce	1 oz	28	do	2.3	.3	.6	1.1
2089		Prepared with equal volume of water	1 cup	240	do	9.6	1.3	2.7	4.6
2090		Prepared with equal volume of milk	1 cup	245	Corn oil, milk, cream	14.2	4.0	4.2	4.7
		Pea, split:							
2096		Condensed:							
		Can and approx. contents:							
	a	Size, 211 × 400 [5] (No. 1 Picnic); net wt., 11¼ oz.	1 can	319	Pork	8.3	2.7	4.0	.8
	b	Size, 404 × 700 [5] (No. 3 Cylinder); net wt., 51 oz. (3 lb. 3 oz.).	1 can	1,446	do	37.6	12.0	17.9	3.5
	c	Cup	1 cup	255	do	6.6	2.1	3.2	.6
	d	Ounce	1 oz	28	do	.7	.2	.4	.1
2097		Prepared with equal volume of water	1 cup	245	do	3.2	1.0	1.5	.3
		Tomato:							
2098		Condensed:							
		Can and approx. contents:							
	a	Size, 211 × 400 [5] (No. 1 Picnic); net wt., 10¾ oz.	1 can	305	Corn oil, cream or butter	6.4	1.1	1.7	2.6
	b	Size, 404 × 700 [5] (No. 3 Cylinder); net wt., 51 oz. (3 lb. 3 oz.).	1 can	1,446	do	30.4	5.1	8.1	12.4
	c	Cup	1 cup	250	do	5.3	.9	1.4	2.2
	d	Ounce	1 oz	28	do	.6	.1	.2	.2
2099		Prepared with equal volume of water	1 cup	245	do	2.5	.4	.7	1.0
2100		Prepared with equal volume of milk	1 cup	250	Milk, corn oil, cream or butter.	7.0	2.9	2.2	1.2
		Turkey noodle:							
2101		Condensed:							
		Can and approx. contents:							
	a	Size, 211 × 400 [5] (No. 1 Picnic); net wt., 10½ oz.	1 can	298	Turkey, egg	7.2	2.1	3.0	1.4
	b	Size, 404 × 700 [5] (No. 3 Cylinder); net wt., 50 oz. (3 lb. 2 oz.).	1 can	1,418	do	34.0	9.9	14.5	6.5
	c	Cup	1 cup	245	do	5.9	1.7	2.5	1.1
	d	Ounce	1 oz	28	do	.7	.2	.3	.1
2102		Prepared with equal volume of water	1 cup	240	do	2.9	.8	1.2	.6
		Dehydrated: [80]							
		Beef noodle:							
2109		Mix, dry form (2-oz. pkg.)	1 pkg	57	Vegetable shortening, egg.	4.2	1.2	2.0	.6
		Chicken noodle:							
2111		Mix, dry form (2-oz. pkg.)	1 pkg	57	Vegetable shortening, egg, chicken.	5.7	1.7	2.5	.9
		Chicken rice:							
2113		Mix, dry from (1½-oz. pkg.)	1 pkg	43	Vegetable shortening, chicken, rice.	2.9	.8	1.3	.6

[5] Dimensions of can: 1st dimension represents diameter; 2d dimension, height of can. 1st or left-hand digit in each dimension gives number of whole inches; next 2 digits give additional fraction of dimension expressed as 16th of an inch.

[80] Weight of packages of dehydrated soup mixes may vary as much as ¼ oz. However, this variation in weight would result in only negligible differences in fatty acid content of soups in ready-to-serve form.

TABLE 2.—*Fatty acid values for household measures and market units of foods*—Continued

[Item and footnote numbers correspond to those in table 1 of this publication. Values in parentheses denote imputed values usually from another form of the food or from a similar food. Dashes (—) denote lack of reliable data for a constituent believed to be present in a measurable amount. Calculated values, as those based on a recipe, are not in parentheses]

Item No. (A)		Food, approximate measures, units, and weight (edible part unless footnotes indicate otherwise) (B)			Principal sources of fat (C)	Total fat (D)	Total saturated fatty acids (E)	Unsaturated fatty acids: Oleic $C_{18}(-2H)$ (F)	Unsaturated fatty acids: Linoleic $C_{18}(-4H)$ (G)
				Grams		*Grams*	*Grams*	*Grams*	*Grams*
		Soups, commercial—Continued							
		Dehydrated [80]—Continued							
		Onion:							
2115		Mix, dry form (1½-oz. pkg.)	1 pkg	43	Vegetable shortening	4.6	1.1	2.3	1.0
		Pea, green:							
2117		Mix, dry form (4-oz. pkg.)	1 pkg	113	do	4.6	1.2	2.3	1.0
		Tomato vegetable with noodles:							
2119		Mix, dry form (2½-oz. pkg.)	1 pkg	71	Vegetable shortening, egg.	5.7	1.5	2.8	1.1
		Souse. See Sausage, cold cuts, and luncheon meats (item 2020).							
		Soybeans:							
		Mature seeds, dry:							
2139		Raw:							
	a	Cup	1 cup	210		37.2	5.6	7.4	19.3
	b	Pound	1 lb	454		80.3	12.1	16.1	41.7
2140		Cooked:							
	a	Cup	1 cup	180		10.3	1.5	2.1	5.3
	b	Pound	1 lb	454		25.9	3.9	5.2	13.4
2145		**Soybean curd** (tofu):							
	a	Piece (2½ × 2¾ × 1 in.)	1 piece	120		5.0	.8	1.0	2.6
	b	Pound	1 lb	454		19.1	2.9	3.8	9.9
		Soybean flours:							
2146		Full fat:							
		Cup:							
	a	Not stirred	1 cup	85		17.3	2.6	3.5	9.0
	b	Stirred	1 cup	70		14.2	2.1	2.8	7.4
	c	Pound	1 lb	454		92.1	13.8	18.4	47.9
2148		Low fat:							
	a	Cup, stirred	1 cup	88		5.9	.9	1.2	3.1
	b	Pound	1 lb	454		30.4	4.5	6.1	15.8
		Soybean oil. See Oils (items 1401z–1401ad).							
2163		**Spaghetti (enriched) in tomato sauce with cheese,** cooked from home recipe:							
	a	Yield from recipe [12]	8⅓ cups	2,095	Olive oil, cheese	73.3	16.8	45.3	5.9
	b	Cup	1 cup	250	do	8.8	2.0	5.4	.7
	c	Pound	1 lb	454	do	15.9	3.6	9.8	1.3
		Spaghetti (enriched) with meatballs and tomato sauce:							
2165		Cooked from home recipe:							
	a	Yield from recipe [12]	7 lb. 1½ oz	3,220	Olive oil, pork, beef, cheese, egg, breadcrumbs, milk.	151.3	43.1	82.1	11.6
	b	Cup (mixture of spaghetti, meatballs, tomato sauce, cheese).	1 cup	248	do	11.7	3.3	6.3	.9

(A)		(B)			(C)	(D)	(E)	(F)	(G)
	c	Pound	1 lb	454	Olive oil, pork, beef, cheese, egg, breadcrumbs, milk.	21.3	6.1	11.6	1.6
	d	Portion, ⅙ of yield (item 2165a)	1 portion	537	do	25.2	7.2	13.7	1.9
2166		Canned (regular or ring-shaped spaghetti):							
		Can and approx. contents:							
	a	Size, 300 × 407 [5] (No. 300); net wt., 15 oz.	1 can	425	Corn oil, beef, cheese, breadcrumbs.	17.4	3.7	5.5	6.7
	b	Cup	1 cup	250	do	10.3	2.2	3.3	3.9
	c	Pound	1 lb	454	do	18.6	3.9	5.9	7.1
2236		**Sunflower seed kernels**, dry:							
		In hull (refuse: hulls, 46%): [2]							
	a	Pound (yields approx. 1⅔ cups hulled seeds).	1 lb	454		115.8	13.9	23.2	73.0
	b	Cup (yields approx. ⅓ cup hulled seeds)	1 cup	85		21.7	2.6	4.3	13.7
		Hulled:							
	c	Container, net wt., 16 oz. (1 lb.)	1 lb	454		214.6	25.7	42.9	135.2
	d	Cup	1 cup	145		68.6	8.2	13.7	43.2
2251		**Sweetpotatoes**, cooked, candied:							
		Piece, 2½ in. long, 2-in. diam. (dimensions before cooking), prepared using ½ of—							
	a	Potato peeled by mechanical methods	1 piece	85	Butter	2.8	1.4	.8	.1
	b	Potato peeled with split-knife peeler	1 piece	105	do	3.5	1.7	1.0	.1
	c	Pound	1 lb	454	do	15.0	7.4	4.4	.4
2270		**Tapioca dessert**, cream pudding [3]	1 cup	165	Milk, egg	8.4	3.9	3.1	.4
		Tuna:							
		Canned in oil:							
2323		Solids and liquid:							
		Can and approx. contents:							
		Size, 307 × 113 [5] (No. ½):							
	a	Solid pack, net wt., 7 oz	1 can	198	Soybean oil, tuna	40.6	7.5	8.2	17.2
	b	Chunk style, net wt., 6½ oz	1 can	184	do	37.7	7.0	7.7	16.0
	c	Flake or grated style, net wt., 6–6¼ oz.	1 can	174	do	35.7	6.6	7.2	15.1
		Size, 303 × 212 [5] (Family):							
	d	Chunk style, net wt., 9¼ oz	1 can	262	do	53.7	10.0	10.9	22.8
		Size, 401 × 205½ [5] (No. 1):							
	e	Solid pack, net wt., 13 oz	1 can	369	do	75.6	14.1	15.4	32.1
		Size, 603 × 408: [5]							
	f	Solid pack, net wt., 64 oz. (4 lb.)	1 can	1,814	do	371.9	69.1	75.5	157.6
	g	Chunk style, net wt., 60 oz. (3 lb. 12 oz.).	1 can	1,701	do	348.7	64.8	70.8	147.8
	h	Pound (all styles)	1 lb	454	do	93.0	17.3	18.9	39.4
2324		Drained solids:							
		Can and approx. drained contents:							
		Size, 307 × 113 [5] (No. ½):							
	a	Solid pack, wt., 6 oz	1 can	169	Tuna, soybean oil	13.9	3.7	2.9	2.9
	b	Chunk style, wt., 5½ oz	1 can	157	do	12.9	3.4	2.7	2.7
		Size, 303 × 212 [5] (Family):							
	c	Chunk style, wt., 7.9 oz	1 can	223	do	18.3	4.9	3.9	3.3
		Size, 401 × 205½ [5] (No. 1):							
	d	Solid pack, wt., 11 oz	1 can	313	do	25.7	6.9	5.4	5.3
		Size, 603 × 408: [5]							
	e	Solid pack, wt., 54 oz. (3 lb. 6 oz.)	1 can	1,542	do	126.4	33.8	26.7	26.2
	f	Chunk style, wt., 51 oz. (3 lb. 3 oz.)	1 can	1,446	do	118.6	31.7	25.0	24.6

[2] Measure and weight apply to food as it is described with inedible part or parts (refuse) included.
[3] Cup measure made on product after it had cooled. See also Appendix B, section on Home-Prepared Foods
[5] Dimensions of can: 1st dimension represents diameter; 2d dimension, height of can. 1st or left-hand digit in each dimension gives number of whole inches; next 2 digits give additional fraction of dimension expressed as 16th of an inch.
[13] Formula used to calculate nutritive values shown in Agr. Handb. No. 8, rev. 1963.
[80] Weight of packages of dehydrated soup mixes may vary as much as ¼ oz. However, this variation in weight would result in only negligible differences in fatty acid content of soups in ready-to-serve form.

TABLE 2.—*Fatty acid values for household measures and market units of foods*—Continued

[Item and footnote numbers correspond to those in table 1 of this publication. Values in parentheses denote imputed values usually from another form of the food or from a similar food. Dashes (—) denote lack of reliable data for a constituent believed to be present in a measurable amount. Calculated values, as those based on a recipe, are not in parentheses]

Item No. (A)		Food, approximate measures, units, and weight (edible part unless footnotes indicate otherwise) (B)			Principal sources of fat (C)	Amount in edible part of foods: Total fat (D)	Total saturated fatty acids (E)	Unsaturated fatty acids: Oleic $C_{18}(-2H)$ (F)	Unsaturated fatty acids: Linoleic $C_{18}(-4H)$ (G)
				Grams		*Grams*	*Grams*	*Grams*	*Grams*
		Tuna—Continued							
		Canned in oil—Continued							
		Drained solids—Continued							
		Cup:							
	g	Solid pack and chunk style	1 cup	160	Tuna, soybean oil	13.1	3.5	2.8	2.7
	h	Pound (solid pack and chunk style)	1 lb	454	do	37.2	9.9	7.8	7.7
2326		**Tuna salad:**							
	a	Cup	1 cup	205	Cottonseed oil, soybean oil, corn oil, tuna, egg.	21.5	5.0	5.5	7.0
	b	Pound	1 lb	454	do	47.6	11.2	12.2	15.5
		Turkey, cooked:							
		All classes, roasted:							
2328		Total edible (flesh. skin, giblets):							
	a	Yield from 1 lb., ready-to-cook turkey	8.6 oz	245		40.2	11.7	17.3	8.4
	b	Pound	1 lb	454		74.4	21.6	32.0	15.6
2331		Flesh only:[31]							
		Cup (not packed):							
	a	Chopped or diced	1 cup	140		8.5	2.5	3.7	1.8
	b	Ground	1 cup	110		6.7	2.0	2.9	1.4
	c	Pound	1 lb	454		27.7	8.0	11.9	5.8
	d	Pieces (1 slice of white meat, 4 in. long, 2 in. wide, ¼ in. thick; wt., 1½ oz.; with 2 slices of dark meat, 2½ in. long, 1⅝ in. wide, ¼ in. thick; wt., ¾ oz. each).	3 pieces or 3 oz	85		5.2	1.5	2.2	1.1
2335		Light meat without skin:							
		Cup (not packed):							
	a	Chopped or diced	1 cup	140		5.5	1.6	2.4	1.1
	b	Ground	1 cup	110		4.3	1.2	1.8	.9
	c	Pound	1 lb	454		17.7	5.1	7.6	3.7
	d	Piece, approx. 4 in. long, 2 in. wide, ¼ in. thick.	2 pieces or 3 oz	85		3.3	1.0	1.4	.7
2337		Dark meat without skin:							
		Cup (not packed):							
	a	Chopped or diced	1 cup	140		11.6	3.4	5.0	2.4
	b	Ground	1 cup	110		9.1	2.7	3.9	1.9
	c	Pound	1 lb	454		37.6	10.9	16.2	7.9
	d	Piece, approx. 2½ in. long, 1⅝ in. wide, ¼ in. thick.	4 pieces or 3 oz	85		7.1	2.0	3.0	1.5
2349		**Turkey, canned,** meat only, boned:							
	a	Can, net wt., 5½ oz. (solid pack)	1 can	156		19.5	5.7	8.4	4.1
	b	Cup	1 cup	205		25.6	7.4	11.0	5.4
	c	Pound	1 lb	454		56.7	16.5	24.4	11.9
		Turkey potpie:							
2350		Home prepared, baked:							

(A)		(B)			(C)	(D)	(E)	(F)	(G)
	a	Pie, whole (9-in. diam.)	1 pie	[7] 698	Vegetable shortening, cream, turkey, butter.	94.2	31.5	41.4	15.8
	b	Piece, ⅓ of pie (item 2350a)	1 piece	232	do	31.3	10.5	13.8	5.3
	c	Pound	1 lb	454	do	61.2	20.5	26.9	10.3
		Veal:							
		Chuck cuts and boneless veal for stew:							
2369		Raw, lean with fat:							
	a	With bone (69% lean, 11% fat) (refuse: bone, 20%).[2]	1 lb	454		36	17.3	15.8	.7
	b	Without bone (86% lean, 14% fat)	1 lb	454		45	21.6	19.8	.9
2370		Cooked (braised, pot-roasted, or stewed), drained (85% lean, 15% fat):							
	a	Yield from 1 lb., raw veal with bone (item 2369a).	8.4 oz	240		30.7	14.7	13.5	.6
	b	Yield from 1 lb., raw veal without bone (item 2369b).	10.6 oz	299		38.3	18.4	16.9	.8
	c	Cup, chopped or diced pieces (not packed).	1 cup	140		17.9	8.6	7.9	.4
	d	Pound	1 lb	454		58.1	27.9	25.6	1.2
	e	Piece, approx. 2½ in. long, 2½ in. wide, ¾ in. thick.	1 piece or 3 oz	85		10.9	5.2	4.8	.2
		Loin cuts:							
2381		Raw, lean with fat:							
	a	With bone (71% lean, 12% fat) (refuse: bone, 17%).[2]	1 lb	454		41	19.7	18.0	.8
	b	Without bone (85% lean, 15% fat)	1 lb	454		50	24.0	22.0	1.0
2382		Cooked (braised or broiled) (77% lean, 23% fat):							
	a	Yield from 1 lb., raw veal with bone (item 2381a).	9.5 oz	269		36.0	17.3	15.8	.7
	b	Yield from 1 lb., raw veal without bone (item 2381b).	11.4 oz	324		43.4	20.8	19.1	.9
	c	Cup, chopped or diced pieces (not packed).	1 cup	140		18.8	9.0	8.3	.4
	d	Pound	1 lb	454		60.8	29.2	26.8	1.2
	e	Piece, approx. 2½ in. long, 2½ in. wide, ¾ in. thick.	1 piece or 3 oz	85		11.4	5.5	5.0	.2
		Plate, breast of veal:							
2385		Raw, lean with fat:							
	a	With bone (58% lean, 21% fat) (refuse: bone, 21%).[2]	1 lb	454		61	29.3	26.8	1.2
	b	Without bone (74% lean, 26% fat)	1 lb	454		77	37.0	33.9	1.5
2386		Cooked (braised or stewed) (73% lean, 27% fat):							
	a	Yield from 1 lb., raw veal with bone (item 2385a).	8.3 oz	237		50.2	24.1	22.1	1.0
	b	Yield from 1 lb., raw veal without bone (item 2385b).	10.6 oz	299		63.4	30.4	27.9	1.3
	c	Pound	1 lb	454		96.2	46.2	42.3	1.9
		Rib roast:							
2389		Raw:							
	a	With bone (63% lean, 14% fat) (refuse: bone, 23%).[2]	1 lb	454		49	23.5	21.6	1.0
	b	Without bone (82% lean, 18% fat)	1 lb	454		64	30.7	28.2	1.3

[2] Measure and weight apply to food as it is described with inedible part or parts (refuse) included.
[7] Yield of formula used to calculate nutritive values in Agr. Handb. No. 8, rev. 1963.
[8] Fatty acid values based on 50% light meat, 50% dark meat.

TABLE 2.—*Fatty acid values for household measures and market units of foods*—Continued

[Item and footnote numbers correspond to those in table 1 of this publication. Values in parentheses denote imputed values usually from another form of the food or from a similar food. Dashes (—) denote lack of reliable data for a constituent believed to be present in a measurable amount. Calculated values, as those based on a recipe, are not in parentheses]

Item No. (A)		Food, approximate measures, units, and weight (edible part unless footnotes indicate otherwise) (B)			Principal sources of fat (C)	Amount in edible part of foods: Total fat (D)	Total saturated fatty acids (E)	Unsaturated fatty acids: Oleic $C_{18}(-2H)$ (F)	Unsaturated fatty acids: Linoleic $C_{18}(-4H)$ (G)
				Grams		*Grams*	*Grams*	*Grams*	*Grams*
		Veal—Continued							
		Rib roast—Continued							
2390		Cooked (roasted):							
	a	Yield from 1 lb., raw veal with bone (item 2389a).	8½ oz	241		40.7	19.5	17.9	0.8
	b	Yield from 1 lb., raw veal without bone (item 2389b).	11 oz	313		52.9	25.4	23.3	1.1
		Cup (not packed):							
	c	Chopped or diced	1 cup	140		23.7	11.4	10.4	.5
	d	Ground	1 cup	110		18.6	8.9	8.2	.4
	e	Pound	1 lb	454		76.7	36.8	33.7	1.5
	f	Piece, approx. 4⅛ in. long, 2¼ in. wide, ¼ in. thick; wt., 1½ oz.	2 pieces or 3 oz	85		14.4	6.9	6.3	.3
		Round with rump (roasts and leg cutlets):							
2393		Raw, lean with fat:							
	a	With bone (67% lean, 10% fat) (refuse: bone, 23%).[2]	1 lb	454		31	14.9	13.6	.6
	b	Without bone (87% lean, 13% fat)	1 lb	454		41	19.7	18.0	.8
2394		Cooked (braised or broiled):							
	a	Yield from 1 lb., raw veal with bone (item 2393a).	8.7 oz	247		27.4	13.2	12.1	.5
	b	Yield from 1 lb., raw veal without bone (item 2393b).	11.3 oz	321		35.6	17.1	15.7	.7
	c	Cup, chopped or diced pieces (not packed).	1 cup	140		15.5	7.4	6.8	.3
	d	Pound	1 lb	454		50.3	24.1	22.1	1.0
	e	Piece, approx. 4⅛ in. long, 2¼ in. wide, ½ in. thick; wt., 3 oz. (cutlets); or 2 pieces, 4⅛ in. long, 2¼ in. wide, ¼ in. thick; wt., 1½ oz. each (roasts).	1 or 2 pieces or 3 oz.	85		9.4	4.5	4.1	.2
2405		**Venison**, lean meat only, raw	3 oz	85		3.4	2.1	.8	.1
		Waffles:							
2409 or 2410		Baked from home recipe, made with enriched or unenriched flour:							
	a	Round, 7-in. diam., ⅝ in. thick	1 waffle	75	Vegetable shortening, milk, egg.	7.4	2.4	3.3	1.1
		Square, 9 × 9 × ⅝ in.:							
	b	Whole	1 waffle	200	do	19.6	6.3	8.7	3.0
	c	Section, 4½ × 4½ × ⅝ in.; ¼ of item 2409b.	1 section	50	do	4.9	1.6	2.2	.8
	d	Pound	1 lb	454	do	44.5	14.4	19.8	6.8
2411		Frozen, prebaked, unheated:							
		Waffle, 4⅝ × 3¾ × ⅝ in.:							
	a	Container, net wt., 12 oz.; 10 waffles	1 container	340	Vegetable shortening, egg.	21.1	5.4	9.8	4.5
	b	Waffle	1 waffle	34	do	2.1	.5	1.0	.5
		Waffle, 3½ × 2¾ × ⅝ in. or 3¾ × 2¾ × ½ in.; wt., ¾–⅞ oz.:							

(A)		(B)			(C)	(D)	(E)	(F)	(G)
	c	Container, net wt., 5 oz.; 6 waffles, 3½ × 2¾ × ⅝ in.	1 container	142	Vegetable shortening, egg.	8.8	2.3	4.1	1.9
	d	Container, net wt., 9 oz.; 12 waffles, 3¾ × 2¾ × ½ in.	1 container	255	do	15.8	4.1	7.3	3.4
	e	Waffle	1 waffle	22	do	1.4	.3	.6	.3
	f	Pound	1 lb	454	do	28.1	7.2	13.0	6.0
2417		Baked from mix (pancake and waffle); made with egg, milk:							
	a	Round, 7-in. diam., ⅝ in. thick	1 waffle	75	Vegetable shortening, milk, egg.	8.0	2.7	3.4	1.2
		Square, 9 × 9 × ⅝ in.:							
	b	Whole	1 waffle	200	do	21.2	7.3	9.0	3.3
	c	Section, 4½ × 4½ × ⅝ in.; ¼ of item 2417b.	1 section	50	do	5.3	1.8	2.2	.8
	d	Pound	1 lb	454	do	48.1	16.6	20.3	7.5
		Walnuts:							
2420		Black:							
	a	In shell (refuse: shells, 78%) [2]	1 lb	454		59.2	3.6	20.7	28.4
		Shelled:							
		Chopped or broken kernels:							
	b	Cup	1 cup	125		74.1	4.5	26.0	35.6
	c	Tablespoon	1 tbsp	8		4.7	.3	1.7	2.3
	d	Ground (finely)	1 cup	80		47.4	2.8	16.6	22.8
	e	Pound	1 lb	454		269.0	16.1	94.2	129.1
	f	Ounce	1 oz	28		16.8	1.0	5.9	8.1
2421		Persian or English:							
		In shell (refuse: shells, 55%): [2]							
	a	Pound	1 lb	454		130.6	9.1	19.6	81.0
	b	10 large nuts	10 nuts	110		31.7	2.2	4.8	19.6
		Shelled:							
	c	Halves, 1 cup (approx. 50)	1 cup	100		64.0	4.5	9.6	39.7
		Chopped pieces or chips:							
	d	Cup	1 cup	120		76.8	5.4	11.5	47.6
	e	Tablespoon	1 tbsp	8		5.1	.4	.8	3.2
	f	Pound	1 lb	454		290.3	20.3	43.5	180.0
	g	Ounce (approx. 14 halves)	1 oz	28		18.1	1.3	2.7	11.2
2428		**Welsh rarebit**	1 cup	232	Cheese, butter, milk	31.6	17.3	10.4	1.0
2457		**Wheat germ,** toasted; used mainly as ready-to-eat breakfast cereal.	1 tbsp	6		.7	.1	.2	.3
		White sauce:							
2469		Thin	1 cup	250	Butter, milk	21.8	12.0	7.2	.7
2470		Medium	1 cup	250	do	31.3	16.4	10.3	1.0
2471		Thick	1 cup	250	do	39.0	21.4	12.9	1.3
		Yogurt:							
2481		Made from partially skimmed milk:							
	a	Container, net wt., 8 oz	1 container	226		3.8	2.1	1.3	.1
	b	Cup	1 cup	245		4.2	2.3	1.4	.1
2482		Made from whole milk:							
	a	Container, net wt., 8 oz	1 container	226		7.7	4.2	2.5	.2
	b	Cup	1 cup	245		8.3	4.6	2.7	.2
2483		**Zwieback:**							
	a	Package, net wt., 6 oz. (approx. 24 pieces)	1 pkg	170	Vegetable shortening, egg.	15.0	3.7	7.3	3.4
	b	Piece, approx. 3½ × 1½ × ½ in	1 piece	7	do	.6	.2	.3	.1
	c	Pound (approx. 65 pieces (item 2483b))	1 lb	454	do	39.9	9.8	19.4	9.0

[2] Measure and weight apply to food as it is described with inedible part or parts (refuse) included.

APPENDIX A.—NOTES ON SELECTION OF ITEMS AND SUPPLEMENTARY DATA ON THE COMPOSITION OF FOODS

Food items selected for a new publication on the nutritive value of foods should be responsive to developments in food production and consumption practices and the changes they induce in the composition of foods. Changes of both types have occurred since data were prepared in 1963 for Handbook No. 8 (*28*), which was the principal source from which the data shown here in tables 1 and 2 have been developed.

The 1963 handbook was prepared to be a basic general reference. It provided data for a wide variety of foods, including some that are not produced and are seldom used in the 48 contiguous States. For these less widely used items, new data on composition or on weights of specified measures have not been developed and the foods are not listed in the present publication.

For various reasons, some other kinds of foods also have been excluded. Products no longer on the retail market have been omitted. Likewise, items have been excluded if the data applied to primary food stocks, such as field corn, which undergo considerable processing in their conversion to customary consumer products. Also, data for many food items in the raw form have been omitted if the food is used only after it has been cooked.

For a large number of items, some adaptation or revision has been made in the values used as the basis of the figures shown or in the description of the items. The kinds of adaptation that have been made are as follows:

- New data where available have been used for the percentages of edible portion and refuse for many foods.
- Unrounded figures for nutrient content rather than the rounded values in table 1 of Handbook No. 8 have been used in calculating numerous food items to preserve an appropriate relationship among the values to be shown for several different measures of an item.
- In many instances numerical values have been provided for nutrients previously indicated as present only as "Trace."
- Terminology for a few foods has been changed to be more descriptive of the products currently used. The data selected from Handbook No. 8 as the basis for the values in the present publication were considered most nearly representative of the product in current use. Possibly some minor change may have occurred also in the nutrient content. New values were not available and the foods were too important to be omitted from this publication.

Most of the revised or new data for items in table 1 are shown in footnotes on the page where they apply if data for only one or a few of the nutrients were changed. It was not feasible, however, to show the revised values in footnotes if the content per 100 g. had been revised for all or even several of the nutrients. These more extensive revised values have been tabulated and are given in table 3.

In the following paragraphs, attention is called to several specific foods or groups of foods for which values have been or may need to be revised.

Breakfast-Type Cereals.—Data for vitamins and mineral elements in the ready-to-eat breakfast cereals have been updated through 1972. In 1974, Federal guidelines for their fortification were proposed and are discussed in Appendix C.

Baby Foods.—Changes made since 1963 in the formulations of precooked baby cereals (items 67–71) have altered their nutrient content. It has become general practice among manufacturers to add several minerals and vitamins. Values for the content of calcium, iron, and niacin in the cereal products vary widely and show slightly greater differences among brands than among the different kinds of cereals made by the same manufacturer. For some cereals, the content of protein is less than was formerly claimed. Bases of the revised data for these items in the present publication are shown in table 3.

Sodium values for the several baby foods listed in Handbook No. 8, except the fruit items, reflected the use at that time of monosodium glutamate as a flavor enhancer and also seasoning with salt at various levels. Since then the use of monosodium glutamate has been discontinued, and in 1970 a committee of the National Research Council (*9*) recommended that 0.25 percent be the maximum level at which salt be added to baby foods. This meant a considerable lowering in the amount of salt added to these products. At present, data are inadequate for providing revised values for sodium in baby foods affected by these alterations and no sodium values are shown.

Likewise, no sodium values are given in the tables for some of the strained and junior fruits listed under the group of baby foods, as data available for sodium content in them are too variable. The items affected and the range in their sodium content in milligrams per 100 g. are applesauce and apricots (item 93) 1–25, bananas with tapioca or cornstarch (item 94) 30–70, peaches (item 97) 7–45, and mixed pear and pineapple (item 99) 2–75 mg. Factors such as the level of sodium in the water used for blanching and in the packing medium or the use of lye for peeling could account for these wide ranges in values.

Omission of salt from the precooked baby cereals (items 67–71) has lowered their sodium values. Lack of uniformity among manufacturers in the use of other sodium-contributing ingredients, such as sodium iron pyrophosphate, brown sugar, and nonfat dry milk, may result in values for sodium that fall in the range of 20 to 200 mg. per 100 g. of product. Data are inadequate at this time to provide revised sodium values for these items.

Fats.—Developments since the early 1960's in production practices for margarines, shortenings, and oils used for salads and in cooking have significantly affected the kinds and proportions of fatty acids they contain. As developments continue, the fatty acids in these products continue to be subject to change in kinds and amounts.

Published sources and unpublished data from manufacturers made available since 1968 have been used to update the fatty acid values shown for the fats used in cooking and for margarine. Revised data for margarines (see information under item 1317, table 2) reflect the increased use of vegetable oils, higher degree of unsaturation, changes in sources of fat, and the introduction of soft and whipped-type products.

Data for cooking fat made from vegetable sources only (item 999) have been included in table 2. In line with the trend in manufacturing practices for products of this kind, the new data given for vegetable shortening indicate a lower content of oleic acid and a higher content of linoleic acid than generally found in cooking fats prior to 1960. Data for shortenings made from mixtures of fats from animal and plant sources have not been included in table 2 because data are lacking for the many products of this type currently available.

Margarine as well as cooking fat is often used as an ingredient in prepared products. The fatty acid values in table 2 for foods containing margarine or cooking fat as ingredients are based on calculations using the revised values for these two fats. The choice of fat used in the preparation of a product may affect the fatty acid content of the finished product. Data in table 2 for some of the prepared products show the differences in fatty acid content in a product when the source of fat is changed. For example, data are shown for mashed potatoes and for macaroni with cheese when made with butter and when made with margarine and for cornbread and corn muffins when made with vegetable shortening and with lard. When a table fat is used in place of a cooking fat, as in home-prepared cookies and cakes, the data are based on the substitution of an equal volume of the alternate ingredient. This is believed to be in line with usual home practice.

The values in table 2 for food products such as cake, in which fatty acids are supplied by several ingredients, reflect the contribution of the fatty acids from each major source of fat. Also, data are given for individual items separately, such as different kinds of cake, whereas in Handbook No. 8 the fatty acid values sometimes were provided only for groups of foods of similar type.

Values in table 2 are not rounded to whole numbers in order to preserve appropriate relationships among values for the several units of volume shown for an item and to account more closely for the total fat content of the item. This should not be interpreted to mean, however, that the figures for fatty acids are necessarily significant to one decimal place.

Frozen Orange Juice Concentrate.—Most of the frozen concentrated orange juice on the retail market in this country is packed in Florida. Values shown for the concentrate and items prepared from it have been revised to comply with the Florida requirement for a minimum of 44.8 percent (by weight) of orange juice soluble solids in the concentrate (*4*). This requirement became effective in October 1965. Values previously published in Handbook No. 8 were based on concentrates having 41.8 percent of orange juice soluble solids, the minimum specified in the USDA Grade Standards (*14*), which are still current.

Enriched Products.—For certain grain products, flour, farina, and breads, new standards of enrichment have been proposed. The adjustments in values that would have to be made if the proposed regulations become effective are discussed in Appendix C.

APPENDIX B.—NOTES ON WEIGHT AND VOLUME RELATIONSHIPS

One of the overall objectives for this publication was to present data for specified measures or units that would be reasonable for practical application in planning or evaluating diets or assessing nutrients provided by foods and food supplies. Processed foods in containers of numerous sizes are available on the retail market and those shown in tables 1 and 2 are the ones in highest production.

Weights corresponding to the various household measures and market units specified in the tables have been obtained from several sources. Some have been based on published data, some calculated from measurements made of specific gravity, and many have been based on unpublished information supplied to or determined in experimentation by the staff of the Consumer and Food Economics Institute.

Wide ranges were often observed in data from different sources for the weight of a given measure or unit of a food product. The wide range is not surprising in view of differences among samples measured and in the conditions and purposes the various investigators had for making the measurements. Attention is called here to the procedures and some of the problems in arriving at the weights of the measures and units of the foods listed. Procedures and problems of the more general type are discussed first and those relating to small groups of foods or individual foods last.

Most of the weights shown for the items have been rounded to whole numbers. As a result, some inconsistency may appear between the weights of different measures or units for the same food in some instances. Likewise, nutritive values shown for one unit of volume for an item may not al-

TABLE 3.—*Data on food composition to supplement tables 1 and 2*

[Item and footnote numbers correspond to those in tables 1 and 2 of this publication. Values in parentheses denote imputed values usually from another form of the food or from a similar food. Zeros in parentheses indicate that amount of a constituent, if present, is probably too small to be measured. Dashes (—) denote lack of reliable data for a constituent believed to be present in a measurable amount. Calculated values, as those based on a recipe, are not in parentheses]

Item No.	Food, approximate measures, units, and weight (edible part unless footnotes indicate otherwise)			Water	Food energy	Protein	Fat	Fatty acids: Saturated (total)	Fatty acids: Unsaturated: Oleic	Fatty acids: Unsaturated: Linoleic	Carbohydrate: Total	Carbohydrate: Fiber
			Grams	*Percent*	*Calories*	*Grams*	*Grams*	*Grams*	*Grams*	*Grams*	*Grams*	*Grams*
	Baby cereals, precooked, dry:											
67	Barley, added nutrients		100	6.8	360	11.0	2.6	—	—	—	75.8	1.3
68	High protein, added nutrients		100	6.6	357	35.0	4.6	—	—	—	46.5	2.6
69	Mixed, added nutrients		100	6.9	372	13.1	4.0	—	—	—	71.1	1.1
70	Oatmeal, added nutrients		100	6.8	386	14.1	7.1	—	—	—	67.3	1.2
71	Rice, added nutrients		100	7.3	382	6.9	4.5	—	—	—	76.4	1.3
370, ftnt. 50, table 1; ftnt. 2, table 2	Ground beef with 21% fat, cooked to well-done stage (oven-broiled, pan-broiled, or sauteed):											
	100 g		100	48.8	320	27.1	22.7	10.9	10.0	0.5	0	0
	Yield from 1 lb., raw (item 369a)	10.4 oz	295	48.8	944	79.9	67.0	32.2	29.5	1.3	0	0
	Yield from 4 oz., raw (item 369b)	2.6 oz	74	48.8	237	21.1	16.8	8.1	7.4	.3	0	0
	Yield from 3.2 oz., raw (item 369c)	2.1 oz	60	48.8	192	16.3	13.6	6.5	6.0	.3	0	0
	Pound	1 lb	454	48.8	1,452	122.9	103.0	49.4	45.3	2.0	0	0
538a, ftnt. 104, table 1; ftnt. 11, table 2	Pound cake, old-fashioned, prepared and baked from home recipe (equal weights of flour, sugar, eggs, fat):											
	100 g.:											
	Made with cooking fat[1]		100	15.6	482	5.5	30.1	—	—	—	48.3	.1
	Made with vegetable shortening		100	15.6	482	5.5	30.1	7.7	14.6	6.6	48.3	.1
	Made with butter		100	19.7	437	5.6	25.0	12.9	8.4	1.4	48.5	.1
	Yield from recipe:											
	Made with cooking fat[1]	3¾ lb	1,694	15.6	8,165	93.2	509.9	—	—	—	818.2	1.7
	Made with vegetable shortening	3¾ lb	1,694	15.6	8,165	93.2	509.9	130.4	247.3	111.8	818.2	1.7
	Made with butter	3¾ lb	1,694	19.7	7,403	94.9	423.5	218.5	142.3	23.7	821.6	1.7
	Loaf (8½ × 3½ × 3¾ in.; ⅓ of yield):											
	Whole (vol., 292 cu. in.):											
	Made with cooking fat[1]	1 loaf	565	15.6	2,723	31.1	170.1	—	—	—	272.9.	.6
	Made with vegetable shortening	1 loaf	565	15.6	2,723	31.1	170.1	43.5	82.5	37.3	272.9	.6
	Made with butter	1 loaf	565	19.7	2,469	31.6	141.3	72.9	47.5	7.9	274.0	.6
	Slice, ½ in. thick (3½ × 3 × ½ in.; 1/17 of loaf):											
	Made with cooking fat[1]	1 slice	33	15.6	159	1.8	9.9	—	—	—	15.9	Trace
	Made with vegetable shortening	1 slice	33	15.6	159	1.8	9.9	2.6	4.8	2.2	15.9	Trace
	Made with butter	1 slice	33	19.7	144	1.8	8.3	4.3	2.8	.5	16.0	Trace
	Cube (1 cu. in.):											
	Made with cooking fat[1]	1 cube	5.8	15.6	28	.3	1.7	—	—	—	2.8	Trace
	Made with vegetable shortening	1 cube	5.8	15.6	28	.3	1.7	.4	.8	.4	2.8	Trace
	Made with butter	1 cube	5.8	19.7	25	.3	1.5	.7	.5	.1	2.8	Trace
	Parmesan cheese:											
651d–h	Shredded		100	25	422	38.6	27.9	15.4	9.2	.8	3.0	0
651i–m	Grated		100	17	467	42.7	30.8	16.9	10.2	.9	3.5	0
958, ftnt. 194, table 1; ftnt. 37, table 2	Doughnuts, yeast-leavened, glazed:											
	100 g		100	26.4	405	5.4	22.9	5.7	11.8	5.0	44.5	.2
	Doughnut, 3¾-in. diam., 1¼ in. high	1 doughnut	50	26.4	203	2.7	11.3	2.8	5.6	2.5	22.3	.1
	Orange juice concentrate, frozen, unsweetened:											
1436	Undiluted		100	55.2	170	2.5	.2	0	0	0	40.7	.2
1437	Diluted with 3 parts water by volume		100	87.2	49	.7	.1	0	0	0	11.6	.1
1629, ftnt. 298, table 1; ftnt. 56, table 2	Pizza, with cheese and sausage topping, from home recipe, baked (in 14-in.-diam. pan):[33]											
	100 g		100	43.0	282	12.9	13.3	3.4	4.7	1.2	27.4	.3
	Whole, 13¾-in. diam., 43.2-in. cir	1 pizza	604	43.0	1,703	77.9	80.3	20.5	28.3	7.1	165.5	1.8
	Sector, 5⅓-in. arc; ⅛ of pizza	1 sector	76	43.0	214	9.8	10.1	2.6	3.6	.9	20.8	.2
	Sector, 1-in. arc	1 sector	14.0	43.0	39	1.8	1.9	.5	.7	.2	3.8	Trace
2448, 2449, ftnt. 395, table 1	Wheat, rolled, instant-cooking (used as hot breakfast cereal):											
	Dry form	1 cup	90	10.1	306	8.9	1.8	—	—	—	68.6	2.0
	Cooked (salt added):											
	100 g		100	83.8	58	1.7	.3	—	—	—	13.1	.4
	1 cup	1 cup	245	83.8	142	4.2	.7	—	—	—	32.1	1.0

TABLE 3.—*Data on food composition to supplement tables 1 and 2*—Continued

Item No.	Food, approximate measures, units, and weight (edible part unless footnotes indicate otherwise)			Ash	Calcium	Phosphorus	Iron	Sodium	Potassium	Vitamin A value	Thiamin	Riboflavin	Niacin	Ascorbic acid
			Grams	*Grams*	*Milligrams*	*Milligrams*	*Milligrams*	*Milligrams*	*Milligrams*	*International units*	*Milligrams*	*Milligrams*	*Milligrams*	*Milligrams*
	Baby cereals, precooked, dry:													
67	Barley, added nutrients		100	3.8	[4]930	825	95.0	([5])	384	(0)	2.47	2.12	[6]22.1	(0)
68	High protein, added nutrients		100	7.3	[4]842	873	[7]80.0	([5])	1,261	(0)	2.37	2.15	[6]15.9	(0)
69	Mixed, added nutrients		100	4.9	[4]977	778	[7]80.0	([5])	309	(0)	2.59	2.47	[6]20.6	(0)
70	Oatmeal, added nutrients		100	4.7	[4]823	768	[7]80.0	([5])	370	(0)	2.59	2.47	[6]20.6	(0)
71	Rice, added nutrients		100	4.9	[4]888	683	[7]80.0	([5])	203	(0)	2.59	2.47	[6]20.6	(0)
370, ftnt. 50, table 1; ftnt. 2, table 2	Ground beef with 21% fat, cooked to well-done stage (oven-broiled, pan-broiled, or sauteed):													
	100 g		100	(1.4)	(12)	(217)	(3.6)	66	304	(40)	(.08)	(.22)	(5.7)	(0)
	Yield from 1 lb., raw (item 369a)	10.4 oz	295	(4.1)	(35)	(640)	(10.6)	195	897	(120)	(.24)	(.65)	(16.8)	(0)
	Yield from 4 oz., raw (item 369b)	2.6 oz	74	(1.0)	(9)	(161)	(2.7)	49	225	(30)	(.06)	(.16)	(4.2)	(0)
	Yield from 3.2 oz., raw (item 369c)	2.1 oz	60	(.8)	(7)	(130)	(2.2)	40	182	(30)	(.05)	(.13)	(3.4)	(0)
	Pound	1 lb	454	(6.4)	(54)	(984)	(16.3)	299	1,389	(190)	(.36)	(1.00)	(25.9)	(0)
538a, ftnt. 104, table 1; ftnt. 11, table 2	Pound cake, old-fashioned, prepared and baked from home recipe (equal weights of flour, sugar, eggs, fat):													
	100 g.:													
	Made with cooking fat[1]		100	.5	19	74	.8	[8]102	61	250	.03	.08	.2	0
	Made with vegetable shortening		100	.5	19	74	.8	[8]102	61	250	.03	.08	.2	0
	Made with butter		100	1.2	25	79	.8	366	67	960	.03	.08	.2	0
	Yield from recipe:													
	Made with cooking fat[1]	3¾ lb	1,694	8.5	322	1,254	13.6	[8]1,728	1,033	4,240	.51	1.36	3.4	0
	Made with vegetable shortening	3¾ lb	1,694	8.5	322	1,254	13.6	[8]1,728	1,033	4,240	.51	1.36	3.4	0
	Made with butter	3¾ lb	1,694	20.3	424	1,338	13.6	6,200	1,135	16,260	.51	1.36	3.4	0
	Loaf (8½ × 3½ × 3¼ in.; ⅓ of yield):													
	Whole (vol., 292 cu. in.):													
	Made with cooking fat[1]	1 loaf	565	2.8	107	418	4.5	[8]576	345	1,410	.17	.45	1.1	0
	Made with vegetable shortening	1 loaf	565	2.8	107	418	4.5	[8]576	345	1,410	.17	.45	1.1	0
	Made with butter	1 loaf	565	6.8	141	446	4.5	2,068	379	5,420	.17	.45	1.1	0
	Slice, ½ in. thick (8½ × 3 × ½ in.; 1⁄17 of loaf):													
	Made with cooking fat[1]	1 slice	33	.2	6	24	.3	[8]34	20	80	.01	.03	.1	0
	Made with vegetable shortening	1 slice	33	.2	6	24	.3	[8]34	20	80	.01	.03	.1	0
	Made with butter	1 slice	33	.4	8	26	.3	121	22	320	.01	.03	.1	0
	Cube (1 cu. in.):													
	Made with cooking fat[1]	1 cube	5.8	Trace	1	4	Trace	[8]6	4	10	Trace	Trace	Trace	0
	Made with vegetable shortening	1 cube	5.8	Trace	1	4	Trace	[8]6	4	10	Trace	Trace	Trace	0
	Made with butter	1 cube	5.8	.1	1	5	Trace	21	4	60	Trace	Trace	Trace	0
	Parmesan cheese:													
651d–h	Shredded		100	5.5	1,221	837	.4	786	160	(1,140)	.02	.78	.2	(0)
651i–m	Grated		100	6.0	1,352	926	.5	870	177	(1,260)	.02	.87	.2	(0)
958, ftnt. 194, table 1; ftnt. 87, table 2	Doughnuts, yeast-leavened, glazed:													
	100 g		100	.8	32	66	[9]1.3	200	69	50	[9].14	[9].14	[9]1.1	0
	Doughnut, 3¾-in. diam., 1¼ in. high	1 doughnut	50	.4	16	33	[9].6	100	34	25	[9].07	[9].07	[9].6	0
	Orange juice concentrate, frozen, unsweetened:													
1436	Undiluted		100	1.4	35	59	.4	2	704	760	.32	.05	1.3	169
1437	Diluted with 3 parts water by volume		100	.4	10	17	.1	1	202	220	.09	.01	.4	48
1629, ftnt. 298, table 1; ftnt. 56, table 2	Pizza, with cheese and sausage topping, from home recipe, baked (in 14-in.-diam. pan):[2,3]													
	100 g		100	3.4	188	205	1.4	668	196	550	.08	.18	1.4	9
	Whole, 13¾-in. diam., 43.2-in. cir	1 pizza	604	20.5	1,136	1,238	8.5	4,035	1,184	3,320	.48	1.09	8.5	54
	Sector, 5⅓-in. arc; ⅛ of pizza	1 sector	76	2.6	143	156	1.1	508	149	420	.06	.14	1.1	7
	Sector, 1-in. arc	1 sector	14.0	.5	26	29	.2	94	27	80	.01	.03	.2	1
2448, 2449, ftnt. 395, table 1	Wheat, rolled, instant-cooking (used as hot breakfast cereal):													
	Dry form	1 cup	90	1.6	32	308	2.9	2	342	(0)	.32	.11	3.7	(0)
	Cooked (salt added):													
	100 g		100	1.1	8	59	.5	295	65	(0)	.06	.02	.7	(0)
	1 cup	1 cup	245	2.7	20	145	1.2	723	159	(0)	.15	.05	1.7	(0)

[1] Vegetable, animal, or mixed vegetable and animal shortenings.

[2] For amount of cheese and proportion of crust to filling, see ARS 62–13 (7, p. 32).

[3] Values based on product made with unenriched flour; with enriched flour, increase values in milligrams per 100 g. of product as follows: Iron 0.6, thiamin 0.10, riboflavin 0.06, niacin 0.7.

[4] Value varies with the brand, ranging per 100 g. from 660 to 1,200 mg. for items 67, 68, and 71; 530 to 1,600 mg. for item 69; 570 to 1,000 mg. for item 70.

[5] See discussion under Baby Foods, p. 262.

[6] Value varies widely with the brand, ranging per 100 g. from 14 to 30 mg. for items 67, 69–71; 4 to 30 mg. for item 68.

[7] Value varies widely with the brand, ranging per 100 g. from 50 to 100 mg.

[8] Applies to product with same proportion of added salt as used for product made with butter.

[9] Based on product made with enriched flour. With unenriched flour, approx. values (mg.) for 100 g. of glazed doughnut are iron 0.5, thiamin 0.04, riboflavin 0.07, niacin 0.4; for 1 doughnut: Iron 0.3, thiamin 0.02, riboflavin 0.03, niacin 0.2.

ways convert exactly to values given for another volume measure of that item. For some of the small basic units where the error from rounding the figures seemed important, weights have been taken to one decimal place. Equivalent weights in grams for units of 1 pound and 1 ounce by weight have been expressed as whole numbers, 454 and 28 g., respectively. Nutritive values corresponding to these units, however, have been based on the unrounded values of 453.6 and 28.35 g.

Liquids and Foods With Large Liquid Component

A wide variety of products are liquid or largely liquid and for them measures are generally expressed in terms of fluid measure. Products usually measured by cup or fluid ounce include milk, fruit and vegetable juices, canned fruits and vegetables, all types of beverages, and the various sirups.

Weights per cup or fluid ounce for many of the liquid products were calculated from specific gravity using the weight of water in a standard measuring cup as 236.6 g. and for a fluid ounce as 29.573 g.

Specific gravity readings used for beer and wines were averages of values reported for them from several sources. Specific gravities used for other alcoholic beverages were those corresponding to their content of alcohol by volume as given in reference table 47.003 of the Association of Official Analytical Chemists (*1*). Reference table 47.008 from this source was used to derive the specific gravity, which corresponded to the content of soluble solids or degrees Brix, for the nonalcoholic beverages, fruit and vegetable juices, fruit drinks, nectars, sirups, and molasses. To facilitate calculating data for measures in addition to the quantities listed in table 1, data have been provided for 1 fluid ounce for the alcoholic beverages, other beverages, and fruit and vegetable juices.

Commercially canned fruits and vegetables are available in many can sizes and styles. Data shown include the most popular sizes and styles for each item. Weight in grams is given for the net contents of the can. These weights are based on the net weights declared on the labels by major processors of each product and may be slightly below the actual weights of the total contents inasmuch as processors may fill the cans to weights in excess of the declared net weight. At times, data are needed for such measures as a cup or other specified portion of fruit or vegetable with and without the liquid. To some extent, information of this type is included in table 1.

The proportion of fruit to liquid in canned fruits varies with several factors, such as the form of the fruit used, the packing medium, and the can size. The various factors that affect the proportions could not all be taken into account and the information in table 1 for the volume and unit measures of fruit and liquid should be considered as approximations. As data for the composition of drained fruits were not available to use with weights of the drained fruits, volume measures for drained fruits could not be included.

For canned vegetables, information is provided for the nutrients in the vegetables drained of their packing medium. Yields of drained solids from the cans are based mainly on the minimum drained weights recommended by the Agricultural Marketing Service, U.S. Department of Agriculture, in their standards for grades set up for many of the canned vegetables. The data shown do not apply to vegetables canned with added butter or sauce.

Nonliquid Foods

Cup measures are shown for numerous foods in addition to those that are liquid or have a large liquid component. Many nonliquid foods are measured by the cup, and this measure and fractions or small multiples of a cup are commonly used. Weights of the cup quantity for these foods apply to weights found for the amounts in standard 1-cup measures of the type that can be leveled off with a straight edge. When the weights of a cup quantity are calculated from the weights of larger volumes, the calculated weight per cup has usually been greater—probably because the particles or pieces of the food packed together more in larger measures—than when the weights are determined for 1-cup quantities. Cup weights shown in the tables may or may not be adequate for determining weights of larger measures such as 1 quart or more. Although specific only for 1 cup, the weights are believed reasonably suitable for calculating nutrients in serving portions that are in the range of from less than 1 cup up to 2 cups.

Many other factors also affect the weight of 1 cup of food. For nonliquid foods, the most important include the physical characteristics of the product, pretreatment of the product as stirring or sifting, the size of particles, the procedure for filling the cup as spooning, scooping, and pouring, and the pressure applied to the product when in the cup. Factors and conditions believed to affect the weight of a cup of product are indicated as part of the description of an item if the information was available, and several are discussed later in this section.

Some cup measures are described in the tables as "not packed" and "packed." "Not packed" refers to lightly filling the cup without pressing down on the food. A "packed" cup represents about the maximum amount of food that can be pressed into the cup without altering its physical structure.

For those foods commonly used in units of 1 tablespoon and 1 teaspoon, weights shown are for the foods measured in those units. Weights obtained in this manner are usually less than the weights derived for them by dividing the weight per cup by 16 (the number of tablespoons in 1 cup) or by 48 (the number of teaspoons in 1 cup). For ingredients like cornstarch that pack easily, pressing a maximum amount of food into the measuring spoons was found to give better agreement between the weights obtained by the two methods. As packing to get maximum amount in the measuring utensil is not typical, weights obtained in this way are not shown.

Household measuring spoons of several styles are on the market. Unpublished data have indicated that the weight of 1 tablespoon or 1 teaspoon of baking powder, salt, or sugar in some spoons may be 10 or 20 percent lower, respectively, than the weight in other measuring spoons. Weight rather than measure by spoonful may be needed if concentrated sources of critical nutrients are to be used frequently in preparing food for individuals on severely restricted diets.

Foods Measured in Pieces, Slices, and Other Units.—For foods consumed mainly as pieces or slices, these measures are shown in table 1. Dimensions used in describing the measures are in terms of common fractions of an inch and are approximate. They are given as aids for visualizing the volume measures in relation to the weights and for estimating the weight of a food item for which only dimensions are known. Such dimensions should not be used to establish weights per cubic inch, particularly of irregular-shaped foods such as pieces of fish, candies, cookies, and slices of bread, or very thin slices of cheese and sausage. A difference as small as one-sixteenth of an inch in thickness would greatly alter the weight per cubic inch derived from the dimensions for a slice.

The specific quantities shown for foods should not be construed as average servings. The quantities specified are those considered reasonable for use in calculating amounts in the various serving sizes commonly used. For example, the measures shown for cooked fish, meat, and poultry items and for a specified count of nut kernels should not be interpreted as typical serving sizes.

Where information was adequate to provide weight per cubic inch of a food, this weight is shown. Data for 1 cubic inch are included for such foods as cakes cheeses, table fats, and candy. Information available did not justify showing different weights by kinds and classifications of cooked meats and poultry or by differences in proportions of fatty tissue or poultry skin present. For these items, the weights specified for the slices of the dimensions shown have been calculated on the basis that 1 cubic inch weighs 18.4 g. This weight per cubic inch was used for all the cooked meat and poultry items except chopped, diced, and ground forms. A weight per cup of 140 g. has been used for the chopped or diced form and 110 g. for the ground form of any kind of cooked meat or poultry.

For items in several groups of foods such as prepackaged baby foods, cheese, sausage, soups, and home-prepared fish dishes, data are provided for 1 avoirdupois ounce.

Units of 1 pound are shown for the raw forms of some fruit, vegetable, and meat items without their inedible portion and for the cooked forms of vegetables and meats. A reasonable yield of cooked food from a given weight of raw food is listed for meat, poultry, fish and shellfish, alimentary pastes, vegetables, and some packaged desserts and baked goods.

Cooked Vegetables.—Weights per cup found by various investigators for the cooked greens, such as collards, spinach, and turnip greens, vary widely. Factors contributing to this are the physical structure of the green (smooth. curly, coarse, tender, size of midrib or stems), maturity, the part used (leaf including midrib and stem or without one or both of these parts), preparation for cooking (left whole or chopped), cooking time, amount of cooking liquid drained from greens before measuring, and method of filling the cup (with or without pressing down on the greens). Weights reported usually are not identified as to these conditions. The cup weights shown in this publication for greens represent a common method for serving them—that is with little adhering cooking liquid and not packed down. If the greens are packed into the cup, the weights per cup would need to be increased by 50 to 80 g.

Frozen Fruits.—Frozen fruits are usually served when partially or completely thawed. To obtain measures of volumes suitable for serving portions, the weights per cup were determined after the fruit had thawed.

Home-Prepared Foods.—The nutritive values for several home-prepared foods have been based on calculations from formulas for lack of satisfactory analyzed values. As indicated by the footnotes in table 1, information is given in ARS 62–13 (7) about the formulas used, the ingredients, and the methods of calculating the nutritive values. Data for the yield of cooked food from these formulas are given in terms of weight and measure in the present publication for cakes, dessert pies, pizzas, potpies, several main-course dishes, and some puddings. This information can be used for estimating portions of several other sizes and also for approximate estimations with products of similar formulation having about the same or unknown yields.

Volume measures that might be used for some foods would be too numerous to tabulate, and for a designated weight of some foods the dimensions could vary indefinitely. Weights and nutritive values for basic units of 1 cubic inch and a 1-inch sector of circular-shaped foods are therefore provided for calculating data for volume measures other than those shown in the tables.

The temperature of the product when the volume is measured affects the quantity by weight of some prepared foods such as macaroni and other pastas, rice, puddings with starch base, prune whip, and souffles. Alimentary pastes and rice are heavier per cup when measured hot than cold. With cooling, the individual pieces become firmer and separate from one another, leaving more and larger air spaces as the cup is filled. For these foods, weights per cup are provided for each condition if the product is commonly served either hot or cold.

Air incorporated in prune whip and cheese souffle is rapidly expelled as these products cool or when a serving utensil is inserted. Weights per cup determined on these two foods when cool are greater than weights based on their volume immediately after cooking. Weight per cup of prune whip is provided on both these bases. Data for cheese souffle represents a collapsed product.

Weights per cup for puddings with starch base and for desserts made with gelatin or rennin were determined by pouring the hot products into the cup to the capacity of 1 cup. Spooning the cooled mixtures into the cup may give different weights, but data on this basis were not determined.

Weight-volume relationships for other desserts, as custard, apple brown betty, bread or rice puddings with raisins, and tapioca puddings, were based on measurements obtained by spooning the cold products into the cup. Weights per cup probably would differ from those shown if other methods of filling the cup were used.

Cereal Products and Foods Made With Cereal Products

Cornmeals and Related Products.—Weight per cup for the dry form of cornmeals, corn grits, and corn flour is affected by the size of the grind and the method of filling the measuring cup.

The size of grind for a specific product varies with different manufacturers, with the same manufacturer, and with differences in consumer preference in the geographical areas where the products are marketed. Products coarsely ground have been found to weigh more per cup than when finely ground. Weights per cup shown for the cornmeals, corn grits, and corn flour are based on products with a grind considered typical for each.

The weights shown represent one method of filling the cup. The method used was to pour the product from container into cup to overflow with as little fall as possible and to level with a straight edge. The weights per cup will differ from those shown if the cup is filled by other methods. Other commonly used methods are scooping from a container with or without applying pressure and spooning the product into a cup applying pressure with the spoon. Approximate increases in weight per cup to be expected by these methods are shown in table 4.

Breakfast-Type Cereals.—For those breakfast cereals that require cooking before eating, the trend has been toward products with a shortened cooking time, 5 minutes or less. In this handbook those products requiring 2 to 5 minutes' cooking have been described as "quick-cooking"; those requiring 1 minute or less as "instant-cooking." To help identify these products, the cooking time is indicated in column B in table 1.

For most cereals, unless specified otherwise, the shortened cooking time has been accomplished by physically reducing the size of particles. This reduction does not change the nutritive values but sometimes has changed the weight per cup of the dry form. For example, whole-meal wheat cereal (item 2450, table 1), which as formerly manufactured had a cooking time of 15 minutes, weighed about 145 g. per cup. The more recent product on the market with a cooking time of about 5 minutes weighs only about 125 g. per cup. For the flaked cereals, such as rolled oats and rolled wheat, weights per cup do not appear to be affected as much by reduced particle size as do the weights of the granular-type cereals.

For some of the products requiring shortened cooking time, directions for proportions of dry cereal and liquid to use have changed from those specified in ARS 62–13, table 3, page 9. This change, however, has not altered the proportion of cereal and water in the cooked product; the nutritive values per 100 g. of the cooked cereal in Handbook No. 8 still apply.

Weights per cup shown for both the "ready-to-eat" breakfast cereals and the dry form of those used mainly as "hot cereals" are also based on the method of pouring the product from container into cup or spooning the product into cup to overflow and leveling with a straight edge. Weight per cup is greater when the cup is dipped into the cereal for filling. This technique results in some compressing of the cereal, especially for those products of small particle size, such as cream of rice, cornmeal, and corn grits.

Breads.—Information on the weight-volume relationships shown for commercial breads (items 444–474, tables 1 and 2) was derived from data for brands considered typical of breads in national distribution. The data were determined on samples of bread obtained from retail stores in the Washington, D.C., area and supplemented by unpublished data supplied by several baking companies in other areas.

The data for the bread items were extremely variable. For each type of bread, loaves of the

TABLE 4.—*Cornmeals and related products: Effect of measurement procedures on weight per cup as shown in tables 1 and 2*

Item No. from tables 1 and 2	Description	Increase in weight per cup [1]		
		Scooped into cup		Spooned into cup, pressed down
		No pressure	Slight pressure	
		Grams	*Grams*	*Grams*
860	Corn flour	---	30	45
862, 864	Corn grits, degermed, enriched and unenriched	10	10	20
883, 884	Cornmeal, whole-ground, unbolted and bolted	15	20	40
885, 887	Cornmeal, degermed, enriched and unenriched	10	20	30
889–892	Cornmeal, self-rising	20	25	35

[1] Obtained by pouring product into cup with little fall.

same declared net weight were found to differ by brand in the actual weight of the loaf, its dimensions, the thickness of the slices, and the number of slices per loaf. Dimensions and weights for slices within a loaf also varied. Loaves of the same type of bread but of two different net weights varied in the dimensions and weights of their slices.

For pan bread baked in the usual shapes, the dimensions shown for the slices are for the center slices. The weights of the slices were determined by dividing the declared net weight of loaves of a specified net weight by the average number of slices, including the end slices. The weight of the two end slices varied considerably, but generally their combined weight was 1½ times the average weight of the center slice.

For breads baked in oval-shaped loaves, such as often found for French or vienna, Italian, and rye breads, it was not feasible to relate the size of the slice to the count of slices per loaf. The information in the tables is for what might be considered a typical slice.

Commercial white breads and whole-wheat breads currently on the retail market are of two main types. The more common type has been described as having a soft crumb. The other is more like homemade bread and has been described as having a firm crumb. For the same net weight the two types differ in size of loaf and in the count, size, and weight of their slices.

Cakes.—Both weight and volume of a cake can vary considerably as a result of differences in many factors, such as formula used, techniques in mixing ingredients, baking temperature, and amount of crumb loss.

The weights, measures, and nutritive values shown in this publication are considered reasonable estimates, but they should be used realizing that specific samples will vary.

Data shown apply to uniced cakes, cake icings, and combinations of cakes and icings. Sizes shown for whole cakes and pieces of cake are limited. However, data in terms of 1-cubic inch portions are given for calculating values for other sizes of whole cakes or pieces of cake. In addition, values for other combinations of the cakes and icings than those shown can be calculated from information tabulated on yields of uniced home-prepared cakes and icings.

The formulas for the home-prepared uniced cakes, the icings, and the proportion of cake to icing used for calculating the nutritive values were those noted in tables 7, 9, and 11 on pages 13–17 of ARS 62–13 (7). In the present publication the weight and volume measure of the baked cakes, prepared icings, and iced cakes corresponding to these formulas have been shown for most of the cake items. For some of the cake items, a weight and volume measure have been tabulated for a size of whole cake other than would be obtained from the formulas in ARS 62–13. The weight and volume of these additional sizes of cakes have been calculated using the same proportion of ingredients in the cakes and the same relative amounts of cake and icing that are shown in ARS 62–13. Footnotes to the items indicate which sizes of whole cake would be obtained when using the formulas in ARS 62–13 and which sizes have been calculated. Sizes of pieces for each kind of cake were selected as ones commonly used and were based on the information tabulated for the whole cakes.

For cakes prepared from mixes, the same weight of baked cake and the same weight of icing were used for both the 8- and 9-inch-diameter cakes. The cakes differ only in their dimensions and the size of their pieces.

The formula in ARS 62–13 for caramel icing yielded a quantity too small for cakes of either 8- or 9-inch diameter. An adjustment was made therefore in the amount of icing in the calculated weights and volumes of the cakes having caramel icing. The yield of the formula for the icing (item 570a, tables 1 and 2) was increased approximately 1½ times to cover the top and sides of the caramel and yellow cakes of 8-inch diameter and approximately doubled for the cakes of 9-inch diameter. It was doubled also for the icing of the honey spicecake prepared from a mix (item 563, tables 1 and 2). These added amounts of icing would result in only minor changes in the data on composition shown for these iced cakes in Handbook No. 8.

Diameters specified in the description of the cakes refer to the measurement as taken at the top of the cake. The length of the arc of a piece of cake was calculated from the circumference at the top of the cake and rounded to the nearest one-eighth inch or common fraction of an inch.

Table 5 shows the sizes, dimensions, and volume capacities of the pans used as the basis for estimating the volume measures shown for baked cakes, except fruitcakes. The formula used for calculating the cubic-inch capacity of pan is as follows:

$$\frac{\pi h}{3}(r_1^2 + r_1r_2 + r_2^2)$$

Where π = 3.1416, h = height of pan. and r_1 and r_2 = radii or one-half diameter of pan at top and bottom, respectively. If the diameter is the same at the top and bottom of the pan, the formula is πr^2h. If the cakes prepared from the formulas given in ARS 62–13 filled the size pans described in table 5, the inside dimensions and cubic-inch capacities of the pans represented essentially the dimensions and cubic-inch volume of the baked cakes. If a cake did not completely fill the pan or if its height was greater than the height of the pan, adjustments were made in the dimensions. The volume of the cake was calculated from these adjusted dimensions.

Information for fruitcakes was based on measurements of commercial products rather than on pan size.

Dimensions for cupcakes were too variable to permit calculation of their cubic-inch volume with any degree of accuracy. For these items, only an approximate measure in diameter has been shown in the tables.

TABLE 5.—*Sizes and dimensions of pans with volume capacities equivalent to yields shown for baked cakes in tables 1 and 2*

Type of pan and outside dimensions	Inside dimensions of pan [1] Diameter at— Top	Bottom	Height	Calculated capacity of pans
	Inches	*Inches*	*Inches*	*Cubic inches*
Layer cake; round:				
9 in. × 1½ in	9	8½	1½	90
8 in. × 1½ in	8	7½	1½	71
Tube cake:				
10 in. × 4 in.:				
Pan including tube space	9¾	8½	4¼	278
Tube	1¾	2⅛	4¼	13
Net capacity of pan	---	---	---	265
9 in. × 3½ in.:				
Pan including tube space	8½	7½	3½	176
Tube	1¾	2⅜	3½	12
Net capacity of pan	---	---	---	164

[1] For tubes in tube cake pans, outside dimensions are given.

Frozen Pies.—Measures and nutritive values shown for frozen pies apply to those with a diameter of 8 inches. Pies of other sizes would have different proportions of crust and filling and different nutritive values. The 10-inch-diameter pie is the more predominant. However, nutritive values were available to include data for weights and volume measures for only 8-inch frozen pies.

Eggs

Federal Standards (*13*) provide for classifying shell eggs by size based on a minimum weight per dozen. The six U.S. weight classes or sizes and the minimum weight (ounces) per dozen for each are as follows: Jumbo 30, extra large 27, large 24, medium 21, small 18, and peewee 15. These minimum weights per dozen are the basis of the weights for the extra large, large, and medium eggs in shell for which data are shown in this publication. These sizes are in most frequent production. To determine the weight per egg in shell for the other sizes not listed in this publication, the minimum weight per dozen could be used. For the weight of the edible portion, deduction for weight of refuse as shell should be made as follows: Jumbo 9 percent, small and peewee 13 percent.

Fruits and Vegetables

Bananas.—Measurements for common and red bananas and plantains, also called baking bananas, are included in table 1. Data are shown for the common banana in four sizes, three of which are usually marketed at retail. The average diameter and average weight for each size increase from small through large with some overlapping in diameters and weights for the three sizes (table 6).

The fourth size, petite, applies to bananas of relatively uniform size and weight packed as single fingers for institutional use. The practice regarding count and size for these bananas is described in table 1, column B.

Bananas vary widely in proportions of skin and edible flesh. The percentage of skin (refuse) has been found to range from as little as 14 to as much as 40 percent. Variations of this kind in proportion of edible part, in addition to variations in weights of bananas, indicate that whenever precise figures are needed for the quantity of banana, the actual weight of the edible portion should be determined for the specific bananas used.

TABLE 6.—*Dimensions and weights of bananas and plantains* [1]

Size	Length [2]	Diameter	Weight
	Inches	*Inches*	*Grams*
COMMON BANANAS			
Large:			
Average	9¾	1 14/32	200
Range	9 and over	1 10/32–1 18/32	161–232
Medium:			
Average	8¾	1 13/32	175
Range	8–9	1 8/32–1 22/32	134–263
Small:			
Average	7¾	1 11/32	140
Range	6¼–8	1 7/32–1 19/32	113–163
PLANTAINS			
Average	11	1 28/32	365
Range	9–14	1 21/32–2 3/32	311–484
RED BANANAS			
Average	7¼	1 17/32	193
Range	7–7½	1 16/32–1 19/32	173–201

[1] Data supplied by United Brands Co.
[2] As measured along outer curve.

Berries.—Fresh strawberries, blueberries, and other berries are marketed in containers with declared net contents of 1 pint or 1 quart. Usually these containers are filled to a volume greater than their declared net contents. Weights in table 1 for these containers of fruit represent containers filled in this manner.

Citrus Fruits.—The weights per fruit shown have been calculated from estimated net weights of shipping containers and counts of fruit in the container. The information was obtained from the U.S. Agricultural Marketing Service (AMS), the Florida Department of Citrus, and the Sunkist Growers, Inc. The calculated weights per fruit represent large, medium, and small sizes shipped in largest quantities for use as fresh fruit.

The Federal and State standards for fresh citrus fruits specify diameters in inches and their counts in shipping containers of specified volumes for sizes marketed commercially. The standards do not give the net weights of the containers because weights vary with the size of fruit, differences in climatic conditions from year to year or within seasons, and time of harvesting during the shipping season. However, estimated net weights for the containers are provided in footnotes for the several fresh citrus fruit items. These weights are considered reasonable and may be used to calculate approximate weights for fruits of diameters and counts not included in table 1.

Tomatoes.—Most tomatoes for the retail market are prepackaged three or four to a carton with a declared net weight of 12 ounces. Conformity to this net weight is difficult because of irregularity in the size and weight of the tomatoes. In a study conducted by the U.S. Department of Agriculture (*27*) on packaged tomatoes in retail stores, the average weight of tomatoes in the cartons was found to be 14 ounces. Data in table 1 for prepackaged tomatoes are based on this average weight rather than on the declared net weight. Although no two tomatoes in a container will be of the same dimensions and weight, the sizes shown are typical. Tomatoes sold in bulk usually are larger than those that are prepackaged. Data for a size considered representative are shown.

Olives and Pickles.—Dimensions and weights for the sizes of olives shown are based on standards for green, ripe, and salt-cured olives specified by AMS (*15, 16, 26*). These standards have illustrations of sizes and specify the average and range in number per pound for all sizes available commercially. Many sizes of dill, sour, and sweet pickles are marketed. The sizes given in table 1 are those in greatest usage.

APPENDIX C.—NOTES ON FOODS

Information is included here on characteristics or particular features of food groups or individual foods too extensive and detailed to be incorporated in the tables but useful as background in understanding the data on nutritive values.

Cereals and Cereal Products

Enriched Foods and Standards of Enrichment.—Items described as "enriched" are those for which Federal standards for enrichment have been promulgated. To be labeled "enriched," these products must contain amounts of certain nutrients within the limits specified for the particular product. In addition, the standards provide for enrichment on an optional basis for certain other nutrients. The quantities specified in the standards for the affected nutrients, both required and optional, are summarized in table 7. These quantities are based on the amounts in 1 pound of product as specified in the standards and in 100 g. as calculated from those specifications. Values for enriched foods in table 1 are for items that comply with the standards for the required nutrients.

Federal standards for enriched rice became effective on February 27, 1958, for all nutrients except riboflavin. The requirement for riboflavin was stayed pending further hearings. If the regulation becomes effective, the riboflavin values in table 1 for the weights of volume measures for the dry forms of rice (items 1871, 1873, 1875) should be calculated on the basis of the minimum level of enrichment shown for 100 g. of rice in table 7. For the cooked forms of rice (items 1872, 1874, 1876), a corresponding value of 0.07 mg. per 100 g. should be used. Meanwhile, or until further action is taken by the U.S. Food and Drug Administration, riboflavin values for enriched rice should be based on the values for unenriched rice in table 1.

The minimum levels stated for the nutrients in table 7 and the values shown for enriched rice in table 1 apply to packaged rice bearing on the label the statement "To retain vitamins do not rinse before or drain after cooking." Values for products without this statement or with directions for washing and draining, to be labeled "enriched," must carry enough of each of the nutrients so that after washing, the rice will contain at least 85 percent of the amounts specified in table 7 for the minimum levels.

Federal standards provide for enrichment of whole-ground and bolted cornmeals as well as for degermed meals and for self-rising cornmeals. Enrichment with calcium is optional. The minimum level required for enrichment is 500 mg. per pound. For self-rising cornmeal, the maximum level allowed is 1,750 mg. per pound, which is approximately 2⅓ times the maximum level of 750 mg. per pound allowed for other cornmeals and corn grits enriched with calcium (*20*). The calcium values in table 1 for enriched self-rising cornmeal represent products containing about 75 percent of the maximum level allowed in the standards. Values shown for these cornmeals have been based on a formula that includes anhydrous monocalcium phosphate at a level of 1¾ pounds per 100 pounds of cornmeal or cornmeal and wheat flour.

Standards of enrichment for noodle products in table 7 also apply to egg pastinas (item 1475, table 1), a type of noodle product.

The minimum and maximum values in table 7 are the amounts specified in the standards that have been effective for several years. Revised standards were issued on October 15, 1973, and further revised on February 11 and June 14, 1974. They specified only single-level requirements with provisions for reasonable overages within the limits of good manufacturing practice (*22*). The revised standards of enrichment apply to thiamin, riboflavin, niacin, iron, and calcium in self-rising flour, white flour, and white bread, rolls, buns, and farina. For the enriched forms, the single-level requirements for those nutrients required and for calcium when optional and required are shown in milligrams per pound and per 100 g. (values in parentheses) as follows:

TABLE 7.—*Standards for enrichment of cereal products: Minimum and maximum amounts of required and optional nutrients specified for foods labeled "enriched"* [1] [2]

Cereal product	Required nutrients										Optional nutrients			
	Thiamin		Riboflavin		Niacin		Iron		Calcium		Calcium		Vitamin D	
	Min.	Max.	Min.	Max.	Min.	Max.	Min.	Max.	Min.	Max.	Min.	Max.	Min.	Max.
	Milli-grams	*Milli-grams*	*Milli-grams*	*Milli-grams*	*Milli-grams*	*Milli-grams*	*Milli-grams*	*Milli-grams*	*Milli-grams*	*Milli-grams*	*Milli-grams*	*Milli-grams*	*Inter-na-tional units*	*Inter-na-tional units*
PER POUND OF PRODUCT														
Bread, rolls, and buns, white	1.1	1.8	0.7	1.6	10.0	15.0	8.0	12.5	---	----	300	800	150	750
Cornmeal; corn grits	2.0	3.0	1.2	1.8	16.0	24.0	13.0	26.0	---	----	500	750	250	1,000
Cornmeal, self-rising	2.0	3.0	1.2	1.8	16.0	24.0	13.0	26.0	---	----	500	1,750	250	1,000
Farina	2.0	2.5	1.2	1.5	16.0	20.0	13.0	([3])	---	----	500	([3])	250	([3])
Flour, white	2.0	2.5	1.2	1.5	16.0	20.0	13.0	16.5	---	----	500	[4] 625	250	1,000
Flour, self-rising	2.0	2.5	1.2	1.5	16.0	20.0	13.0	16.5	500	1,500	---	---	250	1,000
Macaroni products; noodle products	4.0	5.0	1.7	2.2	27.0	34.0	13.0	16.5	---	----	500	625	250	1,000
Rice, milled	2.0	4.0	[5] 1.2	[5] 2.4	16.0	32.0	13.0	26.0	---	----	500	1,000	250	1,000
PER 100 G. OF PRODUCT														
Bread, rolls, and buns, white	.24	.40	.15	.35	2.20	3.31	1.76	2.76	---	----	66	176	33	165
Cornmeal; corn grits	.44	.66	.26	.40	3.53	5.29	2.87	5.73	---	----	110	165	55	220
Cornmeal, self-rising	.44	.66	.26	.40	3.53	5.29	2.87	5.73	---	386	---	---	55	220
Farina	.44	.55	.26	.33	3.53	4.41	2.87	([3])	---	----	110	([3])	55	([3])
Flour, white	.44	.55	.26	.33	3.53	4.41	2.87	3.64	---	----	110	138	55	220
Flour, self-rising	.44	.55	.26	.33	3.53	4.41	2.87	3.64	110	331	---	---	55	220
Macaroni products; noodle products	.88	1.10	.37	.48	5.95	7.50	2.87	3.64	---	----	110	138	55	220
Rice, milled	.44	.88	[5] .26	[5] .53	3.53	7.05	2.87	5.73	---	----	110	220	55	220

[1] Information here, except for rice and self-rising cornmeal, from Federal Register of Dec. 20, 1955 (*17*), and information for rice and self-rising cornmeal from Federal Register of Aug. 27, 1957 (*18*) and Aug. 10, 1961 (*20*), respectively, and became effective for latter on Jan. 27, 1962 (*21*).

[2] Standards for enrichment provide for inclusion of calcium and vitamin D within stated limits as optional ingredients for products here, except self-rising cornmeal and self-rising flour; for these items calcium is required as indicated.

[3] No maximum level established.

[4] When acidified with monocalcium phosphate at specified range of 0.25–0.75 percent of the finished product, calcium levels may range from 680 to 1,165 mg. per pound (150–257 mg. per 100 g.).

[5] Requirement for riboflavin stayed pending further hearings (*19*).

Item	Thiamin	Riboflavin	Niacin	Iron [1]	Calcium
	Milligrams	*Milligrams*	*Milligrams*	*Milligrams*	*Milligrams*
Self-rising flour	2.9	1.8	24	40	[2] 960
	(0.64)	(0.40)	(5.3)	(8.8)	(212)
White flour	2.9	1.8	24	40	[3] 960
	(0.64)	(0.40)	(5.3)	(8.8)	(212)
White bread, rolls, and buns.	1.8	1.1	15	25	[3] 600
	(0.40)	(0.24)	(3.3)	(5.5)	(132)
Farina [4]	6.1	4.2	80.0	129.6	[2] 2,400
	(1.34)	(0.92)	(17.6)	(28.6)	(529)

[1] Requirement for iron stayed pending further hearings.
[2] Enrichment with calcium required.
[3] Enrichment with calcium optional.
[4] Levels at 15-percent moisture content.

Except for iron and the requirements for farina, the effective date specified for the revised standards was January 1, 1975. For iron, the regulation was stayed pending further hearings. For farina, as of August 1974, no effective date has been specified.

The required level for enrichment with calcium is about twice the previous existing minimum levels for these products, except for farina for which it is about five times.

For self-rising flour, the single-level requirement for enrichment with calcium is 960 mg. per pound (212 mg. per 100 g.). If a calcium compound is added for technical purposes to give self-rising characteristics to the flour, the new standards specify that the amount of calcium per pound of flour may exceed 960 mg. per pound if it is at a level within good manufacturing practices. Calcium values in table 1 for self-rising flour (item 2445) and baking powder biscuits prepared with it (item 412) were based on a value for self-rising flour of about 1,200 mg. per pound. This value is higher than the new single-level requirement for enrichment with calcium, but it is permissible as noted here.

The new required level for white flour is also 960 mg. per pound (212 mg. per 100 g.) and for bread, rolls, and buns, 600 mg. per pound (132 mg. per 100 g.).

In the standards issued in October 1973 and revised in February and June of 1974, vitamin D was no longer listed as an optional ingredient.

Values for "enriched" foods in table 1 have been based on the minimum levels of enrichment shown in table 7, except for white bread and rolls. For these items, values are based on data from actual analyses or data calculated from ingredients and represent enrichment at or slightly above the minimum levels listed for white bread and rolls in table 7. For conversion to the new standards of enrichment shown on page 275, values shown in this publication for thiamin, riboflavin, and niacin in the enriched flours will need to be adjusted to 1½ times the existing values and values for iron about three times. Values for thiamin in the bread and roll items will range from 1⅓ to 1⅔ times the existing values, for riboflavin from 1 to 1⅓, for niacin from 1¼ to 1½, and for iron from 2¼ to 3⅛ times.

Specific factors are provided in table 8 for converting the values given for these products in table 1 to the basis of the new levels of enrichment.

Products containing appreciable amounts of the enriched flours also would have their content of thiamin, riboflavin, niacin, and iron increased. The extent of the increase is determined by the amount of these nutrients furnished by enriched flours in relation to the amounts from other ingredients in the products. If flour is the main contributor, the increases will approximate the increases for the enriched flours. For products such as baking powder biscuits, which also contain appreciable amounts of milk, the increases in values except for riboflavin would be about the same as for the flours. For riboflavin, the increase would not be as large as for the other nutrients inasmuch as milk is a good source of this vitamin. Likewise, the higher levels of enrichment specified for the flours would have less effect on products that contain several good sources of the nutrients involved than on products in which flour furnished all or nearly all the nutrients. Foods made with eggs, flour, and milk, such as pancakes and muffins, for example, would have about the same increase in niacin values as the flour but not as large an increase in thiamin, riboflavin, and iron values.

For several home-prepared foods made with enriched flour, it has been possible to estimate the increase in values that would result if the flour used were to be enriched according to the proposed new standards. Factors have been provided in table 8 that can be applied to the values in table 1 for iron, thiamin, riboflavin, and niacin in the specified products to calculate the amounts of these nutrients that would be present if the items were made with flour enriched according to the standards issued in October 1973 and revised in February and June of 1974. Foods have been listed in table 8 in groups. Approximately the same set of factors applies to each of the individual foods in a group.

Breads.—In breadmaking, mold-retarding compounds and compounds to improve handling characteristics of dough are permitted under Federal specifications. Such compounds are usually included by bakers in commercial breads. Calcium and sodium values in table 1 for these bakery items are based on the use of a calcium-containing dough conditioner and calcium propionate as a mold inhibitor. These calcium-containing salts are the ones most commonly used. Although the amounts of these additives are small, they may account for a third or more of the total calcium in bread and roll items.

Values for calcium in breads would be decreased if sodium propionate or another compound that does not contain calcium were selected for these purposes. Higher figures for sodium than shown would be expected for breads containing sodium propionate. Values for the content of calcium and of sodium calculated for bread and roll items made with sodium propionate are presented on a 100-g. basis in table 11 on page 173 of Handbook No. 8.

Breakfast-Type Cereals and Alimentary Pastes.—Salt is usually an ingredient in the manufactured cereal products that are ready-to-serve

TABLE 8.—*Factors for converting values for several foods in tables 1 and 3 to basis of enrichment levels issued, October 1973, and revised, January 11 and June 14, 1974*

Item No.[1]	Description of food	Iron	Thiamin	Riboflavin	Niacin
	Wheat flours:				
2439	All-purpose or family flour				
2441	Bread flour	3.08	1.45	1.50	1.50
2445	Self-rising flour				
	Farina, enriched:[2]				
	Regular:				
991, ftnt. 200	Dry form				
992, ftnt. 200	Cooked				
	Quick-cooking:				
993, ftnt. 200	Dry form				
994, ftnt. 200	Cooked	[3] 10.41	3.22	3.70	5.29
	Instant-cooking:				
995, ftnt. 203	Dry form				
996, ftnt. 203	Cooked				
	Bakery products:				
446	French or vienna bread and rolls	2.50	1.42	1.10	1.33
450	Italian bread	2.50	1.36	1.21	1.27
	White bread, soft-crumb type:				
461	Fresh				
462	Toasted	2.21	1.59	1.16	1.38
475	Breadcrumbs, dry, grated				
	White bread, firm-crumb type:				
463	Fresh				
464	Toasted	2.21	1.48	1.21	1.38
	Rolls and buns, commercial:				
	Ready-to-serve:				
1900	Hard rolls	2.40	1.53	1.06	1.23
1902	Plain (soft rolls or buns)	2.91	1.42	1.34	1.50
	Partially baked (brown-and-serve):				
1907	Unbrowned				
1908	Browned	3.05	1.64	1.18	1.50
	Roll dough and rolls baked from dough:				
1911	Dough, unraised, frozen				
1912	Rolls, parkerhouse, baked	3.12	1.48	1.22	1.50
	Home-prepared foods containing enriched flour:[4]				
382	Beef potpie, baked				
476	Bread pudding with raisins, made with enriched bread.				
	Fruitcakes:				
531	Dark				
532	Light				
533	Gingerbread				
750	Chicken potpie, baked	1.4	1.3	1.2	1.3
	Brownies with nuts:				
813	Baked from home recipe				
814, ftnt. 148, 149	Frozen, with chocolate icing				
837	Made with incomplete mix, egg, water, nuts.				
1346	Muffins, bran				
2350	Turkey potpie, baked				
25	Apple brown betty, made with enriched bread.	2.0	1.3	1.3	1.5
1657	Popovers, baked				
	Biscuits, baking powder, made with—				
410	Enriched flour				
412	Self-rising flour	3.0	1.4	1.3	1.5
1916, ftnt. 335, 336	Rolls, prepared and baked from mix				
415	Biscuit mix, dry form				
416	Biscuits, prepared from mix and added milk	2.1	1.1	1.2	1.3
554	Coffeecake, baked from mix, made with egg, milk.				
	Cottage pudding:				
528	Without sauce				
529	With chocolate sauce				
530	With fruit sauce (strawberries)				
831	Cookies, sugar, soft, thick				
	Muffins:				
1343	Plain	2.6	1.4	1.3	1.5
1345	Blueberry				
1453	Pancakes				
	Waffles:				
2409	Home recipe				
2411	Frozen (commercial)				
	Doughnuts:				

See footnotes at end of table.

TABLE 8.—*Factors for converting values for several foods in tables 1 and 3 to basis of enrichment levels issued, October 1973, and revised, January 11 and June 14, 1974*—Continued

Item No.[1]	Description of food	Iron	Thiamin	Riboflavin	Niacin
957	Cake type, plain				
	Yeast leavened:				
958	Plain	2.7	1.3	1.3	1.4
Table 3, ftnt. 9	Glazed				
1566–1588, ftnt. 289	Pies, baked:				
	1-crust pies	3.3	1.8	1.3	1.7
	2-crust pies	3.5	1.3	1.5	1.4
	Piecrust, or plain pastry:				
1597	Unbaked	3.08	1.45	1.50	1.50
1598	Baked				
1628–1633, ftnt. 297; table 3, ftnt. 3	Pizzas from home recipe, frozen and chilled	3.9	1.6	1.6	1.7
	White sauce:				
2469	Thin				
2470	Medium	2.7	1.2	1.0	1.4
2471	Thick				

[1] From table 1 unless indicated otherwise.

[2] For calcium, use factor of 22.32 for items 991–992 (no dicalcium phosphate added) and 1.12 for items 993–996 (dicalcium phosphate added).

[3] Use this factor for farina, items 991–996, with label claim of 0.8 mg. per ounce (2.9 mg. per 100 g.). For products with label claim of 12.0 mg. per ounce (42.4 mg. per 100 g.), use factor of 0.21.

as purchased. Salt is not ordinarily an ingredient of the dry cereals that require cooking. Usually directions call for adding salt to the water or milk used in preparing the cereal.

Unless otherwise noted, it may be assumed that the data in table 1 for the sodium content of dry cereals that require cooking before they are served apply to products manufactured without added salt.

The data for sodium in cereals purchased ready-to-serve reflect the addition of salt or other sodium compound if either or both are added in the manufacturing practice. For cereals that are cooked after purchase, data for sodium apply to products that have had salt added during preparation in line with package directions.

On June 14, 1974, Federal guidelines (*25*) were proposed for fortification of ready-to-eat cereals with protein and certain minerals and vitamins. If these guidelines become effective, the values in table 1 for the ready-to-eat cereals with added nutrients should be based on the following amounts per 100 g. of cereal:

Protein	22.9	g.
Vitamin A	4,409	I.U.
Thiamin	1.34	mg.
Riboflavin	.92	mg.
Niacin	17.6	mg.
Calcium	529	mg.
Iron	15.9	mg.

Macaroni, noodles pastinas, and spaghetti are ordinarily manufactured without added salt, and the values in table 1 for the dry forms of these products are without salt. Directions for cooking usually specify boiling in salted water. Inasmuch as a representative amount of salt in the drained, cooked products could not be estimated, the data in table 1 for the plain cooked forms apply to the products cooked in the unsalted water. However, the data for mixed dishes, such as macaroni and cheese, apply to products in which salt has been added in accordance with a typical recipe for the product.

Cakes.—The vitamin A values in table 1 for the cakes prepared from home recipes are representative of cakes made with cooking fat that does not contain vitamin A. If table fat (butter or margarine with vitamin A added) is used in preparing these cakes, their content of vitamin A would be higher. To obtain vitamin A values for the cakes made with this substitution of table fat for cooking fat, the values shown in table 9 for 1-g. or 1-cubic inch portions may be applied to the various units of weight and volume in table 1 for the home-prepared cakes made with cooking fat.

Cakes prepared and baked from home recipes have sodium and potassium values based on the use of salt in all cakes and the use of a sodium aluminum sulfate-type baking powder (item 130, table 1) in all cakes except angelfood, dark and light fruitcake, gingerbread, and spongecake. The two kinds of fruitcake and gingerbread were leavened with soda.

Omission of salt and sodium-containing leavenings would considerably lower sodium values of these items. Without salt and with substitution of low-sodium baking powder (item 135), sodium values for cakes, except angelfood, fruitcakes, gingerbread, and spongecake, would be about 11 to 12½ percent of the values shown for them in table 1. The potassium values for these cakes would be increased if made with the low-sodium baking powder preparation. The potassium content would be from 1½ to 3½ with an average of 2½ times as much as the amounts shown in table 1.

Pies.—Sodium values for pies (items 1566–1588, table 1) were based on values calculated from the formulas given for them in ARS 62–13 (*7*). Content of sodium in the following pies represents the customary use of salt in preparing their fillings: Apple (item 1566), cherry (item 1571), chocolate meringue (item 1573), coconut custard (item 1574), custard (item 1575), lemon meringue (item 1577), mince (item 1578), and raisin (item 1585). For other pies, salt was not used in the fillings as it was considered an optional ingredient. If the customary amount of salt is used in preparing fillings for these pies, the sodium values should be increased to 1½ times

TABLE 9.—*Vitamin A values of cakes made with butter or with margarine having vitamin A added*

Item No. from tables 1 and 2	Type of cake	Vitamin A value of cake in— 1 g.	1-cu. in. portion
		International units	*International units*
522	Boston cream pie	3.9	19.5
	Caramel cake:		
523	Without icing	6.6	32.3
524	With caramel icing	5.7	37.0
	Chocolate devil's food cake:		
525	Without icing	4.8	24.0
526	With chocolate icing	4.1	25.0
527	With uncooked white icing	4.3	26.7
528	Cottage pudding without sauce	3.9	17.9
	Plain cake or cupcake:		
534	Without icing	5.4	26.5
535	With chocolate icing	4.4	27.3
536	With boiled white icing	4.1	21.3
537	With uncooked white icing	4.6	28.5
	Pound cake:		
538	Old fashioned	10.1	59.6
539	Modified	7.1	40.5
	White cake:		
541	Without icing	5.2	25.0
542	With coconut icing	3.5	20.6
543	With uncooked white icing	4.4	28.2
	Yellow cake:		
544	Without icing	4.8	23.5
545	With caramel icing	4.5	29.7
546	With chocolate icing	4.1	25.4

the amounts shown in table 1. Sodium values for the frozen pies (items 1589–1594) represent use of salt in their fillings. For all pies (items 1566–1594), sodium values are for pies prepared with piecrust containing salt as an ingredient.

Fruits and Vegetables

Acerola.—Data in table 1 for acerola, commonly called Barbados-cherry and West Indian cherry, are for *Malpighia punicifolia.* This species is an extremely rich source of ascorbic acid, with values from 1,000 to over 2,000 mg. per 100 g. in the ripe fruit. The unripe fruit has even more. The ascorbic acid content is much lower for other species of *Malpighia.*

Apples.—The ascorbic acid values in table 1 for apples have been weighted to represent the content in important commercial varieties, which comprise the major part of the total production. These are winter apples of the varieties Delicious, Golden Delicious, McIntosh, and Rome.

For freshly harvested apples with skin (item 15), the values were based on an average content of about 7 mg. per 100 g. This is typical of the important varieties of winter apples previously mentioned and of important varieties of fall apples, such as Jonathan, Wealthy, and Grimes Golden. However, freshly harvested summer varieties, as Gravenstein, Early Harvest, and Yellow Transparent, would have a higher content, about 11 mg. per 100 g. Also, some varieties of winter apples of minor importance commercially would have ascorbic acid values higher than those shown in table 1 for freshly harvested apples. For example, Willow Twig, Northern Spy, and Yellow Newtown varieties of winter apples would have about 19, 16, and 14 mg., respectively, per 100 g. Values to use for these apples after storage for several months would be about one-half these amounts.

Carrots.—Varieties of carrots differ in their vitamin A value. The amount increases with maturity. For example, Imperator, a leading variety, has a vitamin A value of about 11,000 I.U. per 100 g. at prime maturity for fresh market. At later stages of maturity this variety may contain almost twice that amount. Carrots at more advanced stages of maturity, and thus with higher vitamin A value, are used for processed forms. This accounts for the higher vitamin A values in table 1 for drained canned carrots than for the same weights of cooked fresh carrots.

Chicory and Endive.—The terminology for chicory and endive is often confused. However, they may be easily identified by their structural appearance.

Chicory (*Cichorium intybus*) may be marketed as blanched heads Witloof, as greens, or as the large rooted Magdeburg. Information in this publication is only for Witloof chicory, often called French or Belgian endive. The elongated leaves of Witloof chicory form a small, compact head, which is usually well blanched and resembles a small shoot.

Endive (*Cichorium endivia*) is always marketed as spreading, loose-leaved heads. The leaves vary from deeply cut and deeply curled in some varieties to the broad, slightly cut, and curled leaf of escarole. The outer leaves are green and the center leaves or heart and the midribs are pale green to creamy white.

Citrus Fruits.—Ascorbic acid values for oranges, all commercial varieties (item 1420, table 1), were based on a weighted average, which accounted for such factors as origin, variety, and time of harvest. This average represents data mainly for the commercial varieties shipped as fresh fruit from the California-Arizona and Florida areas. Merrill (*6*) gives additional information about this weighted average and about the ascorbic acid values for the specific orange varieties and for grapefruit, lemons, limes, tangelos, and tangerines.

Citrus fruit is marketed increasingly as chilled juice, sections, and other forms of cut-up fruit, but information on the nutrient content of these forms is scanty. The data in table 1 for raw (or for frozen, reconstituted) citrus juices and cut-up fruit, except the ascorbic acid values, are suggested as suitable for use in the corresponding chilled products. The ascorbic acid values for these raw citrus items would be reasonable estimates to use for chilled products that have had little storage and have been handled under optimum conditions. Present information is inadequate for estimating the ascorbic acid content of chilled citrus held under less than optimum conditions.

Corn, Sweet.—The carbohydrate content of corn varies with the variety and stage of maturity at which the corn is eaten. Carbohydrate increases as the kernels mature and their moisture content decreases. Some varieties may contain as much carbohydrate in the early stages of maturity as other varieties have at more advanced stages. Values shown for sweet corn have been based on data for varieties of commercial importance and presumably at a suitable stage of maturity.

Potatoes.—Ascorbic acid values for raw potatoes (item 1785, table 1) are based on thousands of analyses. The amount in 100 g. ranged from 50 mg. in freshly harvested potatoes to less than 10 mg. in potatoes stored for several months. The values in table 1 were based on a year-round value of 20 mg. per 100 g., the average amount to expect in raw potatoes from the market. This average reflects the relative quantities of different commercial varieties in the market each month of the year, as well as the usual length of storage periods. A footnote to item 1785 provides values to use for freshly harvested potatoes and for potatoes stored for various lengths of time. Ascorbic acid values shown for cooked potatoes and for potatoes used in home-prepared foods, such as potato salad, were calculated from raw potatoes using the year-round value.

Ascorbic acid values for dehydrated mashed potatoes (items 1797–1802) apply to products available on the retail market that do not have this vitamin added to them. The ascorbic acid value for dehydrated potatoes varies widely. It is dependent on the content of ascorbic acid in the raw potatoes used, method of processing, and length of storage of the dehydrated product.

Cut Forms of Raw Fruits and Vegetables; Capping of Strawberries.—A large proportion of the ascorbic acid is readily oxidized in cutting cantaloup and squash, capping strawberries, and shredding and chopping cabbage and lettuce. Ascorbic acid values in table 1 for these items do not allow for this loss. They overestimate the content of ascorbic acid to the extent that dehydroascorbic acid is oxidized further to diketogulonic acid, the inactive oxidized form.

Cooked Vegetables.—Nutritive values in table 1 for the boiled form of raw vegetables, unless otherwise indicated, apply to drained products that have been cooked in small or moderate amounts of water until tender. The values shown take account of important losses of soluble nutrients into the discarded cooking water. They do not apply to vegetables cooked by such methods as steaming and pressure-cooking, which require minimal amounts of added water.

The values used to calculate the amounts of nutrients shown were derived by applying retention factors to the nutrients in the corresponding raw vegetables. The percent retentions for the vitamins were based on published reports of carefully conducted studies of losses—solubility, destruction, or both—expressed in terms of the original weights of the raw vegetables. The retention factors for proximate constituents and minerals were based mainly on the percent distribution of soluble nutrients between the drained solids and drained liquid in canned vegetables as this was the most adequate basis available. Estimated in this way, the content of nutrients in table 1 for cooked vegetables is probably too low for vegetables cooked by methods recommended for conserving nutrients.

Sodium values shown for the cooked forms of raw and frozen vegetables do not apply to the vegetables cooked in salted water or to those seasoned with salt at time of serving. The quantity of salt to use for moderately salted vegetables could be calculated as 0.6 percent, the usual amount in commercially canned vegetables. On this basis, the sodium values in table 1 for the cooked form of raw and frozen vegetables would have to be increased by 236 mg. per 100 g. of product.

Sodium values shown for fresh foods cooked in water may be underestimated if the cooking water has a high natural sodium content.

Canned Fruits and Vegetables.—Data in table 1 on canned fruits are for fruits in the predominant medium used, heavy sirup for most. Fruits packed in water without artificial sweetener have also been included and for some this is an important type of pack.

Two styles of pack are shown in table 1 for most of the canned vegetables. These are labeled as regular pack and special dietary pack (low sodium). Regular pack applies to vegetables seasoned with salt during canning. This amounts to about 0.6 percent of salt in the finished product. Vegetables canned without salt and with special precautions to avoid other sources of sodium are designated special dietary pack (low sodium).

Sources of sodium in processed vegetables, in addition to water of high sodium content used either as the packing medium or for blanching, include lye or other sodium-containing material used for peeling, brine for quality separation, and dilute salt solutions to prevent discoloration of the product.

Frozen Fruits and Vegetables.—Ascorbic acid

values in table 1 for frozen fruits and vegetables were calculated from values that in most instances represented total ascorbic acid and apply to products held under highly favorable conditions. The values for total ascorbic acid include both the reduced and any dehydroascorbic acid present. The values shown for the frozen fruits and vegetables may be slightly higher than would be found in products stored under conditions in which temperatures are less ideal.

Some packs of frozen apricots and peaches contain added ascorbic acid. Because of this difference in commercial practices, ascorbic acid values per 100 g. of fruit can range from 6 to 100 mg. in frozen apricots and from 11 to 76 mg. in frozen peaches. Ascorbic acid values for these fruits in table 1 are based on averages representing both kinds of pack. Footnotes to the items give values for the fruit processed with and without added ascorbic acid.

In frozen vegetables and in some fruits a slight loss may occur in certain of the nutrients as the item thaws. No basis was available for making an adjustment in the data for such losses. The nutritive values shown in table 1 therefore are the amounts in the frozen form.

Sodium values for several frozen vegetables may be higher than shown in table 1. Use of a sodium chloride brine in quality separation before freezing and seasoning with salt significantly increase their sodium content. Values shown are based on a wide range. However, if the maximum value in the range had been used, sodium values for the uncooked frozen vegetables and for the vegetables cooked without added salt would be increased. Values for large or Fordhook lima beans and baby limas would be increased to approximately 2⅔ times the present figures, cowpeas about four times, green peas about 2⅓, peas and carrots about 1½, mixed vegetables about 1⅔, and succotash about 3½ times.

Fruit Products With Added Nutrients.—Nutrients, such as ascorbic acid, are sometimes added to processed fruit juice beverage foods, fruit juices, and other fruit products. Values to use for the products with added nutrient(s) are given in table 1 when different brands of a product have similar levels of the added nutrients. Otherwise reference is made to information on labels for these products.

Meats

Several forms of each of the principal kinds of meat—beef, pork, lamb, and veal—have been included in tables 1 and 2. Raw cuts are described in terms of their physical composition, that is, percentages of separable fatty tissue, lean, and in the case of cuts with either bone or bone and skin, percentages designated as refuse. For beef, data have been included for several retail cuts of choice and good grades. The data for lamb, pork, and veal shown for the retail cuts were from carcasses that were intermediate between those of high and low levels of fat content.

Among different samples of any one kind of cut in the retail meat market, it is not unusual to observe a wide range in proportions of lean, fat, and bone. Cuts of beef from carcasses graded choice would be expected to have a higher degree of marbling in the lean portion and consequently a higher content of fat than cuts from carcasses of a lower grade. Differences in extent of trimming separable fat, however, can greatly alter the proportions of the kinds of tissue in the cut and as a result alter the caloric value and the content of fat and of other nutrients. The composition of the raw retail cuts described are considered typical.

Information on yield in weight and the physical composition of cooked meat to be expected from the raw cuts described is provided for several cooked meat items. Among other factors, the composition of cooked meat is related to the composition of the meat before it is cooked. Other of the more important factors affecting the composition of cooked meat are method, conditions, and extent of cooking. The figures for yield and composition of cooked meat in tables 1 and 2 were derived from data considered suitable for meats prepared in usual ways and, unless described otherwise, cooked to about a medium-done stage.

Procedures for deriving the data for physical composition, proximate composition, and yield of cooked meat items from data for raw meat have been published in detail (*11*). Except for sodium and potassium, the data in table 1 for the mineral elements and vitamins also have been based on procedures used previously (*28*). The sodium and potassium values for most raw and cooked meat items shown in this publication were calculated from factors that the Consumer and Food Economics Institute staff had developed from relationships between these mineral elements and protein. Expressed as milligrams per gram of protein, these factors are as follows:

	Sodium	*Potassium*
Beef, lamb, uncured pork, veal:		
Raw	3.50	16.0
Cooked by dry heat	2.45	11.2
Cooked by moist heat	1.75	8.0
Light-cured pork:		
Raw	51.2	16.0
Cooked	35.8	11.2
Corned beef, cooked	934	60

For calculating the sodium and potassium values in raw corned beef for table 1, the contents of these elements for raw corned beef in Handbook No. 8 were used. For canned cured pork, no data were available to develop specific factors. It was assumed that values for this item approximated those developed for raw light-cured pork.

Fish

Most of the sodium values in table 1 for cooked fish and fish main-course dishes do not include sodium from salt that is commonly used to season them. If salt is added, values for these items would be greatly increased. Explanatory footnotes to these items designate whether salt was included in calculating their sodium values. Salted butter or margarine and bacon when used for the broiled or baked fish items contributed to the sodium values shown for them. The use of these ingredients is noted in the description of these items.

Frozen Desserts

In some States frozen desserts resembling ice cream and ice milk are produced and sold. Data have not been included in tables 1 and 2 for these items as they have not been available everywhere throughout the country and a considerable difference has been observed in the minimum level for some nutrients required by States with standards for these products. For one type of frozen dessert, mellorine, Federal Standards of Identity have been proposed (*24*). The proposed Federal standards allow nonfat milk solids or milk-derived solids of sufficient protein in quantity and quality to the nonfat milk solids of milk, and animal and vegetable fat as ingredients. The standards require a minimum of 6 percent fat and 2.7 percent protein by weight of the food, exclusive of the weight of any bulky flavoring ingredients used. The finished product must contain at least 2.2 percent protein and 4.8 percent fat. Fortification is required to insure 40 I.U. of vitamin A per gram of fat.

To some extent the data in table 1 for ice cream may be useful for estimating some of the values for mellorine. Reasonable estimates for calories and vitamin A values would be made by using the values for ice cream if the fat content is similar to that for the particular mellorine product being used. For the other nutrients, the data for ice cream may not apply to mellorine. The data for fatty acids in ice cream in table 2 would not apply to mellorine.

APPENDIX D.—NOTES ON ENERGY VALUES AND NUTRIENTS

This appendix provides a brief source of information about the energy values and nutrients for which data are given in this publication. For more detail, see Appendix A of Agriculture Handbook No. 8.

Energy Values

Data for energy values in this publication are for physiologic energy values. The data represent the portion of the gross energy value that remains after losses in digestion and metabolism have been deducted. (Values obtained by burning a food in a bomb calorimeter would be in terms of gross calories.) The method of determining the energy values here was developed by Atwater and Bryant (*2*) and has been discussed more recently by Merrill and Watt (*8*). Factors for calculating energy values of foods by this method may be found in Handbook No. 8, page 160.

The energy values in table 1 have been expressed in terms of the large calorie, or kilocalorie, the customary unit used by nutritionists and food scientists for many years. It has been defined as a measure of the amount of heat required to raise the temperature of 1 kg. of water 1° C. The small calorie is one-thousandth of the large calorie. Calorie has often been written with a capital letter to insure that the large calorie was the unit intended. However, except for the very early food and nutrition investigations, only the large calorie has been used in work on food and nutrition, and the practice of spelling calorie with a capital letter has not always been followed. In this publication it has been capitalized when the number of calories has been specified but not when used to refer to energy values in general.

Adoption of the International System of Units (S.I.), which is founded on the metric system, could bring about the use of a different unit, the Joule, for expressing energy values. The practice of expressing energy values in calories would be discontinued. A change from a long-established practice that would involve a wide range of problems and applications in food science and nutrition cannot be made abruptly. During the interim period, energy values will probably be listed in publications both in terms of the familiar calories (i.e., kilocalories) and in Joules, or if this is not feasible, the conversion factor may be provided to show the relationship between the values in the two units. The factor 4.184 for converting data for energy values expressed as kilocalories into kiloJoules has been included here along with the factors needed to convert other customary units to terms more in line with the metric system (see p. 2). Adoption of the Joule does not change the accuracy or precision of measuring energy values of foods but permits more precise expression and a common basis for communication among various scientific groups.

Nutrients

Protein and Nonprotein Nitrogen.—The values for protein used were mostly obtained from data for total nitrogen to which the conversion factors developed by Jones (*5, 10*) were applied. A few foods contain considerable nonprotein nitrogen. For example, nitrogenous matter of nonprotein character accounts for about 15 percent of the total nitrogen in chocolate and cocoa, about 33 percent in mushrooms, about 20 percent in yeasts, and nearly all of that in coffee. Values in table 1 for protein in these foods exclude the nonprotein fractions.

Fat.—Values for fat apply to those components in foods that are insoluble in water and soluble in organic solvents. Some other frequently used terms for the fat content of foods are crude fat, oil, and ether extract. Cholesterol is an important component of the total lipid in foods of animal origin. Data for cholesterol have been presented in a separate publication (*3*). For numerous foods, the same measures and units of food have been used as shown here in tables 1 and 2.

Carbohydrate.—The values for carbohydrate in this publication have been calculated from those that represent "total carbohydrate by difference" and include fiber. For those foods with a sizable content of nonprotein nitrogenous matter, the content of the total nitrogenous matter, protein and nonprotein, was used in calculating the content of carbohydrate by difference.

Minerals and Oxalic Acid.—Values for the mineral elements are based on chemical and physical methods of analyses. The values represent the total amount of each present in a food and not the amount of the mineral element available to the body. Availability is affected by many factors and a multiplicity of conditions about which present information is inadequate.

For example, oxalic acid, which occurs in a few foods, may interfere with the use of calcium or magnesium present in the diets, as it may combine with these mineral elements to form highly insoluble compounds. Small amounts of oxalic acid are present in carrots, collards, kale, leeks, okra, parsnips, potatoes, and sweetpotatoes. Moderate amounts, about 200 to 400 mg. of oxalic acid per 100 g. of food, occur in baking and bitter chocolate, peanuts, pecans, and wheat germ. New Zealand spinach, rhubarb, spinach, and swiss chard have fairly high concentrations. Much higher concentrations, over 1,000 mg. per 100 g. of food, occur in dock, lambsquarters, poke, and purslane. Present information is inadequate for determining the extent to which oxalic acid may limit the availability of the various mineral elements.

Likewise, phosphorus may occur in bound forms in some foods, especially in nuts, legumes, and outer layers of whole grain cereals, and be relatively unavailable. It may occur as a phytate and interfere to an undetermined extent with the utilization of calcium, magnesium, and iron and possibly other nutrients. Iron compounds, including the various forms added to foods, are known to differ in the degree of availability of the iron they contain.

Vitamin A.—The values for vitamin A have been expressed in international units. For most foods of animal origin, the values represent mainly preformed vitamin A, retinol. However, for some foods of animal origin, as egg yolk and butter, part of the value is derived from the carotenoids, which are precursors of vitamin A. In foods of plant origin, the vitamin value is supplied entirely by the precursors, mainly beta-carotene.

Most of the values have been based on physical-chemical determinations of total carotenoids or individual carotenes and cryptoxanthin, a biologically active pigment. Factors have been used to convert results from these studies into international units of vitamin A. Amounts of the various precursors calculated as equivalent to 1 I.U. of vitamin A are 0.6 μg. (microgram) of beta-carotene, 1.2 μg. of other commonly occurring carotenes having vitamin A activity, and 1.2 μg. of cryptoxanthin. Amounts of preformed vitamin A calculated as equivalent to 1 I.U. are 0.3 μg. of vitamin A alcohol and 0.34 μg. of vitamin A acetate.

Yellow-pigmented foods of plant origin, such as oranges and yellow corn, contain appreciable amounts of cryptoxanthin. During heat treatment of foods as in canning and cooking, isomers of the carotenoid pigments may be formed. Cryptoxanthin, the individual carotenes, and their isomers exhibit different biological availability. If the vitamin A values shown in table 1 do not include measurement of cryptoxanthin for a food that contains it, or the values represent only beta-carotene and not its isomers or other precursors of vitamin A that may be present, the vitamin A values may be underestimated.

Some yellow- and red-pigmented foods contain a large fraction of carotenoids that are not physiologically active as sources of the vitamin. Lycopene is an example of such a carotenoid. The values in table 1 may be overestimated if they represent the assignment of the biological activity of beta-carotene to total carotenoid values that include biologically inactive carotenoids and the provitamin A carotenoids of lower biological activity than beta-carotene.

Expression of the vitamin A activity of foods in terms of international units has been criticized because the international unit is based on the vitamin A activity of carotene in the rat. Instead it has been proposed that the vitamin A activity of foods be stated in their equivalent weight of retinol in micrograms (microgram retinol equivalents) so that the values would represent the differences in the biological availability in man of the various forms of vitamin A.

At this time it is not feasible to give a single factor for converting the vitamin A values in table 1 to their equivalent weights in micrograms of retinol. Foods of animal origin differ in the proportion of preformed vitamin A, if present, and in the proportion of the individual precursors of vitamin A they contain. Values for foods of plant origin, as previously noted, are based on averages derived from data that may not always represent each precursor of vitamin A that may be present with proper interpretation of its contribution to the total vitamin A value.

Niacin.—The values for niacin are based on chemical and microbiological assay methods, which measure the free acid following its release by enzyme, acid, or alkali treatments. The niacin values shown were based on data that did not include the niacin value that could be contributed by tryptophan, an amino acid that is a precursor of niacin.

Ascorbic Acid.—For some foods the values for ascorbic acid include, in addition to the reduced form of ascorbic acid, dehydroascorbic acid, as both have vitamin C activity. None of the values include diketogulonic acid, an oxidized form that does not have vitamin C activity but is sometimes included in data reported as total ascorbic acid. Ascorbic acid values shown here for raw, canned, and dehydrated fruits and vegetables are based on data mainly for reduced ascorbic acid. The values shown for frozen fruits and vegetables were calculated from data that represented the sum of the reduced ascorbic acid and any dehydroascorbic acid present in these foods.

LITERATURE CITED

(1) Association of Official Analytical Chemists.
1970. official methods of analysis . . . . Ed. 11, 1015 pp. Washington, D.C.

(2) Atwater, W. O., and Bryant, A. P.
1900. the availability and fuel value of food materials. Conn. (Storrs) Agr. Expt. Sta. 12th Ann. Rpt. 1899: 73–110.

(3) Feeley, R. M., Criner, P. E., and Watt, B. K.
1972. cholesterol content of foods. Amer. Dietet. Assoc. Jour. 61: 134–149.

(4) Florida Citrus Commission of the Florida Department of Citrus.
1971–72. standards for canned, concentrated, and other processed citrus products. Regulations Pursuant to Chapter 601, Florida Statutes as Amended (Citrus Code), Regulat. 105–1.19. 15 pp. Lakeland, Fla.

(5) Jones, D. B.
1931. factors for converting percentages of nitrogen in foods and feeds into percentages of protein. U.S. Dept. Agr. Cir. 183, 22 pp. (Sl. rev. 1941.)

(6) Merrill, A. L.
1964. citrus fruit values in "handbook no. 8," revised. Amer. Dietet. Assoc. Jour. 44: 264–270.

(7) ——— Adams, C. F., and Fincher, L. J.
1966. procedures for calculating nutritive values of home-prepared foods: as used in agriculture handbook no. 8, "composition of foods—raw, processed, prepared," revised 1963. U.S. Dept. Agr. ARS 62–13, 35 pp.

(8) ——— and Watt, B. K.
1955. energy value of foods—basis and derivation. U.S. Dept. Agr. Agr. Handb. 74, 105 pp. (Sl. rev. 1973.)

(9) National Academy of Sciences, National Research Council.
1970. safety and suitability of salt for use in baby foods. (A report of the Food and Nutrition Board.) 20 pp. Washington, D.C.

(10) Orr, M. L., and Watt, B. K.
1957. amino acid content of foods. U.S. Dept. Agr. Home Econ. Res. Rpt. 4, 82 pp.

(11) Pecot, R. K., Jaeger, C. M., and Watt, B. K.
1965. proximate composition of beef from carcass to cooked meat: method of derivation and tables of values. U.S. Dept. Agr. Home Econ. Res. Rpt. 31, 32 pp.

(12) ——— and Watt, B. K.
1956. food yields summarized by different stages of preparation. U.S. Dept. Agr. Agr. Handb. 102, 93 pp.

(13) U.S. Agricultural Marketing Service.
1955. grading and inspection of shell eggs and united states standards, grades, and weight classes for shell eggs. weight classes. [U.S.] Natl. Arch. Fed. Register 20: 677. Amended, Fed. Register 20: 10015, 1955; 32: 8229–8234, 1967. Also in Code of Fed. Regulat., title 7, pt. 56, sect. 56.218.

(14) ———
1964. product description, styles, grades. united states standards for grades of frozen concentrated orange juice. [U.S.] Natl. Arch. Fed. Register 29: 12575–12578. Also in Code of Fed. Regulat., title 7, pt. 52, sect. 52–1582.

(15) U.S. Consumer and Marketing Service.
1967. united states standards for grades of green olives. Issue 2, as amended. 9 pp. Washington, D.C.

(16) ———
1971. united states standards for grades of canned ripe olives. Issue 2, as amended. 11 pp. Washington, D.C.

(17) U.S. Food and Drug Administration.
1955. definitions and standards of identity: cereal flours and related products; alimentary pastes; bakery products. [U.S.] Natl. Arch. Fed. Register 20: 9570–9580. Also in Code of Fed. Regulat., title 21, pt. 15–17.

(18) ———
1957. cereal flours and related products; rice and related products. [U.S.] Natl. Arch. Fed. Register 22: 6887–6888. Also in Code of Fed. Regulat., title 21, pt. 15, sect. 15.525.

(19) ———
1958. cereal flours and related products. [U.S.] Natl. Arch. Fed. Register 23: 1170–1171. Also in Code of Fed. Regulat., title 21, pt. 15, sect. 15.525.

(20) ———
1961. definitions and standards of identity: cereal flours and related products; enriched corn meals; calcium. [U.S.] Natl. Arch. Fed. Register 26: 7223. Also in Code of Fed. Regulat., title 21, pt. 15, sect. 15.513.

(21) ———
1962. definitions and standards of identity: cereal products and related products; enriched corn meals. [U.S.] Natl. Arch. Fed. Register 27: 618. Also in Code of Fed. Regulat., title 21, pt. 15, sect. 15.513.

(22) ———
1973. improvement of nutrient levels of enriched flour, enriched self-rising flour, and enriched breads, rolls or buns. [U.S.] Natl. Arch. Fed. Register 38: 28558–28564. Rev., Fed. Register 39: 5188–5189, 20891–20892, 1974.

(23) ———
1972. milk and cream. proposed revision of existing standards and establishment of new identity standards. [U.S.] Natl. Arch. Fed. Register 37: 18392–18396.

(24) ———
1973. frozen desserts. mellorine, parevine; proposal to establish standards of identity. [U.S.] Natl. Arch. Fed. Register 38: 2150–2152. Rev. Fed. Register 39: 27128–27130, 1974.

(25) ———
1974. fortified ready-to-eat breakfast cereals. proposed nutritional quality guidelines. [U.S.] Natl. Arch. Fed. Register 39: 20898–20900.

(26) U.S. Production and Marketing Administration.
1940. tentative united states standards for grades of salt cured oil coated olives. 2 pp. Washington, D.C.

(27) ———
1952. prepackaging tomatoes. Mktg. Res. Rpt. 20, 58 pp.

(28) Watt, B. K., and Merrill, A. L.
1963. composition of foods—raw, processed, prepared. U.S. Dept. Agr. Agr. Handb. 8 (rev.), 190 pp.

INDEX

DISCARD